W0008618

The Diary of Elizabeth Drinker

The Diary of Elizabeth Drinker

VOLUME I

Elaine Forman Crane
EDITOR

Sarah Blank Dine
ASSOCIATE EDITOR

Alison Duncan Hirsch
Arthur Scherr
ASSISTANT EDITORS

Anita J. Rapone
CO-EDITOR, 1982–1986

Northeastern University Press
Boston

Northeastern University Press

Library of Congress Cataloging-in-Publication Data

Drinker, Elizabeth Sandwith, 1735–1807.
The diary of Elizabeth Drinker / Elaine Forman Crane, editor : Sarah Blank Dine, associate editor, Alison Duncan Hirsch, Arthur Scherr, assistant editors ; Anita J. Rapone, co-editor, 1982–1986.
p. cm.
Includes bibliographical references and index.
ISBN 1-55553-093-1 (set)
1. Quakers—Pennsylvania—Philadelphia—Social life and customs. 2. Philadelphia (Pa.)—Social life and customs. 3. Drinker, Elizabeth Sandwith, 1735–1807—Diaries. 4. Quakers—Pennsylvania—Philadelphia—Diaries. I. Crane, Elaine Forman. II. Title.
F158.9.F89D75 1991
974.8'110088286—dc20 90-14260

Designed by David Ford

Composed in Plantin by Coghill Composition, Richmond, Virginia. Printed and bound by Edwards Brothers, Ann Arbor, Michigan. The paper is Glatfelter Offset, an acid-free sheet.

MANUFACTURED IN THE UNITED STATES OF AMERICA
96 95 94 93 92 91 5 4 3 2 1

Contents

Acknowledgments

These volumes reflect the support of people and institutions whose invaluable assistance has resulted in the publication of *The Diary of Elizabeth Drinker*. Over the years, the National Historical Publications and Records Commission responded with funding that ensured both the existence and the continuation of the project. As important, the staff of NHPRC (Roger Bruns, Mary Giunta, Richard Jacobs, Richard Sheldon, and George Vogt) was always available to discuss problems and to offer general advice. Fordham University contributed time, space, funding, and graduate assistants, and we are grateful for this extensive commitment to the project. The Barra Foundation provided seed money at the project's inception and additional funding at crucial intervals. The Philadelphia Center for Early American Studies funded a leave of absence from teaching for the editor and encouraged participation in seminars in which ideas were generated and debated—much to the benefit of the project. Particular thanks go to Michael Zuckerman, Stephanie Wolf, and Richard Dunn. The Library Company of Philadelphia and the National Endowment for the Humanities awarded travel grants for research in Philadelphia.

The David Library of the American Revolution and the Ellis Phillips Foundation contributed to the project through the State University of New York at Plattsburgh.

In addition to financial support, the administrators and staff of Fordham University assisted the project in a variety of ways. Some of these people are no longer affiliated with the university, but their individual contributions on behalf of the project are acknowledged with thanks: John Algieri, Susan Baer, Francis Borchardt, Barbara Costa, Richard Doyle, Laura Ebert, Judith Ginsberg, Joseph McCarthy, Nancy McCarthy, John McLoughlin, Judith Mills, Martha Pagen, Vincent Potter, Mary Powers, Gerald Quinn, and Jay Sexter.

The editor is grateful to a number of research institutions and their staffs for assistance in compiling the annotation and the Biographical Directory: American Philosophical Society; Augustus C. Long Health Sciences Library, Columbia University (Barbara Paulson); Bucks County Historical Society (Frances Waite and Donna Humphrey); Friends Historical Library, Swarthmore College; Haviland Records Room, New York Meeting Society of Friends (Elizabeth Moger); Historical Society of Pennsylvania (Peter Parker and Linda Stanley); History of Health Sciences Library and Museum, University of Cincinnati Medical Center (Billie Broaddus and Cory Oysler); Library Company of Philadelphia (John Van Horne, James Green, and Mary Anne Hines); Library of the College of Physicians of Philadelphia (Thomas Horrocks); New York Genealogical and Biographical Society; New-York Historical Society; New York Public Library; Philadelphia City Archives; Philadelphia Office of the Register of Wills; Quaker Collection, Haverford College, Westtown School (Alice Long).

The editors are also indebted to colleagues who have lent their special expertise and responded to their inquiries on any number of occasions: Edwin Bronner, John Catanzariti, J. William Frost, Mary Gallagher, Bert Hansen, Craig Horle, Robert Jones, Esther Katz, Elizabeth Nuxoll, Louis Pascoe, Carl Prince, Bernice Rosenthal, Richard Ryerson, Sharon Salinger, Billy G. Smith, Jean Soderlund, Dorothy Twohig, Laurel Ulrich, and Marianne Wokeck.

The project has benefitted from the assistance of graduate students in the Department of History at Fordham University: Donna Cartelli, Kathleen Comerford, David Flaten, Patrick Gillen, Terri Hamacher, Georgia Herring, Elizabeth Lowe, Christopher Mauriello, Catherine Osborne, Gilbert Stack, Theresa Vann, and Scott Wight. A special thanks goes to David Sylvester, who compiled the guide to French phrases.

Because of the nature of the diary, the project relied on the advice of a number of medical and dental professionals: Stephen Baum (virology, epidemiology); James Cohen (oncology); Mark Dine (pediatrics); Henry M. Drinker (epidemiology); Peter Rubin (gastroenterology); Robert Rubler (periodontics); Milton Tarlau (neurology). The compilation of the index was also accomplished by professionals (John Kaminski, and his associates Ellen Goldlust and Charles Hagermann), whose skills streamlined this complex and time-consuming process.

The secretarial support staff was essential to the project: Eileen Didie, Gretchen Susi, Nancy Tulino-Polacci, LaRena Young.

The following people contributed at critical times and in various ways: Ernesta Ballard, Suzanne Cleveland, Andrea Crane, Stephen Crane, Jeffrey Dine, Richard Dine, Henry S. Drinker, David Maxey, and Lauren Wachtler.

Finally, an acknowledgment of the debt to Northeastern University Press, particularly to Deborah Kops who guided this project through the publication process from beginning to end, and to William Frohlich, Ann Twombly, and Larry Hamberlin. The care and thoroughness with which they attended these volumes immeasurably enhanced the final product.

Introduction

On one level, the diary of Elizabeth Drinker has all the ingredients of the romantic novel, a literary genre that soared to popularity late in the eighteenth century. Among the best-sellers of the 1780s and 1790s (many of which appear on Elizabeth Drinker's personal reading list) were sentimental works by Samuel Richardson, Susannah Rowson, and Hannah Foster, all of whom sought to reflect contemporary life through fiction. Nowhere in her long journal did Elizabeth Drinker imply that she was influenced by these writers, yet she recognized that life passed "as a tale that is told,"[1] and the striking parallels between the incidents she recorded and the events depicted by contemporary novelists suggest that the latter had very nearly obscured the line between imagination and reality—which was their intention all along.

Conversely, as Drinker spins her own true life tale—which includes the untimely and traumatic loss of both parents in the span of three months; the young husband who spends too many summer evenings in town with his equally young, unmarried sister-in-law; the pregnant maid who is undone by the servant/coachman; a daughter who elopes with her dashing suitor; another who tragically succumbs to cancer; a third whose unhappy marriage pains both parent and child; a son whose tubercular symptoms constantly threaten his life—she unintentionally tempts the reader to ask where Elizabeth Drinker ends and *Charlotte Temple* begins. This is not to imply that the literary efforts of Elizabeth Drinker and Susannah Rowson are indistinguishable, but rather to argue that if, in some ways, the diary is faintly reminiscent of turn-of-the-century fiction, it is because both Drinker and Rowson were influenced by, and in turn reflected, the social codes of their society. As Cathy Davidson maintains in her study of the American novel, works such as *Charlotte Temple* related to the moral fiber of the new republic and were deeply rooted in contemporary life.[2] The proof of that assertion is the similarity between the lives portrayed in those novels and the lives recorded in Drinker's diary.

To history's good fortune, however, Elizabeth Sandwith Drinker (1735–1807) was no fictional character, and her diary is the single most important document reflective of eighteenth-century life from a female perspective—keeping in mind, of course, that not all the world was Philadelphia, and that women of Drinker's class composed only a tiny fraction of its population. Nevertheless, the extraordinary span of the diary (1758–1807), as well as its sustained quality, makes it a rewarding document to explore for a multitude of historical purposes, as historians have done in increasing numbers since the nearly three dozen manuscript volumes were deposited at the Historical Society of Pennsylvania in 1955.

Elizabeth Drinker appears never to have traveled more than 125 miles from her native Philadelphia, which during her lifetime grew from a mercantile town of approximately thirteen thousand people to a major city of seventy thousand. That same half century saw the Quaker population, of which she was a member, reduced from more than one-quarter of the total number of inhabitants to less than one-seventh, as Philadelphia swelled with immigrants and Friends married outside the faith. A French traveler estimated that there were approximately sixteen to seventeen hundred Quaker families in Philadelphia at the end of the eighteenth century, at which time they constituted only one of fourteen religious denominations in that city.[3]

By 1800 Philadelphia could also claim eight different ethnic groups, among which were a considerable number of African-Americans, whose status had changed dramatically in the preceding fifty years. The proportion of slaves to the total population, which peaked during Drinker's young adulthood, declined precipitously as both she and the century advanced in age. At the same time, the number of free blacks escalated from approximately 250 on the eve of independence to close to 10,000 by her death. Moreover, those years saw the transformation of a labor system that depended on bound servants and slaves to one that relied on free wage labor. In the mid-eighteenth century, 40 percent of Philadelphia's workers were either bound or enslaved; by 1800 these two groups had dwindled to less than 2 percent of the work force.

By most standards, Philadelphians prospered after the Revolution. Yet the affluence of families such as the Drinkers coexisted with urban poverty to the extent that by 1790 more than one-third of the population could not afford to meet even a minimal tax assessment. Residential separation of rich and poor eventually accompanied this economic polarization, as did the geographic segregation of blacks, the incidence of which spiraled upward between 1790 and 1820. Although Elizabeth Drinker had little to say directly about the demographic changes that surrounded her, the diary leaves little doubt of their profound effect upon her, her family, and other Philadelphians.[4]

Elizabeth Sandwith began life in 1735 in the same Philadelphia house in which her mother, Sarah Jervis (1708–56), had been born. The family was of

Irish Quaker extraction, and her father, William Sandwith (1700–1756), "follow'd the seas for many years; 10 years after he married."[5] He eventually remained on shore to pursue mercantile activities. Elizabeth was a middle child; her older sister, Mary (1732–1815), remained single and became a permanent member of the Drinker household after Elizabeth's marriage; the brief existence of a younger brother, William (1746–1747), attests to the hazards of eighteenth-century infancy.[6]

Death also claimed both of Elizabeth Sandwith's parents prematurely and within a few months of each other. Her mother died on January 9, 1756, after "a lingering illness," while death came to her father suddenly, on March 13, during "an apoplectick fit."[7] Of age, but unmarried, Elizabeth and Mary were expected to take up residence elsewhere. As their mother's brother and a respectable Philadelphian, John Jervis might have been the most likely candidate for guardian, but even though he seemed to be on good terms with Elizabeth and Mary (to the extent that he directed their affairs), the two young women did not move in with family. Instead, they boarded with the prominent Philadelphia Quaker Thomas Say (1709–96), whose benevolent attitude toward orphans was well known, and whose already large, child-filled household may have profited from the two extra pairs of hands. There they resided for fourteen months after the death of their parents, and from that house they carried on a trade in feathers with Edward Stephens of Dublin, Ireland, a commerce resulting, perhaps, from the interests of their merchant father. Forty years later, Elizabeth remembered Say as "an innofensive, well minded, patient man . . . an even minded man."[8]

By the time we are introduced to Elizabeth Sandwith through the diary, she and her sister, both in their early twenties, were part of the household of Ann Warner. Though no more related to the Sandwiths than was Thomas Say, the Warners appear to have had a warm relationship with their tenants. That they shared the same attitudes and perceptions about life can be seen in Elizabeth's entry, written with more candor than modesty: "Eight Women Friends dinn'd at AWs which made 14 of the best sort, our selves included."[9] Whether a common affluence, religion, or sex led her to that conclusion was left unsaid.

Elizabeth and her sister lodged nearly four years with the Warners, and it was Ann Warner, as a surrogate parent, who accompanied Elizabeth to the Friends' meeting wherein she declared her "intentions of marriage" with Henry Drinker. Not until that marriage took place did Elizabeth move into a home of her own, on Water Street. Mary moved with her and remained a member of the household (as "housekeeper," according to another contemporary, Ann Warder) until her death.[10] In 1771 that household, considerably larger than it had been ten years earlier, removed to 110 North Front Street on the corner of Drinker's Alley, and it was in this large, three-story brick mansion, next-door to the one in which she and Mary had lived with the Warners, that Elizabeth Drinker penned the rest of her multivolume journal, as well as more than fifty loving letters to her husband, who was incarcerated by the Americans in 1777–78.[11]

Henry Drinker (1734–1809) was a young merchant and widower when Elizabeth married him in January 1761, three years after the loss of his first wife, Ann Swett (a close friend of Elizabeth's). Both were committed members of the Society of Friends, although Henry took a far more public role in Quaker life than did Elizabeth. HD, as she called him, was at various times clerk of the Meeting for Sufferings, elder of the Philadelphia Monthly Meeting, and treasurer of the Yearly Meeting. Elizabeth, on the other hand, only hesitantly served on a committee, and even more reluctantly broke the stillness of silent meeting.

From all indications, Henry and Elizabeth Drinker's marriage was a loving one throughout its forty-six years. Although Henry's wide-ranging interests made him a man "who is always at home and never at home," Elizabeth took pride in his accomplishments and satisfaction in his community standing. And since she was not quick to praise at any time, her assessment of HD's character is all the more noteworthy: "if benevolence and beneficence will take a man to Heaven, and no doubt it goes a great way towards it, HD. stands as good, indeed a better, chance than any I know off." She was willing to accept his "good judgment" and follow his instructions—as long as they did not conflict with her own inclinations.[12]

Henry and Elizabeth Drinker produced nine children during their marriage, five of whom reached maturity: Sarah (Sally), 1761–1807; Ann (Nancy), 1764–1830; William (Billy), 1767–1821; Henry (HSD), 1770–1824; and Mary (Molly), 1774–1856. William was the only child to remain single. At the time of Elizabeth's death in 1807, she and Henry claimed nineteen grandchildren, several of whom were named after their grandmother. Thus, on another level, the diary is a chronicle of this family. Certainly Drinker was preoccupied with their health, well-being, and development. Her belief that "no wife or mother, is more attach'd to her near relative[s]" was scarcely overstated.[13] She maintained a loving and intimate relationship with all her children, and was always available to share their confidences and support them during crises as they passed through their own life cycles.

If the Quakers were sometimes referred to as the "plain people," the Drinkers' personal belongings, surroundings, and life-style counterbalanced, or even belied, that description. Clothing was tailored from the finest silk, velvet, and cashmere, with only the somberness of its colors (dark greens, grays, and blacks) to compensate for the elegance of the fabric. Each daughter possessed a gold watch "caped and Jewel'd with chaines," and Sally, at least, wore a gold chain to set off her gowns. During their courtship HD had presented Elizabeth with personalized "locket buttons set in gold," a gift she wore and treasured throughout her life.[14]

Household furniture was carved from the choicest woods: a walnut dining table and chairs, an imported mahogany card table and tea table, a similarly "fram'd sconce looking glass." To match the indoor opulence, exotic fruit trees such as magnum bonum (a kind of plum), nectarine, and apricot bloomed in the yard and garden.[15] The family employed no fewer than four vehicles—cart, wagon, chaise, and carriage. Eighteenth-century Philadelphia summers being no less steamy than they are today, the Drinkers enjoyed cooler breezes at their summer home in nearby Frankford or, for a short time in the 1790s, at the farm they named Clearfield, five or six miles from central Philadelphia. Judged by the standards of the eighteenth century, life must have been as comfortable for this family as the times would allow.

It was probably no accident that some of Elizabeth Drinker's furniture was mahogany, since her neighbor, Ephraim Haines at 100 Front Street, dealt in that imported luxury wood. Yet not all of the Drinkers' neighbors were merchants, and the absence of zoning regulations meant that many were tradespeople—and probably not of the best sort. Innocuous enough were the feather dealer, fringemaker, and barber, and the flavor of the neighborhood was undoubtedly sweetened by the presence of Christian Hahn, the chocolate maker (even if the chocolate grinding was done with horsepower). Favorable aromas must have wafted by from the large bake ovens of the Prusias and Franks as well, but one can only guess what kind of odor emanated from Gardner's soap house, since even Drinker admitted it was "a disagreeable surcumstance." Such were Elizabeth Drinker's neighbors, although one cannot in good faith call them friends. Indeed, by her own account, twenty years passed before she even noticed Mrs. Hahn, who lived three doors away.[16]

As a member of the Society of Friends, Drinker's outlook on life was shaped by Quaker philosophy, even if she rarely attended meeting. In April 1798 she noted that, except for one occasion, she had not been to morning meeting in Philadelphia for the previous five years, and by 1805 she no longer went to meeting at all. Yet her writings reveal that throughout her adult life she lived by the customs of the Society. Her conversations were punctuated by the *thee*s and *thou*s associated with Quaker speech, and it is even possible that Quaker egalitarianism determined the way in which the diary identifies people. Titles are conspicuous by their absence; men and women were referred to by both first and last names, or by initials. The only exception to this rule were her daughters, who even as adults appear as Sally, Nancy, and Molly, while sons William and Henry are more often than not WD and HSD.

As a believer in the peace testimony, talk of war made her "sick at heart," and she earnestly wished Philadelphians would cease production of frigates. She did not observe Christmas, preferred peace and quiet on July Fourth to celebration, and in general, eschewed parades—except when John Adams and his entourage passed her door, on which occasion she admitted she "should have been pleased to see a little more of it."[17]

The principles of the Society of Friends with regard to slavery affected both the attitude and actions of the Drinker family. Elizabeth and her sister had sold a young female slave, Jude, in 1756, when "there was nothing said against keeping or selling negros," but even at that time she felt regret that they "had sold the child to be a slave for life." Some years later Elizabeth's husband attempted to persuade a subsequent owner to free the young woman, and although HD was unsuccessful at that time, the owner did free Jude at his death.[18]

The sympathy of the family toward escaped slaves must have been well known, since runaways frequently found their way to the Drinkers' door. "A Negro man, named Peter from Virginia, in a tatterd trim called to ask for something to help him out of town—we had very little doubt of his being a runaway—I pittied him a young man." More than money was required when Alice Wright's slave sister, accompanied by her free husband and three of their four children, escaped from Virginia to Philadelphia. Not wishing to be legally compromised by their appearance at her own house, Alice, the Drinkers' sometime laundress, enlisted her employers' aid. Since their owner had "sent persons to hunt them up," Henry Drinker spirited the family away to what was cryptically referred to as "RKs in Jersey—At——n," an apparent reference to Reynold Keen at Atsion.[19]

Quaker values frequently competed with American customs; Elizabeth Drinker found "Friends Children going in companyes to public houses" to be "quite out of character," and even disapproved of them "eating . . . iced cream, or going to the ice'd cream house." The latter censure is somewhat surprising, since the ice cream house was potentially less pernicious than the library, where one could savor Paine, Rousseau, or even Rabelais (who, according to ED, wrote "obscene dirty matter"), but if Drinker found fault with her grandchildren's frequent sojourns to the library, she did not record it. She herself maintained that reading was not the most effective use of time, and she shared with her contemporaries a mild disapproval of novels (as opposed to nonfiction), but her voluminous reading list attests that her expressed attitude had little effect on her appetite for the written word.[20]

Henry and Elizabeth Drinker seem to have adhered more strictly to Quaker doctrine than did their children. HD would not even buy portraits, much less have one painted of himself, but neither HSD nor William suffered such scruples, and both sat for Henry Elouis when they were young men. Her children's small transgressions from Quaker rules appear to have embarrassed Drinker to the extent that she concealed their offenses in another language: "J. Bunting, Jacob, Sally and Nancy spent part of this evening Jouer aux cartes." Dominoes were apparently no more permissible than cards, and because two of her children engaged in such immoderate behavior, ED recorded the event as "Jouant aux Ivorys." Molly was even suspected of having gone to the theater, an infraction so heinous that Drinker could not even commit the entire word to paper: "Je craint elle a ete a la [T]——r."[21]

We know little of Elizabeth Drinker's early education or her appearance: she is silent about her childhood and physical qualities, and the diary does not begin until 1758, when she was twenty-three years old. Nevertheless, her writing style and extensive reading lists indicate a well-educated and well-read person (Oliver Goldsmith was among her favorite authors), while a reference to her "French Master," Peter Papin de Prefountain, and the scattered use of French phrases throughout the diary suggest she had some training in that language. The Quaker educator and abolitionist Anthony Benezet was another of her teachers. Her skills also included needlework, from which she derived great pleasure throughout her life; the lengthy list of items she completed, as well as the variety of stitches employed, indicates she was extremely accomplished in that art.[22]

Although the few personal features revealed in her diary are Drinker's weight (130 pounds in 1776) and hair color (very dark or black), her obituary relates that "in her youth she possessed uncommon personal beauty." Obituaries are notorious for their generosity, but it is still probable she was an attractive woman. With a diary written over the course of a half century as confirmation, there is also no reason to doubt her sweet disposition and gentle temper, which was said to be free of bigotry and "narrowness of feeling."[23] Elizabeth Drinker had biases, to be sure, and her liberality stopped short of support for a proposed temple for Deists, but her quill left evidence of a remarkably evenhanded person, respectful of differing opinions and free of backbiting and gossip.

Her own short list of habits and personal characteristics included an addiction to snuff, a tendency toward timidity, and the enjoyment of solitude, but even if she was reluctant to focus attention on her attributes, the diary indirectly discloses additional information. She cherished nature and took great interest in the biological makeup of creatures such as tree frogs, spiders, and snakes. She loved animals and was sensitive to their suffering. She appreciated order and precision: the sound of clocks striking together pleased her. She was conservative in the sense that she was "attached to old fashons and old things."[24] She possessed both wit and a sense of humor, and even if she tried to suppress them, both escape to the pages of the journal. She was not even above a practical joke. Yet her diary is a cautious document, clearly designed to avoid personal and intimate revelations.

Fortunately, however, not everyone contained his or her opinions or wrote as discreetly as Drinker. Another diarist, Ann Warder, left a judgmental journal in which she spared no one for whom she had little regard, and it is therefore safe to assume that she really was "pleased to discover a very sensible agreeable Woman" in Elizabeth Drinker. Indeed, Warder was quite taken with the entire Drinker family in 1787, asserting that Henry was "a fine Man" who was "blest in his Family which is three Daughters and two Sons." Even Mary Sandwith received a good rating: she was, according to Warder, "a [kind] creature."[25]

The recording of events in the form of a journal, especially in the Quaker community, was commonplace in the late eighteenth and early nineteenth centuries, and many of Elizabeth Drinker's contemporaries left similar, if briefer, documents.[26] The length and continuity of Drinker's diary make it unique, however, and even her obituary mentions its existence as a means of "recording in the evening, her reflections during the day." The eulogist knew that the diary spanned five decades: "nearly from the time of her marriage to the evening preceding her last illness."[27]

Although Elizabeth Drinker began her journal when she lived with the Warners, it was not until the end of 1799 that she fully explained her reasons for and philosophy of diary keeping:

> When I began this year, I intended the book for memorandams, nor is it any thing else . . . as what I write answers no other purpose than to help the memory—I have seen Diarys of different complections, some were amuse-ing, others instructive, and others repleat with what might better be totally let alone—my simple Diary comes under none of those descriptions—the first I never aim'd at, for the second I am not qualified, the 3d. may I ever avoid—'tho I have had oppertunities and incitements, some times, to say severe things, and perhaps with strict justice—yet . . . I was never prone to speak my mind, much less to write or record any thing that might in a future day give pain to any one. . . . [H]ow wrong is it to put on record any thing to wound the feelings of innocent persons, to gratify present resent-ments.

Six weeks later she added, "I seldom make a memorandum of my employments: 'tho generally busyed."[28]

If Elizabeth Drinker intended the diary primarily, as she said, for her "own perusal and recollection," she also knew that at some time or other various people might scan its pages. Thus in 1790 she noted that "this book was intended for memorandans of what occur'd during my Sons absence, for his information." In general, however, she foresaw a limited audience: "as I dont lay out for any one but some of my Children to read my silly writings, am the more free to mention bowels and obstructions, than I otherwise would do."[29] Yet in addition to its use as a record of events for people who had no telephones and who were often separated by long absences, diary reading, as opposed to diary writing, appears to have been a way of socializing. It was a source of evening entertainment among Friends ("Betsy read to Hannah, Nelly, Sister, and self,—Sammy Sansoms Journal") or a friendly gesture among contempo-raries ("Hannah Callender came this morning, dinn'd with us, was so kind as to leave her diary with sister").[30]

The possibility of a wider readership may also explain the nature of the Drinker diary, as well as the personality of its author. The diary is almost devoid of emotional language, even when the most tragic circumstances were recorded. This was deliberate on Drinker's part: "I cant describe how I have felt this day, indeed it is what I do not at any time undertake to do." The most affecting exception to this rule occurred after cancer claimed her daughter Sally at age forty-five, and a grief-stricken mother shared her sorrow with her journal. Elizabeth Drinker survived her daughter by only two months, and the Arch Street Meeting Burial Book recorded that her own death on November 24, 1807, was the result of "lethergy."[31]

The lapse in reserve on the occasion of her daughter's death was exceptional, however, and personal opinions, expressions of piety, potentially damaging remarks, or sensitive information is rarely found in the pages of ED's journal. She maligned no one who might be considered her social equal or better—except Pope Sixtus V, long dead, and Tom Paine, who, from her standpoint, richly deserved it. Servants and other employees might be referred to as foolish blockheads, but they, presumably, did not fall into the category of people whose feelings mattered. Ever so infrequently a mildly critical comment about someone near and dear slipped out—such as an allusion to her daughter Sally's garrulous nature—but a hasty retreat to the inkwell quickly expunged it from the record. For the most part, events, fears, disappointments, pleasures, and satisfactions were committed to paper in a noncommital tone, and other topics were either hinted at or ambiguously worded: "HSD and ED held a correspondence with pen and ink by the fire-side on a subject of great importance." Some information was disguised in schoolgirl French (e.g., "mallhereux fois"), although it is not clear from whom she was attempting to conceal the information thus cloaked.[32]

This is not to say that the diary lacks eloquence, but that where it exists, it was probably unintended. During the yellow fever epidemic of 1802, the Drinkers, and others who could afford it, sought refuge from the disease in the countryside. Reflecting on her empty house in Philadelphia, she noted that the "2 Clocks which were wound up when we left home, every hour give the time to the insects & mice if any there be." And on the occasion of her sixty-ninth birthday in 1804: "I have passed another mile stone this morning the miles seem to shorten as we come near our journeys end." Finally—and possibly prophetically—as the moon set on a November evening shortly before her death: "the lamp going out, so that we were soon in darkness."[33]

The diary is not without humor either. After mentioning a news article that referred to a recently discovered mammoth as the ninth wonder of the world, Drinker added: "I dont recollect hearing of the Eighth wonder, was it Genl. Washington, or Tom Paine." Indeed, we can almost imagine her smiling to herself as she noted that the book, *Girl of the Mountains*, was "a high story."[34]

Elizabeth Drinker occasionally resorted to poetry to express her feelings. Her rhymes always concerned topics of a serious nature: her son's marriage, the passage and use of time, friendship, and on one occasion, her diary:

I stay much at home, and my business I mind,
Take note of the weather, and how blows the wind,
The changes of Seasons, The Sun, Moon and Stars,
The setting of Venus, and riseing of Mars.
Birds, Beasts and Insects, and more I cold mention,
That pleases my leisure, and draws my attention.
But respecting my neighbours, their egress, and Regress,
Their coaches and Horses, their dress and their Address,
What matches are making, whos plain, or whos gay,

I leave to their parents, or Guardians to Say:
For most of those things, are out of my *Way*.
But to those, where my love and my duty doth bind
More than most other Subjects, engages my Mind.[35]

ED saw her journal as a record of events, not a repository for gossip or a treatise on behavior. Her personal guidelines permitted strong opinions about her family and friends, as long as her pen did not immortalize those judgments. Since not all diaries followed the pattern that Drinker laid out for herself, one might conclude that she was an exceptionally private person, unwilling to share her innermost feelings, and one who was sensitive to the feelings of others. By her own appraisal, her accounts were "Trifling" in order to preserve their innocence:

Could I write instead of Trifles;
That which most employs my mind;
All thats here would be ommitted,
Nor should I mark, how blew the wind?[36]

If ED's inclination toward revelation was subverted by her better judgment, and if her purpose in keeping a journal was to prod her memory at some future date, how selectively did she record events? In short, what did Drinker choose to remember? In addition to regular reports on the weather, natural phenomena, and her daily stream of visitors, the inclusion or exclusion of other incidents may have been unconsciously influenced by the social and intellectual forces that shaped her thought processes. Late eighteenth-century theorists publicized the lofty relationship between female virtue and Republican Motherhood, while novelists portrayed scenarios where virtue was constantly under assault. Affected by both literary strains, Drinker may have found the fictional world containing seduction, maternal death, stillborn infants, abandoned orphans, wayward husbands, poor health, and melancholy accidents particularly relevant because this was precisely what was happening in many households in Philadelphia—including privileged ones such as her own.[37]

In this context it is neither surprising that the diary relates such events, nor striking that ED was more likely to omit mention of her household "employments" as she aged. Although she continued to sew, knit, iron, and preserve foods, these chores no longer impinged on her consciousness as an important component of her day. It is also consistent with this interpretation that Drinker's entries are neither analytic nor speculative. And while she constantly tried to reconcile the life she lived with the life she aspired to live, she never passed judgment on herself, but merely expressed hope in her ability to conform to God's will.

In some cases Drinker's omissions are as revealing as her entries, although her forebearance was meant to illustrate her self-declared sensitivity to the feelings of others. In later years her sister Mary is noticeably absent from the journal, with only an occasional criticism acting as confirmation that the youthful affection between the sisters had evaporated over time: "Sister spent this day up stairs, her cough not left her, nor is it likely it will sudenly, the way she manages herself."[38] Similarly, the frequency with which ED noted her daughter Sally's cheerful disposition only underscores the dearth of such remarks about Nancy.

If, by her silence, Elizabeth Drinker sought to conceal intelligence, did she also distort information or present it with less than scrupulous accuracy? The question is more difficult to answer than one might suppose, since a personal diary, by its very nature, is extremely subjective. The mind is programmed to interpret events; the hand merely records what the mind perceives as reality. The path from accuracy to distortion is short, and often traveled inadvertently by those with the best intentions. Would she have deliberately engaged in deception? The answer to that query is a resounding no, given her character as it emerges throughout the diary, and because there is simply no evidence to support such a charge. Neither are there any contradictory entries in the journal, which would lend credence to such suspicion. One might even argue, conversely, that the precision with which she attempted to write reflects a desire to relay her impressions as accurately as possible. In describing a servant, she replaced the expression "good for little" with "good for nothing." And in other entries "most of" was substituted for "all," and "engraved" for "drawn." In June 1805 "several loud, but not very loud claps [of thunder] occur'd." Days and nights were cool, cold, or very cold. Linguistic precision also required conscientious attention to gender: Lydia Hollandshead was a "workwoman."[39]

Nonetheless, Drinker herself may have been unaware of certain exaggerations or stretches of truth. She considered herself a sickly person, and indeed, she seemed assailed with more than her share of eighteenth-century maladies. Yet against what standard does one measure her constant malaise? Did she really suffer a greater degree of poor health than her contemporaries, or did poor health justify activities that she felt were mildly inappropriate to her station? Illness, for example, excused solitude and reading, and Drinker admitted that she enjoyed both, even if her pleasure was tempered by guilt. Moreover, by Elizabeth's standards, her sister Mary consistently enjoyed better health. Thus if Elizabeth were constantly indisposed (or thought herself to be, or even simply indicated such) and Mary were quite well, Elizabeth could justify an increase in Mary's domestic responsibilities, leaving herself free to pursue her much-preferred interests.

Or was her health a function of boredom? After returning to a bustling Philadelphia at the end of a sickly summer at Clearfield in 1794, her ailments were mitigated, and as she assumed a more cheerful disposition her physical mobility increased. Were these scenarios played out subliminally in the diary? Were psychosomatic forces at play? It is impossible to say, yet Elizabeth's own admission leaves no doubt of the end result: "as my Sister chooses looking after the family, I have the more leisure to amuse myself in reading and doing such work as I like best."[40]

From the perspective of the twentieth century, there is little, despite Drinker's protestations to the contrary, that is trifling about the diary. Its length alone is daunting—forty-nine years of entries, during which time both her children and her nation were born and matured into adults. (She worried about both.) There is complete silence for only two years (1787–88), and if, as Henry D. Biddle claimed in 1889, these volumes once existed, they are no longer to be found. Fully three-quarters of the journal was written between 1793 and 1807 and is thus the product of her mature years.

Although her early entries were terse and irregular, by the Revolution Drinker usually added at least a paragraph to her journal daily. She might compile a series of sentences at various times as the day advanced (and record events as they unfolded), or she might wait until late in the evening to summarize the entire day. Sometimes, when an event turned into a crisis and claimed an excessive amount of time (as it did during the birth of a grandchild), she would bring the diary up to date several days later, but would label each day's occurrences separately as if she had recorded them as they took place.[41]

Elizabeth Drinker's diary is rich in history in its most inclusive sense—the history of how people lived and what they did—as it appeared to a contemporary woman. The importance of this extensive resource must be emphasized today: when Biddle published a one-volume abridged edition of the journal in 1889, his definition of history precluded the selection of entries that alluded to "strictly private matters" and, in his opinion, took up "too much space," and thus overshadowed more significant public events such as the Revolution and the yellow fever epidemics.[42] Since the publication of the Biddle edition the distinction between public and private has become increasingly blurred. But even if the definition of both words had remained inelastic, a new concern with what Biddle perceived to be strictly private matters (such as family history), as well as the recognition that women, minorities, and the nonelite are legitimate subjects of historical interest, justifies the publication of the unabridged diary.

At the same time, Drinker did not ignore topics of traditional historical importance. She recorded revolutionary events on a daily basis and in great detail during those tumultuous years. And because she was a member of the Society of Friends, the journal contains a particularly fine account of the activities and tribulations of that group during difficult times. Her diary details the urbanization of Philadelphia over five decades and contains an extraordinarily complete account of the recurring yellow fever epidemics that plagued Philadelphia in the 1790s. Indeed, since Drinker, as a woman, was a primary caregiver, the diary is a singularly complete source for the history of drugs and the professionalization of medicine in eighteenth-century America.

As a reflection of life in the pluralistic middle colonies, Drinker's journal is particularly relevant for scholars who are concerned with the ability of twentieth-century Americans to cope with a multi-ethnic, multi-religious society. Michael Zuckerman argues rather persuasively that since our fate ultimately depends on our response to such diversity, the experience of cities like Philadelphia offers the best historical evidence of the capacity of Americans to deal with heterogeneity.[43]

Although in many ways the journal confirms what we already know about eighteenth-century behavioral patterns, it offers the opportunity to reconsider or enhance our understanding in at least four different historical areas. First, Elizabeth Drinker's record suggests the need for alternative or modified interpretations of topics that historians have plumbed in depth. Second, it provides a more detailed look at the multifaceted and intricate relationships among people: family, servants, neighbors, and community. Third, it fosters a revision of standard and tenaciously held views about women in the world of eighteenth-century Philadelphia and perhaps beyond. And fourth, it opens up avenues of historical inquiry.

The American Revolution, for example, is a subject that historians have seemingly investigated from every conceivable angle. Yet from the perspective of a closet loyalist whose political options were limited even if her opinions were not, the illegal wartime searches and seizures, as well as the excessive number of arrests, executions, and reprisals by rebel supporters, were disconcerting, at the very least.[44]

As a British partisan, Drinker is vulnerable to the accusation that she weighted her words in favor of the English. Nevertheless, her criticism extended to both rebels and royalists, and there is little reason to suppose that her entries were designed to shield the British from censure. According to the journal, both sides committed depredations in their effort to win the war, although it seems to have been the Americans whose revolutionary principles justified quasi-legal means and an excessive use of force to defend liberty.

For two months after the British occupied the city in late September 1777, Philadelphians "experienced great quiate" (despite numerous arrests), but between November 1777 and the British evacuation in June 1778, the English burnt houses, "plunder'd and ill used" the townspeople, and committed theft on a large scale. In December, ED noted that "we daily hear of enormitys of one kind or other, being committed by those from whome, we ought to find protection."[45] Thus the British, according to Drinker, were not without faults.

Yet even before the British occupation it appears that the Americans were determined to use more radical means to achieve their goals. Quakers were sorely tested as they steadfastly refused to take loyalty tests. They were jailed for reading testimony at meeting and arrested on other spurious charges.[46] When Philadelphia came under American control once again in the late spring of 1778, swift and certain reprisals became commonplace. It was evident that the rebel government would brook no dissent as people were arrested "for writeing something they find fault with." In March 1779 Samuel Fisher was detained on the basis of the contents of a letter. A jury twice cleared him of treason, but after being ordered to reconsider a third time, the frustrated jurors returned a verdict of guilty, and Fisher served two years in prison. ED's assessment: "fine Liberty." In terms of gender, Drinker's appraisal was consistent with her socially prescribed role as guardian of public virtue. In that guise, Drinker saw a discrepancy between a liberty that was theoretically inseparable from a just social order and the liberty that was played out daily in Philadelphia. The latter, Drinker implied by her statement, was not a virtuous liberty.[47]

On May 25, 1779, an extralegal public meeting created a committee empowered to take measures against anyone found acting inimical to the interests and independence of the United States. As a result, the following week saw as many as two dozen persons imprisoned for vaguely defined crimes, including Tommy Redman, who was seized "for laughing, as the regulators went by." The arrests continued into 1780 and 1781, as Quaker schoolmasters defied the ban on teaching and merchants refused to omit New York from their ports of call.[48]

Moreover, a concern (bordering on obsession) over the existence of British goods in the city led to a dramatic number of searches and seizures, only some of which were legally sanctioned. In these circumstances the Drinker home was mistakenly rummaged, leading ED to conclude, " 'tis a bad Government, under which we are liable to have our Houses seachd and every thing laid open to ignorant fellows prehaps thieves."[49]

Whereas even in wartime the British showed little enthusiasm for public executions (ED reported only one during the occupation), the Americans had no qualms about the use of capital punishment to set examples and maintain control. Drinker first recorded such an incident on March 8, 1777, when an American soldier was shot on the commons in "a City heretofore clear of such Business."[50] In the same month "a Young Man of the Name of Molsworth was hang'd on the Commons by order of our present ruling Gentr'y"—a sarcastic aside both rare and telling.[51]

After the British evacuation, the American government continued its policy of public executions, and dispatched six men between mid-August and early December 1778. The first was George Spangler, whose unfortunate end resulted from "some assistance he had given to the British army." Two weeks later two deserters were shot on board a ship in the harbor, but with two others reprieved at the same time, it appears that the death penalty was more arbitrary than automatic. John Roberts and Abraham Carlisle were hanged on November 4 for assisting the British during the occupation, and on December 5, ED recorded that "Abijah Wright was executed this forenoon on the commons, for I know not what." Wright had been convicted of burglary and intended murder, but Samuel Rowland Fisher later recorded in his journal that, in fact, Wright had been hanged for acting as a guide to the British army during the occupation.[52] Given this behavior, it is reasonable to infer that the rights to life, liberty, and the pursuit of happiness were not quite as universal, even among white adult males, as historians have made them out to be, and the journal suggests that a more balanced appraisal of "patriot" means and ends might be appropriate.

Diary entries also suggest that historians should reconsider the extent of eighteenth-century criminal activity. A reliance on newspaper reports and court records has led scholars to conclude that the crime rate of early America was not disproportionate to the general rise in population. Yet, although there is little reason to doubt the disparity between urban and rural crime rates, diary commentary indicates that the magnitude of urban crime—if Philadelphia was typical—was vastly underreported. "[H]ow many sad occurances we hear off, of murder, Roberies, that are not published," noted ED in 1806, and the following winter she described in some detail a murder of which there had been "no account" in the papers. Moreover, in preparation for a lengthy summer stay in Frankford, the Skyrin family distributed their valuables, including their furniture, among various relatives who remained in town—the unspoken testimony of a community where burglaries were, perhaps, more frequent than extant statistics indicate.[53]

It might also be timely to review the history of medicine with an eye toward the use of various drugs. Some of the remedies employed by the Drinkers in their never-ending confrontation with disease were concocted at home from a variety of plants and liquids; others were purchased at the apothecary shop. However obtained, these preparations were not arbitrarily dispensed. Each was prescribed in response to a particular disease and some, at least, appear to have been moderately effective. Carolina pink root did combat intestinal worms, and the bark did reduce fever. Moreover, the use of leeches, once thought to be no more than a quaint colonial custom, has proved to be valuable in modern microsurgery, and it is entirely possible that bloodletting itself will prove to have benefits of which we are currently unaware.

As part of the new social history, scholars have focused attention on the great variety and intricate nature of personal associations. Even though Elizabeth Drinker was only one person, and her diary a record of only one family, her account suggests that familial relationships were more complex than have generally been conceived. This was a household in which grandchildren resided with their grandparents for extended periods of time—sometimes for as long as six months.[54] What this meant in terms of the parent-child bond or the relationship between grandparents and grandchildren is yet to be determined, but the fact that Abigail Adams records such lengthy stays in her own home suggests that this arrangement was not unusual. Moreover, if today's parents complain that grandparents spoil their grandchildren, the opposite complaint may have been true in the eighteenth century, or at least in the Drinker household. As one of four children, nine-year-old Eliza Downing "had more of her own way at home," and although she was happy at her grandparents' house, it was "a kind of weaning," since she was under the direct supervision of her grandparents and subject to somewhat more discipline than she was used to.[55]

Although we have long known that unmarried women often resided with married sisters or brothers, the dynamics of these relationships have thus far escaped analysis. In this particular case, Elizabeth showed little warmth toward her sister and, at the end of ED's life, even less interest in her well-being. Nevertheless, through the diary it becomes clear that Mary Sandwith was an integral member of the Drinker household who had specific and well-defined roles to play. It is also evident from family papers that Mary was not a dependent: she was a wealthy woman in her own right who had frequent business dealings with her brother-in-law, Henry, and could have established her own household if she so chose. Though she acted as Elizabeth's surrogate hostess only infrequently, she far more often carried out duties as a household manager who went "maid hunting" and oversaw the cleaning and preparation of summer and winter homes in anticipation of the family's semiannual changes of residence. It was Mary, not Elizabeth, who went to the newly purchased farm with Henry, where she "examin'd and approv'd it," and when Henry and Elizabeth's daughter Molly miscarried on a chilly April night at two in the morning, it was Aunt Mary who attended her niece. Only once did "Sister" balk: when Elizabeth proposed a venture to Lancaster in 1778 to urge the release of her incarcerated husband, Mary at first refused to take responsibility for the children who remained behind.[56] These subtle and intricate connections suggest that the definition of a nuclear family must be evaluated further.

Elizabeth Drinker's diary allows a closer look at the father-child bond, which has received far less scrutiny than has the mother-child relationship, possibly because of a dearth of evidence. Even if the Drinker family is only one example, from which it would be unsafe to generalize, it is interesting nonetheless to watch this father as he takes his children swimming, for cart rides, or on fishing expeditions, with little regard to the sex of the child. Grandfather Drinker took his grandchildren sleighing between business calls. These midweek excursions were made possible in part because of the eighteenth-century attitude toward time, and in part because home and place of business (or production) were frequently one and the same. Fathers who were not subservient to clock or sundial could plan midday activities with their children or even spontaneously embark upon such small adventures as buying a new hat.[57]

And even if mothers were the primary caregivers in times of sickness, it was not unknown for a father to nurse an ill child. More than once ED refers to the role her son HSD played in attending his own children. Fathers were not precluded from emergency care in case of sudden accidents, and when son-in-law John Skyrin mistakenly applied brandy and brown paper to his daughter's head injury (instead of vinegar and brown paper, then a common remedy), his substitution did no harm—and actually was a better disinfectant. Fathers took children to the dentist or occasionally extracted solidly implanted teeth themselves. In either case, their greater physical strength might have been needed to hold the child down for the painful operation or to wrestle with a reluctant tooth. Jacob Downing (Sally's husband) "pulled out two sound large eye teeth from his daughter Eliza. . . . It must have been a great undertaking."[58]

Paternal concern crossed class lines, and it was as common for fathers to indenture their children as it was for mothers to do the same. "Saml. Walker called with his little daughter whom he wanted to bind out"; "Thomas Reynolds brought his little daughter Rosetta, and left her here on tryal." Once indentured, a child's father was as likely to pay visits as the mother. In more affluent families, fathers as well as mothers visited children at boarding school.[59]

Although Drinker was by any standards a member of the elite or "better sort," her diary is also a rich source of information about less affluent Philadelphians, their relationship to the Drinkers, and with each other. Elizabeth seems to have been responsible for the servants in her home, and although her management of them cannot be translated into a generalization for all Philadelphians, certain common customs (such as wages and duties) may be extracted nonetheless. More important, we are permitted a view of the mistress-servant relationship from the perspective of a woman who considered servants family, and for whom she attempted to make decisions and impose standards of behavior—class differences notwithstanding.

The diary makes abundantly clear that good servants were indeed "a valuable acquisition" not only because of the daily chores they performed but because they were the information network of the eighteenth-century city. Coach and wagon drivers brought up-to-date news of the health of family members who lived at a distance, while those who shopped at the local markets also returned with fresh gossip. The relationship between the Drinkers and former servants suggests that even when they no longer worked for the Drinkers, some connection with that household remained: in time of stress they could seek—and obtain—help from their former master or mistress.[60]

While the servants were in the Drinkers' employ, however, there was a delicate power balance in the mistress-servant relationship. If the scales favored the mistress because of her ability to suspend a wage-earning worker ("I dismist AW this evening for some time till it suits better to attend to her work"), circumstances benefited the servant at other times. Commenting on the constant friction between John and Nancy Skyrin, Drinker noted that "where heads of families are unsteady, servants take the advantage." And even if Elizabeth's permission was required for leisure time to visit one's family, she had no control over social calls *by* her servants' parents, sisters, or brothers. Nor, if an urgent message arrived, could she deny time off, despite her suspicions of being manipulated:

> Our Rose's Sister came to say, that their little Brother Tommy is dyeing, he wanted to see Rose very much. . . . I let her go, tho' I did not altogether credit the account. If crying was a mark of the truth, she cryed and so did Rose. . . . Rose came home after night, her little Brother is better.[61]

In their capacity as information gatherers and disseminators, servants also held a potential weapon against their employers. Elizabeth Drinker's inordinate concern with the health of her family made her vulnerable to rumor of illness, and word of mouth collected and delivered by household help could be innocently or deliberately distorted to produce stress in a mistress who innocently or deliberately provoked a servant. "What a common error, is false reports! more's the pity."[62]

Despite what may have been seen as excessive control over their personal lives, live-in servants probably enjoyed a better standard of living than day workers, whose independence was costly in terms of food and rent, and for whom the job market was unstable and upward mobility limited. Although the use of the word *family* with regard to live-in servants exaggerates the closeness of the relationship between mistress and servants, residential help had a roof over their heads, enough to eat, and sometimes wages left over for extras: "S Dawson . . . seems to have a great call for money—to purchase finery, she has laid out £27.6—since she has been free, which is not quite 17 months." Household servants might also benefit from the affluence of their employers, as when the kitchen family, "Betsy, Judah, Rosee and Peter took a ride . . . in the Sleigh" one winter night, or when "4 servants went to see the whale, MS. gave them a Dollar for that purpose."[63]

If the diary allows us to evaluate the relationship between mistress and servant, it also permits a glimpse, at least, at the way in which servants (and former servants) related to each other. "S Brant took tea with our Sally Dawson," and "Rhoads Pompey called to see Peter," recorded Drinker in much the same way that she noted a visit from one of her own contemporaries. "SD. has had a party in the Kitchen this evening—Tea, pound Cake, water mellon, &c—3 young men and 3 girls—it wont do often," she wrote, leaving one to speculate whether it was the mixed company, festivities, or emulation of upper-class customs that sparked her disapproval. Out of sight of the families with whom they lived, "black Baux's and Misses" enjoyed New Year's parties, weddings, and dances to mark happy occasions, and attended each other's funerals in time of sorrow. They carried on clandestine relationships, which became more or less public when one Lothario was found hiding in a privy and the lover of another became pregnant.[64]

Racial differences occasionally overwhelmed class similarities among servants:

> Our maid—Nancy Stewart left us this morning before any of the family were up, she has been in ill humour for some time past, with Peter, Judia and Rose, she would not eat with Negroes which we did not desire her to do—Peter was backward in waiting on her.

The fact that Drinker did not force or even "desire" the integration of her household servants is telling, since it is suggestive of her own attitude toward race, which was quite independent of her position on slavery or, for that matter, on class. According to Drinker, Negros were "usefull" when they behaved well. She deprecatingly referred to servants as "black gentry" or "black quality." Her condescending comments about Absolem Gibbs, who was "a decent sensiable Negro man," and about Jery, who appeared to be "a good natured Negro man," or Dublin Black, "a good-looking Negro man," imply that in her mind, many other blacks did not possess such desirable traits. Her patronizing remarks about "a black man of consequence" or the skills of Samuel Wilson, a black doctor, only emphasize the way race tempered her evaluation of a person's attributes and credentials.[65]

But if color affected Drinker's outlook on people, so did class. That there was a "lower class of people" was indisputable; that they possessed certain inalienable characteristics was just as evident. Among other qualities, the lesser sort "were prone to lieing," they hung together "in a string, as it suits their purpose," and they could be found "shewing themselves" before strangers.

The notion that there were recognizable characteristics separating the Drinkers from people of color as well as from their social inferiors may have obviated the need for geographical segregation until the late eighteenth century in Philadelphia. The "Malato man" who rented a room from the owner of the house next door posed no threat to the Drinkers, nor did the four poverty-stricken families who shared a small four-room house in their alley.[66] Mere proximity could not displace the distinctions that determined social hierarchy, nor was there any chance that the Drinker family's status might be jeopardized by their neighbors. It is possible, therefore, that as class distinctions based on these spurious assumptions were dismissed over time, economic (and thus geographic) segregation became one of the means by which a class structure could be perpetuated.

The constant flow of identified visitors in and out of the Drinker home indicates that neighbors were not necessarily friends or Friends, and that her choice of companions most frequently included people of her class and religion. Both men and women paid calls, and it was customary for a male acquaintance to dine or take tea with Elizabeth in Henry's absence. Clues of this nature, which in a sense are a test of separate spheres, allow a more accurate analysis of gender relations, as does the fact that it was not unusual to find men in the kitchen, cooking over a hot stove.[67]

Finally, with regard to the interpersonal relationships so richly detailed on every page, the diary entries suggest a community where people could be counted on to help each other during emergencies such as fires, but where, on other occasions, the instinct for survival overcame neighborliness. During the yellow fever epidemic of 1793, for example, whole families died in their beds unattended because caregivers feared the spread of the disease.[68]

The diary entries also indicate a need to revise commonly held assumptions about women in eighteenth-century America. Precisely because this is a journal written by a woman about herself and other women, the layers of commentary and interpretation superimposed by male contemporaries and later historians are removed, and what remains is Elizabeth Drinker's world as seen by Elizabeth Drinker. Would that William Byrd's wife, Lucy, and Cotton Mather's consort, Lydia, had left such diaries.

Yet even a diary written by a woman is not automatically untainted by conventional notions about women, and Drinker herself must take responsibility for perpetuating the very gender-based stereotypes that the reality of her life so unequivocally contradicts. Time and again she acknowledges female timidity:

"we are easily frighted I think." And in a rare moment of self-reflection in 1794 she admitted that she perceived of herself as "a compleat Coward," a failing that had always been "a great inconvenience and disappointment" to her. Yet her self-proclaimed cowardice stemmed from a trauma suffered during a riding accident, and nothing more than a healthy fear of loud thunderstorms and strange noises late at night sent her scurrying for company.[69] In contrast, men dusted themselves off and remounted horses, men laughed at natural phenomena, and men investigated unusual sounds in the night.

The diary as a whole attests to the courageous roles women played in eighteenth-century America, ED's protestations notwithstanding. Drinker acted bravely when she pressed the Supreme Executive Council of Pennsylvania for the release of her imprisoned husband. In his absence, and despite widespread robbery and looting during the occupation of 1777–78, Drinker rebuffed attempts to quarter a soldier in her home, preferring to fend for herself rather than take comfort in the presence of a British officer.[70] Similarly, attendance at deliveries in the middle of the night at remote locations required considerably more fortitude than she would have admitted. She never suspected that it took inner strength to decide which medication best suited her daughter Nancy's life-threatening bout with yellow fever. Valor, by eighteenth-century dictum, was something men possessed.

A careful reading of the diary also indicates a need to reassess the entire subject of female political sensitivity and participation in the eighteenth century. Although she saw herself lacking in political perspicacity, Elizabeth Drinker and her female contemporaries were in fact keenly aware of political events and trends on both theoretical and practical levels. Indeed, after reading a biography of Pope Sixtus V, Drinker even translated her reaction to his machinations into a general political philosophy that applied to her worlds as an American and as a woman: "The misuse, or abuse of power, does much mischief in Church or state, in public or private, in republicks or families, and is I think, the greatest calamity that the world labours under." Moreover, no one who referred to "the People" as "the mobility" was politically naive.[71]

Yet even if Drinker was politically astute with regard to the abstract concept of power in sixteenth-century Rome, her diary leaves much unrecorded about power struggles closer to home. In some ways this omission is surprising, given the denominational infighting among eighteenth-century Philadelphians, the volatility of which could hardly have escaped her attention. The Quakers were at odds among themselves at the time, and the Society would eventually be wrenched by schism, but except for casual references to Hannah Barnard, Elias Hicks, and Job Scott, the ongoing tensions receive no space.

Similarly, Drinker could not have been oblivious to the erosion of Quaker hegemony in the Pennsylvania Assembly after midcentury, as Friends resigned from that august body in protest against Pennsylvania's militancy. Their commitment to principle was costly in terms of power, if not influence, yet if Elizabeth Drinker contemplated these problems, she did not commit her thoughts to paper. In terms of her own political persuasion, one would call her a lukewarm Federalist who in 1801 saw more reasons "to lament than rejoice" in independence.[72]

Nevertheless, if politics has any meaning as the art of influencing decisions, surely Elizabeth Drinker and her friends were artful and self-assured practitioners. In March 1778 Molly Pleasants drew up a petition to Congress to plead for the release of those husbands who were jailed in Virginia. "[Her] Mammy . . . added somthing to it," and although Friend Nicholas Waln designed a similar paper to be presented instead, his was "not approv'd." At the same time, in order to assuage what may have been ruffled feelings, Waln was permitted to read the agreed-upon address to an assemblage of Quaker women, who thereafter signed the document. Israel Morris "thought it necessary" to appear as their consort before Congress. The women thought otherwise. So much for deference, at least as it related to gender and politics.[73]

The need to revise perceptions about the place of women in the economy, as well as their role as primary caregivers, also becomes clear in the course of reading the diary. Women whitewashed houses and delivered milk by truck instead of, or in addition to, attending to their domestic duties. Even affluent women were productively employed despite the presence of servants in the household. If Elizabeth Drinker indulged in reading, it was in addition to knitting, sewing, cutting shirts, and making children's shoes. Well into her sixties, she was frequently "very busy all day," as were her daughters. "Nancy Skyrin here forenoon clear-starching caps for me." Sally pounded flax seed while ED sifted it, thus making "fine flour of it." Upper-class women often received compensation for their work: "MS went towards evening to pay Hannah Drinker for quilting 2 bed quilts."[74] In terms of health care, they chose and administered drugs in time of illness—an alarmingly frequent occurrence—and made decisions that had life-and-death implications. Since a plethora of ailments claimed victory over even the sturdiest of Philadelphians, women spent a considerable amount of time caring for the sick.

Taken out of context, ED's own words lend credence to the argument of some historians that women knew little of their husbands' financial affairs. As she put it, "I am not acquainted with the extent of my husbands great variety of engagements."[75] This may have been partially true, because Henry's interests were extensive and varied. At the same time, her comment is misleading, because one journal entry after another proves she was well informed of his dealings.

Business associates constantly called at the Drinker home and stayed for dinner or tea. And even if financial issues were not generally discussed in Elizabeth's presence, her entries indicate that few matters escaped her attention: "BW. was mistaken in his account of the fire at Atsion, it was the Furnice, not the Forge that was burnt, all the wood work, and the Bellows &c—the loss, HD. thinks, including repairs and loss of time, will amount to, one thousand pounds and more money." The details of real estate transactions were known and recorded in the diary: "HD agree'd this evening, with Daniel King for his plantation on the old York road for which he is to pay him £3146."[76] Furthermore, the frequency with which ED "acknowledged a deed" is confirmation of her awareness of HD's property transfers. This is not to say that all women were as privy to their spouses' business dealings as Elizabeth Drinker, but it is also not likely that they were as ignorant as they have been imputed to be.

The Drinker diary also permits exploration of new areas of historical interest. Notwithstanding David Flaherty's pioneering study, the whole concept of personal privacy has not been accorded the attention it deserves, once again because of a paucity of evidence. A moderately serious illness at home, for example, turns out to be a social phenomenon given the cooperative efforts of doctors, nurses, family caretakers, servants, messengers, apothecaries, and solicitous friends. Ailments of an intimate nature stood no chance of remaining a private concern, and all of Philadelphia must have been aware of HD's prostate problem in 1802, judging by the number of people who offered remedies.[77]

Moreover, the nature of communication itself in the eighteenth century raises provocative questions. Members of the Drinker family were in constant touch with each other via their servants, leaving one to wonder if, in the absence of household help, the less affluent only infrequently corresponded with or relayed messages to kinfolk—and if so, whether intrafamilial ties were comparatively weaker as a result. Yet Philadelphia was a compact city, and the fact that two prospective servants arrived to offer their services to the Drinkers only hours after the departure of Nancy Stewart implies that information traveled quickly through word of mouth.[78]

Elizabeth Drinker's immediate concern on any given day was the status of her family's health. Constant inquiries and reports containing the most intimate details fill the journal pages, and it is curious that family members, separated (except for HSD) by no more than a dozen blocks in any direction, felt impelled to inquire about (and in Drinker's case, record) the progression of each headache, toothache, sore throat, and cough. From a twentieth-century perspective, these short-term afflictions are presumably, of no consequence, but in the eighteenth century they could portend a life-threatening situation. It is possible, therefore, that although people hoped for the best, they prepared for the worst, and by keeping an up-to-the-minute health watch, forestalled the shock of an unexpected death. Thus, a side effect of the telegraph and telephone may be psychological: the speed of modern communications allays uncertainty and reduces the anxiety it causes.

Furthermore, even at a distance ED dispensed medical advice to her adult children, with the result that their well-being depended on speedy communication between households. As a by-product of this relationship, Drinker maintained a considerable amount of influence over her children long after they left the parental household. And if the role of long-distance matriarch suited Drinker, it would explain why she thought it so "extrodinary" that her daughter Molly eschewed her advice in favor of recommendations from her mother-in-law when she experienced complications during a pregnancy. Even worse (from Drinker's standpoint), Molly followed her mother-in-law's advice.[79] Communication, health, and the mother-daughter bond were inseparably intertwined.

Historians have noted in passing that eighteenth-century spatial considerations precluded a precise commitment to one's own "space," and to spatial boundaries respected by others. Yet the extent of the diary permits a fuller exploration of the peripatetic character of the eighteenth-century family than has been possible in the past. In Henry's absence, or in times of sickness, it was not unusual for Elizabeth to share a room with William, Sally, Nancy, or a nurse. Females might be bedfellows, males usually occupied a separate bed—a trundle, perhaps—and servants were frequently relegated to the floor. Despite occasional references to "our room" or "Billy's room," little sense of possessiveness of surroundings emerges from the pages. Elizabeth slept in HSD's bed in Billy's room, and HSD slept in his parents' room. Sister might lodge in the nursery, while ED and HD moved for a night to the front southeast chamber.[80] Unrelated families, traveling together, frequently shared both room and bed at the local inn while en route to their destination.

Rooms themselves were abandoned with the changing seasons, as family and furniture moved to southerly parlors in the winter and northerly ones in the summer. If there was great stability with regard to certain aspects of life in eighteenth-century Philadelphia, there was less permanence in others. Moreover, if life itself was cut short with sudden and disturbing frequency, one could, perhaps, more easily accept the transitory nature of one's temporal surroundings.

The rhythms of life and death are played out through the entire diary, leaving the clear impression that if new life was not always greeted with joy by parents (of any class), death almost certainly precipitated grieving. The gaps in Drinker's record when she lost a child (and it was too painful to write of trifles), and the acknowledgment year after year of the anniversary of the death of both parents, are eloquent testimony that the constant companionship of death did not make the loss of a loved one any easier to bear.[81] Sorrow, like humor, deserves a history of its own.

If, however, it is possible for us to share the mental anguish of bereavement, it is more difficult to grasp the significance of physical pain in a society that lacked simple analgesics, much less the ability to cure diseases that are easily treated today. Aspirin and tranquilizers may separate us from the eighteenth century more than the social and political differences upon which historians usually concentrate. Even if Drinker exaggerated her own disabilities (and there is no evidence that she did), the diary offers convincing evidence that physical distress invaded daily life to a degree currently unimaginable.

Some pain, such as that experienced during labor, could be expected to dissipate on its own. And the excruciating distress that Hannah Shoemaker underwent during her "severe opperation" when she "had a Cancer cut from her breast" eventually led to a temporary restoration of health.[82] But pain of this nature was aberrational in the sense that it was both more severe and less frequent than the ordinary physical discomfort that people experienced on a day-to-day basis: "Nancy is in pain almost constantly"; "he never saw any one in such extreem pain"; "Molly Rhoads . . . was really very unwell with toothach and pain in her Face this Afternoon"; "Betty Jervis has been unwell with pain in her side"; "I feel all my old pains in my right side, in my left breast, and obstructed bowels"; Samuel Rhoads "has a pain in his side and has been blooded"; "Nancy Skyrin much troubled with pain in her head and Eye laterly"; "I was up in the Night in much pain—continu'd very poorly all this day."[83]

According to Drinker's record, headaches, toothaches, and stomach or intestinal disorders headed the list of eighteenth-century afflictions. As far as the causes of disease or pain were concerned, although any number of physiological or psychological stimuli might have contributed to a headache, abdominal disorders probably emanated from two basic sources. First, the absence of refrigeration undoubtedly led to excessive bacteria in the food, which in turn created intestinal problems. Second, periodontal disease (and its accompanying tooth and gum pain) was rampant among the population of colonial America. This condition was likely to have created a chain reaction that led to tooth loss, the inability to chew properly, and improper digestion of food, all of which resulted in the prevalent and persistent bowel disorders about which we are told more than we ever wanted to know.

The extraction of teeth by dentist, bloodletter, the bloodletter's wife, or family members appears to have been a more routine procedure than we have realized: "Elizath. had the back tooth in her under Jaw drawn this morning"; "I pull'd out a tooth for HD. this evening"; "HSD. had a tooth drawn this morning by Friedk. Hailers wife"; "HD . . . had a tooth drawn which requir'd a strong pull." Although teeth were occasionally replaced, the lack of a full set clearly affected one's general health.[84]

Despite the severity of the pain that accompanied these various afflictions, treatment usually concentrated on a cure, rather than on relieving immediate discomfort. In brief, elimination of the disease, not reduction of pain, was given first priority, although the latter must have been achieved simultaneously with the former. Yet some treatments, including the questionable practice of bloodletting, could exacerbate the discomfort of disease or injury, and it is little wonder that they were deferred or refused altogether from time to time: "John Haylor . . . fixt 7 Cups on my back, a little below the Neck, and one on each temple, or under—each cup received 16 gashes 144 in all,—those on the side of the Face hurt much worse than the others."[85]

Assuming for the moment that Drinker and her contemporaries preferred less Draconian means of relief, to what other remedies could they turn to mitigate distress? Short of escalating doses of laudanum, an addictive opium derivative, there was little available to alleviate suffering. Laudanum and weaker opium preparations were used in the Drinker household, as well as antispasmodics, such as gum ammoniac, assafetida, and volatile drops. In addition, HD turned to a modest amount of alcohol to help him cope with his "disorder" while ED "took a pinch of snuff" when she felt "unwell and uncomfortable."[86]

Yet the effectiveness of any remedy short of the narcotic compounds is questionable, given the reported persistence of physical distress: William Drinker was "in constant pain all night," Tommy James was "troubled for some days past with a bad pain in his Ear," ED herself was unwell "some time" with a pain in her side and shoulder, and Nancy, overcoming her dread of the procedure, finally agreed to have a tooth extracted after "it had been painfull for months."[87]

Historians have not been oblivious to the presence of disease in the eighteenth century, but they have not considered how the often unrelenting presence of pain might have affected personal reactions, relationships among people, or social interaction in general. Drinker admitted that her sore throat, fever, and need to take pills put her "out of sorts," and offered her opinion that Betty Carmor, the whitewasher, was "very bad tempered, oweing . . . to infirmity of body."[88] It would be interesting, therefore, to consider what this might mean on a wider scale. For example, could low-level but constant pain precipitate child or spousal abuse? Could unremitting suffering encourage suicide? Did excessive sickness affect labor and production? If a person was "out of sorts" or "bad tempered," would she or he be more likely to engage in litigation? Or, as Dostoyevsky theorized, did suffering serve as a common bond that bred compassion and solicitude among people? Did the unavoidability of pain breed acceptance, patience, and resignation?

At the death of one of her grandchildren, Drinker consoled herself with the thought that he was "out of all pain."[89] Given the pervasiveness of physical suffering at that time, this commonly expressed idea may have had more than metaphorical or figurative meaning to the people who used it. If so, the implications of unrelieved pain are a legitimate avenue of historical inquiry.

Despite the obvious differences between Drinker's time and ours, if the diary leaves us with any all-encompassing idea, it is the realization that, with precious few exceptions, human nature has changed almost not at all in the last two centuries. Young children asked the same awkward questions, teenagers and young adults threw parties the minute their parents' backs were turned—even in a Quaker household—and mothers bemoaned the inattention of their negligent children: "here am I tout suel . . . mending Stockings for my Son Henry, who has not thought it worth his while to come to see me, 'tho I have been here near two weeks."[90]

Urban life was beset with many of the same problems facing city dwellers today. Anyone who has endured the inconvenience of present-day transportation will share the frustration of a spiritual ancestor who suffered a horse that refused to move despite the most urgent entreaty, the unexpected repair of a horse whose lameness disrupted a journey, and an animal that was improperly secured and either was stolen or ran off, not to mention the exorbitant price of oats at each refueling stop. The dangers of drunken driving transcend the centuries, as does the custom of trading in a less lively means of transportation for a newer model.[91] As Elizabeth Drinker would no doubt confirm (with variations in spelling, to be sure), *plus ça change, plus c'est la même chose.*

Notes

1. Diary of Elizabeth Drinker, HSP, Dec. 31, 1797 (hereafter cited as Diary).

2. Susannah H. Rowson, *Charlotte Temple: A Tale of Truth* (Philadelphia, 1794); this classic novel was among America's earliest best-sellers. For more on late eighteenth-century fiction, the rise of the romantic novel, and its effect on women, see Cathy N. Davidson, *Revolution and the Word: the Rise of the Novel in America* (New York: Oxford University Press, 1986), 105, 262; Linda K. Kerber, *Women of the Republic: Intellect and Ideology in Revolutionary America* (Chapel Hill: University of North Carolina Press, 1980), esp. chap. 8; Russel Blaine Nye, *The Cultural Life of the New Nation, 1776–1830* (New York: Harper and Row, 1960), 251–54; Jan Lewis, "The Republican Wife: Virtue and Seduction in the Early Republic," *William and Mary Quarterly*, 3d ser., 44 (1987): 689–721.

3. Quaker population estimates are taken from Frederick B. Tolles, *Meeting House and Counting House* (Chapel Hill: University of North Carolina Press, 1948; New York: Norton, 1963), 232. See also François-Alexandre-Frédéric Duc de la Rochefoucauld-Liancourt, *Travels through the United States of North America* (London, R. Phillips, 1799), 2:377.

4. My discussion of slaves, indentured servants, and other demographic changes relies heavily on Gary Nash, "The Social Evolution of Preindustrial American Cities, 1700–1820: Reflections and New Directions," *Journal of Urban History* 13 (1987): 120, 121–22, 129, 130–31, and Sharon V. Salinger, "Artisans, Journeymen, and the Transformation of Labor in Late Eighteenth-Century Philadelphia," *William and Mary Quarterly*, 3d ser., 40 (1983): 64–65.

5. Diary, Apr. 11, 1806.

6. For biographical information on the Drinker family see H. S. Drinker, *Drinker Family*, copy at HSP.

7. John Jervis to Samuel Sandwith, June 2, 1756, Jervis-Sandwith Genealogy, Copies of Letters and Documents, 1641–1808, HSP, 109.

8. Thomas Say, according to his son, "was remarkable for being executor to many estates, and guardian to a number of orphan children, to whom, I have frequently heard him say, he had been a faithful steward." Benjamin Say, *A Short Compilation of the Extraordinary Life and Writings of Thomas Say: In Which Is Faithfully Copied, from the Original Manuscript the Uncommon Vision Which He Had When a Young Man* (Philadelphia, 1796), 10; Comly, *Comly Family*, 775–76. Invoice for goods, Nov. 16, 1756, on account of Mary Sandwith and Elizabeth Sandwith, and account current with Edw. Stephens, Aug. 14, 1756, Drinker-Sandwith Papers, vol. 2, items 34 and 35, HSP. Diary, Aug. 23, 1794; Nov. 29, 1796.

9. Diary, Sept. 26, 1759.

10. Ibid., Nov. 28, 1760; Mar. 3, 1807; July 20, 1798. Diary of Ann Warder, Jan. 15, 1787, HSP.

11. Diary, Nov. 19, 1800; Feb. 11, 1805. The letters can be found in the Quaker Collection, Haverford College Library.

12. Ibid., Sept. 8, 1798; Dec. 12, 1795; Aug. 10, Oct. 15, 1796; Sept. 24, 1800.

13. Ibid., Dec. 2, 1802.

14. Ibid., Oct. 28, 1781; Apr. 4, 1800; May 3, 1796; Jan. 11, 1803; May 14, 1796; Apr. 10, 1800; Oct. 30, 1779.

15. Ibid., Sept. 14, 1779; May 1, 1780; Aug. 31, 1793; Jan. 23, 1781.

16. Abraham Ritter, *Philadelphia and Her Merchants* (Philadelphia, 1860), 120. Diary, Sept. 2, 1793; Sept. 26, 1779; July 20, 1784; Aug. 21, 1806.

17. Diary, Apr. 10, 1798; July 4, 1797; May 17, 1801; Aug. 22, 1805; July 6, 1807; May 10, 1797; July 22, 1806; Dec. 25, July 4, 1795; Nov. 10, 1797.

18. Ibid., Oct. 12, 1807; July 22, 1799.

19. Ibid., Mar. 24, June 21, June 25, 1802.

20. Ibid., May 5, 1795; June 15, 1805; Aug. 9, 1800; Sept. 13, 1796; Feb. 29, 1796.

21. Ibid., Aug. 6, 1796; July 15, 1798; Nov. 9, Nov. 11, 1799; Nov. 2, 1798; May 6, May 15, 1801; May 2, 1796.

22. Ibid., Sept. 4, 1800 (end-of-year reading list); Mar. 5, 1807.

23. Ibid., Sept. 13, 1776; Dec. 31, 1799. Poulson's *American Daily Advertiser*, Dec. 2, 1807.

24. Diary, Dec. 3, 1802; Aug. 1, 1795; Dec. 2, 1803; Apr. 15, Sept. 12, 1806; Feb. 3, 1797; Aug. 26, 1795; Aug. 21, 1799; Dec. 9, 1805; May 31, 1807; Dec. 31, Sept. 13, 1800; July 20, 1798.

25. Diary of Ann Warder, Jan. 15, 1787, HSP.

26. *Similar* is meant only to imply likeness in the broadest sense, since diaries written by Quaker women varied considerably from person to person. For example, Sarah Logan Fisher's journal (1776–95) is like Drinker's in the sense that Fisher records daily events, but it is also more emotional and pious in tone. (The Drinker family is mentioned in Fisher's diary.) Ann Warder's diary, on the other hand, lacks any religious component, is highly opinionated and filled with gossip: "[Jacky] Fry . . . is partial to Nancy beyond her Sister but wether sufficiently so to be serious I know not" (Diary of Ann Warder, June 26, 1786). Hannah Bringhurst recorded her thoughts and meditations during an illness in 1781, while Mary Howell Swett left an account of her European travels between 1797 and 1801. The Fisher, Warder, and Bringhurst diaries may be found at the Historical Society of Pennsylvania, and Swett's in the Quaker Collection of Haverford College Library.

For references to other unpublished diaries see Andrea Hinding, *Women's History Sources: A Guide to Archives and Manuscript Collections in the United States* (New York: Bowker, 1972), and William Matthews, *American Diaries in Manuscript, 1580–1954: A Descriptive Bibliography* (Athens, Ga.: University of Georgia Press, 1974). Published diaries are listed in Laura Arsky, Nancy Pries, and Marcia Reed, *American Diaries: An Annotated Bibliography of Published American Diaries*, 2 vols. (Detroit: Gale Research Co., c. 1983). See also Cheryl Cline, *Women's Diaries, Journals, and Letters: An Annotated Bibliography* (New York: Garland, 1989).

An excellent general guide to archival material on female Friends is Elisabeth Potts Brown and Jean R. Soderlund, "Sources on Quaker Women," in *Witnesses for Change: Quaker Women over Three Centuries*, ed. Elisabeth Potts Brown and Susan Mosher Stuard (New Brunswick, N.J.: Rutgers University Press, 1989), 157–68.

In recent years historians have spent considerable time both editing and analyzing women's diaries of the late eighteenth and early nineteenth centuries. Among the most important of the current works are Carol Karlsen and Laurie Crumpacker, eds., *The Journal of Esther Edwards Burr, 1754–1757* (New Haven: Yale University Press, 1984);

Laurel Thatcher Ulrich, *A Midwife's Tale: The Life of Martha Ballard, Based on Her Diary, 1785–1812* (New York: Knopf, 1990); Terri L. Premo, *Winter Friends: Women Growing Old in the New Republic, 1785–1835* (Urbana: University of Illinois Press, 1990); Nancy Cott, *The Bonds of Womanhood: "Woman's Sphere" in New England, 1780–1835* (New Haven: Yale University Press, 1977); Nancy Tomes, "The Quaker Connection: Visiting Patterns among Women in the Philadelphia Society of Friends, 1750–1800," in *Friends and Neighbors: Group Life in America's First Plural Society*, ed. Michael Zuckerman (Philadelphia: Temple University Press, 1982), 174–95; and Barbara E. Lacey, "The World of Hannah Heaton: The Autobiography of an Eighteenth-Century Connecticut Farm Woman," *William and Mary Quarterly*, 3d ser., 45 (1988): 280–304. For a general overview of the historiography of eighteenth-century Quaker women (and a short extract of an eighteenth-century Quaker diary) see Mary Maples Dunn, "Latest Light on Women of Light," in *Witnesses for Change*, ed. Brown and Stuard, 71–89.

27. Poulson's *American Daily Advertiser*, Dec. 2, 1807.

28. Diary, Nov. 19, 1800; Dec. 31, 1799; Feb. 12, 1800.

29. Ibid., Oct. 28, 1794; Dec. 13, 1805.

30. Ibid., Sept. 16, 1790; May 20, June 2, 1760. See also ibid., Sept. 27, 1793; Oct. 10, 1807; Dec. 31, 1799; and George Vaux, ed., "Extracts from the Diary of Hannah Callender," *PMHB* 12 (1888): 432–56.

31. Diary, Sept. 29, 1803; Sept. 28, 1807; H. S. Drinker, *Drinker Family*, 46.

32. Pope Sixtus V (1520–90) ascended the papal throne in 1585. Drinker disapproved of the means by which he brought order to the papal states. Diary, Jan. 27, 1794; Aug. 10, 1791, May 14, Mar. 27, 1796.

33. Ibid., Aug. 12, 1802; Feb. 27, 1804; Nov. 11, 1807.

34. Ibid., Dec. 30, 1801; Dec. 26, 1805, end-of-year reading list.

35. Ibid., Dec. 11, 12, 1794; Jan. 1, 31, 1795; Feb. 27, Mar. 27, Dec. 13, 1795.

36. Ibid., Oct. 28, 1794; July 15, 1791.

37. See Davidson, *Revolution and the Word*, 105. After outlining the substantive themes of the sentimental novel, Davidson concludes, "This is the focus of the fiction, and it is also precisely what was happening around the corner at one of the best addresses in Boston." In Davidson's view, the novel sustained popularity because its female readership recognized a world "in which women operated and were operated upon."

38. Diary, Oct. 31, 1795.

39. Ibid., Aug. 16, 1804; Feb. 20, June 12, 1800; June 21, 1805; Feb. 9, Mar. 11, 1801.

40. Ibid., Jan. 1, 1802.

41. Ibid., Sept. 18, 1795; Aug. 19, 1796; June 15–16, 1797; Feb. 23, 1805; July 21, 1807.

42. Henry D. Biddle, ed., *Extracts from the Journal of Elizabeth Drinker* (Philadelphia, 1889), 3.

43. Michael Zuckerman, "Introduction: Puritans, Cavaliers, and the Motley Middle," in *Friends and Neighbors: Group Life in America's First Plural Society*, ed. Michael Zuckerman (Philadelphia: Temple University Press, 1982), 25.

44. Diary, Nov. 25, 29, 1780; May 26, 1781.

45. Ibid., Nov. 22, Sept. 29, Dec. 11, 19, 14, 1777.

46. Ibid., Feb. 2, 1777.

47. Ibid., Oct. 20, 1778; Mar. 30, July 23, 1779; Aug. 10, 1781. See Ruth H. Bloch, "The Gendered Meanings of Virtue in Revolutionary America," *Signs: Journal of Women in Culture and Society* 13, no. 1 (1987): 37–58.

48. Diary, May 24, 26, 31, 1779; Mar. 11, 1781; Nov. 22, 1780.

49. Ibid., Dec. 31, 1781.

50. On Nov. 1, 1777, "a poor Solider was hang'd . . . on the Common, for striking his Officer." See also Diary, Mar. 8, 1777.

51. Ibid., Mar. 1777.
52. Ibid., Aug. 14, Sept. 2, Nov. 4, Dec. 5, 1778. See Samuel Rowland Fisher, "Journal of Samuel Rowland Fisher, of Philadelphia, 1779–1781," contributed by Anna Wharton Morris, *PMHB* 41 (1917): 170.
53. Ibid., June 27, 1806; Jan. 28, 1807; June 9, 1803. Douglas Greenberg, *Crime and Law Enforcement in the Colony of New York, 1691–1776* (Ithaca, N.Y.: Cornell University Press, 1976), 135–36, 140. See also Lawrence H. Gipson, "Crime and Its Punishment in Provincial Pennsylvania," *Pa. Hist.* 2 (1935): 3–16.
54. Diary, June 14, 1794.
55. Ibid., Jan. 12, 15, 1799.
56. Drinker-Sandwith papers, esp. vols. 1 and 5, HSP. Diary, Sept. 10, 1796; Sept. 23, May 10, Mar. 26, 1794; Apr. 1, 1778.
57. Diary, Jan. 7, 1799; Oct. 4, 1806.
58. Ibid., Sept. 4, 1797; Apr. 17, 1799; Nov. 5, 1801; Aug. 29, 1807; Aug. 31, 1801.
59. Ibid., Jan. 6, 1797; Jan. 18, Mar. 6, 1802; Sept. 7, 1806; May 25, 1807; Nov. 11, 1801.
60. For a more complete discussion of the mistress-servant relationship in the context of the Drinker household, see Elaine F. Crane, "The World of Elizabeth Drinker," *PMHB* 107 (Jan. 1983): 3–28; Diary, Oct. 19, 1794.
61. Diary, May 9, 1803; Oct. 20, 1801; Jan. 14, 1798; Feb. 23, 1802; July 17, 1803.
62. Ibid., Nov. 7, 1803.
63. Ibid., June 26, 1802; May 13, 1803; Jan. 27, Mar. 17, 1804.
64. Ibid., May 17, Aug. 14, 1803; Sept. 8, 1804; Jan. 1, Feb. 14, 1806; Feb. 19, 1801.
65. Ibid., Aug. 24, 1804; Nov. 18, 1799; Jan. 29, 30, 1798; Feb. 11, May 1, 1801; Aug. 3, 28, 1798.
66. Ibid., July 20, Aug. 26, 1796; May 8, 1807; Sept. 20, Aug. 12, 1798; Sept. 5, 1803.
67. Ibid., Aug. 28, 1794.
68. Ibid., Jan. 26, 1794; see July–Oct. 1793, passim.
69. Ibid., Apr. 29, Sept. 11, Aug. 22, 1794.
70. Ibid., Dec. 19, 1777.
71. Ibid., May 27, 1797; July 29, 1779.
72. Ibid., Feb. 23, 1798; July 4, 1801.
73. Ibid., Mar. 31, Apr. 3, 1778.
74. Ibid., Nov. 5, 1799; Mar. 4, 1800; July 20, Nov. 30, 1798; July 5, 1803.
75. Ibid., Dec. 12, 1795.
76. Ibid., Oct. 2, 1794; Mar. 12, 1794; Mar. 9, 1798.
77. David Flaherty, *Privacy in Colonial New England* (Charlottesville: University Press of Virginia, 1976); Diary, Dec. 5, 1802.
78. Diary, Aug. 24, 1804.
79. Ibid., July 18, 24, 1798.
80. Ibid., Mar. 30, 1793; Jan. 8, 1794; Nov. 1, Jan. 14, 1795; July 10, 1806; Dec. 7, 1797.
81. See, for example, ibid., Mar. 13, 1794.
82. Ibid., May 29, Aug. 2, 1803.
83. Ibid., Aug. 16, Nov. 3, 1801; July 15, 1803; Oct. 4, 1806; Aug. 10, 1803; Apr. 22, 1805; July 1, 1800; May 4, 1781.
84. Ibid., Apr. 17, 1801; May 9, 1805; Sept. 25, 1801; Sept. 24, 1778.
85. Ibid., June 29, 1803.
86. Ibid., June 22, July 31, 1802; Dec. 25, 1806.
87. Ibid., Aug. 26, 1795; July 6, 1778; Oct. 23, 1777; Jan. 12, 1781.

88. Ibid., May 11, 1806; June 19, 1798.
89. Ibid., Nov. 3, 1801.
90. Ibid., Mar. 22, 1800; July 22, 1791.
91. Ibid., Apr. 18, 1796.

Editorial Note

Elizabeth Drinker's diary falls somewhere between a historical and a literary document. Although its primary value is historical, readers can enjoy both content and form. Similarly, it falls somewhere between a private and a public document: private in the sense that it was not meant to be published, public because the volumes were open to the scrutiny of others, both in her time and ours.

The journal, like any other document, presents the usual problems with regard to editorial procedure. The primary task was to ensure a faithful reproduction of the unabridged text without sacrificing readability. This balance required certain textual modifications, but the result is a nearly literal transcription of the original manuscript that retains, with minor exceptions, Elizabeth Drinker's spelling and punctuation.

The modifications are as follows:

Superscript letters have been brought down to the baseline, and common nouns abbreviated in this manner have been silently expanded, with the period below the superscript letter omitted. The words so altered are *about, account, appeared, company, could, daughter, dear, deceased, ditto, doctor, dollars, evening, friend, instant, meeting, morning, neighbor, o'clock, paid, pair, quarter, received, said, should, supped, testimony, ultimo, with, would.*

The superscript letters of proper nouns, including titles such as *Nr.* (Neighbor), *Fd.* (Friend), and *Dr.* (Doctor), have been dropped to the baseline, but the words have not been expanded, on the theory that abbreviated names are ambiguous ("Jos.," for example, could refer to Joseph, Josiah, or Joshua); also, it seems more reasonable to apply a consistent rule to all proper nouns than to expand some and not others.

The few abbreviated words within the text that contain no superscript letters have not been expanded.

The thorn (*ye, yt*) has been replaced by *th* (*the, that*).

Punctuation has been retained exactly as it appears in the original manuscript with the following exceptions:

1. A period completes each daily entry no matter what punctuation mark Drinker used.

2. All dashes within the text that indicate a pause or change of thought are reproduced as em dashes (—) regardless of their size in the manuscript. Dashes to fill an incomplete line or to mark the end of an entry have been eliminated.

3. A colon or comma after the first initial of a name has been replaced with a period. Thus "J: Logan" in the manuscript appears as "J. Logan" in the published version. In the case of names such as *McKean* where Drinker wrote a superscript *c*, the letter has been brought down to the baseline and the period under the *c* eliminated.

4. The period following the *s* in possessive superscript names such as *Jamess* has been deleted.

Elizabeth Drinker's handwriting is extremely legible, and the manuscript volumes are generally in good condition. Nevertheless, use has taken its toll, and there are the usual smudges, holes, and even an occasional tooth mark where a mouse has sampled a page corner. In such cases, letters or words transcribed with difficulty are surrounded by a bracket, and totally illegible ones are represented by an empty bracket. Regretfully, the reader will not know how many letters or words are missing in the latter situation, since this was often impossible to determine. Since ED's capital *I, J, T,* and *S* are almost totally indistinguishable from one another, they frequently appear in brackets when used as initials in place of a name.

Entries on loose pages that were erroneously inserted in the manuscript volumes at some undetermined time have been silently placed in their proper chronological order.

Annotation

The focus of the annotation is explanatory rather than interpretive, the assumption being that the editor's role is to present the text with as little bias and as much neutrality as possible. Toward that end, the annotation seeks to clarify entries where the meaning is elusive, and to expand where the information ED relays is insufficient for the reader to understand a situation. Only words omitted from standard English dictionaries are defined. Since the annotation is intended merely to support, the notes have been written and edited with an eye toward brevity. Many notes, however, include citations that allow the reader to explore a subject in greater detail.

Except for those occasions where Drinker corrects herself by crossing out a word inadvertently misspelled or repeated, her deletions have been restored in the form of annotation, since they represent information that she chose to remove from the reader's view for one reason or another. The deleted words, phrases, and sentences appear in a note rather than at their original place in the body of the entry in order to avoid any interruption to the flow of the text.

In addition to the silent corrections already noted, two sorts of deletions appear in the text. In the first case, Drinker merely excised a word or statement with a line through it in order to rephrase a thought, apply a synonym, or change a name. It created minimal difficulty to restore these deletions. In the second instance, however, she attempted to completely obliterate what she had written. Every effort has been made to reconstruct accurately what in many cases Drinker took great pains to conceal. Where this proved impossible, the editor has noted that material has been crossed out. Words within brackets indicate the editor's best guess as to what they had been. Empty brackets indicate word(s) that the editor was unable to decipher at all. Although the reader will share the editor's frustration at not being able to tell with precision how many words belong within that bracket, the reader may assume that the missing words comprise less than a full line of text. Deletions of a line or more are so indicated.

The note number to indicate deleted material has been placed immediately preceding the expunged text.

Drinker's French phrases are an attempt at concealment as well, and a glossary of French phrases includes them in translation. ED's French spelling is even more arbitrary than her English; her French grammar and sentence structure are nonstandard, to say the least. Some "French" words seem to be her own invention. No attempt has been made to standardize or correct any of her French phrases, and in many instances the English equivalents are merely approximations of what she probably meant. When the French is too fractured to permit any reasonable translation, the word or phrase is omitted from the glossary.

For purposes of easy reference, people are identified in a biographical directory at the end of volume 3.

Abbreviations and Short Titles

Abolition Society. *Papers*
Pennsylvania Abolition Society. *The Papers of the Pennsylvania Abolition Society*. Philadelphia: The Historical Society of Pennsylvania and the Pennsylvania Abolition Society, Microform publication, 1976.

Adams. *Works*
The Works of John Adams. Edited by Charles Francis Adams. Vol. 9. Boston: Little, Brown, 1854.

Alexander. *Render Them Submissive*
John K. Alexander. *Render Them Submissive: Responses to Poverty in Philadelphia, 1760–1800*. Amherst: University of Massachusetts Press, 1980.

Alexander. "Fort Wilson Incident of 1779"
John K. Alexander. "The Fort Wilson Incident of 1779: A Case Study of the Revolutionary Crowd," *William and Mary Quarterly*, 3d ser., 31 (1974): 589–612.

American State Papers, Indian Affairs
U.S. Congress. *American State Papers. Class 2. Indian Affairs*. Vol. 1. Washington, D.C.: Gales and Seaton, 1832.

Annals of Congress
U.S. Congress. *Annals of the Congress of the United States*. 42 vols. Washington, D.C.: Gales and Seaton, 1834–56.

APS American Philosophical Society.

Ashmead. *Delaware County*
Henry Graham Ashmead. *History of Delaware County, Pennsylvania*. Philadelphia: L. H. Everts & Co., 1884.

Augustin. *Yellow Fever*
George Augustin. *History of Yellow Fever*. New Orleans: Searcy & Pfaff, 1909.

Averly. *18th-Cen. Brit. Books*
G. Averley et al. Eighteenth-Century British Books: A Subject Catalogue. 4 vols. Newcastle-upon-Tyne: Wm. Dawson & Sons, 1979.

Bailey. *Universal Etymological Dictionary*

N. Bailey. *A Universal Etymological English Dictionary*. 4th ed. London: 1728.

Baldwin. *Whiskey Rebels*

Leland D. Baldwin. *Whiskey Rebels*. 1939. Rev. ed. Pittsburgh: University of Pittsburgh Press, 1968.

Barbour and Frost. *Quakers*

Hugh Barbour and William J. Frost. *The Quakers*. New York: Greenwood Press, 1988.

Bard. *Compendium of Midwifery*

Samuel Bard. *A Compendium of the Theory and Practice of Midwifery*. New York: Collins and Perkins, 1807.

Baurmeister. *Revolution in America*

Carl Leopold Baurmeister. *The Revolution in America. Confidential Letters and Journals, 1776–1784, of Adjutant General Major Baurmeister of the Hessian Forces*. Translated by Bernhard A. Uhlendorf. New Brunswick, N.J.: Rutgers University Press, 1957.

Bezanson. *Prices and Inflation*

Ann Bezanson. *Prices and Inflation during the American Revolution: Pennsylvania, 1770–1790*. Philadelphia: University of Pennsylvania Press, 1951.

Blackman. *Susquehanna County*

Emily C. Blackman. *History of Susquehanna County, Pennsylvania*. 1873. Reprinted under the Sponsorship of the Susquehanna County Historical Society and Free Library Association, Montrose, Pa. Baltimore: Regional Publishing Co., 1970.

Blackwell. *Curious Herbal*

Elizabeth Blackwell. *A Curious Herbal Containing Five Hundred Cuts of the Most Useful Plants. Which Are Now Used in the Practice of Physick. Engraved on Folio Copper Plates, after Drawings Taken from the Life*. 2 vols. London: John Nourse, 1739.

Blake. "Compleat Housewife"

John B. Blake. "The Compleat Housewife," *Bulletin of the History of Medicine* 49 (1975): 30–42.

BLC *The British Library General Catalogue of Printed Books to 1975*. London: K. G. Saur, 1979–87.

Block. *English Novel*

Andrew Block. *The English Novel 1740–1850. A Catalogue Including Prose, Romances, Short Stories, and Translations of Foreign Fiction*. London: Dawsons of Pall Mall, 1961.

Boatner. *American Revolution*

Mark M. Boatner III. *The Encyclopedia of the American Revolution*. New York: McKay 1966.

Bridenbaugh. *Cities in Revolt*

Carl Bridenbaugh. *Cities in Revolt: Urban Life in America 1743–1776*. 1955. Reprint. New York: Capricorn Books, 1964.

Bridenbaugh and Bridenbaugh. *Rebels and Gentlemen*

Carl Bridenbaugh and Jessica Bridenbaugh. *Rebels and Gentlemen: Philadelphia in the Age of Franklin.* 1940. Reprint. New York: Oxford University Press, 1962.

Brigham. *Newspapers*

Clarence S. Brigham. *History and Bibliography of American Newspapers, 1690–1820.* 2 vols. Worcester: American Antiquarian Society, 1947.

Brinton. *Quaker Practice*

Howard H. Brinton. *Guide to Quaker Practice.* Pendle Hill Pamphlets 20. Wallingford, Pa: Pendle Hill Pamphlets 1943.

Brissot de Warville. *New Travels*

J. P. Brissot de Warville. *New Travels in the United States of America, 1788.* Translated by Maria Soceanu Vamos and Durand Echeverria. Edited by Durand Echeverria. Cambridge, Mass.: Belknap Press of Harvard University Press, 1964.

Brit. Mus. Cat.

British Museum General Catalogue of Printed Books to 1955. London: Trustees of the British Museum, 1959.

Bronner. "Quaker Landmarks"

Edwin Bronner. "Quaker Landmarks in Early Philadelphia." In *Historic Philadelphia: From the Founding until the Early Nineteenth Century, 210–16* Transactions of the American Philosophical Society, n.s., 43, pt. 1. Philadelphia, 1953.

Brooke. *George III*

John Brooke. *King George III.* New York: McGraw Hill, 1972.

Buchan. *Domestic Medicine* (1793)

William Buchan. *Domestic Medicine: Or a Treatise on the Prevention and Cure of Diseases by Regimen and Simple Medicines.* 14th ed. Boston: Printed for Joseph Bumstead by James White and Ebenezer Larkin, jun., 1793.

Buchan. *Domestic Medicine* (1799)

William Buchan, *Domestic Medicine: Or, a Treatise on the Prevention and Cure of Diseases by Regimen and Simple Medicines Adapted to the Climate and Diseases of America, by Isaac Cathrall.* Philadelphia: Richard Folwell, 1799.

Bull. Hist. Med.

Bulletin of the History of Medicine.

Cadbury. "Negro Membership"

Henry J. Cadbury. "Negro Membership in the Society of Friends." *Journal of Negro History* 21 (1936): 151–213.

Carey. *Short Account*

Mathew Carey. *A Short Account of the Malignant Fever, Lately Prevalent in Philadelphia.* Philadelphia: Printed by the author, 1793.

Carroll and Ashworth. *George Washington*

John Alexander Carroll and Mary Wells Ashworth. *George Washington.* Vol. 7, *First in Peace.* Completes biography by Douglas Southall Freeman. New York: Scribner, 1957.

Chandler. *Campaigns*
David G. Chandler. *The Campaigns of Napoleon*. New York: Macmillan, 1966.

Chapin. *American Law of Treason*
Bradley Chapin. *The American Law of Treason: Revolutionary and Early National Origins*. Seattle: University of Washington Press, 1964.

Clarfield. *Timothy Pickering*
Gerard H. Clarfield. *Timothy Pickering and the American Republic*. Pittsburgh: University of Pittsburgh Press, 1980.

Clark. *Peter Porcupine*
Mary Elizabeth Clark. *Peter Porcupine in America: The Career of William Cobbett*. Philadelphia: 1939.

Clement. *Welfare and the Poor*
Priscilla Ferguson Clement. *Welfare and the Poor in the Nineteenth-Century City: Philadelphia, 1800–1854*. Rutherford, N.J.: Fairleigh Dickinson University Press, 1985.

Coleman. "Joseph Galloway"
John M. Coleman. "Joseph Galloway and the British Occupation of Philadelphia." *Pennsylvania History* 30 (1963): 272–300.

Col. Recs. Pa.
Commonwealth of Pennsylvania. *The Colonial Records of Pennsylvania*. 14 vols. Harrisburg, 1852. Reprint. New York: AMS Press, 1968.

Comly. *Comly Family*
George Norwood Comly, comp. *Comly Family in America*. Philadelphia: Lippincott, 1939.

Cooke. *Tench Coxe*
Jacob E. Cooke. *Tench Coxe and the Early Republic*. Chapel Hill: University of North Carolina Press, 1978.

Cope. *Smedley Family*
Gilbert Cope, comp. *Genealogy of the Smedley Family*. Lancaster, Pa.: Wickersham Printing Co., 1901.

Corner. *William Shippen*
Betsy Copping Corner. *William Shippen, Jr.: Pioneer in American Medical Education*. Memoirs of the American Philosophical Society, 28. Philadelphia, 1951.

Craigie and Hulbert. *Dictionary of American English*
Sir William Craigie and James R. Hulbert, eds. *A Dictionary of American English*. Chicago: University of Chicago Press, 1940.

Cullen. *Practice of Physic*
William Cullen. *First Lines of the Practice of Physic. With Practical and Explanatory Notes by John Rothermel*. 4 vols. Edinburgh: Bell & Bradfute, and William Creech, 1791.

DAB *Dictionary of American Biography* (1928–58). New York: Scribner, 1964.

Davis, A., and Appel. *Bloodletting Instruments*
Audrey Davis and Toby Appel. *Bloodletting Instruments in the National Museum of History*. Smithsonian Studies in History and Technology 41. Washington, D.C.: Smithsonian Institution, 1979.

Davis, S. G. *Parades and Power*

Susan G. Davis. *Parades and Power: Street Theatre in Nineteenth-Century Philadelphia*. Philadelphia: Temple University Press, 1986.

Davis, W. W. H. *Bucks County*

William W. H. Davis. *History of Bucks County Pennsylvania*. 3 vols. Rev. ed. New York: Lewis Publishing Co., 1905.

Davis. *Fries Rebellion*

W. W. H. Davis. *The Fries Rebellion 1798–1799*. 1899. Reprint. Doylestown, Pa.: Doylestown Publishing Co., 1969.

DeConde. *Entangling Alliances*

Alexander DeConde. *Entangling Alliances: Politics and Diplomacy under George Washington*. Durham, N.C.: Duke University Press, 1958.

DeConde. *Quasi-War*

Alexander DeConde, *The Quasi-War*. New York: Scribner, 1966.

Dewees and Dewees. *Centennial of Westtown*

Watson W. Dewees and Sarah B. Dewees. *Centennial History of the Westtown Boarding School 1799–1899*. Westtown, Pa.: Westtown Alumni Association and Sherman & Co., 1899.

DNB *Dictionary of National Biography*. Oxford: Oxford University Press, 1967–68.

Doerflinger. *Spirit of Enterprise*

Thomas A. Doerflinger. *A Vigorous Spirit of Enterprise: Merchants and Economic Development in Revolutionary Philadelphia*. Chapel Hill: University of North Carolina Press for the Institute of Early American History and Culture, 1986.

Dorland. "Second Troop"

W. A. Newman Dorland. "The Second Troop Philadelphia City Cavalry." *Pennsylvania Magazine of History and Biography*, 45 (1921): 257–91, 364–87; 46 (1922): 57–77, 154–72, 262–71, 346–65; 47 (1923); 67–79, 147–77, 262–76, 357–75; 48 (1924); 270–84, 372–82; 49 (1925): 75–94, 163–91, 367–79; 50 (1926): 79–87, 179–89; 52 (1928): 372–80; 53 (1929): 283–87, 375–83; 54 (1930): 65–84, 175–85, 374–78.

Drinker, C. K. *Not So Long Ago*

Cecil K. Drinker. *Not So Long Ago: A Chronicle of Medicine and Doctors in Colonial Philadelphia*. New York: Oxford University Press, 1937.

Drinker, H. S. *Drinker Family*

Henry S. Drinker. *History of the Drinker Family*. Merion, Pa.: Privately printed, 1961.

Duffy. *Epidemics*

John Duffy. *Epidemics in Colonial America*. Baton Rouge: Louisiana State University, 1953.

Duffy. *Public Health*

John Duffy. *A History of Public Health in New York City 1625–1866*. New York: Russell Sage Foundation, 1968.

Estes. "Therapeutic Practice"

J. Worth Estes. "Therapeutic Practice in New England." In *Medicine in Colonial Massachusetts*, 289–383. *Publications of the Colonial Society of Massachusetts* 57. Boston, 1980.

Evans. *Am. Bibliography*
Charles Evans. *American Bibliography*. 1903. Reprint. New York: Peter Smith, 1941.

Farmer. *Slang and Its Analogues*
John S. Farmer. *Slang and Its Analogues Past and Present*. 7 vols. London: Harrison & Sons, 1890–1904.

Ferguson. *Power of the Purse*
E. James Ferguson. *The Power of the Purse: A History of American Public Finance, 1776–1790*. Chapel Hill: University of North Carolina Press for the Institute of Early American History and Culture, 1961.

Fielder. *Plant Medicine*
Mildred Fielder. *Plant Medicine and Folklore*. New York: Winchester Press, 1975.

Fisher, D. E. "Social Life"
Darlene Emmert Fisher. "Social Life in Philadelphia during the British Occupation." *Pennsylvania History* 37 (1970): 237–60.

Fisher, S. L. "Diary of Trifling Occurences"
Sarah Logan Fisher. " 'A Diary of Trifling Occurences': Philadelphia, 1776–1778." Edited by Nicholas B. Wainwright. *Pennsylvania Magazine of History and Biography* 82 (1958): 411–65.

Fisher, S. R. "Fisher Journal"
"Journal of Samuel Rowland Fisher, of Philadelphia, 1779–1781." Contributed by Anna Wharton Morris. *Pennsylvania Magazine of History and Biography* 41 (1917): 145–97, 274–333, 399–457.

Foner. *Tom Paine*
Eric Foner. *Tom Paine and Revolutionary America*. New York: Oxford University Press, 1976.

Forsythe. *Historical Sketch*
David H. Forsythe. "A Historical Sketch." In *Two-Hundreth Anniversary of the Founding of London Grove Meeting by the Society of Friends of London Grove, Pennsylvania*. London Grove, Pa.: n.p., 1914.

Franklin. *Papers*
The Papers of Benjamin Franklin. Edited by Leonard Labaree et al. New Haven: Yale University Press, 1959–.

Freemantle. *England, 1806–1810*
A. F. Freemantle. *England in the Nineteenth Century, 1806–1810*. London, 1930. Reprint. Millwood, N.Y.: Kraus Reprint Co., 1978.

Friends H. L. *Catalog*
Friends Historical Library, *Catalog of the Book and Serials Collections of the Friends Historical Library, Swarthmore College* (Boston, G. K. Hall, 1982).

Frost. *Quaker Family*
J. William Frost. *The Quaker Family in Colonial America*. New York: St. Martin's Press, 1973.

Frost. "Years of Crisis"
J. William Frost. "Years of Crisis and Separation: Philadelphia Yearly Meeting 1790–1860." In *Friends in the Delaware Valley: Philadelphia Yearly Meeting 1681–1981*, ed. John M. Moore, 57–102. Haverford, Pa.: Friends Historical Association, 1981.

Futhey and Cope. *Chester County*

J. Smith Futhey and Gilbert Cope. *History of Chester County, Pennsylvania, with Genealogical and Biographical Sketches*. Philadelphia: Louis H. Everts, 1881.

Gardner. *New Medical Dictionary*

D. Pereira Gardner. *A New Medical Dictionary*. New York: Harper & Brothers, 1855.

Gifford. "Botanic Remedies"

George E. Gifford, Jr. "Botanic Remedies in Colonial Massachusetts, 1620–1820." In *Medicine in Colonial Massachusetts*, 263–88. *Publications of the Colonial Society of Massachusetts* 57. Boston, 1980.

Gilpin. *Exiles in Virginia*

Thomas Gilpin. *Exiles in Virginia*. Philadelphia: n.p., 1848.

Goodman. *Benjamin Rush*

Nathan G. Goodman. *Benjamin Rush, Physician and Citizen 1746–1813*. Philadelphia: University of Pennsylvania Press, 1934.

Goodrich. *Wayne County*

Phineas G. Goodrich. *History of Wayne County*. Honesdale, Pa.: Haines & Beardsley, 1880.

Gordon. *Gazetteer New Jersey*

Thomas F. Gordon. *A Gazetteer of the State of New Jersey*. Trenton: Daniel Fenton, 1834.

Gordon. *Gazetteer Pennsylvania*

Thomas F. Gordon. *A Gazetteer of the State of Pennsylvania*. Philadelphia: T. Belknap, 1832.

Goulard. *Preparations of Lead*

Mr. [Thomas] Goulard, *A Treatise on the Effects and Various Preparations of Lead, Particularly of the Extracts of Saturn, for Different Chirurgical Disorders*. Translated from the French of Mr. Goulard. A new edition with remarks by G. Arnaud, M.D. London: P. Elmsley, 1773.

Gould. *Dictionary of Medicine*

George M. Gould. *An Illustrated Dictionary of Medicine, Biology and Allied Sciences*. Philadelphia: P. Blackiston's Son, 1901.

Gragg. *Migration*

Larry Dale Gragg. *Migration in Early America: The Virginia Quaker Experience*. Ann Arbor: UMI Research Press, 1980.

Griffenhagen and Young. *Patent Medicines*

George B. Griffenhagen and James Harvey Young. "Old English Patent Medicines in America." In *Contributions from The Museum of History and Technology*, 218. United States National Museum Bulletin 10. Washington, D.C.: Smithsonian Institution, 1959.

Gruber. *Howe Brothers*

Ira D. Gruber. *The Howe Brothers and the American Revolution*. New York: Atheneum, 1972.

Haller. "Tartar Emetic"
John S. Haller. "The Use and Abuse of Tartar Emetic in the 19th-Century Materia Medica." *Bulletin of the History of Medicine* 49 (1975): 235–57.

Hamilton. *Papers*
The Papers of Alexander Hamilton. Edited by Harold C. Syrett. 26 vols. New York: Columbia University Press, 1961–79.

Hamlin. *Latrobe*
Talbot Hamlin. *Benjamin Henry Latrobe*. New York: Oxford University Press, 1955.

Harrison. *Thomas P. Cope*
Eliza Cope Harrison, ed. *Philadelphia Merchant: The Diary of Thomas P. Cope, 1800–1851*. South Bend, Ind.: Gateway Editions, 1978.

Harvey. *Wilkes-Barré*
Oscar Jewel Harvey. *A History of Wilkes-Barré, Luzerne County, Pennsylvania*. 6 vols. Wilkes-Barre: Kaeder Press, 1909–30.

Hess. *Booke of Cookery*
Karen Hess, ed. *Martha Washington's Booke of Cookery*. New York: Columbia University Press, 1981.

Hinshaw. *American Quaker Genealogy*
William Wade Hinshaw. *Encyclopedia of American Quaker Genealogy*. 7 vols. Ann Arbor: Edwin Brothers, 1936–65.

Historic Philadelphia
Historic Philadelphia: From the Founding until the Early Nineteenth Century. *Transactions of the American Philosophical Society*, n.s. 43, pt. 1. Philadelphia, 1953.

Hole. *Westtown*
Helen G. Hole. *Westtown Through the Years*. Westtown, Pa.: Westtown Alumni Association, 1942.

Hopkins. *Princes and Peasants*
Donald R. Hopkins. *Princes and Peasants: Smallpox in History*. Chicago: University of Chicago Press, 1983.

Hotchkin. *Bristol Pike*
Rev. S. F. Hotchkin. *The Bristol Pike*. Philadelphia: George W. Jacobs, 1893.

Hotchkin. *York Road*
Rev. S. F. Hotchkin. *The York Road Old and New*. Philadelphia: Binder & Kelly, 1892.

HSP Historical Society of Pennsylvania.

Jackson. *Pennsylvania Navy*
John W. Jackson. *The Pennsylvania Navy 1775–1781: The Defense of the Delaware*. New Brunswick, N.J.: Rutgers University Press, 1974.

Jackson. *With the British Army*
John W. Jackson. *With the British Army in Philadelphia 1777–1778*. San Rafael, Calif.: Presidio Press, 1979.

James. *Quaker Benevolence*
Sydney V. James, *A People among Peoples: Quaker Benevolence in Eighteenth-Century America*. Cambridge: Harvard University Press, 1963.

JCC U.S. Congress. *Journals of the Continental Congress, 1774–1789*. Edited by Worthington C. Ford et al. 34 vols. Washington, D.C., 1903–37. Reprint. New York: Johnson Reprint Co., 1968.

JHMAS
Journal of the History of Medicine and Allied Sciences.

Jollife. *19th-Cen. Short Title Cat.*
[J. W. Jollife]. *Nineteenth Century Short Title Catalogue*. Ser. 1, phase 1. 1801–15. 6 vols. Newcastle-upon-Tyne: Avero Publications, 1984.

Jones. *Later Periods of Quakerism*
Rufus M. Jones. *The Later Periods of Quakerism*. 2 vols. London: Macmillan, 1921.

Jordan. *Col. Fam. Phila.*
John W. Jordan. *Colonial Families of Philadelphia*. 2 vols. New York: Lewis, 1911.

Kelsey. *Friends and the Indians*
Rayner W. Kelsey. *Friends and the Indians*. Philadelphia: The Associated Executive Committee of Friends on Indian Affairs, 1917.

Kersey. *Narrative*
Jesse Kersey. *A Narrative of the Early Life, Travels, and Gospel Labors of Jesse Kersey, late of Chester County, Pennsylvania*. Philadelphia: T. Ellwood Chapman, 1851.

King. *Medical World of the Eighteenth Century*
Lester S. King. *The Medical World of the Eighteenth Century*. Chicago: University of Chicago Press, 1958.

Kohn. *Eagle and Sword*
Richard H. Kohn. *Eagle and Sword: The Federalists and the Creation of the Military Establishment in America, 1783–1802*. New York: Free Press, 1975.

Korngold. *Citizen Toussaint*
Ralph Korngold. *Citizen Toussaint*. New York: Hill and Wang, 1944.

Labaree. *Boston Tea Party*
Benjamin Woods Labaree. *The Boston Tea Party*. New York: Oxford University Press, 1966.

LaWall. *Pharmacy*
Charles H. LaWall. *Four Thousand Years of Pharmacy*. Philadelphia: Lippincott, 1927.

Laws Enacted in the Second Sitting
Laws Enacted in Second Sitting of the General Assembly of the Commonwealth of Pennsylvania Which Began at Lancaster . . . (February 18, 1778). Lancaster, Pa., 1778.

Lederer. *Colonial American English*
Richard M. Lederer, Jr. *Colonial Amerian English*. Essex, Conn.: Verbatim, 1985.

Lefebvre. *Napoleon*
Georges Lefebvre. *Napoleon From 18 Brumaire to Tilsit 1799–1807*. Translated by Henry F. Stockhold. New York: Columbia University Press, 1969.

Lewis, W. *New Dispensatory*

W. Lewis. *The New Dispensatory*. 5th ed. London, 1785.

Lewis, W. H., and Elvin-Lewis. *Medical Botany*

Walter H. Lewis and Memory P. F. Elvin-Lewis. *Medical Botany*. New York: Wiley, 1977.

Lowndes. *Bib. Manual*

William Thomas Lowndes. *The Bibliographer's Manual of English Literature*. Rev. ed. London: George Bell & Sons, [1868].

Macalpine and Hunter. *George III and Mad-Business*

Ida Macalpine and Richard Hunter. *George III and the Mad-Business*. New York: Random House, 1969.

McLaughlin. *Matthew Lyon*

J. Fairfax McLaughlin. *Matthew Lyon: The Hampden of Congress, A Biography*. New York: Wynkoop Hallenbeck Crawford, 1900.

McNealy. *Bucks County*

Terry A. McNealy. *A History of Bucks County*. Pt. 1. Fallsington, Pa.: Bucks County Historical Tourist Commission, 1970.

Marcus and Perry. *Supreme Court*

Maeva Marcus and James R. Perry, eds. *The Documentary History of the Supreme Court of the United States, 1789–1800*. New York: Columbia University Press, 1985.

Marshall. *Diary Extracts*

Extracts from the Diary of Christopher Marshall 1774–1781. Edited by William Duane. Albany, 1877. Reprint. New York: The New York Times and Arno Press, 1969.

Martindale. *Byberry*

Joseph C. Martindale. *A History of the Townships of Byberry and Moreland, in Philadelphia, Pa*. Revised ed., edited by Albert W. Duckey. Philadelphia: George W. Jacob, 1875.

Mathews. *Wayne, Pike and Monroe Counties*

Alfred Mathews. *History of Wayne, Pike and Monroe Counties, Pennsylvania*. Philadelphia: R. T. Peck, 1886.

Maxey. "Samuel Preston's Agency"

David W. Maxey. "Of Castles in Stockport and Other Strictures: Samuel Preston's Contentious Agency for Henry Drinker." *Pennsylvania Magazine of History and Biography* 110 (1986): 413–46.

Maxey. "Union Farm"

David W. Maxey. "The Union Farm: Henry Drinker's Experiment in Deriving Profit from Virtue." *Pennsylvania Magazine of History and Biography* 107 (1983): 607–29.

Mekeel. "Founding Years"

Arthur J. Mekeel. "The Founding Years, 1681–1789." In *Friends in the Delaware Valley: Philadelphia Yearly Meeting 1681–1981*, ed. John M. Moore, 14–55. Haverford, Pa.: Friends Historical Association, 1981.

Mekeel. *Relation of the Quakers*

Arthur J. Mekeel. *The Relation of the Quakers to the American Revolution.* Washington, D.C.: University Press of America, 1979.

Miller, J. C. *Federalist Era*

John C. Miller. *The Federalist Era 1789–1801.* New York: Harper & Row, 1960.

Miller, R. G. *Federalist City*

Richard G. Miller. *Philadelphia, the Federalist City: A Study of Urban Politics 1789–1801.* Port Washington, N.Y.: Kennikat Press, 1976.

Millspaugh. *Medicinal Plants*

Charles F. Millspaugh. *American Medicinal Plants.* New York: Dover, 1974.

Mitchell. *Hamilton*

Broadus Mitchell. *Alexander Hamilton.* Vol. 2. *The National Adventure, 1788–1804.* New York: Macmillan, 1962.

Montgomery. *Textiles*

Florence M. Montgomery. *Textiles in America 1650–1870: A Dictionary Based on Original Documents, Prints and Paintings, Commercial Records, American Merchant Papers, Shopkeepers' Advertisements, and Pattern Books with Original Swatches of Clothes.* New York: Norton, 1984.

Moore, J. "Moore's Journal"

"Joseph Moore's Journal." Michigan Pioneer and Historical Society. *Historical Collections* 17 (1892): 632–71.

Moore, J. M. *Friends in the Delaware Valley*

John M. Moore, ed. *Friends in the Delaware Valley: Philadelphia Yearly Meeting 1681–1981.* Haverford, Pa.: Friends Historical Association, 1981.

Moore, S. S., and Jones. *Traveller's Directory*

S. S. Moore and T. W. Jones, *The Traveller's Directory.* 2d ed. Philadelphia: Mathew Carey, 1804.

Moreau de St. Méry. *Journey*

Médéric Louis Élle Moreau de Saint-Méry. *Moreau de St. Mery's American Journey (1793–1798).* Translated and edited by Kenneth Roberts and Anna M. Roberts. Garden City, N.Y.: Doubleday, 1947.

Morris. *Encyclopedia*

Richard B. Morris, ed. *Encyclopedia of American History.* New York: Harper & Row, 1970.

Morris. *Government and Labor*

Richard B. Morris. *Government and Labor in Early America.* New York: Columbia University Press, 1951.

Morton. "Diary"

"The Diary of Robert Morton. Kept in Philadelphia while That City was Occupied by the British Army in 1777." *Pennsylvania Magazine of History and Biography* 1 (1877): 1–39.

Mott. *American Magazines*

Frank Luther Mott. *A History of American Magazines 1741–1850.* 2 vols. Cambridge: Belknap Press of Harvard University Press, 1957.

Nash. *Forging Freedom*

Gary Nash. *Forging Freedom. The Formation of Philadelphia's Black Community.* Cambridge: Harvard University Press, 1988.

Nelson. *Anthony Wayne*

Paul David Nelson. *Anthony Wayne, Soldier of the Early Republic.* Bloomington: Indiana University Press, 1985.

NUC *National Union Catalog. Pre-1956 Imprints.* London: Mansell, 1968.

NYPL cat.

Dictionary Catalog of The Research Libraries of The New York Public Library. New York: New York Public Library, Astor, Lennox and Tilden Foundations, 1979.

Oaks. "Philadelphians in Exile"

Robert F. Oaks. "Philadelphians in Exile: The Problem of Loyalty during the American Revolution." *Pennsylvania Magazine of History and Biography* 96 (1972): 298–325.

Oberholtzer. *Robert Morris*

Ellis Paxson Oberholtzer. *Robert Morris, Patriot and Financier.* New York: Macmillan, 1903.

OED *Oxford English Dictionary.* Oxford, 1933. 2d ed. Oxford: Clarendon Press, 1989.

Ott. *Haitian Revolution*

Thomas O. Ott. *The Haitian Revolution 1789–1804.* Knoxville: University of Tennessee Press, 1973.

Ousterhout. "Pennsylvania Land Confiscations"

Anne M. Ousterhout. "Pennsylvania Land Confiscations during the Revolution" *Pennsylvania Magazine of History and Biography* 10 (1978): 328–43.

Pa. Archives

Samuel Hazard et al., eds. *Pennsylvania Archives: Selected and Arranged from Original Documents in the Office of the Secretary of the Commonwealth.* Harrisburg and Philadelphia, 1825–1935.

Pa. Chron.

Pennsylvania Chronicle.

Pa. Ev. Post

Pennsylvania Evening Post.

Pa. Gaz.

Pennsylvania Gazette.

Pa. Hist.

Pennsylvania History.

Pa. Journal

Pennsylvania Journal and Weekly Advertiser.

Pakenham. *Year of Liberty*

Thomas Pakenham. *The Year of Liberty: The Story of the Great Irish Rebellion of 1798.* London: Hodder and Stoughton, 1969.

Pa. Ledger

Pennsylvania Ledger.

Pa. Packet
Pennsylvania Packet.

Pa. Royal Gaz.
Pennsylvania Royal Gazette.

Parr. *London Medical Dictionary*
Bartholomew Parr. *The London Medical Dictionary.* 2 vols. Philadelphia: Mitchell, Ames, and White, 1819.

Partridge. *Dictionary of Slang*
Eric Partridge. *A Dictionary of Slang and Unconventional English.* 8th ed., edited by Paul Beale. New York: Macmillan, 1984.

Peale. *Selected Papers*
The Selected Papers of Charles Willson Peale and His Family. Edited by Lillian B. Miller. New Haven: Yale University Press for the National Portrait Gallery, Smithsonian Institution, 1983–.

Peirce. *Meteorological Account*
Charles Peirce. *A Meteorological Account of the Weather in Philadelphia from January 1, 1790, to January 1, 1847.* Philadelphia: Lindsay & Blackiston, 1847.

Penn. *Papers*
The Papers of William Penn. Edited by Richard S. Dunn and Mary Maples Dunn. Vol. 2. Philadelphia: University of Pennsylvania Press, 1982.

Pennypacker. *Downingtown*
Charles H. Pennypacker. *History of Downingtown, Chester County, Pa.* Downingtown: Downingtown Publishing Co., 1909.

Philadelphia City Cavalry. *Book of the First Troop*
Philadelphia City Cavalry. *Book of the First Troop of Philadelphia City Cavalry.* Philadelphia: Hallowell, 1915.

Philadelphia Yearly Meeting. *Rules of Discipline* (1797)
Society of Friends. *Rules of Discipline and Christian Advices of the Yearly Meeting of Friends for Pennsylvania and New Jersey.* Philadelphia: Samuel Sansom, 1797.

Philadelphia Yearly Meeting. *Rules of Discipline* (1806)
Philadelphia Yearly Meeting. *Rules of Discipline of the Yearly Meeting of Friends Held in Philadelphia.* Philadelphia: Kimber, Conrad, 1806.

Platt. "Encounter between Griswold and Lyon"
Orville H. Platt. "The Encounter between Roger Griswold and Matthew Lyon in 1798." *Papers of the New Haven Colony Historical Society* 6 (1900): 283–301.

PMHB *Pennsylvania Magazine of History and Biography.*

Powell. *Bring Out Your Dead*
John Harvey Powell. *"Bring Out Your Dead": The Great Plague of Yellow Fever in Philadelphia in 1793.* Philadelphia: University of Pennsylvania Press, 1949.

Powers. "Historic Bridges"
Fred. Perry Powers. "The Historic Bridges of Philadelphia." *City Historical Society of Philadelphia* 1 (1908–16): 265–316.

Redman. *Account of the Yellow Fever, 1762*
John Redman. *An Account of the Yellow Fever as it prevailed in Philadelphia in the Autumn of 1762.* Philadelphia, 1865.

Reed. *Joseph Reed*
William B. Reed. *Life and Correspondence of Joseph Reed*. 2 vols. Philadelphia: Lindsay and Blackiston, 1847.

Rhoads. *Catawissa*
Willard R. Rhoads. *History of the Catawissa Quaker Meeting at Catawissa, Columbia County, Pa. and the Roaring Creek Quaker Meeting near Numidia, Columbia County, Pa.* Numidia, Pa.: n.p., 1963.

Richardson, H. N. *Dictionary of Napoleon*
Hubert N. Richardson. *A Dictionary of Napoleon and His Times*. New York, 1921. Reprint. Ann Arbor: Gryphon Books, 1971.

Richardson, J. D. *Messages and Papers of the Presidents*
James D. Richardson, comp. *A Compilation of the Messages and Papers of the Presidents 1789–1908*. Vol. 1. Washington D.C.: Bureau of National Literature and Art, 1908.

Ritter. *Moravian Church*
Abraham Ritter. *History of the Moravian Church in Philadelphia from Its Foundation in 1742 to the Present Time*. Philadelphia: Haynes & Zell, 1857.

Robinson. *18th-Cen. Brit. Books*
F. J. G. Robinson et al. *Eighteenth-Century British Books, An Author Union Catalogue*. 4 vols. Newcastle-upon-Tyne: Wm. Dawson & Sons, 1981.

Rodger. *Second Coalition*
A. B. Rodger. *The War of the Second Coalition 1798 to 1801: A Strategic Commentary*. Oxford: Clarendon Press, 1964.

Rosenbach. *Early American Children's Books*
A. S. W. Rosenbach. *Early American Children's Books*. Portland, Maine, 1933. Reprint. New York: Kraus Reprint Corporation, 1966.

Rosswurm. *Arms, Country, and Class*
Steven Rosswurm. *Arms, Country, and Class: The Philadelphia Militia and "Lower Sort" during the American Revolution, 1775–1783*. New Brunswick, N.J.: Rutgers University Press, 1987.

Rothenberg. *Napoleon's Great Adversaries*
Gunther E. Rothenberg. *Napoleon's Great Adversaries: The Archduke Charles and the Austrian Army*. London: B. T. Batsford, 1982.

Routh. *Memoir*
Martha Routh. *Memoir of the Life, Travels, and Religious Experience of Martha Routh*. York, England: Alexander, 1822.

Rucker. "Pain Relief in Obstetrics"
M. Pierce Rucker. "An Eigthteenth-Century Method of Pain Relief in Obstetrics." *Journal of the History of Medicine and Allied Sciences* 5 (1950): 101–8.

Rush. *Autobiography*
The Autobiography of Benjamin Rush. Edited by George W. Corner. Princeton: Princeton University Press for the American Philosophical Society, 1948.

Rush. *Inquiries and Observations*
Benjamin Rush. *Medical Inquiries and Observations*. 1st ed. 5 vols. Philadelphia: Thomas Dobson, 1794–98; 2d ed., rev. 4 vols. Philadelphia: J. Conrad, 1805; 3d ed., rev. 4 vols. Philadelphia: 1809.

Rush. "Observations on the Gout"

Benjamin Rush. "Observations upon the Nature and Cure of the Gout." In *Inquiries and Observations*. 1st ed. 5:137–207.

Rush. "Yellow Fever, 1797"

Benjamin Rush. "An Account of the Bilious Yellow Fever, as It Appeared in Philadelphia in 1797." In *Inquiries and Observations*. 2d ed. 4:1–62.

Rush. "Yellow Fever, 1803"

Bejamin Rush. "An Account of the Bilious Yellow Fever, as It Appeared in Philadelphia, in 1803." In *Inquiries and Observations*. 2d ed. 4:131–43.

Ryerson. *Revolution Is Now Begun*

Richard Alan Ryerson. *The Revolution Is Now Begun: The Radical Committees of Philadelphia, 1765–1776*. Philadelphia: University of Pennsylvania Press, 1978.

Sabin. *Dictionary*

Joseph Sabin. *A Dictionary of Books Relating to America*. New York, 1868. Reprint. Amsterdam: N. Israel, 1961.

Sachse. "Wayside Inns"

Julius Friederich Sachse. "The Wayside Inns on the Lancaster Road between Philadelphia and Lancaster." *Pennsylvania German Society* 21 (1910): 1–77; 22 (1911): 1–109.

Sachse. *Wayside Inns*

Julius F. Sachse. *The Wayside Inns on the Lancaster Roadside between Philadelphia and Lancaster*. 1912. 2d ed. Lancaster, Pa.: New Era Printing Co., 1915.

Salinger. *Labor and Indentured Servants*

Sharon V. Salinger. *"To Serve Well and Faithfully": Labor and Indentured Servants in Pennsylvania 1682–1800*. Cambridge: Cambridge University Press, 1987.

Scharf and Westcott. *Philadelphia*

J. Thomas Scharf and Thompson Westcott. *History of Philadelphia 1609–1884*. 3 vols. Philadelphia: Everts, 1884.

Scholten. *Childbearing*

Catherine M. Scholten. *Childbearing in American Society 1650–1850*. New York: New York University Press, 1985.

Scott and Rothaus. *French Revolution*

Samuel F. Scott and Barry Rothaus, eds. *Historical Dictionary of the French Revolution*. Westport, Conn.: Greenwood Press, 1985.

Sellers. *Charles Willson Peale*

Charles Coleman Sellers. *Charles Willson Peale*. Memoirs of the American Philosophical Society 23, pts. 1–2, Philadelphia, 1947.

Sellers. *Mr. Peale's Museum*

Charles Coleman Sellers. *Mr. Peale's Museum: Charles Willson Peale and the First Popular Museum of Natural Science and Art*. New York: Norton, 1980.

Shaw and Shoemaker. *Am. Bibliography*

Ralph R. Shaw and Richard H. Shoemaker. *American Bibliography: A Preliminary Checklist for 1801–1819*. New York: Scarecrow, 1958–66.

Sherman. *Miranda Expedition*
[John H. Sherman]. *A General Account of Miranda's Expedition*. New York: M'Farlane and Long, 1808.

Shipton and Mooney. *Index*
Clifford K. Shipton and James E. Mooney. *National Index of American Imprints Through 1800*. [Worcester, Mass.]: American Antiquarian Society and Barre Publishers, 1969.

Siddall. "Bloodletting"
A. Clair Siddall. "Bloodletting in American Obstetrical Practice 1800–1945." *Bulletin of the History of Medicine* 54 (1980): 101–10.

Simpson. *Cyclopedia of Methodism*
Matthew Simpson, ed. *Cyclopedia of Methodism, Embracing Sketches of Its Rise, Progress, and Present Condition, with Biographical Notices and Numerous Illustrations*. 5th ed. Philadelphia: Everts, 1883.

Skinner. *Medical Terms*
Henry Alan Skinner. *The Origin of Medical Terms*. 2d ed. New York: Hafner, 1970.

Smedley. *Catalog of Westtown*
Susanna Smedley. *Catalog of Westtown through the Years*. Westtown, Pa.: Westtown Alumni Association, 1945.

Smith, J. M. *Freedom's Fetters*
James Morton Smith. *Freedom's Fetters: The Alien and Sedition Laws and American Civil Liberties*. Ithaca, N.Y.: Cornell University Press, 1956.

Smith, P. H. *Letters of the Delegates*
Paul H. Smith, ed. *Letters of the Delegates to Congress*. Washington, D.C.: Library of Congress, 1976–.

Smith, W. G. *English Proverbs*
William George Smith, comp. *The Oxford Dictionary of English Proverbs*. 3d ed. revised by F. P. Wilson. Oxford: Clarendon Press, 1970.

Society of Friends. *London Grove Monthly Meeting*
Two-Hundreth Anniversary of the Founding of London Grove Meeting by the Society of Friends of London Grove, Pennsylvania. London Grove, Pa.: Inness & Sons, 1914.

Soderlund. *Quakers & Slavery*
Jean R. Soderlund. *Quakers & Slavery: A Divided Spirit*. Princeton: Princeton University Press, 1985.

Statutes at Large
Commonwealth of Pennsylvania. *The Statutes at Large of Philadelphia from 1682 to 1801*. Compiled by James T. Mitchell and Henry Flanders. 16 vols. Harrisburg, Pa.: 1896–1911.

Stone. "Philadelphia Society"
Frederick D. Stone, "Philadelphia Society One Hundred Years Ago; or, the Reign of Continental Money." *PMHB* 3 (1879): 361–94.

Stoneburner and Stoneburner. *Quaker Women*
Carol Stoneburner and John Stoneburner, eds. *The Influence of Quaker Women on American History*. Biographical Studies. Lewiston, N.Y.: Mellen Press, 1986.

Stryker. *Forts on the Delaware*
William S. Stryker. *The Forts on the Delaware in the Revolutionary War*. Trenton, N.J.: Murphy, 1901.

Swan. *Plain & Fancy*
Susan Burrows Swan. *Plain & Fancy: American Women and Their Needlework 1700–1850*. New York: Holt, Rinehart & Winston, 1977.

Swarthmore. *Catalog Friends Historical Library*
Friends Historical Library, Swarthmore College. *Catalog of the Book and Serials Collections of the Friends Historical Library*. Boston: G. K. Hall, 1982.

Taylor. *Longstreth Family*
Agnes Longstreth Taylor. *The Longstreth Family*. Rev. ed. Philadelphia: Ferris & Leach, 1909.

Teeters. *Cradle of the Penitentiary*
Negley K. Teeters. *The Cradle of the Penitentiary: The Walnut Street Jail at Philadelphia 1773–1835*. Philadelphia: Temple University Press, 1955.

Teeters. *Pennsylvania Prison Society*
Negley K. Teeters. *They Were in Prison: A History of the Pennsylvania Prison Society 1787–1937*. Chicago: Winston, 1937.

Thacher. *New American Dispensatory*
James Thacher. *The New American Dispensatory*. 2d ed. Boston: Wait and Williams, 1813.

Thayer. *Israel Pemberton*
Theodore Thayer. *Israel Pemberton, King of the Quakers*. Philadelphia: Historical Society of Pennsylvania, 1943.

Thomas, K. *Religion and Decline of Magic*
Keith Thomas. *Religion and the Decline of Magic*. New York: Scribners, 1971.

Thomas, R. *Modern Domestic Medicine*
Robert Thomas. *Modern Domestic Medicine: Being a Treatise Divested of Professional Terms on the Nature, Causes, Symptoms, and Treatment of the Diseases of Men, Women, and Children, in Both Cold and Warm Climates: With Appropriate Prescriptions in English*. New York: Collins, 1829.

Tinkcom, Tinkcom, and Simon. *Historic Germantown*
Harry M. Tinkcom, Margaret B. Tinkcom, and Grant Miles Simon. *Historic Germantown: From the Founding to the Early Part of the Nineteenth Century*. Memoirs of the American Philosophical Society 39. Philadelphia, 1955.

Tolles. *George Logan*
Frederick Tolles. *George Logan of Philadelphia*. New York: Oxford University Press, 1953.

Toner, *Inoculation in Pa.*
J. M. Toner. "Inoculation in Pennsylvania." *Transactions of the Medical Society of the State of Pennsylvania*, 16th annual sess. 4th ser. 1 (1865): 163–82.

Van Doren. *Secret History*
Carl Van Doren. *Secret History of the American Revolution*. Garden City, N.Y.: Garden City Publishing Co., 1941.

Vogel. *American Indian Medicine*
Virgil J. Vogel. *American Indian Medicine*. Norman: University of Oklahoma Press, 1970.

Wainwright. *Philadelphia Contributionship*
Nicholas B. Wainwright. *A Philadelphia Story: The Philadelphia Contributionship for the Insurance of Houses from Loss by Fire*. Philadelphia: n.p., 1952.

Washington. *Writings*
The Writings of George Washington. Edited by John C. Fitzpatrick. 39 vols. Washington, D.C.: Government Printing Office, 1931–44.

Watson, G. *New Cambridge Bibliography*
George Watson, ed. *The New Cambridge Bibliography of English Literature*. 4 vols. Cambridge: Cambridge University Press, 1971.

Watson, J. F. *Annals*
John F. Watson. *Annals of Philadelphia and Pennsylvania in the Olden Time*. 3 vols. Philadelphia: Stuart, 1891.

Watt, *Bibliotheca Britannica*
Robert Watt. *Bibliotheca Britannica*. Edinburgh: 1824. Reprint. New York: Franklin, 1965.

Webster. *Brief History*
Noah Webster. *A Brief History of Epidemic and Pestilential Diseases*. 2 vols. Hartford, Conn.: Hudson & Goodwin, 1799.

Weiss. "More's Cheap Repository Tracts"
Harry B. Weiss, "Hannah More's Cheap Repository Tracts in America." *Bulletin of the New York Public Library* 50 (1946): 539–49, 634–39.

Weiss and Weiss. *Snuff Mills of New Jersey*
Henry B. Weiss and Frances M. Weiss. *The Early Snuff Mills of New Jersey*. Trenton, N.J.: New Jersey Agricultural Society, 1962.

Wetherill. *Religious Society of Friends*
Charles Wetherill. *History of the Religious Society of Friends Called by Some the Free Quakers in the City of Philadelphia*. [Philadelphia]: Printed for the Society, 1894.

Wharton. *State Trials*
Francis Wharton, ed. *State Trials of the United States during the Administration of Washington and Adams*. Philadelphia: Carey and Hart, 1849.

White, *Management of Pregnant and Lying-In Women*
Charles White. *A Treatise on the Management of Pregnant and Lying-in Women* . . . Worcester, Mass.: Isaiah Thomas, 1793.

Whiting. *Early American Proverbs*
Bartlett Jere Whiting. *Early American Proverbs and Proverbial Expressions*. Cambridge, Mass.: Belknap Press of Harvard University Press, 1977.

Wilkinson. "Land Speculation"
Norman B. Wilkinson. "Land Policy and Speculation in Pennsylvania 1788–1800." Ph.D. diss. University of Pennsylvania, 1958.

Wing. *Catalogue*
Donald Wing, comp. *Short-Title Catalogue of Books Printed in England, Scotland, Ireland, Wales, and British America and of English Books Printed in Other Countries*. Rev. ed. New York: The Index Committee of the Modern Language Association, 1982.

WMQ *William and Mary Quarterly*.

Wolman. *"Tale of Two Colonial Cities"*

Roslyn S. Wolman. "A Tale of Two Colonial Cities: Inoculation against Smallpox in Philadelphia and Boston." *Transactions and Studies of the College of Physicians of Philadelphia*. 4th ser., 45 (1978): 338–47.

Woodward and Hageman. *Burlington and Mercer Counties*

E. M. Woodward and John F. Hageman. *History of Burlington and Mercer Counties New Jersey, with Biographical Sketches of Many of Their Pioneers and Prominent Men*. Philadelphia: Everts & Peck, 1883.

WPA. *Delaware*

Federal Writers Project, Works Progress Administration in the State of Delaware. *Delaware: A Guide to the First State*. New York: Viking Press, 1938.

WPA. *New Jersey*

Federal Writers Project, Works Project Administration in the State of New Jersey. *New Jersey: A Guide to its Present and Past*. New York: Viking Press, 1939.

WPA. *Pennsylvania*

Federal Writers Project, Works Projects Administration in the State of Pennsylvania. *Pennsylvania: A Guide to the Keystone State*. New York: Oxford University Press, 1940.

Young. *Little Turtle*

Calvin M. Young, *Little Turtle, The Great Chief of the Miami Indian Nation*. Indianapolis: Sentinal, 1917.

Glossary of French Words and Phrases

Accouchement: delivery; childbirth

allez cet matin chez un person a mon desire: went this morning to the home of a person at my request

allez de: left; went out

a mon Chere: to my dear

a point du purpose: to no purpose

argent: money

a un *parlez* pas agreeable: had a disagreeable talk

ausse tot chagrined: so easily annoyed

avac la argent: with the money

avac les Filles: with the girls

avac moy: with me

avac moy solas: with me alone

avac nous: with us

avec nous: with us

baucoup: much; a great deal

beau coup de parler cett sori entre mon fils a son pare: a lot of talk this evening between my son and his father

Bleu Parlor: Blue Parlor

bruit enhaut: a noise upstairs; a loud noise

brulez son —— cett matin: burned his —— this morning

cet matin: this morning

cette matin [acac] le Fille: this morning with the girl; daughter

Cette une Monde de trestes: It's a world of sadness; an unhappy world

cher-amie: dear friend

chez eux: to their house

chez lui: at his house

chez nous: at our house

ci-devant Servant: former servant

Collecta Argent pour: to collect money for

commence this evening tricotté un pr. de bra[cés]: start(ed) this evening to knit a pair of [suspenders; braces]

dan lure Mason Nett: in their cottage; small house

dans cette Mound: in this world

dans la Salon avac H. D. solas—cette matin: in the parlor with H.D. alone—this morning

dans le Cabinet de Verdierre: in the [green arbor]

dans le maisone: in the house

dans le mamme manner de W.E: in the same manner as W.E.

dans [un pett.]: in a [petulant, irritated mood]

[de] nous Amie: of our friends

Dent artificial, met dans sa bouche: an artificial tooth put in her mouth

dire Adieu: to say goodbye

don. cet sorie, sans efft: gave this evening, without effect

don. mat.: gave this morning

donnez: gave

donnez cet maten: gave this morning

donnez sans eff——: gave without eff[ect]

elle demande plus Argent: she asks for more money

elle parler (parlez) beaucoup: she spoke, talks a lot

en bas: downstairs

en haut: upstairs

en haut et en bas: above and below

en passant: by the way

en Verity: in truth; really

et avec ses instruments et beaucoup deficility, ill la delivera d'enfant mort: and with his instruments and a lot of difficulty, he delivered her of the dead baby

et son frere [ ] parle cette main [ ]: and his brother [ ] speak this morning [ ]

faisant les Mason de Chart, pour les enfant: making a house of cards for the children

fort malade cet matin: very sick this morning

frecas avac: disturbance, dispute with

habilliment pour la noir au jaun illigetemate: clothing for the black or yellow illegitimate

ici: here

il don un coup, mas pas de grace: he gave a blow, but not fatal

il est comme son ouvrage, la, la: he is like his work, so, so

il est dix mois, depuis Molly est: it is ten months since Molly is

ill est un viere de Bray: he is a [?]

ill parle beaucoup—Je lui aime: he talks a lot—I like him

ill parlez avac Nous: he spoke with us

il perlez beaucoup: he spoke, talked a lot

J'ai a weight aux coeur cett soir: I have a heavy heart this evening

J'ai boucoup chagrin touchant mes enfants: I have a great deal of sorrow concerning my children

J'ai eté bien favouré cet matin: I was well favored this morning

janteé: gentle; graceful

Jaune pettet: the little yellow one

Je commence donne: I started to give

Je craint elle a eté a la [T]——r: I feared that she was at the [theatre]

Je craint elle a plus que la infirmité: I fear that she has more than infirmity

Je crois: I believe

Je ete malade tout cet jour don. cet. mat. sans efft: I was sick all this day, gave this morning without effect

Je ete tout la jour fort malade: I was very sick all day

Je donne, aujourdui un lavement to SD. trois a mon mari: I gave SD. an enema today, three to my husband

Je donnez a H.D. un —— cet matin, la premier qu'il a Jamais eu: I gave a —— to H.D. this morning, the first that he ever had

Je donnez a [J]L quelque chose pour un pover francioes: I gave JL something for a poor French person

Je la donnez: I gave him, it

Je l'assista pour payer les expenses: I helped her to pay the expenses

Je lui donne cett matin, Un Lev——t: I gave him an enema this morning

Je lui donne doux Levement: I gave him two enemas

Je lui donne un Levement: I gave him an enema

Je[m']donne —— se mataine: I gave myself —— this morning.

Je m'donnez: I gave myself

Je ne dormiez pas tout hier au sois: I did not sleep all last evening

Je ne suis pas assi bien que Jetais ce matain: I am not as well as I was this morning

Je ne suis pas bien: I am not well

Je ne suis pas dans bonne santé: I am not in good health; I am not feeling well

Je n'etoit pas dans le chamber a le moment Cretical: I was not in the room at the critical moment

Je parlez a Dr. K. touchant un malade, que m'donnez trouble: I spoke to Dr. K. about a sickness that was giving me trouble

Je perlez avac: I spoke with

Je priez prendre C——r O——[l]: I was asked to take [Castor Oil]

Je rien plus dire: I have nothing more to say

Je suis bien mala. (malade): I am very sick

Je suis bien Malade aujour'd'huy: I am very sick today

Je suis, Je suis,—pas en un situation hereux: I am not in a happy situation

Je suis loin de bien: I am far from well

Je suis loin de bien ma mamme: I am far from well myself

Je suis Malade: I am sick

Je suis malaide: I am sick

Je suis meux encore: I am better again

Je suis [Seuls]: I am alone

Jeuant avac son frare: playing with her brother

J'ne suis pas bien: I am not well

Jouant aux Ivorys: playing at dice

Jouer aux cartes: to play cards; playing cards

[jouia au fluet]: play the flute

la jour de ma nativite: my birthday; the day of my birth

le enfant est fort grand et la mere bien pitit: the child is very large and the mother very small

levement [hair au soeps]: an enema [last evening]

Lit dans notre Chamber: bed is in our room, chamber

Livre Francious: a French book

Ma jour natal: My birthday; my day of birth

malade au stomac: stomachache

Mal aux Vantre: stomachaches

Malhereux: unhappy

Mall a V——n——r: [stomach] ache

Mallhereux fois: unhappy times

Mall tems: bad times

Ma pouver fils: My poor son

ma tres Chere: my very, most dear

Matres Chere: my very, most dear

m'donnez un L——: gave myself an [enema]

Mon Esprit fort bas, tout cett Jour: My spirit was low all day

mon esprit fort oppresseé sur beaucoup d'occasion: my spirit is very oppressed on many occasions

Notre chate tombez dans la maison-Nette: Our cat fell in the cottage, small house

notre place: our place

nous etions enhaut ensamble: We were upstairs together

Nous somme tout, bien la la: We are all fairly well

Novoux trist des nos Enfant: Sad news about our child[ren]

occurance pas agreeable: a disagreeable occurrence

Oh! quelle un Monde est cella!: Oh! What a world this is!

ou est mon fils: where is my son

ou est WD.: where is WD

pair de Soulier: a pair of shoes

parle trop a son Pere: spoke too much to her father

parlez a son pare: spoke to his father

parlez avac H.D. pas fort agreeable—comme quelque autres: a talk with H.D., not very agreeable—like some (a few) others

Parlez avac JD. touchant S.R.: Spoke with JD. about S.R.

parlez touchant! *MF:* talking about *MF*

par sas proper main: by his own hand; suicide

pas ensamble: not together

pas la Chose: not the thing

pas tout ensemble, mais l'un appre l'autre: not all together, but one after the other

pour Argant: for money

pour argent: for money

pour entendre: to listen to

pour lui: for him

pour moy: for me

pour quoy, Je ne say pas: why, I don't know

pour rien: for nothing; with no effect

pour son avis touchant quelque chose: for her advice about something

pour son frare: for her brother

pouver Mairia: poor Mairia

pr. Souliers: pair of shoes

pren. heir au soir, med[icine]: took last evening some [medicine]

pren. med[icine]: took some med[icine]

prenez un L—— en vain: took an [enema] in vain

quand le Reine du Ciel: when the Queen of the Sky

que [face à fà]: what a [face to face]

que l'enfant [sont] mort: that the child [is] dead

removez le Litt: removed the bed.

Robe Verd.: Green dress.

sans: without

sans Company: without company

sans un motion, Je las donnez un L——m——t: without a movement, I gave her an [enema]

sa Soeur: her sister

Seurtout: overcoat

solas: alone

solas tout cet apriaz midia: alone all afternoon

solas tout le jour: alone all day

sovenen cela: often [he does] that

Tambour'd muslin et [Trant Gounds]: embroidered muslin and [thirty gowns]

touchant Baubette: about Baubette

toujours: forever; always

tout a fait: entirely

tout cet jour: all day; all this day

tout cett matin: all morning; all this morning

tout ensemble: all together

tout est matin: all morning; all this morning

tout La Monde: everyone; everybody

un bruit enhaut: a noise upstairs; a loud noise

un Dent artificial, met dans sa bouche: an artificial tooth put in her mouth

un frecas avac: a disturbance, dispute with

un levement [hair au soeps]: an enema [last evening]

un Livre Francious: a French book

un occurance pas agreeable: a disagreeable occurrence

un pair de Soulier: a pair of shoes

un parlez avac H.D. pas fort agreeable—comme quelque autres: a talk with H.D., not very agreeable—like some (a few) others

un pr. Souliers: a pair of shoes

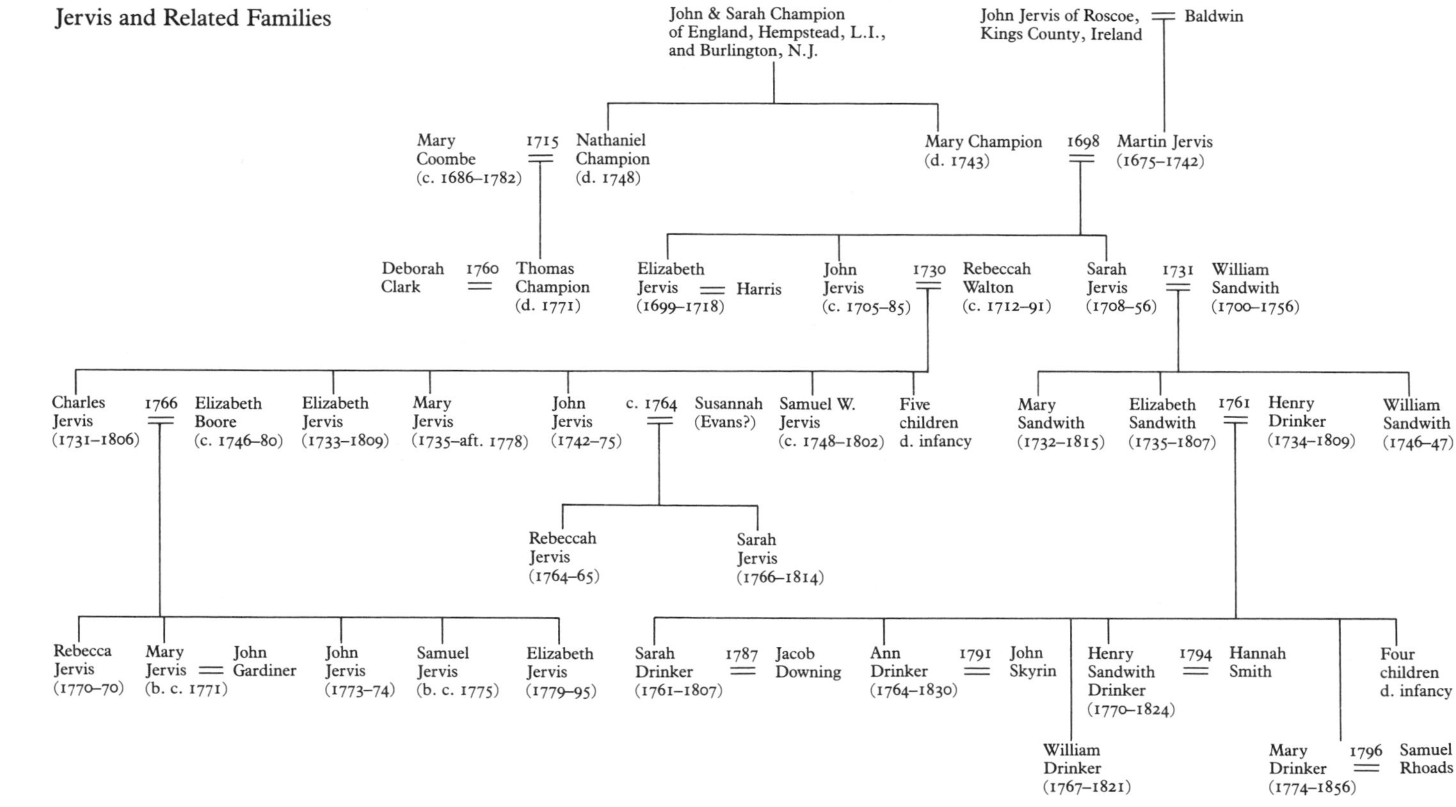
Jervis and Related Families
John & Sarah Champion of England, Hempstead, L.I., and Burlington, N.J.
John Jervis of Roscoe, Kings County, Ireland
Baldwin
Mary Coombe (c. 1686–1782)
1715
Nathaniel Champion (d. 1748)
Mary Champion (d. 1743)
1698
Martin Jervis (1675–1742)
Deborah Clark
1760
Thomas Champion (d. 1771)
Elizabeth Jervis (1699–1718)
Harris
John Jervis (c. 1705–85)
1730
Rebeccah Walton (c. 1712–91)
Sarah Jervis (1708–56)
1731
William Sandwith (1700–1756)
Charles Jervis (1731–1806)
1766
Elizabeth Boore (c. 1746–80)
Elizabeth Jervis (1733–1809)
Mary Jervis (1735–aft. 1778)
John Jervis (1742–75)
c. 1764
Susannah (Evans?)
Samuel W. Jervis (c. 1748–1802)
Five children d. infancy
Mary Sandwith (1732–1815)
Elizabeth Sandwith (1735–1807)
1761
Henry Drinker (1734–1809)
William Sandwith (1746–47)
Rebeccah Jervis (1764–65)
Sarah Jervis (1766–1814)
Rebecca Jervis (1770–70)
Mary Jervis (b. c. 1771)
John Gardiner
John Jervis (1773–74)
Samuel Jervis (b. c. 1775)
Elizabeth Jervis (1779–95)
Sarah Drinker (1761–1807)
1787
Jacob Downing
Ann Drinker (1764–1830)
1791
John Skyrin
Henry Sandwith Drinker (1770–1824)
1794
Hannah Smith
Four children d. infancy
William Drinker (1767–1821)
Mary Drinker (1774–1856)
1796
Samuel Rhoads

Drinker Ancestry

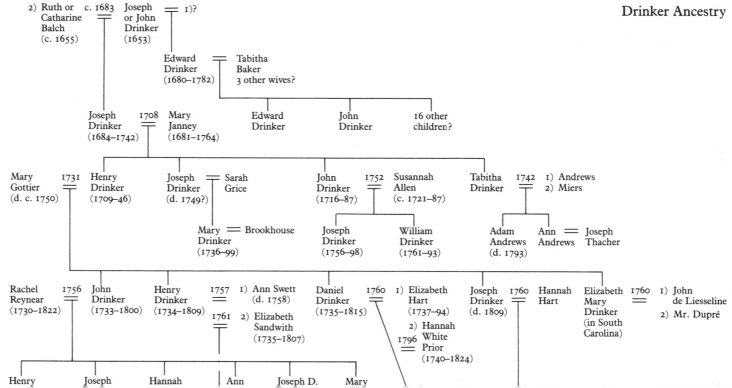

- 2) Ruth or Catharine Balch (c. 1655) = (c. 1683) Joseph or John Drinker (1653) = 1)?
  - Joseph Drinker (1684–1742) [son of Ruth or Catharine Balch] = (1708) Mary Janney (1681–1764)
    - Henry Drinker (1709–46) = (1731) Mary Gottier (d. c. 1750)
      - John Drinker (1733–1800) = (1756) Rachel Reynear (1730–1822)
        - Henry
        - Joseph
        - Hannah
        - Ann
        - Joseph D.
        - Mary
      - Henry Drinker (1734–1809) = (1757) 1) Ann Swett (d. 1758); = (1761) 2) Elizabeth Sandwith (1735–1807)
      - Daniel Drinker (1735–1815) = (1760) 1) Elizabeth Hart (1737–94); = (1796) 2) Hannah White Prior (1740–1824)
      - Joseph Drinker (d. 1809) = (1760) Hannah Hart
      - Elizabeth Mary Drinker (in South Carolina) = (1760) 1) John de Liesseline; 2) Mr. Dupré
    - Joseph Drinker (d. 1749?) = Sarah Grice
      - Mary Drinker (1736–99) = Brookhouse
    - John Drinker (1716–87) = (1752) Susannah Allen (c. 1721–87)
      - Joseph Drinker (1756–98)
      - William Drinker (1761–93)
    - Tabitha Drinker = (1742) 1) Andrews; 2) Miers
      - Adam Andrews (d. 1793)
      - Ann Andrews = Joseph Thacher
  - Edward Drinker (1680–1782) [son of 1)?] = Tabitha Baker; 3 other wives?
    - Edward Drinker
    - John Drinker
    - 16 other children?

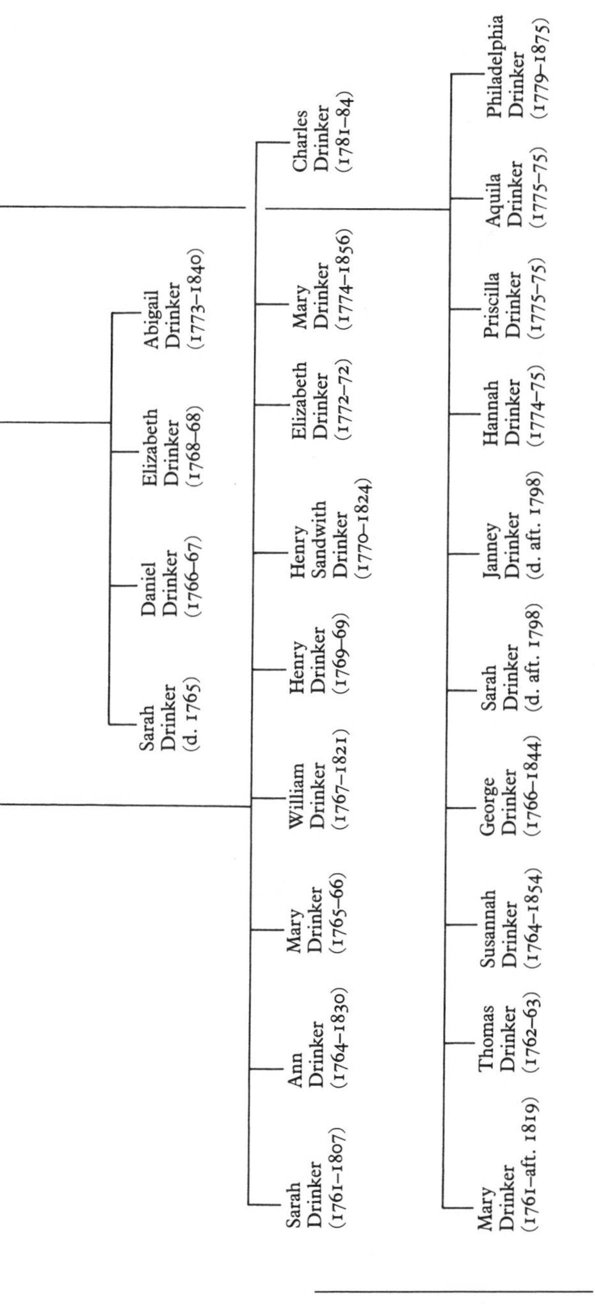
Sarah Drinker (d. 1765)
Daniel Drinker (1766–67)
Elizabeth Drinker (1768–68)
Abigail Drinker (1773–1840)
Sarah Drinker (1761–1807)
Ann Drinker (1764–1830)
Mary Drinker (1765–66)
William Drinker (1767–1821)
Henry Drinker (1769–69)
Henry Sandwith Drinker (1770–1824)
Elizabeth Drinker (1772–72)
Mary Drinker (1774–1856)
Charles Drinker (1781–84)
Mary Drinker (1761–aft. 1819)
Thomas Drinker (1762–63)
Susannah Drinker (1764–1854)
George Drinker (1766–1844)
Sarah Drinker (d. aft. 1798)
Janney Drinker (d. aft. 1798)
Hannah Drinker (1774–75)
Priscilla Drinker (1775–75)
Aquila Drinker (1775–75)
Philadelphia Drinker (1779–1875)

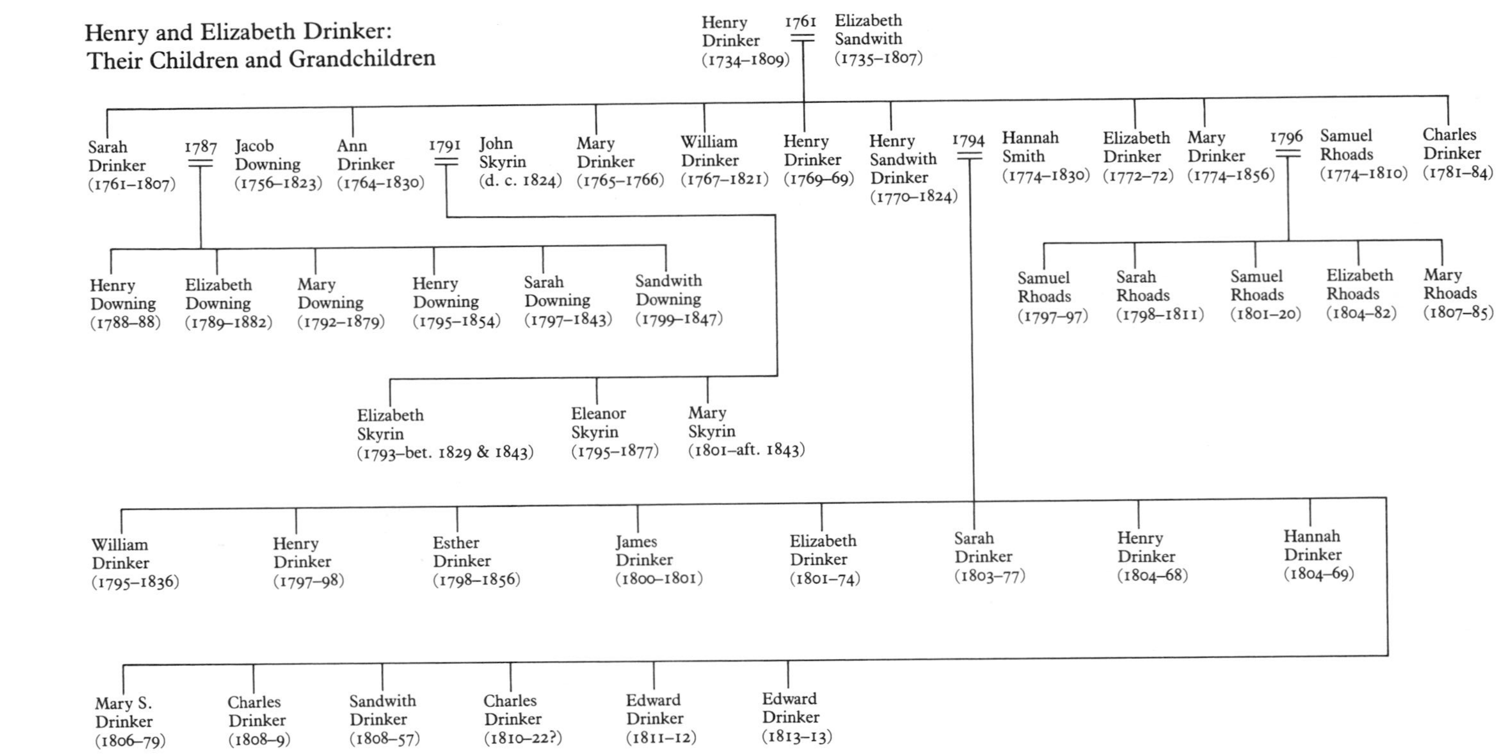

Henry and Elizabeth Drinker:
Their Children and Grandchildren
Henry Drinker (1734–1809)
1761
Elizabeth Sandwith (1735–1807)
Sarah Drinker (1761–1807)
1787
Jacob Downing (1756–1823)
Ann Drinker (1764–1830)
1791
John Skyrin (d. c. 1824)
Mary Drinker (1765–1766)
William Drinker (1767–1821)
Henry Drinker (1769–69)
Henry Sandwith Drinker (1770–1824)
1794
Hannah Smith (1774–1830)
Elizabeth Drinker (1772–72)
Mary Drinker (1774–1856)
1796
Samuel Rhoads (1774–1810)
Charles Drinker (1781–84)
Henry Downing (1788–88)
Elizabeth Downing (1789–1882)
Mary Downing (1792–1879)
Henry Downing (1795–1854)
Sarah Downing (1797–1843)
Sandwith Downing (1799–1847)
Samuel Rhoads (1797–97)
Sarah Rhoads (1798–1811)
Samuel Rhoads (1801–20)
Elizabeth Rhoads (1804–82)
Mary Rhoads (1807–85)
Elizabeth Skyrin (1793–bet. 1829 & 1843)
Eleanor Skyrin (1795–1877)
Mary Skyrin (1801–aft. 1843)
William Drinker (1795–1836)
Henry Drinker (1797–98)
Esther Drinker (1798–1856)
James Drinker (1800–1801)
Elizabeth Drinker (1801–74)
Sarah Drinker (1803–77)
Henry Drinker (1804–68)
Hannah Drinker (1804–69)
Mary S. Drinker (1806–79)
Charles Drinker (1808–9)
Sandwith Drinker (1808–57)
Charles Drinker (1810–22?)
Edward Drinker (1811–12)
Edward Drinker (1813–13)

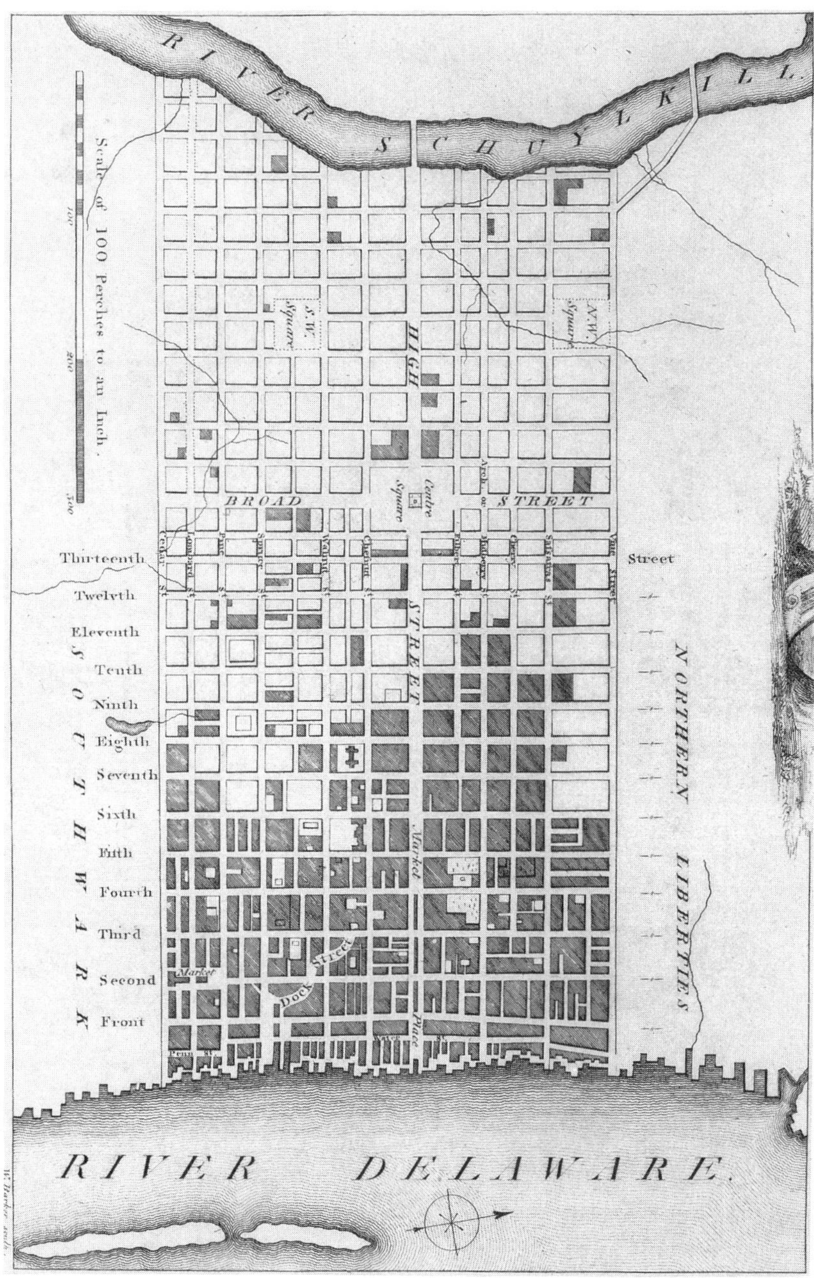

Plan of the City of Philadelphia [1800?], by W. Barker, engraver. Courtesy of the Map Division, The New York Public Library, Astor, Lenox and Tilden Foundations.

Courtesy of the Historical Society of Pennsylvania.

1758

Work[1] done in part of the Years: 175[7,] 1758: 1759: 1760.
Work'd a Irish stitch[2] Pocket Book for Catn. Morgan.
A Double Pocket Book in Irish Stitch for Peggy Parr.
A Irish stich Purse Pincushon for Ditto.
Plated a Watch String for Saml. Wharton.
A Watch String for John Hunt.
Knit a round Pincushon for R. Drinker.
Knit a round Pincushon for R. Coleman.
Knit a round Pincushon for H. Hicks.
Knit a round Pincushon for R. Jervis.
Knit a round Pincushon for R. Say.
A Ditto for self, gave it to Jane Ervin.
Knit a round Pincushon for A. Warner Senr.
Work'd a queen-stitch[3] Purse Pincushon for self.
A Ditto for Polly Sandwith.
Made a Twitcher[4] for Widdow Fielding.
A Ditto for Sarah Fisher.
Work'd a Irish stitch square Pincushon for Sally Wheeler.
Crown'd a Boys cap, for R. Rawle.
Help'd to make Baby Cloaths, for Betty Smith at Point.
Work'd a Irishstitch Tea Kittle holder for M. Parr.
Work'd a large silk Needle Book, in several stitches, for self.
A pair of silk Sleve-strings for Ditto.
A pair of Irishstitch Garters for Ditto.
Plated a Watch string for Josa. Howell.

1. The manuscript volume for Oct. 8, 1758–Oct. 20, 1759, which begins with the following list of needlework accomplishments, has hand-colored floral paper covers. The outside front cover reads, "1758–1759."

2. The Irish stitch, a popular canvaswork stitch in the eighteenth century, is a fast-moving vertical stitch covering three to four squares at once. It acquired several different names at the end of the nineteenth century (Swan, *Plain & Fancy*, 288).

3. Queen's stitch, an elaborate and complex needlework stitch, reached the height of its popularity between 1780 and 1810. Because of the intricacy of the needlework and the cost of the silk yarn generally used, queen's stitch was usually reserved for small items such as pincushions and purses (Swan, *Plain & Fancy*, 91, 98–99, 151–62, 231).

4. A twitcher or twitch was a cord or noose twisted by a stick and placed over the muzzle of a refractory horse in order to control it (Peter Finch, *The New Elizabethan Reference Dictionary* [London: George Newnes, 1955]; letter from Susan B. Swan, Feb. 18, 1988).

Made a Twitcher for Sally Wharton.
Work'd a Queen-stitch round Pincushon for Polly Sandwith.
A Queen-stitch round Pincushon for self.
Work'd a Queen-stitch Pocket-Book for Mary Searle.
Knit a pair of Thread Stockings for Caleb Parr.
Octor. the 21: 1758 Finishd a Irish-stitch Needle Book, for Sarah Sansom.
Finish'd a Queen-stitch Pocket Book for Peggy Parr.
Novr. the 1. 1758. Finish'd a pair of White Wosted Stockings for self.
Finish'd 7 shifts for self.
Finish'd Kniting a pair of blue yarn Stockings, for Susey Georges youngest Child.
Finish'd Kniting a pair of White wosted Stockings for Polly.
Work a round Pincushon for K. Howell.
Decr. the 9 Plated a string for B. Warner.
16 Finishd Kniting a pair of bleu yarn Stockings, for Susey Georges Son.
23 Finish'd a round silk Pincushon in ten stitch,[5] & Queen stitch, for Self.
30 Finish'd footing a pair of thread Stockings for Polly.
1759 Janry. the 9. Finish'd Kniting a pair of Wosted Stockings, for C. Parr.
Plated a string for Rebecca Say.
Feby. the 3. Finish'd Knitting a pair of Ribb'd Wosted Stockings for C. Parr.
Crown'd a Boys Cap for M. Carrey.
Work'd a Irish stitch Rose for Sally Brawton.
Work'd a Bag, for a small Box-Iron, in chain stitch and satten-stitch[6] for self.
Plated a watch string for H. Hicks.
Plated a watchstring for Josa. Howell.
A Knit round Pincushon for Sally Howell.
May the 9: 1759. Finish'd Kniting a pair of fine thread Stockings for Polly.
26th. Finish'd working a Irish-stitch Flower'd Pocket-Book for Self.
Knit, and made up, a round Pincushon for Sarah Walmsley. June.
Knit and made up a round pincushon for Nurse Mary.
Knitt and made up a round Ditto for Catherine Morgan.
1759 Plated 2 Horse-Whip-strings for B. Moode.
July the 19 Plated a Watch-string for Henry Drinker.
Augt. the 31: 1759: Finish'd Kniting a pair of fine thread Stockings for Self.
Septr. the 14 Finish'd 2 Tea Kittle-Holders, in Irish Stitch for.
Octor. Knit a round Pincushon for Sally Walmsley.
Plated a Horse Whip-string for Molly Walmsley.
Knit a round Pincushon for Hannah Hicks.

5. Ten stitch (tent stitch, tenth stitch), a canvaswork stitch that follows a diagonally crossing pattern, is particularly useful for creating intricate designs on fine canvas (Swan, *Plain & Fancy*, 234, 91, 95).

6. In England, satin stitch, an elegant embroidery stitch, was used to cover solid areas, creating a shiny surface effect. In the American colonies satin stitch was used more frequently to fill in small accent areas (Swan, *Plain & Fancy*, 232, 111, and plate 24, p. 143).

Knitt a round Pincushon for Hannah Ward.
November the 1, 1759, Finish'd a pair of Blue Wosted Stockings, for Self.
Decemr. the 31: 1759 Finish'd Kniting a pair of English wosted, Stockings for Self. White.
1760: Janry.
Knit a round Pincushon for Polly Jervis.
Work'd a round Pincushon, in Queenstitch and tenstitch, for H Moode.
Work'd a round Pincushon, in tenstitch and Irish stitch for M Sandwith.
Work'd a round Pincushon in tenstitch and Queenstitch for Self.
Febry. Knitt a Pair of White Wosted Stockings, for Polly Parr.
Finish'd a large Woosted Bible Cover March the.
May the 9. 1760 Finish'd working a Screen, in Irishstitch Flowers.
May the 21, Finish'd Knitting a pair of thread Stockings for self.
May the 30, Plated a Twitcher for Sally Tallman.
June the 17 Plated a Watch String for William Fisher.
June the 27, plated a Watchstring for Henry Drinker.
July: Work a Queen Stitch[7] cover for Polly's twezer-case.
Plated a watchstring for Josa. Howells.
Sepr. finish'd Plating a silk Purse for self.
Knitt a pair of Garters for HD.
Knitt a pair of ditto for M Sandwith.
Decemr. plated a Watch-string for Frances Rawle.
Plated 3 strings for pincushon, for Nancy Warner.
Plated a Watch-string, for Molly Sandwith.
Decemr. the 31. Finish'd knitting a pair white thread Stockings for self.
1761. Janry. the 2. Plated a Watch-string for Henry Drinker.
Janry. the 8, Finish'd Knitting a pair of Silk Mittins for Self.

1758 Octor. the 8 First Day, drank Tea at Jos. Howell's; call'd to see M. Foulk, who was lyeing in; with her Daughter Elizabeth.

9 Stay'd at Home all Day: M Parr Drank Tea with us.

10 Spent the After-noon, with J. Ervin. S. Roberson being from Home.

11 Spent the Afternoon at S. Plumly's.

12 Went to Meeting[8] in the Morning, spent the Afternoon with S. Sansom, at Robt. Lewis's: call'd in the Evening at Danl. Stanton's: and at S. Plumly's.

7. The word "case" crossed out.

8. The Society of Friends was organized around a series of meetings, the smallest being a particular meeting, consisting of a group of individuals who came together for worship at regularly scheduled times (at least once a week on Sunday—or First Day, as Quakers called it—and often more frequently) and to transact corporate business. These local meetings were

13 Stay'd at Home all Day.

14 Stay'd at home all Day.

15 First Day; went thrice to Meeting. drank Tea at Neighbour Callender's.

16 Spent the Afternoon at Isreal Pemberton's, call'd in the Evening at Saml. Sansom's & at J. Foulk's.

1758 Octor. the 17 Went to Meeting in the Morning, spent the Afternoon at S. Sansom's.

18 Spent the Afternoon at Josha. Maddox's call'd in the Evening at Uncle's, sup'd at B. Moode.

19 Went to Meeting in the Morning; spent the Afternoon at A. Mitchell's, call'd in the Evening at Wm. Callender's.

20 Spent the Day at Wm. Parr's; Point, and stay'd all night.

21 came from Point, spent the After-noon at J. Foulk's; call'd in the Evening at S. Sansom's, & at F Rawle's.

22 First Day; Went thrice to Meeting.

23 Spent the Evening at J. Jervis's.

24 Went to Meeting in the Morning.

25 Stay'd at Home all Day.

26 Went to Meeting in the Morning, spent the Afternoon & Evening at F Rawles.

27 Spent the Afternoon & Evening at S. Wharton's.

28 Stay'd at home all Day.

---

also called preparative meetings when they had permanent status and indulged meetings when they had temporary status. (For an example of an indulged meeting in the diary, see the discussions about the Downingtown Meeting.) The members of two or more preparative meetings constituted a monthly meeting, which kept the membership records and had the power to establish preparative and indulged meetings and to receive, disown, and discipline members (Rhoads, *Catawissa*, 8–9; Brinton, *Quaker Practice;* Barbour and Frost, *Quakers*, 77).

29 First Day, Went thrice to Meeting.

30 Stay'd at home all Day.

31 Went to Meeting in the Morning; after Dinner, call'd at Uncles, Drank Tea at B. Moodes; Wm. Parr called.

1758 Novemr the 1 Stay'd at home all Day.

2 call'd at J Maddox's; Went to Meeting; call'd at J Howell's; spent the afternoon at Uncle's; call'd at C. Nicholdson's.

3 Stay'd at Home all Day.

4 Stay'd at Home all Day.

5 First Day, Went twice to Meeting.

6 Stay'd at Home all Day; H Drinker drank Tea with us.

7 Went to Youths Meeting;[9] spent part of the Evening at S. Sansom's.

8 Stay'd at Home all Day.

9 Went to Meeting in the Morning.

10 Stay'd at Home all Day.

11 Stay'd at Home all Day.

12 First Day; Went three times to Meeting.

13 Spent the Evening at Uncle Jervis's.

14 Went to Meeting in the Morning; spent the Afternoon at Saml. Morris's Senr. with R. Say.

9. As the Quaker population in Pennsylvania grew, the Society of Friends became especially concerned with overseeing the behavior of their young, particularly with instructing them in the tenets of the Society of Friends and keeping them from misbehaving at meeting. Following the advice of the Philadelphia Yearly Meeting in 1694, Philadelphia Friends established a special youths' meeting in 1696. The plan called for meetings four times a year, where regular Quaker worship would be augmented by special readings and advice to youth concerning their behavior (Sydney V. James, "Quaker Meetings and Education in the Eighteenth Century," *Quaker History* 51 (1962): 95–99; Philadelphia Yearly Meeting, *Rules of Discipline of the Yearly Meeting of Friends Held in Philadelphia*. [Philadelphia: Kimber, Conrad, 1806], 27).

15 Stay'd at Home all Day.

16 Went to Meeting in the Morning; call'd at S. Sansom's; Esther Smith drank Tea with us.

17 Stay'd at Home all Day.—wrote to Dublin.

1758 Novemr the 18 Stay'd at Home in the Morning; took a walk in the Afternoon with Reb. Rawle; in the Evening Rec'd a Letter from Jamacia; by HDr.

19 First Day; Went to Meeting thrice.

20 Took a Walk in the Morning to Sarah Plumly's; call'd at Uncles; at C. Nicholdson's; & at J. Richardson's; Dine'd and spent the Afternoon at Betsy Moodes: help'd to Quilt: spent the Evening at F. Rawle's.

21 Went to Meeting in the Morning—Spent the Afternoon, at Neighr. Callender's.

22 Stay'd at Home all Day.

23 Went to Meeting in the Morning; Dinn'd & spent the Afternoon at S. Wharton's.

24 Spent the Afternoon at S Plumly's.

25 Stay'd at Home all Day.

26 First Day; Went to Meeting thrice. call'd at S Sansom's; before Evening Meeting.

27 Stay'd at home all Day.

28 Went to Meeting in the Morning: call'd after Meeting at R Rawles; spent the Afternoon at Catn. Morgan's; HD spent the Evening.

29 Stay'd at Home all Day.

30 Stay'd from Meeting in the Morning spent the Afternoon & Evening at Jos. Howells.

1758 Decemr the 1 Betsy Moode spent the Afternoon with us.

2 Stay'd at home all Day.

3 Went to Meeting thrice: drank Tea at J. Howell's call'd at F. Rawle's, before Evening Meeting: First Day.

4 Spent the Afternoon at Neighr. Shoemaker Betsy Moode & HD spent the Evening with us.

5 Went to Meeting in the Morning; spent the Afternoon at S. Sansom's, Sammy Sansom spent part of the Evening with us.

6 Stay'd at home all Day.

7 Went to Meeting in the Morning, spent the Afternoon and part of the Evening at C. Nicholdson's; call'd at Uncle's.

8 Spent the Afternoon & Evening at J. Howell's; Call'd at F Rawle's.

9 Stay'd at home all Day.

10 First Day, went 3 times to Meeting.—call'd at R Rawle's before Evening Meetg.

11 Took a walk in the Morning, call'd at S. Plumly's, at Uncle's, at R Birchall's; at Wm. Brown's, at S. Wharton's; Dine'd and spent the Afternoon at B Moode's; spent the Evening at F Rawle's.

12 Went to Meeting in the Morning.

1758 Decemr the 13 Stay'd at home all Day; Molly Lord and W Parr call'd to see us.

14 Stay'd at home all Day.

15 Spent the Afternoon at T Say's.

16 Stay'd at home all Day.

17 First Day; Went thrice to Meeting.—S. Spavold preach'd.

18 Stay'd at home all Day; Betsy Moode and Nelly; spent part of the Evening with us.

19 Went to Meeting in the Morning, call'd after Meeting with B Moode, at

R. Steel's; call'd after dinner at J. Renold's, spent the Afternoon and part of the Evening at B Moode's.

20 call'd in the Morning at J Renold's, at J. Evan's's, at B. Moodes, and at S. Sansom's.

21 Went to Meeting in the Morning; call'd after Meeting at M Burrows's.

22 call'd at M Burrows's, spent the Afternoon at Uncles; HD spent the Evening.

23 Stay'd at home all Day: W Parr call'd.

24 First Day: Stay'd at home all Day. HD call'd after Evening Meeting.

25 Stay'd at home all Day.

26 Went to Meeting in the Morning, call'd after Meeting at B Moodes; Dinn'd at S Wharton's; went after Dinner to Stores with M Parr, who with Cat Morgan, spent the Afternoon & part of the Evening with us.

1758 Decmr. the 27 Stay'd at home all Day.—M Parr call'd in the Morning.

28 Went to Meeting in the Morning; Molly Lord, spent the Afternoon with us.

29 Stay'd at home all Day.

30 E Moode spent part of the Morning with us; Spent an Hour after Dinner at Neighbor. Callender's.

31 First Day, went 3 times to Meeting.—Drank Tea at F Rawl's.

1759

1759 Jnry. the 1 Went to W Parr's Point no Pt.[1]

2 Stay'd within all Day.

3 Stay'd within all Day.

4 Stay'd within all Day.

5 Went to Frankford Meeting; W Parr, M Parr, MES: Testimonies[2] borne by Sarah Morris, S. Spavold, and two other Friends. Heny. Drinkr. came after Meeting to WP's.

6 Stay'd within all Day.

7 First Day Stay'd within all Day.

8 Stay'd within all Day.

9 Stay'd within all Day.

10 Stay'd within all Day.

11 Stay'd within all Day.

12 Came from Point to Philada. after Dinner.

1. Point No Point is a bulge of land on the Delaware River. Formerly northeast of Philadelphia, today it is within the city limits, north of Kensington (Scharf and Westcott, *Philadelphia*, vol. 1, endpaper).

2. ED uses the word *testimony* in several different yet related ways. In general, Quaker testimony and concerns were public statements that defined the behavioral code required of Society members. Such rules included, but were not limited to, plain dress, pacifism, and the eschewal of oath taking. During meeting, one member might appear in testimony to offer a personal statement of belief (or a concern over the widespread breach of Quaker guidelines), while another member might present a testimonial regarding the exemplary conduct of a particular person. Sentiments could also be expressed by way of testimony at home among Friends or in the form of a letter (explanation courtesy of J. William Frost, Director, Friends Historical Library, Swarthmore College; see also below, Dec. 2, 1777, and Feb. 23, 1778).

1759 Jenry. the 13 Went out in the Morning to buy Wosted; call'd at T. Say's.

14 First Day, went to Meeting in the Morning; came out of Meeting in the Afternoon with the Sick Head Ake, stay'd at Home in the Evening.

15 Stay'd at Home all Day: Began to work a large wosted Bible Cover.

16 Went to Meeting in the Morning; went After Dinner to buy Wosted; call'd at T Say's; HD spent the Evening.

17 Stay'd at Home all Day: Han. Moode call'd in the Morning, for 2 Huming Birds for S Spavold.

18 Went to Meeting in the Morning: S Spavold took leave: Dinn'd, drank Tea & Sup'd at S. Wharton's, help'd Sally to Iron Baby Cloaths.

19 Stay'd at home in the Morning; N Parr & H Callender spent the Afternoon with us. W Parr call'd; went with N Parr in the Evening to S Plumly's; sup'd at J. Foulk's, Betsy & Nelly Moode, call'd while we were out.

20 W & N Parr call'd in the Morning; went with N Parr to Shops; stay'd at home in the Afternoon & Evening.

21 First Day; Went to Meeting in the Morning; stay'd at home the rest of the Day.—HD; call'd.

22 Spent the Afternoon and Evening at R Rawle's; Hannah Hicks call'd their she came to Town the Day before.

23 Went to Meeting in the Morning; call'd after Dinner at J. Maddox's; spent the Afternoon and Evening at J Jervis's.

24 Stay'd at Home all Day; W Parr call'd.

25 Stay'd at home all Day.

26 Stay'd at home all Day.

27 Stay'd at Home all Day.

28 First Day stay'd at home in the Morning; went to Afternoon and Evening Meeting; HD call'd.

29 Spent the Afternoon at S Sansom's, the Evening at F Rawle's.

30 Went to Meeting in the Morning; were invited to the Burial of Wm. Trotter; Dinn'd and spent the Afternoon at B. Moode's.

31 Stay'd at Home all Day:—Hannah Peters Buried.

Feby. the 1 Went to Meeting in the Morning spent the Afternoon and Evening at J. Howells.

2 Stay'd at home all Day; Jos. & Katr. Howell & R Rawles: spent the Evening at Fd. Warner's: (7 to 1, which is often the case chez nous) S Spavold call'd while we were at Super; and left Philada. the next Day but one.

1759 Feby. the 3 Stay'd at home all Day, Hann Hicks call'd in the Morning; Betsy and Nelly Moode spent part of the Afternoon and Evening with us.

4 First Day: Went 3 times to Meeting; James Tasker preach'd from a little after 7, untell nigh 10; Evening Meeting.

5 Went to Meeting in the Morning; it being Quarterly Meeting;[3] call'd at C. Nicholdson, and at Uncle Jervis's; spent the Afternoon at S Plumly's, with E. White, J Kearney, H Hicks; & MS; it being a visit to the Bride, Mary Searson, formerly Lord; S Plumly sick in Bed;—call'd in the Evening at S Sansom's & at R Rawle's.

6 Went to Meeting in the Morning; Youth's Meeting; Spent the Afternoon at J Foulk HD call'd.

7. Spent the Afternoon at T Say's.

8 Went to Meeting in the Morning, call'd after a Jos. Howell's, and at Wm. Fisher's to see the Children, who were in the Meazles; spent the After-noon at Neig Callenders.

9 Stay'd at home all Day; had a Bad spell of the Sick Head Ake.

1759 Feby. the 10 Stay'd at Home all Day.

3. All the monthly meetings in a given area met together four times a year for worship, fellowship, the transaction of business, and the discussion of common problems. They also would undertake projects that needed more support than a local or monthly meeting could muster (Brinton, *Quaker Practice*; Barbour and Frost, *Quakers*, 77).

11 First Day; Went thrice to Meeting—call'd after Evening Meeting a Jos. Howell's.

12 Went in the Morning to Jos. Howell's—to S Plumly's, to J. Pemberton's, to Saml. Wharton's, and to Uncles, Aunt Jervis, Betsy & Polly, spent the Afternoon with us.

13 Went to Meeting in the Morning.—Thunder, Lightning, Snow, Hail, and Rain, in the Night. with Wind.

14 Went in the Afternoon to the Burial of Anna Howell, Daughter of Jos. Howell.

15 Stay'd from Meeting; within all Day. Betsy Moode, spent the After-noon and Evening with us.

16 Betsy Moode call'd in the Morning.—Spent the Afternoon at F Rawle's the Evening at Jos. Howell's.

17 Call'd after Dinner to see Sally Wharton, who was lyeing-in, with her Son Samuel,—spent the Afternoon & Evening at B. Moode's.

18 First Day: Went thrice to Meeting.—S. Sansom Junr. Sup'd with us.

19 Stay'd at Home all Day.

1759 Feby the 20 Stay'd from Meeting; within all Day.

21 Stay'd at Home all Day.

22 Stay'd from Meeting; went in the Morning to Uncle Jervis's (to sign a Deed for a Lot in Mary-Land;) Dinn'd their, went after Dinner to visit S Plumly, who lay very ill; Drank Tea at F Rawle's; call'd in the Evening at Jos. Howell's; Betsy Moode spent part of the Evening with us.

23 Stay'd at home all Day; HD call'd.

24 Stay'd at home all Day.

25 First Day; Stay'd at home all Day.—had one Tooth drawn, in the Morning, and another attempted; suffer'd much thereby.

26 Stay'd at home all Day, Han. Hicks, and Han. Moode, call'd in the Morning: Hannah Hicks, spent the Afternoon with us.

27 Stay'd at home all Day: Betsy Moode call'd in the Morning, before Meeting; she came after Dinner with an intent to spend the Afternoon; but was oblige'd by the Sick Head Ake to go Home: Polly went this Afternoon to the Burial of S. Plumly.

28 Stay'd at home all Day. Jude call'd to take leave of us; as she was going into the Country.

1759 March the 1 Stay'd at Home all Day.—Benja. Swett Senr. Saml. Sansom Senr. and Hannah Callender; spent the Afternoon, at Fd. Warners.—pull'd out a Tooth in the Evening; which the Tooth-drawer had drawn, before and replaced.[4]

2 Spent part of the Afternoon at Jos. Howell's; drank Tea at Uncles; call'd in the Evening at Betsy Moode's, who had been at our House while we were out.

3 Stay'd at Home all Day. B. Moode came home with Polly in the Afternoon, haveing been to the Burial of Sally Howell, seacond Daughter of Jos. Howell; who Dye'd of a Mortification[5] in her Mouth.

4 First Day, Stay'd at home all Day.—HD spent the afternoon, and Evening with us.

5 Stay'd at home all Day; sore Throat so bad, was oblige'd to send for the Doctor after 10 o'clock at Night.

6 Took Physick; stay'd up stairs all Day HD; call'd.

7 Stay'd up stairs all Day: Betsy Moode spent the Afternoon with us: HD call'd in the E.

8 Stay'd within all Day: Betsy Moode call'd in the Afternoon.

4. This was a common practice in early American dentistry. A toothdrawer would reimplant the original tooth into the patient's mouth in the hope that it had enough life to make a good implant and would fit the socket better than an artificial tooth (Samuel H. Willens, "Dr. Nathaniel Peabody and His Book *The Art of Preserving Teeth*," *Bulletin of the History of Dentistry* 28 [1980]: 85).

5. In medical terms, *mortification* meant the loss of vitality, death, and subsequent putrefaction of a part of the body while the rest of the body was still alive. Medical writers differed on the causes and types of mortifications, but agreed that when preceded by inflammation, mortification often meant the forming of gangrene on the affected part, followed by sphacelus, which occurred when the part became brown or black, flaccid, and putrid. Mortification of the mouth, the phrase used here, often referred to pleurisy, an inflammation of membranes around the lungs (Robert Hooper, *Quincy's Lexicon Medicum* [Philadelphia: E. & R. Parker, M. Carey & Son, & Benjamin Warner, 1817]; Parr, *London Medical Dictionary*; King, *Medical World of the Eighteenth Century*, 85–88, 107).

1759 March the 9 Stay'd at home all Day.—Hannah Hicks & Hanh. Moode spent an hour towards Evening; JH, KH, & HD, sup'd with us.

10 Stay'd at home all Day; still unwell; Sarah Mickell call'd.

11 First Day: Stay'd within all Day.

12 Spent the Afternoon at Neighr. Callenders.

13 Stay'd at home all Day. B. Moode call'd after Meeting; HD spent the Evening.

14 Spent the Afternoon at Uncle Jervis's Saw the Grand Burial of Brigadier-General Forbes;[6] who was Buryed after the Milatiary Form: Spent the Evening at Jos. Howell's.

15 Went to Meeting in the Morning—call'd after dinner at J. Searson's, spent the Afternoon at Jos. Maddox's, Polly Wallace was lyeing-in, with her Daughter Nancy, call'd in the Evening, at B. Moodes, and at S. Wharton's.

16 Stay'd within all Day.

17 Stay'd within all Day.

18 First Day. went thrice to Meeting.

1759 March the 19 Stay'd at home all Day.—Thos. Say Junr. call'd in the Evening.

20 Went to Meeting in the Morning; spent the After-noon at Jos. Howell's, call'd at F Rawle's.

21 Stay'd at home all Day. B. Moode, spent part of the Evening with us. A Storm of Thunder, Lightening, Hail Wind and Rain, in the Night.

22 Went to Meeting in the Morning; call'd after Meeting, at A Physicks; spent the Afternoon, at Betsy Moodes, went to Mary Williamss with B Moode; and Bought some kniting Thread: spent part of the Evening at Uncle's: Hannah Hicks came (with an intent to spend the Afternoon) while we were out.

6. Brig. Gen. John Forbes (1710–59), veteran of the Fort Duquesne campaign (November 1758) during the French and Indian War (Morris, *Encyclopedia*, 68).

23 John Storor call'd at AWs in the Morning with John & Mary Armitt, he came to Philaa: the 22 Instant with Saml. Emlen: call'd after dinner at P. Syngs, bought a pair Buckles, spent the Afternoon at Uncle Jervis's: HD spent the Evening with us.

24 Stay'd within all Day. K. Howell, H Callender, and Betsy Moode, spent part of the Afternoon at Fd. Warner's.

1759 March the 25 First Day, stay'd at home in the Morning; had a bad Cold;—went to Meeting in the Afternoon and Evening; half Year Meeting;[7] Jacob Howell & Sarah Wamsley drank Tea at Fd. Warner's.

26 Went to Meeting in the Morning; spent the Afternoon at J. Searson's call'd in the Evening at T. Say's. H Hicks call'd while we were out.

27 Stay'd from Meeting; at home all Day.

28 Stay'd within all Day. Betty Smith, Hannah Callender, Benjamin Swett and Henry Drinker, Drank Tea at Fd. Warners.

29 Stay'd at Home all Day.

30 Stay'd at home all Day; still unwell with a Cold.

31 Stay'd within all Day; Nelly Moode spent the Afternoon at A. Warner's, Tomy Say call'd in the Evening.

April the 1 First Day; Stay'd within all Day; still unwell.

2 Took a walk in the Afternoon call'd at H, Robinson's; at Uncle Jervis's; drank Tea at Betsy Moode's, call'd at S. Sansom's, Sammy Sansom spent the Evening with us.

3 Went to Meeting in the Morning: John & Molly Searson spent the Afternoon with us.

4 Spent the Afternoon at Uncle's; call'd in the Evening at J. Foulk's; Betsy Moode came home with Polly; in the Evening.

7. In 1712 the Philadelphia Yearly Meeting decided to hold a two-day public worship meeting annually in the spring. The meeting was held just for worship and not for the administrative business of the Society of Friends. It was first held in May, but was soon changed to March, six months before the yearly meeting, and thus became known as the Half Yearly Meeting (Mekeel, "Founding Years," 25; Frost, *Quaker Family*, 4).

5 Call'd in the Morning at T. Say's, went from thence to Meeting, with three Trent-Town Girl's, Fd. Say's Couzens; Went After Tea to the Widdow Serle's, to see H. Hicks; call'd at T. Roberson's, at Widdow Mitchell's, to see Nurse Mary; went twice to B. Moodes, who with Nelly were at our House while we were out; call'd in the Evening at Wm. Morris's.

6 Stay'd at home all Day; Rebecca Say, with three of her Neices, vizt. Ruth Potts, Sarah Potts, and Sarah Beeks; spent the Afternoon with us. Hannah Hicks call'd in the Evening to take leave of us, as she was going the Next Day to Oldmans,-Creek.

7 Stay'd at home all Day.

8 Went twice to Meeting; stay'd at home in the Evening. First Day.

9 Took a Walk in the Morning to Catn. Morgan's, and to Thos. Say's; Nurse-Mary, spent the Afternoon with us. Betsy Moode spent part of the Evening.

1759 April the 10 Stay'd at home all Day.—General Amherst[8] came to Philadelphia the 9th.

11 Stay'd at home all Day; was let Blood[9] in the Morning, for a Cough, and cold on the Stomach.

12 Call'd in the Morning at Henry Steel's; went from thence to Meeting; call'd after Meeting at Uncle's; spent the Afternoon at S. Sansom's.

8. Maj. Gen. Jeffrey Amherst (1717–97), hero of the Battle of Louisbourg, July 26, 1758 (Morris, *Encyclopedia*, 68).

9. Bloodletting was a standard treatment for various inflammations, particularly of the lungs, as well as for pneumonia and related illnesses. It was also used as a prophylactic device at certain times of the year such as the spring and fall to maintain the body's balance. In late eighteenth-century Philadelphia it was also used to treat pregnant women. As the tools available to the bleeder became more sophisticated, bloodletting became a widely used therapy in the eighteenth century.

There were two major categories of bloodletting: *general bloodletting*, which involved opening an artery or, more commonly, a vein (usually in the elbow) with a lancet, and *local bloodletting*, which severed only the capillaries and used suction provided by heated cups or leeches to withdraw blood. Each cup held four or five ounces of blood, and several were generally used in any procedure. Because American leech species were considered inferior, Americans frequently imported leeches from Europe. A Swedish leech at maximum efficiency could take an ounce of blood; small children were treated with two leeches, adults with twenty or more.

In England bloodletting had been the special province of barber-surgeons. In the absence of guilds in the American colonies, specialists such as the Hailer family in Philadelphia, often used by the Drinkers, advertised their skills as bleeders. Doctors Kuhn, Rush, and others bled members of the Drinker household themselves or recommended bloodletting specialists (A. Davis and Appel, *Bloodletting Instruments*; King, *Medical World of the Eighteenth Century*, 318–20; Rucker, "Pain Relief in Obstetrics," 101–8; Siddall, "Bloodletting," 101–10).

13 Spent the Afternoon at F. Rawles, were sent for home in the Evening, by John and Molly Searson, who spent part of the Evening with us; HD sup'd Chez Nous.

14 Stay'd at home all Day: Betsy Moode spent the Afternoon with us.

15 First Day; went to Meeting 3 times, HD, call'd after Evening Meeting;— we were Allarm'd by the Cry of Fire at 11 o'clock at Night; (have this last Winter been very much Favour'd on the Acct of Fire).

16 Stay'd at home all Day.

1759 April the 17 Went to Meeting in the Morning, saw Richd. Well's and R. Hill Married; had a satisfactory Meeting, according to my Apprehension of the Matter. Spent the Afternoon at S. Wharton's; Took a Walk in the Evening on the Commons, with Sally Emlen, B Moode, H. Moode, Nelly Moode, and MS, calld after, at B. Moode's, caught a fresh Cold: came home in the Evening, and found Wm. Fisher and Wife, F. Rawle and Wife, J. Howell and Wife with H Drinkr. Chez Nous.

The Fire which happn'd on the 15th. Instant; was a Bake-House of Mark Cooles; which was burn'd down, and a large quantity of Bread distroy'd.

18 Spent the Afternoon at Uncle Jervis's; saw as we were returning Home towards Evening, Neighr. Maddox's—Shop shut, call'd to inquire the Cause, and were inform'd, that (he) Joshua Maddox) departed this Life about half an hour before.

1759 April the 19 Stay'd at home all Day.—a bad Cold.

20 Stay'd at home all Day: B Moode spent the Evening with us.

21 Stay'd at home all Day.

22 First Day, went twice to Meeting, stay'd at home in the Evening.

23 Stay'd at home all Day: Katty & Sally Howell, spent the Afternoon a Fd. Warners, HD, spent the Evening.

24 Went to Meeting in the Morning, went after Dinner to Joshua Howell's, for Deborah Howell, who spent the Afternoon at Fd. Warners: Had a bad spell of the sick Head-Ake, in the Evening.

25 Stay'd at home all Day. Uncle Jervis call'd in the Morning. A North-East Storm in the Night.

26 Stay'd at home all Day,—Betsy Moode spent the Afternoon with us, Jos. Morris call'd to pay for the Lot in MaryLand.

1759 April the 27 Stay'd at home all Day.—Deborah Howell, call'd in the Morning, to bid us farewell.

28 Stay'd at home all Day.

29 First Day; went twice to Meeting, call'd after, Morning Meeting to see Becky Rawle, who was brought to Bed the 28 Instant with her Son William, went home in the Afternoon with Sarh. Sansom, drank Tea, and spent part of the Evening there; B. Swett Senr. came home with me; and Sup'd Chez nous.

30 Spent the Afternoon at Widdow Maddox's; call'd towards Evening at Uncle Jervis's, and at Neighr. Callenders, Saw between 8 and 9 o'clock at Night a large dull star, said to be the Commett.

May the 1 Went to Meeting in the Morning, call'd after Meeting at F Rawle's.—Aunt Jervis, with Betsy & Polly spent the Afternoon with us; HD spent the Evening.

2 Went to Uncle's in the Morning; call'd at S. Whartons, and at B. Moode's, dinn'd at Uncles, went after Dinner to his Pasture, JJ, RJ, CJ, EJ, MJ, SJ, MS, ES, came home in the Evening.

3 Went to Meeting in the Morning, call'd after meeting at J Searson's, spent the afternoon at F Rawles, went to Smiths to Buy cruels. Heny. Drinkr. spent the Evening with us, May the 3.

4 Went in the Afternoon with M Parr, to M. Burrows,s and R Steels, and several other Shops; she came home and drank Tea with us.

5 M Parr spent part of the Morning with us, and drank Tea in the Afternoon, W Parr call'd. Betsy Moode drank Tea, and spent part of the Evening, went part of the way home with her; had a long discourse with B Moode upstairs, in the Dark.

6 First Day; Went 3 times to Meeting HD, drank Tea with us, Joel Evan's call'd.

7 Drank Tea at Neighr. Callender's took a walk after, to Uncles, spent part of the Evening at B. Moodes; came home and found JH, KH, and HD, Chez Nous.

1759 May the 8 Went to Youth's Meeting; call'd before meeting at F Rawle's; spent the Afternoon at Joshua Howells.

9 Spent the Afternoon at T. Say's, was sent for home to B. Moode, who spent the Evening with us.

10 Went to Meeting in the Morning, call'd after at S.Sansom's; spent the Afternoon at S Wharton's, took a long walk in the Evening with B. Moode, from there House, she came home with me, and with Sammy Sansom Junr. sup'd Chez nous.

11 Stay'd at home all Day; HD call'd in the Evening.

12 Stay'd at home all Day, A. Warner Senr. Betsy Warner, Polly; and Henry Drinker, set out for Wm. Walmsleys Buybary[10] in the Afternoon: Betsy Moode call'd in the Evening.

13 First Day; went to Meeting in the Morning; call'd after dinner at Josh. Howell's, and at F. Rawles, went from thence to Betsy Moodes, and with her to the Middle Meeting in the Afternoon, and Evening; came home after Evening Meeting; went back with Betsy Moode, lodg'd with her: drank Tea and sup'd there.

14 Breakfast'd, dinn'd, and drank Tea, at Betsy Moodes; she came home with me towards Evening; went to Sarah Browns silk dyer, return'd to A Warners, spent part of the Evening togeather; A Warner, Polly, &c, return'd from Buybary; this evening.

15 Went to Meeting in the Morning, took a walk after Tea in the Afternoon; with A Warner Senr. A Warner Junr. B. Warner MES; to the Church Burying Ground, read the Tomb Stones.

16 Spent the Afternoon at R Wells's, call'd towards Evening at F Rawles, HD, spent the Evening with us.

10. Byberry was a township in Philadelphia County, north of, although today it is part of, the city of Philadelphia. Settled largely by Quakers, a meeting was established there in 1683, and a wooden meetinghouse erected. Another meetinghouse, north of the first site, was built in 1694; this in turn was replaced in 1714 by a stone two-story building with glass windows, which was enlarged in 1753. From 1702 to 1782 the Byberry Meeting was under the jurisdiction of the Abington Monthly Meeting (Martindale, *Byberry* 35–36, 44, 50, 58; Isaac Comly, "Sketch of the History of Byberry, in the County of Philadelphia, . . ." *Memoirs of the Historical Society of Pennsylvania* 2, pt. 1 [1827]: 177).

17 Stay'd from Meeting, spent the Afternoon at Uncle Jervis's. HD. spent the Evening.

18 Stay'd within all Day, Sammy Sansom call'd in the Evening.

19 Spent the Afternoon at F Rawles, call'd at J Howells, spent part of the Evening at Judah Foulks.

1759 May the 20 First Day; went to Meeting 3 times; call'd before Evening Meeting with Joshua and Katty Howell at their House; HD, came home with us.

21 Took a Walk after Tea in the After-noon, to Uncles, spent part of the Evening at B. Moodes, call'd at Neighr. Shoemakers.

22 Went to Meeting in the Morning; Betsy Moode spent part of the Evening with us.—went home with her, Sammy Sansom with us.

23 Stay'd at home all Day, John & Molly Searson call'd towards Evening, told us Hannah Hicks was in Town, HD, spent the Evening.

24 Call'd in the Morning to see M. Foulk, who lay ill of a Fever, went from thence to Meeting; call'd after dinner at John Armitts, at Jonan. Evans's and at Sally Whartons; drank Tea at Jos. Trotter's, call'd at J. Jervis's, spent the Evening at Frances Rawles.

25 Went to Monthly Meeting, saw Jacob Lewis, and Sarah Mifflin pass;[11] went home with Betsy Moode, dinn'd and spent the Afternoon there; taken very sick there; H Drinker spent the Evening Chez nous.

1759 May the 26 Stay'd at home all Day. Hanh. Shoemaker spent an hour in the Evening.

11. Friends who wished to marry needed the approval of both parents or guardians and their Quaker meeting. The couple was required to appear before two monthly meetings before the marriage was approved. This was called *passing the meeting*. At the first meeting the prospective bride and groom declared their intentions, and either set or both sets of parents offered oral consent if present, or written consent if absent, even if neither party to the marriage was a minor. Moreover, if one of the parties lived within the jurisdiction of another Quaker meeting, he or she had to bring a "certificate of clearness" indicating that the local meeting knew of no impediments to marriage. A committee of overseers was then appointed to investigate potential objections to the marriage. When the couple appeared at the next monthly meeting, the overseers presented their report. If there were no objections, the meeting gave its approval for the couple to marry. At the beginning of the nineteenth century the requirement was reduced to one appearance before the monthly meeting (Frost, *Quaker Family*, 172–73).

27 First Day; went twice to Meeting,—stay'd at home in the Evening.

28 Stay'd at home all Day, Hannah Shoemaker call'd.

29 Went to Meeting in the Morning; went after Meeting, to Sarah Brown's, with Nelly Moode, who call'd Chez Nous.—Betsy Moode came after Tea and spent part of the Evening with us.

30 Stay'd at home all Day; Betsy Moode call'd in the Morning; Peggy Parr with her sister in Law Nancy and Polly, drank Tea with us: Wm. Parr call'd; the first time of our seeing them since their return from Bethelam.

31 MS, came home early in the Morning after seting up all night with M. Foulk. I Went to Meeting in the Forenoon; spent the afternoon at J. Searsons; call'd towards Evening at Uncles; and at Abrahm. Mitchell's, to see Jos. Hicks, who lay ill of the Nerverous Fever:[12] Hannah Hicks there.

1759 June the 1 Stay'd at home all Day.

2 Went in the Evening to A Mitchell's, to see H. Hicks, whose Brother Josey dyed this Morning.

3 First Day; Went to Meeting 3 times. went after, afternoon Meeting to the Burial of Joseph Hicks, call'd after Evening Meeting at S. Sansom's.

4 Stay'd at home all Day: Sarh. Sansom, &c. spent the Afternoon at Fd. Warner's. A hard thunder Gust in the Evening, Several Houses struck with the Lightening; but no great damage done.

5 Went to Meeting in the Morning.—Hannah Moode call'd in the Afternoon. HD spent the Evening.

6 Spent the Afternoon at T. Say's.—came home with the sick Head Ake,—A Thunder Gust in the Night.

12. The nervous fever was generally associated with typhus, after William Cullen, an eighteenth-century British physician famed for his classification of diseases, so described it. The symptoms included a quick, low pulse, chilliness and flushing in turn, giddiness and pain in the head, nausea, and vomiting. There were, however, many descriptions of nervous fevers, not all of which were typhus, and there were also illnesses that presented certain nervous symptoms but were not considered the nervous fever (Cullen, *Practice of Physic*, 1:109–15; Benjamin Rush, "Outlines of a Theory of Fever," in Rush, *Inquiries and Observations*, 1:48–49; Buchan, *Domestic Medicine* [1799], 137–41; Parr, *London Medical Dictionary*; King, *Medical World of the Eighteenth Century*, 130–31).

7 call'd at T. Say's in the Morning.—Took an Emmetic before Dinner.—Rain with Thunder.

1759 June the 8 Spent the After-noon at Joshua Howells, Betsy Moode spent part of the Evening with us; the first time of our seeing her since her return from Egg-Harbour.

9 Stay'd at home all Day, Wm. Parr call'd in the Morning.

10 First Day: Went to Meeting 3 times; Evening Meeting held at the Bank;[13] whilst the Middle Meeting House was altering;—call'd after Evening meeting at Neighr. Shoemakers: HD, spent the Evening.

11 Stay'd at home all Day; John and Molly Searson spent part of the Evening with us.—Took a walk after supper to Josa. Howells.

12 Went to Meeting in the Morning. spent the After-noon at F Rawles,—took a walk after Tea to Isl. Pembertons, walk'd in the Garden; call'd at Betsy Moodes, who came home with me, call'd at S Sansoms, and at Neighr. Callenders.

13 Spent part of the Evening at Neighbour Shoemakers.

14 Went to Pine-Street Meeting in the Morning; Din'd at Betsy Moodes. call'd after dinner at S Sansoms; spent the After-noon at C. Morgans.

15 Went after Dinner to Wm. Fishers S. Fisher going out: spent the After-noon at S. Sansoms.

16 Spent the After-noon with A Warner Senr. Joshua and Katty Howell,

13. When ED began her diary there were three Quaker meetinghouses in Philadelphia. The Bank Meeting, established in 1685, held meetings at a building on Front Street between Arch and Race streets that had been constructed in 1702. This building stood until 1790, when the Philadelphia Northern District built a new meetinghouse at Keys Alley. The High Street Meeting, organized in 1696, erected a new building in 1755 at Second and High (Market) streets. This was the Middle Meeting, and the meetinghouse was sometimes referred to as the Great (or Greater) Meeting House. It was torn down in 1811 after the completion of the Arch Street Meetinghouse, which was begun in 1804. The third meetinghouse, at Pine Street near Second Street, began use in 1753. In 1764 the Society of Friends erected a school at Fourth and Chestnut streets, which was used as a meetinghouse primarily for younger Friends and was known as the Fourth Street Meetinghouse. In 1772 the Philadelphia Meeting was divided into three districts: the Northern District, which met at the Bank Meetinghouse; the Philadelphia Meeting, which met at the High Street Meetinghouse; and the Southern District, which met at Pine Street (Edwin B. Bronner, "The Center Square Meetinghouse and other Meetinghouses of Early Philadelphia," *Bulletin of the Friends Historical Association* 44 [1955]: 67–74).

Beckey Rawle, and Betsy Warr. at their place, at Point no Point. call'd in the Evening at R. Wells's.

17 First Day; Went twice to Meeting, Morning and Evening, Betsy and Hannah Moode drank Tea at A Warners.

18 Polly Howell, and Betsy Flower call'd in the Morning;—spent the after-noon at Wm. Fishers.

19 Went to Meeting in the Morning. call'd in the Evening at Joshua Howells, and at F Rawles.

1759 June the 20 Stay'd at home all Day. Ruth Bonsel call'd in the After-noon.—John & Molly Searson spent part of the Evening with us.

21 Call'd in the Morning at Uncles went from thence to Betsy Moodes. with her to Pine-Street Meeting, dinn'd and spent the After-noon with her. call'd after Meeting at Widw. Mitchell's to see Nurse Mary. B. Moode came home with me in the Evening, who with Sammy Sansom, sup'd at AWs.

22 Step'd over to Neighr. Callenders in the Evening.

23 Stay'd at home all Day.

24 Went thrice to Meeting: Willm. Ricketts, Wm. Callender, and Sammy Emlen, drank Tea at Frd. Warners. JH, KH, and HD, spent the Evening First Day.

25 Stay'd at home all Day; Hannah Ward, formerly Silver, with B, and P, Jervis, call'd in the Morning.

26 Went to Meeting in the Morning, Nancy & Salley Mitchell, spent the Afternoon with us. call'd in the Evening at T. Says.

1759 June the 27 Took a walk in the Evening with Beckey Rawle, HD. call'd.

28 Stay'd at home all Day; H. Callender dinn'd at Fd. Warners, she this day return'd from a journey to New-York. HD. spent the Evening avac Nous.

29 Went in the After-noon to Uncle Jervis, from thence to Betsy Moodes, they were all gone abroad; and to Sally Wharton's who was going out: Drank Tea at Uncles; call'd at C. Nicholdson and at Hannah Hulfords, at Joshua Howells, spent part of the Evening at Ju. Foulks. found when I came home B. Moode, and HD, chez nous.

30 Went in the Morning with Nancy Warner to Wm. Coopers to look for Shoes, call'd at the Stay-makers, at Rebecca Birchalls, at Betsy Moodes, at Widw. Maddoxs, saw John Wallace who lately returnd from England:—call'd at F Rawles, and at Joshua Howells.

July the 1 First Day; Went twice to Meeting; Morning & Afternoon, HD, drank Tea and spent the Evening.

2 Drank Tea at Neighr. Callenders, went with Hannah to severell Shops.—Betsy and Nelly Moode, and HD, spent the Evening with us.

1759 July the 3 Went to Meeting in the Morning, spent the Afternoon at F Rawles, call'd at J. Howells, HD spent the E.

4 Betsy Moode dinn'd at Fd. Warners, John and Molly Searson, spent part of the Evening with us: call'd before Supper at Francies Rawles.

5 Hannah Ward call'd in the Morning—Went to Meeting; Dinn'd and spent the After-noon at S Wharton's; call'd in the Evening at Betsy Moodes; HD, call'd.

6 Spent part of the Evening at Uncle Jerviss. HD, call'd in the Evening.

7 Stay'd at home all Day; HD, call'd.

8 First Day; went to Meeting 3 times, drank Tea at F Rawles; HD spent the Evening; Jos, and Katty Howells sup'd.

9 Went in the After-noon to Uncles Pasture; John Jervis, Reba. Jervis, Betsy and Polly Jervis, ME Sandwith; came after Luke Morris, Chas. Jervis, Thos. Moore, and Thos. Carpenter, call'd in the Evening at Uncles; T Moore came home with us, spent [ ].

10 Went to Meeting in the Morning—Nelly Moode came to spend the After-noon with us, but was sent for home, F, and R Rawles, spent the Evening.

11 Stay'd at home all Day; Nelly Moode, spent part of the Morning; Wm. Parr call'd, Nelly Moode, drank Tea in the After-noon HD spent the Evening.

1759 July the 12 Went to Meeting in the Morning, Dinn'd at S Whartons; spent the After-noon at Thos. Stretch's, went with Molly Stretchs to her Gardan in Straw-Berry-Alley; call'd in the Evening at Betsy Moodes, who came home with us; went back with her as far as F Rawles, call'd their.

13, HD; call'd at dinner-time, to ask us to go to Wm. Callenders place at Point which we declin'd; went to R Steels to buy Silk—Spent the After-noon at T Says, HD spent the E.

14 Stay'd at home all Day; Nancy Mitchell, call'd in the After-noon to Borrow a Pocket-Book, for a Patren; HD; call'd.

15 First Day; went to Meeting 3 times, drank Tea with Hannah Callender; HD; spent.

16 Stay'd at home all Day; Hannah Ward, and Nelly Moode, call'd in the Morning.

17 Went to Meeting in the Morning—spent the After-noon at Saml. Sansoms. call'd towards Evening at Josa. Howells, and at Neighr. Callenders, B Moode and HD, spent the Evening: John Searson and Morton call'd.

18 Stay'd at home all Day. expect'd Wm. Parr to come for us, but was disapointed,—Joshua and Katty Howell and HD; spent the Evening, A Gust with very hard Thunder, between 10 & 11 at Night.

1759 July the 19 Stay'd at home all Day. F & R Rawls drank Tea at A Warners, Hannah Callender, R Smith & HD, call'd in the Evening.

20 Went towards Evening to Thos Says, call'd at Uncles; spent the Evening at B Moodes, took a Walk with her after Super.

21 Went in the Afternoon to George Grays, (at the Lower Ferry) Anna Warner Senr. Sarah Fisher, & MES; drank Tea there. took a ride towards Evening, round by Myomensing:—Betsy Moode spent the Evening with us; went part of the way home with her;—call'd at Frans. Rawles, mett as we came home HD, coming from our House, he went back with us.

22 First Day; Went to Meeting in the Morning and afternoon; stay'd at home in the Evening; Sammy Sansom came home with Polly Sandwith and with HD, spent the Evening Chez Nous.

23 Stay'd at home all Day; Polly Willson, call'd in the Evening: Reba. Say, came home with Polly Sandh. HD, spent the Evening.

24 Went to Meeting in the Morning; went after Dinner to B Moodes, designing to go to Grace Fishers, but as she was out, we went to Janah. Evanss where we spent the After-noon; call'd as we return'd, at John Armitts; and at

Betsy Moodes who with Nelly, took a walk with us in the Evening:—call'd at Uncle Jervis's Charles came home with us.

25 Betsy Moode, Henry Drinker, and David Humpriss, drank Tea with us, B Moode, & B Sandwith, took a Walk in the Evening; mett with Israel Morris, who went with us; sup'd at Betsy Moode's.

26 Went to Meeting in the Morning; spent the Afternoon at Uncle Jerviss; call'd towards Evening at Isaac Howells, at S, Sansoms, sup'd at Francies Rawles.

27 Went after Dinner with Becky Rawle, to Buy Chinia, at Peter Thomsons—was awake almost all Night with a bad Tooth Ake.

28 Stay'd at home all Day.

29 First-Day; Stay'd at home all Day; had the Tooth Ake and pain in the Face.

30 Stay'd at home all Day; Nelly Moode spent part of the Evening. Sammy Emlen, came home with Polly Sandwith.

1759 July the 31 Stay'd at home all Day. Jenny Ervin, with her Couzen Peggy Sharp, spent part of the Morning with me, while our Folks were at Meeting. Sammy Emlen, call'd after Dinner. Betsy and Hannah Moode spent the After-Noon with us.

Augt. the 1 Took a dose of Salts;[14] stay'd at home all Day; Aunt Jervis, Betsy and Polly, with Hannah Ward; spent the After-noon with us.

2 Stay'd at home all Day: Saml. Emlen call'd after dinner; F & R Rawle sup'd, c nous. Danl. Zane a Child of Isaac Zane, was drown'd this day. Ticonderoga and Niagara taken by the English, July the 1759.[15]

14. Many kinds of salts were used medicinally in the eighteenth century. Most, such as Glauber's salt (sodium sulfate), introduced into medical use by Johann Glauber in the seventeenth century, had a cathartic effect on the body, inducing the intestines and neighboring organs to purge their contents. Other salts used similarly were Rochelle salt (sodium potassium tartrate) and Epsom salt (magnesium sulfate). Cathartics were used to treat constipation, colic, dysentery, fevers, and many other ailments. Dr. John Redman used saline purges to treat yellow fever victims in 1762 (Estes, "Therapeutic Practice," 365–83; Redman, *Account of the Yellow Fever, 1762*).

15. In late July Brigadier General John Prideaux and Major General Jeffrey Amherst had captured the fortresses of Niagara and Ticonderoga, two strongholds in French Canadian territory. These victories and the capture of Montreal the following year effectively terminated the domination of Canada by the French (R. Ernst Dupuy and Trevor M. Dupuy, *The Encyclopedia of Military History*, rev. ed. [New York: Harper & Row, 1977], 707; Lawrence H. Leder, *America, 1603–1789: Prelude to a Nation* [Minneapolis: Burgess, 1972], 135–36).

3 Stay'd at home all Day: Henry Drinker came from York, spent part of the After-noon & Evening with us, Sammy Emlen called.

4 Went in the Morning to Uncles; & to B Moodes, Betsy went with me to Jacob Wises, I intending to have a Tooth drawn, but as Jacob was from home we took a walk and came to our House, where Betsy spent the rest of the Morning. Wm. & Sarah Walmsley call'd in the Morning—Wm. Parr call'd in the Afternoon: took a walk round a square with A Warner Junr. call'd at F Rawles, Betsy & Hannah Moode, came to our House in the Evening, went home with them, meet HD, who came home with us.

5 First Day; Went to Meeting three times; Charles Jervis, Tommy Moore; and Sammy Sansom, drank tea with us; CJ, and TM, went with us to Evening meeting; TM came home after meeting with us; found HD there, who spent the Evening.

6 Wm. Walmsley dined at A Warners—spent the After-noon at Uncle Jerviss, help'd to Quilt,—H Callender call'd this Evening.

7 Went to Youths Meeting this Morning. Benny Swett spent the After-noon with us & took his leave—walk'd towards Evening to Betsy Moodes, who came part of the way home with me—call'd at S Sansoms, and at Neigr. Callenders, Saml. Sansom Junr. and Heny. Drinker sup'd at our House.

8 Stay'd at home all Day; S. Sansom Junr. call'd towards Evening, and bid us farewell; B, Swett Senr., and Betsy Moode spent part of the Evening with us, HD call'd.

9 call'd in the Morning at Joshua Howells, and at Francies Rawles; went to Meeting, call'd after meeting at Neighr. Callenders, Katherine & Hannah Callender, drank tea at A Warners;—Sister and self sup'd at Joshua Howells.

1759 Augt the 10 Spent the After-noon at Collonel Whites; call'd at J. Searsons—found at our return home B. Moode, who spent the Evening: Polly, Nancy, and self, went part of the Way home with her. this Evening Frd. Warner & Nancy, returnd from German town where they have been 3 or 4 Days.

11 Stay'd at home all Day; HD spent the Evening—Saml. Sansom Junr. & Benjn. Swett Junr. sail'd from Marcus-Hook, in Snow Chippenham, Edwd. Spain Master, for London; they left Philada. the 10th.

12 First Day; Went to Meeting in the Morning; stay'd at home the rest of the

day; a Gust of hard thunder in the Afternoon: HD, drank tea, and spent the Evening.

13 Stay'd at home all Day; Betsy & Hannah Moode, sup'd at A. Warners.

14 Went to Meeting in the Morning; drank Tea in the After-noon at Betsy Moodes, with Sammy Emlen, and Rachel Reeves; call'd at Billy Morriss, and at Uncle Jerviss, found when I came home, Tommy Moore; who spent part of the Evening;—HD call'd after super,—A Warner Senr. & Polly Sandwith, went to Germantown in the Morning, and return'd in the Evening.

1759 Augt. the 15 Went after–dinner to S Sansoms, who was laying down unwell; spent the After-noon at T. Say's; Joel Evans, and a another young Man call'd in the Evening—HD spent the Evening.

16 Went to Meeting in the Morning; call'd after at S Sansoms, Kasiah Tallman, & Sarah Fisher, drank Tea a A Warners.

17 Wrote this Morning to Hanh. Hicks—drank tea in the Afternoon at S Sansoms, with B Swett Senr. HD and his Brother, call'd after at Uncle Jervis's, went to B. Moodes, who went with me towards Evening to the Widdow Serles to leave a Letter with K. Tallman, for HH, took a long walk, Betsy came home with me spent part of the Evening, bid us Adieu for one long Week, as she intended to go tomorrow to Saml. Cooles, in the Jerseys, HD spent the Evening chez nous.

18 Stay'd at home all Day; Peggy Parr, with her sister in Law, & little Caleb, drank tea with us—HD came in the Evening and inform'd us that the Snow Chippenham in which were Sammy Sansom, & Benny Swett, had sprung a Leak 40 Leagues out at Sea, the 14th Instant, and were Obliged to put back; and that they return'd to Philada. this Evening.

1759 Augt. the 19 First Day; Went to Meeting three times, Hannah Callender, Sammy Sansom, and Benny Swett, drank tea at A Warners, went to Evening Meeting with us. HD came after Meeting.

20 Kathrine Callender drank Tea at AWs—Took a Walk in the Evening with Nancy Warner, to Uncles, and to see Hannah Moode; call'd as we came back for Charley Jervis, who came home with us.

21 Went to Meeting in the Morning; Hannah Ward and HD. drank Tea with us. HD spent the E.

22 Stay'd at home all Day; Wm. Parr, call'd in the Morning,—had a bad

spell of the sick Head-Ake;—Hannah Moode came after Tea and stay'd 'till Night,—Fd. Warner came from Germantown, where she had been 2 or 3 days—with Becky Rawles, and Katty Howell who had spent part of the Summer there, with their Children, as the Small Pox is in Town,[16] and the Weather has been very warm; Joshua Howell sup'd Chez nous; HD. call'd but went away unwell.

23 Went to Meeting in the Morning—call'd after Meeting at Saml. Sansoms—went after Dinner, with Polly, to Shops to look for Pocket Hankerchief's, call'd at Uncle Jervis's, drank Tea at H Moodes, with Nancy and Sally Mitchell.—HD spent the Evening.

24 Stay'd at home all Day; Saml Sansom Junr. came home in the Evening with Polly—and Sup'd with us.

25 Stay'd at home all Day; wrote to Betsy Moode, Doctr. Redman, call'd in the Morning. Hannah Moode spent the After-noon.

26 First Day: Went to Meeting in the Morning; stay'd at home in the After-noon. call'd before Evening Meeting at Josa. Howells, HD came home with us, and spent the Evening.

27 Oston Hicks Junr. call'd in the Morning, to see us—Took a walk to Widdow Maddox's, call'd at Uncle's—went to Betsy Moodes, she came home Yesterday from Saml. Coles—dinn'd and spent the After-noon there. Sally Emlen drank tea there, HD, call'd. Isreal Morris came home with me in the Evening; Josa. & Katty Howell Sup'd with us—Fd. Warner & Nancy gone to German-town.

28 Went to Meeting in the Morning; B. Moode came home with me; Went before Dinner with her to a Dyers, & to C. Brogdens,—HD, call'd after dinner: John Drinker Junr. & little Harry, call'd in the After-noon; Saml. Sansom Senr. call'd, walk'd in the Garden; HD, and B Swett, Junr. spent the Evening & sup'd with us.

16. A smallpox epidemic struck Philadelphia in 1759. Mortality was particularly high among those not inoculated, and it was estimated that five hundred to six hundred deaths were caused by the disease that year. Philadelphia was especially prone to outbreaks of smallpox during the French and Indian War (1756–63) because of the many unimmunized troops and refugees who streamed through the city. During the war years alone there were three major outbreaks, and between 1712 and 1773 Philadelphia suffered ten major outbreaks. According to Benjamin Franklin, there were five "visitations of smallpox" between 1730 and 1752, and Drinker noted several others between 1759 and 1775 (Toner, "Inoculation in Pa."; Wolman, "Tale of Two Colonial Cities"; Hopkins, *Princes and Peasants*," 257; Benjamin Franklin to John Perkins, August 13, 1752, in Franklin, *Papers*, 340–41).

1759 Augt. the 29 Stay'd at home all Day.—HD call'd in the Morning; A Warner came from Germantown, left Nancy; Sarah Sansom & Sammy call'd in the Evening—HD call'd.

30 Went to Meeting in the Morning; call'd after at Uncles; Spent the After-noon at Saml. Sansom's, call'd at Josa. Howells; HD, spent the E.

31 Stay'd at home all Day; HD call'd in the Morning; B Swett Junr. call'd in the After-noon, & bid us a Seacond time farewell. HD call'd. Saml. Sansom Junr. and HD spent the Evening and sup'd with us; Sammy took leave of us again.

Sepr. the 1 Stay'd at home all Day: Henry Drinker came at Noon, and bid us Adieu. he left Philada. after Dinner; several of his Friends accompanying him to Chester or Marcus-Hook, where he designs on the Morrow, with Sammy Sansom & Benny Swett, to embark in the Snow Recovery, Nathanel[17] Falconer Master for Bristol.—Betsy Moode spent part of the Evening with us.

2 First Day; Went to Meeting 3 times—drank Tea at Joshua Howells.

3 Stay'd at home all Day. Joshua Howell, Katty Howell, & Francies Rawle, drank Tea at AW's; Joshua & Katty, W Fisher & Wife, sup'd here,—Saml. Sansom Senr. &c. return'd this Evening from Marcus-Hook, where they have been detain'd longer than they expected, by the Snow Recovery Springing a Leak; which being mended she left the Hook between 2 & 3 o'clock this After-noon.

4 Betsy Moode call'd in the Morning—went with us to Meeting.—spent the After-noon at Uncle Jerviss, went towards Evening to Betsy Moodes, who with Sally Emlen, Polly Sandwith & self, took a Walk. BM. & SE, came home with us.

5 Went in the Morning, to James Delaplains. (Germantown;) Anna Warner Senr. Saml. Rhoads Junr. & MES,—AW & (Nancy who has been there some time) went home in the Evening with Sammy; left us there with RR.

6 Joshua Howell came up and dinned with us, he went home after dinner, with his little Daughter Katty; who has been long unwell.—Becky Rawle & MES, drank Tea & Sup'd, with Molly Foulk, & Betsy Bringhurst, who have been some time at Germantown with the Children. at the House of one

17. The name "Fortuner" crossed out. Although "Falconer" is correct, the latter name may not be in ED's handwriting.

Ming:—Lodged with Becky Rawle, & little Billy, Polly S, in another Bed, in the same Room.

1759 Sept. the 7 Wm. Fisher, Sarah Fisher, & Anna Warner Senr. came to Germantown, before dinner,—After dinner, Wm. Fisher; Anna Warner & Sarah Fisher, Mary Foulk & Betsy Bringhurst with little Polly Foulk, Becky Rawle with M & E Sandwith went to the Paper-Mill,[18] a mile & half from Germantown, came back before tea, WF, AW, & SF, went home after Tea, MF & EB, spent the Evening with us.

On the 31 Ult. the Barn of one Christopher Robins, about twelve Miles from Philada., was set on Fire by Lightning, and entirely consumed in a short time. There was in it about 2000 Bushels of Grain &c.

8 Expected to have gone home, but Rain prevented us, Stay'd within all Day—saw no company.

9 First Day. Frans. Rawle, with his Cousin Sally Rawle, came to Germantown, in the Morning. MESand. could not go to Meeting, for want of Clean Cloaths. Molly Foulk, & Betsy Bringhurst, drank tea with us.—came to Philada. this Evening.

1759 Sept. the 10 call'd in the Morning to Josa. Howells. went to Uncle Jerviss, and to Betsy Moodes, spent great part of the Morning there, Betsy came to our house after Dinner, spent the After-noon & Evening with us. went part of the way home with her—call'd as we returnd at Josa. Howell. Saml. Howell came home with us.

11 Went to Meeting in the Morning. B. Moode came home with me. Received a Letter from ——— went after dinner to Robt. Smiths, whoes youngest Child lay ill in the Small-Pox,—drank Tea at the Widdow Armitts, upon the Hill—calld towards Evening at Wm. Browns, who has lately remov'd from Wallnutt Street, to his New House by the Dock, call'd at Saml. Wharton Sally out of Town with her Children, call'd at B. Moodes,—went before super to Thos. Says.

12 Stay'd at home all Day.

13 Went to Meeting in the Morning, call'd at M Burrows, went after Meeting to Hustons Store with H. Callender &c. call'd after-dinner at R Steels, and at H Steels, to see his son Jemmy who was this Week inoculated for the Small

18. The Rittenhouse paper mill in Roxborough, near Germantown, Pa. (Horatio Gates Jones, "Historical Sketch of the Rittenhouse Paper-Mill, the First Erected in America, A.D. 1690," *Pennsylvania Magazine of History and Biography* 20 [1896]: 315–33).

Pox,[19] spent the After-noon at J. Searsons, call'd towards Evening at Wido. Maddoxs, & at the Widow Graems, who with her Daughter Mc. Knight, & Patty Scanland, lately remov'd, from Trent-Town to Philada.—call'd at Uncle Jerviss & at B. Moodes; Sammy Emlen came home, & sup'd with us.

1759 Sept. the 14 Stay'd at home all Day.

15 Stay'd at home all Day. Joshua & Katty Howell, spent the Evening, avac nous.

16 First Day. Went to Meeting in the Morning and After-noon; stay'd at home in the Evening; John Drinker Junr. drank Tea with us.

Katty Howell was brought to Bed early this Morning, with her Daughter Sally.

17 took a walk in the Evening to see Katty Howell; were sent for home by H. Ward & two other Young Women.

18 Betsy Moode call'd in the Morning. went to Meeting with us. Hannah Ward, with her Mother in Law, and Rachel Knight, spent the After-noon with us, took a Walk in the Evening, call'd at S Sansoms; at B. Moodes, and at S.

19. Smallpox inoculation began in the American colonies in 1721 when Zabdiel Boylston, a Boston physician, learned about the practice from Cotton Mather, who had read about it in the Levant and also learned of it from an African servant. Over half of Boston's nearly eleven thousand persons contracted the disease that year, and almost 15 percent of those infected died. Although only six of the 287 persons Boylston inoculated died, his work excited much opposition on both religious and socioeconomic grounds.

In inoculation, matter taken from a pustule of someone who had caught the disease naturally was placed on several small cuts made by a needle or a lancet in the arm or leg muscles of the person receiving the inoculation. This method produced a milder, less fatal form of smallpox, although the person was still a carrier of the disease.

When smallpox arrived in Philadelphia in January 1731, Benjamin Franklin, who was in Boston in 1721 and whose brother was a leading opponent of inoculation, began a tireless campaign to promote inoculation. According to Franklin, only one of about fifty inoculated persons died. In the 1736–37 epidemic 129 persons were inoculated, again with only one fatality. Franklin reported that by 1752, eight hundred persons had been inoculated, with only four deaths. In the 1750s publications and lectures by physicians urged Philadelphians to adopt inoculation. In 1759 a New Jersey physician opened a house in Philadelphia exclusively for that purpose, and within two years Philadelphia had become a center of inoculation for all the British colonies in North America, attracting patients even from the West Indies. By 1764 a doctoral thesis in Leyden stated that 8,327 persons had been inoculated in Pennsylvania and the adjoining provinces with only nineteen deaths. In 1774 elite Philadelphians banded together to found the Society for Inoculation of the Poor, making inoculation available to a vulnerable part of the population that could not afford the three pounds doctors charged for the preparation and inoculation of patients (John B. Blake, *Public Health in the Town of Boston 1630–1822* [Cambridge: Harvard University Press, 1959], chapter two; Kenneth Silverman, *The Life and Times of Cotton Mather* [New York: Harper & Row, 1984], 339–40; Franklin, *Papers*, 4:341–42; Toner, "Inoculation in Pa."; Wolman, "Tale of Two Colonial Cities").

Whartons, whose Children are inoculated for the Small Pox, went from thence to Uncle Jervis, call'd at F Rawles, who with Becky were gone to our House.

19 Stay'd at home all Day. Wm. Parr, call'd in the Morning—inform'd us of a Melancholy Accident which happen'd in his Family, Vizt. His Man Robert, (who for some time before had appear'd unwell, & low-Spirit'd) was on the 8th. Instant, Missing; and after search, was found, the next day Dead, in the House of Office,[20] where they suppose he had thrown himself. The Jury brought in their Verdict, Non-compas-mentis.—Charley Jervis came home with Polly, & Nancy, this Evening.

20 Went to Meeting in the Morning, call'd after at Joshua Howells, at Judah Foulks, and at Wm. Callenders, whose Wife keeps her Bed with the chills & Feaver.

21 Stay'd at home all Day. Hannah Hicks, came in the Morning, and stay'd Dinner with us, she came to Town last Night.

22 Polly Sandwith sat up last Night, with Neighr. Callender. ES. had Nancy Warner for a Bed Fellow.—Wm. & Sarah Walmsley came to Town this Morning, Breakfast'd and Dinn'd at AWs—went after Tea with Sarah Wamsley to Shops; Betsy Moode spent part of the Evening with us. went part of the way home with her—Wm. & Sarah Walmsley Lodg'd at AWs.

23 First Day. Yearly-Meeting.[21] Sarah Smith from Burlingtown, spent an Hour with us before Morning Meeting, call'd on her at Neighr. Callenders, went to Meeting togeather.—went to after-noon Meeting—Sally Smith came home with us, who with Sarah Walmsley and Becky Rawle, drank Tea chez nous. went to Evening Meeting—Wm. & S. Walmsley sup'd & lodg'd at AWs.

24 Stay'd at home all Day, unwell.—Betsy Cooper and Lisey Barker, dinn'd at AWs—Polly Shoemaker call'd after dinner, Sally Smith call'd in the Evening.

25 Went to Meeting in the Morning, and in the Afternoon to Meeting of

20. *House of office*, a euphemistic term for the water closet or outhouse, came into use in the seventeenth century (Farmer, *Slang and Its Analogues*, 366).

21. In 1685 Quakers who had settled in the Delaware Valley decided to hold their yearly meeting alternately in Philadelphia and Burlington, N.J., in odd-numbered and even-numbered years respectively. This practice continued until 1760, when the last yearly meeting was held in Burlington. Thereafter all yearly meetings were held in Philadelphia (Mekeel, "The Founding Years," p.17; see also the appendix in J. M. Moore, *Friends in the Delaware Valley*, 250, and below, Dec. 14, 1760).

Discipline[22]—Drank Tea at James James's, where we went to see Hannah Hicks, who is unwell with the Ague and Feaver; call'd at Saml. Whartons, to see the Children, went from thence to Wm. Morris's and to B. Moodes. Hudson Emlen came home with us.

26 Stay'd at home all Day. Eight Women Friends dinn'd at AWs which made 14 of the best sort, our selves included.—H. Ward & R. Knight call'd in the Evening.

27 Stay'd up stairs all Day; (not well) reading, writeing & Kniting, F & RR, sup'd with us.

28 Stay'd at home all Day; Polly and Nancy, went this after-noon to the Burial of Sally Lloyd, Daughter of Hannah Lloyd,—Hannah Ward, & R Knight, call'd this Evening.

1759 Sept. the 29 Stay'd at home all Day.

30 First Day. Went to Meeting 3 times—Tommy Moore came home with us from Evening Meeting.

Octor. the 1. Hannah Hicks call'd in the Morning to take leave of us. Betsy Moode came in the Morning. Dinn'd and spent part of the After-noon with us. Went this After-noon to the Burial of Rebecca Rawle, Aunt to Frances Rawle; Sally Smith Spent the Evening with us.

2 Went to Meeting in the Morning, took a walk after, with Betsy Moode, to the Wosted Combers, and else-where, went after dinner to F Rawles (Becky gone out) from thence to Smiths to Buy Cruels. when I came home, found Molly Searson, with Polly, She and Johney drank Tea with us.

3 Stay'd at home all Day, rainy Weather.

4 Stay'd at home all Day.

5 Went this Morning to Monthly Meeting—Saw 4 Couples Pass, Vizt. George

22. The meeting for discipline or the committee for discipline met at the Philadelphia Yearly Meeting to compile the Book of Discipline, the formal compendium of Quaker belief and practice. While work on the book was usually limited to committee members, their meetings were open to all Friends who wanted to attend (Richard Bauman, *For the Reputation of Truth: Politics, Religion, and Conflict among the Pennsylvania Quakers 1750–1800* [Baltimore: Johns Hopkins University Press, 1971], 50; Society of Friends, *Rules of Discipline and Christian Advices of the Yearly Meeting of Friends for Pennsylvania and New Jersey* [Philadelphia: Samuel Sansom, 1797]; earlier manuscript books of discipline are owned by the Friends Historical Library, Swarthmore College, Swarthmore, Pa.).

Dylling and Sally Hill, John Head and Elizah. Hasteings, Nathl. Brown and Matha. Elfrith, William Masterman and Mary Stiles,—Went home with Betsy Moode, after Meeting, dinnd there, call'd after dinner with BM to see Peggy Morris, (who lays in with her Twin Sons, Richard and John) but as she was unwell, we did not go up stairs, drank Tea at B Moodes, Nelly Moode went to spend the after-noon with Polly Sandwith; call'd in the Evening at S Whartons to see the Children who are in a good way to recover; Joseph Wharton Junr. came home with me.

6 Call'd in the Morning at Joshua Howells, at Francis Rawles, and at Uncle Jerviss, went from thence to Betsy Moodes, dinn'd and spent the After-noon there, took a walk in the Evening with B Moode, call'd at Will. Browns, Betsy came home with me, found Hannah Ward with Polly, Betsy stay'd supper with us, went part of the Way home with her, call'd as I came back at Joshua Howells, found A Warner Senr. and Sister Molly there.

7 First Day. Went to Meeting three times.

8 Took a Walk in the Evening to S Whartons, to Betsy Moodes, and to Uncle Jerviss, Charles came home with us.

9 Went to Meeting in the Morning, call'd after dinner at S Sansoms, she went with us to Content Nicholsons, where we spent the afternoon;—spent the Evening at F Rawles.

1759 Octor. the 10 Went in the Morning with Becky Rawle to the wosted Combers, Betsy Moode spent the After-noon & Evening with us.

11 Spent the After-noon at Uncle Jerviss, help'd Quilt.

12 Stay'd at home all Day, rainy Weather.

13 Went in the Morning to S Sansoms, to borrow his Horse, call'd a J Jervis at B Moodes and at S Whartons,—Set out after dinner for Buybary, Charles Jervis, Elizth. Moode, M & E Sandwith—came to Wm. Walmsleys at 6 o'clock in the Evening BM, and BS. lodg'd togeather.

14 First Day this Morning we went to Buybary Meeting, James Thornton preach'd and Pray'd,—came back to Wm. Walmsleys, to dinner, Took a ride in the After-noon to Sarah Titus's, S Walmsley, B Moode, Tommy Waly., Charles Jervis, and MES; mett on the road Tommy Knight a Youth who has past his first Meeting with Molly Walmsley, Eldest Daughter of Wm. Walmsley. he accompany'd us to S Tituss where we drank Tea, return'd in the Evening. to WWs.

15 this Day we intended to return to Philada. but were prevented by bad Weather C. Jervis sett of, for Town after Dinner, designing to return on fourth Day next, to accompany us home.

1759 Octor. the 16 Mathea Walmsley came this Morning from Horseham, where she has been some days, with her Sister, Esther Perry.—Took a walk this After-noon to John Townsends, (S Walmsley Senr. and Junr. B Moode, Mary and Elizth. Sandwith) drank Tea there, return'd in the Evening to Wm. Walmsleys.

17 took a Walk this Morning to the Barn, and up the Lane, Charles Jervis came before dinner; We left Buybary at ¼ past 2 o'clock, and came to Philada. before 6 in the Evening.

18 Went to Meeting in the Morning; came out unwell, call'd at Uncles, came home and stayd up stairs the rest of the Day. H. Moode spent the After-noon with us. John Armitt Senr. brought us a Letter which came from Dublin.

19 Wm. Parr, Charles Jervis, and Hannah Moode, call'd to see us this Morning; spent the After-noon and Evening at F Rawles, Sammy Emlen drank tea there.

20 Went this Morning to Wests to buy Silk, call'd at Joshua Howells; went in the After-noon to sundry Shops, with Becky Rawle, and Nancy Warner.

1759, Octor. the 21[23] First Day. went to Meeting as Usual.

22 Stay'd at home all Day.

23d Stay'd at home all Day, Polly went to the Middle Meeting this afternoon, a Meeting being held before the Burial of Polly Jordan, who departed this life, the 21, Instant—Charles Jervis came home with PS.

24th Went this Morning to Thos. Says, whose Daughter Becky, lays ill, in the Small Pox, which she has taken in the Natural way; and to most that take it Naturaly (at this time) it proves mortal.[24]—call'd at Frans. Rawles, and at

23. The manuscript volume for Oct. 21, 1759–Aug. 14, 1760, has hand-colored floral paper covers. The outside front cover reads, "1759, 1760"; on the inside back cover ED wrote the word "spoke."

24. While most patients who suffered from smallpox eventually recovered, ED was correct in noting the differences in mortality between those who contracted it naturally and those who were inoculated. Accurate statistics do not exist for Philadelphia, but in the Boston epidemic of 1752 almost 10 percent of those who caught the disease naturally died, and in the 1764 epidemic that figure was close to 18 percent. The comparable mortality figures for those inoculated were 1.4 and .9 percent (for a comparative view of English cities see Peter Razzell, *The Conquest of Smallpox: The Impact of Inoculation on Smallpox Mortality in Eighteenth-Century Britain* [Firle: Caliban Books, 1977], 113–37; Hopkins, *Princes and Peasants*, 41).

Josa. Howell's,—had a Meeting this Afternoon at AWs with our good Friends Danl. Stanton, and John Pemberton.

25th. Went to Meeting in the Morning, call'd after at S Sansoms, & at Frans. Rawles, spent the After-noon at S. Wharton's, call'd in the Evening at W Morris's, and at Betsy Moodes.

1759, Octor. the 26 Call'd this Morning on Hannah Callender, who went with me to Monthly Meeting, five couples past; 3 clear'd & 2 enter'd, Isaac Parrish and Sally Mitchel, one of the latter;—spent this After-noon at S Sansom's, Esther Mifflen & Daughter there, went in the Evening to Thos. Say's, whoes little Becky dyed this Morning: Frans. & Becky Rawle sup'd with us.

27th. Stay'd at home all Day, Wm. Parr call'd in the Morning, Polly Sandwith, and Nancy Warner, went this after-noon, to the Burial of Becky Say.

28 First Day: went to Meeting Three times—took a walk down Town in the After-noon, call'd at Uncles, found him unwell with a Fever; drank Tea at Betsy Moodes, went with her to Evening Meeting.

29th. Stay'd at home all Day; J Redman call'd this Morning.

30th. Went to Meeting this Morning, call'd in the Evening at Neighr. Callender's, AW. Lit dans notre Chamber.

31st. Spent this Afternoon at Thos. Says—Tommy very unwell.

1759: Novr. the 1 Went to Meeting in the Morning; took a walk in the After-noon to Bush-Hill,[25] Anna Warner Senr., Becky Rawle, Anna Warner Junr., Betsy Warner, and P and B. Sandwith.—Joshua and Katty Howell and Frances Rawle, came after; view'd the Paintings, and walk'd in the Garden—came home before Evening, drank Tea at Josa. Howell's.

2d. Spent this after-noon and part of the Evening at Betsy Moodes; call'd at Francis Rawles, stay'd out after 10 o'clock, FR, came home with me, A Warner Senr. and Polly Sandwith, went this after-noon to the Burial of Mary Powell Widdw.

25. Andrew Hamilton's Bush Hill estate, located north of Vine Street between the present Twelfth and Nineteenth streets, was the site of the first major art collection in Pennsylvania. As part of the estate, it passed to Hamilton's son, James, in 1740. The art collection and estate gardens were open to tourists (Bridenbaugh and Bridenbaugh, *Rebels and Gentlemen*, 213–19).

3d. Stay'd at home all Day.

4 Went to Meeting 3 times, call'd at F Rawles, before Evening Meeting First Day.

5 Stay'd at home all Day, Posted Accounts.

6th. Went to Youths Meeting, call'd at Preist's for Nitting-Needles, call'd at F Rawles; over took B Moode going to Beulah Clarks, went with her, B Moode call'd after dinner at our House. Beulah Burge and Hannah Shoemaker Junr. spent this afternoon with us:—went in the Evening to Josa. Howells, Katty, and Hanh. Callender came home with me, supped chez nous. Polly Sandwith and Billy Coats, came for me, to see Tommy Say. who is very ill,—I had a bad spell of the Sick-Head-Ake, this Evening. Polly gone to T Says in order to set up with Tommy.

7 Stay'd at home all Day. R Rawle spent the Evening.

8th. Went to meeting this Morning, went home with B Moode, call'd at Uncle Jervis, call'd after dinner at R Rawles, spent this after-noon at Saml. Rhoades's with A Warner Senr. and PS,—A Warner's front Parlour Chimney took Fier this Evening, which much Alarm'd us:—B Swett Senr. who came to assist at putting it out, spent part of the Evening.

9 This Morning Rachel Budd brought us a noat from R Say, requireing (if we had a desire to see Tommy Say in this World) we would come Immeadatly, which we did, and found him very ill, tho in his Senses, he continued untill Evening—when he departed this Life in the 20th year of his age, Rachel Wells spent this afternoon with us.

1759: Novr. the 10, William Parr call'd this Morning M Winter fitted a Body Lining,[26] Betsy & Nelly Moode spent this Afternoon and part of the Evening with us,—Betsy went with me to T Says to see Tommy's corps.—We were Alarmm'd this evening by the cry of Fire, prov'd a Chimney directly oppisite to AWs.

11 First Day. Went to Meeting thrice, after Meeting in the afternoon, went to the Burial of Thos. Say Junr. call'd after at F Rawle's.

12. Took a walk this Morning to several Shops, call'd at F Rawles, at Wm.

26. *Body* or *bodies* was the original form of the word *bodice*, the undergarment also known as a corset, worn by American women in the eighteenth century (Estelle Ansley Worrell, *Early American Costume* [Harrisburg: Stackpole Books, 1975], 73).

Fisher's, at T Says, found when I came home Hanh. Ward with Polly; Charley Jervis came in the Evening home with PS.

13th. Went to meeting this Morning spent the after-noon at Wm. Fisher's, took a walk in the Evening to Josa. Howells & F Rawles—Anna and Billy Rawle were this Afternoon Innoculated for the Small Pox by Docr. Redman.

14th. Stay'd at home all Day, rainy Weather.

1759: Novr. the 15 Stay'd at home all Day, rainy Weather Wm. Parr call'd this Morning pour Argant.

16th. Stay'd at home all Day.

17th. Stay'd at home all Day, Jams. Hamilton came to Town, a large number accompanying him, he was this After-noon Proclaim'd Govener,[27] in the Room of Wm. Denny.

18th. First Day; went 3 times to Meeting.

19th. call'd after dinner at Neighr. Brooks, went to Uncle Jervis's, found him in Bed, bad with the Chills and Fever, spent the afternoon there, Charles came home with us in the Evening.

20th. Went to Meeting this Morning J Head and Betsy Hasteings, were Married, to whome Danl. was led to speak comfortably—spent this afternoon at Neigr. Callenders.

21 Stay'd at home all Day, unwell—Hannah Callender spent the Afternoon and Evening with us.

1759: Novr. the 22 Went to Meeting this Morning, went home with Betsy Moode, call'd at Uncles spent the Afternoon at John Armitt's, M Wister there, call'd in the Evening at F Rawles.

23d Spent this Afternoon at F Rawles the Evening at Joshua Howells.

27. Pennsylvania was a proprietary colony, which meant that the proprietor, in this case the Penn family, had the power either to serve themselves as governor, or to appoint lieutenant governors, often called governors, in their place. Appointed governors were responsible to the Penns to uphold their instructions, but like the Penns, they were ultimately answerable to the Crown. James Hamilton was appointed to his second term in office on Nov. 17, 1759, and served until the end of October 1763 (William Robert Shepard, *History of Proprietary Government in Pennsylvania*, Studies in History, Economics, and Public Law 6 [New York: Columbia University Press, 1896], 474–95; "James Hamilton," *DAB*).

24 Stay'd at home all Day: Peggy Parr, and her sister in Law, spent an Hour with us this morning.

25th. First Day: Went to Meeting 3 times some extracts from the Minuets of the Quarterly Meeting, and advice against going to Fairs,[28] was this Morning read by William Callender in our Meeting.

26th. Stay'd at home all Day rainy weather.

27 Went to Meeting this Morning B Moode came home with me after meeting—wrote this Afternoon to Dublin.

28th. Spent this Afternoon at John Searsons—the Evening at Francis Rawles.

1759: Novr. the 29 Stay'd at home all Day C Jervis call'd in the Evening.

30 Went this morning to Point, set out by the Parish, S Sansom's Horse, A Warner's Chair, Charles Jervis waited upon us, found Wm. Parr's Family all well, but Molato Poll, who was brought to Bed last Evening—took a walk before Dinner round the Meadows, and to Roberts Grave, Billy and Peggy, Charles, Polly and myself,—dinn'd at 3 o'clock, left Point before 4, came home to Tea by 5—spent this Evening very agreeably, with our Friends Elizth. Hannah and Elleror Moode.

Decemr. the 1 Stay'd at home all Day; warm weather for the Season.

2d First Day. Went to Meeting three times, Wm. & Sarah Fisher sup'd. at A Warners—the Wind arose last night at about 12 o'clock,[29] I think tis now as cold as ever I knew it.

1759. Decr. the 3 Stay'd at home all Day, very cold Weather A Carpenter's Shop, on Society Hill, took Fire,[30] this Morning at about 9 o'clock, the Wind blowing Violently at N W; severel Houses were burnt down.

4th Went to Meeting this Morning. Phebe Broom from NewPort, call'd to see us this After-noon—begun to read Pope's Homer; the Iliad.[31]

28. Market fairs, held biannually in colonial Philadelphia for three days each in November and May, featured stalls selling dry goods, toys, millinery, cakes, and confections. In 1775 the mayor and Common Council of Philadelphia persuaded the Pennsylvania Assembly to abolish the fairs, as they were also occasions for drinking and gaming (J. F. Watson, *Annals*, 1:364; Rosswurm, *Arms, Country, and Class*, 37).

29. The word "and" crossed out.

30. See *Pa. Gaz.*, Dec. 6, 1759.

31. Alexander Pope, *The Iliad of Homer* (London: W. Boyer, Bernard Lintott, 1715–20) (*Brit. Mus. Cat.*).

5th. Stay'd at home all Day.

6th. Went to Meeting this morning; call'd after at Widdow Maddox's. Sarah Sansom, and Rachel Drinker, spent this After-noon with us, H. Callender spent the Evening.

7th. Phebe Broom call'd this Morning—spent the Afternoon, and part of the Evening at Betsy Moodes.

8th Stay'd at home all Day: Becky Rawle spent the Afternoon with us.

1759: Decemr. the 9 First Day. Went to Meeting. Morning & Afternoon, stay'd at home in the Evening. dark & rain.

10th. Stay'd at home all Day. Joshua & Katty Howell, spent the Eveing. [Maria] allez de.

11th. Molly Whey came to live with AW—went to Meeting this Morning; went out after Dinner, designing to go to Uncles, but mett Sally Wharton coming to our House, turn'd back with her, she spent the Afternoon with us, we went home with her in the Evening, Sup'd there, George Morgan waited on us home.

12th. Went out this Morning, call'd a S Sansom's, Spent the rest of the Morning, and Dinn'd at Betsy Moodes, went after dinner to Uncle Jervis's, where I found M Sandwith, spent the Afternoon and part of the Evening there.

13th. Went to Meeting this Morning. Molly Foulk, spent the Afternoon with us—we spent this Evening at F Rawle's.

1759: Decr. the 14 Stay'd at home all Day: Hannah Ward spent the Afternoon with us, Becky Rawle part of the Evening.

15th. Stay'd at home all Day: Wm. & K. Callender, and B Moode, drank tea at AWs Hannah Moode, came after, intending to spend the Evening with us but were sent for home—William Callender, stay'd part of the Evening.

16th. First Day: Went to Meeting three times.

17th. call'd for Becky Rawle, who went with me to S Sansom's, where we spent the Afternoon,—Polly went to the Burial of Elizth. Mifflin Morris.

18 went to Meeting this Morning, B Moode came home with me, she dinn'd, spent the Afternoon, and part of the Evening with us.

19 stay'd at home all Day: Nothing occurd.

20th. Stay'd at home all Day. Francis and Becky Rawle, Catty Howell, and S Fisher spent this Evening at A Warners.

1759: Decemr. the 21 Polly and self, went out after Breakfast, call'd at Uncle Jervis's, went from thence, Polly to S Wharton's, self to B Moodes, spent an hour there, then went SWs—Dinn'd, spent the Afternoon and Evening there, Sammy came home with us.

22d. Stay'd at home, spent the Day Drawing—Able James call'd in the Morning avac Argent,—Received this Afternoon, a Letter from H Callender, Burlington.

23d. First Day: went to Meeting 3 times—Sarah Fisher drank tea at AWs.

24th. Stay'd at home all Day: rainy, and slipery.

25 Christmass Day, went to Meeting in the Morning, spent the Evening at F Rawle's.

26th. Stay'd at home all Day.

27 Went to Meeting this Morning. Sarah Mitchel, Married,—spent the After-noon & Evening at Uncle Jervis's.—Polly Jervis's Ancle spraind badly.

1759: Decemr. the 28th Spent the Afternoon and Evening a Josa. Howell's, call'd after Supper at Frans. Rawle's. Mary Cooper inform'd Polly Sandwith this Morning in Meeting of the Death of Mary Allbeson, who dyed some Day this Week.

29th. Ostin Hicks Junr. call'd to see us—went out after Dinner, call'd at Uncle Jervis's. spent this Afternoon & Evening at B Moodes.

30 First Day. went to Meeting three times; this Morning, Benjn. Trotter, M Kirby, preach'd, John Pemberton pray'd,—in the Afternoon, Sammy Emlen and Hesah. William's, preach'd,—in the Evening John Storor, preach'd, Danl. Stanton pray'd, Tommy Moore came home with us, spent an hour.

31st. Rebh. Rawle, and K, Howell, call'd this Morning, agree'd with us to spend this Afternoon, with Polly Howell, at Charles Jones's,—which we did.[32]

32. Word crossed out.

1760

1760 Janry. the 1 Went to Meeting this Morning: S Morris preach'd, John Storor kneel'd down to pray, at which time I was obliged to come out of Meeting, being unwell. Wm. & Sarah Fisher, spent this Evening at AWs.

2d. Went after Breakfast to Francis Rawle's—Becky went with me to Smith's to buy Cruels, nobody at home to sarve us; Dinn'd at FRs went after dinner with Becky, again to Smith's—drank Tea at FRs Francis and Becky, spent the Evening at our House.

3d. Stay'd at home all Day: dull weather, Fifth Day.

4th. Stay'd at home all Day: dull Foggy weather.

5th. Nelly Moode, came[1] after Dinner to desire I would go set with Betsy, who otherwise would be alone, as Hannah was gone over the River, with Mary Kirby; and she (Nelly) was going elsewhere. I call'd at Uncles, then went to Betsy's where I spent the Afternoon and Evening. came home alone.

6th. First Day: stay'd at home this Morning, not well, went to meeting in the Afternoon: B Trotter preach'd—Betsy and Nelly Moode came home with us[2] went to Evening meeting togeather: Danl Stanton and B Trotter, appeard in Testimony, the former concluded the Meeting in Prayer, Tommy Moore came home with us.

1760: Jenry. the 7 Stay'd at home all Day: T Moore, call'd this Morning to know, if we would go, to the Accadamy,[3] to hear the Lectures upon Electricity, did not suit us to go—Johney Searson drank Tea with us.

8th. Went to Meeting this Morning, D Stanton, [H] Willims, & B. Trotter, preach'd, went after Meeting, with B——y Moode, to Paul Chanders's, and to Heny. Groath's—spent this Afternoon at Thos. Say's.

1. Word crossed out.
2. Word crossed out.
3. The College and Academy of Philadelphia was offering a series of lectures and experiments on electricity. A professor of English and oratory, Ebenezer Kinnersley, was the main speaker; admission to each lecture was a half a dollar (*Pa. Gaz.*, Dec. 27, 1759).

9 Stay'd at home all Day: rainy Weather.

10th. Went to Meeting this Morning: Mordecai Yarnal, Benjn. Trotter, and Hezekiah Williams, preach'd. call'd after Meeting at S Sansoms, spent this After-noon at Thos. Robertsons, over the Bridge.

11th. Stay'd within all Day. Jos. & Katty Howell, Frans and Becky Rawle, drank tea at AWs Nancy, went out to set up with the Corps of Hannah Lynn.

12th Went before Tea in the Afternoon, to Wm. Callender's, call'd at Molly Smith's with my Gown, went to Thos Say's with a magnifying Looking Glass, which I had borrow'd, came home to tea.

13 First Day: went to Meeting this Morning, B Trotter preach'd and pray'd, stay'd at home this Afternoon, Polly, went to the Burial of Hannah Clifton, went to Meeting this Evening, Daniel Stanton, pray'd, M.Yarnal, B Trotter, & D Stanton, appear'd in Testimony.

1760 Janry. the 14 Stay'd at home all Day, had the sick Head Ake—S Fisher drank Tea at AWs—extream cold.

15th. Stay'd at home all Day: Betsy Moode, came after meeting, stay'd dinner, spent the Afternoon, and part of the Evening with us.—Polly came out of Meeting this Morning. Mall au V——n——r.

16th. Stay'd at home all Day: Charles Jervis and Hannah Ward, came home with Polly, this Evening.

17 Stay'd at home all Day dull Weather.

18th. Stay'd at home all Day: Hannah Callender and Katty Smith spent this Afternoon at A Warner's, Received a Billet this Evening from RR and CH.

19th Went out this Morning after Breakfast—calld at Patty Powell's, for mittens, stop'd at C Jones's, call'd at S Whartons, dinn'd and spent the Afternoon at B Moodes—call'd in the Evening at Uncle Jerviss—Charles came home with me.

20th First Day: went to Meeting this Morning—Daniel Stanton, and John Pemberton, appeard in Testimony, S Morris in Prayer; In the Afternoon, Becky Jones, [H] Willims & David Estaugh, preach'd—Wm. & Sarah Fisher drank Tea at AWs Joshua & Katty Howell spent the Evening—stay'd from Meeting this Evening, it being very dark & the Streets dirty.

21st Stay'd at home,[4] spent the Day in the Blue Parlor—reading, and darning, dull Weather.

22d. Went to Meeting this Morning. Danl. Stanton, B Trotter, [H] Willims, and Sarah Morris, appeard in testimony: D Stanton in Prayer,—Cadr. Evans, and Jane Owen were Married—call'd after Meeting at Josa. Howells, Dinn'd at Frans. Rawles, came home after dinner—then went back to FRs with Polly, where we spent the Afternoon.

23d. Wm. Parr and Judath Foulk calld this Morning. spent the Afternoon at Uncle Jerviss,—Molly [Wye] a young Woman, who had liv'd a Week, (some time ago) with A Warner; was yesterday put in Jail for Theft.

24th Went to Meeting this Morning, sans Polly—Mary Emlen, S Morris, and D Stanton, preach'd B Trotter pray'd—went home with B Moode, after Meeting, spent half an Hour dans lure Mason Nett, came home to dinner, went after to S Sansom's, found C. Nicholdson there, who came to inquire for Letters from her Son; but mett with none, Wm. and Kat Callender drank Tea there, A James call'd. came home in the Evening, baucoup Chagrin'd. Betsy Moode, according to my wishes, came and sup'd with us.

25th. Stay'd at home all Day: wrote all the Morning. Molly Searson and Hannah Ward, spent, this Afternoon with us. John Searson came to Tea, [H] Ward spent part of the Evening.

26th. Went out this Morning with H Callender. call'd on B Moode, who went with us to Corry's Store to buy Thread, went from thence to view the burnt Buildings on Society-Hill, then walk'd to Uncle Jervis's Pasture, stop'd there, from thence We went to Anthony Morriss Junr. dinn'd there—after dinner return'd to Town, left the Thread at M Willimss, went home with B Moode where we drank Tea, and talk'd over the perticulars of our agreeable Excursions.

27 First Day: B Trotter, and Becky Jones, appeard in testimony, this morning; had a Silent Meeting[5] in the Afternoon;—we were detaind from Meeting this Evening, by rain.

4. Word(s) crossed out.

5. The purpose of the Quaker meeting was to allow the community of Quaker believers to experience the inner light, a spiritual state not attainable by such earthly means as speech and prayer. Quakers distrusted set prayers and an ordained ministry—creations of man's reasoning powers, an earthly faculty—because the personal experiencing of God through the inner light required the suppression of those very qualities. Persons who entered the Quaker ministry did so because they believed they had been moved by the divine spirit to speak; though they both preached and prayed at meetings, their sermons and prayers were expected to be spontaneous and from the heart. Ideally all Quaker meetings would have been held in silence, but in practice only a minority were (Richard Bauman, "Speaking In the Light: The Role of the Quaker Minister," in *Explorations in the Ethnography of Speaking*, ed. Richard Bauman and Joel Sherzer [Cambridge: Cambridge University Press, 1974], 144–60).

Janry. the 28th. 1760 Went this Evening with Sister, to Uncles—stay'd there an hour or two, then we took a Walk with Charles, round by the Buring-Ground—the Moon shone bright.

29 Went to Meeting this Morning: B Trotter, M Yarnal, and B Trotter again, preach'd. Went with B Moode after Meeting to Knotts Shop, engag'd to spent this Afternoon with her, which I did, and Polly, who left me there where I spent the Evening. Isreal Morris came home with me.

30th. Stay'd at home all Day: Caleb Parr Senr. and Billy, call'd this Morning: Joshua and Katy Howell, and Becky Rawle, spent this Evening at their Mammys.

31st. Daniel Stanton open'd the Meeting this Morning, in Prayer, Elizth Stephens; and Thos. Bullard, a Friend from the Country, and Sammy Emlen, appear'd in Testimony. Went after Dinner to Smiths, to buy Cruels. call'd at James Carmalt's to see Suckey, who has been unwell some time:—Peggy Parr with her Sister in Law, drank Tea at A Warners,—Took a walk this Evening to F Rawles, who came home with us.

1760 Febry. the 1 Stay'd at home all Day. Snow in the Morning.

2d Stay'd at home all Day. Sarah Fisher, spent this Afternoon at her sisters AWs.

3d First Day. went to Meeting as usual—Margret Ellis, and B Trotter, spoak in the Morning: Margret dinn'd at A Warners—In the Afternoon, we had a full, but silent Meeting—Tommy Moore drank Tea, and went to Evening meeting with us, where Mary Kirby, and John Storor, appear'd in Testimony, went after meeting, home with Becky Rawle, sup'd there. went after Supper to Joshua Howells, who came home with us.

4th. At home alone in the Morning, writing—all our Foulk gone to Quarterly Meeting. Billy Parr, with his son Caleb, call'd after dinner—spent this Afternoon at George Dyllings,—H Callender call'd this Evening.

5th. Went this morning to Youths Meeting—Mary Kirby, Saml. Emlen, Bennajah Andris, and B Trotter, appeard in testimony, Margt. Ellis, in prayer, after whome, John Storor, appear'd in testimony, D Stanton in Prayer.—Peggy Parr, and little Caley, drank Tea at A Warners.

1760 Febry. the 6th Polly and self, went out this Morning after Breakfast, call'd at Uncles, and at Betsy Moodes,—Dinn'd and spent the Afternoon at Samuel Whartons, little Sammy weanning.

7th. Went to Meeting this Morning. D Stanton preach'd, Mary Evans pray'd. spent this Afternoon at Wm Callenders,—Wm. & Sarah Fisher, Josa. and Caty Howell, spent this Evening at A Warners,—Mon Esprit fort bas, tout cett Jour.

8th. Spent this Afternoon, with Molly Foulk at the Widdow Bringhursts, where we were entertain'd with divers objects in a Micrescope; and with several expediments in Electricity.

9th. Stay'd at home all Day. unwell, with a cold, Josa. and Caty Howell, drank Tea at A Warners, Polly went out this Evening. C Jervis came home with her.

10 First Day. Stay'd at home all Day; Fd. Coleman being also unwell, did the same, spent the Morning reading, the Afternoon writeing—Betsy Moode, and John Drinker, drank Tea at Friend Warners,—Francis and Rebecca Rawle, spent this Evening, chez nous.

1760. Febry. the 11. Billy Parr, and his Boy Sipteo, came for us with the Chaise, before 4 o'clock, this Afternoon, Arriv'd at Point before 6 o'clock, roades very bad, found Peggy, and the Children well.

12 Stay'd within all Day. Peggy, Polly & Self, busy kniting,—one Kellett an Officer, and Judah Foulk, came to Point, before Dinner, with whome Billy, went to Town.

13 Peggy, Polly and self, took a walk after dinner to the great Gate,—John Armitt Senr. and Betsy Moode, came to Point this Afternoon to see us,—walk'd to the Summer House and in the Gardens—they left Point[6] after Tea.

14th. Stay'd within all Day: unwell in the Evening.

15th. Stay'd within all Day: dull rainy Weather.

16 Stay'd within all Day. dull Weather. Eat no meat, this last Week past.

17th. First Day, Stay'd within all Day, John Drinker, Junr. came to Point this Afternoon, he with Thos. Bowlsbys drank Tea with us.—Received two letters from HD, one from Bristol, the other from London.

1760: Feby. the 18th. Stay'd within all Day. cold Weather.

6. The word "[before]" crossed out.

19th. Received a Letter this Morning from Betsy Moode, Billy Parr left home; for Town this Afternoon with Capt. Goodman, and Billy Pearson.

20 Peggy, Polly and self, with the Children, went out after Dinner, walk'd to the Summer House, to Moors Place, to the Retreat, and to Roberts Grave, came back to Tea, very much tired—fine Weather.

21st. Stay'd within all Day: dull weather.

22d. Rain this Morning, clear'd in the After-noon—I walk'd in the Gardens with the Children.—Billy came home in the Night.

23 Received two Letters this Morning, one from Uncle Sandwith Dublin, another from S—— Sansom Junr. Liverpool,—Left Point with Wm Parr, before Dinner, Roads bad—Hannah Callender call'd this Evening—when she[7] left us, we went to Betsy Moodes, spent some time with her, up stairs,—sup'd at Uncle Jervis's.—Johney came home with us.

1760: Feby. the 24th. First Day: Went to Meeting as usual—This Morning Grace Fisher, B Trotter, and Esther White, appear'd in testimony. in the Afternoon, a Young Man, a Stranger, spoke, I Pemberton, Pray'd,—in the Evening divers appeard,—Received a Letter this Evening from HD, Bristol.

25 Stay'd at home all Day: Sarah Sansom sent this Morning to desire, we would come there in the afternoon, but as we expected B Moode could not go: Hannah Moode call'd after dinner to let us know, Betsy was unwell, and could not come,—Hannah Callender, spent the Evening at AWs Received a Letter this Evening from HD London.

26 Stay'd from Meeting this Morning, Naboth Yarwood came this Morning to tell [to] that Uncle Jervis wanted us there, this Afternoon, B Rawle, sent Jacob, of the same Errent,—Polly went after dinner to Uncles. Myself, to F Rawles, where I spent the Afternoon and Evening. Polly came to us to Supper.—Francis Rawle, came home with us.

1760: Feby. the 27th Wrote this Morning to Dublin; H Moode came after dinner to desire us to come chez eux, could not go as we were engag'd to S Sansom, with whome we spent this Afternoon, sup'd at B Moodes, call'd at Uncle Jervis, Charles came home with us.

28th. Call'd before Meeting at Neighr. Burrows that was) and at Becky Steels, went after meeting, home with S Wharton, call'd at Thos. Willimss,

7. Word crossed out.

shoemaker, went after to Bennings the Staymaker, call'd at Betsy Moodes; Dinn'd at S Whartons, went after Dinner with Sally to Leverss to David Barnes, &c drank Tea with Sally, came home in the Evening.

29 Billy Parr call'd this Morning—Anna Warner Senr., Polly, and Nancy, went this After-noon to the Burial of Mary Cooper, I stay'd at home and wrote,—spent this Evening with sister, at Joshua Howells, who came home with us.

March the 1: 1760 Stay'd within all Day: wrote in the Morning, sewed in the Afternoon, read in the Evening.

2d First Day, Went to Meeting 3 times, Widdow Oakham's Daughter, from MaryLand, dinn'd at Fd. Warners, she spoke this Morning at our Meeting, Becky Rawle, Joshua & Katty Howell, Sally Dylling, and Hannah Callender, drank Tea at A Warners, I was taken very unwell this Evening in meeting, was obliged to come out.

3d Stay'd at home all Day: Betsy Moode call'd after dinner, Aunt Jervis, Betsy, & Polly, spent this Afternoon with us, Naboth Yarwood, Hannah Ward, and Charles Jervis call'd in the Evening.

4 Stay'd within all Day, rainy weather, Peggy Parr call'd this Morning, all our People gone to Meeting but myself—Peggy came again in the Afternoon and drank tea with us.

March the 5: 1760 Went this Afternoon with sister to Joshua Howells, drank tea there, with one Goldfrap, and Betsy White, step'd into Becky's towards Evening mett H Callender there, she went back with us[8] to Catys, where we spent the Evening Chearfully, Joa. Howell came home with us.

6 Went this Morning to Meeting, call'd as I return'd at S Sansoms, went after Dinner with Fd Warner to Betsy Moodes, where we spent the Afternoon, Polly and A Warner left me there, took a walk in the Evening with Betsy, call'd at Mary Williams's—R Rawle sup'd chez nous.

7 Spent this Afternoon with Sally Wharton, at Content Nicholdson's, Received a Letter this Evening from HD, Bristol—Wm. & Sarah Fisher, sup'd at AWs.

8th Stayed at home all Day—Sleety Weather.

8. The word "and" crossed out.

March the 9th: 1760 First Day: Went to Meeting this Morning stay'd at home the rest of the Day, Martha Barker from Burlinton, dinn'd at AWs—PS, sup'd at F Rawles, Snow this Afternoon.

10 Stay'd within all Day.

11th. Betsy and Nelly Moode call'd this Morning, went with us to Meeting.—Sister and self, spent this afternoon, at John Searson's,—call'd towards Evening at T Says, whose Mouth and Chin, is very much hurt, by a fall which he had lately.

12 Sister and self, went to Neighr. Brookes's, designing to spent this Afternoon there—but as she was busy'd, we proceeded to F Rawles, drank tea there, Wittness'd FR's Will—went towards Evening to S Sansoms, spent an Hour there, return'd to FRs suped there.

13 Stay'd from meeting, within all Day rainy weather.

14 Stay'd at home all Day, H Callendr. spent the afternoon with us.

March the 15th. 1760 Went out this Afternoon with sister, called at Widdow Maddoxs, then went to Isaac Howells, to leave silk with Polly Parrish to make a Bonnit—call'd at Uncles, then went to Betsy Moodes, drank Tea there, with Sally Morris and Ra. Reave; spent part of the Evening avac les Filles.

16th. First Day: Went to Meeting Morning, and afternoon, stay'd at home in the Evening snow falling.

17th. Snow'd in the Night, and greatest part of this Morning, tis now said to be near 2 foot deep,—Hannah Ward, Hannah Callender, and Katty Smith call'd towards Evening.

18th Went to Meeting this Morning, Betsy & Nelly Moode, call'd after meeting, went after dinner to Smiths to buy Cruells—call'd as I went at Wm. Fishers, spent the Afternoon at Widw. Maddoxs, with Polly Wallace, Widw. Grant, Polly Rhea, a Parsons Wife from the Country & Sister. call'd as we came home at C Parr's, Peggy & her sister gone abroad: they call'd afterwards at our House.

March the 19: 1760 Stay'd within all Day: F Rawle, R, ditto, and Catty Howell, drank Tea at A Warners, Joshua Howell, gone to York—had a spell of the Sick Head Ake this Evening.

20 Went to Meeting this Morning, call'd after meeting at F Rawles, stay'd

dinner there, stay'd at home in the Afternoon—Sister had a turn of the sick Head Ake.

21st. Went out after dinner with sister, call'd at Joshua Howells, and at F Rawles—went to several Shops, Betsy Moode over-took us in Market street, she had been at our House,—sister went to Uncles, where I was to have gone with her, but upon meeting with Betsy, concluded to take a walk, altho tis very muddy, after a long walk, went to Betsys, (nous etions enhaut ensamble) drank Tea there, spent a little time at Billy Morris's, went from thence to Uncles, to Sister, from there we went to Josa. Howells, sup'd there, with Betsy White, and Johney Howell, Catty was obliged to go to Bed, by the Head Ake—went after supper to F Rawles, where we stay'd discourseing, as is customary, untill 10 o'clock, FR, came home with us—I think I have rambled sufficently for one Day.

The violent North-East Snow Storm,[9] which we had on First Day, last, lasted but 18 hours, and considering the Season of the year, there was the greatest fall of Snow, that has been known (it is said) since the settlement of the Provence.—in the Storm, tis said, that 4 Vessels were lost at our capes, the people saved.

22d Stay'd at home all Day, dull Weather.

23d First Day: half Years Meeting, fewer Friends in Town than usual, the roads being very bad, several Men Fds. appeard in testimony this Morning, at the Bank House, in the Afternoon John Storor appeard twice, the Widdow—Sarah Bolton that was, pray'd,—in the Evening Peter Fern, Ellis Hugh, and Becky Jones, spoke, Peter concluded the Meeting in Prayer.

March the 24: 1760 Went to Meeting this Morning: divers Testimonyes deliverd—R Rawle, Catty Howell,[10] Sally Smith, from Burlinton and H Callender drank tea at A Warners—Hannah Hicks, Mary Rhoades, and Anna Pole came after, and spent some little time with us.

25th: Went to Meeting this Morning, John Storor, with several other Frds. appear'd in testimony, Mary Kirby concluded the Meeting in Prayer, went after dinner to Smiths to buy cruels; from thence went to Uncles, and to Betsy Moodes, had a long confab in the counsel Chamber, stay'd tea there, call'd again at Uncles and at Saml. Sansoms, at F Rawles, and at Josa. Howells, then came home, was told that Polly was at Neighr. Callenders, went to her, and stay'd supper there, Bobby Smith came home with us.

9. *Pa. Gaz.*, Mar. 20, 1760.
10. Word crossed out.

26 Spent this Afternoon at Wm. Fishers, with K. Callender, Anna Warner, Senr.—the Evening we spent at Josa. Howells, Josh. Radolph came home with us.

March the 27: 1760 Went to Meeting this Morning, call'd after at Isaac Howells, Hannah Hicks dinn'd at A Warner's, she and George Bound, drank Tea with us.

28th. Went to Monthly Meeting this Morning, 4 Couples past, Vizt., Benn. Swett and Sush. Siddon, Ruban Hanes, and M Wister, Josh. Drinker & H Hart, the other couple unknown by me, call'd after I left meeting at John Searsons, to see Molly who has been unwell,—Betsy & Hannah Moode, came to our house after dinner stay'd but a little time, Hannah Hicks call'd in the Evening, Polly and self, took a walk after she was gone, to Thos. Says—and to Uncles, Charles came home with us.

29 Went out after Dinner, with sister, call'd at Isaac Howells, at Uncle Jerviss, and at Wades Shop, drank Tea at B Moodes, with Nurse Mary: spent part of the Evening there, with Nancy Mitchel &c: Hannah Hicks, Polly Rhoades, and Polly Pemberton, call'd while we were out.

March the 30: 1760 First Day: went to meeting as usual, had a silent meeting in the Morning—in the Afternoon, Mary Kirby appeard, S Morris in Prayer, in the Evening, B——y Jones and D Stanton.

31st. Stay'd within all Day: Hannah Moode, and Saml. Emlen junr. call'd this Morning. Polly went out with them, H Moode, came back with sister,—Peggy Parr call'd after Dinner, stay'd but a little while, she came to Town this Morning in the Boat.

April the 1: Went to Meeting this Morning. M Kirby, and Mori. Yarnal, appeard in testimony, Saml. Emlen, and Mary Kiry. in Prayer,—spent this Afternoon with sister at Isaac Parrishs, AM, there, H Hicks came after Tea to JPs, she had been to our House to bid us Adieu, intending for home tomorrow, took a walk towards Evening with Hannah, call'd after we parted from her, at Coll. Whites, whoes spouse, is ill of the Head Ake,—Peggy Parr, and H Ward, was at our House, while we were out.

April the 2: 1760: Stay'd within all Day, Hannah Ward spent this Afternoon with us, fine weather.

3d Stay'd from Meeting within all Day—unwell with a cold,—read in this

Days Paper, an account of a Terrible Fire, which happn'd in Boston,[11] New-England, on the 20th. or 21st. Ultimo when near 400 Houses &c: were consum'd,—tis remarkable that not one Life was lost, Notwithstanding, the falling of the Walls and Chimneys.

4th. Stay'd at home all Day, very busy—Betsy and Nelly Moode came this Evening.

5th. Hannah Ward, call'd this Morning, I went to Smiths to buy cruels, from thence to Josa. Howells, was present when his 2 children, Caty & Sally, were innoculated, by Doctrs. Redman, and Evans,—spent this Afternoon at Frans. Rawles, went towards Evening to Uncles, and to S. Whartons, call'd as we came home at Saml. Sansoms.

April the 6: 1760 First Day: had a Silent Meeting this Morning, stay'd at home the rest of the Day, Polly went this Afternoon with Debby Morris, to the Burial of John Iden's Wife, J. Storor in town.

7th. Stay'd at home all Day: B Swett Senr. came this Morning to invite Sister and self, to his Wedding, on fifth Day next, declin'd going—H Callender, and Betsy Smith from Burlinton call'd.

8th. Went to Meeting: Mary Kirby, Danl. Stanton, and John Pemberton appeard, Mary, pray'd—Nurse Mary Cosgrave, spent this Afternoon with us.

9th. Stay'd within all Day: dull Weather—F & R Rawle, H Callender, Betsy & Katty Smith drank tea at AWs the Girls spent the Evening.

10th. Stay'd from meeting at home all Day, Unwell, Sarah Fisher spent this Afternoon at AWs—Benjamin Swett Senr. was this Morning married to Susannah Siddon.

April the 11th. 1760 Went this Morning after Breakfast, to Betsy Moodes, who was gone out, the Girls busy in the Garden, went from thence to S Whartons, stay'd a short time there, then came back to EMs. who was not yet return'd, went to Uncle Jerviss, stay'd some time there, went again to Betsys, where I stay'd dinner, and spent the Afternoon, and part of the Evening.

12th. Stay'd at home all Day H Callender, and Betsy Smith, call'd in the Evening.

11. Accounts of the fire that destroyed much of Boston on Mar. 20, 1760, appeared in *Pa. Gaz.* and *Pa. Journal*, Apr. 3, 1760.

13. First Day: went to Meeting as usual—B[T], DS, &c, spoke this Morning, Daniel was led in a particular manner, to speak of tryeing times which Would come upon the people, if they did not soon repent,—in the Afternoon we had silence, went home with B Rawle, drank tea there, with S Fisher—went to Evening meeting, where Polly Pussey, Elizth. Morgan, Ann Widdowfield, J. Storor, and D Stanton, appeard in testimony.

April the 14: 1760 Stay'd within all Day: Betsy Parker call'd this Morning, to fitt a Bodylining Polly went out after tea, H Ward and another young woman call'd—removez le Litt.

15th. Went to Meeting this Morning—Polly Pussey, and John Storor, appeard in testimony, Josey Drinker and Hannah Hart were married,—Saml. Emlen call'd after meeting,—this Afternoon[12] had a fierce Storm of Wind, Hail, thunder and Lightning.

16th. Stay'd at home all Day: took a dose of Glaubers salts, FR, call'd this Evening.

17 call'd this Morning at Judah Foulks, then went to Meeting, Margt. Churchman, S Emlen, J Storor, and John Churchman; appear'd in testimony—call'd after meeting at Uncles, and at several Shops,—call'd after dinner at S Sansoms, and at C Morgans, who was gone abroad, drank tea at J. Searsons, call'd towards Evening at Josa. Howells.

April the 18: 1760 Betsy Parker call'd this morning,—spent the Afternoon, at Neighr. Callenders, Mary Armitt, Sally Morris, Becky Rawle, &c there,—spent this Evening at Joshua Howells.

19th. Stay'd within all Day. took salts, B Moode, dinn'd with us, she was sent for home, after dinner.

20th. Went to meeting as usual, call'd after Evening meeting at Josa. Howells, First Day.

21st. Spent this afternoon, with sister, at Robart Smiths, Lumbard street, call'd as we came home at Saml. Whartons, at Betsy Moodes, at Uncle Jerviss at Widdow Hazeltons—who has lately lost her Father John Wilkinson,—call'd at Widdo. Maddoxs, & at F Rawles. R Coleman, and A Warner, was this afternoon at the Burial of Mary Allen.

22d. Went to meeting this Morning—John Armitt Senr call'd after dinner,

12. The word "was" crossed out.

Sally & Nanny Armitt, spent the afternoon with us, went this Evening to Jonathan Evanss, two of whose children have been Innoculated,—call'd in our return at Samuel Sansoms, and at Thos. Says.

April the 23: 1760 Went out after dinner, call'd at Widw. Childs, spent the Afternoon at C. Morgans, H Ward drank tea with us,—call'd at John Knights where HW boards, and at R Wellss.

24th. Went to meeting this morning. Isaac Andrews, M Yarnal, and J Storor, appeard in testimony—D Stanton in Prayer, Ruban Haines, and Margt. Wister, were married—went from meeting to S. Whartons, dinn'd and spent the Afternoon there, Martha Meridath drank tea there,—went in the Evening to B Moodes, Betsy, and Hannah, Sister and self, took a walk, call'd after we parted from the Girls, at Josa. Howells, found when we came home Frans. and Becky Rawle, chez nous.

25 Sarah Sansom, call'd after Dinner, Rebecca Say, spent the afternoon with us, sister and self, went in the Evening to Josa. Howells, and to F Rawles, took a walk with Becky, round by the late Dwelling of Wm. Griffets—sup'd at F Rawles—Israel Morris, call'd while we were out, to bid us farewell, is he intends, soon to embark for Barbados.

26 Stay'd at home all Day, Peggy Parr with her three children, call'd this Afternoon, Polly gone out, H Ward, came home with her in the Evening.

April the 27: 1760 First Day, went 3 times to meeting, warm weather for the Season, Peggy Parr came home from afternoon meeting, and drank tea with us—John Storor appeared this Evening in testimony. Thunder.

28 Went this morning to Neighr. Callenders, who are busy, moveing to Point no Point, haveing sold their House to Thos. Richee,—spent this Afternoon at Richd. Wellss, Mary Pemberton, Senr and Nanny Lloyd there, call'd in the Evening at Willm. Callenders, Hannah Callendr. and Katty Smith, sup'd and loged at our House,—one Wm. Ricketts, a man, who serv'd Joshua Howells, was this Afternoon drown'd, endeavouring to git up a Hoggshead of Sugar, which had[13] fell in the River—On First Day last, was Buried, Peter Pappin, de pre fountaine, our Frence Master.

29th. Wm. Callender and Wife, Hannah Callender, and Katty Smith, Breakfast'd with us, Hannah & Katty, went after Breakfast to Point,—went to Meeting, this Morning—Wm. and Kattre. Callendr. Dinn'd at AWs—spent this Afternoon at S Sansoms, went in the Evening to Betsy Moodes, Hannah

13. The word "falling" crossed out.

alone, call'd at Uncles, Charles came home with us, Wm. and S Fisher, sup'd at AWs.

April the 30: 1760 Sister and self, took a walk this Morning, call'd at Thos. Says, went to Henry Groaths, call'd at Collol. Whites, spent the Afternoon at Uncle Jerviss. Polly, after we came home, had a spell of the sick Head Ake,—Molly Searson, was at our House, while we were out.

May the 1. One John Jackman, a young man from Barbadoes, Breakfasted, with us, he log'd here last night,—call'd this Morning at S Sansom's, went to meeting, went after meeting, home with B Moode, came home to dinner.—Molly Searson, Polly and Sally Pemberton, and Black Jude, spent the Afternoon with us—John Searson call'd after tea, FR, call'd this Evening.

2d. Spent this Afternoon at Thos. Says, Polly Willson, there, H Ward, call'd this Evening—Betsy Moode, sup'd with us, went part of the way home with her, call'd as we came back at F Rawles, and at Joshua Howells.

3d. Wm. and Catherine Callender, came to Town, the latter, sup'd, and loged at AWs Joshua and Catty Howell drank tea here, Becky Rawle, call'd. sister, and self, took a walk this Evening to Uncles.

May the 4. 1760 First Day. went 3 times to meeting, drank tea at F Rawles, call'd at J Howells,—Saml Sansom Junr., arrived here this afternoon, from London, in Ship Martyla, Balitho master,—Katherine Callender, log'd with A Warner.

5 Betsy Moode call'd this Morning, she went with Polly to Quarterly Meeting,—Hannah Moode spent this afternoon with us, Polly, Hannah, and self, went towards Evening, to C. Marshalls, to buy Ducape,[14] then went home with Hannah, where we stay'd a short time.

6 Went this morning to Youths Meeting—call'd after to see Sammy Sansom,—K Smith dinn'd at AWs she with Hannah Callender, and John Jackman, drank tea at AWs—took a walk this Afternoon with Hannah to look for a Washer-woman—Sammy Sansom, came towards Evening; Polly & self, went with him to Saml. Nobles, to see H Callender; came back to our House. Sammy sup'd with us.

May the 7: 1760 Hannah Ward, call'd this Morning, left her with Polly, went with H Callender—to S Sansoms, to see Sammy's Prospective views, went

14. A plain-woven silk fabric with a soft texture (*OED*).

from thence to Joshua Howells, call'd at FRs left Hannah there, came home before dinner,—spent the Afternoon writeing.

8th. Call'd this morning at Joshua Howells, and at Frans. Rawles, then went to meeting, John ——— something, and Susanna Townsend, were married,—call'd after meeting to see Sarah Fisher, who lays-in, with her Daughter, Elizabeth,—spent this Afternoon, at Jonathan Zanes, who has been disabled, (next October will be five years) by a fall from his Horse,—went towards Evening, to Betsy Moodes, stayd a while there, Betsy and Nelly, came part of the way home with us. I had the Sick Head Ake, after I came home.

9 Billy Parr, call'd this Morning.—spent the greatest part of the Morning, in writeing, spent the Afternoon & Evening at Saml. Burges, H Shoemaker Junr. there, SB, came home with us.

May the 10: 1760 Hannah Ward, spent the greatest part of the morning with us, Thos. Say, call'd in the Afternoon. H Callender came to Town this Afternoon went with her to Abrm. Carlisles, A Warner Senr & Nancy gone to Point, R Coleman, and Polly, gone to talk a walk, Sammy Sansom, came in the Evening, I went with him to B Moodes.

11 First Day, went to Meeting this Morning, John Hawksworth, appear'd in testimony—the first time of his so doing for Several Months past, Sammy Emlen, also appear'd, Katty Smith dinn'd at AWs, John Drinker Junr. call'd after dinner,—stay'd at home this afternoon—Phebe Brown drank tea with us, went to Evening meeting togeather,—Nancy Warner went this Afternoon with Catty Smith, to Point, designing to stay there some Days.

12th. Stay'd within all Day: rainy weather Katherine Callender drank tea, sup'd and log'd with AW.

13. KC, Breakfast'd with us, Sally Morris, call'd before meeting,—went to meeting, Wm. Callenr. dinn'd at our House, Nancy Warner came home this Morning H Callender, Sister, and self, spent this Afternoon & Evening at Joshua Howells, Hannah came home with us, and log'd with her mamy at AWs.

1760 May the 14. K, & H, Callender, breakfast'd and Dinn'd with us, went out after dinner with Hannah, call'd at S Sansoms, from thence went to Wm. Coopers, came back to S Sansoms—drank tea there, went after Hannah left me, to Betsy Moodes, stop'd at Billy Morriss—found sister at Betsys, went up stairs with BM, where we read part of Samy Sansoms journal, which he lent me, went from Betsys with Sally Parrish left her, and call'd at Uncles, Charles, came home with us—Margt. Allen, Wife to our Chief Justice, and sister to our present Governour, was this Afternoon, interr'd.

15 Wm. Callender came this Morning, went with us to Meeting,—Sammy Sansom came this Evening, stay'd supper with us, agree'd to go tomorrow, to Wm. Callenders, at Point.

16 A Warner Senr. went this Morning in WCs Chaise, which was sent for her to his House, she was desireous of Sister or selfs accompanying her, but as we were otherwise engaged could not, were this Afternoon prevented by rain, from prosecuting our intended jaunt to Point—Sammy Sansom came and drank tea with us.

1760: May the 17 A Warner Senr. H Callender, and Betsy Warner—came from Point this Afternoon, went with Hannah to Wests, and to Joshua Howells, came home to Tea, Sally Pemberton, came to Desire me to draw her a Screen, which she left with me, rain this Evening with Thunder.

18th. First Day: Went 3 times to meeting, Elizabh. Shipley appeard in testimony, went After meeting in the Afternoon to see Beulah Clark, who lays very ill—a woman nam'd Gillbart,[15] drank tea at AWs—Mett John Armitt Senr. this Evening who desir'd we would call after meeting to take leave of his Wife, as they intend to set of tomorrow, for Flushing, Rhoadisland, &c.—call'd. to see Betsy Moode, who is unwell, went from thence to John Armitts, sup'd there, Widw. Fielding there, Joshua Crison, came home with us, found H Callender, at our House, were she stay'd all Night.

19 Sammy Sansom call'd before dinner, went with him and sister after dinner to Wm. Callenders, Point were overtaken by rain, Anna Pole there—came home after Tea, Becky Rawle chez nous, Sammy Sansom call'd again, went this Evening with sister to B Moodes, call'd at F Rawles, who came home with us.

1760: May the 20. Went this Morning to Meeting, Peggy Parr, with her children, call'd while we were out,—call'd after Dinner, at J Foulks, to see Peggy—left sister there, and went to Betsy Moodes—who is still unwell, Polly came there to us, sat up stairs, where Betsy read, to Hannah, Nelly, Sister, and self,—Sammy Sansoms Journal.

21 Peggy, Parr, and little Caleb, spent part of this Morning, with us, went this Evening to Becky Rawles, Frances gone to Willingstown, left sister with Becky, went home with Catty Howell, sup'd there.

15. Words crossed out.

22d. Went to Meeting this Morning, went after meeting home with Nelly Moode, who went with me to Corrys Store, Nobody there, came back with her to their House. spent this Afternoon at F Rawles, went down town in the Evening, with Sister, call'd at B Moodes, and at Uncles, mett at our House, Joshua and Katty Howell.

23 Stay'd at home, spent the Day, drawing and reading—Sammy Sansom spent part of the Evening with us, dans le Cabinet de Verdierre.

1760: May the 24 Went this Afternoon to Betsy Moodes, drank tea there, call'd in the Evening at Saml. Kirks at Uncles, and at Joshua Howells, found R Rawle at our House.

25 First Day, went to meeting as usual—Sammy Emlen call'd after morning meeting Wm. Callender, Wife and Daugher, call'd this afternoon, sister and self, call'd after Evening meeting at S Sansoms, Sammy came home with us.

26 Stay'd within all Day, Nelly Moode call'd this Morning, Betsy Parker came in the Afternoon, K Callender, F and R Rawle, sup'd at AWs—Neighr. Clark dyed this Evening.

27th. K Callender, log'd last night with AW—breakfast'd with us this Morning, Hanh Ward came this Morning, left her with Polly, and went to meeting, B Moode, Nelly ditto and Sally Pemberton, came home with me, after meeting, stay'd but a short time, H Ward not yet gone, went after dinner to Betsy Moodes—from thence to Uncles, mett Sister there, spent the Afternoon and part of the Evening there, Thos. Carpenter, C Jervis, Naboth Yarwood, and Joel Evans, came home with us.

28 Went this Afternoon to the Burial of Beulah Clark, Danl. Stanton spoke at the Grave,—went home with Becky Rawle, drank tea there, then came home—went back to Frans. with sister, sup'd there.

29 Call'd this Morning at S Sansoms,—went to meeting, took a walk in the Evening to Wm. Fishers.

30th. Wrote the greatest part of this Morning. went in the Afternoon to S Whartons, took a walk with Sally, to several Shops, call'd at Betsy Moodes, then went home with Sally, drank tea; George Read there.

31 Stay'd at home all Day: John Paul, call'd in the Afternoon, Sister busy ironing—myself makeing up Pincushons.

June the 1: 1760 First Day: had a silent meeting this Morning; in the

Afternoon, Moi. Yarnall—spoak: went home with Betsy Moode who was at our meeting, drank tea there, went with the Girles, to Evening Meeting—call'd after with sister at S Sansoms.

2d. Hannah Callender came this Morning, dinn'd with us, was so kind as to leave her diary with sister,—spent this Afternoon at Widdow Dowars's, our old Neighbour a hansome young widdow, saw a large peice of a bone, which was taken out of the Leg of a little Girl, who boards with her, an extraordinary cure—went to Mary Deals, to look for B Parker, who was at Enoch Flowers, went to her there, from thence to Uncles, who is just come from Pasture, went to S Whartons, Sally gone out, went to B Moodes, saw Sally Wharton at her Aunts, door, she came to us, H Moode, Sally, sister, & self went in the Garden, Betsy came home, Sam——y Emlen with her, left him there,—stop'd with Rachel Wells, Dicky came home with us—Peggy Parr, and John Drinker, call'd while we were out,—began this Morning to Knitt a pair of silk Mittins.

1760 June the 3 Sansoms, Leonard brought me a Letter this morning, from HD, London, Lees Wife call'd, Peggy Parr, with little Caley, she has left her Daughters in town, to go to School, they board with Sally Evans, in Church-Alley,—went to Meeting, Betsy Moode came home with me, we agreed to go on the Morrow to Point, betsy went with me to S Sansoms to borrow his Horse & Chair, look'd at Sammys Prospects—parted with betsy, came home to Dinner, Billy Parr call'd while I was out,—went after Dinner with sister, to Saml Whartons, designing to have gone to Reece Meridaths, but as Sally informs us her Aunt is indispos'd, declin'd going there,—went to Josh. Stampers, over the Bridge, Sally has two pritty Children, a Girl and a Boy—came home in the Evening, like for rain, Samuel Sansom junr. spent this Evening with us, sup'd—rain with thunder.

1760: June the 4 read all this Morning in H Callenders, Journal, went after dinner to B Moodes, to know what detain'd them, desired Hannah to go up to our house to Sister, which she did, they went togeather in a Chair, to Billy Parrs, Point, Betsy and self follow'd 'em, mett Catty Smith by the Bridge, just return'd from Burlington, she desir'd, we would call and lett her Uncle know, that she was come, we did so, K & H Callender, in Town, from thence went to WPs, found our sisters there, spent the Afternoon very Agreeably, Strawberrys, & Cherrys, Galore, Judath Foulk, & several others, there left Point after Tea, came home Frank-ford road,—took a walk with sister in the Evening to John Searsons who is moveing into his New House Parson Sturgon, and Wife there—went from thence to Thos. Says, stay'd a Short time—Betsy and Nelly Moode call'd while we were out.—done no work, this two days.

1760: June the 5 Sister gone this Morning to Meeting myself at home, up stairs writeing—caught cold yesterday, a violent pain in my left Arm,—in the

Afternoon, knitt at my mittings—Nurse Mary, and Betty Farris, call'd this Evening—went near 10 o'clock to F Rawles. Nancy, Sister, and self, A Warner Senr. and little Betsy there, Frances R, gone out of town.

6th. Stay'd within all Day, rainy weather, Knitt at my Mittings.

7 Stay'd within all Day, Betsy Parker, came in the Morning, Becky Rawle, and Catty Howell, in the afternoon—imploy'd many ways[16] this day.

8 First Day: Went to Meeting as Usual, Hannah Callender call'd, Polly went from Evening meeting to Uncles, Charles came home with her.

June the 9: 1760 Stay'd at home all Day: dull Weather, cold weather for the Season Betsy Parker came in the Afternoon to fitt Gowns, Betsy Moode, came in the Evening, stay'd but a short time.

10th. Went to meeting this Morning, call'd after dinner at S Sansoms, went from thence to Uncle Jerviss bid Betsy farewell, as she intends tomorrow to sit of for Cape-May, left Uncles after Tea, went to S Whartons, left sister there, went to Betsy Moodes, stay'd a short time, came back to SWs sup'd there, Sammy came home with us.

11 unwell in the Morning, Becky Rawles sent for us after dinner, went there—spent the Afternoon, Sarah Fisher there, went in the Evening with Becky to see Molly Foulk, who was brought to Bed, last First day, of her Son went back with Becky, sup'd there, Frances came home with us.

June the 12: 1760 call'd this Morning at Josa. Howell's, went to Meeting, call'd after meeting at Uncle Jervis's, at Abm. Mitchells to buy knitting thread, Sally Wharton there, went with her to Leverss. shop, then came home, Wm. Callender and Wife, dinn'd with us—S Fisher, and Richd. Footman's Wife, spent this Afternoon at AWs—took a walk this Evening to B Moodes—call'd as we came back, at F Rawles, and at Josa. Howells, Johey Howell came home with us. H Ward call'd this Morning.

13th. Stay'd within all Day: Betsy Parker call'd this Morning. Fd. Warner & Nancy, gone to Point, Hanh. Moode spent the Afternoon with us.

14th. Peggy Parr, call'd this Morning, I went after dinner, to Betsy Moodes—call'd at Uncles, and at Wades shop—Sister came to me, to Betsys, drank tea there, call'd towards Evening at T Says, Hannah Ward, call'd this Afternoon, while I was out.

16. The word "to" crossed out.

June the 15: 1760 First Day: Hannah Callender & K Smith, call'd this Morning, went to Meeting—had a Silent meeting. Stay'd at home in the Afternoon, not well, went to meeting in the Evening, Mary Kirby and Daniel Stanton, appear'd in testimony, Mary in prayer, call'd after meeting at S Sansoms, Sammy came home with me.

16th. Arose this Morning between 4 & 5 o'clock—went with A Warner Senr. to Wm. Callenders—WC, went to Town after breakfast, came back before dinner, Anna Pole, with him, went after dinner to the Barn, HC, AP, KS, and self, diverted ourselves, reading and talking, took a walk before tea in the Woods, pick'd some very beautiful wild Flowers, look'd like for rain, which caus'd us, to return sooner then prehaps we otherwise should,—rain with thunder did not hold up, till it was too late to think of returning home this Night.—the two Hannahs and self, was much pleas'd with the vast number of Fire-flies, which appeared in the Meadows, after dark, went to Bed before 10, loged with A Warner.

June the 17:1760 got up before 5 o'clock this Morning—A Warner & self, left Point before breakfast, Polly and Nancy, not up when we came home; Sister went this Morning to Meeting, stay'd at home myself, and wrote, Hannah Ward came this Evening to take leave of us, she is going to live in Carlisle.—Sister and self, step'd this Evening to Wm. Fishers, and to Frances Rawles.

18th. Spent the greatest part of this Day, up stairs with sister, looking over accounts, Betsy and Nelly Moode call'd this Evening, Sammy Sansom brought a letter from HD, Liverpool, Sarah Fisher and B Rawle, sup'd at AWs.

19th. prepar'd this Morning for Meeting but was prevented, by signs of rain, the Sun I thought appeard strangely—Went out after Tea this Afternoon, with Sister, took a walk to H. Groaths, call'd at J Searsons, John and Molly going to the Funeral of Saml. Jacob,—call'd at Uncle Jervis, at C. Nicholdsons, and at T Says, &c, set some time this Evening at Neighr. Shoemakers, Betsy and Nelly Moode call'd this Evening,—the Weather is now so cold, that I wore a Cloak, and several people have fire in their Chimneys.

20th. Stay'd within all Day: work'd in the Morning at my Purse, Henry Drinker call'd this afternoon, he arrived here, since dinner from London, in the James & Mary Capt. Friend.

21st Work'd this Morning at my Purse, HD call'd before Dinner, Hannah Callender—Katty Smyth and HD, drank tea at AWs Betsy and Nelly Moode call'd this Evening they had been to the Burial of John Benson.

1760: June the 22 First Day: went to Meeting 3 times unwell all Day, went home with Nelly Moode, after afternoon Meeting, drank tea there, went to Evening Meeting with the Girles, came home in the Evening. HD.

23d. Stay'd at home all Day, rainy weather, work'd at my Purse in the Morning, help'd quilt Nancy Warners Peticoat in the Afternoon.

24 Went to Meeting this Morning B Moode came home with me, Kate. and Hannah Callender, dinn'd at AWs—I went this Afternoon to Betsy Moodes drank tea there, Hannah and Nelly gone out—Betsy and self took a walk after tea by the Negros Burying Ground,[17] Numbers of People out, came home with Betsy stay'd but a short time, call'd at Uncle Jerviss found when I came home Becky Rawle, Francis and B supd—HD. came.

June the 25: 1760 Spent this Morning with sister, up stairs, looking over accounts. B. Moode came after dinner, stay'd till 5 o'clock Molly Foulk sent to desire we would drink tea with her, did so, came home in the Evening, a Gust of Thunder and Lightning, HD, spent part of the Evening.

26 Call'd this Morning at S Sansoms, went to Meeting, took a walk with B Moode after meeting,—HD, call'd after dinner, Sister and Nancy, went this Afternoon to the Funeral of Lydia Taylor.

27 Stay'd upstairs this Morning busy, our Foulk gone to monthly meeting.—went out after tea designing to go to Betsy Moodes, call'd at Frans. Rawles, mett Betsy comeing to our house, she stay'd supper,—HD, came after she was gone, stay'd till past 11 o'clock.

June the 28th. 1760, Billy Parr call'd this Morning, says Peggys unwell, HD, call'd this Evening. after he was gone, Polly, Nancy, and self, took a run to Fs. Rawles, Josa. and Katty Howell there, A Poor unfortunate Wretch, a Young Man, yesterday hung himself in a House, in Elfreths Alley, the cause of his so doing, I dont rightly understand.

29th. First Day: went to meeting 3 times Katty Smith dinn'd at AWs, Frances and Becky Rawle Hannah Callender and Katty Smith, drank tea here—Henry Drinker spent the Evening.

30 Stay'd at home all Day, Jude came this Morning to see us, I am ready to

17. The Negro burial ground, a separate section of the Strangers' Burial Ground, located at what is now Washington Square in Philadelphia, was a popular meeting place for the city's black population, both free and enslaved (Nash, *Forging Freedom*, 13; J. F. Watson, *Annals*, 2:265).

think she has run away, says her Master uses her ill, poor Child—Sarah Sansom, Thos. Williamss Shoemaker's Wife, and Mother, spent this Afternoon at AWs Peggy Parr call'd, she is very desireous that we would come to Point. HD, spent this Evening, Josa. Howell came home with sister.

July the 1st. Went to Meeting this Morning, Elizabeth Morris, Mori. Yarnal appeared—Polly Jervis sent to let us know, that she and Betsy Edgcomb, design'd to spent this Afternoon with us, but as Fd. Warner is busy Whitewashing could not receive them. spent this Afternoon at Frans. Rawles. left sister there, and went in the Evening to Betsy Moodes, Neddy Jones there—sent Patty with a note, to sister, desireing she would premit my stay all Night with Betsy. Sammy Sansom, and sister, came after super to us, Nelly Moode went back with 'em and log'd with Polly at AWs my self stay'd with Betsy Moode.

July the 2: 1760 Spent this day with my Friend B Moode, and tis probable tis the last I shall spend in the house they now are, as they desighn to remove this Week; step'd over with Betsy to Billy Peterss in the Afternoon, call'd in my way home, in the evening at F Rawles, and at Josa. Howells, found when I came home HD, at our house, he spent the Evening.

3d. Call'd this Morning at Josa. Howells, and at Frans. Rawles, went to Meeting call'd after Meeting at Uncle Jerviss—from thence went to S Whartons, where we dinn'd and spent the Afternoon—call'd in the Evening at B Moodes, and at Widdow Howards,—HD, this Evening.

4 Spent the greatest part of this Day up stairs with sister, looking over accounts, HD, came at 10 o'clock, stay'd till past 11, unseasonable hours, my judgment dont coincide with my Actions, tis a pity, but I hope to mend.

5 Stay'd at home all Day, busy, Sammy Sansom spent part of the Evening with us.

6th First Day. went to Meeting as usual, unwell all Day, Joshua & Katty Howell and HD, spent the Evening at AWs.

7 took a walk this Morning, to see my Friends. the Moodes, in their new Habitation, call'd at John Searsons, HD, call'd this Afternoon.—Sister and self left home before tea, with Judath Foulks chair and Horse, Arrived at Wm Parr, Point by 6 o'clock, Peggy well, Billy from home,—Many agreeable hours have I spent at this delightfull place—this Morning was bury'd from Neigr. Mountgomerys a Man who with several others, was drown'd on sixth Day last.

July: the 8. Billy Parr, who came home last night, left Point this Morning with one Crosston, who breakfast'd with us. Peggy—Sister and self, spent the Day at our work, towards Evening we took a walk, then sat chattering untill near 12 o'clock which is usual at Point.

9th. Stay'd within all this Morning, in the Afternoon Robt. Lewiss wife, Spenser Trotter and Wife, one Kelsey and Wife, came to Point, they stay'd till after Tea,—when they were gone, Peggy, sister and self, took a walk; Billy came home this Evening.

10th. Took a walk after breakfast to Frankford Creek, found Billy and his son, there fishing, HD, came to tea with us, walk'd in the Gardens, and to the Summer House, he left Point after 10 at Night.

11 Knitt at my Mittings this Morning—after tea, Billy and Peggy, sister and self and little Caley,[18] took a ride for sake of novelty in the Cart, went as far as A Jamess new road, call'd in our return at Goodman Bowlesbeys stay'd a while there, then, came home, spent the Evening Agreeably.

12 Billy gone to Town this Morning, work'd today at a Watchstring, Peggy, sister, Caley and self, took a walk after Tea as far as Hugh Robartss place, mett the Children, Nancy and Polly Parr, comeing home they came as far as Robt. Hopkins[19] in his Waggon.

13th. First Day: Billy came home last night or rather this Morning: John Wright, his Daughter, and Capt. Roberson came to Point before breakfast, HD, came also, they all spent this day with us, took a walk after dinner to the Summer-House, round the bank as far as the Boat House, some one propos'd going into the boat, which we being of our guard comply'd with, row'd a little way up the Creek, landed at the Horse-Shoe, I don't like such doings on a First Day. walk'd home by the retreat, after tea, our coumpany all but HD—departed, I took a walk with him in the Gardins, to the Summer-House, round the Meadow banks &c—he left Point between 9 and 10.

14 Billy went to Town this Morning with his 3 Children, in the Boat, Peggy, Sister and self minded our work, till after Tea then found ourselves inclin'd to take another ride in the Cart, which we did, Polly and black Arch took turns to drive,—when we had road about 2 miles from home, we had like to have been cast away, by reason of the gears brakeing—thought we should have been oblig'd to walk back, but 2 or 3 honest dutchmen, (for ought I know) who overtook us on the road were so kind as to rectify Matters, and we proceed'd to Wm. Callenders, were inform'd by George Adams the tenant of

18. Words crossed out.
19. Word crossed out.

the place, that WC with his Family, were gone to Town—however we made free to walk in the Garden, stay'd but a short time, remounted our Vehicle, and return'd home, were overtaken by Billy and his Son, who made their deversion of us, spent the Evening as usual,—Billy informs us, of the arrival of some Indians in Town, who pretend to be Quakers.

15 Awoke this Morning before 4, Arose at 5, which is not my usual Costom, took a solitary walk in the Gardens, found Billy up, when I return'd, went with him to see his people Mow Barley—he went to Town before dinner with Crosston, HD, came to Point towards Evening—Peggy, Sister, Henry and self, walk'd in the Gardens, eat Currants and Pares, Henry stay'd all Night. After he was gone to Bed, (which was not till past 12 o'clock) we had a Washing Frolick, for which we had prepar'd beforehand, took the oppertunity of Billys absence, went to Bed between one and two.

16th. Dull rainy weather, HD, went to town this Morning before we were up—Billy Parr came home this Evening.

17 Dull weather, Peggy and self took a walk to the Gate in the Afternoon, HD came in the Evening, took a walk with him to the Summer-House, he stay'd all Night.

18 HD. went to Town early this Morning, Judath Foulk and Thos. Lawrence, came to Point before breakfast, they went a Fishing with Billy, came back to dinner; being willing to leave the Men to themselves we propos'd a ride this Afternoon, set of in Judaths Chaise Peggy, and Polly conceated, before we had road 2 miles, that the Horse did not manage right, so took it in their Heads to return,—took a walk to the Summer-House; JF, TL, and WP. left Point before Tea, we went after tea to Robart Hopkinss walk'd with his Daughter Hannah in their Garden, came home by Moon-light.

19th. left Peggy Solus this Afternoon, came to Philada. Sip waited on us, Betsy and Nelly Moode, and HD, came this Evening.

20th. First Day: Went to Meeting this Morning and Afternoon, stay'd at home in the Evening, on account of rain and the Head-Ake, Sammy Sanson drank tea and spent part of the Evening with us HD, spent the Evening.

July the 21st. up stairs most of the Day—went out after tea with sister, call'd at Josa. Howells, and at Frances Rawles, at S Sansoms, and at Uncle Jerviss went from thence to Josh. Richardson to buy a Thimble, call'd at John Armitts, who last Week return'd from their Boston journey. stop'd at George Roberthorns—HD. spent this Evening.

22d. Went to Meeting this Morning, Hanh. Callender call'd after Meeting, B Moode came home with me, she stay'd Dinner and spent the Afternoon with us, parted with Betsy this Evening at third street corner. Sammy Sansom, sister and self, went to Wm. Callenders, at their new dwelling, up market Street, found HD there, stay'd super, then went round to B Moodes, stay'd but a Short time—Henry and Sammy came home with us, the former stay'd till near 12 o'clock.

July the 23 HD,—call'd this Morning, B. Trapnal, brought some Pine-Appels HD, call'd this Afternoon went out this Evening, call'd at T Says, at Uncles, at S Whartons, Sally gone out, went from thence to B. Moodes, mett Sally Wharton there, came home before 10, Henry over took us, he stay'd till after 11—my Mind has been much distress'd all this day.

24 Went to Meeting this Morning, Saml. Nottingham pray'd and preach'd—call'd after meeting at S Sansoms, Joshua Howell, drank tea this Afternoon at AWs his Wife and Children, with B Rawle are out of Town, H Drinkr. spent this Evening—hard Thunder.

July the 25 Sister went this Morning to Monthly Meeting, we spent the Afternoon at S Sansoms—HD, came this Evening Chez nous.

26 Stay'd at home all Day, Betsy Moode came this Evening, she stay'd till after Super, HD, (who I thought was gone to Burlington) came after she was gone; this Evening I shall never forget.—for tis a memoriable one.

27 First Day: slept none last night, HD, came this Morning, before I was up, had a conferance with sister, he went to Burlington—there is a great similitude this day, between the Elements and my Mind,—stay'd at home all day.

28th. Stay'd within all Day. unwell both in body and mind Betsy Moode, spent the day with us, HD, came in the Evening.

29th. Went this Morning to Meeting—went out after dinner sans sister. call'd at Josa. Howells, the Children unwell, call'd at S Whartons, Sammy not well, went from thence to Betsy Moodes, spent the Afternoon there, Sally Morris drank tea there—call'd towards Evening at Isreal Pembertons, walk'd with Polly & Sally in the Gardens Polly Pembern. and Nelly Moode, came part of the way home with me HD, spent this Evening.

30 HD. call'd this After noon, sister and self went out after tea, call'd at Cate. Morgans, pour son avis touchant—quelquechose, went from thence round by the Church Burying-Ground, to H Groaths, sat a while there, then

went to John Searsons, Hanh. Moore there, came home to Super, took a walk after to F Rawles.

31 rain all Day, set up stairs with sister, looking over accounts, took a Nap after dinner, HD, spent the Evening.

Augt. the 1 Stay'd within all Day, wrote in the Morning, sew'd in the Afternoon, HD, spent the Evening.

2d. Went after dinner to Josa. Howells—call'd at F Rawles,—Catty Howell with her Nurse and Children—Polly Sandwith and Nancy Warner—Anna Warner Senr. and myself,—Joshua on Horseback—took a ride this Afternoon to their Newly purchas'd place, Edge le-Point. I took a walk before tea with AW Senr. and Katty to Skulkill, which runs but a small distance from the House. I was much diverted with Dorothy, a dutch Woman, who lives in a little (adjacent) House, quite alone, has everything aboute her neat and clean, and appears to be as happy, as those that are possessed of Thousands—we came to town before night, stay'd a little time at F Rawles, came home unwell, HD, came between 9 & 10 stay'd till after 11—I had a spell of the Colick in the Night.

Augt. the 3. First Day: Went to Meeting this Morning B Trotter, D Eastaugh, Sally Morris, appear in testimony BT, in prayer,—HD, call'd after Meeting, says he's going to dine at Frankford,—I stay'd at home the rest of this day not being quite recoverd of my last Nights indisposition,—rain this Afternoon & Evening. HD, came at super, stay'd till after 11.

Augt. the 4: 1760 Sister gone to Quarterly Meeting, my self at home all Day, began to knit a pair of thread Stockings for self,—Nancy, Sister and self; strowl'd, after 9 o'clock to Joshua Howells.

5 Went this Morning to Youths Meeting—intended to have gone home with B Moode, but as it rain'd, thought it best to return home, HD, call'd after dinner,—he spent the Evening avac moy.

6th. This Morning we spent writeing, in the Afternoon went to Uncles, Charles has been unwell, a disorder in his Face—came home in the Evening, H Callender, Katy Smith, at our House, HD, came, he went away with the Girles—A Warner, Sister, Nancy, and self, took a Walk after super to F Rawles, Sammy Sansom there—he came home with us,—Henry was chez nous, while we were out.

7 Charley Jervis, call'd this Morning before we were up, with a Letter from

Dublin,—went to Meeting, call'd after at S Sansoms,—Becky Rawle, and Katty Howell, spent this Afternoon at AWs—HD, spent the Evening.

8th. the Weather very warm, stay'd at home all Day, Sarah Fisher, drank tea at AWs HD, call'd this Afternoon, he came again in the Evening.

9 Stay'd within all Day, wrote in the Morning—Peggy Parr and her Son, call'd before dinner, she came again in the Afternoon with her Daughters they drank tea at AWs with us, Sucky Carmalt call'd towards Evening, Sammy Sansom spent part of the Evening Polly and he went to B Moodes &c—HD—came.

10 First Day: Went to Meeting 3 times—Nelly Moode drank tea with us—went to Evening Meeting togeather HD. came home with us, spent the Evening.

11 Stay'd at home all Day; a violent Storm of Wind and thunder this Afternoon—HD. drank tea at AWs he came again in the Evening, stay'd till past 11.

Augt. the 12:1760—Went to Meeting this Morning, Mary Kirby,[20] preach'd—Cathe. Callender, Elizabeth Smith, and Sarah Morris, dinn'd at AWs—KC drank Tea here, Frances Rawle sup'd with us, Becky out of town—HD. came after Super stay'd till near 12—rain with thunder.

13 Spent this Morning up stairs with sister, writeing, A Warner Senr. gone to Edge-la Farme, designing to stay a day or two, Sister and self spent this Afternoon at John Searsons—poor Molly, I pity her—parted with sister, at Market street corner, call'd in my way home at S Sansoms, took a walk with her in the Garden, came home before night.

14th. Went this Morning to Meeting at 9 o'clock, call'd after at S Sansoms—rain most of the Afternoon, HD, spent the Evening—Nancy Warner, went this Morning out of Town with her Brother, to stay till her Mammy returns—so that our Family is smaller than usual.

Augt. the 15: 1760[21] Stay'd within, spent the greatest part of the Day writeing—Fd. Warner, and Nancy came home towards Evening,—HD. spent the Evening.

20. Word crossed out.
21. The manuscript volume for Aug. 15, 1760–May 12, 1761, has hand-colored floral paper covers. The outside front cover reads, "1760, 1761." Inside is a drawing of what appears to be some sort of family seal.

16 Went out after Breakfast, call'd. at Uncle's—went to B Moodes, spent the Day with Hannah, Betsy and Nelly, gone to London-Grove with John Armitt; Sammy Emlen call'd there after dinner—Elizath. and Sally Morris, and Molly Sandwith, drank tea with us—we left Hannah towards Evening—call'd at C. Morgans, came home before Night HD, call'd this afternoon while we were out told R Coleman he was going to Burlington to the Funeral of Josa. Raper.

17 First Day—went 3 times to Meeting—Sammy Sansom, drank tea with us this Afternoon, Joshua Howell and HD—spent the Evening.

18 Sister & self spent this Morning looking over accounts—HD call'd after dinner—spent this Afternoon, with A Warner Senr & Sister, at Neighr. Waln's.—the first time of our being there—sat a little time at Neighr. Shoemakers—HD. spent part of the Evening.

19 A Warner sent for this Morning out of Twon—to Caty Howell, who was taken unwell in the night Sister and self went to Meeting—we spent this Afternoon at Wm. Fishers, HD—spent the Evening.

20 Knitt at my mittins this Morning, went after dinner to Josa. Howells, Caty lay'n down unwell—spent the Afternoon at F Rawles—left sister there towards Evening—went to William Callenders—Hannah bad with a Feaver—Sarah Hunlock there—went from thence to Betsy Moodes who came to town this Afternoon—found Sister and Henry there stay'd supper, came home before 10, HD stay'd till after 11.

21 Went to Meeting this Morning, D. Stanton appeared in Prayer—M Yarnel in testimony—Betsy Moode came with me as far as Becky Steels,—Polly Sim Steel, bad in a Feaver—Sister and self spent this Afternoon at John Armitts, calld in our way home at Uncles—cool agreeable weather—H Drinker spent part of the Evening.

August the 22: 1760 Parr's Robin, came this Morning, to desire we would spend a few days with his Mistress as Billy is gone abroad for some time—spent this Afternoon at Josa. Howells, Becky Rawle there, came home before Evening—Betsy Moode and HD, came, Henry went home with B——y—came back again—Frans. and Becky sup'd at AWs.

23 Stay'd at home all Day—A Warner Senr and Sister, went this Afternoon to the Burial of Sally Owen, who dyed of a canser in her Breast. HD—spent an hour this Evening. he went to see his Brother Joseph who is sick.

24 First Day: went 3 times to Meeting—went home with H Moode, after

afternoon Meeting went to Evening Meeting with Betsy—John Storor in Town—Joshua & Caty Howell sup'd at AWs—HD—came.

25 C. Morgan; Broomwich Staymaker, call'd this morning—Parrs Robin came for us—desir'd him to come again tomorrow—Sister and self took a walk this Evening. call'd on B.Parker, and at John Searsons, Molly in Labour—went from thence to B Moodes Betsy out—call'd at S Whartons—little Sam ill—went to Uncles—several Men from Barbadoes lodging there—Charles came home with us—HD—had been chez nous—while we were out—he came again after we return'd.

26 Went to Meeting this Morning, Mary Emlen, Abraham Griffey, and John Storor, appeared in testimony—HD. call'd after dinner—Billy Parr's Scippeo, came this Afternoon with the Chaise, he drove us to Point, Frankford road, mett J Searson—arriv'd at Point time enough to drink tea with Peggy—Billy gone to the Fort at Shimoken[22]—went to bed after 11 o'clock.

27 Busy at work all the Morning, took a walk in the Afternoon in the Orchard to look for peaches—then went to the Summer-House, sat there some time—Edmund Janney and Henry Drinker came to tea with us—walk'd with them in the Garden—they left Point before dusk,—sat up till near 12.

August the 28: 1760 Arose this morning at 6, o'clock, came to Town a little after 7—pleasant rideing—Went to Meeting this Morning—S Morris, John Storor, appeared in testimony—went this Afternoon with R. Coleman, and A Warner & Sister to S Sansom's—designing to spent the afternoon, but altered my Mind—left them there, and went to see Molly Searson who lays in with her Daughter Sarah, stayed but a short time there—went to B Moodes, drank tea there, with Isreal and Mary Pemberton; came home in the Evening Betsy part of the way with me—HD—spent the Evening.

29. Went this Morning to Monthly Meeting, Widdow Hopkins and John Storor, appeared in prayer, came away after meeting of Worship broak up, call'd at S Sansom's—stay'd till 1 o'clock reading French with Sammy—Betsy Parker call'd after dinner Janey Evans and Sally Evans, spent this Afternoon at AWs Becky and Katty also—HD—spent the Evening.

August the 30 Stay'd at home all Day.—Polly went this Afternoon to the Burial of Dickey Morris, one of Billys Twins—HD spent part of the Evening.

22. Shamokin, a cluster of three Indian settlements located at present-day Sunbury, in Northumberland County, Pa., was the Indian capital of central Pennsylvania until it was abandoned around 1770 (WPA, *Pennsylvania*, 531).

31 First Day: went this Morning with S Fisher, and R Rawle, to the Great Meeting House—Mary Emlen, and John Storor appear'd in testimony, Mary Kerby in Prayer—went this Afternoon to the Bank, where D. Stanton, and J Storor appear'd—Polly Pemberton came home with me, after meeting—H Callender & Caty Smith came afterwards—went all togeather this Evening to Pine Street Meeting-House—where John Storor and Sammy Emlen spoke—HD—came home with us stay'd till past 11.

This Morning was bury'd, one Robt. Scull, a Young Man, who on Fourth-day last was shot through the Body, by an officer, at the Center.[23]

Septemr. the 1: 1760 Spent this Afternoon at Isreal Pemberton's walk'd in the Garden, call'd in our way home at John Searson's—HD—Betsy & Nelly Moode, spent part of the Evening with us—Henry went home with the Girles, unwell with the Head-Ake—he has been today to Chester, with John Storor &c.—where John Embark'd, in the James and Mary Ct. Friend, for London.

2 Stay'd from Meeting this Morning Betsy Moode came home with Sister, dinn'd and spent the Afternoon with us—Hannah Moode came to tea HD—call'd twice, he went away unwell.

3 Stay'd at home all Day: Nancy Morgan, and Peggy Ross, drank tea with us—Sister went out this Evening Sammy Sansom came home with her—Henry Drinker, is as I fear'd ill, of a Feaver.

Sepr. the 4. hard thunder last Night—stay'd at home all Day—received intelligence this Morning, that HD. is better—have not heard of him since—Betsy & Nelly Moode, call'd this Evening—Joshua and Caty Howell, and Becky Rawle, sup'd at AWs.

5 Stay'd at home all Day: Sammy Emlen drank tea with us, our people gone out, H Moode call'd in the Evening—to tell me, Betsy goes tomorrow to Plymouth,—Sister went this Evening with[24] Sarah Sansom, to see Henry who is very weak and low.

6 Stay'd at home all Day: Peggy Parr and Caley call'd this Morning—A Warner and Nancy, set out after dinner, for Merrion, they talk of staying till seacond Day: Rachel Drinker, call'd this Evening to tell us Henry is better—Samy Sansom spent the Evening and supped with us.

23. On Aug. 27 John Bruleman, an officer in the Royal American Regiment, had shot Robert Scull at the Center House tavern while Scull was playing billiards. The attack was apparently unprovoked. Scull, a Philadelphian, died from his wound on Aug. 30 and was buried the next day. Bruleman was convicted of murder on Sept. 23 and hanged on Oct. 8 (*Pa. Gaz.*, Sept. 4, 1760; *Col. Recs. Pa.*, 8:506).

24. "Sammy" crossed out.

First Day Sepr. the 7: 1760. Went 3 times to Meeting—Joshua and Caty Howell, drank tea with us, this Afternoon; Sarah Sansom, informs us this Evening that HD. is so much mended, that he rode out this Morning,—Wm. and Sarah Fisher here this Evening—just as we had sat down to supper, Betsy Warner, came in to acquaint us, that Fire was cry'd;—it prov'd to be a House next the Frds. Burying Ground, at the Sign of the Spread Eagle; a Pot House, and Stable, adjacent, were burnt down.

8 Henry came out to see us this Morning looks very thin and pale—Becky Rawle call'd; Polly preserveing Quinces—Sammy Jervis came to lett us know that his Mammy and Sisters, design'd to spend this Afternoon with us,—Joshua and Frances, Becky and Caty, sent after dinner to desire us, to go over the River with them,—but as we expected Company could not, which I'm sorry for, as the weather is very fine—Aunt, and the Girles, accordingly came, HD—also drank tea with us, Nelly Moode call'd to let me know that they had a Letter from Betsy—Uncle call'd towards Evening—A Warner and Nancy, came home from Merrion, this Afternoon,—Joshua and Caty Howell, and Hannah Callender, came this Evening went home with Josa. and Caty—Sister, Hannah, and self, sup'd. with them.

9 Went to Meeting this Morning—HD drank tea at AWs this afternoon.

10 Stay'd at home all Day: rainy weather Benny Swett, came to see us this afternoon, he arriv'd yesterday at New-Castle, from London, in the Philada. Packet Capt. Buden, with whome came Passengers, George Mason, Jane Crossfield, and Susannah Hatton, all Publick Fds.[25] (Susy Hatton is an Irish woman) H Drinker and Benny Swett drank tea with us Henry came again in the Evening—I hope he is Haply recover'd—he went away before super,—Wm. and Sarah Fisher supped at AWs.

11 Stay'd from Meeting this Morning—set a little time towards Evening at Neighr Shoemaker's doore, HD—spent this Evening.

12 Stay'd at home all Day: Katty Callender dinned at AWs—Joshua and Katy Howell and Becky Rawle, sup'd. with us—Francis out of Town—HD. came, stay'd but a short time.

13 Stay'd at home all Day: HD. call'd this Morning—Sarah Fisher drank tea Hannah Moode, and Sally Emlen, call'd this Evening—HD—spent the Evening.

14 First Day: Went to Meeting, Morning and Afternoon, Sammy Emlen, and

25. These Public Friends were Quakers authorized to travel in the ministry. See below, Aug. 15, 1762.

Henry Drinker, drank tea at AWs stay'd at home this Evening, Henry with me.

15 Stay'd at home all Day: HD—spent this Evening.

Sepr. the 16: 1760. Went to Meeting this Morning, the strange Fds. there,—HD—call'd, and Hannah Moode after Meeting she read 2 Letters to me from Betsy desir'd we would spent this Afternoon with her and Nelly—which we did—call'd in the Evening at Uncles, came home before dark,—Lisey Richardson (a Young Woman from Rhoad-Island) Polly Pemberton, Hannah Callender, Polly Dachler, Betsy Robarts, and Patty Lloyd, call'd this Evening—after they were gone, HD—came, stay'd till 11.

17 Stay'd within all Day: unwell with the Tooth-ach—dull Weather—saw Nobody but our People.

18 Stay'd from meeting—dull Weather and a pain in my Face—HD—call'd after dinner, Becky Rawle sent for us, spent the Afternoon there—HD—came to tea with us at FRs—came home in the Evening call'd at Josa. Howell's—Henry spent part of this Evening. H. Moode call'd while we were out.

Sepr. the 19 Stay'd at home all Day: dull Weather, Francis and Becky, Joshua and Caty—drank tea at AWs.—HD—spent the Evening.

20 Stay'd at home all Day.

21 First Day: my Face ach'd badly in the night:—stay'd from meeting, rainy weather:—HD—call'd after Morning Meeting he spent the Evening with me.

22 Stay'd within all Day: had the sick Head-ach this Morning—HD—call'd before dinner. he came again in the Afternoon, and call'd this Evening—Sister went out this Evening tells me Betsy Moode is return'd—Poor unhappy Josey Jordan, has this Afternoon stab'd Tommy Kirkbride, in the Belly—of which wound, he almost immeadately dyed—Josey is taken to Prison—The widdow Attwood was this afternoon Buryed.

Sepr. the 23 Went to meeting this Morning—George Mason appeared in testimony—Betsy Moode came home with me—spent this Afternoon at Wm Callenders, with A Warner Senr and sister. Hetty White call'd there, desired we would step over to their House, which after tea, we did, drank another dish with her—went back to WCs. for A Warner—came home in the Evening Hannah Hicks, and HD—call'd while we were out—Francis and Becky Rawle, Benny Swett and HD—sup'd at AWs—the latter stay'd till near 12 o'clock.

24 Tommy Kirbright was this Morning Bury'd, the Corps was carry'd to Meeting. I am sorry I was not there—Han. Hicks spent this Morning with us—a more anxious day, I have not experience'd for some time—HD. call'd towards Evening. he is going to meet the Fire-Company—J Jordan was brought to Court this Morning & arraign'd. he pleads not gilty—The City is this Evening illuminated on account of the Reduction of Mount-real.[26]

Sept. the 25: 1760. Went to Meeting this Morning: spent the Afternoon at Uncles, the Evening at B Moodes. John Armitt and HD. sup'd there.

26 Our Foulk gone to Monthly Meeting. Myself at home this Morning,—went in the Afternoon to Betsy Moodes, who goes toMorrow to Burlington, to the Meeting, with John and Mary Armitt,—John Armitt & HD, call'd at our House, while I was out—Sister was sent for this Evening to Cate. Morgan who lays very ill—HD, came at 10 o'clock, stay'd till past 11.

27 Stay'd at home all Day: A Warner and Nancy, went before dinner, in a Boat, for Burlington, to the yearly Meeting:—HD. call'd this Afternoon, he came again late in the Evening.

28 First Day went 3 times to Meeting, S Sansom and B Swett, Junrs. drank tea with us—Benny went to Evening Meeting with me; Sister went to see C Morgan, she inform'd me after meeting, that our old Friend Catherine, departed this life, this Afternoon. HD, I believe is gone.

Sept. the 29th, 1760. HD, came to Town this Morning, he call'd here, Sister and self, went before dinner to see our deceas'd Fd. C. Morgan,—H Hicks, spent this Afternoon with us, HD the evening.

30th. Went to Meeting this Morning—HD, call'd while we were at dinner,—C. Morgan, was Buryed at Noon, we were not at the Burial, being Ignorant of the time,[27] [Joh]ney Jervis, call'd to let us know, his Uncle Michal Walton was dead, Sister went this Afternoon to the Funeral; he was bury'd from Jonathan Evans's—HD spent this Evening.

Octor. the 1st. Stay'd at home all Day: Sarah Fisher sup'd with us, HD, call'd, he went to the Election,[28] came back again, stay'd till near 12 o'clock.

26. When news of the surrender of all French forces in Canada, then in Montreal, to General Jeffery Amherst on Sept. 8 reached Philadelphia on Sept. 24, the city celebrated. At noon the guns of the fort were fired, and at night the city was illuminated, bonfires were lit, and bells were rung (*Pa. Gaz.*, Sept. 25, 1760).

27. The words "of her intearement" crossed out.

28. On Oct. 1 voters in Pennsylvania elected their provincial representatives and their local officials: sheriffs, coroners, commissioners, and assessors (*Pa. Gaz.*, Oct. 2, 1760).

2d. Went to Meeting this Morning: went after, to several shops, Catty Howell with us—call'd at F Rawles—A Warner, and Nancy, came this Afternoon from Burlington, in Able James, Waggon,—HD——call'd, Sammy Emlen call'd—Becky, and Caty, drank tea at AWs—took a walk this Evening, Nancy Warner with me, to N. Moodes; stay'd but a short time—HD—spent this Evening with me.

Oct. the 3d. Stay'd at home all Day; Peggy Parr spent part of the Evening with us, HD—sup'd. and stay'd till after 11 o'clock.

4 John Armitt Senr. call'd this Morning, I stay'd within all Day. HD, call'd after dinner—Peggy Parr, Nancy, and Caley, call'd this Afternoon—HD—spent the Evening—B Moode came home last Night.

5 First Day: went 3 times to Meeting, M Evans, in the Morning, George Mason, Afternoon & Evening. Sister and self drank tea at B Moodes,—Betsy Malhereux—went to Evening Meeting with the Girles—Caty Howell sup'd at A Warners, Joshua gone to New-York—HD—call'd, stay'd but a short time, he has been to day to Plymouth to the Burial of Robt. Waln's Brother.

6 Stay'd at home all Day: Becky Rawle, and Caty Howel, spent this Afternoon with us—up stairs helping to Quilt,—HD—spent this Evening with me.

7 Went to Meeting this Morning—Molly Smith try'd a body lineing, Wm. Callender and HD, drank tea with us, Henry spent part of the Evening.

October the 8: 1760. Stay'd at home all Day: Betsy Jervis & HD—— call'd,—A Warner Senr. was taken unwell, last night, keeps her Room, the Doctor visits her,—Sarah Fisher, Becky Rawle, Katty Howell, came—Benny Swett, and HD—sup'd with us,—John Bruleman,[29] an Officer, was this morning Executed, for the Murder of Robt. Scull.

9 Went out this Morning designing to go to Meeting, but declin'd going, being too late, as we were inform'd it began at 9 o'clock—call'd at Uncles, and at Wades and R Steels shops, HD. spent the Evening with us.

10 HD call'd this Afternoon, Robt. Parrish, came while he was with us, to invite us to a Meeting, Appointed by George Mason—drank tea up stairs, in Fd. Warners, room, B Rawle here, went out towards Evening, call'd at John Searsons, at B Moodes, went with the Girles to Meeting, which was held at the School-House, George appeard in testimony, Meeting concluded before nine, HD—came home with us spent the rest of the Evening.

29. The word "the" crossed out.

October the 11. HD—call'd this Morning, dire Adieu, he's going towards Lancaster, intends to stay, untill seacond or third day,—finish'd quilting—went out this Evening with sister, call'd at Thos. Says, and Nancy Morgans, then went to Betsy Moodes, call'd at S Whartons, and at Uncles—Johny Jervis, and Naboth Yarwood, came home with us.

12 First Day: went 3 times to Meeting, Silence in the Morning,—in the Afternoon, Mary Kirby, Susey Hatton,—the Evening George Mason, in Testimony, Susey, in Prayer,—Polly Rhoades, S. Fisher, Wm. Callender, Wm. Fisher, drank tea at AWs—call'd before Evening Meeting, with [P.] Rhoades at FRs—Francis and Becky [R]awle, Wm. Callender, Wm. Fisher, and Sammy Sansom, sup'd with us.

13th. Hannah Hicks call'd this Morning sister and self spent this Afternoon at S Sansoms, Benny Swett went home with Molly; I call'd at F Rawles, and [J]Howells—Benny spent the Evening at our House, HD—came home this Evening came chez nous—

We were Allarm'd last night after 12 o'clock, by the cry of Fire—prov'd to be McColough's Bake-House.[30]

October the 14. Went to Meeting this Morning—Danl. Stanton, Mary Kirby—Katty Howell, drank tea at AWs Henry Drinker spent the Evening.

15 Spent this Afternoon at Neighr. Shoemakers, she keeps her Chamber—came home in the Evening—I know not whats become of HD.

16 Call'd this Morning at F Rawles,—then went to Meeting—Ann Moore, Mary Kirby appeared in testimony. Mary in prayer, call'd after Meeting at Uncles, and at B Moodes—spent this Afternoon at Thos. Says—came home in the Evening. found Hannah Callender, Katty Smith and HD. here—Henry spent the Evening.

17 Took a walk after dinner, with Sister, call'd at T Says, went from thence to third Street Saml. Burge, would have us in to see Bulah, who has lately come out of a lyeing in—went from thence to H Groath's—call'd at William Callenders, Sally Smith from Burlington there—then we went to F Rawles, where we spent the Afternoon with A Warner Senr. helping Becky Quilt. Hannah Hicks call'd there she had been to our House—came home in the Evening—where I continu'd with Nancy—Sister went back to FRs—HD, came when it was late.

30. McClough's Bake House, located on Front Street, was destroyed by the fire (*Pa. Journal*, Oct. 16, 1760).

Octor. the 18: 1760 Stay'd at home all Day; HD—call'd this Afternoon,—he was been this Morning to Germantown to the Funeral of Derick Johnson—he came again in the Evening.

19 First Day. Went to Meeting 3 times—Sarah Fisher, Wm. Callender, and Benny Swett, drank tea at AWs—HD—came after tea—he went with us to Evening Meeting and came home with us.

20 Stay'd within all Day: Elizath. and Polly Rhoades, Hannah Hicks, Kathe. and Hannah Callender, and Sally Smith, drank tea at AWs Sammy Sansom, spent this Evening ici.

21st. Went to Meeting this Morning—Widw. Scattergood, and Sally Smith, dinn'd at AWs—Sister and self—spent this Afternoon at Joshua Howell's—with Sally Smith and H. Callender—came home HD—spent the Evening he call'd while we were out.

22d. Spent this Afternoon at S Whartons—Sally unwell, keeps her Room—call'd in our way home at Uncle Jervis's, and at S Sansom's—found when we came home Benny Swett—Beny has a mind to our Nancy—No Henry this Evening.

Octbr. the 23: 1760 Call'd this morning at F Rawles—went to Meeting, call'd after at Josa. Howells—spent this Afternoon at John Searsons, Sally Kirbe, there, came home in the Evening which HD spent.

24 Stay'd at home all Day: rainy Weather. HD drank tea at AWs—he came again this Evening.

25th Received a Note this Morning from Betsy Moode, requesting my company for the Day; which I comply'd with, found Nelly unwell—Betsy return'd home, Yesterday, from Chester, where she, with several others, has been, to Meetings appointed by Mary Kirby—who embark'd (on fifth-day last) in the Philadelphia Packet, Richd. Budden Master—for London.—Betsy and self took a walk towards Evening—HD. spent this Evening avac moy.

26 First Day: Went 3 times to Meeting: Henry Reynolds, a country Fd. and John Pemberton appeard this Morning—and in the Afternoon H. Reynolds,—call'd before Evening Meeting[at] S Sansoms, Josa. and Katty Howell sup'd at AWs HD—came.

Octor. the 27. Stay'd within all Day: were just going to Uncle Jerviss, when Hannah Hicks came—she spent this Afternoon with us—HD—spent the Evening Benny Swett came this Evening.

28th. Went to Meeting this Morning David Eastaugh, M. Yarnal, and Polly Pusey, appeared in testimony. Betsy Moode came home with me—she dinn'd, spent the Afternoon, and part of the Evening with us. HD drank tea avac nous—Fd. Warner went this Afternoon to the Funeral of Rachal Pole.

29 Stay'd at home all Day: HD. spent the Evening.

30. Went to meeting this Morning—Jane Crossfield &c. appeared. call'd after meeting at Uncle Jervis's and at S Whartons, Sally ill—call'd at Wests, spent the Afternoon at Uncles—S Sansom and Wife, called at AWs this Evening on busyness with RC. Benny Swett spent part of this Evening. after he was gone HD—call'd.

31 Alone this Morning—our people gone to Monthly Meeting—took a walk with sister, after dinner—drank tea at C. Nicholdson's—H.D. call'd this Afternoon while we were out, he came again and spent the Evening with me—sovenen cela.

Novr. the 1 Peggy Parr, and Caley, call'd this Morning—went with her to several shops call'd in my way home at F Rawles. HD—call'd before dinner—he spent the Evening with us—he's unwell with a cold.

2 First Day: went 3 times to Meeting—Robt. Jones, Benn. Trotter, in the Morning Jane Crossfield, in the Afternoon—George Mason, Margt. Ellis in the [ ]—Francis, Joshua, Becky, Catty, and the Children, drank tea at AWs—Wm. and Sarah Fisher sup'd.

3 Polly received a Letter this Morning from HD informing us—his cold is so bad, he's obliged to lose Blood—spent this Morning at home with sister—she at work, myself writeing—our people gone to quarterly meeting—from whence they did not return till late—dinn'd at 4 o'clock—Sammy Sansom spent part of this Evening.

4. Went this Morning to Youths Meeting—Margt. Ellis, Susy Hatton, George Mason, and Jane Crossfield, appeared in testimony Wm. Brown in Prayer—the Corps of Mary Moore, sister to Dr. Moore, was brought to Meeting—Patty James, tells sister that Henry's better—every body gone out this Afternoon, but R Coleman and self—Betsy Steel married on seventh Day last to James Wallace Scotch-Man.

5 Stay'd within all Day—Betsy Moode, spent part of the Morning with us, Benny Swett part of the Evening.

6 lay'd awake most part of last Night, stay'd from meeting, at home all Day

unwell—Betsy Moode came after meeting to inquire how Henry was,—could not inform her—Nelly Moode spent part of the Evening with us.

7 Stay'd at home all Day—HD, came after dinner he is not yet recoverd—Nelly Moode spent this afternoon and Evening—Betsy came in the Evening.

Novr. the 8. Stay'd at home all Day. Henry called before Dinner.

9 First Day: Went to Meeting this morning Stay'd at home in the Afternoon HD, with me went to meeting in the Evening—call'd after at Uncle Jervis's—Charles came home with us—went afterwards and sup'd at F Rawles—AW, and Nancy there.

10 Stay'd at home all Day, Sammy Emlen, calld after dinner, I had a conference with him, in the Bleu Parlor—touchant Baubette—HD, spent the Evening avac moy hes still unwell.

11 Went to Meeting this Morning—went afterwards, down Town, call'd at C. Nicholdsons—at Uncles &c. spent this Afternoon at Samuel Sansoms, Henry came to us in the Evening—found when we came home, R. Rawle and Benny Swett,—HD—spent this Evening avac moy—I had the Head Ach.

Novr. the 12: 1760 Call'd this Morning to see Sally Howell, who is sick at Joshua's, spent the Day at B Moodes, Henry and sister, call'd there in the Morning—they came in the Afternoon, and drank tea with us. left the Girl's towards Evening. HD—spent.

13 Stay'd at home all Day: Rachel Drinker spent this Afternoon with us, Henry, drank Tea, he came again and spent the Evening.

14 Spent this Day at Betsy Moodes, Rachel Reeve there in the Morning, Mary Armitt, Sucky Hudson, drank tea there,—came home in the Evening John Armitt call'd at our House, while I was out, HD twice.

15 Stay'd within all Day: HD—call'd this Afternoon—he's to be busy at home this Evening.

16 First Day: Went to Meeting, Morning and Afternoon, Nelly Moode, Sammy Sansom, and HD—drank tea with us,—stay'd at home this Evening, Henry with me, he's not yet well of the Cold.

Novr. the 17: 1760 Stay'd at home all Day: snow the greatest part of the Morning: HD—call'd this Evening.

18 Stay'd from Meeting this Morning, within all Day: spent this Morning solas, writeing—Betsy Moode and HD—call'd after meeting—Henry's Brother Daniel, married this Morning A Warner Senr. and Molly Sandwith, went this Afternoon to the Burial of Caleb Parr,—Billys Brother—HD, call'd this Afternoon, Benny Swett spent part of the Evening, HD came after he was gone.

19 Stay'd at home all Day: HD. call'd this Evening.

20 HD—call'd this Morning he came from Betsy Moode, to ask if I would walk this Afternoon to A Morris's, could not go—went to Meeting Hannah Brintnall Junr. Married—went after meeting to several Shops—call'd at Uncles—Peggy Abbercromey spent this Afternoon at AWs—Henry Drinker spent this Evening.

Nov'r. the 21st. Took a walk this Morning—call'd at Francis Rawles, and at Isreal Pembertons and at Betsy Moodes, came home to Dinner—went out after dinner with Sister—call'd at S Sansoms, left silk for a Bonnit, with [James] Edwards—spent this Afternoon at Uncles—left Sister there in the Evening, and went to B Moodes—took a walk with Betsy,—came again to Uncles—then came home—HD—call'd while we were out—Not so easy in my Mind this Evening as I could wish.

22 Stay'd within all Day: HD—call'd this Evening, hes very busy—I spent the Evening plating for Nancy.

23 First Day: Went to Meeting Morning and Afternoon, HD. drank tea with us—I stay'd from Meeting this Evening, read to Fd. Coleman,—Henry came home with Sister, after Meeting, they had been to Uncles—he stay'd till 11.

November the 24 Stay'd within all Day:—HD spent this Evening—Sister's got a bad Cold.

25. Sister stay'd at home this Morning, Unwell, I went with Fd. Warner, to Meeting—Mathew Franklin, from Long-Island, and John Casey, from Rhoad-island, (Companions) appeard in testimony—and others—went After Meeting with Betsy Moode to Paul Chanders's—Betsy came home with me, she stay'd dinner—and spent the Afternoon—Peggy Parr, and little Caley, drank tea with us—HD. spent the Evening.

26 Stay'd at home all Day: Rainy weather—sent a Note to B Moode, requesting her to apply to Sally Morris, on my Account—Henry spent this Evening with me: Sister still unwell.

27 Stay'd at home all Day: dull weather—Betsy Parker, and HD. call'd this Morning—Betsy Moode spent this Afternoon, HD. the Evening—Sister this Evening at Uncles—they are all offend'd.

November the 28: 1760 HD. breakfasted, with us—Went to Monthly Meeting this Morning—A Warner Senr. and Sister, with me, diclare'd my intentions of Marriage with my Friend HD—Sarah Sansom and Sarah Morris, accompany'd us, to the Mens Meeting—Stephen Colling, and Polly Parish, and 2 other couples—past—Betsy Moode, came home with us, she and Henry, dinn'd at AWs and spent the Afternoon, Betsy went home[31] towards Evening.

29 Stay'd within all Day—HD—call'd this Afternoon, he came again and spent the Evening.

30th. First Day Went to Meeting this Morning and Afternoon, Nelly Moode drank tea with us—Henry came—he went with Sister and Nelly, to Evening Meeting, I stay'd at home, and read to R Coleman,—HD—came home with sister, he spent the remainning part of the Evening avac moy.

Decemr. the 1: 1760 Stay'd at home all Day: took a warm-water-vomitt this afternoon, Benny Swett—drank tea with us—Henry spent the Evening.

2 Went to Meeting this Morning, Silence—took a Walk after, with Betsy Moode—came home to dinner,—Henry Drinker spent this Evening avac moy.

3 Dull weather, stay'd within all Day—HD. call'd this Afternoon, he came again and spent the Evening.

4 Polly went to Meeting this Morning, she stay'd dinner at Uncles, HD—call'd while we were at Dinner hes going to Burlington, I dont expect to see him till tomorrow—had the sick Head-Ach, this Evening.

5 Spent this Afternoon and Evening at F Rawles, S Emlen, call'd there—Henry came to Town late this Evening, he call'd chez nous, while we were out, came again after 10 o'clock when we were at home.

Decemr the 6: 1760. Stay'd within all Day: A Warner Senr. from home,—the greatest part of the Day, with Becky Rawle,[32] who was brought to Bed, this Afternoon, of a Daughter,[33] which she calls Peggy.—the 7th. Child born in

31. The words "in the" crossed out.

32. Becky Rawle, born Rebecca Warner, was a daughter of Quakers Anne and Edward Warner. This was the Warner family with whom Elizabeth and Mary Sandwith resided after the death of their parents (Jordan, *Col. Fam. Phila.*, 151).

33. The word "whome" crossed out.

the Family, since our abode in it.—B Moode spent an hour this Evening, after she was gone Henry came he spent the rest of the Evening.

7 First Day: Went this Morning to Meeting the London Yearly Meeting Epistle was read by Wm. Callender—call'd after meeting at Joshua Howell's, and to see poor Becky and the young Stranger—HD—calld before Evening meeting—to meeting he went, left sister and self at home, not being well, he came again after meeting, and spent the rest of the Evening.

8 Stay'd within all Day: Henry call'd this Afternoon, he came again and spent the Evening.

Decmr. the 9 1760 Went to meeting this morning, Becky Jones appeared in prayer—Saml. Notingham in Testimony I design'd to have gone home with Betsy Moode, but think the Weather won't admitt. Winter's now, (I believe) proclaim'd, as Nancy says—We have had, I think, a very moderate Fall—HD—call'd this Afternoon, he left with me, some minutes which he had made at Sea, the reading of them gave me pleasure, he came again, and spent the Evening.

10 Stay'd within all Day: Billy Parr, call'd this Morning, HD. this afternoon—Sister Mollys Throat[34] sore—Henry came again in the Evening.

11 Fine Weather—went this Morning to Meeting with AW, and Nancy, Sister at home unwell, D Stanton appeared in prayer, D Eastaugh, and S Notingham, in testimony—call'd after meeting at F Rawles, and J Howell's, Caty and Children unwell—came home to dinner Henry here twice this Evening.

December the 12. Stay'd at home all Day: Henry call'd in the Afternoon, he came again in the Evening.

13 Fine Weather, for the Season, Stay'd at home all Day: Peggy Parr, and Henry Drinker, call'd this Morning, Sister in the Kitchen Ironing—expected Betsy and Nelly Moode this afternoon, they came not—Henry drank tea with us—said he would come in the Evening, but did not.

14 First Day: Went to Meeting this Morning—Molly at home, her throat not well—The Burlington yearly Meeting epistle[35] was read—HD. call'd while we

34. Word crossed out.

35. The Epistle was the annual report drawn up at the yearly meeting in September to be sent to the London Yearly Meeting, which noted the spiritual condition of the Society of Friends, its achievements for the year, and its future goals; it also contained requests to British Friends for help on certain political issues pertaining to colonial affairs (Mekeel, "Founding Years," 17; see also the appendix in J. M. Moore, *Friends in the Delaware Valley*, 250).

were at dinner—I stay'd at home this Afternoon with sister being unwell myself, which I think is frequently the case—Hannah Callender, drank tea at AWs she, HD, and self, went to Evening Meeting togeather—Henry came home with me, spent the rest of the Evening.

15 Went out after Breakfast to B Moodes, spent the Day with her—HD. drank tea with us, he came home with me after Night—a long walk in the rain—Henry spent the Evening—Joshua and Caty Howell, sup'd with us.

Decemr. the 16. Stay'd at home all Day: sister went to Meeting, rain the greatest part of the day, HD. call'd after meeting, he came again in the Evening.

17 Stay'd within all Day: Polly abroad, busy for me—Molly Smith fitted a Body Linning for sute—HD. call'd—Peggy Parr, drank tea with us, Henry spent the Evening with me.

18th. Went this morning to meeting, George Mason, and D Stanton, appeared in testimony—Mary Emlen in prayer, Daniel took leave of us, he sits out some time this week, with Isaac Zane, for South-Carolina—Samuel Richards (I think it was) and Hannah Townsend, were married, they past meeting with us—I went after meeting home with Caty Howell—dinn'd there—Sister came to us, after dinner—I stop'd in the Afternoon to see B Rawle, went back to tea to Joshuas, Henry Drinker drank tea with us—Molly and Henry went down Town, towards Evening—I came home—B——y Swett came, I think he wont succead—Sister came home, Betsy Moode and HD. with her they spent the Evening.

Decemr. the 19—1760 Stay'd within all Day: T Williams measur'd me for a pair[36] shoes, HD. call'd and drank tea, he expects to be busy this Evening chez lui—therefore I expect not to see him untill tomorrow.

20th. Stay'd at home all Day: HD. call'd towards Evening, he came again while we were at Supper, stay'd till after 11—Polly went this Evening to see Uncle, whome we hear Johnny Searson has in a Passion abbus'd.

21 First Day: rain all Day: Stay'd at home—Henry drank tea with us—he came again and spent the Evening.

22 Went out this Morning with Sister, called at S Sansoms, and at S Whartons, parted with Molly—went to Betsy Moodes, where I spent the Day, S Morris, and George Mason, call'd there after dinner, Elizth. Morris, called,—

36. Words crossed out.

S Morris, Rachel Tory, and M Sandwith, drank tea with us.—left Betsys towards Evening call'd at Uncles, talk'd of John Searson,—stay'd but a short time, then came home—HD. call'd. while we were out—he's busy despatching the Ship, Friendship, Natl. Falkner Master. with whome, George Mason, and Ann Moore, designs on the Morrow to embark, at Marcus-Hook, for London,—George has made but a short stay with us.

23 Went to meeting this Morning, Mori. Yarnal, and T Williams, appeared. HD. and Nelly Moode call'd after dinner; the former came and drank tea with us. fine winter weather—expected Sarah Sansom this Afternoon, but she did not come, her Son Sammy spent part of the Evening at AWs Henry with me.

24 Stay'd at home all Day: Henry call'd—Hannah Hicks, drank tea with us—she came to town on account of her Father's being ill of the Pleurisy—she designs to stay in town till I have changed my Name—Henry Drinker spent the Evening.

December the 25: 1760. Friend Warner, Molly, Nancy & Betsy—gone to Meeting this Morning—R. Coleman, and my-self at home—I spent the Morning writeing—HD. call'd after dinner, expected Betsy Moode this Afternoon but was disappointed—Sammy Emlen, and Henry Drinker drank tea with us, Samy informs me Betsy was prevented by Coumpany—She came in the Evening, which she and H.D. spent with us. Henry went home unwell.

26 Henry call'd twice this Morning—I went to Monthly Meeting, A Warner Senr. and Sister with me—inform'd Friends that I continued my intentions &c.—Sarah Sansom, Sarah Morris, A Warner, and Sister, went up to the Mens meeting with us—Betsy Moode came home with us. she and HD. dinned at AWs—they spent the Afternoon, Henry the Evening—Stephen Collins, and Mary Parish,—one Wells—and—I dont know the Womans name—Henry and myself past the Seacond meeting—Isreal Morris, and Phebe Brown; Molly Holloway, and I know not who, past their first—HD. informs us this Evening of the Death of our good Old King, George the 2d,[37] who departed this life October the 25. 1760,—his grand-son George the 3d. was proclaim'd at Bristol the 27.

27 Sister out this Morning on busyness, HD call'd tells me he's going this Afternoon to his Place, beyond Frankford to have it survay'd—Hannah Hicks,

37. George II had died Oct. 25, and George III was proclaimed king the next day, first at Savile House and then at other places in and around London. News of the death of George II and the ascension of George III reached the American colonies on Dec. 26 (Brooke, *George III*, 73–74, 79; *Pa. Gaz.*, Jan. 8, 1761).

spent an hour with us towards Evening—Henry came to Town after Night, he spent the Evening avac moy.

28 First Day: Went to Meeting this Morning Mathew Franklin, S Emlen, and John Casey, appear'd in testimony—we were invited to the Burial of Sammy Lloyd—who is to be carried to the Great Meeting-House this Afternoon—I stayd at home this Afternoon, and Evening very unwell—Henry went to SLs Funeral—he came afterwards and spent the Evening with me.

Decemr. the 29. 1760. Stay'd at home all day, still very unwell HD. call'd this morning, S Fisher, and Neighr. Walln, spent this Afternoon at AWs Henry called, he came again and spent the Evening.

30th. HD. call'd this Morning before Meeting—I stay'd at home and wrote—keep close House least I should take cold—Betsy Moode came from meeting home with sister—she stay'd but a short time—Sister went out this Afternoon of arrents[38]—S Fisher here—HD. spent this Evening with me.

31 The last of the year 60: stay'd at home all Day Sister out this Morning, Sarah Sansom, Sarah Fisher, and HD. drank tea at AWs Hannah Hicks call'd this Afternoon—I dont expect Henry this Evening—Sister and self very busy.

38. To collect rents (*OED*).

1761

Jany. the 1: 1761 Went to Meeting this Morning, call'd after Meeting at Uncle Jervis's, had a dialogue at the Door, with Aunt, no very agreeable one, call'd to see Becky Rawle—came home to dinner—HD. call'd—Betsy, Hannah, and Nelly Moode, Sammy Emlen, and H——y Drinker, drank tea with us—Henry came again and spent the Evening.

Bad accounts of James Tasker.

2d Stay'd within all Day: HD. call'd this Afternoon, altogeather today in the Bleu-Parlor—Henry came in the Evening, he went to Uncles, to Sister, they also went to Sammy Whartons—came home to super—tells us it snows fast—Moland the Lawyer bury'd.

3 Continues Snowing this Morning: Stay'd at home all Day, Knitt at my mittins, HD call'd before dinner, sister busy Ironing all Day,—Henry spent the Evening with me clear'd up very Cold.

Janry. the 4. First Day, Stay'd at home all Day: sore Throat—HD. call'd after meeting—Hannah Callender, and Nelly Moode, drank tea at AWs—Sister went to Evening meeting with Nelly—HD. came after Evening Meeting.

5 Stay'd at home all Day: Molly Smith fitted my Cloaths, Wm. Callender, Nelly Moode, call'd while she was so doing. HD. call'd before dinner, K Howell drank tea at AWs Sister out—Henry spent the Evening.

6th. Molly Newport call'd this Morning—I stay'd at home all Day: HD. here several times, Sister busy, down at the House in Water-street—this day we began to move our Goods from AWs—Polly went down-town this Evening, Henry spent the Evening with me; went home much tir'd.

7th. Henry call'd 3 times this Morning, Sister gone to Market &c—A Warner Senr. Nancy Warner, Polly Sandwith, Betsy Warner, and HD. went after Breakfast in A James's Sleygh to Frankford, Henry drove—they came home to Dinner—Sister in Water-Street this Afternoon. Aunt Jervis, A Warner Senr. there. Polly and Henry came to AWs to Tea, they went back to the House in the Evening, no body left at home but R Coleman, and myself, knit at my mittins—Throat sore—wish it was well—I know not what B Moode means, by

Absenting herself thus—Henry and Sister, came home after 8 o'clock, he spent the rest of the Evening.

8 Stay'd as usual at home, Sister all Day down at the House, had her dinner sent her, A Warner Senr. and Junr. went to her in the Afternoon, Nelly Moode spent the Afternoon at AWs Henry call'd several times to Day—Becky Rawle, Caty Howell, call'd this Afternoon, the first time of Becky's being here since her lyeing-in—Henry and Sister, came and spent the Evening at AWs.

9 This Day 5 Years, and on the same day of the Week, my Mind was much agatated, tho on a very different Occasion,—May I so conduct myself, in this state of perpetual change, as to arrive at last, to that state of Bliss, never to be again seperated from my dear Parents. Sister and Fd. Warner the greatest part of the Day in Water-Street, prepareing for the important Day—AW came home to Dinner, Pollys sent to her.—HD. call'd several times, he spent the Evening with us—Sister and self, were to have lodg'd this night in the Bleu Chamber (our Bed being remov'd) but Polly had inadvertantly put the Key of the door on the inside, and pull'd it too, which prevented our enterance, were oblig'd to go into AWs Chamber, and sleep, or lay, there—Sister in a little Bed on the Floor, myself between AW, and Nancy.

10 My Throat continues very bad, which gives me great uneasaness, Sister and AW. Senr. busy in Water street, Betsy Moode spent this Afternoon & part of the Evening—Rachel Drinker call'd this Afternoon—Henry went home this Evening with Betsy—Nurse Peggy Grigory came this Afternoon to put up my Pallet,[1] have found no relief thereby—Henry came home with Sister after 11 o'clock, did not go to Bed till near 12.

11 First Day: Sister, and self at home alone this Morning, HD, call'd before I was up—he drank tea at AWs this Afternoon. Sister in Water-street—Henry spent the Evening with me. very cold weather.

12 HD. informs that the River's fast—Pollys gone in Water-street—My Throat not quite well—Betsy Moode, and Hannah Hicks, here this Afternoon—Henry Several times.[2]

1. By "pallet" ED means the soft palate, or uvula, which in a viral illness could become inflamed and interfere with swallowing. The seventeenth-century German surgeon Wilhelm Fabry (Fabricius Hiladanus) fashioned several devices that could be thrust in the mouth either to place an astringent powder on the swollen uvula or to give the patient nourishment when the organs of the mouth were very swollen. See also below, Apr. 14 and Dec. 19, 1806 (Parr, *London Medical Dictionary*, s.v. "palate" and "uvula"; *Oeuvres chirurgies die Hierosome Fabrioe* [Lyon: Chez Pierre Ravaud, 1659], 594–95).

2. ED and HD were married on Jan. 13, 1761.

1761: May the 12. Went to Burlington, with my dear H——y—left home aboute 1 o'clock stop'd at Hall's, proceeded on our journey at 3—cross'd Duncks's Ferry—arriv'd at B Swett's Burlington before 7.

the 13—took a walk this Morning with S Swett and HD. call'd at Edward Catherell's, and at Saml. Smiths, dinn'd at BSs at 1 o'clock, left Burlington a little after—drank Tea at home with Sister and Able James.

Our Friend Francis Rawle, departed this Life, June the 7, 1761, was bury'd the 8th (Sister and self too unwell to attend)—the 30th. Ultimo he received a Gun-Shot at Point in his left Arm, which was the cause of his Death.[3]

3. Francis Rawle was hunting at his country estate when his fowling piece discharged accidentally and wounded him. He died from the aftereffects of the wound (Jordan, *Col. Fam. Phila.*, 1:151).

1762

HD. left home, for Eastown June 16th. 1762,[1] between 2 & 3 o'clock, Afternoon—Mary Cosgrave, Jenny Heaton, and Betsy Fortuner spent this Afternoon with us, Bekey, and Abel James, here this Evening—our Betty gone to stay out all Night, Sally Midling.[2]

17 AJ, call'd, this Morning Sister & Self went this Afternoon to Frankford, to notre place, with Sally, Sally Emlen, Hannah Moode, Call'd this Evening—I wrote this Morning a mon Chere.

18th: Hannah Jones, spent part of this Morning with us,—Sister & self design'd to have gone to Point but signs of rain prevented us, not very well this Afternoon, Betsy Waln, Becky Rawle here; step'd this Evening into Abels—no news from HD.

19. Abel here, I at Abels, B. Oxon brought his Account, let him have 20 S—Sister, Sally, John and self, went this Afternoon, to Quarry-Bank, or Airy-Hill—saw Richd. Wells preparing his Carriage to take a ride, invited him with us—he follow'd with Rachel, they stay'd an hour at our Place, visited the Spring-House &c then left us for Blooms-Berry,—we came home too late, tho I hope no ways injur'd, several to see us while we were out. Betty knows not who—wrote to my H——Y.

20th. First-Day: Sister went to Meeting, This Morning I stay'd at home, Samy Sansom drank Tea with us, I left him with Sister, and went to Evening Meeting Samy and Hannah Sup'd with us.

21st. Mid-Summers Day; Went this Afternoon to Edegla Farm, Sister, Sally, John, and self, Becky Rawle, Catty Howell & their Children there—spent the time till after Tea there, then went to Tench Frances's Place Becky, Caty and 3 of their little ones with us—walk'd in the Garden, the Prospect of Scheylkill, and the oposite Banks is delightfull—they accompany'd us part of the way home the Evening very Pleasant—got out of the Chaise a J Howells Door, to

1. The manuscript volume for June 16, 1762–Apr. 12, 1764, has two-tone blue floral paper covers. The outside front cover reads, "1762, 3, 4—"; deleted numerals appear on the inside front cover.

2. Sally Drinker was born on Oct. 23, 1761.

avoid Arch-Street Hill—calld to see Fd. Warner, went this Evening to Abels, Abel here—a Small pleasant Shower this Evening, without thunder, or lightning—Sister & self well, our dear little Sall indifferent, Isaac and Ben here, John a tolerable good Boy. Betty troubled with a Meagram.[3]

22 I went to Meeting this Morning, Hanh and Nelly Moode, came home with me, they went away before dinner, Hannah came back and went with Molly to Frankford, B & P. Parr there, R Say spent this afternoon with me, Fd. Warner, and Sindry, calld, H Moode went home before Night—Sally well.

23 Anna Warner Senr., Saml. and Sarah Sansom, drank tea with us, B. Walln here with the Child, Richd. came in, Silvia Spicer, Patty, Becky, James, call'd, sister out this Evening looking for a Maid—Nanny Silas Iron'd here, Betty behaves Badly—some talk of an Earth-quake last seventh-Day Night I remember to have heard a Strange Noise—John Drinker Abel Js.—here.

24 the Brig Recovery saild YesterDay: Capt. Reese went down to Day—Abel, Becky James, call'd this Morning Sister and Benny, went this Afternoon to Frankford, Rachey Budd here, she came back to let me know, that HD, was to set out for home [this] Day. John Drinker call'd this Evening.

1762 7 mo. July 22 took up our Aboad during the warm weather, at our place near Frankford, from 22d. to 28th. kept no account. saw but little Company—Sister went to Town the 24th. 28th. She went again in the Morning with my H——y she came back to dine with me, took a ride in the Afternoon, John and Sally with her to B. Parrs, came back to Tea with me. HD. stay'd in Town all Night the first time since we came up; I have my Sister, my Sally; John Burket and Hannah Broom; with me, and did it suit HD, to be constantly here also, I think I could be very happy in the Country.

29th. Billy, Peggy, Caley Parr, came this Morning; Billy went to Town, Peggy & Caley spent the Day with us: HD, Abel James, and John Parrock, came to Tea HD. went this Evening home with MP return'd again to us.

30th. My Henry stay'd with us to Dinner, rain in the Morning; he left us before 2 o'clock, I dont expect him back to Night.

31st. HD. came to Tea with us.

Augt. the 1 First Day Benny Trapnel came up this Morning: HD. and MS went to Meeting. Mary Emlen, Mary Evans, and Aqua. Jones, B Trapnal, din'd with us; they Went away before Tea, HD took a walk to A Jamess Place.

3. A migraine headache (*OED*).

2d. HD left us before breakfast—Charles and Hannah Jones, drank Tea with us HD. came up towards Evening.

3d. HD. and MS. left me for Town this Morning after Breakfast, between 7 & 8 o'clock, John went with them, he return'd at 11 o'clock.—the first time of my dining alone since I came to Frankford—Thos. and Rebecca Say with Benny came up this Afternoon, HD. and MS, came home before Tea took a Walk round the Place, TS. &c went home towards Evening.

4th. Ma Chere went to Town Early this Morn—Samey and Betsy Emlen Hannah and Nelly Moode, spent this Day with us, the Day as Agreeably spent as could be in the absence of my best Friend.

5 HD stay'd in Town all Night,—Richd. Waln, Betsy, and Child, came up this Afternoon—HD. came home at 4 o'clock this Afternoon.

6 HD and MS. with John, went to Town before 7 this Morning; Sister and John return'd before dinner, HD. came in the Afternoon; Isaiah Worrel paid us a Viz—Sallys unwell.

7th. HD. left us soon this Morning Katherine Callender, Sarah Sansom, Samey and Hannah Sansom, spent this afternoon with us, HD. came up in the Evening.

8 HD. Sally and self took a ride this Morning Went to Meeting left sister at home, Robt. Willis, and Danl. Stanton appeard Robt. W. and John Pemberton dinn'd with us—they went this Afternoon for Germanton—Abel with part of his Family up to Day, HD. went this Evening to Abels Place, came home, John Drinker with him—Frankford Meeting a very Small one.

9th. HD. went to Town, [agin] this Morning saw no Company to Day, clean'd House.

10 HD. stay'd in Town last Night—came home this Afternoon.

11 HD. Went to Town this Morning. Robt. Willis, and John Pemberton call'd the former to bid us farewel, as he was on his way home, John inform'd us that Samey and Betsy Emlen were coming up to see us, but I believe rain prevented them; as they did not come.

12 Sister and John went to Town this afternoon, ma Chere came back with them drank, coffee with me, they took Sally to ride a little way—Abel Jamess little Son George was Yesterday Buryed—HD. in Town last Night.

13 HD. stay'd Breakfast with us this Morning, went to Town after, he brought Nancy Warner up in the Chaise after Dinner, A Warner Senr. and Betsy with them, they spent the After-noon with us Peggy Parr, Nancy and Polly also here, We all took a Walk after Tea round by the Creek, HD. went to Town with them, I dont Expect him back to Night, Peggy Parr &c went away soon after them.

14th. Samey and Betsy Emlen came up at 10 this Morning they spent the Day with us, HD came home this Evening.

15th. First Day. HD, and self went to Meeting this Morning, no Publick Friends[4] there, took a Nap in the Afternoon, then went with the Child to ride, round by Willings Place and to the River, came home to Coffee—no Body to see us from Town to Day.

16 HD. went to Town this Morning, no Coumpany to Day, Sister, Sally, John & self went after 4 o'clock to W Parrs and drank Tea there; Billy from home, signs of Rain hurry'd us, came back a little after 6—No Henry to Night.

17th. rain with Clouds, HD came up this Evening, Sister and Hannah went to Meeting this Morning being Frankford Week-Day Meeting, it consist'd of 2 persons besides themselves.

18 We had the pleasure of HDs Company to Breakfast with us, he left us, soon after—came up again in the Afternoon with Abel and Becky James and their 6 Children, Abel &c left us after Tea, HD—stay'd.

19 HD stayd breakfast, left us before Dinner, rainey Day: my H——y came up in the Evening: Sally Unwell.

4. Public Friends originally were Quakers, both male and female, who expressed their faith by preaching to and attempting to convert and reform the larger society. Later the term came to designate the authorized traveling public ministry of the Society of Friends. Many Public Friends appear in the Drinker diary: those from the Philadelphia vicinity who received permission from their monthly meeting to travel to other communities, and those from abroad who visited Philadelphia and the Drinker home. Many of these men and women often held, or "appointed," special meetings for nonmembers. This practice was not so much an attempt at conversion as it was a means of spreading Quaker tenets to the larger society through public preaching. Of equal importance were formal visits to the families of members, which gave Public Friends an opportunity to emphasize the importance of family worship and to discuss Quaker philosophy among small groups (Stoneburner and Stoneburner, *Quaker Women*, xv; Carol Stoneburner, "Drawing a Profile of American Female Public Friends as Shapers of Human Space," in Stoneburner and Stoneburner, *Quaker Women*, 61; Thomas D. Hamm, *The Transformation of American Quakerism: Orthodox Friends, 1800–1907* [Bloomington: Indiana University Press, 1988], 8–9; Jones, *Later Periods of Quakerism*, 1:230–31).

20th: HD. MS. went to Town this Morning Cloudy, Molly return'd before Dinner. We had this Afternoon a voielent Storm of Wind and rain with Thunder: I dont expect HD to Night.

21st. Our dear little one very unwell to Day—HD came home this Evening he took a ride with Sister and Sally.

22 First Day: HD. and self went to Meeting, (we took a ride before with the Child) had a silent meeting—Abel James came up after Dinner brought us a Letter from Joseph Sandwith, which inform'd us of the death of his Father, our Uncle who departed this Life the 24 of 2 mo. Febry. 1762 in Dublin—Abel & Henry took a walk, came back to Tea, then went out in the Chaise. HD. came back solas.

23 My H——y and Sister went to Town this Morning, I have been alone all Day they came home late; Isaac Worrels Wife and Sister here this Evening.

24 HD. went to Town after Breakfast Joyce Benezt and Mary Groath came this Morning: after they were gone, Sister and John went to Meeting—Molly Worrel, Phebe Morris and Joseph Pauls Daughter drank tea with us—HD. came home this Evening.

25 HD. left us, for Town after Breakfast; Mary Armitt, Hannah Logan, Saml. and Betsy Emlen drank tea with us,—HD. came home in the Evening.

26 HD. went away after Breakfast came home in the Afternoon. Johney Drinker with him—several Hands Busy here, hauling Mudd.—Wm. Griffits Bury'd this Afternoon.

27. HD. left us, as usual, he came back in the Afternoon, saw no company to Day, my self very unwell with sick Head-Ach Sister Ironing—We were up in the Night I being [very] bad with my Head.

28th. HD. and MS, went to Town this Morning, rain'd smartly about Dinner-time, my Head not well—they came home at 5 o'clock; call'd in their way to Town at Cummings's saw a Lyoness there.

29 First Day, HD, went to Meeting, Sister and self at home, not very well—[William] West, and Isaac Worrel here this Afternoon—dull Weather.

30, A great quantity of rain fell, last Night and this Morning, [in] so much, that the Road by the Mill was rendred impassable, the Fresh was so great, Oswin Sutton says, the like has not been since his time, at Frankford, which is 40 odd Years—HD, Sister and self, took a walk after Dinner to the Mill,

People were oblig'd to swim their Horses, [accross] the road—HD, stay'd with us till this Afternoon—tis an ill wind,[5] &c.

31 HD. stay'd in Town last Night, came home this Afternoon,—the Lyoness, past this road in the Morning paid 2 S—for Seeing her—a large ugly animel—Phebe Morris here this Morning.

Septr. 1st. HD, left us this Morning Sister, self, John with the Child, walk'd to Fishers this Afternoon; pleasant walk: HD. overtook us, returning home.

2 HD. and MS. with John, went to Town this Morning: Abel and Becky James, and John Parrock, [called] here about Noon did not stay long—Sister and John came home before Dinner: MS. ED. John and Sally went to Wm. Parrs this Afternoon, drank Tea there—came home after Sun-set—I do not expect HD. to Night—the Weather grows Cool—must return to Town e'er long.

Septr. 3: Jacob brought me a Letter this Morning from HD. giveing us an account of the Reduction of the Havannah, by the English;[6]—and of the safe delivery of Hannah Jones who was brought to Bed, on First-Day last of a Son:—Samey & Hannah Sansom, Peggy Parr, Nancy, Polly and Caleb, spent this Afternoon with us—HD. came home to Tea—Isaac Worrel here this Evening.

4 HD. went to Town this Morning—Samuel Sansom Senr. and Wife spent this Afternoon with us—Abel James and Wife came before Tea, a little after them, came HD. and Patty James—they went away after Tea, but Patty stay'd all Night—Slept with Sister.

5 First Day: HD. MS. and MJ. went to Meeting this Morning—Abel & Becky James, with Patty din'd with us—, Benny Trapnel and all Abel's Children, and little Maid came after Dinner—they went away towards Evening, Patty stay'd all Night with us.

6 HD. and Patty went to Town, after Breakfast—HD. came back in the Evening.

7th: HD. went to Town this Morning. Sister and self very busy Ironing &c—preparing for our return home—Took a walk, this Afternoon, MS. ED, SD,

5. Word crossed out.

6. England and Spain were then at war. In June an expedition headed by the earl of Albemarle captured Havana (Howard H. Peckham, *The Colonial Wars, 1689–1762* [Chicago: University of Chicago Press, 1964], 207).

JB, HB—call'd at B. Oxen's, who is bad with a sore-Leg walk'd round by the Creek—call'd at H——y Boozer's, then came home—my HD and Capt. Reese drank Tea with us they came up in Abel's Waggon, left Abel at his Place—they went away at 6 o'clock I dont expect to see HD. again untill tomorrow Evening, weather very fine.

8th. very busy this Morning—Anna Warner Senr. Joshua & Caty Howell, and Becky Rawle came up this Afternoon in their Waggon—HD. came soon after—they took a walk after Tea, left AW, with me—they went away towards Evening Billy Asbridges Sister and Nancy Paul came this Evening.

9 left Frankford this Afternoon Bag and Bagage—found our Frds. at Philaa. generaly well—Hannah Moode, Here this Evening.

10 Abel Becky James here, want us to go with them in the Waggon to Burlington Tomorrow, dont suit, went this Evening to see Molly Searson who is I believe nigh her End—call'd to see our Fd. Hannah and her Young Son—from hence went to S. Emlens, came home in the Evening.

11 Abel and Becky James, Cathern. Callender, Sarah Sansom, [C]atty, Chalkley, Josey—gone this Morning in the Wagon to Burlington—My Henry and Sister went this Afternoon to Quarry-Bank, came home towards Evening.

1762 Septr. A Sickley time at Philada.[7] many Persons are taken down, with Something very like the Yallow-Feaver.

1762 Septr. 19th: First-Day—Ma tres Chere went out of Town this Morning, J. Parrock with him, they intend for Chester Meeting, then farther, dont expect him home this Day or two—John Drinker and Son here this Morning. Sister went to Meeting in the Afternoon, Abel and Becky James here this Evening: Sister left Becky with me, and went to see M Searson &c—Isaac Stroud lodges with B Trapnal.

20th. Within all Day as useal. Polly Guest, Parr's Poll, and Betsy Waln, call'd—had some expectation of HD to Day—but am disoppointed—the Weather good.

21st. Went to Meeting this Morning Nelly Moode came home with me, went

7. Yellow fever struck Philadelphia in August and did not subside until October. The city did not experience another major outbreak until the disastrous epidemics in the 1790s. Philadelphia's first experience with epidemic yellow fever occurred in 1699, when 220 persons, approximately 5 percent of the population, died (Redman, *Account of the Yellow Fever, 1762*; Duffy, *Epidemics*, 142–61; Augustin, *Yellow Fever*, 986–87).

to Abels After dinner, and to Richd. Waln's, my dear Henry came home this Evening.

Septr. 23[8] Received a Letter this Evening—from Samuel Emlen junr. intimating his Wife's indisposition, went there about 9 o'clock & stay'd till near 3 in the morning,[9] when H.D. came to inform of Sal's being Saucy, so came Home, about 5 in the morning (the 24th) E.[10] Emlen was delivered of a fine Boy Joshua junr.

24th. Hannah Moode pass'd Meeting with Henry Haydock, perform'd well, good luck to her.

Octor. the 11: Billy Chancellor died of the Yallow-Feaver—was bury'd in Friends Birying-Grownd. 1762.

Octor. 11: 1762 My little Sally taken unwell with a vomitting and Purging, Doctors Redman and Evans tended her, seems now recover'd, the 26th.

Sister this Evening Ointing Hannah Broom for the Itch,[11] an ugly peice of Work Octor. the 26th. 1762.

Molly Searson departed this Life Octor. the 23: 1762, her Body carri'd to Church, Sister at the Burial—she died of a Consumption.

A Negro of Patty Craddocks, dead at Abel James's of the Small Pox, it proves Mortal to Many. Octor 26: 1762.

HD. gone this Morning to Burlington Abel James with him, in the Waggon. expect them home, tomorrow—stay'd at home all Day myself: Sally got a Cough—Becky James and Betsy Waln here this Evening. Novemr. the 14: 1762.

15th: Went this Afternoon with B Waln to see Rebecca Waln, who lays in with her Daughter Rachel, HD. came home this Evening.

The Small Pox in Town and proves very mortal.[12]

Novr. 17th. two Negroes were hang'd to Day for Roberey[13]—1762.

8. The entries dated Sept. 23 and 24 do not appear to be in ED's handwriting.

9. Word crossed out.

10. The word "Moode" crossed out.

11. The itch, or scabies, was caused by a small parasite known as the itch mite (Skinner, *Medical Terms*, 235).

12. In the last months of this year minor smallpox outbreaks occurred in New York City and Philadelphia (Duffy, *Epidemics*, 97).

13. The two men, identified only as Caspar and Joe in colony records, were convicted of felony and burglary on Oct. 28 at the Court for the Tryal (*sic*) of Negroes in Philadelphia, and sentenced to be executed (*Col. Recs. Pa.*, 9:5–6).

Novr. 18. Neighr. Shoemaker and Beulah Burge here to Day 1762.

Novr. 20th. HD. MS. and SD. took a ride.

the 22, HD, Sally and Self, went to Frankford.

the 23 Abel and Becky James, Sister self and Sally, and little Becky, went in the Waggon to Abels Place, came home to late Dinner.

From the Gazette, Philada. Decemr. 2 1762, Last Week were interred in one Grave, three Children of one Family in this City, who lost their Lives by a most unfortunate accident. It had been proposed, it seems, to prepare their Bodies for the Small-Pox, by giving them some Cream of Tartar, which was accordingly sent for to an Apothecary's Shop; by mistake Tartar Emetic was delivered and administred instead of it which by its Excess of quantity, and violent operation, soon brought on Death. The Grief of the Parents, who have no other Children is inexpressible, "How Carefull ought the Venders of Medicine to be, that none but discreet and intelligent Persons are suffer'd to attend and serve in their Shops.[14]

they were I am told the Children of one Boar.

Decr. 11. 1762 Anna Howel, daughter of Joshua Howel, died of the Small Pox—between 13 and 14 months Old.

Hannah Jones's Son Innoculated for the Small Pox. Decemr. 13: 1762.

Peggy Rawle Innoculated the 15.

the New Brig Concord, sail'd from Philada. Decemr. 14: 1762 Dl. Reese for Barbadoes.

Decemr. 24 Sally Fisher dead of the Small-Pox, her Brother Johny bury'd last Week of the same disorder.

14. ED copied this story from the *Pennsylvania Gazette*. Cream of tartar (sodium potassium tartrate, Rochelle salt) was used as a cathartic (see below, June 17, 1797) and diuretic. Tartar emetic, a preparation of antimony and potassium tartrate, was a popular eighteenth-century emetic, diaphoretic, expectorant, cathartic, and sedative, although it was known to cause poisoning in large doses (*Pa. Gaz.*, Dec. 2, 1762; Haller, and Abuse of "Tartar Emetic," 235–57; Estes, "Therapeutic Practice," 365, 371, 378; see also above, Aug. 1, 1759).

1763

Janry. 6. 1763 Alarm'd by the Cry of Fire, between 1 and 2 o'clock—Duchees Pot House.[1]

Janry. 21st, 1763. HD. MS, E Jervis and ED—went to Quary-Bank, in a Sleigh.

Febry. 6: 1763—First-Day Afternoon very unwell, Miscarried;[2] Sally, Inoculated, last sixth-Day.
8 Weeks gone, when it happn'd.

March, 2: 1763, A Friendly Visit from Robt. Willis and Joshua Emlen.

March the 24. 1763, Rebecca Birchall, my School-mistress, was burried.

March the 25. 1763, HD. went to Thos. Mauls, with several others to accompany the Corps of Content Nicholson to Town, she was burried First-Day the 27 Instant from B. Swetts Junr. HD, and myself at the Buriel.

March 24. 1763, Becky James, last Night Miscarried of a Daughter—HD. was let blood to Day—Hannah also—March 30th, 1763.

March 31: 1763, began this Morning to Ween my Sally,—the Struggle seems now (April 2) partly over.—tho it can scarcely be call'd a Struggle she is such a good-natur'd patient Child.

April the 2. HD, and MS, design'd to have gone this Morning to [Buybarry] to the Burrial of Sarah Walmsley, but signs of Bad Weather prevented.

April the 23. 1763, went in the Waggon to Frankford, AJ, HD, the Children Jacob Spicer Junr. and my little Sall, R James and Sister in the Chaise—Henry, Molly & Self went from Able's place to ours stay'd but a little time there all came home to Tea.

1. A tavern on Chestnut Street (*Pa. Gaz.*, Jan. 13, 1763).
2. Word(s) crossed out.

May the 1: 1763 Wm. Callender departed this life, after a lingring sickness; the 2d Instant accompany'd his Corps to the Water side;—he is to be bury'd to Morrow at Burlington.

May 3 My Henry and Sister, with many others, went to Burlington to the Funeral of WC.

Nancy Jones came to work. May 3: 1763 the 3 day of the Week.

May the 19: 1763, HD—and Thos. Say set of for Brumswick, after Dinner.

20. Becky James, Betsy Waln here—unpleasent Weather.

21 all Day sick, Nurse Mitchell here—Sister Sally and self in at Ables this Evening.

22 First Day—at home all Day bad weather, Able and Becky here this Evening—Betsy Waln here to Day.

May 23:1763, at home as usual, Rebecca Say here this Afternoon Abel here to day; mis'd an oppertunity of Writeing to my Henry. very unwel, Elizth. Pines here this Evening partly Engag'd to[3] hier her.

24 Went out this Afternoon; with Sister, call'd at S Sansoms Junr. drank Tea at C Jones's. Rachl. Budd here to Night says her Mamy has a Letter from her Husband, I'm disopointed in not receiving one from my HD—Peggy Parr here to Day.

25 Went this Afternoon, with Sally, in the Waggon to Frankford, with Abel, Becky and Children, David Franks and Wife, drank Tea with us there; came home towards Evening, Abel received a letter to Day from HD—white Washers here.

26 HD. return'd this Morning.

27 ED. was let Blood; May 1763.

June 20, 1763, little Joshua Emlen was this Afternoon buried, he dyed the 19 of a vomitting purging and cutting Teeth &c.

1763: July 1st. sixth Day afternoon came to Quarry-Bank myself with Abel James in the Chaise John behind, HD. MS, the Child and Hannah in Abels

3. Word crossed out.

Waggon,—left Elizabeth Pines, and B Trapnel, to keep House in Town—Judah Foulks Family moveing up to Widdow Mc. Vaughs new House, so that we shall have Molly for a Neighbour—Abels Family at their Place—myself and Child unwell.

2 HD, went to Town this Morning—sister and self busy all Day; Hannahs Toe sore—HD, return'd in the Evening A James here.

July 3: First Day—H.D. E.D. went to Meeting this Morning, silence—call'd to see M Foulk, came home to Dinner, No Coumpany but our Benjn.—took a ride this Afternoon to Abels,—Ann Throneton, Bulah Coats, Giles Knights Daughters, John Langdell &c there—drank Coffee at home, late.

4th. HD. went early to Town, he came back this Evening, Sister the Child & myself, pay'd a short visit to M Foulk this Afternoon.

5 HD, MS, and John went to Town this Morning; Sister with John return'd to Dinner, My Henry stays in Town to Night—a pleasent rain this Afternoon.

6 Richd. and Betsy Waln with little Josey call'd this Morning, in their Way to Town, from Abington, where Betsy has been some time with the Child, HD, return'd this Evening.

7 H.D. left us this Morning: John Drinker, came after he was gone Breakfast'd here—rain this Morning in the Afternoon, Sister; Sally; John, & self, took a ride to W Parrs, stay'd a short time, call'd at A Jame's, Doctor Evans there; came home betimes—Ma Chere and Abel came this Evening the Weather very pleasent.

8 H.D. went to Town this Morning—Sammy Sansom call'd, in his way to Burlington he Breakfast'd here—Sister; Sally, John and myself, spent this Afternoon at Billy Parrs, Abel James, and Judah Foulk, came there towards Evening;—came home, found HD there before us.

9 HD, stay'd with us untill nine, then went to Town, Sammy Sansom, drank Tea with us, he went away a little before my Henry came.

10 First Day, John Drinker, Wife, and Children spent, the Day with us—JD. MS. and my H——y went to meeting—, after they went away in the evening, we took a walk round our place—call'd at Judah Foulks—Peggy Parr there.

11 HD, went to Town—P Parr spent the Day with us—M Foulk spent the

Afternoon, took a walk after Tea—their Children came in the Evening—Judah and HD came up, drank Coffee here.

12 HD. went to Town, he came back, early this Afternoon, AJ with him HD. went Guning, Doctor Evans call'd, Richd. Waln drank Coffee with us—Made Currant Jelly.

13 H.D. spent the whole day with us. Abel, Senr., Chalkly, and Josy, call'd this Evening,—made more Jelly.

14 Went to Town this Morning, all of us, did not go from home, busy—came back to Frankford before Tea time, Charles West Junr. & Wife drank tea with us, my Henry at Abels, he came from Town with him.

15. HD. went to town this Morning he came back early in the Afternoon, Josey James, and little Abel with him. went to buding Trees—Sister, self, Abel's Children; Sally, and John, took a ride, call'd at Abel's, left the Children at home—Sally Dorsey there—drank a Dish of Tea, took a ride as far as Moore's place—turn'd and came home to Coffee with HD.

16 Ma Chere stay Dinner with us. Sister went with him to Town, came back in the Evening.

17 First Day HD. and self went to meeting this Morning call'd at Judaths door, I rode with M Parr, walk'd back Joyce Benezett and Sally Morris Preach'd, they din'd at Abels—HD. MS. and self, John & the Child took a walk towards Evening—Abel and Becky James, Molly Foulk sup'd with us.

18. HD. went to Town as usual—came up again in the Evening.[4]

19 H.D. went to Town, came up again in the Evening—inform'd us of Bettys being sick.

20 Went all to Town, found Betty in Bed, stay'd at home all Day.

21 Sister went to Meeting, Betty much better, she went away this Morning. Phebe Broom in Town, I visit'd Sally Bond, in her lying in.

22. Sister and self went out this Afternoon, call'd at S Sansoms Junr. at Uncles, at S Emlens, Betsy unwell talks of going to England, Nelly in Town,—went from thence to Chars. Jones's, sat a little time, call'd at A Warners, and then came home.

4. Five lines crossed out.

23 Molly and self went to Market this Morning, call'd at Uncles, and at Reeves, Silver-smith,—bought little Books at Rivengtons—came home found Phebe Broom there. she went away this Morning—we are very busy giting ready to return to the Country—lock'd up the House this Afternoon—HD. MS, the Child and Hannah, went in our Chaise, myself with Abel in his Waggon—& our John &c—call'd at Abels, Edmd. Carneys Wife and Nurse Lloyd there—HD, came for me, came home to Tea.

24 First Day: Abels Family gone to Buyberry. HD. and self went to Meeting, silence; din'd alone—John Lowense; George James and Young Hartshorn here this Afternoon rain with Thunder most part of the Day.

25, HD went to Town after Breakfast. came up in the Afternoon, Abel with him.

26 Richd Waln Breakfast'd with us. HD. went to Town—Becky James Jr. and Patty came here after Dinner. they two, Molly Foulk, Peggy Parr, Sister and self, visited Billy Ashbridges Wife,—HD. came up early this Afternoon, call'd at WAs—we came home before Evening.

27 HD. went to Town as usual—Billy Ashbridge came up this Evening in our Chaise, says we need not expect my HD, to Night—he stay'd Tea with us.

28 HD. stay'd in Town all Night he came up, soon in the Afternoon, saw no Company to Day, took a small walk with HD towards Eveng.

29. Ma Chere went after Breakfast. Sister and self stay'd at home all Day Rain with Thunder this Afternoon and Evening—I dont expect to see my Sweet-Heart to Night.

30th. HD. in Town all Night; James and Hannah Bringhurst with their Son, came to see us this Afternoon, from M Foulks—HD. came up this Afternoon with Dickey Waln, who drank Coffee with us, Betty Claypool here this Evening.

31. First Day. John Drinker Spent the Day here—he, my Henry, and Sister and B. Trapnel went to Meeting—, Molly Foulk and Family came this Evening we went all togeather to take a Walk return'd before night.

Augt. 1 HD. went away as usual return'd soon in the Afternoon.

2 Went all of us to Town this Morning Sister Went to Youths Meeting. I visit'd Rachel Wells in her lyeing in, this Afternoon,—came back to Quarry-Bank in the Evening—several Showers this Day.

3 HD. and AJ, came up early this Afternoon, Saml. Bell and Stephen Reynear, call'd—Abel drank Coffee with us.

4. HD. stay'd with us all day—Molly, Sally, John and my-self took a ride this Morning to Wm. Parr's, calld in our return at Abels. came home by 11 o'clock—John Drinker and Jos. Penock here this Afternoon,—HD & MS went this Evening to M Foulks, Phebe Morris here—James Bringhursts Child dy'd[5] this Afternoon.

5 HD, went to Town this Morning came home at Night, inform'd us of poor Randel. (our Neighbour Walns little Servent Boy) being Drownded—some time yesterday.

6 HD. came up this Afternoon; Dicky Waln's Family gone to Town.

7 First Day: H.D. and myself went to Meeting Benn. Trotter preach'd, call'd in our way home at J. Foulks—din'd without Company—HD. MS. ED—took a Walk towards Evening—cloudy—Abel and Judah here this Morning.

8 The rain which fell last night and this Morning, occasion'd so great a Fresh that People were obliged to go over the road by the Mill in Boats—it detain'd HD with us till sometime after dinner when Abel James, Judah Foulk and ma Chere, went in the Waggon to Germantown, return'd in the Evening—Thunder and Lightning continues—Sally's got cold, which I hope will prove but slight.

9 H.D. and M.S. John with them, went to Town this Morning; Samey Sanson call'd here, in his return from Burlington, where Hannah has been some time with her Child—my Henry, and Sister came back to dinner,—we took a walk this Afternoon to Oxons, drank Tea at J. Foulks.

10 I forgit all aboute it.

11 HD. went to Town this Morning Samuel Sansom Senr. and Wife spent this Afternoon with us—our John busy making Hay—Abel James, call'd here this Afternoon HD. came home after night—we took a walk in the Afternoon. we have had as yet a very moderate Summer, but now grows very warm.

12 H.D. went to Town this Morning Sister and self took a walk as far as Oxons, to see the Haymakers—HD came this Evening.

5. The word "Yesterday" crossed out.

13 HD——went to Town this Morning—he came up [to] dinner, then went to Abels, came back to Tea—a Thunder gust this Evening.

14 First Day HD. and MS. went to Meeting: B Trapnel came up—H and ED—took a ride to Abels Sister and the Child came after—drank Tea there—came home towards Evening—a very heavy rain this Evening.

15 HD. went to Town this Morning. MS. John the Child and myself went to School, which is held at the Meeting House—A Jamess, W Parr's and J. Foulks, Children go there. tis a large School—We call'd in our way home at M. Foulk's—Thos. Bolsbey and Wife there, drank Tea with them; HD. came home—while we were there—the Weather is very cool and Pleasent.

16 HD. gone to Town: W Parr call'd here this Morning—Sammy and Betsy Emlen, & Nelly Moode, spent this Afternoon with us—they went away early, my HD came home late.

17 HD. went to Town: Richd. & Betsy Waln with little Jo. spent this Afternoon with us HD. came to Tea with us.

18 Ma Chere gone:—took a walk this Morning, to Catty Boozers, call'd at M. Foulks: came home with the Head-Ach—Sammy Pleasents came here this Afternoon—HD came home in the Evening.

19 Went to Town, had our Ironing done up, step'd into Richd. Waln's—came back to Quarry-Bank in the Evening I came with Abel; HD. MS. and the Child in our Chaise.

20, HD. went to Town this Morning. John Drinker, his Wife and 2 Children, Thos. Say, Wife, and Son, with Sucky Willson, spent the Afternoon with us—HD. came up to Tea: the Weather is exceeding Pleasent.

21 First Day: HD. and self went to Meeting: we took a walk towards Evening Abel and Rebecca James Supped with us.

22. MS. and John went this Morning (after HD. was gone) to Bowlsbey's to buy Butter &c—they came home before Dinner,—Sister and self with the Child and John, spent this Afternoon at Isaac Norris's, we came home before Night—Abel James came home with my Henry—Molly and self step'd over to Judahs.

23. HD. went to Town—Patty James dinn'd and spent the Afternoon with us—Peggy Parr call'd, several of hir Family unwell, little black Nedd dyed last week of the Flux, which disorder, many are troubled with, in Country and

Town—Alexander Seaton buried some time this Week.—cool Pleasent Weather.

24 HD. went to Town.—Sister Ironing Molly Worrel call'd—HD—came up in the Evening.

25 HD. went to Town before Breakfast, Sammy Sansom, dinn'd and spent the Afternoon with us—Beckey James, and Children, with Sally Crispen, spent the Afternoon—HD. came home late this Evening.

26. HD. MS. and John went to Town this Morning, after Breakfast, MS. and John, return'd by 11 o'clock Noon—put a Gown skirt in the Frame, to Quilt this Afternoon—HD came up this Evening unexpectedly.

27. HD. went away as usual—saw no Company this Day—HD return'd in the Evening.

28 First Day: M Sandwith went to Town by herself.—John Drinker and Son spent the Day here, they went with my Henry to Meeting—I Stay'd at home till Evening then took a Walk with HD, round our place, call'd at a dutch House to look at Grapes—Sister came home, after us—Betsy Emlen in a poor state of health.

29 HD. stay'd with us all Day—Abel James here this Evening.

30 HD. went to Town this Morning—Sister and self finish'd my Quilt this Afternoon—took a Walk to the end of the Lane HD. came home in the Waggon with AJ—Moderate Pleasent Weather.

31 HD. went to Town this Morning—Sammy and Betsy Emlen, Molly Foulk and Children, here this Afternoon, a large number of the People about Frankford troubled with sore-Eyes—another of Billy Parrs little Negros, dead of the Flux;—Abel James here this Evening: says I need not expect my Henry up to Night—the Weather grows cool—expect soon to return to Town.

Such quick regards his Sparkling eyes bestow:—
Such wavy ringlets o'er his shoulders flow!

Sally Drinker's Mouth was sore from the time she was a fortnight old, until she was five months—discover'd her first Tooth November 17th. 1762—she being then near 13 months old.[6]

6. The next seven lines in the manuscript do not appear to be in ED's handwriting.

began to give her Physick 1st. 2 month 1763 & Inoculated by Dr. Redman 4th of 2d month 1763. She was unwell & Feverish 10th Ditto.

11th continued . . . . Ditto.

12th some few appear—as well as to be Expected.

18th are now turning, about 30 in the whole & the Child bravely.

21 gave her a dose Physick—11 doses in all Pills included 9 before Innoculation 2 after—came down stairs the 1st March. she began to go alone at about 16 Mont[hs] old.

Sept 1st. Sister and self. John and the Child went to Ashbridges Mill, walk'd from thence to Abel Jamess, drank Tea There: just after we had set out for home, saw Abel and Henry comeing from Town HD. the Child and self road home, sister walk'd after.—Abel James here this Evening—cool Weather.

2 HD. went to Town this Morning—he return'd after dinner—Sammy & Polly Pleasents, drank tea with us.

3. rain this Morning. HD. stay'd with us till after dinner, then went to Town—Benjn. Kostor here here this Morning.—HD returnd to Tea; Cloudy Weather.

4 First Day: HD. and ED. went to Meeting: silence—no Company to day—HD went this Evening to A Jamess Molly and self to M Foulks—Judah and B— Parr came home with us—HD. sup'd at Jud'h Foulks.

5 HD. went to Town this Morning with Abel in his Waggon—he return'd to Tea with us—Lizey Ashbridge, spent this Afternoon with us—Pleasent Weather.

6 HD. stay'd with us till after dinner, then went to Town; Robt. Waln, Wife, and youngest Child; Sammy and Betsy Emlen—spent the Afternoon with us—John Drinker and Stephen Collins, came towards Evening; HD. came soon after—just as John and Stephen went away Abel James came—fine Weather.

7 HD. went to Town this Morning, he came back in the Evening—Molly Foulk spent this Afternoon with us.

8 HD. and MS. with John. went to Town this Morning—they return'd to Dinner. Abel James here this Afternoon, HD there this Evening—the Brig Concord came in this Afternoon.

9 HD. went to Town this Morning—John went this Afternoon with the Cart to carry the Oats to Town—Sister and self, with the Child, went towards Evening to Medeira's; met John returning—with a load of Shingles—we call'd at Billy Ashbridges—then came home HD. came this Evening.

10 HD. gone to Town this Morning he came up after dinner, John Drinker with him—Abel James here,—My Henry left us this Afternoon on Horse-back at 5 o'clock—designing for Burlington to Night; toMorrow to proceed towards Brunswick, Elizabeth-Town, and New-York.

11 First Day—Benn. Trapnel came up this Morning: he went with me to Meeting—silent meeting, which is very common here—this has appear'd a long day—Ben went away in the Afternoon, wrote by him to E. Emlen, I call'd after Meeting at M Foulks.

12. Peggy Parr, and Children drank Tea with us this Afternoon; Abel James here this Evening his Family generaly unwell—the Weather warm.

13 I was taken (last night) with a smart fitt of the Colick—was ill this Morning—better by dinner-time, tho' unwell and Feaverish all day—worse then I have been since we came into the Country—it was occasion'd by, my Eating Indian-Corn Yesterday at dinner. saw no Company to day,—Sister step'd this Evening over to Judah Foulks,—he came home with her—no news from my dearest.

14 Phebe Morris here this Morning—Sister went over to Rudey Knifes to buy Silk, mett with the Post brought me a Letter from my dear Henry:—Molly Foulk and Betsy Bringhurst here this Afternoon. Myself unwell—they went away early. Molly, John, the Child and myself took a short ride; Sister went afterwards, in the Chaise by herself to see Abels Foulks, she came back, and drank Coffee with me.

15 Sister went to Town this Morning—Molly Foulk with her—she came home before dinner with John—Joshua Emlen, Mary Armitt, Sammy and Betsy Emlen, and Nelly Moode, dinn'd with us—Sammy Betsy and Nelly, Black Cuff, with them, set of at about 3 o'clock on their way towards N. York—Joshua and Mary went to Town soon after—Abel James here this Evening.

16 have reason to belive that some of Oswins Family has got the Itch; at which I am alarm'd design for home tomorrow—My dear Henry return'd home before dinner—he went to Town after, came back again to Tea, A James with him—Molly Foulk and Betsy Bringhurst, with the Children, drank tea with us.

17 HD. went to town this Morning. sent John after, with a load in the Cart—he came back before dinner, We left Frankford this Afternoon, came to Town to Tea: all of us (through Mercy) well—11 Weeks Yesterday since we went into the Country—Moderate Weather.

Sepr. the 19: 1763; Busy all Day: Cleaning House, went this Evening to see Catty Howell, who, Miscarried last seventh Day, and has been very ill.

Septr. the 24: 1763. Antony Morris Senr. Burried this Afternoon.

Sepr. the 27: 1763. Hannah Hulford departed this life; a publick Friend.

Septr. the 30: HD. and MS. went to Frankford: this Afternoon, with the Child. did not go to our House, as they were inform'd, that old John Joyner was dead of the Flux.

October 28, was called up in the Night to Betsy Waln, who was, brought to Bed this Morning, of her Son Nicholas.—1763 sixth Day.

1763 Octor. the 30: First Day—Were Allarm'd by a Shock of an Earth-Quake; ¼ past 4 in the Afternoon—a clear Weather.—went this Afternoon with my Henry to the Burial of Josey Drinkers Son Thomas.

Octor. the 31. 1763 Went this Afternoon to see Jenney Heaton, who lays in with her first Child, who she calls, Mary.

Octor. 31: 1763, John Penn, Proclaim'd Governour—he arriv'd. Yesterday.

Novr. the 5: 1763. My Henry, John Drinker and his Son left home for Burlington, in the Chaise, after dinner—Richd Waln here this Evening, it seems a long one.

6th First-Day; went to Meeting this Morning Molly at home, she went in the Afternoon I went to Becky Rawles, Sister came After Meeting with Sally—came home in the Evening—step'd into Richd Walns he came home with us, spent an hour.

I, was let Blood Nover. 27, 1763.

Decemr. the 3. Becky James Miscarried 1763.

1764

M Sandwith had a Tooth drawn March 10. 1764.

Mary Drinker, my Henrys Grand-Mother, departed this Life March 17. 1764. in the 84th. year of her Age.

HD. was let Blood, April 7. 1764.

HD, left home, for Brumswick, this Morning, April 12. 1764.

13th. Benny and myself took a ride to Frankford before dinner—Abel & Docr. Evans, had our Horse and Chaise this Afternoon—HD. came home the 16.

cut her last stomach Tooth[1] at the age of 2 years and 5 months March 23. 1764—her Eye Teeth some time before. Prattle'd pritt'ly at about 22 months.[2]

1764[3]		1766	1766	M 24
			20	20
Janry.	11	0	16	16
	0	0	12	12
	0	17	7	7
	0	16	3–27	3–30
	0	0	24	26
	0	0	20	20
	0	0	16	16
	0	0	11	11
	0	0	7	7
	0	0		4–30

1. The baby canine teeth of the lower jaw were called stomach teeth because gastric disturbance frequently accompanied their first appearance. The upper canine teeth were called eye teeth because Galen, the classical Greek physician, thought that, with their long roots, they received a branch from the nerve that supplied the eye (*OED*; Skinner, *Medical Terms*, 170).

2. This entry appears on the inside back cover of the manuscript volume.

3. The manuscript volume for June 6, 1764–Apr. 21, 1766, has marbelized paper covers in a pink, yellow, and aqua pattern. The outside front cover reads, "1764, 5, 6." The inside front cover contains the following lists of numerals.

	o	o	
	o	o	1765
			28
1765			22
			19
	o		16
	o		11
	o		5–30
	20		25
	o		22
	o		16
	o		11
	o		5–28
	o		24
	o		
	o		
	o		

My Dear Friend Bettsy Emlen, with her Husband—left Philada. after dinner, for Chester, intending there to embark or board the Ann, George Fortune Master for Bristol—I took leave of them at the Ferry—My Henry and Sister with Several other Friends gone with them to Chester, dont expect them home 'till Tomorrow—June the 6. 1764.

June 10: 1764. My dear HD. with Abel James, Judath Foulk, and Benn. Booth went from home—intending for Amboy &c.

HD. &c. return'd from Amboy. June the 13: 1764.

June 16: 1764, My Henry, my Sister and my dear Sall, went to Burlington after Dinner, they return'd the 18.

Our dear Nancy[4] was left at Sammy Harpers at Frankford, July 3: 1764.

July 4. took a ride this Afternoon to see our little Dear,—drank Tea at A James'.

July 10: 1764, My Henry on Horse-back, Sister, Sally and myself, in the Chaise, went to GermanTown, to Doctor Witts, for Worm-Powder for Sally, the old man sick, got the Powder of a young Man in the Shop—drank Tea with the Widdow Vanaken who I think is in a poor way—then went to Mackenetts where we put up, and than home.

4. Nancy Drinker was born on Jan. 11, 1764.

1764. My Henry and Capn. Rees, went to Burlington. July 14. After Dinner.

HD. left home early this Morning for Mary Land B Booth &c with him—R. and E. Walln here this Evening July 17. 1764.

18th. Becky James here to Day—Sister and self desin'd to have gone to see Nancy, the Mare ready in the Chaise; but rain prevented a heavey rain with wind—B Waln here this Evening.

19. Sister. self, John, and Sally, went this Morning, after breakfast, to see our little dear, call'd at Abels, came home a little after 11; I went this Afternoon to see Neighr. Levy—Sister went down Town with Sally—Betsy, and Richd. Waln here this Evening.

20th: Ironing to Day. Betsy Waln here.

21: HD. came home this Evening. Sister gone with Betsy Waln to see our Nancy; Capt. Reese sail'd to Day.

July 26: 1764. MS. ED. Sally & John, went this Afternoon, over Schuylkill, to S Whartons place came home in the Evening.

July 30, spent this Afternoon at Edge la Farm, Joshua Howells Place.—Joshua, Catty, Becky Rawle,[5] Nancy Warner; Molly Foulk, Janny Evans; Ann Hume, Sarah Fisher,—My Henry, Sister, Sall, and self—came home in the Evening.

Augt. 8: 1764. sent Benny this Morning for Nanny Harper, and our dear Nancy they spent the Day with us, went back in the Evening.

Augt. the 16. 1764, went to the Burial of Josey Sansom.

Septr. the 3: 1764. left home after dinner Seacond Day—B. Booth on Horse back & his man Robt.—HD. and ED. in the Chaise: drank tea at the red-Lyon,[6] 13 miles from Philada. lodg'd at Allexr. Browns 28 miles from Town, good Accomadations—Breakfasted there the 4th. then went to James Morgans

5. Word crossed out.

6. The Red Lion Inn was situated on the Kings Highway, later the Bristol Pike, near the border of Bucks and Philadelphia counties in Bensalem Township, Bucks County. The inn, which had been in operation since 1730 and was known as the Red Lion from at least 1759, was a popular hostelry for travelers to and from the Bristol springs (Terry A. McNealy, "The Red Lion Inn," *The Bucks County Historical Society Journal* 1, no. 6 [1974]: 1–14).

at Derham Iron-Works[7]—48 or 50 miles from home, roads very bad, stay'd there to dinner walkd to the Furnice, where we saw them at work, casting iron-barrs &c—then went to Bethelam, arrived there after Night cross'd the Lehia—very much Fateagued. lod'gd at Jasper Pains, a Publick House.

5th. Walk'd about Bethelam this Morning with Sister Garrison, view'd the many Curiosities there—din'd at Pain's, stay'd there all the Afternoon BB. HD. gone, out. Went in the Evening to Timothy Horsefields agreeable people—I was very sick there lodg'd again at Jasper Pain's.

the 6th. left Bethalam; T Horsefield and Wife, accompany'd us, to Christian-Spring, Nazareth &c—and—to Brother Culver's, where we din'd and parted with them—then proceeded to Eastown, cros'd the Ferry, rain all the rest of the Day came this Evening up a tiresome, long Hill call'd Musconetcong rain all the way—came this Evening—after rideing 30 miles very much tir'd to the Hickry Tavern, where we stay'd all Night and fair'd but poorly.

the 7th. road 9 miles for our Breakfast to one Lipincuts, 15 miles farther for Dinner—then went towards Brumswick, where we arriv'd time enough for Tea at Brook Farmers—roads very good—slep't at B Farmers.

8th. HD. and BB. went done into the mine—came back to Breakfast, I went with them afterwards to examine the mine above—walk'd to the end of the mile run, took a ride to the Stamping-Mill. 2 or 3 miles out of the Town—came back to dinner. then left Brumswick, road through Maiden-Head—KingsTown—drank Tea at Prince Town.—came to Trentown to Supper. at Pontius Stills: where we lodg'd,[8] and left next morning.

the 9th. cros'd Ferry and Breakfast'd at Bristol at one Priestlys—came to Sammy Harpers just as meeting broke up—had the satisfaction to find our dear little Nance well and to hear from home—dinn'd at Abel James at Frankford—came home in the Afternoon.

1764 October 23, sent for Nancy home to Wean, Nanny Harper came with her she stay'd all Night the child takes her weaning Extroydinary well so far.

7. The presence of iron ore in the area of Durham, Pennsylvania, was noted in the early eighteenth century. After purchases of nearly six thousand acres of land by Jeremiah Langhorne, John Chapman, and James Logan between 1715 and 1727, the tract was granted to two trustees, Griffith Owen and Samuel Powell, Jr., in March 1728. The furnace was already in operation by 1727, and from the mid-1750s to shortly before the Drinkers' visit, George Taylor (a signer of the Declaration of Independence) directed the works. The Durham Iron Company was partitioned and sold in 1773, and early in 1774 Taylor returned to Durham to lease the ironworks from its new owner, Joseph Galloway (McNealy, *Bucks County*, 101–2).

8. The words "and Breakfast'd the 9th then left Trentown" crossed out.

1764 Octor. 29 Phebe Morris came to Work—stay'd 11 Days.

1764 Novr. 11 HD. with John Parrock left home after Dinner first Day—going near 30 miles into the Jerseys. expect him home To-morrow—Becky James here this Evening. HD. came home the 12 in the Evening.

Novr. 21. 1764 ED. was let Blood.

1765

HD. MS. myself and both our little ones went in a Sleigh to Frankford stop'd at Nanny Harpers, who was gone abroad then went to Widdow Cummins, stayd a short time, came home to Tea. Janry. the 8. 1765.

Febry. 5. 1765. the Carcase of an Ox or Cow, was this Day roasted on the River, which has been fast 5 Weeks past and seems likely to continue so 5 Weeks to come, this being a remarkable hard Winter. the river open'd the 17 Instant Feby.

Febry. 9. 1765. HD. J. Parrock and some others, left home this Morning for Marcus-Hook;—expect him home tomorrow—return'd the 10.

Febry. the 22. Samuel Mickel Buried 1765.

Rachel Pemberton departed this Life Febry. 24. 1765.

Sally Drinker went first to School April the 8. 1765, to Becky Jones, and Hannah Cathrall.

1765 May 23 ma tres Chere, and Sister with Sally, went to Burlinton this Morning—Molly Moore with me, Abel James here invited me with them to Frankford, I could not go,—HD. &c came home the 26.

Sally Pemberton married June 27. 1765.

June 12. 1765 Came to Frankford, all except BJ, in the Evening, fourth Day.

13th. HD. and B Booth set of early this morning for Brumswick, sally unwell with a sore Throat; hope the Country air may be of service; Abel James call'd this Evening; Sally bad with a vomiting and Purgeing.

14 Sallys hand brused with the Door, nobody here to Day.

15. HD. and BB. return'd from[1] Brumswick, they din'd with me, and went to Town after Dinner. HD. came back in the Evening.

1. The word "[Frank]" crossed out.

16 First Day HD. MS. went to Meeting Molly Moore came home with them. she now stays at Frankford with B——y James who is in a poor state of Health. Abel Booth and Patty came in the Afternoon; our Benny and Billy, here. they all went away in the Evening.

17 HD. MS, John and Hannah went this Morning to Town—so that I have none with me at Present but Agnis and my three Children.[2] Sally, who has been unwell several days past, grew worse this Afternoon, Complains of her Throat, and has a Fever, which increas'd as night came on. I sent to AJs for Nurse who did not come till 11 o'clock.—A James and Patty Accompanied her. the Child bad all night, vomited, freaquently—this has been a tedious long and anxious Day.

18 Sister, John and Hannah came this Morning; Nurse went away before Dinner; MS, John and Hannah went to Town after dinner and took my dear sick Child with them, and now I seem in a manner forsaken: my dear Henry engag'd in Town geting Roberson away—Booths Man Robart came this Evening informing that, there was no reason but to think Sally was better, which seems a mesage calcalated to make me easy—but misses having that effect.

19 waited impatiently this Morning to hear from Town—HD. came in the Afternoon with whome I return'd shuting up the House at Frankford. took Nancy and Polly in the Chaise with us; Agnis walk'd to Town—where we found the Child ill; she had just taken a vomitt, grew worse towards Evening.

20 Sally so bad this Morning that we thought it best to consult Docter Evans, who with Docr. Redman, who before attended her, concluded in the Evening to clap on a Blister,[3] and a large one it was, which we laid on her back, Betsy Jervis sat up with us.

21st. Sally continues much the same. the Blister drawn and runs finely. her disorder the Doctors calls an Apthea Fever,[4] something of the nature of the Melignent sore Throat—her Mouth having several soars in it: she continued

2. Mary Drinker was born on April 20, 1765.

3. A substance applied to the skin to stimulate and promote redness and inflammation and eventually to produce a discharge. Bringing an inflammation to the surface of the skin was thought to have beneficial effects in a variety of illnesses and conditions including fevers, smallpox, measles, hemorrhages, diarrhea, and kidney and bladder problems. One of the most widely used substances in eighteenth-century blisters were cantharides, or Spanish flies (Parr, *London Medical Dictionary*, 254–55).

4. *Apthae* was the term used to describe white inflammations and ulcers of the mucous membranes in the throat. *Apthae* or *aptha fever* was most often used to describe the illness still called thrush, but was sometimes used to denote other common childhood illnesses involving the throat, such as diphtheria (Skinner, *Medical Terms*, 35–36).

bad for several days, when the disorder took a turn for the better: and on the 30 Instant we came back to Frankford: First Day. afternoon.

July 1. HD. and John went this Morning to Town, left Sister and Sally with us. Docter Redman din'd with us: HD—return'd in the Evening, inform'd us, that Becky James (who is now in Town) was this morning deliverd of two Sons, who, as she was not near her time, expired soon after their Birth, and that she was as well as could be expected.

2 HD. MS. Sally, John and Hannah, left me this Morning after breakfast. so that my Family is again reduced to myself, Agnis, and my two little ones. Nancy very poorly all the Morning with a bad lax. she was taken, before we left Town with a vomiting and Purging—the former went of, but the latter continues, she cuts her Teeth with more difficultey then some Children; she seems better this Afternoon—the Widdow Commins and Lizey Ashbridge drank Tea with me—HD. came up this Evening.

3 HD. went to Town this Morning—Nancy unwell till after dinner then grew better—John came this Afternoon for the Cart returnd with the Little Bed and bedstead, he stay'd all Night.

4 up last night with Nancy who was very unwell, myself also, John went to Town this Morning; he came back in the Afternoon with Sister, and Phebe Morris, who came to fit a Body Linning for me, Sister took Nancy to ride, the child very unwell—she intends to stay with me to Night, HD. in Town.

5; Sister and Sally went to Town after dinner, came back in the Evening HD. with them, stay'd all Night—Nancy took Rheubarb.[5]

6 HD. MS. went to Town after Breakfast. came back this Afternoon stay'd all Night.

7 First Day: HD. MS, gone to Meeting—J Foulk and B Booth call'd while they were gone:—dinn'd alone only Benny—I mean our own Family. Stephen Collins and John Drinker with little Henry, spent this Afternoon here, Abel James & Isaiah Worrel call'd—HD and my self took a ride this Morning with our little Nance, who continues unwell, we went up Busbys road, where I had never been before. were HD. MS. constantly here Frankford would be very agreeable to me.

5. Rhubarb was used in the Drinker household for constipation and indigestion. According to one contemporary manual, rhubarb helped purge the stomach, but was also "celebrated for its astringent [quality] by which it strengthens the tone of the stomach and intestines, and proves useful in diarrhorea and disorders proceeding from a laxity of fibers" (C. K. Drinker, *Not So Long Ago*, 9; W. Lewis, *New Dispensatory*, 210).

8 took a ride this morning after Breakfast. with the Children; after which HD. and MS. went to Town.—when Hannah and Sally's here my Family seems large, HD. MS. came back in the Evening.

9 Robart Waln and Wife and little Son came here this Morning, and Abel James—Robart, Abel and HD went to the Burial of Robart Harper, Sister and Sally went to meeting. Becky Waln stay'd with me untill they came back—AJ. stay'd dinner with us, then went to Town with my Henry:—Sister gave the Children a little Airing in the Chaise this Afternoon—Nancy continues poorly, which with the care of 2 Houses, occasions us a good deal of Trouble.

10. Sister, Sally, Hannah and John went to Town, early this Morning:—John came back in the Evening, with a letter from his master, and is to stay all night, Nancy still poorly.

11 John went to Town this Morning—HD. Sally and John came up this Evening: Nany Harper here: Weather very Sultry.

12 HD. and myself took a ride with Nancy this morning, after Breakfast. he then went to Town with Sally and John: Peggy Parr and her two Daughters spent this Afternoon with me—I expect to be alone to Night: as it is now late and nobody come—HD. came unexpectedly at 10 o'clock.

13 HD. went to Town this Morning he came back in the Evening, with Sister, Sally, John. and Hannah.

14 First Day: HD. and MS went to meeting. Isaac Stroud and Suckey James din'd with us. Abel James came in the Afternoon in his Waggon; HD. Sister, Sally, Nancy, and Hannah went with him to Billy Parrs; Isaac drank Tea with me—our People came home in the Evening—a great Gust of wind and thunder this Evening.

15 HD. &c gone to Town this Morning Phebe Morris here this Afternoon fitting a Gown for me, Molly Worrel with Sitgreaves's Baby who she Nurses, were also here: HD. came towards Evening.

16 HD. went to Town early this Morning Phebe with him: she is I expect at Work at our House for Sister: John came by himself this Evening to my great disapointment, many and various, are the Occasions, that will communicate Sorrow to a Susseptable mind.

17 John went to Town this Morning Sister, Patty James, Becky and my Sall, came this Evening, HD. came after them, Hannah and John also so that we

have our Family togeather in the midel of the Week, which is not common, Patty Becky went away after Tea.

18 HD. went to Town Solas this Morning leaving Sister &c with me; he came up again this Afternoon, B Booth with him, they went Fishing: Nany Harper here—HD. BB. came back to Tea: Abel James, Capt Rose, Capt. Rees, and John Parrock here this Afternoon, they went away soon—how exceeding agreeable the Country is when we are all togeather.

19 HD. MS, SD. John and Hannah went to Town this Morning, the Weather is very warm: I alone all Day, which is not very uncommon: John came up this Evening with Sundrys for me sent by my provident Friends in Town, I should have been pleased to have seen my HD. to Night.

20 John went to Town this Morning. Molly Brown, and Betsy Waln came this afternoon little Joe with them HD. MS. and John came after—MB. EW. went away in the Evening.

21 First Day—HD. MS. and Sally went to Meeting this Morning: Ben came up I went this Evening with my Henry and Nancy to A James's to see Becky who is well enough recover'd to come again to Frankford; we took a little ride towards point, and so home.

22 I went to Town this Morning with HD. and my little Polly: took John and Hannah with me: I have not been in Town before this 3 Weeks. we came back again in the Evening. Nancy very poorly, her mouth sore.

23 HD. MS. gone to Town this Morning they came back in the Evening. Sally rejoyce'd to see them.

24 My Henry went to Town this Morning John with him: Sister and Sally with me, Nancy better: HD. in Town to Night.

25 Sister: Sally, John & Hannah, went to Town this Morning. John unwell—I rec'd a noat this Afternoon, from HD. informing that he could not come up, and that John was gone to Bed; so that I expect no one from Town to Night.—We have had 3 days cloudy weather: this last seems long and lonely, to me.

26 HD. came up this Evening.

27 He went to Town this Morning, came back in the Afternoon with B Booth, they went Fishing; Sister, Sally, Hannah and John came up in AJs. Waggon; B Both sup'd with us.

28 First Day: HD. MS. gone to Meeting. Sarah Morris preach'd and pray'd, She, Mary Armitt, and Caleb Crisson dined with us, they went in the Afternoon to Abels—HD. ED. and Nancy took a ride[6] as far as Oxford Church.

29 HD. MS. SD. and John gone to Town this Morning, left Hannah with us, My Henry came up this Evening.

30 HD. gone to Town this Morning: Sister and Sally. Sally Wharton and her Son Dicky came before 11 o'clock. they spent the Day with me; wint home in the Evening: I took a run to the end of the lane at 9 o'clock to look for my best beloved; but saw him not: as the Moon shone bright, I was in hopes it would induce him to come; tho late.

31 I took a walk this forenoon to S Harpers; Nanny came here this Afternoon:—HD. MS. &c came up this Afternoon stay'd all Night.

Augt. 1. HD. went to Town this Morning Sister stay'd with me all Day, we took a walk in the Afternoon all of us.—found HD. on our return home.

2 HD. MS. &c went to Town this Morning; Henry came up again in the Evening:—we have had a remarkable dry time, no expectations of a seacond Crop—our three Children at present, thr'o mercy, in[7] tolerable good health.

3 HD. went to Town this Morning. came up again before dinner, with MS. and Sally: Booth and Capt. Rose, din'd with us, they went Fishing after dinner; We took a walk this Afternoon to S Harpers. Nanny came to Tea with us:—HD. sup'd at Cummins,—Weather warm.

4 First Day: HD. MS. and Sally, gone to Buybarry: Benny the only one that din'd with me: John Drinker and Stephen Collins spent this Afternoon with me—little Hannah Drinker with them—our Foulk came home, after they were gone—they din'd at Gilles Knights.

5 HD. MS. &c gone to Town this Morn'g it began to rain at about 10 o'clock; and seems signs of a good quantity—John came up this Evening—it has left of raining, but continues Cloudy.

6 Saw no Coumpany: Stay'd at home all Day: indeed its very rarely that I go from home—HD. came up this Evening.

7 HD. went to Town this Morning: he came back in the Evening.

6. The word "to" crossed out.
7. The word "pritty" crossed out.

8 HD. went to Town this Morning. Sister, Sally and John came here to dinner and intend to Stay all Night. HD. stays in Town, a pritty shower of rain.

9 Sister here all Day. HD. came up this Afternoon, he went with me and Nancy, to take a ride, towards the river-side, came home to Tea.

10 HD. Sister and John, went to Town this Morning: I expect them back before Night: they return'd this Evening.

11 First Day: rain'd all last Night, a heavy rain. HD. gone to Meeting this Morning no Coumpany at Dinner—Abel James and Booth here in the Afternoon—they say that the rain has done considerable damage in Town: tore up the pavement in some places and spoiled goods, that were in Cellers in Market-Street.

12 HD. MS. Sally and John, gone to Town this Morning, it is pleasently clear'd up: MS, Sally and John came back in the Evening; [they] found me and the Children at Nany Harpers.

13 they went this Morning to Town HD. stay'd in Town last Night. he came up this Evening. Nanny Harper here:—William Plumsted was Burried; Yesterday, he dyed the day before, of a Mortification in his[8] Head.

14 HD. went to Town this Morning: Sister, &c came up this Afternoon intending to stay till sixth Day morning—I dont expect my Hy to Night.—we went this Evening tout ensemble to see Nanny Harper.[9]

15 Sally fell this Morning against a Tub. and cut the back part of her Head. and I am afraid she has fractur'd the Bone—we stop'd the Blood with Turlington;[10]—HD. came this Evening.

16 HD. MS. and Sally gone to Town. Becky James call'd on me this Morning took a ride with her in the Waggon came home by 10 o'clock.—Nancy very

8. The word "Neck" crossed out.

9. The words "s little" crossed out.

10. A British patent medicine, Turlington's Balsam, patented in 1744 by Robert Turlington. Its maker claimed it would cure kidney and bladder stones, colic, and inward weaknesses. The ingredients used in the preparation, a compound tincture of benzoin, had entered into European pharmaceutical practice in the seventeenth century. Similar, if not patented, medications in the pharmacopeia of the time were Traumatic Balsam, Jesuit Drops, and Commander's Balsam. The Drinkers were using it externally to clean and heal a wound (Griffenhagen and Young, "Patent Medicines," 160–61; La Wall, *Pharmarcy*, 414, 282; W. Lewis, *New Dispensatory*, 323–24).

unwell to Day. found several little worms in her Clout[11] about the Eighth of an inch long: went after dinner to Abel James's in hopes of sending word to Town; but as nobody was going from thence I soon return'd: mett Sister &c just by Cummins, got in the Chaise, and rode home.[12] HD. stay'd in Town all Night—took a ride with Nancy this afternoon.

17 Sister went to Town this Morning to speak to the Doctor, as Nancy was very unwell all night. She came back in the Evening HD. with her—the Child all day in a high fever.

18th. First Day: HD. and Sammy Sansom went to Meeting this Morning Sammy spent the Day with us. our dear little Nancy very poorly—she takes powders:—rain this Evening.

19. HD. gone to Town this Morning He came up early in the Evening brought stuff from the Doctor for our dear little Nance: the Weather is now exceeding Pleasent.

20 HD. and John went to Town this Morning:—We gave Nancy a Clyster,[13] composed of Worm-wood, and Tansey,[14] made into a strong Tea; to a Gill of it: put a table Spoon full of Lynseed Oyl,[15] and a little Venice-Treacle;[16]—it is gave with a design of killing the little Worms, that she is troubled with; which

11. *Clout*, a word deriving from Old English, had many meanings, all related to a small piece of cloth or a patch. It could mean a handkerchief, a diaper, a bandage, or a sanitary napkin (*OED*; Farmer, *Slang and Its Analogues*, 2:129).

12. Words crossed out.

13. *Clysters, glysters, lavements*, and *injections* are terms used in the diary to refer to enemas, or more technically, rectal injections for therapeutic or nutritive purposes. There were many types of glysters in use in the eighteenth century, the more common ones including a starch glyster made of starch and linseed oil, opiate glysters made of liquid laudanum, common glysters made with chamomile flowers, and simple glysters made with warm water. Because they purged the intestines of their contents, glysters were often used to treat cases of flux and dysentery. They were also a useful way of introducing a medication, such as cinchona bark, into the body of a person unable to swallow an oral dose (Gould, *Dictionary of Medicine*; W. Lewis, *New Dispensatory*, 618–20, 289; Buchan, *Domestic Medicine* [1799], 445).

14. Wormwood and tansy, perennial plants flowering in August, are noted for their bitter taste. Both were used singly or in conjunction to expel worms from the intestinal tract. Wormwood was also considered a tonic (Thacher, *New American Dispensatory*, 156, 356; R. Eglesfeld Griffith, *A Universal Formulary: Containing the Methods of Preparing and Administering Officinal and Other Medicines, The Whole Adapted to Physicians and Pharmaceutists* [Philadelphia: Blanchard & Lea, 1850], 397).

15. Linseed oil, cold-drawn oil from the flax or linen plant, was a popular remedy for both chest and stomach disorders. It could be administered by mouth or in glysters (Blackwell, *Curious Herbal*, vol. 1, plate 160).

16. Venice treacle was typical of the elaborate preparations popular in the seventeenth century but not as widely used in the eighteenth. Among its ingredients (fifty-five to sixty in all) were alcohol, opium, honey, and squill (J. Worth Estes, "John Jones' *Mysteries of Opium Reveal'd* [1701]: Key to Historical Opiates," *JHMAS* 39 [1984]: 204, 206; W. Lewis, *New Dispensatory*, 582–92).

the Doctor says, are a sort, that always lay at the lower part of the Bowels—HD. returnd in the Evening.

21 MS. and John went to Town this Morning: they came back early in the Afternoon: went rideing with Nancy. Doctor Redman; Sammy and Polly Pleasents drank Tea with us—HD. came up, after they were gone.

22 HD. went to Town this Morning. little Becky James, Polly and Betts Foulk, here in the Afternoon; HD came in the Evening; repeatd the Clyster.

23 HD. gone to Town this Morning he intends to stay[17] there all Night. John came up this Evening.

24 MS. and John went to Town this Morning: came back in the Evening HD. with them: dull Weather.

25. First Day: No Coumpany here to Day: I went to Meeting this Morning with HD. took a ride this Afternoon with Nancy, as far as Hugh Robartss who is building a large New House at Point no Point, call'd as we came back at Abel James; Giles Knight and several others there, came home to Tea—Rich'd Waln call'd.

26 Clean'd House this Morning—Anna Warner Senr. Becky Rawle and little Peggy—Joshua Baldwin, his Wife and four of their Children, drank tea with us—they went away towards Evening:—HD. and John came up in the afternoon, they went to Town this Morning as usual Sister has stay'd with me Several Days past as the Children has been unwell, I hope they are gitting better.

27 HD. and John went to Town—they came back in the Evening—Nanny Harper here.

28 HD. MS. and John went to Town, MS. John came back in the Evening, they gave the Children a little Airing. Daniel Drinker buryed his little Daughter Sally this Afternoon. She died of the Small Pox—I dont expect to see HD. untill sixth Day.

29 We stay'd at home, saw no Coumpany till towards Evening. we went after John came up to Abel Jamess: John draw'd the Children in the little Coach. Sister and self walk'd.

30 HD. went to Town:—Becky James Patty and little Becky, spent this

17. Word crossed out.

Afternoon with us: HD. came home towards Evening and went back with them.

31 HD. MS. &c went to Town this Morning: they did not return till after Night—3 Men were executed at Burlinton the 28. Instant for Threft.[18]

Sept. 1 First Day: Fine Weather. I went to Meeting this Morning with HD.: he left us after Dinner and sit out for Burlington, intends for home tomorrow Evening: Benn. Booth call'd this Evening—A Country Man, sup'd here last Night who came from our place near NewCastle, and inform'd that some one had taken undue possesion of it.

2 Sister, Sally and John went to Town this Morning: they return'd in the Afternoon; Sammy and Hannah Sansom with little Billy here—HD. return'd from Burdington before Tea time.

3 HD. went to Town with John. We took a walk to Caty Boozers, to Nanny Harpers &c. came home to Tea: the Weather very Hott—HD. return'd in the Evening.

4 HD. and MS. &c went to Town this Morning: Sister and John came up after Dinner; I gave Nancy a little Airing: then went to J. Robart's to buy silk; call'd at S. Harpers, came home to Tea: our children all bravely—HD. in town all Night.

5 Dull rainy weather or rather misty—HD. came up this Evening.

6 HD. went to Town this Morning—Samuel Sansom Senr. and Wife, Richd Waln, Wife and 2 Children, spent this Afternoon with us—signs of a Thunder Gust this Evening; which occasion'd Benjamin Levy and wife to take shelter with us. They stay'd supper—H.D. came up as usual—weather very warm.

7 HD. MS. and John went to Town this Morning—they came back in the Afternoon.

8 First Day: HD. MS. and Sally went to Meeting this Morning—Sucky and Abey here at Dinner. Stephen Collins and John Drinker spent this Afternoon with us—they walk'd to Frankford. little Henry with them.

18. Three men had broken into the home of Joseph Burr in Burlington County on July 18 and robbed him at gunpoint. The men, John Johnston, John Maguire, and John Fagen, were captured and later tried on Aug. 20; they were convicted, sentenced, and eventually hanged on Aug. 28 (*Pa. Gaz.*, July 25, Aug. 22, Sept. 5, 1765).

9 HD. went to Town this Morning dont expect him back till tomorrow Afternoon, when he comes for me. Sister gone this Afternoon to see the Widdow Cummins who has been very unwell; she call'd at Billy Ashbrige's Lizey came home with her. Nany Harper here this Afternoon to take leave of Nancy; as we are praparring for home: Sammy and Hannah Sansom call'd here, on their return from Burlington: they and Lizey Ashbrige drank Tea with us. John brought up this Evening a Bantam Cock and Hen: which were sent me, by Pearson Parvines Wife from Barbadoes.

10 MS. SD, AD. John and Hannah went to Town this Morning: HD. came for me and little Polly after Dinner. I went over to see the Widdow McVough who is unwel, came soon back, and between 3 and 4 o'clock bid Adieu to Frankford for a Season.

Deborah Howel (formerly Fred) departed this life Octor. the 1765, at Chester.

Decr. the 6. 1765 Sally was taken ill of a Plurisy was atten'd by Redman and Evans,—was let Blood the 8, and Afterwards grew better.

Decemr. the 16. 1765, began to Physick Nancy and Polly in order for Innoculation. 16 a Dose to Purge, 17 a Pill 18 a Pill 19 ditto 20 ditto 21 a Purge 22 a Pill 23 ditto 24 ditto 25 ditto 26 they were Innoculated by [J.] Redman, Docr. Evans Present: took Nothing that Day, 27 took nothing 28, took a Pill, 29 a Purge 30 at night or 31 in the morning Nancy grew Feverish and unwell which seems very early her Leg has been sore ever since she took the infection, 31 they took cooling Powders, twice.

1766

Janry. 1. 1766 they took Powders, Nancy continues unwell, Polly not yet Sicken'd.

the 2d Small Pox coming out on Nancy.

the 3 Polly sicken'd at Night.

4,5,6, Nancy very few 8 or 10, which seems as if they would come to Nothing—Polly has numbers which I belive will fill—the 10, gave Nancy a dose of Phisick; her Leg sore, Polleys, not at all sore the 12 gave Polly a dose, the 13 gave Nancy a Seacond dose; the Children came down Stairs—they took a third dose of Physick, but were afterwards troubled with breakings-out.

Janry. 22. 1766 my Henry, and B Booth, left home after Breakfast, designing for Virginia &c, the Weather very cool. John Drinker call'd this Morning my Sally very poorly this Afternoon, of a Fever and Vomiting; Becky James here this Evening; Abel went over the Ferry this Morning with HD. &c.

23 sent last Night for the Doctor to Sally whose Vomiting continued all Night, she seems better this Morning, took a Vomit this afternoon, and in the Evening was much mended. R. Warsams Wife, Becky James, and [J] Redman call'd, Peggy Parr spent this Afternoon with us.

24, my little Poll very much broke out like the small Pox—Sally better—Nancy broke out—Becky James, Betsy Waln, [J] Redman, call'd this Morning—Received a Letter from Sammy Harper informing that Nanny had got the Small Pox; Becky James, and Sister went to Frankford to see her, found her bad: they return'd to Tea; snow this Afternoon, weather raw and cold.

25 the Children very fretful with their sores. Sally better; Becky James here this Afternoon Johns Foot Scalded.

26 First Day: Abel James here, This morning: Hannah Jones spent the Afternoon with us, Becky James, and Betsy Waln Here in the Evening:—fine Weather.

27. John Drinker, Molly Brookhouse call'd:—Pollys Face and Ears worse, and very troublesom, Johns Foot bad.—fine Weather for Travelers.

28th. R Warsam here this Morning, Peggy Parr, spent this Afternoon with us, Billy came in the Evening. they stay'd supper warm weather for the Season.

29 Becky James this Morning call'd—Sister and Sally went with her this Afternoon to Frankford in the Waggon, Betsy Waln here in the Evening—Sister gone to By. Rawles: Pollys Face very sore;—pleasent warm Weather.

30. Abel James gone to Bybarry this Morning with Giles Knight, whose Wife die'd suddenly last Night: Mary Armitt spent the Afternoon with us.

1766 Janry. 31. the humour in Pollys Face and Ears,[1] very troublesom, Betsy Waln here this Evening. Doctr. Redman call'd.—Abels Family gone to Bybarry in order to be at the Burial tomorrow—Cloudy this Evening.

Febry. 1. busy Ironing Peggy here—R Warsam's Wife drank tea with us. Charlott and Henny here in the Evening: a fine Clear day, but overcast this Evening no account yet from HD.

2 First Day. Sister at Meeting twice—Betsy Waln here this Evening—John Drinker call'd after Dinner.

3 Elferth's Boy. came this morning to tell us of the death of Nanny Harper who dyed last night—Hannah Jones, and Nancy Mitchel, Sally Parrish and little Nancy Parrish spent this Afternoon with us. My dear little Nancy was taken this Afternoon with a Fever;—wrote this Evening to HD. the weather clear and cool—Abels Family came today from Bybarry where they have been since sixth day last.

4 the Children all better to Day—Docr. Redman call'd; Received a Letter this Evening from my dear Henry. rain this Evening after a long series of fine Weather.

5 Docr. Evans, Chart. Warsam, and John Drinker call'd this Morning; Abel James, Betsy Waln after Dinner, Aunt Jervis, Betsy and Polly spent this Afternoon with us. B. Waln here in the Evening: very fine Weather.

1. Some kind of swelling involving fluids. The Greek humoral theory underwent changes in the late seventeenth and early eighteenth centuries; following the work of Hermann Boerhave, a Dutch physician in the first half of the eighteenth century, *humors* came to mean the various fluids in the living human body (King, *Medical World of the Eighteenth Century*, 59–83).

6 Abel James call'd before dinner, I went with him, his Wife and Daughters in the Waggon to Frankford this Afternoon—Cloudy Weather Nancy took Physick.

7 Nancy unwell and Feverish, John Drinker Docr. Redman, and Becky James call'd.

8 My dear Nancy very unwell, Abel James call'd: cloudy Weather Polly took Physick.

9 First Day Nancy seems to have lost her appetite; Fever and disorder in her Bowels continues; sister at meeting, Becky Rawle and little Anna, and Samy Sansom, drank Tea with us. Weather unseatled.

10 Nancy continues very poorly, Docr. Redman call'd, Betsy and Polly Jervis spent the Day with us, Peggy Parr the Afternoon, cloudy Weather.

11 R Warsams Wife here this Morning—Sally Morris, and Benjan. Trotter call'd—Docr. Redman call'd: Betsy Jervis spent the Afternoon here; Betsy Waln, and Molly Brown here in the Evening, very fine Weather Nancy exceeding poorly.

12 Nancy better. Received a letter from my Henry, by one Mosley, very fine Weather.

13 the Children Indifferently well, Abel James call'd,—sent Benny after dinner to Chester (after a Person, who tis probable may meet my Henry) with Letters for him. Ben. return'd in the Evening: Betsy Waln, Edey Devenshire here—the Weather very fine.

14 took a Walk with Sally this Afternoon to Billy Parrs, call'd at Warsams, and at A Warners. Betsy Parker din'd with us, John Drinker and Docr. Redman call'd this Evening. Sammy and Hannah Sansom spent the Evening and sup'd with us, A James gone to Burlington with Patty, Warsams Girls &c his wife at Bybarry—the Weather exceedingly Pleasent.

15. Peggy Parr spent this Afternoon with us. Phebe Morris call'd,—the Wind very high from the North-East with rain.

16 First Day. Sister twice at Meeting—Betsy Waln here, in the Evening, cold Weather.

17 Docr. Redman and John Drinker call'd. Paggy Parr call'd, Becky James

and Becky Waln here in the Evening—little Jessy Harper, bury'd, Yesterday he dyed of the Small Pox—Snow to Day.

18. Sister went to Meeting this Morning Nancy much Better, cold Weather.

19 Peggy Parr spent the Afternoon with us—my Nancy again unwell, disordred in her Bowels and Feverish—the Weather very cold.

20 Nancy poorly. Fine Weather, R Warsams Wife and John Drinker, calld.

21 Nancy a little Better, Betty Waln, and Danl. Drinker call'd this Evening. fine Weather.

22 took a Walk this Morning, with Sister, Sally, Nancy, and Hannah; call'd at W Parrs, at Uncle Jerviss, at S Pleasents, and at A Warners—came home before dinner,—the Prince-George sail'd after dinner, Capt. Roberson call'd to bid us farewell; I step'd into Wallns—Becky James here this Afternoon, My Nancy still unwell—Weather very fine—A Melloncally accident happ'n'd this Morning at Arch-Street Warf—a Shallop took fire, in which was a Young Man, suppos'd to be asleep, who was burn't to death.

23 First Day. Sister went to Meeting twice—Abel James, John Drinker, and Betsy Walln call'd: rain this Afternoon.

24 Fine Weather, the Children indifferent.

25 Danl. Drinker here this morning to fastning up the Book-Case, John Drinker call'd, Peggy Parr spent the Afternoon, she and S Sansom sup'd with us, Cold raw Weather.

1766 Febry. 26, in the front Parlour to Day Charlott Warsam here this Evening—I step'd into R Wallns, [hazey] Weather.

27 Abel James, Josey Drinker call'd, Polly taken with a Vomitting last night, unwell all Day to Day: good Weather—Nancys Leg heal'd 3 or 4 Days past, Abel rec'd a Letter from HD, Newburn, dated 13 Instant.

27[2] good Weather.

28 Charles Jervis Married last Night to Betsy Boore;—My Henry return'd home this Evening.

2. Word crossed out.

1766. March 15. HD. left home after dinner, cross'd the river, designs for Mount-Holly, MP. sup'd with us.

16 First Day: step'd into Walns with Sally to see their little Polly, who has the Small Pox—cloudy Weather.

17 very stormy all the fore part of the Day, Samy Sansom spent the Evening with us—I expect'd HD home to Day, but the Weathers bad.

[18] HD came home 18.

began to wean my Polly, April 21. 1766 she being a Year and day old, not one Tooth bears weaning extrodinary well—she cut her first tooth July 1 or 2d., being 14 months and 11 or 12 days old, 4 or 5 days before she dyed[3]—could almost go alone, and speak many Words very plain.

Nancy Drinker's first Tooth was perceiv'd Octor. 29. 1764. she being betwixt 9 and 10 Months old, and weaning, which she bears very well.—she went alone at 16 months—she began to talk prittily at 17 months.

21st May.[4] Sally began her Seacond Quarter at School—August 12. 1765.

sent for [J] Redman to Nancy Sepr. the 28 1765 as we think tis the bloody flux she has—prov'd to be a Teething disorder—Sally went to School March the 31. 1766 13 Gammons April 25

	1 Gammon
March 26	1 Ditto
April 25	1 Ditto

Febry 3—2 [ ][5]
Janry 27—3 [ ]
febry. 3—4 [ ]
12—6 [ ]
20—6 [ ]

21.

3. Mary Drinker died on July 7, 1766.

4. The entries beginning "21st. May" and ending "1 ditto" appear on the inside back cover of the manuscript volume.

5. The manuscript volume for Apr. 27, 1766–Aug. 7, 1768, has two-tone blue floral covers. The outside front cover reads, "1766, 7, 8"; inside the front cover are various numerals and calculations, including the following lists.

2/ 2/ 4
3/ 7/ 3
4/ 9/ 6
2/15/ 2
2/ 9/ 0
3/18/ 3
4/13/11
——————
23/15/ 5

John Drinkers Daughter Nancy was bury'd, April the 27. 1766.

Hannah Shoemaker our Neighbour was bury'd May the 2. 1766.

May 3. 1766. My Sall seems now upon the recovery from a bad Cold and fever took some time last week.

5 she took Physick rose [laives].[6]

May 11 1766 MS. was let Blood.

Richd Warsam dyed May the 10. 1766.

May 19 a Vessel from Pool brought the Account of the Repeal of the Stamp Act, the 20th. the Town Illuminated upon the occasion.

May the 25. HD. and MS. went to Darby, to the Burial of Sarah Fordam, who dyed of a Cancer in her Breast.

May 27. 1766. Sister gone to sit up to Night with Peggy Parr, who has been ill for 3 days past, bleeding at the Nose, & Vomitting Blood.

1766 May 31. Govenor Penn & Nancy Allen Married.

MS. and SD. went over the river with M Armitt and C Crisson to the Widdow Hopkinsons, June 21. 1766, they return'd the 23d.

June the 30. 1766, went to Frankford with my Children, Polly very unwell, she

6. Rose petals, common in many English recipe books both for cooking and sweetening and for medicinal uses, were thought to provide a refreshing, cooling quality (Hess, *Booke of Cookery*, 267–68; Blackwell, *Curious Herbal*, vol. 1, plate 73; Blake, "Compleat Housewife," 36).

has been drooping for some time past, but now grown worse, July the 1 she appear'd a little revived[7]—MS. came up this Morning with Sally.

the 2d. took her Polly about a mile to ride, which she boar very ill, but seem'd, better after, the weather being clear—the 3, MS, went to Town, cloudy weather, the Child worse.

the 4. sent John to Town for Docr. Evans who had attended her during her sickness he came up in the Afternoon found her very ill, brought 2 blisters [with] him, which we apply'd at Night to her Ancles as [she] appeard Convulsed, the 5th seventh day, the little dear worse, the blisters rose but badly—brought her to Town this Evening, not quite without hopes of her tho' they prov'd vain—the Weather bad all the while we were at Frankford, except one day—which had great effect on my little Lamb—she cut her first tooth dureing her illness, had [numbrs] in the Gums—which with the lax &c prov'd too much for her.[8]

Isaac Norris, burry'd, July 14. 1766.

Sally began a quarter Schooling—July the 14. 1766.

Ben. Trapnel went to York July 17 1766.

Becky Howell dyed July 22. 1766.

1766 Augt. the 5 came to Frankford, third-day Evening Sister, John, Agnis, the Children and myself, the 6th, My Henry, Abel James, and Patty, Charlotte and Henny Warsam came up in AJs Waggon, they, with Judah Foulk, George James, and Tommy Fisher, Breakfasted with us; I accoumpany'd them to Bristol, in order to meet B Booth and Wife—Betsy Willit whome he married at N. York about 10 days ago we came to Brister a little before them; AJ, HD, [T] F. C. and HW. went over to Burlington—they came back to Dinner to Priestlys left Bristol after dinner came to our House at Frankford to Tea; they went to Town in the Evening HD. with them BB. and Wife lodges at A James.

1766 Augt. 7 MS. Sally and John went to Town, they came back in the Evening.

8 took a ride this Morning with the Children the Weather very warm no body here to day.

7. Words crossed out.
8. Words crossed out.

9 MS. and John went to Town this Morning—HD. came up with them in the Evening.

10 First Day: took a ride with my H——y this Morning to the river side—came back a little after 7. Sister and the Children not up when we return'd: Dicky Waln stop'd, in his Way to Abington to inform us, of Jammy Smiths being very ill occasiond by drinking cold Water last Evening; HD. and MS. went to Town after Breakfast, on his Account B Booth and Wife drank tea here this Afternoon, HD. came up, he stay'd all Night.

11 HD. went to Town this Morning, John came up with our dinner—Jammy much better—saw no Coumpany to Day—HD. came up after 9 o'clock in our New Waggon—bad Accounts, of our Maid Betty.

12 HD. went to Town this Morning came back in the Evening.

13 Ditto Ditto.

14 came home from Frankford,—Jammy gone to Burlington finely recoverd.

15 B Booth and Wife Patty James, HD. and self went to our place at Frankd. in the Waggon to Breakfast came home by 10 o'clock.

1766 Augt. the 17. My HD. left home this Morning with Neddy Penington to go into the Jerseys, dont expect them home till fifth Day—this is first Day—return'd fourth Day.

Thomas Roberson dyed August 16. 1766 of a fit of the Appoplexey.

1766 Augt. 30. HD. and S Sansom left home after dinner seventh Day, for MaryLand—Daddy Swett came soon after, dined and lodg'd here, cool pleasent weather.

31 MS. and Sally went to Meeting this Morning. Sister went after dinner to A Jamess, Becky brought to Bed of her Son Tommy, B Booth and Wife drank Tea with us; Betsy Waln here in the Evening Sister and self took a walk after the Children were in Bed, as far as Uncles—to see Hannah Ward, whose Husband is sick there.

Septr. 1 Betsy Booth here this Morning—Sally and Nanny Armitt spent the Afternoon with us, I stepped in this Evening to see Becky James.

Septr. 2 Sister, Jammy, Sally, Nancy, and John went this Afternoon to

Pennyvilles—Peggy Parr drank tea here; John Startin call'd—Betsy Walln here this Evening.

3 At home as usual, Sally Armitt and B. Waln call'd—No news from my Henry.

4 Betsy Waln, Widdow Warsam and Charlotte call'd this Morning. J Drinker this Afternoon—Sister and Sally out.

5 HD. return'd.

Sally began a quarter Schooling Sepr. 30: 1766.

HD. MS. ED. SD. AD, and John, went to Glouster Point in the Waggon, cross'd the River, walk'd to the Mineral Spring, drank of the water and came home to Tea—third-Day Afternoon, Octor. 14. 1766.

Octor. the 19. HD. ED, SD, AD, Jammy, and John, went to Burlington, in the Waggon—first Day: got there to late dinner; went to Govenour Franklins[9] towards Evening.

Second Day Morning went to Dicky Wells, and George Dwylings, came on rain, dinn'd late, set of from Burlington near 3 o'clock were benighted and overset, tho through mercy none of us much hurt, Jammys wrist, and my thumb, a little strain'd did not git home till 9 o'clock.

Octor. 28 HD. gone into the Jersys: John Parrock with him; Thomas Pearsol from New York here—he came the 25—HD. return'd the 29—1766.

ED. was let Blood Novr. 9. 1766.

Novr. the 24 Sally was let Blood, and took a Vomitt, 25 she took a purge—for a bad cold, Docr. Redman tend her—the 28 the Child much better—1766.

Novr. the 26: 1766. An Irish Vessel in the river, took fire, and was consum'd.

Decr. 1 John went to School 1766.

Decr. the 1 Sally Gardner came to live with us, at 2/6 p Week—1766.

Decr. 1. 1766 Widdow Warsam went away.

Decr. 9. 1766; HD. and AJs. went to Burlington, HD, return'd in the Evening.

9. William Franklin (1731–1813), the son of Benjamin Franklin and the last royal governor of New Jersey, was named governor in 1763 (*DAB*).

1767

Janry. 13. 1767. ED. was let Blood.

John has been sick for 3 Week past, Docr. Evans, tends him, something of the Plurisy and a swelling in his Groin.

EDs Tooth drawn, Febry. 1767.

Molly Brookhouse came March 10. 1767 went away June the.

Lydia Warder was bury'd March 18. 1767.

1767 Sally and Nancy went to School April the 13.

HD. and MS. left home for Burlington seventh Day Afternoon at 4 o'clock, like for rain April 18. 1767 return'd the 19.

1767 May: Billy[1] unwell, a Cold and Fever with disordered Bowels, Docr. Redman tends him—June 4 the Child better: weather very hott.

Agnis Fergusong went away May 3. 1767.

Rosanna came June 16. 1767 at £8—p Ann.

Agnis came again June the 20. wint away [Augt.] the 2. 1767.

Went to Frankford June the 20. 1767 Billy very unwell of a purdging Agnis and Sally Gardner with me. Sister, Sally, and Rossanna in Town HD. and John here and there—Nancy and Billy with me also, seventh Day came up in AJs Waggon: Our old Mare lame, HD. stay'd all Night.

21. First Day Jammy and John came up in the Waggon. HD. and Jamey went to Meeting. Went towards Evening to give the Children an Airing. An unruley Horse in the Waggon occasion'd our gitting out, and walk to Abels

1. William Drinker was born on Jan. 28, 1767.

Place near which we were, from thence home Near Night,—Billy crying all the way, Patty and Becky with us. HD. stay'd all Night.

22 HD. went to Town this Morning Sister and John came up this Afternoon they left Sally at Abels place, not choosing to bring her here, on account of the Hooping-Cough, which numbers of Children near us is troubled with, Patricks Amoung the rest; I keep my little ones, more in the House than is Agreeable: Sister went to Town after Tea, Billy something better, the Weather warm.

23 Saml. Griscom came up before dinner with one of his Boys: he and Ish. Worrel are building a Barn for us. Saml. dined with me: My Billy still poorly, tho' I hope he is mending, fine Weather this day; no HD. to Night.

24 Sister came this Morning with John, after she had sent Sally to School, she went away before dinner, took my Nancy with her; HD. came this Afternoon Abel with him.

25 HD. went to Town this Morning took a walk this Afternoon, myself and Agnis with Billy to Ashbridges—came home before Tea, Becky James with several of her Children came in the Waggon to see me, they stay'd but a short time, a thunder Gust this Evening HD. came.

26 myself unwell for 2 Days past, Billy better, took a walk with Agnes and the Child to Neighr. McVaghs then went to look at the Barn, went up with Isah. to the top Scaffold, John here this Morning with Griscom and his Boys, HD. went to Town this Morning I dont expect him to Night.

27 HD. came up before dinner with John, the Barn rais'd this Afternoon the Workmen had a rump Befef and Gammon &c on a Table set out before the Door at 7 o'clock in the Evening, HD. stay'd to Night, John went to Town with the Carpenters; the Weather dry and Warm.

28th. First Day: Sister, Sally, Nancy Benny and John came up this Morning Patrick and Rose took their Children and spent the day in Town, least ours should take the Hooping Cough HD. went to Meeting—Sister &c went to Town in the Evening HD, stay'd with me, we took a Walk round our Place, like for rain.

29 HD. went to Town this Morning came back in the Evening Benjn. Shoemaker dyed last Week.

30 HD. went to Town this Morning, John came up with our dinner: myself, Agnis and Billy spent this Afternoon at Ables place—fine rain this Evening.

July 1. Sister and Benny came up this Morning they went away before dinner—Becky James Senr. and Patty spent this Afternoon with me. HD. and AJ. came up this Evening in our Waggon, and John. The Thunder, very hard last night in Town, it struck the Moravian House in Race-Street and damag'd it much.

2 Billy unwell to Day, the weather much cooler, Samuel and Sarah Sansom & Lizey Ashbridge spent the Afternoon with me, HD. went to Town this Morning I do not Expect him to Night.

3 HD. came this Evening our Kitchen Chimney took fire Yesterday before dinner but by the help of Isah. and his Men, it was soon put out. Cool Weather.

4 HD. went to Town this Morning Sister call'd to see me this Evening she left the Children at Abels, they came up with his Faimly—I dont expect HD. to Night.

July 5 First Day: HD. MS. Sally, Nancy and John, came up this Morning Stephen Collins, J Drinker and Son, spent the Afternoon with us, they went away in the Evening except HD—Patty and Becky James here this Evening.

6th. Ommitted.

7 Henry D went to Town this Morning one of our Neighbor Children dead of the Hooping Cough, almost all the Children in the Neighborhood bad with it mine in pretty good health, which makes me think of going to Town. HD. Sister, and Betsy Waln here this Afternoon.

8 HD. here most of the day, Sammy and Hannah Sansom spent the Afternoon with us, after they were gone, we shut up Frankford House, and came away. John, Agnis and Sally in the Cart, HD. myself and Billy in the Chair. by Norriss Woods we [mett] the Company returning from Ludys Childs burying. a Yound Fellow on a mad Colt gallop'd against our Mare, with such force as occasion'd my falling out of the Chair, having the Child in my arms, asleep,[2] in endeavouring to save the Child, I fell with all my weight on my right foot and hurt it so much that I was unabel to set it to the Ground for upwards of 3 Weeks, the Child through mercy escap'd unhurt. I have laterly mett with so many frights, that I can[3] not [bear] to think of riding with any satisfaction.

2. Three lines crossed out.
3. Word crossed out.

My very dear Friend, Betsy Emlen, departed this life, Janry. the   1767 in Bristol, Old England, leaving behind her 2 little Sons.

Nancy Drinker cut one of her little fore-Teeth, when she was, between 3 and 4 years of age.

Becky Rawle, Married Novr. 10: 1767.

1768

Charles Jones dyed, Janry. 1: 1768. Hannah came to live with us towards the end of the Month:—she went to Duck Creek, to live with her Father, April 1768.

Phebe Morris, Widdow to A Morris dyed. March, 1768.

Benjn. Trotter was bury'd March the 24: 1768.

HD. was let blood March 22, 1768.

ED. was let Blood March 23. 1768.

May 26. 1768 ED. miscarried.

B Swett Senr. went to live at New, Castle June the 1. 1768.

Janny Evans dy'd last March 1768.

Billy was weand the 6 of Febry. last 1768, cut his tooth April 14 a Jaw Tooth. he went alone at the Age of 15 months.

in the fall 1767 the Children took the Hooping-Cough, it continued some time in the Winter.

June the 3. 1768. Becky James Miscarried.

Catrine went away with Child some time last fall.

1768. July 13. HD. MS. Sally—Nancy, A. Spicer, and John, left home after dinner, for Black Point, in the Waggon—Benny has been from home some time, that our Family at present consists of but 6 persons. The Baker here this Afternoon.

14 Doctors Lad Call'd: Benny came home: Lydia Parker spent this Afternoon with me. Betsy Waln here in the Evening cool Weather.

15 John Drinker, Abel James call'd. B. Booth, & Becky James, drank Tea with me, Billy poorly: Weather cool and Cloudy.

16. Billy poorly: Docr. Redman here this Morning—Abel James also. [I.] Din'd at Abels with his Wife, Patty, C. Evans, Hide, Hazelhurst, Booth, LaMarr,—, Betsy Waln, spent part of this Afternoon with me, Patty James here,—Abel gave me a Letter this Evening from HD.[1]

17 First Day. Billy very poorly—went after Breakfast with Billy, in Abels Waggon, with his Family to Frankford: spent the Day there, Billy very tedious, came home towards Evening Docr. Redman, Molly Moore here; while I was gone.

18 took a ride this Morning with, the Child and Benny: then sent him out with Sall, Doctor here this Morning Betsy Waln, Patty James, here, Molly Moore came and stay'd all Night—Billy still poorly.

19 Nurse and Benny took Billy rideing, fine cool Morning she went away when they came back, John Drinker call'd: received a letter this Evening from HD. black Point—billy seems better; very hott this Afternoon.

20 Molly Moore came after dinner—I wrote this Afternoon to HD.—Nurse rode out this Evening with Billy.

21. I was call'd up last night between 12 and 1. by B. Waln, who made a falls alarm, came home at day break, Billy road out this Morning with Nurse—went thice into Walns to day. Becky Waln here to Night. Weather very hott Billy much better.

22 Nurse here, Patty James, Billy seems well, he road this Morning with Nurse.

23 Billy road with Nurse and Benny—Nurse, went home after Breakfast. Jammy with her; HD. &c return'd before dinner, all well.

Betsy Waln brought to Bed, with her Daughter Elizath. July 30: 1768.

July 31. 1768 Sister went to Frankford with Billy: who is very unwell, Sally Drinker, Eve, and Sally Gardner with her, I stay'd in Town, with my H——y, who is unwell with the Chills and Fever.

1. Words crossed out.

Augt. 1, Went to Frankford this Afternoon with HD. and Nancy came to Town after Tea.

2. Came to Frankford this Afternoon HD. myself and Nancy; MS went to Town with HD, here I have taken up my aboad for some time.

3 saw no body from town to Day but John, Billy better.

4 HD, came this Evening stay'd all Night hard thunder in the Night.

5 HD, went to Town this Morning Lizey Ashbridge here in the Afternoon no body from Town to Day.

6 clean'd house this Morning John Hunt Junr. here, HD. and MS. and Sally came up this Afternoon in James's Waggon, Becky James and 3 of her Children drank Tea with us, HD, MS. &c went to Town this Evening weather very hott.

7 First Day: HD. MS, Sally, John and Harry, came up after Breakfast, HD. Sister and the Children, went to Meeting. Josey Drinker, & Isaac Stroud din'd with us: Charles Jervis and Wife drank tea with us; they, sister, Sally, John and Harry went away in the Evening. HD. stay'd with me.

11111111111111

came from Frankford July the 8—HD went to the [Cap's] July the 31, return'd Augt. the 12—Abl. F[ ]fwood came Augt. 12. 1767—Green Candles Augt. 14.

HD went to Newcastle Sepr. 22, 1767.[2]

Augt. 8. 1768[3] Frankford—HD. went to Town this Morning John came up after night: rain this Afternoon.

9 A dull rainy day, nobody here—John came after night, all well at home; Billy a little better.

10 dull rainy Weather: HD. came this Evening Billy poorly.

2. The entries beginning with a series of "1"s and ending "Sepr. 22, 1767" appear on the inside back cover of the manuscript volume.

3. The manuscript volume for Aug. 8, 1768–Oct. 22, 1771, has marbelized paper covers in a pink, yellow, and aqua pattern. The outside front cover reads, "1768, 9, 1770, 1771 4d." The inside front cover contains some jottings and "March the 26. 46/12/ in the Draw[ ]. 25 Augt."

11 HD. went to Town this Morning rain almost all day, a long spell of dull weather.

12 fine clear weather, Billy bravely HD: came this afternoon, W. Hiron with him; WH. went to Town after Tea.

13 HD. went to Town this Morning Saml. and Sarah Sansom here this Afternoon, none of my Folks from town; tis a Week tomorrow, since I have seen my Sister or Sally: both our Horses Lame. John came late.

14 First Day: HD. MS. Sally John and Harry, came up; HD. Sally and ED. went to Meeting: Josey Drinker and his 2 Daughters dind with us. HD. and Sister stay'd all Night.

15 HD. MS. [went] to Town this Morning Sister came up in the Afternoon, John with her, in the rain, Robt. and Becky Waln with 2 Children here this Afternoon. Sister stay'd all Night.

16 Sister, Nancy and John, [went] to Town this Morning: John came back to dress dinner; Sally and myself went to a Meeting; appoint'd by George Mason; nobody din'd with me;—Neighr. Pollard, his wife and 2 Children, drank Tea with me; no body from Town this night. fine Weather.

17 Abel James set of this Morning he and many with him, are going beyond the Bleu-Mountains: Neighr. Sindry and R Lloyds Wife, B Booth, a Young Man with him, and HD. drank tea with me. HD. stay'd all Night—rain in the Night, Billy very naughty.

18 HD. went to Town this Morning dull weather, Sister and Nancy came up this Afternoon in Abels Waggon,—Becky James and her Children call'd for them after Tea, I expect to be alone this Night. Weather seems clear'd.

19[4] Sister and Aunt Jervis here this Afternoon they went away in the Evening HD. came up after Night.

20 HD. went to Town this Morning Billy very feverish and poorly—Sammy and Hannah Sansom spent the Afternoon with me, & two of their Children: Sister, Sally and Harry came up to stay all Night.

21 First Day: HD. came up this Morning he, myself, the Children and S

4. The sentence "HD. went to Town this Morning Billy very feverish and Poorly" crossed out.

Gardner, went to meeting, no body din'd with us: Becky James and 6 of her Children, Capt. Williams and his Wife drank tea with us.

22 HD. and Sister went to Town this Morning Sister came up after dinner with Betsy Jervis they went to Town towards Even'g, Sally with them: Sammy Sansom call'd, before dinner, he had been to Burlington to Visit Betsy Allisson, who he informs dyed last Night; my Billy better.—a Storm of Wind and thunder this Evening John came up in the midst of it.

23 Nancy and Debby Mitchel drank Tea with me, HD, came this Evening.

24 HD. went to Town this Morning—John Drinker came after Dinner. Sister and HD. and Sally came, Henry and Johny went to Point. Sister myself and the Children went to Sindries drank tea with her, HD, and Sister stay'd all Night with me. fine Weather.

25 they went to Town this Morning, sister came up this Afternoon with Polly Jervis. she took Billy to ride, they went home in the Evening my Sally with them. no body from town to Night.

26 HD. Sister and Sally; came up this Afternoon, they stay'd with me all Night. Weather very warm.

27. HD. and MS. went to Town this Morning Agnis went away. she has been with us 3 or 4 days upon a Visit. HD. and MS. came up this Evening after 9 o'clock, the Moon shone bright.

28th. First Day: John and Harry came up this Morning dinner ready provided in Town for the Boys—HD. myself and the Children wnet to meeting: B. Booth and a Lad who came with him, din'd with us—HD. went in the Afternoon to Ables. took a walk after he came home round by the Creek.

29 HD. MS. and Sally went to Town this Morning Becky James Patty and Becky Junr. drank Tea with me. John came up this Evening.

30 HD. MS. Peggy Parr and my Sally: came up this Afternoon in the Waggon, they went away after Tea. Billy bravly, myself very sick this Evening—I was taken very unwell in the Night, Billy also, with a vomitting and purging.

31 No body here to Day; billy better—HD. came up after Night.

Sepr. 1 HD. went to Town this Morning—Sister and Sally, Sally Wharton and her Daughter Becky, and Neighr. Legay, came up this Afternoon in our

Waggon, Nanny Eve, and her Daughter Sally here also—they all went home towards Evening—our Neighr. Vanderspregle, bury'd this Afternoon.

2 No body here to Day, HD. came up late this afternoon, we took Billy rideing.

3 HD. went to Town this Morning—Sister, Sally, and Benny came up this afternoon, they left Sally with me.

4 First Day: No body here to day but our own Family, from Town: Lizy Ashbridge here in the Afternoon.

5 I came home this Morning with HD—John took the Waggon up this Afternoon, Sister, the Children, Eve and Sal [Gr.] came home.

1768 Sept. 10 My Henry, and John left home after dinner, they are gone for Shihollock, very dry Weather,—Sally and Nancy, both have bad fevers, and Sally a Vomitting; Becky James, Doctor Redman here this Evening.

11 First Day. Sally very bad, Nancy [taken] again very bad this Afternoon it has turn'd out in her, a reagular intermitting fever; several here to Day.

12 Sally very ill, light head'd in the night, Sister and Betsy Jervis set up with her, Nancy better.

13. Sally and Nancy both very ill this Afternoon, high fevers and delarious; Billy but poorly.

14 this is Nancy well day as we call it; Sally was so much better this Morning as to be taken up, to have her Bed made, she was very chearfull and eat some toast and Chocolate, the fever came on towards Evening[5] and by 10 o'clock she was very ill Patty James sat up.

15 Nancy has taken 13 doses of the Bark[6] since yesterday Morning and has

5. The word "with" crossed out.

6. Medication derived from the bark of the cinchona tree, native to Peru. Also known as Peruvian bark, Jesuits' bark, red bark, and yellow bark, it is the basis for quinine, used in the treatment of malaria. First imported into Europe in 1638, it achieved swift popularity because of its efficacy in treating stubborn recurring fevers. It did not become available in the American colonies until the 1720s and then via Europe rather than South America. Sometimes European pharmacopeias included preparations made with barks of other trees in the hope they would prove as useful as cinchona (LaWall, *Pharmacy*, 283–85; Richard Harrison Shryock, *Medicine and Society in America 1660–1860* [New York: New York University Press, 1960], 48; Buchan, *Domestic Medicine* [1799], 115).

mist her fitt to Day—Sally was Chearful this Morning but in a high fever and lightheadd, in the Afternoon; several here—Abby Spicer sat up.

16 move'd Sally this Morning into my Chamber, Docr. Redman call'd on Docr. Evans, he came with him to Visit our dear little Girl; Her Fever has never intermitted but remitts;[7] she has what the Doctors call a double tourchen; every other day it comes on at about 2 or 3 o'clock and every other at 7 or 8 in the Evening—I sat up with her.

17 Nancy keeps clear of the Fitts, she continues to take the Bark; Sally very ill again this Afternoon. Polly Jervis sat up with her.

18 First day: Sally very weak and low this Day. the Doctors have given her a mixture with bark infus'd; her Fever came on this Evening with violence; she has had no Stool since fifth Day last. Sister and self sat up with her.

19 Sally fever very high no sweat to signify, very low all day, she took something to open her body, which had the desired affect, R James, sets up to Night.

20 Sally took 7 doses of the Bark to day was twice up, appeard Chearful her chill came on at 10 o'clock, it appears to be the Worst she has yet had.—Molly Moore sets up with Sister.

21 Sally took 5 doses bark this Day seem'd Chearful, eat Rye Bread and butter, and olives; the Fit came on her at 10 o'clock, was much lighter than usual.[8]

22 Sally better, she sat up longer then she has yet done, Nancy very unwell, I received a Letter from my H——y.

23. The Children through Mercy are now on the recovery; tho Sally's very weak[9] HD. came home before dinner in the rain.

1768 Octor. 1 Hannah Jones came to stay some time with us.

7. Intermittent fevers recur at short, regular periods, remittent fevers at longer, irregular periods. A fever with a three-day cycle was called tertian, one with a four-day cycle quartrain. Though the doctors labeled Sally's fever a double tertian, ED seems to describe a two-day double cycle. Sometimes called agues, some of these recurring fevers were probably various forms of malaria. Medical writers of the era such as William Buchan recognized the connection between the prevalence of these fevers and low marshy areas, stagnant water, and tropical climates. The most common form of treatment was with Peruvian bark (Buchan, *Domestic Medicine* [1799], 112–18, 150–52; Gould, *Dictionary of Medicine*, 468–69).

8. The words "Nancy, very unwell" crossed out.

9. The words "and low" crossed out.

Hannah Jones went to York Octor. 9: 1768.

1768 Octor. 12. Mary Ann Ashman went to New Castle to live with B Swett.

1768, Octor, 17. Jammy Smith has been confind with a fever for a week past. Docr. Evans tends him.—continues poorly.

Sally Drinker began to shed her teeth befor she was 7 years old.

Novr. 4 Jammy Smith continues ill—he has been 3 times let Blood, and Blister'd: Grace, his Fathers Housekeeper, came here to tend him Octor. 31—Redman visits him, with Evans.

1768 Novr. 13. went to the Burial of Danl. Drinkers little Daughter Betsy.

1768 Novr. the 17. our good Friend Sarah Sansom, departed this life.

Novr. 20 Sarah Sansom's Corps was taken to the Bank Meeting-House this Afternoon, from thence to the [Buring] Ground:—Snow all Day: HD. and Sister were at the funeral.

1768 Novr. 25. Jammy Smith after 6 Weeks illness, is so far recovr'd as to go to Burlington; Grace Bauchanan, with him, his Head is still very weak.

My dear little Nancy very unwell with a Fever &c, Evans tends her—Novr. 25, 1768.

Decr. 21. Nancy much better, she has had a tedious fever of the kind of Jammys.

1769

1769 Janry. 11. ED. was let Blood.

1769 Jarny. 21. HD. and MS. went to Germantown; roads very bad.

Janry. 24. 1769. HD. went to Frankford—bought the front Lot of Henry Paul—the Horse fell down with him coming home but through mercy he was not much hurt.

Feby 22: Hannah Jones came from N. York stay'd with us 2 or 3 days, then went to Duck Creek, for her Child whom she intends to take with her to York her father A. Hicks Dyed 2 or 3 weeks past 1769.

HD. went this Morning for Burdentown with Clem. Biddle. March 1. 1769.

H. Jones left us this Morning set of in the Stage for N. York, with [J.] Pearsel and her Son.

March 29. 1769. our dear Billy took a dose Phisick. April 2 took a Pill, the 3 a ditto the 4 a ditto the 5 a Purge, the 6th he rested, seems but week and unwell; tho' in good Spirits—the 7 sixth Day he was innoculated by Docr. Redman—took a Pill in the Afternoon: 8th took a pill—the 9 took a Pill, the 10, he rested: his Leg has been sore from the first; the 11 took a dose of phisick: which did not work him—the 12 took a pill—the 13th. he took a purge—complain'd of the head ake in the Evening.

14 a pretty high Fever, vomited in the Afternoon, tho by intervales, chearfull: 15th. fever all Day, no small pox has yet appear'd, but one on his Leg by the insesion. fever higher to Night.

16 fever all day as usual, 2 or 3 has made their appearance—17. 18. 19th. the Child pritty well tho weak; not above 8 or 10 small Pox in all, which we do not expect will fill; Leg very sore—20. 21 got a little Cold; 22 Billys cold worse—23 he took a dose phisick; 24 his cold better; he came down stairs in good Spirits. the 30th. first Day he took a dose of Phisick: seems bravly; his Leg in a good way.

1769 April the 25 My Henry gone to Burlington to the Burial of Sally Dwyling, daughter of John Smith. she dy'd in Child-Bed, of her first Child. HD. return'd the 26.

1769 April 28 ED. was let Blood.

Dinah Trotter departed this Life May 11. 1769.

May 17. 1769. ED. was let Blood.

June 14. 1769. our dear Billy was taken with a disorder like the Hives,[1] sent for Docr. Redman late at night.

the 15 very ill, was let Blood, and vomitted, Docr. Evans call'd in.

16 he was much better,—many Children in Town taken down with the same disorder, Numbers ill of a sore throat which has taken of several.

June the 21. 1769. HD. and Abel James set of for Shilock;—1769.

June 22. 1769. Harry taken with the disorder like the Hives, with some thing of a sore Throat, Docr. Evans tends him, he was let Blood this Morning.

June 24. 1769, Harry took Physick Rachel took Physick she is better,—Eve was let Blood, very poorly—my Nancy taken ill this Afternoon with a high Fever, and Vomiting sent for Docr. Evans, he tends all.—the Weather very hot.

25 First Day, The weather very hott our Family very unwell;—ED. was taken at 11 at Night with the Collick and Cramp in the Bowels and Stomach to such a degree that at 2 in the Morning we were oblig'd to send for Docr. Redman who administered an anodyne Pill[2] and Mixture of the same Nature, which Lull'd the pain by day brack—the disorder was accompanyed with a violent lax and vomiting insomuch that in 2 or 3 hours I was unable to stand on my feet or hold up my head.

26 lay all day under the effects of the Anodyne;—Nancy bad with the Fever.

1. For an explanation of the hives, see below, Jan. 17, 1800, and Nov. 3, 1801.
2. ED generally uses *anodyne* to refer to any medication containing opium or laudanum (tincture of opium) in pill, liquid, or glyster form (Gould, *Dictionary of Medicine*; W. Lewis, *New Dispensatory*, 315–16, 618–19).

27 ED took a dose Rheubarb, and through mercy is much better than could be expected, considering the voiolence of the disorder.

28 Harry getting better, Eve still in her Chamber, Rachel Fingers sore, I took a ride this Afternoon with Becky James in their Waggon to Frankford, came home early.

29 We seem at peasent so favour'd as to be on the mending hand, only my dear little Nancy, who had a fit of the Fever, Yesterday, Notwithstanding she had taken 11 or 12 doses of the bark, which she still continues to take—She has had 2 spells of bleeding at the Nose this Afternoon Sally Norris was buryed last First Day: she dyed of the Small Pox.

1769 June 30, My dear little Nancy miss'd the fitt of Fever this Day, after taken a large quantity of the Bark—she blead pritty much at the Nose this Evening—weather very hott.

July 1, We are now much better. I took a ride this Afternoon with Becky James to Frankford; HD. and AJ. came home this Evening.

July 1769 the begining of this Month Sally had 3 or 4 fitts of the intermitant Fever; got better by taking the Bark.

July 7. 1769, came to Frankford with our 3 Youngest Children:[3] Sally in Town with her Aunt: Molly Moore, with me, Eve, and Sally Gardner—My Henry came up with me in the Chaise, the rest in the Waggon: HD stay'd all Night.

8 HD. went to Town after Breakfast I was taken this Evening with something of a vomiting &c. Children bravely.

9 First Day. HD. MS. SD.—John Rachel and Harry, came up before breakfast: HD. went to Meeting—they went to Town towards Evening Sally stay'd with us, Nancy went to Town, HD. stay'd all Night.

10 HD. stay'd with us till after dinner then went to Town.

11 ED. taken with the Chills and Fever, in Bed most of the Day Thos. Say and Wife here this Afternoon, HD. came in the Evening.

12 I came to Town with my Henry. John brought Nurse and the Children home in the Waggon.

3. Henry (Harry) Drinker was born May 24, 1769. He died Aug. 20, 1769.

13 I had another bad fit of the Fever, which occasion'd me to be very weak, as I had been unwell so long before.

14 took plentifully of the Bark.

15 mis't the fitt, continue to take bark road out, every Morning with HD.

25 July I hope I have got rid of the Chills and Fever—HD. set of this Morning with S Pleasants, and S Morton for MaryLand, my little Henry not very well.—they return'd the 31.

Augt. the 5. several Houses burnt down, at the Corner of Wallnutt & Seacond Streets—[before] 10 o'clock at Night.[4]

HD. unwell with the Flux—Augt. the 5th & 6—took Physick.—7 he was let Blood; towards the middle of the month he got better.

Sammy Emlen came from Bristol with his 2 Sons, in the Brig Concord.—Augt. 23. 1769.

1769 Augt. towards the End of the Month a large Comet appeard in Philadelphia and elsewhere.

Sally Gardner went away Sepr. 2. 1769.

Billy Emlen dyed of the Flux October 7 1769.

Novr. the 9: 1769: Rachel Wilson. Abel James, and Isaac Stroud—went to Chester: where they embark'd in the Pennsylvania Packet Natl. Falkner Master for London.

Novr. the 29. 1769—Polly Sim Steel was bury'd, she dy'd at R. Steels, of a Consumption.

ED. was let Blood Decr. 4. 1769.

Billy Drinker cut his last Tooth Decemr. 1769. aged 2 years & 10 Months.

4. The fire took place between Second and Third streets. The owners of one of the shops, Messrs. Mayshalls, were accused of housing large quantities of gunpowder, which could have ignited and started the fire. They denied having more than four ounces in their possession; no further action was taken against them (*Pa. Chron.*, Aug. 5, 1769).

1770

Hannah Finney dyed Janry. the 4. 1770.

Hannah Waln dyed Janry. 13. 1770.

our Tenant at Frankford, Patrick McCormish lost his 2 oldest Sons, by the Small Pox, Simon and Dickey December 1769.

John Burket, a Free Man Decr. 9. 1769.

Sammy Emlen and Sally Mott were married Febry. 1. 1770.

E.D. was let Blood Febry. 22. 1770.

John Burket went away March the 12. 1770 Benjamin Ardey came the same day at £20 p year—Benn. went away March 29. John returnd March 28 1770 John went away Octor. 22. 1771.

Sally Stretch Dye'd March 29 1770.

Snow'd all Day the 2 April 1770.

ED was let Blood June 3. 1770.

Sally Gardner came June 26. 1770 at £8—p Ann.

1770 Eve Cathrine Motlin went away June 23: 1770, to live with Docr. Sheubart at the Trap, near Pott-Grove.

Daniel Stanton was bury'd June 29 1770.

Neighr. Le Gay dyed July 1. 1770.

Hannah Jones came July 6. 1770.

ED. was let Blood at Bristol Augt. 1770.

Hannah Jones went away Sepr. 3. 1770.

Rebecca Coleman departed this Life Septr. the 12. 1770, Aged 92 years or upwards.

Peggy Roach came to live with us Sepr. 13 1770, at 11 pounds p Ann.

Rachel Houlton went away Sepr. 10. 1770.

Hannah Jones married to R Stephenson—Sepr. 6. 1770.

Sally Gardner went away Sepr. 26 1770.

Sally Gardner came again Octor. 4 1770, at £8 p Ann.

Peggy Roach went away Octor. 10: 1770.

Octor. 16 HD. was let Blood. 1770.

Maria Singer came Octor. the 17. 1770 at £10 p.

ED. was let Blood Octor. 21. 1770.

Hannah Stevenson came from York Octor. 1770.

Nancy Evans came Decemr. 16. 1770—at 11£ p ann.

Betsy Waln brought to Bed of her Son Richard Decr. 23. 1770.

Peggy McClain came Janry. 4. 1771 at 12£ p Ann.

ED had a Tooth drawn Feby. 5. 1771.

Peggy went away Feby. 6. 1771.

Black Beck came Feby. 18. 1771—she went away Octor. 17. 1771.

Nancy and Billy went to School March 11. 1771.[1]

1771 March 28. Nany Evans went away intending to be Married to one Saml. Butler.

1. The entry "March the 26. 1771, HD. left home with Owen Jones, for Mary Land" crossed out.

ED. was let Blood April 10: 1771.

Sally began her quarter at School April 15. 1771.

Sally Gardner went away April 18. 1771.

Patty Clark came April 18. 1771. at 10£ p Ann. she went away May 1.

Abey Spicer came to work April 18. 1771.

Betty Davis came April 27. 1771 a 10£.

Richd. Penn Governour, arrived Octor. 16 1771. in the Brita. Capt. Foulkner.

Abbey Spicer Married Octor. the 17. 1771, to John Kibble.

Octor. the 7. 1771. MS. ED. and John went to Frankford, before dinner MS. drove.

John Burket went away Octr. 22. 1771.

Septr. 1770: H and ED. John with us left home after Breakfast, din'd at Chester, then proceeded to Concord came to John Brintons in the Evening sup'd and lodg'd there—the next Morning First Day—HD. went to Meeting: I stay'd with Margt. Brinton; went after dinner to their Son in Laws.—came back in the Evening I had a very bad fit of the Colick, which continu'd most part of the Night—next Morning after Breakfast left JBs din'd at Copelands Chester, John Morton and Sammy Sansom din'd with us—left Chester after dinner: drank Tea at Grays with Saml. and M. Pleasent S. and S. Rhoads, Molly Stretch &c—cross'd the Ferry, just before sun set—and came home little[2] before dark.

1769 Sepr. 10.[3] left home after Brakfast First Day Morning for New-York, HD. ED.—John Glover and John Bossley in Company. our John on Horse back din'd at Priestlys Bristol—Thos. and Saml. Franklin, Jacobes Vansant, with their Wives, din'd with us, in their way from NY to Philada. HD. wrote to Sister by T. Franklin—We left Bristol after dinner, and arriv'd at Trenton to Tea, took a walk towards Evening about the Town sup'd and lodg'd at Richd. Williams, at the Royal Oak.

2. The word "after" crossed out.

3. The entries for Sept. 10, 1769, through the line ending "end of June 1771" are entered upside down at the back of the manuscript volume.

11 left Trenton this Morning between 7 and 8 o'clock Beakfasted at Prince-Town at Hicks, Dined at Michl. Duffs, or the White Hall Tavern at Brunswick, & from thence wrote by Cornelius Bradford to Sister; the late North East Storm has done much damage; many Trees blown up by the roots; Bridges carried away by the force of the Water, and the roads greatly hurt by it.—We cross'd the river Rariton, and proceeded to Woodbridg where we lodg'd at Herds' Tavern not very comfortably.

12 went this Morning to Elizabeth Town, and Breakfasted at Broughton Reynolds, at the Lyon: walk'd thro' part of the Town and then continued our journey, thro' New-Ark and Bergon to Powles Hook, Opposete New-York. Near Newark saw about 1500 Sheep belonging to that place and Elizth. Town, attended by one old Shepherd—We cross'd in this Stage, Hackensack or Second River & Newark River—Dine'd at Ellsworths, spent some time there, cross'd the North River and came to Henry Haydocks, about 5 o'clock.—This Evening was Intear'd the remains of Sir Henry Moore, late Govr. of New York, and much regretted by the Inhabitants very generally thro' the Province—at H Haydocks we found Saml. Emlen and his 2 Sons. on a visit there.

13 Saml. Emlen, his Sons and HD. Breakfasted at Thos. Pearsalls—I went to meeting, with Hannah Haydock and Nelly Moode; HD—went also—din'd at HHs.—after dinner H Haydock and Wife, S Emlen and Children, HD. and self Rid the 7 miles round up the East and down the North River; drank Tea at Capt. Clarks, and then return'd home to HHs—Jos. Delaplane, Wm. Richman, and Hannah Jones, sup'd with us.

14 HD. Breakfasted at B. Booths, and afterwards walk'd thro' the City, Fort &c. in Company with Geo. Bowne, Thos. Pearsall, Hannah Haydock, and Hannah Jones, view'd the inside of a new Dutch Church finely Decorated and built upon an Elegant plan.—came to Dinner, H Jones stay'd—after dinner Margt. and George Bowne, (her son) Henry and Hannah Haydock, H and ED, rid out to Hell Gate and return'd in the Evening—after having Drank Tea there at one Waldrons. Yesterday wrote to Sister and received a Letter from B. Trapnell and this Evening another, inclosing one from Sally Drinker.

15 this Morning HD. wrote again to MS, and after Breakfast cross'd the East River to Long-Island in Company H and H Haydock, H and ED went to Gravesend, and down to the Beach or sea Shore—HD went into the Surf—and then Return'd and Dined at Garret Williamsons. from thence Rid to New Utrectch, walk'd down to the Sea Shore, and return'd thro Flat Bush to New York, crossing the East River by Moon Light.

16 this Morning stay'd at H Haydocks. after an Early Dinner, T. Pearsall; H Jones, H.D and self cross'd over to Long Island, and Rid thro' Jamaica to

Richd. Cornells' at Success—Father in Law to T. Pearsall; in this Ride pass'd thro the Edge of the great Plains—Lodge'd at R. Cornells.

17 First Day: this Morning we accompany'd the Cornell Family to Flushing Meeting—after Meeting din'd at Widdow Wilsons, where I was very much disordred in my Bowels: after dinner T. Pearsall Wife and Child, H Jones, HD and self rid to Jamaica and down to Rockway, that Evening sup'd and Lodg'd at the Widdow Fosters.

18 Breakfasted at the Widdows, and then rid down to the Beach, where we all opposed HDs going into the Surf, it being very high, and T.P. apprehending it dangerous from the undersuck of the Waves which break on the Beach.—after some time spent there return'd towards our Inn, and in our way stop'd at an Indian Wig-Wam, and had some talk with the Master and Mistress, two old Indians, from thence pass'd on & by the Inn, and on our Journey to Jamaca, where we din'd at Walter Smiths, Relations of H Jones; first having seperated from T.P. and Wife, who proceeded that Evening to Success.—after Dinner we made some stay at a Tavern to Bait our Horses, and then went on our way to New York, which we came to in the Evening, and cross'd the East River after Dark.

19 Walk'd out this Morning with HD—H Jones and Nelly Moode, to a Number of print Shops, and Booksellers &c. and particularly to Gerardus Duykinks [Medley] Shop, also to Grove Ben's shop—call'd at Thos. Dobsons, spent a little time with Peggy, then HD. E Moode and self went to Walter Franklins, where we dined. in Company with John Franklin and Debby, Col. Curser &c.—in the Afternoon Nelly Moode and self drank Tea at B. Booths.

20 this Morning sent out John over the North River with the Chaise and Horses, and about 9 or 10 o'clock Repair'd to the Ferry in Company Hy. Haydock, Geo. Bowne and H Jones, from whome parted at the Waterside; and with Nelly Moode, little Polly Haydock, and Robart Bowne, cross'd with little wind to Powles Hook, from whence after some delay proceeded, and cross'd the two Rivers—and as it seem'd likely for Rain, push'd forward to Broughton Reynolds at E. Town, din'd there, and then went to Joseph Shotwells at Raway, at whose House we arrived, just as it began to Rain. Here we drank Tea and spent the Evening in Company with Joseph Scott &c—sup'd and Lodg'd there. at JSs.

21 the Weather Lowering and Moist—after Breakfast put forward, and came to Brook Farmers at Brunswick to Dinner. after dinner continued to Prince Town, drank Tea at Hicks, and then reach'd John Thorntons at Trentown Ferry in good time; here we sup'd and Lodg'd.

22 sixth Day Breakfasted this Morning at the Ferry ED. very unwell—left it after Breakfast, and got home to Philada. in good time for Dinner.

for above a 12 Month after my return from New York; I rode very frequently abroad, but neglected making memorand[a]. when and where; being in a bad state of health. But never went in that time far from home, but once to Concord.

Spent 6 weeks of the Summer 70, at S. Merriotts Bristol.

1771

1771 March 9 Removed from John Smiths House in Water Street, (where we had lived 10 Years and near 2 Months)—to our House in Front Street.

1771 March 26. HD. left home for MaryLand, Owen Jones with him—MS. went to Meeting this Morning Nancy Byard and Sally Logan, spent this Afternoon with us, Isaac Hazelhurst and Johanna call'd towards Evening—Becky James Senr. Patty and Becky junr. with Sucky Waln here this Evening—Becky Senr. sup'd with us—Thos. Champions Widdow call'd this Afternoon; says she intends to pay her debt, in a fortnight—Chalkley James here.

27 Docr. Redman call'd this Morning.—Susanna Jaquet call'd—Neighrs. Swift and Waln, with Sucky spent this Afternoon. with us—Polly Ritche Reynolds came in the Evening—she went with us to enquire for a Maid, came back and sup'd with us—We were invited this Afternoon to the Burial of John Smith of Burlington.

28 Betsy Parker here this Morning—Abel James call'd, he intends, with his Wife &c this Afternoon for Burlington—Widow Mountgomerys Maid call'd—Nany Carlisle call'd—our Nancy little Henrys[1] maid lift us this Morning.

29 Neighr. Carlisle spent this Afternoon—Sister and self took a walk this Evening to Abels.

30th. Neddy Pennington here this Morning for Grape Cuttings, Edey Devenshire in the Evening Esther Welkinson call'd.

31 First Day: Unwell of the Colick—Molly Moore sup'd with us.

April 1. Chalkley James call'd, A. James Saml. Emlen: John Drinker—Sister and self took a walk in the Afternoon—Patty Merriott, Polly and Jenny Osborn, and R. James Senr. call'd.

1. Henry Sandwith Drinker was born October 30, 1770.

2d Docr. Evans call'd: Sally Moore and her Daughter, spent this Afternoon with us—C. Evans call'd in the Evening Patty Merriott Abby Spicer call'd.

3d. HD. return'd.

March 20.1771 lent Rachl. Evans 20 S—

5 Shirts)—/1/4½
2 Shifts)

4 Shirts)
1 Shift)——/1/——

1 little Shift)
2 Shifts)——/1/5½
5 Shirts)

2 Shifts)
7 Shirts)——/1/10½
1 little Shift)

3 Shifts)
7 Shirts)——/2/5½
6 little Shifts)

5 Shifts)
8 Shirts)——/2/6

3 Shifts ——/——/6

1 Shift)
3 Shirts)——/——/11½
2 little shifts)

6 Shirts)
5 Shifts)——/2/5
4 little Ditto)

6 little Shifts)
2 Shifts)——/2/1
6 Shirts)

7 Shirts ———/1/5½

5 Shifts)
7 Shirts)——/2/8½
6 little Shifts)

3 Shifts)
3 Shirts)——/1/4½
3 little Shifts))

1/4½
1/—
1/5½
1/10½
2/5½
2/6
—/6
—/11½
2/5
2/1
1/5½
2/8½
1/4½

1/2/2

1770 Sepr. 3[2] Received from Friend Streeton fifty Shillings, for one quarters rent due the 6 of July last

Received the further Sum of —— £ 3—
Received the further Sum of —— 3—
April 1772 Received ———— 1/10

8/3 8
10
28 8d
1/8
5/10
8.2

Opend Barrel Sugar & 1 of Coffee latter end of June 1771.

1771 June 22[3] seventh Day—came to Bristol HD. ED. HD Junr. John Drinker with us—din'd at John Kidds: George Baker drove up Polly Campbell, whome I have hir'd this day to tind my little Henry; George [return'd] to Philada. from Kidds: came to the Widdow Merriotts to Tea—Boarders there at this time; Parson Carter and Wife—Parson Peters—David Halls Wife and Son; Thos. Cash's Wife—their Servants—my self, my little Son, and Maid.—went to the Bath[4] this Evening.

23 First day went to Bath this Morning—HD went to Meeting; after dinner he with JD left Bristol, took a ride this Evening to Bath and little further, Docr. Denormande's Lad Amos with me—my little Henry very poorly.

24 rain this morning I took a walk to Sim Betts where A. Tilghman, and one Goldring and Wife Lodges; road out in the Afternoon with Amos towards the ferry and to the Spring.

25 my little dear something Better then he has been: lost 7 of our Family this Morning R. Peters, Carter and Wife, their Servants, and David Hall Junr. he

2. The inside back cover of the manuscript volume contains numerical calculations and the material contained in the entry "1770 . . . 1771."

3. The manuscript volume for June 22, 1771–May 21, 1773, is covered in brown paper. The outside front cover reads, "1771, 2, 3"; the inside front cover reads: "Tinc Rheu: March 22, 1772 IIIIIIIIIIIII."

4. Bristol, Pa., was noted for its bath springs, located just outside the borough limits. Hotels and boarding houses were built in the 1760s to accommodate summer guests who came for the waters and eventually transformed Bristol into one of the most fashionable watering places in the United States in the years following the Revolutionary War (Doron Green, *A History of Bristol Borough in the County of Bucks, State of Pennsylvania* [Camden, N.J.: Magrath, 1911], 67–68, 73).

road with me this Morning 2 miles up the Trent Town road, stop'd at our door, in our return, took in my little Son and went to Bath;—S. LeGay din'd with us—took a ride this Afternoon with Anna; (S Merriott and M. Hall, went with us.) to the Ferry, and Spring, came home to Tea;—Sucky Waln here to day: Docr. Redman stop'd. he was on his way to Trenttown, with his newly Married Daughter, and others.

26 Foggy Morning Collinson Reed Breakfasted here, M. Hall and myself went in our Chaise to Bath. P. Buckley drove us;—Billy Parr, and Judath Foulk call'd this Afternoon, A Tilghman in the Evening Capt Williamss Wife.

27 Capt. Williams's Child, Nurse, and Negro Girl, took up their aboad with us this Morning The Mornings have been Foggy most of this Week which renders it improper to go out I took a short ride this Afternoon with Anna Sarah Large here, and several others this Day.

28 took a ride this Morning Phines Buckley and my Child, 3 Miles on trent Town road, then to Bath;—Docr. Redman din'd with us,—Ringgold and Wife drank Tea—road none this Evening—my side, Breast and Sholder very uneasy this Day.

29 took a walk this Morning to see Fd. Ringgold, saw Robt. and Hannah Stevenson at Bisonetts, they came home with me, insisted on my going to Dine with them at the Taveren, which I reluctantly comply'd with; being very unwell: after dinner I came home, with them in their Carriage they proceeded on their way towards Amwell;—rain this Afternoon, with very sharp Thunder.

30 First Day; My dear Henry, with our Nancy and Billy, came here last Night a little before nine o'clock; they were detaind at Frankford, by rain; HD. went into the Bath this Morning we took a little ride, came home to Breakfast, the Children with their Daddy took a walk, they then went to Meeting;—S. Merriott Senr. Molly Hall, Anna Humber, and self, went this Afternoon into the Bath, I found the shock much greater than I expected; road the 7 miles round afterwards; came home rather late, our dear little ones went to Bed, this and last Night, very much tired.

July 1 took a ride this Morning to the Bath, had not courage to go in, road up the Trentown road 3 miles came home to Breakfast: rain and wind after dinner, My HD. with his Daughter Ann and Son William, left about 4 o'clock; as did M. Hall. and Cyntha Cash, for Philada. Docr. Denormande here this Evening—Adam Hoopss Corps, taken from Trentown to Philada. to Day: disagreeable Weather.

2 Docr. D and Neighr. Hodge, and her son Billy call'd this Morning—

Richd. Shataford call'd to tell me that My Henry and children got home safe last Evening—rain most of this Day: I have drank 6 half pints of the water.

3 Fd. Ringold call'd on me this Morning went with her, and Betsy Tilghman to Bath;—Capt. Williams and Wife here, they took away their Child, Nurse, and Negro, Girl;—A Ringold, sent after dinner to desire my Company to Tea: I went, mett several others there;—Wm. Parr, Peggy, and their Daughter Nancy came this Afternoon to S. Merriotts, Billy went away after Supper intending for Town early in the Morning I took a ride this Evening to Bath: Patty Merriott with me, where I received a Letter from My Henry, by E. Large.

4 went to Bath this Morning Patty Merriott drove, I carried the Child; we road to the Ferry. at 11 o'clock I went into the Bath; with Fear and trembling, but felt cleaver after it; T Ringold and Wife with B. Tillman, drank Tea with us—I wint with them to Bath: Peggy Parr and Nancy in our Chaise; call'd in our return at Rights to see one Hoffman's Wife from N Yk. who is in a very bad state of Health; came home towards Evening one McColegh from Jamacai took lodgings here this Evening.

5 Foggy Morning I went to Bath with M. Parr about Noon, took the 3d. plunge; came home to Dinner; went out after four o'clock, took Polly and my Son with me, call'd at Sarah Large's; drank with S Hoffman & others, at Widdow Wrights; E. Large drove me and my Son to Bath; mett there, Sl. Allison, H. Sansom, and others from Burlington: went one mile on the ferry road, and then home; Doctor here this Evening as usual.

6 Went to Bath this Morning Patty with me, mett J. Hodge there; as she intended this Morning for Philada. I wrote by her to My Henry—rain almost all Day: HD. came this Evening.

7 First Day: HD. MP. and ED. went to B—Cloudy all Day. my side very unwell—My Henry went to Meeting and elsewhere, I stay'd at home; John came up this Morning.

8 went to B this Morning took a short ride our Horse lame: about Noon I went into the Bath; felt cleaver after it—My HD left us this Afternoon; dull Weather.

9 I went to B this Morning Anna with me we went again at 11 o'clock. I went in—George Morgan call'd to see me,—Peggy Parr and Nancy went riding this Afternoon when they came back it grew cloudy and rain'd with thunder, which prevented my rideing:—John went home this Afternoon by Water: Billy Parr came after 9 at Night.

10 WP. gone this Morning before I was up—Peggy went with me to B, to drink—at Noon I went again with Anna, took a dip, drank a pint and then home—G. Morgan call'd, I wrote by him to My Henry: Peggy, Jack, my little one and self took a ride of about 6 miles, then went to B. came home to Tea: the Sun set clear this Evening which has not been the case for a long time past.

11 Went to B. this Morning before breakfast, went again before dinner and Bathed—Peggy and Nancy Parr, my self and Son drank tea at E. Willims; went in the Evening to Bath; Mett Nr. Hodge their, she told me her Son had a letter for me, from my Henry: but upon inquiry, he had carelessly left it in Philada.

12 Went to B. this Morning had a great many Visiters this Afternoon, TR. and Wife, Sucky Pentard, Sally Hoffman, Budenotts Wife; Serless Wife, Sally Treadwell, Betsy Tillman, Nancy Cox &c—Went to B this Evening—S Le Gay call'd to see me this Morning wrote by him to My Henry;—My dear, came unexpectedly this Evening intending tomorrow for B. Point; as he is not very well.

13 My Henry left me this Morning I have been unwell all Day: I went into the Bath this Morning Dr. D. says I must wean by little Henry or get a nurse for him, either seems hard—but I must submitt. Billy Parr, and Caleb, came up this Afternoon, Billy went to Trent town: I wrote this Afternoon to sister; went to B. saw in my return, R and E. Waln—there is a great number of People in Bristol at present. Pollys Mother call'd here.

14 First Day: Went into the Bath this Morning came home to Breakfast: S. Sansom call'd before meeting—Molly Foulk, with 3 of her Children took up their Abode here took a ride this Afternoon with Molly—went to B. much Coumpany there—Capt. Mershall and Wife: with another woman took lodgings here. 23 persons in the House this Night;—wrote to Sister.

15 Wm. Parr, and J Foulk, went to Philada. this Morning Dull rainy Weather I wrote to Sister—D. Divine came this Evening to S Merriotts—I went into the Bath this Evening—clear Cool Weather for the Season.

16. Took a ride this Morning M. Foulk with me; Docr. De. went with me to Bath into which I went, the weather Cool—took a ride this Afternoon, went in the Evening with MF. to E.Ws. to see Sally Morris. I have been very unwell all day.

17 Went to B. this Morning Dr. D, with me I went in;—took a ride this Afternoon Anna, and my little dear with me went to one Bidgoods, call'd at Sally Oatts, came home to Tea, then went to B [S. Merriott] with me,—MF &

MP gone to dine at John Kidds—Capt. Marshal, his Wife, and, the Widdow Gadd, left us this Morning My Side and Breast painfull.

18th. I had the Colick last Night, call'd up M. Foulk, and M. Parr, better towards, Morning—My dear Sister and B. Trapnell came up this Morning left A. Spicer in charge of our [Chickeness] at home, Sister and MF went with me to Sally Oats; agree'd with her to take my Sweet little Henry to Nurse—then went to Bath, came home to Dinner, Sister and Benny, left us at 4 o'clock for Philada.—took a ride to Shamney with MF—went to B came home after Sunset—one David P Mendez a Jew came to lodge at S. Merriotts to Day.

19 took a ride with M. Foulk in her Chaise, her Children in mine; Peggy and Nancy Parr in theirs—3 Miles up the Trent Town Road—[call'd] at S. Oatts—then went to Bath, came home to Dinner—Went after Dinner, in the same manner, the 7 or 8 Miles round—then to B—came home to Tea—Docr—Evans here this Evening. fine Weather.

20 Docr. Evans, here this Morning—I received a letter from HD. New York,—MF. went with me to Sally Oatts; then to Bath, received a Letter from Sister, by Sucky Waln, went this Afternoon to the Ferry, MF. ED. MP. AP. Tommy Roberson and M. Divine went to Bath; wrote to Sister,—Billy Parr here this Evening very fine [Weather].

21 First Day: Went this Morning to S. Oats, Sarah Merriott with me, then to Bath—MF. MP. AP. MD. &c went to Burlington; My Henry and Billy Parr came here this Evening very fine Weather.

22 HD. and myself, took our little Lamb, after Breakfast to S. Oats, whose Breast he willingly suck'd; stay'd there an hour or 2, then went to Bath, came home to Dinner; went in the Afternoon to see our little dear; found him asleep, he waked in high good humour—but has a little Cough; We then went to Bath; and 2 or 3 Miles up the Oxford road, back again to B: then home to Tea; Wm. Parr, his Wife, Daughter and Jack; went to Town this Afternoon as did M Divine and S Merriott Senr. My Henry and self took a walk this Evening to see Fd. Ringold:—I seem lost without my little dear—the Weather exceedingly fine.

23. Went this Morning with my HD. to see our Child, then to Bath, came home to Breakfast, after which my Henry went for Philada. about 11 o'clock it began to rain and has continu'd so to do all Day. I sent Johny Foulk, in the Evening to see how my Son was, he brought back pleasing accounts—no going out this Evening.

24 I went this Morning John Foulk with me to see my Child; came back to

Breakfast. Josh. Redman here; wrote to my Henry by him; rain all the rest of the Day.

25 rain all Day: I sent Wm. Witherall to know how my Child was, he brought back good accounts. no going out this Day.

26 rain most part of this Day—could not see my little dear.

27 went to B: MF. went with me to see my Child whome I found pretty well; went again to B.—HD. & my dear Sally came to Bristol this Evening.

First Day: 28. My Henry, self and Daughter went this Morning to B: then to S. Oats,—came home to Breakfast: HD & SD went to meeting—rain fell before their return;—HD. SD. and George McCullough went this Evening to see little Henry—Fd. Ringold and M. Redman call'd this Evening—we have had a long spell of rainy weather, very unseasonable.

29 I went this Morning to B. with MF—I went into the Bath: found a difficulty of Breathing for many hours after it—My Henry and Sally left me this Morning after Breakfast;—I went when they were gone, M. Divine with me to Sally Oats—then to Bath—M.F, her Son John, and Daughter Betsy, left us this Morning they are gone to [T.] Ritches rain the greatest part of this afternoon and Even'g with thunder, very unsettled bad weather.

30. Cloudy bad weather; went to B. this Morning and went into it—wrote to HD went in the Afternoon to see my child, S. Merriott with me, clear weather in the Afternoon.

31 Went with M. Divine to B. this Morning went in before Breakfast; and to S. Oats spent this Afternoon with Fd. Ringold, S. Hoffman, Polly Kibles and her Sister there; went in the Evening to B.—A Ringd A Tilghman, Pentards Wife and Serles's at our House this Evening—wrote to HD to Day.

Augt. 1 Went into the Bath this Morning MD. with me then went to see Henry—came home to Breakfast Mary Hall, and her Son Wm. came to Sarah Merriotts before dinner—Patty Merriott went this Afternoon for S. Oats and my Henry. They spent the Afternoon with us, 3 Chaise full of us went home with them,—Weather very warm; M.H is to be my Bed-fellow—pain in my Breast better received a letter from HD.

Augt. 2. Went into the Water before Breakfast. Weather very hott.—wrote to my Henry. went towards Evening to S Oats; all well there.

3 Went into the Bath this Morning road to the Ferry. Dilly Divine with me,

came home to Breakfast, Molly Foulk and her Children are return'd to Bristol; Saml. Morton came to S. Merriotts this Afternoon—I went with MF to Bath—My Henry came up after Night—all well at home.

First Day 4. went this Morning into the Bath, came back to Breakfast, then went to G. Oats, from thence to the Falls Meeting[5] MF her Children, HD. E.D—went after Meeting to Yarleys Ferry, mett Judah Foulk and John Swift there, din'd there, came home in the Evening very hott Weather.

5 My Henry went to Town this Morning Molly Foulk with him; I went this Morning to see my Child. S Morton with me, took him with us a Mile up the road, left him with his Nurse on our return; went afterwards to Bath, MD with me, went into the water,—spent this Afternoon at the Doctors Numbers there—went this Evening to B.—the Weather extreen hott.

6 went into the Bath with M. Divine took a ride afterwards; spent part of the Afternoon at Writes, with S Hoffman &c—S. LeGay went with me to B in the Even'g to see Henry.—G. McCulloch went away this Morning.

7 Went into the Bath this Morning with M Hall—Dilly Divine went away this Morning—as did David P. Mendez—Janny Osburn, a Woman from St.A Cruse and her Daughter and Maid came this Day—spent this Afternoon at Browns, with Docr. Redmans Wife, much Company there.

8 wrote this Morning to my Henry—went with S. Morton, M Hall and her Son, to Trent-Town Ferry. din'd there—call'd in our way home, to see my dear little one. then went into the Bath—drank tea late the Weather much cooler, then it has been.

9. Went this Morning to see my son, gave him a little ride, Anna with me; then went to Bath with M. Hall, went in.—Went this Afternoon with S. Morton, M Hall and her Son to Wm. Penns old Mansion House[6] in the Mannor, came back to Tea Docr. Redman and Wife at our House; went to Bath—very unwell all-day.

10 went to B this Morning went in, then went to see my Child; M Hall with

5. The Quaker meeting in Falls Township, Bucks County, named for its location at the falls of the Delaware River and home to the oldest Quaker meeting in the county, was one of the first five townships laid out there. Quakers began meeting in private homes in the area in 1683 and built a meetinghouse in 1692. A new meetinghouse was erected in 1728 (W. W. H. Davis, *Bucks County*, 1:63, 68).

6. William Penn purchased a proprietary manor of over eight thousand acres called Pennsbury in Falls Township, Bucks County, around 1683. He began laying out the manor and building his country seat in 1683–84 and resided there until 1701 (Penn, *Papers*, 2:524–25; McNealy, *Bucks County*, 40–44).

me—Went to see Henry this Evening then to Bath took a ride towards the Ferry mett HD, P. Morton, Daved Evans, and Wife, coming to Bristol—M. Foulk her son John, Widdow Harrison. 2 of her Children. came this afternoon.[7]

11 First Day: HD and my self went this Morning to see our Child: I went with MH. into the Bath; HD—went to Meeting—took a ride this Afternoon to bid my little dear farewell—then call'd at E. Williams, and to see Fd. Ringold and to Bath—Parson Carter and his Family came this Afternoon we have a House full.

12 left Bristol this Morning HD—ED. MF drove me; her son John road with Debby Saunders; Widdow Harrison &c—Breakfasted at the Red Lyon came home to dinner.

1771 Augt. 19 First Day. went with H.D. to Bristol, [baited] at the red Lyon, Becky Mifflin and A. Powel there—went to S. Oats, found our little dear well—din'd at S. Mirriotts; HD. left me there, and went back in the Afternoon to Philada—Drank tea with B. Mifflin, at S. Betts, went with her to Bath.

20 hir'd a Horse and Chair, and went to see my Child this Morning the Widdow Allen, Parson Carters Sister went with me; Saml. Morton very bad of a Fever at SMs—I slep'd with Dilly Divine.

21 went this Morning the Widdow Allen with me to see my Child, come back to SMs to dinner—came after dinner to Philaa. in the Stage Waggon—the Widdow Supple and her daughter Janney: Polly and Jenny Osburn, with me:—came home in the Evening.

Augt. 22. 1771. left home after dinner fifth Day HD. ED. and John, stop'd at [Roben] Hoods—waited there half an hour for Robt. and Hannah Stevenson, who accompanys us on our tour to Lancaster &c. baited at the Nags Head 12 Miles from Philada. came to Rowland Evanss before 7 o'clock.—wrote to Sister this Evening sent back my Keys, which I had unknowingly brought from home: sup'd lodg'd and Breakfasted at REs road 23 long miles this Day.

23 went after Breakfast from REs his Son Cadr. with us. by way of guide—foarded Schuykill. then went to the Yallow Spring; din'd there took a walk to a spring in the Meadow.—HD. HS. and myself took a duck in the Bath.—set of between 3 and 4 from thence, HD. ED. RS. HS. John and Portuga. their Servant stop'd a minnut at Jos. Bentlys, at the Red Lyon, near Uuchland

7. One line crossed out.

Meeting House—then came to the Kings Arms Pennsburg, on Lancaster road, drank tea there: HD. took a walk to Joshua Bawldwins, half a Mile from the Tavern. Josa. return'd with him—we rode upwards of 18 miles this day and 23 Yesterday, tho we are at present but 32 miles from Philaa. weather very fine, roads very hilly & Stony. RS. HS. HD. and ED—sleep'd all in one Chamber.

24 left Chainys Pennsburg this Morning rode 8 miles to the Waggon Breakfasted there, then went 12½ to the Hat. Jacobss: din'd there—left it at 3 o'clock, rode on, were overtaken by rain but not wett, went 12½ miles father, to Lancaster, were we arrived about 6 o'clock.—We foarded this day 2 branches of Brandy Wine—and Conestogoe Creek—tiresome roads; 33 miles this day—put up at Matts. Sloughs, in Lancaster; at the sign of the Swan; took a walk this Evening through part of the Town, came back to Supper;—lodg'd all togeather again.

25 First Day: Went to Meeting this Morning yearly Meeting here;—din'd at Sloughs; [C]artherington an Officer, din'd with us;—I went after dinner to George Ross's drank tea there.—came back to Sloughs, this Afternoon we examined the Coart-House, took a walk to the New Dutch Church, took a Survay of it inside and out then return'd to our Lodging.

26 Breakfasted this Morning then set off to Wrights Ferry; got there a little after 10; took a walk to James Wrights; stay'd a short time there; had some talk with him and his Sister Susanna:—return'd to the Ferry, where we dinn'd; and were divert'd with a Musical Clock, an organ in it—I had a desire to cross the Suscananna with HD, but the Wind was too high—came back to Lancaster by 6 o'Clock—took a walk after Tea to the Widdow Dowarss. found her door Shut. she abroad; mett her, and her Daughter Betsy at Sloughs when we return'd.

27 left Sloughs Lancaster, after Breakfast cloudy morning rode 10 miles to the Glass-House, at Manheim, saw them make a Wine-Glass &c—din'd at Jarome Hazelmans, near the Glass-House, then set of for Lititz, came there before 4 o'Clock, put up at one Horn's, took a walk to Gasper Pains; he went with us to the Brethern's House and Sisters—mett with Molly Penry there.—left Lititz after 5 o'Clock—continued on 'till we lost our way, hir'd a Guide, and arrived after night at Henry Millers, a quarter of a Mile from Dunkers Town (where we eat a hearty supper of fry'd Beef-stakes, and Chocolate) and lodg'd all in one Room very Comfortably.

28 left H. Millers this Morning after Breakfast went to Ephrata or Dunkers-Town: Peter Miller (a Chief Man amongst them) and Sister[8] Keturah; went

8. The name "Catura" crossed out.

with us about the House &c stay'd there near an hour [then] rode over Cocalico Creek, and by Cocallico Church to RinesTown, and through Adam's Town; din'd in a Mill-House at Peter Pennybakers, boyl'd Mutton, and old Kidney Beans, eat very hearty—proceed'd on our journey after dinner foarded Schuykill, and arrived at Reding about 4 o'clock, put up at Witheringtons—drank tea; then took a walk through the Town. 18 or 19 Miles this day—Phebe and Betsy Shoemaker came towards Evening to see us. they, with their Mother &c came last Week to live at Reding.—David Beveridge and Wife, George Emlen Junr. and their sister Nancy, put up this Evening at the Tavern with us. they came from Bethlehem.

29 this Morning HD. RS. &c examin'd the Coart House, and after Breakfast our Company together with D. B[ar]ridge & his Company P. and B. Shoemaker: John Murry and J. Whitehead, some on Horse back and some in Carriges—began our Journey to the top of the high Hill, call'd one of the Oley Hills, to the Eastward of the Town; after winding the Hill and passing some steep places; deserted Carriages and Horses, and then with great fatigue and labour, and several stops to rest, overcame all obstructions and found ourselves on the Summit of an Eminence, commanding an extensive prospect of the adjacent Country; which was some compensation for the toil of the day; tho we all concluded never again to make the attempt.—In our return discoverd the Young Horse, (rode up the Hill by HD) had broke loose and that the inner part of his Thigh was badly wounded; probably by the Spur of a Tree, it bled fast, which hurry'd us back to the Tavern where a Bath and suitable applications were made: here we dined, and about 3 o'clock after paying an extravagent Bill, we set forward to David Levans 18 Miles from Reding, a Tavern in Manatawny, to this place we got about Dusk, the Wounded Horse soon became stiff and his Thigh swell'd much—This Evening our Landlady, a dirty old Dutch Woman, refused Changing very dirty, for Clean Sheets, tho after much intreaty, she pretend'd to comply, but to our mortification found she had taken the same sheets, sprinkled them, then Iron'd and hung 'em by the fire and placed them again on the Bed; so that we were necessitated to use our cloaks &c & this Night slepp'd without sheets.—with the assistance of our two Servants cooking, we sup'd pretty Well and slep'd better than we had any Reason to expect, all in one Room—our Horses fared well, but the wounded one appear'd very bad in the Morning.

30 HS and self each folded a dirty Sheet Nutmeg fashion, and left then cover'd up in the Beds, for the old Woman;[9] old at; may it be the means to mend her Manners. her Husband is a rich farmer:—from this place to the Widdow Albrights at Macungee Spring we proceeded about 8 miles, and then Breakfasted tolerably for a Dutch House, from hence over several Miles of

9. Words crossed out.

Barrens, we pass'd near Plumsteds place, and pass'd thro. the Town of Northampton, commonly call'd Allenstown, from the Owner of the Lands hereabouts Wm. Allen or his Son James, who has a genteel House built here.—After Riding thro this Town we came to a Creek call'd Jordan, which we forded, and within about ¼ mile we forded the Lehigh first from the Shore to an Island and from thence over the broad and stony part to the other Shore—from hence we had 5 or 6 miles bad and stony Road to Bethleham, which however we reach'd in good time to eat a hearty Dinner—this Afternoon walk'd thro' several parts of the settlement with J.F Oberlin, examined the Single Brothers House, single sisters and Widdows Houses—Water Works &c—and then return'd to our lodgings at the Tavern in Bethleham.[10]

31 After Breakfast our company only, went 11 Miles to Christians Brun, after inspecting the Occonomy of this Fine Farm, the Mills, Brew-House, Dairy, &c and eating of their excellent Butter with Rye Bread, proceeded 1 mile to Nazereth-Hall, on our way our Horse stumbled badly in a rut; I jump'd out of the Chaise and strain'd my foot badly, so that it soon swell'd much and proved very painful—at the Hall Bath'd it, and from thence with a Borrow'd stockings, went to the Tavern, where we din'd with George Mc-Cullouch and [L]augher who we mett with at Bethleham on our arrival there—they accompany'd us as far as this place, and after dinner they set of for Eastown, we for Bethleham.

Sepr 1 This day confin'd to my Chamber, with my foot. RS. HD. and Hannah went to the Childrens Meeting this Morning—they drank Tea at Timothy Horsefields; H Vanvleck and his Wife there.

2d. Rain'd this day which confin'd us all within, only HD drank tea at Oberlins.

3 This Morning HD went to Fish without success in the afternoon, I rid to Horsefields & drank Tea with our Company their Family, HV. and wife.

10. Moravians settled in Bethlehem in 1740 and dominated the community for nearly a century thereafter. Their society was based on the concept of a joint economy in which members resided in communal living quarters and pooled their income to support the missionaries among them. In 1744 a house for single brothers was completed, and four years later when the men were removed to a larger building in order to accommodate their growing numbers, unmarried women made their home in the older structure.

By 1754 the Bethlehem waterworks was in operation. Among the first of its kind in the colonies, the system consisted of a waterwheel that provided power for pumps, which directed the water into a holding tank (information courtesy of Judith B. Claps, Board Member, Burnside Plantation, Bethlehem, Pa.; William J. Murtagh, *Moravian Architecture and Town Planning: Bethlehem, Pennsylvania, and Other Eighteenth-Century American Settlements* [Chapel Hill: University of North Carolina Press, 1967], 36–37, 73).

Sepr. 4 Set our Faces Homewards rode 10 Miles, very bad Roads to Widdow Teters, from thence 7 miles of a very rough tedious way to near Tohiccon where we din'd and after fording the Creek rid about 15 miles to Bartholomews, which we did not arrive at for near an Hour after dark—here we lodg'd and far'd well.

5 Rid 11 Miles to Yunkins at the foot of Chesnutt Hill—Breakfasted and then put forward, reaching home about Dinner time.

left home Sepr. 28 1771 seventh Day Eleven o'clock HD, and ED. din'd at the Red-Lyon Samuel Nottingham and John Bringhurst din'd with us.—Gunners run remarkabley wide.—came to G. Oats in the Afternoon, found our dear Child well; drank Tea at S. Merriotts. Mary Hall the only Lodger there at present—went after Tea to Priestlys;—spent part of the Evening at the Widdow Wrights, with S. Pintard, Sup'd at Priestlys, Micl. Hilligas and Jacob Bright, with us—We lodg'd at Priestlys.

29 Weather chang'd in the Night, very warm Yesterday: very cold this Morning Breakfasted at P——ys—set off about 8 o'clock, M. Hilligas, J. Bright, HD. and myself, stop'd at S. Oats and took leave of our Baby, and then rode on by the Falls Meeting House by Yarllys Ferry—stop'd at T. Yardlys, Baited our Horses and eat a seacond Breakfast there, from thence about 11 o'clock continued on our way to Wells's Falls or Coryells Tavern, the last 3 or 4 Miles excessive bad Roads, the Worst I think I ever pass'd. reach'd there to dinner; found Richd. Stittaford unwell with a Fever—after Dinner, HD—M.H. and J. Bright, Commissioners appointed for improving and clearing the Navigation of Delaware, and whose business to this place was to inspect the Works carrying on at these Falls; they left the Ferry, spent some time on the Water and return'd to me about 5 o'clock, when we again Journey'd on, & about Dusk got to the Widdow Jemmisons, here sup'd and lodg'd; and next morning the 30th set[11] Homewards, Breakfasted after 10 o'clock at the Billet Tavern and from thence reach'd Home without stopping at about ½ past 2 o'clock, to Dinner.

1771 Octor. 26 H & ED. left home, seventh Day. 11 o'clock, din'd at Andersons Red Lyon—Joel & Polly Evans, Adam Hubley, G. Groff, Nancy DeCow and Sally Nicholson, din'd there also—left them after dinner and proceeded on to G. Oats, found little Henry well, drank Tea with S. Oats; then came to Bristol, call'd at S. Merriotts; Nobody at home but Patty and Sally: then drove to Priestlys, their Beds all taken up; calld at Sally Larges; Richd. and Betsy Waln there, they left Philada. ½ hour after us.—stay'd but a short time a SLs then went to Bissonets where we sup'd and Lodged.

11. Words crossed out.

27 First Day: Went after Breakfast to George Oats; stay'd there upwards of an hour; Sally is in trouble conserning the disposal of her Children, Isreal talks of going to sea, Nancy to go home with us—came from G.Os to the Tavern—HD. went to Meeting. I took a Walk to S. Merriotts to Sim Betts, call'd at Docr. Denormandie, paid of his Account. HD. came there to me. dinn'd at Bissonets, set of after dinner, R. and E. Waln with us. baited at Fitz's at the Sheaf of Wheat: came home to late Tea, brought Nancy Oats, home with us in the bottom of the Chaise—found Sally Wharton and Becky Vanleuvenagh at our House.

Octor. 29. 1771; Sally Moore, call'd on me this Morning I went with her to their place at Point; dinn'd there; took a walk to Frankford Creek, back of Hugh Robertss place, on our return, mett Hugh, he took us over his House, out on the Top, the prospect very pritty, the Lands about Point remarkably level; went back to Wm Moores Place, and after dinner took another walk, return'd home in the Evening.

Novr. 5 1771 Benjn. and Susanna Swett came on a visit from New Castle, third day Evening.

Novr. the 7. fifth Day before dinner, H. and ED. took a ride to Frankford.

Novr. 10 First Day HD. and ED. took a ride round by Point and Frankford.

Novr. the 14 Daddy Swett and Wife left us after Breakfast. fifth Day Morning.

Novr. 17 first Day. HD. MS. and Nancy. went in the Waggon, to Bristol, they left home at 10, in the Morning Cuff drove—the Weather very fine—I expect they will bring Sally Oats and my little Henry back with them:—John Drinker call'd after dinner—in the Evening I step'd over to Neighr. Walns; this has been a lonesome day and Evening.

18 HD. MS. Sally Oat and my little Henry came before dinner.

19 and 20 they stay'd with us.

21. fifth Day HD and ED went as far as the Red Lyon, With our little dear Boy, on his way back to G. Oats:—din'd there, and after dinner parted with them—Israel Oat drove his mother and the Child in our Chaise—the Weather very fine.

1771 Novr. 26. third day took a ride with HD. before dinner as far as the 3 Mile Stone.

1771 Decr. 9. HD. AJ.[12] C Evans &c went to Burlington; return'd the 10—HD. cross'd over to Bristol went to see our little HD. found him well.

1771 Decr. 21. the Ship Chalkley. Ed. Spain Master saild, for Bristol. Isey Oat, went in her this is Capt. Spain first [Voi'e.] in her.

Decr. 15. 1771 Billy left of his Frock and shift, put on his Cassock and shirt.

Decr. 24. HD. and John Drinker, gone this Morning towards Trentown &c. in search of HD. JDs Son, who has been missing several Days—1771.

12. The words "[Jos] Galloway" crossed out.

1772

1772 Janry. 1. HD. left home at 8 o'clock fourth day Morning. John Brown with him for Baltimore in MaryLand;—George McColough, call'd this Morning.—Robt. Stephenson, his Wife and Mother spent this Afternoon with us—Sister and self. went this Evining to see our poor Friend Peggy Parr, who was taken this Afternoon with a fit of the Appoplexey; in which she lays: (A very affecting Scene)—Sister sat up all Night with her.

2 I went this Morning to see my Fd. peggy who still continues in the same Malancholy situation:—Sister went there after dinner, Aunt Jervis and the Girles spent this Afternoon with me—Sister came home in the Evening Peggy still the same—Judah Foulk came after 10 o'clock, to desire sister to go to Wm. Parrs, as the Doctor Expected a change e'er long in Peggy; she went accordingly with him stayd all Night.

1772 Janry. 3 Peggy Parr, departed this life, between 38 & 39 Years of Age—dull weather this day—We stayd at home all day, nobody here.

4 Sister and self went this Morning to Wm. Parr's, came home to dinner—A James, call'd this Afternoon.

5 First Day: I stay'd at home all Day—the Weather very cold—Sister and Sally went this Afternoon to meeting; and after to the Burial of our Friend M. Parr—Sister went this Evening in to Neighr. Swifts.

6 Molly Moore call'd this Morning—Sister, self and Nancy, spent the Afternoon at Neighr. Pollards; I went this Evening to Wm. Parrs.—Patty, Becky and Chalkley James call'd this Evening.

7 Stay'd at home all Day—Bad Weather—John Swift and Wife, and John Glover, drank tea with us; Joshua Fishers Wife was buryed this afternoon, AJ received a letter from HD.

8 Stay'd at home all Day. Betsy and Polly Jervis spent the Afternoon with us.—Neighr. Waln here in the Evening.

9 Stay'd at home all Day: nobody here—sister went in the Evening to Parr's, and to see Sally Emlen, who is unwell.

10 Sucky Mason, Docr. Redman call'd this Morning—I stay'd at home all Day—HD. return'd this Evening from MaryLand Richd. Parker buryed this Afternoon.

Janry. 14. 1772. Docr. John Kearsley, the Elder, was buryed aged 88 years.

Janry. 30. 1772. this Morning about 7 o'clock a fire broke out at Thos. West,[1] in second Street which communicated to those of John Wallace, one Smith next door, and to Wm. Saverys—the Roofs and upper Appartments of those 4 Houses, with a great quantity of Furniture & Merchandize were consumed.

Febry. 1. 1772. seventh Day—HD. and MS left home between 11 and 12 near Noon, in a Sleigh for George Oats,—Conrade drove—they return'd the 2, left our dear baby well—ordred Sally Oat to begin to wean him on Second day the 3 Instant.

Febry. the 12 we heard from our baby this Day, and several times by the Post Boy since he has been weaning; he takes it pritty well; and is bravely.

Feby. 17 1772 Benjn. Ardey; Abel Jamess Man was taken up, and put into Jail for taken Goods out of the Store &c. to a large Amount.

1772 March 3. Molly Brown, our Neighr. Walns Sister, dyed Suddenly.

1772 March 3, HD. went to Chester, he returned in the Afternoon, after our Friends Sarah and Debh. Morris with Joseph Oxley had taken Ship for London, Osburn Master.

1772 March 7 seventh Day: HD. ED. took a ride to Frankford, roads very bad.

1772 March 8. between 10 and 11 at Night, Sally Oat brought our dear little Henry home; they came down by Water in John Elwoods boat, First day.—Sally stay'd till the seventh Day following, went away in the Afternoon.

1772 March 13. Polly Pollard our Neighbor departed this Life.

1. The fire spread from the shop of Thomas West, a furniture and merchandise salesman (*Pa. Chron.*, Jan. 30, 1772).

1772 March 14. HD. ED. SD. AD. WD. went past the 4 Mile Stone in a Sleigh.

March the 11. and 13, very Snowy days—the Snow very deep for the Season, we have had very frequent Snows, this Winter past. 1772.

April 11 seventh Day. Benjn. Ardey, was whip'd, at the Carts Tail and this Day week is to be whip'd at the Post—1772.

April 15. 1772 HD. was let Blood.

April 25. 1772 ED. was let Blood.

April 28. 1772 HD. Docr. Moore &c—went to Perkioming after Breakfast, Robt. Stevenson, his Mother and Wife and Sucky Wharton, drank tea with us HD. return'd the 30th.

HD. went to Chester with Saml. Emlen, who embark'd in [Sporks][2] for London—May 1. 1772.

Ann Thornton, was bury'd May 11. 1772.

May 19. 1772 HD. and ED. went to Spring-Feild to the Burial of Morda. Yarnel; a very large meeting. third day. drank tea at Jams. Pembertons.

May 21. 1772 Richard Penn. Govenour was married to Polly Masters.

Billy Drinker put on Coat and Britches[3] May 12, 1772.

Sally Drinker went to Writing School April 22. 1772. to B. Jones.

May 31. 1772 H and ED. took a ride after afternoon Meeting to Frankford, drank Tea at A. James, Jos Scott and Daughter there.

June 5. 1772 HD. ED. took a ride to our place at Frankford, call'd at AJs.

2. Probably the ship *Mary and Elizabeth*, captained by J. Sparks. It had been cleared for London on Apr. 30 (*Pa. Gaz.*, May 1, 1772).

3. In the eighteenth-century Anglo-American world, boys and girls wore similar tunics or dresses from infancy until age six or seven, when the boys began donning breeches or jackets and trousers. At age five, Billy Drinker first wore breeches a little earlier than most boys, as did his brother, Henry (Karen Calvert, "Children in American Family Portraiture, 1670 to 1810," *William and Mary Quarterly*, 3d ser., 39 [1982]: 87–113; Philip Greven, *The Protestant Temperament: Patterns of Child-Rearing, Religious Experience, and the Self in Early America* [New York: Knopf, 1977], 282–86; see above, Dec. 15, 1771, and below, June 25, 1775).

June 7. 1772 Patty Oat. came on a visit First Day.

June 9. 1772. third day Morning Six o'clock HD. ED. took a ride Gloster Point, drank of the Mineral Water, which is brought over, at 4 d. p Bottle, Numbers of People resort there.

Patty Oat went[4] home June 13. 1772.

1772. June 13. HD. ED. AD. WD. HD Junr. [h]arry and Nany; set of in the Waggon for Frankford, but could not get the Horses' cross Race Street corner, they run back and behav'd so ill that we were oblidg'd to get out and stay at home.

1772 June 24 HD. and ED. went in the Chaise, Billy in the Bottom. to Monkton-Hall, to see Robt. and Hannah Stephenson; Robt. has gone there with his Family, out of the Way of the Measels, which is now in Town; and he has never had—Hannah expects to Lye-in there, we drank Tea with them—Polly Stevenson and S. Badger there:—R. Meridoth also.

1772 June 27 seventh Day about 10 o'clock HD. and self began a Journey in the Chaise, stop'd a little time at Fair-Hill, at Wm. Hills, where Rachl. Drinker and her Son Henry join'd us, in their Chaise, and proceeded on the Old York Road untill we came to Moses Shepards, about 11 Miles from Philada. where we stop'd & visited the Mineral Waters opposite his House, where one French has contrived a Bath, the Water tastes pretty strong:—At Loyds Tavern at the Forks of the Roads leading to Horsham and the Billet we stopp'd and dined and John Drinker with us who came there soon after us, his Son returning to Town after Dinner on our Young Horse which his Father had rid up. in good time this Evening we came to the Widdow Jemmisons where we sup'd and Lodg'd; S. Harold &c came in the Evening.

28 First Day: Breakfasted at the Widdows then went to S. Harolds, who with his Wife and her Sister Hannah Russel accompany'd us to Jos. Ellicots House, he being absent in MaryLand, we were amused with his curious four Face'd Clock &c for some time, then proceeded to Buckingham Meeting, said to be the largest House and Body of Friends belonging to it of any Country Meeting in the Province. Saml. Eastburn and Frd. Simpson preach'd—after meeting proceed'd to Howells Ferry 7 miles from our last Lodging, and after Dinner on the Jersey side continued our Journey towards Kingwood, in our way had a noble and extensive view off Robins's Hill, then had to pass about 3 miles through a rough Road call'd the great Swamp; arriv'd at Isaac Horners at Quaker-Town in good time for Tea; this about 22 Miles from Jemmisons.

4. The word "away" crossed out.

29 Breakfasted at I. Horners, then went Amy Horner in Company and visited Robt. Larges Family, his Wifes Mother Elizth. Wildman an Ancient Woman between 90 & 100 Years of Age, retains her senses very perfectly, but is so Paralytic as to be incapable of feeding herself for above [12] Years past, or of seting or lying still one moment, from hence we proceeded to John Emleys, who had in the Morning engag'd us to dine with him at his House about the distance of 3 Miles. After dinner JE. and his Sister Molly accompany'd us down to the River Delaware, about 8 miles, the Men cross'd the River.—we drank Tea at John Sherrads' and then return'd by way of Pitts Town & so to Isc. Hornors about 11 or 12 Miles from the River, supped here on good Strawberrys.

30 Breakfasted and Din'd at I. Hornors, and then set forward on our return, drank Tea on the Pensilva. side of the Ferry, and reach'd the Widdow Jemmisons about Dusk, where John Baldwin & J. Bright had just come by appointment to meet Delaware [Compy.] the former delivered HD. a Letter from Benn. Trapnel inclosing one from each of our Daughters.—Rachel Drinker and self went over in the Chaise to Lodge at Saml. Harolds H & JD. went with us; our Chaise being left at the Door without securing the Horse, he set off with one of SHs. Sons in the Chaise, and soon after was over set on the side of a Hill, without hurt to the Boy, and no great damage to the Carrage—Henry & John D went back to the Widdows to Lodge.

July 1 fourth Day. H. and JD. came to SHs. Henry borrowing Samls. Mare. they went down with their Compy. to the River.

2 this Afternoon they return'd and drank tea with us, they went yesterday down to the River about 12 or 15 miles & Lodg'd last Night at Yeardleys, Ferry & return'd this Morning to Corryells; This Evening they leave us and lodge at the Widdows—Sam. Harolds Wife, Rachel D. and self took a walk this Afternoon to John Hills about half a mile from S.Hs.

3. Jos. Galloway, John Kidd & his Wife, & ——— Gibb Sherriff of Bucks, and his Wife Abel James, & J. Vaux, John and H. Drinker, all Lodg'd at the Widdows, last Night.—This Morning we Breakfasted at S.Hs and after proceeded to the Billet at the Manor of Moreland, where Abel join'd us, from thence turn'd off towards Abingdon and Din'd at VanCourt Tavern, then road round by Oxford Church, drank Tea at Abel James at Frankford; came home this Evening my little Henry taken with a vomitting. the rest well.

July 6: 1772. MS. spent this Day at Mt. Hall, with Hannah Stevenson, HD. went for her in the Evening.

July 8, 1772 HD. on Horse back MS. ED. and Sally D in the Chaise, Harry, with us—went to Frankford after Dinner to our place: Sammy and Hannah Sansom and their daughter Sally, Richd. and Betsy Waln, and John Glover, drank tea with us there, return'd in the Evening.

July 20, 1772. HD. and MS. road out this Morning with our little Henry, which they have done several times lately, as he has been very unwell, with a vomitting and lax, and much troubled with Worms. MS. went after dinner, George Baker with her to Mt. Hall, to see HS. HD. went for her towards Evening they drank tea there.

July 22. 1772 fourth Day Afternoon; HD. MS, Sally, Nancy, Billy and little Heny. and Nany Oat, went over the River, they came home to Tea. S Sansom here.

July 25, 1772 Seventh Day Morning HD, set of for North Wales, with Saml. Neal &c.

July 27. 1772 I was call'd up between 12 and one, this Morning by Richd. Waln Betsy was brought to Bed about. four with her Daughter Rebecca, Second Day Morning.

July 28, 1772 Richard Jolloff was Drownd'd, he was playing in the River, but knew not how to swim.

July 28, 1772. Sally Oat came to visit us.

the 29. MS. Betty Davis, my Nancy and Jacob, went to Frankford, to clean the House, they came home in the Evening—Sally Oat went away this afternoon. My little Henry has voided nine worms this Day. 20 since he came home from Nurse. he has taken the Caro. pink-Root;[5] Rheubarb, and Bark for disordred Bowels.

July 30, 1772. Dickey Jolloff found, and Bury'd, a Bristol Lad, aged 19 years Lived with Abel James.—Henry voided 15 worms this Day.

31 Sister went this Afternoon to Robt. Stevensons, George Baker with her.

Augt. 1, 1772 HD. and MS. took a ride with our Child, he has voided 8 Worms this Day—HD. and self with Billy went to Frankford this afternoon,

5. Carolina pink root or Indian pink root, native to the southern United States, was effective in treating worms in children. Long used by Native Americans and adopted by southern colonists in the mid-eighteenth century, the root was administered in powders or infusions (W. Lewis, *New Dispensatory*, 231–32; Millspaugh, *Medicinal Plants*, 522–23).

spent some time at our Place, then went to Abels, came home rather late; Billy unwell.

Augt. 4. 1772. H Stevenson sent for one of us at 10 at Night, could not go.

5th. MS. went to see HS. she was brought to Bed last night or this Morning with her Daughter Jane; Sister went to ride with little Henry after she came from Hannahs, she went again this afternoon with Billy who has been feverish for several Days.

Augt. 9 my little Henry very Bad all Day, he took a vomitt this Morning.

10 Henry very poorly all Day—Saml. Neale embark'd this day in the Brig —— Curtis Master, for Cork.—Josey Drinkers Daughter buryed this Afternoon, 5 Weeks old.

Augt. 14 MS. and George took a ride before Dinner to see H Stevenson—My little Henry seems mending; he has voided 53 worms since he came home from Bristol 46 or 7 of them within the last 5 or 6 weeks—his Bowels has been greatly disordred and often troubled with a vomitting he is cutting his Eye teeth. Docr. Evans tends him.

Aug. 15 HD. ED. took a ride this Afternoon to see HS. and her little Daughter drank tea there.

Samuel Forthergill departed this Life June the 15, 1772.

Augt. 23 1772. First Day: HD. Abel James, and John Swift went to Bristol, HD. returnd the 24.

Augt. 29 HD. ED. took a ride up Germantown road, and round the Wissahiccon to Robt. Stevensons, where we drank Tea came home after sen set.

Augt. 31. 1772. ED. was let Blood.

Sepr. 1, 1772, Sally Moore calld on me this Afternoon, went with her to Visit H. Stevenson at Mt. Hall.

Sepr. 5. 1772. HD. and Daughter Sally went to Chester, and returnd in the Evening.

Sepr. 15. 1772 HD. went to Josh. Henszeys Wedding.

1772 Octor. 2 the Measels came out on Sally, after being 5 days very unwell she has been for 3 days past, much Afflicted with a reaching to vomitt, &c.

Octor. 6 Sally took a dose of Physick, it work'd her very often; she seems as well as can be expected,—On Seventh Day last the 3d Instant, HD. &c went to Burlington to the Burial of Elizabeth Smith, they return'd First Day at Dinner time.

1772 Octor. 10. H and ED. took a ride to see Robt. and H. Stevenson, drank tea with them, they are now at Re. Meridaths Place, but intend home soon.

1772 Octor. 12. HD. and self went to our Meadow at Point, then went to Frankford, came home to Dinner.

1772 Octor. 15 Nancy has the Measels coming out on her, tho not so kindly as could be wish'd, little Henry they are just appearing on 'tho he has been very unwell for a week past, they are both very poorly; Sally took a dose Physick to Day, and seems, thro' Mercy bravely—Nany Oat, beginning to grow unwell—Docr. Evans very unwell, Docr. Redman tends us.

Octor. 18 First Day: My dear little Henry very much oppress'd, his Fever very high the Mesels have never come out as they should have done; he was let Blood this Evening; Philip bound up one Arm but could not find a vain; struck the Other without success, and at last blead him in the back of his Hand.

19 The Child rather better, Nancy took a dose of Physick, she seems bravely.

23 little Henry took another dose of Physick, continues very poorly.

24 Nancy and Nany took Physick they seem in a fair way of doing well Sucky Wharton dyed this Morning.

Octor. 26 1772 Billy has had a high Fever for 3 days past, but no Mesels has yet come out.

28 Billy very full of the Measels, little Henry continues very poorly.

31 Billy took a dose Physick, did not work little Henry very poorly something of the Flux.

Novr. 1 Billy took another dose of Physick, little Henry better.

4 Billy but poorly his Nose very Sore took another dose Physick to little Purpose.

5 Billy continues very poorly, he took a pill this afternoon, his Nose bad.

7 Billy took a fourth dose Physick Yesterday which did not work him till in the Night he is but poorly.

8. 9. 10. Billy bad with the Bloody Flux greatly pain'd in his Bowels—the Flux better but the pain continues.

Novr. 12 Billy took the 5th dose Physick still continues much disordred in his Bowels.

13 Billy appears to be better.

Novr. the HD. Senr. was let Blood.

1772 Novr. 24 third day. the first Monthly Meeting up Town. HD. chose Clark.

1772 Novr. 30, ED. was let Blood.

1772 Decr. 2. Benn. Swett Senr. came to visit us, he went away the 7th.

1773

1773 Janry. 27 HD. went to Bybary to the Burial of Sarah James, return'd in the Evening.

1773 Febry. the 6 HD. went to Racoon in the Jerseys, returnd the next Day, First day.

1773 Febry. 10 HD. went to MoorsTown &c in the Jerseys return'd the 13.

1773 Febry. 16 Sammy Morton dyed.

1773 John Vansant dyed in Jail of the Small-Pox Febry.

1773 Febry. 25 HD. set of after Dinner for Concord. Notingham &c, he return'd the 28.

1773 March 9 HD. and A James, went after dinner into the Jerseys, rain all this afternoon the 10 HD. return'd, very wet with the Rain.

1773 March 14. HD. and A James went into the Jerseys, they return'd the 17.

1773 March 20, HD. ED. and little Henry took a ride round the Race Ground[1]—3 Miles.

1773 March 24 HD. ED. and little Henry took another ride round the Race Ground—3 Miles.

March 24, 1773. HD. ED. SD. AD. WD. spent the Afternoon at Jams. Bringhursts where we were entertaind with sundry Electrical expirements perform'd by Js. B, road home after Night in the Rain.

1773 March 30 John Brinton and Wife—Samuel Trimble and Wife, with their Sister Rachel Trimble, left us after dinner, they have spent 2 or 3 Days

1. Philadelphia's racing ground was located at Center Square, then west of the settled part of the city and now the site of Philadelphia's City Hall (Bridenbaugh, *Cities in Revolt*, 364).

here.—HD. with Lawrence Salter left home this Morning designing for NewArk—HD. was let Blood Yesterday.

April 3 HD. return'd he has been to New York.

1773 April 2 Went with A James, his Wife, Daughter Becky and Son Jos, in their Waggon to their place at Frankford, drank Tea there came home before Evening—10 miles this is the most foward Spring that we have had for several years past.

1773 April 6 MS. and ED. went to Frankford in the Chaise, George on Horse Back, came home to Tea—10 Miles, HD. went this Morning into the Jersyes, return'd in the Evening.

1773 April 8 HD. ED. and little Henry went to the Chaise to Frankford in the Afternoon—10 Miles.

1773 April 9 HD. and Daughter Sally went round the Race Ground on Horse Back; Sally on the oldest of our Brack Mares, the first of her riding alone, unless, 2 or 3 times up and down our Alley.

1773 April the 11 First Day—After Dinner—HD. Josey James, and myself, cross'd Delaware, the wind pretty high at N W, did not sail—ED. road on the Old Mare as far as Moores-Town, had not been on Horse back for 15 years past—drank tea, sup'd and lodg'd at Josh. Smiths—a good Deal shaken; Breakfasted there next Morning, then set of in a Borrow'd Waggon, with our 2 Mares. for Ansiunc[2] at the Iron-Works, Polly Smith with us; stop'd at Charles Reeds Iron Works 10 miles from Moorestown; then went on 10 miles further to Lawrence Salters, dined there late:—went in the afternoon to the Forge, saw then make Barr-Iron; Lodg'd there at LS.

13th. Went this Morning in L.Ss Waggon, (Dolly Salter; her half Sister, Becky Gordon; Polly Smith and my self) to Goshen 3 miles from the Iron Works, to take dinner to HD. LS. &c who have been the greatest part of this

2. The Atsion ironworks in the Pine Barrens of New Jersey, near Shamong Township, were first developed by Charles Read, a lawyer and political leader of Burlington County, N.J. In 1766 in conjunction with two other partners Read built a forge to convert pig iron into bar iron. He ran into financial difficulties in 1773 and on Mar. 16 sold his interest in the forge to Henry Drinker and Abel James. In a financial reorganization on Apr. 2 Drinker and James became owners of 50.1 percent of the forge and Lawrence Salter, one of Read's original partners, the owner of the remainder. In 1774 the owners expanded the furnace of the forge, making it independent of other forges and allowing the ironworks to exploit the bog ore at the site (Arthur D. Pierce, *Iron in the Pines: The Story of New Jersey's Ghost Towns and Bog Iron* [New Brunswick, N.J.: Rutgers University Press, 1957], 20–35).

Day, survaying the Lands; we examined the saw Mill, then return'd to Atsiunk to a Late dinner, left the Men behind.

14 Went after dinner in LSs Waggon, HD. LS. Polly Smith and ED. to the Seader Swamp, sat in the Carriage while the men went out to examine the Swamp, Josey James with us—rain all the after-noon; call'd in our way back at Ephrime Clynes at Goashan; came back to LSs to late tea;—I was very unwell this Evening.

15 stay'd within all day bad weather I was up 3 or 4 times in the night very much disordred in my Bowles, occasion'd by going last night to the Foarge in the rain, and being out yesterday. [ ] unwell all Day.

The 16th, sixth day: after Breakfast left Atsiunc; Lawrence S—— his, Wife and Sister, with us, made a Short stop at C Reads, lefe Dolly and Becky there:—LS. and HD. went elsewhere on Business; M Smith my self and Josey, continued our Journey, bated at Benjamin Thomas's, then proceeded on, HD overtook us near Moorestown, where we eat a late dinner; and about 4 left them; HD. and myself in the Chaise Josey James on Horseback, he led my Mare, I being too unwell to ride her—cross'd the ferry towards Evening very calm—came home after candle light, found all wall—road 78 miles.

1773 April 20, I went this Afternoon to Frankford with Billy by my side, Harry on one side of the bottom, I drove the Chaise for the first time, call'd at McVaughs and at Sindrys, came home a little after 5 o'clock—10 miles—HD. set of this Afternoon for Bristol—he return'd the 21.

April 21 Went this afternoon to Frankford in A James Waggon, Becky James Senr. Becky Junr. Patty Sucky, Tommy, Polly Jacobs, and myself—drank tea there, came home in the Evening 10 miles.

1773 April 22, went to Frankford this Morning, HD. on his New Horse, my self on the Old Mare—came home to Dinner—10 Miles.

1773 April 23, Went to Frankford and round the Point. rode, with Billy, Harry in the Bottom came home to Dinner—10 Miles.

1773 May 3. HD. ED. and little Henry took a ride this Morning as far as the 3 Mile stone on the old Ferry road—6 Miles.

1773 May 4 HD. and L. Salter set of this Morning for Bristol, HD return'd before six in the Afternoon ED. went this Morning with Molly Foulk, to J. Lawrences Pump, between 6 and 7 o'clock came home to Breakfast, went to Youths Meeting.

1773 May 7. Went to Frankford this Afternoon MS. ED. and Billy in the Chaise, HD on Horseback, came back to Tea, 10 Miles.

1773 May 8. HD. and his Daughter Sally took a ride, each on horseback, before dinner.

1773 May 9 First Day: ED, Nancy, and Harry, went in the Chaise; to the 6 Mile Stone call'd in our return at Frankford, came back to Tea—12 Miles.

1773 May 10. HD. with the 4 Children; Nanny Oat, and Jacob, went to Frankford, in our Company Waggon, bought of [J]P—Jacob drove for the first time, they came home towards Evening.

1773 May 11. ED, Billy, and Harry, went to Point, in the Chaise, mett Caly Parr there, walk'd up to the old Summer House, then went to A Jamess Place, none of the Family there—stay'd but a short time,—mett HD—and his Daughter Sally, each on Horse back, two miles from Town, they turn'd back, and came home to Tea—12 Miles.

1773 May 17 ED, Nancy and Harry, went after dinner in the Chaise to Frankford;—about ½ mile from Frankford; in our return met HD. and Sally on Horse back; went back to our Place with them, stay'd about ½ an hour, then set of for home, ED. on Sallys mare, Sally in the Chaise with Nancy, Harry drove; at the 1 Mile Stone stop'd; Sally again mounted the Mare, ED the Chaise,—came home to Tea—11 Miles.

1773 May 18, ED. Billy and Harry, went this morning in the Chaise the Point and Frankford, round: a cool Pleasent Morning came home to Dinner—10 Miles BS. and EW. married this Day.

1773 May 21.[3] HD. ED. and little Henry took a ride up the Wisahecen Road, and across to Germantown road, came home to dinner,—in the Afternoon ED, and Neighbour Waln, with our Harry went to Frankford, walk'd about there some time, came home to Tea—17 Miles.

4 Shifts[4]	20 Clouts
4 gowns	5 Frocks
7 Aprons	3 Night Gowns
2 Linnen Under Pe[t]icos.	6 shirts
3 Shorts Gowns	6 or 7 Arm cloths
7 Neck Handkers.	4 pair Stockings

3. After the entry for May 21, 1773, ED proceeded from the back of the volume toward the center, concluding with an Apr. 15, 1773, account of HSD's inoculation.
4. This list is found inside the back cover of the manuscript volume.

7 Pocket ditto	6 Day Caps
2 pair Pockets	3 Night Caps
6 Day Caps	
3 Night ditto	
3 pair Stockings	

H——V. Ws IIIIIIIIIIIIIIIIIIIIIIIIIIIIII

7.8	6.8	7.1–9½
7.6	10	6.5–9
1.4	5	11–11½
6.8	2.3	13.19.6
5.6	8	
7.9	8	
12.5	1.3	
7.8	15.6	
8.9	5.3	
4.–	1.	
3.10	6.–	
4.9	2.–	
11.8	6.6	
1.6	3.6	
4.8	4.–	
10.6	5.6	3.3
4.–	5.3	8.8½
2.9	8.10	
3.6	9.2	
12.–	7.7	
1.10½	4.6	
10.6		

Sundries	"	3
Paid for Bringing Box from Shollop	"	7
Paid for Freight for Mattrass	1 "	–
for Bringing it up to the House	"	6
Sundries	"	3
Paid for Washing—	10 "	–
Paid for Bathing ED	3 "	–
Paid for ditto—HD	1 "	–
Paid for a Bath Ticket	3 "	–
Paid for mending Pincushon Hoop	1 "	–
Paid for a Basket	1 "	–
Paid for Washing	9 "	6

Paid P. Buckley. Bath Subscription—	2 " – " –
Paid Widdow Merriott	6 " 15 " –
Paid for Washing	9 " 4
Paid S. Merriott	7 " 6
Paid for a Tea Pot	1 " 6
Paid for Brown Holland	– " 7
Paid Polly Campbell	17 " 3
Paid for her pasage in the Waggon	5 " –
Paid for Pruins	1 " 3
Paid for 2 Bath Tickets	6 " –
Sundries	– " 3
Paid for Paper	– " 6
Paid Sally Hoffman for a poor Man	5 " –
Paid for Silk	2 " 6
Paid for pruens and raisons	2 " –
A Bath Ticket	3 " –
Paid for Washing—[5]	13 " 6
Paid Sarah Merriott	3 " – " –
Paid Peggy at Bath	15 " 11

Dimsdale, M.D. on the Small Pox

about the 7 day from the eruption liquors should be taken in abundance—if

1772 Novr. 16 our old Parrott dyed which we have had near 21 Years.

List of HD. Junrs. Cloths. which, Sally Oatts has, with him—

16 Clouts
2 Night Gowns
3 Frocks
5 Shirts
4 Day Caps
3 Night ditto
4 Arm Cloaths.
3 Dimoty Peticoats.
2 Flannel ditto
1 Long Double Gown
his Jockey Cap &c
1 Pair Worsted Stockings

5. The words "paid [Sally Oat]" crossed out.

Henry Drinker Junr. cut his first Tooth the beginning of Sepr. 1771 at G. Oats.

Henry Drinker Junr. walk'd alone, the beginning of Novr. 1771; just turn'd of 12 Months at George Oats.

HD. junr. began to Chatter in the Spring 1772.

1773 Feby. 18 HD. junr. took a Pill fifth Day, in order to prepare him for innoculation; it made him very sick and vomited him several times.

the 21. First Day he took the second Pill, which also made him very sick.

24 took another Pill, which likewise made him very sick.

27 the Child took a dose of Jollop,[6] which vomitted him several times but did not Purge him.

28 First Day, our little Henry was innoculated by Docr. Redman, between 12 and 1 o'clock—he took a pill this Evening, which did not make him sick as the others has done.

March 2d. he took a Pill; but a little sick with it.

the 3d. he took the 6th and last Pill not much sick.

the 5th. he took a dose Jollop, it vomited him as the other had done but did not purge him.[7] in the Evening he was feverish and unwell, the 6th. continued the same tho at times Chearfull, he has not had a stool for 3 days past.

7 First Day; the Child continues feverish; Molly Moore gave him a Glyster,[8] in order to open his bowels, which had the desir'd effect; some appearence of Small Pox this Evening.

the 8th. 8 or 10 come out; he has been taken in the Yard and to J Howels to Day. and has drank Water from the Pump, several times.

9 Several More has appear'd, he continues feverish.

6. The word "purge" crossed out. Jalap is a cathartic or purgative drug obtained from the tuberous root of a Mexican plant, *Exogonium purga*. The name was also used for purgatives derived from the tuberous roots of native North American plants, such as the wild potato, morning glory, and related species (*OED*; Vogel, *American Indian Medicine*, 324–25).

7. Words crossed out.

8. The words "[which proved a]" crossed out.

10 seems bravely, but very Cross.

11 got a little cold by the damp Weather.

12 and 13 the Small Pox begins to turn, he has about 40, or 50 and is through mercy bravely.

15 he took a dose of Jollop, which did not work.

18 he took another dose of Jollop which [vomited] him once, but did not purge—his Arm is not quite as well as could be wish'd.

April 15. the Childs Arm appears to be heal'd, it has been a long time sore tho not very bad.

Hannah[9]
Sandwith
Notwithstanding
Constantinople
Philadelphia
Sandwith
Sally Sandwith
Sally
Drinker
Billy
Drinker

232 miles[10]

1776 John Salter Dr to 2 pr Shoes—
Saml. Sanson Dr to 1 pr Shoes—
1777 Janry. Robt. Waln Dr to 10 quarts and one pint of old Mederia Wine

May 13: Woodcock dr. to 12 [lb] Coffee.

Received Janry. 1777 from E. Waln 14 ounces of spun cotton, instead of one pound.

9. The manuscript volume for May 22, 1773–Oct. 16, 1777, is covered in brown paper. The outside front cover reads, "1773, 4, 5, 6, 7." In addition to this list of names, there are many faded numerals and some undecipherable words on the outside front cover.

10. The material "232 miles . . . third day" is found on the inside front cover of the manuscript volume.

S. Gardner came to Work 1774 Janry. 5. fourth Day—She came to Work Novr. 22. 1774 third day.

1773 May 22 HD. set of for Bristol, with Clem Biddel, at 4 in the Afternoon, seventh Day—he return'd first Day afternoon.

1773 May 24—MS. Sally and Harry went to Frankford, came back to Dinner—ED. Billy, and Harry took a ride this afternoon past the 4 mile Stone, came back towards Evening 8 Miles.

1773 May 26. MS, Billy, and George Baker, went to Frankford this Afternoon, HD. A James, there.

1773 May 28—ED. Billy and Harry, went this Afternoon to Frankford—10 Miles.

1773 May the 31. ED. Sally. and Harry took a ride this Evening round Point and Frankford—10 Miles.

1773 June 1. ED, Sally and Nancy went this Morning before 6 o'clock to Lawrence's Pump—set of at 8 o'clock for Frankford ED. Nancy and Harry—came home after 10 to Breakfast—10 Miles.

June 2 ED, Sally and Harry went up Frankford, road as far as the black Horse, then turn'd round Kingsington into Point road—4 Miles.

June 3 HD. arose at 4 o'clock this Morning went with Abel James, John Drinker &c to the Iron-Works—return'd the 6th.

1773 June 4. ED. George Baker and little Henry went this Afternoon to Frankford, stay'd some time at our place, then rode up the Road past the 6 m-Stone stop'd in our way home at Billy Ashbridges, walk'd in their Garden, came home by sun set—12 Miles.

June 7. HD. ED. WD. went round point and Frankford Roads in the Chaise—10 Miles.

June 8 HD. Sally and Jo Waln went this Afternoon to Frankford.

June 10 HD. ED. drank Tea this Afternoon with Dorcas Mountgomry at her Place; were overtaken on the Commons by a storm of wind and Rain as we returnd—3 Miles.

June 14 HD. A. James &c went this Morning to White-Marsh. they spent the day there—ED. Nancy and Harry went this Afternoon to Frankford—10 miles.

June 17 fifth Day HD. on horse back ED. and Sally in the Chaise left home after dinner, found it very Hott stop'd at Frankford; stay'd above an hour there, then went on to the Red-Lyon, drank Coffee there.—proceeded to Shamney Ferry, near where the Mare had like to have run away with us,—we came to Bristol by dusk; call'd at Halles to see Docr. Evans, who is very far gone in a Decay I think—Sally and myself lodged at Widw. Merriotts HD. at Bisonetts; Molly Foulk and her Daughters Polly and Debby, at Merriotts. Sally very unwell in the Night with a lax and Vomiting, she had eat to much Fruit. Tommy Giles also there.

18 Went this Morning to Bath HD ED and Sally, came back to Breakfast, then set of for Bybary to the Burial of William Walmsley, we foarded by Redmans went through the woods to Buybary.—we went to Wms house great numbers of Carriages and Horses there, thought it best to go to meeting before the Burial, as it was very Hot and dusty—John Churchman, Wm. Brown and John Hunt appear'd in testimony—We dinn'd at Giles Knights—came back to Bristol by way of the Ferry—drank tea at SMs Sally slept with the Widdow Merriot HD. with me.

19 HD. left us this Morning early went 20 odd miles further. Where the Workmen are clearing the River—Sally and self went this Morning to Sim Betts, Tabby and Becky Fisher, Nancy and Polly Parr, lodge there—ED. SD. went to Bath, came home to Breakfast. Cs. Thomson calld. Molly Foulk gone with Docr. Evans to Jos Galloways ED. SD. drank tea at Ennion Williams, Phins. Buckly went with us to Bath; Becky Chase came back with me like for rain.

20 First Day: HD came [bake] to Bristol this Morning after Breakfast, Sally and my self were at Bath this Morning—we calld at Sarah Larges, Sucky Waln there—Docr. Evans gone this Morning to AJs Frankford—We left Bristol by 12 o'clock, din'd at the Red Lyon—stop'd at Abels to see the Doctor who is very ill—came home in the Evening 61 Miles.

June 24 ED. Nancy and Harry went this afternoon to Frankford, pick'd Rasberries, went to A James's Place found HD. there, he came up with Abel—we drank Tea there, Docr. Evans very ill, HD. came home in our Chaise with Nancy—myself in A James's Waggon—10 Miles.

June 28 ED. and George Baker took a ride this Evening round Point and Frankd. 10 Miles.

June 29 ED. George Baker went this Morning to Frankford—10 Miles.

June the 30. 1773 Docr. Cadwalr. Evans Departed this Life at A Jamess Frankford after a Lingering illness aged 58 years.

June 30. HD. and several others gone this Afternoon to accompany the Doctors Corps from Frankford, to North Wales, where he is to be intearr'd tommorrow morning.

Sally, Harry and self, went this Afternoon to Point no Point, the Mare run with us a little Way, came home Frankford road—12 Miles.

1773 July 3 Sally went on the Mare, with her Daddy, on horse back, John Drinker his Wife and Children in their Chaise, to Utopia.

July 6 HD. John Drinker and Charles Tomson set off early this Morning for Atsion—ED. took a walk with Betsy Jervis to John Lawrences pump.

July 7 ED. and George Baker went to Frankford this Afternoon—10 Miles.

July 10 Went this Morning before 5 o'clock with M Foulk to Lawrences pump; examined John Dickensons New House—then road round the race Ground—3 Miles HD, return'd this Evening from Atsion.

July 13. HD. ED. and little Henry, went this afternoon to Frankford—10 Miles.

July 14 HD. ED. and Billy, took a ride this Afternoon, up Germentown road, the old York road, round by [J] Pleasents place; to Frankford, stay'd there some time, came home after Sun Set—12 Miles.

July 16 HD. on Horse back. ED and Nancy in the Chaise, went this Afternoon to Frankford 10 Miles.

1773 July 21. HD on Horse back, ED. and Billy in the Chaise, went this Afternoon to Frankford—10 Miles.

July 22 MS. and Sally, spent this Day at Abel Jamess at Frankford, Benny went with them. HD. for them in the Evening.

July 24 HD. and John Drinker left home this Afternoon; for Bristol or near it—return'd the 25.

July 26 HD. ED. and little Henry, went this Afternoon in the Chaise to Frankford 10 Miles.

July 29 HD. on Horse back, ED. and Nancy in the Chaise, went this Morning to Frankford 10 Miles.

Augt. 3. HD. ED. went this Afternoon in the Chaise to Frankford—10 Miles.

Augt. 5 B Trapnel & ED. went this Afternoon in the Chaise as far as W Parrs' Gate at Point then went round to Frankford. beyond the 6 Mile Stone, home by Sun Set—15 Miles.

1773 Augt. 6. HD. went to the Iron Works, to Reeds Vandue, he return'd the 7th.

Augt. 8. First Day: BT. ED. went after dinner to Frankford, came back in Meeting time 10 Miles.

Augt. 12. HD. ED. in the Chaise BT. and Sally, on Horse back, spent this afternoon at A Jamess Frankford—10 Miles—tryed Frankss Horse.

Augt. 13 HD. ED took a ride round the Race Ground to try Millers Horse—4 Miles.

Augt. 13 Capt. Allexr. Gillon, his Wife, Molly Newman and Polly Pickering, South Carolina Foulks; who came recommended to HD—set of this Afternoon for New York in our Waggon.

Augt. 15 First Day Evening HD. and AJ. went as far as Moores-Town, on their way to the Iron-Works—B Booth, came the 14 they return'd the 19.

Augt. 17. BT. ED. and Billy went in the Chaise as far as the 8th. Mile Stone; beyond Beggrs-Town stop'd in our return at Hillery Bakers, School, at Germantown; stay'd but a short time there.—came home by sun set—16 Miles.

1773 Augt. 18 George, ED, and little Henry went this Afternoon in the Chaise round Point rode to our place at Frankford came home by sun set—10 Miles.

Augt. 20. sixth Day, about Noon, HD. and ED—left home for Willmington—stop'd an hour at Chester, proceeded on, and arived towards Evening at Willmingn. put up at one Marshalls at the Royal George—drank tea there and intended to Lodge, but James Lee, desired our Company at his House, went over eat super and lodg'd there—HD. left me at JLs in the Morning and went up BrandyWine in search of Plank; heavy rain while he was gone—he return'd to JLs to dinner, after which we set of Homewards, stop'd at BrandyWine Bridge at Tatnals son in Law to J Lee—stay'd there but a short time, rode on to Abraham Robinson, at Nemans Creek; where we alighted just as a Shower of rain came on; about 5 o'clock stay'd there all Night as it continued bad weather, and breakfasted with them next Morning then proceeded. towards Home, where we arrived to dinner, after baiting at Darby—First Day—55 Miles.

1773 Augt. 25. HD. ED, went in the Chase to Frankford, in the forenoon—10 Miles.

Augt. 28. HD. and John Drinker left home early this Morning for Atsion &c—they return'd the 30, after staying to Burlington quarterly meeting.

Augt. [29] John Penn proclaim'd Governor—he came to town Yesterday, from N York, where he arrived with his Wife from London.

Augt. 31. ED. was let Blood—MS. very unwell with something like the fall Fever,[11] Sally, has a sore Eye Docr. Redman tends them.

Sepr. 4. HD. MS. in the Chaise, Sally and Sam Lyon on Horse back, went this Afternoon to Frankford.

Sepr. 7. HD. went to White-Marsh, returnd in the Evening.

Sepr. 8. Sally Parrock, Bury'd this Afternoon.

Sepr. 11. HD. set of for Atsion after Breakfast return'd the 12.

11. Some medical writers in the eighteenth century noted seasonal differences in patterns of disease. John Pringle was one English writer who characterized several maladies as autumnal fevers. Benjamin Rush in his writings on Pennsylvania's climate also noted that after Aug. 20 the quality of air in Philadelphia changed and the wind passing over dams and mill marshes brought the seeds of fevers into the city. Some of the diseases more common in the autumn months included yellow fever, malaria, typhus, dysentery, colic, cholera morbus, and diarrhea. Rush attributed these to the increased miasma in the air caused by food rotting on wharves, green wood, wet paper, wet cotton, stagnant water in privies, and other substances. Certainly yellow fever and malarial fevers were more common in the late summer and autumn months, as were fluxes and dysenteries caused by eating unripened and unwashed fruit (King, *Medical World of the Eighteenth Century*, 132–34; Benjamin Rush, "An Account of the Climate of Pennsylvania and Its Influence upon the Human Body," in *Inquiries and Observations*, 2d ed., 1:111; Benjamin Rush, "An Inquiry into the Various Sources of the Usual Forms of Summer & Autumnal Disease in the United States, and the Means of Preventing Them," in *Inquiries and Observations*, 2d ed., 4:163–72).

Sepr. 17. HD. Nancy and Billy in the Chaise, John Drinker, Hannah, and our Sally, on Horseback, went to Frankford this Afternoon.

1773 Sepr. 19. Sarah Morris &c came from Chester where they arrive'd yesterday in Osborn from London.

Sepr. 21. HD. and JD. set of after dinner for Atsion, they return'd the 23.

Sepr. 24. HD. went to Burlington to the Burial of Josey Smiths Wife; he return'd the same Night, very much disordred in his Bowels—the 25 took a dose of Physick from JR.

Octor. 1. HDs now bravely he has been very unwell all the meeting Week,—Moses Brinton his Daughter Abby, and Son in Law; from towards Lancester, lodg'd with us, as did John Ballderston and Wife: they left us this day.

Octor. 4. HD. ED. and Billy took a ride round Point and Frankford, before dinner in the Chaise.—10 Miles.

Octor. 5. MS. ED. and Billy, went in the Chaise Harry behind, a round aboutway, to Sally Whartons, drank tea there—2 Miles.

Octor. 6. Billy took a Vomitt, he has been unwell several weeks past, a lax and sometimes a Vomiting.

1773 Octor. 8 HD. and JD, went this Afternoon to Atsion sixth Day—return'd the 10, First Day.

Octor. 16. HD. J Drinker, and Sally, went on horse-back, to the Widdow Gordons.

Octor. 19. HD. went after dinner, to Accompany Thos. Goodwin, as far as Burlington—ED. fell of a step at Wm. Fishers, this Evening, and sprain'd her Ancle—Billy Jobb'd a Pen-Knife up his Nose, which occasion'd the Blood to flow so fast, that we sent for Docr. Redman,—[but] happly stop'd it in a little time—HD return'd the 20th.

Octor. 20—MS. and G. Baker went to Frankford.

Octor. 22 Lawrence Salter and Wife came, went away the 28.

Octor. 26. Elizth. Roberson, Mary Lever, Margary Norton, Isaac Zane, and

John Pemberton, din'd with us, after dinner we had a[12] setting with them. they are now visiting Familys.

Octor. 30. HD. and ED. took a ride round Frankford and Point—10 Miles.

Novr. 3. HD. set of for Atsion, before dinner he return'd the 4. in the Afternoon.

Novr. 8 1773 HD. and MS. took a ride this Afternoon to Point and Frankford, try'd S Pleasants Horse.

Novr. 13. HD. ED. took a ride before dinner, round Frankford and Point—10 Miles.

Novr. 22. HD. ED. took a ride before dinner round Frankford and Point 10 Miles.

Novr. 23 ED. was let Blood.

Novr. 24 HD. ED. took a ride before dinner, up the Wissahiccon road, as far as the 4 m Stone 8 Miles.

Decr. 2, 1773. AJ. and HD. sent a paper to the Coffee-House this Evening conserning the Tea.[13]

Decr. 7. 1773. our back Parlor Chimney took Fire this Afternoon, it had been sweep'd but a month and 2 or 3 days; soon put out.

Decr. 10. AJ. HD. and JD. set of this Morning Early, for Atsion—they return'd the 13, second day Morning.

Decr. 14 HD. ED. took a ride before dinner, as far as the 3 M Stone,

12. The word "meeting" crossed out.

13. James and Drinker, like other agents, had posted a bond enabling them to sell dutied British East India tea, the object of great opposition in the colonies. During the autumn of 1773 a popularly chosen extralegal committee of twelve (later augmented to twenty-four) pressured the agents not to sell the tea. Agents Thomas and Isaac Wharton, despite a previous agreement to stand together, yielded to the committee's demands sooner than did James and Drinker, who were caught between their business obligations, their bond, and the popular opposition in Philadelphia to landing the tea. Finally on Dec. 2 the committee of twenty-four secured a pledge from James and Drinker that they would not insist on landing the tea from the ship *Polly* (Ryerson, *Revolution Is Now Begun*, 34–37; Labaree, *Boston Tea Party*, 97–103; *Statement of Philadelphia Consignees to the Committee*, Dec. 2, 1773, in Mss. Relating to Non-Importation Agreements, 1766–75, *APS*; James & Drinker Statement, Dec. 2, 1773, in Drinker Papers [1739–79] at HSP).

return'd home by [the front] of Kingsington, where they are just begining to build a Ship for James & Drinker—6 Miles.

Decr. 13 1773 George Baker went to Germantown to stay a few days with his Mother as he was unwell.

Decr. Saml. Sansom Senr. in a bad way with a sore Toe, which has lately mortified.

Decr. 23 began to Snow last night, and continued most of this Morning, the first Snow we have had this Winter; we have been favourd with a remarkable fine Fall.

Decr. 24. an account from Boston, of 342 Chests of Tea, being thrown into the Sea.[14]

Decr. 25. John Parrock call'd this Evining to inform that the Tea Ship, was at Chester.

Decr. 27. began to Snow, about noon, continued 24 hours, tis' now (the 28) near 2 feet deep.

Decr. [27.] The Tea Ship, and Cargo, sent of this Morning.

Decr. 29. little John Oat Burye'd.

Decr. 31 HD. MS. and the 4 Children went round Point and Frankford in a Sleigh.

14. A special postscript edition of the *Pennsylvania Gazette* on this date brought Philadelphians to their first published accounts of the Boston Tea Party of Dec. 16 (*Pa. Gaz.*, Dec. 24, 1773; for further account of the Boston Tea Party, its background, and its consequences, see Labaree, *Boston Tea Party*).

1774

Janry. 8 [1774] HD. John Drinker and Sammy Sansom set of before dinner for Burlington—seventh Day return'd the 10.

1774 Janry. 19. HD. ED. took a ride after dinner round. Point, to Frankford,—drank tea at A James's—10 Miles.

Janry. 29 HD. in Company with Capt. Harper, and others, left home, this Morning after Breakfast for Baltimore &c in MaryLand, Conrade, waits on him. weather very cold—seventh Day.

Febry. 9. HD. return'd in the Afternoon, from My.Land.

Febry. 17 Early this Morning HD. left home with J Drinker for Atsion, they[1] walk'd over the River on the Ice.—return'd the 18.

Febry. 21. ED. was let Blood.

Febry. 20, last Night a Soap-Boyler Shop down-town took fire and was burnt down.[2]

Febry. 23. our old Friend Saml. Sansom Senr. departed this Life this Morning.

March 1. My little Henry, went first to School; to, R. Jones, and H. Catheral—& Nancy went to Drawing-School—to Ty. Barret.

March 4. HD. ED. took a ride before dinner round part of the Town—1½ Mile.

1774 March 7 HD. was let Blood.

from March the 7 to April the 12, HD. went to Atsion JD. with him, and to Burlington, AJ. with him, while ED—was up stairs.[3]

1. The word "went" crossed out.
2. The shop belonged to Thomas Badge (*Pa. Gaz.*, Feb. 23, 1774).
3. ED gave birth to Molly Drinker Mar. 14, 1774.

April 14. Sucky James Departed this Life—she pass'd the first meeting, with R S Smith the 22 ultimo—Age'd 17 years.

April 20. HD. and JD. set of this Morning for Atsion they return'd the 23.

April the 18. HD. ED. took a ride to the 3 Mile Stone, before Dinner—6 Miles.

April 21 MS. ED. in the Chaise George Baker on Horse back, took a ride round the race Ground and to the 2 mile stone on the Ferry road 4 Miles.

22 MS. ED. GB, took a ride round the race Ground &c—4 Miles.

Nany Oat went to School to H Catherall April 20.

24 First Day: I went with Abel James and Wife; their Tommy and our Billy, in their Waggon to Frankford, after dinner—drank tea there.—10 Miles.

1774 April 25 HD. MS. went to the Burial of Charles Jerviss Son John, aged 5 months.

April 24 or 25. Sucky Linnington formerly Say dyed.

April 2[8] Molly Moore left us, and went to Mayberries at the Iron-Works.

April 27 HD. ED. took a ride to Kingsington, clim'd up to the side of our new Ship which is building there—came home by Charles Wests place—4 Miles.

May 3. Govr. H——h——n, &c, carted round the Town hang'd and burnt in Effigie.[4]

May 4. the Weather was uncommonly warm for the season, the 27 Ultimo[5] the Mercury in the thermometer stood at 84°—and this morning it snow'd very fast: which appear'd odd as the Tulips &c were blooming in the Garden.

on Seventh Day last, the 30, April, were executed, here, 5 persons, 4 men and

4. Massachusetts Governor Thomas Hutchinson's failure to oppose British taxation policies aroused hostility in the major colonial port cities. On May 2 residents of Philadelphia constructed a wooden effigy of him, to which was affixed a plaque describing him as a traitor to his native country. The likeness was placed in a cart, conducted through the streets, and finally burned (*Pa. Gaz.*, May 4, 1774).

5. The words "[and this morning]" crossed out.

a mulatto woman, the Woman, and one of the men for Murder, one for counterfeiting, and 2 for burglary.[6]

May 7 HD. ED. took a ride to the New Ship, and round into Frankford road—4 Miles.

1774 May 10. HD. and A. James, went after dinner to Burlington, returnd the 13 Instant.

May 16 HD, A James, John Drinker and Josh. Smith, went this Morning in our Waggon to Burlington, return'd the 17.

May 27. Sally Drinker and Nany Oat, took a dose Physick; Docr. Redman tends 'em for a rash and soar Throat,—which great numbers are afflicted with at this time, in town—, several have been taken of, with the Putrid soar Throat,[7] of which number were, Abey Howel, and Sucky James.

May 26 we were Alarm'd this Morning between one and 2 o'clock, with a knocking at our door and cry of Fire, prov'd to be at A James's in Sam Lyons Room, it was Happly put out, before much damage was done.

May 28. HD. left home this Morning early, for Atsion, in the Sulkey return'd the 30.

June 3. HD. and his Daughter Sally, went to Woodburry in the Jersyes, on horse-back—Sally dined at John Hopkins, after meeting, Where she went in the Chaise with cosin Sally—they return'd in the Evening.

1774 June the 6, HD. ED. wint in the Chaise, as far as Frankford, between 7 and 8 o'clock—with our Neighbours, Richd. & Elizth. Walln, on their way to their Mill, near Crosswicks where they are going to reside—took leave of them at our Place—Robt. Waln and Wife, went with them to Bristol—HD. and self, call'd at A Jamess Place.—went to the Point Meadows—came home before Eleven o'clock—11 Miles.

6. At the Court of Oyer and Terminer held in Philadelphia in April, five men and one woman had been sentenced to be executed. Joseph Price, Thomas Stephen, and Richard Burch were convicted of burglary, James Swain and a mulatto named Elizabeth were convicted of murder, and Bernard Repton was convicted for counterfeiting colonial bills of credit. Apparently only two of the three burglars were hanged (*Col. Recs. Pa.*, 10:172; *Pa. Gaz.*, May 4, 1774).

7. A serious inflammation of the mucous membrane of the pharynx, the tonsils, and the folds of the palate that resulted in the formation of gangrenous patches in the throat. The illness could be fatal if the eroded blood vessels in this area hemorrhaged (Gould, *Dictionary of Medicine*, 1220, 1063).

June 10, HD. ED. and little Henry, took a ride to the Ship &c—4 Miles.

June 12 First Day, HD. John Drinker and Josey James, went after dinner to Atsion.

June 13. my little Molly taken this Afternoon with a vomit[ing], she is better the 15.

June 14. we were knockd up before Day this Morning by Portugease, his Mistress, Hannah Stevenson, being ill, Sister waited on her; I could not leave my little Molly she being unwell—Hannah Was brought to Bed, about 5 this Morning of her Daughter Hannah.

1774 June 22, Our 4 Children, Nancy Oat, and Nancy Waln, Hannah and Polly Drinker, went in our Waggon to Kingsington, Jacob, and Harry, went afoot to see the New Ship Chalkley Lanch'd, the Seacond of that Name, Belonging to James & Drinker HD. din'd there—the Children return'd and all din'd with us.

June 24. HD. set of very Early this Morning with A James, &c for Burlington return'd the 26, after being to Atsion.

June 28 HD. ED, and little Molly, took a ride near Frankford, before Breakfast, the Child being unwell with a lax—HD. and J Drinker, set of this Afternoon for Mantua Creek, they return'd the 30th—[9] miles.

July 1 Sister and the 3 oldest Children, went this afternoon to Frankford, Jack drove Jacob [and] Nancy took little Molly out in the Chaise, which they have done for several days past.

July 3 B. Trapnel taken unwell—the 4 and 5–6 continues very unwell keeps his Room, with a sick stomach and Fever Docr. Park tends him.—he continued the same till the Morning of the 9th without our being apprehensive of the danger he was in or Docr. Parke; tho' Benny had desir'd him to call in Dr. Kearsley, who did not see him till the 9th. when he was much changed for the worse his fever had chang'd to Billious.[8] he departed this Life about 4 o'clock the Morning of the 10th. First Day—and was so much chang'd by 9 o'clock that the Doctors advis'd by all means to bury him that day which was

8. *Bilious fever* in its simplest definition meant a fever accompanied by a copious discharge of bile. Many writers found this to be a symptom of intermittent and remittant (malarial) fevers, occurring in the summer and fall, but it was also used to describe other fevers (Cullen, *Practice of Physic*, 111–12; Buchan, *Domestic Medicine* [1799], 187–88; Gould, *Dictionary of Medicine*, s.v. "fevers").

accordingly done between 7 and 8 in the Evening—Benny was in his 27th. or 8th. year; much lamented by all of us.

July 15. HD. left home for Atsion—Hillary Baker, lodges here, in the place of our poor Benny, who we miss very much—My dear little Henry, is now I hope, upon the recovery from the Bloody Flux, which he was taken with, during Bennys illness. Docr. Kearsley tends him—HD. return'd the 20th.

July 19. MS. Billy and Harry went this Afternoon to Frankford in the Chaise they drank tea at Abels, came home towards Evening.

1774 July 2[0]. Sally and Nancy, left Hannah Cathrells School.

July 24 First Day: Billy went With George Baker to Germantown, in the Chaise, they spent the Day there.

25: HD. and Sally, took a ride on Horse-back—to Frankford.

30. MS. Billy little Henry, Harry, and Nanny, (who they took up out of Town,) went in the Chaise to Frankford, HD. and Sally on Horse back, Sally rode her Daddys Horse for the first time—they clean'd the House, drank Coffee there, came home by dusk in the Evening.

Augt. 2. HD. ED. and little Henry in the Chise Sally and Josey James, on Horseback, went this Afternoon to Frankford, Oswell Eve, and his Son came there, from our Place we went to A Jamess Place, ED. on Horse-back ED. came home on Horseback Sally in the Chaise—10 Miles.

Augt. 3 HD. ED. took a ride on Horse-back, this Afternoon round the race Ground—3 Miles.

1774 Augt 3 The New Ship Chalkley, Edward Spain Master sail'd this Afternoon, for Bristol.

Augt. 12. MS. Billy and little Henry, in the New Chaise, J Drinkers Horse; ED. Hannah Dingee and little Molly in the old Chaise and Mare—Jacob on Britton—went after Breakfast to Frankford.—HD. and Sally came up on Horse back after dinner; Sally on Noble, HD. on Wilddear the Children and Daddy, went Fishing to the Creeck—came home all togeather after Tea—10 Miles.

Augt. 13 HD. ED, took a ride round Point and Frankford this Afternoon; on Horse back—10 Miles.

Augt. 14 HD. A James and Tench Francis set of after dinner for Raccoon Creek; first Day return'd the 16 in the Evening—J. Drinkers Son Henry slep't here.

Augt. 16. HD. ED. took a ride this Afternoon towards Frankford—7 Miles.

Augt. 19 fifth Day: HD. Sally and Nancy, in the New Chaise, MS. Billy and Henry in the Old Chaise, went after Breakfast to Frankford,—Rachel Drinker, her Son Josey and Daughter Polly—Sammy Sanson and Hannah, with their Daughter—John Drinker on Horse back—went after dinner to our Foulks at Frankford, Becky James with her daughters, and son Tommy and Sally Dukes, drank Coffee with them—the Children were much delighted catching Fish—Jacob and Herry there.

Augt. 20. HD. Sally and Hillary Baker on Horse back—ED. Nancy and Henry in the Chaise—Harry behind—went this Afternoon to Frankford; caught Fish at the Mill-dam—came home little after sun-set—10 Miles.

Augt. 26. Reba. Waln and her Daughter Nancy—MS. ED. Sally, Nancy and Billy, went to see the Wax-Work made by Mrs. Wells,[9] opposit the Royal white Oak.

Augt. 27. HD. ED. took a ride on Horse-back to A James' Frankford—10 Miles.

1774 Augt. 31 HD. MS. Sally, Nancy, Billy, Harry Catter, and Oswel Eve—cross'd the River after Breakfast before 9 o'clock, intending for Atsion—HD. and Sally went on Horse back Sister in the Chaise with Nancy and Billy, she drove Hutchins—it has been a warm day—they return'd Sepr. 2 sixth day—Nancy road on Horse back all the way home, which is 30 miles the way they came she had never been on Horse back before but once, up and down our alley—Sally came home very unwell, sick at stomach and disordred Bowels—eating Huckel-berrys, corn &c.

Sepr. 7 fourth Day: MS. and Billy spent the Day at A Jamess Frankford.

9. Rachel Lovell Wells (d. 1795), born a Quaker, was the widow of Philadelphia shipwright James Wells. In the early 1770s she and her sister, Patience Lovell Wright, began making portraits in wax. The two sisters toured the South with their portraits during the winter months and displayed their work the rest of the year at the Wells's home in Philadelphia and at Wright's home in New York City, until Wright left for London (E. J. Pyke, *A Biographical Dictionary of Wax Modellers* [Oxford: Clarendon Press, 1973]; For a description of Wells's work from 1776 see John Adams's account in Charles Coleman Sellers, *Patience Wright: American Artist and Spy in George III's London* [Middletown, Conn.: Wesleyan University Press, 1976], 119–20, 13–14, 24–43).

Sepr. 7. Sally and Nancy went to Mrs Woods Kniting School.

1774 Sepr 14 HD. ED. and Sally went to Frankford on Horse back; HD. on Wildear, Sally on the Mare ED. on Noble—were overtaken by two of O. Joness Daughters, they went with us to A Jamess Neighbor James and the Girls gone to Jos Knights—came home Point road 10 Miles.

Sepr. 17. HD. took a ride with Billy behind him for the first time they went 6 or 7 miles Billy much tir'd.

Sepr. the ——— John Ballderston spent the Week with us—Mary Moore, Ruth Jackson, and Mary Perkins, lodg'd with us.

Octor. 6. HD. and Sally on Horseback—ED Nancy and Henry in the Chaise, went to Frankford after dinner—went to the Creek fishing—ED. and little Henry, call'd at Nr. Sindrys—Sally fell in the Creek—came hom after Sun-Set—10 Miles.

Octor. 7. R Walln, her daughter Nancy and Son Boby. ED. Sally, Nancy, and Billy, & MS—took a walk this afternoon, to the new Prison:[10] workman very busy there—walk'd in the Negros Burying Grownd, and went in to J Dickinson's new House, came home to Coffee.

Octor. 16. HD. and John Drinker set of this Morning early for Atsion—First Day—they return'd the 17—Jacob with 'em.

Octor. 19 HD. and John Drinker set of about noon for Chester County. they return'd 21st.

Octor. 24. Jacob [Shup] went away to a Taylor.

Octor. 25 our dear Nancy, very unwell with a fever, she had her Throat sore about a week ago, of which she got better, but has been sick at stomach at times sence yesterday and day before, she broke-out in a Rash, which has too suddenly disapear'd;—Docr. Redman tends her.

26 Nancy better.

10. The construction site of Philadelphia's new jail was at Walnut Street near Sixth Street. The old city jail at Third and High streets was overcrowded and underfunded, and it lacked security. While the new jail was able to receive some prisoners in 1775, it was still only partially completed when the British entered the city in 1777 (Bridenbaugh and Bridenbaugh, *Rebels and Gentlemen*, 250–53; Teeters, *Cradle of the Penitentiary*, 17–27).

Novr. 3 ER. and R[J] &c[11] return'd from a Jurney into the Jersys, where they have been 4 or 5 Weeks, Becky had our Mare.

Novr. 1. HD. and Nancy went out on Horseback, road 6 or 7 Miles Nany on Noble.

Novr. 11. HD. Sally, Nancy, Billy, Henry took a ride round Frankford in our Waggon Bill Bowles drove for the first time.

1774 Novr. 12. HD. Sister, Billy, John Drinker and his Wife; set of after dinner, in our Waggon for Chester, (intending for Concord quarterly meeting tomorrow) Bill Bowles drove they return'd the 14th.

Novr. 28. HD. and our Children &c went this Morning to see the Timber-Ship, lanch'd in their way to Frankford, where they stop'd, then went up Oxford road, then home.

Novr. 29. HD. MS. Billy, Henry, took a ride this Afternoon in the Waggon—our dear little Molly was taken unwell this Evening with a Vomiting, which continued all Night and all Day the 29th. Docr. Redman tends her—she is better this Evening the 29th.

Decr. 2. Sally Eve departed this Life.

Decr. 3. HD. and J Drinker set of in our Waggon for NewCastle, in Consiquence of a Letter HD. received Yesterday, from Daddy Swett, informing of his being very ill of the Jundice—return'd the 5.

1774 Decr. 7 MS. went this After noon with Neighr James to Oswel Eve's.

Decr. 8 HD. MS. and Sally went this morning about 9 o'clock for New-Castle, in our Waggon, Black Bill drove—having heard that Daddy Swett was worse, Benny Swett call'd after they were gone, in his way to N Castle dull Weather Received a Letter from Robinson and Sandwith,[12] for MS.—giving account of the Marriage of [J]S.—and the Death of Cozsin Isabella &c.

Benjamin Swett Senr. departed this Life Decr. 8. 1774, fifth day morng—My Husband Sister and daughter, arrived there that Evening—they are not yet return'd, this is the 12th: dady Swett was to be bury'd last seventh day the 10th.—My little Molly has had the Rash since they went away, and Henry is

11. The words "[come home]" crossed out.
12. Robinson and Sandwith was the Dublin mercantile firm with which ED's cousin Joseph Sandwith was associated (see above, Nov. 17, 1758, and Aug. 22, 1762).

now exceeding poorly, with a [sore] throat, fever and Rash Docr. Redman tends them. HD. MS. &c return'd the 13, little Henry very bad—the 14 his fever abaited, and his Throat got better.

Decr. 28. it began to Snow last Night and the Snow, this morning is near 2 foot deep.

1775

1775 Janry. 11—HD was let Blood.

Janry. 25. HD. left home before dinner for Atsion—S. Emlen and Wife, Nancy Potts, Sally Parish and Daughter Debby Mitchel, and Saml. Plesents—drank Coffee with us.—rain this Evening.

26 dull weather.

27 clear weather and warm. S Logan here.

28 received a Letter from HD, given an account of his being unwell which has prevented his return.

29 First Day, HD. return'd (John Tomson the Clark at Atsion) came with him, in LSs Waggon, he was very unwell indeed, of a fever &c, the 30th. he seems better, Docr. Redman tends him.

Febry. 3, HD. better, but trouble'd with a Cough.

1775 Febry. 4. Richd. Waln, sent for our Waggon—which he has bought for 40£.

Febry. 10 HD. was let Blood, he continues very unwell, and Feverish.

15 my Henry still unwell.

21 HD. took a Vomitt in the Evening he is much better this day—the 22 continues mending—fever gone, pain in his back better.

27 HD. went to meeting Yesterday-afternoon; and down to the Store to Day—I hope he is recover'dng.

March 8. New-Ship Chalkley, arriv'd here with servants—in Ballist.

March 10. HD, on Wild-Deer, Sally on Noble, Billy on the Mare, and black

Bill on Brittian, took a ride to Frankford. this afternoon, they came home to Coffee.

1775 March 16, HD. and Billy, went with A James, (in his waggon); this Morning to Frankford; to the Burial of Wm. Ashbridge,—they return'd to Dinner Snow all this Afternoon, Sucky Hall sleeps here.

March 17. John Trapnel dyed.

March 21. HD. and JD. set of after dinner for Atsion,—third-day—return'd, the 24th.

April 1. HD. set of this Morning Early for NewCastle—Nancy is now we hope recovering of a fever sore Throat and Rash—HD. return'd the 3.

April 4 Batchelor's-Hall burn'd.[1]

April 13. Susannah Swett came to Live with us.

April 14. Children went to Chapple. S & A.

April 15. HD. was let Blood.

April 29. R Walker, E Robinson and M Lever, &c. went away.

1775 May the 1. Bill Bolis, was innoculated by Docr. Redman.

May 3. Billy Drinker, went to Shool to. Wm. Dickinson, the first of his going to a Mans School.

May 4. HD. set of for Atsion, return'd the 7 first Day.

May the 5 Benjamin Franklin arrived here.[2]

May 8 Bill Bolis, went to his Lodgings, on account of the Small Pox.

1. Bachellor's Hall, a large, handsome, square building with pilasters and a commanding view of the Delaware River, had been erected in the Kensington section of Philadelphia County, north of the city, in the first half of the eighteenth century. The wealthy Philadelphians who constructed the building intended that it function as a private club. The last survivor of the group was entitled to the premises. The hall, which eventually came into the hands of the Norris family, was the site of many dancing and tea parties. It also earned a reputation as a place "where maidens were inveigled and deceived." It was destroyed by fire on the morning of Apr. 4 (J. F. Watson, *Annals*, 1:432–33; *Pa. Journal*, Apr. 5, 1775).

2. Franklin returned to Philadelphia from London, where he had been serving as a colonial agent (David Freeman Hawke, *Franklin* [New York: Harper & Row, 1976], 227, 349).

May, 11. HD. and John Drinker went to Burlington, return'd in the Evening.

May 18. HD. ED. took a ride to Frankford the first time I road with our Horse King, 10 Miles.

May 24 HD. MS. and Billy, Bill Bolis with them, set of for Flushing after Breakfast—they return'd June the 3.

M. Pleas's.
J. Drinker
H. Lloyd
Doc'r.

1775 May 24[3] HD. MS. and Billy left home this Morning—Abel James, call'd this Morning—talk about Sister's Linnens Niles here—Bill owes him he says 34/—Becky James Senr. here this Evening. Ailce Coats, Rachel Woodcock call'd George Baker opening goods [this] Evening paid 2/6 Tax.

25 Molly fell out of Bed last Night an attemt was made last Night to break open the Jail, to resque one Steuart, who is condem'd for foarging Mony[4]—Molly Gosnold here this Morning for to Borrow Sheets—Sarah Mitchel and Molly Stretch, drank Tea with us—A Lad call'd for HD. to make up a Board. at the School Corporation Saml. Hopkins, call'd for a paper I step'd over to R Walns.

26 John Glover call'd this Afternoon to let us know he had seen HD &c, R James and J Strouds Wife here this Evening—J Drinker call'd S Wallace in the Hospital dead.

27. R. Jones here this Evening.

28th. First Day: S Swett went to Meeting with the Children this Morning myself wint with them this afternoon—R Waln, J. Drinker here.

29. I went out this afternoon to look for Jane,—Ay. Shoemaker[5] call'd.

3. For purposes of continuity, the entries for May 24, 1775, through May 5, 1777, are arranged here in chronological order, even though the manuscript entries do not always follow progressively. Not only were several loose, unrelated manuscript pages sewn together at an undetermined time, but ED herself occasionally backdated and duplicated entries during that two-year period.
4. *Pa. Ev. Post,* May 25, 1775.
5. "Morris" crossed out.

30 went this Morning to A. Taylors—Amos here—I received a Letter from HD. by Post, wrote to him John Drinker call'd—Wm. Brown drank Coffee[6] with us—A James call'd this Evening.

31—Wm. Brown borrow'd the Mare—Neigr. Waln drank Coffee with us—I Went with Nancy this Evening to A James'—very warm weather.

June 1 Becky [Vanlenargh], Betsy Thomson and Nancy [Vanceealaugh] drank Coffee with us. Nancy and. Polly Parr call'd—John Drinker call'd—I received a Letter from Thos. Pearsal.

2 at home all Day—Widdow McKnight and a School Mistress, call'd—this Afternoon.

June 6. HD. ED. SD. AD. went to Jos. Smiths Wedding, who was married this forenoon at the Bank-Meeting-House, to Patty James.

1775 June 15 HD. ED. went to E Stiles this Afternoon—stay'd there 'till towards Evening then went to Frankford 10 Miles.

June 25. little Henry put on Coat and Britches.

July 9 HD. self and 4 Children went this afternoon, to the Burial of little Hannah Drinker, daughter of Jos. Drinker—not 10 months old—they bury'd last week a Son and Daughter (twins) who were born the week before—Aquila & Prissila.

July 11. Third Day. HD. S Swett and our Nancy, left home, at little before Six—for Chester, intending tomorrow for Willmintown—the hotest day this Year—they return'd the 13 Instant.

July 26. HD. set of this Morning with George James. for Atsion &c return'd the 29.

Augt. 2. HD. went after dinner for Burlington, in a Boat, with A James. and Oswel Eve—return'd the 3 to dinner.

Augt. 9. HD. SD. AD. WD. in the New Chaise MS. S Swett, and HD. Junr. in the old Chaise:—Harry on Horseback,—went to Frankford, to spend the Day—fourth Day.

6. "Coffee" written over the word "Tea."

Augt. 16 MS. Janny and little Molly went this Morning to Frankford. HD. Billy and Henry, Robt. Waln and Wife went to them after dinner.

Augt. 18 ED. went with S. Moore to Point in the Afternoon.

Augt. 20 First Day: Billy and Henry went to Germantown with G. Baker.

Augt. 23. HD. MS. SD. AD. WD. HD Junr. Naney Oat and Harry—spent the Day. at Frankford—S & H Sansom went to them after dinner.

Sepr. 5. Ship Chalkley Sail'd.

Sepr. 6. Isaac Hunt, and Docr. John Kearsley were exposed in a Cart, through some parts of the City[7]—the Doctors Hand much wounded with a Bayyonet.

Sepr. [11] HD. set of for Atsion after dinner—return'd 16th.

Sepr. 16 John Jervis junr. departed this Life.

1775 Octor. 2. HD. MS. and Henry went to Frankford, Sister got a bad cold,—Maudlin at Frankford sick.

Octor. 9. Anna Kelly came to us.

Octor. 11. HD. MS. and Henry went to Frankford. before dinner.

Octor. 13. HD. went to Atsion in the Sulkey—return'd the 21.

Octor. 13 1775. HD. went to Atsion—I drank Tea at Uncle Jerviss—stepped over to Nr. Walns in the Evening Robt. Bown and Sam Fisher here in the Evening.

14. A Jame's borrow'd the Mare—Reba. Waln here this Evening—much talk about Men of War.

7. Isaac Hunt was an attorney who had represented a dry goods retailer before the Philadelphia Committee of Observation and Inspection. The retailer was accused of selling goods contrary to rules set up by the Continental Association, which promoted a boycott of British goods, and Hunt, who had Tory leanings, challenged the committee's right to regulate commerce. Hunt was forced to submit to popular pressure, however, and agreed to make a public confession on Sept. 6, when he was carted around the city in an orderly fashion apologizing to groups of residents. Dr. John Kearsley, also a loyalist, observed this procession and fired on the militiamen escorting Hunt. The militiamen then released Hunt and seized Kearsley, who was then carted around the city and subjected to taunts and abuse by its residents (Ryerson, *Revolution Is Now Begun*, 128–32).

15 First Day—All went to Meeting, but ED. this Morning.—in the Afternoon ED. SS. Sally. Nancy and Henry. Becky Scattergood, and S Wharton drank Coffee with us. Sally spent part of the Evening.—Hilling Borrow'd Noble.

16. B. WoodCock Breakfast'd here, I went out for silk this Morning MS. and George went to Frankford this Afternoon—Becky Jones and John Drinker call'd.

17. Becky Waln spent this Afternoon John Drinker here, borrow'd the Mare.

18 Spent this Afternoon at G. Meads Becky James, John Drinker.

19 rain almost all Day.

20 rain Ditto.

E Waln Cr.—
1 Bottle Snuff—
3/4 yard Ribbon—
1½ yard White Persian

John Drinker
C West
J. Bringt

M. Plest.
J. Drink
H. Lloyd
Docr.
A Oat
K Howel
[I] Parish
SE & [JT]
[J]P. SS
RW. K[H]
R[J]

Reba. Waln
John Drinker
S. Penington
B. Burge
C. James
K. Howel
S. Sansom
R.W
[J]D
Docr.
[SS]

Octor. 24. our Friend Sarah Morris departed this Life, Aged about 73 years.

Novr. 15. HD. & L. Salter, went this Morning to Burlington, return'd the 17th.

Novr. 27. HD. was let Blood.

Novr. 30. Thos. Pearsal and D. H. Wickham came here—they went away the 6 Decr.

Decr. 13. Harry went to School.

Decr. 14 HD. went to Radner Monthly Meeting return'd the same Evening.

1775 Decr. 17 First Day. HD. went to Woodberry to the Funeral of our Friend Isaac Andrews.

Decr. 19 third Day—HD. with John and Joseph Drinker set of after dinner for King-Wood, return'd the 23.

1776

1776, Janry. 8. HD. was taken unwell on fourth Day, fifth Day sent for Docr. Redman—was let Blood in the Evening, for an Inflammation &c. continu'd very unwell 'till the 17th. then got better.

Janry. 21. Lydia Parker was Buryed.

Janry. 25 ED—M.

Janry. 26 Judah Foulks was Buryed.

Janry. 30. JD. call'd before the Committee.[1]

Febry. 9 HD and JD. set of about Noon for King-Wood—John Drinker and the Fishers advertised in hand-bills—(from the 11th of this Month, to the 17 ED[2] Chill and Fever, Face much swel'd with St. Anthonys-Fire—).[3]

1776 Febry 9. HD. JD. left home about noon for King-Wood—Paper out from the Committee.

10 A Storm of Rain Hail and Wind in the Night—Josa. Howell—Abel James,—Becky Jones, and B Waln here to Day—Sister went this Afternoon to J Drinkers.

11. on sixth Day Night I had a Chill and Fever—have sence been very unwell with a soreness in my head and Neck[4]—The Children at meeting this Morn-

1. John Drinker and Thomas and Samuel Fisher were called before the Committee of Observation and Inspection for the City and Liberties of Philadelphia on Jan. 30 for refusing to accept continental bills of credit. On Feb. 5 the committee issued a statement condemning them as enemies of their country; the three men neither denied nor appealed the charges. The committee also precluded them from all trade with the inhabitants of the colonies (*Pa. Journal*, Feb. 7, 1776; *Col. Recs. Pa.* 10:486–87).

2. Words crossed out.

3. St. Anthony's Fire, also known as erysipelas or the rose, is characterized by red swellings on the face, the legs and face, or the whole body, and is caused by streptococci. Some forms attacked women in childbearing years (Buchan, *Domestic Medicine* [1799], 188–91; Gould, *Dictionary of Medicine*).

4. Words crossed out.

ing. Sister and the Girles this afternoon. Becky James Senr. Danl. Drinker Caty Howel and Son,—and Nany Carlilse here this Day.

12 had a very bad Night, got up with my Forehead very much swel'd discover'd it to be St. Antoys Fire—sent for Dr. Redman—Jacob Shoemaker call'd, a man for poor Tax—H Sanson, Becky Waln, Rachel and Henry Drinker here to Day:—fine Weather.

13 I arose this Morning with my Face and Eyes so much swel'd, that I nither look'd nor felt fit to go down stairs, therefore stay'd above—Docr. Redman—Rebbecca James Senr. & Junr. here—and Becky [Jones] Betsy Drinker.

14 Henry Drinker Dr. Redman, John Parrock, Saml. Emlen—Reba. James, Rachel Drinker here—My Face badly swell'd and painfull—rain this Evening.

15. Caty Howell, H Catherel Becky James, Reba. Waln, Dr. Redman and Henry Drinker here this Day—The Swelling much abated in my Face Johney Drinkers and the Fishers Stores shet up this Evening by the Committe.[5]

15th. John Drinkers Store shet up by the Committe—. HD. JD. return'd the 18th.

16 Fine Weather, Dr. R— Aunt Jervis and Betsy, Sally Logan here—Sister went to J. Drinkers—I took a Dose Rheubarb.

17. H Drinker, R Jones, John Parish Josa Howel, here this Day—Abel James.

1776 March 2 HD. left home about 10 o'clock for Atsion, returnd the 6th. fourth Day Night, very Stormy, Crossing the Ferry.

1776 March 2. HD. left home Sammy Sansom—call'd,[6] din'd A Benezet; Salors Wife, G. Churchman, call'd—Cheese from Burlington, fell on Sisters Toes—Ellection[7]—MS. out this Morning at R Stevensons &c.

5. On Feb. 15 the Council of Safety directed the Philadelphia Committee of Observation and Inspection to seize all of John Drinker's books and papers and deposit them in a locked and sealed chest or trunk in his ship and to lock up the windows and doors of his stores and warehouses and nail them shut (*Col. Recs. Pa.* 10:486–87).

6. The name "Tommy James" crossed out.

7. A by-election for the seat held by Benjamin Franklin in the Pennsylvania Assembly. Franklin, who had never occupied the seat, resigned on Feb. 27, giving Philadelphians an opportunity to elect another representative to the assembly in his place (Ryerson, *Revolution Is Now Begun*, 159).

3 First Day—Booth in Town—Sammy, Hannah and Sally Sansom—Reba. Waln.

4 Nanny Andrews here, brought a Letter from Jos. Drinker—John Drinker call'd—Saml. Emlen.

John James
David Eastaugh
John Parish
Joseph Yerkas
Becky Scattergood
S. Swett
Jenny Wood
Reb Jones
Betsy Jervis
Polly Ditto
Edw'd. Stiles
Polly Pleasents and Daughter
Sally Logan
John Drinker & Wife supped
James Huchingson
Saml. Emlen
Polly Waln

March 12 HD. Nr. Waln, and Jacob Shoemaker viset'd Fair-Hill School.

March 29 HD set of about Noon, sixth Day for NewCastle &c, return'd April 1st.

April 1st. Robt. Hares Malt-House burnt.[8]

April 13. seventh Day—HD—and Billy—John Drinker and Henry Clifton, set of after Breakfast for King-Wood—the 20th. they return'd HD & WD.

April 25 HD and L. Salter set of after Breakfast in the Chaise—towards Bristol—return'd in the Evening.

April 26. HD. was let Blood.

May 3. HD. SD. AD. and HD Junr in the Chaise—Billy on Horseback—went to Frankford in the Afternoon—S Emlen Wife & Children spent the

8. *Pa. Ev. Post*, Apr. 4, 1776.

Afternoon with us—George Dylwin also—S Emlen appeared in Testimony GD in Prayer.

1776 May. 4—3 Men were hang'd here—one for the Murder of his Wife, the other two for Robery.[9]

May 8th. HD. this Morning Henry Mitchel and Jos James went to Atsion—the Town has been in Confusion this afternoon on account of an engagement between the Rowbuck Man of War and the Gondelows[10]—the 9 another fight below, without much Damage—HD, return'd the 10th—sixth Day.

May 15 HD. and Sally, left home after dinner for Burlington, fourth Day—they return'd the 20th. they spent 2 Days at Richd. Waln's &c.

May 19 Rebbecca Mc.Vaugh, our old Neighbor at Frankford was buryed.

May 21. our Old Friend Joshua Emlen departed this Life.

May 29 HD. in Company with Joseph Meriott, Joyce Benezet and H Catheral left home this Morning intending for Buckingham—return'd June the 1.

1776 June 4 Saml. Notingham din'd with us—he went away, for home after dinner.

June the HD went with John Pemberton and S. Emlen (on their way to Rhoad-Island) as far as Trentown.

June the 10, ED. went with M. Pleasents to Frankford, to A James.

June two or 3 Men call'd to look at our Window Weights,[11] found them to be Iron.

June Sally went with her Aunt and Harry to Neighr. Stiles's Place.

9. On Apr. 11 William Bales and James Jones had been convicted of robbery at Philadelphia's Court of Oyer and Terminer. This capital offense had been perpetrated upon John Cunningham on Dec. 7, 1775. They were executed along with John Woodward, who was convicted of the murder of his wife, on May 4, 1776 (*Pa. Ev. Post*, Apr. 11, May 4, 1776).

10. On this day two heavily armed British ships, the *Roebuck*, a man of war, and the *Liverpool*, a frigate, were prevented from sailing up the Delaware River to Pennsylvania by colonial forces stationed at Fort Island. Fire was exchanged, but neither side was able to inflict much damage (*Pa. Gaz.*, May 15, 1776).

11. On May 7 the Committee of Safety in Philadelphia had passed a resolution requesting all inhabitants of the city and liberties of Philadelphia to send to the Commissary any lead draft weights, window weights, and clock weights so that the lead could be used for defense purposes. A few days later the committee appointed four men to inspect houses in the city and to procure the lead, which it offered to replace with iron (*Pa. Gaz.*, May 8, 22, 1776).

June 25. third day—HD. left home after dinner for the Iron Works—Billy, Henry—and Harry went over the River with him, they return'd before 5 o'clock HD. return'd the—29.

July 2. HD. left home this Morning third day—with Joice Benezet, for Bybary. he return'd in the Evening.

July 6 HD went this afternoon with Anthony Benezet to Bybary.

July—sent to King Wood—in a Hogshead, two Beds 2 Boalsters 4 Pillows, 4 Blankets, 2 Sheats 2 Pillow Cases and 2 Check'd Pillow Cases.

1776 July 13. George Baker left us, and went among the Soldiers.

July 15. HD. MS. (and Billy on Horse back) went to Burlington, to the Funeral of Saml. Smith, return'd in the Evening.

July 16. Friends Meeting-House at Market-Street Corner broke open by the American Soldiers, where they have taken up their Abode.[12]

July 24. HD. and Nancy in the Chaise Dan'l. Drinker, and, Sally on Horse back set of after dinner for King Wood, weather very warm forth day—they return'd the 29. before dinner.

Augt. 7. MS. and Nancy, went this afternoon to S. Pleasentss Place.

Augt. 13. third Day—HD. Nancy and, little Henry—in the Chaise, George James on Horse-back.—left home for the Iron, Works—Nancy to be left at J. Hopkins Haddonfield—An Account this afternoon of 104 sail of Vessels having joyn'd Lord How[13]—Sister went this Afternoon with S Wharton to Visit Joseph Whartons Widdow HD return'd the 17th—Nancy stay'd at Haddonfield 'till the 21st—then came home, with Betsy Mickel and Hannah Hopkins, who, went back in the Afternoon.

12. In 1776 several Friends' meetinghouses in the Philadelphia area were seized by local agencies and used to quarter soldiers and for other military purposes. American soldiers en route to New York from Maryland broke into the Market Street Meetinghouse and seized it for their quarters. After discussions, the officer in charge allowed Quakers to use the meetinghouse for worship, but the army retained possession of it (Mekeel, *Relation of the Quakers*, 167).

13. Philadelphia newspapers reported various sightings of British and Hessian ships off Perth Amboy, Bermuda, and Annapolis in August. Some of these vessels carried the remnants of the British army following its defeat in Charleston and survivors of Lord Dunmore's raids in Virginia. The ships were bound for New York to join Gen. William Howe and Adm. Richard Howe, whose forces had arrived in New York in July (*Pa. Journal*, Aug. 14, 1776; *Pa. Gaz.*, Aug. 14, 1776; Boatner, *American Revolution*, 472–73, 798).

Augt. the 22 fifth Day B. Woodcock and his Daughter came here, they went away the 27 third Day.

Augt. 28. fourth day, Susanna Swett, left us, and went to House-Keeping near Cabble Lane.

Sepr. 12. 1776, HD. ED. and Billy left home fifth day after Breakfast—cross'd the River at the upper Ferry—left the ferry after 10 o'clock, HD. on Horse-back, ED. and Billy in the Old Chaise with the Mare, Din'd at Rancocus ferry at one Wallace's, baited again 7 miles beyond Burlington at Joseph Archers—came to R. Walns after dark, bad roads the last 5 or 6 Miles.

13th. HD. left us at RWs this Morning and went across the Country on Bussiness—Billy very much disordred in his Bowels—walk'd about Richds. Place, Examnin'd the Mill &c ED. weigh'd 130 lb. Billy 56—EW 116.

14 Billy continues unwell—stay'd within most of this day. HD. return'd this Evening very much Feteagu'd.

1776 Sepr. 15 First day: Went in the Waggon with E.W. Nicholas, Dickey, my Billy—HD. and RW. in the Chaise to [E]arneysTown Meeting—came back to RWs to dinner, Billy better, step'd this Afternoon in to [S.] Wrights a near Neighbor.

16 left Walnford[14] after 12 o'clock early dinner Betsy Waln in the Chaise with me, Billy in the bottom, HD. on Horseback, stop'd at Archers, a man[15] there (as we suppos'd, dyeing) of the Flux—came in good time for a dish of Tea to Jos. Smiths, at his House about a mile out of Burlington to where they have this Week remove'd,—lodg'd here this Night EW with ED. Billy with his Daddy.—Breakfasted this Morning with Patty and towards Noon set of home-wards—cross'd the Ferry at Dunck's, din'd at Andersons at the Red Lyon—stop'd at AJs Frankford, came home to Coffee—found our Family well.

1776 Ocor. 3. HD. left home this Morning for PrinceTown, in the Sulkey, fifth Day—returnd the 5.

Octor. 18 HD left home with J Drinker, this Morning for Atsion—return'd the [ ].

1776 Octor. 23. H & ED left home fourth Day about ½ past 7 o'clock & reach'd Neshaminy Ferry about ½ past 10, baited and pursued our journey to

14. The words "this morning" crossed out.
15. Word crossed out.

the second Ferry on Delaware below Trentown Windy crossing, din'd on the Jersey Shore at [Love] Bakers about 2 o'clock, and half an hour afterwards set out, and reach'd Rd. Walns before dark, found RW very unwell.

24 RW. better today, & our prospect is to set out in his Waggon with his Betsy on seventh Day Morning his health and weather permitting—HD wrote a Letter to Sister and the Children in readiness for an oppertunity.

25 spent this day at RWs he very unwell repair'd his Waggon—[J.] Leonards Wife & Sally Lawrence, din'd there with us.—much conversation with the former.

26 As RW. is very Feverish tho' somewhat better, his Wife declines attending Shrewsbury Meeting—We set out in his Waggon, with his Son Nicholas, & his Negro Peter as a Driver, about 9 o'clock—reach'd Monmh.—Court House, at least 20 miles about one, din'd there at the Lower Tavern & then after two proceeded on our way, took the wrong but best Road at the Falls mill, and went directly down to John Hartshorns at Black Point, about dark.

27. HD. went into the salt water this Morning. went 6 miles to Shrewsbery Meeting, after the close there of, came back to J.Hs to dinner, Hannah Hartshorn, her Cosin Betsy Roberson, and Hannah Smith in the Waggon with me HD. in JHs—Saml. Allinson his Wife and her Sister Nancy—H Smith & Johney Morris din'd with us at JHs—walk'd after dinner with SA. and Wife to the Waterside in their way to Robt. Heartsn.

28. HD. went into the Salt Water again. I, drank neare a pint of it, which operated largely & speedily—I attended the Meeting of Worship and then return'd with Lucy Hartshorn and her Daughter in their Waggon—Charles West and Wife din'd there and lodg'd also—about 9 at Night HD. and H Smith return'd from an Evening Meeting held at Jos. Wardels, I sleep't with HS.

29 HD. Bath'd & I drank salt Water which affected me as Yesterday—pach'd up & went to meeting, after which proceeded to Richd. Lawrences Dine'd there spent the Afternoon and Lodg'd, Thos. Dobson and Wife with several other Friends there—wrote to H Haydock.

30 Breakfasted at RLs began our return homewards stop'd sometime at Edmd. Williamss Baited at Monmoh. Court House & came up to dinner about 1½ o'clock to Lawe. Taylor's Mery. Fowler &c din'd with us—left there about 3 and came to RWs about 5, where I am pleas'd to find myself, as I have been unwell ever since I left them, with a disorder in my Ear &c—found Richd. Waln much better.

31st. Rain'd pretty much last Night and this Morning & dull, latter part of the Day—HD. visited Nathn. Wright in the Afternoon—we think of staying here partly or wholly tomorrow unless the weather clears up pleasent.

Novr. 1. Between 9 and 10 this morning, the weather being fine, we left our Friends and proceeded homewards, chang'd to Raw and Cold before we reach'd Jos. Smiths 1½ Clock, there din'd, found Reba. James Senr. there—in the Afternoon H & ED. went in JS. Carriage to Burlington; visited Peggy Morris and Sally Dyllwin, S Allinson, K Callender—and Peter Worrells—and then return'd to JSs H Smith with us—who soon after return'd to Burlington.

2d. Breakfasted at JSs and left them after 9 o'clock—call'd at Rodmans place about Cyder—cross'd at Duncks Ferry and reach'd home about one o'clock—found our Family in good Health.

1776 Decr. 10. HD. and ED. were this Day at the Wedding of P. Hartshorn and S. Waln.

1776 Novr. 15 sixth Day. HD. left home this Morning—with James Thornton, intending for the Grove Meeting—return'd the 20.

Novr. 27. HD. was let Blood.

Decr. 22. HD. Billy and C. West, went to Fair-Hill Meeting, they din'd at [J.] Hunts.

1777

1777 Janry. 25. We had 5 American Soliders quartered upon us by order of the Counsel of Safty[1]—the Soliders named Adam Wise, Henry Feating, these two stay'd 2 or 3 days with us, the rest went of in an hour or two after they came.

Janry. 28. sister went this Afternoon to the Burial of Jane Hodge Senr.

Janry. 31. Capt. Vollans call'd to imform of the Death of Capt. Spain.

Febry. 1. HD. went this Afternoon to the Funeral of Hannah Logan.

Febry. 2. HD. David Bacon &c went to Gloster, to visit: Mark Miller & Thos. Redman,[2] who are confin'd in the Jail; for reading a Testimony from the meeting for Sufferings,[3] and refusing to take the Test propos'd them.

1. In the winter of 1777 various colonial militia groups passed through Philadelphia. As the available barracks in Philadelphia filled up, the Council of Safety on Jan. 22 directed the barracks master to quarter the militia in the private homes of people who had not joined the campaign against England. Quarters in private homes were to be based on the size of the house and the convenience of the families (*Pa. Ev. Post*, Jan. 25, 1777).

2. Thomas Redman and Mark Miller, two New Jersey Quakers, were jailed in Gloucester because they refused to take an oath or affirmation of loyalty, known in Quaker parlance as "taking the test." Redman and Miller had read aloud at the Haddonfield Monthly Meeting an epistle from the Meeting for Sufferings of the Philadelphia Yearly Meeting of December 1776, instructing Quakers to refuse to submit to ordinances compelling them to participate in the war effort and to refuse to take oaths or affirmations of loyalty to the new state governments. In the view of Quaker leaders these oaths and affirmations violated their peace testimony, made them participants in the destruction of one government and the erection of another, and affirmed their support for the military measures adopted by the new governments to enforce their laws. The reading of this epistle made Miller and Redman suspect under the state of New Jersey's first acts establishing a loyalty oath or affirmation and the means for its enforcement, which passed in September and October 1776. According to the law anyone holding a public office was required to swear or affirm his loyalty to the new state government. Furthermore, anyone suspected of being dangerous to or disaffected from the government could be summoned to appear before two justices of the peace, who would then administer the oath to him. A person who refused could be bound over to appear at the next Court of Quarter Sessions. Further resistance or default on the surety could result in confinement until the court met. This is evidently what happened to Redman and Miller.

The situation worsened for Quakers in New Jersey and Pennsylvania in the following years. In 1777 both states passed laws extending the loyalty oaths to all males, with various fines and the loss of many rights as punishment for refusal. In 1778 Pennsylvania adopted a statute requiring all schoolteachers to take the oath, a step that endangered many Quaker schools (see below, Aug. 25, 1778). Friends' meetings in Pennsylvania and New Jersey responded by

1777. Febry. 10 second day. HD and J Drinker left home after Breakfast for Atsion.

1777. Febry 10 HD left home with JD—tax geather'r call'd—Wm. Piatt—Henry Drinker Hannah Drinker. Betsy Hough,—H. Baker slep't here.

11—T. Scattergood, A James,—call'd Sally Zane din'd here—Joshua Howell call'd with M Waln cirtificat[4]—Henry Drinker—Jacob Evans drank coffe with us—Harry wated up on the Weding—S Emlen here this Evening.

11 Charles Mifflin and Polly Waln were this day married—Harry tends table at the Wedding—HD return'd the 15th.

12. spent this Afternoon at S Pleasants who lays in with her Daughter. Elizth. James Logon here this Afternoon.

13. Snow to day, Reba. Waln here—Cadr. Evans call'd.

14 Abel James call'd, Becky James junr. Richd. Brown—Snow a foot deep.

Febry. 17—Betsy Waln and her Daughter Polly—stay'd all night with us.

---

strictly enforcing their testimony against the taking of the test, although they seem to have dealt somewhat more charitably with violaters of this offense than of other war-related offenses. Over the course of the war between 185 and 222 Pennsylvania Quakers were chastised for taking loyalty oaths or affirmations, but only 101 were disowned, compared to a 72 percent rate of disownments for all war-related offenses of discipline (948 disownments of a total 1287 cases). In New Jersey 49 Quakers were dealt with on this issue and 28 were disowned, while two-thirds of all war-related offenses among New Jersey Quakers resulted in disownments (288 of 429 cases) (Mekeel, *Relation of Quakers*, 164–69, 189–213, 334–37; Peter Brock, *Pacifism in the United States from the Colonial Era to the First World War* [Princeton, N.J.: Princeton University Press, 1968], chap. 5, esp. pp. 204–6; *Acts of the General Assembly of the State of New-Jersey, 1776–1777* [Burlington, N.J.: Isaac Collins, 1777], 2, 4–6; David Alan Bernstein, "New Jersey in the American Revolution: The Establishment of a Government amid Civil and Military Disorder, 1770–1781" [Ph.D. diss., Rutgers University, 1970], 263–68; Lois V. Given, "Burlington County Friends in the American Revolution," *Proceedings of the New Jersey Historical Society* 69 [1951]: 196–211).

3. The Philadelphia Yearly Meeting had established the Meeting for Sufferings in 1756 in the wake of the French and Indian War. In response to the worsening condition of Quakers and other frontier settlers suffering from the conflict, the Yearly Meeting changed its Standing Committee on Relations with British Friends into the Meeting for Sufferings, whose responsibilities included corresponding with its British counterpart, representing the Society where the reputation and interests of Friends were concerned, and raising and administering funds for the relief of Friends on the frontier and elsewhere as needed. The Meeting for Sufferings was composed of twenty-eight members from the Philadelphia area, including Henry Drinker, its clerk. Its mandate was extended over time to aid Friends who suffered during the American Revolution and later to Amerian Indians and Friends in need in other countries (Mekeel, "Founding Years," 40–41, 45; Frost, "Years of Crisis," 57).

4. A marriage certificate for Mary Waln and Charles Mifflin (Philadelphia Northern District Men's Monthly Meeting, Minutes, 1772–78, Friends Historical Library, Swarthmore College, 241, 247, 253; all sources at the Friends Historical Library are on microfilm).

Febry. 28. Nancy went home with Betsy Waln, her Daughter Polly &c in a Sleigh to Walnford—sixth Day—Janny Boon went this Afternoon in a Boat to Visit her Aunt at Wilmington—Janey return'd the 12th March—Nancy return'd March 21.

March 5. Thos. Wharton, was proclaimed; Esqr., President of the Supreme Executive Council of the commonwealth of Pennsylvania,[5] Capt. General and Commander in Chief in and over the Same—some call him Governour.

March the 8. Brint Debades, an American Soldier,—was Shot upon the Commons, of this City[6]—a City heretofore clear of such Business.

1777 March 18. HD. and Billy left home after dinner in the Chaise, intending for R. Walns to bring our Daughter Nancy home—they return'd with Nancy the 21.

1777 March the 18. HD. and Billy left home intending for B Waln's, to bring Nancy home—after they were gone we received a Letter from Nancy—another from E. Penington—J Drinker call'd MS. ED. SD. spent this Afternoon at Becky and Hannahs.

19. Saml. Simpson call'd on account of S. Harold, Oliver [ ]oland, call'd, Robt. Willis call'd John Drinker, D. Drinker took the Horse Reba. Walln here in the Evening.

20

March 22. HD. was let Blood.

March a Young Man of the Name of Molsworth[7] was hang'd on the Commons by order of our present ruling Gentr'y.

5. On Mar. 5 Thomas Wharton, Jr., was elected president of Pennsylvania's Supreme Executive Council. Wharton, a merchant, was a younger cousin of Thomas Wharton, Sr., a Quaker who was later exiled to Virginia with HD. Wharton Jr., unlike his cousin, was an enthusiastic supporter of the rebel cause and had been the head of Pennsylvania's Council of Safety, which ran the state from July 1776 until this date, when the new constitution went into effect. The 1776 state constitution created a plural executive branch called the Supreme Executive Council, made up of one representative of the city of Philadelphia and one representative from each county. The representatives served three-year terms. At the head of the council was a president elected jointly by the council and the assembly. Wharton was its first elected president, and George Bryan was the vice president. Five members of the Supreme Executive Council constituted a quorum (*DAB*, s.v. "Thomas Wharton"; Robert L. Brunhouse, *The Counter-Revolution in Pennsylvania 1776–1790* [1942; 2d ptg. Harrisburg, Pa.: The Pennsylvania Historical and Museum Commission, 1971], 10–15, 22).

6. Brint Debadee, a soldier in Pennsylvania's Tenth Regiment, was executed for desertion and perjury (*Pa. Ev. Post*, Mar. 8, 1777).

7. James Molesworth was hanged following his conviction for treasonable practices against the state. He was accused of trying to hire men to pilot the British fleet up the Delaware River (Reed, *Joseph Reed*, 2:30–34; Marshall, *Diary Extracts*, 118, 201; *Pa. Archives*, ser. 1, 5:270–82; *Col. Recs. Pa.*, 11:197).

March Polly Drinker came, went away in a few days.

March Our little Henry was run over by a Horse in the Street, his Knee was Brused, but not meterially hurt.

April 12 Bill Gardiner push'd little Henry of a Carpenters Bench, in Carlilse's Shop, and hurt his arm very much—we sent for Docr. Redman who after examineing it, found the Bones were not broak but the Arm badly strain'd.

April 15 HD. left home after dinner with John Salter for the Jersey; return'd the [ ].

1777 May 5. Nany Oat went this Evening off to her Fathers.

May 6. HD. left home after Dinner, intending to accompany our Friends John Pemberton and S Emlen part of the Way on their Journey towards N. Carolina &c—Sammy Fisher Rumford Daws, G. Napper and [J] Richardson went with them.

the 7th. little Jacob Howell was buried—HD return'd the 13th third day.

May 21 fourth Day HD. and Billy went to Frankford HD left Billy at Neigr. James, and went to Moorestown, return'd home Billy with him the 23 sixth Day.

May 29 fifth day—HD. left home this Morning for Egg-Harbor—he return'd June 2d—Second day.

June the 3 ED. and SD. went to the Burial of our Antient Fr'd Mary Emlen.

June the 5 an Officer with 2 Constables call'd on us for Blankets,[8] went away without any—as others had done 3 or 4 times before.

1777 July 4—the Town Illuminated and a great number of Windows Broke on the Anniversary of Independence and Freedom.[9]

8. On Mar. 12 the Continental Congress had passed a resolution requesting the states to supply blankets to colonial troops. The commissary of the continental army then requested the Pennsylvania Board of War to supply blankets, and on May 2 Pennsylvania's ruling body, the Supreme Executive Council, authorized the requisition of 4,000 blankets from the state, 667 of them to come from the city of Philadelphia, where twelve men, including the artist Charles Willson Peale, were appointed commissioners to collect the blankets. Quakers were apparently singled out for this and other requisitions (*Pa. Ev. Post*, Mar. 13, 1777; *Pa. Gaz.*, May 7, 1777; Mekeel, *Relation of the Quakers*, 167).

9. Quaker shopkeepers refused to close their shops on holidays like July 4 or days appointed to celebrate American military victories. In retaliation, Philadelphians broke the windows of many Quaker shops (Mekeel, *Relation of Quakers*, 167).

July 7. this is the seventh day of the seventh month. 1777.

July 27. First Day—Evening between 9 & 10 o'clock, was seen by many, a Strange appearance in the Sky of Streamers, moveing in regular order, from the East to Westward.

July 31, an account of a large Fleet being within our Capes,[10] they disapear'd the next day.[11]

Augt. 10. First Day Morning HD and John Perish gone to Merrion Meeting they intend tomorrow to Concord quarter return'd the 12.

Augt. 14. We arose this Morning between 4 and 5.—HD. and S Emlen left us about 5 cross'd the up town Ferry, intending for Burlington, on their way to Raway Genl. meeting, the weather very hot. Thos. Fisher confin'd in the Jerseys—Catty Howell brought to Bed with her Son—fifth Day HD and SE return'd the 22.

Augt. 20 or 21 our dear little Henry was taken ill with a vomiting and disordred Bowels, occasion'd by eating watermellon too close to the Rine—he voided in the course of his Sickness, (which turnd out to be an inviterate Bloody and white Flux) 3 large Worms, and vomited one alive—for 12 Days he eat nothing—and is now Sepr. the 6 in a very poor way, reduced almost to a Skelaton with a constant fever hanging about him, tho' the disorder seems to be somewhat check'd, and he has an appetite in the Morning—he has taken 8 Clysters and many doses of Physick—his Body comes down and he is so weak that he cannot sit up alone.

Some day since the illness of our Child, we had a valuable pair of large End-Irons seazed and taken from us, by Philip Mause.

1777 Sepr. the 2 third Day—HD. having been, and continuing to be unwell, stay'd from meeting this morning. he went towards Noon into the front Parlor to copy the Monthly meeting minuits—the Book on the Desk—and the Desk unlock'd, when Wm. Bradford; one [Bluser] and Ervin, entred, offering a Parole for him to sign—which was refus'd. they then seiz'd on the Book and took several papers out of the Desk and carried them off; intimating their

10. Words crossed out.

11. The fleet spotted off the Delaware capes on July 30 was the British fleet under Adm. Richard Howe, which had set sail from Staten Island, New York, on July 23 for the campaign on Philadelphia. The fleet disappeared from view the next day, temporarily obscuring British motives, then headed into Chesapeake Bay, where Gen. William Howe's troops disembarked at Head of Elk (Elkton), Maryland, at the end of August, then proceeded on foot toward Philadelphia (Boatner, *American Revolution*, 858–59, 863–64).

design of calling the next morning at 9 o'clock; and desireing HD to stay at home for that time, which as he was unwell, was necessary; they according calld the 4th, in the morning and took my Henry to the [Massons] lodge—in an illegeal, unpredesented manner—where are several, other Friends with some of other proswasions, made prisoners;—Isreal Pemberton, John Hunt, James Pemberton, John Pemberton, Henry Drinker, Saml. Pleasants, Thos. Fisher, Saml. Fisher, Thos. Gillpin, Edward Penington; Thos. Wharton, Charles Jervis, Ellijah Brown, Thos. Afflick, Phineas Bond, Wm. Pike, Mires Fisher, Charles Eddy, Wm. Smith, Broker—Wm. D Smith, Thos. Comb, &c I went this Even'g to see my HD. where I mett with the Wives & Children of our dear Friends and other visitors in great numbers—upwards of 20 of our Friends call'd to see us this Day—my little Henry very low and Feverish.

5 went again to the lodge, myself, Sister and the Children, at different times—Rachel Drinker spent the Day with us—a day of great distress it has been to me.

6 HD. Breakfasted with us, but left us soon after—we visited him as usual at the Lodge; several Friends here to day.

7th. First Day—received a note this Morning from my dear Henry—desireing as the others have done, that we would not visit them untill the close of the Afternoon meeting—wishing to have this day more particularly to themselves, in stillness. R. Scattergood R Jones, Docr. Redman call'd this Morning I gave little Henry a Clyster he is very unwell, tho' the Doctor says he is mending S Swett, H Drinker, here, H. Morris, D. Morris, John Foreman, J. Parish, and E Drinker drank tea, with us—I went this Evening to the lodge and found my Henry in good Spirits—came home after night, John Drinker, Rachel Drinker, Hannah Elfreth, R. Waln, H Catheral here this Evening H Sansom call'd—H Drinker sleeps here.

8th. my little Henry very unwell this Day could not go to see his Daddy untill the Afternoon, who I found with the other Friends pritty-well. they have sent several Remonsterances to the Congress and Consel,[12] the latter of which,

12. The prisoners sent remonstrances to the Continental Congress and the Supreme Executive Council, protesting that their arrests were arbitrary, unjust, and illegal. They said no political papers had been found on any of those arrested, there were no specific charges brought against them, there was no cause to banish them, and they were being sent to Virginia without a hearing or trial. Upon receiving the remonstrances, the Continental Congress requested that the Supreme Executive Council give the prisoners a hearing. The council replied that in the press of events it had no time to listen to the prisoners' claims. The Congress then disassociated itself from the matter by saying that the prisoners were subject to the Supreme Executive Council and that Congress would not interfere in the state's internal affairs. This exchange set the pattern for the future six-month exile, when neither body wished to claim authority for the prisoners (the remonstrances are printed in Gilpin, *Exiles in Virginia*, 77–85, 96–97, 103–4; Congress's response is in *JCC*, 8:718–19, 722–23; for a discussion of the confusion regarding authority over the prisoners, see Thayer, *Israel Pemberton*, 225–31).

have this afternoon turn'd them over to the Congress, they know not what they'd be at—. gave the Child another Clyster this Evening his Disorder continues, with a Constant Fever, he's in a state greatly reduc'd, and has no signs of amendment but a desire for Food, which 'till lately has not been the case—Nancy unwell with disordred Bowels, I have given her Rheubarb.—John Drinker, Rachel Drinker, Hannah Sansom, Polly Story, S. Swett, R. Scattergood, Josa. Howell, G. Oat, Charles West, T. Masterman, [S] Logan, Danl. Drinker, Docr. Redman, R Say. Huldah Mott, S. Hartshorn—here this Day.

9 Our poor Child after a bad Night, is very low this Morning. very frequent calls to the Pot with fluxey stools,—Sent Billy to the lodge to enquire after his dear Daddys Health he found him well—James Thornton, John Parish, Becky Jones, John Drinker, Jos. Howel, Docr. Redman here this Morning Margary Norton, Molly Foulk, Sarah Fisher, Becky Scatergood, call'd after Meeting. My self Sally and little Molly went this Afternoon to the Lodge, during my stay there, word was brought from the Conscil that their Banishment was concluded to be on the Morrow,[13] the Waggons were preparing to carry them off—I came home in great distress, and after doing the necessary for the Child went back near 10 at Night, found the Prisoners finishing a Protest against the Tyrannical conduct of the Present wicked rulers.—R Waln, H Catheral A Parish J Drinker, Doctor, &c here—'tis now near 11 o'clock, I have just heard a cannon go off.

10th. Our dear Friends continue still at the Lodge—I was there twice to day—the time for their going off is say'd to be tommorrow. at 9 o'clock—My dear Henry spent this Afternoon Evening and stay'd all Night with us—numbers of our Friends here—I gave the Child a Clyster is has a constant Fever, I cant help being happrehensive of his falling into a Consumption.

11 The sending off our Friends is put of till 3 this Afternoon, they find it difficult to procure Waggons and Men—My Henry Breakfasted with us; then went to the Lodge. I went there about 10 o'clock, R Drinker with me, I step'd over to S. Pleasants, then back to the Lodge HD—not there when I return'd—the Town is in great Confusion at present a great fireing heard below[14] it is

13. The instructions of the Continental Congress to Pennsylvania were only to secure and disarm disaffected persons. On September 3, however, Congress noted a letter from George Bryan, vice president of the Supreme Executive Council of Pennsylvania, requesting the approval of Congress for Pennsylvania's plan to send those arrested, particularly Quakers who refused to make any promises or affirmations of allegiance, to Staunton, Virginia. Congress approved the request. Many other prisoners of war were also in Virginia, as the Quaker exiles found when they arrived in Winchester, Virginia, later in 1777 (*JCC*, 8:707–8; *Col. Recs. Pa.* 11:264, 265; Oaks, "Philadelphians in Exile," 309).

14. A reference to the Battle of Brandywine, fought on Sept. 11, at which General Washington unsuccessfully attempted to halt the British advance on Philadelphia from Head of Elk, Md. (Boatner, *American Revolution*, 104–10).

supos'd the Armies are Engag'd, 'tis also reported that several Men of War are [ ] up the River—Jos. Howell, R. Scattergood, S Swett, R Drinker &c here this Morning.—Some time after dinner Harry came in a hurry for his Master Horse for a Servent to ride, informing me that the waggons were waiting at the Lodge to take our dear Friends away. I quickly went there; and as quickly came away finding great a number of People there but few women, bid my dearest Husband farewell, and went in great distress to James Pembertons, Sally with me the waggons drove of about 6 o'clock and I came home at Dusk—S Emlen and wife, R Jones, H Catheral, M Smith, S Swett, R Waln, Patty Smith, Abel James Jos. Howell; J Drinker, D Drinker, Doctor with others here this day. I wrote a Letter this Evening to my dear, to sent by a Man from Gillpins in the Morning.

12 the Letter I wrote last Evening mist of the intended oppertunity, but went by another hand; received a Letter from my HD, this Morning which afford'd me great Comfort, JD, wrote to him—this has been a day of Great Confusion to many in this City; which I have in great measure been kept out of by my constant attension on my sick Child. part of Washingtons Army has been routed, and have been seen coming into Town in Great Numbers; the perticulars of the Battle, I have not attended to, the slain is said to be very numerous.—hundreds of their muskets laying in the road, which those that made off have thrown down—I was a little fluttred this Afternoon by hearing a Drum stop at our Door and a hard knocking succeed; it proved to be, men with orders for HD to appear or find a Substitute—there has been a meeting this Afternoon at the State-House, on what Account I know not—'tis suppos'd that G. Washington is in Town this Evening—the Wounded have been brought in this Afternoon, to what amount I have not learnt.[15] call'd to see us J Drinker and Wife DD. & Wife R Waln & Wife, Wm. Redwood, C. West Dr. Hutchins, Jos. Howell, Dr. Redman, H Sansom, Neigr. Stiles, R. Jones, Wm. Norton, A Parish, Isaac Foster, S Swett, H. Elfreth, S. Fisher, R. Scattergood, E. Scattergood, Sucky Hartshorn—I, understand that our dear Friends, din'd to day at the Black Horse.

13 Wrote to HD. by Isaac Zane Junr.—our Child appears to be better.—they have Chang'd the place of Banishment of our Friends to Winchester, as I understand;[16] Docr. Redman, Enoch Story, Molly Moore, Hannah Catheral, Saml. Sansom, R't. Waln, John Drinker, hear this Morn'g;—Hannah Moore, Betsy and Polly Jervis drank Tea with us, A Carlilse, Abel and Reba. James, Charles West, Betsy Foulk, G. Napper, Reba. Waln, T. Say, Jos. Howel, J. Bringhurst, Jos. Scott R. Jones, call'd, our Child I hope continues to mend,—

15. The words "John [G] lodges here to Night with HD." crossed out.
16. The first choice for the place of banishment was Staunton, Va. (*Col. Recs. Pa.*, 11:290, 295, 296).

JD. wrote to HD—a Number of the Inhabitants are moveing out of Town, John Parish call'd this Evening he went with our dear Friends 23 Miles on their journey, and left 'em all well, yesterday Afternoon.

14 First Day. I ommitted mentioning Yesterday, that C. West brought home the Monthly Meeting Book, and rough Minets, which Timothy deliverd up to him—we took our Child to the Front of the House as we have frequently done since his illness, in order to air his Room; and by that means had an oppertunity of seeing the number of Waggons, Drays, and other Carriages which past; it took of that Solemn appearance that this day ought to ware;—Sally, Nancy and Billy went to Meeting this Morning ED. SD. AD. WD. in the Afternoon; it is say'd that G. Howe is at Chester, and that G. Washington has left this City and cross'd Schullkill this day;[17] M Story informs us, that our best Friend &c lodg'd last night at Pots Grove—Docr. Redman, R Waln, Nurse Wilson, J Drinker, D Drinker, R. Scattergood, M Foulk, R Jones, M Story, S Emlen Wife and Daughter R Say—Hannah Drinker J Green sleeps here with Henry Drinker.

15, I have heard no News from abroad this Morning but Carriages constantly passing with the Inhabitants going away—My poor little Henrys Bowels comes down in a frightfull manner, red, Bloody and inflam'd; his stools are bitter, his appitite craveing, but the Fever continues—last night I heard of several Friends having lost their Horses, taken from the Stables,—for which reason I ordred our Horse, and Cow to be put into the Washhouse, where they at present remain—several of my Sisters in Affliction, have this Day received Letters from their Husbands, I make no doubt but I should also have had one, but for some good reason; I have [however] the satisfaction to hear that my dear is well—great talk of a Habeas-[Corpus] and of our Friends haveing a hearing:—the manner, or the Men employ'd, or something, or other, I hardly know what, prevents my haveing the pleasure in it, that some others express; I trust it will please the Almighty to order all for the best—I have heard from 2 or 3 to day, that the Church Bells, are taking down, the Bridge over Schullkill taken, up, and the Ropes across the Ferrys cut—&c ——— call'd to see us this day: Reba. Waln, Joseph and James Bringhurst Doctor, C. West, Dr. Cooper, Hannah Morris, John & Rachel Drinker Thos. Masterman, Saml. Smith, Saml. Hopkins, Jos. Scott, Mary Armitt, Sally Logan, Sarah Fisher,

17. Following Washington's defeat at Brandywine on Sept. 11 the American army first moved to Chester Bridge, twelve miles east of the battlefield, and then to Germantown. Though the main body of the British army remained camped at the Brandywine, General Howe did send out detachments to Chester Bridge to keep an eye on Washington's army, first on Sept. 12 under Gen. James Grant and then on Sept. 14 under Lord Charles Cornwallis. Washington, seeking a better strategic position from which to defend Philadelphia, moved his troops west on Sept. 14 over the Schuylkill River to White Horse, Pa. (Boatner, *American Revolution*, 859).

Reba. Jones, O. Jones, Nics. Waln, Jos. Richardson, the latter of which, informs; that one of the Waggons that took our Friends; has this Afternoon return'd empty.

16 I read a letter this Morning from my HD to JD—our Stable seller was last Night broak open, and several of Jos. Scotts Barrels of Flour stolen—I rote to my HD. this Morning by Nisbet—our child seem'd better, this forenoon, but more unwell towards Evening a great weight upon my Spirits most of this day: Nancy and little Molly both complaining—this is a Sickly season, many taken down with Fevers. May it please kind Providence to preserve my dearest Husband—Henry Drinker, Saml. Noble, Josa. Howel, E. Story, Dorcas Mountgomery, David Bacon and Wife, Danl. Drinker & Wife, Thos. Scattergood & Wife, Reba. Scatergood, Nancy Pots, H. Mitchel, Deba. Morris, Hannah Steel, Molly Cresson, Bell Cresson, Thos. Holloway, John Drinker, Docr. Redman, Abel James & Wife, S Sansom, Dr. Moore, Josh. Fox, and Robt. Waln, call'd to see us. heavey rain this Evening.

17 Clouds, wind and Rain all Day, I take it to be the Equinoctial Storm.[18]—I understand that our dear Friends mett with[19] a very disagreeable reception at Reding[20]—little Henry very poorly—Richd. Footman, J Drinker, Jos. Scott, Dr. Redman, R. Jones, Reba. Waln, Sally Zane, Hannah Samson Jos. Howel, Henry Drinker, call'd to Day I have not yet received my Letter by R. Adams.

18 this Day has been spent as usual chiefly in the Chamber with our Child, who I think I may say is now better, 'tho 'till this day I could scarcely say so—but where is his dear Father, or how situate'd; at times my thoughts are hard to bare, and at other Times I am greatly favour'd and suported—James

18. A belief shared by Shakespeare as well as ED's contemporaries held that unusually violent weather coincided with the vernal and autumnal equinoxes. Although equinoxes themselves do not cause storms, the seasonal movement of air masses around the time of the equinoxes occasionally cause violent weather. In 1847 Charles Peirce published a detailed meteorological account of Philadelphia's weather over the preceding 57 years. For the period 1790–1801 he recorded a storm or "considerable" and "copious" rain in the middle or latter half of March on four occasions (1790, 1794, 1797, 1799), moderate rain three times (1791, 1795, 1801), and variable weather (including rain) in four years (1792, 1793, 1796, 1800). Only during March 1798 did he note "very little rain this month." Although he did not include the phrase *equinoctial storm* in his weather reports for March, he specifically referred to one such disturbance in Sept. 1790 and alluded to another in his report for Sept. 1791: "There were several very plentiful showers and considerable rain fell about the time the sun crossed the line, but the wind was not boisterous in this vicinity" (Peirce, *Meteorological Account*, 51–53; *Encyclopedia Brittanica*, 11th and 15th eds.; Charles Willson Peale to William Thornton, Apr. 16, 1805, in Peale, *Selected Papers*, 2:822–23; Richard Inwards, comp., *Weather Lore: A Collection of Proverbs, Sayings, and Rules Concerning the Weather*, 3d ed. [New York: F. P. Hayes, 1898]).

19. The word "but" crossed out.

20. Townspeople threw stones at the Quaker prisoners and their escorts as they entered Reading. Later, two local Quakers who attempted to visit the prisoners at the house in which they were confined were stoned and beaten by a crowd (Gilpin, *Exiles in Virginia*, 136).

Hutchens &c who went out with design for Reading, found they could not proceed on account of great freshes, and return'd last Eveng—Saml. Shutt din'd here, I pay'd him one half Jos. for 2½ Cord Oak Wood—Aunt Jervis and Betsy drank tea with us, J. Drinker and Rachel here in the Evening Docr. Redman, John Parrock, Sl. Smith S & H. Jones; the Childs Body came down very badly this Evening which it frequently has done lately—it has cleared up finaly after the Storm, and is now a Serene Butifull Night.

19 Jenny awoke us this Morning about 7 o'clock, with the News that the English were near; we find that most of our Neighbors and almost all the Town have been up since one in the Morning The account is that the British Army cross'd the [S]weeds-Foard last night, and are now on their way heather; Congress, Counsil &c are flown,[21] Boats, Carriages, and foot Padds going off all Night; Town in great Confusion;—But just now, (about noon) I am inform'd that the above report arose from 2 or 3 of the English light-Horse, having been seen recogniting the Foard; a note from E Story, letting me know of an Oppertunity of writeing to my Henry by Levi Hollensworth this Evening.—I accordingly wrote—the Town very still this Evening and very much thin'd of its Inhabitance; John Drinker, D. Drinker, H. Drinker, John Green, C. West, George James, Edmond Richardson, Susa. Swett—M. Foulk Mary. Norton Reb. Scatergood John Parish, Ab. Parish, Reba. Waln.

20 The Town has been very quiet all this day, I believe; it is said that Washingtons Army has cross'd the Foard and are at present on this side—some expect a battle hourly; as the English are on the opposite side—I received a Letter this Evening from my dear, a long letter—J Drinker also received one—dated the 17 Instant they were then at Reading—all the boats, Ferry boats excepted, are put away—and the Shiping all ordred up the River, the next tide, on pain of being burnt, should G. Howes Vesels approach—Our Child very low and unwell this Evening—Weather Cloudy; little Molly disordred in her Bowels—call'd to see us this day—S. Hopkins Anty. Benezet, S. Sansom, Robt. Waln, Reba. Waln; H. Elfreth, A Carlisle, Betty Davis, J. Drinker, Neigr. Stiles, Doctor the Inhabitants continue going out—some returning.

21. First Day. MS. SD. AD. WD. went to meeting this morning The Child appears to be better again—After meeting, Sam. Emlen and Wife, Becky Jones and S Swett call'd—Sammy read aloud my dear Henrys long letter of the 17th Instant and was very much affected thereby.—after which we had a setting togeather, and Sammy was led to speak comfort to us.—In the Afternoon ED. SD. AD. WD. went to Meeting, which was silent—James Hutchin-

21. Members of the Continental Congress, expecting Philadelphia to fall to the British, left Philadelphia on Sept. 19 for Lancaster, Pa. (Boatner, *American Revolution*, 860).

son call'd this morning with a Letter from Saml. Pleasants to his Wife dated the 18 wherein my dear gives his love to us:—this Evening our little sick Son received a letter from his dear Father, which is well worth the store he sits by it, he has ordred it to be put in his Pocket-Book Wile he larns to read writeing—Robt. Waln, John Drinker, Doctor, Joshua Howel, Saml. Smith, call'd—we have been favour'd with quiateness all this day;—rain this Afternoon—prehaps our dear Friends are this day moveing further from us.

22 Molly Pleasants came from her Sister this morning to tell us of an oppertunity to Reading, and as the person was to set off, in less than half an hour, J Drinker who came in, wrote to my Henry, for himself and us—We are inform'd this Evening that they left Reading Yesterday Morning but no perticulars of their treatment. Nanny Oat call'd to day, to demand her freedom dues,[22] and was very impertinent and Saucy—Jenny carried our sick Child this Afternoon up stairs, down in the Parlour, and in the Nursery, for the first time, he can't yet stand, alone, but I hope he is mending. very unwell myself to day. with pain in my back and Head—Sister poorly—many flying reports of various kinds to day but we know not what to depend upon; they have been taking Blankets, Coverlids &c to day from many of the Inhabitance—call'd to see us, Hannah Lloy'd Doctor K. Howell John Parish, Saml. Emlen, John Tomson, S Swett, R Waln R. Jones &c—clear'd up very Cold, wind high this Evening.

23. J.D. wrote a Compy. Letter this Morning to our dear Henry—by Levi Hollandsworth—ED. AD. WD. went to Meeting, it is our Monthly Meeting where my dear was mist, and thought on by many—Wm. Brown appeard in Testimony recommending Faith and Patience with respect to chooseing proper persons to transact the business of the Church &c S. Hopkins appeared he had to Mention something relating to our dear absent Friends.—Billy informs me, that the Clarks business devolved upon Abel James, S Smith and T. Scattergood—Our dear Child has walk'd several times across the Room, with Jennys help to day. those men that collected Blankets &c in our Ward, were this Afternoon at each of our Neighbours, but did not call on us. it is reported and gains credit, that the English have actually cross'd Schuylkill and are on their way towards us,[23]—I received two letters after meeting from my dear Husband; which at the same time that they made my Heart ake, gave me

22. Legislation passed in 1700 by the colonial assembly gave indentured servants two suits of clothes, a new axe, a grubbing hoe, and a weeding hoe as freedom dues (the axe and hoes were eliminated in 1771 legislation), but the actual composition of freedom dues varied greatly over time and place in eighteenth-century Pennsylvania. By the 1770s many indentured servants in Philadelphia received clothes and a cash settlement upon the completion of their service (Cheesman A. Herrick, *White Servitude in Pennsylvania* [Philadelphia, 1926; reprint, New York: Negro Universities Press, 1969], 205–11, 293; *Statutes at Large*, 8:30–31; Salinger, *Labor and Indentured Servants*, 134–35).

23. The word "they" crossed out.

comfort,—many have had their Horses taken from them, this afternoon, some going one way and some another; it is likily from the present prospect of things, that we shall have a Noisey Night, tho' at this time 9 o'clock I hear nothing like it, but we living back and retired escape many hurries, that others are expos'd to; all the Bells in the City are certainly took away, and there is talk of Pump handles and Fire-Buckets being taken also, but that may be only conjecture; things seem upon the whole to be drawing towards great confusion, May we be strengthen'd and suported in the time of tryal—I have had a bad spell of the sick Head-Ake this afternoon it still continues uneasy—S. Swett and E. Norris, dinn'd with us, the latter spent the Afternoon—call'd, Wm. Brown, Chs. West, John Drinker, Han. Drinker, D. Drinker, Abel James, Edwd. Jones, Reb Jones, M. Shaw, E. Armitt, H. Steel, Sally Logan, Saml. Smith, T. Scattergood, Docr. Redman, Lewis the Lawyer, Josey Fox, Reba. Waln, Danl. [Caheb] a tavern keeper from Kingwood—the Atsion Black Smiths Brother call'd yesterday to know, if an account which he had heard, was true, viz that all the Men at the Works were taken up and confin'd, G. James has heard nothing of such matter.

24. Sister all Day bad with the Head Ake, little Henry much better—Josa. Fishers Goods, and others, taken from them, by order of G. Washington[24]—Goods taken from Wm. Lippencot and others from the Substitute fine,[25] return'd to the owners, they continue pressing Horses—Sister and HD. set up last Night, 'till 2 o'clock, as did many others in the City; Cannon plac'd in some of the Streets—the Gondelows along the Warfs, the latter gone of to Day tis say'd with Fishers Goods &c—the report continues of the English approaching us, but know not what to believe, the Sign (Over the Way) of G. Washingn. taken down this Afternoon—talk of the City being set on fire—Joseph Ingel, call'd to pay, for 2 or 3 Tonns of Hay, but as I had not my Husbands papers, could not receive the money—Neigr. Buckleys gone off,—We heard this Evening that our dear Friends, were arrived at Lebanon all well—Hannah Sansom, Susanna Jones and Daughter, Betsy and Polly Jervis, spent the Afternoon with us, heard much News—John and Rachel Drinker, E Drinker, R. Jones, George James, Doctor and Becky Wharton call'd—very fine Weather—little Molly not very well.

24. Goods were taken and horses were impressed as a result of Washington's order of Sept. 22 to procure blankets, clothing, and matériel for the army. Horses were also removed from Philadelphia so that they would not fall into enemy hands (Washington, *Writings*, 9:249–50).

25. The substitute fine, based on legislation passed by the Pennsylvania Assembly in March to regulate the militia, was payment made by nonassociators (those who did not participate in Philadelphia's militia) to officers of their respective units for the cost of hiring and supplying a substitute if they failed to appear or hire a substitute on their own. There were also fines for each day that a man or his substitute failed to attend muster. In September, with the approach of the British, most of Philadelphia's militia units were called out to defend the city. Many men chose at this time not to serve, and those who had not deserted or disappeared were forced to pay the substitute fine, which amounted to at least twenty-five pounds (*Statutes at Large*, 9:75–94; Rosswurm, *Arms, Country, and Class*, 136–37, 143).

25 this has been so far, a day of great Confusion in the City, tho with respect to ourselves we have experienc'd[26] no injury and but little fright; set asside the consideration of the situation of him we love;—Enoch Story (to whome I pay'd 3 half Joes by my dear Henrys order) this morning, was the first that inform'd us, that the English were within 4 or 5 miles of us, we have since heard they were by John Dickinsons place; they are expected by some this Evening in the City—most of our warm people are gone of, tho there are many continue here that I should not have expected. Things seem very quiate and still, and if we come of so, we shall have great cause of thankfullness—should any be so wicked as to attempt fireing the Town, Rain which seems to be coming on, may Providentially, prevent it—a great number of the lower sort of the People are gone out to them—G. Napper also went, and I hear he brings word back that he spoke to Galloway, who told him that the Inhabants must take care of the Town this Night, and they would be in, in the Morning, as it rain'd they[27] fixt within 2 Miles of the City for the Night; it is now near 11 o'clock[28] and has been raining for several hours, which I look upon as a remarkable favour, as tis said that tar'd faggots &c are laid in several out Houses in different parts, with [meschievous] intent;—Numbers mett at the State-House since nine o'clock to form themselves into dfferent Companyes to watch the City, all things appear peaceable at present, the Watch-Men crying the Hour without Molestation,—Sister, Nancy, and Harry sitting up for H Drinr. who is out among the rest;—the Number of the English Troops is not yet assertaind some say—20,000, which I think not very probable;—Our dear little Henrys Shoes and Briches were put on today for the first time since his illness, he cannot walk yet without help.—Jos. Yerkes sent this morning for Billy to tell him, that Nichs Hicks had mett our [Friend] near Lebanon, and his Daddy on Horse-back who gave his love to us, and said he was well; O! that he was but with us. call'd to see us to Day E. Story, J Drinker Robt. Waln and Wife Doctor, John Green, D. Drinker, Patn. Hartshorn, S. Swett, Isaac Catherel, R. Jones, &c.

26. Well, here are the English in earnest,[29] about 2 or 3000, came in, through second street, without oppossition or interruption, no plundering on the one side or the other, what a satisfaction would it be to our dear Absent Friends, could they but be inform'd of it; our[30] end of the Town has appeard great part

26. The word "very" crossed out.
27. The word "continued" crossed out.
28. The words "at night" crossed out.
29. On Sept. 26, three thousand British troops under Lord Charles Cornwallis took possession of Philadelphia. The main body of the British army remained in Germantown, five miles north of the city, where they had camped on Sept. 25 with their commander-in-chief, General Howe (Frederick D. Stone, "The Struggle for the Delaware: Philadelphia under Howe and Arnold," in *Narrative and Critical History of America*, ed. Justin Winsor [Boston: Houghton, Mifflin, 1887], 6:383–84).
30. Word crossed out.

of this Day like the first day of the Week—I understand that Barnhill, Hysham, and some others, are taken up,[31]—it is recommend to the Inhabitance to continu to assist in guading the Town each Night for some time yet—CornWallace came with those troops to day. Genl. Howe is not yet come in—Richd. Adams, brought me this Afternoon, my Henrys Letter from Potts-Grove—Saml. & Sally Emlen sup'd with us, J. & R Drinker, Han Drinker drank Tea, Becky [James] Junr., Reb. Waln, John Parish, call'd—this has been a very fine day. tho rather Cool.

27 About 9 o'clock this Morning the Province, and Delaware Frigets, with several Gondelows came up the River, with a design to fire on the[32] they were attac'd by a Battry[33] which the English have errected[34] the engagement lasted about half an hour when many shots were exchang'd; one House struck, but not much damaged; no body, that I have heard, hurt on shore; but the people in General, especialy downwards, exceedingly Allarm'd, the Cook on board the Delaware, 'tis said, had his Head shot off, another of the men wounded, She ran a Ground, and by some means took fire, which occasion'd her to strike her Colours, the English immediately boarded her; the others sheard off—they took Admiral Allexander and his Men Prisoners—it seems he declar'd, that their intentions were to distroy the Town;—part of this scean we were spectators of, from the little Window in our Loft—We heard to day of the death of poor Meriam LaMar,[35] who lost his life with many others, of Gen. Vaynes Bragade, over Schuylkill,—Billy went this forenoon with Neigr. Howel and his Son, to their [place]. he return'd in the Afternoon—little Henry walk'd alone several times to day, but had two falls—John Drinker, Daniel Drinker, Jos. Howel, Ricd. Wells, Doctor Neigr. Stiles Reb. Waln, Reb. Jones, S. Sansom, H. Drinker, call'd to see us John Glover and C. West, H. Catheral also call'd.

31. Three lines crossed out.
32. "Town" crossed out.
33. On Sept. 27, a day after the British occupation of Philadelphia, British soldiers began erecting batteries to protect the city against the American navy anchored a short distance below in the Delaware River. The British succeeded in mounting only four guns when the American frigate *Delaware*, with Capt. Charles Alexander in command, the ship *Montgomery*, the sloop *Fly*, and four galleys began firing on the British at nine in the morning. The battle lasted about an hour, when the *Delaware*'s foremast was shot away and the ship ran aground. The *Fly* also ran aground shortly thereafter. The other American vessels slipped away safely. The British boarded the *Delaware* and captured those of the crew who did not escape to other vessels or the Jersey shore (Stryker, *Forts on the Delaware*, 3–4).
34. The words "at the upper lower end of the Town" crossed out.
35. The death of Marion Lamar, a major with the Fourth Pennsylvania Battalion, stationed with Gen. Anthony Wayne's division, occurred during the Battle of Paoli. Washington had left Wayne's division south of the Schuylkill River to harass General Howe, but the Americans were surprised in an attack after midnight on Sept. 21 by British soldiers. At least 150 men, one-tenth of Wayne's force, were killed, wounded, or taken prisoner in the attack, also called the Paoli Massacre (Francis B. Heitman, *Historical Register of the Officers of the Continental Army during the War of the Revolution April, 1775, to December, 1783* [1914, 1932; reprint, Baltimore: Genealogical Pub. Co., 1967], 338; Boatner, *American Revolution*, 828–29).

28 First Day: Sister and the Children went to Meeting this Morning this is our Yearly Meeting, and many more Friends in Town than could have been expected, the Situation of things considred,—not one from Jersey—Robt. Vallintine, Wm. Mathews, and Benjn. Townsend, the latter from York County, din'd with us; after dinner Johnny Drinker, Reba. James, Sarah Carry and her Neighr. Watson came in while we were setting in Silence.—the three Men Frds. had each something to say, tho but short; ED. and the Children went to meeting in the Afternoon.—Joshua Baldwin and Debby Morris drank Coffee with us. Sally Penington, S. Swett, K. Howell call'd. Our little Henry taken off his feet again by a pain in his Hams. I fear he has caught some cold—the Weather is cold for the time of year—I hear this Evening that they are building Battrys on the Jersey shore, opposite Arch and Market Streets. The Ameriacans I mean.

29 Went with the 3 Children to Meeting this Morning Silent Meeting—S. Swett din'd with us, S. Logan drank Coffee—Sam Sansom. J. Drinker, Nurse Willson, Henry Drinker Doctor, Robt. Waln & Wife, S. Hartshorn—call'd—Phineas Bond call'd while I was at meeting—some Officers are going about this day Numbering the Houses, with chalk on the Doors—a Number of the [Citysans] taken up, and imprison'd,[36] among whome are, John Hall, Jacob Bright, Tom Leech, Jacob Duchee, Wm. Moulder, &c—reinstated our Horse & Cow,—Received part of a Cord Wood of A. James—G. James call'd.

30 Sister and the Children went to Meeting in the Morn'g and Afternoon;—G. James, D. Drinker, John James, Josa. Baldwin and John Forsyth, call'd—Cate. Greenleaf with Rachel Hollandsworth and Eliza—Jollif, two Widdows who live near Winchester in Virginia, who call'd kindly to see us, that in case they should see our dear HD, they might have to say that they had been to his House—Becky James Junr. (Jessy Waterman, who appear'd in Testimony at meeting this Morning) Joseph Scott, Doctor likewise call'd to see us. Sucky and Hannah Jones came to tell us of the arrival of our Friends in Carlisle last fourth day, but could not inform us who brought the intillegence, Sarah Fisher and Becky Jones drank Tea with us—Giles Knight Junr. & Wife, Chalkley James, and Henry Drinker lodges with us this Night,—Abel James and Family are come to Town, thinking it more safe to be here, as a Number of the Amricans are skulking near and about Frankford—Old Joshua Gibson, whose Son lives at Ashbridges Mill, was last Week taken from thence, by one Horse Man, but was quickly resqu'd by one or 2 of the English light-Horse—Phebe Pemberton has received a Letter from her Husband, dated from Lebanon.

36. Loyalists were rounding up American sympathizers, subjecting them to a "Loyalist citizen arrest," and incarcerating them in the Walnut Street jail. After questioning, British authorities released most of the several hundred persons arrested (Jackson, *With the British Army*, 17).

Octor. 1 Sister and the Children went to meeting this Morning John Parish and Andrew McCoy a friend from Virginia[37] expects if he is favour'd to return home in safety (to see my Henry &c call'd. John Brintons daughter Polly with one Ben James, who she calls her Husband) call'd, with her Father and Mothers kind love to us—Sarah Pile from Concord din'd with us—Josa. Brown from Lancaster County and Thomas Wickery from chester County, Jos. Sermon John Drinker and John Glover also call'd—G. Knight and Wife lodg'd here. Josey James is again very ill in Town, the Americans are lurking about Frankford, several have come out of their way, to Town to day, 'tis said that a large Number of Friends in and near Burlington are taken up; Several fire Rafts which ware sent down the River in order to annoy the Fleet, ran on shore, and were burnt,—fine Weather.

2d. Sally, Billy and myself went to Meeting this Morning—Sister & Sally in the Afternoon—G. Knight and Wife Breakfasted with us—Abel James, Becky Jones, and Tommy Scattergood call'd—Benjn. Hough and Hannah Churchman din'd with us—Sarah Carry and Sarah Janney came after dinner, the latter intends to visit our Friends at Winchester, 'tho it is 40 miles from her own Habittation, Reba. Waln spent the Evening with us. Allexr. Allair and Joel Zane call'd to day to take an account of our Family; as it is intended to Number the Inhabatance, that in case provisions should be scarce each may draw their proportion with the Army, as I understand the matter.—it is said that the English have taken Billingsport, I believe 'tis not confirm'd. I have not yet exchang'd a word, with any one of the new comers—C. James is come to night to sleep with H. Drinker—John Byards Son Jim, was taken up, two or 3 days ago, in the English Camp near Germantown, when he was ask'd his Name, he said it was Howel, he is now confin'd as a Spy, and has wrote to day to Abel James, desireing him to interceed for him, he says he is wrongfully suspected &c—Henry has been downstairs to day; walking about the Parlor and Yard.

3d. Sister and the Girls went to Meeting—the Women finish'd their Business, men not yet done nor very near it—John Drinker wrote last night, to my dear; by an Opportunity that I knew nothing of—Joshua Howel, S. Swett, Caty Howel Sen'r. J. Drinker, Docr. Redman, Nurse Willson, call'd—'tis repoarted to day that Gattes has beat Burgoine,[38] also that Burgoine has beat Gattes;[39] which is the truth we know not, prehaps nither—our little Henry has

37. Word crossed out.
38. The word "and" crossed out.
39. A reference to the first Battle of Saratoga, also known as the Battle of Freeman's Farm, fought on Sept. 19. Gen. John Burgoyne had been leading a British invasion from Canada through upstate New York when he encountered the rebel forces under the command of Gen. Horatio Gates at Saratoga. The Americans commanded a superior position at the start of the battle, but were unable to force the British back. Since the British troops were camped on the

been tottering about to day in the usual manner, weak & feverish, tho I hope mending.

4 this Morning John Parish, Eaneas Ellis, and Andrew McCoy call'd, Eaneas is, from a place call'd Hopewell, and expects to see our Friends at Winchester on his return home—I wrote this Morning to my Henry by A. McCoy, and a few lines by Rachel Hollandsworth,—while I was writeing I heard Connons fire, and indeed before I was up; understood upon enquiry that a party of Washingtons Army had attack'd the English picket guard near Chesnut Hill.—I went before dinner to C. Greenleafs to look for Rachel Hollandsworth, she was gone out, call'd in my return at J. Drinkers—I have not been from home before, except to meeting since my dear left me.—step'd down to Neighr. James's, Josey very ill, Nanny Eve and Gibbons Wife at the Mill were there, they came to Town through fear, the Battle appeared to be near them, and some of the Provincials about Frankford, Joseph Paul and some others, they have taken away—After dinner C. Greenleaf sent me word, that Rachel was at Home, took Billy with me and went again; Thos. Afflicks Wife and several others there, left my note, bid the Friends farewell, (Rachel, and Betty Jollif) and then went round to Chesnut Street, call'd at A Benezets, and went over to S. Pleasants, where we drank tea, mett several Friends there, among the rest Phebe Yarnel who told us, of Clem Biddles violent behavour to her Husband, when he wanted to make his escape, after the Battle near Concord; he held a Pistol to his Breast or head, and Swore he would blow out his brains if he would not show him the road he wanted, &c—came home towards Evening—R. Jones, Reb. Waln, Sucky Jones, Jos. Scott, B. Morgan, J. Drinker, Heny. Drinker, Nurse Willson, & S. Hartshorn call'd—this has been a Sorrowful day at Philada. and much more so at Germantown and thereabouts.[40]—it was reported in the forenoon that 1000 of the English were slain, but Chalkley James who lodges here to night, as Henry is out on guard, tells us, that he has been to day as far is B. Chews place, and could not learn of more then 30 of the English being kill'd, tho a great number were wounded & brought into this City, he counted 18 of the Amiracans lyeing dead, in the lane from the Road to Chews House, the House is very much Damaged, as a few of the English troops had taken shelter there, and was fir'd upon from the road by great

field after the battle, Burgoyne was able to claim victory in this engagement, despite heavy losses. The Americans, however, were still in command of the high ground overlooking the battlefield and were able to obtain reinforcements of both men and ammunition for their subsequent victory at Saratoga on Oct. 7 (see below, Nov. 1, 1777; Boatner, *American Revolution*, 139–41, 971–75).

40. Despite Washington's loss of Philadelphia in September, he was able to mount another attack on the main body of British troops controlling the city, who were then encamped at Germantown. The Americans began a futile attack on Oct. 4, hindered by a thick fog and by a complicated battle strategy, which they were unable to execute and which led to their confusion and retreat. Over a thousand American soldiers were killed, wounded, or missing, of a total of eleven thousand. The British lost less than six hundred of a force of nine thousand (Boatner, *American Revolution*, 426–30).

numbers of the others. The last account towards Evening was that the English were pursueing Washingtons troops, who are very numerous, and that they were flying before them, the Amaricans are divided into three different divisions, one over Schuykill, another near Germantown, and the third I know not where—so that the[41] Army that was with us, are chiefly call'd off, and a double guard, is this Night thought nescesary; it is thought, that it was the intention, that one division[42] should enter the City, while the troops were engaged with the others. The apprehensions of their entering, and fears of the Gondelows & other Vessels in the River, will render this night, greveious to many; Washington is said to be Wounded in the thigh; Friends, and others, in the Jersyes, and indeed almost round the Country, are Suffering deeply—['tis] now past 12 o'clock, and all in the House, except myself I believe asleep the Watchman has cry'd the Hour, and all seems quiet a fine star light Morning.

5 First Day: things appear quiet to Day. MS. SD. AD. WD, went to meeting this Morning Ann Moore and Debby Morris, din'd with us, Anty. Morris Senr. and his Son Thos. Becky Jones and Jonney Drinker call'd after Dinner, in the Afternoon ED. SD. WD. went to meeting; Nathan Yarnel and Wife, Hannah Williams and G. Churchman, drank Coffee with us—ED went to Evening Meeting, which was large as a number of Country Friends are yet with us—Danl. Drinker, Patn. Hartshorn and Wife, Docr. Redman and Jos. Bringhurst call'd. The latter brings word of the Wellfare of my Husband, who with the other Friend, were seen last, Second day, Morning 9 o'clock, within 20 miles of Winchester, Danl. Roberts who came ashore at Willingstown from the Fleet, brings this News from Docr. Whey, who saw the Man that spoak to[43] our Friends.[44]

6 Heard a fireing this Morning; went after Breakfast, to Josa. Fishers to look for Linnin &c as they have open'd their Store mett M Pleasants there talk'd about the Testimony which Friends have lately put out, and 'tis said they are going with to Washington,—Sally Penington and Bulah Burge spent this Afternoon with us. I took a walk down to Abel's this Evening Josey much better, Chalkley came home with me, he tells me that our Meadow at Point is spoil'd by 300 Head of Cattle, which the Americans had there some time—The heaviest fireing that I think I ever heard, was this Evening, for upwards of two hours, thought to be the English troops, engag'd with the Mud-Island Battry,[45]—an Officer call'd this Afternoon to ask if we could take in a Sick or

41. "Soliders" crossed out.

42. More than a line crossed out.

43. The word "the" crossed out.

44. The words "Sarah Fisher sent this Evening to borrow a Bed-Chair, for a wounded Officer, who it seems they have, at their House" crossed out.

45. Mud Island, situated in the Delaware River a little below the mouth of the Schuylkill River, south of Philadelphia, had a commanding position over the navigable channel between

Wounded Captain; I put him off by saying that as my Husband was from me, I should be pleas'd if he could provide some other convenient place, he hop'd no offence, and departed—Our little Henry has been down stairs for 2 or 3 days continus very weak in his Lims, but eats victuals at a great rate—We have had two loads of Hay brought in to day. Reba. Waln, John Drinker, Katty Howell, Saml. Sansom call'd—our Friends from the Country have generally left us, they have fine weather for their return, which has been the case during the Meeting—two of the Presbytearan Meeting Houses, are made Hospitals of, for the Wounded Soliders, of which there are a great Number.

7 Thos. Say, and David Estaugh, call'd this Morning ED. SD. AD. and WD. went to Meeting; Grace Fisher, S Swett, and Nurse Wilson din'd with us, H Catheral drank Tea—R. Waln call'd, S. Moore, stop'd in her Chaise at the Door, [no certain] account of the cause of the heavey fireing last Evening—unless it was the Gondelows.

8 Charles West and John Drinker call'd—this Morning—went before dinner, Billy with me, to Josa. Fishers Store, call'd at Uncle Jervis's, Reba. Waln call'd—Sister with Billy and the two Hannah Catherels & M Pleasants, went to the Play-House, the State-House, and one of the Presbytearn's Meeting Houses, to see the Wounded Soliders.

9 fireing last night, and heavey fireing this Morning from 5 o'clock 'till between 6 & 7, it was the Frigit and Gondelows, playing upon the English, who were errecting a Battry on, or near the Banks of Schuylkill,[46] one Englishman slain and two Wounded, 2 Horses kill'd—Jenney and Harry went this Afternoon in the rain, to the Play House &c. with a Jugg of Wine-Whey and a Tea-Kittle of Coffee, for the Wounded Men. Cloudy all Day, and rain the greatest part, but now, near 10 o'Clock it seems to be clearing with a North Wester,—little Henry up Stairs all day by the Doctors advice, least the weather should affect him, he geathers fles[h] surpriseingly, and strenght, tho he complains still, of his Legs being very heavey, and comes up stairs upon all-fours—Myself but poorly to day; fell down one [pair] of the Stairs Yesterday, and brus'd my foot and Hip,—J. Drinker, R Jones, and D. Drinker call'd.

---

the island and the Pennsylvania shore. American forces built Fort Mifflin there and placed barricades in the river to hinder British vessels. The British, who had entered the lower Delaware on Oct. 4, knew they had to incapacitate the American batteries and river barricades to advance. The gunfire to which ED refers may have had some connection with the British troops who began building batteries on nearby Province Island in the Schuylkill River on Oct. 7. The British hoped that the Province Island location would give them a commanding position over Mud Island so they could silence the batteries at Fort Mifflin and remove the barricades (Stryker, *Forts on the Delaware*, 7–11).

46. An attack by nine American galleys on British grenadiers who were building batteries at Webb's Ferry, a crossing point of the Schuylkill River to Province Island (Jackson, *Pennsylvania Navy*, 143, 139).

10 Sally, Nancy, and Billy went this Morning to Children's Meeting, Jenney and Harry went to the Statehouse with Coffee and Whey for the Wounded Amaricans, Billy went with them—in the long Room at the State house are the Prisoners, Saml. Howel Mercht. among the rest—George James call'd with £30″ 6″—in Jersey money, which he left with me, I pay'd him a half Jo', for some silver which my dear Henry had of him a day or 2 before he was taken from us—I went this Afternoon to C. Whites with Sally and little Molly to be measur'd for Shoes, came home with the Child, and then took Billy with me, to see Hannah Pemberton, who is unwell in her Chamber, call'd at Thos. Says—Saml. Sansom call'd—Humphyriss paper came out to day—the weather has clear'd up cold.

11 Jenney and Harry visited the wounded, again to day, with a double portion—the Battry on Province Island was taken this Morning from the English, and retaken in half an hour, we hear Connon fireing almost every day—Abel James sent us ¾ Cord Wood this Morning.—J. Drinker, A Benezet, Jos. Scott, R. Jones, Reba. Waln, S. Fisher, Patn. and Sucky Hartshorn, call'd. S. Emlen sent us word this Evening that he and the other Friends vizt. Nics. Waln, James Thornton, Wm. Brown, Josa. Morris, and Warner Mifflin,[47]—were return'd, from a visit [paid] to Washington. I apprehend they have no good news, or I think I should have heard it—We were frighted this Evening near 10 o'clock by a terrable cry of Murder, in our Alley—proved to be the Bakers William, who I supose was in Licquor—I have been more distress'd in mind this day, then for some time past, not from any thing I have heard, but my Spirits seem much affected.

12 First Day: We were awaked this Morning at about 2 o'clock, by H Drinker, knocking at my Chamber door, and asking for a light, as there was a cry of fire, it prov'd to be a Stable at the upper end of Second Street, where 3 or 4 Horses were burnt to Death—Sister and the Children went to Meeting this Morning Saml. Emlen, Saml. Smith call'd after dinner, SE. related some perticulars of their reception at Washingtons camp, as I had little expectations from their application, am not so much disapointed,—as little has come of it—S Swett din'd with us—J Drinker, D Drinker, and Robt. Waln call'd after dinner—ED. and the Children went to Afternoon Meeting—Enoch Story and Wife call'd; the latter went to Evening Meeting with me where Nics. Waln appeared in Testimony & Prayer, when I came home found Hannah Sansom and her Son William at our House—HD call'd to let us know, that he was to be on guard to Night, sent down for Chalkley, who is to be engag'd on the same business, so that Abel Junr. lodges with us this Night.—My Ancle, which I sprain'd 2 or 3 days ago, is so swell'd and painful this Evening that I can scarcely walk on it—S. Smiths Wifes Brother was taken by the Amricans,

47. Word crossed out.

bringing provision to Town against our Yearly Meeting, and carried to Washings. camp, where 'tis said he is to be try'd for his life.

13 fireing almost all night and very heavey towards morning, the Gallyes on the men which are employ'd at the Battry on province Island—2 or 3, said to be kill'd—Reba. Waln, Docr. Redman, Amos Taylor measur'd our Sons for a Sute of Cloths each—G Oats call'd and behaved with so much impudance, that I could not agree to give his Daughter her demand—dull weather this day.

14 Sister and the Children went to Meeting;[48] much talk of Wash[s] endeavouring to enter the City, a number of the People greatly alarm'd on that account—Polly Waln dind with the Children.—Polly Pleasants and Daughter, Sally Logan, Betsy and Polly Jervis, drank Tea with us, John and Rachel Drinker Supped.—John James, David Eastaugh, John Parish, Joseph Yerkes, Becky Scattergood, S Swett, Jenney Wood, Becky Jones, Edwd. Stiles; Saml. Emlen and James Hutchingson call'd, the latter with a Letter from Thos. Fisher, wrote in Behalf of the Company at Winchester, with the agreeable account of their all being well, the rest of the Letter, rather gives me pain, than pleasure. Our Harry Catter is free this Day,—My Ancle so swell'd and painfull this Evening that I am oblig'd to have it bath'd—Sister and Sally went to the Burial of Edy. Devenshire.

15. Nothing material occur'd this Day that I know of—Josa. Howel call'd to enquire for some paper respecting the School, Board, I could not find it—Reba. Waln, Saml. Emlen, Nics. Waln, and John Glover call'd.

16 I step'd over to Neigr. Walns this Afternoon and drank Tea with them, Robt. appears to me to be more unwell than he has been for a long time past[49]—a man was Yesterday kill'd with the Bursting of a Cannon which is was trying—last night one of the Hessian Guards who stood on Race Street Warfs, was fired at, from, or nearly from, A Jamess back store—Joseph Bringhurst, John Drinker, C. West, call'd—the inhabitance have mett to day, and Yesterday, to regulate a Nightly Watch, which has been drop'd for some time, but is thought to be again Nesessary—5 Weeks this day since my dearest Henry left us, the thoughts of the approaching cold season, and the uncertainty when we shall meet again, is at times hard to bare; yet at other times I am sustain'd with a Lively hope, that I shall see that time, and prehaps it may be sooner than we seem to expect. Sister has been busy to day in the Garden, planting out [the] Roots—Our dear Children are all present pretty well; but little Henrys face and Belly somewhat Bloated, which I hope he will run down e'er long.[50]

48. The words "a great deal of" crossed out.
49. The words "there was" crossed out.
50. Several of the entries on loose, mispaginated leaves in the manuscript volumes that follow the words "e'er long" have been inserted in the printed volume in chronological order.

our little Molly went alone when she was, between 14 and 15 months—May—1775.

little Molly began to Chatter, when she was about 20 months old.

Novr. the 20. 1775. second Day, I began to Wean my little Molly—she is very good natur'd, and bares it well, tho' she seems in trouble about it—20 months old and upwards, when she was Wean'd.

Nancys[51] Buckles Octr. 30, 1773
HD. 15 Shirts Novr. 1773
WDs new Hatt Novr. 14, 1773
HDs new Gs. Janry. 28. 1774

Barrel of Coffee, March 1. 1774
Barrel Sugar July 28. 1774
New S[l]ips—Bleu, put on Novr. 20. 1774
Sallys New Buckl Decr. 1774
Thimble Janry. 2, 1775

1777, Janry, 31 parted with the Calf: and used our Cows milk for the first time.

Purple Shoes, and Black Shoes, put on the Middle of Janry. 1777.

Keeper dye'd. June 28, 1773.

Tinc Rheu Octr. 23. 1774.

Tinc: Rheu April 13. 1776.

New Castle
Philadelphia
1773 1772 1774
Dublin
Constantinople
Abracadabra Most Men
Sally
Germantown
London
Burlington
Many Men of many minds
Lay wh[ ] asside, ill nature & Pride

51. The material "Nancys Buckles . . . Tinc: Rheu April 13. 1776" is written on the inside back cover of this volume. The outside back cover contains random jottings, including the alphabet, numbers, and the list beginning with "New Castle."

500[52]
75
54
27
21/4
15/–
30/–
45/–
30.
60
10/19

895/3

Moster Man Man

1777 Octor. 17. Becky Jones call'd this Morning with Mary Pembertons Letter from her Husband, of the 6th Instant for me to read; and to send Billy with it to Sally Penington.—I sent for J. Drinker, who read it, and went with it to SP,—Isreals Letter has afforded me, much more pain than Comfort,—Billy Compton call'd after Dinner, as did Robt. Waln, the former read great part of Dr. Smith's Journal to us—I paid him 36/– for 24 lb Candles—there is talk today, as if, the English Troops had left Wilmington,[53] but I know not the truth—S. Swett drank Coffee with us, Johney Drinker spent the Evening—my ancle still painful, and my right Ear stop'd for several days—the careful attendance on our little Son, during his illness, with other trouble, has left me very much relax'd, and weaken'd, cloudy Weather.

18th. Isaac Catheral paid us a visit this Morning—we hear abundance of news, but know not what to depend on—Saml. Emlen, S Sansom, and Josey James, call'd this forenoon, the first time of Joseys coming out since his illness—Docr. Redman call'd while we were at dinner, Saml. and Sally Emlen, spent this afternoon with us—had a setting togeather, when Sammy was led to speak a few words to us—Robt. Waln and Wife and Johnny Drinker, spent part of the Evening with us—Elizth. Shipley we hear is dead—The Troops at Germington are coming within 2 or 3 miles of this City to encamp—provisions

52. The manuscript volume for Oct. 17, 1777–Jan. 27, 1778, has light blue covers. The front cover reads, "1777 & 1778"; the following list and words also appear on the front cover.

53. The departure of British troops from Wilmington had already begun. General Howe, during his advance on Philadelphia, had kept some of his troops and his hospital ships in Wilmington; these he began evacuating after securing his position in Philadelphia, even before the aborted attempt by American forces on Wilmington. He sent the hospital ships to New York on Oct. 12 and later sent the remaining troops upriver to Chester to help with the destruction of American fortifications along the Delaware River (Baurmeister, *Revolution in America*, 123–25).

are so scarce with us now, that Jenney gave 2/6 p. lb. for mutton this Morning—The people round the Country dose not come near us with any thing, what little butter is brought is 7/6—The fleet not yet up, nor likely to be soon, I [fear]. Jenney and Billy, went this Afternoon, with coffee and whey for the Soliders.

19 First Day: MS. and the Children [went] to Meeting this Morning—Sammy Smith & Wife call'd before dinner, her Brother is releas'd—ED. and the Children went this Afternoon to Meeting, Silent—C. West and Wife drank tea with us—as did Daniel Drinker—J.D. came home with me from Evening meeting—Chalkley James lodges here to Night HD. not here—The troops have come this afternoon within a mile of us; J Hunt's family I hear have mov'd to town, and many from Germantown, the Amricans have stop'd several who were out, and returning, home, and have sent 'em back again, M Hains is one, as we hear, A James and Wife &c who went to Frankford, to bring away their Cloaths &c. were told while there, that some of the Provincials were at J Dickensons place, which intiligence occasiond them to get into the Waggon and come home Point road as fast as they could, a great fireing below today.

20th. Chalkley James Breakfasted with us—Billy began a quarters Schooling, whole Days, at Joseph Yerkess the first of his going since his dear Daddy left us, and for a long time before, Henry went this morning for the first time since his illness, little Molly also, I put to school with Henry, to H. Catheral, the first of her ever going unless on a visit—Docr. Park call'd to tell us of a Letter he had received from his Father in Law, James Pemberton dat'd the 10th Instant four days since the last, no fresh intilegence that concerns the friends—I step'd down to Abels, Thos. [Loozley] there, whose 2 Sons are taken from him by the Amricans, and he oblig'd to leave home—I went out this Afternoon, was stop'd at S. Burdges, S. Penington there; stay'd about half an hour, H. Moore call'd me over, stay'd about a quarter of an hour there—then went and drank tea with Mary Pemberton, and T. Gorthrope, step'd into S. Pleasent's, Polly has lost their Waggon and 2 Horses, and Negro Boy—also a Negro Man, who was hire'd to go with them to Germantown, to bring some things, away from Isreals place, were all taken by the Provincials; a Waggon stop'd that was loaded at J Hunts door with his Goods, and obliged to unload; A Morris and son Billy, who went to wait on R Hunt, were stop'd and their Horses taken from them, they escaped themselves with some difficulty—there has been a Skirmish this Morning between Germantown and Philada. the Perticulars of which I have not learnt,[54] and very heavey fireing below, great part of the Afternoon, know not yet upon what occasion,—16 or 18 flat bottom Boats came up last night, got safely by the Gondelows and Battry, but

54. On Oct. 20 British troops were withdrawn from Germantown and moved into Philadelphia (Washington, *Writings*, 9:413).

were fir'd upon by some of the English who did not know 'em and kill'd one Man—if things dont change 'eer long, we shall be in poor plight, everything scarce and dear, and nothing suffer'd to be brought in to us—Tom Prior taken up today, on suspicion, as 'tis said, of sending intiligence to Washingtons Army—Johny Drinker, Nics. Waln, Becky Jones, Robt. Waln and Wife, Saml. Emlen, Docr. Redman and D. Drinker, call'd—Danl. came to borrow our Horse for a few days, to bring home his Potatoes &c from his place, he lent his Horse and Cart yesterday to Thos. West, to bring his Goods to Town, they were taken by the Amricans, so that Danl. has met with a loss, T. West, himself got off, but his Son is taken.

21 Sammy Smith call'd this Morning for the Queries—[J].D took the papers concerning Slaves, Yesterday—ED. and the Children went to meeting—Thos. Gothrope, and John Gracey & S. Swett din'd with us—Saml. Emlen call'd to let us know that there was a person in Town who was going to Winchester, and that I could get information of him at Isaac Zanes—I sent Billy after Dinner to learn his Name, and when he went, he brought word from Sarah, that he was a Wild Irish-Man, who wanted friends to get him a pass, and she thought, not fit to be trusted—his name John Gibson. I went in the Afternoon to Hannah Pembertons (who has been very ill) to hear more about this Man, she could tell me nothing conserning him. I call'd at O Joness where he has been this Morning and expected again this Evening they are to let me know Tomorrow, wheather they conclude to write by him or not—Sucky Badger and Abel James, drank tea with Sister, John Drinker and Wife, Betsy Drinker, Hannah Saunders, Becky Scattergood, Reba. James, Becky James Jr. Reba. Waln, call'd—John [G]racey, who has been threaten'd, has left his home on that account.—2000 of the Hessians were landed in the Jersyes this day, tis supposed their intinsions are against the Mud-Island Battery &c—we saw, a Number of them crossing in the flat Bottom'd Boats, from our Garret Window—there has been applycation made by the English for Blankets, as the Fleet is at a distance, and they lost a number in the Battle near Germantown,—as I was not in the way, Sister came of with that excuse.

22. J. Drinker wrote a few lines this Morning to my HD. by the Person spoke of yesterday—Amos Taylor (who was here trying on the Childrens Cloaths) informs me, that Richd. Waln is taken up, and sent to New York, he had his choice of 3 things, either to go to Jail, take the Test, or go within the English lines, the latter was chose—Joseph Scott and Hannah Drinker drank tea with us, Phines Bond, Abel James, Becky Jones, John Drinker, Reba. Waln, Taba. Fisher, Becky Fisher; call'd.

23 this day will be remember'd by many; the 2500 Hessions who cross'd the River the day before yesterday, were last Night driven back 2 or 3 times, in

endeavouring to Storm the fort on Red Bank,[55] 200 slain and great Numbers wounded, the fireing this Morning seem'd to be incesant, from the Battry, the Gondelows, and the Augustia Man of War, of 64 Guns, she took fire, and after burning near 2 hours, blew up, the loss of this fine Vessel is accounted for in different ways—some say she took fire by accident, others, that, it was occasion'd by Red hot Bullets from Mud-Island Battry—another English Vessel somewhat smaller, it is said is also burnt, Many of the Inhabitance of this City, are very much Affected, by the present situation and appearance of things, while those on the other side the question are flush'd, and in Spirits—old [H]unt De Nope, is said to be among the slain—it was between 11 and 12, near Noon, when the Augustia blew up, many were not sensable of any Shock, others were, it was very plain to most who were at Meeting, as this is fifth Day—and appear'd to some like an Earth Quake—Abel James Oswald Eve, and Chalkley James, went on the top of our House this Morning with a Spy-Glass, but could discover nothing but Smoke, Sammy Emlen, Joshua Howel call'd—S Sansom and John Drinker sup'd with us—S Logan drank Tea—I step'd over to Nr. Walns after dinner,—Robts Health bad, and Spirits low—the Weather cool and clear—The Hessians and other of the British Troops are encamp'd in the Jersyes, this Night, we can see their fiers for a considerable distance along the shore—I have been unwell some time with a pain in my side, Sholder Blade &c.

24. We have heard a few Cannon fir'd this day. but cannot tell the occasion—S Swett din'd with us, Josey Bringhurst, Nr. Stiles, Becky Jones, call'd, Robt. Waln & Wife, spent part of the Evening; Cloudy.

25 Saml. Emlen call'd this Morning Samuel Coats came to ask for Room in our Coach House, for John Reynolds Carriage, I agree'd thereto, Abel Jamess Waggon is already there, brought this Afternoon—An Officer call'd to Day to know if Genl. Grant could have quarters with us; I told him as my Husband was from me, and a Number of Young Children round me, I should be glad to be excus'd—he reply'd, as I desir'd it, it should be so—Tom Kite tells me, that Neighr. Stiless House near Frankford, was broak open, the Night before last, and much Plunder'd, by the Amricans—Johny Drinker call'd this Afternoon, he was going to the Funeral of Saml. Bell, who was bury'd from John Parrocks—a few Cannon was heard this day—cloudy all Day.

55. A reference to the Battle of Fort Mercer on Oct. 22. Fort Mercer, another of the Delaware River fortifications (see above, Oct. 6), was located at Red Bank in Gloucester County, N.J. Four hundred American troops led by Col. Christopher Greene repulsed an attack by three battalions and one artillery regiment of Hessian soldiers. The Hessians suffered many casualties. The naval action concerning the *Augusta* took place on Oct. 23 in the vicinity of Fort Mifflin at Mud Island, where a five-hour battle transpired between the British and American fleets (Stryker, *Forts on the Delaware*, 15–26).

26th. First Day: Sister and the Children went to Meeting this Morning Myself with them in the Afternoon, the first time of our little Henrys going since his recovery—John and Danl. Drinker, call'd after dinner—Hannah Drinker, Sam. Hopkins call'd—Katty Howel and Reba. Waln spent part of the Evening—S. Swett drank Coffee with us—Molly Moors Mother, bury'd this Afternoon, at Frankford.

27 Wind at N.E. rain all the fore part of the Day—and very Stormy this Evening A. James call'd this Morning. he disir'd me to speak to Mary Pemberton for some Wood, as she has some to cut within the lines; he design'd to have supply'd me, but that now, is out of the Question; J Drinker call'd for the Yearly meeting minuets, which are not in our possesion—Robt. Waln and Wife drank Coffee with us, Saml. Emlen call'd; he has had a quantity of Hay taken from him, by the Soldiery and a House up Town, much abused—Edwd. Jones call'd to inform us, that one Thos. May, who lives beyond Winchester, was to set of, next day after tomorrow, Becky Jones call'd this Evening.

28. Wind Easterly, rain all Day and Stormey, Sister went to Monthly Meeting Sammy Sansom and Jonny Drinker here this Afternoon, Heny. Drinker Breakfast'd with us, I wrote this Evening to my HD.

29 this is the third day of rain and NE wind, J. Drinker and Saml. Emlen call'd, a few Cannon heard, this Afternoon, the tide so high to day as to come into the Cellars in Water Street. JD. wrote to HD.

30 About 2 o'clock this Morning Henry Drinker knock'd at Sister's room door for a light, as he thought he heard somebody tampering with the middle room Window in the Alley, Sister and Harry got up, but could discover nothing, I went this Afternoon, Sally and Nancy with me, to Owen Joness John Nancarrow came home with us, Sarah Fisher and J. Drinker drank Coffee with Sister, Robt. Waln & Wife here this Evening. John Parish and John James call'd, they have Concluded (after the Quarterly meeting at Concord, to visit our dear Friends at Winchester,—Aurther Thomas, lodges hear to Night, with Henry Drinker.

31. I went[56] this afternoon out with Sally and Nancy, call'd at Uncle Jervis's, took a long walk to see Sally Wharton, who has been confin'd for a long time with a bad Leg—came home towards Evening Robt. Waln & Wife here—talk of a Flag from Red-Bank-Battery this Afetrnoon Jo Blewer one that brought it, I know not for what.

Novr 1. Uncle and Aunt Jervis spent this Day with us, the first time of his

56. "Yesterday" crossed out.

being in this House, they inform us that O Jones has received a Letter from his Daughter Lowry, which tells them, that our Friends are gone from Winchester to Isaac Zanes, Abel James call'd this Morning with the same account, and further, that he has received a Letter from G. Morgan who is at Frankford, wherein he mentions my dear Henry, and E. Penington &c &c being well. Georges busyness is with a Flag, for his Wife, Becky James junr. and Gibsons Wife went to day to frankford, and were stop'd by the Amrican Light Horse, and might prehaps have been detain'd, but for Capt. Craige, who after some Apologies, suffer'd 'em to return. Isaiah Worrels Son with many others, were taken this Morning at Frankford and brought to Town, by the English Light Horse: accounts in Town to day that Gen. Borgoine with 5000 men have surrender'd &c.[57] this account seems to gain Credit—a poor Solider was hang'd this Afternoon on the Common, for striking his Officer; The Hessians go on plundring at a great rate, such things as, Wood, Potatoes, Turnips &c—Provisions are scarce among us—Sammy Hopkins, Robt. Waln and Wife, call'd—Jos. Scott drank Coffee with us, and Hanh. Drinker I had a spell of the Sick Head Ach last Night.

2d—First Day: The Children Sally excepted went to Meeting; myself and the 4 went this Afternoon, H Catheral calld this Morning Elizth Morris din'd with us—S Swett, Nany Eve, Nurse Moore, R. Proud, J Drinker and D Drinker drank tea with us—Myself & Sally spent part of this Evening at A. Jamess the Hessian Count is not dead, but wounded, Saml. Emlen and Wife call'd after Morning Meeting.

3 S Swett came this Morning Nancy went to quarterly Meeting with her, she spent the rest of the Day with us, Sister has a bad cold, myself sick at Stomach Nancy [Carlile] and Nr Catheral drank [Coffee] with us, Sucky Jones came over from R Walns to aquaint us, that P. Hartshorn, had just [parted] with Docr. Whay, who had a Packet of Letters from the Friends at Winchester. I sent Harry to enquire after one, but found that there is none come, but from the Pembertons—Jos. Howel & Wife, and Robt. Waln here this Evening John and D. Drinker, and C. West call'd—fireing heard, to day and Yesterday, dont know the cause—E.D. took a cardas Vomitt[58] this Evening—C. James lodges here, HD. with the Night Watch—very fine Weather.

4. The 4 Children went to Youths Meeting—my self went, Sally and Nancy

57. British general John Burgoyne formally surrendered his army of approximately five thousand men to Gen. Horatio Gates on Oct. 17 after his defeat at Saratoga, N.Y., on Oct. 7 (Boatner, *American Revolution*, 971–80; Fred J. Cook, *Dawn over Saratoga: The Turning Point of the Revolutionary War* [Garden City, N.Y.: Doubleday, 1973], 158 and passim; Rupert Furneaux, *Saratoga: The Decisive Battle* [London: Allen & Unwin, 1971], 222, 241, and passim).

58. The cardues, a thistle, was used in ED's time as a bitter tonic. A decoction of its leaves would provoke vomiting (W. Lewis, *New Dispensatory*, 117–18).

also, to the Burial of Jenney Hough, I went afterwards to P. Pembertons, drank tea with her, & spent part of the Evening, fine Weather—I wrote twice this day to my dear Henry Becky Jones, Sammy Hopkins, John Parish, John Drinker, Reb. Waln, Sally Zane, Patterson Hartshorn and Wife, Sally Jones, call'd—Jos. Scott and Sally Logan, drank tea with Sister.

5 Jammy Morton call'd this Morning with Israel and James Pembertons Letters, which I read, and was pleas'd therewith—A Solider came to demand Blankets, which I did not in any wise agree to, notwithstanding my refusial he went up stairs and took one, and with seeming good Nature beg'd I would excuse his borrowing it, as it was G. Howes orders, Saml. Emlen and Wife, J. Drinker Reba. Waln and Hannah Drinker call'd—Sammy Sansom drank Coffee with Sister, I spent part of this Afternoon at A James, Josey again unwell,—I wrote this Evening to my Henry by Docr. Way,—rain this Afternoon and Evening—We have not bought a pound of Butter for 3 or 4 weeks past all we get is from our Cow, about 2 pound a week, and very few of the Citizens have any; JD. wrote this Morning to HD.

6. John Parish and John James came this Morning to take leave of us, they intend to set of tomorrow, on their way towards our dear Friends, John Drinker and John Redman call'd—spent this Afternoon with Becky and Hannah; G. Napper call'd this Evening it has clear'd up very cold.

7 The Weather to day very fine, and moderate. No occurance worthy note, C. Carmalt call'd to give notice that the Insurence of our House should be renew'd before the 17 Instant,[59]—Grace Fisher Eliz Drinker S Swett, Rachel Drinker and Hannah Drinker, drank tea with us—John, Rachel and Hannah spent the Evening and sup'd with us—Docr. Way, call'd this Evening, I added a line or 2 to my Letter, which he took with him—Becky Jones, Becky Waln Senr. Abel James and James Logan call'd—Sally and Nancy went this Afternoon with Han. Drinker and Nancy Waln, up to Philipss Rope-Walk, to see the Redoubts which are errected thereabout I have been much disordr'd at my Stomach, for some weeks past; our dear Children have enjoy'd their Health since their dear Fathers Absence, as well as ever I knew them [for] so long a time.

8 We had a Stove put up in the back Parlor; this Morning Wood is so very scarce, that unless thing mend there is no likelyhood of a Supply, and we have

59. Caleb Carmalt was the clerk of the Philadelphia Contributionship for the Insurance of Houses from Loss by Fire, with which HD first insured the Drinker home on Nov. 7, 1770. The policy was renewed four times at seven-year intervals (correspondence from Carol Wojtowics, Curator/Archivist of the Philadelphia Contributionship, Mar. 19, 1986; Archives of the Philadelphia Contributionship, policy numbers 1454–57; Wainwright, *Philadelphia Contributionship*, 64–96).

no more then 4 or 5 Cord, in the Celler,—a fine Morning rain this Evening I dont recollect one single person calling on us to day—HD. informs us this Evening that a Brother of John Balderstons who left home some time past, to get out of the way of the Amrican Army, has from a kind of Necssity enlisted with the English Light-Horse, and is now in trouble for so doing. D. Drinker borrow'd our Horse Yesterday, J. Drinker had him the day before; S Sansom has him today, to Haul Wood from his place; we have mov'd into the little front parlor, where we expect to stay for some days.

9 First Day: Sister and the 4 Children went to Meeting this Morning my self with Sally, Nancy and Henry this afternoon—Billy went to Evening meeting—A. Benezet, David Eastaugh, and John Glover, drank Coffee with us, Reba. Waln spent part of the Evening.

10 dull weather with rain, fireing below to day, began very early in the Morning and continu'd untill Noon, S. Swett, din'd and drank Coffee with us, Saml. Sansom drank Coffee, and spent the Evening John Drinker call'd, he has our Horse to day.

11 Grace Eastaugh, Saml. Emlen, and Jenny Lowerymoore, call'd this Morning Sister, Sally, Nancy and Billy went to Meeting, Saml. Hopkins and John Drinker call'd, myself and little Henry, went this Afternoon to Hannah Pembertons, drank Coffee there Polly Pleasants, Debby Morris there,—I call'd at Nancy Powels, she has been to Reading and was bringing a Number of Letters, from our dear friends at Winchester, which were giving her by the Widdow Shoemaker, at whose house they had lain for some time; Sam. Mifflin accompany'd Nancy and his Daughter, who was with her, some miles on their way, he said he was bound in Honor, not to suffer them to take any seal'd Letters to Philada., which oblidg'd her to give them up; it is two months this day since my dear Henry left me, and I have not heard directly from himself since he left Reading, except one Letter from Carlile to J Drinker, there has been very heavy fireing this Evening, tis supos'd they are attacking the Battrys below, as the English open'd several[60] Yesterday on Mud-Island; Provisons of all kinds grow daily more scarce, I this day bought the Early kind of potatoes for to feed the Cow, at 6/– p Bushel. Robt. Waln call'd this Evening—Tis now near 12 o'clock, I have just clos'd a letter to my dear, which I expect will go in the Morning—a fine Moon light night, cannon now fireing below.

12 great part of last Night and most of this day at times, we have heard the Cannon below; Mud-Island Battry not yet taken.—they say that it is reported in the Country that 5/– is given here for a Rat: it is bad enough indeed, but far

60. "Battrys" crossed out.

from being so, I trust it will not—Robt. Waln, C. West, and Edwd. Drinkers Widdow, call'd this Morning the latter I sent for, as I had heard she was in want. gave her Beef and Biscuit &c—Hannah Elfrith, Rachel Drinker, David Bacon drank Coffee with us—they except David, with Sammy and Hannah Sansom, Reba. Waln Sucky Hartshorn, spent part of the Evening I sent my letter to HD this Morning to Geo. Morgans Wife who expects to go, to day or tomorrow. poor Beef is now sold for 3/– p lb. Veal 4/– Butter 7/6—Chocolate 4/6—Brown Sugar 6/– Candles 2/6 Flour what little there is, at 3£ p [ ]—Oak Wood as it stands 17/– to 20/ p cord—and scarcely possible to get it cut or Haul'd—We are told that our Friends J. Parish and J. James, were stop'd on the other side Schuy kill, and taken to Head-quarters,—but were soon dismist with being told that they should not return to the City.

13. Sister and Sally went out this Morning to D. Drinkers for Bowls, &c, I went this Afternoon to G. Morgans Wife, she has lain in a Month and Sets of tomorrow, with Becky James junr. for Frankford, to stay at Abels place with her Children 'till her Husband comes back from Pittsburgh, where she says he is call'd on exroidanary busyness. call'd on Caleb Carmalt, in my way home, he was here this Evening, I paid him four Dollars to renew the Insureance on our House, J. Drinker here this Evening he tells us that a Company of Soliders have taken possession of our House in Water Street, near Vine Street—Johnny call'd on them, they promis'd to take care that nothing is distroy'd—no news from the Battry; fine clear cool Weather.

14 Hannah Elfreth, Dorcas Mountgomery—Mary Armitt, R. Jones, and Robt. Waln, call'd this Morning D. Drinker drank Coffee with Sister Saml. Emlen call'd—Heavey fireing this Morning, and at times all day, Nothing of Concequence done,—I went after dinner down to Abels, to see Josey, who is again in his Chamber, took a walk to Uncle Jerviss—drank Tea at John Drinkers, call'd at Neigr. Stiles and at Nr. Walns—JD. here this Evening.

15 Becky Wharton, Sally Gardner, Joseph Bringhurst call'd this Morning, Jos. Scott, Reba. Waln, J Drinker this Evening—The fireing to day has been like thunder, comparitevely speaking, from the Vigilant and Sommerset Men of War, on this formidable Mud-Island Battry, which is not yet conquer'd, tho Greatly damag'd,—I had the great Satisfaction this Evening of receiving two Letters from my dearest Henry, the first I have received from him since he left Reading, he mentions 2 others, wrote before these, that have not come to hand, several since I doubt not,—if I can judge of my dear by his Letters, he is in good Spirits, which thought is pleasing to me, I went, Billy with me, this afternoon to Uncle Jerviss and to S. Pleasants, Polly she sent me her letter of the 17th Ultimo this Morning gone out, we came home to tea—a fine Moon light Night this.

16 First Day: Sister and 3 Children went to meeting this Morning the Children all except Sally who has her Face very much swell'd with the tooth ach, went in the Afternoon; the Mud-Island Battry is at length taken,[61] the Amricans left it last night about 12 o'clock, when it is supos'd the English ware about to storm it; other perticulars I have not yet heard—Abey Parish, J Drinker and D Drinker, drank Coffee with us, M. Pleasants came after tea spent the Evening with us—Jammy Morton came this Afternoon to inform us of an oppertunity to Winchester tomorrow, R Waln & Wife, Josa. Howel and Wife here this Evening; a little spiting of Snow to Day.

17 J. Drinker, Billy, and myself wrote to day, to our dear HD, at Winchester, Dorcas Mt. Gomery Spent this Afternoon with us—Hetty Fisher and Neigr. Waln call'd this Evening, the latter brings us a sorrowful account, that our dear Friend Betsy Waln lays so ill that her life is dispair'd of, her mammy is sent for, but cannot easyly get to her—the British troops are busyly employ'd geting up the Chevaux-de-Frise,[62] cold and raw.

18 D. Drinker call'd this Morning S. Swett spent the day with us, Saml. Emlen call'd after meeting he read my Henrys letters, seem'd much pleas'd with 'em, spoke Exellently to the Children &c by way of testimony; express'd great regard for their absent Father—Molly Pleasants junr. came to know if I would go with her Sister to visit S. Penington, I sent Harry to know if it suited SP. who brought word that she is not well, we put it of at present—I took a walk this afternoon, to Uncle Jerviss read my HDs Letters to them and Peggy Smith,—came home to Coffee—J. Drinker call'd—Nanny Oat came while I was out, to ask pardon for her former conduct, which has been vastly impudent—the weather clear and cold, English Troops very much taken up, but private in their [movements].

19 Isaac Zane call'd this Morning I pay'd 30 pounds for 4 Loads of Hay, at 8£ p load, forty Shillings allowd for a difficiency in one of them—John and Daniel Drinker call'd, they are trying to purchase some Wood for themselves

61. The final bombardment of Fort Mifflin on Mud Island began on Nov. 9. The small American force guarding the fort was attacked by British batteries on Province Island, as well as by heavy artillery outfitted on English ships in the river and by riflemen posted on the top masts of one of the English vessels. On Nov. 16, after their fortifications were destroyed and their ammunition had run out, the Americans evacuated the fort and rowed over to the New Jersey shore. During the week-long siege an estimated 250 Americans were killed or wounded (Stryker, *Forts on the Delaware*, 32–39).

62. In the summer of 1776 the Pennsylvania government, concerned about an attack on Philadelphia, made plans to place barricades at several points in the Delaware River, including areas near Billingsport, N.J., and below Red Bank between Fort Mercer and Fort Mifflin on Mud Island. These barricades, called *chevaux de frise*, were constructed of large pieces of heavy timber securely bolted and jointed together, with sharpened iron spikes facing downstream to pierce the hulls of hostile vessels. Heavy stones used as anchors kept the chevaux de frise hidden at low tide (Stryker, *Forts on the Delaware*, 4–5).

and us—Sally Logan spent this Afternoon with Sister, I spent it with Sally Penington, B. Burge there—R. Waln and Wife here this Evening—G. Corn Walace left this City the Day before Yesterday at 2 o'clock in the Morning with 3000 men,[63] as its said—he was fire'd at, out of a House near Darby, when some of his men rush'd in, and put 2 men to the Sword, and took several others prisoners—he designs for the Jersyes—A Number of the Amaricans were seen this Afternoon in the Jersyes, opposite the City, and in other parts.

20 that 2 men was put to the Sword Yesterday is a mistake, but that one of the English was shot is true, the person who did it made of—it is said, and credited that Red-Bank Battry is taken, the Amrircans left it, and it is thought they have blown it up, they have also, distroy'd one or two of their Vesels—I saw a great Smok[ing] from our little Window—John and Dl. Drinker call'd, the former told me that M. Pleasants had received 2 Letters from her Husband, and that there was one for me, I made some enquirey but could not find mine 'till Evening when Wm. Jackson and Benjn. Mason call'd and brought me two letters from my dear Henry—dated the 1 and 11th. Instant—tis a great comfort to know that he was so lately well—they left others litters for us poor women; at 3 several places, at Josa. Pusys at the Grove, at Willmington and at Darby—they thought it best, not to take all, least they should be taken from them—Jos. Scott, Josa. Howel call'd as did Becky Jones—Wm. Jackson gave me a Letter from my dear to G. Churchman, with an account of their situation—We have a small quarter of Beef, came home to day—spaird us by Nr. Stiles, I went to bed very sick at my Stomach, as I have frequently been laterly, with a Vomiting—little Molly has had a bad cough for several Weeks.

21st. I was awaken'd this Morning befor 5 o'clock by the loud fireing of Cannon, my Head Aching very badly; All our Family was up but little Molly, and a fire made in the Parlor, more then an hour before day—all our Neighbours were also up, and I believe most in Town—The Amricans had set their whole Fleet on fier,[64] except one Small vesel and some of the Gondelows, which past by the City in the Night; the fireing was from the Delaware who lay at Coopers Point, on the Gondelows, which they did not return; Billy counted

63. Lord Cornwallis left Philadelphia with two thousand troops to attempt another assault on Fort Mercer (see above, Oct. 23). After the fall of Fort Mifflin on Nov. 16 further defense of Fort Mercer was untenable, and Col. Christopher Greene evacuated the fort the night of Nov. 20–21, thus opening the Delaware River to British shipping (Boatner, *American Revolution*, 383).

64. ED was not the only Philadelphian who thought that the Americans had set their own navy on fire. Robert Morton, another Quaker diarist, reported that the ships were "burning with the greatest fury." The Americans did not destroy their whole navy, however: the burning of the ships was part of the destruction of Fort Mercer, the last outpost on the lower Delaware River, which the Americans demolished on the afternoon of Nov. 20 rather than leave for the British. The remnants of the American fleet sailed north and anchored at Bristol, Pa. (Morton, "Diary," 29–30; S. L. Fisher, "Diary of Trifling Occurrences," 457; Jackson, *Pennsylvania Navy*, 275–76, 282–83).

8 different Vessels on fire at once in sight, one lay near the Jersey shore, opposite our House; we heard the explosion of 4 of 'em when they blew up, which shook our Windows greatly—We had a fair sight of the blazeing Fleet, from our upper Windows.—We have heard this Morning of Skirmishing in many places, at the Black-Horse on Frankford road, and in different parts of the Jersyes.—Isaac Wharton, with another man, call'd, to tell me, that his Brother Thos. had mention'd in a Letter to him—a sum of mony, lent to an Hessian Officer a prisoner, in Virginia,[65] by my HD. &c. that 2 half Joes was coming to me, which David Franks was to pay, and he intended to call on him for it.—An inferior Hessian Officer, an elderly man who lodges at the Bakers next door, insisted on putting his Horse in our Stable, which I refus'd, he came in this morn'g and ask'd for Harry. I call'd him into the Parlor; he either could not, or pretended he could not understand English; but told Harry in Dutch that he must and would put his Horse in our Stable. A. James who came in some time after, was kind enough to go to Jos. Galloway and get a few lines from him, which he took in next door, and had some talk with them, which I hope will settle the matter; J Drinker, Danl. Drinker Jos. Bringhurst and Becky Jones were also here before Dinner—C. West Saml. Smith and Reba. Waln, the last came late in the Evening she is afraid to go to Bed, as there is talk of Washingtons making an attack or the City before Morning—this has been a Day repleat with events, very hazey weather, my Head Achs.

22 Fireing again this Morning Cannon and small arms,—an Amrican Schooner burnt in our river this morning by the English, partly oppsite our House—An Earthquack was felt this Morning between 7 & 8 o'clock, by a great number of the inhabitans, not one in our Family was sensible of it—these are tremendous times indeed—there has been Skirmishing to day several times between the Amercians and the Picquet Guards and tis said 7 or 8 have lost their lives,—five Vessels have turn'd the Point this Afternoon—one thousand Men, attack'd the Picquet guard[66] this Morning about 11 o'clock, they drove them off, when some took Shelter in J. Dickensons House, and other Houses thereabouts, the English immeadatly set fire to said Houses and burnt them to the Ground,—the burning those Houses tis said is a premeditated thing, as they serve for skulking places; and much anoy the Guards. They talk of burning all the Houses &c within four miles of the City, without the lines—J. Dickensons House; that in which C. Tomson liv'd, Jon. Mifflins, Widdow Crawstons, and many others were burnt this Afternoon—R. Waln and Wife, Josa. Howel and several others, went on top of our House to day, where they

65. During the course of the war large contingents of Hessian soldiers were captured and confined in the western parts of Maryland and Virginia. A group of Hessians had been transferred from Pennsylvania to Winchester in September (Klaus Wust, *The Virginia Germans* [Charlottesville: University Press of Virginia, 1969], 87–88).

66. A small detachment of troops sent out to watch for the approach of the enemy (*OED*, s.v. "picket").

could see the Houses burning, and the Ships coming up—those two days past have been big with events, and Alarms; 'till now, we have experienc'd great quiate since the English came in, I have heard the Noise of a Drum, but twice[67] since they came,—R Waln was ask'd in Market within this day or two 30 s—— for a very small Turkey; Butter 12 s—— I gave 3 half Joes to day for £60 Conti[68]—Sally Emlen, John & Danl. Drinker call'd, weather warm and Hazey.

23 First Day: Sister and the 4 Children at Meeting this Morning myself with them in the afternoon, Wm. Jackson came home with us after meeting, he, J. Drinker, S Swett and D Drinker drank Coffee with us—after which, we had a setting togeather, when Wm. was led to speak encourageingly to us—Becky Jones, Reb. Waln Sucky Hartshorn here this Evening—William Jackson proposes, paying a visit to Winchester next month, he leaves Town tomorrow Morning I gave him this Afternoon £61. 11. 3. Continenl. Cury.—and 2 pair of worsted Stockings for my dear Henry—The Widdow Crawtsons House said to be burnt yesterday proves a mistake,[69] its said is burnt to the Ground, all that was in it—H. Catheral just now informs me that D. Williams is not burnt, but that, the Widw. Taylors, John Byards, and A. Hodges are burnt, with many small out Houses, Barns, &c—I have just heard that poor Docr. Kersley died lately in Carlile jail. wrote a Letter this night after the Family was retir'd to rest, to my dear Henry.

24 Wm. Jackson call'd this Morning to let me know, that he was not free to take the continental money with him, I must therefore seek another conveyance, I took a Walk to Mary Pembertons, Billy with me, to alter that part of my letter concerning the money—a number of Friends there—I went in to M Pleasants, read her's and my Litters, the last we received—call'd at Uncle Jerviss read Charless Letter to his Father—came home to Dinner, Cate. Greenleaf, Becky Jones and Hannah Catheral, drank Coffee with us—Saml. Emlen, Nancy Jones, Cristr. White and J Redman call'd; it is an agreeable sight to see the Warfes lin'd with Shippin, and number has come up to day—the poor people have been allow'd for some time past to go to Frankford Mill, and other Mills that way, for Flour, Abraham Carlile who gives them passes, has his Door very much crouded every morning—Gen. CornWallace is said to be in the Jersys, some say that he has taken a number of Prisoners, others say

67. The word "this" crossed out.
68. Portuguese gold coins called johannes (after King John V of Portugal) were popularly known as joes and half joes in the American colonies, where they were widely used. Before the Revolutionary War, half joes were worth sixty shillings or three pounds in Pennsylvania currency. At the time of ED's writing they were trading at nearly seven times their previous value because of the depreciation of both Continental bills ("Conti") and Pennsylvania's paper currency (Bezanson, *Prices and Inflation*, 24, 35).
69. The words "but Daniel Williamss" crossed out.

this afternoon, that he is taken himself &c—we know not what to believe—I saw a general Letter to day from Winchester sign'd by Thos. Fisher, with a line in my dear Henry writeing; giving an account of his Wellfare.

25 Sister and the 4 Children went to Monthly meeting. Rachl. Hunt came home with 'em and din'd and stay'd all the Afternoon. Dr. Moore drank Coffee with us, S. Hartshorn came over this Morning to go on the top of our House to see the Fleet come up; 2 or 3 twenty Gun Ships and a great number of Smaller Vessels came up today—Becky Jones, Robt. Waln and Billy Compton call'd—We have seen fire and Smoak in several places in the Jersys to day, it is said that Gloster is Burnt, and several Houses in Woodberry—We were very much affrighted this Evening before 9 o'clock, Jenney happen'd to go into the Yard, where she saw a Man with Ann—she came in and wisper'd to Sister, who immediately went out, and discoverd a Young Officer with Ann coming out from the little House, Sister held the Candle up to his Face and ask'd him who he was, his answer was whats that to you, the Gate was lock'd and he followd Ann and Sister into the Kitchen, where he swore he had mistaken the House, but we could not get him out,—Chalkley James who happen'd to be here, came into the Kitchen and ask'd him what busyness he had there he dam'd him and ask'd whats that to you, shook his Sword, which he held in his Hand and seem'd to threaten, when Chalkly with great resolution twisted it out of his Hands and Collor'd him—Sister took the Sword from Chalkly and lock'd it up in the draw in the parlor, all his outcry was for his Sword, and swore he would not stir a foot untill he had it. I then sent in for Josa. Howel, when he declar'd that he knew we were peaceable people, and that he gave up his Sword on that account out of pure good natur'd, which he had said to us before. he told Chalkley in the Kitchen that he would be the death of him tomorrow,—Josa. got him to the door, and then gave him his Sword, expecting he would go of, but he continu'd swaring there, where Josa. left him and went to call Abel James; in the mean time the impudent Fellow came in again swareing in the entry with the Sword in his hand. Sister had lock'd Chalkly up in the Middle Room, and we shut ourselves in the parlor, where he knock'd, and swore desireing entrance, our poor dear Children was never so frightend, to have an enrag'd, drunken Man, as I believe he was, with a Sword in his Hand swareing about the House, after going to or 3 times up and down the Entry, desireing we would let him in to drink a Glass of Wine with us—he went to the end of the Alley—when Harry lock'd the Front door on him, he knock and desir'd to come in, when J. Howel, and A James whome Josa. had been for, came to him, they had some talk with him, and he went off as I supose'd—I had all the back doors boulted, the Gate and[70] Front door lock'd, when in about 10 minuts after Harry came out of the Kitchen, and told us he was there I then lock'd the parlor door, and would not let Chalkley

70. The word "back" crossed out.

go out, Harry run into Howels for Josa. who did not come 'till some time after the Fellow was gone, and Ann with him he came over the Fence, and they went out the same way; 'tis not near one in the Morning and I have not yet recoverd the fright,—Ann call'd him Capt. Tape, or John Tape—Henry Drinker and C. James lodges here.

26, S. Swett spent this day with us, R. James, Nr. Stiles, John Drinker, S. Clark, Deby. Norris, Sally Jones, Henry Drinker, Ra. Waln, Josa. and Catty Howel, An. Carlile and A. Oat call'd, No News to day from Ann, and her Gallant—I have not yet got over last Nights fright, but have been in a flutter all day: there is near one and 2 hundred Vessels in Port, and several hundred more, they say to come,—I received a Letter this Morning from my Henry dated the 17th. last month. it came from Wellmington Saml. Clark brought it to me—fine Weather.

27 Nurse Wilson din'd with us, I with Sally Nancy and Henry, spent this Afternoon with M. Pleasants,—call'd at Jonathan Zanes to know when his Son John Farris goes to Willmington—we went in the Evening into M. Pembertons, to see Thomas Gathrope, who intends to leave us in a Few days, in a Packet also G. Napper—John and Rachel Drinker Patn. and Sucky Hartshorn drank Tea with Sister, Josa. Howel, C. James call'd—the Aurora Borrilaes or Northern Light appeard greater to Night than ever I remember to have seen it—Lord Howe 'tis said is in Town to day[71]—moderate Weather.

28 sent Harry to M. Hains, with 9 Bottls of Sider for Thos. Gothrope, Sally Logan spent this Afternoon with us—Nr. Waln and myself took a walk this Morning to see Polly Brown, we call'd at Sally Lewiss at Eliza Armitts, came home to dinner, I took a walk in the Afternoon to Uncle Jerviss came home to Coffee,—John Drinker, Chalky. James, Owen Jones, Reb. Waln, Sally Jones, Molly Pleasants, call'd—Jessy Waln at Roberts. The Light which appear'd last Night in the Sky, is thought by many, to be unacountable—the Vigilant Man of War and a number of other Vesels, came up to Day Reba. Waln spent this Evening with us.

29 last Night we had an Easterly Storm; and rain the greatest part of this Day: Sammy Sansom spent the Evening and sup'd. their has been some signs of a Fair, held in the Market Place, tho' it was but just the appearance—little to sell.

71. Admiral Lord Howe commanded the British transports that were trying to remove the blockades in the Delaware River. The transports succeeded in making their way to Philadelphia unchallenged through the main water channels by Nov. 23. Howe arrived in Philadelphia on Nov. 26 and established his quarters there (Gruber, *Howe Brothers*, 260; Morton, "Diary," 31).

30 first day: Sister and the Children went to meeting, morning and afternoon, S. Swett, Robt. Waln, Paterson Hartshorn, Josa. & Katty Howell, Abrm. Carlile and a Young Man of whome I bought a Barrel of Flour, at 3£ p hogshead call'd—Hanh. Drinker drank Coffee with us,—clear'd up finely—I received 2 letters this Afternoon from my dear Henry, JD. received one of the 16th Instant.

Decr. 1 there is talk to day, as if a great part of the English army, were making ready to depart, on some secret expedition, S. Sansom and Son call'd this Evening, Joseph Scott drank Coffee with us.—Ann Kelly had the ausurance to come to our Stable Yesterday Morning and desir'd Harry to give her Buckels &c.—the old Wind Mill on the Island was pull'd down, some day last Week.

2 Thos. Gothroap, and G. Napper, went yesterday in a Boat for Chester, intending to embark on board a Packet for London—S Smith &c went with 'em to Chester; Wm. Cowper officiated I believe as Clark at the Adjournment of our Monthly Meeting a Young Man of the name of McNickle call'd this Morning his busyness was to seize Horses, but understanding to whome ours belong; said if we had ever so many, not one of them should be touch'd Our Saucy Ann came while I was at meeting desereing to know what I would take for hir time and she would bring the money in a minuit Sister told her she did not know, but that she heard me talk of puting her in the Work House, she reply'd if you talk so, you shall neither have me nor the Money, Sister then ordred her to come again at 12 o'clock, but she has not been since—M. Story call'd to borrow, for Joseph Galloway, (who is going to House-keeping) some Bedding End-Irons,—Tables &c—some of which articles we agree'd she should have. myself, Sally, and Billy went to meeting this Morning Nancy and little Molly have both got cold—Rachel Drinker, Hugh Roberts call'd before dinner,—Thos. Lightfoot, Ben. Hough, George Churchman, Warner Mifflin, and S. Swett, din'd with us—a little before dinner Saml. Emlen came in, and after reading my Henrys Litter of the 17th. 10 mo, he speak to us, by way of Testimony, beginning with, What shall be done to the Man, whome the King delighteth to Honour &c[72]—The Friends stay'd talking with us and smokeing their pipes 'till after 3 o'clock, some of them intend to visit Winchester, and they now are calling on; each of us poor Women whose dear Husbands, they expect 'eer long to see—they went from hear to S. Peningtons—myself Nancy and Molly, spent the Afternoon at Jonney Drinkers—John Glover, John Elliott, Josa. and Katty Howell, Reba. Waln and Becky Jones and Charles West call'd.

3d. William Loague call'd this Morning he lives in Chester County and

72. A quotation from Esther 6:6.

came, to Town with, Flour Butter &c—Debh. Elwell Jannys Mother din'd with us—Sally and myself took a walk to S. Peningtons, read her Letter from her Husband then went to M. Pleasants, did the same there, call'd at Uncle Jerviss came home to dinner, Aunt Jervis, Betsy and Polly and Peggy Smith, spent the Afternoon with us—Chalkley James, J. Drinker, and Thomas Lightfoot call'd this Evening; the latter came to borrow my Henrys Letter to G. Churchmans, with an intent to send a Copy of it to S Neale in Irland,—I wrote this Evening to my dear. A great number of the British troops, went out of Town since Night, with stors & Bagage.

4th. the Troops which were ordred out of Town last Night, it seems are countermanded, why I know not—Wm. Loage, and Ann Kelly call'd this Morning Ann came to know what I would take for her time, Sister told her 20£; she did not see me, being again out—I went with Nancy to H Pembertons, to carry my Letter &c to T Lightfoot, I sent lap'd up in[73] HDs Shirts £61. 11. 3 in Conti—We calld at O. Joness at Uncle Jerviss—came home to dinner, Suky and Hannah Jones call'd while I was out, S. Swett din'd and spent the Afternoon, M. Pleasants came with her Children, spent an hour, then went to Tea with Becky and Hannah, Molly Pleasants, Debby Norris, Hannah Sansom, Isey, Sally and Sammy Pleasants, and S. Sansom drank Tea with us, MP, return'd towards Evening—John Drinker, Daniel Drinker, Robt and Reba. Waln, here this Evening I wrote this Evening to my HD.

5 I took a Walk, Sally with me, to see Phebe Pemberton, who is unwell in her Chamber, there I understood by one of JPs letters that my dear Henry was unwell the 20 of last mo: call'd at Uncles; came home before dinner—Saml. and Sally Emlen, and J Drinker, drank Coffee with us—Dl. Drinker call'd—A Number of Troops are actualy gone out of Town, and tis said they are this Afternoon at Chestnut Hill—fine Winter Weather—I wrote this Evening to my dear Henry.

6 I took a walk, Nancy with me, to Benj Chews, to deliver a Letter to Dr. Way, (who lodges there,) for my Dear Henry,—then went to M. Pleasants, who was gone to Shoemakers Mill—call'd at Uncles, then went to A Jamess came home to Dinner;—Our Neighr. Stiles sent over this Morning to borrow our good Horse Tomsom, but as he was not shod, we deny'd him, she sent again and we lent him to her to go to Frankford, her Boy Sam with her,—she return'd in the Evening on foot having lost her Chaise and our Horse; they were taken from her by 2 light Horse, just as she was geting in the Chaise at their place—they have been Plundred at their Country House lately, of all the Valueble Furniture, Provisions, Coach, Chariott, Horses 8 or 10 Negros &c &c to a great amount,—John Drinker, C. James, Edwd. [Stiles] call'd to Day.

73. The word "his" crossed out.

7 First Day Sally, Billy and Henry went to Meeting this Morning Sister and Nancy not very well; I went this afternoon with Billy, Nancy and Henry—I drank Tea at Neigr. Howell's who was last Night Robed of a Bed from one of their 2 [p'r.] Stairs Chambers, the Fellow being surpris'd got of, without the rest of the Bootey which he had lay'd out of the Drawers ready to take away—there has been many roberies committed lately in Town. fireing has been heard to day, but no certain account of the cause—Reba. Waln, Becky Jones, Abel James junr. S. Swett; John Drinker, call'd—dull rainy weather to day, tho not very cold, we have but [9] Persons in Family this Winter we have not had less then 13 or 14 for many years past.

8 John Morton brought me a Letter this Afternoon, from my Henry, it came from Willmington, I spent this Afternoon with Abby. Parish,—Robt. Waln here this Evening—Uncertain accounts from the Army—very damp giving Weather.—We are inform'd since 10 o'clock this Night that part, if not all the Army are return'd, which carrys no very agreeable appearance with it. Chalkley and Tommy James lodges here to Night.

9 Wm. [Shirtclift] call'd this Morning to see us, he is going to Winchester—Sister and the Children went to meeting this Morning R. Scattergood S Swett Katty Howel, John Drinker Danl. Drinker, call'd after meeting; I took a walk after dinner to Bartrams Shop in Market Street, call'd at Owen Joness Saml. Smith and Wife spent the Afternoon with us, H. Catheral also—Hannah Moore call'd While I was out, to read some letters from George Dwyling, things seem to ware but an unpromissing appearance at present. but the absence of my dear Husband is worse to me than all the rest put togeather—Nothing will pass at this time, unless with a Few, but Gold & Silver, which is hard upon those who have a quantity of the old paper Money, by them; the fence of Boards &c round our House in water Street, is pull'd down, and I suppose burnt;—Sally Howard and two of her Daughters came here this Evening she came from the Jersys this Afternoon, and brought us a Bottle of Snuff from Betsy Waln, who is much recover'd of her late indispossion—Neigr. Waln sent a Horse and Chaise here this afternoon to put into our Stable, which Pattersons 2 Sisters came with, from Bristol—C James & Tommy lodges here again to Night, as H Drinker is gone a Forageing—I wrote to my dear Henry to day, by [I.] Star of Willmington; who goes out of Town tomorrow.

10th. I took a walk this Morning Sally with me to M. Pleasants, who is unwell up stairs, calld at Uncles, came home to dinner—I spent this Afternoon with Lydia Gillpin, went first to Thos. Fishers, but she was gone out—call'd in my way home at J. Drinkers—Neigr. Stiles, John Drinker, Reb. Waln, call'd C. James, Jos. Bringhurst also call'd.

11 Catty Howell came in to show us, some things that she had purchas'd, Sister went out upon the Strength of it and bought a piece of Lennen &c, its a long time since we have done such a thing—goods will soon be plenty in all probobility, nothing but hard mony will pass; 40 or 50 Sail below with goods: A Vessel run on the Chevaux de Frize [lately] with a Cargo, worth 40,000 pounds, made a hole in her botton and sunk:—Myself Sally and Nancy, spent this Afternoon at Josa. Fishers Hetty read her Brother Sammys Letter giveing an account of the scarcety of Salt there—where 36 Bushel Wheat is given for one Bushel and 300 weight of pork for like quantity Isaac Zane call'd here this Morning to see us. he is going to Winchester to see our dear Frds. he takes no letters, I sent by him a under Jacket and pair Gloves, and lap a letter up in them from Billy—Sally Logan and Chalkley James drank Tea with Sister, Molly Foulk and her Daughter Betsy, John Drinker call'd; at near 10 o'clock this Evening who should come in but Richd. Waln, he came from New York in a Vesel with a number of others,—he's harty and well—these are sad times for Thiveing & plundering, tis hardly safe to leave the door open a minuet—Danl. Drinker was lately offronted by an Officer; a number of Friends to Gouvernment about the Country have lately been plunder'd and ill used by the British Troops. things ware a very gloomy aspect at this present time.

12th. I went to a Store this Morning Sally with me, to look for Cloth for Harry; mett Rd. Walln, who advis'd me to stay some time longer, till a number of Vesels, which are below, comes up. Abel James, John Drinker, Robt. Waln call'd. Some of the Troops are gone over Schuylkill, Fireing heard to day, JD. wrote to my HD.

13 S. Emlen here this Morning with a Letter he had received from Hh. Haydock. Danl. Drinker John Drinker, Richd. Waln Reba. Waln, Nancy Waln, Hannah Drinker here to day, I went Nancy with me to M Pleasants, call'd at Uncles—Wm. [Sikes] came home with us—I have heard it hinted to day, that our Friends John Parish and John James were confin'd in Lancaster Jail—John Gillingham was lately stop'd in the Street, after Night, and his Watch taken from him. we daily hear of enormitys of one kind or other, being committed by those from whome, we ought to find protection.

14 First Day: Sister and the 4 Children went to Meeting this Morning myself went with 'em in the afternoon, S Swett drank Tea with us, R. Scattergood Reba. Waln, Reba. Jones, Henry Drinker, D. Drinker, Richd. Waln, Thos. Savery, and Thos. Eddy, call'd—the latter brought word that Drewet Smith was return'd from Winchester, which news at first much surprisd and flutter'd me; I have not yet seen him, but am told that my dear Henry and those with him, have the same liberty, but many of them are not free to take it, so that I know not yet what to think, but am [loath] to be too Sanguine, or to give way to such pleasing expectation as would naturly occur on a certainty of their

being set properly at liberty;—we are told to day, that the people of York Town got togeather in numbers, and fir'd on the Congress who were setting.[74] wounded one of them badly;—Wm. Loage came to Town to day with Flour, Butter &c to sell, on his own account—as his prises were high and hard mony demanded, I did not deal with him,—J Drinker R. Drinker and H Sansom sup'd with us.—We were a little fright'n'd before 11 o'clock by seeing 2 fellows peeping into Becky Joness Yard and climeing on the top of her Gate, Watch bark'd and Harry went into the Yard,—they went off it causes me to recolect last night, about one o'clock I heard a noise against our fence the Dog bark'd voilently, I awak'd Jenney, who look'd out of the Window and saw 2 Men in the Alley, who went out of sight. I often feel afraid to go to Bed—I wish Wm. D Smiths coming away, may in no shape injure our dear Friends which he has left behind.

15th. last night about 11 o'clock when we were going to Bed, we saw 2 Soliders in the Ally, standing by the Fence, we went down Stairs again, and into the Yard, ask'd Harry aloud if John and Tom were yet in Bed, Harry answered yes, Sister ordr'd him to untye the Dog and then come in; while we were contriving in this manner down stairs, Jenney saw them, from my Room Window, move off with a large Bundel which she took to be a Bed,—after we had been in Bed about an hour we heard a great Noise in the Alley. Janey Sister and the Children run to the Window, and saw the Baker next door runing up the Alley in his Shirt only a little red Jacket the rest of his Family with him; we did not discover the cause of the uprore untill this Morning when we found the Baker had been rob'd of some of his Wifes cloths &c— which we supose was the Bundle the Fellows went off with some time before— I wrote this Morning to my dear, Sister took the Letter, with one that she had wrote Yesterday herself, to Mary Eddys, who objected to mine, as I had mention'd the arrival of W D Smith, it was what I had some thoughts of myself, and approv'd of her bringing it back; Peggy York call'd this Morning with a Letter which she had received from her Husband, from London, acknowledging the kindness he had received from Pigou and Booth, in consiquence of a Letter from James and Drinker, for which he returns thanks.— she had on the highest and most rediculeous Headdress that I have yet seen[75]—

74. The Continental Congress had been meeting at York, Pa., since Sept. 30 (Boatner, *American Revolution*, 267).

75. Among the many merchants and artisans who came to Philadelphia with the British in November 1777 were hairdressers who advertised the latest in London and European hairstyles. These coiffures, which featured masses of curls piled high on the head, were considered an affectation by Americans and were ridiculed for their association with Toryism (advertisements for hairdressers can be found in the *Pa. Ev. Post*, the *Pa. Ledger* and the *Pa. Royal Gaz.*; D. E. Fisher, "Social Life," 247–48; Frederick D. Stone, "Philadelphia Society One Hundred Years Ago, or the Reign of Continental Money," *PMHB* 3 [1879]: 363–64, 368; see also the cartoons in Donald H. Cresswell, comp., *The American Revolution in Drawings and Prints: A Checklist of 1765–1790 Graphics in the Library of Congress* [Washington; Library of Congress, 1975], 289, 291).

Polly Reynolds, formerly Ritche, with 2 other Woman call'd before dinner, she is here to solicit the General on account of her Husband, who has been a Prisoner in the Jersyes, ever since last Christmass; S. Swett and J Drinker call'd before dinner. I took a walk with Sally, to E. Jerviss and hir Neigr. Betsy Smiths they were both in trouble on account of Oifficers who had been there and threatned to quarter themselves on them—we call'd after to see Thos. Afflicks Wife,—found when we came home, Richd. Waln, Becky James junr. Sucky Jones, Hannah and Nancy, at Tea with Sister,—Becky Jones, Josa. and Katty Howell, Saml. Sansom, Daniel Drinker here this Evening—SS, read his journal to us, that is to DD, MS, ED and the Children—Sarah Fisher call'd—Henry Drinker tells us this Even'g that W D Smith has been call'd before the General to day.—Friends have had several meetings lately, and have agree'd to send Orders to Sundry Merchants &c in London for a Cargo of provisions and Coal, as from the present prospect, the Inhabitance will stand in need of such a Supply—the Oifficers and Soliders are quartering upon the Families [Generaly]. one with his Servant are to be fixt at J. Howells, I am in daily expecttation of their calling on us. they were last night much frightned at Isaac Catherals, by a Solider, who came into the House,—drew his Bayonet on Isaac, and behav'd very disorderly,—Anthony Morris, Son of Samuel, said to be dangerously wounded.

16th. Saml. Clark, and Vincent Bonsel call'd, the latter from Willmington with a mesage from B. Woodcock, that he can purchase Flour for us at 35/ p [ ] in Conti. if we can contrive the manner of bringing it away, J. Drinker call'd, I left it under his consideration—Sister, Sally, Nancy, and Billy, went to meeting this Morning—a rainy day so far Joseph Scott and Reba. Waln drank Coffee with us, Docr. Redman, Saml. Emlen, call'd.

17 Charles West, Daniel Drinker and Neigr Stiles call'd; I drank Tea at Neigr. Walns, Jessy Walns Wife and Jenny Hartshorn came their this Afternoon, from Millford, Robt. sent the Horse to our Stable, as he had done once before,—Jessy's Wife informs me, that Joseys Drinkers Family is well, that he has had lately, taken from him, his Waggon, a Horse and our Mare,—Hannah Drinker's near lying in.

18th. we have had dull weather for 3 days—S Swett drank tea with us, Richd. Waln sup'd with us—J Drinker brought me a Litter from my dear, and Betsy Smith sent her little girl with a letter from her Husband with a few lines from my Henry, Ezekeil Edwards[76] is returnd from Winchester, I have not seen him, but am told that he brings very disagreeable intillegence, that he has heard it hinted that there is a design of sending our dear Friends to Stanton, which would be sorrowful indeed, should it so happen, but it may not,—An

76. "I am told" crossed out.

Oifficer who calls himself Major Carmon or Carmant, call'd this Afternoon, to look for Quarters for some Oiffecer of distinction, I plead off, he would have preswaded me that it was a necessary protiction at these times to have one in the House; said I must consider of it, that he would call in a day or two, I desir'd to be excus'd, and after some more talk we parted, he behaved with much politeness, which has not been the case at many other places; they have been very rude and impudent at some houses,—I wish I may come of so; but at same time fear we must have some with us, as many Friends have them, and it seems likely to be a general thing. This has been a trying day to my Spirits—E. Edwards had a number of Letters stolen from him, which was for us poor destitutes. I have just finish'd a Letter to my dearest tis now past 12 o'clock, and Watch has put me in a flutter, by his violent barking, as if some one was in the Alley, which I believe was the case—hail since Night.

19. Rd. Waln, Jacob Shoemaker, and Abey Parish call'd this Morning the latter very sick while she was here, Sister went out to know how Polly Pleasants and her Mother had manag'd the matter, they have had their Doors mark'd with respect to takin in Officers, they had been to Jos. Galloway; but E. Story seem likely to settle the matter with the quarter Master General one Roberson—while Sister was out, Major Cramond came to know if I had cunsulted any of my Friends upon the matter, I told him that my sister was out on that Busyness, that I expect'd that we who were at present 'lone women, would be excus'd, he said he fear'd not, for tho I might put him of (as it was for himself he apply'd to me) yet as a great number of the Forign Troops were to be quarterd in this Neighborhood, he believ'd they might be troublesom; we had a good deal of talk about the Mal Behaveour of the British officers, which he by no means justify'd, I told him how I had been frightend by the Officer, that thief like stole my servant girl over the Fence, and of many other perticulars of their bad conduct that had come to my knowledge; he said that Yesterday I had told him what sort of a Man, would suit in my Family, if I was oblidged to take any, that he was concious some of those, qualities were his, (which were early hours and little Company &c) that there was very few of the Officers he could recommend, that Mr. Galloway knew him very well; that he would call again tomorrow to know my mind further—so went off;—I am straitend how to act, and yet determind; I may be troubld with others much worse, for this Man appears much of the Gentleman, but while I can keep clear of them, I intend so to do—they have taken up part of several Houses, mark'd the Doors of others against their consent, and some of the Inhabitance have look'd out for Officers of reputation (if any such there be) to come into their Families, by way of protection, and to keep of others—Becky Waln junr. pick'd up 2 Letters for me to day from my dear, old dates, but welcome to me as they add to my valueable treasure; Neigr. Waln, Hannah Cartheral, Auther Howel, call'd—John Drinker sup'd with us, E Story call'd this Evening says he thinks he shall be able to get us, whose Husbands are gone from us,

clear of the mellitary Gentlemen—he says they are much chagrin'd at the difficulty they find in getting quarters, and the cool reception they have mett with, or something to that effect—that several Young Noble-Men are at this time oblidg'd to sleep at Taverns, on board Ships or in the Redoubts—for which I think they may in great measure thank themselves, tho' at same time it appears to me that there was a backwardness, shown towards them, prehaps too much in the beginning—we are told this evening, that, Owen Joness Family have been very ill used indeed, by an Officer who wanted to quarter himself, with many others on them, he drew his Sword, us'd very abusive language, and had the Front Door split in pieces &c.—Mary Eddy has some with her, who they say will not suffer her to make use of her own Front Door, but oblidges her and her family to go up and down the Alley—Molly Foulk has been affronted and so has many others—we have come of as yet wonderfully well,—my resolution and fortitude has fail'd me much of late; my dear Henrys absence, and the renew'd fears on his account with the sittuation we are in hear and thoughts of our dear Children, my health but very midelleing; all togeather seems at times hard to bear up against;—Lord C. Wallace has embark'd for England, which occasions various conjecttures—Lord Howe going to New York,—Gen. Howe intends its said to winter with us,—I hope he is a better man, than some people think him. it has cleard up very cold, tis now between 12 and one o'clock, high time for me to go to Bed, tho I seem sleepless.

20 Sl. Emlen call'd to see us this Morning he read my dear's Letters which I last received after reading 'em (as is usual with him) he spoke to us for a considerable time, mention'd how many comfortable seasons he had, had in this parlor,—Cramond call'd a third time with the same story over again, I put him of as before, he said he would call again tomorrow,—after he was gone Sister went down to consult Abel James, Abel went to Enoch Storys, and came here in the Evening belives we shall not be able to free ourselves from them, Mary Pemberton and M. Pleasants, have been in [trouble] about it to day, J. Drinker went this Evening for our information to Mary Pembertons to know how she had come off—she had promises of being excus'd, on account of her being an ancient Woman, her Husband from her, and a Meeting held in her House[77] as the 4th Street Meeting House, is taken up with the poor, who are turnd out of the House of Employment, for the Soldiers,[78] for the above

77. The words "being on account of" crossed out.

78. On Dec. 20 General Howe took over the House of Employment (also known as the Bettering House or almshouse) for the exclusive use of the British army as a hospital, forcing the poor who resided there to find other quarters. Howe had previously notified the managers of the almshouse that he could no longer supply the poor with food or supplies nor lend money to the managers to buy food. Those who were unable to leave the almshouse before the British takeover found shelter in the Friends' Fourth Street Meeting House and in the Carpenters' Company Hall (Jackson, *With the British Army*, 86–87; Rosswurm, *Arms, Country, and Class*, 150–51).

reasons she was to be excus'd provided it could be got from under the hand of General Howe;—so that upon the whole I fear we shall have our Family, disagreeably incumber'd—we must trust in providence on that and all other accounts,—William Canby of Willmington call'd this Evening—Abel James appear'd to me, to be dull and low spirited—the times are truly alarming and Josey so poorly that Abel says he has giving him over, a slow fever attends him and Chills, tho he is [about] House, I hope he is not so bad as his Father thinks, I have expeirence such a time, and was favour'd to get better, tho' at present I am very poorly, and my Mind, much oppress'd; my dearest Husbands present doubtful situation afflicts me much, as there is some reports in Town, that young Owen Jones is put into close confindment, and that it is concluded in Congress that our dear Friends should be sent to Stanton, this is as much as I can geather, but I fear there is something more as I hear Ezekiel Edwards is going back to Virginia, and he has not been to see me: I hear that he should say that my dear Henry has had a Cold and disordred Bowels, but that it was wearing of, and that he was Chearfull, I fear he is more unwell, than I was led to think, I have not been out for 4 or 5 days past, but intend to endeavour it tomorrow or to send for Ezekiel Edwards to know on what account he is going back, I wish I could compose my mind, and feel more easy.

21 First Day our 4 Children went to Meeting this Morning myself with them in the Afternoon. Jessy Waterman appear'd this afternoon in Testimony—D Drinker drank Coffee with us—R Drinker spent this Evening and supped with us. Neigr. Waln, S Swett R Jones, and J Drinker call'd—No Officer here to day—M Pleasants I hear has got of, but S. Penington has two—the Northern Light appeard learge to Night.—Mary Eddy call'd this Afternoon in much Affliction, she wanted Sister or myself to go to A. Jamess with her and to desier him to accompany her to some Head Officer to make complaint of the Insolence of one who has quarter'd himself on her, and a woman who he calls his Wife, but Mary thinks otherwise, he has insulted her, and behav'd very abusesive, Abel advis'd her to go to Galloway—it is said that a large number of the Troops go out to Night.

22 Joseph Warner of Willmington call'd this Morning to disire we would send if oppertunity offer'd for some Flour which BW. has purchac'd—Thos. Pleasants and Ezekill Edwards, came this Morning stayed [above] an hour, conferms the Sorrowful account that my dear is to be sent further from me, Sammy Sansom Sally Emlen, Robt. Waln, Abel James, call'd—I went out to buy a peice Linnen call'd at Joseph Yerkess School for Billy; call'd at Owen Joness they appear Chearful, I believe they have not heard the distressing accounts relaiting to their Son—John Molsworth who was executed here last

Summer, was Yesterday taken up, and Buryed in Friends Ground[79] follow'd by a number of people—a foolish notion in my oppinion—10,000 of the best Troop are gone over Schuyckill; the Comanding Officers with them their intention unknown here. Rd. Waln drank Coffee with us—we heard a noise last night in the House, Janny and Harry got up, but made no discovery. the night before, I heard somebody down stairs, upon enquiry found it was Harry who had been up; every[80] noise now seems alarming, that happns in the Night.

23 Monthly Meeting Sister and the 4 Children went to meeting this Morning—David Eastaugh and Jennys mother call'd,—I wrote to my dear Henry to day—Sister mett Ann in the Street, who promis'd to pay for her time—the Soliders Wife who lives in our House in Water Street came to me this Morning to inform that some were taring down the Shed &c. Sister went down after Meeting and desir'd 'em to desist, they said they would not for it was a Rebels House, she assur'd 'em it was not, and after more talk, proms'd if she would let 'em take the large Gate they would desist, she agreed thereto, and came [away]. We sent Wm. Wells and Harry, with Wells Waggon, for the Boards, they brought one load; and said that the Soliders and the Children in the Neighborhood, were pulling down the rest as fast as they could—John Drinker and I Catheral call'd—the Letter I wrote this Morning went too late by an hour, Isaac Hains set off at 11 o'clock, and P. Pemberton sent me word this Morning at 9 o'clock, (which was the first I had heard of the opportunity) that he did not go till 12 o'clock. Sister went out after dinner to look for Cloath, for Cloaks for the Children, Neigr. Waln with her—G James brought me £12: 5″—for our share of some Stoves that they have sold for Gold;—Sammy Smith here this evening, wishes for my dear, to ease him of his employment as clark, Debby Morris drank Coffee with us.

24. John Brintons Daughter Molly call'd this Morning her Father and Mother talks of coming to Town on busyness, Sammy Trimble she says is ill, and not likely to recover; I went this Morning Sally with me to young John Elliots, to give my Letter to Job [Harvey], but found he was gone—we call'd at Uncles and at J Drinkers—Sally and Nancy spent this Afternoon at their Uncle Johns, Jams Logan, Reba. James, Junr Reba. Waln and Jessys Wife call'd. this is Christmas eve', and the few Troops that are left in this City I fear are Frolicking.

79. Although the reasons for the reburial of Molesworth (a non-Quaker; see above, March 1777, note 7) are unclear, certain commentators looked upon this act as another demonstration of Quaker support for the British, even as they continued to claim neutrality. An anonymous correspondent in the *Pennsylvania Packet* charged in September 1778 that the Quakers gave Molesworth a grand reburial "to shew their loyalty to what they call the best of the Kings, and agreeable to their neutral principles, trample under foot the laws and authority by which they expect to live" (see below, Dec. 22, 26, 1778; Reed, *Joseph Reed*, 2:30–34; Marshall, *Diary Extracts*, 201; *Pa. Packet*, Sept. 1, 1778).

80. The word "thing" crossed out.

25 I heard Cannon I thought about 12 o'clock last night;—last Evening there was an attack made on the lines, but did not succeed, a Cannon Ball came as far as the Barracks,—'tis said that the Amaricans are very Sanguine, and talk of coming soon into the City—Janny Maxel the Soliders Wife who lives in our Water Street House, came to disire I would make a pair Stairs for her to get into the House, I put her off and desir'd she would take all the Care of it that was in her power, which she promis'd,—Hannah Sansom spent this Afternoon with us, Robt. Waln part of the Evening, Sister & Sally was out this Afternoon, and were told that Thos. Pike was come home from Winchester, I supose in the same manner that Wm. D Smith came; it gives me some concern, least their elopement should injure our dear Friends that they have left behind. J Drinker heard to Day that a Man who left Winchester, about 2 weeks ago, says that the sending our Friends to Stanton was giving over, by the influence of Isaac Zane junr.

26 The Philada. monthly meeting was held at the Bank, as the Fourth Street House is taken up with the Poor—Sister and Nancy went to it—Susey Jones and her Daughter Hannah call'd after Meeting—John and Daniel Drinker call'd—M Pleasants and her Cosen Tommy Spent this Afternoon with us—I step'd over this Evening to Neighr. Walns—I find that this afair of taking up Mollsworth and Burying him in Friends Ground has giving many great uneasyness, myself among the rest, thay have made it a meeting matter for which I am very sorry—cold with rain this Evening a man knock'd down last night, and robbed of his Watch.

27 I wrote this Morning to my Henry, Sammy Sansom spent the Afternoon with us, he and Richd. Waln spent part of the Evening—there has been a work among our Friends about Mollsworth, some are for taking him up again, others more wise are against it, some for turning the Friends who granted the order, out of their office, some for putting out publications,—I wish they would let the matter rest; the dispute does not I beleive proceed from a right Spirit—the putting him into our Ground was a rediculous foolish Act; the making a fuss about it, now it is done under a pretence of regard for our dear absent Friends, makes the matter much worse, 'tis Strange that men of understanding should act either the one part or the other.—a certain something a peice of Clockwork, a Barrel with Gunpowder, &c was found in our River, which blew up near the Row-Buck Man of War, and distroyd a boat near it[81] several others they say are found, thought to be the contrivance

81. The clockwork explosive device was associated with the Battle of the Kegs. Americans under the guidance of David Bushnell built a number of underwater mines, which they connected with buoys or kegs and placed in the Delaware River. They hoped the action of the water would lead the mines to explode against the hulls of ships. The attempt failed, but inspired a patriotic ballad by Francis Hopkinson (Jackson, *With the British Army*, 179; Boatner, *American Revolution*, 63–64).

of some designing evel minded person or persons, against the Shiping—the fuss that is made about reburying this man, gives me more pain then the foolish act itself.[82]

28th. First Day: it begun to Snow last night, and has snow'd great part of this day, Sister and the 4 Children went to meeting this Morning A. Parish din'd with us, Sister and the Children Sally excepted went this Afternoon, J Drinker call'd, Joshua and Katty Howel, and Hannah Catheral drank Tea with us—R Jones call'd—our ancient Fd. Esther White dyed lately at Willmington, this day more like winter, then any we have yet had.

29 very clear and cold, Cramond here this morning, we have at last agreed on his coming to take up his aboud with us, I hope it will be no great inconvenience, tho I have many fears, he came again in the Afternoon with a servant to look at the Stable, stay'd Tea, Thos. Masterman also, C. West and Reba. Waln here, the Troops are all return'd from Forageing—tis now 19 days since the date of my dears last letter; my mind is greatly troubled.

30 R Jones call'd this Morning Abel James S Smith, Saml. Emlen and Josh. Bringhurst call'd after meeting—Major Cramond took up his aboad with us to day; one servant is to be with him here, two others he has boarded at our Neighr. Well's in the Alley, he has 2 Horses and [o] Cows which are to be put in our Stable J Drinker here this Evening.

31st. J. Cramond who is now become one of our Family, appears to be a thoughtful sober young man, his Servant also sober and orderly; which is a great favour to us—Joshua Howel call'd—[Ricd] Waln and JC. drank coffee with us—Robert Veree came towards evening he and J.C. sup'd with us—James Logan, Robt. Waln, an R Jones call'd, a number of Vessels run ashore the Ice being in the way—they were set on fire, I know not by which party; I am fearful something disagreeable is going on, by the many mesages sent this Evening to J.C.—J. Veree sleeps here with H Drinker.

82. The words "moderate clear weather" crossed out.

1778

1778 Janry. 1st. Josa. Howel call'd this Morning he has bought a Ferkin of Irish Butter for me, Robert Veree Breakfasted with us—Richd. Adams, call'd of whome I have engag'd a quanty of Pork, Betsy Drinker, Hannah Drinker and J.C. drank tea with us—Rachl. Drinker D. Drinker and Abel James call'd, J.C. supped with us—the Soliders were call'd out in order to day, which look'd alarming—many are fearful of an attack from the other side the water—I wrote to day to my Henry. I feel very uneasy on account of J. Parish who is not yet return'd—weather more modderate—Cramond has 3 Horses 3 Cows 2 Sheep and 2 Turkeys with several Fowls, in our Stable, he has 3 Servants 2 White Men, and one Negro Boy call'd Damon, the Servants are here all day, but away at Night. he has 3 Hessians who take their turns to wate on him as Messengers or orderly men as they call'd 'em so that we have enough of such sort of Company.

2d. Saml. Emlen call'd 2 or 3 times, he Breakfastd with us, Richd. Adams call'd, Isaac Wharton and P. Bond also call'd, they bring us flattering accounts; tis reported that Edwd. Bonsel who has lately come to Town from John Nixons, where he heard him, and several other men of like consiquence say, that our Friends were discharg'd, a Letter from Moore-Hall to P.B. seems to confirm the first account should it be so in reality, it will be cause of Joy, but it seems a doubtfull matter with me, J Drinker here this Evening—J.C. has had 5 Hanspachers[1] to dine with him, he spent the Evening out, came home before 10.

3 Sl. Emlen, Ricd. Adams, R Jones, and J Drinker call'd, G. James, came with a note of hand of my Henrys, to James & Drinker, on account of E. Edwards, which I answer'd with 9 half Joes, and 2 Dollors, I also parted with 7 half Joes to R Adams, for Pork and Flour; Ricd. Waln and Jos. Scott, drank Coffee with us, Josey Waln Neigr. Waln and Nancy Waln, here this Evening J.C. also.

1. In February 1777 Margrave Christian Friedrich of Brandenburg-Anspach-Bayreuth signed a treaty with the British promising to send hired troops from his states to aid against the rebels. These troops, named for their state of origin, served in Philadelphia during the British occupation (Albert W. Haarmann, "The Anspach-Bayreuth Troops in North America, 1777–1783," *Military Collector and Historian* 19 [1967]: 48–49).

4 First Day: I forgot to mention Yesterday, that I had a conferance with the officer who took away Ann; I stop'd him as he past the door—and after desiring him to stand still, 'till a noisey Waggon which was going by had past, (as he said he was in a hurry) I then adress'd him; if thee has no sense of Religion or Virtue, I should think that what you Soliders call Honor would have dictated to thee what was thy duty after thy behavour some time ago in this House, who me! Yes I know thee very well, I have as yet been carefull of exposeing thee, but if thee dont very soon pay me for my Servants time; as there is officers quarterd among Numbers of my acquaintance, I will tell all I meet with, he stutter'd and said I han't got your Servant, I dont care who has her, it was thee that stole her; well said he a little impudently if you'l come up to my quarters up Town, I told him If he did not bring the Mony or send it soon he should hear further from me; well, well well said he and away he went seemingly confus'd. The 4 Children went to meeting this Morning Sister and self stay'd at home, but had a meeting afterwards in our parlor, with Saml. Emlen and Wife, who call'd after meeting; Danl. Drinker, John Drinker, S. Swett, Rebeca Scattergood, call'd, I went to meeting this Afternoon with the Children, and afterwards went little Henry with me to S. Pleasants, her Son Israel is ill of a Fever; Polly has a Officer quarter'd on her, of the name of Foard—I drank tea with her, and came home before dark.

5 J.C. had 11 or 12 Officers to dine with him to day, they made very little noise, and went away timeously—Saml. Sansom spent this Evening and sup'd with us—R Jones, J Drinker and HDr call'd—most of our acquaintance seems much taken with our Major. I hope he will continue to deserve their good oppinion, he tells us this Evening that a Sassation of Arms is concluded on, that Gen. Lee is out on his parole,—every thing I hear, (is it makes for the continu'd confindment, or deliverance of my dearest Henry,) has its effect on my Spirits—a numbe of those floating Barrels of Gun-Powder continue coming down the River, they have been frequently fireing at 'em to day, the weather is much moderated, so that most of the ice out of the river, some Vesels came up to day.

6th. Reba. Jones, A. James Josa. Howel, C. James, Rachl. Evans, call'd this Morning—Ricd. Waln din'd with us, I am inform'd that S. Penington has received a letter from her Husband,—Katty Howel who was here just now says it is a mistake—Sister and the Children out this Afternoon, [T] Pleasants call'd to bid us farewell intending to set of tomorrow; I received 2 letters this Evening from my dear, one dated the 19 the other 27 Ultimo they had not then received an answer to their memorial, so that I hope the late account by P. Bond &c may not be without foundation. This Evening S. Emlen, R. Waln, and Wife, C. Howel and Daughter & R. Jones were here, after reading my dears letters and setting a time in Silence S.E. had somethings to say to us Generaly and to some separately—J.C. came home in good time after dineing at headquarters.

7 J Drinker, D. Drinker, David Bacon, Josa. Howel, call'd, S. Swett din'd and spent the Afternoon—K Howel and my self went this Morning to see Isey Pleasants who continues very ill; [T] Pleasants who was to have gone Yesterday, stays till tomorrow to see if any alteration for the better may take place in the Child—I gave him a few lines to my Henry—Snow this Afternoon, rain this Evening—J.C. drank Coffee.

8 I wrote to my Henry this Morning Saml. Emlen call'd, sister lent him Six half Joes—Abey Parish spent this Afternoon with us—John Drinker Abel James and Ricd. Waln call'd—J.C. had 8 to dine with him to day I have not seen him to day but en passant he has not yet come home and it is near 11 o'clock; I shall soon be tir'd of such doings.

9 Saml. Emlen call'd this Morning I went to know how I Pleasants was, found him very ill—call'd at Uncles and at S. Peningtons, H Catheral there this Even'g she informs us that Isey P—— is worse, and that his disorder is turn'd to Putrid, I am much concern'd for his dear Mother—S Swett call'd, as did J Drinker—there is orders given out that no person shall be out after 8 o'clock, without a Lanthron.

10th. I went this Morning to H Pembertons found her smokeing her pipe with 2 officers one of 'em is quarter'd there, after they were gone Hannah and myself were comparing notes, and reading our last Letters, we were neither of us so happy in our expectations as some others—I left Hannah near 1 o'clock and as I was returning I mett Susanna Jones and Richd. Wister talking together. I stop'd and heard him tell that he had just parted with Billy Lewis who told him that Andrew Roberson was come from Lancaster this Morning, and assures him that our dear Friends were actualy discharg'd—I have heard the same report several times since Morning and I know not what ails me that I cannot believe such good news—so much has however laid hold on me that I shall be grievously disoponined if it should fall through, a Letter from my dearest confirming it would rejoyce my Heart. S. Swett drank coffee with us, R Jones, Ricd. Waln Josa. Howel, call'd, Sam Sanson J. Drinker and J.C. spent part of the Evening very warm for the Season—Ricd. Adams call'd while I was out and paid Sister 25/– which he was over paid for the Pork. we were alarm'd this evening by a voilent cry of fier very near us—it prov'd to be a Chimney in Water Street which was soon put out,—we have been much favour'd this Winter on account of fire.

11th. A very bad day on account of weather, Snow and rain, Sister and Billy went to meeting Morning and afternoon, the rest of us stay'd at home—Becky James Senr. call'd—Hannah Catheral drank Coffee with us, she had been to the buryal of Magdaline Brown—before we had done Coffee who should come in but Jn. Brinton his wife, his Brother Georges Wife and his Daughter Esther

Trimble, John brought me a Letter from my Beloved dated the 13 and 15th. Ultimo they are come to stay with us 2 or 3 Days, they were very wet when they came.

12. Ra. Waln C. West and D. Eastaugh call'd—M. Brinton her Sister in Law and Esther Trimble din'd and drank Tea with us—sup'd and lodg'd, and Breakfasted with us.

13th. it is 17 years this day, and the same day of the week since my marriage with my dear Henry.—J Brinton &c din with us. they set of for home after dinner. S Swett also din'd with us—S. Emlen, J. Drinker, E. Drinker, R Scattergood, R Jones call'd—James and Sally Logan and J.C. drank Coffee with us.

14 Sister and Nancy went out this Morning R. Say call'd while they were out, Ricd. Waln Robt. Waln and J.C. here this Evening it is likely to be a very cold night—I am constantly wishing for some fresh accounts from my Lover, something cartain, I want this good news confirm'd—little Molly has a very bad cough, Billy has been unwell for 2 days past.—Isey Pleasants continus very ill. his mamy very unwell.

15. I spent this Afternoon with R Hunt at her Sisters; Reba. Waln, S. Hartshorn, Josa. and Catty Howel, and William Temple here this Evening—no news of my Henry; the hopes that I had from the late accounts begins to fail, prehaps we may hear something tomorrow or next day.

16 Wm. Turner brought us this Morning a cord of Oak Wood, which Robt. Waln had engag'd for us—Molly Pleasants here with our girls—Isey very ill, S. Swett and J.C. drank Coffee with us—Rot. Waln here this Evening Sister in at Becky Joness—no intiligence yet from my Henry. J.C. stay'd out last night till after 12 or nearer one.

17 S. Emlen, Abel James, J Drinker, call'd—Saml. Sansom and J.C. drank Coffee with us—dull rainy weather—we are inform that one Jones who was last week at York Town says that the memorial which our dear Friends sent to Congress, was under consideration, and was thought by most, that they would be acquited, so that the former accounts of their being deschargd and on their way home, is all come to nothing. Becky Jones call'd this Evining.

18th. First Day the children (all but Billy who is a little indispos'd) went to meeting.—S. Swett, R. Scattergood, A. Parish, S. Penington John and Daniel Drinker, drank Tea with us. this being the Queens birth Day, there has been fireing of Guns from the Shiping and the collers flying—fine moderate Weather.

19 This Morning our officer mov'd his lodgings from the bleu Chamber to the little front parlor, so that he has the two front Parlors, a Chamber up two pair of stairs for his bagage, and the Stable wholly to himself, besides the use of the Kitchen, his Camp Bed is put up—I went out this Morning to Christr. Whites, where I heard a sorrowful account which at that time I did not believe, Christor. told me that John Tomson had received a letter from Reading, informing of the death of our Beloved Friend John Pemberton, and that our Friends J Parish and J James were in Lancaster Jail. I then went to Uncle Jerviss where I heard the latter part of this distressing intiligene they not having heard the former—I call'd at J Drinkers then came home, where I found Abel James who had heard Peter Tomsons letter—I step'd into Becky Joness they had also heard the mournful news last Night, I went out after dinner to O Jones, stay'd but a little time and came home,—S. Fisher Saml. Emlen and S. Hopkins here this Evening We are some of us willing to hope that this account may be a mistake should it prove true, what a loss will it be to my dearest Henry at this time of Afflicting tryal—Isey Pleasants very ill, a sorrowful Family is theirs at this present time, poor Hannah how I feel for her.

20 the sad news of Yesterday is not yet imparted to H. Pemberton; many are led to beleive it is false, as some say it was reported in Reading 3 week ago; and the 28th Ultimo the accounts from Winchester are that J.P. was then in good Health, I begin to think the time long since I have heard from my dearest—Sister and the Children went to meeting,—myself all day within with a bad cold, on my Breast, Sister and Nancy went out after dinner to M Pleasants, Isey thought to be a little better—S. Logan came home with them she drank Coffee with us—D. Eastaugh, Thos. Masterman, S. Hopkins, R. Jones, John and Racl. Drinker, Josa. and Katty Howell, Robt. and Reba. Waln, call'd—J.C. here this Evening. The play-House was open'd last night for the first time, our major attended, he came home a little after 10 o'clock; cloudy weather—sister call'd this afternoon to see Abey Parish—who[2] appears in great distress.

21st. a house on fire in pewter platter Alley this Afternoon which was soon put out, S. Swett din'd with us, Sally Emlen, Jos. Scott, Richd. Waln, & Sucky Jones, drank tea with us—Betsy Jervis, and Charless Wife, Saml. Emlen, Robt. Waln, D. Eastaugh, call'd—none of us from home to day.

22 I took a walk this cold afternoon to M. Pleasants call'd at Uncles—J Drinker call'd I lent him ten half Joes—J.C. here in the Evening—very cold.

23 Charles West paid us a Morning visit, M. Pleasants junr. and Sally P. part of the Morning with our Girls, dull weather, snow this Evening.

2. The word "seems" crossed out.

24th. Molly Pleasants junr spent this Day with our Children they were teaching her to knit a Purse—Charles Logan Call'd—Dr. Parke, John Drinker and Becky Jones call'd—Sally Zane brought a letter this afternoon for me to read, from Allexr. White to her Sister H.P. informing that the memorial sent to Congress by our Friends had not yet had a final hearing;[3] and by what I can geather from his Letter it is not likely to be favourbly received at least I fear so—Sally Jones brought us a Letter from Hannah Churchman to her Mother,—giving an account that John James [had] din'd with her the 22d Instant—and that he and John Parish might be expected in Philada. on 2d. day next; so that the account Peter Tomsom respecting them is false; as I hope the rest is—but the situation of my dear Husband &c. at this time, I fear is very distressing, to me I am sure it is.

25 First Day; the Children went to meeting this Morning Sister with them in the afternoon. I stay'd at home all day—Charles West and Wife with their little Son and Peggy Baldwin drank Tea with us,—S. Swett, J Drinker, R James Senr and Chalkley call'd—J.C. in the Evening.

26 S. Swett spent the day with us—R Drinker drank coffee—Danl. Drinker John Drinker, Owen Jones, Abel James Hetty Fisher, Becky Jones and Robt. Waln call'd—this has been a Gloomy day to me, not for any perticular rason more than common, but my mind is much oppress'd, and I labour under Bodyly weakness which is distressing at times.

1778 Jan 27—Sister and the 4 Children went to Monthly Meeting—John James came to Town this Morning, he call'd here after meeting, stay'd but a little time as he was going to dine with Saml. Emlen, he gives us very little hope to expect otherwise than that our dear Friends will be sent to Stanton, cruel orders—John Pemberton was well, wh[en] he left him, so that the whole of P. Toms[on] account proves false—J. Parish with [I] Zane and 2 other Friends were to go to Congress, which is the reason of his not returning with JJ, he brought Letters for several, but none for me, as he says my Henry was employ'd when he came away, writeing something that was necessary for the

3. A memorial, or memorandum, from the Quaker prisoners at Winchester was delivered to the Continental Congress and the Supreme Executive Council of Pennsylvania by Alexander White, a Virginia lawyer sympathetic to their plight. The memorial, dated Dec. 19, 1777, among other concerns protested the planned removal of the prisoners from Winchester to Staunton, one hundred miles farther away. The Supreme Executive Council heard the memorial on Jan. 5, 1778, but claimed that the prisoners were under the jurisdiction of the United States and not the state of Pennsylvania. Opposition and lack of time prevented White from delivering the memorial to Congress, and it was presented instead by Isaac Zane, Joseph Janney, Benjamin Wright, William Jackson, John Parish, and Joseph Wright on Jan. 22. It was subsequently referred to a committee of William Ellery, John Henry, and Abraham Clark (Gilpin, *Exiles in Virginia*, 188–93, 198–200; see also *Col. Recs. Pa.*, 11:395; *JCC*, 10:85, 98; Jonathan Bayard Smith to Timothy Matlack, Jan. 19, 1778, in P. H. Smith, *Letters of the Delegates*, 8:615, n.3).

Friends, I went this afternoon to M. Pleasants she has no Letter from her husband, but JJ informs us they were well, I drank Tea there, and came home toward evening afraid all the way I came, Saml. Sansom and Molly Pleasants junr. drank tea with Sister, John Drinker, Hannah Catheral call'd, very cold to day, I wrote this Morning to my Henry, Sally and Billy also wrote—the Troops have been out these two days Forageing, it is amazing to see the great quantitys of Hay they have brought in,—70 odd loads I am told they have taken from Abel James—what will they do when the present suply is gone, large as it seems, I am told it will last but a little time, if they use as 'tis said 24 Tons p day.

28 Danl. Mifflin call'd this Morning he took charge of my letter wrote yesterday to my dear and one from Sally another from Billy, he intends as far as Nottingham—I wrote another Letter to day which I send by Sally Bond as far as Baltimore—I belive I did not sleep ½ an hour dureing the whole of last night. My mind was so disturb'd, I arose this Morning with a Bad Heak-a[ch] which has continu'd all day:

R[J][4]
[J]B
[J]D
DD

8/ 6/ 3
11/ 6/ 5
39/ 7/ 9
40/ 9/ 1
17/ 4/ 8
[72]/10/ 7½
21/13/ 2
12/12/ –½
16/15/ 7½
11/16/[ ]½
11/19/ 3½
―――――――
264/ –/ 11[½]

Philadelphia
72
15 – 7½

4. The list of initials appears on the inside back cover of the manuscript volume. ED penned the material beginning "8/6/3" and ending "10 2 3" on the outside back cover of the same volume.

Mc.M
A.K
H.R

TH
TL
G.C
W.M
S.S
M.S
R.D
S.E
[J].G
[J].E
[J.]H
K.H
C.W
R.[J]
R.W

264

9	2	10½
1	15	7½
7	7	3
2	15	
10	2	3

S. Logan drank [tea] with us,[5] Reba. James Senr. spent part of the Afternoon and Evening[6] John Drinker call'd, he paid me the 30£ which he had some time ago—Chalkley James, Patn. Hartshorn and Sucky, call'd—SH tells us that Edward Catheral is dead at Burlington; weather more moderate.

(Jany.) 29 Isaac Cathral went over the River this afternoon, but was not sufferd to go to his Fathers Burial—a warm rain this Morning, J Drinker Robt. Waln and Sl. Emlen call'd—our Major stay'd out last night 'till between 12 & one. at a Concert at head quarters, I fear he will do the same to Night as he is gone to an assembly—I have been unwell all day.

30 John James, John and Danl. Drinker Saml. Emlen, Sucky Jones, Richd.

5. The manuscript volume for Jan. 28–Oct. 5, 1778, has brown paper covers. The outside front cover reads, "(commencing Janry. 29/78)," but part of January 28 begins the volume.
6. The words "with us" crossed out.

Waln, and Docr. Redman call'd—SE. spake to us, he went over afterwards to Neigr. Walns where he found Sister, they had a setting there also and Sammy something to say to them. J Parish not yet come, R. Hunt I understand has received a Letter from her Husband of the 16th. Instant.

31st. Docr. Parke call'd this Morning to let us know that he intends to set of on 3d. day next for Winchester or Stanton to see our dear Friends, Sammy Sansom spent the Afternoon and part of the Evening with us [J.]C. drank Tea—rain and Foggy all Day.

Febry. 1st. First Day: the Children went to meeting this Morning I went with them in the Afternoon, mett E. Morris at the meeting House door, who inform'd me that she had just read a letter from Peggy Byard to her Son, telling him that his Father had mov'd in the House of Asembly to have the Banish'd Friends releas'd and that it was answer'd in the Afermitive. I have but little dependance on this news or the Chanel thro' which it comes; and yet the possibility of its being true is somehow pleasing; E Morris, Mart. Porter, John James and S. Swett and Richd. Waln, drank Tea with us—Saml. Emlen and Wife, Sarah Fisher and Rachl. Drinker, myself Sister, and our 4 Children had a Evening Meeting in our parlor,—R Drinker and her Son Henry sup'd with us—John Drinker and Hannah call'd—J James read a paper to us this Afternoon, from Friends in pike Creek to our Friends at Winchester—our major has Company to sup with him to night, it is now near 12 o'clock and they are not yet broke up—moderate weather.

2d. Jammy Morton call'd this Morning before I came down stairs, he intends going with Docr. Parke tomorrow, I wrote to my dear and took the Letter to M. Pleasants, where I mett the Doctor and several others, drank Tea there—Robt. Veree, Molly Pleasants junr. and John Nancarrow call'd—Moderate.

3 Wm. Brown call'd this Morning he intends setting of to morrow with his Daughter Sally to go as far as Notingham; I have heard since he was hear that he intends a visit to our dear Friends, which he mention'd to me as a thing at a distance—I have wrote this evening to my Henry by [S] Bond. as Dr. Parke has taken that I wrote by her before—our 4 Children went this Morning to Youths Meeting Nancy came home very unwell with a pain in her Face and Ear—very sick at Stomach and a bad Head Ach, she has been poorly for a week past, with a sore throat, but was got better, I hope she is not breeding the Fever, which many have lately had—I took a walk this Morning to see Hannah Pemberton; stay'd till near dinner time mett Sucky Jones in my return who told me her mammy wanted to speak with me; she intends to go before long to G. Washington, on account of her Son; she hinted as if she would like me to go with her,—which I think will not suit me; tho' my Heart is full of some such thing, but I dont see the way clear yet—Hannah Drinker and

[J.]C—drank Coffee with us. John Drinker also, he has heard this Afternoon by some round about way, that our dear Friends are actuly remov'd from Winchester, I fear it is too true—David Eastaugh brought a Letter here this Morning which he had wrote to John Pemberton, Sister seal'd & Superscrip'd it for him, we sent Harry with it to Dr. Parke, who with Jemmy Morton set of this Morning John Allen Son of Wm. Allen was bury'd this Morning—the weather is remarkably moderate, and agreeable, to such whose Hearts are at ease.

4 I took a walk this Morning Sally with me, to Thos. Fishers, mett Saml Emlen there, stay'd but a little time, S.E. came away with us—call'd at his request at J. Logans,—parted with him at Chestnutt street—call'd at Uncle Jerviss and at J. Drinkers, came home before dinner, C. Jerviss Wife and Sister Betsy, call'd, as they had been up town, and stay'd Dinner with us—J.C. drank Coffee with us. Reba. Waln, Saml. Smith call'd, [J.] Howel sent word in, this evening that J. Parish was return'd, S. Smith went to see him and brought me from him, a Letter from my Henry, the first I have received since the 27 Decr. he tells us that our dear Friends are not to be remov'd from Winchester, which as they are not suffer'd to return to us, is an Agreeable peice of intilegence—Major Coats and Capt. Swift with some others were brought in to day as prisoners—they are going on at a sad rate in the Jersys, Parson Odells Family, are to be sent to him hear, and Rd. Waln is apprehensive of the same.

5 Sister went out this Morning she call'd at Rl. Whartons; Molly Carry call'd—S. Jones and her daughter Sucky call'd, James Logan, and [S.] Hartshorn drank tea with us, John and Rachel Drinker, Danl. and Elizh. Drinker, and John Parish here this Evening I cannot rightly understand Johns account but when we can get him by our selves shall be more satisfied prehaps—but this is clearly understood that our dear Friends are to be continu'd at Winchester 'till further orders, and that the Congress have again offred them their Liberty on taken a Test,[7] which is all sham, as they know they will not do it—John also tells us that John Hough and [Coll.] Gillpin have undertook to apply to Congress in their behalf—that a number of the Hott-Ones appear to be softned &c &c—Molly Pleasants junr and Sally Jones here this Morning Sally spent this Afternoon at S. Swetts, Nancy much better than she was, but not well enough to go abroad, little Henry has a bad cough.

6 Dull with rain all day, Saml. Smith and Robt. Waln, call'd this Morning—

7. On Jan. 29 the Continental Congress ordered the release of the prisoners on condition that they take an oath or affirmation to the state of Pennsylvania whereby each man agreed to be "a good and faithful subject" (Gilpin, *Exiles in Virginia*, 188–93, 198–200; see also *Col. Recs. Pa.*, 11:395; *JCC*, 10:85, 98; Jonathan Bayard Smith to Timothy Matlack, Jan. 19, 1778, in P. H. Smith, *Letters of the Delegates*, 8:615, n.3).

Katty Howel & Sammy Sansom and J.C. drank tea with us, Jos. Bringhurst call'd—, little Henry, Nancy and Jenney all unwell, as numbers now in Town are, with colds & Fevers.

7 little Henry very poorly all day; towards evening he grew worse, with a Head-Ach & Vomitting; rather better when he went to Bed—I took a walk this Morning with Sally to M. Pleasants—call'd at Uncles—Betsy Hough and J.C. drank tea with us. Wm. and Sarah Fisher here this Evening the first time of WFs ever being here—John James, Saml. Emlen call'd—I have been much distress'd at times, when I have thought of my being still here, when prehaps it might be in my power to do something for my dear Husband; which uneasyness I communicated to MP. who then show'd me a Letter from her Father; intimating something of the kind to her Mother and herself—I hope it will please the Lord to direct us to do that which is right. it would be a tryal on us to leave our Young Familys at this time, but that I belive, if we could conclude on the matter we should leave, and trust in kind providence—it is now between 11 and 12 o'clock, and our Officer has company at Supper with him; the late hours he keeps is the greatest inconvenienc we have as yet suffer'd by having him in the House.

8 Snow all day; First day—Henry appear'd well all day, but in the Evening he was taken down with a Fever sick Stomach and Head-ach—Billy and Sally went to meeting this Morning my self and Billy in the Afternoon, I cannot recollect one person calling to see us this day—the Major drank tea with us.

9 Clear weather this morning Snow 12 or 14 Inches deep; J. Drinker call'd; little Henrys fever came on again this Evening tho' rather lighter.

10 none but Billy went to meeting. John Parish call'd after, he shou'd us the memorial which our dear Friends sent to[8] the Govr. Virginia and the Copy of the order of the Consel of War, for sending them to Staunton[9]—S. Swett, and Polly and Betsy Jervis din'd with us—they with J.C. drank tea with us—Becky Jones, David Eastaugh, C. West and Reba. Waln call'd—Billy Wilson brought

8. "Congress" crossed out.

9. A reference to the Board of War's resolves, sent to Congress and the Supreme Executive Council of Pennsylvania in December 1777, to move the Quaker prisoners to Staunton, Va. The Board of War had based its decision on uncensored, intercepted letters and on reports of currency speculation by Owen Jones, Jr., one of the prisoners. Reports also circulated that the Quakers undermined local confidence in American currency. The memorial of the Quaker prisoners protesting these charges was sent not to the governor of Virginia but to Congress and the Supreme Executive Council of Pennsylvania. In Virginia, the prisoners negotiated with the local military officials assigned to guard them in order to delay implementing the removal orders until Congress could act on their memorial. On Jan. 21, 1778, the Board of War rescinded the removal order (Gilpin, *Exiles in Virginia*, 185–87, 199–200, 204; *Col. Recs. Pa.*, 11:383).

me a letter this Evening from my dearest. it has began to Snow again this Evening and promises to be Deep—Henry still very poorly.

11 dull rainy weather and a great thaw, very foggy—several in our Family and in many other Families have got Colds—Robt. Waln and J. Drinker call'd—J.C—drank Tea with us—5 month this day since my dear Henry left me.

12 I have not been out for many days—Henry continues poorly,—John Drinker, Jos. Scott, Sammy Sansom and Mary Eddy. drank Coffee with us—Abel James and Jos. Howel call'd—cleard up fine weather.

13. S. Swett spent the Day, Docr. Redman din'd with us—Molly Pleasants junr. spent the Afternoon; Jos. Howel, S. Sansom, D. Drinker and Sammy Emlen call'd—Nancy, Henry and Molly all unwell. I received a Letter from my Henry this Afternoon.

14 I went this Morning to M Pleasants to enquire after Wm. Askew who is going to Winchester, call'd at M. Pemberton, at Uncles, at Ben Hootens to pay for Veal, when I came home found John Parish and John James at our House—Robt. Waln and J.C.—here this Afternoon Nancy seems something Better, Henry poorly, little Molly had a Chill this Afternoon and is gone to Bed in a High Fever;—I wrote to my dear Henry this Evening—I am out of all patience with our Major he stays out so late almost every Night.

15 First day little Molly very poorly indeed all Day, a High Fever in the Afternoon, Janny also gone to Bed very unwell, which occasions us to be the more put to our Shifts having so little help, Sally and Billy went to Meeting in the Morning Sister, Sally, Billy and Nancy in the Afternoon; Nancy and Henry are nither of them well—Becky Scattergood, S Swett, John Drinker and Becky Jones call'd—Hannah Sansom, her Son Joe and J.C—drank tea with us—hail this Evening we have had a long spell of unsettled weather, which tis likely has been the occasion of those winter fevers, so many are seiz'd with.

16. Molly ill again this afternoon a high fever, Sally and Nancy went this Afternoon with Molly Pleasants and Sally Jones, to visit Debby Norris—Wm. Loage told Billy to day in the Street, that our Summer-House at Frankford had been broke open by the British Trops and that they had taken 2 Cows from Joseph, Janney's fever came on her again this Evening Sammy Smith and Wife, Reba. Waln, call'd David Eastaugh and J.C—drank Tea with us.

17 Sally and Billy went to meeting; Docr. Moore, Nics. Waln, and Saml. Emlen, call'd after meeting; Sally Penington, A. Potts, Nics. Waln drank tea with us—Josa. Fisher Richd. Waln and Becky Jones and Isaac Penington

call'd—NW. read to us this Afternoon 8½ sheets of paper or 17 pages, wrote by our Friends at Winchester and sent here for the consideration of Friends.—our major had 8 or 10 to dine with him, they broke up in good time, but he's gone of with them and when he'l return I know not, I gave him some hints 2 or 3 days ago, and he has behav'd better since—Jenny is much better to day—Mollys fit of the Fever rather lighter this evening little Henry is poorly, Nancy also, very unwell, clear weather—part of the Army went out last night they have sent in great quantities of Wood and Hay—I want much to hear from Winchesr.

18 No body call'd to see us to day but Robt. Waln; and J.C—Nancy, Molly, and Henry still unwell—my Heart is very heavy.

19 I step'd into J. Howels, and over to Neigr Walns, Boby has got the Measels—Neigr Carlile sent me word that there was a Young Man there, who had come from Winchester lately, I went to him, his Name John Hains, of Evesham, he inform'd me that my dear Henry was well about 10 days ago, that he had some talk with him about the Iron-Works, that he left Isaac Zane Senr. at the Grove, who had a Packet of Letters for us—but as there was a committe to be appointed from that quarter to wait on the Presedent and Counsel of Pensylvaa.[10] to whome the Congress, he hears has given our Friends over[11] if he Isaac Zanes should he be nominated would return to Lancaster, and send the Letters forward by some other hand, this J. Hains had no thoughts of coming to Philada. when he left him—prehaps Wm. Brown may bring them tomorrow or next day. Taby and Becky Fisher, Polly and Betsy Foulk, spent this Afternoon with us—John Drinker, Josa. Howell, and Hannah Catheral call'd—dull rainy Weather Reba. Say spent this Afternoon also with us. our dear Nancy is very unwell with a pain in her side and Neck with a hard Cough—little Molly still poorly, Jenny and Henry much better,—The Army has brought in a great quantity of Hay, with Jos. Galloways Wife, Goods and Chattles.[12]

10. Word crossed out.

11. The words "to them" crossed out. The question of authority over the Quaker exiles was confusing from the start. The Continental Congress first ordered the arrest of some of the men, after which the Supreme Executive Council added other names and then sought and received permission from Congress to banish them. When Congress subsequently ordered a hearing, the Supreme Executive Council refused, and Congress left the affair in the hands of the state of Pennsylvania. Once the prisoners were exiled, matters became even more disorganized, since prisoners of war came under the direction of the Board of War, which was under the authority of the Continental Congress. As it became clear that the Quakers posed no threat to anyone's security, the issue of their exile embarrassed both Congress and the Supreme Executive Council, and both bodies denied responsibility for the prisoners until March 1778, when the Supreme Executive Council finally took control of the men (Thayer, *Israel Pemberton*, 225–31; Gilpin, *Exiles in Virginia*, 158–71, 178–79, 216–20; Oaks, "Philadelphians in Exile," 315–20; *Col. Recs. Pa.*, 11:395, 427; see below, Mar. 10, 1778).

12. The British sent the army on foraging expeditions to the countryside in order to supply

20 dull weather this Morning rain and Snow in the Afternoon, John Parish, John James, John Drinker and Saml. Sansom, drank Coffee with us—Nancy had a very bad Night with a high fever, and is very poorly to day, little Molly something better—Nichs. Hicks, and Leonard—call'd here yesterday with a Subscription paper for the poor, I gave them 2 Dollars—there was 18 or 20 prisoners brought in from ———.

21st. Reba. James Senr. and J.C— drank tea with us—Nancys cough still bad.

22 First Day: Billy went to Meeting this Morning Sister and Billy in the Afternoon, Sally unwell with a Cough and pain in her face, a little touch of the times—Ricd. Waln and J.C— drank tea with us—Reba. Waln Senr. here in the Evening—dull this Morning rain the Evening.

23 little Henry went to School this Morning the first of his going since he has been sick, Molly not well enough yet to go—Nancys cough very bad in the Night, but better in the day, Billy has been very hearty all Winter, this forenoon John James brought me a Letter from my dear Henry—our Hopes all Crush'd for the present—they have again offer'd the Test to our Friends—Robt. Waln, Jos. Howel, and John Drinker call'd—James and Sally Logan and Sally Penington drank Tea with us—Becky Jones came in for my Letter for to read to Sally and Hetty Fisher, I sent it with Sally Peningtons; She left with me one from TF to his Wife and one from TF to his Sister another from [T]F to Hetty, which we read here, we also had the reading of one from T Fisher to J. Logan—Henry slip'd out to day and got himself wett above his knee I chang'd his cloths as soon as I knew it, but he complains of a pain in his Breast this Evening—it has again clear'd up.

24th. Sister and Billy went to Monthly Meeting S. Swett, S. Penington and Rachl. Drinker call'd this Morning—John Parish, Benn. Hough, Isaac Jackson and Wm. Harvey din'd with us—after dinner, I. Jackson read to us the Epistle from Pike Creek Meeting to our Fds. at Winchester, after which they had each of them somthing to say by way of Testimony—Sammy Smith likewise spake to us—Josa. Howel here during the setting—they went from here about 4 o'clock to S. Peningtons—Molly Pleasants, Sally Jones and Debby Norris, spent this afternoon with our Girls—Reba. Waln Senr. and Sucky Hartshorn part of the Evening with us—Danl. Drinker and Richd. Waln call'd, this has been a very fine day—130 head of Cattle and Several prisoners brought in

---

Philadelphia with such necessities as hay. On one of these trips they apparently escorted Grace Galloway from her Bucks County home to Philadelphia, where she joined her husband during the British occupation (Ousterhout, "Pennsylvania Land Confiscations," 328; Jackson, *With the British Army*, 89–93).

to day, taken as they were going to G. Washingtons Camp[13]—Nancys Cough very bad to night, with pain in her Sholder.

25 S. Swett spent the Day with us—C. West & Abel James here before I came down stairs; I am very much broke of my rest by the Childrens being unwell, and other troubles—I did not mention Yesterday that Sally Zane was here with a Letter from JP. to Hannah, in which my dear Henry had wrote a few lines to me; Josa. Howel came in this Afternoon and desir'd me (with a smiling Countinance) to prepare to here News; which prov'd to be the return of Docr. Park, who he had mett as he came to Town, I received 3 Letters from my dear Husband, and one for JD another for AJ and one to our Son Billy, my dears indispossion gives me more pain, then I felt when they were ordred to Stanton, or at least I think so. Oh! how anxious shall I be untill I hear again. Josa. and Catty Howel, Becky Jones and Hannah Catheral here this Evening John, Rachel and Hannah Drinker came after 9 o'clock—Joseph Bringhurst call'd and J.C. came in. a British officer is in Custody on suspision of being concern'd in a plot lately discoverd to set the Play-House and several other parts of the Town on Fier. &c—I have not heard the whole of the matter—Nancys cough very bad.

26 Docr. Parke paid us a long visit this Morning he has made me somthing easyer on account of my Henry, tho not much—Richd. Waln, Janny Morton and J.C. drank tea with us—Saml. Emlen, Heny. Drinker, Robt. Waln call'd—Becky James junr. was here yesterday, she had heard nothing of our Summer-House being broke open, but say'd she would enquire Billy went round to give his Daddy love to the Friends he had mention'd in his letter to him; as it was a damp foggy day he came home unwell and is gone to Bed, after having a spell of the sick Head-ach—Nancy coughs very bad every night after she goes to bed—Sister went to Becky Joness this evening and brought home a little Trunk that had been deposited. we had the reading to day of a paper drawn up by Allexr. White which he presented to Congress, with reasons why our Friends should be set at Liberty, on the score of Humanity, justice and good Policy; but all in vain. those are things they seem unaquainted with—the talk of Sammy Pleasants coming home on his parole gives me some concern, tho we know not what's for the best; we dont know how or when we shall hear next from Winchester.

27 Abel James call'd this morning he read my Henrys Letter, and promis'd to send me his to read—John Drinker and Saml. Sansom drank tea with us—

13. Washington had sent Anthony Wayne on a foraging expedition to New Jersey to bring cattle back to the encampment at Valley Forge. British dragoons and loyalist troops intercepted the detachment and captured the American troops and 130 head of cattle near Skippack, in Bucks County, Pa. (Jackson, *With the British Army*, 180–81).

Josa. Howel call'd—rain all night and Snow great part of the day—going into the Kitchen to night, I met Heritta the Hession Stable—Boy, in the dark, I ran against him and hurt my Eye, my Cheek is much swell'd and painful,—the Major tells me this Evening that there is great news from England—that 80,000 Troops are to embark by the 1st. March, for America, and that the French have seiz'd all the Rebel Vessels, by desire of Great Britian.

28th. Rain and Snow all day, clear to night the Blood has settled round my eye, and it looks very ugly, my Cheek much swell'd. Capt. Harper Son from Alexandria call'd this Morning said that he was at Lancaster 3 Week ago, and heard then that the Friends at Winchester were well—Becky Jones call'd this Evening—a Number of the Troops are gone in to the Jersys, tis said that the Rebels there, are burning and destroying all before them.

March 1st. First Day: Sally and Billy went to meeting this morning—Nancy still unwell with a cough and pain in her side, little Henrys face swell'd with the Tooth Ach—Abey Parish, S. Swett, Jos. Scott, Danl. Drinker, Anthony Benezet and the Major drank tea with us—Sarah Fisher and her Son James here this Evening—a fine clear day, Moonlight evening a Snow Storm Since night—a number of prisoners brought from the Jersys to day, 18 or 20 they say.

2d. David Eastaugh calld this Morning Molly Pleasants junr. spent the Morning with the Girls—M. Pleasants spent the Afternoon with us, she and the Major drank Tea with us, J. Drinker and the Widdow Gordon call'd, Billy went to MPs—Billy stay'd at home Yesterday Afternoon to write to his dear Daddy, the first time he has mist going to Meeting since we were left—Nancy wrote also—clear all Day, snow this Evening two men were lately brought to our Niegr. Wellss in the Ally, at different times, Sick, from a Ship, they did not appear very ill when they came there, but dyed, one in a days time, the other in a few hours after, they came, Sister sent for Wells to talk to him about it, he say'd he would take no more in and appear'd alarm'd about the matter. J.C. went home with MP. this Evening.

3 Abel James, here this Morning—Josh. Harper Son of Capn. Harper came for a few lines I wrote to my Henry, Charles West and J.C— drank tea with us—Snow most of this day; I have wrote a long letter in order to send by the Friends, but they are gone of this Morning and I am disopointed Billy went to meeting this Morning J. Parish spent an hour with us after meeting.

4 John Drinker call'd—Owen Jones and J.C. drank tea with us—Joshua and Caty Howel spent part of the Evening Nancy seems to be getting better, clear.

5 Sally Moore came to see us this Morning she has not been before since

my Henrys departe she tells me they have had 50 or 60 Tons of Hay, and 20 odd Head of Cattel &c taken from them by the British Troops, for which they expect no recompence—Thos Pike also call'd, he gave us an account of his journey—from Winchester &c—said that my Henry was but little indispos'd when he left him,—Old Edward Drinker and Robt. Waln call'd—it has been clear all day; which has not been the case for a long time past.

6 Sally Logan spent the Afternoon with us—Docr. Redman call'd, I apply'd to him on account of a weakness, I labour under, Saml. Emlen Abel James junr. call'd—Lidia Gilpin sent me a Letter to read, from George Gilpin to her, informing that he had been able to do Nothing with Congress towards their release, but expected when the Assembly set, something would be done towards it—J. Drinker received a Letter this evening from my Henry dated the 11 Ultimo, read and forward'd by order of Counsel, sign'd Ty. Matlack—as my Husband does not mention me in his Letter to JD— I have rason to believe there was one for me, which I fear they have detain'd; fine weather.

7 I wrote to day to my dear—S. Emlen call'd; he read my Henrys last letters—J. Drinker call'd; M. Pleasants junr. spent this Afternoon with our Girls—we had our plate brought from JDs where it has been deposited, rain again to Day.

8 First Day. Sally and Billy went to Meeting this Morning Sister, Sally, Nancy and Billy this Afternoon—S. Swett drank tea with us—I step'd over to Nr. Walns this Evening Anna has the Measels,—I have not been out of the Front Door for a long time before, I have been much troubled lately, With a pain in my Back.

9 Snow almost all Day, Nobody call'd to see us—Major drank tea with us.

10 Sister and Billy went to Meeting, John Parish and John James din'd with us—Sammy Sansom, John Parish and J.C—drank Tea with us, Isaac Zane and J Drinker hear also—in the Evening we had a setting, when IZ and [J]P, had each of them something to say to us—Cloudy & rain,—IZ tells us that the Congress and Counsel, have turn'd our Friends over to the Assembly,[14] who mett the 24th. Ultimo so that we may soon expect to hear something.

11 half a year this day since we were left, Richd. Waln spent the Afternoon

14. On Mar. 7 Thomas Wharton, Jr., president of the Supreme Executive Council of Pennsylvania wrote Henry Laurens, president of the Continental Congress, requesting that the council be given authority over the prisoners in Virginia. Congress granted the request and on Mar. 16 ordered the Board of War to give control of the prisoners to the Supreme Executive Council of Pennsylvania (*Col. Recs. Pa.*, 11:460; Oaks, "Philadelphians in Exile," 322).

and part of the Evening with us, rain all day—things seem to have a very gloomy aspect. Docr. Cooper and Ebenezr. Robinson call'd with a Subscription paper for the Poor,[15] I Gave them 4 Dollars.

12 a warm giving day, rain in the Evening, Josh. Scott and J.C. drank tea with us—I step'd into Becky Joness this Morning.

13 a very heavy air warm, foggy, and damp, J. Drinker call'd—Abel James, Sucky and Hannah Jones, drank tea with us, Polly Pleasants spent part of the Evening Abel left my Henrys Letter to him, with me—Sally very ill this Evening with the Sick Head-Ach—a few days past, 2 or 3 Vessels were taken near Willmington—a number of the British troops are since gone down the River, with what intent we know not, some think they heard fireing this Afternoon—we hear that James Thorntons Barn is burnt &c.

14 I took a walk to H Pembertons before dinner, Our Major din'd with us to day, for the first time; Saml. Emlen, Chackly James, call'd—Molly Pleasants junr. spent this Afternoon with our Children—I call'd while I was out this Morning at O. Jones, Susy full of the notion of going to Congress, gave me several broad hints, which I could not give into—I call'd at Benn. Hootens to pay him for a [quarter] Veal—the first fine day we have had for a long time past.

15 First Day: the 4 Children went to Meeting this morning, Sister with the 4, in the Afternoon—I have not been to meeting for several weeks past, on account of Sickness among the Children my black Eye &c—David Eastaugh drank Coffee with us, S. Swett, Reba. Waln, Saml. Emlen Katty Howel and J Drinker, Debby Norris, Sally Jones and Isaac Norris call'd.

16 dull weather, C. James came with Taffities, J Logan at Tea with us—tis a month to Day since the date of my Henrys last Letter, which inform'd of his Indispossion.

17 a great Croud of Irish Soldiers went by this Afternoon,[16] with one on Horse-back representing St. Patrick—Watch was very noisey all night, Drunken Fellows as we suppose passing and repassing—Saml. Emlen, Saml.

15. During the British occupation of Philadelphia the normal channels of funding poor relief were nonexistent. None of the Overseers of the Poor were in the city, and by mid-February the funds distributed by the British for the support of the poor had been used up. General Howe permitted Joseph Galloway, chief civil officer in the city, to authorize private subscriptions and collections for the almshouse (*Pa. Ev. Post*, Feb. 14, 1778; D. E. Fisher, "Social Life," 247–48).

16. Many other British troops and Philadelphians joined the Irish grenadiers, part of the British forces stationed in Philadelphia, for their St. Patrick's Day procession (Jackson, *With the British Army*, 216; S. L. Fisher, "Diary of Trifling Occurrences," 462).

Sansom, John Nancarrow, John Parish and Wife, and Danl. Drinker call'd—I. drank tea this afternoon at Neigr. Walns, Sally and Nancy at their Uncle Johns.

18. Josa. Howel here this Morning he bought a [quarter] Beef at 16d p. of which I had half—Sally Penington, John Drinker call'd—Becky and Patty Wharton drank tea with us, our Girls spent this Afternoon at M. Pleasants.

19th. John Drinker here this Morning he bought a peice of Linnen for me, to make Shirts for my Henry—Robt. Waln and wife Josa. Howel call'd—Our Major has had a Concert this Evening 11 of them in Company; it was carrid on with as much quietness and good order as the nature of the thing admitted of, they broke up, between 11 and 12 o'clock—fine Weather.

20 Charles West, Dorcas Mt. Gomery and her Son, Hannah Pemberton junr. Molly Pleasants junr. called this Morning Chalkley James, Abel junr. with another young man, went on Top of our House to discover the cause of a Smoke near Frankford, but could make out nothing—A James sent for me after dinner, Sister went down, he had kill'd a Beef, of which we are to have part.[17] Sally Penington, Phebe Pemberton, Polly Story, Sally Logan, and Sally Wharton spent the Afternoon with us—our Major took it into his Head to dine to day in the Summer House, with another Officer, he had 2 or 3 to visit him while they set there, so that when the House is kept open, I supose we shall have them passing and repassing, which has not been the case hitherto; they behave well and appear pleas'd—but I dont feel so—fine weather to day—Isey Pleasants, spent this Afternoon with Billy.

21 Josey Bringhurst call'd this Morning Sally and Nancy went to Saml Emlens to know how the Children were, who have been unwell—they heard there, that a Friend who is in Town says that Thos. and Susanna Lightfoot, Robt. Vallentine and Wife, with some other Friends, waited on the Assembly on account of our dear Friends at Winchester—that they had a hearing and were favourably received—that two were appointed from the Assembly, and one from the Govenor and Counsel, to go to Congress to know whose prisoners they actuly were, that if it was left to either of the two aforasaid Bodys, they would release them—the mesengers were not returnd when this Friend came away—Saml. Sansom, M. Pleasants Senr. M. Pleasants junr. and J.C—drank tea with us—Reba. James Senr. and Nurse Willson call'd. Reba. Walln Senr. spent part of the Evening—it is wisper'd about, that Thos. Gillpin is dead, I cant find who it is that brings the news, I hope it is not true—fine weather this day.

17. The word "of" crossed out.

22d. First Day: Sister unwell all day, the Girls went twice to meeting, Billy 3 times, myself in the Afternoon and Evening—Wm. Jones call'd—his Bror. Benjn. and George Dylwin have not been heard of, for 5 months past—there are but few Friends at this Spring meeting compar'd to former times, tho' concedering the Difficultys there are many—we hear that Thos. Lightfoot Robt. Valentine and Josa. Balldwin are confind in Lancaster Goal—Sarah Carry, S. Swett and JC—— drank tea with us—Wm. Blakey, Jos. Dingee and R James Senr. call'd—fine cool weather We were in great expectation that some Friend would have brought us Letters, but to our great disapointment, we have none.

23d. Myself and the 4 Children went to Meeting this Morning Wm. Jackson and S. Swett din'd with us—Sarah Fisher drank tea with us—John Drinker, Danl. Drinker, Abel James junr. Becky James junr. Isaac Coats, Isaac Horner, John Field Jonan. Daws, Dorcas Mountgomery, call'd—very fine weather.

24 Sister has not been to Meeting this Week being unwel, our 4 Children went this Morning—G. Churchman and Wife, Mary Cox and S Swett din'd with us—after dinner MC spake to us in a very comfortable manner, D. Morris who was here, went with her to Sally Penningtons, Mary intends to visit our dear Friends at Winchester—Molly Pleasants junr. and J.C. drank tea with us—Jessy Waterman, Debby Norris, Wm. Clifton, Warner Mifflin John Cowgill, Ricd. Waln and Reba Waln Senr. call'd to see us—fine Weather—I am told that, John Roberts has a Letter from one May—informing him of the death of Thos. Gillpin, and that John Hunt Miers Fisher and several others of our dear Friends are unwell, I have great reason to fear that my beloved Henry is one of them, I shall have little comfort untill I hear from him—I have wrote this Evening to him.

25th. Dr. Parke call'd this Morning he seems to think it somthing strange that we have no letters—Caty Howel here after dinner—Phebe Pemberton, M Pleasants, R. Drinker, Hannah Drinker, Polly Drinker and Sally Pleasants, drank tea with us—PP. and MP. came to consult me about drawing up somthing to present to those who shall acknowledge our dear Friends as their prisoners; I had sometime ago mentiond JD. as a sutiable person to assist us in such an undertaking—We went in the Evening to JDs.—he appeard rather reluctant, but tis likely he will think of it—our intention is, tho we do not yet say so, to take it ourselves, 2 or 4 of us—when we can hear how, matters stand with our dear absent Friends, the Friends that are hear from the Jersys, have had word sent them, that there are several laying in wait to take them up, on their return—our Hay is out, and I beleive I must sell our poor Cow,—Cloudy tonight.

26 rain most of this day: Thos. Ross, John James, Abel James, Robt. Waln &

Wife, Capt. Spain's Widdow, call'd—Samuel Esborn paid us a religious visit, and spake encouragingly to me and the Children,—Docr. Cowper accompany'd him—Jane Shaw, an irish Friend up Town, call'd to day to let us know she had been rob'd of almost all her wareing apparel, I gave her several things to help her—Josa. Howel and Wife and Polly Swett spent part of this Evening with us.

27. Josey Bringhurst call'd this Morning—Sally Penington came while we were at dinner. I appointed to meet her at 5 o'clock at M Pleasants, in order to take a Letter I wrote this Morning to Mary Cox at D Morriss—George Churchman and Wife, and Warner Mifflin set with us a little time this Afternoon, after they were gone I went to M Pleasants, who was gone out I went and set an hour with Mary Pemberton, while I was there, Rachel Hunt sent her a Letter to read, from Thos. Wharton to R. Hunt, confirming the account of the death of Thos. Gillpin, and the illness of her Husband JH. and of the indispossion of several others, my dear Henry and S Pleasants are mentiond as having been very unwell, but were getting better. There is no Letters as I can find from Winchester, Tommy Eddy came while I was there and read a Letter from his Brother Charles, in which my dear Husband and SP. are mention'd, and not in TWs as I have said—they have no medicines, Wine, Sugar, Vinager, nor many other necessary articles at Hopewell, nor I fear at Winchester,—it is 3 weeks since the date of those Letters, and the thought of what may have happend in the Intrim distresses me much—I went from MPs to D Morriss met S Penington and M Cox there—left my Letter and we came away, call'd at O Joness they have a Letter, but were gone out with it—came home towards evening—G. Churchmans Wife Warner Mifflin, John Cowgill, Becky Wright and Mary Stevenson, had a Meeting with us this Evening—Sally Penington was here during the setting, she brought her Husbands Letter for us to read, Warner Mifflin read it, he says John Hunt is dangerously ill, but not one word of my dearest—John Drinker and Billy Rawle call'd and Becky Jones—dull Weather.

28 I went out this Morning to enquire if Rachel Hunt intended to go to Winchester, met Rachel Wharton and Billy Smiths Wife, in Market, we went into the Meeting-House, to read T. Whartons Letter, in which he expresses an expectation of a release e'er long; in what manner I dont rightly understand. but it seems to me, by an extract of a Letter from his Cosen Tom to him, it is talk'd of a forfiture of their Estates, or by acknowledging themselves to be Subjects of the King of Great Britian.[18] this is not the words of the Letter, but

18. Thomas Wharton, Sr. (1731–82), one of the Quaker exiles in Virginia, had written in January to his cousin, Thomas Wharton, Jr. (1735–78), president of Pennsylvania's Supreme Executive Council, complaining about the harshness and injustice of the banishment of the Quakers. Wharton Jr. did not reply directly, but later sent Wharton Sr. a letter about actions the state government was planning to take against those who cooperated with the British. Wharton Sr. sent excerpts of this letter to his wife, Rachel, who shared its contents at the meetinghouse (James Donald Anderson, "Thomas Wharton, Exile in Virginia, 1777–1778," *Virginia Magazine of History and Biography* 89 (1981): 425, 443).

what I think may be inferd from it. I then went to M Pleasants, talk'd a while with her about sending necessarys to our dear Husbands—we went togeather to see poor R. Hunt, who we found writeing to her Husband, she is in a great deal of trouble, has no thoughts of going untill she hears further, least she should hear of her Husbands Death on the Road, which would be more than she could bare, I feel greatly for her; P. Pemberton and myself went from RHs to M Pleasants, had some talk about Susy Joness going to the Assembly; I came home before dinner, my mind much distress'd—Sammy Sansom, Richd. Waln; and J.C. drank tea with us—two of Owen Joness Daughters call'd this Morning while I was out with their Brothers letter, in which he says that my dear Henry had been unwell, but was getting better,—Dorcas Mt.Gomery, Molly Pleasants junr., Saml. Emlen, John Parish, Saml. Smith; Reba. Waln, John Drinker, Becky Jones, and Josa. Howel call'd—Mary Eddy and her Son George came this Evening to consult about sending provisions &c to our Friends John Drinker went to O Joness to consult him on the matter—Our Children are all through Mercy in good Health at present—but little Henry swallow'd a pin Yesterday which adds something to my uneasyness.

29 First day: Stormy Wind and rain greatest part of the Day—our Sons went to Meeting but none other—J. Drinker call'd, he says that upon talking with Owen Jones about sending provisions to our Friends, they concluded it was best to wait a while longer, I forget what his reasons were, and I feel uneasy at the delay, I wrote a third letter this Afternoon to my dear Henry, to go by the Friends who are still here, I sent a quire of Paper some spice, Rheubarb and Herbs, I want to send some old wine but fear they cannot carry it—I'll try further tomorrow.

30. The Equinoctial Storm, as I take it, has done much damage among the Shiping &c. one Ship stove in peices and Sunk, others hurt, some of the Warfes broke, a Chimney in Arch-Street blown down—and two women said to be drownded—Robt. Waln, John and Danl. Drinker call'd—Josa. and Katy Howel, spent part of the Evening.

31 Reba. Scattergood, Josa. Howel, Rd. Waln Thos. Scattergood, Saml. Emlen call'd, John Forman din'd here, H Sansom & JC—— drank Tea—Sister and Billy went to meeting—M. Pleasants sent for me before dinner, I went, she showd me a paper drawn up to send or take to Congress, she had drawn it up, and her Mammy had added somthing to it, Nics. Waln had also made out one for us, which was not approv'd—in the Afternoon O. Jones came to desire I would meet the rest of the Women concern'd at 5 o'clock at M. Pembertons, which I did, they were all there except R. Hunt, Hetty Fisher and T. Afflicks wife—Josa. Fisher O. Jones, A. Benezet, J Drinker and Nichs. Waln, were also there—Nicholas read the Address, and the Women all sign'd it—it is partly concluded that Sush. Jones, P. Pemberton M. Pleasants and E.

Drinker is to take it—I wish I felt better both in Body and mind for such an undertaking. A person is set of I beleive to G. Washington, for permission for a Waggon to pass with Stores for our dear Friends, Docr. Parke has undertaken to supply the Medicines—E. Story is to conduct the other Matters.

April 1st. Charles Logan call'd to let us know that he intended for Winchester on seventh or first day next; Josey James here this Morning the first of our seeing him since his recovery, Neigr. Waln call'd with Polly Mifflins Child—I sent Billy for John Burket, who came, I demanded the Money which has been so long owing, he promis'd to pay it next seventh Day—I took a walk to look for Shoes, but did not succeed—Sally Logan drank Tea with us, I step'd down to Abels to ask for J. Burkets account he say'd it was not in the Company Books—Sally Zane Becky Jones call'd—I had promisd to meet R Pemberton and M. Pleasants at H. Pembertons this Afternoon, but Sister declin'd taking the weight of the Family on her during my absence, which prevented my meeting them according to Promise, and distresses me much—Charles Logan came this Evening at 9 o'clock to inform me that the Friends from Winchester had wrote to their Wives, they have all received letters, this evening at 7 o'clock, myself excepted, he says that in one or more of the letters my Henry is mention'd as recover'd, which if tis so, is joyful news—We all think he must have wrote, but as the letters came through Washingtons camp, are fearful it is stop'd, which gives me great uneasyness—as the Letters were all open'd Isreal Pembertons excepted; and S. Pleasants was seal'd again they were forwarded by Elias Bodinott—no hints in any of them that CL heard, of a release—J Hunt very ill.—to hear that my Henry is better is comfortable, but yet I shall go to Bed, with a heavey Heart, having mist of my Letter, disturbs me much.

2d. Josa. Howel, C. West, Saml. Emlen, Ricd. Waln, Becky Jones; call'd, Molly Pleasants and Sally Jones came with S. Pleasants letter while I was out—I went to Rachl. Hunts who I found writeing to her Husband, she had flattred herself from some of the letters that he was getting better and that his disorder had terminated in a Rumitisam. when I came from their door, Patty Hudson call'd me, and told me, that John Hunt was no more—that the Account of his death was just come to Town, I then went to M. Pleasants, who had sent for me, to meet at O. Jones, to settle matters for our journey; I had reason to think that it would be no easy matter to get of, therefore say'd but little about it, but concluded in my mind, that to the care of kind providence, and my dear Sister I must leave my dear little ones, and the Family generaly—it will be a great care on Sister, as we have an Officer and his Servants in the House, but I hope she will be strengthen'd—M.P. and myself went into Mary Pembertons, found Joyce Benezet, with her—Mary concluded to send her letter to R. Hunt, wherein her Husband is mention'd as being dangerously ill; she[19]

19. The word "concluded" crossed out.

thought it would serve to prepare her; after which Joyce and Mary went to brake the sorrowful news to her, Polly and myself went to Joness stay'd their above an Hour then went to H. Pembertons where we mett M. Haines—a number of our Friends are employ'd to look for sutable Horses and drivers for us, we stay'd and din'd with HP.—I call'd as I come home at R Wisters to buy a Bottle to put Vinager in to send to Winchester—and at [T] Speakmans for Sunderis, came home in the Afternoon. Augustine Hicks, din'd with Sister—J.C. drank tea with us—Nichs. Waln call'd with the Address to Congress for me to sign, Mary Pemberton had coppy'd it afresh with some small addition on hearing of the Death of our dear Friend, J.H—Jammy Morton came this Evening to know if I had enquird of A James for Horses, I had, and he knew of none Abel James spent this evening with us, and the Major. he stay'd 'till near 11 o'clock—A Storm of thunder and Lightning, wind and rain, this Evening—it is say'd that Wm. Rush is dead—a man was kill'd on Frankford road yesterday or the day before.

3 S. Swett spent this day with us—Jammy Morton came this Morning with a mesage from his Mother.—O. Jones call'd to tell me, that Isreal Morris had been to offer himself to accompany us on our journey, Owen seems inclin'd to favour his applycation, for my part I do not approve of it, however we are to meet at 3 o'clock at O Jones to consider of it. Johnny Drinker call'd—and Josey Fox—I went accordingly after dinner to O. Jones mett the other women there—it was agreed to except of Isreal if he would come into our terms, he was sent for, and came, said that he had had a concern for some time to go to Congress on account of our dear Friends and that he look'd upon this as the proper time, we told him that, we could not agree to unite with him in the busyness, we spoke very freely to him, that is MP and myself—that if he could be willing to escort us, and advise when we ask'd it, we should be oblig'd to him for his company, to which he consented—but hinted that he thought it necessary that he should appear with us before Congress, which we by no means consented to—and he acques'd—I hope that his going with us, may turn out more satisfactory then it at present appears to me—we drank Tea at O Jones—and came away in the evening—John Nancarrow came home with me—I found when we came in, Sarah Fisher and her Son James, Saml. Smith and Wife here—Molly Pleasants junr. drank tea with our Girls, Joseph Scot, J. Drinker, and Becky Jones call'd while I was out, it is cold and very windy to day—while we were at OJs this Afternoon, Thos. Pike came in, and mention'd the names of 4 prisoners that are hear, and which they propose to exchange for E. Penington, T. Wharton, O. Jones junr. and C. Eddy—I dont rightly understand what they were about, or ment by it—I wrote this Evening to my dear, did not go to Bed till after one o'clock.

4 I went this Morning to visit our Friend Rachl. Hunt, who appears to be compos'd tho in great affliction—I then went to M Pleasants, we agree'd to be

Bed-fellows during our journey, call'd at Uncle Jerviss and then came home, S. Swett spent this day with us—Abel James, C. Logan Hannah Lloyd Sam Emlen, R James junr. Sammy Sansom Richd. Waln, T. Masterman Charles West, Josa. Howel call'd this Morning John Burket came and paid me 17 Ginues £29..15—out of which I gave him 3/– Borrow'd of J. Howel 160 Dollars, or £60—in Continental currancy, which we are to pay in the same coin—it is on account of myself, S. Jones, & M Pleasants I received a Letter from my dear Henry this Afternoon, which has very much disconcerted me, dated the 24 last month, he then kept his [chamber] and from the appearance of his writeing he is very poorly yet, tho he says he is much better—what with this Letter: the preparing for our journey, the inpossibility of my sending him such things as is necessary for him, with the number of Friends that are calling constantly, my Heart is afflicted and fluttred very much—S. Emlen and Wife Mary Armitt, J. Drinker and Wife, Chalkley James, Abel James, M. Foulk, Isaac Penington, J. Bringhurst, J. Parish, R and R. Waln, K. Howel, here this Afternoon—Sucky Hartshorn the 2 Hannah Catherals and Becky Jones here this Evening I am told that Dr. Moore and Wife were had up at Head quarters to day—for sending Letters out—our address to Congress is to be wrote over the third time, as it was altred on account of the supos'd death of our Friend John Hunt—I wrote to my dear Henry this Evening with a great number round me, clear weather.—this has been a day of great hurry and comotion with me, we talk of setting of tomorrow. may the Almighty favour our undertaking.

5 First Day: I arose early this Morning sent for Dr. Redman who I consulted on my dear henrys case, he said as it was so long since he wrote, and would be longer before we could send him any directions, that the case would be altred so that we could form no judgment [how] to advise—A Benezet, S. Hopkins, Isaac Catheral, J. Drinker call'd—A great number of Troops went out last Night I left home after dinner went to M. Pleasants where were a great Number of our Friends mett to take leave of us, We took Coach at about 2 o'clock, S. Jones, Phebe Pemberton, M. Pleasants and Myself—with 4 Horses, and two Negros who rode Postilion, Mary Pemberton, Hannah Pemberton, and Owen Jones accompany'd us to the Ferry, over which we pass'd without much difficulty or interuption, James Stevens attends there, we went no further then John Roberts Millers, about 10 miles from home, we did not meat with above 2 or 3 persons on the road—we were kindly entertain'd by the Woman of the House and her Daughters, the Owener being at this time a Refugee in Town, in the Evening came a Scouting party of near one hundred men, 2 of their officers came into the House saying that they had heard there was Ladys from Philada. ask'd how many Miles it was theither—they were Strangers, that had lately come from New England, behav'd civiley and stay'd but a short time. they were about the House and in the Barn when we went to Bed—which leaves us under some apprehersion concerning the Carriage and

Horses,—Israel Morris accompanys us on this Journey as an Escort—it is what he appears desireous of.

6 left J. Roberts after Breakfast, and proceeded on to the American Picket guard, who upon hearing that we were going to head-quarters, sent 2 or 3 to guard us further on to another guard where Colll. Smith gave us a pass for Head Quarters where we arriv'd at about ½ past one;[20] requested an audience with the General—set with his Wife, (a sociable pretty kind of Woman) untill he came in; a number of Officers there, who were very complient, Tench Tillman, among the rest, it was not long before GW. came and discoarsd with us freely, but not so long as we could have wish'd, as dinner was serv'd in, to which he had invited us, there was 15 of the Officers besides the General and his Wife, Gen. Green, and G. Lee we had an eligant dinner, which was soon over; when we went out with the General Wife up to her Chamber, and saw no more of him,—he told us, he could do nothing in our busyness further than granting us a pass to Lancaster, which he did, and gave a Letter to Il. Morris for T. Wharton, after dinner, as we came out of the dining Room, who should we see, but Isaac Penington and Charles Logan, who had been taken up Yesterday at Darby, put into the Provo last night, and now brought to Head Quarters they were soon acquited, we have reason to belive that they fared the better by meeting us there, they delived up the Letters for Winchester and the rest of their Bagage to us, and are to return to Philaa. tomorrow, for which the General has given them a pass: We came all togeather to James Vauxs with JV himself who came over to invite us, cross'd the large Bridge over Schuylkill, just by his house—drank tea and lodg'd there, Rowd. Evans and Wife, came to see us in the Evening—Isel. Morris and the Lads, went to lodge with 'em, as they live near—We found the roads very bad to day. MP. and ED. often out of the Carriage—good Weather.

7 left James Vauxs after Breakfast, chang'd one of our Horses for C. Logans, found the roads exceeding bad, some of us frequently in & out, din'd at a kind Friends nam'd Randel Mellon, left his House at about 3 o'clock, and went on through deep rutts and mudd, to Robt. Valintines, where we drank tea and lodg'd, our Friends are very kind to us, making Fires in our Bed Rooms, which is comfortable, as we are but weakly, and the Season rather early for Traviling—MP. and ED. a little indispos'd this evening—a warm evening with IM.

8 left R Vallintines after Breakfast, Jacob Parke escorted us 8 or 9 miles, thro' the worst roads that we have yet mett with, to one Thos. Trumans, where we din'd on the usual fare, Bacon & Eggs—left them after dinner, and so

20. General Washington and the American forces spent the winter of 1777–78 and the spring of 1778 at Valley Forge, Pa. (Boatner, *American Revolution*, 1136–37).

journy'd on to James Moores in Sadsbury Lancaster County, where we drank tea Sup'd and Lodg'd.

9 this Morning we were visited by Becky Moore and her Husband, who Breakfasted with us—We set of after on our journey till we arrived at James Gibbons, where we din'd, his Wife is lyeing in, while we were at Dinner JG. and several other Friends came there from meeting, James Webb and Wife amoung the rest, with whome we went home and took up our aboad for a short Season, here we understood that our Friends were by an order of Council to be brought to Shipensburgh, and there discharged—this day we foarded three large Waters, Conostoga the last, which came into the Carriage and wett our Feet, and frighten'd more then one of us—it was near 5 o'clock when we came here, as soon as we had dry'd ourselves and wip'd out the Coach, we set of to Lancaster, 1½ mile, and drove directly to Thos. Whartons door, we were admitted to him and a number of others, but desird to speak to him by himself—we had about ½ hour conversation with him, not very satisfactory, as they were agoing to Coffee. we drank a dish with his Wife and the rest of the Company, then came back to J Webbs by Moonlight—where we drank tea and lodg'd—Timy. Matlack paid us a visit here this evening—S. Jones and PP. sleeps togeather, MP. is my Bed Fellow—the weather continus favourable.

10 we arose by times this Morning dress'd ourselves, and after Breakfast, went to Lancaster, several Friends went with us, I. Morris also—We allighted at Thos. Poultnys, where we din'd, Sally Greff alias Nicholson, Nancy and Polly Parr, Polly Morgan, and Sister, Saml Meredath, Moses Brinton and a number of other Friends call'd here to see us—we were this day waited upon by T Matlack, who undertook to advise us, and prehaps with sincerety—we paid a visit to 3 of the Councilors, vist. Colll. Hart,—Edgar, Hoague, and another who was not at home, we were at Timothys where one of them lives, Nelly seem'd much pleas'd to see us,—we were stop'd by numbers in the street, and at every place we came, Docr. Phile, Young Banton &c &c—after the council had set some time, T.M. came for our address, which was sign'd by all the Women concern'd, he say'd he would come for us, when it was proper, but after above an hour waiting, he inform'd us, that our presence was not necessary, and put us of in that way. We sent for Capt Lang who is one of the Guards that is to conduct our Friends to Lancaster, or any place nearer home, that we shall chuse, Shippensburg was to have been the place, but to oblidge us it was chang'd—we came back towards evening drank tea; wrote Letters to our Husbands, and to Philada.—MP. and ED— were not in Bed till near 2 o'clock in the Morning.

11 Stay'd within all day, dull weather, all but S Jones, who went to Lancaster to procure a pass for Billy Webb, T Matlack consulted Council thereon, and inform'd her on his return, that Wm. Webb could not be permitted to go

on our busyness, as he had not taken the Test. this was a great balk to us, all things being ready and Wm. booted to set off—TM. read to SJ. a copy of the orders to go with Lang, which were favourable—she came back to dinner; after consulting our Friends here, we heard of one John Musser, a Menonist, who had taken the test, and was willing to go on our erant—and as sutable as any we could find, we pack'd up the things in his Sadel-Bags and he set of before dinner, with a pass, under the lesser Seal of the province, sign'd by T. Wharton, and T Matlack,—several call'd to see us this day—Robt. [T]ewel among the rest.

12 First Day—dull rainy weather, James Webb and Wife, S. Jones, and M. Pleasants, with I. Morris, went to Meeting—P.P. and ED. stay'd within, they came home to dinner, in the Afternoon Parson Barton and Wife, Owen Biddle and Wife, and some others, came to see us—John Brown call'd.

13 Wind with clouds, James and Abraham Gibbons, Wm. Downing, and Wm. Marshal came to have some talk with us, they tell us that Benn. Mason is going to Philada. to the Meeting for Sufferings—Wm. Parr and wife, came to visit us—Thos. Dorsey came to know if we had heard of a mesenger, if we were not provided, he knew of one—it was on first day that yound Musser set of, and not on seventh day as is inserted—We went after dinner to Lancaster, with design to wait on G. Brion, Stop'd at Timy. Matlacks, who told us, if we would stay and drink tea with his Wife, he would hurry Council on their busyness, and prehaps he might bring G. Brion home with him,—when he was gone, we went over to Chrisr. Marshals Senr. who lives opposite to Timothy, stay'd there long enough, came back with Nelly Matlack, and drank tea:—Timy. on his return inform'd us that G.B. had no inclination to see us, and he believ'd[21] our visit to him might as well be omitted, We return'd to James Webbs near Evening, I. Morris who has spent this day abroad, came home this evening with very sorrowful inteligence, that he had seen Jos. Reed, who inform'd him of a Letter which he had seen, from our Friend James Pemberton, to Charles Tomson, giving an account of the death of our worthy Friend John Hunt and dangerous illness of Edwd. Penington, and further Isreal could not tell us—this has been a day of Gloom, espesaly the latter part of it,—Stormy Night.

14 went to Town before Breakfast, to look for Jos. Reed, who we mett with at one Attleys, with Thos. McClane and 2 others,—he conferm'd the account of the death of J Hunt &c—we discourc'd with 'em for some time, they appeard kind, but I fear tis from teeth outwards—T McClain went with us to G. Brions Lodgings, who was gone out, we mett with Genl Green, Clem Biddle, and several others there, they all make a show of favour—we went after

21. Word crossed out.

to Billy Parrs, where we Breakfasted,—from thence to the Presidents, set half an hour with his Wife and Sister, then came to J. Webbs, where after getting ready to depart, we bid them farewell for some days, and set of for Moses Brintons, stop'd in our way at James Gibbons, where we din'd and stay'd some time After, set of in the Afternoon and road thro' the rain, which did not incomade us to M. Brintons, where we propose to spend a few days, as we are kindly invited so to do—when Bed time came, tho the Room was clean and nice, the Beds were so damp that we were fearful of going into 'em, the Windows having been open during all the rain,—in our journey to day we found the roads so bad, that we walk'd part of the way, and clim'd 3 fences, to get clear of the mud, Isreal has enough to do with us.

15 Stay'd within all day: at Mos Brintons rain most part—in the Afternoon, Abm. Gibbons came to see us.

16 rain almost all day, it will be a Week to morrow, since we have seen a clear day: M. Brinton I. Morris and S Jones, went to Lampater meeting, the rest of us stay'd within, they return'd to tea.

17 cleard up with wind this Morning we stay'd at M Brintons till after dinner, then took Coach for Abrm. Gibbons, where we mett with Is. Morris and M Brinton who had been to meeting. Elenor Brinton and her Son Joseph accompany'd us to A Gibbons, where they left us in the Afternoon, here we continue for a time, four Soliders took up their lodging in the Kitchen this Night, who had guarded 5 men to Lancaster Jail, who had been taken up near Philada. we slep'd here Comfortably.

18 Stay'd within all day, tho' fine weather, I. Morris who lodges at M Brintons since we left it; spent this day with us; James Webb came this Morning to see us and brought 2 letters; from O Jones junr., one to his Parents, the other to T Matlack, informing that our dear Friends were generaly well, E. Penington excepted, and he geting better, they were dated the 11 Instant our Hearts feel rather lighter this evening than usual, cloudy.

19 First Day: thunder last Night, fine clear weather this morning were disturb'd in the Night with our own, and each others Dreams,—Billy Webb came this morning with a Letter to PP— from her Husband, as he thought, who he say'd was in Lancaster, which put Phebe into such a flutter that she could not read it,—it prov'd to be from Thos. Afflick who had left the company and come to Lancaster to solicite his release, to return home to his Wife, who is very ill—We went to Lampater meeting and return'd to A Gibbons to Dinner, after which set of for James Webbs; Tommy Afflick mett us at Conostoga Ferry, we were glad to see each other, and to hear of the wellfare of our dear Husbands, we came to Tea at JWs where were a number of

Friends from Lancaster &c—here we took up our lodging again;—TA. at T Poltneys Lancaster.

20 fine clear windy weather such as will dry the roads,—Billy Lewis, Owen Biddle, T. Afflick, and Danl. la Fever came this Morning to JWs After dinner John Musser return'd from Winchester with Letters from our Husbands, giving us expectation that they would be with us, here, the latter end of this Week—after we had read our Letters over and over, we went with Becky Parke &c and drank tea with O Biddle and Wife (she is Jane Webbs Daughter) T. Afflick Timy. Matlack, and I. Morris were also there, we came back to JWs in the Evening.

21st. We went to Town directly After Breakfast, alighted a Poultnys, where we mett with T. Afflick, and P. Bush our Husbands late Landlord at Winchester, he was going to Philada. on business—we took a walk to Thos. Whartons, had a conference with him, not altogeather agreeable, we call'd before we went to him on G. Brion, who appeard well dispos'd, we call'd at S. Graffs, Molly Rheas, Polly Morgans—din'd at Danl. Whitelocks, went after dinner to Parson Bartons, where we drank tea, and spent the Afternoon, came home towards evening—while we were at Whitelocks, T. Matlack came with our dear Friends sham release, and said that was the conclusion Council had come to, (of this order we each took a Copy).

22d. this has been a Holy day hereaway,—We stay'd within all day, had several visiters, T. Barton call'd—Thos. Afflick, Timy. Matlack, and David Rittenhouse drank tea with us—S Jones went with Jane Webb to Lampr. Meeting, they returnd in the Afternoon, I. Morris with them, a storm of wind and Hail this Evening.

23 Philip Bush, call'd this morning in his way to Philada.—we gave him our letters and a Packet for the Wives in Town,—Henry Hill, Thos. Dorsey and T. Afflick, came to see us,—Jams Webb went to Lancaster, brought home with him, an act of Parlament, much in favor of America.[22] We hear that a number of the British Light Horse, have lately been to Bristol, where they have taken

22. In order to forestall an American alliance with France, Lord North had introduced into the House of Commons in February a series of proposals that included the repeal of the Tea and Coercive Acts, a pledge that Parliament would not impose any revenue taxes on the American colonies, and the appointment of a peace commission to negotiate with the American colonies; these proposals passed the House of Commons on Mar. 16. The commission, known as the Carlisle Peace Commission after the earl of Carlisle, had the authority to agree to the suspension of all acts passed by Parliament since 1763 concerning the colonies (a draft of the bill appeared in the *Pa. Ledger*, Apr. 22, 1778; Morris, *Encyclopedia*, 116; the Carlisle Peace Commission is discussed in detail in Van Doren, *Secret History*, 59–116; see below, June 6, 1778).

many Prisoners[23]—We stay'd within all day, intended to have gone to Town, with a fresh address, but many things concur'd to hinder us—P.P. and myself not very well, it has been remarkably windy for a day or two, where are our dear Husbands this Night.

24 James Gibbon call'd this Morning—we went to Town after Breakfast, drove directly to the Coart-House, where we mett with George Brion and Tim Matlack, going up to Council, we presented our second address, (requesting a pass for our Friends) as the first was not answ'd to our minds, GB. said that all was granted that could be, he would not feed us up with false Hopes, we desir'd they would reconcider the matter, which he did not refuse; we had more talk with Timothy at the Door,—then went to Thos. Poultnys, and then to the week day meeting, which is held at D Witelocks—after Meeting took a short ride—towards the river,—then came to Thos. Poltneys, where we din'd, with Thos. Afflick who lodges there, while we were at dinner, TM came from Council, saying he was sorry to tell us, that nothing further could be done, towards granting our request,—We stay'd Tea at TPs—then took a walk to the Prison, intending to have visited the Prisoners, Charles Dingee and others, but could not gain admittance, as the Keeper was from home,—came to J Webbs towards evening Abm. Gibbon call'd just before night; James Pembertons negro Man Richard, came in, as a forerunner of his Master, who with Saml Pleasants, soon after entred—as I did not expect my dear Henry yet, I was not so much disapointed, as I should otherwise have been—they tell me that he is well but not able to travil so fast as some others as present, we sat chattering togeather, till after 10 o'clock—I change my Bedfellow, and now lodge with S Jones,—fine weather.

25 I can recollect nothing of the occurances of this Morning—about one o'clock my Henry arrived at J Webbs, just time enough to dine with us; all the rest of our Friends came this day to Lancaster; HD. much hartier than I expected, he look fat and well.

26 First Day: we went to Lancaster this morning where we mett with the rest of our Friends all well but E Penington, and he much mended—they had a Consultation before meeting, of Worship; which geathered about 11 o'clock, at D Whitlocks, Thos. Whartons Wife and Sister with some others were at meeting, which was not usual,—John Pemberton pray'd, We came back to JWs to dinner, my Henry din'd in Town,—the Friends mett this Evening—

23. While the main body of the American army spent the winter and spring at Valley Forge, colonial militia detachments took up positions near Philadelphia to prevent food and supplies from coming into the city. Periodically the British sent out raiding parties to attack the militia and keep food supply lines open. In a foray on Apr. 18–19, the Pennsylvania Dragoons and light infantry encountered the Bucks County Militia near Bristol and captured forty-four men, including the watch and some officers (Baurmeister, *Revolution in America*, 166).

and agreed on a applycation to send tomorrow to Counsil—Billy Lewis came this Evening—according to the request of us Women,—fine Weather—PP. MP. Wm. Webb, Becky Parke, and myself, took a walk towards Lancaster this Evening as we had done Yesterday Evening.

27 We women stay'd all day at James Webbs, were visited by several menonists, and many others—Ellenor Brinton, Josey Brinton, Becky Moore, Wm. Downing &c &c—our Friends apply'd to Counsil this Morning for a proper discharge, which was not comply'd with, but a permission to pass to Potts-Grove, in the County of Philada. was all they would grant—Isreal Pemberton, Thos. Wharton, Thos. Afflick, Charles Jervis, Charles Eddy, the 3 Fishers, Owen Jones, and Elijah Brown, left us, and went homewards, we and our Husbands continue this Night at J Webbs.

28 Wm. Parr and Wife call'd this Morning to see us, before we went, Ed. Penington and Wm. Smith set off this Morning—about 8 o'clock we took leave of the Family and turn'd our Faces homewards—I. Morris and James Pemberton went with us, Saml. Pleasants soon overtook us—My Henry stayd behind with John Pemberton, we mett Becky Moore, Wm. Downing, Abrm. Gibbon and Wife, on the road going to visit us—the two later turn'd back, with us, as far as James Gibbons, the two former went to meet JP. and HD—— who went with them the Sadsbury road; we took Lancaster, so that I did not see my HD untill evening when we mett at Robert Valentines, where we lodg'd and were very kindly entertain'd, except John Pemberton who stay'd at Thos. Pims, a mile or two distant,—our part of the Company din'd to day at one Millers.

29th. detain'd at R Valentines somtime after Breakfast, to repair the Carriage, which had given way the day before; MP and ED, step'd over to Richd. Downings where we stay'd but a short time, had a meeting at RVs with Thos. and Susaa. Lightfoot, Thos. Pym, Richd. Downings Wife and Sister, ourselves and the Family, Susanna appear'd in Testimony—We left Downingtown about 10 o'clock; proceeded on to Robt Joness above 17 miles, where we din'd, JP. and HD. did not join us (having stop'd at Randel Mellens) till just before we arriv'd at Robt. Joness here I. Morris came to us, from Washingtons Head Quarters to which place he went in the morning and brought a pass for all our Company Horses &c—after dinner we went on to J. Roberts being frequently stop'd by Guards, poasted on the road in diferant places,—at JRs we are now going to Bed.

30 After Breakfast we had a setting at John Robertss John Pemberton, speak to the Family, we set of after 8 o'clock, and traveled on without interuption, were wellcom'd by many before, and on our entrence into the City—where we arrived about 11 o'clock, and found our dear Families all well, for which favour and Blessing and the restoration of my dear Husband, may I ever be

thankful—We have had such a number of our Friends to see us this day, that it is not in my power to enumerate them.

May 1st.[24] cloudy weather, too many of our Friends here to day; for to perticularize.

May 2 visitors from Morning to Night—my HD. not very well, fine Weather.

3d. First Day: HD. MS. and the Children went to meeting this Morning myself in the afternoon, Several Friends at tea with us.

4 Went to Quarterly Meeting, call'd at Uncle Jerviss and at several Shops,—went out again after dinner to Shops, bought merceals Quilting[25] for Peticoats for the Girls—Campany here this Afternoon.

5 went to Youths Meeting this Morning Company in the Afternoon.

6 Stay'd at home all day: S Swett din'd with us, S. and M. Pleasants, spent the evening, partly settld our acct of journey, much company here to day, fine weather.

7 visitors this Morning John and Hannah Pemberton here this Afternoon, which prevented me from going to Jas. Pembertons according to appointment, I went however after tea, found My Henry, Saml. and M. Pleasants there, came home in the Evening.

8 Stay'd within all day: Israel Pemberton, Thos. Fisher, Saml. Fisher, Abel James, Joshua Howel, Edwd. Penington, Sam. Emlen, Becky James junr. here this Morning Richd. Waln, Isaac Hornor and S Swett din'd with us—Sally Moore and Daughter John Drinker, M. Pleasants junr. call'd—we had a meeting here this afternoon,[26] of the Friends who are visiting Families, Sam. Emlen, Sam. Smith, C. West, David Eastaugh, Margy. Norton, and Mary Cowper, the two Samuels, and David had something to say—broak up about Dusk, Sammy Sanson and J.C. spent the Evening—it is reported that War is declared with France,[27]—the situation of things at present is far from agreeable.

24. The word "fine" crossed out.

25. Cloth associated with Marseilles, France, a center for fine quilted petticoats and coverlets consisting of two layers of cloth, with backing in between for the raised pattern on the quilt or petticoat. Similar cloth, known as Marseilles, Marcella, or Marsella, was also imported from England in the eighteenth century (Montgomery, *Textiles*, 289–92).

26. The word "with" crossed out.

27. The war between England and France did not begin formally until June 17 (Boatner, *American Revolution*, 400–401).

9 Stay at home all day; fine cool weather, Ay. Benezet and J.C. drank tea with us, John Drinker, R. Jones, Abel James, [Wr.] [Shes] Wife, and Sally Pancost call'd—General Clinton, arrived here Yesterday[28]—Isaac Catheral's Shop was rob'd, last seventh day Night, of goods amounting to 100£ in value—my Henry has been unwell for several days past, with disordred Bowels.

10 First day: I went to meeting this Afternoon, step'd over to Neigr. Walns after tea,—Wm. Brown, John Parish, John Hill, Becky Jones and Hannah Catheral, drank tea with us—a part of the Army that went some days ago, up the River; are return'd, they have burnt several Houses and a number of Shipping; what more has not yet come to my knowledge.

11 I spent this Afternoon with poor Lydia Gillpin, who is under great Affliction—several here this day.

12 Went to Meeting this Morning—spent the Afternoon with Rachl. Hunt, Sam. and M. Pleasants, here this evening.

13 HD. was let Blood this Morning a very fine day: stay'd at home; but little Company Jos. Bringhurst, spent part of the Evening.

14 Sam Emlen, J. Bringhurst, and A James call'd this Morning I spent part of the afternoon at Neigr. Walns,—Wm. Ford and Molly Pleasant drank tea with us—J.C. had a Consert this Afternoon, 7 or 8 officers with him, Docr. Knowles one of them, came into our Parlor, and had some talk with my Henry—Richd. Waln call'd—John Drinker and Sam Sansom sup'd with us—there is some movements in the Army, which we do not rightly understand, the heavy Cannon are ordred on board the Ships, and some other things look Mysterious—it is very fine weather.

15 spent this Afternoon at Jos. Howels—HD. and Colll. Gordon who quarters there drank tea with us—I went down Town this Morning to look for Silk, warm weather, Owen Jones, and John Nancarrow, call'd I took a Cardas Vomit this Evening having been disordred at Stomach all day.

16 I stay'd at home all day: Wm. Smith Bror. here this morning a fine Shower this Afternoon; some of the Officers have orders, to pack up their Bagage &c.

28. Gen. William Howe's resignation as commander of the British army had been accepted on Feb. 4. Gen. Henry Clinton, who was appointed to replace him, arrived in Philadelphia on May 8 (Gruber, *Howe Brothers*, 224–303).

17 First Day: John Forman din'd with us—Richd. Waln, and D. Drinker, drank Coffee.

18 this day may be rememberd by many, from the Scenes of Folly and Vanity, promoted by the Officers of the Army under pretence of shewing respect to Gen. Howe, now about leaving them—the parade of Coaches and other Carriages with many Horsemen, thro' the Streets towards the No. Liberties, were great numbers of the Officers & some Women embark'd in three Galleys, and a number of boats, and pass'd down the River, before the City, with Colours display'd, a large Band of Music, and the Ships in the Harbour decorated with Colours, saluted by the Cannon of some of them; it is said they landed in south wark, and proceeded from the waterside to Joseph Whartons late dwelling, which has been decorated and fitted for this occasion—in an expensive way, for this Company to Feast, Dance, and Revel in,—on the River Sky-Rockets and other Fire Works, were exhibited after Night.—How insensible do these people appear, while our Land is so greatly desolated, and Death and sore destruction has overtaken and impends over so many.—this Morning M. Pleasants and Debh. Norris call'd, in the Afternoon, Wm. Norton, Wm. Cowper and Edward Penington, Betsy Waln came to Town this Afternoon,—Ducks hatch'd Yesterday.

19 Went to Meeting this Morning step'd over to Neigr. Walns to see Sucky who is unwell, Sally Zane came here this Morning to invite HD. and myself to dinner with John and Hannah Pemberton, we went, Sally Dr. with us—HD. left us after dinner my Sally and self spent the Afternoon there—Johnny Pemberton came home with us, found De Demarsan Anspach Officer, who quarters at Folwells at tea with sister &c—a large number of the British Troops march'd out this evening the Light Horse and Cannon, also—wether they expect an attack from Washington, or wether they are going after him, remains unknown, we have heard firing since Night, somthing is going [f]oward, which I must confess raises my apprehension.

20 the large body of Troops which went out last night, return'd to day: about 2 o'clock having done nothing to purpose,—Our Major who went this Morning at 5 o'clock—came home to dinner—Richd. and Betsy Waln din'd with us—I went out after tea with Betsy, call'd at Bent. Dorseys, and at Nany Powels, parted with BW at Chesnut street, and went to Sam Pleasants, stay'd but a short time there, came away with Tommy and Sally Fisher thro' a small rain, parted with 'em and came home before night—Sammy Fisher spent this Evening with us—Martha Harris appear'd in a very particular manner at the Pine-Street Meeting to day, as she did Yesterday at our Meeting House,—Sam. Emlen, Abel James call'd.

21st. HD. went this Afternoon to the Burial of Phineas Pemberton, Myself

Sally and Nancy spent the Afternoon at Owen Joness Grace Galloway there—HD. came to us after tea, we went togeather towards evening to Benjn. Poltneys, where we stay'd but a short time—Our dear little Molly was taken unwell last Night, and continues so to day, disordrd Stomach and Bowels, with a fever—the weather warm—M. Harris appeard to day at the Middle Meeting as at the two others.

22 Molly all day very feverish and unwell, the Officers have orders to put their Bagage on board the Vesels, our Major pack'd up his matters to day for that purpose—Molly Pleasants, Becky Jones &c call'd.

23 little Molly sick and feverish, her Mouth sore this evening I am fearful of an Aptha Fever which she was bad with while I was absent last Month at Lancaster—the Army tis thought are going in reality to leave us—to evacuate the City[29]—some hope tis not the case, tho' things look like it—many of the Inhabitants are preparing to go with them,—Robt. Waln, Reba. Waln, Richd. Waln, Abel James, Saml. Emlen, Reba. Jones, Molly Pleasants, Sucky Jones, here to day—fine weather.

24th. First Day: I stay'd at home all day—little Mollys fever continues,—the Officers Bagage going on board all day, the people talk confidently now of their leaving us—Sammy Shoemaker, Danl. Cox, and many others, are preparing to go with them—Abel James, John Drinker, Wm. Smith, Docr. Redman, Richd. Waln, Henry Drinker, Caty Howel, Becky Jones, Han. Catheral, Rach. Drinker, S. Swett, and a man from the Iron Works call'd—the weather warm.

25 a Number of the Cityzins are in great distress, on account of this movement of the British Army; My dear little Molly very poorly, she took a vomitt this evening which work'd but little, her fever is not quite so high as, heretofore,—HD. went to Kingsington this Afternoon to meet Lawe. Salter, whome he has not seen for a long time our major sent his things away this Morning he is at a loss, or appears so, as are many others, what to think of the present appearance of things amongst us—Abel James, Reba. James, and Becky James, John Drinker, Docr. Redman, Jos. Howel, Widw. Gordon call'd.

26 I stay'd at home all day: Molly very poorly, Sister out at Shops—John James din'd with us—My Henry, Sister and the Children went to Monthly

29. After negotiations with colonial forces, the British army, under the command of General Clinton, agreed to turn control of the city over to General Washington and withdraw their troops on June 18 (George M. Wrong, *Washington and His Comrades in Arms* [New Haven, Conn.: Yale University Press, 1921], 196).

meeting—many in Town are in much affliction, at this time, some quite otherwise,—Richd. and Betsy Waln, Reba. Waln, Robt. Waln, Edwd. Penington, Sally Penington, Billy Smith, Docr. Redman, Thos. Fisher, Sally Fisher, Becky Jones, Wm. Coopers Wife from the Ferry—Sammy Emlen junr. Dan Drinker Jos. Scott, Miers Fisher, Sam Sanson, Molly Pleasants, and Wm. Foard call'd, Heavysides Wife drank tea, with us, a visitor of the majors—fine moderate weather.

27 little Molly continues very poorly we remain in suspence with respect to publick affairs—Docr. Redman, Wm. Smith, Neddy Penington, Hannah Catheral, Jos. Howel, call'd Sammy Smith, deliver'd up the monthly meeting Book to HD—rain this Evening.

28 I stay'd within all day, Molly took a purge, which work'd her very little, Abel James, John Green, J Drinker &c the weather very cool.

29 so cold this Morning that we have a fire in the Stove, Molly something better, little Henry taken with a lax and vomitting, which continu'd all the forenoon, in the Afternoon he seem'd a little better, Molly took a small pill this evening—HD. went to the Burial of our Neigr. Well's Child, who dy'd of the small-Pox—Abel James, Jos. Howel, Robt. Waln, James Logan, John Drinker Docr. Redman, Saml. Emlen and John Parrock call'd; Sister out this Afternoon.

30 Henry better, Molly still poorly—tis reported that the British Army are giving the remainder of their Stores of Wood and Hay, to the poor, which seems to prove they intend 'eer long to leave us—John Head and one Hurst, John Green, Sammy Sansom, Israel Pemberton, C. West, Richd. Waln, Dr. Redman, John Drinker, Becky Jones, Reba. Waln, and Sucky Jones call'd—very cool for the Season.

31 First Day: Stay'd within all day: cold with rain, Rich'd. Waln, John Drinker Docr. Redman call'd—J.C. din'd with us—little Molly took a pill this evening.

June 1 rain almost all day: Saml. Pleasants John Drinker, Docr. Redman, John Burket call'd.

2d. fine weather, I went to Meeting this Morning S. Swett din'd and drank tea, Sally Logan spent the Afternoon, Robt. Waln, Sam Sansom, Thos. York and Andw. Roberson, Jos. Howel, Becky James junr. &c call'd.

3d. No News to day. all things quiet, Owen Jones and Wife, Sucky Jones, Robt. Proud and J.C— drank tea with us—Thos. Fisher and Wife, Hetty

Fisher, Thos. Roberson, John Drinker, Christr. White call'd—little Molly still poorly—Dr. Redman here, fine weather.

4 Nancy and myself spent this Afternoon at Saml. Emlens, Richd. Waln, and J.C—drank tea with Sister, Reba. Waln here this Evening Christopher Kenat and Jack, busy making fire works to Celebrate the Kings birth Day—Molly still unwell, cloudy and cold.

5 several call'd. I took a walk in the Afternoon call'd at S. Pleasants.

6 The Commissioners are arrived to day:[30] from England, Ld. Corn Wallace also—they bring accounts tis said, that there is no likelyhood of a War with France, &c. a visit from Gen. Washington, is not so soon expected, as a day or 2 past, or does it look so likely that the British Troops will so soon leave us—a Vesel is below with the Cargo of provisions, which our Friends wrote for, and permision is granted for her coming up, Any. Benezet, Davd.[31] Bacon, Docr Redman, and J.C—drank tea with us—James Bringhurst, Jos. Howel, Robt. Waln, and Wife, Becky Jones, John Drinker, call'd—the face of things seems again chang'd—Chalkley and Josey James lodges here to Night, Molly still unwell, the weather rather cool for the Season.

7 First Day: I went to Meeting this Afternoon, my little one better, S Swett din'd and drank tea with us, Molly Pleasants, Sally Jones, and Debby Norris, with our Girls this Afternoon, several call'd.

8 orders this day for the 2 Regments of Anspachs to embark, Our Major, goes with them,—I went this Afternoon, Nancy with me, as far as Nany Powels, the Troops appear all in motion talk again of their leaving us intirely, the Major very busy sending the remainder of his things on Board, Jack gone with them—Major Williams, and Capt Ford call'd to bid J.C adieu—Abel James, John Drinker, Henry Drinker &c call'd—Harry Catter left us to day, he has undertaken to drive a Waggon in the Army, I wish the poor Fellow may come to no harm,—Molly Brookhouse brought her Daughter Nancy to day, I beleive she is too little and too weakly to be of much use—J.C. sup'd. with us—he is gone to Bed, to be call'd up at one o'clock—to go of with his Company—Christopher and [Rillard] here, I intend to set up 'till they are gone.

30. The members of the Carlisle Peace Commission were the earl of Carlisle, William Eden, Adm. Lord Richard Howe, Gen. William Howe, and George Johnstone. The Howe brothers were already in America, and the other commissioners sailed from Portsmouth, England, on Apr. 16, arriving in Philadelphia on June 6. Lord Cornwallis, on board the same vessel, was returning to Philadelphia to become General Clinton's second-in-command (Van Doren, *Secret History*, 59–85).

31. The name "Drinker" crossed out.

9 The Major left us at a little past one, this Morning, was very dull at takeing leave,—Sister and self stay'd at the Door untill the two Regiments, (which quarter'd up Town) had past—J.C. bid us adieu as they went by—and we saw no more of them, a fine moon-light Morning—HD. busyely employ'd for a day or 2 past, on committes to settle properly this Cargo of provisions—Saml. Emlen, Ed. Penington, Richd. Waln, John Drinker, Abel James, Reba. Waln, call'd—Major Williams here to day for J.C.s Horse, which he left for him,—Christopher and the Hessian stays here till another party of the Army goes of by Land to take J.C. Horses—one or 2 Regiments went this Afternoon.

10 Charles West and Wife, Peggy Hart, Sammy Hopkins Saml. Noble, here this Morning—they mett here, in order to visit some Families in this Neighbourhood—Jessy Waln, Polly Pleasants Senr. Abel James, Elijah Brown, Saml. Coats, &c call'd—Christopher and [Rillard] came in this Afternoon with a Story, that the 2 Anspach Regiments were taken, somewhere where they had landed—I step'd into J Howels to ask Colll. Gordon, what he thought of the report, he was gone out—I find this evening it does not gain Credit—my H——y was taken this evening with a Collicey paid in his Bowels, is gone to Bed, very unwell—rain this evening.

11 HD. unwell all day took Rheubarb—Colll. Starling and another Officer call'd this Morning to enquire for the Major: I am surpris'd they did not know he was gone; Richd. Waln drank tea with us—C. West and John Drinker sup'd with us—Saml. Rhoads, Robt. Waln, Reba. Waln call'd, the latter says that she heard the Anspachers were coming back, I think it is a Mistake, a Shower this evening.

12 Cool pleasant weather, Molly Brookhouse here all day, Cleaning House—HD. something better, 'tho not well, Abel James, Saml. Pleasants, O.Jones jun Sammy Fisher, Reba. James, Saml. Smith, John Drinker, Any. Benezet &c call'd—I feel myself very forlorn this Evening.

13 a very fine day: 'tis reported that the Troops are to leave us, on second day next, if we may judge from appearances, it dont look unlikely; Jos. Howel, John Drinker, Richd. Waln, S. Emlen, Wm. Norton call'd—Saml. Pleasants drank tea with us, I went home with him, and spent an hour with Polly, call'd in my return, at Uncle Jerviss and at Saml. Sansoms, HD— is unwell, myself not extrodinary.

14 First Day: remarkably fine weather, Richd. Waln din'd with us, he seems at a loss how to determine, wether to stay or go—Our Harry took leave of us to day, he is gone into the Jerseys where a large number of the Troops are encamp'd—opposite the City, I wrote a few lines to J.C— in order to send by Christopher, who expects to go early in the Morning—I step'd in to Neigr.

Howels, this Evening and over to Neigr. Walns—I went to meeting this Afternoon, Eliza. Morris came home with me, she and Robt. Proud drank tea with us—Sister went with her towards evening to visit E. Norris who is very poorly.

15 3 Regiments of Hessians pass'd our Door to take Boat up Town—I have felt myself very poorly all this day. as have many others,—Richd. Waln, Samy. Emlen, Jessy Waln, Reb. Waln Wm. Ford, Molly Pleasants, call'd—we have had many fine days, I mean good weather—Christopr. is to go tomorrow, poor fellow is much affected.

16 The Troops Moving all day, Christr. and [Rillard] made a Second attempt with the Majors Horses, to cross the River, but came back in the Evening so that we have them another Night in the House—I went to meeting this Morning Sally went with me before dinner to Nanny Powels—Isaac Zane, S. Smith, Sl. Emlen, Nics. Waln, Richd. Waln, Jessy Waln, John Drinker, Wm. Ford S. Swett, Becky Jones, Aunt and Betsy Jervis, Jos. Howel call'd—Sally Logan, drank tea with us, Enh. Story took leave of us, he and his Family are going with the Fleet—fine Weather continues.

17 Troops still crossing the River, vast Numbers are gone over, and many continue with us yet—HD. [J]P. IZ. & SS— endeavour'd to day to speak to the General, he had not time to attend them—Capt. Ford and Richd. Waln, took leave of us to day, as did our John Burket, Sammy Shoemaker and Dan Cox is gone on board one of the Vesels, and many other of the Inhabitants, J. Drinker Reba. Waln, &c call'd—the Weather is very warm to day:—engag'd Black Peter to take care of the Cows.

18 last night it was said there was 9000 of the British Troops left in Town 11,000 in the Jersyes: this Morning when we arose, there was not one Red-Coat to be seen in Town; and the encampment, in the Jersys vanish'd[32]—Colll. Gordon and some others, had not been gone a quarter of an hour before the American Light-Horse enter'd the City, not many of them, they were in and out all day A Bell-Man went about this evening by order of one Coll. Morgan, to desire the Inhabatants, to stay within doors after Night, that if any were found in the street by the Partrole, they should be punish'd—the few that came in today, had drawn Swords in their Hands, Gallop'd about the Streets in a great hurry, many were much frightn'd at their appearance.—Richd. and

32. After withdrawing from Philadelphia on June 18, Clinton began to move his troops through New Jersey toward New York. Washington broke camp at Valley Forge on June 19 and pursued the British forces (William B. Willcox, "British Strategy in America, 1778," *Journal of Modern History* 19 [1947]: 110).

Jessy Waln, went away early this Morning J. Drinker Jammy Logan call'd—fine weather.

19 The English have in reality left us—and the other party took possesion, again they have been coming in all day, the old inhabetance, part of the Artilery, some Soliders &c—Washington and his army are not come, 'tis said they are gone otherways—Robt. Waln & Wife Benn. Mason, D. Drinker, J. Drinker and S. Emlen call'd—rain last night.

20 rain: George Morgan, Hilly. Baker C. West, S. Smith, J. Drinker, Jos. Howel, and S. Emlen call'd.

21st. First Day: R Jones, J. Drinker here this Morning Becky and Hannah din'd with us, Robt. Proud drank tea, Danl. Drinker call'd. many reports conserning the British Army, but nothing to be depended on.

22 dull rainy weather an account of a Battle in the Jersyes, the perticulars not known, no great one—the Store and Shop-keepers, orderd to shut up, and render an account of their goods[33]—Reb Waln and John Drinker call'd.

23 Bancroft Woodcock came here to day, from Willmington, he lodges with us, S Swett din'd and spent the Afternoon James Logan, John Drinker call'd—the British Troops are said to be near Trentown, the fleet near Reedy-Island we are troubled this Summer, for abo't. a week past, with an unusual number of Flies—Cloudy cool weather, Billy went to Edgely with Neddy Howel.

24 The Sun was eclypts'd this Morning 11½ Digets,[34] almost toutal, it was not so obscure as I expected—B. Woodcock sup'd and lodges with us—he goes away tomorrow morning—Robt. Waln, D. Drinker John Drinker Jos. Bringhurst, Sucky Hartshorn call'd—Betsy Drinker and Abey drank Tea with us, fine weather the dealers are forbid selling their goods so that it is very dificult to get any thing. We had this Morning a very plentiful market, but as the Country People could not get goods for their produce, tis to be fear'd it will not be the case much longer, Saml. Arolds Son call'd.

33. On June 4 Washington had ordered that once Philadelphia was occupied by American troops, measures should be taken to prevent the removal, transfer, and sale of all British goods and merchandise in the possession of the inhabitants. Gen. Benedict Arnold, who became the city's military governor following the American reentry on June 18, issued these orders as a proclamation on June 19, in effect closing all private shops until individual owners could make lists of their goods. The shops reopened a week later (*JCC*, 11:571; *Pa. Archives*, ser. 1, 6:606; Scharf and Westcott, *Philadelphia*, 1:385–86).

34. A unit of measure one-twelfth the diameter of the sun or moon (*OED*, s.v. "digit").

25 John Hopkins, Sammy Fisher, Saml. Sansom, drank tea with us—warm weather—Black Peter left us this evening he is going to make Hay.

26 warmer than Yesterday: O Jones jun. Caty Howel, Robt. Waln, Benn. Swett, call'd—Small Frogs, some call 'em Toads, are remarkably numerous about the No. Subburbs of this City—I have heard much talk of them—a great fireing has been heard to day by many, which lasted several hours, tis very warm weather for such dreadful busyness.

27 it is repoarted that it was thunder, that was head yesterday, and not the fireing of Cannon as many thought,—a diffrent Story is told by others that many were slain near Crosswicks,[35] the truth of the matter is not yet come out—the thomometer is to day 5 degrees above Summer heat, I spent this Afternoon at Neigr. Walns—Sister went to see Sally Wharton, who is bad with a sore Leg—John Kibble, Zacy. Vanluvenagh, O Jones junr. J. Drinker, Sarah Mitchel, Molly Pleasants, here to day—Billy has larnt to Swin, as I discoverd to day, by his wet hair.

28 First Day: I went to meeting afternoon and Evening HD. myself and Billy sup'd at Saml. Pleasants—S. Swett, John Parish and Wife, drank tea with us—exceeding warm to day—Molly Roberthom, R. Waln, call'd.

29 Sammy Trimble came to Town this Morning he lodges with us—Nanny Oat call'd,—Sister told her to come tomorrow evening for her Cloths, Reba. Waln, John Pleasants &c here this Afternoon—the report of there having been a Battle is contradicted.

30 very warm, Robt. Valentine, Becky Jones, Sus. Lightfoot, Saml. Trimble, Sam Emlen, here before meeting. I went to meeting—SL—and S Emlen appeard in testimony, James Bringhurst and Hannah Peters were married—Lawrance and Dolly Salter din'd with us—Nany Oat here this Evening—gave her part of her Cloths—she is to call again for the rest,—Reba. Waln, and Capt. Spains widdow call'd—it is said that there has been a great Battle on First day last,[36] that great numbers of the British Troops were slain and taken, a young Solider that is disorderd in his senses, went up our Stairs this Afternoon, we had no man, in the House: Isaac Catheral came in and went up after him, found him in the entry up two pair Stairs, saying his prayers—he readly came down with him. Jenny up stairs all day, unwel with the Collick.

35. A battle between Hessian troops and American forces took place at Crosswicks, N.J., on June 23 (WPA, *New Jersey*, 571).

36. The Battle of Monmouth, N.J., June 28, in which each side lost approximately three hundred men. More than six hundred British soldiers deserted and made their way to Philadelphia (Boatner, *American Revolution*, 716–25).

July 1 The Thromomoter this Afternoon up to 91—Jos. Howels at 96½—Lawrence and Dolly Salter bid us farewel Sister and Sally out after tea.

2 The Congress came in to day: fireing of Cannon on the Occasion—rain and thunder this Afternoon. I hope it will be cooler—Reba. Waln drank tea with us Wm. Smith [Bror.] call'd—a Man with a Letter from Hannah Stevenson to Sister, which she answr'd this evening Sally Zane call'd.

3d. George Mead call'd this Afternoon John Balderston sup'd an Lodg'd here, rain almost all day.

4 Ezekel Cleaver, Wm. Smith, S. Emlen, S. Pleasants, Suky Hartshorn, Becky Jones, John Drinker, call'd. Jos[] Burr. and John Balderston din'd with us.—A great fuss this evening it being the Annaversary of Independance, fireing of Guns, Sky Rockets &c—Candles were too scarce and dear, for Alluminations, which prehaps sav'd some of our Windows—A very high Head dress was exhibited thro the Streets, this Afternoon on a very dirty Woman with a mob after her, with Drums &c. by way of rediculing that very foolish fashon—a Number of Prisoners brought in to day: moderate weather.

5 First Day: Saml Harold breakfasted with us, Sam Emlen, Sam. Hopkins, C. West, Debby Norris, Sally Jones, call'd—Any. Benezet and Molly Pleasants drank tea with us—I went to meeting afternoon and evening—went to the Burial of Wm. Smiths Child, Nancy with me, call'd at Uncles, and at Wm. Fishers—step'd this Evening into Jos. Howels, Neddy has had somthing of the Flux, fine weather.

6 My Henry unwell with disordred Bowels, he took Rheubarb, as the Flux is about, I am uneasy on his account—Sally is also complaining in the same way—we hir'd Black Isaac to day Billy gone to Frankford this Afternoon with Tommy James, he has been troubled for some days past with a bad pain in his Ear. I went this Afternoon little Henry with me, to Saml. Pleasants Polly gone abroad, stay'd a little time there, talking with Joice Benezet, call'd at Townsends Speakmans for medicines—came home to Tea, James Logan, there—Saml. and M. Pleasants sup'd with us—Sarah Watson from Bucks County, and Suky Hudson here this Morning—Jams. Berry, Wm. Clarke, Patty Smith, Becky James, J. Drinker, Wm. Parr, Robt. Waln, and Jos. Howel call'd.

7 Went to Meeting this Morning unwell while there, a Wedding at meeting Plankinghorn and Hart, Nics. Waln and S. Emlen appd.—S Swett came home with me, she spent the day—Sally very ill all day, with a vomitting and Flux—sent for the Doctor this Evening My Henry continus poorly, tho' he attended the adjournment of the Monthly meeting—myself bad this Afternoon with a

Head Ach and vomitting, and paind Bowels—am better this Evening—the weather warmer.

8 very warm to day: Sally very ill, with the vomitting and Flux, above 30 stools to day, she took a vomitt this Morning and I gave her a Clyster this Evening she has a great deal of fever,—HD. continues disordr'd in his Bowels, I have been realy ill in that way myself this day: and tho not well, am better this evening—Jenney taken with a vomitting this evening—Billy came from Frankford this afternoon, S Swett, R. Drinker, Reba. Waln, Betsy and Polly Jervis, Be[c] Jones, Robt. Waln, J. Drinker, Saml. Emlen, Dd. Eastaugh and the Doctor call'd—numbers in the City are ill with the Flux. I wish I could get Molly Moore, but find I cannot—Sally takes Anodynes.

9 our dear Girl continus very ill, the vomitting not left her, Flux very bad—weather very warm, she took a dose of Rheubarb, which partly came up, I then made 2 pills of Rheubarb, which stay'd down, and work'd her in the Afternoon twice,—she took an Anodine again, slepd but very poorly—Sister and myself up all night, a number of our Friends here to day.

10 exceeding Hott my poor Child very ill, continues sick at her Stomach, and frequently vomitts quantities of dark green Boile, which as the Weather is so warm, gives me great uneasyness, she took to day 3 Spoonfulls of Castor-Oyl—one of which she vomitted up, it work'd her twice, she is very low this evening—I have not had my cloaths of since 3d. day Night, and tis now sixth day: little Henry and Billy are both unwell,—Lidia Stretch was bury'd Yesterday, she dy'd of the Flux,—Robt and Reba. Waln, Caty Howel, H. Catheral, Molly Pleasants, Sally Logan, Sam Emlen, Dr. Redman, Charles, Betsy and Polly Jervis, Saml. Pleasants, Reba. Jones, &c here.

11 Sally continus very ill, tho the calls are not so frequent, she complains of a great oppression at Stomach, and sickness; Reba. Waln, Becky Jones, Katty Howel, John and Abey Parish, Wm. Smith, Docr. Cowper, John Drinker, Docr. Redman, E. Clever call'd—John Vangeasel Breakfasted here—rain with thunder.

12 First Day: weather more moderate Sally not much better, she took Castor-Oyl which makes her very sick, it work'd but once, and the Disorder seem'd to increase after it was over I gave her a Clister last night, which flutter'd her very much, the oppression has not left her—cool to day: Aunt and Betsy Jervis, S. Swett, R. Scattergood, R. Jones, Betsy Drinker, Sally Zane, Sally Jones, Betsy Hough, John and Rac Drinker, Docr. Redman, D. Drinker, Josey Waln, call'd—Betsy Jervis sets up to Night, I have not been fairly in Bed, since 3d day night last; only laid down in my cloaths.

13 Sallys disorder is scarcly check'd, tho we hope she is something better, the fever being less—Billy unwell this evening with pain in his Bowels and bloody Stools we gave him Mollasses and Butter, cloudy, with some rain, Abel James, John Pemberton, Edwd. Drinker, Doctor, Sally Pleasants, Debby Norris, Sally Jones, Isaac Norris, Robt Waln, Neigr Catheral, Becky Jones, call'd, S Sansom drank tea.

14 Sally appeard better this Morning but in the Afternoon, her disorder returnd, and fever increas'd—the weather very fine—Saml Esborn din'd and drank tea with us—Saml. and Sally Emlen, Reba. Say, Reba. James, Saml. Pleasants, Molly Pleasants, Patty Smith, Doctor Davd. Eastaugh, John Drinker Sam Smith, Jos. Howel Hannah Carthral Senr. call'd—C. West and Wife, Lydia Noble, Isaac Jacksons Wife, Nics. Waln, Aunt Jervis, Betsy and Polly, Sally Logan, and Parson Murry and Wife, drank tea with us—Wm. Fisher was had up Yesterday before the Council, for saying something inemical, and secuerity was given.

15 Sally took a dose of Rheubarb to day she is still very bad, the Flux continues complains of an inward coldness, takes Anodines every Night, and yet in some respects appears better—My Henry has been for several days past engag'd with other Friends, visiting Families, Esther Trimble, Rachel Trimble, din'd with us, John Pemberton, Bob. Stevenson, Wm. Smith, C. West and Wife, Lidia Noble, Saml. Esborn, Nics. Waln, James Logan, Becky Jones, Han. Catheral, Polly Pleasants, Reba Waln call'd.

16 Sally much as Yesterday—complains of a fullness in her Throat—Bob Stevenson here this Morning he took several things for Hannah, which Sister had bought for her,—Betsy and Polly Jervis, S Swett, Debby and Isaac Norris, Sally Jones, Abel James, Ephram Blain, John Parish, Betsy Drinker &c call'd.

17 The weather very fine for our Sick Child, she is I hope on the mending hand,—the accounts from Backwards are, that the Indians are committing great raviges there[37]—Dr. Redman, Hannah Catheral, Becky Jones, Reba. Waln, Josey Waln, Hannah West, Ly. Noble, Molly Cowper, Peggy Hart, C West, Nics Waln, Docr. Cowper, [S] Esborn, Robt. Proud, John Drinker, Isreal Pemberton, D Eastaugh, call'd—Samuel Emlen and Thos. Evans din'd here.

37. The Wyoming Valley Massacre took place on July 3–4, when Maj. John Butler, commanding a force of approximately 1,000 Indians and loyalist volunteers, attacked the rebel fort in the Wyoming Valley, a twenty-five-mile area of Pennsylvania along the Susquehannah River below the mouth of the Lackawanna River that includes modern-day Wilkes-Barre. All but 60 of the 360 American soldiers were killed; many were also scalped (Boatner, *American Revolution*, 1221–28).

18 a number of Friends here to day—Sally neither better nor worse.

19 First Day Sally very feverish and her Stools bad—several call'd.

20 Sally more unwel to day, with greater pain in her Bowels, and vomitting—many call'd to day.

21 Sally had a bad night, sick at Stomach and fever, she took a dose of Rheubarb, which had a good Effect—and she seems better this Evening—S Swett din'd with us—Sam Pleasants Thos. Fisher, John Pemberton, Reba. Jones, Reba. Waln, Rach. Drinker, Ben[n]. Shreve from Winchester, Dicky Wharton, Doctor.

22d. I am sorry to say that our Child does not yet appear to be on the recovery.—tho I hope she is not worse, cloudy dull weather—Doctor here this morning—Becky Wright, Betsy Drinker, Rachel Drinker, Han. Catheral, Saml Hopkins, John Drinker, Joseph Bringhurst, and Auther Howel call'd—the latter had something in the preaching way, to say, to our Children down Stairs—Sally better this evening.

23 Sally lay doseing untill near 4 this Afternoon, the Anodine last night did not lull her, she lay awake almost all night, she set up this Afternoon and seems better, Sally Logan spent the Afternoon, Reba. Waln Molly Pleasants, Hannah Drinker, Hannah and Patty Jones, James Logan, John Parish, Nics. Waln, Robt. Waln, Jos. Bringhurst Molly Gesnold, and Docr. Redman call'd, I spent great part of this day writeing, was very sick at my stomach this morning and again this evening—they have taken an account Yesterday or the Day before, of Sammy Shoemakers and Joseph Galloways property, and several others, with design to Confiscate,[38] moderate weather.

38. In September 1777 the Council of Safety, which acted in emergencies when the Pennsylvania Assembly was not in session, had passed a confiscation ordinance, appointing commissioners with wide powers to examine witnesses and papers, break open doors, jail those who resisted their authority, and call for civil and military personnel. The council specified in October that persons who joined the British or fled to a place under British possession might have their personal estates seized. The commissioners for Philadelphia city were William Will, Sharp Delaney, Jacob Schriner, Charles Willson Peale, Robert Smith (hatter), and Samuel Massey. On Mar. 6, 1778, the Pennsylvania Assembly added the right to seize real estate as well and gave the Supreme Executive Council the right to accuse suspect persons of treason and order them to appear for trial. Those who did not surrender were pronounced traitors and had both their personal and real property confiscated. The British occupation of Philadelphia prevented any action on these measures until the summer of 1778, when the appointment of the commissioners was reconfirmed by the Supreme Executive Council and officially announced in the *Pennsylvania Packet* on July 9. Estates slated for confiscation were inventoried, and newspaper notices announced dates of auction. The estates of 118 Pennsylvanians, 79 of whom were Philadelphians, were confiscated. Joseph Galloway, who had been the chief civil officer in Philadelphia under the British occupation, had left with the British army, as had Samuel Shoemaker, a Quaker and former mayor of Philadelphia who

24 Sally more unwell than Yesterday—John Drinker, E. Clever, Saml. Esborn, Docr, Nancy Waln, Nics. Waln, C. West and Wife, Peggy Hart, call'd—Robt Willis din'd—John Balderston call'd—HD. went to the Burial of the Widdow Gordon, who dyed of the Flux, we did not hear of her sickness or death, untill invited to the Funeral—warmer to day, our little Molly went to meeting for the first time, with her Sister Nancy, to the Childrens meeting, which is held at the Bank.

25 Sally awake almost all night, doseing all the forenoon, better towards evening—Saml. Pleasants, Lawrence Salter, John Drinker, Sally Jones calld—cloudy.

26 First Day: Sally much as usual—several call'd to day—Rachl. Catheral Nancy Waln and Betsy Hough with Sally.

27 Sallys disorder continues bad, tho' something abated,—Aunt, Betsy and Polly Jervis spent the Afternoon, Caty Howel, Polly Pleasants here this Evening—HD. went this afternoon to the Burial of John Hollowel—the Overseers mett here this Evening—as they frequently do.

28. Monthly Meeting—Sally not wors this Morning—the weather very close and warm, Becky Jones, S. Swett, Doctor, Reba. Waln call'd—Saml. Lee and Saml. Hughs, from towards Reading, din'd here—Reba. Moore, Debby Morris, Becky Jones & H. Catheral, drank tea with us—Sally better to day.

29 Sally not quite so well as Yesterday—H. Catheral, S Swett, Polly Howel, Saml. Emlen, Robt. Waln, Sally Jones, John Salter &c &c—the weather warmer, talk of a Battle with Gates.

30. Sally has less fever, but the Disorder in her Bowels, bad yet,—Reba. Waln here this Afternoon, Reba. James in the Evening.

31 Sally took Rheubarb, and has been very poorly all day—she spits much, and I am at times very uneasy about her—Hannah Sansom, Caty Smith, M. Pleasants here this Afternoon—Sally Jones &c call'd—the weather is very warm.

Augt. the 1st. The weather very warm,—our Neighbor Abraham Carlile was

---

served as a magistrate of police under Galloway. Both had been named traitors in the Pennsylvania Assembly's Act of Attainder, passed in March (*Col. Recs. Pa.*, 11:329–31, 479–80; *Laws Enacted in Second Sitting*, 102–10; *Pa. Packet*, July 9, 1778; Ousterhout, "Pennsylvania Land Confiscations,"; Peale, *Selected Papers*, 1:282–92; Coleman, "Joseph Galloway," 274, 288–89).

yesterday taken up, and put into Jail,[39]—several here to day—Sally, not much change in her.

2 First Day: Saml. Emlen, John Lloyd here this Morning—Isaac Wright and Wife,[40] Mordica Lees Wife and Jos. Pennrose from near Reding & S. Swett din'd with us—Danl Drinker & John James Reba. Waln, Anthony Benezet, Sally Gardner, call'd—Ann Moore, Alice Jackson, Hannah Williams, Wm. Mathews, James Thornton, George Churchman, and Benj. Hough, drank tea with us—very warm; Billy carried, or help'd to carry Miers Fishers child to the Burying Ground, this Afternoon; the first time of his officeateing in that manner—two of Osweld Eves Sons, were Yesterday put into Jail—Sally appears better to day, she has [tacken] Suit, Milk and Loaf Sugar, boyld togeather, which I hope will be of service.

3d. Sally much better, she eat her Breakfast down Stairs—Robt. Veree &c call'd—Abram. Leddon din'd with us, rain and thunder this Afternoon—Ann Carlile call'd, she had been to the Old Prison to visit her Husband.

4 HD. most of this day at diffirent meetings, Sally not so well as Yesterday—Reba. Waln spent the Afternoon with us—Thos. Watson sup'd and lodges with us—Hannah Hopkins here, Sally Gardner &c call'd—very sharp lightning and Thunder this day about noon, it is said, a Man was yesterday kill'd, on the Commons with the Lightning.

5 HD. at meeting most of the day: Thos. Watson Breakfasted with us—Jas. Logan at Tea—Wm. Smith, Warner Mifflin, John Drinker call'd—weather more moderate—Sally very weak, her Bowels still disordred—S Swett and Doctor call'd—tis a month tomorrow since Sally was taken ill.

6 Sally very poorly this Morning—but better in the Evening—Abey Parish drank Tea, Saml. and M. Pleasants, John Parish, George Churchman, Wm. Smith Robt. Waln, call'd—John Drinker sup'd with us—Nancy, Billy and myself went this evening to hire a Maid next door to S. Pleasants—call'd there, and at Uncles, a fine Moon light night, tis near five Weeks since I have been over our door sill till this night—fine Weather—little Josa. Howel has the Small Pox.

39. Abraham Carlisle, a Philadelphia Quaker, was first named as a traitor in May 1778, along with more than fifty other Pennsylvanians. Against the advice of Friends, he had accepted a post from the British to grant passes in and out of the city (see above, Nov. 24, 1777; *Col. Recs. Pa.*, 11:481–86, 603–605; Mekeel, *Relation of the Quakers*, 193; notes on Carlisle's trial and petitions on his behalf are in *Pa. Archives*, ser. 1, 7:44–52 and 53–58, respectively).

40. The name "Anthony" crossed out.

7 Sally with her Daddy took a ride this Afternoon about 4 miles.—Nancy & Billy went to Bush-Hill, to see the Aloes Tree, whose rapid groth lately, has been the subject of much Conversation—a report prevails this Evening of a great fire having happn'd on first day last at New York—fine weather to day—Wm. Smith, Reba. Waln, Doctor &c call'd—Isaac brought the mare from Frankford.

8. very busy all day—Robt. Waln &c &c call'd—J.D. RD. HDr call'd.

9 First Day: I went to meeting this Afternoon S Swett, Reba. Waln, call'd Becky and Patty Wharton drank tea, Wm. Smith sup'd with us—cloudy.

10 cloudy weather, Sally down stairs, she is still very weak—Docr. Redman, Reba. Waln, Saml. Emlen call'd.

11 Clouds with rain this Morning very Stormy about noon and after—Edwd. Penington John Drinker call'd—HD. Isreal Pemberton and S Hopkins waited on G Arnold, on Account of some prisoners, for whome they procurd a release—Sally much better—the York Paper mentions the fire that happn'd there on the 2d Instant[41] 64 Houses were burnt. and on the 5th a Vesel with a quantity of Gun-powder on board, was struck by Lightning, and blew up, which damaged most of the Houses, and greatly shocked the Inhabitants—a great quantity of goods was consum'd by the fire.

12 it has cleard up cooler, since the Storm of Yesterday, Wm. Norton, Wm. Webb from Lancaster &c call'd—they are pressing Waggons to day; for what purpose I know not—the lamps have not been Lightn'd for some time past, nor does the Watchmen call the hour as usual.

13 rain almost all day—Billy Webb, Breakfasted with us, Jos. Burr din'd—Sammy Sansom drank Coffee—Docr. Redman, John Drinker call'd.

14 rain the greatest part of this day—S. Swett spent the day with us—Wm. Smith spent the Evening—Reba. Waln call'd—our little Molly gone to Bed very feverish—one George Spangler was executed here to day for some assistance he had given to the British Army &c[42]—he has left a Wife and several Children—J. Drinker call'd.

15 little Joshua Howel died this Morning of the Small Pox, aged one year—

41. *Pa. Packet*, Aug. 11, 1778.

42. George Spangler, convicted of spying for the British, was hanged following a court-martial ordered by Gen. Benedict Arnold (Scharf and Westcott, *Philadelphia*, 1:394).

Josey Bringhurst, Sucky and Nancy Jones, John Drinker, Reba. Waln, two of Judaths Daughters call'd—Bant. Woodcock supped and lodges here.

16 First Day: went to Meeting this Afternoon, and after to the Burial of little Joshua Howel—many of the Company set in our House—Sally Zane and Molly Pleasants drank Tea with us, B Woodcock sup'd and lodg'd—rain this fore noon, and heavy rain this Evening. We have had a long spell of rainy weather.

17 many Showers of rain to day—I went out after dinner, call'd and spent an hour at Wm. Fishers, drank tea at S. Emlens, Samey gone to Raway Meeting—came home after candle light—Wm. Smith, &c call'd—B Woodcock sup'd and lodg'd with us—Tom James breakfastd here.

18 BW, breakfasted, and then took leave—I. went to Meeting, S Swett came home with me and spent the Day—I went out after dinner call'd at [T] Speakmans for medicine—and at J Drinkers, at Uncle Jerviss at Rd. Footmans, then went and settled an account with A. Powel—call'd at S Pleasants—came home in the Evening Robt. Waln, Parson Murry, &c. calld here many Showers to day, with sultary weather—a fleet from England, said to be[43] on their way.

19 many Showers to day with Sun-shine—HD. went over the river, with T. Masterman and I. Catheral this Morning—I spent the Afternoon at Neigr. Walns—Parson Murry, Wm. Smith, Polly Gordon, Lawrence Salter &c call'd—Sister went down to Abels, for a peice Linnen and some Tea—Janney Boon left us this Evening and went to stay a week with her Cozin Jacob James's wife, and then to go to her aunts at Willmington who has wrote for her—she has been with us, 3 years and near nine months—Molly Lahew came to day in her place—a great noise last night or the night before at the Bakers, William crying Murder, while the Baker beat him.

20th. Grace Galloway turn'd out of her House this forenoon,[44] and Spanish Officers put in—this is the first day we have had without rain for 8 or 10 days past—Sally went abroad for the first time since her[45] illness—I spent this

43. The word "near" crossed out.

44. After Joseph Galloway fled with the departing British, his wife, Grace, remained in Philadelphia in the hope of protecting family property. Their home on Arch Street had been the subject of negotiations between Grace Galloway and Charles Willson Peale, one of the confiscation agents. Another confiscation agent, however, rented the house to Don Juan Miraille̱s, the ambassador from the court of Spain to the Continental Congress. Peale and two other agents were forced to break open the kitchen door and evict Galloway on August 20th. Miralles and his retinue (not Spanish officers, as ED reported) then acquired the house (*Pa. Packet*, Aug. 15, 1778; Raymond C. Weiner, ed., "Diary of Grace Growden Galloway," *PMHB* 55 [1931]: 46–47; Peale, *Selected Papers*, 1:290–91, n. 37; *Statutes at Large*, 9:325–26).

45. The word "recovery" crossed out.

Afternoon at Neigr. Howells—several reports concerning the Frence Fleet, it looks as if there was some disagreeable news for the people here, but what I connot say—many Children have died of the Small Pox lately, taken in the natural way—we were alarm'd this evening by the cry of fire. a brew-House up Chestnut Street, back of Dickinsons, which was much burnt.

21st. I spent this Afternoon at Willm. Fishers, he is still in his Chamber, tho much better—James and Sally Logan drank tea with Sister, & S Swett, Polly Pleasants, Jon. James, Danl. Drinker and Wife, Jane Boon, Chars. West &c call'd—Billy help'd to carry Wm. Norton junrs. Child to the Grave this Afternoon, Becky Shoemaker was again ordred out of her House last night[46]—many are ill in Town of Fevers—HD. unwell to day in his Bowels—nobody is allow'd to go to N York without a pass from Congress.[47]

22d. very cool this afternoon & evening—Saml. Emlen, Reba. Waln, J. Drinker, Jn. Pemberton, call'd—HD. unwell, tho' he goes abroad.

23d. First Day: I went to Meeting Afternoon and evening—call'd after evening meeting with Saml. Pleasants, to see Becky Shoemaker, who is to leave her House tomorrow—Any. Benezet and John Drinker drank Coffee with us—David Eastaugh din'd here—the weather cool.

24th. I spent this Afternoon at [J.] Fishers, Tommy came home with me, found Wm. Smith and Becky Jones here; A Parish drank Tea with Sister—S. Swett Din'd with us—M. Pleasants here this Morning she had been with Becy Shoemaker to Thos. [McKim]—fine weather—Sammy Pleasants has had 6 good Mohogany Chairs taken from him for the Substitute fine.

25 Went to Monthly Meeting this Morning 3 Couple past, vizt. Jonan. Knight, and the Widdow Baldwin, George Smith and Elizth. Roberts, Danl. Mifflin and Debby Howel,—Fireing of Connon to day, and other demonstra-

46. The day after Charles Willson Peale and other confiscation agents took possession of the Galloway home, they acquired the Shoemaker home on Arch Street and ordered Rebecca Shoemaker out. Many years later, Peale recalled that the confiscation agents began with the property of those "who were of most consideration among those named in the Proclamation" and so accordingly they went first to the Galloway and Shoemaker homes (Coleman, "Joseph Galloway," 288, 289 n. 51; "Memoirs of Charles Willson Peale: From his Original Ms. with Notes by Horace Wells Sellers" [1896], typescript, Peale-Sellers Papers, APS, Philadelphia, 67).

47. The Continental Congress resolved on Aug. 13 that only Congress or General Washington could issue passes to New York, then ordered Benedict Arnold, military governor of Philadelphia, to recall all unused passes he had previously issued. The resolution was in effect through Aug. 21, when Congress gave the executive and the local military authorities in each state responsibility for passes, although the Aug. 21 resolution made no specific mention of New York. By Aug. 22 the Supreme Executive Council in Pennsylvania was issuing passes to New York (*JCC*, 11:779, 825; *Col. Recs. Pa.*, 12:560).

tions of joy, on the annaversary of the French Kings Birth, Saml. Emlen Breakfasted with us, Saml. Fisher and John Nancarrow, S Swett, Reba. Waln call'd my Henry and Sammy Emlen left home at about 4 this Afternoon, intending for Bybarry James Thorntons, this evening—and then to proceed to the Falls Meeting &c—I do not expect them home untill some time in next week—Joseph Yerkes was had up yesterday before a Magistrate for keeping School;[48] his School is stop'd, and our Son Billy is at a loss for employment, as well as many others, in consiquence of it; sad doings—the weather very warm again.

26 Capt. Harper, Henry Van-Valk, John Drinker, Josa. Howel, call'd—our Isaac and Man he hired, have been busy to day at the Stable, taken in 2 loads of Hay—Billy Sansom came this evening to know if his Father could have a load—My self, Sally and Nancy spent this Afternoon at James Logans, call'd at Uncle Jerviss, Sammy Jervis very ill—very warm.

27 Spent this Afternoon at Edwd. Peningtons, Reba. Waln here this evening—rather cooler—2 loads of Hay brought in to day—the Girles out this Afternoon. Tomy. Lloyd came home with them.

28 Stayd within all day—John Pemberton and S. Hopkins stop'd as they road by this Afternoon going to Burlington, by whome we sent our love to HD—Reba. Waln spent this Afternoon with us,—Davd Eastaugh din'd with us—Sarah Goodman and Parson Murry call'd—Billy went to the Philada Monthly Meeting two loads of Hay brought in to day, one went to Sammy Sansoms the other to E. Peningtons, we sent one Yesterday to A Parish, which she sent back; they made shift to get it into our Stable, which is very full—cooler.

29 Easterly wind with some rain: Reba. Waln; John Salter, Jane Boon, & J. Drinker, call'd—J. Logan at Tea,—Caty Howel Senr. here this evening—many ill with the neaveous Fever.

30th. First Day: I was unwell this Morning and again this evening disordred Bowels—went to meeting this Afternoon which did not geather 'till after 3 o'clock, on account of a heavy shower—drank tea at O Joness Billy with me—went to evening meeting, and Sup'd at S. Pleasants [S]ammy came home with me.

48. Joseph Yerkes was called before a magistrate because he did not conform to legislation passed in April requiring all schoolmasters to take an oath or affirmation of allegiance. Those who failed to do so by June 1 could be removed from their positions and subject to a penalty of five hundred pounds plus costs. Yerkes was not the only Quaker schoolmaster who ran afoul of this legislation: some Quaker schoolmasters were imprisoned (*Laws Enacted in the Second Sitting*, 127–30; Mekeel, *Relation of the Quakers*, 189–90, 180, 187 n. 40).

31 Sally Barton from Lancaster call'd this Morning—Sally Moore drank Coffee with us—John Drinker, Boby. Moore call'd—I went after Tea, little Henry with me, to Nanny Powels—call'd to see Hannah Pemberton, and at O Joness &c—the weather cool to day: many reports of Shatterd Fleets: and waggons being taken; but nothing that can be depended on.

Sepr. 1 Stay'd at home—Fredrick the Smith from the Iron Works, brought a Letter for HD—Sister step'd out this evening to Wm. Fishers—Molly Pleasants and Sally Fisher spent this Afternoon with our Girls—J Drinker, Reba. Waln call'd—Sister and the Children went to meeting this Morning—the weather very cool.

2d. stay'd within all day: S Pleasants, Sl. Fisher, Jane Boon, John Drinker &c call'd—HD— came home this Afternoon to Tea, Josey Drinker with him—I expect he will stay some days with us—Reba. and Becky James here this Morning—Sister & Sally went home with them this Afternoon in the Waggon to Frankford, where I expect they will stay some time—two men of the names of Lyons and Ford, were Shot about Noon to day on board a Gondelow for Desertion, 2 were repreved.[49]

3 Tommy James brought a Letter this Morning from Sally, which Nancy answer'd—Billy Smith, Saml. Emlen, Thos. Shore, C. West, Josey and Daniel Drinker call'd—Wm. Smith and Thos. Shore drank tea with us—Saml. Pleasants, Saml. Smith &c call'd—John Drinr. and Henry Clifton supd with us, cool and pleasant—our Family seems small, we miss Sister and Sally; Isaac lock'd out.

4 Henry Clifton breakfasted with us, John Drinker, Abel James, Josh. Bringhurst, &c call'd. Saml. Sansom drank tea with us, John and Jos. Drinker sup'd with us—Nancy wrote to Sally—pleasant cool weather H.D. received a Letter yesterday from Richd. Waln dated from Walnford, we are pleased to find he is with his Family, but do not yet know upon what terms.

5 Saml. Emlen, John and Danl. Drinker, Philip Bush, Wm. Smith, &c call'd—Tommy James brought a Letter from Sally—which Nancy answer'd—fine weather Josey Drinker went away this Morning—stepd over this Afternoon

49. Samuel Lyons and Samuel Ford, lieutenants in the Pennsylvania navy, were two of four men charged with perjury and desertion during the Battle of Fort Mercer, Oct. 22, 1777. The other two men were reprieved, but Lyons and Ford, despite petitions on their behalf, were shot on Sept. 2, 1778 (*Pa. Packet*, Sept. 3, 1778; Marshall, *Diary Extracts*, 198; *Col. Recs. Pa.*, 11:564–66).

to Neigr Walns—a Letter from Gen Sollovan with an acct of a Battle, on Rhoad-Island &c &c.[50]

6 First Day: HD came out of meeting unwell; tho he went again this Evening—Matha Harris made her appearance again to day about 11 o'clock at the Bank and Great meeting Houses—where she told Friends, that a very trying time was near at Hand &c—Myself, Nancy and Billy went this Afternoon, HD stayd at home, Sammy Fisher, Wm. Shipley, Becky Jones and Hannah Catheral call'd, very fine weather—no accounts from Frankford.

7 Isaac left us this Morning and went as he said to John Parishs—a number of Friends here this morning with HD—a Negro Woman brought a Letter this Morning for Jane Sibal, formerly Boon; so that Janny is I supose married to Philip one of the Majors orderly men; Reba. Waln, myself, my two Sons, Bob Waln, Neddy Howell and Anna Waln, took a walk this Afternoon to Springsbury to see the Aloes Tree[51]—stop'd in our return at Bush-Hill and walk'd in the Garden,—came home after Sun Set, very much tired—R Waln drank tea with us—found Sister and Sally at home when we return'd—they came in Abels Waggon—the weather is rather warmer, tho' very fine.

8 HD. Sister and the Children went to Meeting—Sammy Shoemakers goods &c sold to day at Vandue[52] 'tis said that Molesworths Body is again taken up, I have not yet heard by whose direction—Phebe Pemberton spent the Afternoon

50. Newport, R.I., had been occupied by the British since December 1776. During the summer of 1778 a joint assault on the town was planned that included the French fleet, commanded by Adm. Charles Hector, Comte d'Estaing, and land forces serving under Gen. John Sullivan, the Marquis de Lafayette, and Gen. Nathanael Greene. D'Estaing arrived on July 29, but Sullivan's troops were not gathered until Aug. 8. A British squadron was sighted shortly thereafter, and d'Estaing sailed out to confront Admiral Howe and his reinforcements on Aug. 10. Before the engagement even commenced, a hurricane scattered and damaged both fleets; Sullivan, left to lay siege to Newport without naval reinforcements, was forced to retreat at the end of August. Sir Henry Clinton brought in four thousand troops and naval reinforcements to protect Newport from further attack by Franco-American forces (Sydney V. James, *Colonial Rhode Island: A History* [New York: Scribner, 1975], 355–56).

51. Springettsbury Manor, a tract of land along the Schuylkill River in Philadelphia County, held two large country homes: Bush Hill, built by James Logan, and Springettsbury, built by Thomas Penn in the 1730s. A popular place to visit, Springettsbury was noted for its flowers, formal gardens, and greenhouse where the great American aloe tree was nurtured (J. F. Watson, *Annals*, 2:478–79).

52. The contents of Samuel Shoemaker's house brought in over twenty-five hundred pounds at auction; the contents of Joseph Galloway's house brought in close to nine hundred pounds (auction announcement in *Pa. Packet*, Sept. 1, 1778; inventories of the Shoemaker and Galloway estates and their value at auction are in Pennsylvania Archives, record group 4, reproduced in *The Collected Papers of Charles Willson Peale and His Family*, ed. Lillian B. Miller et al. [Millwood, N.Y.: Kraus Microform, 1980], series 2A, card 6; the real estate properties of Shoemaker and Galloway are listed with the dates and value of their sales in Anne M. Ousterhout, "Opponents of the Revolution Whose Pennsylvania Estates Were Confiscated," *Pennsylvania Genealogical Magazine* 30 [1978]: 244, 250).

with us, she and Charles West drank tea—J. Drinker, call'd—very fine weather.

9 rain all the Morning cloudy the later part of the day—Sammy Fisher, and John Drinker drank tea with us—Wm. Smith, Reba. Waln, John Parish, Saml. Hopkins call'd—I went to Josa. Howels and spent an hour after tea—George Morgan and another[53] Breakfasted with us Yesterday.

10 I spent this Afternoon at Sarah Lewiss Sally Logan drank tea with Sister,—we are reduc'd from 5 Servants to one, which wont do long, if we can help ourselves, it is the case with many at present, good Servants are hard to be had, such a time was never known here I beleive in that respect.—Abel James, &c call'd—fine weather.

11 HD. Isaac Zane Senr. John Parish, Wm. Smith, Thos. Masterman &c took a walk after Breakfast to Frankford they din'd. at Abel Jamess came home by 4 o'clock—Wm. Smith and Capt. Harper, drank Tea with us—Sister and Sally out—Tabatha [Mires], J. Logan, John Drinker, George James, &c call'd—we have a new Cow came home to day, for whome HD paid 45£—to Parson Stringer—fine weather.

12 Clouds with rain—Wm. Smith, Reba. Waln, Sucky Hartshorn, &c call'd—we sent our two old Cows to day to the point medow to fatten.

13 First Day: HD, Sister and the Children went to meeting this morning I went in the Afternoon, Saml. and Sally Emlen with their two daughters came home with me, they with John Forman, Josh. Bringhurst, John and Danl. Drinker, and Molly Pleasants drank tea with us—Sister went this Evening to see Neigr Carlile—HD. supd at Iseral Pembertons—cool weather.

14 I spent this Afternoon at John Drinkers, Sally and Nancy with me, Saml. Pleasants drank tea with Sister—the overseers mett here after dinner—Caty Howel here this evening—raw cold weather.

15 Becky Jones, Saml. Fisher call'd—Sally Moore came and went to meeting with me,—Gaberal Jones and Isaac Zane junr. both from Virginia and Sally Moore din'd with us—Reba. Waln came over; with her I went to the Burial of my old Friend and aquaintance Nancy Potts formerly Mitchel, whome I much valued, she dy'd of the Neverous fever—M. Pleasants came with my Henry and drank Coffee with us. she spent the Evening and sup'd. HD. went home with her—the weather is very cool.

53. The words "which I" crossed out.

16 Robt. Stevenson Breakfasted with us—John Pemberton, Saml. Emlen, John Drinker, Wm. Smith, Reba. Waln call'd—Saml. Sansom drank tea with us—Sister gone out to buy a peticoat for Hannah Stevenson—cloudy with some rain to day, east'rly wind, Stormy this evening—myself not well to day.

17 Sister out this Morning—Sally Zane drank tea with us—Robt. Stevenson spent part of the Evening—HD. most of the day at different meetings—unsettled weather.

18th. Sally and Nancy, went this Afternoon to Springsbury &c. with Sally Zane, her Brother Isaac, and Gaberal Jones—they came home in the evening Isaac Zane junr with them—John and Danl. Drinker call'd—I step'd over to Neigr. Walns—pleasant weather.

19. stay'd within all day: Edwd. Penington, Wm. Smith and Benjn. Morgan, call'd—Becky James junr. drank tea with us—she informs us that, Oswd. Eves Goods &c were sold Yesterday, for the use of the State.

First Day: went to meeting this afternoon, drank tea with Neigr. Waln, went with her to the Burial of the Widdow Many—call'd at Wm. Fishers—Sally and Nancy were this Afternoon at the middel meeting and afterwards at S Pleasants—good weather.

21 I spent this afternoon at Abram. Mitchels,—HD. had a sumonds sent this afternoon desiring his to meet the 2[5]th. Instant with his arms and accouterments &c[54]—Wm. Smith, Reba Waln, Edwd. Penington, Hannah Catheral, call'd.

22 went this Morning to Monthly Meeting, stepped over after to Neigr. Walns—went out towards evening Billy with me, to Amos Taylors and Ann Powels, on busyness—call'd at S Pleasants—cloudy &c, Raw—James Thornton here this Morning many since.

23 Stay'd within all day—cloudy with rain—Robt. and Reba. Waln, Wm. Smith, call'd—HDs allmost all night awake with the toothach—which he had had greatest part of the day.

24th HD. sent for Fredrick this Morning and had a tooth drawn which requir'd a strong pull; Neigr. Waln spent this Afternoon helping me to cut out

54. In early September Washington notified the Supreme Executive Council that he was withdrawing Continental troops from Philadelphia to join the main army. The council responded by calling up various militia units for garrison duty in Philadelphia. Those who refused to serve in the militia paid fines (*Col. Recs. Pa.*, 11:568, 581; Rosswurm, *Arms, Country, and Class*, 162).

a Satten Cloak for Nancy; she and Josh. Scott drank tea with us—cleard up—Charles West, Jane Sibel, Sammy Fisher, John Drinker call'd.

25 Abraham Carliles tryal came on to day and is not yet concluded, are at a loss to judge how it will go with him—Sammy Smith, Mires Fisher, George Mead, Molly Moore, Reba. Waln, Wm. Smith, John Parish, John Field, John Drinker, call'd—James and Joseph Stear, from Virginia, came this evening to stay with us during the Meeting—HD. at home all day, a pain in his Face—I step'd over to Neigr. Walns, good weather.

26 HD stay'd within all day,—the two Steers Joshua Baldwin, and Sammy Trimbel breakfasted with us—Sammy and John Balderston are come to stay with us—Joseph and Hannah Drinker came this Evening they lodge at her Sisters, they with 6 others sup'd with us—Reba. Waln, Betsy Waln and Daughter Polly, Molly Pleasants, Hugh, Elli and John John Drinker, John Parish; Andw. McCoy, Wm. Smith; Thos and John Hough, &c &c call'd—I went in this Afternoon to visit our depress'd Neigr Carlile, whose Husband they have brought in gilty of High treason, tho' it is hop'd by many that he will not suffer what some others fear he will—fine weather—AC. sent in this evening for HD—old Benjn. Mason was Yesterday bury'd at Fair Hill—a year this day since the British Troops entrd.

27 First Day: the two Stears, John Balderston, Saml. Trimble, and Jos. Drinker Breakfasted with us—went to meeting this Morning Robt. Vallentine & Wife, Josa. Baldwin and wife came home with me—they with seven others din'd with us—Thos. Ross, Wm. Jones J. Balderston, the Stears, with 3 or 4 I do not know;—Warner Mifflin, Sarah Watson, call'd—9 drank tea, Sarah Carry, Rachl Watson, Hannah and Jos. Willson, John Brinton and Wife who lodges here, one Simsom, with several men, whome I do not know—Becky Jones, Josa. Gillbert, call'd—our six lodgers sup'd with us, and no others—the weather cool and pleasent.

28 Joseph Jenney with our Lodgers and several others breakfasted with us—twelve din'd—Thos. Watson and Wife, Robt. Moore & wife, &c &c—Robt Varee, &c call'd Esther Trimble and Josey Brinton came this forenoon. They and John Brintons Sister Temple lodge here, we have nine with us this Night a great number in and out to day—I went to meeting Morning and Afternoon, several came home to tea with me—fine weather.

29 several of our lodgers, Danl. Smith &c Breakfasted with us—13 din'd. Richd. Downing and Wife, Abrm. Gibbons and Wife, R Dowgs Daughter Trimble, Thos. Lightfoot, James Thornton, George Churchman, David Eastaugh, John Hoskins, &c &c Robt. Pleasants, Wm. Smith, Mary Cox, Wm. Downing —— Hollandshead, Jessy Waterman, &c call'd Wm. Jackson,

[ ] Thomas, 2 or 3 woman Strangers, Alice Jackson, call'd—Molly Moore here this Afternoon and evening—good weather.

30 3 or 4 whose names I cannot recolect, breakfasted with us—8 din'd, Wm. Cox & Mary Cox, Sarah Merriot Prudance Jackson, Joseph Moore, &c, Sally Dillwing, Reba. James, drank tea with us—Esther Trimble went home this Afternoon—our own lodgers sup'd with us and T. Watson—several call'd I was at meeting this Afternoon, fine weather—Black Peter and Molly Brookhouse, are here every day this Week, assisting in the kitchen—John Roberts Millers tryal came on to Day. I have not heard, how it goes on, Abraham Carlile is to be try'd again they say on seventh day next as the Lawyers have made a demur.[55]

Octr. 1. 5 or 6 Breakfasted with us, 14 din'd—Malon and Sarah Jenney, Jos. Janney; Jerh. Brown, John Balderston, Jos. Brinton &c &c—Jos. Knight Mary Moore &c call'd—I went to meeting Morning and Afternoon, our own lodgers sup'd with us—John Robertss tryal not over—fine weather. Martha Harris at the Mens Meeting this Afternoon this is thought to be the largest Yearly Meeting ever known here; our Maid behaves badly.

2. I went to meeting Morning and Afternoon, am very unwell this evening with the Head ach—our own lodgers at Breakfast, 8 at Dinner; 10 at Supper, many call'd—John Roberts is brought in gilty at which some are surpris'd as they did not expect it, who had attended the court—there is some demur in his case, as I understand this evening—very fine weather—some Friends are gone home—Saml Brown and Wife, from Winchester, [J] and Edey Sharpless, Becky and Hannah, [S.] Watson, Sarah Carry, and Daughter Reba. James, with 20 others.

3 James Gibbon and Benn Pearson with others at Breakfast—Danl. Browns wife, Polly Wallace and another woman with her, and others calld this Morning. Sally Moore, Janny Sibal, call'd—Abraham Gibbons and wife, Sammy Trimble, Isaac Everit, Josa. Bawldwin, &c &c din'd with us—I went to meeting this afternoon Mary Moore came home with me, she and Robt. Moore with our lodgers sup'd with us. Daniel Mifflin also—he came in to invite us to his wedding, which is to be on 3d day—next—Josey Brinton left us this

55. Carlisle's attorneys, James Wilson and James Ross, brought a motion after his conviction to arrest the judgment. They sought to prove that the indictment against him was "vague and uncertain" and therefore faulty. The court heard the motion but ruled for the state on Oct. 5 (A. J. Dallas, *Reports of Cases Ruled and Adjudged in the Courts of Pennsylvania, before and since the Revolution* [Philadelphia: T. Bradford, 1790], 1:35–38; [(Dallas, *Reports*, First ed. vol. 1);] Chapin, *American Law of Treason*, 69; see also Henry Campbell Black, *Black's Law Dictionary*, fifth ed. [St. Paul, Minn: West, 1979], s.v. "demurrer").

evening—the womans meeting is concluded,[56] the Men have adjornd till second day—which I never rembember to have been the case before,—talk that the English Troops are at Egg Harbour, spioling the Salt Works that a number of the Conti [   ] this Afternoon, towards them.

First Day John Brinton and Wife, Sl. Trimble, J Balderston, James and [Josu] Steers, with some strangers, breakfasted with us—Sarah Watson call'd to bid us farewel—John Brinton and wife, Saml. Trimble, Joseph Wilson, Sarah Mickel, Hannah Hopkins, Benn. Swett, and 4 or 5 strangers dind with us—Polly Swett and Sally Maul &c call'd—10 drank tea with us—[Caterine] Callender, Hannah Sansom; Sl. Smith and wife, Hannah Drinker, 5 others—I stay'd within all day unwell—rain this Morning cleared up in the Afternoon—after dinner we had a Setting when Josa. Willson spoke to the Children; another Friend a few words—Isaac Hornor, Isaac Pickering & John Parry, dind.

5 very unwell all day, had a chill which was follow'd by a fevar, a fit of the Collick with a vomitting and lax—[J.] Branton and wife, John Balderston with the others that are here breakfasted Betsy Waln and Thos. Carlton, [S.] Trimble din'd with us—Thos. Poltney and Wife, Sally Dillwyn, Nancy Dillwyn, Jos. and Hannah Drinker, Danl. Drinker, Henry Drinker, Josa. Baldwin, Phebe Morris, Susanna Brown, Grace Buchanan, John Clifford, Reba. Waln, Wm. Smith, —— Gillingham, S. Hopkins, Jos. Steer, James Steer, some sup'd some drank tea, and others call'd—fine weather.

6. [T.] Branton and Wife, the 2 Steers, J. Balderston, S. Trimble, all left (1778)[57] us this Morning the Mens Meeting concluded last night—I was very feverish and unwell all night, often up—Ruth Jonson Sally Biddle, Jos. and Hannah Drinker Becky Jones, Wm. Smith, &c call'd this Morning HD gone to Meeting, he is with Robt. Waln, to attend the marriage of Dl. Mifflin and Debby Howel, Sally Zane, and 5 or 6 of the wedding Guest came here after meeting,—we were just inform'd that our poor neighbor Abram. Carlile, has received sentence of Death. Robt. Willis, Wm. Jones, and John Parish drank

56. The Society of Friends, believing strongly that women's faith and gifts in the service of the church were as valuable as men's, set up parallel women's meetings to the men's monthly, quarterly and yearly meetings. The difference in these meetings supposedly related to function rather than status, but in practice, women's meetings, at least in Philadelphia, had less power over discipline than the men's meetings. They were required to obtain the approval of the men's meetings before disowning women for marrying out or accepting their statements of apology before readmitting them to full standing. In neighboring Bucks County, the women's monthly meetings appear to have exercised full disciplinary functions without the approval of the men's meetings (L. Hugh Doncaster, *Quaker Organization and Business Meetings* [London: Friends Home Service Committee, 1952], 17–18; Frost, *Quaker Family*, 55–57; on Bucks County see Jack D. Marietta, *The Reformation of American Quakerism 1748–1783* [Philadelphia: University of Pennsylvania Press, 1984], 28–29).

57. The date "(1778)" is an interlineation.

tea with us—Nics. Waln, John Drinker, C. West, Polly Brown, Betsy Waln, Polly James, call'd—Edd. Penington call'd this evening. fine weather.

7 Several Friends mett this morning in the front Parlor. Jane Webb spent the day with us—she with John Wallace and wife drank tea with us—George Dillwyn, Sammy Emlen and John Drinker sup'd, Neigr. Shippen and her Daughr. Kitty, Edd. Penington, a young woman of the name of Derham with M Wallace, Warner Mifflin, Sammy Smith, Becky Jones,—&c very fine weather,—I not very well today, tho' better. Myself and Nancy spent this afternoon at Saml. [S]ansoms,—Edd. Penington, C. West, Wm. Smith, Dr. Moore, [Ab]bey Kibble, Morg. Dobson from Raway, Hanh. Richardson, [ ]mmy Smith, Saml. Pleasants, call'd—fine weather, [sev]eral Friends went today to visit Neigr. Carlile in the Dungon.

9 Myself with Sally and Nancy spent this Afternoon at James Pembertons; I spent part of this Evening at Josa. Howels, James and Sally Logon here this afternoon, Wm. Smith, Saml. Emlen, Betsy Waln. &c our Sons went with their Daddy this morning to a meeting for Children, appointed by G. Dillwin some rain to day—Miars Fisher here the morning.

10 dull morning rain all the Afternoon and evening a settled rain—G. Dillwyn call'd, Willm. Smith spent the Afternoon and part of the evening—HD. went this Afternoon to the Burial of Jonathan Zane—Sen'r. rain most of the night.

11 First Day. rain all day: HD. and the four Children went to meeting morning and afternoon. John Drinker drank Coffee; Robt Waln called.

12 Stay'd within for several days past. Sister ill last night with the sick Head Ache. Myself up often in the Night with a sick stomach and vomitting—George Dillwyn, Docr. Moore, Willm. Smith, David Eastaugh, Tommy Fisher, Reba. Waln &c call'd—Debby Norris and Sally Jones spent the Afternoon with the Girles—little Moll went this Morning with Nancy as far as Uncle Jerviss She has never been so far before but once to visit her Daddy when a prisonr. in the Lodge—clear'd up last night—tis now fine cool weather—A Carlile is removed from the Dungon, into the Room in which he was before confined.

1778[58] Octor. 17. Wm. Hambleton was this Day try'd for his Life, and

58. The manuscript volume for Oct. 17, 1778–June 10, 1780, has dark blue covers. On the inside front cover ED wrote, "[H]nn Drinker."

acquited.[59] John Robarts Miller condem'd to die,[60] Shocking doings!—I spent this Afternoon with R Waln &c at Neigr. Howels, on a visit to Debbe Mifflin.

18 First Day: John and Abby Parish, Peggy Morris and Hannah Sansom came home with me after meeting they stay'd tea—HD. and myself call'd after Evening meeting at Mary Armitts to see Thos. Dobson and Wife—'tis reported and Credited that England and France have accomodated matters, and that the French are call'd home; A Carliles Irons are taken off.

19 I went out this Morning call'd at Docr. Parkes, at uncle Jerviss at Benjn. Poltneys to see Jane Webb—at Owen Joness—went this Afternoon with H. Sansom to the Funeral of Thos. Coombs Wife, who dy'd soon after she was deliver'd of twins—the Corps was taken to Church, and afterwards to the burying ground in arch Street.

20. HD. C. West and David Eastaugh, visited John Roberts and A. Carlile in Prison. Sally and Nancy took a walk this Afternoon with Molly Pleasants and Debby Norris &c to Springsbury and Bush-Hill—David Franks taken up;[61] and put into Jail for writeing something they find fault with.

21st. went this Afternoon with S. and M. Pleasants, [T.] and S. Fisher to see Sally Shepherd, Joseph Scotts Daughter—who is going with her Children and Father to set off tomorrow for N. York—a Young Man of the name of Latham, one of our Society, has appeared lately in the publick streets, warning the People to repent &c.

24 John Robarts and Abm. Carlisles Death warant was sign'd today and read to them—HD went this Afternoon to the Burial of William Norton junr.—

59. William Hamilton, charged with high treason for aiding and assisting British troops while they were in Philadelphia, was tried on Oct. 16, and a jury acquitted him within minutes (*Pa. Ev. Post*, postscript, Oct. 17, 1778).

60. John Roberts, a Quaker miller from Merion who had originally sought the intervention of the British because of his distress over the banishment of the Quaker exiles, had been forced to act as a guide and informer for the British, then advancing on Philadelphia. Roberts was tried with Abraham Carlisle at the Philadelphia Court of Oyer and Terminer on Sept. 27, 1778; both men were found guilty of treason and executed on Nov. 4 (*Col. Recs. Pa.*, 11:481–86, 600–605; petitions for Roberts in *Pa. Archives*, ser. 1, 7:21–43; Mekeel, *Relation of the Quakers*, 193; Judge Thomas McKean's pronouncement of the death sentence despite the jury recommendation for mercy is in *Pa. Packet*, Nov. 7, 1778).

61. David Franks, the commissary for British prisoners, was able to purchase supplies for British prisoners held by Americans under arrangements worked out by both armies. Considered a loyalist, he was arrested on the orders of the Continental Congress after his letters to Moses Franks of London were intercepted. Congress charged that his letters revealed a "disposition and intentions inimical to the safeties and liberties of the United States," and that he "endeavoured to transmit the letters by stealth within British lines," thus abusing the "confidence reposed in him by Congress." The jury returned a writ of ignoramus, by which they refused to indict him, on Dec. 12 (*Pa. Packet*, Oct. 22, Dec. 12, 1778).

Peter Chavilleor was bury'd 2 or 3 days past, 'tis reported this evening that the British Troops have evacuated New-York, it appears rather too sudden to be true.

28. That N York is evacuated, proves a mistake as also, that, France and Great Brintian have settled matters: at least we have no proof of it—Jane Roberts, wife of John Roberts, Owen Jones and Wife, and James Thornton were here this morning HD. and self went with them to visit our neighbor Ann Carlile; when James had something to say to the afflicted women, by way of Testimony, which I thought encourageing—the time for the execution of their Husbands, is fixt the 4th. next month. The Destress'd wives have been with the Men in Power and several petitions are signing by different people to send in to the Council or Assembly—tis hop'd and beleived that their Lives will be spard, it would be terriable indeed should it happen otherwise—HD. and Sister went yesterday Afternoon to the Funeral of our Ancient Friend Mary Pemberton, the Corps was carried to meeting—she departed this Life on first Day morning the 25th. Instant—The prevailing report of this day is, that the British Troops, who lately left Egg Harbour, have return'd there again with a reinforcement.

Novr. 3 This afternoon I spent at Catre. Greenleafs, the Evening at S. Pleasants, where I was inform'd that preparations were making this evening for the Execution of our poor Friends tomorrow Morning—Notwithstanding the many pertitions that have been sent in, and the Personal appearance of the Destress'd wives and Children; before the Council,—much Compy. here. I am still of the mind, that they will not be permitted, to carry this matter to the last extremity. Billy went to Frankford with Tommy James, the 28 last month; he return'd this Morning. George Dillwyn about leaving us, for Sh. Carolina &c.

Novr. 4. they have actually put to Death; Hang'd on the Commons, John Robarts and Am. Carlisle this moring or about noon[62]—an awful Solemn day it has been—I went this evening with my HD. to Neigr. Carliles, the Body is brought home, and laid out—looks placid & Serene—no marks of agony or distortion, the poor afflicted widdows, are wonderfully upheld and suported, under their very great tryal—they have many simpathizing Friends.

5 HD. left home this Morning after Breakfast with Saml. Smith and Docr. Cowper for Radner meeting,[63] intending tomorrow for Merrion, where I

62. *Pa. Ev. Post*, Nov. 6, 1778.

63. Radnor, a township in northern Delaware County bordering on Montgomery and Chester counties, was first settled by Welsh Quakers in 1683; by 1686 Friends were conducting meetings in private homes. In 1693 the first meetinghouse was built, and in 1718 Friends began building a new, larger meetinghouse, which was completed after 1721 (Ashmead, *Delaware County*, 678, 687).

expect they will be at the Funeral of John Robarts—Isaac Catheral, Samuel Noble, C. West, Molly Shippen, Katty Howel, John Drinker, Reba. Waln, call'd this Morning—our back parlor was fill'd this afternoon with Company who came to the Burial of our Neighr. Carlile,—Myself and 4 Children went, Sister Stay'd at home,—it was a remarkable large Funeral, and a Solemn time; George Dillwyn and S. Emlen, spake at the grave, and the former, pray'd fervently; Sally Wharton and Daughter S. Swett came after, and drank tea with us.—HD. return'd the 7th.

Novr. 13. HD. with [J.] Parish &c. went to Merrion Meeting; they return'd the 14th.—much rain last night.

15 First Day G. Dillwyn who has not yet left us din'd with us to day, his Wife also—very cold to what it has yet been—many People have lately drop'd off.

Novr. 18 HD. had a fit of the Collick last night, is better to day—Reese Meridath bury'd this Afternoon.

19th. Nancy and Polly Parr, din'd and spent the Afternoon with us—Patty Smith and Becky James, sup'd and lodg'd with us—I had a fainty fitt this morning which lasted 10 or 15 minits, and continued poorly afterwards.

Novr. 23 HD. John Drinker, Saml. Sansom, Josey Drinker, Josey Sansom, Billy and Henry Drinker took a walk to Frankford; they had two Horses in Company, on one of which little Henry road 2 miles for the first time, he came home very much tir'd—they din'd at A. Jamess Becky Parke din'd with us.

24th. I went to monthly meeting this morning Molly Stevenson, Becky Wright, Benjn. Hough, Joshua Gibbs, John Parry, Sam Emlen, John Pemberton, Reba. James, Hannah Catheral, Becky Jones, were here after meeting, several of them dined with us, and set of after dinner for Middeltown meeting;[64] a good deal of company here to day.

Novr. 25. HD. left home after dinner with Charles West &c for Middletown

64. Although Middletown was the home of the second oldest Quaker meeting in Bucks County, it was the first town in the county to build a meetinghouse (1690). Like Falls Township, which had the oldest organized Quaker meeting, Middletown was one of the first five townships laid out in Bucks County. Quakers began worshiping in private homes there in 1682, and the first monthly meeting was held in 1684. The Middletown Meeting was known as Neshaminy Meeting until 1706 (W. W. H. Davis, *Bucks County*, 132–33; McNealy, *Bucks County*, 54).

meeting, and has some thoughts of going to Crosswicks,[65] after—I have been all day very ill with the sick headach—Betsy Waln here while I had lain down—several call'd—Rt. Waln here this evening.

26. Headach all day; fasted for the last 24 Hours, Sally Moore &c call'd this Morning S. Swett din'd with us, a man call'd to pay some money to Mountgomerys Estate—our girls at Norriss this afternoon,—Reba. Waln spent the Evening—Debby Norris, Molly Pleasants, Sally Wister, Sally Jones, Isaac and Josey Norris came home with the Girls—Cloudy raw weather—Sister has been very busy all day in the Kitchen with Isaac Catheral and Molly, cutting up and salting a Beef—rendring the Tallow, [&c.]

27. Sally Jones, P[ ]cy Jackson call'd—I step'd in this evening to see Neigr. Carlile—[J.] Logan here this Afternoon; cold and raw.

28. [J.] Parish took down the stove in the back Parlour this Morning with a view of putting it up more comodiously,—found the Chimney very foul, could not get a Sweep; so we have fixt ourselves in the little back Room for the present—S Smith call'd this evening he is return'd from middletown meeting, and informed me that HD. intends for Crosswicks meeting—very cold this Evening, a chimney in the alley on fire this afternoon—many more 'tis fear'd will be ere long, tis so dificult to get Sweeps—tis the opinion of many that the British are actualy leaving N York.

29 First Day: I went to meeting this afternoon with the 4 children; Abel James junr. din'd with us—Robt. Waln here this evening. I spent part of this evening with Billy at Neigr. Howels—our maid Molly went out last night, and has not return'd yet, so that we have had none other than little John Pope, to assist us this day; we were never so situate before; tis the case with many others—moderate, rain this Evening.

30 John Parish call'd, rain this Morning, cleard up this evening Reba. Waln spent part of the evening—2 men call'd for the Lamp and watch Tax;[66] C. Sowers wife call'd—to borrow a Horse.

65. Crosswicks, a village in Chesterfield Township, N.J., was originally settled by Quakers in the early 1680s, and a meeting was organized in 1684. The first meetinghouse was completed in 1692; a new one, built in 1706, was later replaced by the meetinghouse erected in 1773. The Crosswicks Meeting was also more formally known as the Chesterfield Friends Meeting (Woodward and Hageman, *Burlington and Mercer Counties*, 286–89; WPA, *New Jersey*, 571).

66. During the Philadelphia campaign and the occupation and eventual withdrawal of British forces, regular tax levies for the night watchman and street lamps had not been collected, and the wardens were forced to borrow money to pay salaries and buy oil. The Supreme Executive Council allowed private levies for support of the watch and maintenance of the street lamps until new legislation could be passed for a regular tax levy (*Col. Recs. Pa.*, 11:559; *Statutes at Large*, 9:390–92).

Decr. 1. [J.] Parish put up the Stove in the back-Parlour—he drank tea and sup'd with us—Betsy Watson spent the Afternoon, S. Emlen M. Smith, Jos. Knights Daughter, J Logan, call'd—appearances of great rejoysing all day: on choosing a President, Josh. Read is said to be the man;[67] ringing of Bells and fireing of cannon,—moderate weather.

Decr. 2. HD. not return'd—[J.] Parish, finishd putting the stove in order, he din'd with us—Sally Logan spent the afternoon, [T.] Fisher and J. Drinker call'd—moderate weather.

3. a pleasant warm day for the season—Thomas Smith, Wm. Norton, S. Swetts, &c call'd—Hannah Drinker and Nancy Parish spent the Afternoon—Reba. Waln calld—HD. return'd home this evening.

4. Wm. Norton, Josa. Howell, Edd. Penington, Saml. Smith, Thos. Lightfoot, Susa. Lightfoot, Reba. Jones, Abl. Parish; several girls—call'd—Abel James din'd with us—J. Drinker drank tea—Danl. Drinker call'd—Saml. Emlen—fine weather.

5. very busy all day.—several in and out, a Chimney on fire this Afternoon, next Door but one, where Marshall liv'd—and one over the way yesterday—Sl. Emlen drank tea with us—Becky and Hannah here—a Vesel this Afternoon from Nantz brings an account, that England and Franch are likely to come to an accomodation, &c—rain all day—Abijah Wright was Executed this forenoon on the commons, for I know not what.[68]

Decr. 12. a Chimney took fire next Door to Follwells at the small House, and burnt with violance for a long time.

13 First day: Several Friends here to day: Wm. Smith din'd with us.

14 HD. left home this Morning about 8 o'clock to accompany Saml. Emlen a few miles on his way to Fairfax in Virginia, he intended to return after dinner, or in the Evening at farthest, but is not yet return'd, and it is now near 10 o'clock. Saml. Noble, Charles West, Thos. Masterman, Docr. Cooper, Isaac Catheral, Wm. Norton, here after dinner: Susanna Jones and her Daughter

67. Joseph Reed, an attorney, was elected president of the Supreme Executive Council on Dec. 1. His election was celebrated with a military procession down Market Street with regimental music, and with a festive dinner at the City Tavern, where thirteen toasts were given, each accompanied by the firing of cannon (*Pa. Packet*, Dec. 5, 1778).

68. Col. Abijah Wright was charged with burglary and felony for breaking into the house of Andrew Knox. It was charged that Wright, armed when he broke in, intended to murder Knox. Samuel Rowland Fisher later wrote in his diary that Wright was hanged for acting as a guide to the British army while the British controlled Philadelphia (*Col. Recs. Pa.*, 11:631–32; *Pa. Packet*, Dec. 8, 1778; S. R. Fisher, "Fisher Journal," 170).

Sucky spent the Afternoon with us—Jonathan Jones and Reba. Waln here this Evening about 130 Light Horse came into Town yesterday—G. Washingtons Wife in Town—a grand entertainment at the New Tavern.

15. HD. return'd this evening he went with Sammy and his companion B Dorsey, as far as Thos. Pims 36 or 7 miles from hence where he lodg'd last night—Several here to day.

16 talk of the English being at Monmouth—and that the Fleets arriv'd at Carolina, HD and MS spent part of the evening at Wm. Fishers the evening HD. returnd—Saml. Trimble and his Mother in Law Phebe Trimble came here with their Horses—they sup'd and lodg'd with us—went away next morning after Breakfast—Betsy Stedman, Neigr. Carliles old maid, came yesterday to live here.

Dec. 18 Josa. and Caty Howel and their Daughr. Caty spent the Afternoon with us—HD—received a Letter from J. Cramound—our new Maid has had a visitor all day and has invited hir to lodge with her, without asking leave, times are much changed, and Maids are become mistresses.

Decr. 19. P. Pemberton and M. Pleasants sent Molly this Morning to ask my Company with them, to see G. Washingtons Wife:[69] which visit I declin'd.

Decr. Robt. Smith from Egg-Harbor sup'd and lodg'd here.

69. The word "the" crossed out.

1779

1779. Janry. 4—S Swett and Abel James din'd with us—Several Young Folke here this Afternoon and Evening with our Girls—a young man came this evening from Atsion with a Waggon, for HD. and J.D—he lodg'd here.

5 3d. day HD—and JD—left home after Breakfast for Atsion very unfavourable weather—they cross'd the river partly on the Ice—unsafe crossing. Snow all day—S. Swett call'd—Reba Waln spent part of the evening—I have reason to believe that I swolled a pin this evening.

6. stay'd within all day, nobody here; the calf kill'd this morning in full view of the Cow, which I think a cruel way of manageing—little Molly unwell in her Bowels, as she has been great part of this Winter, she is often up these cold nights—cleard up.

7. rather dull weather—Jenny Heaton spent this afternoon with us—Robt. Waln part of the evening.

8. Jenny Heaton spent this day with us—Sammy Emlen call'd this Morning he returned yesterday evening from Virginia—John Parish, John Balderston &c call'd—HD return'd this Afternoon from Atsion After candlelight—cloudy.

1[4] HD. and the Girls went this Afternoon to the Funeral of Hannah Shoemaker, daughter of Saml. Shoemaker—who has been upwards of a year confin'd.

19. Snow allmost all day: E. Morris din'd and spent the afternoon.

1779 Janry. 23—our Maid Elizabeth, has been in Bed all day, with the ague and Fiver, Sister is very much taken up in the Kitchen, having none but little John to help, Molly Brookhouse occasionly.

24 First day: HD. was let blood—S. Swett din'd and drank tea—Becky and Hannah spent the Afternoon and part of the evening.

Febry. 4 fifth day—HD. and JD—left home this Morning for Atsion, HD.

unwell—a man brought cheese and lard from Newbolds—Reba. Waln here this Morning—Sally and Nancy out, bought mantua for Gowns at £7– p yard—S. and M Pleasants and Molly Pleasants, spent this Afternoon, with us.

5. Saml. Sansom spent this Afternoon, Saml. Emlen, Reba. Waln, Suky Hartshorn, R. Jones here in the Evening—clear and cold.

6 a fire broke out this Morning a little before day, in front street or water street, opposite to Mary Armitts, and consum'd 3 Houses.[1] Abraham Sharpless brought a Letter from Saml. Trimble, he took the sugar for him—a Letter from L. Salter—Betsy Jervis spent the day with us, and lodg'd here—A fuss this evening on the Commons, fireing of Guns, &c, on the Annaversary of the Alliance with France.[2] Snow this Afternoon.

7 First day: stay'd at home all day—E. Jervis has been with us[3]—S. Swett spent the Evening—Sarah Fisher here—Reba. Waln—dull weather.

8. Sally ill in the Night and this Morning with a vomitting—better in the Afternoon, Sally Logan, E Jervis and D Drinker drank tea with us—10 Barrels Flour from R. Waln—Molly Moore, D. Eastaugh, call'd—raw—a Letter from HD.

9 S. Emlen, R. Waln, Polly Smith; Ed. Stevenson from towards Kingwood, call'd Aunt Jervis and Polly spent the afternoon; Catty Howell call'd for Sister, who went with her to Becky Shoemakers.

10—spring like weather—several call'd—HD. return'd this Evening—Betsy Jervis went home—she has been with us ever since seventh day.

11 step'd in to see our Neighr. Carlile, who is very much agitated by the visit of Smith and Wills, who came there this Morning to take an account of Abrahams Effects—Sister out this Afternoon; moderate weather.

Febry. 18. we have had much Company in the last week. 4 or 5 young Girls to see our Daughters this afternoon. Phebe Pemberton and M. Pleasants in the Evening. Benn. Mason sup'd and lodgd.

19 Nancy very poorly with sore throat &c—Nancy and Hannah Hopkins

1. The fire broke out on Front Street near Chestnut (*Pa. Gaz.*, Feb. 10, 1779).

2. Two treaties between the United States and France, one recognizing the independence of the United States, the other forming a military alliance between the two countries, had been signed Feb. 6, 1778. The second treaty went into effect when war broke out between England and France on June 17, 1778 (Boatner, *American Revolution*, 400–401).

3. The word "over" crossed out.

here this Afternoon—I spent it at Molly Foulkes, R Waln here this evening she propos'd my being an Overseer with her at C. Howel approaching Nuptals,[4] she is to pass meeting on third day next, with Johns Hopkins from Maryland—moderate weather.

20 Nancy still poorly—little Molly has been most of this winter disorderd in her Bowels, up 2 or 3 times almost every night, tho' bravely in the day time, Wm. Smith, C. West, Benn. Swett, &c here this Morning, Hannah Hopkins, Jos. Howel, John Drinker, Saml. Wallace, Josh. Bringhurst—Wid. Rusel to measure the Girls for Stays—Becky Jones and Katn. Howell call'd, the latter desird my attendance at meeting with her Daughter on third day—I have not refus'd—but dont seem desireous of offices of this kind—cooler today.

21 First Day. Nancy better, step'd this Morning into Neigr. Howels, finding some scruples arise in my mind respecting this (to me) new office, but came away without any change in the matter—went to meeting this Afternoon, Molly Moore and Danl. Drinker drank Tea with us. S. Swett call'd—temperate.

22. Spent this afternoon with By Jones, my Henry and Sally, at Saml. Smiths.

23. went to meeting monthly this Morning with Johns Hopkins and Caty Howel, Reba. Waln is my partner on the occasion, felt a little comical on going into the mens meeting[5]—Molly Pleasants jun'r. John James, David Eastaugh and a Friend from the Country din'd with us—S. Logan, J. Logan, &c &c here in the afternoon, step'd over to Nr. Walns in the Evening.

24 Spent the Afternoon, Nancy with me, at Grace Galloways, she lives with Debby Morris, a good deal of Company there, went to Nr. Howels this evening—fine weather, too much so for the Season we have had Crocusses blown in the Garden 3 or 4 days past—newspapers full of matter.

4. To ensure that marriages between Friends were conducted in good order, a monthly meeting would appoint two male and two female overseers to attend the marriage and the festivities that followed. The overseers were responsible for seeing that everyone behaved properly and went home at a respectable hour. They were then obliged to make a report in person at the next monthly meeting and to make sure that the marriage certificate was recorded (Philadelphia Yearly Meeting, *Rules of Discipline* [1797], 67).

5. Overseers for weddings made their reports to both the men's and women's meetings. ED reported to the Philadelphia Northern District Men's Monthly Meeting that Caty Howell and Johns Hopkins were being married according to proper Quaker procedure (see above, Feb. 19; Philadelphia Yearly Meeting, *Rules of Discipline* [1797], 67; Philadelphia Northern District Monthly Meeting, Men's Minutes, 1772–78, p. 351, microfilm, Friends Historical Library, Swarthmore College).

25 spent this Afternoon with Hannah Morris, remarkable fine weather—took a walk this morning Nancy & Henry with me to Sally Whartons, call'd at 2 or 3 Shops.

26 dull weather stay'd all day at home—Reba. Waln and her Daughters, Sucky and Beckey, and P. Hartshorn drank tea with us—our great men, or the Men in Power, are quarreling very much among themselves.

28 First Day: Wm. and Sarah Fisher and C. West drank tea with us—the 2 former stay'd part of the Evening and Becky Jones—a Friend from the Country, deliver'd something remarkable; this Morning at the middle meeting House—of a vision or something like it that had appear'd to him lately—it is many Years since we have known a Season so forward as this—the weather has been for several weeks past very moderate, we have had Crocosses blown in our Garden for a week past, and this day persian Irises are also blown—the Apricott Trees are in Blossom.

March 4—last night at near 12 o'clock a fire broke out in second street nearly opposite to Uncle Jerviss at Capn. Rancons, some wooden back buildings were distroy'd—HD. went this forenoon to Frankford. moderate weather—Billy began his first quarter yesterday with John Tomson to learn Latin—took a walk this Afternoon.

March 15th. little Henry went to School to Jos Yerkes, the first of his going to a mans School.

23. went this Morning to monthly meeting, Caty Howel past her second meeting—E. Morris and R. Hunt. din'd with us—we have lately had several snows and some hard frost—which 'tis to be suppos'd has kill'd the early fruit, if no more—changable weather.

27 a number of Friends here to day, at the Spring meeting—S. Trimble and John Balderston lodges here—Robt. Valentine, B. Swett, Abm. Gibbons, &c. &c.

28 First Day: stay'd at home this morning went to meeting afternoon and Evening—S. Swett, Wm. Jones, Robt. Willis, Abm. Gibbons and Saml. Trimble din'd with us—After afternoon meeting Thos. and Susa. Lightfoot, Danl. Smith—Wm. Smith, Saml. Fisher, Rachl. Hollandsworth, Ruth Jackson, Sally Brown, Jos. Janney, Wm. Mathews; Rachel Watson, John Balderston, Saml. Trimble, 10 or 12 more, came home with us, they did not all stay tea—we had a Setting, when Susy Lightfoot appeard in testimony—Warner Mifflin and Jessy Waterman call'd[6]—good weather.

6. The word "fine" crossed out.

29. Sammy and John Breakfasted—Isaac Pickering Tommy James din'd—Ruth Jackson, Polly James, Oliver Paxton, Polly Waln, John Allsup, Saml. Hopkins &c call'd—A. James and Wife, Josa. Brown and Wife, Saml. Trimble Polly James sup'd with us—J Balderston went away this Afternoon—Samuel Burdge was bury'd yesterday afternoon.

30 went to meeting this morning Sammy Trimble went home—one Friend only din'd with us—Mary Eddy spent the Afternoon—the Wid Hartshorn from Bristol, Neigr. Waln, Geo. Churchman, Jacob Shoemaker, Reba. James &c &c call'd—Tommy Fisher and John James, who were this Morning at Timy. Matlacks on a visit to his Son, were beat by Timothy with a Cane, in his Entry and in the Street—until he broke the[7] it—Sammy Fisher taken up, and had before the Chief Justice, on account of a Letter which 'tis said he wrote—little Becky Follwell, who was yesterday at play with our Molly and several other Children, at Neigr. Howels door, fell of the Poarch and broke her Arm, very moderate weather—Billy went to Day a foot to Frankford, with Tommy James, [J.] Gilpen Isey and John Pleasants, came home in the Evening.

31 Benn. and Polly Swett their Son, Wm. Bleakey and another man, Breakfasted with us—Rachel Hollandsworth, Ruth Jackson and Sarah Brown, and Sammy Pleasants, Debby Morris also, din'd with us—HD. sup'd with them at S Pleasants—Sally Maul, Sammy Hopkins, &c call'd—warm.

April the 1 HD. went with the Virginia Friends as far as Darby, return'd in the Evening—Josa. Howell his Wife and Daughter spent the Afternoon—a great noise this Afternoon with poor Watch. Robt. Waln very angry, his naughty Son, has almost spiol'd the Dogs temper, by tormenting him—good weather.

2d. HD—left home after dinner, for Willmington—Betsy Waln and her two Daughters din'd with us—they and Polly Brown spent the Afternoon, Abel James, Josey Smith, Nancy Hopkins, Polly Howel, Becky Jones, Robert Stevenson Reba. Waln call'd.

April 3—a Letter from Law. Salter, [Js.] Kendle, Becky Jones, &c call'd—Wm. Smith also—Betsy Jervis here very warm.

4 First Day. went to meeting this Afternoon, the weather much chang'd, cool with rain—B. Jervis lodg'd here last night, spent this day, and continues with us.

7. The word "stick" crossed out.

5 Susy Jones and her daughter Sucky, Docr. Redman, John Drinker, Danl. Drinker, &c call'd—set up till after 12 making Candles. very fine weather E [J.] here.

5 Saml. Emlen, Danl. Drinker, Han. Jones, &c call'd, S. Swett and B. Jervis din'd with us, Sarah Lewis, Polly Mifflin, Reba. Waln, Nancy Waln, Molly Pleasants and Sally Zane, spent the Afternoon here—Cs. Mifflin, HD. came home this Afternoon—Sammy Fisher was put in Prison on Second day Night last—cold this evening.

April 18. there has been greater transitions (for these two months past) from cold to heat, and heat to cold, than I ever remember to have remark'd—first day afternoon the 11th. Instant was as warm as midsummer, and on the next day we sat by a good fire comfortably;—the 13th. attended the marriage of Johns Hopkins and Caty Howel, upwards of 60 persons at Wedding,—Samuel Garrigus and James Stevens who were accused of High treason, were clear'd at coart, some time since[8]—Sally and little Molly were taken unwell the night before last with a vomiting, are now better; HD. unwell.

19 Abel James and Lawrence Salter din'd with us—Aunt Jervis, Betsy and Polly, and Sally Wharton spent the Afternoon with us—Becky Jones, Reba. Waln, Wm. Smith &c call'd.

20—John Payne and Wife here this Morning they din'd with us on sixth day last, Virginians, went with 'em to meeting—S Swett din'd here, Sally Moore spent the Afternoon—Sally Penington, Saml. Pleasants, John Drinker calld—all our Fruit in the Yard and Garden spoild with the Frost—fine weather this day.

22 John Payne and wife din'd with us—I spent this afternoon the Girles with me, on a visit to our Neighbor Caty Hopkins—several young women there—our Friend Israel Pemberton departed this Life early this morning—I am told this evening that there is a Bill found against Sammy Fisher.[9]

8. Samuel Garrigues the elder, a clerk of the market and trader, and James Stephenson, a baker, were among the more than fifty men charged with treason in a proclamation issued by the Supreme Executive Council on May 8, 1778. Garrigues was thought to have employed spies to work for the British during the attack on Red Bank (Fort Mercer) in the fall of 1777. The two were acquitted in April 1779 (*Col. Recs. Pa.*, 11:481–86, 513–18; Marshall, *Diary Extracts*, 143; *Pa. Packet*, Aug. 26, Dec. 12, 1778; the acquittal of Garrigues Sr. and Stephenson is noted in Christopher Marshall's diary, Apr. 17, 1779, HSP, quoted in Rosswurm, *Arms, Country, and Class*, 341 n. 42).

9. Samuel Rowland Fisher had been ordered to appear before Judge Thomas McKean on Mar. 30, 1779, on charges of conducting a correspondence inimical to the interests of Pennsylvania and the United States, and conveying intelligence to the enemy. Fisher, who refused to post bond or let any of his friends do so, was placed in the city jail. A grand inquest in April found enough evidence to indict him, but because the state was not ready to proceed to trial in the April session he was released from jail on Apr. 24 (S. R. Fisher, "Fisher Journal," 145–57; see below, Apr. 24).

April 23 Robt. and Nancy Jones spent this Afternoon with us.—Nancy related some things (tho' I believe not quite candidly) that Susannah Lightfoot had said to her, at their Door touching her Head-dress &c—Caty Howel, HD. and myself, went this evening to see the remains of our friend Israel Pemberton found several Friends there.

24 fine weather—Billy and [J.] Gillpin had a super this evening in the Kitchen, of Fish of their own taken, and were much pleased—Sammy Fisher sat at Liberty, his tryal put of 'till next Court—several call'd.

25 First Day. HD. and Billy attended the Funeral of I. Pemberton before morning Meeting—very fine weather, went to afternoon and evening meetings.

May 2 First day—in the last week past several things occur'd which I have omitted,[10] call'd in that time to see, M Pleasants after the death of her Father:—Jos. Burr, lodg'd here, one or 2 nights—on third day last at monthly meeting, Hannah Catheral made a miniut (that one of the Friends who attended the mariage of Johns Hopkins &c, reported, that it was orderly accomplished)—which as Reba. Waln, was the person who spoke—and I only stood up, made it necessary for me to repeat, what she had before said, or to the same effect—which was something trying to me; as I do not remember an instance of it being requir'd of both,—as my appearance fully assented to what RW. deliver'd—a number of Friends have been here in and out for some days past, as HD has been preparing for his departure for Virginia &c with S Emlen—he has been very unwell of late with some pain in his breast and rising of Phlegm &c—yesterday John Brinton and wife came here, stay'd with us till after dinner this day—many friends here this morning—went to meeting this morning—S. Emlen appear'd in testimony—HD. read the Epistle from Irland[11] several came home with us—my Henry appears rather better in health today than for some days past, I wish he may be favour'd with health sufficient to prosicute the Journey, I have been much pain'd lately on that account—he took leave of me and the Children after dinner, and went to S. Emlens, Sister and Billy &c with him, on Sisters return she inform'd us that HD, and SE &c set off a little after 2 o'clock, they have a fine day—sent John this afternoon

10. The words "being taken up with" crossed out.

11. The 1778 epistle of the National Half-Year's Meeting held in Dublin, which was to be sent to all the meetings in Ireland, decried the spiritual decline of the Society and contained testimonies against vanity, ambition, and greed. The Philadelphia Meeting for Sufferings printed and circulated the document among their own meetings (*An Epistle from the National Half-Year's Meeting Held in Dublin 3/5/1778 to 3/7/1778* [Philadelphia: Philadelphia Meeting for Sufferings, 1779], in pamphlet group 1, Society of Friends, Ireland Yearly Meeting, Friends Historical Library, Swarthmore College; for a general discussion of the epistles and contacts between the Meeting for Sufferings and British and Irish Quakers during the Revolutionary War, see Kenneth L. Carroll, "Irish and British Quakers and Their American Relief Funds, 1778–1797," *PMHB* 102 (1978): 437–56).

to Johney Pembertons with Mare—Sammy Smith, Becky Jones, Josa. Gillpin and Sammy Hopkins call'd, the latter at near nine this evening—he has been as far as two miles beyond Darby with my Henry, he says he left them as well as usual—[Wm. Longe] call'd.

3 paid Wm. Smith 15 half Joes, for a bay Horse, on whome HD. is gone abroad—Sister, Nancy and Billy gone to quarterly meeting this morning—I stay'd at home with the little ones,—Norris Jones, from Pottss Slitting Mill call'd this Afternoon to inform us that HD &c lodg'd last night at his House, and left it this morning at 7 o'clock—Sister and Nancy went this Afternoon to the Funeral of M. Franklin—Amos Weeting, John Drinker, Reba. Waln &c call'd, [J.] Gillpin and Tommy James drank tea with Billy, warm to day.

4 S Pleasants, James Thornton, Jonas Cattle, Josey James, Saml. Hopkins, [J.] Parish and wife call'd—Docr. Redman here this morning consulting about Innoculating our dear little Molly—he has sent three pills for her to take preparati[ve] theretoo—one of which she took this evening—the Children went to youths meeting, except little Henry who has a hard cough—Becky James junr. din'd with us, Billy din'd at Josh. Gillpins—Subscrib'd for a B—— £1"2"6. [T.] Scatergood call'd to extract[12] minuets from the monthly-meeting Book, for himself and C. West—Sammy Smith call'd to borrow our Chaise for Becky Jones and Hannah Catheral—Sally Logan spent the Afternoon with us—our Girles at Isaac Zanes—warm weather.

5. Caty Hopkins call'd this morning to bid us farewell as she was just seting off with her Husband for[13] Maryland—I took a walk before dinner to M. Pleasants, four of her little ones the young[er] were innoculated on second day last—our Child was ill in the night, occasion'd by the Pill she had taken, vomited 8 or 10 times &. is better this morning—one David Wright here with an order from L. Salter—John Pemberton, J. Drinker, Josey Potts came this afternoon with a Letter from my Henry, he accompany'd him as far on the way as Wm. Millers 40 miles from home; he is better in health then when he left home—Caty Howel spent part of the evening with us—Debby Norris and Isaac, the 2 Wisters and Sally Jones, call'd—Lawrence Salter here towards evening—fine weather for travelers, but rather windy—a packet arriv'd at New-York, much news in the Papers.

6 Sammy Smith, J. Drinker, Docr. Redman call'd—this is called a day of fasting and prayer[14]—I gave my little Molly a second pill this evening—Sister

12. The word "some" crossed out.
13. The word "Virginia" crossed out.
14. On Mar. 20 the Continental Congress proclaimed May 6 to be a day of fasting, prayer, and humiliation (*JCC*, 14:272, 342–44).

and Billy spent this Afternoon at S. Emlens the Girles at D. Norriss—moderate weather.

7 Saml. Smith, Josa. Cresson, Benj. Dorsey, Reba. Waln, call'd—Mary Armitt spent the afternoon, Molly Moore came in the Evening and Lodg'd with us, I gave the Child a third pill this evening—fine weather.

8 John Drinker and John Balderston, call'd Debby Morris and M. Moore and Docr Redman drank tea with us, the latter continues here M.M—fine weather.

9 First Day: gave my little Molly a purdge of Rheubarb.—before 11 this Morning she was innoculated by Docr. Redman in her Arm—Sammy Hopkins, Joshua Howel, Reba. Waln, call'd—Phebe Pemberton and [Po]lly Lewis came this evening after Molly Moore—Danl. Drinker and MM. drank tea with us—Nanny Carlile and MM sup'd with us[15]—very fine weather—[J.] Gillpin Jo Sansom.

10 went this morning to S. Pleasants, call'd at J. Jerviss &c—Betsy and Polly Jervis spent the afternoon—M. Moore is still with us—received a Letter from HD—gave little Molly a powder this evening her arm is a little inflam'd—very fine weather.

11 S. Swett spent the day with us—Wm. Rush call'd twice to speak with M. Moore—I went after dinner to Amos Taylors and George Guest—Docr. Redman, Bell Cresson, J. Elliotts wife, D. and E. Drinker—Saml. Smith &c call'd—gave Molly a powder this evening—she has been very feverish all night which adds to my anxiety—is better to day—Henry has a very bad cough—received two letters to day from my Husband—warm weather.

12 one of the name of Pickering call'd this Morning for a fine, left it as HD. is out of Town—Jams. Logan, Josa. Howel, S. Sansom, &c call'd—Docr. Redman thinks by the appearance of our Childs arm that she will sicken the sooner, she continues a little feverish—Henrys Cough very bad, cloudy to day, rain this evening which is much wanted—M. Moore who has been out all day, came back this evening.

13 rain all day—little Molly[16] unwell in the night—bravely to day—MM, with us all day—Isaac Catherals wife here this evening—a bad night for our poor Cow, who is missing.

15. The words "the child [ ] very fine weather" crossed out.
16. The word "very" crossed out.

14. James Pemberton, S. Pleasants, J. Drinker, R. Drinker, [S.] Fisher, K. Howel, Josa. Howel—Reba. Waln, S. Hartshorn, a man from atsion, and one for a Tax call'd—MM. still with us—Isaac Catheral call'd, he was so kind as to go with John to look for the Cow, but found her not, B. Hugens much to blame for not bringing her home—our dear Molly very unwell all last night, a rash broak out on her this morning—a high fever this Afternoon—she was better in the evening complains much of her arm—took a dose of Rheubarb which work'd—'tis said that 30 or 40 sail of Vesels have been seen up Chesapeak-Bay, with in these few days—British. fine clear moderate weather, for our dear Child.

15 the report of yesterday, appears doubtful to day—little Molly full of a rash again this Morning—feverish tho' chearfull all day; the Doctor thinks her Fever yesterday, was not of the small-Pox—I am of a different oppinion as her arm run, and her breath was very offencive, she is gone to Bed with much fever; after having been very cold—Aunt Jervis and Betsy spent the Afternoon S. Swett and MM also; D. Drinker who had been looking for his stray'd Cows thought he had seen ours, little John went with him to the place, but she was gone—Billy went about Noon with Josa. Gillpin to Frankford intending to stay with Tommy James, untill Second day, Morning—Josey Drinkers Boy brought some dry'd peaches this afternoon—says the Family came to Town last Night, J. Drinker here this Morning—he is gone with S. Pleasants to the Grove-Meeting[17]—Butter from Jonas Cattle, Josa. Howell and Sammy Emlen junr. call'd—very fine weather.

16 First Day—the Childs fever high in the night; no other eruption then the rash has yet appear'd, her arm very painful—Sally Moore, S. Swett, Hannah Catheral, Senr. Wm. Norton and Wife, call'd—Danl. Drinker, Becky Wharton and little John R. Cox drank tea with us—Molly Moore call'd away this Morning to Polly Mifflin—I went to meeting only in the Afternoon—Doctor and K. Howel this evening—the girles went to see their Cousins—fine weather—found the Cow.

17 went out this morning—Molly had but a restless night, tho' not so much fever as the 2 preceeding nights—little Henry very bad with the Cought, it seems like the hooping cought—I slept none 'till after day—30 or 40 small-Pox made their appearance this morning—she has been bravely all day, but complains much of her arm—Abel James, Willm. Norton, Charles West, Isaac Catheral, Reba. Waln, Patty Anderson &c called—Billy came home this

17. London Grove was a township in Chester County, Pa., settled by Quakers in 1701. A meeting was established there in 1714, the same year its first meetinghouse was built. The meetinghouse was replaced by a larger one in 1743 (Forsythe, "Historical Sketch," 20–31).

morning JG. with him—fine weather—heard to day, that HD. was well some time since at West river, the Girles out this Afternoon.

18 I was awake with the Children almost all Night a few more small pox out on Molly this Morning they itch very much, which makes her restless—Debby Morris, Rachel Drinker, Hannah Drinker Senr. J. Logan, Josa. Bringhurst, Nics. Waln, Molly Smith, Hannah Saunders, Katty Howel, Docr R— call'd—Patty Smith, Becky James junr. D. Eastaugh, and E. Sindry din'd with us—Aunt Jervis spent the Afternoon—cloudy this evening.

19 little Molly bravely, Henrys Cough very bad—rain last night, this morning and evening—Molly Pleasants junr. drank tea, J. Drinker, D. Drinker, Doctor and Tommy Redman, call'd—I received this Afternoon £40/5– for one English Guinea—Taylor here.

20 Molly continues bravely—upwards of an hundred small pox made their appearance but not above 6 or 8 have come to perfection, John Elliott Senr. call'd to inform of a Letter from his Son, when near Curles, giving an account of the wellfare of my HD. &c—Sally Logan, drank tea with us—Docr. Redman, Josa. Howell, Sally Zean, S. Swett, D. Drinker, Becky Jones, call'd—cloudy; children at meeting this morning, Hannah Jones married.

21 Chalkley James, din'd with us, Patty Smith, Becky and Josey James, drank tea—Wm. Norton, J. Drinker, D. Drinker, Sammy Fisher, Betsy & Molly Jervis, call'd—cloudy most of this day.

22 Henry has not been to School or meeting for 2 weeks past, on account of his Cough, which increases—John has the same, tho not so bad. Sister and Sally out this afternoon,—Sarah Fisher, here—S. Stapler call'd with a Letter from [T] R—clouds, and sunshine—thunder this evening—many are apprehensive of a Mob rising on second day next—with a view of discovering monopolizers &c.[18]

18. Philadelphians were agitated throughout 1779 over the fall in value of Continental currency and the scarcity and high price of foodstuffs and supplies. On May 12 an artillery company of the Philadelphia militia sent a complaint to the Supreme Executive Council about inequities in pricing. In the following week a ship, *Victorious,* arrived with dry goods, which sold for exorbitant prices, and flour prices increased precipitously. Many citizens accused Robert Morris, then a private citizen who had an interest in the vessel, of transgressing market regulation laws already passed by the Pennsylvania Assembly. Christopher Marshall, a leading radical who belonged to Philadelphia's Constitutional Society, came to Philadelphia from Lancaster for the express purpose of organizing a town meeting to create a price-control committee. On May 22 he issued a call for a meeting on May 25 (Foner, *Tom Paine,* 161–66; Rosswurm, *Arms, Country, and Class,* 172–78; Hazard, *Pa. Archives,* ser. 1, 7:392–94; Oberholtzer, *Robert Morris,* 54–55; Clarence L. Ver Steeg, *Robert Morris, Revolutionary Financier* [Philadelphia: University of Pennsylvania Press, 1954], 28–34; Marshall, *Diary Extracts,* 217).

23 First Day: S Swett din'd—A Parish came from meeting with me and drank tea—Wm. Miller and Jemmy Emlen, Owen Jones Senr., Hannah Catheral D. Drinker, call'd—my little Molly took a dose of Phisick to day:—Docr. call'd—warm to day—Abel James junr. din'd with us—heard cannon fire.

24 S. Swett spent the day—she and Nics. Waln junr. din'd—threatning hand-Bills pasted at the corners, with a view to lower the prises of provisions &c[19]—Thos. Masterman, C. West, Jon. Drinker, S. Pleasants, Isaac Catheral, Reba. Waln, &c call'd, Betsy Waln, her daughter Polly and Josey, drank tea with us—George Baker borrow'd the Chaise—an northernlight appear'd this evening—they have had this Afternoon a general muster or review—a thousand or fifteen hundred men of the Militia were drawn up, between Race and Market Streets, a sight by no means agreeable to me—several Persons, were taken up to day a put in Prison. Rich'd. Mason, Joseph Hensey, John Wall, and Abram. Kintzing are committed—a Town meeting propos'd to morrow at the State House[20]—Accounts to day that Suffolk is burnt, a Storm seems to be geathering on all sides, happy for them, that are prepar'd to meet it—our dear little Molly is very unwell this evening—feverish and her Arm very painful—Henrys Cough so bad that he frequently vomitts when he coughs—weather very warm to day—Joshua Fisher call'd—no accounts from HD.

25 the Bell-Man was about this morning proclaiming a meeting to be held at the State House.—Saml. Smith call'd for the monthly meeting Book[21]—Katty Howel, Polly Smith, Docr. Redman, call'd—Sister and the 4 Children at meeting this Morning—Rachl. Hunt din'd with us, she and Becky Jones drank tea,—Richd. Wister and Levi Hollandsworth, put in prison, have not heard on what pretext—a great concorse of people assembled at the State

19. On the night of May 23 someone had posted a broadside throughout the city that threatened to bring down prices by force to where they stood at Christmas. The broadside, signed "Come on Cooly," read: "You that have money, and you that have none, down with your prices, or down with yourselves. For by the living and eternal God, we will bring every article down to what it was last Christmas, or we will down with those who opposed. We have turned out against the enemy and we will not be eaten up by monopolizers and forestallers." As a result of the broadside a number of people were threatened, paraded through town, or jailed the following day. That afternoon the militia held its exercises at 4 P.M. at the State House Yard, then dispersed to prepare for the town meeting on May 25 (Rosswurm, *Arms, Country, and Class*, 178–79).

20. Signers of the handbills circulated on May 24 to promote the next day's town meeting pledged themselves to support any measures the Continental Congress might take to restore confidence in the currency (Bezanson, *Prices and Inflation*, passim; Morris, *Government and Labor*, 107–11, 118–19; Marshall, *Diary Extracts*, 217–18).

21. HD, clerk of the Philadelphia Northern District Monthly Meeting, was out of town and therefore could not attend the monthly meeting on May 25 (Philadelphia Northern District Men's Monthly Meeting Minutes, 1772–81, pp. 12, 369, 1782–89, p. 110, microfilm, Friends Historical Library, Swarthmore College).

House by appointment at 5 this afternoon,[22]—Men with clubbs &c have been to several Stores, oblidging the people to lower their prises—one of the name of Panter from Point call'd here to know if he could hire or buy the meadow there—Tommy Redman the Doctors prentice, put in prison this afternoon for laughing, as the regulators past by, fine weather.

26 Thos. Mastermen call'd this morning tells us that Billy Compton is put into Jail—two men from Tuckehoe, call'd by desire of Wm. Tomlins to inform us that some persons were cutting down the Cedar &c desireing a drought of the Land—, Benn. Humphriss takeing forceably out of his Bed a 12 o'clock last night, rob'd of his hard cash, and put into prison—S. Sansom here this Morning—I went this Afternoon to see Uncle Jervis who is unwell, has become suddenly hard of hearing—call'd at John Elliotts junr. and at M. Chaveliers—Hannah Sansom, Reba. Say, Reba. Waln, Danl. Lawrence from Baltimore and a Man with him; the two later and John Parish drank tea with us, Isaac Catheral, call'd—heard while I was out, that David Franks, John Evans, Nics. Brooks, and Several others were taken to Prison, they went after Rt. Jones, G. Morgan bail'd him, his wife has been in fitts—many are much frightned—Primas came to day and began to whitewash—cloudy to day.

27 Mollys arm painful, gave her a dose Physick, John Parish took down the Stove—received a Letter dated near Curles—Wm. Smith, J. Drinker, call'd Sammy and Hannah Sansom spent the Afternoon, rain last night, cool to day—Thos. Story and several others, put in Prison.

28 Doctor call'd this morning discover'd a swelling under our dear childs

22. The May 25 public meeting at the State House Yard was the first extralegal public meeting to create a price-control committee. In fact, two somewhat overlapping committees were created: one to set prices at their May 1 level, another to investigate Robert Morris's business practices. The resolves passed that day included a statement directing the committees to "take measures" to ensure that anyone "who by sufficient testimony can be proved inimical to the interests and independence of the United States not be allowed to remain among us." In practice, this meant that radical militia members or others could seize people and put them in jail for unspecified crimes. The only documentary evidence for the arrests comes from sources such as ED's diary, Christopher Marshall's diary, Sarah Bache's letters and other personal correspondence, and Joseph Stansberry's historical ballad. From the sources available it appears at least twenty-one men were arrested between May 24 and the end of May, nineteen of whom can be identified.

On May 28 the Supreme Executive Council, disturbed by these extralegal arrests, ordered the city magistrates to determine if there was sufficient evidence to bind over those arrested for trial at the next court of quarter sessions. Those for whom there was enough evidence could be bound over, but could also post bail and be released until their court date. Those for whom there was not sufficient evidence were to be released. The council's action apparently had the desired effect, for the arrests ceased after May 30 (Rosswurm, *Arms, Country, and Class,* 181–83; Alexander, "Fort Wilson Incident of 1779," 597–98; Stone, "Philadelphia Society," 383; Joseph Stansberry's ballad is quoted in full in J. F. Watson, *Annals,* 2:304; Foner, *Tom Paine,* 145–68; Hubertis Cummings, "Robert Morris and the Episode of the Poleacre Victorious," *PMHB* 70 (1946): 239–57; Bezanson, *Prices and Inflation,* 28–34 and passim; Morris, *Government and Labor,* 107–11; Marshall, *Diary Extracts,* 217–18).

Arm, which he has ordre'd to be bath'd with vinager, and talks of more purdgeing—George [Shloser] and a young man with him, came to inquire what stores we have; look'd into the middle Room and Seller, behav'd compl[as]ant[23]—their Athority the Populace—one Runnion from Kingwood brought our Beds this morning—I went this Afternoon to S Sally Emlens, who has been frightn'd by a mobb that surrounded the House at past one in the morning the day before yesterday, after making a noise for some time, went away,—I call'd at Wm. Fishers, S. Fisher unwell in her Chamber—the Inspectors I find have been at most Houses to day: taking account of Stores and provision—Wm. Norton, Betsy Huff, Nany Carlisle, Hannah Drinker, Isaac Catheral, J. Drinker—call'd—good weather.

29 very busy all day; our dear little one, very feverish and restless most part of last night, the swelling to day much the same—S Swett, Reba. Waln, three weeks tomorrow, since the date of HDs last Letter.

30 First Day: Doctor J. Parish, J. Drinker, Sally Moore, call'd before morning meeting—Polly Wells, Paisy Jackson, and [Mordeica] Moores daughter call'd after meeting. I went to meeting this Afternoon and Afterwards designed to go to O Jones—but was stop'd by rain and went with T. and R Say to their Son Benjns where I spent the Afternoon, came home towards evening found at our House, Hannah Lloyd and two of her granddaughters Hannah and Sally Pemberton—our Childs Arm very painful this evening the swelling increas'd, & feverish.

31 Molly took a purdge to day, it work'd well, she appears better her Arm not so painful, tho the swelling continues—a very heavey shower this afternoon, C. West, Sarah Goodman, Joseph Drinker, J. Drinker, Reba. Jones, call'd—S. Nobles Family allarm'd in the night by a Mob; some persons put into Jail to day, others let out.[24]

June 1st. [T.] Scattergood, Jenny Clark, Doctor S Swett &c here this morning—put a poltice to the Childs Arm, James and John Pemberton, Sammy Fisher, call'd after meeting Sally Emlen also; (a young man from Leesburge, by desire of Joseph Jenny) has inform'd her, that our Husbands were gone forward to Old Neck in North Carolina, and were to be at Fairfax meeting[25]

23. Words crossed out.
24. Words crossed out.
25. The Fairfax Meeting was established in 1744 in Waterford Township, Fairfax County, Va. In 1757 Waterford became part of Loudon County. The meeting, founded by Quakers moving south into Virginia from Bucks County, Pa., also included the Monoquesy Valley or Cold Spring Meeting, which was just north of it on the Maryland side of the Potomac River. In the years preceding and immediately following the Revolutionary War it was one of the fastest growing meetings in Virginia (Hinshaw, *American Quaker Genealogy*, 463–64; Gragg, *Migration*, 38–41, 60).

the 20 Instant Sammy Trimble and S Swett din'd with us—paid Jonas Cattle for 20 Butter—, Polly Swett, Han Catheral, Hulda Mott, Sucky Jones, Reba. Waln call'd—Sally Emlen and little Betsy spent the Afternoon with us, our Girls went this afternoon with Hannah Sansom, her daughter &c to their Place, came home much tir'd—received three Letters from HD. and SE—wrote this evening to my Henry—I was pleas'd to hear the watchman cry the hour last night, as they had discontinud it for above a week past, for what reason, I have not learn'd—very fine weather HD. is not gone as we thought, to No. Carolina.

2d. I went down Town on errants, M. Pleasants hear part of the morning—Hannah Moore spent the Afternoon with us—Sammy Hopkins, Eliza. Sindry, Wm. Norton, Josa. Howel call'd, very fine weather—'tis said this evening that the British Troops at Carolina are beat, &c &c.

3. Molly Pleasants, Doctor call'd this Morning—Danl. Drinker and Betsy, drank tea with us Sammy Hopkins was busy here this evening Sally and Nancy spent the Afternoon with Debby Morris—very fine weather Molly [Lahew] Wm. Heysham call'd, to settle some matters relateing to Henry Moore at Cranberry.

4 one Cresswell from Chester County call'd to talk about some Land—Sally Logan, Dr. Redman, Sammy Pleasants, Sammy Sansom, and John Parish, drank tea with us—Sammy Smith &c call'd.

5 Betsy and Polly Jervis spent the day with us—Isaac Hough call'd—James Parker from Kingwood call'd—Sally Fisher, Doctor, Charles West, Tommy Fisher, Katty Howel, John and Daniel Drinker, Tommy [James] drank tea, very warm to day.

6 First Day: the swelling under the Childs arm does not appear to be near ripe, tho I have by the Doctors order chang'd the Poltice, she is often in much pain—I stay'd at home all day, Sister and the Children went to meeting:—S. Swett, the Doctor[r] John and Rachl. Drinker, Hannah Catheral, Sr., Nanny Carlile call'd. Sammy Emlen junr. din'd here—Sister and the Children went out this afternoon. John Drinker, yesterday had before the committe, for refusing to show what provision he had.

7 one Jacob Franks call'd for the Continental Tax[26] but as HD. was from

26. In November 1777 the Continental Congress, which did not have the power to tax directly, had requested a specific amount of money from each state to support the war effort and had passed legislation to procure supplies. As a result, Pennsylvania's projected contribution was set at four million dollars. The Pennsylvania government apportioned this sum by city and county; Philadelphia's share was £497,596 16s 7p. All real and personal property including silver plate and unimproved lands was taxable (Ferguson, *Power of the Purse, 32–34; Statutes at Large*, 9:230–35, 360–72; see also below, June 11, 28, 1779).

home, said he would call again—Saml. Wharton junr. call'd to ask if we had Bees-wax to sell—Isaac Catheral, &c call'd—Girles out this afternoon, very warm busy all day whitewashing and cleaning Rooms.

8 our dear little Molly walks very crooked giving way to her sore Arm—James Logan, Sammy Smith (brought home the Book) Polly Smith, Elizh. Drinker, Danl. Joseph and Hannah Drinker, Hannah Drinker junr. Sally Johnston, Sally Fisher, Joshua Gillpin, Hannah Catheral call'd—a man call'd for the lamp Tax—Sam Jervis brought me a letter from my Henry, which he had of Cruthers.

9 a thunderstorm in the night, Molly very much pain'd with the geathering, but releiv'd by its breaking this morning—Henrys cough much better, finish'd whitewashing—a heavy gust with lightning this evening—Danl. Drinker, Reba. Waln, John Drinker Doctor—call'd.

10 Caty Howel call'd for me to go with her to Wm. Fishers, where we spent the Afternoon, Sally Logan drank tea with Sister—Abey Parish, Danl. Drinker call'd for our Chaise—fine week—different are the repoarts of the day, some good some otherwise—nothing to be depended on.

11 I went to S. Emlens this Afternoon, came home with the Headach—H. Catheral, J. Drinker Wm. Smith Doctor &c call'd.—they have been to several persons to day, taking an account of their Plate—much talk of the British being beat and overcome at South Carolina,[27]—Sister expected HD—this evening—I think tomorrow more likely—cool weather to day.

12 Billy went over the river to Swim this afternoon with Josa. Gillpin &c—John & Danl. Drinker, Caty Howel, John Parish, Abel James call'd—Becky Waln borrow'd the Chaise—cool,—look'd out this evening for HD. in vain—step'd over to Neigr. Hartshorns for the first time.

13 First Day: A smart shower this Afternoon, with thunder which they say struck M. Norriss House, S. Hopkins, Reba. Waln, call'd, J. Drinker call'd this morning he is sit of for King-wood.

14 John Elliott Senr. brought a Letter this Morning from Saml Emlen informing of their expectation of being home on 4th. day next—we had the Taylor next door (and several of our Alley neighbors) here, bleeding and

27. American forces had won victories at Beaufort, S.C., on Feb. 3 and at Kettle Creek, Ga., on Feb. 14, though the Philadelphia press did not report them until June (*Pa. Gaz.*, June 9, 16, 1779; *Pa. Packet,* June 8, 12, 1779; Boatner, *American Revolution,* s.v. "Southern Theater," 1034–35).

cooking up the Cow for the Staggers[28]—Isaac Catheral, Danl. Drinker, Doctor call'd—I spent this afternoon at S. Lewiss on a visit to Polly Mifflin who lays in with her second Daughter came home in the rain, stop'd at A. Warners—much thunder and Lightning this afternoon and evening—the Girles out at their Uncles—I went out this morning to shop with Nancy—calld at J Logans and at uncle Jerviss.

15 John Pemberton, S Swett, K Howel call'd this morning—the latter read part of a Letter from her Daughter mentioning HD &c—Sister & the Children gone to meeting—Debby Morris & S. Swett din'd with us—Hannah Moore, Jenny Clark, Wm. Smith, call'd—Zachy. Andrew call'd to pay a grownd rent,[29] which Sister refus'd—Sarah Mitchel, Sally Parish, Debby and Hannah Mitchel spent the Afternoon with us—George Pickering came this Afternoon for the Nonassosiation fine,[30] which came to 13 pounds, which is 13/– as the Money now is exchang'd 20 for one—he took a Looking-Glass worth between 40 and 50/– 6 new Fashion'd Pewter Plates and a 3 qt. pewter Bason, little or nothing the worse for the ware.—the Girles took a walk out of Town to Jacob Shoemakers place with Hannah Drinker &c—Hannah Catheral Senr. here this evening—cool weather.

16 rain most part of this day: a few lines this morning from SE, was received repeating their intention of being with us this evening—Benny Swett, Billy Sansom, and several others call'd—HD. came home this afternoon in the rain, was oblidg'd to change his cloaths—but has not I hope caught much cold—several here this evening.

25 many thunder Gusts in the last weeks.—Katty Howel, her Daughter Betsy, my Nancy and little Molly with myself, went this afternoon to Josa. Howels place on Schuykill, in their waggon; Joshua & HD—on Horse back—spent the Afternoon their—a Storm of wind and rain while there—which towards evening seem'd to abait; we set off, but were presently overtaken by a

28. *Staggers* in this context could mean either stag hunters or, as a slang expression, persons who look out or watch (*OED*).

29. A ground rent was an income reserved by the grantor of land in fee-simple to himself or herself and his or her heirs out of the land conveyed. As a freehold estate held in fee-simple a ground rent was created by deed and was perpetual by the terms of its creation (John Bouvier, *A Law Dictionary, Adapted to the Constitution and Laws of the United States of America and of the Several States of the American Union: With References to the Civil and Other Systems of Foreign Law* [Philadelphia: Lippincott, 1883], 1:723).

30. Nonassociation fines were paid by those who refused to serve in the Pennsylvania militia. The people who first established the militia were known until 1777 as the Associators, or the Association. On Apr. 5, 1779, the Pennsylvania Assembly increased the fines for failure to serve in the militia from £40 in paper currency (about £2.5 in hard coin) to £100 in paper currency (approximately £6 in hard coin) (Rosswurm, *Arms, Country, and Class*, 46, 49, 163–64).

very heavy Shower, with thunder and lightning all the way—we got safe home a little before 9 o'clock.

26—the Bell-man went about the City at near ten this night—desireing the people to arm themselves with guns or Clubs, and make a sarch for such as had sent any Flour, Gun Powder &c out of town, with great threats to the Torys; said it was by order of a Committe.[31]

June 28 Second day: HD. gone this morning to Abington monthly meeting,[32] with S. Pleasants—I took Molly to School to Betsy Devenshire—Christopher Baker and call'd to take an account of our property, in order to lay the continental tax; plate among the rest.

July 5 the annaversary of independence (which was yesterday: it being the first day of the week, did not suit for such doings) was kept this day, with fire works &c.

7 Sister and Nancy went this afternoon to the Funeral of Elizath. Norris, who dy'd yesterday.

8 Sally and Nancy[33] went this morning to the marriage of Charles Logan and Molly Pleasants; spent the rest of the Day at Saml. Pleasants, where the wedding was kept—came home at near 11 o'clock at Night.—our maid Molly Hensel, left us on third day last to go to her Parents in the Countrey—so that we are now without a maid servant.

9 a heavey Shower, with hard thunder early this morning.

19 on sixth day last the Well in our Yard was open'd in order to repair the Pump, which has been long out of order, and this day a new tree put down, and the well closed again which gives me satisfaction; as I always look'd upon open wells of any kind very dangerous whe[re] there is young Children—an

31. This call, one of several issued by the price-fixing committee urging direct action against those who evaded price control regulation, received little public response (Rosswurm, *Arms, Country, and Class*, 186–87).

32. Abington Township, in Montgomery County, Pa., was patented in 1684; its Quaker meetinghouse was begun in 1697 and completed in 1700. Abington, north of Philadelphia, was also the site of a regional monthly meeting, which in 1779 consisted of Abington, Byberry, Germantown, and Horsham meetings. In 1785 it became the site for a quarterly meeting (Theodore W. Bean, ed., *History of Montgomery County, Pennsylvania* [Philadelphia: Evarts & Peck, 1884], 682–85).

33. The words "spent this day" crossed out.

account to day of a Fort at Stony-Point being taken by the Americans,[34] by surprise and [5]oo of the British taken Prisoners—on which account the Bells have been ringing most of the Afternoon—H Catheral sup'd with us—Sister gone to sit up with Patirson Hartshorns Son Robt. who is ill, he is near 5 weeks old—Billy went this afternoon after tea to Frankford on foot with Josa. Gillpin and Tomy. James, intending to stay some days—second day.

22 fifth day: this Morning after Breakfast; Sally cross'd the river with Benn. and Molly Swett, to go with them in their waggon, as far as John Hopkinss where they leave her, to spent a few days—very fine weather.

23 Billy return'd this Morning from Frankford; little Henry has giving me great uneasyness lately, by several times going into the river and attempting to Swim, which he knows nothing of:—living so near the river, the example of other little Boys, joyn'd to his own inclination, makes it hard to restrain him—he brus'd his fore-Finger of his right Hand badly this Afternoon between two Boats—Billy carried at a Burying. Sammy Fisher was this day try'd at Coart, and brought in giltey of mispresion of Treason,[35] for which they say he is to forfit half his Estate and suffer imprisonment during the war—the Jury brought in verdicts to clear him twice, but being sent out a third time, they return'd with an opposet Verdict—fine Liberty.

24 S. Fisher rec'd sentence this day, and is imprison'd.—rec'd a Letter from Sally by Billy Sansom.

25 First Day, rain most of this day: Hannah Catheral din'd with us,—little Henry poorly, he took a dose Rheubarb.

29 rain every day since seventh day last—which will take of part of the satisfaction Sally would otherwise have enjoy'd in the Country—Jemmy Smith

34. American forces won an important victory at Stony Point on July 16 after losing it to British control on June 1. Stony Point was one of two ferry anchorages at King's Ferry below West Point, N.Y., and the closest place on the Hudson River to New York City where American forces were able to operate barges safely and maintain east-west communication lines. It was also the opening to the highlands of New York State. In a midnight raid commencing on July 15 Gen. Anthony Wayne captured the fort and approximately five hundred prisoners along with equipment and stores. The Americans suffered few casualties (Boatner, *American Revolution*, 1062–67).

35. *Misprison of treason* was defined as speaking or writing in opposition to the public defense; attempting to carry information to the enemy; advocating resistance to the government or a return to British rule; discouraging enlistment; inciting disorder; propagandizing for the enemy; and opposing or trying to inhibit Revolutionary measures. The jurors failed twice to convict Fisher, but the state prosecutor sent them back until they returned with a verdict that pronounced him guilty of holding correspondence inimical to the United States (Thomas R. Meehan, "Courts, Cases, and Counselors in Revolutionary and Post-Revolutionary Pennsylvania," *PMHB* 91 (1967): 29; S. R. Fisher, "Fisher Journal," 164–65).

drank tea with us Yesterday, he has not been to see us before since he was apprentice—M Pleasants here this [aft]ernoon—the Town meeting has Concluded more quickly than many expected—tho they are differig much amoung themselves, which may be one reason why peaceable People are left quiet—Johney Drinker, Robt. Jones and 6 or 8 others were nam'd at the State House as Persons against whome they pretended to have found of matter.[36] this was address'd to the People or the mobility, but nothing has, as yet come of it—. our little Henry has been very unwell for many days past with a hard cough and fever, he took Physick to day.

31 upwards of 400 British Prisoners past by our Door this morning guarded, in their way to the New Jail—they were taken some time ago at Stony Point Fort.[37]

Augt. 4. 1779—HD. left home after dinner for the Valley and Concord[38]—H Catheral &c with him. little Henry is better; he wrote to day to his Sister Sally—it seems to be clear'd up, after a long spell of wett weather.

5 ringing of Bells, and other demonstrations of Joy—on account of the taken of Grenada;[39] and Adml. Birons Fleet being much shattred—I spent this afternoon at S. Pleasants, my little Molly with me, several here to day.

6 Sally Maul brought us a Letter from Sally—I spent this afternoon at S. Sansoms—rain in the Afternoon, Becky Jones here in the Evening.

7 Norris Jones call'd for J. Brintons Salt, he left HDs Saddle—Saml. Emlen &c call'd—Billy went over the river with [T] & M Fisher &c Nancy and self wrote to Sally—rain in the night and this day.

8 First Day: the Children went to Meeting this Morning—Sister Myself and

36. At a divisive public town meeting held by the price-fixing committee on July 26 and 27, a group of citizens ultimately withdrew to another location to hold a separate meeting. At this meeting, the committee read the names of those who had violated its resolves, although no decision about punishment was made. The list of eight or ten names included John Drinker and Robert Jones (tentatively identified as Robert Strettel Jones by Rosswurm, *Arms, Country, and Class*, 189–91, 182 n. 37).

37. The prisoners were probably en route to Easton, Pa., the site of the American army's stores (Henry P. Johnston, *The Storming of Stony Point on the Hudson, Midnight, July 15, 1779* [New York: White, 1900], 87, 44, 53; see above, July 19).

38. The name "Becky Jones" crossed out.

39. Adm. Charles Hector Theodat, Comte d'Estaing, was the commander of the French fleet sent to aid the rebel Americans in 1778. After some embarrassing failures near the continental United States in the summer of 1778 he sailed to the West Indies and on July 5, 1779, succeeded in capturing the island of Grenada. The British fleet under John Byron began a counterattack on July 6. The British were outnumbered and their leading ships suffered heavy damage when the French unaccountably withdrew (Boatner, *American Revolution*, s.v. "Byron," "d'Estaing," and "West Indies").

3 youngest in the Afternoon, Nancy and John at home; Docr. Cowper call'd for look at a minuet in the monthly meeting Book—Sarah Fisher Josa. and Caty Howel drank Tea with us—M. Pleasants spent the evening.

9 Thos. Say, one Barns with a Letter call'd I spent this Afternoon with M Pleasants at C. Logans—Furniture taken this afternoon from S. Pleasants for a Tax—we have had no Maid Servant for some weeks past but Molly Brookhouse who comes before dinner and goes away in the afternoon, so that now HD. and Sally are absent, we have but 7 in Family, Billy and little John are our Men, which makes it rather lonesome of Nights, in this great House—no account from Sally since last third day—very warm.

10 I went to Meeting this Morning Grace Fisher, Elizath. Drinker, S Swett, A. James junr din'd with us—J. Logan and SS. drank tea, I took a walk towards evening down Town, call'd in my way home at A Warners, who has lately had a fall and hurt her knee—found HD. at home, he return'd this evening—very warm weather—a very hard thunder Gust in the night of the 12th. instant.

Augt 14 HD. left home this afternoon with James Pemberton, for the Grove quarterly Meeting[40] the weather very warm.

15th. First Day: went to Meeting with little Molly, this afternoon, Billy carry'd at the Burial of Bittles child over the way—I went with Neigr. Waln this evening to see Sally Penington who has been unwell—Becky Jones call'd.

16 Frederick Mauses Wife and Son, call'd to pay a debt of upwards of 40 pounds—which I refus'd to take—Sally Logan spent the afternoon, D Salters cousen call'd.

17 I went to Meeting this Morning S Swett came home with me and spent the day—J. Drinker and [R.] Jones here this evening—cloudy with rain.

18 Sally came home this Morning her Daddy this afternoon.

Augt. 22 First day: Billy went after meeting this afternoon with Sammy Emlen junr. on Horseback, to Abington, to visit his mother S. Emlen, (who is

40. In 1758 London Grove, in Chester County, Pa., became the site of the quarterly meeting for the western district of the Pennsylvania Yearly Meeting, which oversaw monthly meetings from London Grove, Centre, Kennet, New Garden, and Fallowfield (Forsythe, "Historical Sketch"; see above, May 15).

there on account of her bad Health, drinking the waters)[41] they came home on second day morning before Breakfast.

23 great rejoycing, with fire works &c, this being the French Kings birthday.

27 Billy went to Frankford this Afternoon on a visit to Tommy James, Josa. Gillpin went with him, they went on foot.

30 HD. left home this Morning after Breakfast for Abington—Billy return'd from Frankford—An advertisement pasted at our Front Door this Morning mischevious and rediculous in its kind, with a view to enflame the People—sign'd, come on warmly—S. Emlen drank tea with us, went with me on the top of the House; fine weather.

31 at Meeting this Morning—a marriage there, C. Barnes, S. Fisher, H. Sansom call'd—S Swett din'd with us—cool to day—C. West drank tea, [J.] Parish call'd, D Drinker borrowed the chaise—the Girles at R. Wellss.

1779 Sepr. 4 Billy went to Abington with Sammy Emlen junr. they return'd the 6th. Second day morning.

7th. I went with Sally this Afternoon to the Burial of Nancy Murdoch, Sister to Phebe Pemberton.

8 Spent this afternoon with Sucky Jones Nancarrow who was married on fifth day last—I have been several times lately troubled with a disagreeable sensation in my head, accompany'd with something of a giddyness,—fine weather.

14th. this morning in meeting time (myself at home) Jacob Franks and a Son of Cling the Vendue master, came to seize for the Continental Tax; they took from us, one Walnut Dining Table, one mahogany Tea-Table, 6 hansom walnut Chairs, open backs crow feet and a Shell on the back and on each knee—a mahogany fram'd, Sconce Looking-Glass, and two large pewter Dishes, carrid them of, from the Door in a Cart to Clings.

18 HD and Sister went to Frankford, found old Joseph our tenant, ill in

41. The mineral springs at Abington, located twelve miles north of Philadelphia along the Old York Road, were first described by Benjamin Rush in 1773. The springs were popular with Philadelphians from 1774, when William French, the owner of the plantation on which they were located, first advertised their medicinal virtues in the newspapers, through the beginning of the nineteenth century (Benjamin Rush, *Experiments and Observations on the Mineral Waters of Philadelphia, Abington, and Bristol, in the Province of Pennsylvania* [Philadelphia: James Humphreys, Jr., 1773], 6, 7; F. H. Shelton, "Springs and Spas of Old-Time Philadelphians," *PMHB* 47 (1923): 222–24).

Bed; ordr'd some of our Furniture to be brought to Town, they call'd at A James, came home to Dinner.

20 heard this morning of the Death of Jos. Mires our Frankford tenent, Jos[h] Redman Buried—Sammy Mickels Wife call'd to bid us farewell, she has been some time in Town, under the Doctors care, being in a bad state of Health, she is sent for home on account of the illness of her only child.

24 HD. Nancy and little Molly went this Afternoon to Frankford—Sally Logan here—Peter Worrel &c call'd—James Steers wife from Virginia took up her lodgings with us, John Tomson from the Iron-Works [stop'd and] lodg'd here.

25 Sarah Carry and Rachel Watson from Bucks Cy—Sammy Trimble from Concord—John Willis, James Mott and Elias Hicks from Long-Island came this morning to take up their aboad during the meeting.

26 First Day—our Lodgers Breakfasted with us; ten din'd—great numbers call'd—John Willis who was most part of yesterday in Bed ill of a fever, is bravely to day—our Neighbour Franks the Baker, dy'd this morning of a Fever which at present prevails much in the City and Country, and many are taken off.

27 went to meeting morning and afternoon 30 persons din'd with us—John Willis ill last night again—and this Evening he was taken ill at the pine-Street meeting and went to Bed at Elijah Browns—where I expect he must stay all night.

28 went to meeting this Afternoon 16 din'd with us, John Willis stay'd at home all day he took the Bark and mist the fitt—Docr Cowper visits him.

29 I stay'd at home being unwell, Elias Hicks very poorly, 12 din'd with us—a large number come to visit the long-Island Friends.

30 went twice to meeting, 10 or 12 din'd with us, many at Breakfast—a great number of people ill of a Fever—many taken off—B. Woodcock went home this afternoon very unwell, scarcely a House but some one or more are indespos'd.

Octor. 1 went to meeting this morning—6 or 8 at dinner many more at Breakfast, Ellias Hicks taken very ill to day—in Bed all the later part of the day. Docr. Cowper tends him 7 or 8 sup'd with us; I went in a hurry this Afternoon to see M Pleasants, who has lately miscarried,—cloudy weather.

2 stay'd within all day Elias Hicks still very poorly—John Willis, James Mott and our Billy went this Afternoon to Frankford—J. Mott came back very unwell, went to Bed and took a Sweat—we have had much company this day—the womans meeting finishd to day—mens not yet—fine weather.

3 First Day: E. Hicks very ill, took a vomit this Afternoon. I went to meeting this Evening—a great number of Friends here to day—Abagall Seers left us to day.

4 Ellias Hicks who appears something better left us this afternoon with an intent to go a few miles on his way—John Willis stays 'till tomorrow—Sarah Corry and Rachel Watson also left us, and Sammy Trimble went home, Betsy Waln and Hannah Hartshorn with many others spent this day with us, Cousin Sarah Mickel is here Polly Waln sleeps with her to night—Johnny Drinker was taken up to day by a Mob; (part of the Militia) as he came out of meeting where he had been sitting six hours, at the conclusion) they allow'd him to go home to eat his Dinner, and after took him, with Buckrige Sim and Tommy Story and[42] led them about the Streets with the Drum after 'em beating the Rogues March, they then stop'd at the Door of Willson the Lawyer who they Intended to take, but mett with opposition, Jos[a] Read at the Head of many of the Light-Horse came up and a Battle ensued, when 2 or 3 lost their lives and many were wounded[43]—they rescu'd the Prisoners, but though proper to send them to Prison, where they are this Night—it seems the intent was or is to take up a number of the Inhabitants who they call disaffected and send them off to some other part; prehaps New York—a guard is set at the prison, and the Light Horse partroling the Streets.—we had a setting this evening in the parlor with our Friend John Willis who expressed his regard to the Family in a very Affectionate manner and the satisfaction he had felt in being with us—with good advice to the Children.

42. The word "[Drum'd]" crossed out.

43. In what came to be known as the Fort Wilson riot, a group of Philadelphians, mainly militiamen, marched through the streets of Philadelphia in response to a broadside posted the night before naming a number of men who were to be forcibly exiled from the city. During their march, the militants seized John Drinker, Buckridge Sims, Thomas Story, and Mathew Johns, parading them through the streets to Burns's Tavern, where radical leaders such as Charles Willson Peale and Dr. James Hutchinson had earlier tried unsuccessfully to deter the demonstration. The militia then marched again to James Wilson's house, where several persons had already barricaded themselves, fearing themselves to be targets of the militia because of their opposition to price controls and Pennsylvania's constitution, and because Wilson had defended people accused of treason. Gunfire broke out, killing six or seven persons and wounding seventeen to nineteen. While the militia was marching, Joseph Reed, the president of Pennsylvania's Supreme Executive Council, turned out with Philadelphia's elite First City Troop of Light Horse to put an end to the riot. Twenty-seven militiamen were arrested, and the captives of the militia were jailed for their own protection (Alexander, "Fort Wilson Incident of 1779"; Rosswurm, *Arms, Country, and Class,* 205–27; C. Page Smith, "The Attack on Fort Wilson," *PMHB* 78 (1954): 177–86).

5. J Willis left us this Morning no lodgers left but cousin S Mickel a great deal of Company here to day—J. Drinker still in Prison—Wm. Lewis the Lawyer taken up and put into Jayl to day, but is out again this Evening. the Mob has taken a number of the Militia out of Prison, who were confin'd Yesterday.

6 Betsy and Sally Waln spent the Afternoon HD. went this morning to Prison to see Johney Yesterday he was not admitted.

7 a Proclamation put out by J Read[44]—an appearance of quietness to day—J Drinker still in Prison—Sarah and Nancy Mickel, Saml. Smith Henry Drinker Jos[h]. Bringhurst Betsy Waln and Polly Waln, Patty Smith Becky James, Elisha Hopkins, D Drinker, &c here—cleard up.

9 S. Mickel left us to day.

10. First Day: 'tis said that the Assembly (who are now setting) are makeing a Law to send of all the dissafected, at the request of the malitia.

13 several Friends visited Jos Read on account of J Drinker—he was this afternoon releas'd from Prison.

Octr 27 Reba. James Lodg'd with us.

30 Sally recover'd a gold-chain which she lost 4 or 5 weeks ago; Hannah Drinker Joseys wife, found it in the Street.

Novr. 2 Robt. and Hannah Stevenson came to Town this afternoon—they make their home with us.

3 the Roof of David Bacons House caught fire occasion'd by the Chimney—and in the Evening the Shop of one Emsley, near the Dock took fire—the Shop or Stable with 2 small Brick Houses were nearly consum'd—wind high.

Novr. 4 HD was let Blood this Afternoon he has been unwell for some time past, with stitches about his Breast &c.

6 Robt. and H. Stevenson left us this forenoon.

the 9 Katty the Dutch woman from the IronWorks, came this evening stay'd all night; a large Northern-light appear'd between 10 and 11 this night.

44. The proclamation condemned the Fort Wilson riot and called for "Law and good Order [to] prevail" (reproduced in Foner, *Tom Paine*, 177, and in *Col. Recs. Pa.*, 12:122).

12 an account of a Battle near Georgia Sh. Carolina, came lately—tis said that a large Number of the French and Americans were Slain and their whole Army beat off—the Newspapers say that upwards of [100] were kill'd; others say 1500 Count Polascai lost his life; and D'Estange was wounded—particulars are in Town.[45]

16 HD. left home after dinner with David Bacon for Bucks County—S Swett spent the Day.

17 stay'd at home all day—had a Beef cut up—S. Sansom spent the afternoon, S Swett, Hillory Baker Senr. &c call'd—60 or 70 Cabbages brought in—cloudy weather.

18 stay'd within all day—Abel James junr. Tommy James dind—Josh. Howel, Caty Howel call'd—Sally Emlen spent the Afternoon—fine weather—little Molly poorly.

19 stay'd at home—Abey Parish drank tea, Peggy Hart, John and D Drinker—call'd.

20 Cloudy to day—Molly Grifits spent the afternoon HD. return'd this Evening.

30 HD. attended as oversere the Mariage of Isaac Bartr[am] and Mary Steel.

Decr. the 3 sixth day HD—left home after Breakfast for the Iron works—Sam Emlen, Bob Moore &c call'd, cold weather, Betsy Jervis came in the afternoon and stay'd all night—Oliver Paxton call'd.

4 Aunt Jervis and Polly spent the Afternoon Saml. and Israel Pleasants call'd—put their Chariot in our Coach-House—Is[c]. Catheral cut up 4 Hoggs—B Jervis here all Day.

5 First Day—Snow'd the greatest part of the Day—Sister and the Children went to meeting.

45. On Oct. 9 a combined Franco-American assault attempted to recapture Savannah from the British. Although the rebel forces had superior numbers and the support of the French fleet under Admiral d'Estaing, the attack failed. The French and Americans suffered heavy casualties; different sources give figures ranging from 750 to 1,200 killed and wounded. Among the dead was Count Casimir Pulaski, the Polish volunteer who led a cavalry legion. Admiral d'Estaing, seriously wounded, returned to France in early 1780. The report of the American loss reached Philadelphia in November (Boatner, *American Revolution*, s.v. "Savannah," "Pulaski," and "d'Estaing"; *Pa. Packet*, Nov. 13, 1779; *Pa. Gaz.*, Nov. 17, 1779).

6 several hundred Soldiers came to Town to day.

7 went to meeting this morning—Saml & Hannah Sansom, John Drinker drank tea with us—Wm and Sally Moore, Thos. Scatergood, Saml. Emlen &c call'd—Betsy Jervis still here, Saml. Harolds Son brought a letter—cold—R Waln here this evening.

8 HD—not yet return'd—stay'd at home all day, which I have done every day for 7 or 8 weeks past except once or twice a week to the Bank meeting—T James here to day, he lodges with Billy—B Jervis here.

9 this day is set apart by the Congress for fasting and prayer—HD. return'd this evening—B Jervis went home.

Decr. 12 First Day—Joseph Fox Buryed—Josey James, Jessy Waterman din'd with us Hannah and Becky & S Swett drank tea—rain most of the day—or cloudy.

16 fifth day Sister went to the Funeral of Sarah Roberson, late of Nemans-Creek—Benjamin Mason lodg'd here.

28 third day a violent East'rly Storm, our House, as was most others, very much try'd by it, most of the front Rooms very wett—our maid abroad since seventh day last—Caty Hopkins brought to Bed yesterday morning—with her son Joshua—Josey James lodg'd &c here for near a week past he writes at the Store.

1780

1780 Janry. 2 Richd. Penns large House up Market Street took fire last night, and this Morning is consum'd all but the lower Story,[1] a most violent Snow Storm this Afternoon, and all night—a very foul Chimney in Water-Street opposite the Bank Meeting House—took fire this evening—and occasion'd a great Hubbub—First Day—on sixth day last Decr. the 31—Sam. Lewis a little Boy from Sleepy-Creek—came to live with us—he has the Itch; for which I basted him on seventh day night with Brimstone.[2]

Janry. 4—Sally, Nancy, Billy Sansom, and our little Molly, with Josey James, gone to Frankford in a Sleigh to Abel Jamess—with intent to stay all night. they return'd the 5th.

8 Billy gone this evening home with Josey and Tommy James, in a Sleigh.

9 First Day. HD—and J. Drinker took a walk this cold morning—(Jessy Waterman with them) to Frankford, to see A James who is unwell.

15 Nancy went with J[a]mmy Hopkins to Haddonfield in a Sleigh, HD. and all the Children went over the river with them on the Ice—little Molly very much tir'd with the walk when she return'd—the river has been fast for some weeks past.

1780 Janry. 19. A James sent a Sleigh for HD and self—we left home before dinner—found Abel very unwell as he has been for several weeks past—N Waln. Jos[h] Bringhurst John Foulk &c there in the Afternoon—HD return'd in the Evening with 'em to Town, left me at Abels,—little Henry with me.

20 severely Cold, stay'd within all day.

21 went this afternoon, (Becky James junr. and Josey, with me) to see Sally

1. The house was occupied by Jean Holker, the French consul to the United States (*Pa. Packet*, Jan. 4, 6, 1780).

2. A combination of sulphur and rum used in treating skin diseases (Lois K. Stabler, ed., *"Very Poor and of a Lo Make": The Journal of Abner Sanger* [Portsmouth, N.H.: Peter E. Randall for the Historical Society of Cheshire County, 1986], 560).

Moore at Point, drank tea with her—and come home after Night—the full Moon shining Beautifully—very cold—John Thompson.

22 stay'd within all day—A James better.

23 First Day: went to Frankford Meeting this Morning in the Carriage—Becky Josey, Abel junr. Tommy my Henry Jessey Waterman &c, some in the Sleigh—Jessey appear'd in Testimony—a pretty full meeting the cold weather considred—Sammy Pleasants and Docr. Parke up this afternoon.

24 left Frankford after dinner—G. James and Josey came with us—came here to Tea left A James very Poorly—Nancy returnd from Haddonfield on sixth day last—Molly Moore went back in the Sleigh with Jos James.

Febry. the 1st. HD. left home after dinner, for Atsion, cross'd the river in the Sleigh—C. James, Billy Sansom and Billy Drinker with him—they return'd the 4th. sixth day.

7 ED taken poorly this Morning could not attend quarterly meeting tho' appointed.

8 James Thornton and George Churchman sup'd and lodg'd here.

10 HD. went to Frankford to see A James who continues unwell, he attended their general meeting, and return'd in the evening—Sister went this morning—with Benjn. and M Swett, in [J.] Howels Sleigh, over the river and to John Hopkinss where they left her, and she spent the day, on a visit to cousin Sarah Mickel who has been very ill—Hannah Hopkins came here this Afternoon intending to spend some days with our Children—Sister came home in the evening—I dismist my maid Caty Paterson this afternoon, on her return home after 2 or 3 days frolicking, our old maid Molly Hensel is to Supply her place tomorrow.

11th sixth Day HD. left home this Morning for Havourford Meeting,[3] he returnd the 12th.

13 First Day: little John Pope left us this afternoon—he has been here about 16 months.

3. Haverford, then in Chester County, Pa. (it later became part of Delaware County), was founded by Welsh Quakers, who settled in the area known as the Welsh Tract. They erected a meetinghouse in 1688–89 and added onto it in 1700; the original building was replaced a century later (Ashmead, *Delaware County*, 563–68, 574).

16 Hannah Hopkins left us before dinner—they are apprehensive that the Ice on the river grows weak—Ostan Jones here.

26 seventh day HD went to Frankford to visit A James, who is still confin'd—by indesposition, Chalkley, Josey, Jessy Waterman, Abel, Tommy here this afternoon they came to the Funeral of Robt. Hopkins—HD. sent for clean cloths for Tomorrow as he has concluded to stay this Night at Frankford.

27 First Day—HD—returnd this Evening.

March Polly Parrock dy'd some time in last month at whose funeral we were—Billy spent a day or 2 at Frankford some time in this month—myself and Daughters went to the Burial of Polly Shoemaker the 28th. Instant—Sarah Carry and Rachel Watson made their home with us this meeting as they did last Fall, which was the first time—we have had as much company as ever, at a Spring meeting.

March 31 sixth Day: Peter Barker caus'd great disturbance in the middle monthly-meeting this Morning—by his Crazy behavour.

April 1st. Saml. Emlen and Wife and G. Dyllwyn spent the afternoon with us—after Tea we had a silent setting for some considerable time when SE spake to us and GD. had something very remarkable to say to J.D—who came in a little time before he spake.

April 3 HD took a dose Salts, he has had a sore Leg for near 2 Weeks, it is now seemingly worse.

April 10 HD. was let Blood this Morning he has been unwell for several days past, with stitches in his breast, and feverish—his Leg continues sore—Abel James Senr. din'd here to day, he did so last week several times, being the first[4] of his coming to Town since his Sickness—he's now geting better—Iron seiz'd for a Tax at the Store this Afternoon, by Daniel Drais.

11 John Duncan and Betsy Shipley married this morning—Sally & Nancy at Wedding.

12. HD. went to Frankford with Abel James stay'd all night—return'd the 13th.

23 HDs Leg we hope is nearly well.

4. The word "time" crossed out.

April 24 Billy went to School to Robt. Proud to learn Latten.

30 First Day—HD. MS. and Billy, went to the Burial of Elizah Jervis Wife of our cousin Charles Jervis—myself and Daughters would also have gone, but for a heavey shower which fell about the time—and not being very well.

May 1st. Jerm[h]. Baker took a mahogany folding or Card-Table from us this morning for a Northn. liberty Tax, amounting to about 18/– the Table worth between 3 & 4 pounds—Bancroft Woodcock and Daughter Rachel came this Morning to stay some time with us—quarterly meeting, many in and out.

2d. several of A Jamess family and others—BW. went this evening left Rachel to spend the rest of the week here.

3 HD. Sister and Sally left home about 10 this Morning for Atsion; J Drinker with them—L. Salters Waggon came to Coopers ferry for them, but 7 of us now in family. RW. makes 8—Billy Sansom lodges here, I was taken very unwell before dinner, sent for Molly Moore, who lodges with me,—was better towards evening.

May 6—three Men were executed for theft—on the Commons.[5]

7 First Day: R Woodcock left us to day, she went with D Drinker for Concord—, J Drinker return'd this evening from the works, left HD Sister and Sally well.

9 Billy cut off part of his little finger Nail it blead badly, and continu'd sore for many days.

10 B Woodcock sup'd and lodg'd here, he came for his Horse, which had got out of D Drinkr Stable some days past; but since found.

11 Robt. Stevenson, his wife, Children & Servants came this Morning—they are come to settle in Town, from the Jersys—Robt. Hannah and Child din'd with me, the rest went to their House, where their goods &c are.

18th. HD. sister and Sally come home before dinner—I have been unwell for many weeks past,—in great pain all night.

19 Patty Smith and Becky James lodg'd here[6] [Rtn'd home].

5. Denis Carrag(h)an and Marmaduke Grant were hanged for burglary, and John Hill for highway robbery (*Pa. Packet,* Apr. 25, May 23, 1780; *Col. Recs. Pa.,* 12:329).
6. Words crossed out?

20 they went home; myself in my chamber, where I have expected for some time to be confin'd—am thankful it is so far over, as it is what I had reason to expect.

May 22 began to Shingle the House, the Kitchen first.

June 6 HD. gone this Afternoon J Parish with him to Frankford.—his Leg not yet quite well tho' it appears to be nearly so—as it did when he left home for Atsion but came back with it much worse, and has been allmost ever since confin'd—many accidents have lately happen'd of the sorrowful kind—Josh. Morgans Wife of the Jersys, Mary Roker, and another Woman were drown'd, by the overseting of the Boat—a Young Man of the Name of Morgan was since drown'd in Scuilkill—and two Children said to be lost in the common-sewer.

June 10 James Pickering a Capt. at the Corner of race street—and 6 or 8 others with Bayonets fixt—came and demanded our Horses—after some talk they went and broke open the Stable took a fine Horse bought some time ago of Wm. Smith for 16 half Joes—and a Mare belonging to J Drinker—they took Horses from many others.—they now act under a Martial Law—lately proclaim'd[7]—by a N York Paper we have an account of the taken of C. Town S. Coralina the 12 last month[8] the People here, some of them affect not to believe it—repoort of a Skermish near Morris Town between the British and G. Washingtons Men.

HDs junr Shoes Octor. 3[9]

1779 Molly went to School Octor 4

Ann Drinker 1775

1779	1780
AD	0

7. Joseph Reed declared martial law on June 9, acting on a resolution passed unanimously that allowed the president or vice president of the Supreme Executive Council to declare martial law, if necessary, while the assembly was not in session (*Col. Recs. Pa.*, 12:383–84; *Pa. Packet*, June 10, 1780).

8. British forces numbering almost nine thousand soldiers and five thousand sailors left New York in December 1779 under the command of Gen. Henry Clinton, bound for Charleston, S.C. By April 1780 they had succeeded in besieging the rebel defenders of the city. Gen. Benjamin Lincoln, the commander of the American army, accepted Clinton's terms of surrender on May 12. The Americans gave up the town and all their troops, shipping, and military stores and installations. The captured forces numbered close to fifty-five hundred, although fewer than half that number were active in the defense of Charleston (Boatner, *American Revolution*, 205–14; *Pa. Packet*, June 10, 1780).

9. The manuscript volume for June 25, 1780–Dec. 31, 1781, has brown paper covers. The outside front cover reads, "(commencing June 1780)"; the inside back cover contains the jottings and columns of figures reproduced here.

Febry.	19	25
	26	19
	0	[ ]
	0	5–28
	24	
	0	
	0	
	17	
	10	
	0	
	3–27	

June 29 [ ] this afternoon [ ] by ba[d] management was overset near Drawbridge in a Squall—but thro' the [ ] quickly sent. all were sav'd except one woman.

25 First day—a Friend from the Country [ ] name of Roberson, in publick Testimony this morning at the Bank House, said amo[ng] other things) that Pennsylvania [once] the flower of Amarica, was now [ ] a Den of thieves.

27th. Nancy took a ride this morning [ ] about 5 o'clock on the mare, who ca[ ] yesterday from pasture, Billy San[ ] on Horseback with her.—we have [ ] Taxes at a great rate almost daily coming upon us—Yesterday was [s] but not yet taken from us—by Adam Lapp and Henry Snyder, a walnut Dining Table, 5 Ditto Chairs and a pair large Kitchen End-Irons—as our part of a Tax for sending 2 men out in the Militia—10 half Joes were ta[ken] from Abel James for the same Tax.

June 27, 1780 I took leave of [ ] with several other woman wives of those [ ] who are with the English, are ordred [ ] of this State by Counsel[10]—She left Philada. for New York the 14 Instant. [Gr]ace Galloway and Sally Cox I bid farewell [ ] are not yet gone away—[ ] confirmation of Charles-Town being [ ]ed and falling back again under [ ] English Government came about this time [ ] Salter and wife left us, after spending [ ] of yesterday and this day with us—[ ] Dolly seems in a bad way, and it is to [ ]ear'd she has

10. On June 6 the Supreme Executive Council had ordered the wives and children of men who had joined the enemy to leave the state within ten days. The resolution stated that those who departed after that date would be subject to proceedings against them as enemies of the state. The council wrote that the presence of the women and children "had at all times proved incovenient to the public interest" and that it had now become "too dangerous to be longer permitted or connived at." This resolution followed earlier demands made in the summer of 1779 by radical militia groups in Philadelphia to deport the women and children because the women were suspected of engaging in illegal correspondence (*Pa. Packet*, June 10, 1780; Rosswurm, *Arms, Country, and Class*, 209).

neglected the complaint of her [br]east too long to be now effectually help'd [ ] Docr. Jones who has been consulted—[ ] feel much for her.

[ ] st John and Rachel Watson lodg'd the [la]st two nights with us—and return'd home [th]is morning Rachl. brought home our [ ]mbrick and thread, well bleachd [ ] visited A James at Frankford—[ ]llop put of this afternoon for Oldams.

1780 June 29, little Henry went this Afternoon to Frankford with C and [J.] James in their waggon.

July 1st. he returnd.

3. Lawrance and Dolly Salter come before Dinner, Becky and Josey James with them—Docr. Jones examen'd DSs Breast, found little or none alteration in it since his last visit, he drank Coffee with us.

5. I spent this afternoon at Nics. Walns, very warm weather—A gust this Afternoon—was very ill this night[11] of a very bad fitt of the Collick—had no sleep 'til after day—L. and DS went away.

6 very weak and unwell all day.

7 on third day last Adam Lapp came for the goods he had seiz'd some days past, said the Sub-Leutenent[12] told him he had not taken sufficient, he, however left the Table without giving any reason—but came this Morning and seized for the same Tax (having sold the Kitchen Endirons and 5 Chairs for 96£) the Dining Table before mentioned Six walnutt Chairs, a Ditto Tea Table, a pair Brass End Irons and 2 Brass Kittles [ ] the amount of the Tax: £235[ ]/15 Conti [ ].

from Josa. Howel whose Tax was upwards of an hundred pounds more then ours) they seiz'd several peices of Furniture, but as he made some stir in the matter, they sold only one pair End Irons, Shovel and Tongues and a small Looking-Glass. Becky, Chalkley and Josey James came before Dinner—Becky and Josey din'd with us—they came to the Funeral of Capt. Donne, who was this afternoon Buried—Josey Knight sup'd and lodg'd here.

8 HD—and S. Emlen went this Afternoon to Frankford to visit Abel James who is still very unwell—a young Man yesterday drown'd in Frankford Creek.

11. The words "with a" crossed out.
12. Word crossed out.

9 First Day: went this Afternoon to the Burial of a Child of Meirs Fisher, a sudden Gust of Wind oblig'd M Pleasants and self with many others who were at the Funeral to take shelter at Docr. Redmans—little [ ] with me—after the Gust 'twas [ ] Evening meeting, went with MP. to Molly Logans who lays in of her first Child[13] who they call James.

10th. HD left home after dinner with John Parish and Saml. Hopkins and C West to visit Some Friends over Schuylkill: expect him home tomorrow or Next day—weather has been very warm for many days past: Several have been suddenly taken off and many seiz'd with violent colickey complaints. HD return'd the 11th.

14 Sally and Billy Sansom went to Frankford this Afternoon, on Horse Back—I have been often uneasy this Summer on account of little Henry, who is endeavoring to learn to swim—about 3 months past I hurt my left Breast by cutting a hard bak'd loaf of Bread, have had a pain in it at times ever since, it is through mercy better at present.

15 HD. was let Blood this Morning—he has been troubled for some time past with a swiming in his Head.

19 HD. and Sam Emlen left home this Morning by 4 o'clock for Burlington, on a visit to G. Dillwyn who has been unwell—they return'd the 20th. fifth day by 9 o'clock the Morning.

July 20 ED went to the Burial of Jemmy Morton—Robt. Willis, Thos Carlton and S Emlen spake at the Grave.

21st. Nancy, Billy Sansom, Sally Sansom and Betsy Hough went to Frankford,—fresh orders lately concerning those Women who still continue here, whose Husbands are with the English. Molly [Blans] serv'd with a warant sign'd by TM—ordering her to the Common Work-House or to find security, the latter was comply'd with.

24 Billy went to Frankford with Tommy James,—L. and D Salter came—Dollys Breast no better—they and Josey James Lodg'd here—second day.

25 DS was blooded in her Foot this morning—appear'd to be faintey after it.

26 L & D S left us this afternoon, Billy came home in the Evening—I visited S. Moore.

13. The word "which" crossed out.

27 Billy went this Morning with T. James to visit Josa. Gillpin at Schuylkil—came home in the Evening I spent the Afternoon at Docr. Redman.

Augt. 1 little Henry went with Neddy Howel to their place on Schuylkil—the French fleet which arrive'd lately at Rhoad-Island,[14] is said to be surounded by the English—Polly Wallace call'd to see us this Afternoon—one Stackhouse a plasterer, fell of a scaffold last week, and lost his life by the fall—on sixth day last a little Boy who was fishing of a warf near Pine Street, fell in and was drownded—and the next day a Woman was drownd'd near the same place.

Augt. 22 L. and D Salter came they stay'd 2 or 3 days with us, Dollys Breast worse, I went with her to Dr. Jones who was unwell, he did not say it was worse, but it is obvious to me—since I wrote last, Billy has been to Frankford, several of AJs Family here Abel appears to be much better—we have had and continue to have so far, a very warm Summer, many remarkably effected by drinking cold water, our 3 Youngest Children favour'd with health Sally generaly so, tho she has lately been ill of a vomitting &c—Nancy often unwell.

25. Nancy bad last Night with a vomiting better this Morning—she left home after Breakfast with her Daddy and Rachel Drinker, in A Jamess Waggon, for John Salters, where they expect to meet Lawrence and Dolly, who left us yesterday—from thence they intend to cross the river and go in LSs Waggon to Burlington; Rachel Drinker intends going with Dolly to Kingwood Lawrence with 'em, to ask the oppinion of a certain Docr. Willson, who 'its said has knowledge in Cansers; I fear poor Dolly will receive little comfort by the journey—HD. and Nancy proposes staying at Burlington during the quarterly meeting—this being the French Kings birth day, we have had a fussy day of it, ringing of Bells, fireing of Guns—fire-works &c—Josey James din'd here.—Billy Sansom and Tommy James lodges here to Night.

26 Billy S. and Tommy J. Breakfasted with us, the latter went home this evening—a new born infant was taken out of the river this Afternoon with a wound in its neck—suppos'd to have been murdre'd—Sally wrote to Nancy.

27 First Day: went to Meeting as usual, company here, which is as usual—I took a walk towards evening, Billy and Henry with me, down to Sally Whartons, who I have not seen for a long time, considering our intamacey—she has been confin'd most of this Summer by a sore Leg, which has been bad at times, between twenty and thirty years, occasion'd by a hurt she received in her laying in with her first Child. Sally received a Letter this Afternoon from

14. Jean de Vimeur, Comte de Rochambeau, commander of the French army in the United States, arrived with the French fleet in Newport on July 10 (Boatner, *American Revolution*, s.v. "Rochambeau"; *Pa. Packet*, Aug. 1, 1780).

her Husband who is now in France, where he arriv'd within these few months from England—he has been absent from his Family, the first of next Febuy will be 12 years; she expects him home next month.—I call'd at Tommy Fishers whose child is ill mett Polly Pleasant there, we came away together, stop'd at Jammy Logans, where we sup'd—found R and H Stevenson at our House on my return—very warm.

28. a Vindication put out by Friends, confutting the Spank-Town forgery &c[15]—spent this Afternoon at S Pleasants.

29 received a Letter this morning from HD—informing of his intention of going to Bucks Quarter held at the Falls, and of leaving Nancy at Burlington.—Sally Pemberton Breakfasted with us—she, Sally Zane, and Sally Drinker went after Breakfast in our Chaise, SD. drove to visit Charles and Molly Logan at Stanton, our Amos waited on them; they did not come home 'till long after Night—heard from HD. this evening by Saml. Hopkins.

30 little Henry fell into the River this Afternoon, and after a quarter of an hour remaining in his wet cloaths, came home very cold and coughing, we strip'd him, and after rubing him well with a coarse towel, put on warm dry cloaths, gave him some Rum and water to drink, and made him jump a rope till he sweated—he is bravely this evening.

31 an express came with an account of the defeat of G. Gates near Carolina,[16] the perticulars have not learnt—A Carliles Dog Lion, bit Henrys Eye lid and Eyebrow 'till it blead, it was swell'd and sore for a day or 2, then got better.

Sept. 3. First Day. HD—return'd in a Sulkey left Nancy at Burlington—She

15. The Philadelphia Meeting for Sufferings was engaged in a long dispute with the legislature over the imprisonment of Quakers who had refused to perform military services. On Aug. 12 an article had appeared in the *Pennsylvania Packet* accusing Quakers of sedition and promoting disaffection. The article reprinted a three-year-old letter from Gen. John Sullivan to the Continental Congress containing an allegedly traitorous report of the Spanktown Yearly Meeting on troop movements. This "intercepted" (but fabricated) report had sparked a controversy in the summer of 1777 and had exacerbated the hostile feelings of the rebels toward the Quakers. It also led to the arrest and exile of Henry Drinker and others that fall.

Spanktown, a small village near Rahway, N.J., had never been the site of a yearly meeting, nor could the troop movements mentioned in the letter have taken place on the dates of the alleged meeting report. In order to counter the negative effects of the publicity of the newspaper article of Aug. 12, 1780, the Philadelphia Meeting for Sufferings wrote a reply on Aug. 24 and published it in the *Packet* on Sept. 2, stating that the reports of the Spanktown Yearly Meeting were spurious and presenting evidence of the Friends' innocence in the affair (*Pa. Packet,* Aug. 12, Sept. 2, 1780; Mekeel, *Relation of the Quakers,* 198–99).

16. A reference to Gen. Horatio Gates's disastrous campaign and defeat at Camden, S.C., on Aug. 16 (Boatner, *American Revolution,* s.v. "Camden Campaign" and "Battle of Camden," 159–70).

came the 4 with James Bringhurst and wife in their Waggon—second day dinner time.

Sepr. 7. this Afternoon was buried, Willm. Allen, formerly Chief-judge of this Province.

11 Nancy and myself went this Afternoon to the Burial of a Child of Thos Fishers, went after to see S. Emlen who is unwell—2 or 3 different kind of Fevers are at present prevalent in this City. numbers are taken off. there are very few Houses, but one or more of the Familys are unwell—in some the fever is thought to be puterid.

15 sixth day, HD. and myself went this Afternoon to Magnolia to John Salters, on a visit to Dolly Salter, who is there, under the care of a Quack Doctor who is employ'd on account of her sore Breast—we call'd at Abel Jamess—drank tea at J Salters—did not come home 'till after Night.

16 HD. and the Children went this Morning to the Funeral of Sarah Zane Senr.—Josey James has been here 2 or 3 days past posting Books—little Molly very feverish and unwell all day, she had a high fever all last Night—HD—unwell this afternoon.

17 First day: Daddy and the Child both better to day.

Sepr. 18 HD—went to the Burial of Saml. Howel Joshuas Brother—L Salter sup'd and lodg'd here.

3d day 19th. Josh. Reeds (the present Governor) wife, was this morning Buried—L Salter din'd with us—our little Henry went with him this afternoon to Magnolia intending tomorrow for the Iron-works.

Octor. 1 First Day John and Rachl. Watson and Sammy Trimble left us to day the last of our lodgers—Sarah Carry John Balderston, James and Grace Steers, and B. Woodcock went yesterday, John Brinton and Wife and Jessy Richardson the day before H Bornsel—12 lodgers—and daily much Company at meals &c—tho' not so many as last Year—many of the Country Friends are taken down with this fever which at present is much among us—tho' none that I have heard of dangerously ill.

2 went to Bed last night between 10 and 11, arose at 7 this morning without having slept one moment, 'tho as well as usual—it is what I have often done in the course of my Life.

the 3d. David Sands a publick Friend from New-York Gouvernment, Josey and Becky James, drank tea with us—Yesterday the 2d. our Sammy cut his Ancle badly and little Molly her Finger—this Afternoon was bury'd Anthony Morris Senr. and Patty Hudson—some day last Week was bury'd our little Neighbor John Folwell, and David Frankss Wife and Many others—a very sickly time.

4 this Afternoon David Sands, Sammy Emlen, Edward Hallock and John Parish drank tea with us; towards evening we had a setting, when each of them had something to communicate, [ ] extract of a Letter to Congress—that a scene of the blackest villainy had been just disclosed, that Arnold was gon off to the enemy:[17] that Coll. Andrie, Genl. Clinton's principal aid and confidant was apprehended in disguise in the camp: that West-Point (where Arnold commanded) was to be the sacrifice, and that all the dispositions were made for delivering it up last Monday the 25th. ult. at night—it is further said that G. Washington arrived at West-Point just after the plot was discover'd, he lodg'd there that night, and was to have been giving up with the Fort—G Arnold was by his orders, pursu'd but without effect,—Coll. Andrie 'tis also said was condem'd to be hang'd—on seventh day last the 30th. ultimo was exhibited and poraded through the Streets of this city—a ridiculous figure of Gen Arnold with the two faces; and the Devil standing behind him pushing him with a pitch-fork, at the front of the Cart was a very large lanthorn of gre[ ] paper with a Number of inscriptions, setting fourth his crime &c—several hundred men and Boys with Candles in their hands—all in ranks; Many Officers; the Infantry; men with guns and Bayenetts; Tag, rag, &c.—some where near the Coffee-House they burnt the Effigey (instead of the Body as was said in the papers).

Octor. 7 seventh day: went to the Bank meeting this morning a meeting appointed by Hannah Wheeler an Ancient Friend from New England, she had a meeting Yesteray at the fourth Street House, and the day before at Pine-Street; with the particular members of each meeting:—George Bowne breakfastd, din'd and drank Tea with us, Becky Jones din'd, A Jamess 3 Sons & [I.] Morris drank tea, David Sands, Ed. Hallock and Saml. Emlen sup'd with us, David stays all night here—it is said that two of the Franklins of New York and several others are taken up there; on account of some information given by

17. While serving as the military governor of Philadelphia in 1779, Benedict Arnold had agreed to help the British assume control of West Point in return for twenty thousand pounds. General Washington discovered Arnold's scheme when he arrived at West Point on Sept. 25, 1780. Col. John André, the British officer to whom Arnold had given the plans for West Point, was caught and hanged as a spy on Oct. 2. Arnold escaped. His letter to Washington exonerating his wife, the former Peggy Shippen, and his two aides Richard Varick and David Franks from knowledge of his conspiracy was printed in the *Pennsylvania Gazette* on Oct. 4 along with details of Gen. Nathanael Greene's letter to the Continental Congress notifying it of Arnold's treason (Boatner, *American Revolution*, 35–43; *Pa. Gaz.*, Oct. 4, 1780).

Gen. Arnold[18]—many here are also taken up and confin'd; David Franks and Wm. Hambleton are among the rest.

8 First Day: HD. gone to Frankford Meeting with S. Emlen; D Sands & Ed. Hallock.

10 Third Day: HD. gone this Morning to Harford meeting with David Sands &c.—Nancy had a Blister laid last night behind her Ear, for the Toothach and pain in her face, with which she has been troubled for 2 or 3 month past at times—little Henry not yet return'd from Atsion, it is 3 Weeks this day since he left home. HD return'd this evening little Henry also.

12 fifth day: Sister &c went this afternoon to the Burial of Betsy Scatergood wife of [T] Scatergood. Patty Smith and Becky James came to Town this morning intending to stay some days, they make their home with us—Nancy confin'd to her Chamber with the pain in her face, and soreness of the Blister—Patty, Becky, and Joseph Burr lodged here.

13 Childrens Meeting this Morning Billy and Henry gone, rains to hard for little Molly. Josey James here writeing, Polly & Becky gone out.

14 Patty Smith, Becky and Josey James left us this Afternoon.

17 third day: James Thornton, David Sands, George Dylwyn, Edward Hallock, Wm. Bleakly, and Polly Waln din'd with us David and some others are visiting Families in our Neighbourhood.

18. HD. and Josey James left us this Morning after Breakfast for Atsion—Nancy is still up stairs with pain in her Face and Tooth-ach, Docr. Baker, the famous Dentist, lanced her Gum this morning—he thinks she ought to loose a tooth, but leaves it at present.

18. Benedict Arnold had earlier attempted to learn the details of the pro-American Townsend-Woodhull spy ring in New York. After his defection and the arrest of Major André by the Americans, British General Henry Clinton arrested approximately twenty alleged rebel spies and placed them on prison ships. It is not known if the arrests included Quakers John Franklin, his wife, Deborah Morris, or their son, Anthony—good friends and possibly relations of the spies, and well known for their generosity to American prisoners of war on board the prison ships in New York harbor. Clinton released the arrested persons ten days after André's execution on Oct. 2, but he banished the Franklins from New York on Nov. 21 (Morton Pennypacker, *General Washington's Spies on Long Island and in New York* [Brooklyn: Long Island Historical Society, 1939], 1:168–71, 184–91, 2:34–35; Thomas Jones, *History of New York during the Revolutionary War and of the Leading Events in the Other Colonies at That Period,* ed. Edward Floyd de Lancey [New York: New-York Historical Society, 1879], 1:382–83; Robert C. Moon, *The Morris Family of Philadelphia: Descendants of Anthony Morris, 1654–1721* [Philadelphia: Robert C. Moon, 1898], 1:366–71).

19 S Swett spent the day S. and M Pleasants drank tea, the latter stay'd the evening—Amos went home this morning sick.

20 HD. return'd home about dinner time very unwell, and feverish; grew worse towards Bed time, J James lodges here.

21 I set up 'till after 3 this morning HD ill most of the night. he is better to day.

22 First day: HD. stay'd within all day very poorly, tho better than yesterday.

24 went to Monthly Meeting, Jane Webb came home with me and din'd—Sally Wharton sent in meeting time her Son Richd. to inform Sister and self that her sore Leg was mortify'd, and desir'd we would come to see her—sister went this Afternoon—S Emlen and wife and several Girls drank tea with us and D. Sands—B Woodcock and Daughter came towards evening to spend some days.

25 I went this Morning to visit S Wharton, found her setting up tho' very poorly, her Spirits remarkably good, considering her situation—the Doctors, Bond and Clarkson, dress'd her leg while I was there; said the Mortification was stoping—she has taken the Bark for several days.—the old sore has been heal'd up for some time, which has often been the case before) and the mortification has taken place in an Issue,[19] which had been in her Leg for 12 or 14 years.

26 [B] Woodcock and the Girles abroad, several here.

27 BW. and Daughter went away this Afternoon—I went to see SW. who I hope continues to mend—very fine weather.

30 Second day HD. went this Morning with David Sands and S Emlen to Abington, returnd the 31 to Dinner.

Novr. 5 Abel James and wife came to Town lodg'd &c here.

6 went this Morning to quarterly Meeting, sat five hours, had the head Ach—Abel and Reba. James went home this Afternoon.

7 Becky, Josey and Tommy came this Morning gone with our Children to Youths Meeting they went away in the Evening.

19. An incision or artificial ulcer made for the purpose of causing a discharge (*OED*).

9 HD. went early this Morning with S Emlen over the ferry intending for Evesham meeting.

10 Abel James Senr. came to Town before dinner stay'd all night—HD. SE. and Peter Yarnel returned from Evesham, drank tea with us.

Novr. 12 First Day: a little before 12 o'clock this night, we were alarm'd by a hard knocking at the front Door,—while we were preparing to go down stairs; Josey James (who happned to lodge here with his Brother Chalkley in the front Room) came to our Chamber door and inform'd us, that Thos. Lawrencess Negro-Man was waiting at the Door, he say'd that Several Men had broke open the store on the Warfe; belonging to J & Dr. Chalkley and Josey went quickly down but the thieves were gone off; they had broke the Lock and Door, and opend the Windows,—but not any thing missing that they could then discover; as there was nothing but Iron in our Store, it is supos'd that their design was to have rob'd the Store over ours, in which Math[w] Clarkson had a large quantity of Prize-goods.

Novr. 17 numbers of People from the Iron Works here to day: among the rest, Sally Lewis our Sams Mother with her Baby, she lodg'd here, last night and went home this Morning sixth day and Sammy with her, on a visit to his Father &c—Dolly Salter rather worse than better—had a little Stove put up in the back Parlor the day before Yesterday.

19 Josey James lodg'd here.

20 little Henry went over Schuylkill with Billy Sansom to King[sess]; in the Chaise with our young Horse, I spent this afternoon with my Girls, at Joseph Stampers—Billy S. and Henry return'd towards evening Henry has been unwell for several days with a bad cough and fever.

21 Abel James and Wife and 2 Sons came to monthly meeting.

22 Joseph Stansberry, Saml. Clark, John [Commins] and several others put into Jail for trading to New-York.

23 a Committee of Merchants, as they are call'd, lately mett, and came to a resolve, that the Continental Money, (which now passes at upwards of 100 for one) should pass at 75—and that debts &c should to paid at that rate.—they have appointed men to go round the City to the Inhabitants with a paper to

sign to the above effect—those who refuse, are to be held up to the Populace as enemies to their Country—the committee are to meet weekly.[20]

Novr. 25 seventh day—two Men were hang'd this forenoon on the Commons[21]—Saml. Emlen came here before dinner he had a setting with us, and something to communicate;—he took leave of us, as he sets off this Afternoon for Virginia &c—HD. gone part of the way with him—[Jams.] Hopkins dinn'd. our little Sam came home yesterday—there has been lately, frequently red appearances in the Sky, with streamers.

28 H.D—Sally, and Billy left home this Afternoon, (the 2 former in the Chaise, Bill on Horseback) intending for Bucks quarter tomorrow, they expect to lodge this Night at Buybarry—third day.

29 a man was executed this fore-noon, on the Wind-Mill-Island; being accused of Piracy.[22]

30 Chalkley and Becky James came to Town this morn. they din'd sup'd and lodg'd here, Becky sleep'd with me.

Decr. the 2 HD. and Billy return'd from Bucks County, he parted with Sally yesterday at Middle-Town Meeting, she went home with Thos. Watson and wife, in their waggon.

Decr. 5. Isiah Paxton, his Brother Jacob, and Jacobs Son Joshua lodg'd here &c.

Decr. 12 third day: David Sands, G. Dyllwin, David Brook, his Companion and Jn. Foreman, din'd with us.

20. The value of Continental paper currency, which the Continental Congress had first issued in 1775, began to drop sharply in 1779. As war costs climbed, Congress authorized larger and larger emissions, from $6 million in 1775 to $63.4 million in 1778 and $124.8 million in 1779. At first the currency depreciated slowly. In Philadelphia at the beginning of 1779 Continental bills circulated at a ratio of 8:1 per their value in specie. By the end of the year the ratio climbed to 42:1 and July 1780 to 64.5:1, reaching the 100:1 mark in November and December of 1780. The currency continued to depreciate through the spring of 1781, when Congress stopped issuing the bills. On Nov. 20, 1780, a committee of merchants headed by Frederick Muhlenberg, Speaker of the Pennsylvania Assembly, agreed to fix the ratio at 75:1. It also created a committee of thirteen to draw up a petition of association to be circulated among all householders and traders in the city for their signatures (S. R. Fisher, "Fisher Journal," 325–26; Rosswurm, *Arms, Country and Class,* 241; Ferguson, *Power of the Purse,* 25–47; see also above, June 15, 1779).

21. Richard Chamberlane of Gloucester County, N.J., was hanged for passing counterfeit bills, and David Dawson of Chester County, Pa., for treason (*Pa. Packet,* Nov. 28, 1780; *Col. Recs. Pa.,* 12:535–36).

22. James Sutton had apparently commandeered a rebel privateer to take it to Bermuda (*Pa. Packet,* Dec. 3, 1780; *Col. Recs. Pa.,* 12:535; S. R. Fisher, "Fisher Journal," 327).

13. HD. left home after Breakfast for Bucks County, in order to bring our Daughter Sally home—they return'd the 15th. sixth day.

Decr. the 19. John Simson Breakfasted here—we had a setting before meeting, when he had to speak to the Children 3d. day.

Decr. 24 First Day—HD. was let Blood.

30 HD and little Molly went before dinner to Frankford to A Jamess came home before evening—Josey and Tommy James lodg'd here this Night—HD. has been very unwell for several days past, spitting blood &c—tho' he keeps about as usual.

31st. First day: went this afternoon to S Emlen's came home after Night, little Molly with me, several guns fired off very near us—the Bells ringing according to the old foolish custom of ringing out the old year.

1781

1781. Janry. 2.[1] third day morning Abel James and wife came to Town; Josey and Tommy gone home.

1781 Janry. 2 went this afternoon with R James and Nancy to G. Meads, rain in the Evening.

3 A and R James out to day, came home in the evening.

4. HD. left home after Breakfast for Jos[h]. Burrs in the Jersyes—intending to morrow for Atsion, he is poorly, and the weather damp—Abel and Becky went home after dinner, they and S Swett din'd with us.—Robt. and H Stevenson drank tea and sup'd.

9 HD. return'd, something better in health.

11 David Brooks, Seth Coffen and S. Hopkins din'd here—after dinner had a meeting with them; and some of the overseers of our district—Sammy Smith, T. Scatergood. C. West, Peggy Hart and Hannah Yerkes, the Men all—Seth excepted—had something to say—several stay'd tea—went away in the Evening there is a general visit in hand of the overseers visiting one another.

12 Nancy had a tooth drawn this Afternoon by Fredrick, it had been painfull for months, about this time 2 men were executed on this side Trentown [Ferry], say'd to be spys, and giving up by the rioters—on the 5th. Instant or thereabouts, an express came to Town with an account that 1500 or 2000 Men under G. Wayne had mutined and were on their way to this City[2]—many

1. The word "[second]" crossed out.
2. On Jan. 1 the units of the Pennsylvania Line of the Continental Army, then at Morristown, mutinied against their officers over the interpretation of the terms of their enlistment. Many of them thought they were eligible to be discharged, and others wished to reenlist at higher pay. The soldiers who demurred from joining the mutineers were threatened by artillery cannon, until all the units of the Pennsylvania Line left the camp and marched to Princeton. The mutineers eventually negotiated with Joseph Reed, the president of Pennsylvania's Supreme Executive Council, and were allowed their discharges (see below, Jan. 25; John B. B. Trussell, Jr., *The Pennsylvania Line: Regimental Organization and Operations 1776–1783* [Harrisburg: Pennsylvania Historical and Museum Commission, 1977], 18; Charles Royster, *A Revolutionary People at War: The Continental Army and the American Character, 1775–1781* [Chapel Hill: University of North Carolina Press, for the Institute of Early American History and Culture, 1979], 302–8).

hundreds of them have since been discharg'd by their own request.—it is thought that the matter is not yet settled—J Reed, the Light-Horse and some others, on the first alarm went out to them; there is no knowing how the matter stands,—it has not yet been mentioned in the Papers.

21st First day—a very remarkable redness in the Sky, between 8 and 9 this evening, to the Eastward; and towards the North-East, it appear'd like the morning-dawn.

23 third day: a violent storm last Night from the North East: of wind and rain: it shifted round to the N-W towards morning—blew down a Nectrine, an Apricoat, and 2 Snow Ball Trees, in our Garden: an Old Stable belonging to E Stiles, in our Alley—and 2 or 3 Vessels were drove on the sand-Barr, but no considerable damage done any where that I have heard of—Monthly Meeting. James Simpson lodges here.

24 J James came with the Waggon,—(his Mother and myself had concluded to set off this day, on a visit to Dolly Saltar, but RJ. as well as myself concluded that the change of weather would make the journey rather difficult, so put it off 'till another oppertunity Josey went home in the afternoon by himself.

25 by an order from Counsil; they are now Billiting (chiefly on Friends) the Officers who commanded the Soliders that were lately discharg'd;[3] two French Men, who were call'd Capts. came here with an order from Saml. Miles, requiring decent Quarters for Leut. LaRoy & Servant—they behav'd very respectfully; but on HDs representing the impossition, as he thought it, fully to them; say'd they could not lay in the Street, and would call again the next day: but we have seen no more of them; LaRoy has since taken up his aboad with Sammy Sansom and behaves well—the next day but one, we had a Second application of the same sort for Leut Robt. Kennry & Servant but got clear of him also—he behav'd complisant they find it very difficult to get quarters.

Febry. 1st. Charles Mifflin and his Pupils mett in our little Front Room; he has lately undertaking to improve a few young Girls in writeing: teaching 'em Grammar &c—Hanh. Redwood, Sally Fisher, Caty Haines and Sister, Betsy Howel, Sally and Nancy Drinker, are his scholars at present—are to take turns at the different Houses; they began at Ruban Haines, the 8th. Ultimo when Sally first attended—Nancy being unwell, did not go 'till the 18th.

3. On Jan. 23 the Supreme Executive Council had ordered the deputy quartermaster to find billets in private homes for the officers of the Pennsylvania Line, who were then in the city. The officers were quartered in the homes of Quakers and people suspected of loyalist tendencies (*Col. Recs. Pa.*, 12: 605; Mekeel, *Relation of the Quakers*, 167).

Febry. the 17 seventh day, Sammy Wharton return'd to his Family, after upwards of 12 years Absence, he came last from France, he lost his eldest Son; Joseph, on the passage, by a melancholy accident; they had several English prisoners on Board, whome they susspected of designs to meeting, which occasion'd the passengers &c to keep under Arms—Josey Whartons Pistol, 'tis said, went of by accident, and shot him through the Head, of which wound he immediately expir'd; this is the story they tell, but some think; that as they were actuly engaged on the passage with an English Vessel, that he lost his life in the Engagement.

18. Sally Wharton sent for Sister and Self to come there, Sister went in the afternoon.

19 Isaac Wharton came this morning, desireing we would go to there House, Sally being in great Affliction, the death of her Son not having been disclos'd to her 'till this Morning. I went about Noon, din'd with them—and went in the afternoon to the funeral of Sarah Armitt widdow, Sally Logans mother.

20 Jacob and Isiah Paxton, sup'd and lodg'd.

Febry. 25. First Day: HD. left home this Morning with Hannah Catheral in our Chaise; Saml. Pleasants and Molly Smith in his—for Burlington quarterly meeting, intending for Frankford this morning—they return'd the 28th. fourth day.

March 5 Molly Payne spent the day and lodg'd with us. she and Son Walter Breakfast the 6th.

10 HD. and MS. went this morning to Frankford, to visit R James who has been unwell for sometime past, and in trouble—they came home in the evening.

March the 11. Billy Drinker and Sammy Emlen junr. set off this Morning early, intending for Bybarry meeting—and after for New-Town, with a release for 2 Friends, (Schoolmasters) who have been confin'd for several months past, in that Jail; for following their calling, and not having taken the Test re-quird.—First Day.

23 Sarah Carry, Rachel Watson, Jon. Balderston came to our house, to attend the Spring meeting.

24 Saml. Trimble and John James, and Tommy James &c came, they lodge with us.

28 they left us, we have had Company as usual.

April 1 Jammy and Hannah Hopkins from Haddonfield spent part of the day, and lodg'd here. on 3d. day last the 27 Ultimo our Sally, and Sally Fisher attended Becky Shipley to monthly-meeting, where she declar'd her intentions of marriage with John Ming.

April 4 fourth day: HD. Billy and self, cross'd the River in a wherry, set off from Wm. Coopers after 10 o'clock, in S Pleasants Chaise. Thos Scattergoods blind Horse; our own Horse and Chaise being lent, Billy on our Mare; found the roads but midling, much rain having lately fell; din'd at 3 o'clock at Benn. Thomass arriv'd at Atsion at about 6 o'clock; found Dolly Salter in Bed, tho' not so ill as she has been some time past. I found myself much fatigued this evening.

5 I was very poorly in the night, sick at Stomach, vomitted much, eat no Breakfast or Dinner; took magnezar and Rheubarb, took a walk with HD to the furnace—saw DSs Breast dress'd, an affecting sight—HD. LS. and Billy went after dinner to the Ceder-Swamp.

6 very sick again last Night, fasted most of this day—spent great part of it with poor Dolly—she takes annodines twice in the 24 hours, which much relieves her pain, tho' at times she is in great distress; and at other times sets up and talks very chearfully—she is favour'd with one of the kindest of Husbands, in this her great affliction.

7 left Atsion after Breakfast, a misty Morning eat a late dinner at John Hopkinss Haddonfield—the first time of my being at his House—came to the ferry some time before Night; was indulg'd to cross without Sails, tho' the wind was not high; got safe home to Tea—Billy came over in the Horse-Boat with 2 drunken Ferry Men, they got a ground on the Barr; but he came home soon after us.

9 Company to Breakfast, dinner, Tea and Supper—the owners of the Union Saw Mills, mett.

10 they mett here this Morning again—Josey Smith, James Verree, James Jess, Wm. Burr and one or 2 others din'd with us, A James here also.

22 First Day: our good old Dog Watch, who has been a prisoner near 2 years; dyed this Afternoon of a disorder in his Throat, which prevented him from swollowing, that he seem'd in a manner starv'd;—he sarv'd us faithfully for upwards of 7 years—a good deal of Company here within the last Week or 10 days—lodgers from the Country &c.

24 monthly meeting Sally spent most of this day at Wm. Shipleys, whose Daughter Becky past her second meeting.

25 much talk in Town of the British designing for Philada., 'tis thought that they actualy intend for our Bay.

27 Polly Newgent was this afternoon Bound to[4] us by her mother, she has been with us a week, and appears cleaver, brought the Itch with her, which I hope we have nearly cur'd—received a Letter this evening from J. Crammond New York—and another from L. Salter, informing of the Death of his Wife; her Corps is now at John Salters Magnolia; and to be brought here to morrow Morning to be bury'd from our House in the Afternoon.

28 seventh Day: HD. went this morning to Magnolia after Breakfast; return'd about 10 o'clock, with Docr. Edwards, and the Body of our deceas'd Friend Dolly Salter; Wm. Wayne had brought the Coffin an hour before; he and Nanny Perdeux, remov'd her, out of that in which she came, into the other; and screw'd it up, concluding it best so to do—I did not see her, tho Sister thought she appear'd much like herself, considering what she had suffer'd—Lawrence and the rest of the Family came after Dinner; HD. and Docr. Edwards have been busy'd all the morning preparing for the Funeral, she was interr'd in the Church Burying Ground at 6 in the Evening—the Family came back to our House; and several others, 15 or 20 drank tea with us—they went back to Magnolia-Grove in the Evening. several of A Jamess Family here.—it was a sort of a Friendly Burying; tho the Parson attended and the Bell rang—two of our Publick Friends assisted to carry her to the Grave; and two thirds of the company, I believe, were of that People.

29 First day: S Swett din'd, Isaac Stroud sup'd and lodg'd here.

30. Betsy Test came this morning to sew for me—John Saltar and George Gordon came before dinner, HD. and Henry went with them in their Carriage after dinner to visit LS. who is still with them—HD and Son intends to lodge to night at A Jamess.

31 HD. and Henry return'd this Morning in A James Waggon; Henry brought home with him a young Dog, a present from Chalkley, for our yard, they call him Watch.

May 3 HD. was let Blood; myself very unwell all day.

4. The word "searve" crossed out.

4. I was up in the Night in much pain—continu'd very poorly all this day—John Brinton and Wife came before Dinner, they lodge here to Night.

5 JB. and Wife went away after Breakfast, the Continental Money has past for some time past at 200 for one; yesterday and to day it goes at 6 and 700 for one, but few will take it at that rate, the State Money at 3 and 4 for one; this fall occasions great confusion among the People Generaly.

8 the Sailors getting togeather by hundreds with Clubbs, cursing the Continental Money, and declaring against it—state Money goes 6 to one.

9 Sally took a ride on Horse back this Afternoon, with Caty Hains and Brother—she went with them last week to their place at Garmantown—great feasting this Afternoon on board a frensh Frigate, fire Works &c [exhibited].

10 HD. arose early this Morning set of after Breakfast, with G. Churchman for Evesham. return'd the next day.

16 ED. was let Blood, had not been bleed for seven years and upwards.

17 hard thunder this evening. Sarah Merriott and Jos[h]. James lodges here this night.

18 sixth day: HD. set off early this Morning with Robt. Valintine and Thos. Ross, for Salem meeting,[5] he proposes going to Maurices River before he returns home.

19 Sally and Nancy went to Josa. Fishers Place on Schuylkil—little Henry went with Neigr. Howel to their place,—return'd in the Evening.

22 R James and Son Jos[h]. in Town—Monthly meeting—C. Cresson acted as clerk in HDs absence. S Swett &c din'd with us.

23 RJ and Josey din'd here—a poor Fellow who had been condem'd to be hang'd and Gibbeted, was this day repreav'd.

26 three Men were this Morning hang'd on the Commons for theaft &c[6]—J

5. Friends in Salem, N.J., first organized a monthly meeting in 1676. They erected a meetinghouse in 1688 that stood until 1700. A new meetinghouse built in 1700 was replaced by a larger one started in 1770 and completed in 1772 (Joseph S. Sickler, *The History of Salem County New Jersey* [Salem, N.J.: Sunbeam, (1937)], 66–67; Thomas Shourds, *History and Genealogy of Fenwick's Colony* [Bridgetown, N.J.: George F. Nixon, 1876], 391–404).

6. John Dobbins and James Byner ("Byrnes" in Fisher's journal) were hanged for burglary, and Thomas McGee for robbery (*Col. Recs. Pa.*, 12:730, 735; S. R. Fisher, "Fisher Journal," 426–27, 428).

Scott din'd here.—a cool spring so far with much rain—Billy went home this afternoon with Jos[h] and Tommy James in their Waggon.

27 First Day: stay'd from Meeting all day—troubled with a vomiting and otherwise unwell, Billy returnd this afternoon with Josey & Tommy to Tea.

28 HD. return'd home about dinner time.

29 Joseph Scott took leave of us this Morning—he is going to New York to look after his Grand-Children, who have lately lost their Mother—John Ming and Becky Shipley were this Morning married—our Girls at the wedding, &c many other Young People.

June 1 many Dogs said to be mad in Town; Robt. Wharton lately bit by one supos'd to be mad.

[7] fifth day: HD. and Sally left home this Morning [for] Middletown, they lodg'd at John Watsons, return'd the 9th. went on Horse back.

9 I went this Afternoon, Nancy with me: to the Burial of Mary Hall, widdow of David Hall. She dy'd of a Canser in her Breast.

10 First Day: Billy and Sammy Emlen junr. set off early this Morning intending for Bristol meeting, and after to Trent-Town, on a visit to Sally Emlen, who has been some days there, HD. went this afternoon to the Burial of a West Indian of the Name of Cadett.

11 Billy came home this Evening, 34 miles since 12 o'clock, fatigu'd.

19 James Jess lodg'd here, he went, HD with him the 20th. into the Jersyes, travle'd between 30 and 40 miles, and return'd in the evening—HD return'd.

20 little Abey Wilson; Jacob Coopers Grandaughter, on a visit this afternoon to our little Molly, got badly hurt in Neigr. Howels front yard by a fall of the Fence, she cut her chin and brus'd her Face. she came in bleeding and much frightned, I dress'd it with Balsam-Apple, and sent her home towards evening, the Doctor has tended her for several days, has had her bleed, &c—she is now the 24th. got bravely.

24 First Day: Chalkley and Josey James lodg'd here this night.

June 27th. I was up from 12 'till 2 this Morning occasion'd by a sharp Thunder Gust;—tis said one or 2 Houses were struck, but nobody hurt: on sixth day last, Sister fell of a high Chai[s]e strain'd her left wrist, and brus'd the other Hand.

29th. Rachel Watson and her Brother Johnathan Paxton, came before dinner, Rachel lodges here—. Jenney Sibbel formerly Boon, my old maid—) with her Baby came this afternoon, she lodges in the Nursery.

30 RW &c went home.

July 1 First day: Jenney and her Child went away this Morning—I stay'd at home all day, which seems likely will be the case for many weeks to come (should I be spar'd) being unwell, and not in fitt trim to go abroad.—, Joshua Howel and Family have yesterday left our Neighbourhood; intending to reside for the Present, at their Place on Schuylkill,—a Deligate in Congress is to take their place next Door, I dont know his name; am not pleas'd with the change of Neighbours—several accidents have lately happn'd—a Boy of 13 years from Willmington who had never been at Philada. was killd on the Deck of the Shallop as soon as it arrived—by the wading of a Gun from the Franklin Privateer, and a little girl of 6 years lost her life in a nesessary, into which she had fell—two little Children in the Jersyes some days ago, wandred out of their knowledge in the woods, and were not found 'till the third day—one is likely to recover, the other not—Billy went this Morning to Frankford with Tommy James and Sammy Emlen, expect them home this evening.

6 HD went to Frankford this Evening returnd the [ ]th early in the Morning.

7 C. Mifflin broke up School, the weather being hott, and the Girls tir'd.

10 Josey James went home early this Morning he lodg'd here last night—HD went after Breakfast to Frankford, intending for Burlington, with A James &c—Abel is going on his way towards Black-Point in hopes that change of Air &c will be conducive to his better health—third day.

11 fourth day. HD. return'd this evening from Burlington, which place he left at ½ past 4 o'clock A.M.

13 little Henry took a walk this Morning to Ja. Howells, return'd on foot in the Evening—Sally Drinker, Sally Fisher and Billy Sansom went this Afternoon on Horseback to Frankford they return'd after Night.

14 Billy and Jo Sansom, went to Frankford return'd in the Evening.

15th. First day: I have been confin'd for some weeks at home, and likely to be for many more, not so tedious to me as it would be to some others, being no great goer abroad at any time; but I am at times very unwell, and often up in the Night; try'd with sickness &c, Brother Joseph Drinker who has been ill for 3 weeks past, of a violent nerveous fever; appears to be better to day.

19 Sally, Nancy, and (Sammy in the bottom of the Chaise), went this afternoon to Josa. Howells—no body else with them; they took a walk on the Banks of Schuylkill, were caught in a Shower, and much wet—returnd home in the Evening T Pleasants din'd here.

20 sixth day Polly Smith and Nancy Drinker in our Chaise, Sally and Billy Drinker on Horse-back, set of this Morning between 5 and 6 o'clock, for Thos. Watsons in Bucks County—a gust last Night has coold the Air—pleasant riding—B Swett lodgd here last Night—Dorcas Mountgomery call'd this morning to bid us farewell—she expects to set off tomorrow or next day for Chester, there to embarke, with her Son Robt., in a Vessel, Bound to   in France, Sally Logan and Molly Logan spent the Afternoon.

22 First Day: I have been very poorly for several days past, with pains &c—Polly Smith and our Children return'd this Evening.

25th. the Children went this afternoon to the Burial of little Joshua Hopkins.

26 ED—was let Blood.

Augt. 1. HD. little Henry and Molly went this Morning to Frankford, came back to Dinner.

2 WP.s Son Caleb put in the Hospital.

5 First Day: HD. poorly this Evening myself very much so—one Townsend and Joseph Throne from the nine Partners lodg'd here.

6 Abel James and Wife came to Town, lodg'd here.

Augt. 7. R. James junr. came this Morning—to Youths meeting, Abel and wife went home—hard thunder to day or yesterday—Becky James and Warner Mifflin lodg'd here.

8 B James here this day and Night.

9 she went home—ED. very poorly.

10. HD. went to Dr. Edwards near Byberry this morning—return'd in the

Evening—Sammy Fisher was releas'd from Prison some time in last Month, after having been confin'd there 2 years and 2 Days.

12 First Day: very unwell all Day.

13 in pain at times all last Night. hard thunder and sharp lightning and exceeding heavey rain most of the Night.

14 HD was let Blood—myself greatly distress'd, Mind and Body for several days past.

First Day Octor. 28—two days after the last memorandum my dear little Charles was born, on the 16th. Augt. towards evening; was favour'd myself beyond expectation, but my poor Baby was alive and that was all—did not expect he would survive many days; but he is now between 10 and 11 weeks old, and appears to be thriving, which is wonderful, considering how unwell I was for near a Month before his birth, and much falling away; the Child little more than Skin and Bone—Occasion'd prehaps by a cold I caught,—the first 7 or 8 months of my time, I was heartier and better than ever I had been in like situation—and am at present through mercy favourbly recover'd, so as to be able with the help of feeding to Nurse my little one—Nurse Molly Morris was with me near 2 weeks, her Sister Sally Stanberry near 4 weeks, both good Nurses—when the Child was 5 days old he was taken with a sore mouth which prevented him from sucking for nine days: in which time my capacity for Nursing him was much lessen'd—agree'd with Rachel Bickerton a shoemakers wife next door to come in 4 or 5 times a Day to suckle him: which she did for 4 weeks—and with what little I could do in that way we made out for that time, having in the intrim been disapointed of several Nurses; when Rachel was taken with the Ague; and I left to Nurse him myself, which (having geather'd more strength and not geting a Nurse to my mind) I was favour'd to do much better then I could have expected—I had engag'd one Nancy Pool a Young Widow who liv'd or had liv'd at Bristol, but she was prevented coming by Sickness—I then sent for Elizath. Scott from Haddonfield, who was taken the next day she came with the chills and fever, she stay'd with me in my Chamber 4 days had 2 smart fitts, and several after she left us—I then hir'd one Betty Larkey who stay'd here but 5 or 6 days when I dismist her as she by no means sutted—it is a favour to be able to do that offece oneself—as there is much trouble with Nurses. Sister was much fatigu'd during my confinment, as we had much company in and out—and my Nurse call'd away in the hight of our Yearly Meeting—we had but nine lodgers, and those our old ones. Sarah Carry, John Brinton and wife; John Watson and wife, Sammy Trimble Wife and Daughter Peggy, and John Balderston, the meeting concludid with the week, I made shift to get out 2 or 3 times there—HD junr. went home with John Watson junr. who came on sixth day with his Parants, and went back on

14 Sally and Nancy, Becky, Nancy and Robt. Waln junr. went this afternoon to our place Frankford.

16 HD. &c returnd from the Seaside—yesterday and this day, so cold that we, and many others had fire in the Parlors and People wore cloaks abroad.

22, 23 and 24 the weather was extremely warm, many dyd drinking cold water.

23 Sally and Nancy went with John Hopkins junr. to their House Haddon Feild—intending to stay some days.

24 Billy all night at Frankfd.

26 Molly Brookhouse lame of her right hand, bad geathering.

29 Sally and Nancy returnd, Hannah Hopkins with them.

Augt. 5: Hannah Hopkins went home; she was sent for, her little Sister being ill.

7 HD. went to the Funeral of Mary Maddox Aged 102 years.

8 Sally, Nancy (Polly Haydock from New York) Tommy James and Billy went to Frankford on Horse-back—drank Tea at Neigr. Jamess.

11 Molly went first to writeing School, to Becky Jones.

12 John and Rachel Watson came before dinner lodg'd here.

13 they went away after dinner.

14 James Hambleton our former Governour, dyed—Joseph Turner dy'd sometime in last month.

21st. HD. went to the Burial of Amy Jones, aged 88 years.

Augt. 22 HD. din'd at A Jamess, Frankford, with Matw. Cowper his Wife and 2 Daughters &c.

23 little Henry went this morning with Wailing the Mate of the Ship Brothers, Capt. Haythorn—to S. Sansoms to Breakfast, seventh day—he has form'd an intimate acquaintance with said Mate. Sally Drinker and Polly Haydock left our House before 10 o'clock this Morning intending to dine with R. James at

seventh Day—Henry stay'd there near two weeks, when his Father went for him. on the second day of the yearly meeting when Sally and Nancy was about dressing, they mist 6 Silk Gowns, all nearly as good as new, which had been taken out of a Draw in the bleu Room, by whome we could give no Guess—but before Night Wm. [R]ush who is a Majestrate; inform'd us, that six such gowns as we describ'd were then at Benjn. Paschals who is also a majistrate, they were found on first day morning thrown over a fence, and taken to Paschalls by the Constables who had taken up a woman that had got privately out of Jail, on seventh day Afternoon, where she had been confin'd many months, she had not been above 3 hours at Liberty before she was taken up, and sent back for her old misdemenor, she had in that time committd this thift, so that we recover'd the Gowns with no other trouble than sending for them—Sucky Hartshorn and Caty Hopkins, were both brought to Bed the day before myself—Sucky of a Daughter, Caty a Son, both seven months Children—now well and thriving Some time during my Confinment, prehaps about the begining of Sepr.—past through the City a French Army, consisting 'twas say'd of about 5000 Men[7]—they were in whats call'd good order; well accouter'd and hearty,—going to the Southward—HD. Sally and little Henry went to Atsion some time in September—account of a Bloody Battle to the South-ward.—heard from New York of the Death of our old acquaintance and near Friend Nelly Moode; also of the Death of Js. Crammond a young Officer who had liv'd 6 months with us, while the British Troops were in this City, and Behav'd so in our Family as to gain our esteem, he dy'd after 8 days illness; have not heard the time exactly of either of the above Deaths—Prince Wm. Henry arriv'd at New York in Digbys Fleet[8]—Sally Drinker, Ed. Stapler and [J] Houghs Daughter from Virginnia, Sally Fisher Sally Sansom &c went out on Horse-back. Peter Barker has been very troublesome, this fall and last Summer, at our Meetings, meetings of Disipline perticularly, threatning Violently, thumping with an Hammer &c &c.

Octor the 12 HD. John Head and [I] Parish went with Robt. Valentine before Councel—Robert intends 'err long for Ireland.

Octor. 14 First Day, when our Family was at meeting this Morning—myself and the Servants excepted—the little Back-Room Chimney took fire, and was near blaseing out, but by good management was prevented.

7. French troops marched through Philadelphia on Sept. 2 and 3 en route to Yorktown (Boatner, *American Revolution*, 1236).

8. British Rear Adm. Robert Digby was ordered to take command of the North American Squadron on July 9 and arrived in New York City at the end of September. In his fleet was the midshipman Prince William Henry, the future King William IV (John A. Tilley, *The British Navy and the American Revolution* [Columbia: University of South Carolina Press, 1987], 245, 265–66).

Octor 15. an ox that had been drove hard got loose at the Ferry, and run mad through the Streets, he aim'd at HD—who providentialy excaped him; but afterwards hurt a Woman badly.

19 Sally went out on Horse back, with Sally Sansom and Jacob Downing our Children have frequently rode out this fall.

the 17th. of this month Octor. Genl Cornwallace was taken; for which we grievously suffer'd on the 24th. by way of rejoyceing[9]—a mobb assembled about 7 o'clock or before, and continud their insults untill near 10; to those whose Houses were not illuminated scarcely one Friends House escaped we had near 70 panes of Glass broken the sash lights and two panels of the front parlor broke in pieces—the Door crack'd and Violently burst open, when they threw Stones into the House for some time but did not enter—some fard better and some worse—some Houses after braking the door they enterd, and distroy'd the furniture &c—many women and Children were frightned into fitts, and 'tis a mercy no lives were lost.

Octor 30 HD attended the Mariage of Jos. Bacon and Sarah West.

31 Josh. Scott call'd, lately return'd from New York; HD left home this Morning for Atsion; return'd the

Novr. 10: HD left home seventh day morning for Bucks County return'd the 13th.

the 11 First Day: a Fire in Market Street, occasion'd by a Chimney, caught the Ruff of 2 or 3 Houses.

17 Gave Sally Smith warning: dont like hir Conduct towards Henry Briggs, she left us this Morning.

Novr. 24 Sally Smith went away—Polly Moore from Atsion came.

27 our old Friend Jos. Scott departed this life, at Patty Roberts—He very

9. The allied French and American siege of Yorktown had begun in early October. After several days of skirmishing and an unsuccessful attempt to cross the York River to avoid being surrounded, Lord Charles Cornwallis opened negotiations for surrender of his army on Oct. 17. News of the British surrender at Yorktown on Oct. 19, which effectively ended most of the military operations of the Revolutionary War, reached Philadelphia on Oct. 22, and on Oct. 24 Philadelphians celebrated the surrender and illuminated the city. Once again Quakers were singled out by mobs for refusing to participate in the celebrations. Many Quaker residences were damaged (Boatner, *American Revolution,* 1230–50; Mekeel, *Relation of the Quakers,* 199).

frequently din'd and drank Tea with us for several years past, was a judicious sencibble old gentleman.

Decemr. 31st some time in this month Sally Drinker was very [ill] of a vomitting for 16 hours, with short intervails—about the middle of this month our little Charles was very ill of a disorder like the Hives; very much oppress'd, and troubled with a Coughing he is now bravely, I have Nurs'd him carefully for upwards of 4 months, have been but 4 or 5 times out of the House in that time and but once as far as Arch Street corner Josey Smith, Josey James &c &c have lodg'd here on seventh day the 22 Instant one Johnson, an Under Sherif, and one Brown or Ritche, who did not seem free to tell his Name; came as they say'd with an order to sarch our House for British Goods; which they accordingly did, examining draws, Trunks and Closets, Presses &c—They had nearly finish'd their search, being in the garret when HD came home, and order'd them out of the House, when they produc'd their order, sign'd by SB [ ]ith—John Drinker's Son Henry was the person ment by the order and John Thomas, so that our House was Rumag'd by the mistake of the Sherif &c—Henry Drinker hearing that they were at our House had time to hide his Goods, if he had any—but they did not go to look after them; being as I suppose asham'd of the mistake they had made, as well they might, and[10] afraid too.—while they were in our entry up two pair Stairs, Billy Sansom came up, and said somthing provoking to this Ritche, who immediately laid two Pistoles on his hand and offr'd one to Billy; who not taking it, he put them in his Pocket again;—'tis a bad Gouvernment, under which we are liable to have our Houses seachd and every thing laid open to ignorant fellows prehaps thieves,—HD. had he been so disposed; could have made them [paid][11] for their mistake.

Decr. 30, Polly Moore Shew'd Sister several things, such as, Handkerchiefs, Ribbons, Buckles, Pad-locks &c &c—giving her by our little Sam Lewis, to keep for him, 'till he had an oppertunity to sent 'em to his Parants, pretending he had bought them with his own Money—but upon being examin'd by his Master, own'd that he had taken 9 pieces of silver out of the Desk-drawer—by the account he gave of the things he had bought, they amounted to near £5—, so that he made a false confesion—HD. talks of sending him home to his Parants.

Decr. 31st. my HD. in but a midling state of health, tho not worse than at many other times; myself better than I could expect, considering my late tryal, and present confindment; Sister in good health; Sally and Nancy in health tho' not very Strong; Billy a growing thriving lad, tho' far from robust, Henry much the same; Molly [ ].

10. Word crossed out.
11. Word crossed out.

1782

1782 Janry. 1st.[1]—Isey Pleasants came this morning to acquaint us, that his mamy was brought to Bed, at 6 this morning of a Son—who they call James.—their 10th Child; all living.

2 HD. and Son Henry left home after Breakfast, for Atsion—Josey James and Billy Sansom Lodg'd.

3d. WS—here to night.

4 HD. &c return'd this Evening.

7 and 8th. Josey James lodg'd here.

10th. HD left home this Morning Saml. Hopkins with him—for Burlington &c—Billy Sansom lodg'd here.

11 HD—return'd this evening Sammy Trimble came before dinner, lodg'd here.

12 S Trimble went away after Dinner.

14 Lawrance and John Salter came to Town with Dr. Edwards, they din'd with us Lawrance and John lodg'd.

15 they din'd and lodg'd here.

16 fourth day LS—din'd with us,—after dinner he with George Gordon and our Son Henry went to Magnolia in our Chaise—George and Henry are to return tomorrow Morning. Billy Sansom, Issey Pleasants and George Gordon, tend at our Iron-Store, as Apprentices to HD.

17 HD junr. and GG—return'd.

1. The manuscript volume for Jan. 1, 1782–Feb. 26, 1784, has light blue paper covers. The outside front cover reads, "1782–3, 4." On the inside front cover ED wrote, "Novr. 3. Novell Soliars."

24 Nancy had a bad spell of sick Head-ach.

29 third day: Sally, Nancy, Sally Sansom Billy Sansom, Jacob Downing and John Head—went this Afternoon to Frankford in a Sleigh—the coldest day by far that we have had this Winter.

30 the River fast: about 2 weeks ago the fields were green with growing Grass, & M Norris pick'd a Flower out of her Garden. two or 3 very cold days has fastn'd the River.

31st. Jos. Hampton sup'd lodg'd & Breakfasted here.

Feby. 3 our little Charles very unwell oppress'd and Feverish.

5 the Child beter—HD. and MS went after Breakfast to Frankford to visit R James, who has been for some time past indispos'd—they return'd towards evening. Sally, Nancy, Nancy Waln, Jacob Downing, Ezra Jones and Billy Sansom; went over the River on the Ice—before dinner.

10 First Day: HD. Sally, Nancy & Billy, went to the Burial of Grace Galloway, who dyed last fourth-day, on which day John Morris Senr.[2] was buried. this day 4 or 5 persons were drown'd crossing the River; pushing the Boat off the Ice into the water—the wife of one Little: daughter of Thos Williams was one.—HD return'd this Morning from the Jersys, where he yesterday went, Jos James, J Drinker and Billy Sansom with him.

Febry. Josh. Smith and his son Saml sup'd lodg'd and Breakfasted here.

21 Atsion Poll Moore went away she has been near a quarter here, and is now near lying in, I was glad to get rid of her.

22 Patty Smith and Becky James lodg'd with us.

24 First Day: HD and his daughter Nancy, left home this Morning on Horse-back for Buckingham—intending this day to Abington Meeting Nancy

2. The word "departed" crossed out.

is going to [T] Watsons, HD. to Writestown Meeting[3] he is very poorly, and has been so for some time past—Billy Sansom lodges here.

25 Nancy Rubins came to work.

26 a Soap-Boyler Shop burnt last night, near the Dock.

March 3 First Day: HD. and Nancy return'd, while I was at afternoon meeting.

15 Lawrance Saltar lodg'd &c here.

18 and 19 James Jess lodg'd here.

22 Sarah Carry, R. Watson, John Balderston came.

23 Sammy Trimble came, they stay'd till the 26. after dinner then went away—less company at this Spring meeting than usual.

27 sharp lightning this Afternoon, John Dickinsons House, where the French Ambasador lives was struck and much shattered a Man who set in one of the Chambers was so much hurt that his life is dispair'd of.

28 a Meeting in our Parlor this evening G Dillwyn, S Emlen, [T] Ross [T.] Scatergood, C. West, HD. R Jones and myself—[T] Ross and S Emlen had somtthing to say to us the others were silent—these Men Friends with several others, had spent the afternoon with HD on Business they went away after 9 o'clock.

29 HD. was let Blood—little Molly went to Frankford with A James and Wife—came back before dinner with Abel.

31 B Woodcock came from Willmington to accompany the Corps of Lidia

3. Wrightstown, in Bucks County, Pa., was settled in 1684 by Quakers, who began meeting in private homes in 1686. Under the jurisdiction of other Friends' meetings in Bucks County, Wrightstown Friends received permission in 1721 to build a meetinghouse, which they completed the next year. In 1724 the meeting shared a monthly meeting with nearby Buckingham, and in 1734 it was granted its own monthly meeting. As the Quaker population grew in the county Wrightstown became one of the locations for the quarterly meetings that rotated after 1735 between Falls, Middletown, Wrightstown, and Buckingham. Wrightstown was also the site of general prayer meetings held at harvest times and of youths' meetings. Wrightstown Friends built a new meetinghouse in 1787, but discontinued all meetings in 1811 (Charles W. Smith, "A History of the Early Settlement of the Township of Wrightstown," an appendix to William J. Buck, *History of Bucks County* [Doylestown, Pa.: John S. Brown, 1855], 8, 21–23).

Farris, formily Zane, she had been marrie'd 12 or 14 years without having had a Child, and was now within a week or 2 of her time, was upwards of 24 hours ill but not deliver'd, when she dyed—she was big with twins, which the Doctor took from her soon after her Death, by opening her, a Boy and Girl, who were bury'd in the same Coffin with their Mother. Bancroft lodges here.

April 2 Betsy Waln spent the day with us—HD left home this afternoon for Bucks County.

3 B Woodcock went homewards HD. return'd this Morning. Sally took a ride the day before yesterday on horse-back, with Billy Sansom—she has a bad Cough.

4 HD and self were at the Marriage of Henry Drinker and Polly Howel, at the large Meeting-House—the weding was kept at Jonan. Shoemakers in Elbow-lane; near 30 persons there—we came home after tea—fifth Day.

April 5. HD and J Drinker set of after Breakfast for Atsion, HD in a Sulkey—Sally and Nancy spent this Afternoon and Ev'ing with the Bride, with many other young persons, who were not invited to the Wedding her Uncles House being small.

7 First day: HD returnd.

18 my dear little Baby has been ill near a week, much oppressd and very feverish, I have been the greatest part of 3 Nights up with him, his disorder at times like the Hives—I have a heavy cold myself—Sallys Cough bad—little Henry very poorly with a Cough and fever—'tis in the Air I believe. HD. and Son Henry went yesterday to Spring-Field, they returnd in the Evening. the 14 Instant Billy and Sammy Emlen junr. went to Burlington they return'd the 15th. second day.

27 seventh day: HD and Sally went to Woodbury where HD had Business, on their return he left Sally at John Hopkinss and came home himself in the evening—C. James call'd this afternoon, he return'd this week from Sh. Carolina, where he has been near 6 months—Sally went out yesterday, on Horse back with Sally Fisher, Hannah Redwood, Caspr Hains and Billy Sansom—on forth day last she went with Molly Logan, John Pleasants and our Billy to Docr. Logans at Stanton.

April 29 second day, Abel James and Wife and Patty Smith, call'd on me this Morning I went with them in their Carriage to visit Becky Shoemaker who has lately return'd from N:York, by permission—her Husband and Son Ewdw. still there—after seting a while with Becky we went to see Amy Jones, who has been Bed-rid (as it is call'd) for near 5 Years—by the Palsey in her left side—she is in her 87th. year, her memory good—she was much pleased to see us.—Abel, his Wife and Patty, din'd with us.

May first, fourth day, Betsy Test came to work here—Josey James lodg'd here last night.

May:3 sixth-day: Nancy went out on Horse-back, with Polly Wells, John Morris and Benjn. Morris.—My little Charles very Poorley—the Painter at work this Week—painting the Ruff of our House, and back Buildings with Brick-dust.

4 my child very restless last Night slept none myself, till after day—a report prevails at present, that independence is granted:[4] beleived by many.—John Hopkins junr. din'd with us, he says Sally is well at their House, but cannot tell when she may return home.

8 spent this Afternoon, Nancy with me; at Wm. Fisher's—it is the 3d. time that I have drank Tea out of our own House, for upwards of 11 months past.

16th. fifth day. Sally return'd home this Afternoon; Nancy and Hannah Hopkins with her; she was, while at Haddonfield, at the funeral of Mary Champion, widdow of Nathaniel Champion, Brother of my Grand mother Mary Jervis—aged 96 years I was pleasd Sally happen'd to be there at the time; she being her great great Aunt by Marriage.

19 First Day: HD. set off after Breakfast in his Sulkey for Salem Meeting—intending before he returns home to go to the saw mills at Maurices river.

20 Sally and Nancy went to the Burial of Sally Biddle from Ruth Johnsons, Henry went to Schuylkill with Neddy Howel—returnd in the Evening.

May: 22 Sally Nancy, Hanh. Redwood, Tom Wister, Ben Morris and Casper Hains went over Schuylkill to James Joness on a visit to Caty Hains who is there for her health:—W Sansom lodges here.

23 Our wicked Neighr. Pantlif in the Alley beat and brus'd Black Tom Thos. Shamefully, (a negro man we have lately hir'd) his Wife set their Dog at him, who bit his Thigh in 2 or 3 places, because he had throne a stone at the Dog, who had run at him some hours before.

4. A special postscript edition of the *Pennsylvania Journal* on May 4 announced the British government's decision to cease hostilities and end the fighting in America (*Pa. Journal,* May 4, 1782).

24 Black Toms lame with the wound and under the Doctors care, he had Pantlif up, before Wm. Rush, who bound him over, 'till next Coart, but by no means humbld him—this Man and his Wife are two of the most Wicked Spiteful revengfull persons I think I ever knew they are dutch Foulk.

25th. HD returnd from Maurices river—seventh day.

May 28 third day—went to Frankford with R James, in their Carriage, Sally and little Charles with me, intending to spend some time there on account of the Childs health—Josey and Patty Smith there.

29 J and M Smith with his Son Sammy, left us, for their home—We stay'd at Frankford 11 days, in which time we were visited by most of our Family and many others, Hannah Hopkins came with our Nancy and Tommy James, she has been some time at our House—John and Rachl. Watson din'd at AJs on their way home from her Brother Oliver Paxtons weding—he was married to Ruth Johnson the day week that I left home—three of his Brothers with their Wives, his Sister Rachel and her Husband, lodg'd 2 nights at our House—H Hopkins also.

June 8 we return'd home, left R. James very poorly with a rumatic pain in her arm, for which she was let Blood &c—C. James came home with us he lodg'd here.

10 I went this evening with HD to take leave of [J.] Pemberton, found their back Parlor and Entry nearly filld with Company—they were seting in silence—several appear'd—after the meeting broke up we took leave of JP—who set of the next Morning on his way to New-York, intinding—from thence to take shiping for Great-Briten.

June 15. our Son Henry with Sam Parish and 2 other little Boys, went to our place at Frankford, seventh day—when they clim'd on the limb of an old Chery-Tree, which gave way. Henry being badly hurt was taken to James Streets our Tenant,—Tom Kite being there, went quickly home and informd Becky James junr. who went directly to him and did what she could for him—[Sam] Parish came to Town to let HD know, who went immediately with the Chaise for him, he mett T Kite bringing him home, I knew nothing of the matter 'till I saw him with his Daddy enter the Parlor; Docr. Redman was sent for, who upon examineation found his collar bone was broke, and his sholder brus'd. I assisted the Doctor to set it, (which as I was favour'd with resolution) was no hard matter—he was much better after it was over then I could have expected, consedering how much hed suffer'd from the first.

16 First Day: Henry walks about with a Bandage on, and his arm in a

Sling—Hannah Hopkins went home this Afternoon—Billy went to Frankford with J. Pleasants and Tommy James.

21st. sixth day: HD senr. SSD. AD WD. MD: Rachel Drinker, her two Daughters 2 Sons, and Sons Wife,—Billy Sansom, [J.] Thomas, and our Black Thomas—went a Fishing—took provision with them—din'd at John Saltars—came to Tea chez-nous.

22d. ED. a bad fitt Colick last night—little Charles very poorley. towards the end of this month or the beginning July, Lawrance Saltar lodg'd here, Josey James also—and Billy Sansom lodg'd here the Night his Father and Family moved out of Town, where they intend residing for a time 2½ miles from the City, at a place of theirs on Shulkyl.

July 8th. HD left home for Haddonfield monthly-meeting, intending after for Atsion. Billy Sansom lodges here during his Absence—he rides out every morning with Sister and little Charles, who has been very poorly for some time past.

11 Pantlifs Dog Bit [I.] Hazelhursts Negro Boy in the thigh, worse then he had some time ago bit our Tom. Hazelhurst had the Dog shot.[5]

July 12: HD. return'd home.

15 Great doings this evening at the French Ambasadors, (who lives at John Dickinsons House up Chesnut Street) on account of the Birth of the Dauphine of France—feasting Fire-Works &c, for which they have been preparing for some weeks.[6]—C. James and our Children were part of the evening on the top of our House, where they could see the Fireworks—Chalkley lodg'd here.

19. AJ. very poorly and low spirited—his Afairs going contrary to his wishes—HD. busy endeavouring to settle them—Bancroft Woodcock and Son Isaac came here early this morning they lodge here.

20 seventh day—Billy went with BW. and Son in a Shallop for Willmington, set off about 10 fore-noon.

5. The words "and threatend the master and mistress" crossed out.

6. The first son and second child of Louis XVI and Marie Antoinette, Louis Joseph Xavier François, had been born on Oct. 22, 1781. The Chevalier de la Luzerne, the French minister to the United States, formally announced the birth of the dauphin to Congress on May 13, 1782, and gave this fête in his honor (Madame de la Rocheterie, *The Life of Marie Antoinette*, trans. Cora Hamilton Bell [New York: Dodd, Mead, 1893], 1:242–44; Scharf and Westcott, *Philadelphia*, 1:420–21).

23 Josey James lodg'd here.

24 Sally went this Afternoon on Horse-back with Billy Sansom to his Fathers place—Billys Horse threw him, and hurt his leg badly.

25 Billy return'd, B. Woodcock and Son with him, they lodg'd here.

26 BW. went home, left his Son, who is to stay some time at Josh. Richardsons—some time within this last month, Charles Crage (eminent for his humanity without the Lines, when the British held the City) shot himself through the Head at Redden occasiond by some Family decensions—and on the 24th. Instant a French Officer at the Indian-Queen, was guilty of the same crime, dissapointed in Love, and Money Matters.

27 HD. went this morning to the Funeral of Wm. Smith Broker.

29 HD. went to Abington with H Catheral, in our Chaise.

Augt. 1 Sally and Nancy, went with C. James in their Chaise to Frankford—Chalkley lodg'd here last night) they returnd in the Evening.

2 Billy went to S Sansoms place.

3 Billy went to Frankford.

7 Nancy went to Haddonfield with Jemmy Hopkins.

9 Sally went to H Roberts place at Point no Point, with Billy Sansom &c, return'd in the Evening.

10 Billy Drinker went to S Sansoms with Isaac Woodcock after dinner, returnd in the evening.

Augt. 12. HD. and Abel James in the Chaise, Abels Man Saml in a Sulkey, left home this Morning at 6 o'clock, for Virginia. Billy Sansom lodges here.

13 A Flag from London, said to be below,—talk of peace & Independence—. little Henry went to Frankford this afternoon Betsy Test lodg'd here last Night she finesh'd work here to day.

14 Nancy return'd from Haddonfield.

15. Sally went to Frankford with Tommy James—Wm S——n seemingly derangeé.

16 very uneasy on WSs Account.

17 Billy took a ride to Frankford with Tommy James—Isaac Woodcock lodges here this night, WS. gone to Burlington—little Henry went this Afternoon to our place at Frankford with S Parish &c.

Augt. 18. HD. return'd from Virginia &c. ED. keep't Chamber the latter part Augt. with Chills and Fiver &c Nurse Molly Morris with me 4 days, little Charles very poorly, look'd out for a Nurse for him, have found none yet to my mind.

Sepr. 8. HD. was let Blood having been unwell for some time past, which is generaly the case with him, Spring & Fall.

14 HD. went to Frankford, to visit Chalkley James, who has been ill of a Fever &c for several weeks past, but is now better—Thos. Watson, came here this Afternoon, from Bucks County, he is one of the meeting for Sufferings, who are summond here by Friends on account of a petition sent into the Assembly sign'd by Isaac Howel and White Mat[lack], in the name of disown'd Quakers—, claiming a share of Friends property pretending to a right thereto[7]—the end of last Month or beginning of this, the French Army march'd through this City towards New-York 'tis said.[8]

Sepr. 15 little Molly unwell with sore Throat and fever—Sister has been

7. Meetings in the Philadelphia area often disowned members who actively supported the American cause during the Revolutionary War, took oaths of allegiance to the new state governments, or both. Rather than join other Protestant denominations, many disowned members banded together under the leadership of Samuel Wetherill, Jr., to found a society based on Quaker principles, but which supported the laws and military efforts of the new states. Calling themselves the Religious Society of Friends, they were also known as the Free Quakers and the Fighting Quakers. In 1781 they petitioned the Society of Friends in Philadelphia for use of a meetinghouse for worship and the right to share the burial ground for their members who wished to be buried with their ancestors. The Philadelphia Meeting turned down their request, and the Free Quakers then sent a petition signed by White Matlack and Isaac Howell to the state legislature on Aug. 21, 1782, claiming they had been denied their rights in consequence of obeying the laws of the state. Though the petition and counterpetitions aroused a great deal of public interest and forced the state legislature to consider the question of religious freedom versus compliance with state laws, the legislature ultimately tabled the issue (Wetherill, *Religious Society of Friends*, 5–42, esp. 33–37; the petitions are reprinted in appendixes 3–6, pp. 53–82).

8. Following Cornwallis's defeat at Yorktown, the French army remained in Virginia until the end of June, when it received orders to march northward to meet with Washington and the American forces then at Kings Ferry on the Hudson River in New York. The French army passed through Philadelphia in early August, reaching Kings Ferry on Sept. 17 (Howard C. Rice, Jr., and Anne S. K. Brown, trans. and eds., *The American Campaigns of Rochambeau's Army 1780, 1781, 1782, 1783* [Princeton: Princeton University Press, Providence, R.I.: Brown University Press, 1972], 1:72–78, 159–65, 2:172–86).

afflicted for two weeks past, by a Felon in her Thumb, which has been very troublesom—I fear tis not near well yet, tho I hope 'tis better.

16 HD. and a number other Friends near 20—mett a Committee of the Assembly at the State-House—T. Matlack takes upon him to be speaker for the Apostates; Nicks. Waln for our Friends—they broke up before dinner—are to meet again on fourth Day.

18 The Committee of Friends went according to appointment to the State-House, were inform'd, the case was put of 'till the next Session.

20 The Woods have been on Fire in the Jersys, for some weeks past, and done considerable damage—we have had a remarkable long dry spell of weather—Sally and Nancy went this Afternoon to the Burial of James Bringhursts Second Wife—sixth day evening and no friends yet come to the yearly meeting Lawrence Salter was Married to Sally Howard the 22 Ultimo.

Octor 1 Yearly Meeting concluded on seventh day last, much Company but not so many lodgers as at some other times—Sarah Carry left us to lodge with her Daughter Walker, who has lately come to reside in Town.

6 First day—HD. E Stapler and S Emlen, left our House after Breakfast, for New-Town in the Jersys, intending afterwards for Burlington &c—I went to meeting this Afternoon the first time for many months, George Gordon lodges here during HDs absence.

7 Lisey Plumer from Mt. Holly came this morning with intent to suckle my Baby, but not having Milk sufficient, not so much as myself—she undertook to tend him &c at 10/– p week.

8. [J] James lodg'd here with G G.

10. HD return'd.

12 about this time a Negro Man was executed, for murder—and some days past Jemima Wilkingson left this Town a woman lately from New-England who has occasiond much talk in this City—she, and those that accompany'd her, (who were call'd her Deciples) resided some short time in Elfriths-Ally, where crouds went to hear her preach and afterwards in the Methodast meeting-House—her Dress and Behavour, remarkable.

13 James Jess lodg'd here.

14 Joseph Smith & J Jess lodg'd here I received a perticular letter from WS.

15 Bancroft Woodcock lodg'd here.

17 J. Jess went away.

Octor. 18 B. Woodcock left us.

19 HD. and MS went Frankford.

22 went this Morning to monthly meeting with Becky James—she declar'd (or ment to do so) her intentions of marriage with John Thompson—the Family mett this Morning at our House—Nancy Jones and Betsy Foulk were also here, they being Brides-Maids—Sarah Fisher and Myself were appointed overseers for the mariage they left the meeting when they had past, stay'd a short time at our House, and went to Frankford to Dinner—John Tomson Potter also past meeting, with Kasiah French.

23 HD. left home this Morning with H Catheral for Burlington to the Burial of her Sister Craff HD. went into Bucks-County on Business, left HC at Burlinton, but return'd with her the 24 in the evening—Josey James lodg'd here the 23 24 and 25—My little Charles, who was all Summer very unwell, and at times ill, has since the cool weather altred much for the better; am in hopes from the present prospect, I shall be abel to suckle him myself this winter—he eats and sleeps well.

Novr. 1. Billy came home about dinner time, his Face much Brus'd, had been Boxing with one of the Lattin School Boys,—an exercise that by no means suits him.

3 First day—went this evening over to see Neigr. Waln, who has had bad Collick.

Novr. 4. Nancy, Billy and Tommy James, began to learn French, they are taught by one Bartholemew at 4[½] Dollars each p month, and 6 Dollars each for entrance money—they occupy our smallest front Parlor, on second-day fourth day and sixth day evenings, from 6 o'clock, 'till ½ past 7. AD. received a B——l d——x from [JJ].

5 HD. left home, about 10 o'clock this fore-noon, in his Sulkey expecting to reach Richd. Walns this evening—little Henry went to Frankford, Micajh Churchman lodg'd here.

7 M Churchman went away—HD. returnd—John Dickinson proclaim'd Gouvernor.

Novr. 10 First Day: HD. and Daughter Sally, left home after Breakfast, in the Chaise—for Darby Meeting[9]—intending for Concord, and afterwards for Willmington—Billy bad with the Tooth Ach—Fredrick lanc'd his Gum—G Gordon lodges here—Owen Biddle appeard this Morning at the Market-Street Meeting.

12 Nancy went to S Sansoms, on Horse-back, with Sally Parish Tom Wistar, and Casper Hains, the two later with Josey James spent the evening—Josey lodg'd here with George Gordon—I received a Letter this evening from W S——n.

14 J Drinker came from Willmington to Day, brought a Letter from Sally to Nancy, She and her Daddy, lodges at Bancroft Woodcocks.

15 [J.] Parish put up the Stove in the back Parlor—I went this Afternoon to H Stevensons, HS gone out, from thence to S Whartons, came home in the evening. have not walk'd so far from home for upwards of 18 months—Tommy Moore was married last Night to Sally Stamper—AD. wrote this evening to JJ——s Betsy Watson spent the Afternoon and lodg'd here.

16. HD. and Sally return'd.

19 HD. and Billy went to the Burial of Edwd. Drinker Great Uncle to HD. said to be upwards of 100 years of age.—My left Breast and Shoulder more than commonly painfull for several days past.

26 this Morning John Tompson and Becky James, past their marriage the Second time, our House the Rendez-Voose as before—my little Charles very poorly with a lax and vomiting, found it Difficult to leave him during the meeting,—My Girles and Billy went with them to Frankford to dinner—R James Senr. Ditto junr. Patty Smith and the 2 Brides-Maids went in the Coach, A James Senr and JT in a Chaise; Abbijah Daws and Sally Drinker in another, C. James and Nancy Drinker in another, [Joh.] Fox and AJ junr in Ditto Tommy and Billy on Horse back—the two last return'd late in the evening, expect the Girles will stay all Night.

27 the Girls return'd this Morning after Breakfast with Josey Fox in [J.] Smith's Carriage, Nancy Jones with 'em.

Decr. 3 Cloudy misty morning my Baby better than for several days past; set

9. Quakers started a meeting in Darby, a township and borough in Delaware County, just south of Philadelphia, in 1689; their meetinghouse, completed in 1701, stood for over a century (Ashmead, *Delaware County*, 521–22).

of about 10 o'clock for Frankford, to the marriage of JT and RJ—Wm. and Sarah Fisher call'd for me in Joshua Howels Cariage myself and Son William went with them, Sally and Nancy with Nichs. Waln, in his Chariott, HD in the Chaise solus, and Black Toms in the Sulkey—on our coming near AJs saw the Family moving towards the Meeting House, where we went without stoping beforehand had a Silent meeting,—between 12 and one, the Ceremony performd, HD. read the Certificate, company mov'd on to A Jamess weather clear'd up, Sun Shone—din'd about 3 o'clock, an elegant, tho' not large Wedding not more than 32 or 3 persons besides the Family—could not attempt to stay Tea, the days so short—came away as soon as the Servants had din'd, Nichs. Waln and myself first; the rest of the Company soon after except HD. and some of the Young People; who stay'd all Night—. it was some time after Candle-light when I reach'd home, cloudy and hazey—George Gordon and Enoch Evans lodg'd here; found my Baby bravely.

4 HD return'd this Morning the Girles before dinner, Josey James with them, in their Carriage.

7 Charless Nurse Lizey Plumer went this Morning for Mt. Holly to spend a few days with her Child &c.

8 First day: an old Stable took fire this Afternoon, at the back of B Shoemakers House at the upper end of Market Street, and was burnt down, our Polly Nugent who went out after dinner intending as she said, to go to Chapple, went to see the fire, near which place she was thrown down, and run over by a Man on Horse-back and badly hurt. she got some one to assist her to Dunlaps in second street, where she expected to have found her Mother, but she had left the place some days before—they had her Bleed as she appeard ill—and sent us word of her situation—Sister and Black Thomas went to Dunlaps, where they found her, better then she had been at first coming there. Thos. and another man brought her home in an Arm-Chair—her left Leg is much swell'd and bruisd by the Horses Foot—after proper care was taken of it she appeard bravely, but will not be well very soon, I beleive.

9 Thos. taken with the Chills and fever this morning—so that with Lizeys absence Pollys hurt and Thos. sickness—we have none at present but little Sam Lewis—HD. junr. went before Dinner to Frankford to visit the Bride—he return'd towards evening.

15 First day: [S] Sansom sent a note to Billy desiring him, to go home with him and spend the night with his Son Jos. Billy went and was detaind all the next day by snow. Snow, after 11 o'clock this night, Sally and myself not being in Bed, observed a fire break out, next yard but one to Hazelhursts, presently

heard em cry fire, it was soon put out,—heard next day that it was occasiond by hot ashes being put in the yard near the wood.

16 Snow all day.

17 Lizey came home this evening Billy returnd from S Sansoms before dinner Josey James lodg'd here. Becky James alias Tompson mov'd to Town, they are settld in water-street in a House of Buch[ ]. Sim's near Chestnutt Street, the Girls had 2 or 3 invitations to go Sleighing, but they [d]eclind em all.

19 Thos. Lightfoot lodg'd here.

Decr. 22 Josey James lodg'd here first Day.

25. Sally, Nancy, Hannah Drinker, John Thomas, Jacob Downing and Tomy Wister, walk'd after Breakfast, to Par-la Ville, Samy. Sansoms Dwelling near Schuylkil, they din'd there and return'd home before evening.

1783

1783 Janry. 6. Josey James lodg'd here.

9 Jacob Paxton lodg'd here.

14. Sally, Nancy, Polly Wells, Abby [Dorsey], Willey Morris, Docr. Morris, Ben[n]. Morris, Toms. Wister, John Dorsey, Sally Greenleaf and Caspr Hains, went out Sleighing in the Afternoon return'd, at 9 at Night, Moon light.

1783 Janry. 16. little Molly went out with S Emlen Daughters, in a Sheigh about Dinner time—return'd between 3 and 4 o'clock Lawrence Saltar has been in Town several days past, on account of a bruse on his toa; was apprehensive of a mortification—but is now in a fair way of gitt[ng] well.

18. George Churchman lodg'd here.

26 Josey James lodg'd here.

Febry. 8 Lawrence Saltar, HD. and little Henry, went after Breakfast—10 Miles up the ridge-roade—returnd towards evening.

13 this day was printed the Kings Speech to both Houses Parliment Decr. 5th.—bespeaking peace, and Independence;[1] I fear they will not long agreed togeather with us.

1783 Febry. 16 First Day: up Stairs all day, unwell,—Joshua Fisher departed this life about the begining of this Month, Jeremiah Warder some weeks before, Three Men were yesterday executed, one of the Name of Stackhouse, A Molato and a Negro.—for robing Balls House, near Kingsington.

25 HD. was let Blood.

March 10 a fire broke out about two o'clock this Afternoon, in front-street,

1. The text of George III's speech of Dec. 5, 1782, reached New York on Feb. 9, 1783. Most Philadelphia newspapers published the speech on Feb. 15. ED's Feb. 13 source is unlocated (*Pa. Journal, Pa. Packet,* and *The Independent Gazetteer; or, The Chronicle of Freedom,* Feb. 15, 1783; *Pa. Gaz.,* Feb. 19, 1783).

at the Corner of Norriss Alley, the House Thos. Coomb formerly liv'd in, was almost consum'd, and the two next Houses, towards Walnut Street, much damag'd—Sally Drinker, Hannah Redwood Thos. Wistar and Benny Morris sat up with the Corps of Catey Greenleaf, second daughter of Catherine Greenleaf, she died of a Consumption—the first time Sally set up all Night.

11 Saml. Lewis taken unwell.

12 discoverd he had the Measels Docr. Redman tends him.

13 Saml. Harris and [Lamuel] Wright, of the Sect call'd Nicolites; lodg'd here.

20st. little Molly taken unwell simptoms of the Measels.

23 First Day: measels out on Molly, and has been for 2 or 3 days hope she will have 'em favourably, our Spring meeting, not much Company here as yet—S. Trimble J. Balderston, B Woodcock &c.

25 A James junr. lodg'd here.

31 James Jess lodg'd here.

April 3 our little Charles unwell.

4 the Measels coming out on him.

6 First Day: the Child pretty full a good-deal fever, but h[ ]t-whole HD. and his Son Henry left home, after an early Breakfast intending to morrow for King-Wood—HD in the Sulkey little Henry on Horse-back, his Daddy bought a Horse for him Yesterday.

7 up with the Child most part of last night, he is ill to day—the Measels struck in, gave him a Levament, and Bath'd his feet. Sally Nancy, Sally Parish, Walter Payne and Billy took a walk to S Sansoms.

10 HD. and Son return'd home.

13 First Day: the Child appears to be geting better; last night was the first of his laying in Bed for a Week past—Charles Mifflin died some time past Henry went to Latin School May 5[2] Charles ill of a vomiting awake with him all night the 11th.

2. The words "May 5" crossed out.

May 11 First Day HD. and Son William, left home after an early breakfast, intending for Reding &c—a great number of Soliders prisoners, in different company have past thro' this City, within those few weeks, for New-York.

14 A Remarkable Hail-storm between 11 and 12 this fore-noon such as I never saw the like—from the N:W—the hailstones as big as Hickery-Nutts, broke 51 pains of Glass, in the back of our House, and crack'd 12—HD. and Billy return'd the 15.

June 4 Walter Payne went for Virginia.

5 HD. and C West went in our Chaise to Chester, a number of other Friends went also, to attend Nichos. Waln who expects to take Shippen there, for Great Britain &c HD. &c return'd in the Evening, the Ship left Chester after dinner.

9 Sally, Nancy in the Chaise, Billy on Horse back left home after dinner about [1] o'clock—second day—intending for Thos. Watsons, Bucks-County—HD and MS. went yesterday to Frankford Meeting, spent the rest of the day at A Jamess.

14 HD. and little Molly, left home after dinner for Middle-Town, seventh day,—to Visit our Children, at John Watsons.

16 Daddy and Molly returnd, Sally Nancy and Billy, were to leave Middle-Town this day for Richd. Walns near Crossweeks in the Jersys.

28th or threabout the Children return'd from R Walns.

July 4 Masons Grand Exebition.[3]

July the 9:—HD. Lawrence Salter, Charles Howard, Tommy James Sammy Emlen, and Billy Drinker left home after Breakfast for Summers [pont] near the Seaside—John Paynes Family came to reside in Philada.

13 Josey James lodg'd here with G Gordon—storm in the night, up with the child who was ill.

3. In an evening torchlight procession, a platform carrying a sofa by Mason & Co., a Philadelphia upholsterer, embellished with portraits of George Washington, the Comte de Rochambeau, and Horatio Gates, was pulled by eight white horses and accompanied by thirteen young girls dressed in white and boys carrying torches. A band playing music led the procession (Scharf and Westcott, *Philadelphia,* 1:432).

Frankford, and to set off after dinner for Burlington, they were to have set off early this Morning but were disopointed of the Company of S. Emlen the younger, who was to have escorted them—our Son William left home before 11 o'clock for Frankford intending to wait on the Girls to Burlington; it is one of the hotest day we have had this Summer.

24 First day: Billy returnd to Frankford this Morning with Tommy James, whom he mett with at Burlington he stay'd at Frankford this day, lodg'd there, and returnd home, Tommy with him on second day morning the 25 HD. and Henry left home for Glouster, the latter put on Board the Brothers, who lay at Anchor there; they soon after set sail for Bristol, put Henry on shore, where he waited the return of his Father from the Jersys, came home togeather.

28 Fifth day: Sally and Polly Haydock return'd from Burlington, Isey Pleasants with them.

29th. John Thomas and Hanh. Drinker past their first meeting: Sally Drinker waited on Hannah as Brides-Maid—she came home before dinner with the sick-Head-ach.

Sepr. the 1st. & 2d. Josey and Patty Smith Lodg'd here.

3 Sally Drinker, Becky Waln and Robt Waln went to Frankford, Richd. Waln here this evening—Polly Haydock took leave of us, intending homeward tomorrow—Abel James engaged for some time past in a great hurry of Business—HD. unwell for upwards of a week past disordred in his Bowels.

4 Nancy came home this evening very unwell, went to Bed with a chill on her was before Morning in a high fever.

5 Nancy very ill.

6 still very ill sent for Dcr Redman—she took a vomitt our valued Friend Lawrance Saltar departed this Life at Atsion, after 10 days illness; appeard to be a Billous Fever.

7 First-day: L. Saltar Buried from John Howards this Morning before meeting Sally Drinker came from the Funeral very poorly with the Head-Ach and fiveres Nancy still very ill a high fever, Sick Stomach and pain in her Bones—Billy came from evening Meeting, where he had a smart Chill, which was follow'd in the night by a high fever.

8 Nancy and Billy very ill. this evening[4] Silas Downing a publick Friend, and Refine Weeks, from West-Bury on long-Island, came to our House where we expect they will continue for several weeks.

9 Billy took a vomitt.

10 Sally, who has been very poorly ever since first Day—this day took to her Bed—high fever and Sick Stomach.

11 She took a vomitt, they are all three very ill—Docr. Rush apply'd to—to consult with Docr. Redman about this times Sister was taken ill; a violent fitt of the Chill and Fever, having been much fatigued and taking a nap on the foot of the Bed, with her Head towards the Chimney; she Had almost lost her hearing—the fever went of with a great sweat—she took the Bark,[5] had no other regular fitt but continu'd very weak for upwards of a week then recover'd her hearing and health—while Sister was unwell, S Moore sent us word, that if we had would see our Friend H Stevenson alive, we must loose no time;—Robt. had sent us word some days before that she was brought to Bed of a Daughter, and was extreemly ill—the situation of our Family had prevented our going before—HD took Sister in the Chaise, she found Hannah very low—her disorder a violent Bloody Flux, which she was afflicted with several days before her delivery—she continu'd several days after Sisters visit.

12 Nancys fever gave way and she set up, the Doctors had propos'd Blisters that evening, but she through Mercy continu'd mending from this time—some time in this Week Henry Post, companion to Silas Downing, who had been left unwell at Burlington) came here intending to make our House his home, but so many of our Family being ill, some other Friends House was recommended—he, and Refine Weeks were a week or two very ill at Sammy Hopkins—Refine recoverd first—but Henry Post was taken to James Pembertons where he continud ill some time longer—Silas, who was favour'd with health stay'd with us—soon after Nancy got better little Molly was taken with the Chill and fever had one smart fitt, took a dose of Phisick and got better—the day that H Post come here my dear little Charles was ill of the second fitt of chill and fever, he had three afterwards 5 in all, I gave him a large dose of the Bark divided into 8 parts, in one day, which stopd the fitts—but something of a Bloody Flux follow'd, but did not continue above a day or two—Billys fever from the first of his being taken continud 5 days without remition it then intermitted and he had 2 regular fitts took the Bark and recoverd tho but slowly—during his fever he was light-Headed, and Blead twice at the nose—after Nancy and Billys getting better, little Henry come from School

4. The words "or the evening of the 9 instant" crossed out.
5. The word "she" crossed out.

with a Chill on him, which was follow'd by an high fever and sick stomach, it went off by a Sweat—gave him a dose of Phisick the next day—and with the help of bitter Tea, he soon recover'd. Sallys fever continud without intermition 12 days in which time she had 4 Blisters, took 2 doses of [Nataral] Salts &c &c nothing that was administred operated properly—the 2 first Blisters did not rise at all, the others not very will, but I belive they were of service—she was longer recovering than any of the others—the Doctors call'd the disorder the fall Fever, of which many in the city are ill—some of neverous and some of putrid Fevers—tho they dont say it is a very sickly Season [or] not a very mortal one; so much sickness in our Family and amoung our acquaintance made appear so to me—before our Children were ill, our Man John McCahan had the fall fever and was Nursd at home by his Wife, our Girl Polly Nugent had it lightly, by drinking Billers Teas and taking a dose of Phisick soon got better—great numbers of People up Town have been ill—Nurse Jenny Mullin was with us 2 week—Betsy Test was here all the time in the Day—Molly Hensal came 2 Weeks before the Meeting and remains still with us—Polly and Sucky Drinker, Becky Griscomb, and Becky Waln set up, each one night with Sally—I was also with them,—I had not my cloaths of for upwards of 2 weeks, only to change them—when the Yearly Meeting came on, our Family was getting better, but we were much worn down by the time it was over—had not so much Company as usual to lodge with us—our Fd. Hannah Haydock sister to my Beloved Fd. E Emlen, was several times here, she lodgd at S Emlens I had not seen her for near 13 years.

Our dear Friend and old acquaintance Hannah Stevenson departed this life, Sepr. the 19 1783 in Child-Bed, in the 51st. year of her Age—the child a Daughter who they call Susanna.

Octor. 1 call'd up in the Night to S. Hartshorn; the child was born just before I entred the room a Daughter, nam'd Rebecca—it dyed in less then 2 Days.

7 Silas Downing left us—Refine Weeks went also—H Post follow'd a day or 2 after.

9 John Thomas and H. Drinker were married at the Market-Street Meeting-House—HD. myself and Billy at the Marriage—Sally and Nancy came to dinner not being sufficiently recoverd to set in a damp Meeting House, the day before having been very stormey and much rain.

Octor. the 12 HD. was let Blood.

15 HD. and John Saltar went to Atsion fourth day,—G. Gordon lodges here.

18 HD. &c returnd from the Works.

23 HD. went to the Funeral of John Heads Wife, his 3d. wife.

25[6] seventh day morning WP. spake to HD. on account of Nancy.

Novr. 6 fifth Day: HD. Jos. Smith and John Saltar left us after Breakfast, for Morices River—Saml. Cornells four Daughters viz Molly Edwards Widdow, Hannah and Sally Cornell, Betsy Bayard, Wm. Bayard her Husband—Abel James and Son Chalkley dined with us—and little Susan Edward they lodg'd at Frankford at AJs are on their way from N York to N. Carolinia, Sally and Nancy went with them to Several places, Chalkley also—to Simiters, to see Peels paintings to view the Wax Works &c[7]—they went back to Frankford after Night,—G Gordon lodges here.

8 the Same Company din'd here the Widd. Edwards other little daughter Becky—4 Servants they took leave of us between 3 and 4 in the Afternoon, C. James attended them to Chester where they propose lodging.

12 or 13 HD. &c return'd.

Novr. 24 Sally Emlen spent this Afternoon, discorse conserning pouver WP.

26 HD and Son Henry left home after dinner for Bybary intending tomorrow for Middeltown G Gordon lodg'd here returnd 29th.

29. An Alarming Shock of Earthquake.

1783 Decr. 2 third-day Morning—had Conversation with WP. Hannah Watson came this evening intending to stay some-time here Jonan Paxton and Jos[a]. Ahurst lodg'd here.

8 George Churchman lodgd here.

6. The word "sixth" crossed out.

7. Pierre Eugène du Simitière was a Swiss-born collector of American and West Indian historical materials and natural curiosities who also painted portraits. In May 1782 he opened his American Museum, located on Arch Street near Fourth Street, to display his collection. Six months later, Charles Willson Peale opened a skylighted gallery at his house on Third and Lombard streets to display his paintings of Revolutionary War heroes. The waxworks display the young Drinkers and their company viewed has not been determined (Paul G. Sifton, "A Disordered Life: The American Career of Pierre Eugène du Simitière," *Manuscripts* 25 (1973): 235–53; William John Potts, "Du Simitière, Artist, Antiquary and Naturalist, Projector of the First American Museum, with some Extracts from his Notebooks," *PMHB* 13 (1889): 341–75; *Pa. Packet*, Nov. 14, 1782, Nov. 6, 1783; Sellers, *Charles Willson Peale*, 1:219–22).

10 Hannah Watson went away, I spent this Afternoon at AWs.

13 Molly P. spent the Afternoon HD. went to Chester with Patience Brayton &c—She and Becky Wright embark'd for Irland—HD returnd the evening.

14 First day HD. and Children went to the Funeral of Josey Waln, eldest Son of Nics Waln dy'd of the putrid sore-Throat his Father in Europe.

30 S.E. spake freely of WP. at an adjurnment of the monthly meeting.

Decr. 30. HD. went to the Burial of Rebecca Steel.

1784

1784. Jenry. 2. HD. left home after dinner sixth day for Moores Town, intending tomorrow for Atsion—the Committee of Friends oppointed to visit Families mett here this Afternoon. S Emlen, S Hopkins, Billy Savery, C. West, and Caleb Cresson, Magry. Norton, [Merry] Smith, H. Catheral, and R Jones.

9 HD. return'd—the river fastned last Night, HD walk'd over it.

13 Our Old Aquaintance and Neighbor M Walace was Buried from Bradfords.

1784 Jenry. 13 Third day—little Betsy Pleasants Buryed.

18 First day fire cry'd in morning meeting time, the Roofs of 2 Houses in Chesnut Street burnt—Josey Fox went out this Morning for Frankford on a Skitish Horse, who threw him over his Head against a Post at the upper end of third Street, his Body voilently brused, he was taken home on a Couch, sufferd great pain 'till some time in the Afternoon when he dyed.—James Mendinghall lodgd here.

1784 Jenry. 20. John and Sally Hopkins, their Son and Daughter dind here; John and his Daughter Hannah went to the Funeral of J. Fox, as Relations.—Hannah has been here since seventh day last.

21st. HH went home.

22 The Grand Fire-Works, which were to have been exibited this evening and for which the Assembly vouted £600—, (paintings and other preparations have been a long time about) the first thing to be done was to light up the Lamps sudenly, which in performing by some accident the oyl'd pictures took fire and immediately communicated to the powder; blew up the whole affair, so as entirely to spoil all the sport—several lives were lost by the sudden going off of the Rocketts.[1]

1. The Pennsylvania Assembly commissioned Charles Willson Peale in December 1783 to make a "triumphal arch embellished with illuminated paintings and suitable inscriptions" for

26 Henry Waddey a Young Man from Irland came with memorandan from Roberson & Sandwith recommending him; about a year after this date, in his return home he was knock'd over board by the Boom of Ship and drowned[2]—A Comet has lately appeard the river fast the 9th. Instant.

29 a fire broke out in third street about 3 in the Morning and comsum'd the Store of one Epley, near [J.] Parishs.

Feby. 5 a Carpenters Shop in Race Street near front Street corner took fier about 4 in the Morning and was burnt down, Rigleys Shop.

8 a note from A James to HD first day—in much trouble.

14 little Henry went to Haddonfield returnd the 19.

21st. WP. went to Virginia.

22 HD and MS. went to Frankford First day.

Feby. 22 Isaac James lodg'd here—John and Jonathan Balderston lodg'd here some time ago.

23 Daniel Haveland a publick Friend from Oblong, came here intending to stay some weeks with us.

26. our Son Henry went to Haddonfield to visit the School—return'd the 27.

Feby. 18, 1783 my little Charles cut his first Tooth, being 18 months and 2 days old.

Octr. 23 began to wean him at upwards of 2 years and 2 months old.

[S] S D[3]	A D
1783	1783
18	21

---

the celebration of the Confederation Congress's January 1784 ratification of the peace treaty between the United States and Great Britain. An errant rocket fired during the parade caused one of the thirteen transparent paintings hung on a fifty-by-forty-foot wooden arch to catch fire, destroying Peale's work. One person was killed, several were trampled in the rush to get away, and Peale and a servant suffered burns (Sellers, *Charles Willson Peale,* 1:223–34; Peale, *Selected Papers,* 1:396–401, 405–7).

2. The preceding clause is an interlineation written in a different-colored ink.
3. The inside back cover contains these two columns of figures.

9	11
6	7–28
1–	21
18	14
11	8–28
4–31	18
–	
–	
22	

1784 March 2[4] Saml Trimble lodg'd here.

3 HD. wrote to [B]W—about this time Sister bad with a Rheumatisem in her left Shoulder, could not dress her Head for above a week,—after giting better a Spell of damp weather came on, when she was taken with a chill and fever and pain in her side, kept her Chamber 'till the Spring meeting Sally and Nancy at the same time or before had very bad Colds—my Husband, Molly and our dear little Baby had also bad Coughs.

13 HD. was let Blood—it has been a very cold unsittled winter—our dear little one after dilegint nursing had out grown most of his weekness and promissed fair to be a fine Boy, became much oppress'd with phlegm, insomuch that Docr. Redmans oppinion was that unless we could promote some evacuation he could not live, he ordred what he thought might prove a gentle vomitt, agatated him much, but did not work, and in little more then 20 minits from the time he took it, he expired aged 2 years 7 months and one day—about a week before he was fat, fresh and hearty—he cut a tooth a day before he dyed—thus was I suddenly depried of my dear little Companion over whome, I had almost constantly watchd, from the time of his birth, and his late thriving state seem'd to promise a [reward] to all my pains—he dy'd the 17 march, fourth day.

26 Docr. Bond departed this life—I had this evening a conference with Becky and Hannah.

27 HD continues poorly has not been this day to meetig Margret Branton, her daughter in Law, Rachel Watson and John Balderston came last night—Nancy and little Henry took a ride on Horse back this Morning seventh day. the 19 this month Spring[ ]bury was burnt, partly, the 20th. Rachel Watson lodg'd here, she went home the 21st.

4. The manuscript volume for Mar. 2, 1784–Apr. 30, 1786, has brown paper covers. On the front and back outside covers are numerical calculations. On the inside front cover ED wrote, "parted with the Cow July 14, 1784."

28 James and Ann Willit from Egg Harbour lodg'd here.

29 John Crew, was bury'd.

31st. Friends left us, who came to the Spring meeting—little Henry cut his Toe badly runing against a sharp Adds.

April 1st. Thos. Ross, G. Dillwyn Saml. Emlen, Becky Jones, H Catheral and several others mett here.

6 HD. an overseere at the marriage of John Bartram & H [Steel].

10. last night, or early this Morning seventh day, Abey Bowne, wife to George Bowne, departed this life very sudenly, but few hours ill, of something like the Colick, she was within 2 or 3 weeks of her time.—they came this week from Burlington to reside here—HD. who has been unwell for near 5 weeks of a bad Cold, and rheumatic pain in his Sholder, is now better. A James came to Town this Afternoon after having been unwell at Frankford for several Weeks—his affairs in very bad situation. HD. much concerned thereat.

14 John Parish C. West, S. Hopkins, and D. Haviland, who are visiting Families had a meeting here; Daniel Haviland, express'd himself—in a very perticular manner.

20. S. Emlen and Wife D. Eastaugh, Margt. Porter, M. Pleasents, Maht. Jinkens, Becky Jones, and Hannah Catheral din'd here.

21st. Sally Drinker, Dolly Payne and HD junr. went on Horseback to Frankford.

22 this Afternoon a Laboring Man lost his Life, who was diging a Seller up Town—by the bursting out of an Nesesary against which he stood.

23 George and Sally Dillwyn James Thronton and John Cox breakfasted with us—many Friends mett here this Morning to conclude on setting of tomorrow in different companys &c—Thos. Ross, George Dillwyn and wife [R.] Jones, M. Jenkins, S Emlen and Son, calld to day to take leave of us, as they have taken their passage for Great Britian—Charlotte Prettyjohn from Barbadoes paid us a visit this morning.

April 24 seventh day: HD. and Son William left home this morning after Breakfast, to accompany our Friends S. Emlen and Son &c to New Castle, they expect to dine to day at Chester,—lodge at Willmington and proceed to

Morrow to Newcastle where our Friends expect to embark on board the Ship Comerce Truckson Master, bound to London.

26 HD. and Billy return'd.

May: 2. First day. HD. and J.D left home after breakfast, before 6 this morning for Evesham meeting intending this evening for Atsion—Josey James lodges here during his absence—little Henry went this Afternoon to S Sansoms, with Wheling.

3 Molly began a quarter at A Marshs School—first of her going there.

May 4. between 3 and 4 o'clock this Morning—Sally, Nancy and Billy were all awakned ('tho in different Chambers) by the light of a Pot-House on fier in Elfriths Alley, our Familey were all soon up, a lane was made to our Pump—Gardners, Pantlifs and other fences were pull'd down—the Pot-House is burnt, several others Houses damaged—our much valued Friend and School-master Anthony Benezet departed this Life yesterday afternoon, after a short illness.

5 Billy went to the Funeral of AB it was very large, a great number of Blacks attended—WP. came from Virginia.

6 Betsy Test came to work—Sally, Nancy, Henry, Becky and Nancy Waln, Jacob Downing, [I]sra Jones, Billy and Sally Sansom—drank Tea at our Place at Frankford this afternoon.

7. Sister mett the Committee of 12,[5] this Afternoon for the first time.—she went to the Burial of Widow [Laniar], Aunt to Sarah Lewis.

8 W Byard from N. York and C. James drank tea—I went to G Bowns and J Tompsons to visit their Children in the small Pox—Dicky Bown—and little Jonah Tompson they were innoculated.

9 HD. return'd towards evening. First day.

10 Paintings Exhibited in the Triumphant Arch[6]—as 'tis call'd.

5. The Committee of Twelve was made up of four representatives from each of the three Quaker monthly meetings in Philadelphia (the Northern District, the Philadelphia Monthly Meeting, and the Southern District). It administered the common property of the meetings and joint accounts for taking care of the poor, and provided other services to the Philadelphia Quaker community as well as to non-Quakers (Philadelphia Northern District Men's Monthly Meeting Minutes, 1771–78, microfilm, Friends Historical Library, Swarthmore College, 131–32 and passim).

6. A private subscription helped Charles Willson Peale raise the funds necessary to rebuild his triumphal arch for the May 10 parade honoring the proclamation of the definitive peace treaty between the United States and Great Britain (Sellers, *Charles Willson Peale*, 1:223–34; see above, Jan. 22).

11 Billy Byard din'd drank tea and took leave of us, intending for N York tomorrow, then to Carolina.

12 Storm of Wind and thunder this evening—Sally Burge Rawle and Sally Mickel, who were on a visit to our Girles—lodg'd here, on account of the weather.

16 First day, meeting broke up about 11 o'clock by the cry of fier-sparkes from a Chimney opposite the Bank meeting House; had caught the Ruff of an House, it was soon put out.

20 the Barn of Joshua Cooper, which stood near the Delaware, on the Jersey shore opposite to this City, was entirely consumed by lightning, together with a Horse, 2 Calves, and some Hay, which were in it—a Hog passing by the road at little distance from the Barn, was kill'd by the same flash.

23 Billy help'd to carry little Hannah Howel to her grave.

28 Joseph Palmers wife much hurt by falling out of the window; she has lost her sight, and been other wase disordred for some time past.

June 1 heavy thunder Storm this Afternoon; Jacob Streeker and Sons Houses, both struck, on opposite sides the Street in Second Street.—a woman kill'd in one of them—Saml. Whartons House struck.

6 First day: Sister ill of the Chills and fever, has had 3 fitts.

8 and 10 each of these days she had a fitt of Chills and fever, stopd it with Centry tea[7] taken every hour Docr. Redman tends her—one Patrick Dowling an Irish lad whome HD purchased out of an Irish vesel the 5th. Instant: he stay'd with us untill the 6th. first day morning then went in [L]owel Claytons Shallop for Mouricie's River, where he was to have served his time; we since heard that he was drown'd endeavouring to Swim, which it appeard he did not understand.—a very pritty innocent Lad he appear'd to be, between 17 and 18 years of Age.

the 2d. Instant Sally went on Horse back with Tommy James to Frankford stay'd all Night—Betsy Hough lodg'd here, on account of a thunder Gust in the afternoon.

the 5th. Instant Billy and Henry went to Joshua Howells Place on [Schuy Kill].

7. The American centaury, a bitter herb, was commonly used to alleviate remittent and intermittent fevers (Millspaugh, *Medicinal Plants,* 514).

21st. Sister had a slight fitt of Chill and fever.

23. John McCagan, Polly Nugent and little Molly, went in the Chaise to Frankford.

last fifth day week, Betsy Moore married to a French gentleman of the name of MarBois.

26 very hott weather, a man dyed drinking cold water.

30 HD junr. went with Robt. Bowne to Burlington, in the Stage Boat—fourth day intending to stay some days.

July 2 Bancroft Woodcock lodg'd here, he went away the 3d.

3 Billy went this evening to Frankford on a vist to [T.] James.

4 First day: HD. MS. gone to Frankford, expect 'em home in the evening with Billy.

7 fourth day Nancy went home with Sally Sansom to Par la Ville.

8 Billy went this evening to Frankford with [T.] James,—3 of our children absent. from home—last evening the 7 Instant a most horrid murder was committed, between 9 and 10 o'clock, on George Fitler a Shoemaker, in Arch near Front Street, he was sitting at his door, smoaking a pipe, when a Villain in a check-shirt came up, and run him through the Heart with a Knife or dagger, of which he died in a few minutes after.

9 sixth day: Billy return'd this Morning from Frankford—Henry this afternoon from Burlington.

10 Sally Drinker and Walter Payne, Billy Sansom and Polly Wells, Jacob Downing and Dolly Payne, went to our place at Frankford—Sally and Josey Sansom and Nancy Drinker (from Par la Ville), mett them there. A Squable—Nancy return'd home in the Evening with her sister &c.

12 this morning about 2 o'clock our Neighbour Robt. Waln, departed this Life, after a lingering illness, Aged 63 years. second day.

July 12 second day: ED. went to Frankford this evening with Patty Smith in her Carriage, little Molly with me.

13 Becky Thompson and little Jonah who is unwell, came to Frankford.

14 fourth day: came home this evening Becky and her Child came to Town with us.—Sister had a fitt of Chill and Fever yesterday.

15 Sister had another fitt of Chill and Fever.

16 AJ. call'd his Creaditors togeather.

17 two Men were Executed for Robing and wounding Cap. Hustons wife, at Night in the Street—an Air Balloon was this Afternoon sent up from the new Jail Yard. it took fire, (when it was thought by some to be near a mile high) and consumed—the first sight of the kind that I have seen.[8]

July 18 First day: this Morning before one o'clock we were alarm'd by the cry of fier Billy and little Henry went to it—prov'd to be a Hatters Shop belonging to Benjn. Hooten in Second Street.

19 WP. went for Virginia.

20 Nancy and Henry took a ride this Evening on Horse back—Cadwr. Evans writes in our front Room, busy setling accounts he has been here some weeks—eats with us—this day at dinner, cutting a piece of Bread, the Knife slip'd and cut the Thumb of my left hand badly. H. Catheral here, third day—several alterations in our alley within the 2 or 3 last months, the House wherein Becky Jones and H Catheral liv'd, is now occupi'd by one Dows a Sailmaker,—A large quantity of stoleing good were found in Pantlifs house, for which he was taken up and put in Jail. E. Stiles bail'd him out, and he has run off—his Wife and Children gone I Know not where we are at last reliev'd from a very troublesom Neighbor—Strangers occupy that house—and this month our Neigr. Gardner has finish'd a large Soap House; directly opposite us—a disagreeable surcumstance.

July 24 seventh day: HD and ED. and Henry left home after dinner for middletown in Bucks County—came to John Watsons towards evening just before a Gust.

25 First day: went to mideltown meeting—din'd at JWs S Carry and several others din'd there—cloudy afternoon—[ ]lly Paxton a relation of Rachel Watsons, a young woman about 22 years old, Boards with them, she has lost

8. The Montgolfier brothers had built the first practicable hot-air balloon in France in 1783. In 1784 a Mr. Carnes demonstrated his American aerostatic balloon in cities in the United States. He scheduled his flight in Philadelphia for the late afternoon of July 17, taking off near the new workhouse. While in flight the balloon caught fire from its heating apparatus and descended near the new playhouse. Mr. Carnes was not seriously hurt (*Pa. Packet,* July 15, 17, 20, 1784).

the use of her limbs ever since her infancy: sets in an arm-Chair with wheels, which they push about occasionly—she can use her Hands so as to sew and knitt a little.

26 left J Watsons after dinner, HD and self in the Chaise Henry on Horseback Called at Bussel Town at Willm. Roberts who married Becky McVaugh—where we stop'd on seventh day—he has lost the use of his Limbs, so moves about with Crutches.

30 Polly Drinker, Betsy Hough and Nancy Drinker in a Chaise, Sally Drinker and our Sam Lewis on Horseback, went this afternoon to Germantown and to the falls of Schuykill—came home in the evening—Sally had a bad spell of sick Head ach after she came home.

Augt. 1 First day HD was let Blood, he is very unwell with pain in his Breast and Shoulder—Nancy very ill this night up with her 'till one o'clock. violent pain in her Head and sick Stomach &c.

2 ED very unwell this afternoon disordred Bowels &c—last first day week while I was out of Town, Sister had another fitt of the chill and fever—but none since.

Augt. 5. a fire broke out in front Street between race and vine Streets, on the Bank side, about nine in the Morning burnt 'till after 10—the Ruffs of 2 Houses were burnt and other damage done.

6 sixth day: HD. Sally and Billy, went this morning to Horseham, return'd in the Evening.

11 Sister had a fitt of Chill and Fever.

12 HD. Sally, John and Hannah Thomas in A Jamess Waggon; (J Downing & Nancy in his Chaise); left home after Breakfast about 8 o'clock for Raw-way, fifth day intending also for New York, HD poorly—Henry went this Afternoon to J Howels—the Horse threw him, rub'd the Skin of his Knuckle against a Post, which he fell [near.] G Gordon lodges here.

13 Sister had a fitt of Chill and Fever. Michel Donely an irish Servant from Atsion, came here this evening at a loss for Lodging—kept him here all Night least he should loose himself being a stranger in town.

Augt. 14 Cry of fier this morning Bells rang. Apothycarys Shop, in market street—our Polly Nugent unwell, sick Stomach and fever—gave her a puke this evening.

15th. Sister had a slight fitt of Chill & fever. Jemima Welkinson in Town; preaches in the Arch Street meeting House; built by those who call themselves freequakers.[9]

18 a young man was Bury'd Yesterday, who lost his life the day before, helping to heave-down a Vesel.

23 we were awakned about 2 this morning by the cry of fier—saw a great light, and smelt the burning—G Gordon Billy and Henry went out—it prov'd to be a Stable in Spruse-Street, which was burnt down, and 3 Horses burnt in it—we have had very frequent fiers lately, considering it is summer—and most of them in the day time—a little before 7 this morning before I was up, S Heartshorn sent for me;—she was deliver'd about 8 of a fine Girl,—who they call Susanna; I breakfasted there, came home about 9—second day.

Augt. 24: Sister, Billy and Molly went to Monthly meeting. Sally Johnson past meeting—Mary Armitt and J. Hopkins junr. din'd with us. most of John Hopkins Family, have been lately ill of a putrid fever sore Throat, but are now nearly well.

25th. John Hayworth call'd this morning he is lately return'd from Ireland—Our Friend [J] Pemberton, has lately gone through close tryals in that Kingdom.

26th. HD. our Daughter &c return'd home this evening in pretty good health fifth day during their stay at New-York, about the 19th. Instant Nancy was taken ill of high Fever and sore Throat,—at H Haydocks, Docr. Jones attended her—she kep'd Chamber, 2 or 3 days—came home as well, seemingly, as when she left it.

29 HD and sister left home after dinner, in our Chaise for Burlington; first Day: Cadr. Evans lodges here.

31 HD. return'd this evening left Sister with Neigr. James at Frankford.

Sepr. 1. little Henry had a large Jaw-Tooth drawn this morning.

2 Billy went this Afternoon to Frankford for his Aunt, they came home before Evening, stranger in [tow].

9. After the Free Quakers were denied use of a meetinghouse by the Society of Friends in 1783, they began construction of their own building at Fifth and Arch streets. It was completed in June 1784 (Wetherill, *Religious Society of Friends,* 5–42; see above, Sept. 14, 1782).

Sepr. 4 HD. and Billy went to the Funeral of our Ancient Friend John Reynold—seventh day.

7 Johney Hopkins came for our Girls, they went with him to Haddonfield cross'd the river about 5 o'clock, third day, this evening about 9 Polly Thomson and Ephrim Cline came from Atsion, with an account of Joseph Saltars being very ill, of vomitting &c—Polly lodg'd here, Ephrim was sent to Magnolia late as it was, to inform John Saltar of his Brothers illness.

8 J Saltar Breakfasted with us, then went with Docr. Jones to Atsion—return'd the 9th with an account of his being better:—WP went to V.

13 on third day last the 7th instant a most shocking murder was committed on the Body of one Timothy McAuliffe, at his House in Water-Street, opposite John Thompsons, in the Afternoon of that day, his servant Boy (about 17 years old) was observe'd to shut up the House, and after locking the door, went off, giving out that his master had gone to Jersey, and that he was going somewhere else to Work, untill his masters return. The three following days people in the neighbourhood were exceedingly incommoded by a most disagreeable smell, which seem'd to come from McAuliffes house; on seventh day it was so offencive that some persons determined to enter the house, and accordingly got in at one of the Windows, when they beheld a Spectacle too shocking for description—he had been murdered in his Bed, supposed on third day,—and remain'd in the same situation ever since, was overrun with vermin. By a mark on his skull it appear'd that the deed had been committed with an hammer, as one was lying near; a reward is offered for the Boy, on suspicion of his being the murderer; which seems highly probable, as no person besides him and his master was seen in the House, during that time, and the deceased having a sum of money by him, some time before; seems to confirm this suspicion.

Sepr. 15th. Sally and Nancy return'd from Haddonfield fourth day Afternoon.

16th. HD. and Son Billy left home about 11 o'clock before dinner, for Atsion fifth day. Henry went to Point no Point—Cad Evans lodges here.

17 Equinoxal Storm.

18 HD. and Billy return'd towards evening—seventh day.

19 First day—Jenny Boon alias Sibald, with her little Son Henry came here this Afternoon from New-port.

21st. Bancroft Woodcock from Willmington came this morning—he lodges here—Thos. Irwin, a young Man from Cork in Irland, call'd this Morning—he came recommended by S Neal.

22 BW. went homewards.

23 Dorcas Mountgomery and her Son Robart, paid us a visit this Afternoon they lately arrived from England and France.

Sepr. 24 Jenny and her child went home to Newport—Sixth day—this evening came to lodg'd with us during the Yearly Meeting—Jacob [J]enny and wife, Thomas Grigg and wife and Casper Saybalt; from Virginia.

25 Our Son Henry went this Morning to Haddonfield—Mary Jackson sister to John Willis, her Daughter Mary Seaman and Saml. Willis, from Jerico on Long-Island; came to lodge here—also Sammy Trimble.

26 First day: Hannah Hopkins and her Brother John came to lodge here.

27 John Hopkins went away—John Balderston came.—this Meeting I constantly attended which I have not done for several years before.

Octor 2 seventh day Thos. Watson here this morning had some discoarse with him conserning my Breast which I brus'd between 4 and 5 years ago—he alarm'd me much—began to diet myself—this day several of our Company left us.

4 Mary Jackson &c left us this morning after Breakfast.

6 fourth day—consulted Docr. Jones conserning my Breast which I have had a pain in for a long time—he nither encouraged or discouraged me by words—but ordred a Strict regiman, and to leave of Stays—on First day night last George Churchman and wife lodg'd here this afternoon I went with HD. to the Burial of Billy Fisher—little Jonah Thompson was also Buried this afternoon to whose funeral my Husband and Children went.

Octor. 7 HD. went to the Burial of John Houghton—and on third day last Jos. Richardson was also Buried—many have been lately taken off—Charles West has been very ill of nervous fever—on fourth day last Hannah Hopkins was sent for home, her Father and mother both being unwell.

16 seventh day: this fore noon 4 Men were executed, one of them the Boy

that murdred McAuliffee[10]—Charles Wharton and Hannah Redwood were married the 13th Instant—Robt. Morton and Hannah Pemberton were married the 14th. instant.

22 sixth day Rachel and John Watson came here—they went away the 23 after dinner.

27 fourth day Henry began a quarter at Josh. Sharplesss Night School, writeing &c.

29 HD was let Blood.

30 the Girles went to Molly Newports feast Seventh day evening—little Henry went to Frankford this Afternoon.

Novr. 7 first day: HD. went to Haddonfield & returnd in the Evening—Charles Reeds Wife and two Children &c din'd here.

11 Sammy Lewis left us, being fifteen Year's of Age: fifth day: he went into the Jersyes.—Henrys Leg sore, have kept him from school a day or 2 to [poltice] it; he hurt it against the meeting house steps—B Woodcock came here this day.

14 he went away.

16: third day: Sally and Nancy at the Marriage of Ezra Jones & Becky Waln.

19 sixth day: HD. George Bown, Josey Smith, and John Saltar, left our House after dinner, for Maurices River &c.

22 little Ned. Fifer came upon tryal; his mother is desirous of binding him to us 'till he is 16 Years of Age, he is now[11] between 8 & 9. Docr. Jones paid me a visit to day: discourageing, as I thought it—Cadr. Evans lodges here.

29 David Evans lodg'd here, Cadr. out of Town—HD. &c return'd this Afternoon, second day.

Decr. 7: Peter Wallover came to us—a dutch Boy about 12 years of Age, purchased from on board a Ship.

10. The four men executed were James Bourke for murder, Peter Brown and Richard Williams for highway robbery, and George Crowder for burglary (*Col. Recs. Pa.*, 14:227–28).

11. The word "about" crossed out.

10 Ned. Fife went home to his parants being to small for our busyness.

12 First day: this morning about 2 o'clock, we were awaken'd by the cry of fier—none of our Family went to it, it being beyond south street, back of Sammy Whartons, 3 or 4 small Houses were burnt.

14 Henry Waddy bid us farewell, he sails to morrow for Dublin.

Sammy Rhoades dyed.

Thos. Wharton dy'd.

Betsy Test dyed.

little Sally Saltar dye'd.

23 Jonathan Hood lodg'd here.

26 First day: this evening Waltar Payne took leave of us, intending to set of early to morrow morning for Virginia, and in a few weeks to embark there for Great Britain.

1785

1785 Jenry. 8 seventh day—Molly Williams, a young woman from Sadsberry, came here, with a Letter to John and Henry Drinker, from William Downing, desiring them to recommend her to some place in Town, for a few weeks, while she visited her Brother, who is in Jail here, he was taken up in South Carolina as a refugee, and brought here for the reward offerd.—his name Amos Williams—entire strangers to us; the young woman not knowing where to go, and not having had the small pox, we invited her to stay with us 'till she could get a Place nearer to the Prison where she every day took vituals &c to her Brother.

9 First day: HD. and J Drinker left home after Breakfast, for Bybarry meeting; intending after for Burlington, and then for Atsion,—Nancy and self visited Hannah Thomas this Afternoon, who lays in with her Son Aurther—Cad. Evans lodges here—evening meeting broke up by cry of fier.

11 David Evans lodg'd here—Cadr. out of Town little Henrys sore leg, which I have dress'd, every day for 3 months; appears to be now well, or near it.

12 fourth day: HD. return'd.

the 5th. Instant Jemmy Fisher was married to Hannah Wharton at Pine street meeting House—the marriage had been put of some weeks, on account of the Death of her Father Thos. Wharton—Sarah Fisher as she was getting into the Carriage at the meeting House door after her Son's marriage fell down, (it being slipery) and broak the small bone in her left Arm, she is in a fair way of recovery—they have had much trouble in their family of late, on account of Death and Sickness &c.

18 third-day: HD. went into the Cold-Bath for the first time; after having ommitted it upwards of 15 years.

20 Molly Williams left us, she went home in a Waggon after dinner fifth day.

Febry. 2 fourth day HD. MS. Nancy, Henry and little Molly—left home after an early dinner, in our Sleigh, for John Watsons Middle-town:—Sally Billy and myself seem lonesome without them. Cadwr. Evans lodges here.

3 Docr. Jones paid me a visit; gave me little or no, encouragement, respecting the disorder in my Breast—I think I never saw the Trees look[1] prittyer; not even in the Summer Season, then they do this day, so beautifully bespangled with frost—were I in perfect health I should enjoy it much.

4 HD. &c return'd home before dinner Sally and Nancy Drinker, and Nancy Waln, Jacob Downing and [T.] Morgan, went Sleighing this afternoon—we were up 'till 1 o'clock, with little Henry who was very ill for an hour or 2.—he was much bound in his Bowels, had been eating a quantity of Chestnuts, which made him sick at Stomach; gave him 2 pints of warm water at several times, and as much strong Cardas-tea; which had no other effect then to swell his Stomach—and increase his pain—I then gave him a Levement, which after some time had the desired effect, and he got better.

Febry. 7 Billy went to Frankford—with Tommy James, Charles Howand &c in a Sleigh—stay'd there all Night—came home in the Morning to Youths Meeting.

14. Polly and Hannah Wells, Henry and Polly Drinker—Polly Drinker, Nancy Waln and Thos. Morgan, Jacob Downing sup'd with our Children in the front Parlor.

18 Polly Nugent left us—sixth day—she has been free 5 weeks—went away to attend the Jublie.

27 First day: HD. was let Blood—he has been unwell for some time past—first of a slight sore Throat—which soon got better—a day or 2 after he was taken unwell with pain in his Face and felt heavey, a cold in his Head and much spitting of fleighm—Dr. Redman tends him—numbers are unwell in Town at present, of like disorder.

28 Molly came from School very unwell, sore Throat &c—Uncle Jervis taken ill—they sent for us—Sister went—left him seamingly better the 23 or 24 Instant Febry. B. Woodcock came—he lodges here.

March the first Coleman Fisher departed this Life.

5 B Woodcock left us this morning—this afternoon—Sister and Billy, Nancy and Henry—went to the Funeral of our Uncle John Jervis, our mothers Brother, he departed this Life on fourth day last in the afternoon, being the 2d. instant Aged Eighty years and about 3 Months, a Docr. Henry Moyes, who has been blind since he was 16 or 18 months old, is now in this City

1. Word crossed out.

exhibiting Lectures &c on natural Philosophy &c—Sally, Nancy and Billy attends them.

9 fourth day: Abijah Daws and Sally Fisher were married—Sally and Nancy were at the Wedding.

31st. HD. was let Blood, he is now better, after 5 weeks indispossion.

April 10 First day: Billy and Henry went to Radnar meeting, came home in the Evening: din'd at John Joness.

April 12 third day: HD. left home after Breakfast for Atsion,—Cad. Evans lodges here.

13. Sally D. and Robt. Waln on Horse back, Ezra and Becky Jones in Chaise, Nancy Waln and J. Downing in another, took a ride this afternoon.

14 HD. return'd.

28 Nancy and Henry went in a Chaise to Frankford.

Un bruit enhaut, could not account for it: fifth day Afternoon.

29 A Rumpus with Peters Mother.

May: 2 Saml. and John Wilson came lodg'd here.

3 they went away—parted with Peter W[alager] to Fredrick Sh[ield]s who keeps a paper mill over Schuylkill.

10 Nancy had a Tooth drawn.

11 Fourth day: HD. and John Saltar in a light waggon, Billy on Horse back, left home after an early dinner, for John Evanss, intending for Shoholac—C Evans lodges here.

15 First day: Sally Harrison very perticular. at the Middle meeting House, a young woman very much affected by what she deliver'd.

17 went with Neigr. Waln to the Funeral of Polly Garrigas, formerly Mitchel.

19 Sammy Wharton struck with the Palsey.

20 J. Downing and Sally Drinker, Robt. Waln and Nancy Drinker, T.

Morgan and Nancy Waln, B. Morris and Polly Wells—Henry Drinker and Hannah Wells, and Gidion Wells on Horse back, the rest in Chaises, went to our place at Frankford,—this has been a remarkable wett Spring.

25 HD &c return'd in the afternoon—he brought home with him a little Boy[2] about 10 years of Age, nam'd Daniel Foster,— the 13 Instant Dorcas Mt. Gomery and her Son Robt. call'd: they intend'd to set off the 14th for New Castle to embark for Great Britian, intending for France.

June 18 Seventh day: Nancy and myself in the Chaise, HD. on Horse back, took a ride, a little after 5 this morning to the lately discover'd mineral Springs near Frankford—came home to breakfast—some time in this month, or towards the end of last, HD. and myself took a ride to S Sansoms, near Schuykill, the first time of my being there—on fourth day the 1st. Instant Benjn. Andrews, being employ'd to do some work about the press of a paper-mill, the ketch unfortunately broke, and the bar of it struck in his forehead, with such violence that it fractured his Skull, and he dy'd the second day following—sometime in this month, Jenny Clarke departed this life, she had been ill for upwards of 6 months.

30 fifth day: Nancy and self went to Frankford little Henry drove us in our Chaise, got there to tea, Henry left us towards evening—we intend staying some days with R. James, who is much alone—myself very poorly.

July 2 HD and JD. breakfasted there.

3 First day went with R James, Josey and Tommy[3] to Frank meeting.

5. Chalkley and J Tompson came up, Chalkley just return'd from Newburn NC, where he has been for several months—HD. inform'd us of the deaths of Edward Stabler, Joseph Stamper and Jos. Morris.

July 7 fifth day. Nancy and self return'd home in AJs carriage.

10 First day: HD. JD. C. Evans, M Sandwith and Molly Drinker, left home after Breakfast, for Haddon Feild, the Men intending for Atsion, Sister and Molly to spend some days with cosin Sally Hopkins—Henry junr. left home after 10 o'clock for Burlington in the Stage Boat,—so that half our Family are from home—no one lodges here but what is left of our own Family.

14 George mifflin dy'd Sudenly—Jacob Downing, Nancy Waln and Sally

2. The words "between 9 and" crossed out.
3. Words crossed out.

Drinker in one Chaise, Robt. Waln and Nancy Drinker in another went to our place at Frankford.

17 First day: HD. MS. Molly &c return'd. Docr. Moore bury'd this Morning.

18 Henry return'd from Burlington—William Norton bury'd this Afternoon he dy'd Sudenly.

19 Tabitha Mires Aunt to HD. was bury'd this Morning HD. Sally, Billy and Henry at the Funeral.

23 Sally and Nancy and Henry, and Parkers Girls took a ride to the Spring, early this Morning.

July 25, second day visit from Dr. Jones; as usual very discouraging, advis'd me to go Shrewsbery and bath in the Salt water.

26[4] third day sent for Dr. Kuhn, told him my trouble, he was much more encourageing then Jones, tho' I fear it proceeded more from his humanity then his better Judgment.—Nancy Thomas was this afternoon buryed from Neigr. Walns she has been a long time very ill, and suffer'd more than any one that has come within my knowledge, of a disorder of the nature hers was.—about this time one Francis Courtney was executed, for using a young woman very ill,[5] near Frankford.

28th. fifth day: left home after dinner, H and ED. in the Chaise Nancy and Henry in another, [called] at Martins arrived at Josey Smiths in the Evening near Burlington, lodg'd there and stay'd till after dinner next day.

29 came to Richd. Walns before dusk—should have got there sooner, but were delay'd some time on the road, about 3 miles from RWs, by the oversetting of the Chair Henry drove, occasion'd by Nancy and himself carelessly talking, instead of minding a Stump in the way. found RWs family well.

30th. Betsy Waln and her daughter Polly set of with us after dinner for Shrewsbury—HD. EW, HD junr and ED—in RWs Waggon, Nancy Drinker and Polly Waln in our Chaise, [stop'd] at Lawrence Taylors, then proceeded to Haggermans at Freehold where we lodg'd.

31st. First day: left Freehold after Breakfast, where we were visited by Saml.

4. The word "fourth" crossed out.

5. Francis Courtney was executed for rape on July 22 (*Pa. Gaz.*, July 26, 1785).

Fermen &c—journey'd on to Lippencuts at Shrewsbury 11 o'clock—HD. his Son and the Girls went to meeting—EW and self stay'd at the Tavern—where we din'd—left it after dinner and came to John Corlass near Black Point, where we took Lodgings for some time—George Eddy and Wifee there—rode down to the Bath house in the evening—Polly Waln and our Nancy went into the water.

Augt. 1: EW. myself and our daughters went into the Bath this morning—came back to Corlases to Breakfast—Capt. Karney din'd here—John Fry came about dinner time, he lodges at Wardels—he left Philada. on seventh day last, he brought us the afflicting account of the death of our Neighr. Walns daughter Becky Jones—who we suppose dyed on fifth or sixth day last, as she was ill, and her mammy with her when we left home—drank tea this afternoon at John Hartshorns—little Henry out most of the day with G Eddy.

2 went into the water this morning—HD. and Son: John Corles and his Son went this morning fishing off the Banks—came home to late dinner—took a ride this evening to the North River.

3 Went into the Bath this Morning as usual it becomes rather more easy—Robt. Hartshorn came after dinner, My Husband and Son, and Nancy, Polly Waln and Hetty Eddy—went with him over the river to his House—they came back in the evening—received a letter this evening from J Drinker.

4 went to Bath this morning—Bose Reeds wife &c there before us, as they generly are—they lodge at Wardals—We set of after Breakfast for long branch on the Sea Shore—HD. EW. and ED. went round in the waggon—George Eddy and wife, Nancy, Henry and Polly Waln and John Fry, went in a Boat, we mett at one Brindleys to dinner—many others din'd there also; Jacob Morris and wife, Isaac Wicoff and wife, and Daughter—Saml. Ferman &c &c—took a walk to the Sea Shore which was very near the House—came back to Corlass to Tea before Sun Set.

5 Betsy Waln and Daughter G Eddy and wife left us this morning for their respective homes—HD. John Fry, Henry Nancy and self—went to Bath this Morning We shall miss Betsy Waln very much HD and Henry left us after dinner, to go by water to New-York, John Fry and Jacob Morris went with them, it is about 40 miles—Nancy and myself are left (as it were) alone, John Skyron and John Pleasants calld to see us this evening, they left Philaa. the day before yesterday Broomfield and wife calld this Morning.

6 rain this Morning within all day—a very lonesome day to Nancy, mist bathing.

7 First day: went to Bath this Morning Betsy White a young woman who lives in the House, went with us—John Skyron, John Pleasants, Nancy and self, went in the Waggon to Shrewsberry meeting, Asher Corlas drove; came back to dinner,—went this Afternoon to visit at John Hartshorns, John Skyron, J Pleasants, Nancy and self, drank tea there, came back by Sunset.

8 very cool this Morning mist bathing HD. JF. and HD junr. return'd from New-York after dinner—HD. and Nancy took a ride to J Hartshorns, this evening—Rachel Corlas wife to J Corlas sick a Bed—she has been unwell ever since we have been here.

9 went into the water this morning set of after Breakfast for Middle-Town—14 miles from B: Point, the roads very bad—din'd there at a Tavern, came back to Tea, John Hartshorn and John Fry here this evening—little Henry very bad till 12 at Night with lax and vomitting and pain in his Bowels—very busy tending him and preparing to return homewards tommorrow—received 2 letters one from our Son Billy all well at home, another from Betsy Waln, giving some perticulars relating to poor Becky Jones; she was in labour tho' not strong labour on the night of the 28 Ultimo brought on by the Colick, she was not deliver'd, but expired on sixth day morning the 29th and was buryd the same evening—she had something of the cramp a little before her death.

10. Henry better this morning—left John Corlass this Morning—J Fry accompany'd us a mile or 2 on our way—[called] at Isaac Vandikes—din'd at Hagermans at Monmouth—[called] again a L. Taylors—arrive'd at Richd Walns towards evening 40 miles, found Bell Marshall, P. Lewis and T Wister there—Ricd. Waln gone to Philaa. with our Horse and Chaise, which detaind us there a day longer then we intend'd.

11 spent this day at RWs, Richd. return'd home this evening—bringing us word that all were well at home.

12 left RWs after Breakfast, came to Josey Smiths to dinner—JS Patty and Becky Thompson, with her little Son gone to Mores-Town they return'd towards evening—Tommy James here also.

13 Seventh day. left Josey Smiths after Breakfast, cross'd at Dunkss—stop'd at A James Frankford—HD and Son proceeded homewards, left Nancy and self, as it was the heat of the day, to dine with H Elton, Reba. James being gone to Bybary, we came home after dinner in AJs Waggon—found all well at home. A remarkable hard clap of Thunder in Philada. while we were absent.

15 second day Nancy and myself taken this Afternoon with Chill and Fever.

17 we had each of us another fitt of Chill and Fever, worse then the former, sent for Docr. Kuhn, took the bark, stop'd it in me, Nancy had a 3d. fitt, but by takeing bark in larger quantity stop'd it. A Carpenter working at Neighr Gardners shop in our Alley, fell from the second story, and was so badly hurt, that he dyed the next morning the 18th. Instant.

Augt. 24 Sally attended Betsy Hough as Bride-Maid, she pass'd her first meeting at Pine-street, with John Olden.

26 sixth day: HD. and Sally in the Chaise, Danl. Drinker on Horseback, left home after breakfast, for Atsion, intending to attend Burlington Quarterly meeting. Nancy took a walk out this morning—went with Jacob Downing to Frankford in the Afternoon—she seem'd bravely—but about 10 at night was taken again with chill and fever—Billy went to Frankford with Tommy James, stay'd all night.

28 First day she had another fitt, and the 31 another, took the bark in pills.

the 29 or 30 instant HD. and DD. return'd, left Sally at [J] Smiths near Burlington.

Sepr. 10. HD. was let Blood, seventh day.

12 Sally return'd from Burlington, with Josey James—some day this week Nancy had the seventh fitt of Chill and Fever, stopd it by the bark.

18 First Day: HD. poorly, he went with J Drinker to Darby meeting, return'd in the evening; JD. who came back in the Sulkey, by some missmanagement run against a Post, frighten'd the mare, and overset; he excap'd unhurt—the mare run away with the Sulkey, which was very much damaged. The 13th. Instant John Storor, John Townsend, and Thos. Colley &c din'd with us—they arrived here last week, from Great Britian, with Nics. Waln &c.

20 Sally attended Betsy Hough, who pass'd her second meeting—Billy went this Afternoon with Jacob Downing to Jane Robarts over Schuylkill intending to stay all night.

22 Billy return'd.

23 Casper Sybald came this afternoon to yearly meeting—Rachl. Woodcock this evening Nancy had a fitt of Chill & Fever.

24 Margt. Branton[6] Grace Steer, Saml. Trimble, his Daughter Peggy, Rachl. Watson Debby Balderstone, Betty Gest, and Ann Lupton who came with Grace Steer, lodgers.

25 First Day: Henry junr. went this Morning to Haddonfield.

26 Debborah Gest lodges here.

29 John Watson and his Daughter Hannah came—we have 13 lodgers.

Octor. 1 they all went away except Casper Sybolt, who stay'd till next day—Nancy unwell most of this week with Chils and Fever and pain in her Face.

Octor. 6: Sally attended Polly Wells, as Bride-Maid. She pass'd her first Meeting with Benny Morris.

7 Nancy had her Teeth clean'd by Docr. Baker—by the desire of Docr. Kuhn—Sally Ashbridge at work here.

8 seventh day: Dr. Jones and Dr. Kuhn visited me; they did not appear to come to any certain conclusion about the matter; to me at least—some day this week, Sally, drove Lizey Haydock out to the falls, her Brother Silas [Titas] with them—they have been in Town during the yearly meeting, and often visited us—their home is New-York. Jenny Sibold or Sivile, formerly our Jenny Boon, came to stay a few days, with us—she has her sucking Daughter Anne with her—they live at East-Town, and is on her way to New-port—on Busyness for her Husband.

10 After missing several fitts, Nancy was taken again this evening with the Chills & fever—she has had 12 or 13 fitts within the last 8 weeks.

12 Nancy another fitt of Chill & Fever.

14 a slight Chill, follow'd by Fever.

15 seventh day: Henry junr. Johnny Hopkins and Tommy Pearsal, went this Afternoon to Frankford, they din'd here, and Thos. Pearsals 2 Daughters from New-York, John Hopkins lodges here to night.

18 Billy Saltar from Atsion lodg'd here.

19th. fourth day evening JD. spake to HD—on account of Sally.

6. The name "Ruth" crossed out.

23. Seventh day: HD. left home after Breakfast with Charles West for Bybary—to stay 'till tomorrow or next day—C.Evans lodges here—return'd on first day.

Octor. 24 second day: Thos. Watson came—he stay'd with us two nights, went home the 26th.

28th. Sally all day at R Wellss Polly past her second meeting. Saml. Emlen and Son arrived this day, from Great Britian.

Novr. 3 fifth day: eat a small peice of meat at my dinner, the first I have tasted for upwards of 13 months.

7. 8 or 9th. Sally and Nancy went with J. Fry and R. Parker, Lidea and Sally Parker and Ellison Perott to Danl. William two or 3 miles from the City, came home after Night.

11 Sally, went with Benny Morris and Polly Wells to S Sansom's, Par la ville. Sally and JD. dit Adieu, about this time.

15 Joseph Saltar lodg'd here or the 22.

24 Benny Morris and Polly Wells were married at the Great Meeting House, Sally at the Wedding.

25 Sally and Nancy spent this Evening at R Wells, with a large Number of Young People.

Novr. 27 Sally went to meeting with M Morris she is to be there every day this week.

Decr. 7 fourth day—HD and Son Henry and T. Mountgomery, set of this afternoon for Haddonfield, intending to proceed tomorrow to Atsion. C. Evans lodges here.

9 S Sweet lodg'd here.

10 HD. returnd, left Henry at Haddonfield.

12 Henry returnd from Haddonfield.

23 sixth day: Capt. Isaac Robinson arriv'd here from Dublin &c[7] he lodg'd here—his Brother John Robinson married my Cosin Isabella Sandwith.

7. Isaac Robinson was captain of the *Robinson*. The ship's arrival in Philadelphia from Dublin was noted in the *Pennsylvania Mercury* on Dec. 30, 1785.

28 fourth day HD. and Saml. Emlen Capt. Robinson and S Emlen junr. left us before dinner for Burlington.

29 Capt. Robinson and S Emlen junr. returnd, they left HD and SE at Burlington they intend tomorrow for Mountholy, &c David Evans lodg'd here.

31 HD and SE return'd.

1786

1786 Janry. 15. HD. and Billy on Horseback, Capt. Robinson and Nancy in the Chaise went to Frankford meeting, dind at A Jamess S Emlin came home with them.

Janry. 28 seventh day: HD. and JD. left home after dinner for the Iron-Works—Capt. Robinson lodges here.

30 Patty Smith lodg'd here.

31 Ditto Ditto.

Febry. 2d. HD return'd.

8th. fourth day: HD. left home after Breakfast for Burlington, Patty Smith with him. Capt. Robinson lodges here—Sister has a swelling under her Arm. Docr. Kuhn tends her.

9 HD. return'd from Burlington.

10 HD. was let Blood. Children went aboard Ct. Robinsons Ship.

11 seventh day: Sally, Nancy, Billy, Henry and Molly—Capt. Robinson John Hopkins Nancy and Hannah Waln went this evening to see Peals Exibetion and Paintings.[1] John Hopkins lodg'd here.

12 First Day Isaac Robinson, Billy and Jacob Downing went to Haddonfield, they return'd in the evening Joney Hopkins went home this afternoon.

14 Sally, Nancy, Billy, Molly, Capt. Robinson and Sammy Emlen went

1. An exhibition, "Perspective Views with Changeable Effects; or, Nature Delineated in Motion," opened in Charles Willson Peale's gallery at his home on Third and Lombard streets in May 1785 and continued through 1786. The series of painted transparencies, displayed twice weekly on an illuminated stage, included views of Philadelphia, Revolutionary War battles, and a scene from *Paradise Lost* (*Freeman's Journal*, Feb. 15, 1786; Peale, *Selected Papers*, 1:428–37; Sellers, *Charles Willson Peale*, 1:242–49).

round point and Frankford road in Sleighs—came home to Tea. B Woodcock lodges here.

March 4 the Ship Robinson set sail this Morning Henry junr. went in her for Chester, where they expect the Captain tomorrow.

5 First day: Capt. Robinson left us this Morning Billy Drinker, Richd. Adams went with him from our house, after Breakfast. Sammy Emlen junr. Jacob Downing and Tommy Roberts, also went; the latter goes with him passenger for Dublin; we expect the others home this evening and Henry with them. ED. had a fitt of Chill & Fever on sixth day last she had a fitt.

April 1 snow'd all day.

2 a violent Storm last night, two or three vessels sunk at the Warfe, and much damage otherwise done.

9 ED had a fitt of Chill & fever.

10 Ditto—Ditto—Sally Drinker and Tommy Morgan, in one Chaise, Nancy Drinker and Bobby Waln in another, went to Magnolia John Salters; coming over the fording place on their return; TMs Horse fell down, after plunging about for some time he overset the Chaise, Sally was completely duck'd, TM almost as bad, they got safely out, tho' very much frightn'd, went back to J Saltars, where they chang'd their cloaths, &c—came home after Night, Sally took a [dose] of warm tea &c and went to Bed, we hope no material harm will ensue; Nancy was very much Affected on her Sisters account.

24 William Blakey and Jos[h]. Knight lodg'd here, second day.

30 HD. was let Blood first day Afternoon.

1789

July 3.[1] sixth day—89—the two or three days past have been remarkable warm, Billy has been very busily engag'd, preparatory to a short voiage in the Ship Mary[2] Japhat Fletcher Comander, getting the Sailors togeather &c—which this day was partly accomplish'd—the Captain, Ben Wilson and himself—din'd early here, they then bid us adieu and went on board with the wind against them, weather very hot, which may probably bring about a gust)—they intend for Baltimore, which I suppose is 5 or 600 miles where the ship is to load for Amsterdam. Benny and Billy intend returning from Baltimore in the Stage.

With wind ahead, and threat'ning Storm
We part,—to meet we know not when,
My heart at times with anguish torn,
For dearest Bill, and Cousin Ben.

Jacob and Sally Downing drank tea here, Saml. Emlin, Neigr Waln here in the evening. I was reading in the Merror this Afternoon a peice on "the danger, incident to men of fine feelings, of quarrelling with the world."

4 I step'd into [J] Whartons last evening when it began to thunder and lighten, and a hard tho' short shower of rain fell, after which I returnd home—it continud to lighten from all quarters from 8 o'clock 'till after 12, when I retird to Bed—this morning arose a little after 5 to go with Nancy to Harrowgate but she declin'd it—Molly went with me, the Horses (Mares I mean) and Benjan. behav'd very well—HP. sent for me, did not go—took a walk a very warm one, to Sallys this morning John Skirin here this evening—it began to thunder and lightning about 7 this Evening we went up stairs about 11, still contin[us] lightning very much.

Tho' the voiage my seem short, and the danger not seen
yet the heart of a parent bodes ill.
with the thoughts of what possibly may intervene,
Keeps my mind from being tranquil and still.

1. The entries for July 3–25, 1789, are written on unbound leaves.

2. The *Mary*, owned by Robinson, Sandwith & Co. of Dublin, arrived from Cadiz in early July. HD, as the Philadelphia agent for the ship, contracted for a cargo of Maryland tobacco and lumber products for the return trip to Europe, where delivery would be made to a consignee in Amsterdam (Henry Drinker to Robinson, Sandwith & Co., July 11, 1789, and Henry Drinker to Thomas & Saml Hollingsworth, July 24, 1789, Henry Drinker Letterbook, 1786–90, HSP).

5 First Day: from 7 o'clock last evening 'till two this morning it thunderd and Lightend very much, I lay down about 12, got into a dose, but was awaken'd by a loud clap of thunder, went into Sisters Room stay'd there till after 2—Nancy very poorly, I am not pleas'd that cousin BW. is in the way of meeting with any difficulties, but I am much pleas'd that Billy has him for a Companion, as I look upon him as a thoughtful worthy young man—Jacob and Sally din'd here, I was taken this afternoon with a very bad fit of the Colick sent in the evening for Docr. Kuhn Neighr. Waln here—got ease about 11 o'clock—a pilot bout came in some time this day, she had her mast shatter'd by the Lightning, she past by the Mary near New Castle—two Houses in sixth street, were much damag'd by the Lightng.

6 Saml. Emlen, Cad.Evans call'd this morning—a vessel came up which pass'd by the Mary near Bombay Hook[3]—John Hillborn din'd here—and drank tea with us—this evening A Horton, R. Vaux, J Hilborn, daddy and Henry were looking over maps—Neigr. Waln, Jams. Logan John Skirin here—Isaac Stroud and another man call'd—Neigr. Waln inform'd me that a Stage Boat with 30 persons in it, was struck with the Lightning and that every one on board was blind for a considerable time. M Bushs House was struck, and several others in Germantown, I dont recolect too such tremendeous nights this long time; this is a fine clear night, I trust Billy and Benny are contemplating the Beauties of this evening with minds at ease—Vaux-Hall set up this afternoon at Horrowgate—J Hilborn Lodges here.

7 Colicey[4] all this day: S Emlen here before meeting—Tench Francis, Tench Cox, John Nicholson and J Hilborn here early this Morning they Breakfasted with us—Isaac Melcher also here.—fresh accounts to day of damage done by the late awful thunder Storms—A house and a Vessel at Burlington were struck and some others that I do not recolect. Letters from FP. London—£1900 Stirling for J Parrock, obtain'd—Nancy and Molly took a ride, they stop'd at Sallys on their return—and spent the evening there—Sarah Fisher and her 2 Daughters call'd, Polly Drinker, Amy Horner, Patty Wharton call'd—Isaac Whartons daughter came to town this afternoon,—John Hancock spent 2 hours with me this afternoon—Anna Waln &c call'd—John Hillborn sup'd and lodg'd—Jacob and Sally Downg. here to day—J Skirin came home with the Girles.

8 J Hillborn din'd—J Field call'd—Sally and Nancy took a ride this After-

3. An island off the Delaware coast in Delaware Bay, separated from the mainland by Old Duck Creek and situated in Newcastle County, Del. The name is a corruption from the Dutch *Bompies* or *Bompties Hook* (WPA, *Delaware,* 486 and endpaper map).

4. The words "and unwell" crossed out.

noon—I took a walk this evening to H Pembertons.—Jam's Pemberton came home with me—Neigr Waln here a very fine night to be at Sea. AJ junr.

9 S Swett here this morning she informs that on sixth day last, a Barn near Spring Mill was burnt Down by the lightning, and 2 Cows and a Horse kill'd by it, at North Wales—took a ride of about 9 miles this Morning with HP—Neigr. Waln and Sister were going this Afternoon to visit RJ. at Frankford—but were prevented by rain—Jacob, Sally, Nancy & Molly went towards evening to try the new Waggon or Coacheé—Nancy poorly.

10 very heavy rain with some lightning last nigh before 12—arose this Morning about 5—. HD. and his Daughters Nancy and Molly, set off in the New Carriage Benjn. Oliver drove—for near Trentown—intending for John Watsons this evening and home tomorrow fore-noon. Sally Downing here this morning—I took a ride again this morning with HP. Neighr. Waln, James Logan hear in the Afternoon—G Baker—we are now but 5 in family, much reduc'd.

11 fine cool Morning Jacob Downg. here paid S Griscomb 1″10″ on account Meeting House[5] Neigr. Waln and Sister went this Afternoon to visit R James at Frankford, J. and SD. here this afternoon. Daddy and the Children returnd before dinner—John McCahan very poorly—Dr. Kuhn, J Skirin here this evening Sarah Fisher dangerously ill.

> I'm tired and weak, and to Bed will repair,
> For 'tis now past eleven at night,
> Prehaps not to sleep, but to think when I'm there
> just at present no more can I write.

12 First day: Jacob and Sally Downing—Nancy and Molly Drinker, in the new carriage with BO to drive them—set of this Morning for Downings Town,—very heavey rain about 11 o'clock—poor Nancy is very unwell I fear the damp may affect her—Josey Downing here—Daddy and Henry were busy this Morning writing to Dublin S Swett din'd and spent the afternoon thunder ghust this afternoon, poor girls Josey Downg. eats here, lodges at Jacobs—Dan. here all day, at home at Night—Benny and Polly Morris, and J Drinker call'd—Daddy wrote to Billy.

13 hot and Sultry: [Noak] came for me took a short ride with HP. caught in the rain—soon return'd—Cad Evans and Jo D—dind with us, another gust this afternoon of wind and rain, but no thunder that I heard—Neddy Brooks in danger of a Lock-Jaw—by a small wound in his foot—step'd this Evening into [T] Whartons, S Swett here.

14th. Henry and JD—marketed this morning a fine cool morning wind at

5. The new meeting house at Key's Alley (Bronner, "Quaker Landmarks").

NW—I wish much to hear from Baltimore and from Downings-town—S Emlen here this morning S Swett call'd—Ben Ayers was bury'd yesterday—Caty Gravil gave up the key of Jacobs House this morning she is gone on a visit to her relations—Little Dan came this morning with a load on his back. Not a Pig in a poke; but a cat in a Sack—so that we have Dan and the white cat added to our little family—a Smart shower of rain this Afternoon—'tis not pleasant to have our Children scattred about the world, this very unsettled gusty Season—Neigr. Waln. S Swett &c here this evening cloudy and like for rain; the post arriv'd this Afternoon from Baltimore and no account of our dear lads—what a tedious time must they have had.

15 took a long ride this Morning with HP—H Cathral din'd and spent the Afternoon. A [Horton] drank tea with us Eliston Perott call'd—I wrote to the girles—fine cool pleasant weather.

16 S Swett spent the day—John Muckelroy call'd—Aunt Jervis and Betsy in the Afternoon—Betsy Fordem—the Pilot who took down the Mary brought us a letter this afternoon from our Son, the Baltimore stage is again[6] come in, and no account of their [arrival], is 10 feet draft of water, for a Ship of 250 tons, sufficient to venter to sea? The Sailors were some of them disabled—and perhap may have behaved refractory & sulkey—I am realy very uneasy this evening on account of my absent Children—Casper Morris and Kitty Wister here this evening—Neigr.[7] has received a litter from Tommy from the cape of good hope—Sister has been busy two days past in the garden with the Gardener &c.

17 HD. and Cad. Evans left us this Morning after breakfast for Atsion, so that we have now 5 of our family absent—one Hall from the Delaware Works call'd—Betsy Fordham at work here—a young man of the name of Fisher brought paper mony from G Bowne—Jessy Kersey call'd to borrow a horse—Isaac Milcher call'd—[J] Goram, John Hopkins and Dan Williams calld. I call'd this evening to see Sarah Fisher—No news this day of Son or Daughter paid an order from Jos. Saltar in favor Saml. [Pen] £5:12:6 JH lodges here.

18 paid S Griscomb four Dollars on account of New Meeting house—received a Letter from J Downing with the agreeable intilegence of their all being well—the Baltimore post again and no news from Billy—took a walk this Afternoon call'd at M. Armitts and at Aunt Jerviss. Sally Dickinson alias Williams died this morning after a short illness—step'd this evening to Isaac Whartons.

6. The word "[arrivd]" crossed out.
7. Two words crossed out.

19 First Day: Sister, Henry, and Josey Downing gone to meeting, myself according to custom at home alone—SE—call'd this Morning HD and C Evans return'd from Atsion just as we had done dinner S Swett din'd here, Neigr Waln and [SS]—drank tea with us—they were to the funeral of Sally Williams—rain this afternoon—after I return'd from meeting—T Scattergood call'd to bid farewell—J Drinker call'd.

20 seventeen day are past, and no account from my dear Son—one Camel call'd about the Boilers—Richd Thomas din'd with us—brings us the agreeable account that he left our daughters all bravely on seventh day last, that Nancy increas'd in weight two pounds in one week—Sister gone out this afternoon, Little Sall and myself, as is common togeather—Henry and Josey Downing went to Harrowgate, Henrys horse fell down with him at the corner race Street the horse hurt more then the rider—Ricd. Thos. sup'd here, he lodg'd with Josey at Jacobs—R Shoemaker here.

21 [ ] Henry set of this Morning early for Atsion, so that our family at present consists of daddy Aunty and myself—no of our Children at home I took a ride this morning with HP—we went to Philip Prices over the lower ferry about 6 miles from Town, stop'd at Grays, where I had not been since the improvements[8] were made I took a short view of the walks and think them very pritty—we stay'd about ½ hour at PPs—came home about noon—Cad Evans here S Swett, SE. call'd—Daddy informed that a man who came from Baltimore on seventh day last says that a large Ship was in the Bay when he came away, supos'd to be the Mary—the most agreeable news I have heard for some time. Daddy and Aunty out again this Afternoon, myself alone—on first Day night last, a House near Darby was struck by lightnig and much damag'd in many parts an Hog who lay at the door was kill'd—the family who were all in their beds, escap'd unhurt, I dont recolled ever hearing of so many places being struck in one summer as this—received a Letter this evening from our dear Son, which was a great satisfaction to me,—but there is no joy, [sans allay]—his being indispos'd after his Arrival makes me desirous of soon hearing from him again—this evening Saml. Emlen, Wm. Savory, [J.] Parish here with daddy—he wrote to Billy by Tench Cox, who sets of early tomorrow.

22 S Swett din'd—C Evans tea'd—Neigr. Waln, J Logan &c call'd—Henry return'd this evening from Atsion—Hannah Baker call'd—she and MS. went to Wm. Saverys.

23 Cloudy, wind at NE—Aunty gone this afternoon to Jacobs House—myself alone, step'd over this Morning to Hartshorns—Jacob Downing and Molly Drinker came home this Afternoon drank tea with us. They left Sally

8. The words "as they call em" crossed out.

and Nancy at Jane Roberts intending to go for them on first Day next Docr. Foulk and wife here this evening the Baltimore Stage in come in this evening no litter from our Son,—his being unwel when he last wrote makes me fearful that he is more indispos'd than he was.

24th. warm again—Danl. Trimble din'd with us—Jacob and Josey also—James Logan in the Afternoon.

25 very heavy rain this Afternoon post came in without a letter, I am in hopes we may see them this evening late as it is—R Vaux, H Drinker here this evening—Josey Downing bid us farewell this evening he goes with Jacob (or intends it) tomorrow morning as far as Jane Roberts, and then home wards—Jacob proposes bringing Sally and Nancy home tomorrow evening.

1790

1790—14th: Sept.[1] third day John Hillborn and Wm. Drinker, left us this morning after breakfast, about 8 o'clock—intending for the beach woods—I went to Sallys and from thence to meeting—[J] Pemberton Neddy Howel and Ailce Needham apper'd [S] Emlen also—the first time of my hearing [J]P. since his return—took leave of the old meeting-House, the new one is to be open'd on first day next—'tis 29. years and 8 months this day since I was married, in it—[P]B here; he says that the Equinoctial storm will be over, before our Son leaves the inhabited part of the country.—Betsy Watson—Nancy and Molly, left home after dinner—for Buckingham, in Jacobs Carriage Benja. Oliver drove it—drank tea at Neighr. Walns thunder—lightning and rain came on about 6 this evening, and 'tis probable none of our children are arrived at the end of their days journay.

15 Cloudy morning tho the wind is at N.W. cleard away about 9 o'clock, and promises a fine day—Neigr. Waln here in the Morning I call'd at Fishers at Jacobs—spent this afternoon at Thos. Says,—Hetty David died this morning—heazey weather.

16 I went this morning with S Fisher, C Howel and M Smith, to look at the New meeting-house, which I think is a hondsom plain convenient bulding—This book was intended for memorandans of what occur'd during my Sons absence, for his information, not a diary of my own proceedings—but as it is the method in which I have been accostomed to write, and know my own movements better then any others—it must serve for an apology—a beautiful day for travelers—Abraham Cadwalader din'd with us Sally and Eliza at Tea—Nancy & Molly return'd from Bucks to Tea—I went with Neighr. Waln this evening to visit Ellenor Foulk, who lies in—very cool this evening.

17 S Fisher and Taby here, I went with them to visit H Baker.

18 Tommy Stewardson din'd with us—S Emlen, [J] Parish here in the evening—Jacob, Sally and the little one in the Afternoon went to ride Nancy and Molly also—Jacob drove; Benjn. Sick—Docr. Clarkson dead—a Stranger of the name of Constable, bury'd from Nany Sagess—Wind at N.E.

19 First day—went to meeting this morning—Wm. Savory open'd the New

1. The manuscript volume for Sept. 14, 1790–Sept. 14, 1791, has no covers.

Meeting in prayer, S Emlen and WS. appear'd in testimony—Jacob and Sally din'd with us—Daddy went after dinner with W Savory to a meeting appointed by him at Chesnut Hill, came home after dark—Jacob Sally and John Skiren drank tea—Sally Zane, and Saml. Emlen call'd.[2] Neigr. Waln here this evening.

20 I wrote a few lines yesterday Morning to my Son, intending to send by W Coper, but on enquiery found that the Burlington boat had left town early in the morning—Jacob and Sally din'd here.

21 Went to meeting this morning—Seamor Hearts daughter[3] hansel'd the new House, she past with one [Shupherd] Sally Downing, Molly and self drank tea at S Emlen's.

22 John Cannon breakfasted with us.

23 Jacob and Sally went to Jane Roberts's their mother Downing and [T]ammy—came back with them in the evening.

24 Received a Letter from B Wilson—M. Penry Mary Downing, Jacob and Sally, Tammy Thomas and Joseph Horsefield, drank tea with us—Wm. Bleakley wife and Daughter stop'd here, John and Rachel Watson came with them—I went with Rachel this evening to John Pembertons, Mary Ridgway and Jane Watson there—clear and cool.

25 many here this day—S Trimble and wife, Joseph Hampton Deborah Guest Ann William and another Ann Williams and John Hopkins lodg'd with us.

26 First day—went to Meeting this morning—16 din'd with us—J Balderston came to day—rain this evening.

27. 28. 29—a good deal of trancient Company sixteen at dinner, one day the same number at breakfast another day, some times but one or two—very heavy rain the 27 at night. received a few lines the 29 from Billy, dated the day[4] after he left us.

30, fifteen breakfasted here, 17 din'd.

Octor. 1 [or] 2—good deal Company James Thornton B Swett and wife din'd

2. The word "and" crossed out.
3. The word "past" crossed out.
4. The word "before" crossed out.

and several others—Ann Hamton and Joseph Moore lodg'd here, several of ours gone.

3 John Gordon brought us a Letter from Billy, with an account of his being in better health, J Thornton went home with our Mare & chaise.

3 First day—Went to meeting this morning after all our coumpany was gone but Ann Williams junr.—Mary Downing, Jacob and S Downing, Tammy Thomas, Sally Hopkins—Dick Downing, John Rierson one of our Lodgers, Zillah Thomas, Joseph Moore Ann Williams &c din'd here—Sarah Hopkins came after dinner—went to afternoon meeting—S Swett, Anthony Woodcock, Saml. Emlen, William Canby, Sally Hopks. Betsy Emlen drank tea here—Capt. Thos. Roberson here this evening—and John Skyrin.—James Logan.

4 Ann Williams and her brother breakfasted with us, she went away after breakfast—A Norton din'd with us.

5 Neigr. Waln here this morning went to meeting—Peter Yarnal din'd here, W Savory call'd—Capt. Roberson drank tea—went down town call'd a D. Bacons and at Aunt Jervis this evening at Nr. Walns, english babys—Jacob and Sally and Eliza, went this fore-noon with their mother Downing and Tammy, to Jane Robertss—return'd towards evening by themselves—Neddy Howel very ill again. P. Vaux nearly blind—Henry received a letter a day or 2 past, from Ben Wilson with irish papers.

6 Sister went with Becky Scatergood in the waggon to the Hospital &c. to visit Betsy Devenshire, saw Caley Parr there—John Hopkins lodg'd here last night—Docr. Kuhn call'd to see sister—Sally Downing and her little chattering lively baby here in the morning—on first day morning last very early, John Watson and Wm Bleakey left our house to go on foot to Frankford, where their wives had gone in a waggon the night before, we suppose [Tarter] follow'd them, for we have never seen him since.

7 one Tucker Esqr. Breakfasted with us—S Swett din'd here,—James Pope, John Talbert, S Swett and Billy Saltar drank tea with us—Joseph Saltar and wife was here several times last week—Billy Salter lodges here. John Skyrin here in the evening—little Eliza, Betsy Emlen &c—32 sail of Vessels came up with [T]R on first day last I believe it was.

8 W Salter breakfasted—Sally Hopkins and WS din'd—SH. and Betsy Watson drank tea—John Skyren here in the evening.

9 WS. breakfasted and then went homeward Esqr. Tucker din'd—rain most of this day—we are in hopes that a fresh will bring a Letter.

10 First Day: nobody gone to meeting but HD. and HD[5]—stedy soaking rain most of the night and all this morning—JS. neigr. Waln.

11 Betsy and Becky Waln spent the Afternoon Sammy Sansom the Evening—J Logan, John Nancarrow, John Skyrin, Sally and Eliza Betsy Emlen call'd—clear'd up in the Night. Sucky and Robt. Hartshorn call'd.

12 went to meeting. Alice Needham and Hannah Catheral din'd here—J Logan and Several others call'd, John Simpson, Gardr. Erle.

13 began to rain at 10 o'clock, continud all day and most of the night stedy heavy rain.

14 appeard clear, wind westerly—wrote to Billy, without knowing of any oppertunity to send—H Pemberton here this Afternoon everybody out this evening but myself—Jammy Logan call'd.

15 Cloudy—Hannah Warder and her two sisters, Nancy Morgan drank tea with Nancy and Sally Downing—Jacob Dg—Tommy Morgen, Docr. Foulk and Wife, John Skyren, Sally Hopkins call'd.

16 fine clear North-wester—Capn. Roberson and wife, din'd with us—they and Hannah Thomas drank tea.

17 First day: very fine weather—went to meeting morning and evening—Sally Downing John Skyren drank tea, the latter sup'd with us—Neigr. Waln call'd HD. and self call'd at D Drinkers after evening meeting his wife returnd from New England—call'd at Jacobs.

18 Jacob and Sally din'd with us Molly Foulk and her Daughter Betsy spent the afternoon—I took a walk this Morning call'd at Aunt Jerviss and at Sam Sansoms—fine weather.

19 I was let blood this morning—Gardner Earl din'd with us—S Swett spent the afternoon—HD and Sister sup'd at Jacobs—Neigr. Waln call'd no news from William.

20 John Penn breakfasted, S Swett din'd—J Skyren spent the Evening J Logan call'd.

21 Abraham Cadwalader din'd B Burge spent the Afternoon.

5. The word "heavy" crossed out.

22 Reading Howel breakfasted—spent this Afternoon with D Mt.Gomery—JS here in the evening—Nancy gone to set up with Bell Wister—Moon eclipced.

23 Wm. Cooper breakfasted—took a walk with Molly to S Whartons—found the family in great distress—call'd at Gideon Wellss at Aunt Jerviss who is very unwell—found M Penry at our house when I return'd, she din'd with us—our Son William returnd from the woods this Afternoon in better health (through Mercy) then when he left us—Sally Emlen, Betsy and Sally Saltar drank tea with us—Wm. Cooper Sup'd. and lodg'd—JS—very fine weather indeed.[6]

6. Lines entered upside down reading "Molly returnd to town with Peggy—Jacob and HSD. came up this evening—Plunket Fleason bury'd this Afternoon or yesterday—" crossed out (see Aug. 23, 1791).

1791

1791 June 17 sixth day fore-noon our [dear] Son William left us for Germantown, where his Sisters now reside—he intends for bucks county &c,—in search of the greatest blessing that mankind can enjoy in this world, next to a good conscience—the latter I hope he in good measure possesses, the former may it please the Lord to grant, is my dayly prayer. Jacob Downing and Jn. Skyrin, have taken a House in Germantown belonging to M. Clarkson, Jacob Sally and their little one went there on fourth day last, with their two Girls; Dan is left with us—Sam JSs boy also went—Nancy who has been very unwell stay'd one night with us—John and Nancy their maid Polly went on fifth day their going to spend the hot weather out of the City is on little Eliza[s] account who has been for several weeks disordred in her bowels—and Nancy having been unwell for some time past, it was thought it might be of servece to her.

18 William lift home yesterday in a newly purchased Sulkey and our old Mare—which John Skyrin drove home this morning the mare lame and not fitt to proceed on a journey[1]—HD. brought a little horse of [S] Pleasents which J Skyrin drove to Germantown this evening.

19 first day HD. and MS—and HSD, went after afternoon meeting to Germantown—HD. and Son returnd in the evening. left MS there who stayd all night—a very heavy rain fell about 2 o'clock, which has changd the air very much.

20 Sister came home this morning—with Jermy. Wardner and J Downing J Skyrin walk'd to town, Billy concludes to stay a day longer as it is now damp, and cold enough to set by a fier—there are a number of Philadelpians at Germantown Patk. Hartshorns family—John Periots family—Jery Warder and Jessy Wallns &c &c.

21 Jacob and John came as usul to breakfast—inform'd that Billy left Germantown between 7 and 8 intending for John Watsons—I was concern'd to hear that WD. with little Eliza in his arms fell down stairs yesterday—hurt Williams hip, and brused the Childs face—he had boots on which were too large for him, and were rendred slipery by walking on the grass—the stairs

1. Word crossed out.

were narrow and he weak. I fear he was hurt in mind as well as body, as I know he dearly loves the Child—I went to meeting this Morning—JD—JS—din'd with us—Sister out this Afternoon—Molly gone with Betsy Emlen to visit Jenny Stevenson—HD. John Drinker—Jacob and John—gone this evening to Germantown, where I expect they will spent this night—Peter Yarnal and Samey Emlen jr call'd.

22 HD. JD. JD, and JS came to town between 6 and 7 this morning breakfasted—[J]D. JS. and Peter Yarnal din'd with us—PY. says, that some time ago he, by coughing, broak a small blood vessel, and discharg'd ½ pint blood, he had been very unwell for some time before, but has been much better since—he further says that some years ago, he was so ill with a cough and fever &c that when he set of for New-England, his friends here never expected to see him again—but the riding about, the change of air, and his manner of living in New england occasion'd such an alteration as was nearly superising, he return'd home I think he said well—the rye bread and Indian bread, with the preserve'd barbaries put into water for drink, prov'd very salutary—barbaries are very plenty there—when I told Peter that the Doctor had advis'd thy going to New hampshire—he said he had no doubts but it would be of great service to thee or restore thee—Jenny Stevenson, Sally Wharton and B Emlen were here this afternoon visiting Molly—I step'd in this evening to Isaac Whartons.

23 Jacob and John at breakfast Jacob din'd with us, and John at John Hopks. I took a walk this evening to S Emlens Sammy came home with me—Docr. Jones died this morning—wind at SE—after a cool spell 'tis now much warmer.

24 John and Jacob came after breakfast, Neigr. Waln here this morning—John and Jacob din'd with us—Thos. Morris and his Cozen James Morris here after dinner executed a Deed febore the latter, for the place at the [Trap], to JD. We were invited to the funeral of the widdow Willing—upwards of 80 years of age. *Notre chate tombez dans la maison-Nette* Betsy Jervis spent this Afternoon and part of the evening—fine shower this evening.

25 John Skyrin lodg'd here last night he and Danl. Trimble breakfasted with us—Jacob and Sally—Caty and little Eliza came to town this fore-noon, they with Thos. Arnold from New England, John Skyrin & Danl. Trimble din'd with us,—[Jacob], Sally, JS. and the child went back in the eveng—left Caty Da[l]ton to stay with us this night—she intends to Birlington to morrow, to stay a fortenight—Sally Hopkins junr. spent this Afternoon.—Hannah Waln & Molly Pleasents call'd—we received a letter last evening from our WD—dated 22 instant he says nothing of the state of his health which I do not like—Robt. Hooper call'd.

26 First-day went to meeting this Morning Molly Smith, Abigail Parish S Swett and H Catheral din'd here—Abey and Nr. Waln drank tea with us—very heavy rain this Afternoon—no account from William.

27 I went this morning with Sally Emlen in her Carriage to visit our Children at Germantown My Husband and Jacob Downing came up to Tea—a fine shower this afternoon—Nancy came to town in the Carriage with her Father—we came home before night Billy Hopkins and Hugh Roberts calld this evening they intend setting off tomorrow towards Bethelam—think 'tis possiable they may meet with our WD—but I dont expect they will—[Josh] Needham (and Brother call'd this evening—John and Nancy staid with us this night—On returning home this evening after the Shower, the prospect was delightfull, every thing around seem'd refresh'd.—the Settng Sun, and a butiful Rain-bow added charmes to the scean.

28 Jacob Dowing came to town this Morning a little after 7 o'clock, on foot—John and Nancy din'd with us—received this Afternoon a pleasing letter from our Son, from Kingwood—Docr. Griffith and a grand Man of Colour call'd this afternoon—John and Nancy Skyrin, Jacob Downing and Molly Drinker went this evening to Germantown, Thos. Arnold drank tea with us—HD. son of John, came this Afternoon from Stockport, Betsy Watson, Polly Drinker call'd—about 7 this evening we had a storm of wind and heavy rain, but no thunder—John Hopkins senr. din'd with us.

29 Jacob this Morn—a Man from stockport lodg'd here last night and breakfasted this morning—Ben Wilson call'd—he returnd from New York this Morning—JS. JD. and B Wilson din'd with us—Robt. Stevenson, Sally Hopkins call'd—Bells muffled for Sally Ritche[2]—Jacob and John went out town 6 o'clock John says, Nancy was very poorly last Night—I drank tea with Neigr. Waln—John Pemberton in a letter to his Brothr. James, mentions having seen our Son, on seventh day last at Kingwood, I expect it was at his instigation that the young-man accompany'd William.

30 Jacob and John at breakfast—Ingle left us this morning for the beach woods,—JS. din'd—Jacob and John set of after tea P. Hartshorn with them, by Wanes Shop the new Horse run a nail in his foot near an inch and half deep, Abraham pull'd it out, and returnd back, the horse very lame—JD and

2. Sarah Riche, the wife of Thomas Riche, a leading merchant and trader in prerevolutionary Philadelphia, was interred in Christ Church's burial yard at Fifth and Arch streets (Edward L. Clark, *A Record of the Inscriptions on the Tablets and Grave-Stones in the Burial-Grounds of Christ Church, Philadelphia* [Philadelphia: Collins, 1864], 14; Doerflinger, *Spirit of Enterprise*, 146–48; James H. Soltow, "Thomas Riche's 'Adventure' in French Guiana, 1764–1766," *PMHB* 83 (1959): 409–19).

JS. went at 8 o'clock in the Stage—Neigr. Waln, Ruth Paxon call'd—Bob Mountgomery call'd.

July 1. Jacob and John came to town on foot this morning—Robt. Mt.Gomery and John Warder call'd—cool this morning clear'd up, wind at NW—remarkable change of weather, heavy rain this Afternoon, cloudy in the evening—John and Jacob din'd with us, Jacob went to Germantown this evening on our young mare—John in Jn. Frys Sulkey—James Wilson Lawyer—Joshua Howel call'd—Sister out all this afternoon and evening—American Musiem and Collumbyan Magizine came in this day for WD.[3]

2 John and Jacob as usual—they din'd here also—Jenny Sibeld and her Son Henry here—Jacob and John gone to Germantown in [Jessy] Walns Carriage. received a letter from our Son, his Father wrote to him—Henry Drinker here this evening received another letter from Billy by Wm. Lee.

3d. First-day, clear 'tho the wind at NE—HD. John and Rachel Drinker and Hannah Thomas gone in the waggon to Germantown, the old mare and young—I stay'd at home all day, and most of the day by myself, which is common—B Wilson calld after meeting this Morning Henry, who had been to Church to hear Parson Ben, went weth BW to Kingssington to dine with George Baker—HD. &c return'd after 7 o'clock.

4 Jacob came to town on foot breakfasted here. Nr. Waln calld this morning inform'd that a Son of Guiers, a Lad—is to be buried this afternoon, his death was occasioned by a brick falling out of a Hodd on his head at Fishers buildings, which brought on a lock-jaw, of which he died—James Logan calld—Jacob din'd—Dan gone off—Jacob found him in the Street, brought him home and gave him a triming—Jacob and Paterson Hartshorn went in our waggon this Afternoon to Germantown—Neigr. Waln, Thos. Morris call'd—rioteous doings at Grays ferry, breaking of windows &c.

5 Jacob, John and Molly Drinker came home this morning to breakfast Ruth Paxon, Grace Eastaugh, Jacob and John din'd with us. I wrote to Billy by

3. The *Columbian Magazine,* started in 1786, was noted for its engravings, fiction, agricultural and mechanical articles, biographical sketches, and articles about the history of the Revolution. After several changes of ownership it became known in 1790 as the *Universal Asylum and Columbian Magazine.* In 1787 Mathew Carey, one of the original proprietors of the *Columbian Magazine,* started the *American Museum,* which soon had over one thousand subscribers. Besides reprinting essays from other sources such as Tom Paine's *Common Sense,* it also published medical essays, antislavery tracts, belles lettres, and poetry, and inclined toward support of Federalist positions in politics. Both magazines were discontinued in 1792 after the passage of the Post Office Act, which was interpreted in Philadelphia to mean that magazines were subject to the same postal rates as letters, making their postage prohibitively expensive (Mott, *American Magazines,* 1:18, 30, 94–103).

Wm. Lee—Sister, Jacob, and P Hartshorn went in our Waggon to Germantown this evening.

6 Jacob and John &c came to town, left MS. with the girles—they din'd with us—HD. and John Drinker left us after dinner for Atsion—John Balderston call'd this Morning—Nr. Waln drank tea with Molly and myself—Ellinor Foulk here this evening—J Skyrin lodges here this night, having been detaind on a jury, and as there is nobody but Henry, Molly and self at home it happn'd very opportunely—warmer to day then it has been for a week past.

7 Ben Wilson, John Skyrin, Henry, Molly and myself—breakfasted togeather—Jacob and Sister came to town before 8 o'clock—John Pemberton call'd, he and Hannah return'd third day evening—he appear'd kindly solicitous on account of our dear William—S Swett spent the day, she and Jacob din'd with us. Sally Hopkins spent the Afternoon—Jamey Logan drank tea—Nr. Waln, Betty Newton, Saml. Leeds wish'd to see HD—things goes wrong at Mari[us]-river—Sam. Skyrin came to town near 11 at night, his master had forgot to shut up his house in town, which he had open'd to air, upon enquiry we found his clerk had done it—Sam lodges here—no news from Willm. since the 1 Instant—a fine clear day—I was much surprisd when I heard Sam stuttering at the door to night, I thought some of the family at Germantown was ill; went to bed at 12 o'clock.

8 Jacob walk'd to town—he BW, breakfasted John came afterwards—Fanny Edwards paid us a morning visit—Docr. Griffits call'd for maple-seed—BW. JD. JS. din'd Molly went this evening with Jacob in the Wagon to Germantown. John went with Jery Warder—very warm this evening The thermomoter up to 82—received Letter from HD—this evening.

9 HD. &c came home from the Jersyes by 8 o'clock—Jacob, John and Nancy with little Eliza came after Breakfast, no news from William, several of our children very unwell—Jacob & his daughter went with P Hartshorn—John and Nancy, B Wilson and Henry went in Jacobs Waggon, Molly is already there—Sarah Fisher drank tea with us—T Morris, Casper —— [Saml.] Taylor and HD. in our back parlor this evening—setteling a dispute between TM, and Casper—had they call'd in P Heart, and innocent neigr. Tompkins, they might have felt such a tenderness for the accuser, that the affair might perhaps have been settled otherwise then it was.

10 First Day: all our Children abroad—HD. MS. and self went to meeting this morning—R[S]. din'd with us—I felt very disagreeably in meeting, was taken very sick at dinner, drank warm water and was a little better—weather very warm—Thermometer 84.

11 Jacob and Henry came to town on foot this hot morning John Molly and B Wilson in the waggon—Thermometer 87—left home after 6 this evening HD. ED. JD. JS—in the waggon, came to germantown to Tea. Caty Wister, Polly Eddy, and Dr. Wister there—HD. stay'd all night.

12 HD. JD. JS. and P Hartshorn left us this morning about 6 o'clock—so here am I with my 2 daughters, sewing this morning—lay down before dinner, Nancy was taken suddenly with the nettle rash or hives—very poorly for near an hour, then got better—took a walk this evening Sally, Nancy, Peggy and Eliza, and Self—came back to late Tea—HD. JD. and P. Hartshorn came up in the waggon. A Letter from our Son of the 4 Instant from Kingwood.—Catys husband over the way, next door to Neigr. walns, died to day—John Skyrin stays in town this Night—Lightening, but no rain.

13 HD. &c went to Town early this Morning Sally, Nancy, and self took a walk towards eveng in the Orchard &c—Isreal Wheling &c came up with JS. and JD. this evening—JS. Nancy and self—took a walk after 9 this evening—as far as the french Mans Gardens—rather cooler to day.

14 Jacob John and Paterson went to Town this morning—we were very busy sewing this fore-noon—little Eliza unwel.—Sally, Nancy, Peggy & the Child, and myself—took a walk after 5 o'clock to P. Hartshorns—drank tea there—JD. JS and PH came there to us in the waggon towads even'g—they all rode home except JS. and myself; we walk'd—they brought me a letter from my dear Son dated at Morris-town, the most agreeable that I have yet received—Nancy taken very bad this night, about 10 o'clock with that rash and itching accompany'd with an oppression, she had been eating green plumbs—she was better in an hour or two—her maid Polly rather saucy and sulkey—very warm in the house tho' a good air blows abroad.

15 JD. JS. went to town—Polly Wheeling din'd and spent the day with us—Sally Parker, Molly Newport and her niece Lisey drank tea with us, Jery. Warder call'd—John and Jacob, came up in the evening as usual, brought Caty, Elizas Nurse with them—the actual heat very great, tho' there is a fine air—

Could I write, instead of Trifles;
That which most employs my mind:
All thats here would be ommitted,
Nor should I mark, how blew the wind?

I have heard of people who have had so much work to do, that they knew not what to do first and so did nothing there is such a weight such a complicated weight upon my [Spirits] that words cannot express.

16[4] John and Jacob went to Town Nancy very bad this fore-noon with nettle rash and oppression—sent for Docr. Bensel who ordred her to bath her feet in warm-water, and to take wine-whey;[5] which was accordingly done—she became better after 2 or 3 hours, but continues week and poorly. Sally Emlen and her daughter with our Molly, came up before dinner in their carriage—after dinner rain came on, and continued most of the afternoon and evening—insomuch that our husbands came not up—Sally, her daughter and Molly stay'd all night with us.

17 First Day: HD. Jacob and John came up before breakfast—Rumford and Abbigal Daws, their Nephew Hearvey and little Son Capt. Somebody and Henry Drinker junr. call'd before meeting—HD. myself, Jacob and Sally Downg—Betsy Emlen and Molly Drinker went to Meeting—Nancy Skyrin and Sally Emlen stay'd at home.—SE. and Daughter and Joseph Drinker din'd with us—SE. EE. and MD. left us after tea—Neighr. Waln, Sucky Heartshorn and Robt. came towards evening—we took a walk with them towards their aboad—weather very cool and pleasant—Ellenor Matlack was buried this afternoon in philada—old Isaac Zane, and Charles Williams preach'd this morning at Germantown meeting.

18. HD. Jacob and John left us about 6 this morning—Sally Nancy and myself took a walk as far as John Perotts, his wife and Children are fixt at the House, formerly Pestori[o]us's Tavern—we call'd at Polly Wheeling in our return I step'd over to see Nancy Smock who is very low in a consumption they think. Hannah Shoemaker &c are with her, next door to Docr. Bensels—mett Sally Zane there, she had left her Sister Hannah—at our house—HP—and SZ. left us a little before dinner received a letter from HD. informing that Danl. Williams junr. had seen our Son on 5 day last, that he continu'd mending and talk'd of seeing us in about 2 weeks—Sally and self paid a short visit to our vis a vis Neighbor Justice Foxs wife, walk'd in their garden, Nancy and self—took a walk this evening in the orchard and up the lane—John & Jacob came—Docr. Logan spent this evening with us.

19 Jacob and Sally Downing, J Skyrin and little Eliza, went to town this Morning Nancy and self left solas—we took a walk to Paterson Hartshorns, return'd at 11 o'clock din'd by ourselves—Neighr. Waln calld in the evening took a walk with us in the orchard—Billy Sanson, Jery Warder call'd, HD.

4. The words "First day" crossed out.

5. Wine whey was a popular remedy made by boiling milk, adding wine until the mixture looked clear, and boiling the mixture. After the liquid had been removed from the heat and allowed to curdle, the whey was poured off and combined with boiled water and sugar (Buchan, *Domestic Medicine* [1793], 265, 476; Maria Rundell, *A New System of Domestic Cookery* [London: 1818], 288).

Jacob, Sally, John, Eliza[6] came up this evening—a Letter from WD. New-York—very cool and pleasant.

20 our Husbands left us early this Morning—busy ironing before dinner—Nancy & myself[7] drank tea at Jessy Walns, he came home with us in the evening—Jacob and John came up later then common—Jerry Warder and Billy Parker with them—the weather is uncommonly pleasent for the Season.—the wife of one Miers a baker in Philada: fell into a Necessary on seventh day last, and continu'd there for ¾ of an hour before she was found: they got her out with great difficulty, and it was thought, when R Waln came up here, that she could not live long—she was sunk up to her Shoulders, and had not the flore, which went down with her) suported her, she would in all probability have been dead when they found her—how careful should every family be, frequently to examine those places, that they are secure—to prevent these very terable accidents which too often happen.

21 this is a delightful morning for WD—to travil, our men gone as usual—we busy at work—Sally and Nancy went visiting to Casper Haness—Jacob came up on Billys Mare—John in his own Chair, the young mare lame—Jacob informs me that Joseph More, who din'd with him at our house in Philada. told him that he saw our W.D—near King-wood, on first day last, and that he told him that he expected to be at home the later end of this week—warmer this[8] evening then it has been for some time.

22. Nancy went to town this Morning in their Chaise with her Husband—Jacob went earlyer—Sally and myself went to preparative meeting,[9] 16 women and about the same number of men—din'd by ourselves—we expect William here this evening or tommorrow—Jacob came up about 5—in our Chaise and Billeys Mare—no Company here this day.—John Thompson who was formerly Clerck at Atsion, was bury'd this Afternoon; the invitation to his funeral, was to meet at our House; the relations &c with the Corpes, stop'd at our door, at the time appointed, when Bishop White and the few others that were in waiting accompanyd them to the burying ground—a smal shower this Afternoon, but not sufficient to lay the dust—no Willm. yet, I am afraid he will give us the slip, and instead of coming here as I have expected, go to Philada.

6. The word "and" crossed out.
7. The word "spent" crossed out.
8. The word "week" crossed out.
9. Preparative meetings, initiated in the Philadelphia area at the beginning of the eighteenth century, dealt with disciplinary problems on a more local and informal level than the monthly meetings, in hope of resolving disputes without recourse to formal proceedings (Rufus Jones, Isaac Sharpless, and Amelia M. Gummere, *The Quakers in the American Colonies* [1911; reprint, New York: Norton, 1966], 251, 534–35).

sixth day night, 11 o'clock, here am I tout[10] suel, sitting in M. Clarksons parlour Germantown, all in the house (for aught I know) sleeping, but myself, and I here of choice busy thinking, and mending Stockings for my Son Henry, who has not thought it worth his while to come to see me, 'tho I have been here near two weeks.

23 Sally and self alone all this day—took a walk in the garden and orchard towards evening—Jacob came up in the Stage—HD. and Nancy in our Chaise—John on horseback—our dear William came to Philada. last evening, not much better I fear, tho' no worse through mercy then when he left us—expect to see him tomorrow.

24 First day—HD. went to town this morning Billy and Henry came to breakfast with us—WD. is better, looks better, and I trust will continue mending—E Perrot call'd—Jacob, John and Nancy, Henry and myself, went to Meeting, Sally & Billy stay'd at home, Betsy Howel din'd with us—Johns and Caty Hopkins, Neddy Howel, John Fry and Jerry Warder drank tea with us—Our Sons. and Neigr. Howels family left us about 7 o'clock—about 9 the two lazy couple here, servants and all went to bed—and here am I alone past 10.

25 Jacob went very early, John after Billy Drinker came up to spend the Day Sally and Nancy went to visit Polly Perrott—Ellis Yarnal and wife call'd. WD. went away towards evening. Jacob and John came up in the Carriage went for their wives—Dr. Logan here this evening, Molly Drinker came up this evening with Jacob and John.

26 Molly went to town this Morning with Nancy and John—Jacob went on foot—W.D. came up at 8 or 9 o'clock, S Swett with him—they stay'd 'till 6—JD. and Nancy came up towards evening left JS, in town. I sleep't with Nancy—Ah. me,—Je suis &c.

27 Jacob went to town this morning—Nancy and self drank tea this Afternoon at Dr. Logans—HD. and J Downg. came up before we went visiting—the young mare lame—John Skirin came up on Horse back.

28. HD. and Jacob, went to town this morning early. John stay'd breakfast—we have not seen WD—these two days—Sally and Nancy went to visit Jerry Warders wife—Jacob Downg—Richd. Thomas, Ben Wilson and W Drinker came up this evening—they all lodg'd here—JS. in town.

29 All the men left us but WD—he stays with us—No Company this day—

10. Word crossed out.

William and myself walk this evening an hour in the garden, I step'd over to Justice Foxs—J Skyrin came up this evening—we have had a long spell of dry weather, otherwise very pleasent.

30 JS. went to town—JD. there last night—WD. here no Company,[11]—Billy and self took a walk this evening—Jacob and John came up this evening—in the Waggon.

31. First Day: John, Nancy and self went to meeting this morning Jerry Parker din'd with us—. John Pemberton and Hannah Yerkes drank tea with us—JS. WD. Nancy and self took a walk this evening to P. Hartshorns—Jacob and Sally went to Weelings—warm dry time.

Augt. 1st. John, Jacob and Billy Drinker went to Town in the waggon this fore-noon, Abraham brought it up for them—Sally intended to have gone with them, but was prevented by indispossion—I burnt my hand last night with the snuff of a candle, which hinders my working this day—very fine air to day: mon esprit fort oppresseé sur beaucoup d'occasion.

2 JD. JS—went to town as usual—Saml. and M. Pleasants and Son Jammy here this morning—Sister, Betsy Jervis and WD—came before dinner, all but WD, left us after tea—Sally Wharton, Molly Waln here towards evening—J Skyrin and HSD came to lodge with us—pleasant weather.

3 JS. and H.S.D. left us early this morning—Billy stays—he read to us, while we sew'd—John and Hannah Pemberton din'd with us—Billy went to town with them in the Afternoon, No HD. no Jacob this evening John Skyrin came up in the Chaise solas—mornings and evenings begin to be cool—we took our usual walk, in the garden and orchard—Sally & Nancy both unwel.

4 John and Nancy went for town after breakfast—Sally not risen, we have been disturb'd for 2 nights past by Eliza, which is not common in the dear little one. Docr. Edwards call'd this morning—HD. came up this evening with JS.—JD. in town on Jury—Justice Fox spent part of this evening—Nancy came up with P. Hartshorn—WD. came up on Horse-back.

5 HD. and JS. went to town[12] this Morning after breakfast—we have been favour'd with a fine rain for several hours—Billy spent this day with us—the Maids busy washing little Eliza unwell,—Nancy very poorly with the Cholick, I am uneasy on her account—HD. JD. JS—came up this evening—Jerry

11. Two lines crossed out.
12. The word "early" crossed out.

Warder call'd twice.—we have 4 men to night. 'tis now between 10 & 11 at night, and raining very hard—a great favour, after a very dry time.

6 HD. Jacob and John went to town early this morning—Henry Drinker son of John here this afternoon—JD. and JS. came up in the Afternoon—clear'd up fine evening.

7 First day: HD. Molly Smith, R. Jones, and WD—came up before 10 o'clock—went to meeting, silent—MS. and RJ. din'd with us—W Savery call'd in the Afternoon. they went away after tea, WD. with them HD—stays—a very fine moon light evening—que [face à fà].

8—HD. John and Jacob went to town as usual, Je ne dormiez pas tout hier au sois—Sarah Fisher, Tabby Fisher Beckey Ditto—Sammy and his wife, and little William, spent the Afternoon avec nous—JS. JD—WD. and Molly Drinker came up this evening—they lodge here.

9 Molly went to town this Morning with the Men, William stay'd with us, rain this Morning and in the evening—much has fallen within these few days—J Warder Warder, call'd—Sally Parker and R Spencer call'd—JS & JD. came up this evening in the Chaise—Billy sleeps this night on the floor in my room.

10 John and Jacob went to town this morning left Billy with us the weather being cloudy—Sally went with Caty and her child to Polly Whalings—Billy myself went over to Justice Foxs he show'd us his printing types, which he makes himself—while we were there, My Husband, with Jacob Tomkins and wife, and Peggy Heart—came up—they stay'd tea with us—then went on to Joseph Potts at Pos Grove, intending to return tomorrow—Jacob came up this evening John stays—in town—Nancy dismist her maide Mallhereux fois, very warm weather.

11 Billy went to town in Hartshorns Carriage, John Skyrin came up before dinner in Chaise, Nancy went to town with him in the Afternoon—Sally and myself, by ourselves—Jacob came in the evening—Jerry Warder and Spencer call'd—Jacob came up this evening.

12. Jacob went to town with Jerry Warder Sally and self alone to day—Jacob in the Evening Molly with him.

13. they went to town this Morning—I dont recolect the occurances of this day and perhaps they are not worth it, find myself more unwel then for some time past. My husband, Jacob and Molly came up this evening—John Skyrin and WD—left Philada this Afternoon for Haddonfield—intending for Atsion—May he return with health improved, and enjoying peace of mind.

14 First day.[13]—Abraham came up this morning with the Carriage for his master, who left us after breakfast to attend our own meeting in Philada. Jacob, Sally and Molly went to Meeting we din'd by ourselves, which has not been the case on a first day before, sence at germantown—Molly and self went over towards evening to Justice Fox walk'd in his garden.—John Periott Jerry Warder and Jerry Parker call'd Neigr. Waln, and Sucky Hartshorn here this evening—fine weather.

15. Jacob and MD—left us early—we were looking this fore-noon for Sister and S Emlen—but were disapointed. Neigr. Waln and Becky Waln drank tea with us—Jacob and MD came up in the evening—fine weather.

16 JD. and MD. went to town—my husband came after 11 this forenoon, he with Nicholas Waln are settling some matters at Stanton between G Logan and Thos. Fisher, stay'd some time with us, then went back to Docr. Logans to dinner—rain this Afternoon—H.D. Jacob and Nancy came up this evening—Nancy poorly—little Eliza not well—Joseph Salter wrote word that JS. and WD. were to leave Atsion this Morning.

17. HD. JD. went to town this Morning P. Hartshorn with them—Nancy with us—Sally Fisher with 3 of her Children, call'd to see us this morning—JD. came up after dinner in the waggon—he went with Sally, Nancy Eliza and self. Dan also, to Joshua Howels where we drank tea, took a walk towards Schuylkill, beautiful prospect—John Skyrin and my Son Henry came to us there—John and Billy returned this Afternoon from Atsion, John says that WD. is better than when he left home—John and Nancy went to Philada. Henry came with us to Garmantown sup'd with us on fry'd Fish—The roads were bad; at least to me, they seem'd so; and I beheaved, as usual, very sily—Henry lodges here tonight—Isaac Wharton, Peggy and their Children, came to see us, while we were [out].

18. Jacob and Henry went early this Morning—Sally and self busy sewing this fore noon—George and Polly Drinker, John and Hannah Thomas, Johns Polly, and Anna Wilson, and little J Thomas, came up in Benn. Olivers Waggon—they spent the Afternoon with us—Jacob and Henry came towards evening. Cloudy and appearance of rain.

19th. Jacob and Henry left us this morning rain—a gloomey time altogeather—very very gloomey—Jacob came up by himself in Chaise—rain—we sup'd on Fish.

20. JD. went to Town—Sally & self Eliza and Dan, walk'd to S. Hart-

13. The initials "HD." crossed out.

shorns—came home to Dinner—HD. Jacob, WD. and Molly came up this evening.

21 First Day: John Skyrin and Nancy and HSD: came up this morng Sallys maid Peggy Lowry, and our little Sall, came also—H Drinker junr. also here—ten of us went to Garmantown meeting. Sister in town by hirself or nearly so—they all left us this evening My husband and Molly excepted—Joseph Yerkes and Jacob Tomkins junr. Justice Fox and his wife drank tea with us—HD. JS. WD. HSD. ED. and M.D—took a walk this Afternoon round Bowmans lane and by P. Hartshorns—calld there to rest a while, came home tir'd, I mean myself.

22 HD. and Jacob went to town between 5 and 6 this Morning too early for the Season MD. still with us—Robt. Stevenson and his Son—John and Hannah Pemberton paid us a visit this morning—Molly and self took a walk this afternoon down town about ½ mile, came home to Tea—Docr. Logan here this evening—Jacob and P. Hartshorn came up in our waggon—WD. on horse back, he stays with us to night.

23 Jacob and Molly went to town in waggon WD. on horse back—Sally and self very busy this morning—Sucky Hartshorn here this Morning Peggy Wharton with her 3 Children and Molly Drinker came up this Afternoon—Docr. Logan Debby and their son Gustavius, also, drank tea with us—Molly return'd to town with Peggy Wharton—Jacob and HSD. came up this evening—Henry [jouia au fluet]—Plunket Fleason was bury'd Yesterday or this day.

24 Jacob and Henry left us early. Abraham brought up this Afternoon George Baker Hannah Baker and their Son Richard—and B. Wilson they left us towards evening—our dear WD. left home about 4 this Afternoon, John McCahan with him, intending (Jacob thinks) for widdow Millers this evening, and tommorrow for Richd. Thomass—cloudy this evening wind NE.

25 Cloudy and Showery—Billy on his way to Muncy. S. Wallace's place. Sammy Sanson spent an hour with us, his wife and Daughter went to see Polly Perots who is laying in at Germantown—Jacob and Molly Drinker came up this evening.

26 Jacob and Molly went after breakfast—thunder and lightning this Afternoon, but little rain here, one very hard Clap thunder, kill'd a hen and several chickens at a very little distance from this house—HD. and Jacob came up to Tea—James Sterne very so so in the night, 'tho he did not disturbe us—poor old man, I pity him.

27 HD. and Jacob left us early this morning—fine clear morning—very warm day—Billy Sansom his wife, John and Nancy Skyrin drank tea with us—HD. Richard Thomas, Isl. Weeling and Jacob Dowg came up this eving they drank tea—Richd. and HD. and Molly Drinkr. who came up with P.H. and Nr. Walln, lodg'd here.

28th. First Day: HD. went to town this Morning by himself—Jacob, Sally, and Molly Drinker gone to meeting, RT—gone abroad—I stay'd at home—a rumpus cette matin [acac] le Fille—No company din'd with us this day—Jacob, Sally, Molly and self—we all took a walk this evening RT with us to Jessy Walns, mett Neigr. Waln and Sucky coming to see us, they turn'd back—came home near night.

29. R Thomas, Isreal Weeling, Jacob Downing and M. Drinker went to Town after breakfast—Many in Germantown last night observ'd a fier in Philada.—we were inform'd this morning that a Stabl in which was Robt. Waln's Chairiott was burnt and the Chariott very much damag'd but no other mischief done no horses there—no company here to day—the warmest I have felt this year, after walking above half an hour in the garden, Sally and self went a little way down town, mett Jacob and I Wg. coming up in the carriage, near night. HD. received a letter this day from our Son—dated on sixth day last, at Richd. Downings he informs us that he got wett, as I fear'd, it was so gusty the day after he left us. but received no damage therefrom.

30 Sally and self alone as usual—Jerry Warder and Rob Wharton call'd this morning—Jacob, Molly and Sally Hopkins came this evening they lodg'd here, a fine shower this evening—our little Eliza very poorly with a lax.

31 Jacob, P. Hartshorn, Molly Drinker & Sally Hopkins, went away after breakfast, Jacob and Daddy came up this Evening.

Sepr. 1 HD. and Jacob went to Town, Molly and Jacob came up this evening two more letters have been received from William, the last 17 miles beyond Downingstown, Saml. Wallace din'd with him—says he is as well as usual.

2d. Jacob and Molly went away this morning—HD. came up by himself to dinner with Sally and I—we spent this afternoon at Laural-Hill S Shoemakers 3½ miles from germantown—Beckey S. poorley—the place beautiful—come back by dusk—Sally went in the waggon to see Polly Perot—come back after night—HD. stays with us this night Jacob in town which is very uncommon, this has been a very fine cool day.

3d. HD—went to Town—cold, cloudy, raw morning—rain'd fast about noon—girls ironing—Jacob Downg. Richd Thomas Ricd. Downg. and Molly Drinker came up this evening—dull weather.

4th. First day: rain almost all day: no body went to meeting but JD—G Logan came this evening.

5. Ricd. Thos. and Ricd. Downg. and Molly Dr. Jacob also—went to Town this morning—rain most of the day JD. came up this evening.

6 Jacob went to town[14] in Stage clear'd up after two days rain—Sally and self went this fore-noon with S. Hartshorn to uper end of Germantown, call'd to see Polly Perott—while we were there our WD. past by in Sulkey, J McCahan with him—he is return'd sooner then we expected—he told [Dan] that he was as well as usual—Jacob came up alone this evening—inform'd us that HD. was unwell—Molly not very well cloudy this afternoon—unseatld weather, the Philadelphiens here, are turning their faces homewards.

7 JD. went to town this morning—H.D. Sister and Hannah Catheral spent this day with us—and Nancy—they all went home but HD. he stay'd all night—WD. came up this evening with Jacob in the Chaise.

8 HD. and JD. went to town in Chaise, Sally, and her maid Peggy, and WD. Dan. also went in the waggon, Sally intends to have her house clean'd—in order to return home—Molly Dr. came up this morning to stay with me, we took a walk down the lane—Jacob Sally, and WD. came up this evening.

9 Jacob and Sally went again to town this morning WD. on Horse back was sprinkled with rain, but I hope he received no damage—Molly stayd with me—Eliza very poorly with a fever and sore mouth—Docr. Griffiths and wife and little Daughter—call'd this Afternoon, J. and S. came up in the eving—P. Hartshorns family, gone home this day.

10 Jacob—and Molly Drinker went to town this morning—Eliza still continus very poorly—Becky Waln, Jessy's wife, spent this Afternoon with us—Jacob, and Molly, and Peggy came up this evening—cloudy most of the day.

11 First day: rain rain nobody went from hence to meeting but Jacob—a very small meeting—John Periot call'd—Abraham drove empty to town this morning—our little girl better—cloudy with rain all the afternoon Jacob Sally Molly and myself—no company this day—two months since I came to Germantown and have not been once to Philada. in that time.

14. The words "with Peterson [ ]" crossed out.

12 Molly and Jacob went as usual, no company here this day—WD. came up in the Chaise with his little Horse,[15] took Sally to Jos. Spencers, who serv'd us with Butter, they came back to tea—Jacob came up alone in the waggon—WD. lodges here to night, the poor Eliza has a sore mouth, a fever, and troubled with worms we think—fine settled weather—Clarksons Tenants in the house were we now are, consist of 4 persons vizt. James Steen, a poor intemperate labouring old man—his Wife, a good sort of woman, their grand Children a young woman and little Boy. Elizabeth and Zackariah Bowman.

13 Jacob, and WD. left us this morning—took part of our movables with them—Sally, her child and Caty and Dan, left Germantown, took as much as they conveinently could with them—they went in the waggon Abraham Dull drove them he has been our driver this Summer—Billy and Molly came up this afternoon to stay with me—HD. at [Jos] James wedding.

14 Abraham came up with a large waggon to take the Furniture to town Jacob in a Chaise—I came away with WD. in our Chaise before dinner as it look'd likely for rain. it rain'd a little most of the way but did not wet us—Jacob and Molly came to late dinner, we have bid adieu to Germantown, for the present, I have been 2 months and 3 days there, never so long from home before since I was married, nor in all my life.

1791 Sepr. 20.[16] third-day: our dear William left us again this morning—to take a journey in search of health, the weather fine tho' rather too warm, as he is on Horse back, Jacob Downing and Ben. Wilson accompany'd him in our Chaise, intending as far as Trent-town, they to return tomorrow, it is uncertain how far WD will go towards the Eastward—may he return in peace.[17] John Skyrin and Nancy call'd Neigr. Waln call'd—cloudy this evening drops rain—HD. Sister, Henry Molly—out this evening—my self with little Sall. at home—rather dispirrited, thinking of my son &c.

21 Henry lodg'd last night at Sallys, Jacob being absent—Molly and self busy all the morning putting up Curtins—Docr. Rush, and one of the Pragers here towards evening—Nancy Skyrin drank tea—John Cannon, J. Drinker call'd—J Downing and B Wilson return'd this evening left Billy about 2 o'Clock on this side trenton ferry—he intends lodging this night at Princetown—the Insurrection of the negroes in Cape-Francoies,[18] has occasion'd the rise of many articles here, such as Sugar, Coffee &c—cloudy this evening.

15. The words "to [tea] with us" crossed out.

16. The manuscript volume for Sept. 20–Oct. 5, 1791, has brown paper covers with "1791" written on the outside front cover.

17. Two lines crossed out.

18. On the night of Aug. 22, 1791, black slaves in the French colony of Hispaniola besieged the city of Le Cap François, killing many whites who had taken refuge there. The insurrection spread throughout the country and culminated in the Republic of Haiti's independence in 1804 (Ott, *Haitian Revolution,* 3–65).

22 John Cannon breakfasted with us, Saml. Emlen senr. call'd—Neigr. Waln call'd, I went with her this afternoon to visit S. Penington who has lately lost her daughter Nancy Smock—went this evening with Molly to Nancys—John came home with us—cloudy all day—heavey rain this evening—wind NE—our dear William perhaps 60 miles from home, where he may possibly be confin'd at an inn for some time if this should prove a equinoctial storm, was he in health, my anxiety would be less—the Ship Marquis de Fiatte lost at Sea.—an account of the death of Enoch Storys only Son, who was drownded, at some port near Jamacia, aged 23 years.

23 continues cloudy wind at east—A Clifton call'd this morning, gave him the grapes left by WD—Wm. Ellis, Betsy Emlen, call'd—Josa. Baldwin call'd. Wm. Bleakey and wife, John Watson & Wife and Son, Wm. Bleakey junr. and S Carry, din'd here—rain this afternoon—W Saltar &c drank tea—John and Nancy Skyrin and James Ross call'd—John Drinker also—John and Rachel Watson and young John—and Billy Saltar lodges here this night.

24 five or 6 breakfasted with us—several call'd to pay their quotoas—John Watson junr. went home with their waggon—Saml. Trimble and wife came—no body din'd and sup'd but those we call our own family, James Moon excepted. cloudy most of this day, 3 or 4 heavey showers this evening, where is our Wm.?

25 First Day: Billy and Hannah Newbold took up their abode with us for this week—5 or 6 at breakfast, 6 or 8 at Dinner, not many at tea—John Gant, John Needles—Jacob and Sally here this evening—Mary Downing in the afternoon—Sally Dg. fell down over their Sill and hurt her Ancle—I went to meeting this Afternoon, but no other part of the day cloudy, some rain wind at NE—our new Horse very much hurt, he was sent to the ferriers blooded and [J]ump'd, wether his leg was out of joint or the cramp or any other thing remains undecided—ou est mon fils?

26 I stay'd at home all day—very little company I forget who, John Balderston came, we now have but 7 lodgers—cloudy and rain.

27 cloudy this morning cleard up in the Afternoon moon changes this evening wind at NW. I hope we shall have a spell of settled fine weather, very little company this day—G Churchman and Jos. Moore din'd with us and no other—received a letter this evening from Billy from New York, I dont like the complection of his letter—but must hope for the best—Epheram Blane &c drank tea[19]—we have not quite as large a yearly meeting as usual I beleive—Joseph Branton &c call'd.

19. The word "I" crossed out.

28 very fine morning no meeting untill the Afternoon, our lodgers all gone out after breakfast—Nancy Skyrin and little Eliza call'd—Ben Oliver has lately returnd from waiting on the afflicted Doble family, the account he gives is realy affecting—he took Thos. Benjah and his Sister Doble some time since to Amboy, (she being in a bad state of health) in hopes of ammendment—, sometime after, the children hearing that their mother was worse, set off in Bens Carriage, to visit her, and on the road they mett the Corps of their deceas'd mother,[20] their distress'd Uncle and others accompaning it to Bristol buring-ground, Ben says, he never was witness to such a scean of affliction and Grief in his life—Peter Doble one of the Sons, fainted in the grave yard, he left them at their country Seat near Shamany—when Sickness and grief visits a family, who love one another, it must be by great exertion and the favour of the Lord that the survivours get the better of it—Two or 3 years ago 10, of this family came (I beleive in good health), from Irland—They have had almost a continual scean of nursing and sickness since their arrival, the remaining children have lost a Father, a Mother, a Sister and a Brother[21]—Their Uncle and Aunt, Brother and Sister to their mother, are with them—I have spent a long afternoon by my self, in the back parlor, where I have spent many a painful solatary hour *solas*, and some,[22] thro' divine favour otherwise—six persons drank tea with us—the committee for setting yearly meeting accounts mett this morning in front parlor.—Jemmy Thornton, Hannah Thornton widdow,—Walton, S. and E. Trimble &c sup'd with us—Jacob Downing here this evening.

29 by deviating from the path of rectitude and eating super 4 nights successively, which is what I very rearly do—and last night after super I drank a small draught of New table beer and eat some grapes after it. about 3 this morning I was seiz'd with a sevear fitt of the colic, which lasted for an hour or 2—I am much better this morning thro' mercy, 'tho unsetled & weak—fine weather—I spent most of this day alone—Thos. Latham din'd, our lodgers sup'd—cloudy this evening.

30 no strangers to breakfast—H & A Clifton din'd with us—R James and R Tompson spent part of this morning—solas tout cet apriaz midia—John and Nancy Skyrin, Nancy Hopkins and Joseph Moore drank tea with us—Joseph buryed his wife,—about 3 weeks since—he took away by mistake last yearley meeting our second vol: of Goffs History,[23] instead of the memorials.—our

20. The word "with" crossed out.
21. The words "the 4 children that remain are [ ] in their health" are crossed out.
22. The words "by chance" crossed out.
23. John Gough, *A History of the People Called Quakers. From Their First Rise to the Present Time. Compiled from Authentic Records, and from the Writings of That People*, 4 vols. (Dublin: R. Jackson, 1789–1790; Friends H.L. *Catalog*).

own lodgers and Billy Ellis sup'd—clear to day 'tho the wind inclin'd to the Eastward.

Octor. 1 P. Yarnal and several others breakfasted with us—I attempted this morning being alone a Letter to Billy—expect the meeting will break up to day—after dinner five left us—Wm. and Hannah Newbold stay untill tomorrow—John Cannon, John and Nancy Skyrin drank tea with us. I went in the evening with John and Nancy Henry and Molly, to Jacobs—have not been over the door sill before, since last first day morning—cry of fire I Beleive it was a Chimney, clear fine weather, feels like what is call'd a weather breader—hazey this evening.

First-day Octr. 2 went to meeting this morning Silas and another friend from Carolina with Sister Downg. din'd with us.—Robt. Nesbet a Scotch man a public friend, much thought of by many, appeared in testimony this morning G Churchman also din'd here—stay'd at home this Afternoon and wrote to WD. JS. AS. JD. and [SS]D. call'd—J Drinker and Sammy Taylor call'd—John Wayne to be bury'd this afternoon—John and Nancy Skyrin and Betsy Emlen drank tea with us—rain this evening wind NE—George Churchman and 4 others sup'd here 2 of them from Carolinaians.

3d. Saml. Emlen Senr. breakfasted with us, Jacob Linley call'd—James Needham call'd—young McKean here this Morning—cloudy Bancroft Woodcock call'd—John and Nancy drank tea, George Churchman call'd—Billy Savery, Thos. Scatergood in the evening.

4. went to meeting this Morning—after meeting was over, Robert Nisbet, appointed a perticula meeting on second day next to be held at the North House, for young persons only, except ministers and Elders—Molly Foulke din'd with us. This Afternoon R Waln and self went to visit A Skyrin.—Nancy upstairs she had heard of letters from R Bowne of New York, giving an account of WDs being ill at H Haydocks, he had ruptur'd a blood vesel in his lungs and was thought to be in danger—I went directly home, found several young girls with Molly who soon went away,—I set about preparing for a journey, had a sleepless night, and next morning the 5 set out for New York[24] fourth day.

2 loads wood[25]
1 quire paper
1 ditto waste Ditto
Poastage of several letters

24. The words "fifth day" crossed out.
25. These two lists are on the inside back cover of the manuscript volume.

3 Bottles pyemont water
8 Phials—

Prunes

paid R a guina	1/15/–
ditto——	15/
Ditto——	15
in his hands	8/6 NY

1792

March 4. 92[1] first Day—we mov'd into the front parlor, intending to stay'd there a week or two, as our dear William has been confind all this Winter and thee last also, thought it would be more lively to be near the street &c—Grace Eastaugh din'd with us—S Emlen junr. and J Downing call'd.

5. William Cooper came before dinner. John and Nancy Skyrin here in the evening Nancy drank tea with us, Cooper sup'd and lodges here—WD. wrote to New York.

6 Many persons apprehend that they felt a slight shock of an Earthquake yesterday morning, a few minutes before 5 o'clock, thunder with very sharp flashes of lightning accompany'd with hail and rain, both preceded and follow'd the earth-quake—Wm. Cooper and John Adlum breakfasted here—HD. MS. and MD. went to meeting, it has clear'd up with a mild North-wester—Wm. with Sally Downing and little Eliza took a ride this fore-noon—Sampson Harveys store on race street warf, took fier yesterday morning—unaccountably, some say it was by the lightning, which I do not believe as it broke out several hours after the storm. no one but little Eliza din'd with us—I took a walk after dinner to S Swetts—in second street on the other side Vine Street in a muddy spot my foot turn'd, I fell down bruis'd my hip and hurt my ancle and foot, which is very painful this evening Wm. Cooper, Rudolph Tilliase and B. Emlen drank tea with us.—E Shoemaker, Caroline and Betsy Giles, Docr. Rush and Henry Drinker, here this evening.

7 WC. breakfasted with us—he went away after an early dinner at 11 o'clock.—Jacob and Sally Downing din'd with us, Sally and her two Daughters spent the Day, the first time of little Marys being here, she is now turn'd of 5 weeks old, a very fine child—Molly gone visiting with Betsy Emlen.

8 wind strong at N.East with rain, continu'd almost all day—nobody here this day, but our own family.

9 B Wilson din'd, W Sansom call'd—W Saltar came this evening to tea, sup'd and lodg'd here.

1. The manuscript volume for Mar. 4, 1792–May 22, 1793, has no covers.

10 Another North East Storm, continu'd all day—J Field call'd—W Salter here.—HD. at home great part of the day.

11 First day: all our family as usual gone to meeting except William and myself—it is finely clear'd up—I have been very unwell for a long time past, and think I am worse instead of better—W Saltar din'd, he went after dinner to visit his uncle John Saltar, Ben Wilson and John Skyrin call'd Betsy Emlen also.

12 Wm. Saltar return'd before breakfast, he din'd here—A Skyrin, S Emlen, Jams Logan Wm. Saltar drank tea, John Skyrin Arthur Donaldson, John Drinker here—Hannah Smith also.

13 W Saltar went homewards after breakfast—Hammond His Britannic Majestys Plenipotentiary,[2] and P. Bond call'd—HD. from home—sent the Carriage for Ruth Woodcock—who with John James, R Jones and H [Catr] din'd with us—Ruth, John and Rachel James, and Clayton Earl drank tea with us—James Logan and Jacob Downing in the evening.

14 Billy and Sally and little Eliza took a ride this fore-noon—Ben Wilson din'd with us—near 50 Indians, chiefs[3] from six nations, arriv'd in town this Afternoon, escorted by the militia with Drum and fifes.[4]—Thos. Stewardson drank tea with us—my Throat very sore—Neigr Waln here before dinner, the first of her going out since her illness, which has confin'd her for 6 weeks, during her illness I sat up one night with her.

15 My throat still sore; Sister mett with Doctor Kuhn at J Downings, and desir'd him to call on me.—our dear little Eliza on seventh day night last, put a peice of a nutt shell up her Nose, which continues there yet—the Doctor has made an attempt to take it out, with an instrument but without success, they bound her eyes, and held her fast down, she cry'd so, that nothing could be done—wind at NE stormey with snow—S Swett here in the Afternoon, John Cannon sup'd here.

2. George Hammond, the first British minister to the United States, had arrived in America in October 1791 (DeConde, *Entangling Alliances*, 79).

3. The words "of the" crossed out.

4. Leaders of the Iroquois Confederacy (the Six Nations) came to Philadelphia at the invitation of Postmaster General Timothy Pickering, formerly a special emissary to the Seneca Indians, to discuss plans for sending instructors to the Indians at federal expense to teach basic literacy and handicrafts. The Washington administration, however, had a different agenda: to persuade the leaders to act as intermediaries between the U.S. government and warring tribes on the northwestern border. The conference ran from Mar. 13 until the end of April (see below, Apr. 5) (Clarfield, *Timothy Pickering*, 116; Francis B. Taylor, *Life of William Savery of Philadelphia, 1750–1804* [New York: Macmillan, 1925], 57–58).

16 The Doctor has ordre'd Sally Downing to syringe the childs Nose with warm water—and afterwards to put Oyl in it—she is terrified at the sight of the Doctor and will not suffer him to examine it, Thos. Stapler, Joseph Churchman call'd, John Ryerson din'd with us.

17 Billy and Molly took a ride this forenoon, R Stevenson call'd B Wilson drank tea Jacob Downing came for oyl, the dear little girl continues as yesterday—HD. Sister and Molly gone there this evening—Jos. Churchman call'd.

18 First Day: All gone to meeting myself and Billy excepted—Docr. Shippen who Kuhn call'd in, try'd with an instrument to take the nut shell out of the poor dear childs nose, but could not effect it—S Swett din'd here—rain this eving.

19 J Logan &c call'd—John and Nancy here this evening Mall tems.

20. Molly had company this afternoon Robt. S. Jones, bury'd—yesterday at Burlington.—cleard up fine weather—the Doctors made another vain attempt to extract the nut-shell.

21 William Sally Downing and dear Eliza took a ride this fore-noon, they din'd with us,[5] Eliza is chearfull, tho' I beleive feels a constant uneasy sensation, Dr. Kuhn call'd this Afternoon, says he hopes it will rot away, advises syringing with warm water and using oyl, to keep it sweet and to prevent a polipus from forming—An Indian Chief who dy'd here lately, was this Afternoon bury'd with great parade—David Dishler died yesterday, and this day Hannah Morris formerly Mickel departed this life Billy more unwell for two days past than usual—P. Hartshorn errecting a new building in his yard—Henry went this morning to woodbury, return'd before dinner—very fine weather.

22. Patty Wharton, Jane Watson, Jessy Coapland, and Peggy Wharton, call'd—our little Eliza here this morning I could plainly discover when she kiss'd me, that her nose was offencive—I went home with her before dinner, stay'd dinner there—after dinner her Father made an attempt with the silver hook, to no purpose but to make her Nose bleed, she screaming violently all the time, it being a case of so much consiquence he was loath to give out, and with three to hold her fast down, try'd again and was favour'd to releive the dear child—he brought away with the hook half of a ground ground nut shell—which has been there near two weeks,—it has taken one burden off my mind, had it continu'd, the consiquence might have been distressing indeed.—

5. The word "and" crossed out.

call'd to see S Fisher in my way home, she has lately had a fall in the Street and hurt her foot which is better—this is the first time I have been abroad since the same accident befell myself—Betsy Emlen call'd.

23 Joseph Smith call'd—Zebalan Hestan, Sarah Smith and Ann Hamton from bucks county came this Afternoon, the women lodg'd with us.

24. Molly Drinker and Sally Brant have a cold, and sore throats—but little coumpany.

25 First day: family gone to meeting—myself as usual busy in my Sons Chamber 'till after 11 o'clock—No lodgers but the two women—Peter Yarnel, Even Thomas, W Savery and another here after dinner—Hannah Hopkins came to dinner, to the funeral of Hannah Morris, who is to be buryed this Afternoon—Hannah Hopkins lodges here—H Catheral drank Coffee with us this afternoon—H Wells call'd clear fine weather 'tho the wind is at N East, little Eliza unwell of a cold and sore throat.

26 several here to day.

27. some din'd, some at breakfast &c call'd—George Churchman, Jacob Downing, John and Nancy Skyrin, Jos. Scattergood, Hannah Hopkins, Jos. Trimbel and Wife, Joshua Gibon, —— [Cogil], William and Sarah Bleakey and their Daughter Polly—Ann Hampton, Sarah Smith, Zebalen Hesten, Neigr. Waln, Sucky Hartshorn—Oliver Paxon &c—myself much oppress'd with a cold and hard cough—Sally little girles have the same disorder which I beleive is epidemic—friends of the [select] meeting [generaly] left the city this afternoon.

28. G. Churchman and H Hopkins breakfast here—Nancy and H Hopkins, din'd here Hannah went home this Afternoon—thunder-gust this evening—my cough troubelsome.

29.30.31, Very much oppress'd with the cough the 31 seventh day I was let blood fine weather.

April 1 First day: fever and cough continues, John and Nancy din'd with us Sally call'd, Robt. and Polly Stevenson and little Susan drank tea with us.

2 Rachel James call'd—H Catheral spent the Afternoon—Hannah Yerkes calld—Docr. Kuhn call'd—a Number of friends here this Afternoon to think with or for Sam. Emlen on his intended voyage—to Great Britian—Neigr. Waln call'd—S. Emlen Senr. SE. junr. Thos. Fisher, Saml. Fisher, Nics. Waln—Thos. Morris, Saml. Smith, C. West, Thos. Scatergood and Henry

Drinker—G Dyllwin, John Parish also—John Elliott G Dwylin, J Parish, S Emlen, T. Scattergood and H Catheral, and John and Nancy, drank tea here—James Logan call'd.

3. HD. MS. MD. gone to meeting. Billy, Sally Downing and little Eliza gone riding—Docr. Kuhn call'd, my cough very hard—Neighr. Waln, R Jones, S. Walace call'd—S Swett din'd with us—Sarah Fisher and daughter Becky call'd after meeting[6]—[S] Pleasants, J. Cannon and John Adlum here this evening—HD gone to Supper to J Downings.

4 Docr. Kuhn, J Parish,—I took a walk by the Doctors advice, call'd at Nancys and at Sallys—my cough very troublesome—Ben. Wilson din'd with us, John Cannon drank tea—WD. MD. and Eliza took a ride morning.

5 Dr. K—we had 20 persons to dine with us besides our own family—Isaac Zane and his Daughter Sally, John Parish, W Savery, Ben Wilson, 13 indians and 2 interpaters—they din'd in the back parlor, and had a talk after dinner in the Garden—went away about 5 o'clock IZ and Sally drank tea with us, went home in our Charriot—J Logan A Skyrin, S Downing Billy Saltar and several others here.

6 my cough very bad—several here to day—Wm. Simpson din'd here.

7 Dr. K. talks of laying a blister tomorrow on my breast, I have done many things but cannot as yet break the cough, Dr. Redman call'd to see us this fore-noon he has been confin'd all winter by the Rheumatism—S Emlen call'd—Hannah Wells, Sally Downing, Polly Drinker Henrys wife, John Adlam Jacob Downing, drank tea with us, Gidion Wells, Richd. Thomas, Richd. Downing Cadr. Evans and his Cosen Cadr. Edward Black, John Drinker &c call'd—the weather at present very fine.

8 First Day: very unwell S Emlen junr.

9 Sally and Nancy &c.

10 in my chamber by the Doctors orders, he talks of laying a blister on my breast. Polly Smith, Neigr. Waln, Nancy Skyn, James Logon came up to see me.

11 my cough rather better, John Adlum din'd, several call'd, Docr. Kuhn.

6. The sentence "HD. gone this Afternoon to Isaac Zanes to Tea with the Indians" crossed out.

12. Ben Wilson din'd—Charles Jervis S Emlen, Sarah Fisher, Becky Thompson, Jacob and Sally call'd, J Logon also my throat a little sore this evening, cough rather better.

13 my cough worse then yesterday—I wrote to M. Haydock, sent 5 pair Locket-buttons and Pincushon—Dr. K. call'd.

14. Dr. K. Neigr. Waln and P. Wharton.

15. First Day: John and Nancy din'd here, R Jones call'd S Swett drank tea on third day past the 10 instant was bury'd in friends burying ground Abigal—Physick formerly Syng,—she has within 2 or 3 years past become a member of our Society—an old aquaintence and Schoolmate of mine, my cough this day much as Yesterday.

16 Dr. K—H Yerkes drank tea, E Emlen call'd.

17 Dr. K—&c.

18 Ditto—Neigr. Waln spent this afternoon.

19—Dr. K. took his leave for the present—my cough much lessen'd—S Swett B Wilson din'd with us—Sally Zane here after dinner.

20—J Downing call'd Sally has a bad cough—wind at NE—we have had a long spell of dull weather HD junrs throat sore—Molly unwell.

May 6 first day 92. at home all day as usual—S Swett here—Molly Newport buryed this Afternoon.

7 quarterly meeting, Ann Hallowell din'd here—Phebe Pemberton, B. Emlen Ben Wilson and John James drank tea here—Molly Swett &c call'd—Billy has taken several long walks laterly.

May 25—Nancy Skyrin is now I hope getting better, she has been for upwards of 2 weeks very unwell in her Chamber—Dr. Kuhn attended her—a voilent sickness and pain in her Stomach—very little appetite and very frequent [ ]achings, I have been every day more or less there and stay several Nights with her—perhaps it may end in what is call'd a natural cause—'tho she has been worse then that generaly comes too in the begening—we are busy white-washing and cleaning house, have had a dry spell of weather after a long wett one—very dusty.

1792. May 26th: seventh day—HD. and Thos. Morris left home early this morning for Dover &c—expecting to be absent a week or 10 days—step'd over this morning to Neigr. Walns, where I have not been for several weeks.—Michael Callanan call'd here this forenoon, he arriv'd this morning in the Pigou from London—he brought a Letter of recommendation from ——. I invited him to make this his home,—he dines with his fellow passengers at the Tavern—he did not say wether or not he would except the invitation—John Skyrin call'd to borrow a horse, says Nancys better—Billy rather weak and languid—he took a ride with Jacob and Sally this Afternoon. Eliza unwell—John and Nancy drank tea here—a note from E Penington this evening—he mett HD. &c two miles beyond Chester—M. Callanan came this evening to take up his aboad with us.—Neigr. Waln call'd—cloudy.

27 First day: heavey rain last night, intended to have gone to meeting but fear'd the damp—Jacob Downg. call'd, Sister, Molly, and Henry went to meeting, William and self at home, Ben Wilson and Michl. Callanan, din'd with us—H. Catheral here in meeting time—John Skyrin, Nancy, and Sally call'd—Molly and self spent some time this evening at Isaac Whartons, clear'd up cold—Henry wrote to his father.

28. cool and pleasent wind at N.W—one Henry Stewart call'd to talk about land. MC. din'd—a man call'd to inform that the Committee respecting the Cannal—sets of tomorrow—Sally Hopkins this Afternoon, Billy went out to ride with J and S Downing—R Jones drank tea, [ ] Gibbs negro man came to hire [ ] Betsy Emlen here this evening.

29 I went to meeting this morning where I have not been before, since the 12 mo Decr. last—took a walk after to Sallys and Nancys—Billy Henry and M Callanan went to Frankford, John Lamsback drove them, James Logan and A Skyrin drank tea with us—Little Polly Garragas bury'd this Afternoon, S Downing and her two little ones here in the afternoon—J Skyrin here. Neigr. Waln call'd.

30. C. and B. Giles here this morning Docr. Redman call'd—Jo. Gibbs a negro man came, S Downing call'd—MC. din'd abroad—Betsy Fordham at work here—Billy went with S Downing and her Children to take a ride—Henry and self went this evening to [J] Pembertons—Hannah sick in her Chamber, call'd to see S Emlen, and to J Downings—John and Nancy, Neigr. Waln, Gidion and Hannah Wells &c here when I came home and Betsy Emlen.

31 J Skyrin call'd.—very warm—Molly Drinker, Caroline and Betsy Giles, in our waggon—Betsy Emlen and the 2 Smiths in Emlens Chariott, Jo Waln and Michel Callanan in a Chair, Ned Shoemaker and Henry S Drinker in an other—went to our Summer House at Frankford, where they drank tea and spent the Afternoon—came home after moon light, Ben Wilson here this

evening William walk'd out with him, the first time of his being out of an evening since last summer—no news from HD.

June 1st. HD. &c return'd before dinner, yesterday I gave a L——, the 31 May 'tis now the 5 June, I hope there will be no more occasion unless 'tis by chance.

June 13. wrote to M Penry.

1792 Augt. 25. seventh Day. after an early dinner, HD. set off for Atsion—Jacob Downing din'd with us—Sister is at his house seeing it clean'd, as his wife and Children are to return home from Downingstown next week, they have been there between two and three months. Nancy Skyrin has been at Haddonfield two weeks this day—John Skyrin removed from Ann Vaux's house in arch street, to a house at the corner of Water and chestnut Streets, beloning to James Pemberton the last day of last month. Our Son Henry is I hope recovering from a cold and fever, which has confin'd him for 4 or 5 days past—William continues bet weekly—'tho I trust not much worse then usual—Docr. Rush has visited HD. for some time past on account of a disorder in his left eye, which there is reason to fear is a fixt *Fistula lachrymalo*[7] [I] William and Henry took a ride in the Chaise—Sammy Emlen and J. Logan call'd—fine moon light evening.

26 First day—MS—and MD—went to meeting—J Dowing and S Swett din'd with us—Wm. and Henry took a ride this afternoon as they are both invalides—the two Giless Betsy Emlen and E Shoemaker drunk tea with Molly S Swett with us—MS. went to E Peningtons. they have lately bury'd their Son Benjn. he had been for some time past in a destress'd way—J Downing sup'd here—fine weather.

27 Sister gone to look after the cleaning of Sallys house, Docr. Kuhn here, I have had a uneasy sensation in my eyes for some months past, a twitching or what is call'd fitts in the eyes,—and a strain in my right thumb, occasioned by a fall last spring—the Doctor advis'd bark for my eyes, is it is a nerveous affect [ ] and to rub my thumb with Spirits turpintine, hire'd a dutch woman this morning nam'd Maudelena, she is to come to morrow—received a Letter HD—a young man nam'd [Burk] from Bay of Hondoras, call'd to enquire for M Callanan—Sucky Gelenham and John Kenseys wife called with Letter for HD—J Skyrin here this evening.

7. Fistula lachrymalis is a hole or ulceration in the lachrymal sac causing a continuous discharge of fluid (tears). The term, however, was widely used to cover many diseases involving the lachrymal passage (see below, Dec. 30, 1803) (Bailey, *Universal Etymological Dictionary;* Gardner, *New Medical Dictionary*).

28 A Letter from HD.—Maudlin came at 6/ p week—Sister and R Waln gone to Morning meeting J Downg. din'd with us—HD. return'd.

29. Nancy Skyrin spent the Day here she return'd from Haddon-field this Morning Molly Gosnold was bury'd this Evening from the House of employment, S. Oat—bury'd this Afternoon, Sister at the funeral.

30. Jacob Downing set of this Morning very early with B Oliver's Waggon one our Carriage Horse, being lame) for to bring home his family, Henry went with him on horse back—Joseph Moore din'd here—Billy went this Afternoon by himself in the Chaise to Germantown or beyond it.

Sepr. 1.92. seventh day evening Jacob Downing return'd from the Vally, with his family, all favour'd with health; they have been there 11 weeks this day—Nancy Skyrin spent this Day with us, and was let blood, being oppress'd with a cold &c—cloudy in the evening she lodg'd here.

1793

Janry. 20—1793 first-day morning—HD. and John Drinker left home after breakfast for Evesham meeting,[1] intending for Atsion this evening Wm. and myself at home this morning as usual—Sister, Henry and Molly gone to meeting—EE. EG drank tea with Molly. Sister went to Nancys.

21st. S Preston and Ben Wilson dind with us—I spent the Afternoon at J Skyrins, with M Pleasents, Nancy Pleasants—R Jones there—Rachel Watson and Wm. Blekey come here this Afternoon Wm. left the horses in our Stable, went himself to S Pleasents to lodge, Rachel with us—this has been a very uncommon moderate winter, remarked by everyone.

22 RW. din'd, Sister and her went twice to meeting Neigr. Waln, S Swett, and R Watson drank tea—much cooler than usual this day, but fine winter weather received a letter from HD S Downing calld this morning.

23d. received a letter from HD—Henry lay awake all night without knowing why—RW. gone to pine Street monthly meeting, her Son John lodg'd here last night, went away early this morning—Sister gone to dine at Nancys.

24th. John Saltar breakfasted with us—R Watson went out after breakfast—I drank tea at J Skyrins, RW, also—we call'd at J Downings—William Blakey &c call'd.

26th: Seventh day R Watson and Wm. Blaky let Philada. HD return'd this Afternoon, he lost the Old Mare—she was brought home some days after.

Feby. 3 first day Nancy Skyrin with her little daughter Elizabeth and Nurse Wilson din'd here the first time of her coming out since the birth of her Child who was four weeks old last night—Richd. Nisbit and J Skyrin also din'd with us.

4 Ricd. Nisbets left us this Morning for the beach-Woods—he has been two days with us.

1. The Evesham Meeting was located outside the village of Marlton in Evesham Township, Burlington County, N.J. This small meeting, established c. 1760, was also known as the Cropwell Meeting (Woodward and Hageman, *Burlington and Mercer Counties*, 316, 323).

1793 March 30. seventh day—HD. and John Saltar left us after tea this Afternoon, intending to Morrices River &c—Sally Downg. call'd—I lodge in henrys bed in Billys Room, Henry in our Room.

31 First day: MS. Henry went to meeting Myself Billy & Molly at home, Molly not well—Nancy with her child and maid came before dinner, they spent the day with us. S Swett and Nancy din'd here—Neigr. Waln Nancy Morgon call'd—after meeting in the Afternoon Sally Downing her 2 Daughters and maid Caty came they with, R Thomas Danl. Drinker, Betsy Emlen drank Tea with us—fine wathe this afternoon J Skyrin call'd.

April 1. A Skyrin came this Morning she went with me to S Emlens,[2] call'd at J Downings—JS. Sally D.—here[3]—R Waln and self went this evening to see Neigr. Rundle, they are abot moving out of this neighbourhood.

2 Nancy here this morning making a Hat for her little Elizah.—S Swett dind—S Fisher and Mary Swett call'd after meeting—S Fisher, Betsy Fisher and Becky Fisher spent the Afternoon Sammy came in the Evening—I went after they were gone with Sally Downg. and Molly Drinker to John Skyrins—call'd at Jacobs—George Baker fell down in a fitt on the warfe this afternoon—hurt himself in the fall—but is better this evening—John Broadhead call'd—Billy went out this Morning on Horse back about 2 miles, and in the Afternoon in the Chaise—he is languid and poorley.[4]

3. William, J[o] with him are gone out on horse back this morning—he went out with Henry in the Chaise in the Afternoon, E Jerves spent the day, she and Nancy Skyrin and Sally Hopkins din'd with us—Saml. Parkes call'd—Sally and Children, Neigr. Waln, J Logan, J Skyrin, call'd—Jacob here this Evening bottling Cyder—James Lee calld this evening brought a letter from HD—went to DDs for mill Saws—Debby Morris was bury'd this Afternoon—warm to day.

4 S Swett spent the Day—J Skyrin drank tea, I went home with him in the evening Nancy had a bad spell of sick headach last night, her baby has a sore eye, got cold going home yesterday—Caty with Sallys children here—Jos. Moore came this afternoon, left his Horse—Betsy Emlen, Jenny and Hannah Stevenson here in the evening—Northeast wind.

5 rain—Joseph Moore, Mary Downing.

2. The lines reading "to tell Sally something relating to little Dick Scott who liv'd some weeks with us and [now] is with them" are crossed out.

3. The words "S. Swett din'd with us" crossed out.

4. The words "B [Wilson] calld" crossed out.

6 Joseph Moore here for his Horse &c Neigr. Waln, Ben Wilson, Eliza Giles call'd—Ben. din'd with us—Sally Downing and her Children call'd, Elliston Perott calld—Molly and self went after tea to Nancys, came home in a heavy rain, chang'd our cloaths, caught no cold.

7 first day HD—return'd.

April 18, 1793 fifth day morning little Elizabeth Skyrin was innoculated by Docr. Kuhn for the Small Pox.

19. HD. and many others went to Chester to accompany G Dillwyn and wife and Elizabeth Drinker who embarkd in Ship Grange for Great Britian—HD &c return'd in the Evening.

23 HD. and James Pemberton went to Bybary to the funeral of James Thorntons Wife—returnd in the Evening—S Swett, B Wilson. M Callanan and Joshua Cliborn a young man lately from Dublin, din'd with us.—Nancy myself, and the above young men, and HSD—[stop'd] to see two Panthers, who are exibeted in an alley between us and Arch Streets.

Near a week after the Grange left Phia: she was taken by a french Friget and brought back, 'tis not yet determind wether she is a lawful prize or not.[5]

May 12. First day: HD. went after breakfast in our Waggon, with R Jones and Caty Haines to Bristol &c.

13 Molly Drinker sits up to night with Nancys baby, it has the Hooping Cough and as it is but 4 months old they are fearful of its strangling if neglected,—Eliza and Mary Downing also have it, Eliza getting better, Mary poorly. Abel Thomas, John and Nancy Skyrin Charles Williams &c call'd, JS. and WD went to Germantown to look for lodgings for Nancy and her Children &c, as change of air is recommended.

17 sixth day Nancy with her baby and her Maid Hope [Sharp] and Sister went to   beyond Germantown where they have taken lodgings.

5. The English merchant vessel *Grange*, which had left Philadelphia in mid-April, was seized by the French frigate *L'Embuscade* on Apr. 25 near the Buoy of Brown in Delaware Bay and brought back to Philadelphia. Though France had declared war on Great Britain on Feb. 1, the British protested the seizure, claiming that the *Grange* had been in territorial waters and under the jurisdiction of the United States. The U.S. government concurred, requesting that the crew be liberated and the vessel and its cargo restored to its owners, to which the French government complied by the end of May (Charles Marion Thomas, *American Neutrality in 1793* [New York: Columbia University Press, 1931], 1–43, 91–98).

18 Sister came home; Molly and her Daddy went, he left her there.

19 or 20 William went, stay'd all Night.

22 Billy went this Morning—rain this afternoon dont expect him home tonight George Dyllwin and Richd Nesbet[6] drank tea hear, Richd. and and Michl. Callanan din'd with us.

1793, July 8,[7] second day: came to German with John Pemberton and H Drinker, stop'd at John Salterbals where Hannah Pemberton has taken lodgings for the warm season—drank tea there with JP. HP. HD. John De Breom and wife, Isaac Zane and his daughter. Sally—came after tea to[8] George Hessers, near 8 miles from Philada. where Nancy Skyrin has taken up her abode with her Daughter for the Summer, mett Sally Emlen and her Daughter with Huldah Mott there, they reside at one Sniders half mile from Nancy, nearer the City—they left us towards evening HD. stay'd all night.

9 HD. went to town this morning William came up, Nancy Molly and self, took a walk to S Emlens, mett Billy as we return'd—he stay'd 'till after dinner, it likely for rain, he left us about 3 o'clock, rain this afternoon; Jenny and Hannah Stevenson and Clifford Smith here this Afternoon—Nancy and Molly took a ride towards evening with Betsy Emlen.

10 William came up after breakfast,—Neighr. Waln, Nancy Morgan and Daughter Anna Wells, paid us a viz this Morning Billy went away before Tea;—John Fry and John Skyrin drank tea here, then went to town; Nancy, Molly and self took a walk to S Emlens, came back after 8 o'clock—a very fine evening.

11 No Company to day—from Town. un'till evening, John Skyrin came up, Betsy Emlen drank tea with us—the night before last, Molly Drinker had reason to think[9] she swallow'd a pin or pins, which she has felt at times ever since in her Throat, untill this evening she does not[10] feel it—rain this afternoon.

6. The word "dind" crossed out.

7. The manuscript volume for July 8, 1793–Dec. 31, 1793, has brown paper covers. The outside front cover reads, "1793 / Book of Mortality," a reference to the numerous deaths ED recorded as a result of the 1793 yellow fever epidemic. On the inside front cover she wrote, "Send to Lbry. for an English translation of Lavater on Physiognomy," and on the inside back cover she jotted, "Plain [ ]lanets £ 11" (Johann Casper Lavater, *Essays on Physiognomy Designed to Promote the Knowledge and Love of Mankind*, trans. Thomas Holcroft [London: G. G. J. and J. Robinson, 1789]; *Brit. Mus. Cat.*).

8. The word "John" crossed out.

9. The word "that" crossed out.

10. The word "now" crossed out.

12 S Swett and Billy came up after breakfast—they spent the day with us, went to the Barn and had a swinging bout—Becky Waln, Molly Wharton, Becky Waln junr. and Polly Tallman drank tea with us—I went this evening Sam Sprigs with me to S Emlens, to wait on Molly home, who went there after tea—very fine weather.

13 took a walk with molly as far as the 8th mile stone and back, is ½ mile, came back to breakfast—eat hearty—set down to dinner with little appetite, taken very sick while eating, was in measure reliev'd by vomitting—have been unwell ever since—Nancy, and Molly and little Elizath. went with H Mott and Betsy Emlen to Flower Town 5 miles from hence—came home too late. HD. came up this evening in the Sulkey—the weather cool, which after the reverse suddenly closes the pores, occasion'd myself, and prehaps many others being unwell.

14 First Day: John Skyrin and William Drinker came up after Breakfast,—HD. and his Daughter Molly, JS. and wife, went to Meeting; Billy and Myself staid at home. No Strangers din'd with us—Betsy Emlen drank tea—HD. and Billy left us about 6 this evening Betsy Emlen Molly and self took a walk to 8 mile stone, after sunset, a very cool evening—I have been unwel all day, JS. and MD gone home between 9 & 10 with EE.

15 John Skyrin left us this morning after breakfast, cloudy with some rain wind easterly—no body here this day but Betsy Emlen.

16 rain[11] in the night fine this morning, Huldah Mott and Betsy Emlen here this fore-noon—Henry S. Drinker came up this Afternoon, He went With Nancy, Molly, and Betsy Emlen to Polly Perotts, they drank tea there, HSD. left them in the Evening for Philada.—I spent the Afternoon with Sally Emlen, Sammy Emlen, Sally Waln jr. Polly Tallman there—John Perott with my Children call'd after 9 o'clock there for me, we came home by fine Moonlight—a Man went through Germantown this Afternoon with something in a barrel to Show which he said was half man, half beast, and call'd it a Man[de], we paid 5½ for seeing it I believe it was a young Baboon, it look'd sorrowful, I pity'd the poor thing, and wished it in its own Country—our dear William left home this morning with Jacob Downing for the Valley.

17 Molly and myself went After—breakfast to Jacob Spicers, they live at Mount Airey, formerly belonging to William Allen, about ½ mile from G. Hessers, came back about noon, John Skyrin came in the Afternoon, he went with Nancy and Molly to Visit Nancy Morgun and Anny Wells, who are at one Becks in Germantown. I spent the afternoon with Hope and the Child.

11. The word "this" crossed out.

18 John Skyrin left us this morning, Hannah Pemberton and Hannah Yerkes call'd this morning nobody here in the afternoon, Nancy and Molly went over to Molly Whartons in the Evening.

19 Nancy, Molly, and self took a little walk after breakfast—John and Hannah Pembern. stop'd, for me to go home with 'em, it did not suit just then—Noke came an hour afterwards with their Carriage, I spent the day with them only that I went from their house to see A Morgan and H wells, who are but a little ways from 'em—much wind this Afternoon and a gust of wind and rain towards evening John Pemberton came home with me.

20 Huldah Mott and little Harriott here this morning I have been more unwell than usual since this day week—H Mott and E Emlen spent the Afternoon, Nancy, Molly & Betsy went to the Rose, to hear Musick—Our dear little Elizath. taken this evening with a vomitting, she is feverish—John Skyrin came up this evening—all well at home. Jacob and Billy are not return'd from Downing-Town, a fine moon-light Night. Warm. two or 3 Showers this Afternoon.

21st. First Day: I prepar'd to go to meeting this morning but could not get a suitable conveience being fearful of going with [JS.]s Mare—our little one better to day—Ben. Wilson and HSD. din'd with us. they and Jo Waln drank Coffee here—we took a walk this evening to S Emlens. came home by Moonlight.

22 Molly Drinker went home this morning with John Skyrin, she has been here 7 or 8 weeks, two since my arrival.—HD. came up this evening himself Nancy and [I]. took a walk this evening to S Emlens, a delightful full-moon light night, stop'd at Lebarts and bought a bottle Oyl, to make oyl of St. Johnsworte,[12] this being the proper time[13] to make it.

23 HD. left us between 5 and 6 this morning Huldah Mott and Betsy Emlen here before dinner—no other company to day—Nancy and self, Sam with little Elizabeth took a walk this evening.

24 John and Hannah Pemberton here this morning—our little Elizath.

12. Saint-John's-wort (*Hypericum*) was long considered a remedy in the treatment of bruises and wounds. Its preparation included stamping the leaves, flowers, and seeds and placing the pulp in a glass with olive oil. The mixture was removed to the hot sun for several weeks before being strained, renewed with fresh ingredients, and sunned again. The resulting oil took on a bloodlike color, which according to Paracelsus's theory was a sign that the plant was efficacious in closing wounds (Millspaugh, *Medicinal Plants,* 114; Gifford, "Botanic Remedies," 265, 267).

13. The words "of year" crossed out.

disordred in her bowels—the girls busy ironing. Nancy, myself, Sam Sprigs and Elizath. spent this afternoon at S Emlens—John Skyrin and Molly Drinker came up while we were there the child had a very bad fit of crying our dear William is return'd from Downing-town rather better than when he left home, Sally and her dear little ones in health.

25 John Skyrin and M Drinker went early to Town—Billy came up between 9 and 10—Hannah Pemberton call'd, I took a long ride with her, stop'd at their present dweling—call'd after 11 for S Emlen who was to have dinn'd with us, as her Sister and Daughter are gone to town, but she was too unwell—Nancy myself and William din'd togeather, she left us about 6 o'clock,—AS and ED—took a walk—HD. came up this evening with Huldah Mott and E Emlen—inform'd us of the death and burial of William Moore, read a letter from S Stapler to HD—she is deranged. the weather very fine.

26. HD. went to Town this morning with Tommy Morgan, I paid visit to Betty Flew, an old 'loan woman near Hessers, who took me into her Garden, and amused me with as much of her History as I had time to hear.—Hannah Yerkas, Jacob Tomkins and wife and Child—Sally and Betsy Emlen and H Mott, drank tea with us—Nancy took a short ride with Huldah and Betsy towards evening—G. Hesser who had been to town with his wife, were just return'd, he took S Emlen home in his Chaise she being very unwel—their Carriage returnd soon after—this has been a very pleasant summer day.

27 took a walk this morning with Nancy to S Emlens, and to the Shoemakers, bespoak a pair Shoes—din'd by ourselves, J Skyrin came up this evening, Sam also, who went to town this morning—rain this evening.

28 First day—Jacob Downing William and Molly Drinker came up this morning We all went to meeting, left the little one to the care of Hope Sharp—B Emlen and Sammy here this afternoon, Billy and Jacob left us at 6 o'clock, Molly stays to night—John Perott call'd—silent meeting this morning 'tis long since I was there.

29 John Skyrin and Molly Drinker left us this morning—Sally Wharton, M Sandwith, W Drinker, came up in the waggon. Jo. Gibbs drove them—rain came on in the afternoon which oblig'd them to stay all night, Billy lodg'd in the front parlor by himself. SW. with me in the Trundle bed, Sister with Nancy, little Elizath. in her cribb, all in the back room we had rather a restless night, the Child fretful, the flies very troublesome.

30. SW. MS. and WD. left us about 9 o'clock this morning—Polly Perott and Christopher Marshal junr. here this morning—Nancy and myself took a walk to a Frog-pond this Afternoon, Betsy Emlen here in the evening.

31 Solas tout le jour, John Skyrin and Molly Drinker came up this evening rain with them. Nancy busy this day painting &c.

Augt. 1. John, Nancy, Hope and Child went to Town this morning—Molly stays with me here—Anna Wells came this morning to inform that Nancy Morgan was unwell and likely to M s——y —Betsy Emlen din'd with us we took a walk before dinner to frog-pond, towards evening took another to Wevers—HD. came up this evening, very cool.

2. HD. left us this morning after breakfast, Molly went with Anna Wilson and Betsy Emlen to Chesnut Hill—weather cool and fine—when they return'd I borrow'd the carriage to visit A Morgan, mett Anne Wells coming for me, Nancy Morn. continues poorly—I came home before one o'clock took a walk by myself to the frog-pond which is not a quarter mile from the house—before dinner, John and Hannah Pemberton, Sally Emlen Huldah Mott, Betsy Emlen and Anne Wilson here this Afternoon at Tea,—Nancy &c not return'd, so that MD. and self spend this night by ourselves—MD. dabling in Water.

3. Molly troubled with tooth-ach and pain in face, in consequence of last nights dabling—I took a long walk by myself, before dinner, no visiters this day—Nancy, Hope and Child, my dear Willm. with them came up this evening in Waggon, John Skyrin came after them in the Chaise.

4 First-Day: Nancy and myself went this morning to meeting in the Chaise, Sam drove, John Skyrin and M Drinker troubled with the tooth-ach—John Pemberton and E Howel appear'd in meeting—Sammy and Betsy Fisher din'd with us—and spent the Afternoon, John and Hannah Pemberton, Jerry Warder —— St. John, and Jerrys little son, here this Afternoon, Billy, Molly and self, took a walk towards evening to S Emlens—Samuel Lewis departed this life yesterday morning after two hours sickness.

5 John Skyrin and Wm. Drinker went to town this morning in the Chaise, Molly went with Anna Wilson in S Emlens Carriage—AS. and ED. drank tea at S Emlen's—no body up this night.

6 Nancy went riding this Afternoon with S Emlen &c—HSD. came up this Evening he stays here all night—fine weather.

7—HSD. went to town this morning. Wm. and Mary came up in the Chaise—E Emlen and H Mott here in the forenoon, HD. and John Skyrin came in the Afternoon in the waggon, Jo drove Billy and Molly home, HD. and JS. stays all night—John and Nancy took their little one riding—HD. and self took a long walk came back to Tea—weather fine.

8. HD. JS. left us this morning no body here this day—Nancy and self went towards evening to S Emlens, mett Betsy coming to our house, the wind easterly, a storm this evening.

9. No body hear to day, except J and H Pemberton stop'd, and Betsy Emlen in the evening—Nancy and self took a walk. cloudy most of the day. rain in the Afternoon, clear in the evening.

10 William and Mary, came up this Morning John and Hannah Pemberton paid us a morning visit—Saml. and Molly Smith spent the Afternoon with us, Nancy and child and Molly, went riding with Sally Emlen &c—HD. and JS. came up this evening—we went after night to S Emlens; Molly stays there all night—Wm. Shipley died this week.

11 First day: Billy went home last night—he return'd this morning with his brother in the waggon—Billy was more than usualy unwell last week, was let blood on fourth day last by order of Docr. Kuhn, he is better at present. HD. HSD. JS. MD. and Betsy Emlen gone this morning to meeting. Nancy, William and self, stays at home, no body din'd with us but 7 of ourselves—Wm. Wilson and Sammy Emlen call'd after dinner, towards evening we took a walk—HD. and his Sons, left us towards evening JS. and MD. stays. Nancy Morgan and Anna Wells drank tea with us—H Mott and E Emlen came, JS. and Molly went home with them—new moon shines—cool evening and morning.

12 sans Company—took a walk towards evening to S Emlens—the family here were invited to the burial of Antoy. Williams—under my Eye swell'd this Afternoon and is a little inflam'd—moon light.

13 no body here this day save H Mott and Betsy Emlen who calld for Nancy to ride with them, she returnd after sun set, I took a little walk during their absence—my Eye bad all day cover'd with an Handkerchief, so that I could not work or read, but little—I fear Billy was injur'd by the walk we took last first day Afternoon, it rain'd while we were out, the Sun broke out very hott afterwards, and we came home heated by walking fast &c—'twas that hurt my Eye, I beleive—warm this day.

14 little to be done by me, as my Eye has been cover'd all day 'tho better—cloudy most of this day—I have been more uneasy than any day since I have been here, not having heard from home since first day last—was much releiv'd this even'g by the arrival of JS. and HSD. who reported all were as well as usual at home—they came in a heavy shower in the chaise—Sam with 'em it was some time before they were chang'd and dry, fitt to set down to a good cup of Coffee—we spent the evening as agreeable as could be.

15th: JS. and HSD. left us after breakfast, cloudy continu'd so all Day—no body here but H. Mott and Betsy Emlen who paid us a short visit towards evening.

16 din'd alone, that is AS. and ED—John and Hannah Pemberton here this Afternoon—towards evening H Mott and E Emlen came, HD. and Molly came this evening we all went home with HM and EE—John Gillenham was bury'd on second day last—'tis a sickly time now in philada. and there has been an unusual number of funerals lately here.

17 HD. and MD. left us at 6 this Morning no Company, morning noor or night no body from Town—I took a walk with Nancys Maid Betsy Hardy after Sun Set, to the Frog-pond, Hope Sharp complaining.

18 First day, I prepared this morning to go to meeting if an oppertunity offer'd, JS. and WD. came after 10, in the Chaise, Billy has been disordr'd several days in his Bowels, I did not leave him, no Company this day—a very heavy Shower this Afternoon with some thunder, Jacob Downing left Philada. last evening to attend the funeral of George Thomas brother of Richard Thomas who died of a lax and vomitting—the rain prevented us from going abroad this evening John and William stays with us to night.

19 JS. and WD. left us after breakfast, William had a good night and seems better—I went this Afternoon to S Emlens, Nancy and her Daughter went riding with Huldah and Betsy they came to SEs we drank Tea there, while there HSD. came up in Chaise he stopd there sent the Mare and Chaise to Hessers by Sam—We came home after Night, rain sprinkling—Henry stays with us to night, 'tis seldom any one of the Family comes to stay a night with us, but[14] they bring an account of the death of one or more of our Citeicnes, Henry informs of the death of Richard Blackham and Peter Aston son of Peter Aston.

20 HSD. left us this morning after an early breakfast—he came into our Room at 4 this morning a pain in the pitt of his Stomach, was sick in the evening Nancy gave him mint-water—he was better when he went away.—Nancy & self took walk this morning call'd at Betty Flew's, and at the Widdow Rigers, a poor woman with three Children, who lost her Husband a week or 10 days ago. we then went to S Emlens, came back by 10 o'clock—Neighr. Waln and Anne Wells paid us visit this morning says 'tis very sickly in Philada. H Mott and B. Emlen here before dinner—Nancy and self took a walk to the Meadow just before sun set—I dont know that I ever saw a more beautiful Evening, the House we are at lays open in front to the Westward, the

14. The word "that" crossed out.

Sun set without an interweneing cloud, the Sky remain'd red for near an hour afterwards, the full Moon riseing towards the back of the house, added Charmes to the scene, the weather very temperate. I did little else for near an hour, but walk up and down the Entry making frequent stops at the front door to see if one of our family were coming up, but in that am dissapointed; were all well, that I call mine, I think I should feel this evening, a little as formerly.

21. H Mott an E Emlen here this fore-noon—Willm. and Mary came before dinner—8 or 10 persons bury'd out of water-street, between Race and Arch Streets, many sick in our Neighbourhood, and in the City generaly—HD. unwel of a Cold, HSD. better—EE. spent the Afternoon. WD—took a ride towards Chestnut-Hill—we took a short walk—JS. came up this evening—the young people very chearful to night metamorphosing. Molly went home this evening with EE lodg'd there, we had 2 beds in the front parlor, William lodg'd in one myself in the other—fine evening.

22. Billy and Molly went to Chesnut Hill after breakfast—JS. Nancy and the Child to M Periotts. JS. from thence to Philada. Wm. when he return'd from the Hill, went for his Sister and the Child to Perotts—they came back before dinner.—this Afternoon we were agreeable surpris'd by the Arrival of HD. MS. and HSD—so that we have had all our family here to day—they stay'd but a little time with us; Wm. and Mary went home with them—so that Ann and myself are again left Solas. My husband and Henry both better than they were, Jacob Downing unwell at our House—the weather seems fine, 'tho the wind is Easterly—many sick in Town.

23 the wind shifted to South-west—alone all day—in the Evening HD. and WD. came up—I have been unwell all day—Betsy and Hope have also been unwel but by proper applications are better. My husband informs of the Death of Ruban Hains Senr. who died this morning rather suddenly—many have gone off within these few days—Benn Wilson continues very low, is again blister'd—My husband and Son William have something of the influensia, which great numbers have at present in Town and Country—and a fever prevails in the City, perticularly in water-street, between race and arch streets of the malignant kind, numbers have died of it, some say it was occasion'd by damag'd Coffee, and fish, which was stor'd[15] at Wm. Smith, others say it was imported in a Vessel from Cape-Francoies which lay at our warfe, or at the warfe back of our Store; Docr. Hutchinson was ordred by the Governor or employd to enquire into the report, he found as 'tis said upwards of 70 persons

15. The word "by" crossed out.

sick in that square, of different disorders; several of this putried[16] or billous fever,—some are ill in water street between arch and market streets, and some in race street—'tis realy an alarming and sereous time—HSD. has brought the Books up to the house, that he may be as little a possiable in the lower street. Docr. Kuhn tends Jacob Downing at our house, he caught cold returning from Downing-Town, siting at a door in the Air, after being heated—he left Sally unwel of a cough and pain at her breast, she caught cold going to George Thomass funeral—Billy very feverish and a little chiley this evening HD. poorly gave them wine-whey at going to bed—myself better this evening.

24th. HD. had a midling-night, Billy a bad one, he slep'd none 'till after 5 o'clock, had a high fever, sweat towards morning; they made but light breakfasts then left us, they would have stay'd with us all day, but 'twas thought best for William to see the Doctor no body here untill evening when HD. and JS. came up, it had rain'd here some time when they came, JS was wett, found it nesessary to change his cloaths—William seem'd better when they left home Jacob not worse—an Easterly storm came on this evening.

25. First-day: Wind and rain all night & all this day, so much that HD. went not to meeting, he is getting better of a heavy cold—this Storm may, if it please kind providence so to order, abate the alarming fever now prevalent—HD. and JS. spent this day with us, wind and rain all day and all this evening we spent our time in front parlor.

26. Easterly wind with rain all night; no rain this morning 'tho the wind is in the same quarter—HD. and JS. left us after breakfast, we have not heard from home since seventh day, when John Lambsback was taken ill and left the store,—Jo Gibbs came up by Sisters orders to desire HD. and JS not to return as the weather was dull, and Jacob and William better; Jo mett his master and JS. near the City, he brought us 4 Ducks &c. informs that John Lamsback is also better. Betsy Emlen came and spent this afternoon with us—We have been rendred very uneasy this evening by hearsays from the City, of a great number of funerals that have been seen this day there, hope and believe that the number is greatly exaggerat'd wind at east and cloudy.

27 John Skyrin and Molly Drinker came up this morning 'tho the accounts

16. Putrid fever, associated with pestilence, plague, and highly infectious epidemics, was thought to occur in large towns and cities, particularly in the poorer sections, because of a lack of cleanliness. General symptoms included sudden weakness, nausea, sometimes vomiting of bile, labored breathing, and stomach pains. Specific symptoms of putrid fever were a low pulse, dejected state of mind, dissolved state of blood, the presence of purple spots known as *petechiae,* and the putrid smell of excrement. In this instance, the putrid fever was later identified as yellow fever (Buchan, *Domestic Medicine* [1793], 132–39).

we hear'd last were not true, yet there is great cause of serious alarm, the yallow-Fever spreads in the City, many are taken of with it and many with other disorders—Jacob Downing is better, my dear Billy very poorly, I am much distress'd that any of our family continues in town; Dicky Downing has gone home, without consulting his Uncle, he was much frighted—and will I fear occasion great uneasiness to my poor Sally, who continues with her little Girles at Downing-Town—Wm. Burket and his Son, Lamagers wife Wm. Starmen, Ingle at the ferry, 3 or 4 out of one house in water street, Sally Mifflin in walnut Street, and one Molly Mifflin, Hodges Maid, and the Servant Maids of many others, &c &c—have gone of within these few days. they have burnd Tar in the Streets and taken many other precautions,[17] many families have left the City—William and Henry came up this evening, Billy proposes to stay with us, Henry goes to Town tommorrow, intending to go with J Downing to the Valley.—A carriage stop'd at Hessers door to day enquiring for lodgings. they could get none here, went further up the road. John and Polly Perott here this evening.

28. HSD. left us at about 6 this morning I gave him a small spoonfull of Duffys Ellixr and Vinager in a spunge, and a sprig of wormwood[18]—JS. went after breakfast, useing the same precautions—this has been a serious thoughtful day to us. We have some reason to hope that HD. and Sister will leave home & come up to us, if they do not I must go to Town, as HD. does not seem quite free to do so—This Afternoon our Carriage, drove by a white man, a stranger, came up, with Mattrasses &c Blankets &c—and Sally Brant behind,—poor black Joseph gone away sick to some Negro House, where they have promis'd to take care of him, and Dr. Foulk is desir'd to attend him—we have hopes it is not the contagous fever that he has; Sister and HD. came up in the evening Docrs. Kuhn and Rush both advis'd it—as there is a man next door but one to us, who Docr. Kuhn says will quickly die of this terriable disorder—Caty Prusia over against us is very ill, and a man at the Shoemakers next door to Neigr. Waln's, some sick in our ally, we know not what ails them—Isaac Wharton and family are mov'd out of Town. P. Hartshorns family and Neigr. Waln are also out, the inhabitance are leaving the City in great numbers, poor John Lamsback died yesterday.

29. HD. and William went out this Afternoon in the Chaise, JS. on Horse-

17. Tar was thought to prevent yellow fever. Many Philadelphians carried tarred ropes on their persons in an attempt to ward off the disease or lit bonfires in front of their houses to purify the air during the epidemic (Powell, *Bring Out Your Dead,* 22–24).

18. Daffy's Elixir, a popular patent medicine concocted around 1650 by a British clergyman, was a tincture of senna leaves, jalap root, coriander seeds, and alcohol. It was a favorite tonic during the yellow fever epidemic, but was more commonly used to relieve colic and flatulence. Wormwood, also a tonic, was thought useful in preventing yellow fever as well (W. Lewis, *New Dispensatory,* 318; Powell, *Bring Out Your Dead,* 51, 23; *OED,* s.v. "wormwood").

back, they went to procure Cat-Fish and to take a ride, they calld at J Salters on J and H Pemberton and at S Emlen, Sammy Emlen is come up—the Malencholy accounts of this day are, that the disorder spread in the City—that John Morgan who married Smiths daughter Woodrope Sims, one Lumbart, and Vanuxems daughter, one of the name of Duncan and many whose names we did not hear, have dyed since yesterday—Caty Wistar here this evening she left the City this morning lodges at McClanagans—the weather is warm, wind at SW.

30. HD. went this fore-noon to J Pembertons Noke brought him a letter from J Drinker in Answer to one he wrote yesterday, informing of the Death of Peter Tomson Senr. who dy'd 'tis said in some degree of the gout, several others have die'd, whose names we have not heard; Thos. Edmundson, who was Clark to Jacob Downing was left to sleep in our house, he yesterday gave the key to J Drinker, and is gone into the Country—our House is left, fill'd with valuables, no body to take care of it—the Grapevines hanging in clusters, and some of the fruit Trees loaded—but those are matters of little consequence—JD. mett our Jo. in the Street, he is better, has had the pleurisy, was let blood, and thereby releived—HD hier'd a Man to day to take care of our Horses, we have 4 here the sorril Horse gone with JD. and HSD. to Downings town—it must be very very hott in the City this day—Jerry Warder and his family went up the road this afternoon in a light waggon, another with blankets &c with them—to a place of his 6 or 7 miles further up—Nancy and Billy took a ride this afternoon, JS also, on horse-back—after their return, HD. and Sister rode down town, the accounts they geatherd were more favourable then usual, that 'twas thought fewer had dyd this day than heretofore—Hope Sharp who tended Nancys Child, left us this morning, she has a brother and Sister both young in the City, on whose account she has been uneasy, and is gone to take them home to Haddonfield—Molly Drinker lodg'd at S Emlens.

31. The accounts this day from the City are many and various—some 'tis said die of fear, one or more have died in the Street or on the rode, those reports are not arsertain'd, J. and H. Pemberton were here this forenoon, HD. and ED. went in the Chaise to J Pemberton this Afternoon drank tea there—John and Mary De Bram there—several families have movd up to Germantown—HD. received a Letter from JD. informing of the death of several persons, with whom we are not acquainted—some naughty person or persons have broke into our yard, and stole the grapes & magnumbonums,[19] and broke the limbs off that beautiful tree—if they do not get into the house we will forgive them—I call'd on our return home at S Emlens, HD. drove home, Sammy

19. The magnum bonum is a large yellow cooking plum (*OED*).

Emlen walk'd home with me, JS. went to Philada. this morning S Emlen returnd with him this evening the weather continues very warm.

Sepr. 1. First day HD. MS. in one Chaise, JS. and M.D. in another, went to meeting this morning HD. hired a man nam'd Jacob—to take care of the Horses and drive the Carriage, the latter he attempted this morning but could not make out, he could not manage the Horses, was under the necessity of leaving them, and going otherwise—Nancy, William and self, stay'd at home—we have not heard from Town this morning—no body din'd with us.—HD. and AS. WD and MS. went this Afternoon to Lewsleys, E Emlen spent the Afternoon with us—she Molly and myself took a short walk, our foulk return'd to Tea—a large number of Philadelphians at Germantown meeting this morning—we have heard of the death of 3 or 4 in our neighbourhood, and many others in other parts of the City. A man was found dead a day or 2 ago on the ridge-road, who lay there a day or two unbury'd—a Frigate lays in our River opposite the sweeds-Church, with many ill on board—the weather continues warm.

2d. HD. and William went down town this morning—JS. left us about 10 or 11 o'clock, on horseback, to take a ride up the Country, he talk'd of going to Reding or to Downings, to stay 2 or 3 days, 'tis my beliefe he will return tommorrow—Neighr. Waln and Nancy Morgan came to visit us this forenoon RW. stays with her Son Robt. they inform'd us of the death of our poor Neighbors Caty Prusia and her Husband, Christian the biscuit baker, both nearly opposite our house, Christopher the Barber near the corner, and a fringemaker, on this side him—two in water street, near RWs—Hetty Mifflin another of S Lewiss Neices—Josey Stansbery an apprentice of Richd. Wellss[20] HD and WD, went after dinner down town again, soon after they were gone, our Son HSD, come to see us from Downsings town, brings the agreeable intilegence, that Jacob, Sally and the dear little girles are well, and all the families, Dickey Downing excepted who he says is very ill of a billious vomitting, the Doctor who tends him or the family are under no apprehension of its being any thing infectious; had they [heard] as much of the present greivous disorder as we have, and recollected that it was but 8 days from the time that he left water Street 'till he was taken ill, they would be very much alarm'd, as I rearly am on their account A Negro man came here this fore-noon of the name of Richd. Hill, at whose house our Joseph is, he brought a letter from E. Robersen, says Jo is very ill, of the pleurisy and has a bad cough, has been blooded 3 times. HD. wrote by him to JD—[21] gave directions concerning him &c.—received Letter this evening from JD. he says Jo is better, and informs of the death of a Son of Capt. Mason, and others—, we

20. Word crossed out.
21. The words "by him" crossed out.

have heard this day of the death of a poor intemperate woman of the name of Clarey, who sold Oysters last winter in a Seller in front street a little below Elfriths Alley—she was taken out of her sences and went out of town, was found dead on the rode—John Perott here this evening—Nancy and her dear little Babe both unwell of a cold and some fever—Sally Emlen &c call'd for Molly to take a ride with them she return'd before dark, the wind has chang'd to NW, the weather cooler.

3 HSD. left us this morning for Buck County, HD. and WD. took a long ride, Billy had a fine nap after it—we have heard this day of five persons who died in one house in Chestnut street, at the corner of an alley that goes into Carters alley, The phicisians have giving it as their opinion that the disorder spreads in the City, and the Assembly who have lately mett, talk of breaking up—the square opposite us in Water-street, appears to be depopalated by deaths and flight—a vessel in the River below, coming up with 2 or 3 hundred passengers from Irland, an infectious fever on board, orders sent them by the Governour not to come up tis said that one or more of the passingers have venturd nevertheless—A Letter from JD. says Jo is better—WD. and myself took a mile walk before sunset, as we were returning a man at a Door stopt us, to ask if we had heard the bad news that several hundred french soldiers Arm'd were coming to Philada. from New York—and that 5 Negros were taken up for poisoning the pumps, those are flying reports, and most likely to be false—Huldah Mott and Betsy Emlen here this Afternoon, Nancy and Molly went home with them, and as far as John perotts along walk.

4 We were up last night with Nancy 'till after one this morning, she was very ill, of a vomitting and neverous head-ach—is much better to day. Hannah Pemberton and Sally Zane here this morning HD. and Wm. took a walk—Nancy and Molly gone this afternoon to ride with Emlens they have the Child with them, and stay too late, A Man here this afternoon informs of the death of one Stevens in Chestnut Street who bury'd 5 of his family mention'd yesterday, he was a Sadler, it is said that many are bury'd after night, and taken in carts to their graves—tis thought by some that the present tremendeous disorder is a degree of the pestelance, may we be humble, and thankful for favours received—We were told a Sad Story indeed, to day, if it be true, it was repeated by different persons and every thing considred it seems not unlikely, of a young woman who had nurs'd one or more in water street, who dy'd of the disease, she being unwel, the Neighbours advis'd her to go somewhere else as none of them chose to take her in, she went out somewhere, I did not hear in what part of the Town it was, and lay down ill at a door, a majastrate in the ward, had her sent in a cart to the Hospital, where she was refused admitance, and was near that place found dead in the cart next morning.

5 Our little Elizabeth Skyrin has been lately poorly, we last night discover'd her first tooth, WD. and MS. gone this morning to Saml. Fishers, he with his family are some where on the old York-road, they came back before dinner, James Fisher came there from the City, while MS and WD. was there, said his Brother Sam was unwell, we have since heard that he and many others were taken ill—I took a walk with HD. to the meadow to see 'em bind flax—Molly Drinker spent this day at S Emlen, Ellstone and Sally Perott, Jose Sansom and Polly Perott paid us a visit this Afternoon, did not stay tea—HD. ED. WD. and AS. took a walk the mile round as I call it—the weather warm but not hot, wind S.W. [J]S. nor HSD. yet return'd.

6 HD. WD. took a ride down town, mett B Oliver driving a family out, he told them that two of Steels Children in our Alley are dead, and several sick in the Ally—'tis said that the Schools are all broke up,[22]—HD. MS. MD. gone to meeting this morning—Anna Wells paid us a morning visit,—HSD. came before dinner from Bucks County—a fuller meeting this morning then some times on a sixth day—J. Pemberton and T Scattergood, here this Afternoon, we had a meeting in the front parlor Tommy had something to say, JP. silent—Caleb Hopkinson T Scattergoods brother in Law, died this morning of this raging fever, Docr. Hutchinson is also gone, 'tis said he got the disorder by putting a young woman in her Coffin who dy'd at his house, not being able readly to procure any one to do that office—the ringing of Bells for the dead is forbid for several days past.—John Cannon, one of the counsel drank tea with us, as he had business with my husband, he took this in his way home, as the Counsel and Assembly have broke up, on account of this very affecting Dispensation,[23] the officies are almost all shut up—and little business done,—the doors of the Houses where the infection is, are ordrr'd to be mark'd, to prevent any but those that are absolutely necessary from entering—such is the Melancholy and distresing state of our poor City.

7. No body has been hear to day, but HM and Betsy Emlen who drank tea[24] with us, Henry and Molly went with them this evening over to Hessers to see Molly Wharton, who has return'd here with her Baby 4 weeks old—to be more out of the way of the fever—and her mother who assisted to Nurse Hetty Mifflin is gone to King-woods—she inform'd MD—that about a week past a little son of Tommy Wister who was at his Grand-fathers Richd. Walns, was unfortunately drown'd in the Mill-pond—HSD. took a walk this evening to J. Perotts, and heard there of the Death of one William Hays, who liv'd near John Skyrins in Water-Street, and of the death of John Hockley a young man apprentice to Jamey and Sammy Fisher.

22. The words "that many [are carried] to their graves in carts after night" crossed out.
23. The Pennsylvania House of Representatives adjourned on Sept. 4 (*Dunlap's American Daily Advertiser*, Sept. 4, 1793).
24. The word "here" crossed out.

8 First Day: HD. and MS. in our Chaise Nancy and Molly with E Emlen in their Carriage went to meeting, Nancy who has been unwell for many days past, was taken ill in meeting, she and Molly came out. Betsy Emlen follow'd them, they came togeather in the Carriage, Nancy was so ill before they got home, as to loose her sight and was near fainting. George Hesser brought her into the house in his Arms, We laid her on the Bed, gave her Sal: Volitile[25] and rub'd her limbs, she broak out with the Netle rash,[26] was very sick, and her head Ach'd badly—continues ill for an hour or 2 then was favour'd to get better, the disorder work'd off.—Joseph and John Saltar and little George Saltar came from Magnolia, they din'd with us—John Skyrin return'd after dinner, he has been to Reding and to Downsing town &c—brings us the agreeable intelligence that Sally and her Children &c are well. Dickey Downing recover'd—HD received Letters and Newspapers from the City—A fier broke out this Morning at 4 o'clock on the East side of Second Street, near Chestnut street and burnt several back buildings &c, Dobson the Bookseller has lost to considerable value—2 or three[27] persons lost their lives[28] at the fire, by a wall falling on them.—Wm. Whiteside, tea merchant die'd this morning at a place that he had taken for his family near the Germantown road, he came out of the City ill,—'tis remarkable [that] not one Negro has yet taken the infection. they[29] have offered to as Nurses to the sick.[30]—Ephrim Sandford

25. Sal volatil was the popular name for aromatic spirit of ammonia, a cordial that contained cloves, musk, salt of tartar, spirit of wine, and several other ingredients. It entered European pharmaceutical practice around 1650 (C. J. S. Thompson, *The Mystery and Art of the Apothecary* [London: John Lane, The Bodley Head, 1929], 244–45).

26. Nettle rash, also known as urticaria, is today called hives (Gould, *Dictionary of Medicine*, 1582).

27. The word "Men" crossed out.

28. The word "assisting" crossed out.

29. The words "are appointed" crossed out.

30. ED apparently saw the announcement placed by Mayor Matthew Clarkson in newspapers on Sept. 7 that the African Society would furnish nurses to the sick. John Lining, a Charleston physician, had first noted in the 1750s that blacks did not seem to contract yellow fever. In Philadelphia the leading exponent of this view, widespread throughout the Americas, was Benjamin Rush, who was proved wrong, however, when blacks in that city started contracting and dying of the disease. Figures from the black community indicate a mortality rate of 13 percent during the 1793 epidemic, not drastically different from the 18 percent mortality rate for the white population unable to leave the city. Still, the experience of some southern U.S. cities in the nineteenth century lends support to a theory of a greater tolerance of yellow fever among blacks. In the Memphis epidemic of 1878, for instance, over two-thirds of the whites who remained in the city died, while the black mortality rate was less than 7 percent. Historians and epidemiologists have advanced various explanations, none conclusive, ranging from genetic predisposition to early childhood exposure among African-born blacks (C. K. Drinker, *Not So Long Ago*, 119; *Federal Gazette* and *Dunlap's American Daily Advertiser*, Sept. 7, 1793; Powell, *Bring Out Your Dead*, 95–100, 254; Carey, *Short Account*, 62–63; Nash, *Forging Freedom*, 121–24; Richard Taylor, "Epidemiology," in *Yellow Fever*, ed. George K. Strode [New York: McGraw-Hill, 1951], 427–538; Todd L. Savitt, *Medicine and Slavery* [Urbana: University of Illinois Press, 1978], 240–46; John H. Ellis, "Disease and the Destiny of a City: The 1878 Yellow Fever Epidemic in Memphis," *The West Tennessee Historical Society Papers* 28 (1974): 87; Kenneth F. Kiple and Virginia Himmelsteib King, *Another Dimension to the Black Diaspora: Diet, Disease, and Racism* [Cambridge: Cambridge University Press,

drank tea with us, he came from G Roberts Point no point—HSD. went this afternoon to Parleville to E Perots, to meet his Uncle John there, brought a Letter to his father—Docr. John Morris dead—and several others who we dont know.

9 Ephraim Sandford here this morning several Carriages stop'd to talk with HD &c—were inform'd of the Death of Josiah Elfrith, who was buried as many others are in 2 or 3 hours after his departure—HD. din'd at G Roberts's Point. WD. din'd at J Pembertons—None of our family have been to the City for upwards of a week past: I went this fore-noon with J and H Pemberton beyond the 10 M. Stone, we were inform'd by a passenger, of the death of a Son of Saml. Garrigus, Said that the disorder increases—J. and H. Pemberton here this Afternoon, told us of the Death of Willm. Waring, & Peter Beck the Shoemaker, and more taken down the last 24 hours then has yet been known. John Skyrin was abroad this Afternoon and brought word home of the Death of[31] Mathew Parker, and Nancy Warners Maid Servant.—JS. went this evening to S Emlens for MD. who has been there this Afternoon, she concluded to stay there all Night, as they had heard of a Man who came from the City, who lay ill in a field near the 8 Mile stone, that the Overseers would not go near him—We have also heard this account but 'tis not known whether the poor Man is sick or in liquor; such are the fears of the people—weather warm.

10 HSD. left us this morning after breakfast for Downings-town—H Mott and EE here this morning, Josiah Lusbey who is with Jacob Baker at one Weavers, at a little distance from us, with their families, was here this fore-noon, inform'd us that he was in the City yesterday, that it was thought on first day last from 50 to 100 had die'd, the disorder having greatly increas'd, that in arch street between front and second, many had dy'd, and many were ill—[32]the widdow Budd John Coburns daughter are dead Tommy Morriss Son Anthony thought to be near his end, one Abrahams a Schoolmaster, and one Johnson a printer, and great numbers taken down—we have also heard to day that the dead are put in their Coffins just as they die without changing their cloths or laying out, are buried in an hour or two after their disease—that way is made to enter freinds burying-ground with the Herse to the grave; that graves are dug before they are spoke for, to be ready—the Inhabitants leaving the City in abundance—Nancy and Molly went this afternoon to ride with EE—Epm. Sanford here this evening HD. paid him a sum of money—William and myself took a walk this afternoon to S Emlens—wind Easterly—The sick

---

1981], 31; Kenneth F. Kiple and Virginia H. Kiple, "Black Yellow Fever Immunities, Innate and Acquired, as Revealed in the American South," *Social Science History* 1 (1977):419–36).

31. The words "Benjn. Thaw Taylor" crossed out, but underneath is written, "he is since dead."

32. The name "Capt. John Burrow" crossed out.

man who lay down in the field[33] yesterday continu'd there all night, the overseers this morning went to take him away; he arose and walk'd with them.

11 William took a ride on Horse back, wind Easterly, Joshua Whitney came from the City this morning, he had business with HD—says he saw two burials go into friends burying ground at 7 o'clock, and many graves dug—The poor sick man that has lain two nights in the fields, was found this morning by the 7 mile stone vomitting; he had now got among the Inhabitants; J Perot and others rais'd 4 Dollars, for which sum a man took him away in a Cart—Neighr. Waln, Gidion—and Anna Wells, here, informs of the Death of Antony Morris, and the [Mill]-stone maker & two of his Sons, in our Neighbourhood; our Jo. Gibbs came up this fore-noon, looks very pale and weak, we would have been as well pleas'd if he had gone else where, but he wanted to be with us. John and Nancy took a ride before dinner—George Hesser appears unwilling that Jo should stay in his house, as he came out of the City and has been sick, HD. sent him back with a letter to J Drinker, he came upon foot, he has gone back on one of our Horses, to return tomorrow with some Bed cloaths for us—he says that a Man and his Wife named Eweing that liv'd in our Alley, were taken to the Hospital at Bush-Hill, and died there; Govenr. Hambletons House at Bush-Hill, has lately been us'd as an Hospital for those infected by the present prevailing fever.—Jacob Wendolph, the man HD hir'd to take care of the Horses, was thrown by one of them, he pretended to be a good Horsman, but we have reason to believe he is far otherwise—he either was or appear'd to be badly hurt, and left us.—Billy and Molly went this Afternoon to S Emlens, Molly stays there all night.—Daniel and Polly Dupee call'd this Afternoon they have been in Germantown some time, were looking up the road for a residence for some of their friends who wish to leave the City. they told us of a woman who lay very ill of the putrid fever, about a mile higher up, she had been lately in Philada. in a family where the disorder was, and came home[34] 'tis probable to die.

12 we have an account this morning that the poor woman is dead.—Jo brought a letter &c this morning from City is gone to Trent-town for some time; where his relations are—John Drinker writes that the widdow Davis near him is dead, and we have heard of the death of her Sons wife—we were inform'd 2 or 3 day past that two or three dead bodys were thrown into friends burying ground over the wall.—H Mott and Betsy Emlen here this morning I took a walk with my Son William near a mile—Nancy poorly—things appear'd more favourable yesterday, not so many deaths, or so many taken ill—Sally Emlen, H Mott, and Betsy Emlen spent the Afternoon with us—Sally Waln here in the evening she stays here with her Sister M Wharton—Wm. went on

33. The words "last night" crossed out.
34. The words "with it" crossed out.

Horse-back to Chesnut-Hill—We have heard this Afternoon of the Death of a young man who died at Pittfields, next but 2 Doors from our House, and of one Richd. Gardner; the weather is cooler now.

13 Wm. rode out this morning—John Keys stop'd at the door, he saw Jacob and Sally Downing the day before yesterday and HSD. yesterday they were all well—HD. MS. MD. gone to Meeting—John and Deby Field and Sally Parish din'd with us—we hear of the Deaths of Benjn. Oldens wife, Libert an Apothacary, Whitealls Wife, Dupont a french Consel and many taken ill—HSD came to us from Downingstown just after dinner, he left all well—Jacob Shriner in second street dead, Joseph Shoemaker son of Jonathan John Reynold clark to Mountgomery,—Mathew Parkers Wife, he dy'd himself last week—Joseph Hopkins, some time last week—HD and WD went down town this Afternoon, I took a walk to S Emlens, MD. stays there to night—Our dear little Elizah. taken this evening with a Vomiting and Lax, was better about 11 o'clock.

14 Nancy and Molly gone this morning to Ct. Hill with HM and EE—HD. and his Son WD. gone in the Chaise down-town—the Sickness in the City by no means abated—Bertier and others dead, 'tis said that W Sansom is near his end, that his Coffin is bespoke and his grave dug, a common thing now, Nancy, William, Molly and self took our usual walk, went very near the spot where the sick man lay two or three days ago—We have heard this evening of the death of Wm. Antony, Son of Capt. Antony, and of one Vincent M Pelosi—fine weather.

15 First Day: HD. HSD. AS. MD went in our Carriage to meeting [JS.] drove—The report of yesterday concerning Wm. Sansom proves to be a mistake, he has been ill, but is better—A Son of Daniel Thomas Miller, was bury'd this morning at Chesnut Hill of this fever, he came lately from the City, several sick in Germantown, but 'tis not certainly known what ails 'em—we have heard this day of the deaths of Parson Murry; the wife of one Pratt, Isaac Barnet joyner, and one William [T]oplif,—John Hampston din'd with us he came to Philada. on sixth day last in a pilot-boat from the Capes, where the Vessel he came in from Liverpool was aground, could not get a lodging and stay'd in the court House, came on seventh day to John Feilds, to whom he is recommended. he brought him this morning to Germantown to meeting, and left him with HD. to get him a lodging, which he has done, at Hessers Tavern over the road a little below us—HD. WD. JS. [A]S. and the little one gone out in the Carriage this Afternoon.—William Zane's Wife dead—one Stine next door to the Buck over the road, not the 8 of a mile from us is to be bury'd this evening.

16 what little we have heard from the City to day, was gloomy and distress-

ing, of the deaths of several that we did not know—one Lewis a french man who has for some time past constantly attended our uptown meeting—JS. AS. WD. MD. went out in the Carriage this Afternoon, inform'd on their return of the death of a prentice lad of Knoxs Mont Mollin,[35]—John Drinker writes of the death of Michel Minier—G Hesser told a sad story, of Robt. Ross Broker that he died in the night of the Yallow fever, no Body with him but his wife who was taken in labour while he was dying, she opend the window and call'd for help, but obtain'd none, in the morning some one went in to see how they fair'd, found the man and his wife both dead, and a new born infant alive, further I heard not.—I took a short walk this evening with Saly. Brant; loaded waggons coming out of the City, a menencholy sight—Last week was the time we had appointed to return home if[36] things had been as usual, as next week is the time of our yearly meeting.

17 HD. JS. and HSD went this fore-noon to J Saltars at Magnolia—grove—did not return untill the evening—Nurse Waters din'd with us—John Hampson here twice—S Emlen, Hul Mott, Sammy Emlen, and Betsy Emlen, here this afternoon, MD. went out with them in their Carriage—WD. and AS. rode out this morning in the Chaise—The grieveous accounts of this day are, that Abby Morris widdow of Dr. John Morris who dy'd a week or 10 days ago, is also gone, Isaac Parrish Son of Isaac, Sammy Morris Son of Saml. Cornalius Barns, A man and wife[37] known to S Emlens, Polly a little Girl who liv'd with R. Jones, are said to be dead of the malignant fever—very cool this evening wind at N.W—and very clear Doctor Kuhn gone to Bethalem, Dr. Rush unwell—Docr. Wister better,—we have heard since night of the death of Polly Wilson, widdow.

18 WD. AS. MD. ED. walk'd this morning to S Emlens—HD. went to J Pembertons intending to dine with them, Isaac Zane and his Daughter Sally come up.—the people moving in crowds from the City—JS. AS. MD. WD. gone out this Afternoon in the Carriage HSD. on Horseback we have heard this fore-noon of the death of Isaac Taylor and wife, and of Henry Shaw, who died some days past,—Sally Emlen, H Mott Sammy and Betsy drank tea with us.

19 Tommy Fisher and Son here this morning HD. JS. AS. MD. and little one gone out this forenoon in the Carriage, WD. on Horse back—Jacob Baker call'd, he says that he has been inform'd, that there was 40 odd burials in the

35. The words "Jacob Shri[n]ers Wife, he died some days past" crossed out.
36. The word "all" crossed out.
37. The words "who live back of" crossed out.

Lutherine burying ground[38] and upwards of 30 in the Potters-field,[39] on third day last, if so, how many must have been in the City!—Joseph Potts and Jos Moore came home with Billy—the latter din'd with us, he is on his return from the Indian treaty.[40]—a small frost last night, cool and pleasant this day—two funerals past by this doore to day, one was Sabastine Miller an Antient-man, a very great company follow'd, the other a Child who died of the Hooping cough—J Pemberton here this Afternoon, he, HD. and Joseph Moore went to Edmund Randolphs, who is at present with his family on the York road—Sammy Emlen here, Molly Drinker out this Afternoon riding with HM. and EE—she went home with them, intends staying there all night—we have heard to day of the death of one Wigton and his wife, a Schoolmas'r in fourth street, of the wife of one Colll. North,[41]—there is a Doctor Warner said to be very ill at present in Germantown of the Yallow fever—otherwise the people hear are generaly healthy—my Spirits have been greatly[42] oppress'd this evening HD. has concluded to send Sam Skyrin to Town tommorrow morning on an arrant—and intends to go himself next day to the select meeting—JP. talks also of going—this is a very fine evening.

20 William Savery and young marshal call'd here before meeting—Wm. just return'd from the treaty—HD. MS. JS. AS. HSD. went to meeting, a large meeting—MD. who I expected was also gone to meeting with EE. came home, they had been much alarm'd at Neighr. Sniders where SE lodges, by one of the overseers calling over the door, "be upon your guard, for the Doctor says that the woman over the way has the Disorder, and that very badly"—SE. &c are so disturb'd that they intend moving further off.—Nancy, Molly and self took a walk this Afternoon, M. Livezey and her son Joseph spent the Afternoon and took tea with us—Dr. Lusbey here this Afternoon says he has heard,

38. The first Lutheran burying ground was located on the northeast corner of Fifth and Cherry streets in Philadelphia. Following the British evacuation of Philadelphia in 1778 the congregation bought another burial ground, a square block between Seventh and Eighth streets and Race and Vine streets. The Lutheran congregation, which worshipped at two churches, St. Michael's and Zion, lost 625 members during the epidemic (Watson, *Annals*, 3:312–13).

39. Philadelphia's potter's field was located at what was then South East Public Square, now known as Washington Square, between Sixth and Eighth and Walnut and Spruce streets. Over a thousand people were buried there during the epidemic (Watson, *Annals*, 1:405–7; Powell, *Bring Out Your Dead*, 275).

40. One of six Quaker observers who attended the conference in July between U.S. commissioners and representatives of the Western Confederation of Indian tribes, held at present-day Sandusky, Ohio. The conference failed to resolve the two governments' differences, and no treaty resulted. Upon Moore's return he stopped in Germantown with Joseph Potts and visited the Drinkers (J. Moore, "Moore's Journal," 632–71, esp. 664; Reginald Horsman, *Expansion and American Indian Policy, 1783–1812* [East Lansing: Michigan State University Press, 1967], 96–98).

41. The words "one of those young women in race street of the name of North who keep't shop" crossed out.

42. The word "affected" crossed out.

that since second day, morning, 390 or upwards have been bury'd and we have this evening been inform'd of the deaths of Docr. John Penington, another Son of Jacob Morgan, a Son of Moses Bartram, Saml. Taylor, Jacob S. Howel,[43] also a Son of Mordica Lewis—HD. is preparing this evening to go to the City J [P.] with him tommorrow morning—Sam, came back from the City this morning in good time—brought a Letter from J Drinker informing of sickness in his family, but not supossed dangerous.

21 HD. left us after breakfast, Sam drove—Sally Emlen with all her family have mov'd from Christian Sniders to White-Marsh—they hir'd a Waggon of Leonard Stoneburner to take their goods &c—'tis said that several persons are ill in Germantown—HD. return'd from town—about 5 o'clock 50 persons at the select meeting, they have adjorn'd to next 3d day. he saw but 2 or 3 burials while there—heard of the death of Polly Pusey who dy'd in the Hospital, and of the Daughter of James Star, and their maid—John and Nancy took a ride, received a Letter from Jacob and Sally, they are mercyfully well—HD. also heard of the deaths of Stephen Maxfeilds daughter and Edward Brookss Wife, in Cabble Lane—poor S Swett, how she must be alarmed, as she lives directly opposite—or nearly so, fine clear weather.

22 First Day: HD. MS. AS. ED. went this morning to meeting—weather warm—J Pemberton appeard in prayer, W Savery preach'd and pray'd. took a walk this evening ED. AS. MD—J. Hamson call'd. Lusby, and J Perot call'd—we have heard of the Deaths of one Shive and his Wife, of one Smith and several of his family, and of Benjn. Poultney, Thos. Lea, and one Glover &c JS. went this Afternoon to Peter Blights, who is out of Town—WD. rode this morning on Horse back upwards of 10 miles, which is further then he has for a long time—James O'mahoney merchant dead.

23 the poor woman opposite to Sniders is dead. nobody but her husband and several little Children with her—the disorder rages in the City.—HD. and JP. gone this morning to Philada. Sam drives the Carriage—Jacob Baker and Josiah Lusby call'd. they say that parson Blair[44] has remov'd his family,[45]—Christopher Kucher is dead above us, about the 11 mile stone, he came from the City some days past; one major More a keeper of a Ly. Stable is dead, one Mayo, an English Merchant also gone. Billy Gardner, our neighbors Son, and Dick Follwell, stop'd at the door this fore-noon. WG says that his Father and family are gone to Christiania Bridge, and have shut up the House, there is scarcely a family in our square but are gone, he says that 7 persons have die'd

43. The words "Paschal Hollandsworth, son of Levy" crossed out.
44. The word "McCl[enagan]" crossed out.
45. The words "and that T Forest is about doing the same—from Germantown into the Jersyes" are crossed out.

in one of the little houses in our Alley.—the widdow of one Stine who died here about a week ago, went after her husbands death to the City where she also died—Robt. Roberts, Betsy Follwells husband and his Neice are said to be dead.[46] JS. din'd abroad, returnd towards evening, tell us of the death of William Tharpe &c—no HD to night, I earnestly wish that the meeting may adjorn to morrow morning.—Our dear little Elizabeth frightned us very much this evening, Molly was giving her something to drink out of a sauser, it either went the wrong way, as it is call'd, or went up her Nose, which appear'd to strangle her, she strugled for a time unable to make any noise, but by shaking she recoverd, soon after laugh'd and play'd as usual—cloudy this evening.

24 we discovered a large blister on the Childs arm when she was asleep, and concluded it was a burn from the Candle or from the snuffers, that occasion'd her to strugle and hold her breath, a fitt of coughing prehaps coming on at the same time, as she is not free from the relics of the hooping cough.—'tis hard to ascertain the real disorders of young Children.—C. Kuchers body was carried by this morning in a Hearse, about 4 o'clock, to be interr'd in the City.—The woman that dy'd opposite Sniders was bury'd yesterday, they say, that nobody would assist, and her husband was under the necessity of putting her in the Coffin and that into the Hearse, then a Man took her to the Grave—Last night about 12 o'clock, we were all awakned by a loud raping at the Door with the brass Knocker, G Hesser and JS. went to the window up stairs, but saw no body.—HD. not return'd, JS. gone out.—the New York stage past this door to day—they are endeavouring to stop the communication between us and N–Y—they are not permitted to cross at Trenton &c.—JS came home to dinner,[47] Willm. and self took a short walk up the road, found HD. at home when we return'd; he lodg'd last night at [I] Zane's,—our Neighbourhood is diserted, and two of our Girls went away to their relations in the Country when HD and Sister came up—Jo Gibbs not return'd. meeting of Ministers and Elders concluded, but not the meeting of business,[48] who have not adjorn'd as I wish'd they would. The two Sons of Caty Mullen an Apprentice lad and maid are dead—Fred. Hailers wife, Robt. Sowerby black Smith, William Young, and Benn. Catherals Son are also dead—Richd. Humphrits also. many ill.

25 Jo Gibbs came this morning from Trenton, he appears to be recovering.—

46. The words "Peter Ozias dead" crossed out.
47. The words "has heard of the death of Jacob Parke" crossed out.
48. Meetings for business, held monthly, could be attended only by members in good standing. A clerk defined the agenda of the meeting and often appointed committees to investigate reports of misbehavior and wrongdoing among Friends. Discussion would continue until a consensus view or "sense of the meeting" emerged. The clerk would then read the "minute" or decision that had been agreed to (Brinton, *Quaker Practice,* 35–39; Barbour and Frost, *Quakers,* 110–11).

HD. gone again to Town—John Pemberton not gone,[49]—Richd. Morris and Anna Wells here this morning they inform us of the deaths of Jacob Catheral son of Isaac, Jabez Fisher son of Miers, Chrisn. Kuchers Son, Andrew Clow, Benjn. Poultneys Widdow, James Gilchrist merchant, Peter Astons widdow, Christian Hahn near our dwelling in front street; William and myself took a walk this fore-noon, A second student of Docr. Rush also dead. J Skyrin gone out this morning—John Thompson here this Afternoon—JS. and HSD. rode out after dinner—they came back to Tea, have been to visit S Emlen at white-marsh,—we hear that Charles Beam Fredk. Hailers Eldest prentice, another of his prentices a little Boy, and a Sister of the latter are dead.[50]—William and myself took another walk this afternoon.

26 The mournful acounts last evening from the City of increasing mortality, affected our Landlord G. Hesser so, as to keep him all night awake, on acc't of HD. being in the City.[51] James Galbrath and a Docr. Linn, said to be dead—JS. mett on the road, Thos. Masters Cooper, with a sick son of his in the Chaise, a young Man, who was very yallow with the disorder, He brought him out of Town, will find it very difficult to get any admittance anywhere in the Country. HD. came after dinner, the meeting concluded—'tho he told us of but one death that we had not heard of, as he was not in the way of hearing much, yet 'tis generaly thought that there is little or no abaitment of the disorder—Isaac Miller dead, many taken down—William and myself took a walk in the Afternoon—the weather pleasant, 'tho very dry and dusty.

27 Joseph Moore here this morning he read parts of his journal to us, which he keept while at the Indian treaty—MS. MD. and HSD. went to meeting. HD. thought it might be of use to lose a little blood, he sent for Justus Fox, who open'd a vain for him, J Skyrin, and Betsy Hardy were also blooded. I was very unwel great part of this day with disordred bowels. better in the evening 'tho far from well—Sammy Emlen and John Perott call'd to see us. 'tis generaly agree'd that this very alarming disorder is as bad or worse than ever. S. Coats told some one in Germantown to day, that there was 10 graves open'd in Friends burying Ground this morning.—I heard yesterday that Coffins were keept ready made in piles, near the State-house for poor people—Jacob Bakers man, was this evening in Hessers kitchen, he says that his mistresss Brother has been in town to day, and reports that matters are better, and rather an abaitment, so say some others—prehaps they build upon a change that has taken place in the weather it has rain'd somewhere, and the air is much cooler—J Perott heard that they dig trenches in the poters-field, to bury the

49. The words "says his Landlord will not permitt him" crossed out.
50. The words "and also Parson Sproat" crossed out.
51. The name "John Leamy" crossed out.

dead,—Deaths. Samuel Griscomb and[52] Daughter Chrisr. Hanson and wife, Saml. Fishers wifes sister, from Rhoad-Island, a Clerk of Benn. Dorseys and a Clark of Meradath the Tanners, a third of Docr. Rush's Puples—James Smith in third street—Philip Clumburge barber, he dy'd some days ago.

28. a fine cool morning William and Henry set out after breakfast 8½ o'clock in the old Chaise, for bucks county, HD. and MS. left us at 9 in JSs Chaise for G. Roberts at point no point &c—JS. gone out on Horse back, Nancy, Molly, ED. and Child left at home—head ach this morning—Michel Pragers a mercht of Philada. dyed this morning in Germantown of the Yallow fever, was refus'd a burying in the burying-places, and was intear'd in the Orchard back of the house where he dy'd—a few hours after his desease. HD. MS. JS. return'd to dinner—the second sister of Caleb Lowans is dead—13 were buried yesterday in friends burying ground—Elizath. Brogden sister to Molly England dead some days since.—JS and AS. rode out this afternoon. HD. MS. MD. and ED took a walk as far as Daviss—J Baker & J Lusby stop'd at the Door, they say that they have received a Letter or Letters, informing that the Sickness in the City has greatly abaited. I wish it may be so, but from accounts received of deaths and burials fear it is otherwise; G Hesser tells us this evening that Philip Cares wife is dead—, J Drinker in a Litter of this morning to HD. says nothing of an abaitment. cool and very pleasant.

29 First Day: HD. JS. MS. and AS. gone to meeting—MDs face swel'd by a cold—H Pemberton call'd in meeting time, wish'd me to go with her to Jacob Spisers, we went, she agree'd with 'em to remov'd tommorrow to their house—J Salters not being convenient. we mett Anthony Morris as we were returning he inform'd us, of the death of Saml. Powel, but said that it was hop'd that the disorder was lessned, as there was but one person bury'd yesterday in freinds burying ground—Our people heard after meeting, of the deaths, of Saml. Parkers wife, Joseph Bispham hatter, a Daughter of Owen Biddle, a Daughter of Benet. Dorsey, &c. John Hampson din'd with us—Eliston Perott bury'd his youngest Child a Son, this morning in the Germantown burying-groung, it was not suppos'd that it dy'd of the yallow fever—his family are at Sansoms place call'd parlaVille.—this is the fourth Child out of five that they have lost within 3 years, 2 Sons of the putrid sore throught, a little Daughter was over lay'd by her Nurse, they have one Daughter remaining. I have heard since dinner, of the death of Richd. Mason and Son. Tommy Fisher, and son Billy drank tea with us, he inform'd of the death of Hannah Dawson, wife of Daniel—JS heard of the death of one John Brown Distiller—cool evening.

30. we have frequently heard within the last 48 hours that the sickness

52. The word "wife" crossed out.

abaitted in the City, but by Letter from J Drinker of this day, we understand that many are near their end, and many others taken down; occasioned prehaps by a foggy morning, and increase of heat, the weather being much warmer to day then for many days past. William and Henry return'd before dinner from Bucks County, they lodg'd at John Watsons; Robert Stevenson and family left the City five weeks ago, they are fixt at present 3 or 4 miles from John Watsons, in B. County. Willm. and Henry drank tea with them.—Neigr. Snider call'd they have been this morning to visit S Emlen at white marsh, they are well—J. and H.P. remov'd this morning from J Saltars to Jacob Spicers—. we hear of the Death of Joseph Budd wife—Jos. Lion came up this Afternoon with a letter from Ben Wilson to HD. another from Capt. Wetheral to JS.—Josey was by no means an acceptable visitor, as he acknowledges that he is daily with one who is ill of the Yallow fever—he says it is frequently the case that a person is dead and buryed and their next door neighbour know nothing of it for many days after, occasion'd as one may suppose, by their keeping close house, and publick burials no more attended to—Polly Gillingham dy'd, some days ago—William Hopkins here this evening, from him and JS. who has been down town, we hear of the following Deaths vizt. Benjn. Pittfield next door but two to our house, Saml. Fisher Hatter in market street, Jacob Hiltzeimer, and[53] Sons and a Daughter. G. Hesser hears this evening that one Trautwine a Wigmaker, was murder'd by his Son,—he liv'd somewhere in second street.—Henry SD. and myself took a walk about sunset. HD. &c preparing to set of tomorrow, for Downingstown to visit our Children there. cooler this evening P.T. Fentham writer at the post-office dead.

Octr. 1 third day: H Drinker; Daughters Nancy and Molly, and little Elizth. Skyrin, Sally Brant, in the waggon drove by Jo; left us between 7 and 8 o'clock after breakfast this morning for Downingstown—foggy; JS. set off between 8 & 9, to meet Captain Wetheral within a mile of the City—Fredrick Hailer past upwards this forenoon, could give no account of the state of things, but his having lost four of his family,—John and Hannah Pemberton call'd Jacob Baker call'd, he intends leaving Germantown with his family for New-Castle—informs of the death of Charles [S]ing and Andrw. Adgate; An English woman who keep't Shop at Danl. Dawsons is also said to be dead. The people continue moving from the City, two or three Waggons loaded have past the door this day. JS. return'd in the evening he heard of several deaths—G Hesser tells us this evening of the death of Peter Mikle Butcher, and one Hicks a Skinner near Nobles—the weather chang'd this evening blows hard from S.E. HSD. lodges in parlor with Billy, JS. up stairs, Sister with me in the back Room.—unwell.

53. The words "Jacob Morgan, who lately lost two" crossed out.

2d. very high wind north: William and self attempted to take a walk, but were blown back, JS. went abroad after breakfast John Warder and Son call'd—Nurse Waters din'd with us, She mention'd the death of one Docr. Dodd; J and H.P. stop'd, said Joseph Hewlings dead, G Hesser says Henry Darrok's dead, JS. return'd towards evening Parson Sprouts daughter some time ago, Henry M[a]yers wife, also dead.—Looking over a list of persons bury'd in friends burying Ground I mett with several names that I had not before heard of, among them were the following Jane Warner, from the Almshouse, Hannah Cadwalader, Morri[s] Dickinson, Shoemaker, F. Hoops, Eliza Austin, Widdow Peters and 2 Children, A Daughter and Aprentice of B. Olden, Jos. Hill, Enoch Taylor, and Daughter, Abigail Taylor, Danl. Trotter junr., Benn. Holton, John [St]all junr. Charles Smithfield, Aaron Kimber, Edwd. Rease, Eliza. Volans, Nathaniel Banes Wife, Anthony Sharp, Geo. Cribs, Joshua Pearson, from Almshouse, Sarah Briton, Widdow Jackson, William Boices Wife, &c—William and self took a walk this afternoon.

3 a fine clear morning No Equinoctial storm as yet, I fear, if I may so say, that it has past over for this season—Docr. Lusby call'd, he says Jonathan Shoemaker is dead.—John Weaver open'd a vein this morning for William, and took 6 or 7. ounces blood.—he is not much more unwell then usual, but felt some symptoms that he thought indicated want of bleeding.—Becky Waln, Jessys wife, came to see us, she inform'd us of the death of several persons whom we do not know,—JS. has been downtown and there heard of the deaths of Jacob Tomkins junr.[54] Francis Finley, and Kay, Clows partner, JS. and HSD. took a ride upwards, MS. and Sam. Sprigs, downwards, to Germantown, in the Afternoon, I took a walk by myself—Our Foulk return'd to tea. they heard of the deaths of many in our distress'd City, thoes whom we knew were the following vizt. John Todd Senr., [Tos.] Speakman, Margt. Haines, Anthoy. P. Morris, John Reedle taylor, his Daughter and Son in law, one Cameron, Sellers the printer, and Son, James Stocks Brother, some say this disorder is the Pestilence.

4 I find myself very unwel this morning Molly Forbes came to see us, after her came [T] Fisher, his Wife and 3 Children, S. and M Pleasants, J. and H. Pemberton, & W. Savery. we hear from them and others of many deaths, Abraham Cadwalder he dy'd in the Country, Edwd. Parish, the second Son that Isaac has lost by this fever, Stephen Maxfield Wife, Isaac Folwell, J. Hallowel miller, Penman a Coachmaker, [T.] Moyer potters wife, John Lamborns wife, John Bartholomew Grocer, Alexr. Lawrence, & others that I do not recollect; Billy Ashby and Jacob Baker call'd.—Lusbys Clark dead.—Our family return'd from Downings Town between 3 and 4 this Afternoon, they left Jacob, Sally the little ones &c all well, Thos. Lightfoot ill, suppos'd to be

54. The name "Docr. Glentworth" crossed out.

the Malignant fever. Nancy Skyrin came home very ill, Head-ach and sick stomach, she broke out with the Netle rash, occasion'd in measure by putting a small peice of Camphire in her mouth,[55] it happn'd so once before—she was better before Bed-time,—Saml. Macey and Jacob Wilson dead, The Accounts from the City this day, seem to be worse than has yet been, We were inform'd that dead Bodies have been found in some houses, in the City, who have been forsaken in their illness, and not discover'd for some days after death.

5. Nancy 'tho better, is far from well, HSD—took a walk this morning with a Segar in his mouth, which he smoak'd out, and soon after found himself very sick and in a sweat, he made shift to get into G Hessers Orchard, where he discharg'd his Stomach, he was fearfull of doing so on the road, least he should be suspected of having the prevailing disorder, he came home sick and pale, and after it had opperated both as an emetic and a cathartic, he was better.—HD. and MS. went this morning to Jacob Spicers, ED. and WD. took a short walk before dinner—HD. and MS. went down town in the Chaise after dinner—Saml. Coopers Son over the ferry dead—and a little girl call'd Polly who liv'd with John Thomas dead at the Hospital, WD. and ED. MD. took a walk this Afternoon, call'd at a Isaac Beners a weavers not ½ mile from G Hessers—It is told to day that the day before—yesterday 40 persons were sent to the Hospital and a vast number bury'd, yesterday not so many laid in the Earth, but many sick—to day 'tis said that there is an alteration for the better, this has been a fine clear cool day. I have remark'd that 2 or 3 times when we have heard of an abatement of the disease, that the weather was cool. [S]inox a trunkmaker in chestnut Street, and one Austin a Bricklayer dead—'Tho bodily weakness is experience'd by some in our family, we have[56] great cause of thankfullness. It is said that some day this week, 80 persons were bury'd in the potters field—if that be true, 'tis indeed alarming to a great degree.—The day before yesterday a sick man at Chestnut hill was put into a cart to be taken to the Hospital, but dyed before they arriv'd there.

6 First Day: My husband and Sister gone to Abington meeting 5 or 6 miles from hence—J. and A. Skyrin MD. and HSD. gone to Germantown meeting. WD. gone to take a walk in the meadow. J Pemberton call'd as he went to meeting, he has heard nothing very perticular from the City to day—I went after dinner JS. with me to J. Spicers to visit H Pemberton, William came to me, H.D. came also, both families well—we heard as we return'd that a young man lays dead, opposite the house where the widdow Mullen resides—which is near us—HSD. went this Afternoon to Isaac Whartons, he has purchas'd a place near [I] Howels on the Wissahicon—JS. AS. MD. visited Polly Perot who

55. The word "as" crossed out.
56. The word "yet" crossed out.

has lately been hurt, falling out of Chaise. Davis, J. Skyrin's Clark din'd here, he came out of the City—eat in the back room. Emanl. Walkers wife dead, another daughter of James Star, and a Docr. Goss, also. JPs Oronako drove up this afternoon Isaac Zane and his Daughter Sally, who have taken lodgings at the widdow Livezeys.

7 HD. and Son William rode out this morning, J Pemberton call'd, Nurse Waters din'd with us—John Warder and Son, Dr. Lusby call'd.—weather warmer—we have heard this day of the deaths of a Son of Eml.[57] Walker,—Edward Lowrey and Wife, Huston Langstraw, Jacob Howel lawyer, one Lewis a taylor and his Wife, who dyed in the same Bed, and about the same time[58]—the Lad that dyed over the road yesterday Afternoon was bury'd last night.—JS. heard of the death of Sarah Coltman.[59]

8. William and Henry gone out this morning in the Chaise.—HSD. went on Horse-back to look for Wm. Ashby taylor—after dinner—and HD. JS. AS. MD and child went in the Carriage to the Widdow Livezeys to see Isaac Zane and Daughter J. and H.P. here this fore-noon—'Squire Shits was buryed this Afternoon in the Church grounds near us—a large company attending.—William and self took a walk in the meadow, before Sun-set.—we have heard to day of the deaths of Jonathn. Sergent lawyer, Richd. Courtney taylor, Isaac Buck[by] Hatter, and Major Franks also—Fleming the Roamish Priest. sunset clear, weather temperate, 'tho rather warm for the season.

9. William walk'd a mile down town to Hubbss Store, to purchase Cassamer—HD. AS. MD. and the Child, gone this morning to white-marsh on a visit to Sally Emlen. JS. gone to Jerry Parkers on the Wissahicon, Letter this fore-noon from JD.—the Gloom continues in our City, The Awful disease by no means lessen'd—may we endeavour for preparation and resignation:—one Hay a tavern keeper in third street dead &c—HD. and those that were with him din'd with S.Emlen, and return'd home before four o'clock—Neighbor Snider call'd here she expects SE and family back to their house again sometime this week—J Lusby call'd—a Son of John Peters baker dead—JS. came home towards evening he says he has been to the uper end of market street, to meet Capt. Witheral, he had better mett him here, if it was absolutely necessary to meet him at all.—taking a walk this evening with HD. towards the meadow, by a cornfield that had been lately plough'd, the narrow road fill'd in places with stubble that had been thrown out of the field, my foot turn'd under me when I fell down, and was so strain'd and brused that I

57. The words "a Daughter of [Isc. Parish]" crossed out.
58. The sentence "William and Henry gone in the Chair to Livezeys this Afternoon" crossed out.
59. The words "hope is may be a mistake" crossed out.

could scarcely step with help—my husband and G Hesser made a Chair with their hands, and brought me home on it, with my Arms round their Necks, as I have seen Children carry one another—I had it bath'd with Opodeldock and wrap'd up in flannel, and 'tho tis[60] painful this evening 'tis not so bad as I expeted it would have been by what I felt when first hurt—a very clear evening. it will be 7 weeks next first day, since we have had any rain more than what we call a sprinkling—we see very few lately from the City, but have reason to fear there is no amendment.

10 the pain in my foot keep'd me all night awake, dosed a little after day, 'tis much swel'd and painful—HD. AS. MD. &c gone to meeting, 'tis youths meeting or general meetings; held here once a year on fifth day—Wm. Savery, [T.] Fisher &c here before meeting—They inform of the Deaths of Joseph Moore, Thomas Lightfoot, Owen Jones Senr., George Baker, and a Son of Huston Langshaw—There was a marriage at meeting, Danl. Thomas and Agnes Johnson; marriage is solemn at all times, and doubly so at present—Joshua Morris and Wife, Tommy and Nancy Morgan, Neighr. Waln, and Jacob Paxon, din'd with us.—I have been most of this day on the Bed only while the Bed was making had my foot on a Chair as I cannot put it to the ground—we have heard of more deaths this day, than any day yet, and 'tis said that 150 were bury'd in the City yesterday—Betsy Howel told after meeting that Docr. Rush has wrote to Willm. Lewis "that the disorder was now past the Art of man or medicine to cure, that nothing but the power of the Almighty could stop it." or to this effect. Since Morning we have been inform'd of the deaths of[61] the wife of Wm. Trotter Butcher, Aaron Roberts, John Peters, Becky Folwell,[62] Son, Emanuel Walker, This evening my husband went home with Neigr. Waln and Anna Wells, who spent the Afternoon with us, he heard while out of the death of Roland Evans, Son of John,—This day has been repleat with deeply affecting intilligence. clear warm weather. John Skyrin brings account from down town of the death of Charles Williams, who dy'd and bury'd to day.

11 I show'd my foot this morning to Docr. Lusby who desir'd me to chang my method of heating it, which was vinager and opodeldoc, and afterwards I bath'd it with Oyl of St. Johns-Wort, but he orders lead water alone, twice a day: My husband and Son William took a long ride this forenoon, they stop'd at McColls at Isaac Whartons, and at John Fields.—Billy Sansom stop'd at our door on Horse-back, he is finely recover'd. as he just came out of the City, we did not invite him in—he says that 11 persons were yesterday buryed in friends burying ground—that Caleb Attmore and 2 of Sellers Sons are dead.

60. The word "very" crossed out.
61. The name "John Heart" crossed out.
62. The words "John Elliots Wife and" crossed out.

HD heard while out, of the death of Daniel Offley and the widdow Kepley.— HD. and MS. went down town this Afternoon, got some Comfry to make poltice for my foot—Nurse Waters spent the Afternoon—Jerry Warder &c. call'd; received a Letter from JD. another Daughter of James Star dead— Molly and Henry went to see S. Emlen, they are return'd to Christian Snider.

12 HD. went down town, JS. and AS rode out—Nurse Waters spent the day with us—John Pemberton drank tea, Joseph Potts call'd—Benn. Wilson came here this Afternoon, he appears to be finely recover'd.—On fifth day last 40 were sent to the Hospital, which with those there before amounted to 302 persons, 'tis now so full, that another is said to be preparing—17 graves 'tis said were dug in friends buring ground yesterday, 'tis very afflicting to walk through the Streets of our once flourishing and happy City, the Houses shut up from one corner to another, the Inhabitance that remain keeping shut up, very few seen walking about—The disorder now 'tis said rages much in the South part of the City, that great numbers dye in that part call'd Irish-town— The deaths that we have heard of this day, are the following, Major Sproat,[63] Susanna Meredath, Mary Todd, Flickwer and Wife Confectioners, The weather is much chang'd this evening, it blows hard at N.W. and is very cold— may the change be favourable, my Foot to day rather more painful, more swel'd and darker coulor'd, Sister disorder'd—the rest thro' mercy bravely [&c.] well as usual.

13. First Day: Wind lul'd, a beautiful pleasant fall-day—Dr. Lusby here this Morning he has been well inform'd that on one day, the middle of last week, 200 persons were buried in the City. Sammy Emlen call'd this morning HD. JS. AS. MD. HSD. went to meeting, MS. unwell. John and Hannah Pemberton and S Zane, here this Afternoon, W Savery also—HSD went this Afternoon to [S] Shoemakers—Molly gone to S Emlens stays there all night. deaths heard of this day, Daniel Richards, John M Jones's Wife, Pelotiah Websters Wife, a Child of Josiah Coates 7 years old, a Grand Child of Edward Penington.

14 very poorly last night with my foot &c—This morning HD. and Wm. Savery set of after breakfast for Darby, on a visit to J Parish who with his wife &c are there residing.—WD. and HSD. gone to take a ride—MD. doing the same with EE—a very fine day. Lusby, Samey Emlen, and John Stroud call'd—J. and H. Pemberton call'd; Huston Langstroth's wife and child dead.—Jerry Warder here the forenoon,[64] Sally Emlen, Huldah Mott, and Betsy Emlen, here this Afternoon.[65] Peter Millers Wife dead at Abington—

63. The words "William Millhouses wife Chester County" crossed out.
64. The sentence "Jos. Howel brother to A[u]thor, said to be dead" crossed out.
65. The words "Mathew Clarksons Wife dead" crossed out.

HD. return'd after Candle-light, he heard while abroad of the deaths of David Franks, and John Morrison, we likewise hear'd of the death of Adam Hubly, and William Evil Brother in law to our Sally. Neighr. Snider and Sammy Emlen here this evening An extract from a late London paper says "that the Queen of France was lately try'd and condemn'd to suffer, in the same manner that the King her husband had done, that on returning to a common prison, the mob took her from the guard, and tore her in peices;"[66] There appears to be but a very poor prospect of crops of wheat, occasiond by the drought. Disolation, Cruelty and Disress, has of late resounded in our Ears, from many quarters.—Another added to the list of deaths this evening an[67] elder Son of John Hoskins—Nurse Harrison also gone. clear and cool.

15 EE. J and H.P. call'd this morning, Ben. Wilson also; Deaths, Abigal Wilson wife of William, and sister to Sally Emlen, Betsy had but just left us, when we heard of her Aunts desease.[68]—Joseph Inskip and Caleb Kimber, both were schoolmasters in our Society.[69]—It began to rain about noon and continu'd raining 'till after sunset, if kind providence should order no more at present it will have the good effect Of laying the dust, and weting the roofs of the Houses; had fire happen'd in our City during the drought, and Present want of usual help, 'twould in all probability have been terriable—cloudy.

16 HD. took a walk to JP.s he afterwards went to John Fields to look for a letter from JD. which we received while he was absent—HD. Henry and Molly took a ride in the Carriage after dinner. Billy Sansom stop'd at the door while they were out—we did not ask him in, as he just came out of the City—he informs us of the death of Docr. Says Wife and Daughter, that he saw a great number of funerals this day—John Perott here this Afternoon—David Bacons Wife, and James Wilson in Arch street dead—clear and cool, frost. 'Tis a week this afternoon since my foot has touch'd the floor, unless by accident when geting of the Bed on a chair to have the Bed made, I set all day on it, working, or reading when able—the swelling is abaited but the foot very black. To sit so long in one possition is very tiresome, but patience alleviates most afflictions.

17 HD. and Son HSD—went out this morning to visit Nichs. Waln &c—M. Livezley and her daughter Nancy here this morning H Pemberton and Sally Zane here also—John Cook, W Savery, call'd—Billy took a walk to J Pembertons—return'd before dinner. Annabella Cr[o]sson dead—the widdow Livezley or rather her daughter by her order put a plester of the white of Eggs on [top] on my foot and anointed it with the oyl of St. Johns Wort, it has felt very

66. The words "was I think the Words" crossed out.
67. The word "other" crossed out.
68. The name "Fredrick Hailer" crossed out.
69. The words "Josh. Thatcher dead some days past" crossed out.

warm ever since—it may prehaps be right,—My husband and Henry return'd towards evening, they paid several visits, and from all they could learn, and from accounts to this place from the City the fever is considerably abaited, we have not heard this evening of any death, how great the favour, may it continue—Samuel Shoemaker Son of Benjamin of Abington who dyed some time ago of the Melignant fever, was thought dead by the attendant, who went out for his Coffin, and on his return into the Room where the Corps lay, found him sitting on the side of the Bed endeavouring to put on his Shoes, he ask'd him where he was going; was answer'd to take walk, but being desired to lay down and rest himself he comply'd, and dyed in reality about an hour after. had he remain'd as he was first found a quarter of an hour longer, A Livesley, who told the Story, think he would have been screw'd in his Coffen—Peter Browns Clark told my husband to day as he was returning home, of the death of three young women, Daughters of a Man in Kingsington who went home to their parants one after the other sick of the fever, from the City—some time after their deaths the Father and Mother, were so thoughtless as to lay in the Bed wherein they dy'd, and both were taken with the fever and died also. Seven persons Men and Women were this morning Baptiz'd or dip'd in a Creek about 1½ miles from this place, they are of the Society of Dunkers,[70] they differ from the Annabaptis's, who are laid in the water on their backs, those kneel in the water and are dip'd with their faces downwards as I am inform'd, great numbers went to see the performance—JS. AS. HSD and MD. went this evening to the Dunkers meeting.

18. HD. JS. AS. HSD. went to meeting—Nurse Waters, Hannah Pemberton and Betsy Spicer here this morning—WD. took a ride this fore-noon as far as white-Marsh—he went there again this afternoon with his Father to Wm. Ashby taylor—my husband heard yesterday when at frankford, of the death of Joseph Morgans Wife and Daughter in the Jersys, and of Elizh. Sindry who dyed 7 weeks ago at Frankford 'tis likely of Old Age—Nancy Livezly brought me some sweet majoram to make a bath for my foot. A young woman dead, who was left to take care of Tommy Fishers house in town—John Pemberton and Maria Spicer here, Elizah. Stine who liv'd at Clarksons house in German-town 2 years ago when my Daughters were there, call'd to see us, she has lost her husband since, and now lives at Hainess—John Drinker in a letter to HD. informs him of the death of Joshua Whitney who was here on busyness with HD. the 11 last month he then came out of the City where he had been a day or two, he took the disorder and died at Hellers in his way home my foot not quite as well to night as yesterday, Molly has a boil on her Cheek, the rest as well as usual, a fine clear moon light night.

70. The Dunkers or Dunkards, also known as German Baptists and later as the Church of the Brethren, believed in adult trine baptism, full immersion three times in the names of the members of the Trinity (Donald F. Durnbaugh, ed., *The Brethren Encyclopedia* [Philadelphia: The Brethren Encyclopedia, Inc., 1983–84]).

19 warm this day, and 'tho the report of an abaitment of the disorder is not contradicted, yet by the accounts of deaths this morning fear that there is not much dependence to be put on it.—HSD. went this morning to John Fields, heard there of the Death of Benn. Smith and Docr. Phile, and by a note from Debby Field to MS. we are inform'd of the deaths of 4 in Friends Alms-House vizt. Mary Biles, Susanna Burden, Joshua Brown's wife, and Thos. Burden, 'tis said that many die at Kingsington,—Thos. Morgan call'd—'tis reported that Parson Sprout is dead.—Billy Ashby here this Afternoon putting buttons on HDs Coat. WD. took a ride to visit J & H Pemberton. Dr. Lusby was saying here this Afternoon that we may depend on it, that the fever is less in the City, so few have been taken into the Hospital for 3 or 4 days past in comparison to the numbers that were before admitted, that it is the best rule to judge by. this amendment is since the rain on 3d. day last. Deaths heard of this afternoon—John Ingle from England, Lawrence Allman Mason, Lesher Inkeeper, a little rain fell this afternoon.

20 First Day: My husband and Son Henry, set of after breakfast for Bucks county—John and Nancy gone to meeting with Betsy Emlen. Molly Drinker not well—Betsy Emlen spent this Afternoon with us, Accounts from the City to day are very favourable, but few die, and few taken ill, comparatively speaking—A letter this evening from Michl. Callanan, he appears to be much alarm'd, as he says two or three persons have died in Bristol of the melignant fever—JS. gone home with EE.

21st. A delightful cool frosty morning—I have been very poorly since 4 o'clock this morning rather better by 11. JS. AS. MD. gone to visit S & E Fisher—mett Tabby and Becky Fisher there, 'Tis generly agreed that the fever is very much abaited, Our neighbor John Haltzell, dyed some time ago—A little before noon, the Chimney of the back Room, where I am fixt, and likely to remain for some time longer, took fier, and roar'd with violence, The first thought that occur'd to me, as twenty years ago on[71] a like occasion, was an Earth-quake, but that was the thought of a moment, we soon discoverd what it was, and presently put it out,—Sammy Rhoades sup'd last fifth-day night at Jacob Downings, he say they were all well—Dr. Lusby here this Afternoon tells us of the death of James Reed his Daughter and Servant maid, some time ago—Jerry Warder and Jerry Parker call'd—A Flag fixt on the Hospital, but 3 persons buryed from thence yesterday and one 'tis said this day. wind high, and cold this evening.

22 JS. AS. MD. gone to white-marsh to visit Nancy Morgan, John and H Pemberton, Sally Zane, and Nancy Livezly here this morning, also John Hamson—HD. and HSD. return'd from B. County before dinner—Danl.

71. The word "the" crossed out.

Williams junr. here, says his Father is ill of the fever, he does not allow that the amendment is so great as many think—Billy gone this afternoon to J Pembertons, Nancy and Molly to S Emlens—JS. and HSD. elsewhere—Wm. Forbes and Son call'd—G. Roberts also—John Pemberton here this Afternoon, came with William—HD. went to S Emlens came back to tea JP. stay'd tea—Elijah Weed Jailkeeper dead, Parson Smiths Wife, and Joshua Cresson also, and Docr. Ingham of Bucks County.

23 William took a ride on Horse-back to Chesnut Hill, Molly Forbes came to see us this morning Nurse Waters din'd with us, Betsy Emlen spent the Afternoon and Evening—John Field, Dr. Lusby here to day. Polly Lowry Becky Thomsons Maid dead, but little intillegance from the City to day, but that several are very ill—clear pleasant weather, my foot getting better—Miles Mervin Schoolmaster said to be dead,—HSD. went home with EE. Sammy Emlen had been this Afternoon to Marshals Elarbotery[72] where he saw Casper Hains, who left the City about 1 o'Clock, he said that at that time there had not been any funerals, or one grave open'd in friends buring ground.

24 last night between 11 and 12 o'clock, as I had not been asleep, I heard the cry of fier at a distance, on its nearer approach,[73] the family were soon alarmed, George Hesser pronounced it to be John Livesly house or mill, he went with his Buckets,—They have a fire Company here and one Engine, which was soon on its way, and the people some on foot, others on horse-back were very numerous, but as it is two miles from Germantown, the mill which was almost new, was burnt down, about 200 Barrels Flour 500 or 600 a quantity Salt and gin[d]er Busls. Wheat &c—'tis thought their loss will be near 3000 pounds. John Pemberton, my husband and William went this morning to visit the Suffers, found 'em pretty well, and much compos'd considering. Isaac Zane and his Daughter Sally were pretty well, they lodge there—John Perott, Jerry Parker here this morning—Dr. Lusby also—by a letter from J Drinker of this day, we are inform'd that the Malignancy of the disorder is much lessn'd, 'tho many are still ill—we have heard of no death this day—it does not follow that none have died, 'tho a proof of an amendment[74]—a false report Tremendoes times! Wars, pestilence Earth-quakes &c—it seems as tho Great part of the world is in commotions—our friend Jos. Moore, the last time we saw him, which is the last time we shall ever see him in this

72. Either a laboratory or a munitions factory, probably the former (Lederer, *Colonial American English,* s.v. "elaboratory").

73. The words "Nancy who lodges at [ ] with my [ ]" crossed out.

74. The following material is crossed out: "G Hesser was told this Afternoon, by a young woman of the name of Savage, who boards at Beners the next House above us, that her Brothers partner who came today from Chester mett with a young man lately from South-Carolina, who inform'd him that one half of Charles-Town was Swollow'd by an Earth-Quake."

world—told us that in that part of the country where he was a week or ten days before his arrival here, they felt a small shock of an Earth-quake.

25 HSD. set off after breakfast for Downings-town cloudy. HD. JS. AS. and MD. went to meeting—sun broke out before noon—Thos. Wright of Wilks-berry calld, he inform'd us of the Deaths of Camel Dick and John Todd—wind very high about noon, no signs of rain—T. Wright din'd with us. John Hamson call'd—Mierken sugar baker,[75] dead—Polly Perott, Gidion and Anna Wells drank tea with us, Gidion show'd us a list of burials in friends ground in which were a large number that we have not heard of before, among them were, John Guest Senr. James Goram, Grace Eustaugh, Sus. Kribner, Margt. Langdale, Lydia West.—J. Pemberton Wm. Savery here, Danl. Williams junr. and Sally Rhoads call'd—HD. and W Savery went this to [Tommy] Fishers &c.—Isaac Collings from Trenton here this evening HD. wrote, and sent a sum of Mony by him to Ml. Callanan.

26 A man to be bury'd this Afternoon, not far from us, who 'tis thought died of the Yallow fever, and two women have lately dy'd near us—'tis remarkable, that no one has been known to take the infection in the Country of those who came out of the City disorder'd and die—I have not heard of an instance where it has spread. HD. and Son William gone this Morning to Joshua Howels, Nancy and Molly gone to S Emlens—Isaac Zane and Daughter John Pemberton and wife, paid us a Morning visit—J Hamson call'd—JP. here this Afternoon while HD was out—Jacob Downing came this evening to our great satisfaction, he left Sally and the dear Children well—HD. and Billy came home after Candle-light, too late, they din'd at E. Perotts, Sammy Emlin drank tea with us—warm to day, we have not heard of one death that has occur'd this day.—HSD. return'd from Downingstown a few minuits after Jacobs arrival, they mist seeing each other.

27 First Day: HD. gone to meeting with JP. in his Carriage—HSD. and MD. with B. Emlen, Jacob Downing JS. and AS. in our Carriage JD. heard of the Death of Azriah Horton,—cloudy and raw, looks like for Snow, David Cummins and Saml. Gomly din'd here.—Sammy Fisher here this afternoon. HD and Jacob Downing gone this evening to visit John Perott. The swelling in my foot not gone down, nor the blackness gone off, 'tho both better, I am not yet able to bare any weight on it—a hot itching in it to day perhaps owing to the many poltices us'd.

28. Jacob Downing and John Skyrin went after breakfast to visit Elliston Perott—John Pemberton call'd, William went with him to John DeBreams—Molly gone to spend the day at S. Emlens, Huldah Mott and Betsy Emlen

75. The words "and Conelly the Auctonear" crossed out.

came for her, I read a letter from WW to SE. relative to his deceas'd Wife, which was very affecting.—Sally Parker and John Warders Daughter and Dr. Lusby call'd.—took physick, have had but a poor day. very cold. Richard Downing and Thos. Edmunson came here before John and Jacob returnd after sun-set—Molly stays to night at SEs.

29 B Emlen came home this morning with Molly and spent the day with us—R Dowg. lodg'd last night at T. [F]orests he and Jacob left us this morning after breakfast John and H. Pembertons and widdow Livezly here this morning the latter kindly apply'd a plaster of Rosin and Lard to my foot, Billy sent this morning for Docr. Shippen to look at my poor foot, as it makes[76] still a disagreeable appearance, he was not at home, I have not seen him—Neighr. Waln and Anna Wells here this Afternoon, Thos. Fisher and Lusby call'd, Sister went out before dinner, stay'd[77] all night at S Emlens—we have heard this day of the deaths of Sidney Paul who dy'd some time since, and of Patience Howel, The fever appears to be nearly at an end, for which we cannot be too thankful, the newspaper says that the 11th. of this month 2730 odd had dyed of the Yallow fever, on that day dy'd more than any preceeding day, and great numbers since[78]—very cold—The last 24 hours have been to me rather distressing.

30 MS. came home before dinner—J. and H Pemberton here this morning—I cant say that I walk'd, but that I got along to the fire-side with the help of two of my Children, it is three weeks this afternoon since I saw the Sun-set, which I was gazing at, when I made a false steap and hurt my foot.—MS. gone this afternoon to J. Pembertons—HD. AS. and MD. gone to S Fishers, and JS. gone in his Chaise, I know not where—HSD. set of after dinner for Bucks-County. William, little Elizath. myself &c left at home. H Mott and little Hariott spent an hour or 2 with me this Afternoon—JS. been to the City, came home late—I have been unwell all day: cloudy.

31 Cloudy for two days past and seems likely to Snow[79]—HD. went this morning to JPs—John Hamson here, JS went to J Howels—it began to rain about two o'clock this Afternoon and has rain'd steadily, ever since tis now 7 o'clock.

76. The words "but a [ ]" crossed out.
77. The words " 'till late in the even" crossed out.
78. The beginning of October saw the highest mortality of the yellow fever epidemic, with 119 deaths recorded on the peak day, Oct. 11. Mathew Carey, using cemetery records, recorded a total of 4,044 dead out of a total population of roughly 40,000, of whom 17,000 fled during the epidemic. Powell considers Carey's figure to be an undercount (Carey, *Short Account*, 65 and passim; Powell, *Bring Out Your Dead*, 281 and passim).
79. The words "Je priez prendre C——r O——[l]" crossed out.

Novr. 1 It rain most of last night, and 'till noon this day, cloudy ever since, HD. went to JPs—talks of going to town tomorrow—, Jo. went with Justis Fox to Joshua Howels, to bleed some of the family, HSD. not return'd, William not as well as at some other times—myself la la. J Lusby call'd, Capt —— drank tea.

2d. HD. gone this morning to the City, it is our quarterly meeting—J. Lusby went with him; I had the agreeable intiligence from my Children, that the Waggons were taking the people and goods back to the City—it is clear'd up this morning with a fine frost—what a favourable reverse, which calls for humility and thanks—Thos. Fisher, Jos. Waln, and Isaac Wharton, here this morning Nancy Levezley came to see me—JS. gone to Philada.[80]—one Shaffer a Sugar baker dead, and Copeland who keep't a beer house also—a burial hear to day of an antient Man; the weather[81] warmer then could be expect'd so soon after rain and frost, 'twas cold this morning Thomas Clifford Senr. dy'd yesterday at his place out of the City of the gout in his stomach—HD. returnd about 3 o'clock in the Afternoon—Wm. Drinker Son of John Drinker Deces'd., dyed lately in lawrel-Court, Philadelphia. HSD. return'd to tea, from Bucks County. JS. return'd in the evening from the City—Polly Haydock was married some time in last month to Edmund Prior New-York.

3 First Day: Extract from the Federal Gazette of 1st. instant "It gives great pleasure to the Editor to hear, from every quarter of our city, that universal health prevails in a degree equal to any former period in the history of this country. At the Hospital on Bush-Hill, for the last 24 hours, only one person died—and he died of the Flux." HD. MS. MD. HSD. gone to meeting: Cloudy and high wind this morning J Pemberton, [S] Zane, and J Lusby here before meeting—Antony Johnson and an English Man who brought letters for HD—were here after dinner—John and Mary DeBrem spent the Afternoon with us Mary is preparing to go to South Carolina to visit her Children there. Hulda Mott and Betsy Emlen also drank tea with us, my foot uneasy most of the day. we have heard of the death of Speel who was our Baker, and of little Dick Scotts Father and Brother, who dy'd some time since—cloudy this evening.

4 HD. gone to the City to meeting, HSD. gone to white marsh with HM. and EE—rain in the night, clear and warm this morning—William and Nancy took a ride, Molly gone to A Wells—Charles Jervis call'd this morning his family are at Watermans, Bucks County. Molly heard from Richd. Morris who came from Downings-town this morning that little Mary Downing was, unwell—Sister and William set off to enquire more perticularly, while they were

80. The sentence "Seymour Heart dead, he had been ill two weeks—" crossed out.
81. The words "very warm, more so" crossed out.

gone J Pemberton paid me a visit—and just before their return William Ashbridge came with a letter from Jacob Downing informing of Mary having the Flux, and desireing that Docr. Shippen would come or send directions &c—Sister went back into Germantown to the Doctors he is gone to Potts-Grove but expected home this evening. HD. return'd this evening from the City J Skyrin gone to Philada., C Jervis din'd with us, he inform'd that the Widdow [T]ellfare who went into the City last fifth day, is since dead in the Country—Dr. Shipn. not return'd and Dr. Bensel Senr. ill, Wm. Ashbridge who brought Jacobs letter, lodges here to night—remarkably warm for the Season.

5 this day did us'd to be distinguish'd by fireing of Guns, ringing of Bells, Bonfires &c.—which since the revolution hath been ommitted,[82] Wm. Ashbridge left us after breakfast with every thing proper that was in our power to send, the Doctor excepted, who is not yet return'd to Germantown. HD. received a Letter from S Emlen London, he went this morning to JPs—HSD gone with WA to Chest. Hill, to get if possiable some venice-treacle—HD. din'd with J Pemberton—at 3 o'clock this afternoon Richd. Downing stop'd on Horse-back at our door, he came on business to the Governor who keeps his Office in Germantown, he brought us the agreeable intelligence that dear little Mary was much better since yesterday, HD. wrote again by him to Jacob, HD. and HSD. went this afternoon to George Logans and to [T]. Fishers—A Misty rain all day, and heavy shower this evening, wind blowing hard at north east.

6 north-East storm continues with rain—HD. and HSD. gone down town to the Washington tavern on busyness—myself unwell—The inhabitants of Philada. were fast moving into the City before this storm, 'tis said there were upwards of 20,000 had left their dwellings, and retired into the Country—Pembertons Noke came this morning from the City, he says that the day before yesterday, there was no burial in Friends ground, Yesterday three, one of them was the wife of Saml. Garrigas, and that, this day there was no grave open'd there—The widdow Durdan din'd and drank tea with us, HSD. waited on her to the Inn where she lodges to night, HD. has purchased upwards of 200 acres of Land of her, part of Pennsbury Manor, for a farm for Henry, after raining all day, it has clear'd up this evening.

82. Guy Fawkes Day commemorated the discovery and foiling of the plot by Guy Fawkes and others to blow up the British Houses of Parliament on Nov. 5, 1605. In colonial Boston, where it was called Pope's Day, it became an occasion for anti-British and anti-Catholic demonstrations in the years immediately preceding the Revolution (A. B. Wright, *British Calendar Customs: England,* ed. T. E. Lones [London: William Glaisher, 1940], vol. 3, *Fixed Festivals,* 145–56; G. B. Warden, *Boston 1689–1776* [Boston: Little, Brown, 1970], 152, 163, 170, 218; Alfred F. Young, "Pope's Day, Tarring and Feathering, and Cornet Joyce, Jun.: From Ritual to Rebellion in Boston, 1745–1775" [paper presented to the Anglo-American Conference on Comparative Labor History, Rutgers University, Apr. 26–28, 1973]).

7 a fine clear day, 'tho warm for the Season, HD. and JP. gone to Abinton quarterly Meeting. Sally and Becky Parker here this fore-noon;[83]—Huldah Mott and Betsy Emlen here before dinner, MD. went home with them—our dear William seems poorly to day, and I am very far from well myself—HD. return'd to tea—S Emlen H Mott and E Emlen here this Afternoon, MD. went home again with them, intending to stay all night—HSD. spent the evening there. JS. abroad to day, he heard of the death of Matw. Conard tavernkeeper, and others, Sam Sprigs was in town to day, he saw a funeral in Friends ground, with about 6 persons attending, and a Herse in front Street nere Elfriths Alley.

8 HD. took a walk down town, William took a walk to S Emlens and waited on his Sister home, John and Nancy gone this forenoon to visit Josa. Howels family—Sally Zane and Nancy Livezley came after we had din'd from Abington youths meeting, they din'd here, Jenney Heaton and Patty Lewis drank tea with us, they came from the ridge-road, where Wm. Lewis with his family are—HD. JS. AS and the little one gone to S Emlens—Jenny Heaton informs of the deaths of Widdow Batt, Robt. Lloyd and Danl. Baldwin—It is 4 months this Day since I came to Garmantown, where I have ever since continu'd—I have walk'd across the room yesterday and to day, without Shoes, and with Sisters help—if nothing more than the disorder in my foot aild me, I beleive I should now soon get bravely.

9 HD. went this morning to JPs—he went after downtown in the Chaise with William, John Perott, Huldah Mott and Betsy Emlen were here this forenoon; it is a month 31 days since I have been out of the back room, this day I din'd in the front parlor;—HD. and son William din'd at J. Pembertons;—Nurse Waters din'd with us—JS. AS. and MD. went this Afternoon to visit Anna Wells, Polly Perott and E Emlen with them. Our disturb'd City has been this day in great confusion on account of the Arrival of a French Vessel with 400 passingers a considerable number of them ill of the Yallow fever. HD. went this evening to J Lusbys to enquire concerning the report, he says that he has seen a person from the City this Afternoon, who thinks 'tis not so bad as here reported—Sam went in the evening with the Chaise for John & Nancy, the others walk'd home—Neddy Howel & Josey Hopkins here this Morning, warm.

10 First Day: wind very high at S.W—HD. JS. AS. MD. HSD. went to meeting. MS. stay'd at home with me, as I have taken medicine—WD. also at home—John Parish and Daughter John Pemberton and Jos. Sansom, din'd with us.—we hear that Joseph Elam, and James Durkinderen, both noted

83. The sentence "Edward Pole who mov'd into the City last week, is since dead" crossed out.

Characters are dead.—Sammy Emlen here this evening HSD. drank tea at Docr. Logans, Docr. Parke there, whose oppinion it is, that those who have mov'd out of the City may safely return, 'tis the sentiments of several other physicians as I have heard, within the 2 or 3 last days—nothing to day relating to the infected french Vessel.

11 A fine clear cool day: HD. and J Pemberton gone this morning to Abington, where the English friends are said to be, Deborah Darby and M Young, HSD. and George Hesser gone to Philadelphia—JS. gone there also, Polly Perott paid us a Morning visit—HD. and JS return'd in the evening preparing for HD. MS &c to go to the City tomorrow to get the house ready for the family. Nancy and John are to go with us, I can scarcely make shift to step on my foot without a Shoe,—'tho it is getting better.

12 My Husband and Sister, Jo, Sam, and Sally, went to Town this morning intending to stay a day or two—HSD. went to Pennepac to look after Stone to build a Barn, he returnd in the evening, and went home with H Mott and E Emlen who spent the Afternoon and evening with us, S Emlen spent the Afternoon.

13 When we arose this Morning, it was snowing fast, the houses and trees cover'd—how much more butiful the appearance then in the City?—and what in the Country is not?—cloudy all the Afternoon, no body call'd to day, received a letter this evening from HD.

14 Betsy Emlen spent the day, with us—J Pemberton, call'd—very fine weather.

15 J. and H Pemberton call'd this morning as it is a very fine day, I wish'd to have gone home with William as I am lame and he not very well, I sent to borrow JPs Noke and their Carriage, JP. rote me a note that Oronoko was in the City, but if I could trust Aaron, I was welcome to the horses and Carriage—but being a great coward I did not except the offer—Sally Emlen and Huldah Mott Betsy Emlen spent the Afternoon with us—a farewel visit—HD. came up this evening with Joe and the Carriage in order to facilitate our departure, MD. unwell—Mary Briggs and her Nephew Isaac Jones call'd hear to see S Emlen—HD. settled with GH. paid him £ our expenses here for other things have been considerable, for provisions, Horses &c.—I wrote a short note to Maa. Livezey—fine moonlight night.

16 very busy preparing for our departure, J Pemberton call'd.—after one o'clock Noke came with their Carriage, William and myself left Germantown with some of our lugage—the roads but middling—we arriv'd at home between 2 and 3—found things in Statu-[quo], HD. with Nancy her little one and

Molly came half an hour after us in our Carriage, Sam drove Betsy Hardy in the Chaise. We are all through mercy, 'tho not in perfect health highly favour'd—Ben Wilson, John and Danl. Drinker call'd—we mett John Skyrin on the road, going to Germantown, he turnd back with us. most of the Philadelphians are return'd to the City, J and HP. and Sally Emlen are still at G—but I expect they will return next week—Neighr. Waln here this Afternoon, she expects her Daughter Sucky next week from Bristol, where they have spent the Summer—Nancy and her little one stays with us, untill their house is clean'd, cloudy this evening.

17 First Day: all Day in my Chamber, very poorly—HD. MS. JS. AS. HSD—went to meeting—WD. MD. stay'd at home, HD. invited 'this morning in meeting' to the funeral of Luke Morris, one of our oldest Citizens, born in the year 1707—rain all the Afternoon and evening—Billy Saltar came before tea, he lodges here.—How thankfull we ought to be, that we are return'd in safety to our own Habitation, If Jacob Sally and their dear little ones, were likewise well fixt at home, it would add to my Satisfaction, I trust 'eer long 'twill be so.

18 It continu'd to rain all night, clear'd up this morning with a smart NorthWester—John and Nancy Skyrin, John Hampson and Billy Saltar, din'd with our family, I am rather better this day than yesterday, 'tho not fitt to leave my Chamber—received a letter from Jacob Downing, informing of Marys being on the recovery 'tho weak, not able to stand on her feet, and of Eliza's having had the Flux also, 'tho not so violently as her sister. JS. AS. Billy Saltar, John Drinker and Robt. Stretal drank tea here, There is a report circulated that the Indians have beat the Army that went out against them, and that General Wayne is kill'd[84]—what pity 'tis peace was not made with them.

19 William Saltar left us after Breakfast—HD. MS. &c went to meeting it was very small—Caty Mullen here to day, in great trouble; she came over from Irland a poor widdow, when her 2 Sons were small, she work'd industreously for their and her own maintannance, put them apprentice, took great care of them during that term, they have been some years free, and have work'd at their trades with reputation; she hop'd that they would be her support in the decline of Life, but how uncertain are all human prospects? they were both taken this fall with the prevailing desease, and died, one the day after the other, the poor mother 'tho very ill at the same time surviv'd them, and may

84. The report of Gen. Anthony Wayne's death was false. Wayne had taken command of the Legion Army in the Northwest, following Gen. Arthur St. Clair's defeat in 1791. His troops were involved in a skirmish with the Indians near Fort Jefferson, Ohio, on Oct. 15, 1793, which may have served as the basis for this report, though he was not injured. Wayne went on to defeat the Indians in the Northwest at the Battle of Fallen Timbers in August 1794 (Nelson, *Anthony Wayne*, 225–27, 245–46, and passim).

be truly call'd a 'lone woman.—After her came poor Crissy Lambsback widdow of John who work'd for us—she says he did not die of the Yallow fever, as was reported, but of the pleurisy, he had a violent pain in his side, she could not prevail on the Doctor to bleed him, but he gave him wine, which he said he was sure hurt him,—after his death she went with her Children into the Jersyes, and on her return to the City, found the house where they had liv'd open, and most of her small property stolen, she is near lyeing-in, and has four small Children—how many are the instances of deep distress, that have this fall occur'd?—Joseph Drinker, Polly Cope with her young Son &c. here to day—Jacob Downing came this Afternoon, he lodges with us—J Skyrin has the rheumatesim in his shoulder—Betsy Hardy, Sam Sprigs &c are cleaning their house, Nancy went down this fore-noon for the first time, John has lodg'd there since our return—J and H Pemberton came to the City this fore-noon—Emlens Lawrence brought a letter from Betsy to Molly, they talk of returning very soon—I wrote this evening to S Downing, her Mary continus but poorly—Docr. Foulk and Ben Wilson down stairs this evening Charles West, and Nathan Shepherd also. A Woman in market this Afternoon took Sister for Betsy Dawson, a very common mistake, they have been taken for each other for 12 or 15 years past, sometimes 3 times in one day, at other times every day in the week, her Children and my Children have at first sight made the mistake.

20. HSD. went this Afternoon to Germantown—several down stairs and in and out, I know not who'—Neighr. Waln spent this evening with me—she mention'd many affecting Circumstances that have lately occur'd—Everead Boltons wife dy'd some time ago, she was a Daughter of Saml. and Rebecca Griscomb who are both also gone—I have heard of many since my return home, that had not before come to knowledge—Polly Chapman, who liv'd some Years ago at service with us, came here yesterday to tell her troubles, she has lost her husband (a poor thing) and left with two young Children, Our maid Jenny, who went out of town a little before our family, came here this evening but talks of returning to the country again.—good Servants at this time are very scarce—rain or hail this evening Wind at N.E.—No day passes, without some Grief. was a copy I wrote when a schooler to Anthony Benezet.

21 Michel Callanan here this morning he is return'd from Bristol where he has spent most of the Summer—Betsy Grenudle came here this morning Nancy has hired her to tend her Child &c—JS. AS. JD. and David Cummins din'd here, the same and John Rireson drank tea—Sister has been this Afternoon to Jacobs House, ordering it clean'd for their reception—upwards of 30 persons have died in that square—clear this evening.

22 M Callanan; Gilbart Prichard farmer and wife from Great Britian, recommended to HD. by the Barcleys, din'd here, and others. Docr. Kuhn call'd

to see us, Nancy gone this afernoon to her house—Prichard and Wife lodges here, MD. gone this Afternoon to visit E Emlen, they return'd yesterday—clear this evening.

23. JS. AS. JD. GP. and Wife Breakfasted here, and din'd after dinner JS. and AS. went home intend to send this afternoon for the dear little one, Gilbart Prichard and wife set off in our Carriage HSD. with them for Docr. Logans, I have not seen them, having been up stairs ever since my return from Germantown—we shall seem lonely this evening having parted with so many—Doctor Redman, John Pemberton, Nurse Waters, Hope Sharp &c call'd—Crissey Lambsback was here, HD. gave her an order to receive share of monys subscrib'd for poor widdows, renderd so by the late Sickness.—I wrote a note to S Swett. HSD. return'd with GP. and wife, George Logan being from home, they are strangers, and know not where to go, 'till a suitable place is found for 'em. two young men of the Name of Alsop, Brothers, lately from Great-britian, who keep school in the Jersys, drank tea here. Saml. Preston arrived here this evening from Stock-port. It appear'd after dinner, as 'tho we should have been left to ourselves this night, but it looks now far otherwise. JS. AS. and their foulks took tea here, they are now gone to settle at home.

24 First Day: Jacob Downing left us just at Sun-rising—G Prichard and Wife, the two Allsops, lodg'd here last night, they went this morning to meeting, they din'd here, Jn. Collens also—the Alsops set off after dinner for the Jersys—J and AS. came before meeting, she left her babe and its Nurse with me, call'd for them after meeting—HD. MS. HSD. at meeting this morning WD. MD. and self at home—Molly gone this Afternoon to Atsion her Sister Ann, in putting things to wrights.[85] Neighr. Waln spent part of the evening. MD. observ'd while at her sisters this Afternoon, a Coffin in a Cart, and 10 or 12 persons walking on the pavement as attendents, 'tis to be fear'd that the Yallow fever is not intirely over, I have heard of one or two last week who it was thought had it. S Preston lodges here, I can hear him amplifying below as I set alone up stairs.

25 the usual Company at Breakfast, I this fore-noon put on Williams Sliper: next day after tomorrow will be 7 weeks, since I hurt my foot, it continues to be much swell'd, the blackness not quite gone, it continus to mend 'tho slowly—I have been in my Chamber ever since I came home untill this morning after breakfast, went down stairs and spent the day—Gilbert and

85. The following verse crossed out:

To be alone, I mean sans company
To me is oftimes greatfull:
Not that a tast for sweet society
In me is lacking—But when not to be obtain'd
To be alone is pleasent.

Francis Prichard, S. Preston and Mary Savery din'd with us—Betsy Emlen and H Mott call'd for Molly to take a ride with 'em,—William has rode out 2 or 3 mornings on the Old Mare—EE. spent the Afternoon, several Men call'd on business. Nancy here this Afternoon with her little one. Molly and Betsy E. went to Nancys this evening received a note this afternoon from J Logan, M Savery inform'd of the Death of our old neighbor Sally Garraway.—clear.

26 clear and cold this morning a smart N.Wr. Joe set off very early with the Carriage to Downings town for Sally and the Children—Samuel Preston left us this morning after Breakfast—HD. MS. MD. gone to monthly meeting: G.P. and wife who now seem part of our family, H. Catheral and S Swett din'd here—they have both had, as they think, a touch of the disorder—Nurse Waters, Sammy Emlen and others here—John Drinker sup'd with us—Jacob Downings Man Anthony came after night, he and R Downings driver have brought a Waggon load of JDs things, which they have left at a Tavern for this Night—Anthony lodges here[86]—cloudy and temperate.

27 cloudy most of this day: H Mott E Emlen, Nancy Skyrin and Child, Anna Wells and Child, and James Logan were here this day—my foot much swell'd this evening.

28 a raw morning wind easterly—disagreeable traveling for our Children, especially as the young ones are Invalids,—besides our present family, M Callanan, Thos. Edmundson,—began to rain about dinner time, continu'd all the Afternoon and evening—before 5 o'clock, the Downing family arrived here, they have had rather a heavy journey, Sally very well, Eliza bravely, little Mary but poorly—'tho I hope recovering—so soon after very many of our old friends and Neighbours are laid in the dust, to see our own family all mett togeather, is cause of great thankfullness and humiliation, after spending some hours in Company, I have laterly retired to my Chamber much fatigu'd, being inwardly week, I feel then, from under a restraint, can set and think, and bath my foot, and conceit I can do as I please.—our dear William is better than he has been for 3 or 4 years past at this time of the year, 'tho a great weakness at his breast continues, and a cough at times—I beleive the sweet clear air of Germantown has been useful to him.

29 rain all night, continues raining this morning lay awake greatest part of the night—our Children have I trust, taken the right time to return—small rain all day, harder this evening John and Joseph Drinker here, several others. we are just now 17 or 18 in family—I have been more than usualy unwell this day—the fier treads Snow, as 'tis[87] said—last Night and the night before, we

86. The word "clear" crossed out.
87. The word "call'd" crossed out.

heard the cry of fier, our family were not generaly alarme'd, it dyed away—and upon enquiery do not find that any damage of consequence has happen'd.— little MDs disorder still continues, 'tho measurably cheeck'd.

30 Clear'd up—Nancy Morgan and Widdow Durdan call'd—we have lost, or parted with nine of our family to day—Gilbart and Francies Prichard; Jacob, Sally, Eliza, Mary Downing, their servants Catty Antony, and Anna, they went to their House. Nancy, her little daughter and childs Maid, Caty Halzell, daughter to our old Neighbour John Hazell taylor, who dy'd of the Yallow fever, were here this Afternoon—We are at present but eight in family, but expect on second-day next an addition of two.[88]

Decbr. 1. First Day. In my Chamber most of this day, which was very unusual for me, before my present indispossion, it is many years since I have spent a day in my Chamber, on my own account, 'tho often sufficiently unwell but but I lik'd it not, and to me it was formerly very disagreeable, but at present I have no objection to retirement, when necessary, 'tis rather pleasing. John Skyrin, H Mott and E Emlen call'd—little ES. and her maid spent the Morning with me, while her Mother went to meeting—S Swett B Wilson and A Skyrin din'd here. they drank tea, JS. E Emlen and Joshua Cliborn also— Sally, Eliza, Jacob, here, John Drinker sup'd with us.

2 this day spent as usual laterly, I cannot yet walk but little having my Sons shoe on—made a pair Shoes for my grand Daughters ES.—G Prichard walk'd to town from Docr. Logans, left his wife there, he is disapointed of a place there, has still to look out for one, he lodges here S Swett, C. Evans, A Skyrin, M. Callanan called MD. went with EE. to visit Anna Wells HD. at meeting four time this day.

3 AS. left her nurse and Child with me, while she went to meeting—S Swett, Gilbart Prichard, and Nurse Waters din'd with us—GP. went after dinner on foot to G Logans.—HD. MS. MD. out this Afternoon WD. and self at home HSD. writing in the uptown front Room which HD. proposes to use as an Accounting House this winter—Snow this evening Jacob and Sally, Michl. Callanan here to day.

4 Snow Storm blew hard all night; Snow appears to be 16 or 18 inches deep on a level—M Callanan, Ben Wilson &c here to day.

5 fine clear weather G Prichard here to day, he lodges here—Thos Falliot writing in the front Room—Nancy Skyrin call'd, Sally Downing also, H Mott and E Emlen here this forenoon, Molly went home with them and Spent the

88. The word "more" crossed out.

day, S Emlen came with her in the evening—J Skyrin call'd—Sally Dawson came upon trial, her Father intends binding her to us, she is 9 years and ½ old—a pritty looking Child—her mother dead, not long since.

6 A Carpenter Shop a little above vine Street took fier about 10 o'clock this morning and was consumed—H Mott, EE. and MD set off in a Sleigh for Germantown, found the roads so bad they turn'd back—Joe went in our Sleigh with GP. to bring his wife from Docr. Logans, they return'd to dinner, Jo[h]. Saltar din'd here also—HM. EE. AS. and her little one spent the Afternoon with us, Nancy and Child went away with them after 8 o'clock in their Carriage—from their departure untill Bed time, a trying time to me—heavy rain, melting Snow.

7 No Company here to day, GP. and wife excepted—rain—much indispos'd all day.

8 First Day: stay'd up stairs this morning under an apparent absolute necessity to take medicine, which if it could be avoided, suits me not—After midnight this morning a Storm of thunder lightening, wind and rain, and as I thought hail, lasted about an hour—Wind high and Cold this morning, which is common after winters thunder—Nancy Skyrin call'd after meeting—Robt. Stevenson junr. drank tea with us—Saml. Coates and John Drinker call'd, Saml Fisher here in the evening to talk with GP—whom, if they can agree, he proposes to employ on his plantation.—cold and windy all this day, I have been unusualy unwell, or rather more than common, with weak bowels.

9 M Callanan, A Skyrin and Daughter Sally Downing and Eliza, Docr. Redman call'd. John Cannon and G.F.P. din'd with us—Polly Drinker and her little Girl here.

10. Tabby and Becky Fisher and E Foulke, call'd after meeting, S Swett and the Prichards din'd, Sucky Hartshorn and Son here in the Evening—Sister and Molly out, A Skyrin here before meeting—Betsy Dawson sister to our little Sall, came to Nancy on trial—it is very pleasant winter weather.

11 HSD. and Richd. Thomas, set of after breakfast for Bucks county to visit Henrys Farm, and to call on Danl. Trimble—Sally Emlen, Betsy Jervis and James Logan drank tea here, John Cannon and two or 3 others also—Sally and the Children here this morning.

12 This day set apart by the Gouvenor for prayer and thanksgiven.—unwell all day and for a long time past—Neighr. Waln, Doctor Griffits here this morning—Michl. Callanan the Prichards, and Nichs. Depugh, din'd with us—A Skyrin also—Hannah and Sally Hopkins came this evening, they lodge

with us—Nancy Hopkins married about a month past to Marmaduke Burr—clear and cold—Billy went after 8 o'clock to Jacob Downings 'tis long since he was out in a winters night.

13. I have been troubled this day with an inward and outward trembling, occasion'd I believe to the obstruction in my bowles—several at breakfast, the usual company and N. Depugh at dinner, John Cannon the Prichards &c at tea—HSD. return'd from Bs. County—Nancy Skyrin and Child, B. Emlen and her Cosen Wm. Mott, Hannah Smith, Ellinor Foulk, Isaac Wharton, John Hopkins, Phebe Whay &c here to day—Hannah and Sally Hopkins lodge here.—Sally Stapler was here last night, appear'd in much trouble.

14 Hannah and Sally Hopkins went home this Afternoon, Gilbert and Francis Prichard left us after dinner, went to their intended residence at S Fishers place—very few call'd in the back parlor this day—Nancy Skyrin here, our people very busy geting in wood, and salting pork.

15 First day: the family at meeting, William and myself excepted—S Fisher call'd after—S Swett and Anthony New, a Virginia Deligt. din'd with us—Eliza. Downing came this day to spend a week with us, if it should so happen,—she went twice to meeting with her Aunt Molly—Betsy Emlen call'd after meeting the fore-noon—Neighr. Waln spent the evening I have been better this day then usual—M Callanan here.

16 several transient persons here to day—I sent for Docr. Kuhn, had a long confab with him.

17 took one of Joness powders last night and two this day, by Dr. Kuhns order, a point du purpose. Robt. Stephenson and Daughter Susan, paid us a morning visit. George Parish here this fore-noon, Hannah Catheral din'd with us—S Downing and her two Daughters A Skyrin and Daughter M. Drinker and Daughter M Cope and Son, John Skyrin, T. Cope, &c drank tea here, James Thornton and T. Scatergood, in the front Room this evening—Saml. Sansom spent the evening. I spent this Afternoon and evening in my Chamber. prenez un L—— en vain—very moderate weather.

18 The moon full'd yesterday Afternoon, last evening it was hazey, this morning when I awoke it rain'd hard, and has continu'd to rain more or less all day. Docr. Kuhn, and Gilbart Prichard call'd—spent the latter part of this day in my Chamber very poorly.

19 this morning came Wm. Blekley, Samy. Smith, John Simson and James Moon and Rachel Watson, they put up here if I may so call it, were gone before I came down stairs, Nancy Skyrin and Child came this fore-noon and

spent the day with us, she and Jon. Adlam din'd with us—Rachl. Watson and Saml. Smith lodges here—Sally Downing, J Skyrin &c call'd.—John Hopkins here this evening he took leave of us, is going to settle in Charlston South Carolina.

20 Wm. Bleakey, Rachl. Watson &c here the Morning Rachel and William din'd with us, they left us after dinner—Sally Zane call'd—I acknowledged a deed before Isaac Howel, he was so kind as to call on me for that purpose—Sally Dawson was this day bound to us, by her Father Thos. Dawson, for the term of Eight years from this day—James Moon Nancy Skyrin, and Jacob Downing call'd. Saml Smith lodges here, Dr. Kuhn, Oliver Paxon calld this fore-noon—the weather temperate for Seas.

21 John Simson here this morning Saml Smith breakfast'd with us, and then went homewards, the two Alsops call'd—G Prichard and Nancy Skyrin din'd with us, John Cannon, Jacob and Sally Downing drank tea here—very cold this day, the shortest and coldest this winter. Debby Daws call'd she lost her Husband in the Yallow fever.

22 First Day: Wm. myself, and little Eliza at home, the rest of our family gone to meeting—Jonathan Paxon breakfasted here, John Cannon and Thos. Stewardson din'd;—Molly Drinker and Eliza[h] gone to dine at Jacob Downings, ED. under the necessity of spending most of this day in her Chamber—Warner Mifflin and John Drinker drank tea with us—John and Nancy Skyrin call'd after morning meeting. Among the many calamitous occurances of last summer and autumn, I heard of one yesterday that was truely affecting, A Man and Wife of the name of Lewis, who liv'd up town in front street, and had been married about a year, were ill of the yallow fever, (as it is call'd) lay in the same Bed, with only a little Girl to attend them, one morning a Neighbour (who knew they were very ill the night before) went in to enquire how they were, she found them both dead, and an infant partly born dead also—she was 7 months gone with child—Several circumstances, simelar to this, occur'd during the three distressing months that the fever prevail'd in this City.

23. No body at breakfast, Sally Downing din'd with us—John Simson, John and Nancy Skyrin drank tea—Neighr. Waln here in the evening—our three little grand Children spent great part of this day with us, Richd. Thomas call'd this evening.

24. HD. MS. HSD. gone to monthly Meeting Cad Evans call'd—S Swett din'd, A Skyrin call'd—Betsy Emlen and Paggy Mott SS. drank tea with us. Molly Drinker took a ride with EE after dinner—Wm Mott &c here this evening S Downing call'd; warm.

25 Christsmass, so call'd, keep't by some pious well minded people religiously, by some others as a time of Frolicking—Thos. Stewardson din'd with us—rain and cloudy all day; clear'd towards evening.

26 a great transition in the weather, day before yesterday warm for the Season, yesterday temperate, this day very cold, in so much that it is thought if the wind should abait that the river will be fast before tomorrow morning—Richd. Thomas, Betsy Fordham, Betty Newton &c call'd this Morning Nancy Skyrin came after dinner with her little one, this very cold time, too much I think for such a young one—Molly took Eliza to dine with her at her Fathers—came back like a good child in the evening—Charles West call'd, John Adlam and Jacob Lindly sup'd with us, John Elliott here—wind very high this evening.

27 HD. at the middle monthly meeting—John Drinker call'd, sans Company to day, cold.

28. Sally and Nancy here to day. S Swett spent the day with us—Ben Wilson, Jacob Downing here this evening—Nancy Rice formerly Corry call'd on Sister—to excuse herself from paying her ground rent, she has lost her Son, an only child aged 15 years, and Nursed her husbands brother and his wife, who both also died of the late fever.—Docr. Redman here at noon—HD. went this morning with those friends who were at the Indian treaty,[89] to wait on the President,[90] to have some talk with him, touching the Indian War &c.

29 First day: all gone to meeting, Wm. and self excepted—din'd alone—Eliza din'd at her Fathers—Nancy came with her maid and Child after dinner, she left them with us, and went to meeting—Wm. Saltar and A Skyrin drank tea with us—Saml. Smith call'd Anna Wells and Betsy Waln call'd—John Skyrin in the Evening Wm. Saltar lodges here—weather more temperate.

30 WSr. breakfasted. Wm. Simpson and Nurse Waters din'd, W. Saltar at Tea—J Downing here this morning left little Mary with us—John Drinker call'd—and J. Skyrin this evening informing that Nancy complain'd of sore mouth &c. The Trustees of Union-Farm[91] mett in front Room. Nancys Girl here this evening her mistress poorly—William Saltar lodges here.

89. Six Quakers had attended the meetings at Sandusky in July: Joseph Moore, William Savery, John Parish, John Elliott, Jacob Lindley, and William Hartshorne. Moore, who died Oct. 7, could not have attended this later meeting (J. Moore, "Moore's Journal," 632, 668; see above, Sept. 19).

90. The word "dinner" crossed out.

91. Union Farm was founded in 1792 by HD and a group of investors on Little Equinunk Creek and the Delaware River in what is now Manchester Township, Wayne County, Pa. The purpose of the farm was to produce sugar from maple trees and thus help free the U.S. from its dependence on West Indian sugar and the slave trade. By 1795 the project had collapsed, but HD, who owned the land, continued to pay real estate taxes on the property until his death (Maxey, "Union Farm," 607–29).

31 We were disturb'd between one and two this morning by Henry knocking at his Aunts Chamber door, Eliza who sleeps with him was taken with a sick stomach and pukeing, Sister was up with her near two hours, she is bravely this morning Billy Saltar went away after breakfast—Betty Newton fitted a gown on me.—Our dear William who has been more then usuly unwell for some days past, observ'd some blood in the phlegm that he brought up, two or 3 times this fore-noon, we sent for Docr. Kuhn, who ordred him blooded, it was done by Michel, Fredricks prentice, he seems better this evening—T. Stewardson sup'd with us, John Cannon drank tea—Molly spent the afternoon with Nancy, she continues rather unwell.—They are now practizeing the foolish custom of fireing out the old year, may the next be spent to good purpose, by those who are spair'd to see the end of it.—the wind high this night—HD. is at present favour'd with as good a share of health as I ever knew him—the Lachrymal Fistula which took place in his left Eye, in May ninety two, continues as it was when the swelling first subsided, neither better nor worse—MS. highly favour'd with a continued state of good health, much better than some years past. ED. far from enjoying a state of bodily health, Jacob Sally and their little ones much favour'd. Nancy at present but poorly, JS. and the little Elizabeth, well, she is a very promiseing Child. Our dear William, who has been in a low state of health for upwards of four years, is at present as well as could be expected considering what he has past through, it is four years this last fall since he had the Epidimic cold, call'd the Influensia, and had been drooping for a twelve month before, all our family had it, and I beleive every family in the City, and Country also, more or less, William was the worst of us, and longer getting better, he had another attack the spring following—was poorly all summer. The fall after, he went into the beach woods, was from home about 6 weeks, lay out in the woods, one night, and but little better many other nights—he return'd home much recover'd—but on the 9th. of Novemr. was taken with a sore throat, he had smok'd a Cagar the evening before in the store in water-street with some young men, not being us'd to it, found himself sick, and in a sweat, went out into the cold air, and walk'd as far as walnut street—the next day the 9th. he went with his father to visit R James, Abel James very lately dead.—had a chilld in the Evening the next day we sent for Dr. Kuhn, who said he had a touch of the Quinsey, but it turn'd out much worse than the Doctor expected, he was many days that he could not speak,—and when the disorder in his throat was better he lost the use of his limbs, so as not to be able to walk alone, or to button his Jacket, he was four months confin'd to his Chamber,—in the spring he rode out in a Close Carriage, seem'd to geather strength in the Summer. in the fall 91, he went on Horse-back towards new England—but was stop'd at a place call'd Rye 30 miles beyond New York, with a fever and spitting of blood—hir'd a Chaise and Man to bring him back to N-Y—where he was ill at Henry Haydocks, brought up two quarts of blood from his lungs in 3 days, Dr. Jones was sent for, who call'd in Dr. John Bard; Robt Bowne wrote an account to

HD. of Billys having broke a blood vessel, and of his dangerous situation, he and self, set off the next day for NY. Nancy was to have gone with us, but having sleep't none the preceeding night, was rendred uncapable by the head ach[92]—John and she follow'd us the next day—I fully expected to have found my dear Boy a[93] Corps on our arrival at NY—the journey to me was in truth an anxious one—we walk'd from the Elizath. Town ferry, and on approaching HHs house I look'd up to the Chambers windows which I found was rais'd up, as I expected, supposing, my son was laying in the front Chamber, on crossing the Street, we were mett by HH junr. who coming up to me, said "friend Drinker Billy is better," 'tho while on the journey it had frequently occur'd to me, that 'while there was life, there was hope', and that I might hear on our arrival there, that William was better, yet I had so little expectation of it, that when I heard it, I seemd in a torpid state, uncapable of takin in the full force of the words, and prehaps it was better for me that it was so—William who expected our coming, had fortified himself all in his power, to see us, the discharge of blood had ceas'd for near 24 hours, he had been twice bleed in his Arm, before we came, and twice after upon a small appearance of a return of the complaint, he had a hard cough, which was much against him, he keep'd his bed for 3 weeks by Dr. Bards direction—by that means and other judicious [percrecptions] the cough wore off, and he graduly became better—'tho amazinely week;—Nancy stay'd with me 4 weeks, she then returnd home, mett her Sister Molly on the road coming to assist me, as they expected Nancys return—Molly was 5 week with us—The particular care of our good Doctors Bard and Jones, with good nurseing and the kindness of the[94] family we were with—brought William so forward as to attempt a journey home-wards—My husband had visited us two or 3 times, HSD once or twice.—We left H Haydocks on the third of Decemr. and arriv'd at our own dwelling on the 6th. after dinner, I believe I may say with thankful hearts. he was confin'd to the house most of the winter, very poorly in the spring, but re[ ]uted again in the Summer—in the fall 92, he caught cold staying too late in the evening at Frankford—was 8 or 10 days ill of a plurisy—after that something of the fall fever, so that what little health he geather'd during the summer, was generly overturn'd by a cold in the fall—he is now, the many pullbacks consider'd, as well as might be expected. the Doctors encourages us to hope, that if he can survive his Eight or nine and twentieth year, he may still become a healthy Man;—Our Son HSD. just turn'd of 23, is at present very well and hearty, it is remarkable in him that he looses flesh considerably in the Summer season, grows fatt and hearty in the winter—his chief complaints are a sick stomach at times, and two or 3 times in the coarse of his life a stitch in his side, a small obstruction in his liver, he is on the whole favour'd with good

92. The words "to go with us" crossed out.
93. The word "dead" crossed out.
94. The word "good" crossed out.

health & spirits. He is employ'd improving his farm which his father lately purchas'd and gave him, part of the Manor of Pennsbury, where he expects to spent his days as a farmer. May it please kind Providence to direct his steps—in that, and another undertaking of greater consiquence, which 'tis likely he will 'eer long be thinking, off—our Daughter Molly was born the finest and healthyest of 9 Children, she has been for several years at times complaining, 'tho far from sickly, and if she manages herself with care, may make a fine healthy Woman.

1794

1794.[1] Janry. 1 fourth day:—poor R——n H——s was bury'd yesterday at Potts-Grove, he has been much disturb'd in mind for a long time past.—Docr. Kuhn call'd this morning upon seeing Williams blood which he lost yesterday by his order, thought that he would be better for it—he inform'd us of the death of a Son of Alexr. Willcocks who dy'd abroad of the Yallow-fever in one of the Islands:—T Stewardson and Saml. Stanton din'd with us—James Logan, Betsy Emlen, Billy Mott, Nancy Skyrin drank tea with us—John Skyrin, Jacob and Sally Downing, and John Pemberton &c call'd.

2d. Sally Downing, John Skyrin, Ben Willson, call'd, John Drinker drank tea, Dr. Kuhn call'd this morning advis'd William to walk out, he is better, and the day very fine, Polly Noble call'd, Neighr. Waln here this evening—Richd. Waln call'd this morning I have not seen him for a long time past.

3 Joseph Knight and Sam Stanton breakfasted, Molly Foulk din'd, Anna Wells drank tea: Sally Downing, Betsy Foulk, John Skyrin call'd, Molly rode out with Betsy Emlen, HSD. went to Chester and return'd this day.

4 Jacob and Sally Downing call'd, Joseph Townsend, Jessy Hollandsworth, Ben Wilson and Richd. Trimble din'd here, Sam Stanton Tea'd with us, warm for the Season.

5 First Day: S Swett din'd, HD. took Physick, he stay'd all day at home, John Parish, John Drinker, Jacob and Sally Downing, John and Nancy Skyrin call'd.

6 A fier broke out this morning about 8 o'clock on the south side of Race street, between front and second streets which damaged 3 Houses, A Skyrin din'd here, her little one all day: J Skyrin, Sally Downing, Anna Wells, Charles West, Eliston Perot call'd.

7 HSD. set off early this morning for his intended Farm expects to lodge at

1. The manuscript volume for 1794 has light blue covers. The outside front cover reads, "1794." On the outside front cover ED also wrote, "came from town near 17 yards yard wide linnen."

Danl. Trimbles to night,—My dear WD. discovr'd blood in his spittle this fore-noon, he does not appear low spirited, but I am sure it must affect him. S Swett, John Cannon, and Wm. Simpson drank tea with us—Jacob and Sally, J Skyrin, H. Catheral, Molly and Susan Stevenson and Docr. Redman call'd—very cold morning.

8 I lodg'd last night with Eliza. in the front room in Henrys Bed—William and Henry lie in one room in different Beds,—I caugh cold by the change, and have been unwell all this day, John Pemberton, H Catheral &c call'd—J Cannon and Wm. Simpson drank tea.

9 Nancy and her Child din'd here—Sally Rhoades, and Huldah Mott spent the afternoon—Sarah Fisher, M. Callanan, J Drinker &c call'd—HSD. return'd this evening from Buck-county—Hannah Yerkas &c call'd—heavy rain in the night, My dear mother 38 years dead.

10 No body din'd or tea'd with us, which is very unusual, Jacob and Sally, John and Nancy, here this evening, WD. very unwell, the weather warm for the Season.

11 Billy Shotwell, his Wife and Nancy Skyrin, din'd with us—John Skyrin, Warner Mifflin &c call'd—an Affecting account in the paper of this day, of the trial and Death of the Queen of France, beyond discription cruel—she was beheaded on the 16 October last.[2]—Sally Shotwel informs of the death of Sally Cambell, daughter of Thos. Pearsal Merchant of New-York.

12 First Day: little or no Company this day: WD. but poorly, weather cold.

13 The Anneversary of our marriage 33 years—S Swett drank tea, Hannah Smith call'd &c—William continues raising bloody phlem, sent for Docr. Kuhn, he order'd Ellexer of Vitrol[3]—heavy rain this evening.

14 Jacob and Sally, Richd Thomas, and Nancy Skyrin drank tea with us.

15 I am still under the necessity of wareing my Sons Slipper, morn'g and evening my foot being still very weak and Swell'd—it is 3 months and a week

2. A long account of Marie Antoinette's death appeared in *Dunlap and Claypoole's American Daily Advertiser*, describing her as the "unhappy victim of democratic fury" (*Dunlap and Claypoole's American Daily Advertiser*, Jan. 11, 1794; see also Beatrice F. Hyslop, "American Press Reports of the French Revolution, 1789–1794," *New-York Historical Society Quarterly* 42 (1958): 343).

3. Elixir of vitriol, a filtered combination of oil of vitriol (sulfuric acid) and an aromatic tincture of sugar, spices, and wine, was once considered a valuable medicine in case of "weakness and relaxations of the stomach and decays of the constitution" (W. Lewis, *New Dispensatory*, 249–50, 326–27).

since I hurt it.—My dear William is very poorly.—John Cannon and another drank tea, S Downing &c call'd—cold weather, it snow'd the night before last.

16. Nancy and the Child spent the day with us, Neighr. Waln, Nancy Morgan, Sally Downing, Nancy Skyrin and John Ryerson drank tea with us—A Wells &c called.

17. our Girls spent this afternoon with H. Thomas—John Watson junr. lodges here to night. J Nicholdson Comptroler call'd, he has purchas'd A[J]s place at Frankford of Cacardo, the French Gentleman who bought it of the Trustees.

18. very few persons here to day; I mean in the parlor, Jacob Downing and Jacob Lindly call'd, ED. unwell.

19. First Day: Thos. Stewardson din'd here—Becky Thompson and 3 of her Children here after dinner.

20 The weather very warm for the season, The Thermometer up at 50—E. Emlen here this Afternoon, Molly rode out with her.

21 Dr. Redman &c call'd, MS. MD. abroad, ED. unwell.

22.23.24. Omitted 25. several here to day.

26 First Day: William and self at home the rest of the family at meeting, took medicine unavoidably. last night, or rather this morning a little after 12 o'clock, the wind very high, I heard the bells ring, and afterwards the cry of fier, some of our family arose, but discoverd that it was at a considerable distance the people down town had been long before alarm'd, so that they did not go out—We understand this morning that there is three Houses burnt and 2 damaged, at the South-west corner of second and pine Streets.

27 Docr. Redman &c here to day, HSD. and ED—held a Correspondence with pen and Ink, by the fire-side, on a subject of great importance.

28 Our dear Williams birth day—several call'd—Daniel Trotter here to borrow our bed-Chair, for the use of Allen or David Ridgeway, they were both run over by a Horse and Cart yesterday, one had his Leg broke, the others Head badly hurt. J Logan drank tea with us—Sister gone to S Emlens, Molly to J Frys with Nancy her little one here all day—An account in this days paper

of the trial and Excution of Brissot, de Warville and 20 other arrested Deputies in Paris.[4]

29 Joseph Saltar and Son left us after breakfast—HD. set off about 10 this fore-noon for to take a view of a Plantatiton which is for sale about 6 miles from the City, between the old york road and Germantown soon after his departure it began to snow, he went but two miles then return'd, the roads bad and his Horse not properly shod, it has snow'd ever since, and is this evening pretty deep,—We were invited this Morning to the burial of the Widdow Bonham, 'tho numbers have undoubtedly died in this City, yet I do not recollect our being invited to a funeral before since our return from Germantown, it has been an uncommon healthy winter so far, tho the weather has been unsteady.

Janry. 30. A Snow storm last night, when we retired—this morning clear and cold, snow 9 or 10 inches deep—Sleighs flying about in great numbers with Bells at the Horses [e]ars a measure which took place last winter on account of the danger of a Sleigh coming unawares, and not being heard—when the pavements are slip'ry the people walk in the streets.—Moses Brown, William Rotch junr. Saml. Rodman, Thos. Arnold, David Buffam and John Morton din'd with us, those friends John Morton excepted, with John Collins (who is this day at the Marriage of his brother Stevens Son Zach. Collins to S. A. Marshal) are a deputation from Rhode-Island Yearly meeting to Congress, with a memorial on the subject of the Slave-trade.—our little Eliza Downing, spent this day at her Fathers, she generaly dines there once a week.

31 HD. HSD. MD went this fore-noon in the Carriage, to the funeral of Robt. Stevensons Sister Kannady, who was at her Brothers on a visit she dy'd of a pleurisy, after about a weeks illness, and was bury'd in friends burying ground—a Dozen or 14 Carriages attended, none on foot. Jacob Downing, John and Nancy Skyrin din'd here, after an early dinner HD. JD. JS. and Eliza went in the Sligh to Gilbort Prichards, where they left Eliza, while they went to the farm which HD has had thoughts of purchasing—they return'd to tea, Nancy and her little one stay'd with us 'till nine at night. Sally Downing here before dinner. Benjn. Wilson came this evening intends to lodge with us,

4. Jacques-Pierre Brissot de Warville was a French journalist who had spent some time in Philadelphia in 1788 during his visit to the United States and had written a memoir of his travels. He became a leading political figure of the moderate republican Girondist faction during the French Revolution. The Girondists eventually fell out of favor, and the arrest of Brissot, along with twenty-nine other members of his group, was ordered on June 2, 1793. He fled, but was captured soon after and executed on Oct. 31 (*Dunlap and Claypoole's American Daily Advertiser*, Jan. 28, 1794; Scott and Rothaus, *French Revolution*, s.v. "Brissot de Warville, Jacques-Pierre").

for some time, HSD invited him, as Hannah Baker with whom he boards and lodges, expects soon to be confin'd to her Chamber.

Febry. 1. Jacob, Sally, Molly and the two little Girls went after dinner Sleighing—this sharp weather agrees illey with our dear William, he has spit blood for some time past, and feels a great weakness at his breast.—Alexandr. Wilson here this evening.

2d. First day: ED. WD. and Eliza at home, the rest of the family at meeting; Ruhamer John Alsop lodged here last night BW. also—A Skyrin call'd before afternoon meeting—We came this morning into the front parlor, it being much warmer and more lively then the back—Joseph Drinker drank tea with us, the weather very cold—Thos. Stewardson sup'd here.

3 Quarterly Meeting. Thos. Lightfoot of Reding and Danl. Drinker din'd here, Josh. Drinker here after dinner—J Logan drank tea, Saml. Dupee and Jos. Bringhurst call'd Neighr. Waln spent the evening the weather more moderate.

4 James Logan, Nurse Waters call'd—Docr. Redman also—James Harris din'd with us—John and Nancy Skyrin drank tea.

5 Dr. Kuhn call'd being sent for, as William continues to raise blood in small quantities, he was apprehensive that his Lungs were ulcerated, but the Doctor says 'tis nothing like it, he has none of the Symptoms of an ulcer.—Caty Decon brought little Mary Downing to visit us to day, she has been unwell for some time past, with a sore mouth and fever. [S]D. unwel last night.

Febry. 6 Dr. Redman, John James, Betty Newton here this morning very cold, snow this evening—David Ridgway, one of the two Brothers that were hurt by a runaway horse in a Cart, is dead, the other ill.

7 WD. poorly, ED. also, weather rather more moderate, no one call'd today in the parlor, but Jacob Downing—Isaac Wharton and 4 or 5 others in the Counting-room this evening.

8 HD. and Sammy Smith set off after breakfast in our Sleigh for Bucks County—J Drinker, Robt. Stevenson junr., T Stewardson, Christor. Smith call'd—the Snow melting fast away.

9 First Day: Snow'd most all day—HD. return'd about 10 o'clock.—Ben Wilson and Saml Bound from N York din'd with us, J Downing, call'd, Elijah

Pound drank tea, sup'd and lodg'd here, he is come about taking the Quibletown[5] mills.

10 E. Pound went away after breakfast, E Emlen spent the Afternoon—A Committee this evening in front room, they concluded to purchase Langhorn-Park for a publick School.[6]

11 very warm for the time of year—Nancy Skyrin spent this day with us—Jacob and Sally, John and Nancy, their 3 Children, James Logan, Ben Wilson, and Thos. Arnold drank tea here, WD. ED. poorly—M. Callanan & S Emlen junr call'd.

12 Dr. Kuhn, Betsy Foulk, Jacob and Sally Downing call'd Foggy weather for some days past.

13 Febry. 13. John Hillborn, John R. Alsop, and B Wilson, lodg'd here, Sam Preston drank tea and sup'd S Downg. call'd.

14 John Hillborn, S Preston din'd with us—Nancy Skyrin spent the afternoon.

15 John Pemberton drank tea, several call'd.

16 First Day: Sally Rhoads, [S] Downing, A Skyrin call'd.

17 John Hillborn left us this morning Pegey Wharton spent the Evening. John Ruhamer Alsop came as a Clerk to HD—he lodges and Diets in Elfreths Alley. James Logan, Betsy, Sally and Molly Jervis and Betsy junr. drank tea here—Ben Wilson and Saml. Preston sup'd. R Jones &c call'd, fine weather.

18 Anna Wells, James Logan, Nancy Skyrin here this morning Esther Trimble and her daughter Peggy with Jenny Richards here also—spar'd Peggy 11 yards Lutstring for a wedding Garment, Anna Wells, A Skyrin, Patr. Hartshorn, En. Evans, here this evening—A shop burnt, in 3d. Street last evening heard nothing of it 'till this day—S Preston &c call'd.

19 unwell all day: J Logan, Sally Downing.

5. Quibbletown was the former name of New Market, N.J., a village in Piscataway Township, Middlesex County (Gordon, *Gazetteer of New Jersey*, 117).

6. HD and several other Friends purchased Langhorne Park, a tract of 450 acres of land on Neshaminy Creek near Bristol, in Bucks County, Pa., in expectation that the Philadelphia Yearly Meeting would establish a Quaker boarding school there. The purchase took place before the 1794 meeting in order to forestall an exorbitant selling price should the site be selected (Dewees and Dewees, *Centennial of Westtown*, 1–29; Hole, *Westtown*, 20–28).

20 Saml. Smith of Bucks County, came to meeting for Sufferings he din'd and lodges here—Josey Sansom spent the evening hard rain with a great fog.

21st. Saml. Smith left us after breakfast—Nancy Skyrin Ben. Wilson, Hannah Catheral and Bancroft Woodcock din'd here, Richd. Nesbet drank tea—George Churchman, Neigr. Waln and 2 of her grand Children, Robt. Stevenson S Preston &c call'd—J Cannon, James & Sl. Fisher and several others in the front Room this evening.

Febry. 22. HSD. and Ben Wilson, set off after an early dinner for Atsion and Mount holy, Huldah Mott and Betsy Emlen here this morning Jacob and Sally, John and Nancy and Molly went this Afternoon to Tea with James Logan—T Stewardson call'd—Neighr. Waln Sucky Hartshorn and her daughter Hannah here in the evening—S. Preston sup'd.

23. First Day: when we arose this morning it was snowing fast—and continu'd to snow 'till after dinner—then turn'd to rain and thaw, it is now this evening very sloppy—Richd. Nesbit din'd and drank tea with us, Saml. Preston sup'd—J Downing, and T. Stewardson call'd, myself and William poorly—[J.]W. in Limbo—put there by [J]F.

24 S. Preston din'd here—HSD. and BW. return'd from the Jersys, Wm. Saltar with them to tea, they lodge here—Saml. Smith here this evening.

25 HD. MS. HSD. gone to monthly Meeting John Pemberton call'd, S Preston drank tea, Jacob Downing took Eliza to visit her sister who is weaning at two years and one month old. Billy Salter left us after breakfast—the Dam at the Works has given way—and the Furnace stop'd.

26 Jemmy Thornton and his sister, Hannah were here this fore-noon, they came from the Jerseys, she took an early dinner, and went with one of her Neighbours in a Sleigh, Docr. Redman call'd, Gilbert Prichard din'd with us—Nancy Skyrin, James Logan, and Betsy Emlen, drank tea with us—Sally Rhoads, Betsy Fisher Taby. Fisher, Sammy Emlen, and Ben. Wilson here this evening.

Febry. 27. EDs birth day: very unwell, S. Preston and A Skyrin din'd here—we had the 3 Children most of the day with us—Jacob and Sally, John Skyrin, Ben Wilson, Docr. Redman, J Logan call'd. BW. continues Lodging here.

28 Ben Wilson din'd, T. Stewardson tea'd—John Cannon, Sally Downing, Betsy Fordham call'd.

March 1. G. Prichard din'd—S Downing tea'd—Jacob Downing, S.Preston calld.

2d. First Day: din'd alone, that is our family—A Skyrin drank tea, Wm. Simsom and S Preston sup'd—John Skyrin, Jacob Downing call'd—Molly went after meeting to S Emlens, she sent Dick Scott after night for her night choaths, intending to stay there as it rains fast.

3 took medicine, unwell as usual—Thos. Fisher drank tea, Thos. Morris call'd—S. Preston, Willm. Ellis and John Adlum sup'd, S.W. Fisher spent part of the evening.

4 HD. MS. MD. HSD. gone to meeting—S. Preston din'd here—MS. out this Afternoon, MD. gone with her Sisters to visit T. and R. Fisher, Molly Lewis Widdow, bury'd this Afternoon.

5 Wm. Coopers Sister &c here, S Preston drank tea.

6 Several call'd.

7 J Logan, A Skyrin drank tea.

8 Betsy Emlen and others call'd—Betsy Jervis spent the day with us—she, A Skyrin, and Isaac Howel drank tea with us.

March 9. First day: Jacob, Sally, John and Nancy here—S Swett call'd—HD. gone this Afternoon to the funeral of Isaac Zane Senr. he died on fifth day morning last.

10. Becky Shoemaker, Dolly Rundle and her Cosin, Sally Downing Nancy Skyrin call'd this fore-noon, T. Stewardson din'd, S. Preston, John Pemberton called a very fine day, Wm. and self spent some time in the Yard—'tis said that a Vessel has come up from the west-indies with the Yallow-fever on board.

11 the report of yesterday concerning the Yallow fever being on board the Brigantine Sally—is this day contradicted—Joshua Edwards call'd, BW. and WD. went out in the Carriage this 'fore-noon, Hannah Catheral din'd here S. Preston, Jacob Downing &c call'd.

12 It seems as if most of our world, is in comotion, wars and rumors of wars.—a very fine day, Nancy and her Child, William and Henry, took a ride to the middle ferry, AS. din'd with us—Sally, Nancy and Molly, visited this Afternoon for the first time at Jos. Smiths, Elizabeth Dawson and Joseph Richardsons wife call'd—M. Pleasants and her Daughter Molly drank tea with

us—J Skyrin, J Downing call'd—HD. agree'd this evening, with Daniel King for his plantation on the old York road for which he is to pay him £3146—it is between 5 and 6 miles from the City.

March 13. It is 38 years this day, since the death of my dear Father.—Sally Hopkins junr. din'd with us—Neighr. Waln spent the evening—poor Hannah Baker brought to bed of her sixth Child and first Daughter, she lost her Husband last summer, Charles Jervis &c call'd.

14 S. Downing and little Mary here in the Morning Becky Wharton call'd in the Afternoon, H. Mott, Betsy Emlen, Philip Van Coartland, Saml. Preston, John and Nancy Skyrin drank tea with us. HD. at Jammy Smiths this Afternoon.

15 Nancy Ward formerly Quick here this morning with her little Daughter—John and Nancy Skyrin and John Shoemaker din'd hear—rain this evening S. Preston &c call'd.

16. First Day: family except ED. and WD—gone to meeting—Wm. Ellis din'd; S Swett drank tea—Molly Smith, Betsy Watson S Preston, Peggy Wharton and little Hannah call'd—and John Drinker—received a litter from M Penry—very warm for the Season, sprain'd my left wrist lifting HW. off the Table.

17 Sally Smith, S Downing, A Skyrin calld—sent for Docr. Kuhn, he order'd William to loose 6 oz Blood, as he continues spitting phlegm of a sanguinary appearence, Michel perform'd the opperation at four o'clock in the Afternoon—the blood a little inflam'd. Molly Drinker with many others gone this Afternoon to visit Betsy Fisher—Nicholas Waln call'd.

18th. March. Docr. Kuhn call'd. examin'd Williams blood; approv'd of his having lost it.—Sally and Nancy call'd before and after meeting,—little ES stays here to day. ED. took medicine, Hannah Catheral and Becky Jones din'd here—Sally Downing, and Nancy Skyrin drank tea. S Preston here, Mary Tippet call'd this afternoon, she is one of the single Sisters of Lititz, lived in the house with M. Penry. A Committe of the Mapple Sugar Company, mett this evening in the front Room.

19. S Downing, A Skyrin here this Afternoon little ES. with us most of the day, S. Preston drank tea—J Skyrin call'd—Sally and Nancy went this Afternoon to H Yerkass—HSD. with S. Fisher to his and our place.—fine weather J Logan &c call'd.

20 pleasant weather, Becky Thompson and her two Daughters call'd—S

Swett din'd, A Skyrin and SS. drank tea, Neighr. Waln and her two Waln grand-daughters call'd—Saml. Preston, MD. unwell yesterday, better to day—Betsy Emlen, Molly Mathews from White Marsh and Billy Mott, spent the evening with Molly.

21. Spring meeting: Wm. and Sarah Blakey, John and Rachel Watson, Sarah Smith and Ann Chapman came here after dinner, W and S Bleakey went to S Pleasants, where they lodge—the others lodge here, Sarah Fisher call'd, Sally Stapler also, Joe put a bushel of lime in our Masonett, and a like quantity in one of Stiless in the alley, out of which house several dyed—and several were taken to the Hospital.

March 22. None but our family and lodgers, breakfasted with us or din'd—Enouch Evanss wife and Daughter, Thornton &c drank tea—Neighr. Waln here—Ann Chapman and Sarah Smith went to their old lodgings, left their horses with us—Saml. Trimble, John Balderston and Molly Moore, came here to lodge—Sharpless &c sup'd—ED. very unwell this Afternoon oblig'd to lay down.

23d. First Day: Our lodgers, Wm. Newbold and others breakfasted—Wm. and self stay'd at home, Molly also—John Lloy'd, Mark Reeve, Warner Mifflin, William and Sarah Blakey, John and R. Watson din'd with us—Hannah Catheral, R Jones, Saml. Trimble, widdow King from New-York, her Son Ray King, at tea—John Balderston left us this evening—his wife being unwell—a fine day—Becky Wharton Anna Wells, call'd—A Skyrin and Child—Abraham Gibbons and Wife, Danl. Smith &c sup'd here.

24. Caleb Pierce &c din'd—Saml. Smith here in the evening, S. Trimble, S. Preston, Oliver Paxon, John and R Watson &c at supper—A Skyrin and Child here—MD. out to day 'tho unwell—Jenny Heaton call'd for grape-cuttings.

25. 8 or 10 at breakfast—our lodgers left us—this fore-noon—Martha Livezly and James Thornton here before meeting: Martha din'd with us—G. Prichard also, Patty Smith call'd—S Preston, Joseph M Lawrie sup'd—his wife call'd—Nancy Skyrin here.

26th. HD. and MS. went after[7] breakfast to the place lately purchas'd, examin'd, and approv'd it.—came back to dinner:—My old friend Sally Moores black woman Ruth, call'd to see us—J. Logan, S Preston, A Skyrin &c call'd—very poorly all day: weather much cooler—Molly Pleasants, E Emlen, A Marshal visited Molly this afternoon.

7. The word "noon" crossed out.

27. John Cannon breakfasted here, Janny, Hannah and Susan Stevenson and Carolina Shoemaker here this morning Nancy Murry formerly Morgan, whose Husband Parson Murry dyed of the Yallow Fever last summer, spent this afternoon with us, she seems in much distress, weather cold.

28. A Skyrin here this morning with her Child—she and Hetty Smith drank tea, Jemmy Smith and Neigr. Waln here in the evening cold.

29. Sally Downing unwell, several in and out, S Preston and Wm. Simpson sup'd here.

30. First Day: SD. m s——d yesterday, she seems pretty well to day considering—S Swett din'd here, I went after dinner to see Sally, the first time that I have been out of our front Door since my return from Germantown—fine weather—I wrote this evening to M. Penry—S Preston here, H.S.D left us after dinner, for his Farm in Bucks County.

31. March: prenez Med[icine] This Afternoon it rain'd, Lighten'd and thunderd—cleard up this evening—with a very high wind, march is going out like a Lion—Honor Fry and A Skyrin drank tea with us—J. Skyrin and J Fry here in the evening.

April 1st. S Preston gone homewards. J Logan drank tea—HSD. return'd this Afternoon—John Pemberton, Docr. Redman, H. Yerkas, Hannah Tomkins call'd.—Daniel King brought us two Chickins and a bunch of Asparages, this forenoon from the farm 'tis early for both, he has taken pains to raise them.

2. Jacob Downing awaken'd us this morning at two o'clock by knocking at the Gate, Sally was ill, and what we thought was settled on first day last happend this morning: Sister arose and went with Jacob, she stay'd there 'till I went before dinner and releas'd her, I came home toward evening—Sally is at present as well as may be, after being so ill last night and this morning—Joshua Edwards & Nancy Skyrin din'd here.—HD. AS. Jacob and Eliza, MD. Betsy Emlen and Anna Wilson, were this afternoon at our new-purchase—Sister lodges this night with Sally—Our dear William has this day brought up bloody pleghm, the first since he was let blood, 'tis not clear blood but a mixture.

3. Sister all day at J. Downings with Sally, she is better—A Shower of rain with Lightning and thunder this Afternoon—Molly gone to Nancys, No Company here to day.

4. Eliza went to Childrens meeting this Morning with Sally Brant, Hannah and Sally Hopkins, here in the fore-noon—HSD. went after an early dinner to

penny-pack, return'd to tea, Jacob Downing call'd. ED took as usual [Medicine].

5. Sister came home this fore-noon from Sallys with whom she lodg'd last night—MD. has been unwell for a fourtnight past, sent this morning for Dr. Kuhn, he order'd her spiced Rheubarb—Richd. Thomas din'd here—he and Sammy Fisher went with HD. from hence to the new-purchace—Molly Stevenson and her neice Susan, Benedict Van Pradelles, R. Thomas, and A Skyrin, drank tea with us—Neighr. Waln in the evening James Logan call'd—BW. as usual. cool.

6. First day: the Family at meeting, except WD—and ED. they at home as usual—R Jones call'd, S Swett, Hannah Catheral, Widdow King & Son from New-York, din'd with us—SS tea'd—John, Nancy and their little one, here this Afternoon and evening—rain and stormy, towards evening a boat overset and immediately sunk about the middle of the river, nearly opposite the Swedish church, by which accident, seven persons were drowned, three Women, two Men, and 2 Children. two women and one Man were saved by some persons who pushed off in a boat from a wharf opposite the distressing scene.

7. a very fine day, 'tho rather cool, G. Prichard says there was a smart frost this Morning, Michel Callanan, Sally Parish, Hannah Mitchell, before dinner, John, Nancy and Child after—Jacob Downing and Ben Wilson gone to Downing Town—Sister out this Afternoon—George Roberts the Fishers &c—in the Coumpting Room this evening.

8 This morning about 4 o'clock a fire broke out in a Brewhouse above Vine street, between second and third Streets, the house was burnt to the ground, but by the exertions of the Citizens the adjoining buildings were not much injured[8]—A Brewhouse on the same spot was consum'd by fire upwards of 40 years ago, then in the tenure of Preserve Brown.—No Company to day but Betsy Emlen,—William din'd with Hannah Pemberton, her Husband gone to bucks County—cold to day, John the Gardner at work in our Garden—ED—prenez M——.

9 Saml. Wallace breakfasted here, Betsy Fordham, and Betsy Foulk call'd this morning Hannah Baker borrow'd the Carriage to take her little Daughter to the Grave—Sister this Afternoon at S Fisher—J Cannon sup'd.

10 Billy Sansom call'd this fore-noon—Nancy and her Daughter spent the

8. See the *Philadelphia Gazette and Universal Daily Advertiser*, Apr. 8, 1794.

day with us—Elizh. Dawson drank tea, her Son came for her in the evening very cold—very cool for the season.

April 11. James Logan call'd—S Swett and Henry Atherton din'd here—SS spent the day try'd on a gown for me—Thommy Stewardson, Betsy Emlen, and Billy Mott here this Evening—cold—Molly Robertham formerly Burrows our old Neighbor was this Afternoon bury'd.—Jacob Downing and Ben Wilson return'd this evening.

12. James Logan, Jenny and Hannah Stevenson call'd—HD. MS. Sally Downing and WD—went this fore-noon to Newington[9] of our newly purchas'd farm, givin it by Daniel King—Nancy Skyrin here, J Frys Child—our people return'd before dinner, Sally dind and spent the Afternoon with us—John Cannon the evening.

13. First day: Prenez—William and self at home, the rest gone to meeting—Thomas Jinks din'd S Swett also,—Joseph Drinker drank tea, he is going with S Hopkins to build pot ash works for John Nicholdson, Edmund Phisick, Nancy Skyrin, Jacob Downing call'd—MS. went this Afternoon to Jonathan Evans to see Polly Hubley who is in a low stat[h] of health, she went to Jammy Smiths the first time—HSD. went off after breakfast, in the Burlington Boat, to wait on HS. home, who is at present there—this has been a fine day, clouded over in the evening R Thomas came home with Molly the evening.

14. Betsy Fordham came this morning to work for me, Sally and Nancy drank tea here—Neighr. Waln here in the evening—J Skyrin call'd—HSD. return'd from Burlington this evening HS with him—MS. went this afternoon to visit R James at John Tompsons.

April 15. Nancy and Child here in the forenoon, Molly had her Teeth filed by Gardet, at Sallys; Sammy Trimble's were cleand—, I went this Afternoon, Henry S with me to Nancy's, where I had not been before since our return from the Country—from thence HSD. and self went to James Smiths where I spent the Afternoon, HD. came to tea—call'd in the evening at Jacob Downings, Sally out, John Drinker and John Cannon here in the evening HD. and J Drinker went early this morning to the Farm, came home to Breakfast.

16. Sally, her two Children and William took a ride this morning—S Swett &c din'd—Nancy and her little one here—Sally and Molly gone this Afternoon to pay Polly Perot a lying-in visit—after a spell of fine weather, this evening

9. The words "the name" crossed out both here and after the word "farm" below.

'tis chang'd—a disagreeable Easterly wind. I made a quantity of peach blossom syrup[10]—Richd Thomas sup'd with us.

17. Easterly wind and little rain, cleard up in the evening James Moon came with a message from Jos. Thornton who is very ill of a Billious disorder—Sally Downing call'd—MS. and MD. out this Afternoon, our front Room being the Coumpting room, takes off a number of transient visitors.

18. William, Nancy and her Daughter went out this fore-noon in the Carriage, Nancy din'd here, HSD. and Ben Wilson set off after Breakfast for Henrys farm—Jacob and Sally, John and Nancy, Molly and Hannah Smith went to our place and to Jammy Smiths—this is good Fryday as it is call'd. a very fine day.

19. Jammy Logan read a small volumn to us this morning—HD. WD. Sally and her two Daughters went this fore-noon to the New Purchase—Sally din'd with us. Jacob and R Thomas call'd. Robt. Stevenson and Betsy Jervis drank tea—Henry and Ben Wilson return'd this evening—the former well beplash'd with mud by a mad or Drunken fellow frightned his Horse riding quick up to his Sulkey. Sally Hopkins junr. din'd here, clear fine weather sent for Dr. Kuhn to day as Billy seem'd rather more unwell, he order'd him Gum Arabac, Nitre and Conserve of roses[11] powder'd and mixt—Two Bearded Men, Minonests,[12] drank tea here yesterday—Rachel Drinker and Polly, Henrys wife, call'd to see our Gardan.

First day. 20. William and self at home, the rest of the family at meeting, Mary Savery din'd here S Swett also—I am generaly employ'd on a first day morning busyly, my Son and self both being unwell—in the Afternoon I can retire if I choose it.—Sally and Nancy drank tea with us, the Children here—Jacob and John call'd—Hannah Thomas and her two Sons calld our Daughter Nancy is complaining, and looks unwell, she is troubled with the sick head Ache.

10. The word "for" crossed out.

11. Conserve of roses was made by beating rosebuds and sugar to a very fine consistency. Roses were used in many medicinal preparations, mainly for their cooling qualities. In this case, gum arabic was used to bond the ingredients. For nitre, see below, June 4, 5, 1799 (Hess, *Booke of Cookery*, 278, 267).

12. The Mennonites, a Dutch-German-Swiss sect that grew out of the Anabaptist movement of the Reformation, take their name from Menno Simons, an Anabaptist leader of the sixteenth century. Mennonites began settling in Germantown, Pa., in 1683. Their settlements expanded into Lancaster County and other parts of Pennsylvania in the eighteenth century. Mennonites, who, like Quakers, opposed slavery and refused to serve in the military, were noted for their plain dress and their men's long, untrimmed beards (C. Henry Smith, *The Story of the Mennonites*, 4th ed. [Newton, Kans.: Mennonite Publication Office, 1957], 1–114, 302–14, 537–52).

21. April pres—Thos. Fisher in the Morning R Jones drank tea—Nancy, Sally, John call'd—Thunder this evening—Billy, Molly Eliza took a ride before dinner—fine morning rain this evening—Honor Fry here she and AS. went out togeather.

22 rain most of the day—little company.

23. Patrick Casady breakfasted—clear'd up this afternoon, Dr. Kuhn call'd—S Downing spent the Afternoon—WD. and ED. unwell.

24. N.E. wind and cloudy. J Logan call'd.

25. HD. John and Danl. Drinker went to Bybarry to the funeral of our friend James Thornton, who departed this life early yesterday morning, heavy shower this Afternoon—wind continues Easterly—HSD. lodges at Jacob Downings, he being gone to Downings town, set off yesterday.

26. fine clear weather—HD. and MS. went to the farm this Afternoon, bought a new black Horse try'd him and lik'd him—J Logan call'd—Betsy Fordham left us this afternoon, she has been near 2 weeks at work for us, Sally and Nancy hear—our dear Billy very poorly.

27. First Day: HD WD. MD. ED. at home, Molly broke out with a rash, great numbers have had the same complaint this spring—Sally and her Children din'd with us, S Swett also, JD not yet return'd—they stay'd 'till evening, John and Nancy here—and Saml. Fisher—fine weather, Saml. Smith here this evening S Brant went to visit her mother, 2 miles.

April 28th. HD. Saml. Smith and Thos. Fisher set of at 6 o'clock this morning for Lang-horn Park intending to return to morrow—John Kinsey and John Saltar call'd—I went this Afternoon to visit Sally Emlen who has been unwell, HSD. waited on me there, as I continue a little lame yet, it is the Second visit that I have paid in town for a 12 month past.—Sally, Nancy, Jenny and Hannah Stevenson drank tea here, Polly Noble and her 2 Children, Anna Wells and Son &c call'd—John Kinsey lodges here, Ben Wilson also as usual—fine weather.

29. MS. gone to meeting—S Swett din'd—Hannah Baker, call'd—Jacob Bakers wife also—Sally, Nancy, their Children here—Dr. Kuhn call'd HD &c return'd this evening—they were overset[13] received but little hurt—J Kinsey BW. lodg'd—Last night or rather this morning Molly who lodg'd with me, heard a noise in the house, I also heard it, but was not so much alarm'd—she

13. The word "but" crossed out.

could not rest satisfied unless an examinnation was made—I call'd up BW. who went down stairs with me, we found all, as far as we went, in statu quo, but discover'd this morning that the plastering which had been newly put on the top of the front Celler, had fell off which doubtless occasion'd the noise.—took [Medicine].

April 30. H. Pemberton sent Noak with her Carriage for William and self, this fore-noon—Willm. was gone out with his Brother in the Chaise, did not suit me as I was unwell to go. Sally, Nancy and their Children din'd here and spent the Afternoon—John Kinsey din'd. A Committee of the Owners of the Union-Farm[14] mett this Evening in our front Parlor.

May 1st. John Kinsey left us this morning early. John R. Alsop took him in the Chaise to H. Williams at point no point, where he was to meet his B. County friend with whom he went homewards—William and Henry went to the Farm this forenoon, WD. appear'd better for the Ride—Hannah Cathral din'd with us,—James Logon, Nancy Skyrin drank tea here—I step'd in this evening to Isaac Whartons, after taken a walk with my Daughter Nancy to S Swetts—John Skyrin call'd—Jacob Downing return'd this evening from the Valley—clear, fine weather—Molly and Eliza, visited at J Smiths.

2. William and Henry went this fore-noon to the Farm, HD. went there after dinner Gilbert Prichard who din'd here went with him—Molly and S Downing spent this Afternoon at J Skyrins, James and Hetty Smith and their 2 eldest Daughters there—A young Man of the name of Chapman who has lately had a Cancerous Wen cut out of his Eye-lid spent part of the evening, S Fisher call'd—a fine day—warm.

3. Jacob and Sally went this Afternoon to the Farm in the Chaise to try a Horse which Jacob—has lately purchas'd—Molly spent the day with Nancy who is very poorly—Dr. Redman, Sally Downing, Dr. Foulk, Jacob Downing call'd—HSD. and his intended went on Horseback to J Smiths place—fine weather—took [Medicine].

4. First Day. Jacob and Sally, John and Nancy, Joseph Pearsal from New York, Peggy Wharton, John Drinker, S Swett, Children &c here—a very fine day—William better.

5. Quarterly meeting—George Bowne from N Y—— breakfasted with us—William and Henry gone this forenoon to Germantown &c—wind N.E—Nurse Waters, and John Skyrin call'd in meeting time—Nancy had a bad night much oppress'd—Samuel Hughes, Thos. Lee and Wife and Willm. Ellis din'd

14. See above, Dec. 30, 1793.

here—I went after they were gone to visit Nancy Henry went with me, found her rather better—a[15] Ship came up while I was there under full sail, a beautiful sight—There was a rumpus at the wharf with a small Vessel, which 'twas said was going to take provisions or to carry intelligence or some thing else to the English fleet, I could not rightly understand the tale, but they took out her Main-Mast, and drag'd it with ropes up the bank, a mob collected, when J Dallis and others appear'd to put a stop to their proceedings.—I was really distress'd and have been at other times when at J Skyrins, to see the cruelty of the Dray-Men to their Horses, in forceing them to drag loads to heavy for them up the Hill—they whip them unmercyfully and are frequently after many vain exertions oblidg'd to unload.—I have long look'd on the treatment of Carters and Draymen &c to their poor dumb servants, a crying Sin that ought to be perticularly noticed.—came home after night; Huldah Mott, Betsy Saltar, Sally Saltar, John Adlum and Billy Ellis drank tea here—Polly Pleasants call'd—Molly was cup'd[16] in the back this evening on account of a small inflamation in her Eyes—cloudy, raw Easterly wind.

6. Cloudly all day—wind Easterly, took [Medicine]. Dr. Kuhn, Danl. King, James Logan, a Son of G. Churchman, Josa. Fisher, David Potter &c call'd—Molly spent this day with her Sister Nancy—little E. Downings fingers pinch'd by the desk lid. Polly Cope, John Drinker call'd.

7. HD. and MS. went after dinner to the Farm, took up with them several Boxes with China &c as D King is moving away, and we expect soon to take up our aboade there—Nancy & child din'd with us, JS. JD &c call'd—our 3 Daughters spent this Afternoon at Joshua Howels, Neighr. Walns old Negro Man Anthony or Tony was bury'd this Afternoon. clear'd up cool.

8. H Pemberton sent Joshua Cliborn to ask me to take a ride with her tomorrow morning—We sent a waggon load of furniture to our place:—Sally & Nancy call'd—Saml. Sansom drank tea with us—Neighr. Waln this evening—Sally and Molly at S Emlens afternoon.

9. Rachel Griscomb work'd here yesterday, she made up a Bed tick and put in the feathers, preparatory to our going out of town—Betsy Jervis, Sarah Fisher drank tea with us, S. Downing, Docr. Redman, call'd—fine cool weather—Jacob, Sally, John, Nancy and their Children went this Afternoon to the Farm—I step'd this evening into Sally Rhoadess.

15. The word "vessel" crossed out.

16. I.e., bled. In cases of inflammation of the eyes, William Buchan recommended that the bleeding be done as close as possible to the eyes. If the jugular vein was not convenient, then the arm or another part of the body was suitable for the task (Buchan, *Domestic Medicine* [1799], 194–96).

10. MS. Sally Downing, Anthony, Joe, and Anna, went this fore-noon to the Farm, where they spent this day cleaning the House &c—Becky Hopkins, call'd—Nancy Skyrin and Daughter spent this day with me—John here in the evening—Betsy Fordham &c call'd. I took Rhue: very poorly all day, fine weather. John Parish call'd—HD. received Letters this evening from Bay Hondoras, by Capt. Eve, with two little Boys, Sons of Potts, consign'd to his care—HD. preparing this evening—to sett off tomorrow for New-York, which will in some measure retard our leving home for the country.

May 11. First Day: two little Lads, James and Robert Potts came here this morning HD. engag'd Benn. Catheral to take them to board with him—S Swett and the boys from the Bay din'd with us—HD. went after an early dinner to T Scattergoods from whence they sett off in a Stage waggon for New-York, where Thos. Scatergood intends to embark for Great Britian on a religious visit—HD. Thos. Fisher, Thos. Stewardson and others accompany'd him, we expect HDs return towards the end of this week—Jacob and Sally, Ben Wilson, call'd—B Catheral call'd for the Boys and took them home with him this evening—very fine weather.

12. William and his Uncle John went out this fore-noon in the Chaise—MS. SD. and Sally Brant, Anthony and Anna gone to the Farm to make clean &c—Michl Callanan calld—William came home much fatigued, by the heat, they went to the Farm where they stay'd 'till Eleven o'clock, and came home at high Noon. MS. SD. &c. return'd to late tea, John and Nancy drank tea here, Jacob also here—This Morning was very warm wind at SW, 'tis now, this Evening, cold, and the wind Easterly, such are the sudden changes we are liable to and which the weakly ought to guard against; The scarlet fever is said to be rife in the City—Anna Wells and her Son, here this Afternoon. HSD. wrote to his father this morning p post.

May 13. B. Catheral call'd this morning to inform of the wellfare of the Pottss said that if little Robt. was to be innoculated for the small pox the sooner the better, as there was some in his neighbourhood in the disorder. I sent for Dr. Rush as HD desired, he promis'd to visit the Child this evening, and if proper, perform the opperation. William with his Uncle John rode out this Afternoon—HSD. went out of town with B. Wilson, Ben W and Michel Callanan din'd with us—Sally, Nancy their Children and Hannah Smith drank tea here, the first time of Hannah's being here since Henry paid his court to her—Jacob and John here, Betsy Emlen, Betsy and Sally Saltar spent part of the evening—Extract of a Letter, in this evening paper, dated at New-York yesterday, says, that the Ship Ohio in which sailed John Jay,[17] left

17. John Jay was chief justice of the U.S. Supreme Court when he was appointed on Apr. 19 to be envoy extraordinary to the court of George III. He sailed for England on May 12 with

the Wharf at 9 o'clock in the Morning If so, TS. will probably be dissapointed as they did not expect to reach N.Y 'till about Noon.

14. Mathias Tyson from Concord call'd this Morning he promises to bring £100 this day week, towards paying off David Browns Bond.—MS. SD. with the usual serviteurs, Sam Sprigs added to the number, gone to the Farm to continue the business of clensing—HSD. and B Wilson set off after breakfast for Chester. Betsy Emlen and the Saltars call'd for Molly to take a ride with them, so that all our family, WD and self excepted, are out of Town this fore-noon—Henry mett the person that he had expected to see at Chester 4 miles from the City, which shorten'd the business, they returnd by 10 o'clock. I received a note from John Pemberton enquirring, what news from HD. &c, but as I have received no Letter, could not satisfy him, Jacob and Sally, John and Nancy, James Logan, John Drinker and Sally Rhoads, here this evening—took [Medicine].

15. William rode out this fore-noon with his Brother, in the Afternoon with his uncle, Saml. Smith of B. County put up his Horse and din'd with us—meeting for Sufferings broke up early, he left us in the Afternoon—Henry received a letter from his Father, informing that T. Scatergood, follow'd the Ship in a pilot Boat and got on board timeously—Sally and Nancy here to day—little Eliza very poorly with a fever and violent cough—sent for Dr. Kuhn who order'd her a anodyne to night and gentle purge in the morning—HD. returnd this evening, and retired early to rest, having travel'd 80 miles this day, he found our friends in N York generaly in good health—I step'd into Isc. Whartons this fore-noon, they have retired to their Country seat this Afternoon—on the Wissahicon road—warm weather.

May:16. MS. Sally Brant, and Sam Sprigs went to the Farm, spent the day there, we sent up two Chimney Sweeps, they also had white washing done, a day or two more will 'tis suppos'd finish cleaning the house from top to bottom.—Dr. Kuhn call'd this morning he order'd the Child a purge which was given, of peach blossom suryp, it work'd kindly—but this evening 'tho she had seem'd better to day than for 2 or 3 days past, after a spell of Coughing she brought up some blood, which to us is very alarming, 'tho I hope it proceeds from the soreness of her breast rather than any thing fixt.—Wm. Clifton call'd to see Billy, Jacob Sally, John Nancy, here to day: The 14 Instant a small French Schooner, in attempting to cross from Gibbet-Island,

---

instructions to conclude a peaceful settlement with Great Britain over issues remaining unresolved from the 1783 peace treaty and to seek compensation from the British for the injuries they caused to American shipping during the ongoing Anglo-French war (Marcus and Perry, *Supreme Court,* 1:7; Frank Monaghan, *John Jay* [New York: Bobbs-Merrill, 1935], 361–70).

during the severe gust, was over-set and sunk, and all who were on board perished, being ten in number one of whom was a doctor, five officers belonging to the french Vessels in that harbour and 4 Sailors, The above particulars are stated agreeably to the information of a ferry-man, who left the Island a few minutes previous to the Schooner—and was one of those who went in pursuit of her, but could neither find the vessel men or any thing belonging thereto.—from the evening paper—HD. T Stewardson, [T]Fisher &c., were on the river at the time of the Gust, and saw the vessel over set.

17 May: HSD. left home after breakfast for[18] Jinkentown—I expect he will dine with his Aunt at our place, where she went this morning, Sally Brant, Sam and Joe with her—John and Hannah Pemberton call'd this fore-noon—Sally Downing spent the morning with us.—Eliza better—HD. and WD. went after dinner to the Farm in the Chaise, old Mare drew them—they came home to tea, Sally here this Afternoon, her Daughter Eliza much better cool—Henry brought home three Strawberries and 6 or 8 ripe Cheries from the Farm, it proves this to be a very early spring, as I do not recolect seeing any before the Spring Fair, and I dont remember but once their failing at that time. half a Dozen ty'd to a stick for a penny.

18th. First Day: Jacob and Sally, Dr. Kuhn, B. Wilson and Betty Carr call'd before Morning meeting.—Joseph Christy from Fredricksburg, Virginia and Ben Wilson din'd here—Nancy Skyrin and Jemmy Logan drank tea, Neighr. Waln and Becky Jones call'd—Billy and myself poorly—very cold to day, we set by a good fire—we have had frequent changes of the weather this Spring—from heat to cold.

19. HSD. set off this morning for Richland or North-Bank, intending to stay a day, MS. Sally Brant Anna and Joe went to our place and finish'd the rummage effectualy—HD. and Son William paid them a visit there after dinner there, came home before sun set—Dr. Kuhn, John and Nancy call'd—John Saltar, G. Prichard, &c in the morning—Sammy R. Fisher here this evening—poorly took med[c]—Eliza very unwel, pain in her limbs.

20. S Swett din'd here—Sally, Nancy and John Skyrin and Ben Wilson drank tea—Nancy and William went this Afternoon to the Farm.

21st. Rachel Watson din'd with us, she is on her way to several meetings with many others, she left us after dinner, HD. John Drinker, Thos. Stewardson WD. and Eliza went this afternoon to the Farm—John Nicholdson Huldah Mott, Sally Saltar, Ben Wilson &c call'd [TS.] drank tea—HSD. return'd this evening—Nancy and her little one here this evening—John Skyrin here, he has

18. The words "White marsh or Chesnut hill" crossed out.

the Jaundice 'tho not in a great degree—We sent up a load of furniture this morning to our intended dwelling—grows warm again.

22. Tommy Fisher &c call'd—This Afternoon I spent at Jacob Downings, Jammy and Hetty Smith their two eldest Daughters drank tea with us there, Between 5 and 6 o'clock came on a most violent storm of thunder and lightening, accompanied with a heavy rain, and shower of the leargest hail stones that has been known for several years past in this City. The hurricane seem'd to be from the north-east and it lasted for about two hours; it did not hail for that length of time, but heavy rain thunder &c. Great numbers of pains of glass 'tis said were broken, One house at the corner of south & sixth streets, was struck on the roof by the lightening and much damaged, some of the hail stones weighed half an Ounce; and were from two inches, to two inches and an half in circumference—Our people geatherd up after the storm upwards of half a peck of Necterines Apricots and plumbs, that had been beat off the trees in our yard—great numbers of bunches of young grapes beat off, and the vines much cut. the water fell in such quantity that the pavement in Arch street look'd like a river.—We did not get home 'till near 10 at night.—I remember a hail storm in 82 or 83. June, that came siddenly on in a [v]ain, 'tho it did not last so long, as this, if I remember right, the hail stones were larger, the wind higher and more mischief, as it is call'd, done—We had at that time upwards of 60 pains of glass broke and crack'd in our back windows.

23. several here this day—I took [medicine] WD din'd at John Pembertons.

24. HD. MS. and Sally Brant went to Clearfield. the name which HD. has given to the Farm, as James Fisher has a place that has been call'd Newington for many years past, 'twas thought best to change the name.—HD &c came home to tea they brought some green peas, and some Strawberries.

May 25. First day. HSD. set off early this morning in the Trenton boat, for his Farm, having appointed to meet some person there tomorrow morning, the wind ahead NE—cloudy, rain in the evening, HD. din'd at J. Pembertons. S Swett and Reba. Scatergood din'd with us—Dr. Kuhn here this morning in meeting time—took [medicine] very poorly all day—John Cadwalader Lawyer here this morning.—I am thoughtful of HSD.

26. our dear little Girl seems to be recovering. her apetite returning, she has lost much flesh since her indispossion, 'tho she has not been so ill as to be intierly confin'd—John and Nancy drank tea and Sally, their Children also; Jacob here—Isaac Howel here this morning to execute a Deed.—I lodg'd last night in Williams Room, where Sister or myself, generly does when Henry is absent,—a very heavy rain a little after midnight—much has fallen within these 3 or 4 days, 'tis drizling this evening wind NE. I have been unwel ever

since we returnd from Germantown, seem to loose flesh every week a great weakness in my bowels, which I have reason to think grows worse, instead of better—HD. out most of the day, as is usual: John Pemberton preparing to leave us, much talk of War, may it be averted, with Great Britian.

27 May: HD. left us after breakfast to accompany John Pemberton to Chester or New-Castle, where he intends to embark on board the Adriana, for Great Britian, James Pemberton, S Pleasants, Thos. Fisher &c went also;—Polly Smith call'd before meeting—Sam came after dinner for to desire Molly to come set with his mistress as she is unwel and little Elizath. got the nettle-rash—rain all the afternoon and evening—Sally Rhoads spent the Afternoon and evening with us, Saml. Rhoads here this evening—Sam came for Mollys night-cloaths, as she doth not chuse to come home in the rain—so that we shall be 4 out of family this night—HD. HSD. MD. and Joe Gibbs.

28. when I awoke this morn it was raining hard—and has continu'd so to do most of this day, a great quantity of water has fallen within the last week—John Coo[ ]rtney our Gardener, brought from the plantaton this morning about 1½ peck green peas, and 3 pints of Strawberries—there is a bundence of both, either waisted or perishing there, but it does not suit to leave home while the weather continues dull—Molly not yet returned from Nancys—Our Friend J Pemberton took Shiping at New-Castle this morning 9 o'clock. HD. &c return'd this evening they have had a wet time of it—HSD. not return'd or Molly.

29. rain all night and all this day—some say, that they never knew such a long spell of wett weather in this month, but I rather think that their memories fail them, and that they may have said the same before.—but certain it is, we have had much rain since the hail storm, which was this day week—No HSD. or Molly to night—Sister very poorly—Ephrim Clinot brought us some as fine Garden Strawberries as I have seen, from Atsion—B.W. still lodges here—Good accounts by the Pigou this Afternoon, which seem to promise Peace.

30. Cloudy last night and all this day, with some rain—Molly came home this morning—Sally here—R Jones spent the Afternoon—HD. and his daughter SD went to the burial of a Son of Joshua Smith. John the Gardner brought us some pease and Strawberries, hurt by the rain. Henry Atherton here this fore-noon, he brought some, Solomons Seal,[19] for William.

19. Solomon's Seal (*Polygonatum*), a perennial herb native to the northern hemisphere, derives its name from the reputation of its gnarled roots, which were thought to be efficacious in sealing wounds. American colonists used Solomon's Seal to mend broken bones and to stop bleeding, vomiting, and ruptures (Ann Leighton, *Early American Gardens: "For Meate or Medicine"* [Boston: Houghton Mifflin, 1970], 393–94).

31. We expected to have been in the Country two or 3 weeks ago, but are as yet detain'd by the weather &c—cloudy all night, rain most of this day—HSD. return'd home this evening much to my satisfaction. he came in the Stage, the waters are so high that many places are impassable—bridges carried away—A Man and Horse drownded at one of the ferries yesterday—Je [m'] donne[20]—se mataine—the Strawberries which John brought this morning from Clear-field, were almost spoil'd by the rain the fruit generally damaged.

June 1 First Day. rain this Morning clear'd up this evening 'tho the wind continues at the N. East—Benn. Catheral and his pupil Jams. Potts, call'd—Robt. Potts recovering of the Small Pox—Sally, Nancy and their Children here this Afternoon—Edwd. and Caroline Shoemaker and Joe[e] Waln here in the Evening—William discover'd blood in the phlegm that he rais'd to day—I prepar'd the medicine before us'd.

2d. William and Henry took a ride this Afternoon; Sally and Nancy, [T]ammy Trimble and Polly Thomas, here this morning—Jenny and Hannah Stevenson and Betsy Mifflin here in the Afternoon, Bob Stevenn. in the Evening—Je m'donnez, ce matian.

3d. HD. went early this morning to Clear-field—came home to breakfast,—they are mowing there. Dr. Kuhn call'd this morning he ordred William to loose 7 oz. Blood—which was accordingly done, he bled more freely than usual, and when Michal stop'd it, he was very near fainting—I never saw him before so affected, when he came too he broke out in a sweat, complain'd of being sick, but laying down and being rub'd with vinager he recover'd.—Huldah Mott and Betsy Emlen, Reba. Say and Elizath. Bartram and Betsy Foulk call'd after meeting—S Swett and Hannah Catheral din'd with us—Becky Ash, her Daughter Polly Crage and her Sister Esther Wilkinson call'd this afternoon, SS. and Nancy Skyrin drank tea—Nancy Murry and Nicholas Depuis here this afternoon—I went this evening, S Brant with me, to Jacob Downgs. and call'd at [S.] Fishers, where I have not been for upwards of two years.—a fine evening. from the Daily Advertiser—The tide on Thursday last was higher in our river by 3 inches than it has ever been known to be by the oldest inhabitants. Many stores have been filled with it, and goods to a considerable amount damaged. The wind also, on the night of Wednesday, did some injury along the wharves; and the meadows near the river, in the neighborhood of the city, have been chiefly covered with water. New-York, May 27th. Singular variations of weather. On Wednesday the 14th. May the mercury in Fahrenhite rose to 91 deg. The Saturday night following there was a most severe frost throughout the country. The next Tuesday and Wednesday the mercury rose to 85 deg. for six days last past the thermometer

20. The words "moy [m]—un L——" crossed out.

has been nearly stationary, varying only from 60 to 64 degrees—a constant easterly wind, with rain or mist. Before the present rain the earth was parched with droughth; and crops appear'd likely to suffer—'Tho this appears to be a fine moon light night, it does not seem to be fairly clear'd up—a burr round the moon and the wind inclining to the Eastward.

June 4. Sally Downing, Docr. Redman in the fore-noon, Sally Hopkins din'd with us—HD. his Son William, Eliza and Mary Downing, went in the Carriage to Clearfield—Jenny Downing and [T]ammy Trimble call'd after dinner—Je m'donne cette matain—Sally and Nancy in the Chaise J Skyrin on horse-back also went this Afternoon to the Place. they return'd towards evening—John Cox of Burlington drank tea with us—cloudy.

5. our dear William seems better for bleeding. the spitting of blood has ceas'd—Dr. Kuhn call'd—I spent an hour this morning at Neighr. Hartshorns they are going to spend the Summer at their new purchas'd place, call'd Summer Hill—Billy went out this fore-noon on horse-back without his Seurtout, was caught in a mist or drissel, but I hope has cought no cold—Thos. Speakman call'd this morning by desire of John Brinton, with a message of love to us, Johns Wife very poorly—Michel Callanan call'd—cloudy all day—smart shower rain this Afternoon, little Thunder. I have been very weak and poorly all day.

6. HD. MS. Sally Downing, Sal Brant and Joe, Benn. Wilson in the Chaise with HD. the rest in the Wagon—went to Clearfield, to spend the day there—James Logan call'd—John and Nancy & Child, din'd with me—Betsy Jervis spent the Afternoon, JS. AS. BW. [S]D. drank tea. Jacob call'd—he paid a Boat-man[21] 1200 Dollars which were in a Bag, and going on board his foot slip'd, or by some other means he fell into the river, where he left the Money, but saved himself, it happend in the fore-noon, they have been most of the day endeavouring to recover it but in vain—Nancy and self went this evening to J Smiths found Molly there, came home after 10 o'clock, 'tis very rare for me to be out at night, or in the day either lately—Je me donne cet maitain—clear to day.

7. sometime during last night, Emanuel a Negro man, whom J Downing had employ'd with his man Anthony, to watch on the wharf, that no one might take the advantage of night and obtain the Cash,—drew it up with a Hook and brought it home, for which he receiv'd 100 Dollars reward, the Sum stipulated, and indeed, sufficient.—William and Henry went this morning in the Chaise to Clearfield, return'd to dinner—Jacob Downing, Thos. Fisher, William Mickles Widdow, call'd this fore-noon—HD. and self went this

21. The word "with" crossed out.

evening to H Pembertons call'd at J Downg. Sally has had a bad spell of sick head-ach—Nancy Skyrin came from Jacobs home with us—H Smith here, she went with Molly to visit Caroa. Shoemaker, a very clear and pleasent day, this has been—Benn. Cathral and little Robt. Potts here in the fore-noon.

8th. First Day: when we awoke this morning it rain'd very hard—HD. and Son Henry went to meeting, none other of the Family out this fore-noon, Jacob and Sally and their Children and B Wilson din'd with us—BW. went yesterday in Wms. Sulkey to Newport on business for J Downing, returnd this morning, Josh. Sansom and Sally Downing drank tea here—very heavy rain again this evening our Hay that is making at Clearfield will fare but poorly—Je m'donnez.

9. Joshua Cliborn the largest, here this morning he and his Cozen Jo[s] talk of going home—John Watson junr. din'd here, T Stewartson drank tea—A Skyrin call'd this evening. heavy rain this morning—Je m'donnez.

10. S Swett came home with MS. she spent the day with us—J Logan call'd Dr. Kuhn visited little Eliza who is weak and poorly—heavy rain this evening with Thunder Lightening & hail, prehaps a clearing up shower, after so much rain cloudy weather and Eastery winds.

11 William went out on horse back this morning Neighr. Waln, John and Nancy Skyrin drank tea with us, Michel Callanan, H[e]nor Fry &c call'd—I step'd to see Sally Rhoades this evening.

12 this is the day, that when I was a young Girl we call'd the first of June[22]—we expected 'eer now to have been settled in the Country, but it does not appear yet to be clear'd up—wind easterly—HD. and John Alsop in the Waggon, WD. and HSD. in the Chaise went after breakfast to Clearfield to look after several Acers of Hay, that has been mow'd near a week, and maybe perishing—they took their dinner with 'em—WD. return'd home and din'd with his Aunt and myself, we three were all at Table—Molly gone to dine with Nancy—Eliza to spend the day at home, where she has not been for upwards

22. Until 1752 England and her colonies used the Julian calendar, a solar calendar with 365 days per year (366 every fourth, or leap, year). Because it differed from the solar year by 11 minutes 14 seconds, discrepancies occurred over long periods of time. In 325 the Council of Nicaea had set the vernal equinox on Mar. 21; by 1582 it had drifted to Mar. 11. In that year Pope Gregory XIII reformed the calendar by omitting ten days and ordaining that the last year of a century be a leap year only if it is a multiple of 400. Reluctant to follow the practice of a pope, non-Roman Catholic countries finally began adopting the change in the beginning of the eighteenth century. England and her colonies switched from the Julian to the Gregorian calendar by declaring that Sept. 14, 1752, immediately follow Sept. 2 (Wolfgang Alexander Schocken, *The Calculated Confusion of Calendars* [New York: Vantage Press, 1976], 9–14; *Encyclopedia Britannica*, 15th ed., macropedia, s.v. "calendar").

of three weeks—Ben Wilson &c call'd this fore-noon—HD &c came home to tea, John and Nancy & Child here this evening—WD. rather more unwell than usual—fine clear night.

13. John Alsop and Joe, spent this day at the place, trying to recover some of the Hay—Thos. Stewardson and S Swett din'd with us—Sally, Nancy, their Children and J Skyrin drank tea with us—Je m'donne—Dr. K. call'd this fore-noon—clear full Moon this Eve.

14. Sally Downing call'd this morning, our dear little Eliza left us after dinner and went home, she has been with us 6 months one day lacking—Ben Wilson Breakfasted, John the Gardner came this afternoon with the Cart and old Sorrel, took up a load of Necessaries, HD. and ED, in the Chaise, with our good old mare, Billy, Molly, and Sally Brant in the Coachee, Joe drove them. We arived at Clearfield before 6 o'clock, a very beautiful and pleasent place it is—how delighted and pleas'd would many women be, with such a retreat—and I hope a good degree of thankfullness is not wanting in me for the many favours we are bless'd with—should our dear William be restor'd to a comfortable state of health by our removal into the Country, the end would be abundantly answer'd in my view—Molly, Sall and self have been very busy this evening in arrainging matters here, we have left our dear Sister and Aunt to the care of seeing a large house clean'd in the City—but as she is not very fond of leaving home, she is more in her element.

As I am but weak and poorly and very sildom ride out, the coming up here and the bustle since has fatigu'd me, and as all of our little family Sall and self excepted have retir'd, I think 'tis time we should do so too—moon light.

15. First day. As Molly did not conclude to come with us yesterday 'till just before we set off, she neglected bringing a change of raiment, HD. went to meeting solas—we four din'd togeather—after dinner HD. and ED. walk'd into the garden, found a land Tortoise in a Straw-berry bed—which one of us brought into the house—William cut the Initials of his name and the date of the year, on the under shell WD. 1794—I have read some where of some one doing the like, and the Tortoise being found 50 years or upwards afterwards.—This appeard to be a full grown old fellow—Benjamin Buck, Gilbert and Francies Prichard drank tea with us—HD. and his Son took a ride this Afternoon to SummerVille, Jammy Smiths place, found all shut up none of the family out—Sam Sprigs favour'd us with a visit, he din'd and spent part of the Afternoon—donnez.

16. Joe came up this morning between 6 and 7—HD. went to Town after breakfast about 7 o'clock in the Carriage, left the Chaise and Mare for Williams use—he rode 4 or 5 miles on horse back, this fore-noon—and went

out on foot at 11 o'clock came not home 'till after one, saunter'd about and sat on a stump looking at the workmen who are building a barn for Sammy Fisher I was very uneasy at his stay, as it was in the heat of the day 'tho cloudy—he eat his dinner with a good appetite—No Company hear this day—rain this evening, engag'd to take 6 [lb] butter p week of Spencers, they are to bring the first tommorrow, had a fire in the old parlor this afternoon—[cool].

17 June. Cool this morning had a little fire—warm towards noon,—lodg'd last night in Williams Room—Molly and Sally in ours—WD. seems better since we came out of the City, his pulse considerably reduced—J. Courtney brought in a land Tortoise this fore-noon, with William [T]—June 18, 1789, carved on his undershell, the surname not intillagble, we replac'd him, as that of yesterday, near the spot from whence he was taken—WD. MD. and self, din'd this day on Eggs and Bacon and green pease—John and Nancy Skyrin, Sally Downing, the three Children, Caty Deacon came up after dinner—HD. came afterwards, James Fisher and Son, and Sammy Fisher came over from their place, they all drank tea here, left us before sunset.—William rode out a few miles this Afternoon, HD. stays with us to night—[23]—donnez cet matin; we went on the top of our house this afternoon, the top is almost flat and rail'd in, the prospect from it is beautiful, the Church Steeple plain to be seen, if the wood that intercept the sight were cut away, I beleive we could see it in the New Parlor—I went this morning to Beackleys, our Tenant, to settle some matters relative to butter Eggs &c, his Sister Betsy Beckley keeps his house—yesterday I visited poor John Courtney Wife, she expects some time this summer to lay in with her seventh child, has had but one that was born alive, a fine little girl, now between 3 and 4 years of age, whom they have with them, by her own account, poor woman, she has suffer'd greatly, I feel much for her,—to be sick and poor is hard indeed.

18. HD. left us after breakfast about 3 o'clock, in the Sulky—about 11. came Sally, Nancy, and their 3 Children, their Maids, Anna and Betsy—Joe Gibbs also—they din'd with us, on good Beef Stakes, neats tongue, veal broath for the Children, and Goosberry tarts, made by Ann Skyrin—Sally Brant is our Cook and performs very well—they stay'd with us 'till the Sun was in the Horizon, half an hour too late, they have no man with 'em but Joe—William too, went out on old mare after[24] five, did not return 'till 8 o'clock, an imprudent fellow, the Sun had set above ½ an hour, and dew fell, I hope he has received no injury, it has been a very fine day and evening.—We have made great havock of Flies and Cockroaches by setting traps for them.—Geathered Thyme and Camomile. Leonard Stoneburner buryed this Afternoon at Ger-

23. The word "cloudy" crossed out.
24. The word "tea" crossed out.

mantown—John Courtney brought up in the Cart, 8 more Chairs and another Table &c.

19. L. Stoneburners death was occasion'd by an accident, in driving a waggon through a Gateway, he was jam'd against the post, his ribbs were broke, and otherwise so hurt, that he expired soon after.—we were busy most of this fore-noon, doing little—William took a walk rather than ride, we heard the Garmantown Church Bell distinctly at our door, I cannot yet tell exactly how the wind blows here—went a Vane put up,—Took a walk with Molly this evening as far as Woodfield, [S] Fishers—none of the family there, HD. came up after Sunset, he brought us many good things—I spent half an hour in the Garden picking Rasberries for his Supper, a letter from S Preston received this day, informs of John Kinsey being so ill, as his life is dispar'd of.—very warm this day. Donnez.

20. HD. left us after breakfast, Oliver Paxon call'd in his way home—WD. and self took a walk to Woodfield, soon after our return, Hannah Pemberton and Sally Zane came, they stay'd an hour, went about 12—Sammy Fisher din'd with us—he call'd again in the evening—Our HSD. came about dusk, intending to lodge with us—he has been this Afternoon to Summer-ville with young Company—I have been very unwell this Afternoon and evening.

21. very cool for MidSummer, there must have been rain, as I amagine not far from us—HSD. and MD. left us after breakfast, our family is reduced to three at present, WD. ED. and S Brant, 'tho 'tis not likely that it will continue so long—William and self, walk'd in the Garden after they were gone, on our return he discover'd blood in the phlegm that he rais'd, 'tis three weeks this day since he has perceived any thing of that kind—he has been blooded since, and took Gum Arabec &c, he has taken of it to day.—he imputes it to the long ride which he took on fourth day evening last, and the sudden change in the air since yesterday,—he has been more unwell since that ride than for some time before—HD. arrived here about 5 this Afternoon, he and William went in the Chise to Germantown, return'd to tea, they call'd at Summer Ville.—Jacob Downing Sally and Children, Caty and Anna breakfasted this morning at our house in Town, set off after for Downingstown, where they expect to spend the Summer, Jacob excepted—HD. took a walk this evening to S. Fishers, his family is come up this Afternoon.

22. First Day: HD. and Son William took a ride of 3 or 4 miles in the Chaise after breakfast, during their absence, Thos. Fisher and Son James paid us a viz—HD. went to meeting, came home solus—I expect our Son Henry set off this morning for his farm, by water,—My husband and Son William took a ride of 8 or 9 miles before tea—Sammy and Betsy Fisher came here while they

were out, they stay'd 'till their return and drank tea with us—J'ai eté bien favouré cet matin, for which may I be thankful.—very cool for the Season.

June 23. HD. left us after breakfast, John went to town with the Cart to bring up Nancys necessaries—William and self took a walk before dinner to Sammy Fishers—a very pleasent day—Settled with Betsy Beckley—John and Nancy Skyrin their Child and Girl Betsy Dawson came up before tea Joe drove them—John Courtney brough up a load of their[25] Beds &c—Nancy informs of the illness of Jammy Smiths youngest Son, thought to be dangerously ill.

24. Nancy chose the two Chambers in the Old part of the house, as they were contigeous, and convenient for themselves and servants—I lodg'd on the little bed in Williams roome, he was up twice in the night, his late long ride, which affected him, and a little cold he has taken, fell as I suppose on his bowels—he is much better this morning—The dawn was just opening when I[26] first arose, and a Charming morning it was—J. Skyrin left us before breakfast.—Huldah Mott and Betsy Emlen paid us a fore-noon visit—They with Sally Emlen, have taken up their aboad for the Summer Season at Christn. Sniders, their former lodgings at Germantown, so that we are Neighbours again 'tho not so near, as last year. our dear little Mary Downing was unwell with a sick Stomach and vomitting, when her father left 'em, we shall be anxious 'till we hear again from them—between 5 and 6 this afternoon came up, Hannah and Sally Smith and M. Drinker in our Carriage—James Smith & his Son Charles, James Logan with them in JSs—they drank tea with us, and went away after sunset—J Smiths little Son better. Polly —— a widdow, who liv'd formerly—with JS. came up with the Girls, Nancy Skyrin has hired her to tend her Child &c. Daniel King call'd this Afternoon, I walk'd with him in the Garden, he pointed out several things to me, that had escap'd my notice.—I am mercy-fully better in some respects, than I have been since I left Germantown, or since I hurt my foot—'tho still poorly—this has been a delightful day & evening—No HD. to night.

25. We are not very regular in riseing in the Morning or retireing at night, 6 or 7, 10 or 11. this morning between 6 and 7, busy after breakfast making Curant Jelly.—John brought in a Mole he found in a potatoe patch that he was laying out. A mole is, on examination a curious creature, but what shall we call it? it is nither Man nor Beast, Fish or Fowl, Insect or Reptile, prehaps it is of the[27] class of Vermin, 'tho I hardly think that proper.,—'tis an underminer, of whom there are many, that bare a different name, as blind as the mole itself.—HD. and S Swett arriv'd here before 5 o'clock, Othniel Alsop came after them

25. The word "goods" crossed out.
26. The word "was" crossed out.
27. The word "race" crossed out.

on the old mare, they stay'd tea, OA, went to town with SS. in the Carriage, HD. stays with us—he went this evening to Thommy Fishers, it has been a fine day, rain the evening O. Alsop has taken his Brother R. J. Alsops place in HDs Compting house—RJA, is employ'd at present by Jacob Downing.

26. Cloudy. HD. and Son William left us after breakfast, I remonstrated against the departure of the later, he went notwithstanding, it rain'd fast, before they could, as I think, reach the City—busy again making Jelly, for S. Downing—Nancy and self din'd—G. Prichard call'd—rain with thunder and lightning this Afternoon, William will, I think, regrett his having left Clear-field, as 'tis unlikely that he will return this evening;—Nancy had a very bad spell of the sick head-Ach, she was oblig'd to go to bed, left Sammy Fisher with me, he stay'd tea, his wife and oldest Son in town, the Child unwell—Tis now near 11 o'clock, Nancy has been an hour asleep, after having been very ill—I intend seting up 'till she awakes, our little family consist this night of 3 Women and 3 Children it rains at present, very hard, Polly is up stairs setting by her mistress, the little one asleep in the Cradle. Sally Brant and Betsy Dawson are also fast, they are in the Old parlor with me. how many soleumn hours of watching, have I had in the course of my life?—I have been endea-vouring to amuse myself by reading Moors Journal while in Paris,[28] if it can be an amusement to read of so many absurd and unheard of cruelities as have been practis'd there.

27. Nancy awoke about midnight much better, it had been raining very hard, and Sall and myself heard a noise we could not account for, but upon going down the Celler stairs for something we wanted for Nancy, we were surpres'd to see what a torrant of water had run into the Celler through a window which had been carelessly left open, we push'd too the window with a brush stick, but could not go further, Sally stood on the lowest step and put her hand into the water, it was as high as her wrist.—The ground slants towards the house, instead of from it, HD. intends to have it reverst.—After all things was settled in Nancys room, Sally and self retir'd to the front Chamber of the New-house where we lodg'd by ourselves, found the rain droping into that Chamber, we went a story higher, found it leaking by the side of the Chimney, made the best we could of it, and went to bed much fategu'd—arose this morning between 7 and 8, after breakfast made 3 pints more Jelly—rain most of this day, No body from town—Kings people at work here this Afternoon, as they have not yet remov'd their work shop meterials, we have keep'd close house to day, and no one has call'd to see us—Nancy bravely, myself unwell, still cloudy.

28. John Moore, M.D., *A Journal, during a Residence in France, from the Beginning of August, to the Middle of December, 1792 . . . in 2 volumes* (Philadelphia: Rice, 1793 [Evans, *Am. Bibliography*]).

28. Nancy her little one, SB. and myself lodg'd last night in Billys Chamber—a few stars made their appearrence, but it was cloudy this morning the Sun[29] shone for a few minuits this fore-noon, all the rest of this day cloudy—one Collans a Gardener call'd—HSD. came to Dinner with us—HD. MD. and John Skyrin came up this Afternoon, they with Sammy Fisher drank tea here. HD. return'd to the City towards evening—JS. and MD. stay'd HSD. sent to town—[S]F. spent the evening—Edward Garragus came up this Afternoon to see what is to be done in the Carpenters way.—MD. informs of the death of Polly Hubly formerly Evans, she was buried two weeks tomorrow.—WD. not yet returnd, as it appears to be clear'd up this evening, hope we shall see him with his father tomorrow.

June 29. First Day:—No strangers here to day—John Skyrin, Molly Drinker with us, we took a walk this Afternoon, found my Husband and Son William here on our return—they inform of the departure of Michel Callanan who embark'd this morning on board the Pigou for London—I mark'd a young Tortoise, as I thought him, this Afternoon, with ED 17.94 and three + + + s.—then let him run.—Billy seems poorly—not quite as well as when he left us. he had his teeth cleand while in town by Gar[olet]—they look well.—John S gone somewhere visiting this evening I suppose to [S] Fishers—clear this evening and warm.

30. Foggy morning HD. and JS. left us after breakfast.—William seems poorly, his breast very weak—no company this day.—Joshu Horner came this evening, some hours after John came with the Cart—William took a walk out before tea, 'tho it was Cloudy, he was caught in the rain, and was in it for near half an hour, 'twas near or after sun set and John was just coming—I ordred him to put the mare in the Chaise, and go look for William, while he was preparing so to do, he enter'd the Gate, as slow and delibrate as if he was walking in a flower Garden in a fair day.—he was prudent in so doing, for had he hurried it might have been more injurious then being, for a time wett, he chang'd his cloaths 'tho not very wett, and I hope he has not taken cold—it is not quite clear, a few stars appear.

July 1st. No Company the fore part of this day—took a walk this Afternoon with William he is better than for several days past,—Nancy and Molly went towards evening to Saml. Fishers, return'd to tea, HSD. came up to tea with us, says that his father has been blooded this morning on account of some blood that he observed in his spittle, the weather is I think much too warm for such an opperation, he intends being up hear tomorrow morning with some others to have this place survay'd &c.—poor H——y. C——p——r, put an end to his life, this morning with a pistole, I know not why—A French Man,

29. The words "made its" crossed out.

has been exhibiting fire-works this evening in the City, we saw the Sky-Rockets here.—[S] Fisher here this evening—busy this day making Current Jelly &c.—warm.

2. HD. Reding Howel, Sally Rhods came up in our Waggon,—the later went to her Daughters—RH. HD. HSD. &c[30] spent the day Survaing, they din'd and drank tea with us, HD. stays to night, expects R Howel again tommorrow as they have not finsh'd—HSD. went home in the Sulkey, he sets of tomorrow morning for North-Bank to stay there a day or two—RH. [S.] Fisher, [S] Rhoads and Molly Drinker went to town[31] with Joe—they set off after 8 o'clock, cloudy—rain most of the Afternoon, while they were out survaying—RH threw one of the Skuers that they make use of and struck Joes leg, near the Ancle bone, I drest it as well as I could, but cannot form a Judgment yet, how it may be, hope not very bad—Dl. King here twice to day—I feel weak & poorly this evening—continues cloudy.

3d. HD. stay'd this morning in expectation of Joe's coming up with Reding Howel, about ten Othnial Alsop came with several letters, he inform'd that RH thought the weather would not suit him,—and that Joes leg was too bad for him to drive up.—HD. left us before noon—we made more Jelly Yesterday, and black Currant Jelly to day, and have, I hope, done for the present—Nancy, WD, and self took a walk towards evening—mett John Skyrin coming up, turn'd back with him—a little rain towards evening 'tis now clear—donnez.

4. We heard the Guns from the City plain this fore noon—a rainey day, frequent showers with thunder and lightening, two very bad claps.—a little before Sun-set there was an appearance of clearing up, all around look'd charming, the trees, wash'd by the rain, show'd to double advantage, a faint Rain-bow which soon disappear'd. the sight of a rainbow always occasions, or ought to occasion humble, greatful sensations, when we reflect who it was, that set his bow in the clouds, and for what purpose. heavy rain again this evening—in the midst of it HSD came in, he had been riding two hours in the rain, and had scarcely a dry thread about him, chang'd his cloaths, eat a hearty supper and appears well, he is on his way home from his farm, came a round about way on business—We have seen no one from the City this day, Henry informs us, that Joes ancle was swel'd and painful yesterday morning before he left home, I have been very thoughtful of those at home to day.—S Emlens Lawrence[32] call'd.

30. The word "&c" crossed out.
31. The words "in our" crossed out.
32. The word "here" crossed out.

5. rain most of the day; HSD. left us after dinner, he rode home in the rain—We have been closely confin'd for two days past—HD. and JS. came up to tea, they inform us that Jacob Downing set off this Morning to visit his family, our Joes leg is so swell'd and inflam'd that Docr. Physick was sent for, who prescrib'd bleeding, a purge, poultices, and abstaining from meat, under which regimen 'tis to be hop'd poor Joe will mend, he is very faint-hearted when ailing.—The account which HD brings of the present situation of our valu'd friend and old Acquaintance, Sally Wharton, has very much empress'd my mind this evening, in all probability she is now no more, in this world of trouble,—Sister set up with her last night, the Doctors pron. her bowels to be mortified, she was clear from pain when HD. heard last from her, MS. continu'd there;—her Son R——d, has lately been sent from home, being unmanageable,—great and many have been her troubles, which I trust are now near at an end—her mind was calm and much resign'd.—unwell this evening, which is common to me—donnez.

6. First Day: HD. and his Daughter Nancy in the Chaise, John Skyrin on horse back, went to Germantown meeting this morning—they saw none from the City—JS. and AS. walk'd out this Afternoon, HD. and Son William took a ride—John and Nancy drank tea at Saml. Fishers, H. and ED. went out just before Sun set to take a walk, found it damp, and cut it short, the walk.

7. HD. stay'd with us 'till near noon, then went to town, William with him, Joshua Horner and John Courtney hauling dung. Gilbert Prichard at work here, he diets with us—JS. went after breakfast with [S] Fisher.—John Kinsey of the Union-farm, is on the recovery from a severe fitt of Sickness—A child of Josh. Budd was drownded within[33] a few days past—it will be an additional trouble to T. and R. Say.—HD. and Son came back to tea with us, they bring good news, our family well, Joe out again, and our afflicted friend SW. better.—Sister ask'd the Doctor yesterday or the day before, how long he expected she could live? he reply'd two or three hours. The mortification is stop'd, and they have hopes of her, so have not I, knowing so much as I know, of her situation, and preceeding infirmity, I think 'twill be a miracle if she survives—Our people here have been busy to day, washing, we hir'd a dutch woman nam'd Rosanna, to assist—washing at home is a new business to me, having been in the practice ever since we were married to put out our washing—a fine clear day—D King call'd this morning—his wife in the Afternoon.

8. HD. left us before noon, stay'd at home all day, busy Ironing, no one call'd but Gillbert, and Sammy Fisher, Nancy has begun to day to wean her

33. The word "these" crossed out.

dear little Girl, she is very good natur'd 'tho full of trouble—a fine moon light night.

9. Cloudy. Gilbert gone home unwell; the weaning of Elizabeth overset for the present, her mother could not withstand her good natur'd importunity, and after near 24 hours indulg'd her.—Sally Fisher and two of her Sons, spent an hour this Afternoon with us—Hetty Smith and her daughter Sally drank tea here, HD. and JS. came to tea—towards evening Nancy and William went to [Sammy] Fishers, HD. and self took a walk came home by dusk, Sammy Fisher spent the evening—clear moon light night.

July 10. HD. and JS. went to town after breakfast—William took a walk to the potato-patch, Betsy Dawson out this fore-noon helping to plant potatoes—After dinner who should make an appearance? but Sister, HD. with her, Joe driving, his Ancle almost well—Sally Dawson came with 'em—Sally Wharton continues better to all appearance.—Sarah Fisher, Sally Rhoads, Becky Fisher, Sammy and Betsy Fisher, and little William, drank tea with us, HSD. also, he came from J Smiths where he had din'd, he went home in the evening in the Carriage with his Aunt—HD. stays with us—fine weather—HD. Nancy, William and little Elizath. went the fore-part of this Afternoon to Germantown to S Emlens, at Sniders, came home before tea.

11. HD. went to town before breakfast, early—a cloudy day with some rain—geather'd baum—and Hypericon,[34] rain this evening.

12. Cloudy with rain most of this day: settle'd with Betsy Beckley, for milk cream &c. donnez. HD. and Molly came up this Afternoon, JS, at ten at Night—a cool summer so far.

13. First day: John and Rachel Drinker came up this morning in our Waggon, HD. went with them to meeting. JS. and Molly in the Chaise. JS. and MD. went after meeting to visit S Emlen, came back to dinner—Ben[n] Wilson also din'd here,—Ben, has left us, and lodges again at Hannah Bakers, as M Callanans absence left a vacancy for him,—John Jones and Jonathan Roberts, Neighbouring farmers, and S. Fisher call'd.—J. and R.D. left us after tea—JS. AS. Molly and B. Wilson went to [Tommy] Fishers this evening S. Brants brother Billy lodges here to night, in his way to visit his mother—My dear WD. was taken sick and brought up his dinner, he has been more than usualy unwell for two days past.—heavy rain early this morning now clear.—Finish'd reading Lavater on Physiognomy, I believe there is a great deal in

34. Baum tea or balm tea, prepared from fragrant garden herbs, is used as a diaphoretic, to reduce fever, and for internal disorders. *Hypericum* is Saint-John's-wort (*OED*; see above, July 22, 1793).

what he advances, and am not of the oppinion of those who say, he is a madman, or out of his sences, yet I think he carries some things much too far, and has rather too much conceit of his abilities.

14. JS. went to town before breakfast, HD. and his daughter Nancy after.—essaying again to wean the dear little one; Molly Drinker spent most of this day up stairs with the Child and her Nurse—warm to day, WD. poorly; myself also, donnez sans eff—Williams phlegm mixt with blood again, he is better this evening then in the Morning—he and I took a walk towards evening—HD. and Nancy came to late tea—S Wharton continues better—Dr. Foulke very ill, Molly Foulke din'd with Sister.

15. HD. and William left us after breakfast—WD.s going to consult Docr. Kuhn, he is sensible of more weakness and soreness in his breast then for some time past.—HD. went this morning to Germantown, bought us Mutton and Eggs.—Elizabeth has not suck'd since early yesterday morning Sally Emlen, Huldah Mott and Betsy Emlen, spent an hour with us this Afternoon, Betsy Fisher and Molly Thomas drank tea, [Sammy] Fisher and Jemmy Morton call'd—HD. and William came up before Sun-set, William had lost while in town 6 ounces blood by Dr. Kuhns order, finds himself reliev'd by it—Dr. Foulke is better, he has vomitted a great quantity of blood, and been very ill, JS. came up after night with SF. donnez.

16. HD. and JS. left Clearfield early this morning rain most of the day, no one here—HSD. came after 10 at night from Summer Ville to lodge here. Nancy and Molly were up stairs retireing when he came, he soon brought 'em down child and all; by the sound of an instrument he had with him, the dear little one was so delighted, 'tho in trouble, that she keep'd time with her legs head and feet for a considerable time and went to bed in a good humour, she finds it hard to be deprived of that nourishment, which has so long been her chief support.

July 17. rain in the night, cloudy with rain most of this day—Henry left us after breakfast, Nancy had a Conspute, as Mother Lock call'd it, with her maid Polly Wiggins this fore-noon, William went out twice to day, on the Mare 'tho damp and cloudy, which he would not have done had he felt better.—Hetty Smith and her daughter Hannah drank tea with us, they went away between 7 and 8, had not been gone many minuits before, it rain'd thundred and Lightned, by which HS. is generaly much effected.—J Skyrin came up on Horseback in the rain after Candle-light.—HS. inform'd us of the death of Charles Logan who died lately in Virginia.

18. We were disturb'd last night, near midnight, by Beakleys horses, they got out of the Stable, and run about voilently, and were gilty of some trespasses,

John Skyrin and John Cortney, arose and call'd up George Beakley, and after some time they got them put up.—JS. went to town before breakfast—HD. came up after breakfast, with Edward Garrigas Carpenter, who put up stalls in the Stable, made us an Hen-coop &c—EG. din'd with us, and went to Town after dinner, HD. stays here to night, H Smith sent their Carriage for us this Afternoon not knowing that our own would be up, the pole by some means got broke, not far from Clearfield, Joe Gibbs went to assist in mending it—Nancy, Molly and William, set off in JSs Carriage, but as I knew not by what means the accident happen'd did not chuse to accompany them, and went in our old Chaise with HD—we spent the Afternoon there, Docr. Logan and wife, Jacob Downing and HSD. drank tea with us.—we left Summerville a little before sunset, came home in good time—there is an ugley stoney hill in the way.

19. poorly this fore noon, donnez,—HD. left us after breakfast, WD. and self walk'd a little time in the orchard—No Company here this day—but Jessy Hollinsworth, whom I paid. 11/3. for 3 weeks parkage of a Horse—WD. went 2 or 3 miles this evening on old mare—he feels better then usual—warm, HD. comes not this evening—Our dear little ES. has given up her doating peice, and after many conflicts appears to be nearly weaned. Joe came up this morning with the Carriage for his master, he brought several necessaries which Sister had kindly collected.

20. First day. last night or this morning between 2 and three, William came into my Chamber, he was[35] disordered at Stomach and bowels, occasion'd I expect by the heat of the weather, I stay'd with him an hour, left him somthing better, he has been poorly all this day—little or no appitite, chearful this evening—John Thomas and wife, their two Sons, Arthur and John and HSD. came up in our carriage,—JS. AS. MD. and one of the little boys went to meeting. Henry drove his brother out in the Chaise; this fore-noon, they din'd with us, HSD. excepted, he went to dine at Summerville—poor HT. has the Jaundice,[36] I think I never saw Eyes and skin so Yallow.—it rain'd several times to day, they left us after tea—Sammy Fisher call'd towards evening.

21st. Billy up in the night, and disordred this Morning—he took 9 drops liquid-ladanum, seem'd better for it—he sleeps but little, his appetite poor.—Dagney who owns the next plantation call'd.—Sister and HSD came up after dinner, Henry went to [J] Smiths—Our dear William went to Town with his Aunt before tea, hopeing the ride, and change may be benificial, Nancy and Molly spent the afternoon at Sammy Fishers, pleasant weather—donnez.

35. The word "much" crossed out.

36. Eighteenth-century physicians recommended vomits and purges for the treatment of jaundice, which they recognized to be a symptom of yellow fever, a much more serious disease (Buchan, *Domestic Medicine* [1793], 252–54; for a situation in which jaundice was diagnosed instead of yellow fever, see below, Oct. 22, Dec. 24).

22. HSD. came here last evening about 10 o'clock from Summer-ville, about two miles, I dont like those lonely night walks—he left us early this morning—AS. MD. and self, took a walk in the meadow towards evening.—HD. has not been here since seventh day morning I expected WD. with him this evening but am disapointed.—setting rather disconsolate, behold HSD. enter'd just at the close of day, with the agreeable intillegence, of the wellfare of his father and amendment of his brother, after giving little ES two or three tunes on the flute, he went betwen eight and nine to visit [S.] Fisher, intending to lodge here to night.

23. Henry went from us early this morning breakfasted at J Smiths, then went home—our foulk have been busy washing to day, Saml. and M. Pleasants and their Son James spent this Afternoon with us.—HD. and Son William return'd before tea, Ben Wilson[37] also a very pleasant day—A Wilcockss wife bury'd this day, HD. having business in town went back after sunset by himself in the Carriage, Joe only with him, as it is concluded that Molly stays another day.

24. H. Mott and Betsy Emlen paid us a morning viz. they came again in the Afternoon—HD. came up with [To]mmy Fisher, he expected to have mett his wife here, but mett her not, he went home and return'd with her towards evening, they spent an hour with us—HM went home in their Carriage by herself, Betsy lodges here this night with Molly.—[Sa]mmy Fisher and wife, James Fisher and his Sister Tabby, intend setting off tomorrow morning to Downings-town, on a visit to our daughter Sally—our dear William feels himself better, he has been a *little* out of temper lately, which is not usual in him, some say 'tis a good sign, if that could be arsartain'd I should be willing to bare ten times as much as we have ever experienced from him, but I think the reverse, is more generaly the case, good health does or ought to occasion Chearfullness donnez.

25 July. Joe came up this morning for his master, they left us between 9 and ten, HD. MD. WD. and Betsy Emlen, they are to take Betsy to Germantown and then to proceed to the City, I fear the heat will be too much for William, as the Sun is hot and but little air stiring—spent an hour this Afternoon in the Garden geathering Baum and weading—John Cortney brought a load dung from town, he says that none of the family will come up to night, so that our little family here consists at present of three, in the parlor, Nancy her babe and myself, wrote this evening to Sally Downing by Betsy Fisher, who did not go as they intended this morning but propose it tomorrow.

26. It began to rain last evening, continu'd all night, as I think, and all this

37. The word "with" crossed out.

day, our Celler is deluged, and the roof of our house leaks, so that we have water enough, above and below—Nancy and self din'd &c. without other company. John Skyrin came up this Afternoon in the rain, he is complaining, has a touch of the Jundice, a disorder that he had in the spring—he has not been hear since yesterday week, has been busy dispatching a vessel—he brings me word that my dear William has been more unwell since he left us, then before, almost an intire loss of appetite, but that he is better to day.

July 27. First day: rain in the night, cloudy and misty all day, the Sun appear'd bright through the trees a few minuets before setting—cloudy and misty since; Moon chang'd yesterday, at a dull season—I watch the weather on Williams account, HD—and John Parish came up this morning, report, that William is better, but dont think it proper to venture out while it continues so damp—Joe Gibbs and Sam Sprigs are also here—HD. JP. [S.] Fisher and J Skyrin went to meeting. JS. went to dinner with [S] F. JP. din'd and spent the day with us—he and HD went after dinner to Benjn. Bucks. JP. went to town towards evening HD. JS. stays.

28. HD. unwell his Cheek swell'd. he went to town with [S.] Fisher, JS. also unwell, he went on horse back—G. Prichard, and Joshua Horner, mowing here to day—no one here to day—Gillt. Prichard excepted who din'd and drank tea with us—John Skyrin came up this evening unexpected, he says HD is unwell. WD. continues better, they both intend coming up tomorrow, star-light.

29. Arose this morning nearly, with the Sun, Gillbert mowing again to day, diets with us—heat'd our oven this morning for the first time—baked, Bread, Pies, rice pudden & custards—J Skyrin went to town this fore-noon with [S.] Fisher. HD. and Son William came up after dinner; HD. not well, but better than yesterday—he was engag'd to return back this evening, and left us in about an hour, Billy looks poorley, says he is better then he has been since he left us—he stays with us—Nancy & self took a walk to S Fishers, Betsy poorly, her mother SR. came up while we were there—we came home to tea, mett WD. on the road. cool this evening I have been poorly to day.

30. HSD. went on second day last in the Stage to his farm, return'd yester-day afternoon to Philada: WD. walk'd a mile this fore-noon. MS. and M Foulke in our waggon, H.D and Thos. Stewardson in the old Chaise, came up and din'd with us—Hetty Smith her Daughters Sally and Susan came in the Afternoon.—MS. MF. and TS. left us soon after tea, HS. &c, some time after, HD. stays with us, Nancy, William went with their Father after dinner little Elizath. also to Germantown, they return'd to tea,—HD. ED. WD. took a walk about sunset, to the clover field where they are mowing—we parted on our return, HD. went to [T.] Fishers WD. ED came home, HD. return'd after

night. Betsy Fisher &c. set off this day for Downingstown, it has been a fine day and evening.

31. very unwell, took [medicine]—HD. WD. went to town after breakfast—Gilbert, Joshua and John, making hay—our little maids, Sally Brant & Betsy Dawson, help'd to day, to turn the Hay—finish'd reading the farmers friend, by Enos Hitchcock DD.[38] some say this book is trifling, and only fitt for Children. The stile is plain and familiar, the maxims better known than practised,—and if parents, as well as Children, would read it with proper attention, they might be much benefited thereby.—John Skyrin and Ben Wilson came up to tea with us, BW. left us in the evening JS. stays all night—Saml. Fisher, Toms brother, and wife stop'd to enquire the Charecture of a girl, that had liv'd with us 4 or 5 years ago.

Augt. 1. rumpus.—JS. left us about ten this forenoon—H Pemberton and M. Pleasants paid us a morning visit—it is very warm to day, and WD. in town—a peice of nice corn'd Beef which we intended for part of our dinner, stole out of the Spring-house.—Thos. Wright call'd this morning—William and Henry came up this Afternoon, Jacob Downing and J Skyrin in the evening, "It cant rain, but it showers," a silly old adage, to have four men to lodge with us is very uncommon, we are frequently without one—HD. will be detain'd in town for some days by the quarterly meeting—WD. laterly often lodges there—Jacob and John paid [Sammy] Fisher a visit this evening came home to supper—JD. and HSD. loged in the New back parlor,—read, W. Huttons Journey from Birmingham to London.[39]

Augt. 2. Jacob and John left us early, William and Henry stay'd breakfast, then set off—fine air this morning or 'twould be very warm—Pattison and Suckey Hartshorn, their 4 Children and M.A. Warder, paid us a morning visit.—Je suis bien Malade aujour'd'huy; my health very precarious, and has been for a long time past, 'tho I keep about and appear tolerable.—H Smith sent us a basket of large ripe apples, fitt for dumplings, they came very opportunely, as we have no pies made, and only Chicken and Bacon for dinner having lost our peice beef. Nancy gone this Afternoon to Thos. Fishers, 'tis as warm a day according to my feeling as we have had this summer, and my Son William in the hot City. Nancy return'd from TFs before tea, their Son Joshua is ill of the nerveous fever, HD. and WD—came up before tea, they complain of the heat of this day. John Skyrin came after Candle light, he walk'd part of

38. Enos Hitchcock, *The Farmer's Friend; or, The History of Mr. Charles Worthy* . . . (Boston: I. Thomas and E. T. Andrews, 1793 [*NUC*]).

39. William Hutton, *A Journey from Birmingham to London* (Birmingham: Printed by Pearson and Rollason, and sold by R. Baldwin, and W. Lowndes, London, 1785 [*Brit. Mus. Cat.*]).

the way up—WD. is better than he has been—for some[40] weeks past. HD. appears quite fatigued, sitting four hours in quarterly meeting of which he is Clerk, and many other things to attend to, I fear will be almost to much for him. Vanhorn, blacksmith call'd with his account.

Augt. 3. First day, I did not sleep 'till after two this morning the weather excessively warm, or more properly, exceedingly warm, we retir'd with doors and windows partly open. I was apprehensive of Williams taken cold, as I frequently heard him cough, the wind arose in the night, and towards day when I had fallen asleep, HD. was disturb'd, which is not common, by the loud ratling of a window, which is loose, he was twice down stairs before he[41] found out the right, or rather the wrong window.—discover'd another theft this morning of a large peice of beef fine roasting ribbs, brought up last evening for our dinner to day, and two pounds of exellint Butter, so that we must put up with the old resource, of Bacon and Chicking, for which may we be thankfull; HD. went to town this morning I dont expect to see him un-'till 3d. day—'tis very warm, and to attend long sittings very trying—Ja. Downing and Molly Drinker, and [S.] Fisher came up to breakfast—John and Nancy, Jacob and Molly went to meeting in open Chairs, with Umbrellas—JD. JS. AS. MD. WD. ED. din'd togeather, Jacob and Molly left us after seven o'clock,—John and Nancy took a walk after[42] night by moon light to [S.] Fishers—I took a short walk with S Brant towards evening.

4. HSD. went yesterday morning by water to his farm—JS. for want of a proper conveyance to town stay'd with us 'till 6 in the evening then went on the black horse—busy baking &c to day—Huldah Mott B. Emlen and D. King here this forenoon,—donnez sans efft.—this has been a very warm day—WD. and self took a walk towards even'g ½ mile out.—AS. underwent, and went under, a shower bath this evening she fixt herself in a large tub, the girles pour'd water thro' a[43] Cullender on her head—she has felt very pleasant since.—Saml. Fisher spent the later part of the evening with us—John and Joshua have been mowing the meadow before the door to day, they make but a slow progress—moon light.

5. HSD. did not go, as I was inform'd on first day by water to his place, but he went on Second day morning in the Stage,—HD. came up this morning to breakfast with us, he return'd after to town, William with him.—John and Joshua mowing, very warm, took [medicine]. HD. dip'd little Elizabeth in a tub of water, the first time that opperation has been preform'd, she bore it

40. The word "days" crossed out.
41. Word crossed out.
42. The word "moon" crossed out.
43. The word "large" crossed out.

better then expected—HD. and William return'd this Evening Dr. Kuhn and his two little boys, call'd to see us this Afternoon, he was going to visit [T] Fishers Son—Lightning and thunder, not sharp or heavy, the air chang'd cooler. Nancy repeated the Shower bath, this evening.

6. HD. and self up again last night 12 o'clock, to quiet a noisey window, he left us this morning after breakfast, John and Josa. mowing.—Joe came up this Afternoon empty, brought a note from his master informing that he could not be with us this evening he left the Carriage here, a new one being finish'd in town,—Gidion and Anna Wells, their Son and Neigr. Waln drank tea with us, Wiliam and self took a walk towards evening AS. bath'd again, HSD. return'd home about dinner time—WD. and ED. went on top of the House between 9, and 10, a most delightfull moon light night, the prospect beautifull.

7. Washing to day,—Sammy Smith call'd in his way to Abington meeting. H. Mott and E Emlen and Harriott paid us a morning vizt.—HD. came up about 10 o'clock, he set off soon after for Abington, Billy went with him, he left his father there, came back by himself in the Chaise.—Hannah Smith came by herself in the Carriage, spent an hour with us—D. King call'd—Our pump taken up this forenoon, in order to re place a new one—the weather very cool and pleasant. William took a walk this morning before he went to Abington. HD. return'd to tea with us, J Skyrin came up towards evening HD. ED. WD. took a short walk—Sammy Fisher and Betsy here this Afternoon, she &c return'd yesterday from Downingstown to Philadelphia, says, that Sally and little Mary were well, but our dear little Eliza is very poorly, a Cough, a cold in her head and pain in her breast.

8. HD. Billy and the little one left us after breakfast in the Chaise, JS. on horse back—Nancy and self Ironing all the fore-noon, the new pump put up, the Well was clean'd which was very dirty, a number of dead frogs &c taken out of it. 'tis a fine spring of water from a rock.—HD. and Sister came up this Afternoon in our New Carriage, little Elizabeth, with them, William and Henry in the Chaise—W. left H. at J Smiths, then came solas to us—Henry came about 9 o'clock at night from Summer Ville to Clearfield. I have been for a week past under great anxiety of mind on account of our poor little and I fear miserable SB—'tis *possible* I may be mistaken, 'tho I greatly fear the reverse.

August. 9. HSD. left us after breakfast—rain in the night, cloudy and rain most of this day—I talk'd very closely and pointedly last night to SB. but I fear to little or no purpose—JS. came up this evening before tea—this has been a trying day to me.

10. First day: HSD. came up in the Chaise by himself his father being a little

disordred in his bowels—he went alone to meeting, that is HSD. from thence to J Smiths.—J Skyrin, Nancy Billy and self din'd, sent the Chaise by John Cortney for Henry after 4 o'clock—he return'd to Clearfield, and from thence, William with him to Philada.—Nancy and self had another conference with poor Sall but nothing clear or candid could we bring fourth—I have been, as is usual, very unwell all this day.

11. The full moon arose last night very red, which I look'd upon as a mark of dry weather, it occur'd to me while looking at it, that it was to be eclipsed this morning totally for about two hours,—it was late when I retir'd to my Chamber, and later when I went to sleep—the thoughts of the unhappy Child that lay on a matrass at the foot of my bed, who does not appear to feel half so much for herself, as I do for her, keep't me wakeing,—about two o'clock, as near as I could guess, I was awaken'd out of a dose, by very sharp lightening, it rain'd heavely, the thunder rumbling, and more constant and regular than hard claps generaly are; it continu'd 'till I suppose the eclipse was over, during the storm I arose, lighted a candle by the lamp, which we have[44] keep't burning every night, in one or other Chamber in our house since the birth of my first Child, and went into John and Nancys room, stay'd with 'em half an hour, then retern'd to my room, wak'd Sally and went up stairs to wipe up the water which had leek'd from the top of the house, then desended into the cellar found that overflow'd—shut too the windows, which the wind had blown open—then went to bed,—arose this morning by times, set John to work digging a trench to carry off the water at a future time.—Sun shone this morning through flying clouds, weather warm,—J Skyrin left us before dinner with Saml. Fisher, he bid us adieu expecting, before we see him again to set off for New-York and Connetecut.—our little Elizath. was dip'd in cold water the fourth time this morning H Mott and E Emlen call'd this forenoon, AS and her Daughter went with 'em to take a ride, they return'd here before dinner, then left us promise to spend the day with us tomorrow,—Nancy gone this Afternoon to visit Molly Thomas, who has been very unwell for some time past with a broken breast &c.—unwell donnez. HD. and Son William came up this Afternoon, David Cummins and Peter Yarnals Wife drank tea with us in their way home,—H. and ED. had a trying Conversation, if a conversation it could be call'd, with SB—poor poor Girl, who could have thought it?—J Skyrin heard Cannon fireing in the City, this morning early—to commemorate, it is said the Massacre of the Swisse guard in Paris.—read a small volume of Langhorne.

12. a fine cool morning, as is common at this season of the year, cool mornings and evenings. HD. and William went to town after breakfast.—John Courtney, his Wife and Daughter dressd prehaps, in their best, set off in the

44. The word "always" crossed out.

Cart for the City to prepare for the little womans confinement &c it appears to be a grand expedition. Sall wak'd us up between 12 and one, for lint and ladunem for an aching tooth, William, who had taken wine whay for a little[45] cold he had,[46] arose to know if any one was sick—we have been frequently disturb'd in the night laterly—Betsy Emlen spent the day with us, EE. AS. and ED. were all that din'd togeather here—Thos. Fisher paid us a morning visit—Hetty Smith and her daughter Hannah, H. Mott, B. Emlen, and Anna Wilson, Charles Smith also drank tea here.—Sammy Fisher paid us an evening visit. No body from town to night, Nancy, myself and the little one, Polly, Sally and Betsy are the whole of our family just now—a fine clear moon light night.

13 Augt. a very fine day, neglected mowing for want of Sythes—Ben Wilson din'd with us. Joshua Howel and Son call'd this fore-noon, Sally Rhoads, Betsy Fisher and BW, drank tea with us—I am dissapointed, seeing no one of our family up this evening Baked to day.—we have a good baker supplies us with bread from Germantown, and good butter is brought to us twice a week from Spencers.

14. Joshua and John mowing, cool, pleasent, none of our family have made their appearence here, since third day fore-noon—washing to day; Donnez cett matin, and took a dose C. Oil after—Joshua and Caty Howel, their Daughter Betsy, my Husband and Son William came to tea with us. Neighr. Howel &c left us a little before sun-set—my dear Billy more unwell then usual, loss of appetite &c. J Skyrin came up after night.—about nine o'clock this evening we observ'd a considerable fire which we concluded to be in the City. H.D. William and self, went on top of the House, where we could very plainly see it. they concluded it to be at the west end of the town, it continu'd, after we first saw it, burning for upwards of an hour—clear moon light night, very poorley this day, which is no new thing—finish'd reading, Youngs Centaur.[47]

Augt. 15. HD. went this morning to Germantown, to purchase Sugar &c after breakfast, return'd and went to town William with him, J Courtney complains of the conduct of George Bickley, our tenant, and I beleive with reason.—HSD. went on third day last, by water to his farm, return'd yesterday—The fire which we saw last night and suppos'd to be in the City, was not so, but we immagine brush burning to the westward.—An account in the paper of this day, of the Massacre of upwards of 700 French white people, by the Negroes, at Fort Dauphin an Island belonging to the french and Span-

45. The word "cough" crossed out.
46. The word "taken" crossed out.
47. Edward Young, *The Centaur Not Fabulous: In Six Letters to a Friend, on the Life in Vogue* . . . (London: A. Millar and J. Dodsley, 1755 [*NUC*]).

iards.[48] HD. and WD. came up this evening, William seems rather better—ED. taken sick at tea, have had a disordred stomach frequently of late—in consiquence of obstructed bowels.—Henry came here between 9. and 10. from J Smiths.

16. HD. and William left us after breakfast for the City. Henry set off for Newtown B. County. Nancys maid Molly went to town on a visit, so that AS. and ED. Sally and Betsy, with our little, on constitute our family at present. John complain'd again to day of George Bickleys encroachments, I sent for George, and laid matters before him; As guilty persons are generaly Cowards, he had little to say for himself, at least to any purpose; and I hope it may have *some* effect on him. began to rain about 3 o'clock, rain'd heavely most of the afternoon, Henry return'd here towards evening, he has rode 40 miles this day, was so wett as to make it necessary to change his cloaths—it has been the case 2 or 3 times this summer, after taking a dish of good tea &c, he felt himself refresh'd, and appears not to have taken cold. He lodg'd in Williams Bed, Nancy in my room.

17. First day, HSD. left us after breakfast, cloudy. John Skyrin and Molly Drinker came up, in a Chaise, John and Nancy went to meeting—no one here this day but John Smith son of James, & Billy Fisher—John, Nancy and Molly went this evening to Tommy Fishers.—this has been a very serious day to me, as are many others. Jacob Downing and S Swett set off yesterday for Downings-town.—donnez.

18. Sammmy Fisher breakfasted with us, then went with J Skyrin to the City, John took leave of us a second time, intending for New-York &c—a fine clear cool day—H. Mott and Betsy Emlen came this morning for Nancy, Molly and little Elizath. who went with 'em to spend the day—so that I am alone, as an Irishman would say, with Sally and Betsy—din'd by myself, Nancys maid Polly return'd this Afternoon—the same company that our girls went with this fore-noon, came back with them this evening,—Molly return'd with them again to Germantown, where she intends spending a day or two, with S Emlen &c. at Sniders—HD. and William came up this evening Billy continues poorly, bowels disorder'd.

19. HD. went this morning to Germantown, return'd to breakfast—went to

48. Following the upheavals of the French revolution and the black rebellion in Hispaniola (then Saint-Domingue), Spanish and English troops had invaded the island in 1792. The Spaniards, acting in collusion with the black rebel leader Jean François, encouraged French whites who had fled the colony to return and rally behind the king of Spain. On July 7, 1794, the Spaniards allowed François and his troops to enter the town of Fort Dauphin, where they slaughtered 742 whites (*Phil. Gaz. and Universal Daily Advertiser*, Aug. 15, 1794; Ott, *Haitian Revolution*, 81–82).

town by himself—Thomas Fisher call'd—H Mott and EE. and MD. came this fore-noon, for Nancy to go with them to Jemmy Smiths, Huldah stay'd with me 'till their return. Molly went back with them to Germantown—Danl. King call'd after dinner—WD. took a walk forenoon, he seems better, pleasent weather—donnez.—Joe Gibbs, was yesterday morning dismiss'd from our service, we suppose he is gone towards New-England, he has left, if we mistake not, a Memorial behind him.—HSD. came up about 4 Clock Afternoon, order'd his horse put up, and walk'd over to Summer Ville—James Logan and Sally Smith drank tea with us—HD. came up towards evening, while he drank tea, William and self took a short walk, sun set clear, if a tolerable share of health was afforded me, and those I love, I should enjoy the country in a supreme degree.—Henry came home at 10 minuets after 10 o'clock, his father and brother had been in bed ½ hour, I waiting for him, and not a little uneasy; when young men go a Courting so far from home, they should make their visits shorter, and not walk two miles in a dark night alone; the resk of meeting with mischevous persons, or of taken cold this season of the Year, should have some weight with 'em.—I have my Husband and both my Sons with me this night, which is not common.

20. HD. and Son Henry went to town this morning donnez sans efft. William walk'd to Thos. Fishers—John Courtny gone to town for a Waggon, Joshua busy weeding in the Garden, I wish he may not do as much harm as good, as he appears not to understand the business—Nancy withdrawn up-stairs. 'tis not unusal for me to be alone—Billy went with Joshua Fisher and Nurse Waters to Nicholas Walns, Joshua is recovering of a nerveous fever, they parted at our gate,—Ben Wilson came before dinner din'd and spent the day with us—rain this Afternoon—Ben stays with us to night—cloudy—WD. and ED. both poorly.—I could not have thought, that a girl, brought up from her 10th year, with the care and kindness that SB has experienced from our family, could be so thoughtless and hardned, as she appears to be on such an melencholy occasion.

Augt. 21st. John Cortney went to town this morning, with the Cart, Polly Wiggins Nancys maid gone with him, Nancy dismist her yesterday—Joshua weeding weather warm. HSD. came up about 11 o'clock, a new driver with him, James Dunning he was hired yesterday—they brought us Chickens peaches &c—stay'd about an hour, then William with 'em went to town—John return'd about 3 o'clock, brought up iron barrs for the Kitchen Chimney.—took med[icine] C.O. HD. and William came up to tea, [S] Fisher spent part of the evening—Nancy took a walk this Afternoon to see Molly Thomas who continues very unwell—I have been much disordred most of this day—weather very fine.

22. HD. Nancy and her Child went to town. Sammy Fisher breakfasted with

us, Nancy was to have rode with him, but as William concluded to spend the day with me SF. went in his own Chair by himself—fine day. William walk'd out this morning—he and I din'd togeather, we laid out for a walk to Benn. Bucks, but were prevented by the arrival of H Mott. E Emlen and MD—soon after them came HD. AS. ES. and [S.] Fisher in our Carriage—HD. prevail'd on me, much against my feelings to take a ride of two or 3 miles,—(Rosanna hear to day weeding the Strawberries) I mett with so many frights in my younger days with my Children when they were little ones, that I cannot get over and I may say that I am a compleat Coward, it has been a great inconvenience and dissapointment in many ways to me—on our return we found John and Honor Fry at our house, Mett SEs Carriage going home MD. with 'em.

23. HD. WD. and Sammy Fisher went this morning after breakfast—No body here this day but Betsy Fisher who drank tea with us—Nancy and John Courtney went home with her just at dusk.—No body up this evening—Nancy, myself, our two girls, and the little one, we have not been one night, that I recolect quite so distitute but once—read Tom Pains new peice, entitled, the Age of Reason.[49]—John and Joshua made 2 Barrels Cider to day—a Jonathan Carmalt, grand Son of Thos. Say, was lately grievously abus'd on the Frankford road, who the person was that beat him I have not heard, his wife and Children were with him in a Carriage, he was pull'd out of the Carriage and beat with a horse whip 'till he was, as related, in a gore,[50] one of his eyes beat out, and hung on his Cheek, and otherways much injur'd, he put his eye in the socket with his own hand, but turn'd the pupil inwards, the Offence was, entering a gate by mistake—belonging to a person who was a stranger to him, he is since taken up and put in prison—I dont know JC. but feel much for his old grandfather, in whose house my Sister and self boarded 14 months after the death of our dear parants,—he is near 85 years old, and has lately mett with several tryals.—donnez sans efft.

24. First day: heavy rain all this morning have given over expecting any of our family this fore-noon, or provision for dinner, which is generaly brought us on first days. We are favour'd to have sufficient without it.—We are invited to the Burial of Willm. Buck, son of Benjan. Buck, tomorrow at 9. fore noon—a lad who has been for some time past troubled with fitts &c—Nancy and self din'd by ourselves, rain this evening, this has been what is call'd a dull day.—no news from home.—finish'd reading, The Life of Mahomet &c. by Humpy. Prideaux D.D.[51]—I expected Sam Sprigs this evening.

49. Thomas Paine, *The Age of Reason,* Part 1, *Being an Investigation of True and Fabulous Theology* (New York: T. and J. Swords, 1794). Paine's work was also published that year in London, Paris, Philadelphia, and Boston. Part 2 would appear in 1796 (*DNB, NUC*).

50. The words "of blood" crossed out.

51. Humphrey Prideaux, *The History of the Life of the Great Imposter Mahomet* (Philadelphia: Stewart and Cochran, 1697 [*NUC*]).

25. Sam Sprigs came up this morning with paint and brushes to black and red our harths. the two new parlors he put in order, the old parlor yet to be [ ]ivated—H Mott, Betsy Emlen, and Molly Drinker came fore noon, they spent the day with us. HD. and William came before tea, HSD came up after dinner, he went seven miles further, return'd towards evening and lodg'd. with us,—My Husband and 4 of our Children with me, which is not common, Sister and Sally Downing absent.—Hannah and Hitty Fisher and Sammy Emlen junr HM. and EE. drank tea with us, went all togeather towards evening in SEs Carriage, MD. stay'd with us, after spending a week at Germantown with EE—James Smith and HSD. went on sixth day last to North-Bank, return'd on seventh day.—warm to day—donnez.

26. HD. WD. and HSD. left us this morning after breakfast—a fine shower about 10 o'clock, AS. and ED. din'd.—George Fox and wife, and Betsy Fisher took tea with us—John Courtney went to town, brought up the heavy waggon he went once before for, and a peice of beef for us—no body from town this evening. donnez sans efft.—we may in measure become innured to bodily pain, 'tis rarely I pass an hour, without uneasy sensations.—This time twelve month our fellow Citizens were dyeing in numbers, with the malignant fever—not soon, I trust, to be forgoten, but remember'd by survivors with humble thankfullness—and amendment of Life.

Augt. 27. Sam Sprigs drove William up this forenoon in Chaise—our people busy Washing. Sam got dinner—Hannah and Sally Smith, and Sally Large stop'd on horse back, but did not alight. HSD. came after dinner, left his Horse for Sam, and went in the Chaise to Summer Ville to take his *Amie* to Town this evening William stays with us—Henry gave us expectation of his Fathers being here this evening but it is not so. Jacob Downing and Molly Drinker left Philada. after dinner for Downingstown on a visit to Sally—this has been a fine day. I have felt rather better than usual—Different persons have different tasts, their likes and dislikes vary, to me the noise of insects is amuseing, the locust, the Cricket, the Cateydid, as it is call'd, and even the croaking of Frogs.—'tho their notes are inferior, they are pleasing.

28. Sam, came up this morning busy Ironing, Sam cook'd dinner, Rosanna here weeding—received a note by Sprigs from HD. informing that Sally Johnson, our Salls mother, and my Sister intend paying us a visit tomorrow, poor Woman, my heart achs for her. HD. came up after dinner, Polly Drinker and her Son and Daughter with him—Hetty Smith her Daughter Sally, and Sally Learge, and Thommy Morris junr. drank tea with us—WD. came up with his Father &c—they all except William left us towards evening.—HSD. came up this Morning about 8 o'clock stay'd but a few minuets, went forward to middletown Bucks County, intends returning here tomorrow evening—donnez.

29 Received a note this morning inviting to the burial of James Thornton, who departed this life yesterday morning and is to be intered' tomorrow at Bybarry—his Father and Mother lately dy'd, and Brother, within these few years.—Danl. King and Thos. Fisher here fore-noon, Sam Sprig drove William to town in the Chaise. H Mott and Betsy Emlen paid us morning visit, Hannah Pemberton and Sally Zane also,—HP. prevail'd on me to go to town with them, we arriv'd at our house just as HD. and MS—were going to dinner, the first time of my going to town, since I left it on the 14th. June, home and all things there, looks agreeable—we din'd early, set off soon after HD. ED. MS. WD. for Clearfield, where Sister had appointed to meet me, and our unhappy girls mother; she came at 3 o'clock, and was much affected at the sight of her Daughter Docr. Logan his Wife and Son Algernon, drank tea with us, I did not see S Johnson when she went away, having company with me. G. and DL,—HD. and MS. left us after tea, Billy stays with us to night. I have been very poorly this day, especialy in the fore-noon—donnez cet matin—Sister has engag'd OG. for SD. begining April next.

30. Augt. William and self took a short walk after breakfast, a cool pleasent morning no body here this forenoon. Our little Elizath. disorder'd in her bowels, and a little freting, her Stomach and Eye teeth appear to be pushing forward.—A Dismal looking object came to the back door, this forenoon to ask charity, our young people were frighted by his appearence; a middle ag'd man, very lusty, with a staff in his hand, mouth and Nose much larger than the common size, long and thick matted yallow hair, a long beard of the same hue, his cloaths very dirty and raged; I ask'd him, why he went about the Country so frightful a figure, he said he had just recover'd from a fitt of sickness, (of which no symptoms remain'd) and I imagine he is troubled more with lasiness then Sickness, I gave him victuals, but no money, and desir'd him to go quickly off, and to shut the gate after him, to alter his appearence or I thought there was a likelyhood that he would scear many, and have the dogs set on him, I felt afraid while talking to him, and wish'd him further, he said he intended to change his appearence before he entred the City.—I have observed, it is much more common to see those ill looking vagrants about the Country, then in the City, and suppose they are fearfull if they enter a Town in such a figure that they will be taken up and confined.—HD. came up about 4 o'clock Afternoon in the light Carriage, took William, Nancy and the little one airing, I could not muster up courage sufficient to go, but during their absence took an hours walk, with Betsy Dawson for to lean on if necessary, went to the potatoe patch, and strol'd in the Garden &c HD. &c went to J Smiths, they came home to tea, after 7 this evening Nancy went with her Father to Sammy Fishers, just at dusk, return'd between 8 and 9—fine starlight evening.

31. First day: how quick the weeks pass over.—HD. WD. little Elizath. and

Nelly Courtney went out rideing, between breakfast and meeting time.— HD. and Daughter Ann went to Meeting William and self stay'd at home, Thomas Cope and Charles Brown, and Benn. Wilson din'd with us—Cope and Brown went away about 3 o'clock, HD. and BW, took a walk to Tommy Fishers.—they return'd about the close of the day—Tommy Fisher and Son with them, who stay'd an hour with us—BW went off after moon light— Huldah Mott and Betsy Emlen drank tea with us—

who could have thought, that the Season was past,
Or that time roll'd so swiftly away,
When on a review from the first to the last,
Finds this is the last Summers day.—

I have thought that days spent for a length of time in a sameness, appear'd shorter than when a variety took place.

Sepr. 1st. HD. and William left us as usual after breakfast.—Gilbert Prichard here this fore noon. B Dawson with the Child, Nelly Courtney and self paid Betsy Fisher a morning visit, the Sun was under a cloud when we went, the walk was pleasent, but quite otherwise returning, 'twill be a warm day I [judge] William and Henry came up this Afternoon they lodge here to night, fine weather.

2. William, Henry and James, left us after breakfast—busy tout est matin mending Stockings &c.—warm day, far from well—donnez—Took a walk with Sally and the Child, before tea, Sally Fisher and her Son Joshua took tea with us, they were alarm'd some nights past, by ill designing persons as they thought about the house after 11 o'clock,—Rachel Spenser and Jenny Edge call'd after dark, in there way home from town—RS. says that their Spring house was rob'd last night, or the night before of 12 pounds of butter—Our girls saw, or conceited they saw a man passing more then once by our Spring-house, which is opposite the parlor window, where they could easily descern that we have no man with us,—we sent for J Courtney, who with a stick in his hand, and Sall with a Candle, (a fine way to take a thief) went in search of the man, but found him not, but as some of us feel a little cowardly, John has offer'd to sleep on the carpet in the Kitchen, which is agreed to.

Sepr. 3. Sam drove William up in the Chaise this fore noon, it was rather late, the Sun hot, no top to the Chaise, was most too much for Willm. Sally Johnson, her Son in Law and Daughter with their Child, his name Adam Franks, they came to visit, and talk about, poor SB[52]—they went away at 5 o'clock, it look'd likely for rain, has continu'd cloudy all this evening, none others here to day, Sam left us at dusk, WD. stays here to night, donnez cet

52. The words "after dinner" crossed out.

matin sans efft.—Jacob Downing and S Swett return'd from the Valley on second day last, left all there pretty well.

4. A strong Southeast wind this forenoon which threaten'd sprinkling, William Notwithstanding would go to town with Sammy Fisher—Nancy reading, myself busy about many things, we have a very silent time, and little family—spent an hour up'stairs as is common attending to my own weaknesses—donnez—Tommy Fisher paid us a morning visit Our girls were last night disturb'd a second time, by shadows, about the Spring house, which amount to nothing. John Courtney went to town this fore noon for a load of dung, with a Cart and two horses, he took a note and some things from me,—[Sa]my. Fisher call'd after moon light, to inform us, that poor John had mett with a sad accident, the Horses had run away with him, and that one or two of his ribbs and Collar bone were broken, he was taken into a house at the opper end of the City, a Barbers, HD. was sent for, who immediately look'd out for a nurse, and employ'd Docr. Physick to attend him, his thigh is also hurt and [S] Fisher thinks by accounts he is in danger—this accident prevented HD. from coming up this evening as he intended—he desir'd SF. to call and let us know what had happend. We are worse of this night than ever, having no man with us, nor John to call upon in case of any emergancy—I thought it best to make the matter as light as possible to Mary Courtney, who is near lying in—I told her the Horses had run away and John had hurt his knee or thigh, that my husband thought it would not be proper for him to return to night, she made very little enquiry and appear'd less alarm'd than I expected—Our dear little one is much disordred in her bowels.—This is a world of trouble; 'tho much at same time to be thankful for, many mercies.

5. HD. William and James Kinneers wife, came up before dinner, my husband brought her to visit Mary Courtney being an old acquaintance of hers—and as she had been with poor John since he was hurt, could give her a particular account of his situation. HD. and MS. went last night to see him, Docr. Physick was then with him, had him twice blooded in the course of the day,—he was much releived by the second bleeding, and appear'd this morning better, 'tho in a doubtful situation.—B. Wilson came up before dinner, he, HD. WD, and J Kineers wife, din'd with us, they and Benjn. Bucks wife, and Francis Prichard, took tea with us—all left us soon after tea except BW, who took a short walk with me about sunset, he went away after Moon light, and we are again left solas. Rachel Lewis formerly Wharton, paid us a morning visit, she is out with her Children this Summer at the next plantation, but one, to us—HSD. and Hannah Smith set off early yesterday morning in a Chaise for Downingstown.—A number of young men of our society, have lately been with the Elders of the 3 monthly meetings, two have been with HD, to propose a more easy method of passing marriages, than has hitherto been in practice—They propose that a friend shall be appointed to make mention

of the intentions of AB. and CD.—and that the parties may be excused makeing a publick appearance. I am apt to think this scheme will not take place.

6. Septr. I was favour'd with a good night, void of fears. 'tho that is not the case with all of us, when alone as we call it—donnez cet maten.—John Shoemaker call'd.—our little Elizath. appears better,—settled with Betsy Bickley—paid Dillworths Man for ½ cord Hickory Wood deliver'd here, 1.2.6:—finish'd reading Addisons Evidences of the Christian religion, with additional Discourses on elevn different subjects, by the same excellent author.[53] Those who are capable of much wickedness, are, if their minds took a right turn, capable of much good.—and we must allow that T.P. has the knack of writing, or of putting his thoughts or words into method.—and was he rightly inclin'd, he could, I doubt not, say ten times as much in favour of the Christian religion as he has advanc'd against it. And if Lewis the 17th. was set up as King of France, and a sufficient party in his favour, and TP. highly brib'd or flatter'd, he would write more for a Monarchical Government than he has ever wrote on the other side. A time serveing fellow.—Nancy visited Betsy Fisher this Afternoon.—James drove WD. and Sally Rhoads up, she went to her Daughter William stays with us to night—James return'd directly back with the Carriage neglected leaveing our provision which was sent for tomorrow, meat fruit &c—it so happens that we can do without it having sufficient by us.—Huldah Mott and Betsy Emlen, took a ride to see us this Afternoon, Betsy has been to Burlington to visit her intended Sister Sush. Dillwlyn—HSD. return'd from Downingston yesterday, left HS. there, and Jacob set off to day—John Courtney much better after a third bleeding, I went this evening to see Mary, she appears in good spirits every thing consider'd. cool and pleasent 'tho cloudy.

7. First Day: began to rain in the night, continues raining this morning, clear'd away afternoon, moonlight evening—saw no one 'till towards evening Sammy Fisher call'd said that HD. was coming up after evening meeting. he accordingly came to tea, and brought with him the ribbs beef, design'd for this days dinner ready roasted, it will serve for tomorrow; Peaches, grapes, mellons &c &c. John Courtney better—able to walk about.—HSD. went off yesterday for Bristol, he is to meet Richd. Thomas, who goes with him to his farm—William, Nancy and self, spent this day seriously togeather,—perused two Books in manuscript, belonging to Sally Fisher—donnez cet matin.

53. Joseph Addison, *The Evidences of the Christian Religion; To Which Are Added, Several Discourses against Atheism and Infidelity, and in Defense of the Christian Revelation* (London: 1730 [G. Watson, *New Cambridge Bibliography*, 1102]).

How various and shifting, the scenes of this life,
To HD. and Harry his Son;
While William and self, like a Cat and his wife,
Contentedly tarry at home.—Or rather make a virtue of necessity.

Sepr. 8. HD. William left us this morning 8 o'clock, after breakfast, they call'd for Sally Rhoads who went to town with them.—it has clear'd up with a smart northwester and is realy cold—paid Barnard Vanhorn blackSmith £2.12.—he lives within a Mile of us—Nancy, her Child, Betts Dawson and little Nelly, went this fore-noon to visit Betsy Fisher, donnez. Nancy and self din'd togeather,—Elliston and Sally Perot, William Sansom and Daughter Polly Perot and two of her Children drank tea with us.—none of our family up this evening expected WD. and Sam, am disapointed that they came not—a very fine full, moon light night.

9. I lodg'd last night in Nancy's room, Arose early this morning spent the fore noon reading and mending the old Carpet.—just as Ann & myself wear seated at dinner, B Wilson made his appearance, he din'd with us, spent the day and lodges here to night—After dinner Sister and William came up, they stay'd but an hour or two, went home to tea—Huldah Mott and Betsy Emlen came, Nancy and Child took a ride with them, she came home to tea—while they were absent BW. and ED. took a walk—we amus'd ourselves this evening moon and Stars gazeing with a spyglass—this night is very like the last, most beautiful—we have had the advantage of two full moon light nights—which does not often occur, the Moon full'd this morning about 8 or 10 o'clock, and 'rose this evening near the same hour, so that it was last night, and this, equaly near the full.—HSD. went off this morning early, for Downingstown.

10. BW. left us early this morning—Rossanna here washing. Sam Sprigs came up fore noon with the new Chaise, brought with him a young woman, recommended as a Nurse for Mary Courtney by Js. Kenni[ns] wife—we are furnish'd as usual, with provision fruit &c from home.—Peter Yarnel smoked a pipe with us, on his way home from meeting for Sufferings—he inform'd us that, David Bacon, John Parish, Willm. Savery and James Emlen, were appointed a Committe to go back among the Indians. commissioners are also going, Timoy. Pickering &c—The Indians desir'd, that some of their old friends the Quakers would attend the Treaty, and the President, approv'd it.[54] they are to set off in a few days. My husband and Son William paid us a

54. In 1794 the U.S. government sought a neutrality treaty with the Six Nation (Iroquois) Indians, who were being encouraged by British interests to go to war against the U.S. in the wake of growing Anglo-American tensions. Timothy Pickering, who had been a special emissary to the Senecas (members of the Six Nations), led a government delegation in September to Canandaigua, N.Y., accompanied by four Quaker observers: William Savery, David Bacon, John Parish, and James Emlen. The policy of sending Friends to observe Indian treaties was an outgrowth of the Quaker peace policy adopted in seventeenth-century Pennsylvania to safeguard the interests of the Indians. After the creation of the republic, the practice was extended nationally and continued into the nineteenth century (see above, Sept. 19, 1793; Clarfield, *Timothy Pickering*, 149–52; Kelsey, *Friends and the Indians*, 89–90).

short visit this Afternoon, went back to tea, rather too late, the Sun being nearly set, Sam went also, we are 5 females in the house our little one counted.—Lancake at Frankford was bury'd this morning 'twas he that was so troublesome to Cacardo the french Gentleman who liv'd at A Jamess late Dwelling—, and I understand that it is his Son who is in prison for lately abusing Jonathan Carmalt.—donnez.

11 Sepr. went to bed last night in the room over the Kitchen, next to Nancys room, but was disturb'd by a noise could not account for, went to Nancys bed, and spent the remainder of the night with her and Elizah. we are easily[55] frighted I think—busy Ironing this forenoon, donz. our dear William came up with sam about 11—din'd with us, the phlegm he raises is a little discolor'd, redish, he left us between 5 and 6.—after they were gone, B Dawson with the Child, little Nelly, Romeo, Prince and myself, took a walk to our Lands end and return'd by sunset. a fine clear moon light night.—finish'd reading a large Volume pamphlets, on different Subjects—not very instructive or entertaining.

12. favour'd with a good night—No William this morning he intended coming up with Sam:—as he spit something like blood yesterday I fear that he may be more unwell than usual,—Huldah Mott and Betsy Emlen paid us a Morning Visit—Nancy and self din'd by our selves—Danl. Kings people are making Sider here this Afternoon. Jacob Downing and Molly Drinker, Henry SD and Hannah Smith, return'd the night before last from Downgtown—HD. and Son William came this afternoon to ask us, how do ye, HD. being under engagements in town soon left us, WD. stays this night, he and self took a walk about a mile, before tea, he is better than yesterday.—We amused ourselves again this evening looking through a spy glass at the *Spangled heavens*.

13th. a good night through mercy.—William went after breakfast, to town with Sam[y]. Fisher. a pleasent day, fine air, donnez et matin—Nancy and self din'd ensemble,—We spent this Afternoon, Bets Dawson and the Child with us, at Wakefield, Thos. Fishers place, came home after tea, about sun set, Joshua Fisher with us. None of our family up this Night.—fine weather.

14. First Day: HD. and William came up this morning James and Sam with them.—Nancy went with her father to meeting—Gilbert and Francis Prichard came home with them and din'd with us—HD WD. AS. and the Child, took a ride after dinner,—Jammy and Hetty Smith, their Son John, Benjn. Buck, Sammy Emlen drank tea with us, HD. went to town after tea, William stays with us—J. and HS. &c left us about sun set.—a very fine day and evening—

55. The word "soon" crossed out.

took med[icine]—the Committe sets of tomorrow, for the Indian Country—upwards of three Hundred miles.

15. after a good night, am favour'd to feel rather better then usual—took a pleasent walk with my Son William up and down the road—the air agreeable, after a foggy morning. About noon HD. Thos. Stewardson and Sally Savery, came here unexpectedly, they had been as far as Germantown with the friends, who are on their way to the Indian treaty—they din'd with us—left us about 3 o'clock—William went with them. Our Son Henry, was yesterday taken with a Chill, a fever follow'd it, he was very unwell all night, but rather better this morning. I shall be uneasy 'till I hear again from him which I expect will be this evening,—My Husband expected, Sam, with John Courtney up in the Chaise while he was here, having so order'd it, and when he went away desired me to send Sam back with the Chair for him to come up again this evening Evening is come, but no Sam, no John, nor no one else—Mary Courtney poorley, tho not bad, I hope she will continue as she is 'till tomorrow, as we have no man to send out on any occasion, Huldah Mott and Betsy Emlen drank tea with us, they left us after sunset,—past 8 o'clock, wind high and easterly, looks as 'tho a storm was geathering,—All things consider'd and put togeather, the appearence is rather gloomey, but that which bears with the most weight on my mind at this instant is the situation of my Son Henry—'tis best not to anticipate trouble; by tomorrow noon[56] those things that now seem to threating, may wear a different aspect.

In hopes of the best,
We'll retire to rest:
But if she lays still,
As Id fain hope she will,
We shall feel more assur'd, by the light of the day.
But if poor Mary calls, We'll the summons obey.

Sepr 16. After a very indifferint nights rest, arose by times this morning, a Storm from N.E. rain all the fore noon, clar'd away, measureably, after 12: Mary sent to let me know that she had been very poorly, at times all night, wish'd for the necessary woman from the City, said she should not be easy to be another night without her—nor indeed should I. she was willing to wait untill noon or after dinner to see if any of our family would come up, I cannot imagine what has prevented, but I sent for G. Bickley, and desir'd of him to go, he said he was oblig'd to meet a number of men at a tavern about a mile off, being drafted—we were welcome to his Horse and Chair, I then sent for Benjn. Buck, who was kind enough to go, he set of about ½ past two, in Bickleys Chair for a Mrs. Stevenson in lumbard street; I feel much releiv'd by his going, shall hear from home, as I desir'd BB. to call with a note at our

56. The word "every" crossed out.

house. Last night between 10 and 11, we heard the beating of Drums, concluded it was in Germantown, Betsy Bickley inform'd me just now, that there was a great bustle in the City yesterday Afternoon, on account of a number of Arm'd men who were coming down from the back Country[57]—I could not rightly comprehend her information—Hannah Smith and her brother Charles drank tea here, Sam came up with John Courtney in the Chaise, he is better than could be expected, yet looks miserably,—Sam gave me a letter from my Son William informing of his Brother being much indispos'd, 'tho he does not say so, Dr. Kuhn was yesterday sent for, he orderd 12 or 14 ounces blood to be taken from him, and a dose salts given; this morning was so clear of fever as to take an ounce bark, the fever nevertheless return'd again this Afternoon, and the Doctor has ordred Jamess powders[58] to sweat him—My Husband came up this Afternoon in Sulkey, after the fever had return'd on Henry. I cant tell how he made out to take so much bark in the interville, I shall be anxious 'till I hear tomorrow evening, from home, would go in the morning with my husband if could I make it suit, he has a good Doctor and a kind aunt with him—B Buck return'd with Stevenson about 5 o'clock, so that poor Mary has three more with her then common, her husband her Nurse and the old woman—I belive matters will not be settled with her this night—cloudy—the story of arm'd men coming down, amounts to nothing—they have been Druming about the City, to collect the Militia, to go against the Insergents in the Western Counties of this State,[59] a large army is likely to be rais'd.—All Wars are dreadfull, but those call'd civil wars, more particularly so.

Sepr 17. HD. left us this morning after breakfast.—John came in for liquid ladanem for his wife twenty five drops he ask'd, which I concluded would do no harm, if it did no good, as she had been us'd to take it, I went in some time after to see her and gave her, by her own urgent desire 50 drops more in about an hour after the 25—I then left her, in hopes it would still those useless pains that she suffer'd—it appear'd to have little or no effect; the wid-wife inform'd me that le enfant est fort grand, et la[60] mere bien pitit, it was her

57. In mid-September, following riots in Carlisle, Pa., and Hagerstown, Md., over the federal excise tax and attempts to enforce it, rumors swept through Philadelphia and Baltimore that armed men from the west were marching on military stores and magazines in the east (*Dunlap and Claypoole's American Daily Advertiser*, Sept. 16, 1794; Thomas P. Slaughter, *The Whiskey Rebellion: Frontier Epilogue to the American Revolution* [New York: Oxford University Press, 1986], 209–12).

58. James' Powders, first prescribed in 1747, consisted of one part oxide of antimony and two parts phosphate of lime, to be used as a sedative and diaphoretic in cases of fever (Haller, "Tartar Emetic," 236).

59. After fifty-two hundred militiamen had departed for western Pennsylvania on Sept. 9 to suppress the Whiskey Rebellion, volunteers were still being mustered in the following week to form additional companies should they be needed (Baldwin, *Whiskey Rebels*, 185–222; Kohn, *Eagle and Sword*, 157–70).

60. The word "mear" crossed out.

oppinion que l'enfant [sont] mort, that she wish'd I would send for a Doctor I wrote a note to Dr. Bensal of Germantown and sent Sam with the Chaise for him—while he was gone, John and Hannah Thomas came to dine with us. Hannah continues very poorly, they are going to Kingwood by short stages in hopes the journey may be of service to her, just after dinner Sam came with the Elder Dr. Bensal, I left John and Hannah who proceeded on their journey about 3 o'clock intending to lodge at David Commins 8 miles further, and went with the Doctor to poor Mary—terrible was the succeeding hour to me, how must it have been to the poor sufferer? the Doctor confirm'd what the mid wife had said, et avec ses instruments et beaucoup deficility, ill la delivera d'enfant mort, the first male child of seven, a very fine lusty baby—6 of the 7 dead born—Je n'etoit pas dans le chamber a le moment Cretical, poor Mary appear'd very thankful that all was over—I think her a patient well inclin'd woman.—the Doctor came home with me, where we found Ben Wilson, and soon after came my Sister and Son William, they inform'd me, to my no small satisfaction that Henry is better and were in hopes he would miss the fitt, Sam took the Doctor home about 5 o'clock. Stevenson went to town with Sister, William and Ben Wilson stays with us to night—H Mott and E Emlen came this forenoon expecting that I would go to Germantown and spend the day with SE—but as I could not, Nancy and her Child went with them—they came back with her in the evening but did not alight.—Our Son William is drafted for the Militia, was he a fighting man, he is at present very unfitt for the business.—A number of young friends, 'tis said, are going, to the no small grief of many of their Well-wishers. This has been a very pleasent day. BW, WD. and self, took a walk about sun set, don, cet mat. paid Casper Moyer for Bread—£3.5.8.

18. B. Wilson left us early, Sam Sprigs dug a grave this morning in the meadow, beyond our garden, by the side of the fence that incloses Sammy Fishers woods, Sam carried the square seder Box in which the child was depossited—the father and myself attended—I was desierous of seeing it properly done, as John Courtney is almost blind, Sam had dug the grave with great propriety, about 3 feet deep, he let it down with a rope in great order, he was the chief hand in burying the poor little one, who had never seen the light, about nine this morning, before ten, Sam drove William to town.—donnez ct mat. J Skyrin return'd from New England just before dinner, he has not yet been in the City.—Read with attention and pleasure, Creation, a philosophical poem, by Sir Richd. Blackmore M.D.[61]—JS. AS. and ED. walk'd to the clover patch; on our return, at the lanes end mett our Carriage, HD. and Son William coming up—they took little Elizath. in, we all came home to tea.—it lighten'd this evening from all quarters, almost without intermition—William

61. Sir Richard Blackmore, *Creation, a Philosophical Poem, in Seven-Books* (London: S. Buckley and J. Tonson, 1712 [*NUC*]).

seems weak and poorly, Henry much better—I went this Afternoon to see poor Mary, it may be truly said that she is better than could be expected, we have three men lodgers to night,—it looks very likely a gust may come on before morning.

19. Arose about 6 o'clock, HD. went to clover patch after breakfast. Je me don.—I went to town with my husband and William, arrived at our House between 10. and 11. found Henry much better, his mouth and Chin broke out, occasion'd by the feaver, he has taken a great quantity of bark, his fever is a intermittant, 'twas taken I trust in time—many have had the Autumnal fever, some the putrid fever, 'tho it cannot, I believe, be call'd as yet, a sickley fall with us—it is said that the Yallow fever is at present, prevalent in New-York.—Molly Smith call'd chez nous—I went after dinner with HD. to Isaac Howels in fourth Street, between race and vine Streets, to acknowledge a Deed—call'd at two shops for a little book and some cotton. set off for Clearfield about 5 o'clock, William with me, left M. Foulk at our house on a visit to Sister—came here about sunset, sent James back with the Carriage, J Skyrin came up after Candlelight. this has been a very fine day.

20. Took a short walk after breakfast up the road with William—JS. left us about 10 o'clock, don sans eff. Nancy, William and self din'd togeather, Our whole family, SB. excepted, walk'd down the road towards sunset, mett Sam Sprig marching by the side of the Cart with a load boards, we turn'd back, with him and came home to tea, 'twas after 6 when Sam arriv'd, he was to have return'd to town this evening with Beds &c.—by the time his load was ready it was past 8 o'clock, and look'd like for rain, we concluded to send him early in the morning JS. came up after Candle light—I order'd E Dawson, this Afternoon, by HDs desire, to pour a large tea-kittle of boiling water, on the lower part and root of a sickley apricot tree, not with a view to kill it, but in expectation of a contrary effect. 'tis said that it was once done by an ill designing person with an intent to kill the trees, but it only kill'd the grubs or warms, and the trees, throve the better for it.

Sepr. 21. First Day: Sam went as ordre'd this morning early to Town, with Beds &c. as our yearly meeting is approaching, we are necessitated to part with our two spare Beds &c. About 10 o'clock HSD. came up, Sam and James, Henry I hope is recovering, 'tho he looks thin and pale,—JS. and AS. went to meeting—My two Sons stay'd at home with me, No Company here to day but our own family, who are very agreeable visitants when ever they please to favour us—William and Henry left us about 4 o'clock, being both invalides, John and Nancy went with them as far as Thos. Fishers intending to go from thence to Dr. Logans, they mett Debby Logan &c there, where they stay'd tea, and return'd about dusk, JS. went to Sammy Fishers after night—a very fine 'tho cool evening. don. cet. mat.

22. A most delightful clear morning 'tho cool, we had a little fire in the parlor chimney—John Skyrin and his man Sam, left us after breakfast, Rosanna washing here—took a walk in the afternoon with Betts and the Child, found it very cold, soon return'd—HD. and Daughter Mary came up to tea, Molly has not been here since her return from Downgtown before—they stay with us to night—HD. informs me of the death of Debby Balderstone, who dyed sometime this Summer.

Sepr. 23. My husband inform'd me that our dear William lost 6 or 7. ounces of blood yesterday. Dr. Kuhn who call'd some time after the opperation was perform'd approv'd it, Henry has had something of the Collick, occasion'd by his eating hard pear or apple, the day he was up with us.—HD. and Molly, left us, after breakfast this morning—it has been cloudy all this day, looks as 'tho rain was coming on—I visited poor Mary Courtney this forenoon, found her as well as could be,—loosen'd Johns bandages, which were so tight, as to occasion sores under his Arm, the broken bones I expect, by this time, are knitt, but his sight is not yet restor'd, 'tho much better.—I beleive there are few, so low, who do not at times feel satisfaction and comfort, and none so high, as not to experience[62] anxiety, trouble, and distress.—yet I am of oppinion that a tranquil mind is attainable, if rightly sought after.—since our Father and Molly left us, we have been most of the time busy'd ironing—little ES. but poorly.—Thos. Fishers family and Billy Lewiss went yesterday,[63] to the City, many others have mov'd in—Jammy Smiths is also gone.—I have concluded to stay here with my Son William, if he is well enough to return, during the hurry of our yearly meeting, my health being very precarious, Billys the same, and as my Sister has kindly undertaking that trouble, if any one should ill naturdly undertake to sensure me, on their own head[ ] may it lay.—the Army, rais'd to go against the Insergents to the westward, left the City yesterday, many mothers wives and Sisters &c. are left with aching hearts—J Skyrin came up before tea,—don ct. mat.

24. [S.] Fisher call'd this morning to tell us, that he had seen my Husband last evening who inform'd him that William and Henry were both better. John Skyrin left us after breakfast—A little before noon Billy and Henry came up, we had the pleasure of their Company to dinner, with us. My poor dear Billy, has spit more blood since a vain was open'd, than he did before, 'tis occasion'd, I fear, by the cool weather[64] affecting his weak breast, They left us about 3 o'clock,—Nancy, with her Maid and Child, are gone this Afternoon to visit Betsy Fisher—'tis too cold to walk out towards night in the Countary—The Yallow fever said to be in our City, several have died of it, but it is hop'd it

62. The words "at times" crossed out.
63. The words "with their fa" crossed out.
64. The word "being" crossed out.

will not spread. The nights grow long, and when all our Men are in town, it seems rather lonely. don sans efft. S.F came home with Nancy, after candle light, in his Chair, I have been poorly this evening.

25. Nancy and her little one, and SB. lodg'd in my chamber last night. Betts in the little front room, to be as much togeather as possible—Nancy had a trying contest with Elizath. to oblige her to lay down, she held out for a long time, but the mother at last conquer'd, it was late when we retired, and near 8 o'clock this morning, when we arose—between ten and eleven William came up, he feels better then some days past, 'tho what he brings up, is still ting'd. Nancy, her Child and Girl went about 11. to[65] town to procure some necessarys which she stood in nead of, intending to return in the evening—Sam came soon after they were gone, with a load of scantling, which is intended to repair a tenement adjoining to John Courtneys dwelling, for a Gardener to reside in—Sam went back in less then an hour—HSD. left home this forenoon for his farm, the weather was fair, but rain came on in the Afternoon, which has made me apprehensive he may take cold and occasion a return of the fever, he has so lately been troubled with—if William had not come up, to stay with me, while his Sister went to the City, I should have been with SB. only—as the rain has prevented her return, or any other of the family—we are this night but three in the house, one less then ever, yet find ourselves comfortable. Marys Nurse came in this forenoon to tell me that John was ill of a pain in his side &c—I went to see him, found him in Bed, and poor Mary up, I desir'd her to bed again, and found on enquiry that he had been this morning to Germantown on foot, to get blooded again, without advice, he has been for some time past hearty, and was getting better, but very careless—he said the walk had occasion'd a great pain in his side, and he wanted something opening to take—I gave him a large spoonfull of Daffys Ellixer, and have heard nothing from him since.

Sepr. 26. it rain'd in the night, clear'd up this forenoon, a very fine day, after an agreeable rain—A Chimney Sweep call'd this morning very oppertunely, as we wanted our Kitchen Chimney swep'd.—A Young Man from Dl. Kings came for a seed-box that was left in the Garret, they were hardset to get it down stairs—About dinner time Timothy [T]owse, his Wife and Son Charles a child about 11 months old at her back, call'd, they are descendants of the Antient inhabetants and owners of the land, reside at Edgepelek in Evesham, near our Iron-works—they call'd to sell baskets, and get a dinner, don. cet. ma. After dinner came up, Ben Wilson, and Nancy &c return'd, her husband and Sally Rhoads with her, Sally went to her Daughter they inform that a putrid or Yallow fever is prevalent in the City, many have died of it—and the inhabitants much alarm'd,—JS. S. Rhoads and my Son William went to town

65. The letters "wards" crossed out.

about 5 o'clock. HSD. arriv'd here in Sulkey from his farm, after his brother had left us, he and BW. took tea with us, after which BW. left us, Henry stays to night—I have been unwel this Afternoon, under the necessity of taking medicine—call'd to see John, found him, his wife and Daughter[66] in bed togeather, they are better. Joseph Colemans Wife and Servant &c dead of the fever.

Sepr. 27. rain most of this day: the Sun made its appearence once or twice for a short time—foggy in the evening, stars appear to night,—some wind, and lightening this Afternoon, prehaps this may be the Equinoxial Storm, and may be of advantage to those in a fever in the City, should it so happen, 'twil be a great favour. We were busy this forenoon baking &c. most of this Afternoon I spent reading—Henry spent this day with us, and lodges here to night, his Chin is much broke out with sores, occasion'd by his late fever—he set off for home after dinner, but soon return'd, finding his horse lame—Sarah Carry, John Watson and wife, arriv'd last night at our house, to the Yearly meeting, and there may be many more to day. I could wish myself, on some accounts, there, but if it suited me in all other respects, what could I do with SB. in her present appearence, with a croud of company?—I have been poorly all day, my head not well, and stagnation of blood in my feet, occasion'd by obstructed bowels—but through great favour my mind is calm, and I keep about, have as much appetite as is good for me, and sleep better than I could expect.

Sepr. 28. First day: rain[67] or cloudy all day, John Skyrin came up about 11 o'clock—he and Henry din'd with us—about 3 o'clock our Carriage came with William, G. Prichard, James and Sam, WD. has heard very little talk of the Yallow fever since Yesterday, JS. heard this morning of a Man in Water street who is dead by it—James took Henrys lame horse to Oliver Wilsons—to pasture, we should not have sent him to day, but we have no one here to take care of him, Sam took potatoes and apples &c to town—they left us about 5 o'clock Henry went with them, and William finding we had JS. with us, and not likely to be alone, chose to return home as it looks likely for more falling weather.—A grandson of Jacob Dillworths call'd this Afternoon to tell us, that he and his brother were to have mow'd one of our lotts tomorrow, but as the weather would as he thought be unfitt, they would come the first fine day—I wrote this evening to Sally Downing, Jacob intends to sett off for the Vally on 3d. day next.—S Trimble and his daughter Nancy, Robt. Moore and his Daughter, and some other, lodge at our house. S. Trimbles Son, a very young man, is gone off with the army, to the great grief of his parients. Billy Brinton is also at our house,—Our good old mare, whom we have had in our possession about 10 years, she was said to be 6 years old when we purchas'd her, and has

66. The word "all" crossed out.
67. The word "and" crossed out.

never had to our knowledge a Colt, in her life, when James enter'd the Stable,[68] yesterday morning, he found her with a fine Colt by her side, a come by chance, quite unexpected.

29. Still Cloudy with rain, JS. left us after breakfast, clear'd up about noon, warm, no body from town to day, don. cet. mat.—Nancy lodges to night with her Child, and Betts in Billys room, Myself and Sally in mine—when the Men are all away, we seem rather lonely, as the nights are much longer, I have not been one minute this day free from very uneasy sensations in my bowels.

30. Sall and self, spent some time this morning murdering between 20 and 30 Wasps, who had errected their nest on the inside window shetter of our Chamber, 'tho I have a dislike to distroying even noxious animals, yet to be attac'd in ones sleep by an Army of foes, would be rather a disagreeable curcumstance, I was amus'd by the curious manner that they had built their nest.—there is sildom a day passes in the country, without some lesson of industry, patience, fidility and Chearfullness &c.—exhibited by the insects, birds, and brute creation, as they are call'd, 'tho this is no new remark, yet 'tis but little attended to by many, by which neglect, they miss, both instruction and delight.—James came up this forenoon with the old mare and her Colt, of which he says she is remarkably fond. I think, to travil 6 miles at the age of three days, was rather too much.—James brings no perticular message from any of our family, which I dont altogeather like, they were prehaps chiefly, gone to meeting when he came away, William if well enough, might have sent a line or two. Our SB. appears to be as full of Glee, as if nothing ail'd her, but what was right, I would not wish to see her miserable, but rather more steady thoughtfullness, would become her better.—Nancy and self, Bettsy with the Child walk'd down the road beyond [T.] Fishers lane, mett JS. coming up, AS. and Child rode back with him, Betts and self walk'd after, came home to tea. I have been very thoughtful this Afternoon of my dear family at home, and of Sally abroad—several have been taken off within a few days by a putrid fever—'tis very cold this evening don. cet. mat.

Octr 1. Cold and raw, the east wind blew, when we came down this morning and has continu'd so to do all this day, with frequent fine rains—we have set most of this day by a good fire, B. Wilson din'd with us, he says that people are less apprehensive of the malignant fever, then some days past.—'tis hop'd that the cool weather and rain has put a stop to it.—very unexpectedly, Sister came up about 4 o'clock in Carriage by herself, she was desireous to see how we fared and to bring us an account of their wellfare at home and to bring us several necessaries—she did not stay above ½ an hour. BW. left us nearly at

68. The words "some days past" crossed out.

same time. JS. left us this morning after breakfast don sans. efft. John Balderstone and Daughter lodge at our house, ten or 11. in all—Deborah Darby and Rebecca Young, publick friends from Great Britian, lately came to our City, it is about a twelve month since their arrival at New-York.—rains fast to night. BW. inform'd us of a considerable loss we have mett with lately at Atsion by the distruction of the Forge House and its contents, by fire, the Bellows and all gone, the perticulars of when or how it happen'd he had not heard, nor at what the loss was esteemated.—the cry of fire is very frequent at an Iron-works, but as they are, or ought to be, always ready, it is generaly soon extinguished.

Octor. 2. I went to Bed last night, with very uneasy bodily sensations—did not sleep 'till several hours after—it rain'd hard, and wind very high. cloudy this morning clear'd up about noon, 'tis now a fine moon light night.—Our Son Henry call'd on us about 11. this fore-noon in his way to White Marsh, went there, and came back to dinner with us—he left us after 4. Nancy, myself, ED[r]. and Child took a walk after he was gone, the Sun was setting clear and butifull, but the ground was so damp that we made our walk short. better this evening then common, we sat by a good fier working and reading.—don. cet. mat. bon efft. BW. was mistaken in his account of the fire at Atsion, it was the Furnice, not the Forge, that was burnt, all the wood work, and the Bellows &c—the loss, HD. thinks, including repairs and loss of time, will amount to, one thousand pounds and more money—Sally brought in, this evening after dark, a luminous insect, or rather a reptile, in form somewhat like a millepe, but rather longer and flater, if it was a Glow-worm it is very different from the idea I have had of them, nor did I know that we have any in this Country.

3. A fine clear cool day. paid for ½ Cord hickory Wood £1.2.6. Nancy, myself, ED. and Child, little Nelly, went to Sammy Fishers, Betsy is preparing to leave the country tomorrow morning, we had a pleasent walk home—din'd by our selves—William and Henry came up this afternoon, Henry soon return'd to the City, William stays with us, JS. came up before tea—Violet, a black woman who has lived in Uncle Jerviss family as long as I can remember, was bury'd last seventh day.—don.cet.mat—The Board of Health, and 10 or 12 of the Faculty, mett on third day last, in order that from their Communications a just state of the health of the City, might be obtain'd. After compareing notes &c, they seem to conclude, that there has not been that cause of alarm as many injurious reports have circulated, and that at present there is not one case of a contagious nature apparent.—I believe there has been many, and that the worst has been made of it, but 'tis no wonder that the people should be alarmed.

4. John and Nancy Skyrin went to town after Breakfast, Nancy went to

meeting, and din'd at our house, where 16 others din'd, the Yearly meeting concluded this Afternoon and a number of friends left the City, John and Nancy return'd to tea, AS. with a bad head ach, rideing in the wind in an open Chair. a fine cold day, wind N.W. don. cet. mat. William and self took a walk this forenoon to the potato patch, came home to dinner, which was waiting for us, WD. was taking with sick Stomach while he was eating, lost what little he had eat, I judge he had taken too long a walk in the cool air, and set down to dinner too soon after it, he is bravely this evening.

Octor. 5. First Day. clear cold day. Nancy unwell pain in her bones, and face—better this evening John Skyrin and Ben Wilson din'd with us—they went away before tea, William took a long walk in the forenoon, I walk'd out with him Afternoon, G. Prichard call'd,—HD. came up this evening to tea, he has not been here since week before last. he informs that David Evans junr. who went with the Army, hurt his leg by accident, with a Bayonet, which occasion'd a lock-jaw of which he dyed.—don cet mat.

6. The above account of D. Evans I have this day heard contradicted, he was badly hurt by a Bayonet, but is not dead.—We were early up, Rossanna here washing, HD. WD. and little Elizath. went after breakfast, don after dinner Nancy and self, sat down to Iron our small cloaths, when J Logan, Hetty Smith and her Daughters Hannah and Sally came up, my Sons W and H, came soon after, with our little one, they came by desire of their father for to bring me home to acknowledge a Deed, we stay'd tea at Clearfield, and came away between five and six, J Skyrin at our house when we arrived, desir'd him to set off as soon as may be, or Nancy would be alone; Neighr. Waln call'd this evening it seems agreeable to spend an evening by our fire side in the City, Sister gone this evening to see Becky Fisher who has been ill.

7. Isaac Howel here this morning to take my acknowledgment of a Deed,—HD. MS. HSD. MD. gone to meeting this morning William walk'd out, myself at home alone as usual on meeting days.—no Company at dinner—WD. took a walk forenoon, as far as Robt. Stevensons—J Logan call'd 'fore dinner, A Silver Coffee pott from J. Richardson, cost 20 guineas, a present from H.D. to [J. C——ne]—Sett off for Clearfield with my Sons, arriv'd here about 4 o'clock—they left us about 5, William by himself in the Carriage, Henry in Sulky with black horse, which he sent James to O Willsons for, intending to go soon to his farm—I found Nancy and her little one well, JS. left her this morning after breakfast—Tommy Morris, Sammy Smith, John Drinker & HD. at our house in town[69] after meeting. Joshua Wooleston, brother to Molly Smith, has lately mett with a heavy loss, his Saw-mill, Grist-mill, Fulling-mill &c, burnt down in Bucks County. Samuel Emlen has, I

69. The words "this for" crossed out.

expect, arrived this day at his own dweling, from Great Britian, by the way of Boston and New York—the Sun set clear, sky very red, 'tho 'tis now, after night, cloudy, wind N.E—Our audacious Joe, was seen to day at our Stable in town, I suppose the Yallow fever has drove him from Baltimore, should he have the impudence to come up here, I should be angry indeed.—we must endeavour to keep a good look out, as there is very little appearent contrition in the white party concerne'd.

8 Octor. Cloudy, and rain, most of this day—I paid Mary Courtney a visit this forenoon, no one up, our men all in town, we staid all day in the house, no one call'd on us, but in truth, a Sturdy beggar, who enquir'd if he was in the way to New York, being answer'd in the Negative, said he had lost his way, wish'd for something to eat, and a draught of Cider, which having obtain'd, walk'd off. we were carefull to see him fairly out of the gate. A small family in the Country, after the Equinox, generaly, I beleive, find the evenings rather more dreary than in the Chearful months of May and June—Our Watch stop'd this evening at 80. and as we received no hint from Somnus, sat up 'till, we knew not what time.

9. last night we set our watch by guess, and this morning found by its variation from Bickleys clock, that it was near one o'clock when we retir'd, we were busy'd making habilliment pour la noir au jaun illigetemate, but that was not the occasion of our tardiness.—William came up before dinner, intends staying with us 'till tomorrow, James went back with a cart load straw, return'd with load of dung, then, toward evening, went with another load Straw—WD. and self paid a short visit after dinner to Benjn. Bucks, came home to tea—Je ete malade tout cet jour, don. cet. mat. sans efft. HSD. set off this morning for his farm. fine weather.

10. A beautiful clear morning walk'd a mile with WD. before dinner, James came up with a loaded Cart.—about noon, went back with the Carriage, William with him between 12 and one—Nancy and self walk'd about a mile after dinner—we have been industrious with our needles this day—JS. came up before tea—fine seasonable weather.

11. JS. left us after breakfast,—about 10 o'clock HD, Reading Howel, Othniel Alsop, and WD. came up, to finish survaying our land at this place—they din'd with us—HSD. came after dinner from North Bank in his way home, they all, WD. excepted, left us betwen 5 and 6.—walk'd out with William, before and after dinner, weather cool and clear. George Fry and his wife came here this afternoon, he is said to be a complete Gardner, as such HD has hired him, they reside at present in the house with John and Mary—

An account in this days paper, of the death of Baron Frederick Trenck,[70] whose life I am now reading,[71] a second time, and could have wish'd, that after so many grievous sufferings as he past thro', he could have been allow'd to have died a natural death, he was beheaded lately in Paris, if the paper says true, in the 69. year of his age. In his youth, 'tis obvious by his writings, he possessed a large fund of vanity, but what he was in advanced life, I do not recollecd having heard. I have since read, and by his own account he was a cleaver fellow.

12. First day: came down stairs last night between eleven and 12. with Sally, in my dishabille, to call up John Courtny, whose cow was in the meadow eating of a heap Apples, laid there ready for grinding, I fear'd she would injure herself if she continu'd all night at that business, I increas'd a cold I had before taken, and have been much oppress'd by it to day. HD. Hannah Thomas, her two Sons, and HSD. came up this morning about 10 o'clock, they all, but Hannah, went to Germantown meeting, she stay'd with me &c J Skyrin came about 12. they all din'd with us.—HD. JS. WD. stays here to night,—the others left Clearfield about 4. After they were gone, William and self walk'd as far up the road as to the place that formerly belong'd to Thomas Nedro, about ¾ mile from us, came home to tea. don. cet. mat.

13. HD. and JS. left us after breakfast.—About noon James came up with Joshua Smith, who pointed the Chimneys to prevent the roof[s] leaking. they went away in half an hour; WD. and self took a short walk—William has been busy this forenoon geathering pears and spreading 'em in the garret—Daniel King call'd—Nancy poorly—Josha. Smith inform'd us of the death of Stephen Collins, and of Patty Evans wife to Robt. Evans.—Not a day passes without, *memento mori*, being sounded in our ears.—we have been favour'd with fine weather for several days past.

Octor. 14. One third of a year, since we came here,—George and John, Betsy Dawson and two or three other little foulk, busy to day, bringing in potatoes—Billy and self went after dinner to Edwd. Simmons, who lives between us and Benjn. Bucks, in a house belonging to a John Prefountain, Son in Law to B Buck, and Son to my French Master, Pepter Papin de prefountain many years

70. A Hungarian nobleman who had commercial and literary ties to France, where he resided in 1774 and 1777. He returned to Paris in 1791, but was arrested on suspicion of being a Prussian spy and beheaded at the end of July 1794 (E. Boursin and Augustin Challamel, *Dictionnaire de la révolution française* [Paris, 1883]; *Dunlap and Claypoole's American Daily Advertiser*, Oct. 11, 1794).

71. Baron Friederich von der Trenck, *The Life of Baron Friederich Trenck, Containing His Adventures; His Cruel and Excessive Sufferings, during Ten Years Imprisonment, at the Fortress of Magedeburg, by Command of the Late King of Prussia; Also, Anecdotes,* trans. Thomas Holcroft (London: J. Murray, 1788; Philadelphia: Spotswood, 1789 [*Brit. Mus. Cat.;* Evans, *Am. Bibliography*]).

deceased—we came home to tea, very fine day—James came up this Afternoon with the little black horse, which HD. has lately purchased of Joseph Drinker, the same that WD. bought upwards of three years ago of Saml. Pleasants, and sold to Watkins. James says all are well at home—don. mat.

15. fine weather, unwell tout cet jour; pren. med[icine] [ED.], took water gruel in the Afternoon, brought it up, I am often surpris'd at my self, and think I have great cause of thankfulness, considering, how indisposed I am, that I can keep about as usual, and be chearfull—Sister and Betsy Jervis, came up about 11 o'clock, I was pleas'd to see 'em, they din'd with us, but went away a little after four, William with them, he has been rather better for some days past—Huldah Mott, Betsy Emlen and my dau'ter Molly drank tea here, they left us about sunset—J Skyrin came after candle light,—our dear little Elizabeth has been uncommonly commical and merry this evening Our people still busy bringing in potatoes—'tis now near 12 o'clock, Sall and self in the old parlor, Sall asleep, nothing to be heard but the noise of insects, and a mouse nibling in the closet.

Octor. 16. J Skyrin left us after breakfast—I did not come down 'till after 8 o'clock, later than usual—Nancy and self set off about 10. to go to Jacob Bekeys, a Shoemaker at Miles town, the fineness of the day induced us to take the walk, it is about a mile and quarter from our house. I stop'd short of the intended rout by ⅛ of a mile, and Nancy went on, the place I stop'd at belongs to one John Shields, who does not live there, there was no body but an old Dutch woman, name'd Nany White, she was busy spining tow, about three score and ten years old. I ask'd her if she was spining to make cloath for her own ware, oh no! I take it in, at a 1½ d a cut, how many cuts dost thou spin in a day? she was not willing to tell, can thee spin twelve? oh no! six? No. 3 then? maybe so, then thee earns 4½ d a day? yes some times;—I had but a nine penny peice in my pocket which I gave her, and say'd if she would except of it, she might venture to take a days rest, as that was two days earning, she was much pleas'd and gave me many thanks. Well, thought I, to use the words of an Old Author, This is one of the *commoditys that comes of infelicity*, to be delighted with so trifling an acquisition,—Nancy soon came to me, and we had a pleasant walk home, but found ourselves a little fatigued, James arrived with William, while we were absent—stay'd dinner, but left us between 4 and 5.—William inform'd me that his brother has had another fitt of chill and fever, it was but slite, he is taking the bark again, it is a wrong time for Henry to be unwell, if it could be help'd.—One Henry Young call'd this forenoon for taxes—John and George still busy gitting in potatoes—This evening between 9 and 10. as near as I can judge, as we have no watch here at present, Betts Dawson, who had been at the pump, came in frightened, said she saw a great black thing as big as our James, standing with its face towards our kitchen window, it occur'd to Nancy and self, that it might be Joe Gibbs who had the impudence to skulk about after dark, Nancy and I went up in the dark to look out of a Chamber Window, but it was too dark to see if any person was there, instead of a black thing, we observ'd a light under the barndoor, which alarm'd us, fearing there might be fire in the Barn, we prevail'd on the girls to go out and call up George Fry, who soon came to us, he found on examination that G Bickley was sorting his potatoes in the Celler under the Barn, which occasion'd the light we saw, but saw not, nor I who went with him, the black figure that frighed Betts—I retired about midnight as I judg'd by the riseing of the Moon—Nancy went to bed an hour before, all without fear.

Octor. 17. Nancy and self busy sewing this morning I took a walk out by myself before dinner, we din'd early, soon after the table was remov'd HD. and Willm. came up, they had been at Germantown and had not din'd, Sally soon prepar'd a dinner for them, Geo[ ] and John making Cider to day—Nancy, little Elizabeth, and S Brant, were taken sick after dinner so much as to bring up what they had taken—B Dawson was, or pretended to be also sick, we have not yet discover'd wether any thing they had eat occasion'd it, if it was accidental, it was rather remarkable,—my husband came up for me, wishing I would accompany him and William tomorrow to Downingstown, I found myself much at a loss to determine, being in some respects much indispos'd, at same time earnestly desireous to make the visit—I, however came to town, but feel myself less inclined to proceed then when at Clearfield, we came before tea, Danl. Trimble, Jacob Downing here this evening—Jacob lodges and diets here, in the absence of his family—T Stewardson took tea with us.—An account lately received of the death of Elizabeth Drinker wife to Brother Daniel, she left us about 18 month past, on a religeous visit to Great Britian, departed this life the 10 of 8 mo last, at a friends house of the name of Smith, in London.

18 Octor. Danl. Trimble, Jacob Downing breakfasted with us. My Sister kindly took my place in the Carriage and set off with my husband and Son William after 10 this fore-noon for Downingstown—they have had a fine day to travil—two Young Men from G. Britian who came over with S Emlen, call'd this Morning with a Note from E Emlen to Molly, desireing her to go with them this Afternoon to Clearfield. They accordingly call'd on her After dinner, Molly is to stay there with her Sister untill my return, as I am to stay here untill HD. MS. &c comes from the Valley.—HSD. has been taking bark to day. I hope he will miss the fitt tomorrow, as he seems bravely—Neighr. Waln spent part of this evening with me, I dont recollect our family so small as just now in the City, before. Henry has taken a little Black Boy on trial, nam'd Cipio Drake, he came here this Afternoon—he has been to several other places, but has run away from them to his mother, who lives with M[ ]. Fisher, MF. thought it best to put him in prison, where he was when Henry sent for him, he ap[pe]ars very sulkey, is about 11 years old, I cant say I like

him—J Skyrin was here this Afternoon. he set off for Clearfield, took several things with him for Nancy &c.

Octor. 19. First day: J Downing went to meeting. HSD. stay'd all day at home taking the bark, and nothing else, he fasted 24 hours and has mis'd the fitt, which is prehaps as much oweing to the medicine—as the fasting: he took a large quantity, double doses. Sally Rhoads and S Swett came after meeting, the later din'd and spent the day,—Ben Wilson and Jacob Downg. sup'd with us—Ben din'd at Clearfield, says Nancy is very unwell, much oppress'd by a Cold. I am very uneasy on her account. Betsy Emlen lodg'd there last night with Molly, the two young English men who went up with them yesterday, drank tea with them there this Afternoon, and Betsy came to town with them, their names are, I think Henry Hendal and[72] Joseph Merryfield—black Scipio, who sup'd and lodg'd here, arose early this morning, got his breakfast, was then order'd to clean the knives, he took them in the yard, and there left 'em, and set off; in the Afternoon his father, a good looking Negro man, brought him back, he is sadly teas'd with his Son, he advis'd and threatned him, wishd us to keep him, he had eating nothing since morning we gave him his supper and sent him to bed, MF. gives him a good Character, but if he goes off tomorrow, I hope he will not come back to us—a good servent is a valuable acquisition, the want of such is at present a general complaint.—our little family are[73] gone to bed, 'tis now 11 o'clock, I'll go also. [Jimmy] Smith call'd.

20 Octobr. Jacob, Henry, and self breakfasted togeather, Henry set off on Horse back for his Farm, having appointed to meet several workmen there, the wind is chang'd to N.E. 'tho this is a fine moderate day it looks as 'tho it would not last long, Henry has taken a quantity of the bark with him, I could wish it had suited him to stay at home for some time longer, John Skyrin came from Clearfield forenoon, he gives but a sorrowful account of Nancys health, she is much oppress'd by the Cough &c—spits a little blood, is feverish and lost appetite,—John goes up again after dinner, I am the only one of the family, servants excepted, at present at home, or would go immediately to Nancy, Henry Kendal call'd, Nancy Morgan call'd with her little daughter becky, aged 10 weeks. Molly Lippencut also call'd S Swett din'd and spent the day.—My husband Sister & Son William return'd to tea this Afternoon, they left Sally and Children and families well—J Skyrin went Afternoon to Nancy.—a shower about noon—I step'd over this Evening 'tho unwell to Neighr. Walns to see little Hannah Hartshorn who has been in an ill state of health all Summer. I have been more then usualy unwell to day, donne. S Swett fitted a mantua gown on me, which I had provided in the Summer, she is so kind as to do what little I want in that way for me, I beleive I never had a

72. The name "John Merryman" crossed out.
73. The word "all" crossed out.

gown better made in my life, and she is now within about seven weeks of 73 years of age, to work so neatly at such an age is the cause of my making the memorandum.

21st. Octor. Sister gone to meeting this morning HD. stays at home being disorder'd in his bowels, and somewhat oppress'd by a cold—J Skyrin came to town forenoon, says Nancy continues very poorly, I sent for Docr. Kuhn, advis'd with him on her complaint, he orders her loosing 10 oz blood, as soon as may be;—Samuel Emlen, Thos. Morris John Drinker, Josh. Merrifield and Henry Kendal, call'd after meeting,—After dinner William and self set off for Clearfield—found Nancy very poorly, not so oppress'd as I expected nor does she spitt any blood, for which reason, I did not send for Justis Fox to bleed her as I intended. she is very sick, can scacerly hold up her head without reaching, her skin is yallow and a very feverish heavy smell about her—I sent James home with a note desiring Dr. Kuhn might be sent to us tomorrow forenoon, I had her mov'd from the Chamber over the old parlor, to my Chamber in the New House, hoping the change might be beneficial, she set up by the fier a little while this evening but was very sick, and complain of a pain in her back—she eat part of a very good pear, which stay'd on her stomach, and has taken off an ill taste in her mouth which she has been for several days troubled with, and no wonder, as she has eaten scarcely any thing—Rosanna washing here to day.—we brought black Scipio to Clearfield with us, he has behaved very well since his father brought him back on first day last.

Octor. 22. John Skyrin came up this[74] morning with the Carriage to take Nancy to Town if she was able to go—Dr. Kuhn could not come this fore noon, but would try, if she was realy ill, to see her here, Afternoon, I sent word back that we must see him if possiable—Nancy continues very sick, can take no sustinance, and is very Yallow. I think 'tis the Jaundice she has taken, John is but lately releiv'd from it, 'tho I dont know that it is infectious. My Son William, little Elizabeth and self, were taken sick while eating our dinner as five days past:—William had been in the fresh air, the sun shines at noon full in our parlor and we had a little fire, I expect the sudden transition affected his Stomach as once before, for myself I can, I think, account having taken medicine, which I am frequently necessitated to do, for an obstruction in my bowels. B Dawson, was again or pretended to be sick after she had done her dinner—I hope and beleive it is not from any thing that we are in the daily practice of eating—Dr. Kuhn came after dinner, said Nancys disorder was billious and ordre'd spic'd Rhubarb, said he would come again tomorrow. Nancy took a dish Coffee and piece dry toast, more than for several days past,—J Skyrin came up after candle light, he tells us that Dr. K. said at our house that it is a confirm'd Jaundice Nancy has—he brought me a few lines

74. The word "evening" crossed out.

from my husband, who has been confin'd for 2 or 3 days with something like the Influenzia, but hopes to see us here sometime tomorrow. several of our family are at present indispos'd, may we endeavour to be truly thankful for the good we receive, and resign'd to what is call'd the reverse.

Octor 23. Sally Downings birthday. Nancy had but an indifferent night, extremely sick this morning HD. came up to dinner with us, he is better.—Dr. Kuhn came about 3 o'clock, advis'd a continuance of the medicine yesterday prescrib'd &c. Thos. Fisher and Charles Jervis here this Afternoon; Betsy Dawson who was sent upstairs to stay with her mistress while Molly and I were necessarily engag'd below, after setting in silence for some time fell out of the Chair on the floor, Nancy who was in Bed call'd to her, thinking she had been asleep, she then made a noise and seem'd to strugle, her mistress bid her get up and call me, which she did, she said she had a fitt, was formerly subject to them, I gave her a dose of Assafotida,[75] she has been as well since as ever, how it realy was we do not know, but her father told Nancy when he bound her, that she had, had fitts, this is the first we have seen—Nancy has taken the Rhubarb and spice reguarly all day, and twice &c, to no good purpose as yet, the obstruction, I fear, is very obstinate—'tis now past the noon of night, all in bed but myself, Nancy sick at stomach, John Skyrin came before tea brought some snakeroot[76] &c—the weather has been fine for several days past. I have been very unwell all this last day, 'tho I am setting up to night. don. cet sorie, sans efft. William went home with his father after dinner, Molly intended to set up to night with her Sister, and if things had turn'd out as I wish'd, she would have done it, I did not feel easy to have her, and Molly went to bed to little Elizah.

Octor. 24. past two in the morning Nancy has had some sleep, 'tho not of that refreshing nature I could have wish'd, but indeed it is not to be expected in her present situation, I have just given her another dose of the medicine, and am surpris'd it has not taken effect before now, as she lays still, I hope it will not sicken her.—I beleive there are but few, who have no more bodily strength than myself, who can make out with so little sleep, many have been the nights, before I was married and since, that I have continued awake from the time I lay down untill I arose in the morning at the usual hour, or rather sooner, in health, both of body and mind, and can no otherwise account for it than by getting into a train of thought, that I could not, or would not break off, and after a light breakfast felt as much refresh'd as if I had enjoy'd a good nights rest. and very frequently when I have set up all night, and not rested

75. An antispasmodic. For its uses see below, July 24, 1798.

76. Virginia snakeroot (*Aristolochia serpentaria*) is native to the eastern U.S., particularly Virginia and the Carolinas. In a variety of medical preparations, especially infusions, it was used to treat fevers and epidemic diseases and as a gargle for putrid sore throat (W. Lewis, *New Dispensatory*, 229; Thacher, *New American Dispensatory*, 149).

the next day, I have felt as lively the following evening as usual.—and many an anxious waking night have I also had.—I do not say, that being broke of my rest never hurt me, I beleive it has, and not a little, when attended with anxiety. but that I can do, or have done, with as little sleep as most folks I believe I may say. let me retire at what hour I may, I do not, I believe, once in a twelve month sleep before midnight, and often one or two o'clock—Since we have been at Clear-field, I have lost one of my amusements, as I cannot hear how the time passes. when at home in the City, the hour is often repeated in my ears, by the two Town-clocks, our own Clock, and the watch-men.—I never was much disturb'd by common noises in the night, as many are, if they were such as I could account for, and not excessevely loud. The chief that occurs here are, the market waggons, the barking of Dogs, and the Crowing of Cocks—

Tho I cannot say I exactly know,
The time of the first, or the second crow.

yet I have generly a good gess at the time of night when I hear nothing.—E Dawson went down early this morning on a arrent, after her return to the Chamber, I went to see if she had shut the outward door—Aurora had open'd the curtain of the east, and morn appear'd, much sooner then I look'd for it—at 6 o'clock Molly arose to 'tend on her Sister, I went to her bed, came down at 10, J Skyrin had just departed, Nancy appears better this morning not so sick but very Yallow, eat a little breakfast—After dinner Dr. Kuhn came, he order'd pills, Calomel[77] &c to be given every two hours 'till they opperated, Sister and William came just after the Doctor left us, brought us many necessary ingredients, MS. went away before sun set, William stays to night with us, he has received a letter from cousin Jos. Sandwith Ireland, with a present of a large Seal set in Gold with the Arms of the Sandwiths engraved on it, and a drawing of the same Coat of Arms—Nancy very sick this evening brought up the pills that she had so long taken, disolved, I was much at a loss how to act, as the obstruction had not given way, and she could take no more, was too sick, had taken 9 at 3 doses—Molly went to bed with the Child about midnight as her sister at that time lay still, she was too ill for me to leave her.

Octor. 25. between midnight and 3 in the morning my poor dear Child was extremly ill, with excessive hard reachings and pains about her, an uncommon tast and sensation in her mouth and stomach; by her consent I call'd up George Fry at 3 this morning sent him to town with a note to JS. and HD—A

77. A common treatment for jaundice (Buchan, *Domestic Medicine* [1793], 254; C. K. Drinker, *Not So Long Ago*, 122–27).

little before 4 she seem'd rather more easy. I laid down in my cloaths on a bed on the floor by S Brant. Nancy laid still and I dosed near two hours, at 8 o'clock George return'd with a letter from my Husband—JS. came soon after, the Doctor order'd castor Oyl, one dose of which she took, but could bare no more, a little while after a large discharge of green boil was evacuated, a very dark green, it lay so long in the bowels, the Doctor said who came up this forenoon, it was occasiond by the pills, the discharge I mean, at 12 gave by his desire 10 drops laudanum, repeated it 2 or 3 times this day, the reaching continued violent. I apply'd spice and brandy in a flannel bag to her Stomach, and pounded mint to her wrists, she took 2 or 3 doses Daffys Ellixer in coarse of the day, all to no purpose, brought up most that she took, she was very ill most of the evening, with hard and continu'd reachings, distressing sensation in her throat and stomach, 2 or 3 active medicines were administred to day, without effect, at 9 at night, too much spent, and very averse to take the powders the Doctor had order'd in case the other medicines fail'd, and as she now lays still, I am loath to urge or disturb her—Sister who came up to day, set up with her all night. she did not vomitt much in the night, and sleep'd well towards morning.

Octor 26. First day: one of the most stormy days I ever knew, and a trying day it has been.—Nancy much against taking medicine, and hard to [me] to urge it, but as her case was desperate, thought it best to persist,—she had less reaching this morning but a constant sickness, said her Stomach and throat felt as if she had been eating Allum, we were much at a loss what to do, the Doctor had sent several sorts medicine, that if one fail'd the other was to be try'd, JS. came up with perticular directions, the storm so hard that the Doctor did not come, he ordr'd, if no change took place for the better, to lay a blister on her Stomach, said if what he had order'd did not succeed he could do no more, if the pills did not answer she was to take powders of Jalap, if they would not stay on her stomach, Senna was to be given in an infusion,[78] if the sickness continu'd and the obstruction did not give way, the blister was to be apply'd—William was for the calomel pills, which she had taken off before; JS. for the powders, she would take nither, but agreed to take the Senna, of which she took 4 doses, about 11 at night it opperated, from one 'till near 4 she lay still, and dos'd a little, she had in the day two [injections] without effect—she was frequently up in the night, a painful urging, sick stomach but no reaching—the disagreeable sensation in her throat &c better, she discharg'd a quantity of dark mucus, felt cold, with pains about her. I gave her a tea cup of Chicken broath, instead of a dose of Senna, find myself at a loss whether to

78. All the medications recommended are cathartics. Senna, of the genus *Cassia*, was introduced into European medical use by Arabs in the ninth or tenth century. Its use by native Americans antedates the historical record (Estes, "Therapeutic Practice," 369, 373, 377; W. H. Lewis and Elvin-Lewis, *Medical Botany*, 282).

continue or omitt it, Nancy chose the latter, I call'd Sister up,[79] HSD. came home to day, watch'd a slatch when it did not rain, and rode 8 miles—he had been detain'd 24 hours by the Storm, he has had no return of the chils and fever since he left us, which is a pleasing circumstance—storm continu'd all night.

27. Nancy 'thro 'mercy much better to day, I received litter from HD. another from HSD. MS. and WD. left us after dinner, JS. came up in the evening clear'd up—I was up last night, and have not lain down to day, could not, 'tho I find my self much fatigued, Molly sits up with her sister to night.

28. JS. went to town before breakfast; my poor Child, is to day much better, 'tho very Yallow, she has taken nourishment several times to day, and set up, rather longer then I thought proper, my husband and Sister came to see us, rather late in Afternoon, it was our monthly meeting.—Our HSD. desired a minute on account of marriage, directed to the m: meeting of Philada: I have not seen him since his return from North Bank, Sister informs me that William is much as when he left me yesterday—Molly went home with her father and Aunt, to prepare to attend on her intended Sister on sixth day next.—two or three days ago it did not look unlikely but that a very different scene might have taken place, at present our dear Nancy bids fair, with proper care, to recover; JS. came up this evening—We discover'd a day or two ago, that black Scipio had contracted acquaintance while in Jail, that was realy too disgusting to be easy under, we had enquir'd, and made a search, before he left the City, but found none, but since we came up, Sall, after strict scrutiny found three, which was three too many to be born with, the difficulty was, he had no change of raiment, linnen excepted, I had him strip'd, and wash'd, from stem to stern, in a tub warm soap suds, his head well lathered and when rinc'd clean, pour'd a quantity spirits over it, then dress'd him in Girls cloaths, 'till his own can be scalded &c, he appear'd rather diverted, than displeas'd—Trifling as are the incidents which I insert, they are occurances at Clearfield, and I trouble not myself with other peoples business,—but am amus'd, or otherwise, with what comes before me, and look out for little else at present, and as it is only for my own perusal and recollection, 'tis little matter how 'tis said or done.

29. Nancy 'tho much better, is far from well—she took senna this morning we have been alone to day, except a short visit HSD. paid us this Afternoon, he prevail'd on me, without much difficulty, to sign him over to Hannah Smith, under my hand which is to be published on next sixth day—as it dont suit me to attend the monthly meeting, My daughters indispossion would

79. The words "and after some time went to bed [myself]" crossed out.

prevent, were I well enough myself. JS. came up after candle light, our little Elizath. not well, George made cider to day.

30. My Son Henrys birthday. 24 years—J Skyrin left us before breakfast.—I wrote a few lines to Hetty Smith. I lodg'd last night in Williams bed, little Elizath. with me, SB. in the room, Nancy and her maid, in my Chamber—the child had a high fever all night, very restless, and full of talk between sleeping and wakeing, she is much oppress'd by a cold, broke out with a kind of rash I gave her a dose castor oyl this morning—very unwell myself and no wonder—about noon HD. and Willm. came up, they din'd with us—the day being fine, my husband propos'd taking Nancy to town, I knew not how to deny, or how to suffer her to go—being, as I thought, fitt only to be in her Chamber, and the child had taken phisick, but as the day look'd like what is call'd a weather breeder, thought it best not to stand out, as Nancy was willing, and HD. as the Lady said of John Haywood, like—not to be deny'd, they according went, HD. Nancy, her child and girl Betsy—William stay'd with me, he, myself, S Brant and black Sip, are our present family—I have been more than commonly distress'd this Afternoon by my old complaint, don.

31. I seem'd lost yesterday afternoon and this morning after a time of steady nurseing, felt as 'tho I had nothing to do, nor could I, for some time set about any thing, should I, by rest and retirement, recurit a little health, it will be cause of thankfullness. Sally Johnson and her daughter Franks came here before dinner, on a visit to her daughter SB. they stay'd an hour or two, eat dinner, then went to Germantown, she left herbs to make tea for SB. said it was good to procure an easy.——William and self took a walk about 3 o'clock, a very warm day for the season—My husband came up in carriage by himself, says Nancy's rather better since she went home, to our house the child also, which I look on as a great favour. HSD. and HS—perform'd well at meeting this morning Sister went with them, William return'd with James to the City, HD. stays to night. the wind high and cloudy, looks like change of weather.

Novr. 1. William came up after breakfast, my husband left us about 10 o'clock 'tis quarterly meeting, Nancy continues mending, the child poorly—rain in the night, the Sun shone out this forenoon warm, William and self set with the door, in the old Parlor, wide open, and little or no fier,—towards evening we shut the door, had a fire made up, and were just going to tea, when we heard a Man scraping his feet at the back door, who can that be?—and who should it be, but HD. unexpectedly this evening which we spent, HD. writeing—William reading, myself mending Stockings, Sally sleeping on the Couch, Sip in bed, fine weather.

2d. First day morning fine, beautiful moderate. HD. went to Germantown meeting by himself, William took a walk, self at home alone—HD. went to town after dinner, having letters to write &c—WD. and self took a walk after, as far as end cornfield, spent the evening Solidly togeather.

3. cloudy morning, about noon came on Storm from N.E. I have felt myself very poorly this Morning George Bickly busy'd with his boys, putting up a fence between Dagney and us, I know not if 'tis with or without HD.s orders, he is useing old rails. nine at night, continu'd storm all this day, and no abeatment as yet, it has appear'd rather dull to day, with our little family, was I in health, which is far from being the case, I could reconcile much greater difficulties then any we at present experience,—'tho A seperation from several branches of my beloved family, would not set so easy on my mind, as it seems to do, was it not from a sence, that I shall shortly be seperated from them forever in this world, unless it should please the Lord to do that for me, which p[er]haps I have no right to expect.

4. Clear'd up, a sweet pleasant day, wind N.W. but moderate, B Bucks son call'd, Jacob Morris a Negro man in Neighborhood, ask'd to grind his apples at the mill, he has been busy about it this morning. We had an agreeable visit from Sister, Nancy and her little one, she is finely recoverd, for the time, they din'd with us, but went homewards before 4 o'clock, took some of Nancys accoutrements with them, she has not yet left our house, as the weather has been 'till to day unfavourable,—it is now a clear calm, serene evening, I am better than yesterday, don. cet. mat. our dear WD. has been better, for a week or 10 days past then all Summer, which I look on as a great favour—HSD. was to set off this forenoon for North-Bank.

5. cold Northwester this Morning William walk'd out after breakfast, spit blood, which he also did Yesterday, it is past a doubt that the cold air very materially effects his lungs—it is now the middle of the day, much warmer, he is employ'd with George in the Garden, which employment I should much approve of, if the weather was warmer.—Sam Sprigs came up about one o'clock, took home a Cart load of their furniture, said all were well at home, his mistress and Molly gone out walking, which I think was rather presuming in Nancy such a cold morning—Sam left us after dinner, a little after 2 o'clock. about 4 Afternoon William and self took ½ an hours walk, it was pleesant 'tho cool. This day 5. Novr. was always commemorated with us, 'till indipendance was declar'd, by ringing of bells, fireing of guns &c. on account of the discovery of the powder plot, a great deliverance it was. Benjn. Buck was to have taken a load of Hay to our Stable in town, and brought back load Dung, but as we have seen nothing of him, nor[80] any one this evening from

80. The word "nobody" crossed out.

home, I sent George[81] to enquire of BB, he return'd with account that, they had not sent the hay to day, but had been to market, that on returning the horses were frightned and had run away, that the driver was badly hurt,—I expected HD. this evening but [82] suppose, as is frequently the case, he has been call'd on and hindred—don. cet. mat. A very pretty female Cat, intruded herself on us this evening we did not make her welcome at first, but she seem'd to insist on staying, Sall then gave her milk, and very soon after, she caught a poor little mouse, and is now laying on the corner of my Apron by the fireside as familiarly as if she had liv'd with us seven years. William reading, Sall asleep on couch, Sip in kitchen, Billy has read more in the past week; than for a twelve month before in that time, he is deprived by the great weakness in his breast, of that pleasing employment.—a beautiful evening clear moon light.

6. this has been a very fine day, William and I have taken 2 walks of a mile each, half mile down the road in the fore-noon, the same upwards, Afternoon, on our return we saw a young Gentleman & Lady on top of our House, who should they be, but Henry and Hannah, they just stay'd to take a dish Coffee, and left us about sun set. Henry return'd yesterday from North bank—James set off this fore-noon with the carriage for Downingstown, Jacob Downing with him, to bring home Sally, Children &c—don. cet. mat. Benjn. Bucks team brought us up this Afternoon a load of posts for the fence betwen Dagney and us.

7. very poorly this morning don. sans. efft.—went before noon in to Marys, John gone to O Wilson for the little black Horse,—as my mind is now turn'd homwards, I settled matters with Mary, concerning our poor Sall, who I intend leaving with her, 'till her grevious business is settld, I look on Mary as a well minded and well disposed woman, and who, with our help, will take the proper care of her—J Logan paid us a short visit before dinner, he is engaged to dine with Thos. Fisher, with whom he came up, at his place. black Sip. this morning, without my knowledge, took up hot ashes and threw them behind the Stable, near the barn, several hours after a Smoke was seen, some combustibles had taken fire, which was soon extinguish'd, how he came to do it, I cannot tell, but if he had liv'd longer with me, he would have known that I suffer not such as he to undertake a business of that nature, I have ever since we have been here, sent the Ashes early in the morning when cold, by J Courtney, to the dung-hole, and order'd them cover'd up—walk'd a mile or more afternoon with William, on our return saw a Chaise at some distance, waited at the gate for its arrival, it proved to be, as we expected, my husband.

Novr. 8. it was overcast last night, but clear'd away before I retired, so that I

81. The words "this evening" crossed out.
82. The word "expect" crossed out.

had a view of the full moon, the fifth since we came here, we have the pleasure here of seeing the Sun and moon &c in all their glory, which to me is truly delighting. this is as fine a morning as perhaps can be, it is very agreeable being in the country in the fall of the year, as the weather is so often at that season fine. William went to town after breakfast with his Father, intends returning after dinner, this is a fine day for Sally and her little girls. I hope they will embrace it.—being left *tout sule*; about noon I took a pleasent 'tho solitary walk, din'd comfortably by myself, 'tho agreeable company would have been more pleasing. I expected my Sister and Hetty Smith to dine with me, but they came not. S Brant has been for two days past, at times, sighing and crying with the tooth-ach, a natural consiquence with some, I know what it is, and pity her,—G. Fry gone to town for rails. J. Courtney gone to Germantown to loose blood, for a pain in his side—before 4 afternoon William and Henry came up, to pass this evening and night with me—very warm at noon, cool evening.

9. First day. morning and a Charming morning it is. 'Tho all days are alike[83] with the Lord: yet I have thought that there was a solemnity in this day, somewhat different from others, and when I was young, I have thought, that if I had been asleep for weeks, and awakend on this day, that I should know it was first day, by the shineing of the Sun, 'tho this is ideal, yet the silence and quiet, that generaly reigns, may give things a different appearence. Henry went after breakfast to B Bucks, to engage wood for his use here, this winter, as he proposes after he is married, resideing here 'till his own House at North bank is finish'd—About noon Ben Wilson and Joshua Cliborn major, came up, so that I had four Young men to dine with me—Ben inform'd us, of the safe arrival of Jacob Downing and family at our house last evening—HSD. left us after dinner, expecting his father would be up this evening and want the horse and Chaise.—Josa. Ben. Willm. and self, took a walk to Benn. Bucks, my business was to enquire if there was not a useful woman in Germantown, they told me of one, who was helpful in their family, of the name of Ingle, lives near Dr. Bensels, this information has taken a weight off my mind, the having a good one so near.—we return'd ½ hour before sunset, Josa. and Ben. soon after bid us adieu, and it looks now, being night, as if William and self shall spend this evening without other company. pren. heir au soir, med[icine].

10. cloudy: looks likely for change of weather, I wish we were all well settled at home, but do not see the way clear as yet—William and self took walk before dinner as far up, as Thos. Nedros late dwelling—expected on our return to have found some of our family, but were disapointed—William has brought up to day, clearer blood than I have known him do, for a long time past, 'tis the coldness and rawness of the weather I beleive—he keeps himself,

83. The word "to" crossed out.

rather, too much out of doors—paid Mary a visit after dinner, about dusk HD. came up, all well at home except Nancy who has a fresh cold with cough, rain this evening.

11. cloudy morning cleard away about noon, my Husband left us before breakfast, Sally was almost raveing last night with the tooth ach, I was apprehensive that something else was the matter, she was in such a terriable taking. I gave her 15 drops laudenum, and put some of the same, on lint, to the tooth, I was up an hour later then usual with her, she had a good night I beleive, as she lay late, and when up, had no complaint, A pedler call'd this forenoon, I purchas'd some of his merchantdise 'tho dear, and I did not stand in need of the articles at present, there was a value received and if he gain'd a profit, he was wlcome thereto, said he was too old when free, at 21, to learn a trade, which was the reason of his present employment, made a breakfast of bread and Cider, and went away apperantly very happy—with his pack at his back, he put me in mind of[84] Bunyans pilgrem, 'tho he was not so heavely laden, for he appear'd to have a light heart, and the other requisite to go *through the world*.—A Mary Baley, a poor Woman, spent an hour in the kitchen, she has been here once or twice before, says she has a daughter, a criple, which perhaps is true, but she told two or three fibs, as I beleive, for which I like her none the better, William out most of this morning in the Garden with George.—was walking out with Billy before dinner when we saw a neighbouring taylor, whom I had sent for, going to our house, we turn'd homewards and had Sip measur'd for a new Coatee, I have been busy this forenoon mending his overalls, and underments, to make him fitt to appear when we go to the City, for he looks now like a compleat Ragamuffin—A short visit paid us this afternoon by M. Sandwith and H.S. Drinker, they brought us many things, and took many away with them, stay'd about an hour, cool afternoon. wind at N.W.

12. a clear pleasent morning walk'd after breakfast with William as far as Nedros, a strong Westrly wind—settled several accounts this day—paid Spencers £8.12.6. for Butter, settld with Mary Courtney for milk, with Betsy Bickley for Cream &c—sent John to pay the Shoemaker at Milestown, have a few other small matters to settle tomorrow, which will finish—we fully expected some of our family up to day, but no one from the City have we seen, sun set under a cloud, but 'tis clear star light at present—William rather better, myself 'thro' mercy not worse.

13. fine weather, settled with baker, paid Taylor, left necessaries with M Courtney, for Sally, expect to be ready tomorrow or next day at furthest to go home, after putting things to rights and cleaning a little more, as we have

84. The name "[Buttlers]" crossed out.

chiefly done that business[85], William out in garden this forenoon,—after 11 o'clock H.D. came up with the Carriage HSD. in the Chaise, with full purpose of taking us home, it put me in a hurry all the rest of the time we stay'd—we din'd about one:—I believe the flies are as numerous in our old parlor, in the Country on this day, as they are in the month of June at our house in town, after dinner, I disclosed to our Sarah my intentions of leaving her with Mary for some time, she wep't and appear'd in trouble[86] but before we left her seem'd reconciled, about four we bid adieu to Clearfield and arriv'd at home to tea, found Molly Foulk at our house, Jacob and Sally came soon after and dear little Eliza, what a favour! to see my Children again in health, it is very near five months since I have seen Sally and her Children—clear night—it will be a year three 3 days hence, since we left Germantown; On seventh day evening last, the eighth instant Clifford Smith was married to Hannah Stevenson daughter of Robt. Stevenson, her mother, Hannah Stevenson formerly Hicks, was an intimate and dear friend of my Sister and self.

Novr. 14. Sister was preparing this morning to go to Clearfield, HSD. to North bank, but they were prevented by the falling of Snow, it snow'd fast most of the day, turn'd to rain towards evening the first snow this year. We came home, I trust, in the right time, it realey appears so, I beleive we did not stay a day too long, or come home an hour too soon.—John Drinker call'd forenoon, Joseph Merryfield took tea with us, Sammy Rhoads spent the evening—five months to day since we went to Clearfield, and had we been favour'd with health, it would have been a pleasent time.

15. Snow this forenoon, cloudy most of this day—Jos. Merryfield call'd—he, Betsy Emlen, Sally Smith and others spent the Afternoon in front parlor with Molly, unwell myself all this day: prennez med[icine]—Extract of a letter in a late paper, from London—dated Augt. 18: gives an account of a dreadful fire that lately happen'd there, in the suburbs of that metropolis, which laid four or five hundred houses in ashes, Since the fire in London, in 1666, there has not been a conflagration so great.

16. First day. cloudy with a raw air, HD. MS. HSD. at meeting. ED. WD. MD. at home—Jos. Merryfield din'd with us—Jacob, Sally and their two daughters, Nancy Skyrin and her Daughter call'd before afternoon meeting—Hannah Smith came in meeting time she went with Henry to Sallys—HD. drank tea with Neighr. James at John Thompsons, Sister went this evening to Sammy Fishers, Betsy very unwell in her chamber—Isaac Morris Son of Saml. call'd this evening—I have been three days in the house, it was not so in the country.

85. The words "is done" crossed out.
86. The words "for some time" crossed out.

Novr. 17. My son Henry set off after breakfast for his farm, Sister went by herself to Clearfield—brought several things back with her in the Carriage. Sally, while Sister was there, finish'd cleaning—she sent John to town with potatoes &c in the Cart, she return'd to a late dinner—Betsy Emlen Ezekel James, and James Pemberton call'd—Elijah Waring, a young man lately from G. Britian, lodges at S Emlens, din'd with us—Neighr. Waln spent the evening—Betsy Fordham came this morning to[87] work, clear day—Sally and Nancy here in forenoon—William has past this day without bringing up blood, which he atributes to his having been for 3 or 4 days past confin'd, and out of the cold air, he was twice abroad this day.

18. HD. MS. at meeting—Nancy Skyrin and child here this morning Jams. Logan call'd S. Emlen call'd—G. Fry put up the fig—tree and cover'd the grapes in garden. Docr. Edwards and Wife, a young English woman Mary Clarkson who came lately over from London with them, din'd with us, S Swett also—they stay'd tea—I went this evening with my Husband to J Smiths, spent an hour there—call'd at J Downings in our return, Sally at our house—the first time that I have past through Arch Street since the hill was dug away and the street new paved—Hannah and Sally Hopkins lodges here to night—unwell tout le jour, clear and cool, I beleive some frost.—Sarah Fisher call'd fore-noon—fire works exhibited Aron Burr Senator, and daughter call'd.

19. Foggy morning clear'd up before noon fine and temperate—MS. and WD. sett of after breakfast for Clearfield, took a little Sweep-Chimney behind the Carriage, to officiate, at the place, in his way. Hannah and Sally Hopkins went out after breakfast, Sally Smith, little John Armett Cresson &c call'd. Peggy Saltar din'd with us, MD. went out after dinner with her, MS. &c came home to a late dinner, Sally Downing and N. Skyrin, and Docr. Edwards call'd, Thos. Stewardson took tea with us—HSD. return'd from N. Bank this evening, warm for the Season—A Stable in Strawberry-alley on fire last night.

20. Sun shone[88] a short time this morning then clouded over, and has continu'd cloudy ever since with rain this Afternoon, stormy and rain heavy this evening S. Swett spent the day, Jacob Downing, Sally Lea[r]ge and several others call'd—Saml. Smith from B. County and H. and S. Hopkins sup'd and lodg'd here.

21. Saml. Smith left us after breakfast, clear'd up in the night, a fine morning James Logan, Sally Downing and Nancy Skyrin call'd, Jos. Merrifield din'd with us—Molly Cresson Billy Saltar, and Hannah Hopkins took tea, HH. SH. and WS. sup'd and lodg'd here—HSD. went to Clearfield this

87. The word "sew" crossed out.
88. The word "for" crossed out.

afternoon, to see a load of new furniture put into the house, prepatory to his and Hannahs going there.

22. clear weather—W Saltar went away after breakfast—H and S. Hopkins din'd at J Downings, Nancy Skyrin and Jos. Merrifield call'd—little Peter, a negro boy, aged 7 years, came to us to day, from Virginia he has not had the small pox, and appears weakly, otherwise well disposed, we are to give, if we keep him, fifteen pound for his time—wash'd him this Afternoon in a tub of warm soap suds, his head with lark spur and rum, and changed his apparel.—E. Fordham still at work here. Jacob Downing came home with Molly and sup'd with us.

23. First day: clear and cold. HD. MS. HSD. MD. at meeting. WD. and self at home, S Swett din'd and tea'd with us, our Cousins the Hopkinss din'd at J Skyrins, Jacob and Sally call'd before meeting. little Mary Downing and Eliza Sansom stay'd here in afternoon meeting time, Sukey Sansom and Sally Downing call'd for them after meeting, HD. stay'd at home this evening writing, Peggy Wharton spent the evening here, Josh. Merrifield call'd to bid farewell, he setts of tomorrow for New-York.

24. find myself unwell all day, after a poor night. this has been a fine, clear, cool day, I have been but once over our door sill since my return from Clearfield. Saml. Emlen and two young Frenchmen nam'd   were here this morning they left France about two years ago, have resided since in Gret. Britian, Seven months past they heard of the death of their father, or I should rather say, they saw the account in a Newspaper that he had suffer'd under the Guillotine, and his estate confiscated, which was considerable, they are at present, in possession of no more than one or two hundred pounds, wish to buy a small quantity land, which they propose to cultivate; appear to me, to be very unfitt for the business, the eldest is about 23 years of age, the other near 22, My husband advis'd them, not to be in a hurry to make a purchase, but to go into the Country, 'till they saw their way more clear, They came over in the Roebuck, were boarded by a french Frigate, or Government Ship, who took all the english passengers prisoners, as has been their practice for sometime past, those young men, put on the habits of seamen, and fain'd themselves Swiss Salors, by which means they perhaps sav'd their lives, for had it been known that they were french emigrants, 'tis thought, they would have been immediately shot.[89]—Sally Downing here this fore-noon, Jas. Logan, Docr. Redman, Sally Smith and Sally Large call'd—Saml. Emlen junr. here in the evening, HD. sign'd an order this evening for the interment of Betsy

89. The cantons of Switzerland were officially neutral during the Anglo-French war, as they had been for two centuries (William Martin and Pierre Beguin, *Switzerland from Roman Times to the Present,* trans. Jocasta Innes, 6th ed. [London: Elek Books: 1971], 100–101, 142–51).

Howel, formerly Burge; Beulah Burge has lost, within little more than twelve months her Son in Law, three grand Children, and now her Daughter—Hannah and Sally Hopkins, and Molly Drinker, after spending the day abroad, came home to late supper. My dear William has caught cold, the weather pinches him much.

25. clear morning Willm. oppress by his cold, HD. & M.S. at monthly meeting. S Downing call'd, HSD. went to Clearfield, Jacob Wayne with him, to put up bedsteds G. Prichard din'd here, the girls din'd at Nancys, H. and S. Hopkins, and Sally Smith took tea here, and spent the evening—H. Smith, S Large, M. Lippencot and her brother, Sally Rhoads and her Son here also in the evening John Drinker, S. Roland Fisher, and J Logan call'd.

Novr 26. clear blue sky. HD. left home after an early dinner, J Drinker with him in the chaise for Byberry intending for bucks county quarterly meeting and to call at Langhorn park, then to proceed to Henrys farm,—Molly went with Hanh. Smith M. Lippencot and Molly Kelly to Clearfield, to put up Curtains &c. they took dinner with 'em, Henry went to them after dinner, they return'd after candle light—Saml. W. Fisher here this evening HSD. received a letter from M. Callanan London—S Downing call'd,—William beleiv'd that the loss of a little blood might be of[90] relieve him, sent for Docr. Kuhn this fore-noon, the Doctor said bleeding was not necessary, but ordrd him to continue taking deluteing food and drink for a day or two, he is better this evening—Sister went this Afternoon, with Sally Rhoads to the funeral of Betsy Howel widdow.

27. delightful day: wind S.W. Caty Dennis mantua maker, and Betsy Fordham at work here, Hannah and S Hopkins din'd with us, Sally Downing, Nancy Skyrin and Elijah Waring took tea with us. JS. JD. call'd—HSD. went to Clearfield this Afternon-widdow Durdin paid us a morning visit. Account in the evening paper of the Carnage of 1200 men, in Flanders, war.[91]

28. Moderate weather, Dr. Kuhn and Nurse Waters call'd—our Son Henry made his second appearance at monthly meeting with his cher-amie—he came from meeting before 11 o'clock, took an early and light dinner, then set off for his Farm, to meet his Father there, by appointment—Sister and Molly were the only persons of our family that attended at the passing—I wish I could with propriety have been there myself,—but we must endeavor to submit,

90. The word "service" crossed out.

91. According to the reports, the city of Liège was in ruins, and twelve hundred men had been killed or wounded as the French advanced over the Meuse River. On Dec. 2 a report would claim that "there was not a doubt of Holland being entirely in possession of the French" (*Philadelphia Gazette and Universal Daily Advertiser,* Nov. 27, Dec. 2, 1974; see also below, Dec. 2).

where we cannot perform—M. Clarkson, wife to our present Mayor was buryed this Afternoon, she was a pretty girl, when Polly Boud, I went to school with her—S Downing call'd forenoon, Nancy Skyrin after meeting, Molly Lippencot call'd after dinner for Molly to go to J Smiths to tea with the Bride, may not a young woman be call'd a Bride after she has declar'd her intentions of marriage publickly? I think she may with propriety,—Eliza Downing spent this afternoon with us, her mother gone somewhere visiting with her Sister—J Logan took tea with us—Neighr. Waln spent the evening, Sammy Emlen came home with Molly—William took a long walk this forenoon, rather too long, as he appears fatigued after it.

29. Hannah and Sally Hopkins, E. Fordham and Tayloress, breakfast'd and din'd as usual—Becky Hopkins call'd, the girls went home with her after dinner—the mantua maker left us also this evening HD. and Son Henry came home this evening Sammy Smith call'd, Saml. Fisher and George Fox here this evening Tommy Fisher call'd—John Fields Son, came for an order for the interment of Daniel Williams, who departed this life, some time to day.—Hannah Hopkins and our dear William went this forenoon to Clearfield, he is more unwell this evening than common, sick stomach.—Dunlaps paper, of this day, mentions, a conspiracy against the life of the King of Great Britian, which was to be carried into execution at the Theater, by means of a poisoned arrow.[92] Shocking doings.

30. First day: fine morning cloudy Afternoon—Daniel Drinker, Jacob Downing and Daughter call'd, WD. took a walk in meeting time, no one din'd with us—J Logan, Thos. Morris called—Henry and Hannah gone to day to Clearfield—Jacob and Sally call'd after meeting for little Mary, who stay'd with us while they were gone—R Jones and her girl call'd in evening meeting time—rain this evening—The Commissioner, Timy. Pickering, and the friends, who went to treat with the six nation Indians return'd yesterday or the day before, and think they have settled a permanant peace with them, much to be wished.[93] The greatest part of the army, also, are returning from the Westren Counties of Pennsylvania, A body of the troops are left behind to enforce the Laws, they have taken some of the ringleaders, and active rioters.

Decr. 1. cloudy with rain, very damp in house, Sun shone out just before

92. A letter from London dated Sept. 29 reported a foiled plot to kill George III. Four men had been arrested, after which it was revealed that they had fashioned a poisoned dart and a blowgun device with which they were planning to murder the king. No motivation was suggested for the assassination (*Pa. Gaz.*, Dec. 3, 1794).

93. Pickering successfully negotiated a treaty with the Iroquois Confederacy at Canandaigua, N.Y., which called for the Indians to maintain their neutrality in the current disputes between the U.S. and Great Britain, revised certain boundaries in the Northwest, and guaranteed the Indian nations financial and technical assistance from the U.S. government (see above, Sept. 10; Clarfield, *Timothy Pickering*, 149–52).

setting, beautifully, with appearance of a rainbow—Peter Yarnel dined with us, Ben Wilson drank tea, very fine evening John Drinker sup'd.

Decr. 2. Peter Yarnel call'd before meeting, Nancy Skyrin and S Swett din'd with us, Betsy Emlen spent the Afternoon, Saml. Emlen took a pipe with us this evening—Molly Smith and Abigal. Parish here this Afternoon Collecta Argent pour R. N——t. An account in this days paper of the taking of Amsterdam by the French—J.C. came this forenoon to inform us, that S.B— was this morning about 6 o'clock deliver'd of a daughter, the mother and Child both well, we sent him to her mother SJ. who went with him after dinner to visit Sall—John had been out in the Night for the old Woman, disturb'd two or thee families before he found her, he is but an awkward body at best—Danl. King call'd this morning David Evans was here last evening he ownes a place near ours, by Logans Mill, wish'd HD. and others would wait on the Grand Jury to solicite the building of a Bridge over that bad part of the road.[94]

3d. pleasent and cool, very temperate as yet. I have spent this day as usual dans le maisone, John Courtney came to town with the Cart, he took back for Henry a barrel flour, Beef, Pork &c—Sally Zane drank tea with us—[Sa]mmy Smith here in evening Jacob Sally, John Nancy call'd, the three girls visited Pegy. Wharton, this Afternoon little Eliza also, fine moon light.

Decr 4. clear and cool, I took a walk this forenoon to J Smith, Hetty Smith has straind her thumb, which at this busy time she feels not only painful but inconvenient, stay'd there 'till after one o'clock, Molly with me, donnez a [S]F. deu ecú pour HL——s widdow—call'd at C Jerviss and at Jacob Downings—a Man of the name of Grothouse din'd with us,—Docr. Edwards here this evening.

5. Cloudy: HSD. and Sally Smith went off after breakfast for Burlington, Henry intends leaving SS there and going to his farm,—J Downing, here fore noon,—John Hillborn din'd with us,—J Logan, [S] Downing, Docr. Edwards, and Thomas Stewardson took tea with us.—Jerimh. Warder has lost a little Daughter by a very melancholy accident, between 2 and 3 years of age, she was left alone last night for a short time, and fell into the fier, when the girl returnd to the room, she found the Child in a blaze, which was soon put out, but she expired before morning Young Children should never be left alone, nor should they were cotton by a fire—poor Hannah Warder, who now lays in with

94. According to "An Act for the Erecting of Bridges and Maintaining Highways," passed Nov. 7, 1700, county courts with the concurrence of a grand jury were responsible for appointing a person or persons to build bridges in their respective counties (*Statutes at Large*, 2:73).

twins, is much to be pitied, had she been well, it probably would not have happen'd.

Decr. 5. while at dinner, Molly rang the Bell upstairs, she sent for me being ill of Something like a severe Colick, she had been setting in her Brothers room over a little fire, reading, for an hour or two, with her feet on a cold hearth, I think, I never saw a living face look paler, she was in great pain and cold sweat, I gave her a little geneva and water sweet'ned, and us'd friction some time after a draft of Cap-nip tea,[95] which all togeather had the desired effect, she is bravly this evening—I do not altogeather approve of spiritous medecines in the Colic &c. unless some perticular indication call for it, such as wind &c—in most cases it should not be often repeated, 'tho I have known Daffys Ellixer sometimes do good.

6. John Hillborn breakfasted, he lodges here, Sister and William went this fore noon to Clearfield—they found S.B. and her bantling well, Sally weep'd when she saw MS—and cover'd her head with the bed-cloaths—The Child is very Yallow for one so young—they return'd to dinner, Nancy here this Morning Ben Wilson drank tea—Jacob Downing, Docr. Edwards and J Hilborn here in the evening A Negro boy of the name of Peter Woodard, came this Afternoon to us, from one of the lower Counties, Kent I believe it was, sent here by Warner Mifflin, he was raged and lousey, having been for upwards of a week on board the Vessel, and in poor trim before, fifteen pounds is said to be the price for him, WM. writes that he is 11 or 12 years of age, he says his aunt told him he was going in 14. he looks to be between the two.—has not had the small pox. before he had been here ½ an hour, I had him in a tup of Soap and water, well wash'd, afterwards rum, in which larkspur was mix'd pour'd on his head—dress'd him in Scipios old Cloaths, I beleive he suffer'd coming up with cold &c. for after he had warm'd himself and eat something, he look'd like another creature, his appearence at first was rather formidable; being as I thought, hard favoured &c—one of our Daughters is to have one of the three little blacks that has lately come under our care. I feel much for the poor little fellows, little Peter has no parents here, the other two have finish'd reading two octavo volums of Hogath Illustrated, by John Irland.[96]

7. First day: very temperate John Hillborn went away early this morning HD. MS. went to meeting, S Swett din'd, Anthony New and young Elliot call'd after meeting. Betsy Emlen, Peggy and Hannah Saltar also call'd,

95. The dried leaves and flowering tops of the catnip plant (*Nepeta cataria*) were used in hot infusions to relieve muscle spasms of the stomach (W. H. Lewis and Elvin-Lewis, *Medical Botany*, 276).

96. John Ireland, *Hogarth Illustrated (A Supplement to Hogarth Illustrated; Compiled from His Original Manuscripts, etc.)*, 3 vols. (London J. E. J. Boydell, 1791–98 [*BLC*]).

William walk'd out twice to day, he is poorly—HSD. return'd from Burlington &c. to a late dinner. Elijah Waring took tea with us, Jacob and Sally sup'd hear, their daughters were with us this Afternoon—Hetty Smith very poorly, a pain with swelling, in her Hand and foot—Neighr. Waln, Sucky Hartshorn, her daughter Hannah, and Jos[h]. Waln, spent part of this evening with us.

8. last night between 11 and 12. the Sky was illuminated by an aurora-Borealis or northern morning.—cloudy this morning with some rain, HSD. and MS. went about 11 o'clock for Clearfield, to arrange matters there—O. Alsop took out this forenoon, several of the marriage Cards or Wedding tickets for fifth day next—Reba. Jones, who has been visiting the families of this district for some time past, visited us this Afternoon, J. Downings family also, Hannah Yerkes, Jane Snowden, and Caleb Cresson accompanied her, MS. and HSD did not return 'till after they were gone.—I went with HD. this evening to Jams. Smiths, Hettys foot so swell'd that she cannot walk, is apprehensive she shall not be able to attend her Daughters Marriage—call'd at Jacobs in our return, HD. sup'd there, found Jos[h]. Sansom at our house, Dr. Edwards call'd. Betsy Fordham finishd work this evening.

Decr. 9. Cloudy Morning clear'd up about noon, pleasant and moderate, too much so, I think, to last long at this season. HD. MS. went to meeting—Sally Smith, Huldah Mott, Peggy Saltar, Jas. Logan, Saml. Emlen, John Parish call'd—Nancy and her Child here, William walk'd out this forenoon. John Courtney came with the Cart, took a Cask of bottled porter, and some kitchen Utensils up to the place—John Hillborn return'd from Bucks county to our house this Afternoon, he and Sally Downing took tea with us, My poor S——y is remarkably lusty for the time, I am thoughtful on her account Jacob came for her in the evening Molly spent this afternoon and evening at S. Emlens, fine moon light night.

10. delightful weather, HD. and Son William set off for Clearfield about 11 o'clock, Sister out forenoon Molly at J Smiths helping to prepare for the important tomorrow, May it be blest, to the[97] persons concerned—The bells ringing and guns fireing on the arrival of the troops this forenoon, from the western expedition. Sammy Emlen, Sammy Bowne from New York, and J Downing call'd, there was an unusal concourse of people assembled to see the entry of the troops, Josa. Edwards who has been out with the army drank tea, and spent this evening with us. Anthony Woodard, Father of black Peter, came this morning to see his Son, whom he had not seen for eight years before—he took him home with him to see his Mother, has not return'd since—J Hillborn bid us farewell before he went to bed, as he intends going away early in the morning.

97. Word(s) crossed out.

Decr. 11. A delightful moderate Morning, Azure Sky, favourable for my Sons marriage, and to enable me, who have not been to meeting for a long time, to attend it,—

> If the Lord, in condescension,
> Deigns to hear a Mothers prayer,
> He will attend this mornings Meeting,
> And be with my Harry there;
> Great indeed's the undertaking!
> When we give our selves away,
> But if he approve the action,
> Blessed is the Nuptial day.

Hetty Smith being too unwell to accompany her daughter, I went with my husband, from our house to the Market-Street Meeting House, Henry and Hannah &c. were but just seated when we enter'd, the meeting was large, and agree'd by every one, that I heard speak of it, that it was a favour'd time, Nichs. Waln and Samuel Emlen, were the only Ministers who had any thing to communicate—Henry and Hannah spoke very distinctly and in a proper key—were much commended for their conduct and beheaviour.—Robt. Coe read the Certificate.—Henry and Hannah went to, and from Meeting in a Carriage, and the Brides Maids in an other, the rest of the company walk'd, there was about 50 persons at the Wedding—our dear William came about 11 o'clock to meeting, being desirous to be a witness to his brothers marriage, the day was spent agreeably, nothing occur'd to cause displeasure or uneasiness, that I heard of, as sometimes does in large companys—A very plentifull and elegant dinner well serv'd after three o'clock, Supper at nine, tea omitted, indeed there was no time for it the days being so short—My Sister and William left us towards evening, the latter much fatigued.—the company broke up about 10. James and Phebe Pemberton, William Lippencot and wife were overseers.—I past the day better then I expected, having been for a fortnight past favour'd to be better, than for many months before, 'tho great weakness at times still attends me. there are some sufferings that by long bareing we become measurably reconciled too, when not very acute.

12. Sally, Nancy, and Sally Smith call'd this morning Nancy din'd here, her Child also, William and self had concluded to dine with Hannah Pemberton, he had taken cold, that we did not go out 'till about noon, Hannah, who did not expect us, was rideing out, we took possession of the parlour, sometime after she came home, Hannah Yerkes and her little grand-son with her, they, Sally Zane, and John Wilson din'd there also—Sally Pemberton, Molly Morris, and my husband took tea there, William left us at three o'clock being unwell, he is better this evening HD. and self came home after night, the first day that I have spent out of our own house for a long time past, Yesterday excepted, I have not seen Henry or his bride to day. fine weather.

May they, quite free from anxious cares,
Disturbing thoughts, distressing fears,
Live happy to advanced Years.—

and may they live so, as to deserve an exemption from many cares or fears—

There is a lesson worthy notice,
  Which requiers our frequent care,
In every scene of life, that's trying,
  Learn to bear, and to forbear;
Youth too seldom mind this maxim,
  But when arrived to riper years,
Experience shows, it is effectual,
  To alleviate cars and fears.

13. Henry here this morning he, Hannah, Molly, Richd. Smith gone before dinner to Clearfield—John Courtney came for a load which he took in the cart, he says Sall's child is sick, her Mother was here this morning wishes we would bring her home, as she is fearful she will be too fond of the poor yallow Child.—her fears are natural, but we have not yet concluded what is best to be done in that case. Benn. Cathral call'd to inform us, that James Potts is ill of a pleurisy, they had sent for Dr. Rush, wanted a nurse, HD. advis'd him to look out for one, Sister went afternoon to see him, found him very poorly, but they thought him better,—three companys of Light-horse past by our door before dinner, the first were in bleu uniforms, the second in green, 3d. bleu and buff,[98] a large body of the troops came to town to day, a great croud colected to see the entry, those that came in some days past were the Volunteers, a number yet expected with prisoners.—As our Son Henry was desireous of having the young people invited here after his marriage, this Afternoon was appointed, 'tho we are not fond of such parties, yet could not deny so innocent a request, they came about 5 o'clock, Henry and Hannah Drinker, Abey Marshal, Molly Lipencot, Sally Smith and Molly Drinker, bride Maids, Sammy Emlen grooms Man, the other two, Isaac Morris, and [Josh.] Waln, were absent, James Logan, Sally Downing John and Nancy Skyrin, Sally Large, John Smith, Richd. Smith, Saml. Bowne,—they had Cakes, Wine, Coffee, tea, Almonds, Reasons, Nuts, pears, Apples &c—they spent the evening very inoffensively, I beleive, in our front parlor, but made rather too

98. Three companies of cavalry, or light horse, returned from western Pennsylvania, where they had been instrumental in putting down the Whiskey Rebellion. The troops in blue, led by Capt. John Dunlap, were part of Philadelphia's elite volunteer corps, the First City Troop. Those in green were from Capt. Matthew McConnel's Volunteer Greens. Those in blue and buff formed Capt. Abraham Singer's Second Volunteer Troop. Militia and volunteers in Philadelphia met these troops, along with other units, and accompanied them into the city (Scharf and Westcott, *Philadelphia,* 1:479; Philadelphia City Cavalry, *Book of the First Troop,* 53–57; *Dunlap and Claypoole's American Daily Advertiser,* Sept. 12, 15, Dec. 13, 15, 1794; Hazard, *Pa. Archives,* ser. 6, 5:545–48).

much noise—seperated about ten o'clock;—William took a walk fore noon to S Swetts, she had been unwell which prevented her coming to the Marriage, Docr. Edwards call'd this evening after 10, about some business with HD. who was too poorly to attend to it, having been chilly and sick at Stomach for an hour before, he complain'd of a stitch in his left side, and was a little feverish—took a draught of Cat-nip tea, and had his feet beth'd in warm water by the bed side, a fire made in the Chamber, a little moisture came over him after in bed, Nevertheless he had a very restless night, could scarcely turn in bed, the pain in his side was so bad.—I expect it is the pleurisy, believe he took cold in the store under front parlor Yesterday morning, where he spent some time with Othniel packing up goods to send to Atsion.

14. First day: the weather continues remarkably fine, uncommonly so, what a great favour is good weather, with a sufficient degree of health to enjoy it. My Husband was very unwell indeed this morning chilly and sick, Jammy Smith, HSD. call'd before meeting.—sent for Dr. Rush, who order'd bleeding, as we expected, and opening pills[99] after, Fredrick was sent for, who preform'd the operation, in about ½ hour afterwards he was sick and faintly, puck'd and was in a cold sweat, lay down on the Sofa, sleep'd near two hours, and arose better, 'tho he has been very heavy, and seemingly lethargic all day—Sally Downing and HSD. took tea with us—John and Nancy call'd after meeting, Joseph Drinker Senr. and Sammy Bowne here this evening One McCree, a broaker, who liv'd next door but one to Jemmy Smith, put an end to his life, some time this day, with a pistol.—William din'd at J Smiths, I have been mercifully, better then usual, for above a week past, untill this day, being unabele this morning to attend to myself as I ought to do have suffer'd all day—Dr. Rush this evening said when he look'd at HDs. blood, "I hope we have nip'd it in the bud"—he said he had less fever &c. I sent James with the bowl to empty in the river, in preference to the necessary, I do so generaly when convenient, not that I have and fixt, or good reason for doing so, but having heard M. Penry say, that they, at Bethlehem were in the practice of throwing [their] blood into the Lehigh. HD. took four more of the opening pills, which work'd well, J Drinker call'd this evening.

15. HD. considerably better, Dr. Rush, Anthony New, Owen Biddle, John Drinker Danl. Drinker, James Logan, Huldah Mott, Betsy Emlen, the two Saltars, and Nancy Skyrin, call'd this forenoon—James took up to Clearfield in the Carriage, Molly Lipencot, Sally Smith and Scipio behind, with some necessaries, A waggon loaded, is also is also gone up to day, with furniture from Jams. Smiths.—William took a walk to H. Pembertons before dinner,—

99. Any of a variety of preparations intended to open the bowels, from mild stomachics to stronger purgatives (*OED*, s.v. "opening"; Buchan, *Domestic Medicine* [1799], 459–61; W. Lewis, *New Dispensatory*, 574).

after dinner, our dear Henry came to bid us farewell, he, and his Hannah, sett off early this Afternoon for Clearfield, where they expect to reside, 'till his own house at North Bank is finish'd, which will not probably be, 'till some time in next summer;—John Morton, Margt. Porter, James Cresson, Saml. Clark, Saml. Emlen, Joseph Bringhurst, Nichs. Waln and John Skyrin call'd—Nancy drank tea with us, Peter Woodards mother brought him back this Afternoon, After paying them a weeks visit.—Dr. Rush, Jacob Downing, Joseph Drinker, Docr. Edwards, and a young Englishman of the name of Watkinson, call'd this evening—Moderate, clear and pleasent, My husband I hope is recovering.

16. MS. MD. gone to meeting, HD. not well enough to venture out, Saml. Emlen, Elijah Waring, Thos. Morris, R. Jones, James Logan, Docr. Rush call'd—gave William a dose, for the first time, of Norriss drops,[100] which have been strongly recommended. HSD. sent John to town with the Chaise to take up a hier'd servant girl.—Sally Rhoades spent an hour after dinner, Sammy Bowne here this evening Molly out as usual—Cadr. Evans and another person with him here on business.—John Cannon took tea here. J Skyrin came home with Molly—this has been a very warm day, remarkably so for the Season.

17. John Drinker return'd from the Billet, 16 miles off, where he and his Son Joeh. on business for HD. and himself, HD. not being well enough to go, they lodg'd last night at Clearfield. Docr. Rush, Thos. Stewardson, Sally Downing here this morning. Saml. Smith Bucks County, put up his horse, and lodges here, William Blakey his Wife and Son and Rachel Watson din'd here, Rachel lodges with us—J Courtney came to town with the Cart, for several things wanted there, this has been a busy morning—HD. 'tho better, is far from well, Saml. Emlen call'd after dinner, HSD. came to town with Sally Smith Afternoon, sett of after 5 o'clock with his Sister Molly, in his Chaise, just dark, they will not get to Clearfield 'till long after night, her going so late, was much against my will,—they are to have a Company of young foulke to dine with them tomorrow, W Drinker seems, throgh mercy, much better—Wm. Ashby's partner call'd to tell us, of a Tayloress who would come into the House to work for our little black boys—John Cadwalader lawyer, drank tea with us—Saml. Howell from Kent County, John Drinker, Elliston Perot, Jacob Downing call'd, R. Watson and Saml. Smith spent the evening and lodg'd. weather continues warm, roads good.

100. Noriss's Drops were an English patent medicine with an antimony base. Dr. Noriss or Norris claimed that his medication relieved "inflammatory fevers, putrid fevers, scarlet fevers, putrid sore throats, bilious complaints, nervous headaches, gouty habits, rheumatism, scurvy, coughs and colds, asthma, complaints of the bowel, convulsive spasms, and indeed most medical conditions" (Lederer, *Colonial American English,* s.v. "Noriss's Drops"; *Dunlap's American Daily Advertiser,* Aug. 26, 1793).

18th. Saml. Smith left us, this morning early, he is gone with others of a Committee, to examine some land near Concord, as 'tis not yet settled where the intended boarding School shall be fixt.[101] R. Watson breakfasted, Docr. Rush, John Drinker, Peggy and Hannah Saltar, &c call'd, HD. continues mending, 'tho not yet recover'd—Docr. Rush gave William great encouragement this morning thinks him much better, and quite likely that that he will continue to mend 'till quite recover'd. I have the same hope, yet expect that interruptions, or pull-backs will at times occur. 'tis the case in all cronic complaints—HD. William, and our two Downing grand daughters went about 11 o'clock for Clearfield, they return'd to dinner. Robt. Stevenson spent an hour this fore noon with me. we are favour'd with the company of little E. Skyrin for the day, as her mother expects company. Sally Downing, Docr. Redman, James Logan here before dinner, Nancy Skyrin in the Afternoon, she, Sally, and some others, going to visit S. Perot who lays in. J.S. came this evening with B. Dawson for his little daughter No Molly to night, looks likely for rain, A dozen, or more young people, din'd to day at Clearfield. H.D. read this evening to RW. &c. an account of Elizath. Drinkers dyeing saying &c. sent by her companion Sarah Rudd. cloudy evening.

19. A large Committe of the yearly meeting now in town. Wm. and Sarah Bleakey, G. Churchman, and R. Watson, din'd with us. R.W. S.B. Benn. Swett, and Willm. Newbold took tea here. Oliver Paxon, Henry Clifton, Joshua Woolson, and Jn. Drinker call'd. wind N.E. heavy rain this Afternoon, Sally Bleakly stays here this night with R.W. she and husband generaly lodge at Saml. Pleasants,—no account from Clearfield to day—our dear William has caught some cold this damp day, and is poorly this evening.

Decemr 20. I sleep't none last night, I was unwell and thoughtful on Williams account half past three my husband awoke, and was keep't wakeing by the riseing of phlegm—he sleep'd none after but arose soon after day-break, and I soon follow'd him. William much better this morning It rain'd at three o'clock this morning very heavy, and continued raining 'till near noon—Willm. Blakey came to breakfast, his wife was not come down stairs, RW. and she breakfasted after he was gone—sun shone out about noon, WB. and wife and Son Thos. with RW. eat an early dinner—then had their Horses, which were in our Stable, put too, and set off about one o'clock,—Willm. Richardson, Oliver Paxon and James Logan call'd this forenoon—J Logan and J Smith din'd yesterday at Clearfield they left our Children well, HD. went to meeting this Afternoon, the first of his going abroad since his indisposision on seventh

101. At its first meeting, on Dec. 17, the Philadelphia Yearly Meeting's school committee apparently voiced some objections to Langhorne Park, since the meeting was adjourned until Dec. 20 while members examined other potential sites (see above, Feb. 10; Dewees and Dewees, *Centennial of Westtown*, 29–30; Hole, *Westtown*, 24–28).

day last. rain again this Afternoon. Robt. Stevenson junr. call'd after dinner, the first time of seeing him since his return, he has been absent three months in McPherson's company of Volunteers, call'd by some, the Quaker Company, as several under our name were with them,[102] he gave me an account of some particulars of their expedition &c. Robert is not yet 19 years old—Saml. Smith of B. County, return'd this Afternoon from Chester County, where he has been with others to examine a tract of land belonging to Js. Gibbons, whether that, or Langhorn park, is to be the place for the boarding school, is not yet fix't—He, John Drinker, and HD. went from our house to meeting on that business this evening—Samuel Emlen and Daniel Drinker took a pipe here, H.D & SS. came from committee, they inform that they have fix't on James Gibbons tract in Chester County for the school,[103] so that one sixth of Langhorn Park belongs to HD.

21. First day: cloudy morning, a little snow before noon, about noon the Sun shone out wind S.W. and warm, Saml. Smith breakfasted and went homeward before we came down stairs—HD. MS. gone to meeting, WD. and self at home, Molly not yet return'd from Clearfield. Betsy Emlen and the Saltars call'd after meeting. MS. went this afternoon to Jacob Downings. Nancy Skyrin and Child here afternoon, Thos. Dawson call'd for his Daughters to go with him to visit his New Wife, their step mother, Betts being here they went with him. John Skyrin call'd, Nancy stay'd tea, John Drinker, R. Jones, Sammy Fisher call'd this evening. Thos. Dawson and wife waited on the girles home. cloudy. HD. stay'd at home this evening, writing to England—blew up stormy, wind at N.E. it looks likely for cold weather.

22. clear, wind N.W. moderately cold—no frost, it looks as if we should have no winter *this year*, Sammy Smith and Jacob Downing call'd—Henry and Hannah came to town fore noon, in the Chaise, with lame black Horse, Our valuable old Mare, has mett with a bad accident, which has rendered her unfitt for use,—going into the Barn which was left open, she cut her legs in several

102. William MacPherson, a former Revolutionary War officer active in Federalist politics in Philadelphia, had formed a volunteer militia of more than sixty "respectable citizens" to quell the Whiskey Rebellion. The company, known as MacPherson's Blues, was the first of many volunteer companies active in Philadelphia in the last decade of the eighteenth century and the first decade of the nineteenth. Counting a number of birthright Quakers among its elite composition, it was known for its distinctive uniforms, which included blue pantaloons and fur hats covered with bear skins and adorned with black cockades and buck tails (*Dunlap and Claypoole's American Daily Advertiser,* Sept. 16, 1794; R. G. Miller, *Federalist City,* 155, n. 7; J. F. Watson, *Annals,* 1:331–32; St. Andrew's Society of Philadelphia, *An Historical Catalogue of the St. Andrew's Society of Philadelphia, 1749–1907* [Philadelphia: Printed for the Society, 1907], 263–65).

103. After a subcommittee recommended purchasing six hundred acres of a farm belonging to James Gibbons in Westtown, Chester County, the school committee chose that site over Langhorne Park (Dewees and Dewees, *Centennial of Westtown,* 29–30; Hole, *Westtown,* 28; see above, Feb. 10, Dec. 18).

places, with a sharp cutting knife that lay in the way. HSD. George Churchman, and Eliza Downg. din'd with us. Hannah Drinker at her Fathers,—they went away after sun set, roads not good, Horse lame and skitish, I like not such doings—Molly alone at Clearfield all day—Sammy Howell from Kent, and Ben Wilson drank tea with us—Jacob and Sally Downing sup'd here—Isaac Potts, Sammy Pleasants, and Anthoy. Curthbart, call'd, the latter inform'd of the illness of Samuel Leeds, at Maurices River.

23 Decr. HD. MS. gone to monthly meeting. Hetty Smith sent to know if I would go with her to Clearfield to see our Children. 'tho unfitt, and not altogeather willing, I wish'd to go, as the day was remarkably fine, and we might not have many such before winter set in, therefore agreed to go, she call'd before 11 o'clock, her little daughter Abby with her, Jammy Smith had set off before us on Horse back. We arriv'd there after 12.—the parlor in which they set was so very warm by the Sun shining into it, that we, coming out of the fresh air, could scarcely bare it. I never remember such fine warm weather, so long togeather at this season of the year. HSD. had left home some hours before we came, for North Bank, he mett Peter Williamson about 8 miles on the Frankford road, having been first to town, he being the person he wish'd to see, talk'd over the business he had with him, and return'd to us before we din'd, which was rather late. Docr. Logan call'd there before dinner—They appear to be agreeably settled, and very happy. I left them, well pleas'd and satisfied—call'd at John Courtneys just before we came away. S.B. is very well, and in rather too good spirits, everything considered, she had nam'd the Jaune pettet, Hannah G——bs, I disaprovd it, and chang'd it to Catharine Clearfield, with which she appear'd displeas'd—we came home a little after sun set, mett with a little fright, A heavy waggon near the Bridge in second street, the driver having no reins to his horses, who were four, I think, in number, we were near the edge of the bank, and his waggon wheels almost touch'd ours, he came down the Hill with force, hollowing to his horses,[104] whom he could scarcely stop. Ceaser made shift, after both Carriages had stop'd, to get safe along—'the miss of an inch, is said to be as good as a mile, but it frighten'd us a little—Molly Drinker came home with us, little Abey stay'd behind with her Sister,[105] mett at our house when we came in, Edwd. Garragus, and his apprentice John Collins, a rumpus between them, which they call'd on HD. to settle—John Cannon took tea with us—Pattison Hartshorn, Thos. Fisher, Sammy Smith and Billy Sansom, mett here this evening to settle matters conserning Lang-horn Park &c. I went after tea to pay an evening visit to our Neighr. Sally Rhoads, she was at her daughter Fishers, who is poorly, thither I went, and spent upwards of an hour, 'tis seldom that I go abroad, 'tho I have been favour'd lately to get out rather more

104. The word "which" crossed out.
105. The word "found" crossed out.

then has been common for[106] several years—A fine clear star light night—S Swett and Elijah Waring din'd here to day. Betsy Emlen and Pegy Saltar call'd.

24. Wind S.W. hazy and warm, HSD. came to town this forenoon. MS. went out on errends. I had an hours chat with our old friend Docr. Redman, which is not a thing unusal, S. Downing and her Daughters call'd. Henry went homeward before sunset. Othniel Alsop, our Clerk, took tea, Jacob Downing call'd. Patty Wharton was hear, while I was abroad yesterday, she inform'd sister that her mother was so well as to go frequently abroad and sometimes to meeting—her recovery, as far as she is recover'd, comes as near a meracle, as any thing that has come under my knowledge—Neighbour Waln hear this evening—I have been led to think, I may say to conclude, on reading Docr. Rush's account of the Yallow fever,[107] that my daughter Nancy had it towards the later end of October last, at Clearfield—and do suppose that Docr. Kuhn, who attended her, knowing that we would steadily attend her, be it what it would, kindly endeavourd to conceal it from us—he say'd it was the Jaundice and some thing of the fall fever—it is possible it may be so but as it has pleas'd kind providence to restore her, I intend at a sutable oppertunity to tell the Doctor my opinion of the matter, and I have no doubt of his candour on the occasion,—I suspected it while nurseing her by many of the symptoms, and finding many others in Dr. R.s book, seems a confirmation.

25. Such a Christmass day is but seldom known, 'Tho I wont attempt to say, I n'er saw such a one—a green christmass it is, but I trust it does not follow that we shall have *fatt Church Yards*.[108] It may please kind providence to give us frost enough yet, to sweeten and clear the air, which cannot be said to be otherwise at present, from appearances, which are often falacious, we may have a moderate winter. HD. and daughter Skyrin, set off about 9 o'clock in the Chaise for Clearfield, Sally Downing her two daughters, and Maid Anne, WD. with them, follow'd.—Deborah Derby and her Companion Rebecca Young, are to be this forenoon at Germantown meeting. little Elizah Skyrin, and S Swett spent the day here,—Our family return'd home a short time after sunset, Sally, Nancy, S Swett took tea with us, in back parlor, E Emlen and the two Saltars with Molly, in the front, S Emlen junr. here in the evening a Hazy night, very temperate. HD. daughter Ann, HSD. and Wife went forenoon to Germantown Meeting—Sally, her Children, stay'd at Clearfield,

106. The word "many" crossed out.

107. Benjamin Rush, *An Account of the Bilious Remitting Yellow Fever, as it Appeared in the City of Philadelphia, in the Year 1793*, vol. 3 of *Inquiries and Observations*, 2d ed. (Philadelphia: Thomas Dobson, 1794 [*Brit. Mus. Cat.*]).

108. An English proverb dating back to the seventeenth century held that a green Christmas leads to a fat churchyard; i.e., a mild winter leads to high mortality (W. G. Smith, *English Proverbs*, 337).

Jacob and John went up to dinner with them—some of us up 'till midnight, as James was busy in the Washhouse cutting up 6 Hoggs.

26. rain last night, clear this morning. very moderate, almost warm, 'tho the wind is at N.W. Henry and Hannah came to town, they, William, and Molly din'd at Jac. Downings, My husband and self, din'd by ourselves, which I do not recolect occuring before—Sister busy—James Yard &c call'd. Polly Wiggins brought Nancy Walns, I mean Morgans, little fatt daughter Becky, to see me, or rather for me to see, a fine baby. yesterday a troop of the Jersey Horse, came to town, having in custody twenty prisoners arrested in the Western counties of this state, charg'd with treasonable practices against the constitution and laws of the united states. The prisoners were put into the jail of this City.—I have been for some weeks past busy every night bathing my little maid Sally Dawsons, face for a swelling, and dressing her knee for a sore, I have had much to do for the little black boys also, those small foulk ought to be of service when they grow bigger, for they are very troublesome when young, to those who have their good at heart. Henry and Hannah went homeward between 4 and 5.—Robert Stevensons black girl Jenny, came to let us know that Hannah Smith,[109] lately Stevenson, was in town,—John Drinker, Molly Lipencot, call'd—Setting in back parlor reading near 8 o'clock, we were alarm'd by the noise of a fire Engine, and ringing of Bells, but had not heard the cry of fier, our house being deep, and Entry long—upon going out at the back door, saw a great fier at some distance, HD. went out, and on his return, inform'd us, that it was the unfinish'd steeple of the German Church in fourth street, where the Vestry were us'd to meet,—Our maid Polly, gone out to night, to set up with Benn. Catherals neice who is ill. between nine and ten, when we thought the fire was extinguish'd, heard the bells ringing again and soon discover'd the fire had got a head, I am apprehensive, by the appearance, that that great and superb building, the new German Lutheran Church, call'd Sion Church,[110] will be entirely consum'd, in which is an Organ, that cost the society 3500 pounds.—I never saw so much of a fier before, never having been out of the house to see one, and so favour'd, as never to be very near a house on fier.—the sparks came over our house, and fell on the pavement, before our door. some 'tis said fell in the river, and many fleaks fell on our grass plott, Isc. Wharton came in, he thought it was necessary to examine our Stables, as the Neighbours over the street, were watering the tops of their houses—I have little doubt, but that the light will shine in the chamber windows at Clearfield, Henry will be uneasy 'till he knows where it is,—'tis now near 11 o'clock. My Husband, who was in bed arose, and is now

109. The word "formerly" crossed out.

110. The Zion Lutheran Church, located on the southeast corner of Fourth and Cherry streets, burned to the ground. The fire started in a box in the vestry room in which hot ashes had been placed (John T. Faris, *Old Churches and Meeting-Houses In and Around Philadelphia* [Philadelphia: Lippincott, 1926], 142–43).

out with Isaac Wharton,—William was so imprudent, as to go as far as fourth and Arch Streets corner, he did not stay long, but the night air was hazardous, he saw the fire bursting out of the lower windows of the Church,—we had a full view of it, out of our long room up three pair stairs, could see the mighty blaze, and were senciable when the roof full in.

Decembr 27. fine moderate weather.—My Sister and self, did not retire to our Chambers 'till between one and two this morning it was near one, when James came from the fier, when I went to bed, it appear'd to burn with a degree of fierceness, could see the light and smoke from the window, and this morning I pick'd up in our yard, a number of peices of burnt shingles, some as big as my hand, the wind was S.W. and little or none, had it been high, the Houses to leeward would have stood but a poor chance. This Church is said to be one of the most splendid in the Union, and suppos'd to be worth 1500 pounds—Sally Downing, the two Saltars, Sally Smith and Sally Large call'd—Sally Johnson came again, to urge our takeing S.B. home, we have not yet come to a conclusion how to do in that matter, 'tho my oppinon is that she would be better here than any where else—John Watson junr. came after dinner, he lodges here, George Fox, and [S.] Fisher call'd this evening cooler then for some time past.

Decemr. 28. first Day: the last in the year.—John Watson left us, after breakfast. S Swett din'd with us—Sally Rhods spent an hour in Afternoon meeting time. M. Jones, daughter of Thos. Wharton deceased was buryed this Afternoon, Sally Downing and her Children and S Swett at tea.—Sarah Goodman alias McElroy was bury'd last week at Bristol Bucks county, she married at 69 years of age, a yound Man of 23.

29. After dinner, yesterday, MD. went to J Smiths, she and several other Lasses, and Lads, went to Clearfield, where they took tea, and stay'd 'till after night, moonshine. I like not those excursions on first days, or being out of town after night.—she informs me that her brother was absent, having left home after an early dinner for his Farm. Betsy Fordham came this morning, to sew for me. I took a walk this forenoon to visit my old friends Beulah Burge and Hannah Shoemaker, at their present dwelling in Arch street above fifth street,—came home to dinner, I have not takeing such a walk in the City for a long time past. William walk'd out also,—Jacob and Sally Downing, Molly Drinker and several others, din'd to day at John Skyrins, Sallys maid Caty Deacon, came from Burlington while they were out, she din'd with the Children here, then took them home, Thomas Stewardson took tea hear, I spent an hour this evening at Isaac Whartons—Sammy Rhodds here this evening.

30. John Mears here this morning I intended to have gone out with HP. but

am prevented by rain. Wind N.E. all day, Neighr. Waln spent the Afternoon, Molly Lippencott and Walter Bowne here this evening.

31. Another year past over, and our family mercifully keep't togeather—How many calamities have we escaped? and how much to be thankful for;—

Within the space of one short year,
How many changes do appear,
Things oft occur, that's least expected,
And what's most dreaded, oft's averted,
That power which life and health imparts,
Should be adored with thankful hearts
And wills resigned.—

Of the many favours and blessings, bestow'd on us in this life, the greatest, and from which flows the most comfort, Joy, and consolation, is risignation to the divine will—'Tho tis hard, very hard, in many cases to effect, yet, I firmly beleive it atainable, and what I think conduces most to this desirable state is a steady dependence & confidence in the Almighty. Samuel Emlen breakfasted and call'd in the Afternoon—one Devenport who lately run off with, and married a daughter of Thos. Brantenham, a friend in New York, call'd here on business,—Molly Drinker, Sally Smith and John Smith went to Clearfield, they dined there, Henry and Hannah came back with them, they spent the evening at Edwd. Shoemakers, with near 30 young people—'tis not the way I could wish my Children to conclude the year, in parties—but 'we cant put old heads on young shoulders'—Jacob and Sally Downing sup'd with us—Molly came home a little after ten, Henry and Hannah lodges at her Fathers.—Our maid Polly Betton in bed all day, came down in the evening better. There is very little alteration in the disorder in HD.s Eye, if any, 'tis, I think, for the better—he is troubled with a suppression of urine at times, and his old complaint, a riseing of phlegm sometimes in bed—he is otherwise well, and appears to be in good health.—MS. favour'd to be, almost in prime health—Myself, thro' Mercy, rather better for five or six weeks past, than for a long time before, WD. appears stationary, 'tho I hope upon the whole he is better,—HSD. is in good health and I trust a happy husband—MD. bravely. S Downg. all things consider'd, in good Spirits and hearty—Nancy, 'tho low in flesh, and looks pale, says she is bravely—the rest of the family Jacob, John, and the dear little ones, much as usual.[111]

111. On the outside back cover of the manuscript volume are the following notations:

$5 \overline{\smash{)}450}$

90

Occurances at Clearfield &c.

On the inside back cover are a few random jottings.

1795

January the first, one thousand seven hundred and ninety five,[1]
How many hundred's in their grave, that, this day twelve month were alive,
And what numbers now are living, of comely form, and good address,
Who 'err another year'l' be settled, in the land of fixedness.

Cloudy, wind at N.E. Henry and Hannah were here this forenoon, they din'd at JSs James drove them home after dinner, Jenny Stevenson and her Sister Hannah Smith were here this morning Sally Downing spent the Afternoon, she, Nancy Skyrin and J Logan drank tea. Jab. Downing, John Skyrin and Ben Wilson here this evening.

2d. Snow in the Night, wind N.E. in the morning N.W. this evening fine clear moon light. I spent this day at my Daughters Sallys, 'tis I beleive upwards of two years since I have so done, My Husband and Ben. Wilson din'd there also. Jacob and Sally came home with me near 10 o'clock. Sammy Fisher at our house his wife brought to bed the day before yesterday of her third Son. Nancy and Molly spent this Afternoon at Ebenr. Large's.

3d. A most beautiful winter day: HSD. came to town on horse back, he din'd with us, went home before dark. Saml. Emlen call'd, Elizah. Skyrin din'd here—Sally Downing call'd, William walk'd out twice to day—Huldah Mott and Betsy Emlen here this evening, HMs niece, Anna Wilson, was married on new-years day, to Ray King.—Sister out this Afternoon.

4. First Day: Snow in the night, sleet this Morning. William and self employ'd as usual, HD. MS. gone to meeting—clear'd up moderate wind at S.W.—I took cold the day I spent at Jacobs, have not been quite so well since, din'd without company, we miss our Son Henry at meal times, and in an evening more than at other times,—No person, our family excepted, has been here this day that I recolect, which is rather an uncommon circumstance.

Janry. 5. E. Skyrin two years old this day. Sally Zane came in her sisters Carriage for me, to spend the day with them. I went with her, and afterwards rode with HP. several times to the middle ferry. mett a number of Carriages

1. The manuscript volume for 1795 has brown paper covers. The outside front cover reads, "1795."

doing the like, that road being remarkably good, and the day very fine, when we came back to H. Pembertons found WD. there, he, HP. SZ. John Wilson and E.D. din'd there. several persons call'd. Js. Cresson spent part of the evening with HP. and E.D.—W.D. left us at four o'clock—I came home about nine, J. Wilson waited on me, a fine full moon light night.—Sally and Nancy spent this Afternoon at Pattison Hartshorn's. Molly at S. Emlens.—I heard this evening of the deaths of two of Molly Paynes sons, Temple and Isaac, the latter offended a man in Virginia, who some time afterward shot him with a pistol, of which wound he dyed.—Betsy Jervis and Benn. Swett took tea here while I was out. Daniel Drinker, Sally Downing, John and Nancy Skyrin here this evening.

6. HD. MS. MD. at meeting this forenoon—Saml. Parker brass founder, and Sally Howel, were married at meeting, he is so deaf, that he uses a machine, call'd by some a Trumpet, when any one preaches, but to day he omitted it—James Smith call'd in meeting time, S Swett and HSD. din'd here, Henry came to town about 11 o'clock, went homeward about dusk. SS. and Thos. Stewardson took tea with us. [little] E Skyrin here this Afternoon, her mother call'd, she and Molly, with Betsy Emlen, Saltars girls &c. at S. Downings this Afternoon—A Cozen of our James Duning, whom he has not seen for 15 years, lodg'd here with him to night. I made a memorandum some time ago of Amsterdam being taken [by the french, which prov'd premature, 'tis now confidently reported.][2]

Janry. 7. heavy rain in the night, and this morning cloudy the rest of the day, after five days absence, Betsy Fordham came again to work. J Logan, Jacob Downing call'd. Nancy Skyrin, Betsy Emlen and the two Saltars, took tea here, Molly had been out riding with the three latter. John Skyrin and S. Emlen junr. call'd.—Edith Draper, formerly Gardner, Sister to our Sally Gardner, a girl who liv'd with us four years, she came to us a few weeks before Billy was born, was never bound to us, Edith came to Sister for part of John Joness legacy—which is the annual rent of a house in this City, it is[3] given every winter in small sums to such as are thought to stand in most need of it,

2. The French government had declared war on the Dutch Republic in February 1793, but did not invade Dutch territory until the winter of 1794–95. Though Amsterdam had not yet capitulated to French troops, city magistrates, following the fall of Utrecht on Jan. 17, would surrender on Jan. 18 to Dutch revolutionary leaders, who supported the French, and French troops would enter the city on Jan. 19. An accurate report of the French entry would not reach Philadelphia until Apr. 1 (Scott and Rothaus, *French Revolution*, s.v. "Batavian Republic"; Simon Schama, *Patriots and Liberators: Revolution in the Netherlands*, 1780–1813 [New York: Knopf, 1977], 189–91; *Philadelphia Gazette and Universal Daily Advertiser*, Apr. 1, 1795).

3. The word "deliverd" crossed out.

and is of great service to many.[4]—James took up in the Chaise to Clearfield after dinner, one Molly Evans, an english girl, who came over with Tommy Cliffords family, she is hired for Henry and Hannah.

8. Clear and cold: I was up this morning before day, being unwell, observ'd a burr round the Moon, the wind being easterly, it looks likely we shall have change of weather, William Brown from Mifflin county, John Cannon and James Harris took tea. Sally Downing John and Nancy Skyrin and Child, Peggy and Hannah Saltar Ben Wilson &c call'd. Sally and Nancy spent the Afternoon at Tomy. Morgans, Molly at Jos. Whartons, a Cry of fier about 7 o'clock this evening we were inform'd that a window curtain had caught fire, some said it was a Chimney, it was soon out—One Crook from Stockport din'd hear early.

9. cloudy all day. 39. years since the loss of my dearest and nearest female friend, and the same day of the week—I spent this Afternoon with Neigr. Waln, have not paid her a visit for a long time past—HD. took tea there with us—Jon. Connor and J[n]. Cadwalader here this evening Henry Silverthorn din'd here early.

Jany. 10. rain in the night, cloudy morning clear'd up afternoon, wind N.W. more like winter to night than it has been this year before, HSD. came to town forenoon, Docr. Redman paid us a visit at noon.—Judge Brown, Judge Cannon, Lawyer Cadwalader, James Harris Esqr. Survayor and HSD. din'd with us—Saml. Walace, William Ellis, Thos. Stewardson and A. Skyrin took tea here.

11. First Day: A fine winter Morning calls for thanks—Isaac Parish call'd to desire my Husband to invite to the burial of Daniel Tyson. HD. MS. MD. went to meeting—Henry Shotwell from Rahway, din'd here. we heard some time ago, of the death of Baltas Vanclick, an apprentice of Henry Haydock of New York—he liv'd in his house when I was there attending on my Son, he set up with William before I arrived there, had the appearance of a healthy blooming young Man,—Joseph Merrifield drank tea and spent the evening he

4. No legacy from a John Jones to the Society of Friends has been uncovered. When one John James, a carpenter, died in 1791, however, he left a bequest of fifty pounds "To Joseph Russel, John Drinker & Henry Drinker" to be "placed out on Interest or invested in the Purchase of a Rent Charge and the Interest or Rents accruing to be applied Yearly to the Use of the poor of the Society of People call'd Quakers in Philadelphia & to be under the discretion of their Monthly Meetings." This is not the only time that ED appears to have confused the names Jones and James: in addition to other references to this legacy, see her comment about the use of "Joness" powders on Mar. 25, 1798 (will of John James, signed June 23, 1791, and proved July 6, 1791, Register of Wills, City Hall, Philadelphia; Misc. Papers, Philadelphia Northern District Monthly Meeting, microfilm, Friends Historical Library, Swarthmore College).

and Thos. Stewardson sup'd—This day has been rather tedious and painful to me, being unwell, and confin'd, without anything to do, but sat with Company.

12. Snow last night, sharp this morning wind North West, 'tho not as cold as may be, Henry came to town forenoon, he and John Tateam din'd with us—J Logan and Jams. Wilson Esqr. call'd—Rich'd Thomas and John Gilbert took tea with us, the latter, a young Man from Great Britain a Taylor by trade, came over with Saml. Emlen—Henry left us before tea—Willm. Simpson, Saml. Emlen and Elijah Waring call'd.

13. This day of the month, and of the week also, I well remember, it being one of the coldest days I ever felt, 34 years ago, Saml. Emlen often recollects the coldness of our wedding day—colder to day, than yesterday, snow forenoon,—Josa. Pusey and Jo[sh.] Hampton, breakfasted here, MS. MD. at meeting, HD. on a Committee revising the dissipline.[5]—Huldah Mott, Betsy Emlen, Peggy Saltar, Sally Rhoads call'd after meeting. Joseph Trimble and Jos Sharpless din'd here, HSD. came to town forenoon, went out after dinner.—William Richardson, Ezra Comfort and Josh. Merrifield took tea with us—a number of friends from the Country, now in the City,—John Watson junr. call'd.

14. We removed this morning into our front parlor, as the back is more expos'd to the North west wind, and otherwise not so warm a room, in the depth of winter the Sun is excluded by neighbouring back buildings—the front more lively.—Saml. Wallace breakfasted here. George Williams near Abbenton and John Bunting din'd with us. Sally Large, Sally Smith, Sally Downg. Nancy Skyrin and Child, and J. Wilson Esqr. call'd—MS. gone out this afternoon, Molly spent it at S. Emlens.

15. rain in the night, and this morning pavements very slippery—Cadr. Evans. Thos. Clifford call'd. We had 7. Men unexpectedly to dine with us—Abraham Gibbons, William Richardson, John Smith, Samuel Canby, Nathan Coope, John Stabler and Samuel Collins—they went to meet the Committe at two o'clock—Snow this Afternoon and evening Sammy Rhoads and Joseph Merrifield spent the evening.

16. A very fine day, snow six inches deep or more. Sleighs flying too and fro,

5. In September 1794 the Philadelphia Yearly Meeting, at the request of the Meeting for Sufferings, of which HD was a member, had appointed a committee to revise the Quaker discipline. In September 1795 the committee would recommend printing a digest of the new rules, which would eventually be published in 1797 (see above, Sept. 25, 1759; Philadelphia Yearly Meeting, Men's Minutes, 1780–98, microfilm, Friends Historical Library, Swarthmore College, 296, 318).

Henry and Hannah came to town in their Chaise, intend staying 'till tomorrow, Hannah din'd with us, Molly went this Afternoon Sleighing, with Sally Smith, Sally Large, George Benson, John Morton, and Thomas Tylee. The Sun shines most of the forenoon in our front Rooms, which renders them much more pleasent and lively then the back of the house—Reba. Jones took tea, George Robarts and George Fox call'd this evening—Joseph Sansom and Jonathan Paxon also. This forenoon at about 11 o'clock a fier broke out in a wooding building in Eighth street, and partly consum'd it, the paper-hanging business was carried on there, we heard nothing of it 'till it was over.

17. A very fine winter day: several here this forenoon A Skyrin call'd, Joseph Bringhurst din'd with us—James Logan, Roger Hunt from New York, Hannah S Drinker, took tea with us, Nancy Skyrin left her Child and maid here, she went to J Frys—Saml. Emlen call'd, John Morton junr. Thos. Tylee, and George Benson, the two latter are young men from England, call'd on Molly this morning John and Nancy here in the evening they, the Child, and Sam went away at nine.

18. First day: exceedingly cold, HD. HSD. and Molly went to meeting, MS. stay'd at home, it being slippery—Joseph Merrifield and HSD. din'd with us—Henry and Hannah went home after dinner in our Sleigh, left their Chair here—Jacob Downing and Sally Smith went with them, they found the Snow so gone, that Jacob and S. Smith return'd from Clearfield in Jacobs Carriage, which has been left there, since our new one has been in use. Jacob, Sally and their two Children, John, Nancy, and their little one, Betsy Emlen, the two Saltars and Samy. Rhoads, Billy Mott, George Benson, Tomy. Tylee, and Sammy Emlen junr.—here this Afternoon or evening—our dear William has brought up blood with the phlegm owen to the severe cold weather.

Janry. 19. very cold. Jacob Downing, Docr. Redman &c here this forenoon, Hannah Catheral din'd with us, Saml. Emlen, William Ashby, John Gilbart, Docr. Rush, John Drinker and Joseph Bringhurst call'd, Jacob Downg. came home with Molly this evening—I read to day a satyrical pamphlet, intitled, a Bone to Gnaw, for the Democrates, by, I know not whom.[6]

20. Jos Sansom call'd—HD. MS. MD. at preparative meeting—Saml. Emlen, Sally Rhoads, Molly Smith call'd after meeting—The river has been fast, three or four mornings, but gave way in the course of the day—HSD. walk'd to town this fournoon,—James gone up to leave Jacobs Carriage at Clearfield, as there is no room in our Coach-house—Henry left us before five in his Chaise—

6. Peter Porcupine [William Cobbett], *A Bone to Gnaw for the Democrats; or, Observations on a Pamphlet, Entitled, "The Political Progress of Britain"* (Philadelphia: Thomas Bradford, 1795 [*NUC*]).

J. Downing call'd, Neighbour Waln spent the evening—John Watson junr. here this evening we purchas'd some marketing of him,—Our Maid Polly Bitton, left us this evening as she sets off early tomorrow morning for her fathers in Bucks county, she has a weakness in her right wrist, which requires rest, and attention—MD. spent the Afternoon at S. Emlens.

21st. John Watson junr. breakfasted here, Henry came to town after breakfast, understanding that his father in Law James Smith and Jacob Downing were going to dine with him at Clearfield, he return'd home—Caty Dennis here to day makeing a collico gown for Molly, J Logan call'd—Peggy and Hannah Saltar, Maria Saltar and Molly Clarkson, call'd on Molly this fore noon—I made an assent before dinner into our Cock loft, to take a view of the river, which is broken up, before the City, large cakes of ice floating, Boys were yesterday Skaiting on them, to day the weather is much moderated—Sally Downing din'd with us, she and her Aunt, set off after dinner for Clearfield, intending to bring S.B—home with them—Nurse Waters call'd. M.D. went out with E. Emlen &c in their Carriage. Sister, and Sally return'd before tea, Sall with 'em. Benjn. Swett, T. Stewardson, and Sally Downing took tea here, Jacob &c stay'd tea at Clearfield, they brought Samuel Preston to town with them, he had spent the day at Henrys—I read this day, a sermon, preach'd last July, at the Opening of the African Church by Samuel Magaw DD.[7] this church is in fifth street, between walnut and spruce streets built within these two years—Richd. Smith junr. and Sally Smith came here this evening to consert measures with MD. to go tomorrow to visit Hannah.

22. weather very moderate, cloudy most of the Day. Jos. Sansom and John James call'd—Molly went after dinner, with Sally Smith and Sally Large, in Js. Smiths Carriage;—Betsy Emlen and the two Saltars with T. Tylee in S. Emlen's, to Clearfield, MD. is to stay there 'till her Brother returns from his farm, for which I expect he set off this morning. Saml. Preston took tea, spent the evening and sup'd with us. Betty Newton here, fitted a gown on me—H. Pemberton sent Noke, this forenoon to know if I would take a ride with her, I could not go, William not so well yesterday, and to day, as usual.

Janry. 23. Cloudy and moderate, George Churchman, Jos. Sansom call'd.—Saml. Preston din'd and spent most of the Afternoon—Sister din'd at Jacob Downings and waited on Docr. Shippen on SDs account—William Savery call'd after dinner—John Cannon took tea here—Joseph Bringhurst in the evening snow fore part of this evening turn'd to rain, wind high at N.E. Henry

7. Samuel Magaw, *A Discourse Delivered July 17th, 1794, in the African Church of the City of Philadelphia, on the Occasion of Opening the Said Church, and Holding Public Worship in It the First Time* (Philadelphia, 1794). The full name of the church was the African Episcopal Church of St. Thomas. Samuel Magaw was the rector of St. Paul's Church (Nash, *Forging Freedom*, 127–29).

and Molly both from home,—between 8 and 9 a great cry of fier in our Neighbourhood, some run up town, others down, we could not discovery where it was, or whether any where.—HD. out this morning with W Savery and Jos Sansom, raising supscriptions for boarding School.

24. Northeast Storm in the night and all this day.—I was surpris'd to see John Courtney came to town, was fearful Hannah or Molly was ill, but when I found he had brought the Cart for some things that they wanted, but could have done without, I concluded they had thoughtlessly sent him or that he had business of his own to transact, had Henry been at home I beleive we should not have seen John to day.—S. Preston din'd with us—Joseph Bringhurst and John Drinker here after dinner, William but poorly, owening in measure to confindment and unfavourable weather—I should have been much vext and unhappy yesterday and today, had I given way to it, but find it best for me, to bare and forbare.

25. First day: began to snow in the night, has continu'd all day, is now prehaps 12 or 14 inches deep, none of our family at meeting but HD.—Jacob Downing call'd—Saml. Preston sup'd, continu'd snowing in the evening slippery—Rumford Daw's wife fell down coming out of evening meeting, and hurt her foot badly, HD. and others with some difficulty help'd her home.

26. A most beautifull day. temperate, clear sky.—upwards of forty Sleighs past our door, between breakfast and dinner. Tommy Morris came this morning for an order to bury his Cousin Cadr. Morris—S. Preston paid us three visits this day, Jacob Downing, Josey Sansom, John Drinker and Wm. Savery call'd—Hannah Yerkes drank tea with us—Molly Drinker came home this Afternoon in a Sleigh with Hetty Smith and two of her Children. Henry arriv'd at Clearfield on seventh day last in the storm, so wett he was oblig'd to change his cloaths, a common case with him, he had, in my oppinion, better stay'd at North Bank 'till fairer weather.

27. Clear and Moderate, HD. MS. MD. at monthly meeting. Sally Rhoads call'd and went with Sister, Reba. Griscomb[8] said to have been very trouble-

8. A Rebecca Griscom (1747–98), daughter of Samuel and Rebecca (James) Griscom, was disowned by the Philadelphia Northern District Monthly Meeting in 1785 for drinking strong liquors to excess. ED probably refers here to her first cousin, also named Rebecca Griscom (1745–1807), a mantua maker in Philadelphia in the 1780s and early 1790s who in 1794 requested permission to move to the Quaker almshouse. In 1795 the monthly meeting began proceedings against her for her disorderly conduct in meetings, which included using reviling language and calumny about other Friends, interrupting ministers at meeting, sitting at time of prayer when others were standing, making indecent and offensive noises during meeting, and in general having an evil demeanor. She was also accused of "neglecting the proper means of procuring a livelihood." Griscom, after "being long and tenderly treated with," was disowned on Nov. 24 (see below, Sept. 22; William Timmins and Robert Yarrington, *Betsy*

some there—S. Preston call'd, Saml. Wallace din'd with us—Richd. Smith, Sammy Rhoads, and Walter Franklin call'd before[9] meeting—I suspect Molly is gone out this afternoon with company in Sleighs—Henry came to town before dinner, Hannah has hurt herself by lifting a heavy table, I hope not essentially; I sent a note to Hy. Smith, Henry left us before dark—two Menists with long beards here this evening Johnny Smith, Benjn. Tucker schoolmaster &c. call'd.

28. Clear and moderate. WDs birthday and the same day of the week, The Anniversary of the death of my dear mother, Our marriage, and Williams birth, have fallen out this year, on the same day of the week that they happen'd, which generaly occurs once in seven years, 'tho not invariably so. Dr. Kuhn call'd this morning HD and James Logan went before dinner in our Sleigh for Clearfield—I believe this day will finish that business as it thaws fast, and the Snow is almost gone, they din'd there, and did not return 'till towards evening Hetty Smith and George Benson with them, Hannah continues poorly, talks of being let blood tomorrow, and of coming to town next day. Sally Downing and her two little girls spent this Afternoon with us. E. Skyrin also here—Jacob and Sally sup'd with us—John M[usser], Jos. Sansom, Saml. Wallace Neigr. Waln &c call'd—Betsy Emlen and the Saltars call'd on Molly to take a ride with them, Nancy Skyrin poorly malade au stomac,—Our SBs mother call'd at the door on horse back, to know if she was yet return'd home.

29. This has been a *proper* Stormy day, wind at S.E., The word proper has been much in vogue, and very improperly us'd for a few years past, in the country, and in most kitchens in the City, is has crep't also into the houses among the Children, Some say, I am proper sick, others have purchas'd something that was proper dear &c—Jacob Downing call'd, No News to day from Clearfield.

30. After a Stormy day and night, it continues this morning the same, wind variable, clear'd up this evening temperate, a beautiful serene evening, I expected it would have been very cold—James Logan, Peggy and Hannah Saltar here forenoon, Sally Zane here after dinner, John Parish, James Harris took tea—I sent our James after dinner, with a note to Clearfield, to enquire

---

Ross: The Griscom Legacy [Salem County, N.J.: The Salem County, N.J., Cultural and Heritage Commission through the auspices of The Salem County Board of Chosen Freeholders, 1983], 73–79, 112, 114, 117, 232; *Philadelphia City Directory, 1791;* Philadelphia Northern District Women's Monthly Meeting Minutes, 1779–86, microfilm, Friends Historical Library, Swarthmore College, 193, 201, 203, 209, 212, 219–20; Philadelphia Northern District Women's Monthly Meeting Minutes, 1791–1796, microfilm, Friends Historical Library, Swarthmore College, 155, 235–36, 243, 249).

9. The word "dinner" crossed out.

how Hannah was, he brought back a letter from Henry informing that she was yesterday let blood by Justus Fox, was near fainting after the opperation, that the pain she complain'd of was rather increas'd then lessen'd, he wishes that she may come to town tomorrow, if well enough, I sent the letter to Hetty Smith—Molly gone this Afternoon to visit Nancy, she has been very unwell with disorder'd bowels a perfect bloody flux, she is now better, we did not hear 'till to day, how poorly she had been.

Janry. 31

More then one twelfth of the new year already gone and past,
The other eleven certainly will fly away as fast,
Then let us daily keep in mind, what we at School were taught,
That every moment of our time, is still with mercy fraught.

'Every moment of time, is a monument of mercy' was a copy, we used to write at A. Benezets School—A fine temperate morning quarterly meeting.—James was preparing to go to Clearfield for Henry and Hannah, he left the Horses ready put too, under the care of one in the Alley, by some means they took fright, and run off with the Carriage, over turn'd a Cart and Horse in second street near the market, which brought them up, the Carriage much damag'd, 'tho the injury it may be to the Horses, which have been a very fine pair, is of more consequence,—'tis a favour no one was hurt, Jemmy Smith went up for our Children, they return'd after dinner, Hannah better—Anna Shoemaker and Sally Smith call'd this forenoon, Saml. Emlen, Benn. Wilson, and HSD. took tea with us.—We were invited to day, that is HD. and self, by a Wedding ticket, to dine next fourth day with Abigail Drinker and Peter Barker; on which day their marriage is to be solemniz'd at the pine street meeting-House—Molly spent this Afternoon and evening at J. Smiths—Sammy Fisher here this evening.

Febry. 1. First day: A sweet day it may be call'd, clear and cool, HD. MS. MD. at meeting—T. Stewardson, Henry and Hannah Drinker, Peggy and Hannah Saltar din'd with us, Jacob Downing, S Emlen junr. and Betsy call'd, A meeting appointed this evening by Deborah Derby and Reba. Young, to be held at the North Meeting House, for people of other religious Societies—Arthur Howel call'd, he went to it with HD. I expect it will be very crouded, by the numbers that have past our door—Robt. Stevenson junr. call'd he expected to have mett his Aunt and Sister here, supposing they were at this evening meeting—S. Preston who has been to visit his friends in bucks county, return'd to day, and sup'd here.

2d. Jacob Downing and Saml. Emlen call'd before meeting, the quarterly meeting is held up town—S. Emlen had a letter from London, giving an account of the death of William Logan, grand Nephew to our James Logan.

William Newbold breakfasted here, HSD. call'd, HD. MS. MD. gone to meeting. Sally Downing spent an hour in meeting time, John Courtney call'd he is going home, has been two or three days in town under the Doctors care for his eyes—the 2 Saltars call'd—Meeting held 'till between 2 and 3 o'clock, Deborah Darby, Rebecca Young, Ruth Ann Rutter, H. Cathral and R Jones, Daniel Drinker and Saml. Emlen din'd with us, in back parlor, after dinner we had a meeting in the front, when DD. RY. SE. RJ. and HC. had each something to offer to us, not in the terrific and threatning order, but rather the reverse[10]—Saml. Smith, Polly Pleasants and Sally Rhoads, came in during the setting.—the friends left us between 5 and six, and went down to Leonard Snowdens. HD. went there with the Carriage to wait on Deborah and Rebecca to their lodgings, which is at Samuel R. Fishers—M. Pleasants and Sally Rhoads took tea with us, and spent part of the evening—John Drinker and Joseph Sansom call'd—cloudy, moderate for the Season.

Febry. 3. rain this morning, Youths Meeting—Molly did not go, Henry came this forenoon, informs that his Hannah was yesterday let blood, twelve ounces taken, and was order'd to Bed, by Docr. Kuhn, where he wishes her to continue for a week or more, being apprehensive of something of a rupture takeing place, as ever since she strain'd her side by lifting the table, she has had a pain and swelling in the part, and felt at the time as if something had giving way, she is in good spirits, not knowing what is fear'd on her account—Henry has been here three times this day, he feels much for his patient innocent girl,—Sam Preston din'd here. Sally Downing and Jos. Sansom drank tea, Jacob, Sally, and Ben Wilson sup'd. William Savery call'd—Sammy Rhoads spent part of the evening—We heard to day of the death of Jonathan Evans Senr. said to be in his 81st. year, When my sister and self were Children we call'd him and Wife, Uncle and Aunt Evans, she being Sister to our Uncle Jervis's wife—There is a french man some where in our Neighbourhood, that serenades us frequently in an evening by a hand Organ, 'tho for a very short time—I beleive it is a very good instrument, and he a good hand on it, as it is very Agreeable, and I will own, that I am fond of hearing what is call'd good musick.—the Moon eclipsed 7½ digits this evening.

Febry. 4: HD. gone to the marriage of his niece Abby Drinker, it is to be a small Wedding, Uncles and Aunts and a few other friends only, invited—I us'd

10. Rebecca Jones, a noted minister and teacher who belonged to Philadelphia's Northern District Monthly Meeting, had decided in the beginning of 1795 to pay religious visits to families in the meeting. She was joined by Deborah Darby and Rebecca Young, who were visiting families affiliated with the Pine Street Meeting (Rebecca Jones to Esther Tuke, Jan. 25, 1795, and extract from the diary of Katherine Howell, in William J. Allinson, comp., *Memorials of Rebecca Jones* [Philadelphia: Henry Longstreth, (1849?); in History of Women series, New Haven, Conn.: Research Publications Inc., 1975], pp. 220, 222, microfilm reel 213, no. 1412).

some exertion to attend my Sons, but find it does not suit me at present to go out, and set a meeting—Sister gone this forenoon to visit Hannah, it is damp and cold, or I should not omitt going to see her myself—Henry here; says he thinks she is rather better—little Oliver Wadsworth here on a errand from Nancy Skyrin—Betsy Emlen and the Saltars call'd—Jessy Hollandsworth also, he has lost by two great fires, 'tis said near 10,000-pounds, he appears to bare the loss, like a wise man, and a good Christian—little E. Skyrin spent this day with us—sister gone this Afternoon to the funeral of Jonathan Evans, Sally Downg. call'd—HSD. sett off after dinner on foot for Clearfield, the Air sharp, and cold, he intends staying there all night.—Esther Lewis, lately Fisher, is this day number'd with the dead:—how frequently are those hints revived? the death of acquaintances and coevals.—Sally and Molly &c. gone this Afternoon, to visit Anna Wells, John Cannon and Sam. Preston took tea with us, Owen Biddle call'd—I feel anxiously concern'd for our dear Hannah, as Sister, who has been there this Afternoon, informs me, that Doctor Kuhn had this day, mentioned her complaint as something that might be of a lengthy nature, 'tho she may get better.

Feby. 5. cloudy. Our dear William spit blood to day he talks of having a vain open'd—Saml. Emlen, and Billy Ellis here, Polly Stevenson paid us a morning visit—the two Saltars call'd—HSD. came to town about 11 o'clock, I went with him to J Smiths,—found Hannah, as I expected, in Bed, in very good spirits, and hearty, her apprehension of ill, do not run high; she leaves it to others to think for her, or at least appears so to do—I stay'd upwards of an hour, when my daughter Nancy came there, with whom I went home and din'd—J Skyrin came home with me after[11] dinner, the air to day is what's call'd sour, I am so little accustom'd to go abroad that after I was home, I took a nap in my chair, Old woman like,—Sally and her Children here fore noon,—She, Molly, Huldah Mott, the Saltars &c spent the Afternoon and evening at John Skyrins. HSD. din'd and took tea here.

6. clear and fine, William unwell last evening of a griping up in the night, observed that[12] he had evacuated blood of a fluxey appearance, continues so this morning sent for Docr. Kuhn, he is out, not expected home 'till four this Afternoon,—We prepar'd mallow tea,[13] and Chicken broath,—HSD. and Peggy Saltar call'd, Nancy Skyrin unwell,—Saml. Emlen and Phineas Bond here forenoon, James Harris, Saml. Preston and HSD. din'd here—little E. Skyrin spent the day with us, she is a well behaved Child.—Sarah Fisher and John Adlum took tea—Tench Cox, James Fisher here in the evening—Thomas Stewardson also—Our dear William continues poorly, Dr. K. here in

11. The word "noon" crossed out.
12. The word "what" crossed out.
13. Actually, marshmallow tea. See below, June 5, 1799.

the Afternoon, order'd him 15 drops liquid Laudanum going to bed, and Castor Oyl tomorrow.—in this World we shall have trouble.

Febry. 7. clear morning cold and cloudy evening wind easterly. William took the Oyl, which has had the desir'd effect—and he seems better,—Dr. Kuhn, James Logan, Sally Hopkins, Saml. Emlen, Saml. Preston, here fore noon—HD. went Afternoon to the burial of Esther Lewis. James Harris, Saml. Preston, Sally Downing, John and Nancy Skyrin, HSD. and Eliza Downing, who spent the day with us, drank tea here, Jos. Sansom, William Savery, Saml. Fisher, Jacob Downing &c. call'd.—Molly spent the Afternoon and evening at James Smiths, Hannah, we hope, is better—Isaac Howel was here in the morning—HD. and self, acknowledg'd five deeds before him.

8th: First day: cloudy, temperately cold, wind N.E. HD. MS. HSD. and MD. at meeting. Susanna Swett din'd here—Dr. Kuhn call'd in meeting time, says WDs pulse are good—Molly Lipponcott, Sally Smith, Sally Large, Ben Wilson and George Benson call'd after meeting—several of them are going this afternoon, Molly with them, to Lippencots—S Swett drank tea—Peggy Wharton spent the evening.

9. Snow'd in the night, and all this morning very fast, left of about dinner time, and will quickly pass away, Saml. Preston spent the forenoon and din'd with us—HSD. also,—the latter went after dinner to Clearfield in a Sleigh, to enquire how his Man and Maid fair's in their absence—Saml. Emlen and T. Stewardson call'd—WD. still disorder'd in bowels—Henry was but about two hours absent, found all well and in good order—he, John Adlum, and Wm. Ellis, took tea with us. T. Stewardson spent the evening.

Febry. 10. Snow in the night, and all this morning—this has been a lengthy 'tho not a violent storm, wind NNW. HD. at the Adjournment of monthly meeting—HSD. and Saml. Preston din'd here—Molly gone to spend the evening with her Sister Sally—William better.—Saml. Emlen here twice to day, Neigr. Waln spent evening.

11. continues cloudy. Snow melted away, weather very moderate, Wind Northerly—We were particularly invited this morning, to the funeral of John Penn, formerly our Governor, grandson of William Penn, he dyed at Andrew Allens near the Neshaminy, and is to be buryed tomorrow morning from his late dwelling in pine-street—HSD. set off between 10 and eleving for North-Bank. William and Molly took a ride of about 4 miles this forenoon in J Downings Carriage—Elizath. Skyrin spends this day with us—William Ellis, Saml. Emlen call'd forenoon, HD. din'd at Hannah Pembertons—Molly spends this Afternoon and evening at J Smiths, cloudy. Benjn. Wilson drank with us.

12. A fine temperate morning wind N.W. Saml. Fisher breakfasted here. Billy and Molly call'd on Nancy to take a ride, Sally Downing spent the Morning my Husband went to the burial of John Penn, he was interred this forenoon inside Christs Church, so called,—Jemmy and Hetty Smith, Hannah S. Drinker, the first time of her being abroad since her indispossion, John Cannon and HSD. who came to town this Afternoon, took tea with us. William Savery, Isaac Coats and his brother, and Samuel Emlen were also here—Silence took place, and S. Emlen had something to communicate to both Old and Young, of the Company—JS. &c went away after night in their Carriage—Sally Rhoads and her Son spent the evening with us.

Febry. 13. a fine pleasent day, 'tho a little raw, wind N.W. Isaac Coats and Brother, William Savery, Ben Wilson, James Logan, Nancy Skyrin, Saml. Emlen Senr. and S Emlen junr., Saml. Preston and HSD. here this forenoon—Molly strain'd her ancle coming down stairs, not so bad as to hinder her from going with her brother William to call'd on their Sister Sally to take a ride, they return'd to dinner—E. Downing spent this day with us—Patrick Casody, John Drinker, call'd—Geog. Benson came in E Emlens name to ask Molly to visit tomorrow the two Saltars, who are at present at their Uncle John Saltars, at Magnolia-Grove, nine miles from the City.—read a pamphlet entitled Observations on the Emigration of Dr. J. Priestly &c[14] and finish'd reading, A Comparative View of the state and Faculties of Man with those of the Animal World. by John Gregory, M.D. F.R.S.[15] a sensible writer.—A meeting appointed by Deborah Darby and Rebecca Young, was held this evening, at the Pine street meeting house, for persons of different religious professions, and denominations.—Samy. Fisher here this evening.

14. A fine clear cold day. Wind N.W. Sam Emlen call'd, George Fry, our Gardner at Clearfield came to town, our good old mares leg not yet well he says,—Priscila Deavs came from H. Pemberton to ask me there.—G. Benson call'd—Jenny and Susan Stevenson paid a morning visit—intercepted a letter to day, from J.G. to our S.B.—, John Saltar din'd here, Molly went this Afternoon with Sally Smith, Betsy Emlen, G.Benson, R. Smith, and T. Tylee, to J. Saltars, they did not return 'till after nine at night, very dark, wrong doings, John Cannon and Sally Downing, took tea, J. Downg. W. Ellis and Sally Zane call'd, T Stewardson here this evening.

Febry. 15. First day. clear cold morning over cast about noon, as two or three days past, Wind N.N.W.—HD. Sister, HSD. MD. at meeting—Jacob

14. William Cobbett, *Observations on the Emigration of Dr. Joseph Priestley, and on the Several Addresses Delivered to him, on his Arrival at New-York* (London and Philadelphia, 1794 [Averley, *18th-Cen. Brit. Books;* Sabin, *Dictionary*]).

15. John Gregory, *A Comparative View of the State and Faculties of Man, with Those of the Animal Kingdom* (London, 1765, and subsequent editions [Averley, *18th-Cen. Brit. Books*]).

and Henry call'd—no one din'd with us—Joseph Drinker Senr. took tea—HD. went to tea at Sarah Fishers, with the Europeian woman friends &c—little Elizath. Skyrin paid us a visit this very cold day,—Molly went after the Afternoon meeting to Jacob Downings, where she expected to meet Henry and Hannah, who din'd there.—Saml. Preston here this evening Joshua Lippencot came home with Molly—this is thought to be the coldest night we have had this winter.

16. Clear and cold, wind N.W.—S. Preston, and Anna Wells here forenoon, Judge Cooper and Farmer Drinker, din'd with us, J Downing call'd, William Cooper comes down next Session as member of Congress from Ossego, he urges William to go next spring to Coopers-town, seems assur'd it will be of use to him—Saml. Preston Esqr. took tea here, Sister spent the evening at Neigr. Walns—William Simpson sup'd here—Joseph Kite invited yesterday to the burial of one Elliots wife, who was lately deliver'd of twins and died soon after, Sister desired him to miss Jacob Downings House, as our dear Sally reckons in about a month or 6 weeks, she is very lusty, and generally at that time of distress, is peculiarly tried, she has hitherto been favour'd with good Spirits, 'tho by no means void of apprehension—John Skyrin left the city this morning in the Stage for New-York, he will have a cold journey—HSD. has been busy writing in Counting room most of this day, Othnial in Jersyes.

Febry. 17. Snow in the night, and again this forenoon, wind S.W. HD. MS. gone to meeting, Saml. Preston and Saml. Bowne from New York, call'd in meeting time, S. Preston and HSD. din'd here. I have been pleas'd and entertain'd by the perusal of Doctor Rush's Medical Inquiries and Observations, in two Octavo Volumes,[16] which I finish'd this Afternoon, Sister gone to Sallys, Molly to Nancys—clear'd up about noon, Saml. Emlen and our Son Henry took tea with us, Oliver Paxon, William Savery and Ben Wilson here,—Willm. Cooper, Sammy Bowne and Jacob Downing here this evening—Deborah Derby, her Companion, and two or three other friends, held a meeting this forenoon in the Jail of this city, with, 'tis thought two hundred prisoners.

18. Clear and cold, wind N.W. HD. this morning on a Committee, Henry and Hannah and Sally Smith here forenoon, Hannah much better—Molly gone out with them, John and Ezra Comfort din'd with us, Sally Downing and her daughter Mary in the Afternoon—Henry and Hannah went home to Clearfield after dinner, they have been in town between two and three weeks—

16. Benjamin Rush's *Medical Inquiries and Observations* was a multivolume series that flourished through several editions. ED's two volumes could have included vol. 1 (Philadelphia: Prichard & Hall, 1789; 2d. ed. Philadelphia: Thomas Dobson, 1794), vol. 2 (Philadelphia: Thomas Dobson, 1793), or vol. 3, *An Account of the Bilious Remitting Yellow Fever . . . 1793* (Philadelphia: Thomas Dobson, 1794 [Evans, *Am. Bibliography;* Goodman, *Benjamin Rush,* 386]).

Sally, Nancy and William Cooper took tea with us—the two former spent the evening—Jacob Downing here.

19. Clear and cold wind N.W. Saml. Smith of Bucks county, came to Breakfast, he left his horse and went to meeting for Sufferings—This day is sett apart by the President, for prayer and thanksgiving for the blessing of peace &c &c.[17] 'Tho an Ordinance of Man, yet I beleive there are many pious persons who have past the day, measurably as they ought, or as they thought it their duty to do—many others, as is too common, on what they call Holy-days, spend it in dissipation;—I was pleas'd to see many of what is call'd the establish'd Church, and presbyterians, going in a solid manner to their respective places of worship—it had the appearance at least, of their unity with good government, and I hope more,—Sammy Bowne call'd this forenoon Patrick Casady also—Josiah Bunting din'd with us, Jacob Linley call'd—Molly Lippencott here after dinner—Molly Drinker gone this Afternoon with E.E. to visit Molly Field—Sally Johnson came this afternoon to see her Daughter Henry Clifton here this Afternoon—Richd. Thomas, Jacob and Sally Downing and the two Children went this Afternoon to Clearfield, came home after night—John Cannon, Wm. Newbold and brother here this evening.

20. a very fine clear temperate Morning, wind S.W. William Newbold breakfasted here, he is going to attend on Deborah Darby and her Companion to Burlington &c they do not expect to return here for some time, as they expect to visit a number of meetings in the Jerseys—William mett here Letitia Woodrow, sister to William Cooper, she is about binding her Son Benjn. a Child of 5 years of age to him—Isaac Potts call'd—William and Mary went out in the Carriage after eleven o'clock intending to call on Nancy, to take a ride, HD. at meeting revising the discipline—Warner Mifflin, Joshua Pusey, George Churchman and Joshua Sharpless din'd with us,—Saml. Smith of B. County, Jacob and Sally Downing, Neighbour Waln and four of her grand-daughters, call'd—Molly gone to Nancys—Alice, a yallow woman, who has taking our cloaths in to wash for some time past, came here before dinner, in great distress, her Child in her Arms, her husband John Wright, a negro Man, and a white Girl, attended by a Constable, who was taking them all to Jail, for keeping, as he said, a disorderly or riotous House—As we knew nothing of the business and but little of Alice, could say no more in her favour but that we hop'd she was honest,—he took them off, I expected we should loose our Linnen &c that was in her Custody, a dozen quite new Shirts and Aprons and many other things, as they had left their house open and nobody in it—in

17. On Jan. 1, in thankfulness for the restoration of domestic tranquillity following the suppression of the Whiskey Rebellion and General Wayne's victory over the Indians, President Washington had set aside Feb. 19 as a day for public celebration of peace (Carroll and Ashworth, *George Washington,* 226–29, 235; the text of the declaration is in J. D. Richardson, *Messages and Papers of the Presidents,* 179–80).

about an hour after she return'd in good Spirits, informing that her Husband and self had procur'd bail, but the white Girl was put in Jail—soon after she brought our Linnen home, nothing missing. John Cannon and James Logan took Coffee here.

21. Clear and temperate, wind S.W. Sally Downing, Nancy Skyrin, Docr. Redman, Saml. Fisher, our old maid Betty Burrage &c. call'd—Saml. Smith came to bid farewell, he did not lodge with us this time—Henry walk'd to town, he din'd here, James went to Clearfield to exchange the Carriages, as my husband &c intends going tomorrow into Chester county—William took a walk out this forenoon, he calld at J Skyrins and at C. Jarviss, he walk'd out again in the Afternoon—Two or 3 days ago, HD. overtook Joe, a few doors from our house, he laid his cane over his back, and told him, if he found him sculking about our neighbourhood he would lay him by the heels, he look'd sheepish, and walk'd off without reply. Molly spent this Afternoon with her Sister Nancy. Saml. Preston, Sammy Smith, Thos. Stewardson, Jonan. Evans, Owen Biddle, T. Morris here this evening arranging matters for their journey tomorrow—John Adlum call'd—Hazey evening.

Febry. 22. First Day: early cloudy, Sun shone out after—wind N.E.—HD. Tommy Morris and Sammy Smith, sett off in our light Carriage for Darby or Chester-Meeting, intending after, to go 25 miles from hence into Chester county to James Gibbons, where the boarding school is to be fixt and to examine the premises, there are many other friends, also, gone Saml. Preston, Saml. Wallace here this Morning MS. MD gone to meeting, Jacob Downing call'd in meeting time, William walk'd out about 11 o'clock—J Logan here after meeting, S Swett din'd here—Sally Downg. Nancy Skyrin, their little girls and SS. drank tea here. Neighr. Waln spent the evening—Jacob Downing and Richd. Thomas here evening—'tis reported that a sickly Vessel is below—cloudy and moderate. George Churchman came in meeting time the afternoon, for his Horse, his Son Mordecai with him.

23. Cloudy. with some rain this morning wind N.E—Saml. R Fisher call'd, A man about land—Henry came to town forenoon, he din'd with us, went homeward Afternoon—Easterly Storm towards night—heavy Sleet, this has been rather a lonely day.—not favourable for my Husband or those that are with him.

24 rain'd most of the night, perhaps all, sun shone out before noon, clouded over after, wind variable.—MS. went to monthly meeting. R. Griscom troublesome and talkative there as usual.—Saml. Emlen call'd—HS.D. came to town forenoon, went home afternoon, HD. &c, return'd from Chester county about 4 P.M. John M[u]sser took tea here, Hannah Yerkes call'd on Sister, who went with her to visit Sally Downing. Molly gone with Betsy Emlen and the

Saltars, to visit Anna King, formerly Wilson, Nancy Skyrin call'd—she has had a rumpus with her maid Betsy, thought herself under the necessity of applying to her Father, who was far from advocating her, but on the contrary highly disapproved her conduct—HD. gone this evening to the Coffee-house to attend the sale of Langhorn-Park—Sammy Smith call'd, we were invited, to day, to the burial of Joseph Paschal, in Market street, to morrow Afternoon.

25. last night when we retir'd, the stars shone bright—when we arose this morning behold a mighty snow-storm, wind Westerly.—about 10 A.M. sun broke out beautifully, wind very high—many Men in the Office this forenoon as is common, of whom I take no account. Joshua Pusey and Caleb Jones call'd. Saml. Preston din'd with us—Jacob Downing call'd—'tis thought to be as cold this afternoon as at any time this Winter. We expected Henry in town to day, but he came not. Molly and Sally Downing gone this afternoon to visit Nancy Skyrin, where they expect to meet Nancy Morgan, Anna Wells, Dolly Large &c &c, I think such a very cold day, home might be the most proper place for most women, SD. especially, unless they had some very urgent affairs to call them fourth, Yet, doubtless, there are many other Gossips going too and fro like themselves.—Isaac Howel here Afternoon, Acknowledg'd a Deed before him.—Commencè 'lier l'Histoire Naturalle par O.G.[18]

26. Clear and very cold. wind high at N.W.—Henry came to town forenoon, he and Eliza. Downing din'd with us—Saml. Emlen, Jos. Sansom, Jacob Downing, Neighr. Waln, Sally Smith and S. Preston here before dinner, Saml. Emlen junr. &c after—Sally Downing, Peggy and Hannah Saltar took tea here, and spent the evening—Wm. Savery, Jos Sansom, Willm. Ellis here this evening HSD. lodges with us to night—the account in the paper of there being a sickly Vessel below, is this day contradicted, Capt. Roberson who died aboard his Vessel, was the only sick person of the Ships company—The Thermometer was lower this morning than at any other time this winter, of course 'tis colder—A poor Puss, at the time of her distress, went into our Oven in the wash-house some time to day, She was found this evening with four of her kittens frozen to death, not the Cat.—these two last cold days William has brought up blood with his spittle.

27. Clear and very cold, as yesterday, wind N. West—Thermometer at 9 or 10.—mon jour natal—

> May I, each Year, that it occurs, be thankfull for the past,
> And spend my time, as tho' assur'd, that it would be the last.

18. Oliver Goldsmith, *History of the Earth and Animal Nature*, 8 vols. (London: J. Nourse, 1774); see below, Dec. 13 (James Hall Pittman, *Goldsmith's Animated Nature* [New Haven: Yale University Press, 1924], 8).

Henry very unadvisedly, at least by me, sett off for North Bank about 11 o'clock A.M. he put on supernumerary habilliments, and thought that might secure him from the cold—Molly, in consequence of his going, went with Sally Smith to Clearfield to spend 24 hours with Hannah.—Saml. Emlen took a pipe here this forenoon. James Fisher, S Preston call'd. Benn. Wilson drank tea with us.—A chimney took fier towards evening, in second street near vine street, and burnt with great violence, by the long continu'd cry of fier, I was fearful it was something more.

28. continues clear and very cold, wind N.W. S. Preston, and little Auther Thomas call'd—James went about three, afternoon to Clearfield for MD. and SS. the weather is much moderated since morning they came home at 6. P.M. left Hannah Sola.—Sally Downing and O. Biddle took tea with us—An account came in this Afternoon, of a probability of peace with the Hostile Indians, should it take place 'twill be no small favour—Tench Cox, Jacob Downing here this evening.

March 1. First day: Clear, much more temperate than for several days past. wind N.W.—HD. MS. MD. at meeting this morning—Jacob and Sally Downing din'd with us, Nancy Skyrin, Sally, and the three Children, took tea with us—Jacob and Sally, John and Nancy, and Saml. Preston sup'd with us—John Skyrin return'd last evening from New-York—Henry came to Clearfield to day from N. Bank, George Fry brought his horse to town to our Stable, there being a distemper among the horses there. fine moonlight.

2. a very pleasent day: wind N.W.—HD. gone to a meeting of Ministers and Elders, which he has attended for many years past, between 20 and 30, I believe—at 11 o'clock second day A.M.—S. Preston call'd. Dr. Redman call'd at noon, Willm. Wilson also—S Smith call'd on Molly who went to walk with her—I have been unwell all day, which is often the case, 'tho sometimes favour'd to be better than at other times. William, Mary and self spent the evening ensemble—Molly reading some elegant poetical quotations, she reads well, 'tho not perfectly well.

3d. temperate but lowring, clere afternoon wind S.W. H.D. MS. at meeting—WD. and MD. went out in the Carriage they intend to call on Sally. J Logan call'd—Patrick Casody din'd here, Peggy Saltar call'd—Molly spent the Afternoon at Sallys with several others. Saml. Emlen, William Savery, John Drinker &c. called Sally Rhoads here in the evening, Billy caught a little cold riding out this forenoon—Thos. Afflick buryed this Afternoon, he was one of 22, who were sent into banishment with my Husband in Sepr. 1777. S. Emlen call'd—he return'd from Burlington to day, where he has been, to attend his Son's first appearance at monthly meeting with Susanna Dillwyn, daughter of Willm. Dillwyn, who now resides at Bristol, old England.

March 4. clear and pleasent—wind S.W.—Henry and Hannah came to town between 9 and 10—Sally Smith call'd for Molly to go walk with her—little Charles Smith suppos'd to have the measels, our three grand Children and two Negro boys have not had them—Sally Downing here forenoon, she and William &c rode out togeather, Molly din'd at J Skyrins, she, Nancy and the Child, were here after dinner—Molly went back with her to spend the evening there. HD. and MS. went after dinner to Clearfield in the Chaise—James took Sally in the Carriage to Israel Whelens—I took a walk this fore noon with William into our little Garden—the first time this year, as the snow lays long there, and tis generly damp, many flowers are peeping out of the ground.—Polly Noble, formerly Nugent call'd Afternoon with two of her Children, she has had four, all Daughters, I am pleas'd to see her look so fat and fair, hearty and reputably—she served her time with us, four years, has, as she says, and I believe, an industrious husband.—About a mile on this side Clearfield my husband and Sister mett Joe, he had the impudence, as M Courtney told MS. to come up into her room, she ask'd him what he wanted, he reply'd, to see something you have got here, and then look'd into the Cradle—she ask'd him if he own'd it, he say'd No, and further this deponent sayeth not.—If he had not seen the Child, he had all reason to belive it was his, but the colour was convincing, he had frequently boasted of it, but was fearful of the expences that might accrue.—As HD. and MS. were returning home, within a mile or two of the City, they observed a flight of Crows, going from the N.E. to the S.W. such a vast number he never saw, there was many thousands, they could not see an end of them.

March 5. rather warm, wind S.W.—HD. unwell by a cold taken yesterday, staying too long in the Garden at Clearfield.—Richd. Smith junr., Neighr. Waln &c call'd—R.W. and self spent this Afternoon at Jacob Downings, it was a rarity Sally said—James Logan and John Saltar took tea here.—Sally Smith, Molly Lippencott, My. Drinker and Sammy Rhoads in our Waggon.—Betsy Emlen, the two Saltars and Richd. Smith in S Emlens—went after dinner to Clearfield—return'd by moon light.

6. Clear. 'tho the wind is north east. This morning about 5 o'clock we were awaken'd by the cry of fier, soon discover'd it was at a considerable distance, none of our family went out, indeed it did not suit them, we understand that it was a Coachmakers Shop that first took fier, in pine street almost opposite friends meeting house, the Shop was burnt down and several Carriages in it, two adjoining houses were almost consumed.—Jacob and Sally with their two daughters Nancy and hir's, Betsy Emlen, and Peggy Saltar, Saml. Preston, Docr. Redman, &c here this forenoon.—Nancy, William, and little Elizath. rode two or three times to the middle ferry which is much the [Top], as it is generally a good road—Frederick Hailer took 6 or 8. ounces blood from HDs arm before dinner, as he is still oppress'd by a cold—Neighr. Waln here this

forenoon, she and MS. went out to Shops, call'd at Ewd. Peningtons, who has been unwell many weeks—I finish'd reading this evening The Memoirs of James Lackington, Bookseller London.[19]—We must have but a poor opinion of the Methodists, if all he says relating to them is true,—his education consider'd, he is a very extraordinary genius, much wit and humour, shews his tast by his quotations &c. and appears to be candid, and a man of integrity, 'tho by no means without his faults.—A Docr. Jardine and a Mr. Porter, as p card left, call'd here forenoon, they are from G. Britian, enquir'd for HSD. informs us that he Dr. J. or both of them, I know not which, have purchas'd of the Widdow Durden, that part of Penns mannor adjoining to Henry, where they intend to settle and follow farming &c. the Doctor is a married man, and has a young family, I hope they will prove good Neighbours, which is a matter of great consequence in the Country.

7. Cloudy, wind Easterly. Stormy forenoon, rain after. HD. took medicine, Saml. Emlen and Peter Yarnel smok'd a pipe here, Thos. Stewardson and Saml. Fisher call'd—After dinner S. Emlen and P. Yarnel came again, when we had a meeting, or setting togeather, P.Y. S.E. HD. WD. MD. and self—they both had something to say, particularly to the younger ones, wholesome advice, and kindly offer'd—J. Skyrin, J. Cannon, and a deputy Surveyor here this evening. still stormy from the S.E—The hand Organist, continues his nightly Sarenades.

8. First day: cold and raw, wind S.W. HD. 'tho unwell, MS. and MD. went to meeting this morning. Willm. Sansom call'd after meeting. HD. stay'd at home afternoon, MS. gone to see S Downing, MD. at meeting—after dinner, William lay down on the Sofa, my husband Molly and self were reading, all quiet, when HD. rang the Bell, little Peter came at the summons, bring some Soldiers, said HD. wood I mean; he was reading of soldiers in the Apocrypha; mistakes of this kind are common, especialy when reading; the Eye is fixt on a word, the idea on the mind, and the tongue utters it. 'tho it means something else—had HD. took his eye off the book and look'd at the fier, he would have said wood—Sally Rhods spent an hour in meeting time, Saml. Emlen call'd after meeting—S Swett, Sally Downing and her two Children took tea with us—Jacob and Sally sup'd—the weather has been variable to day, which is common this month, "March, many weathers," it lightened last night, and snow'd for a short time to day,—Molly spent this Afternoon with Nancy, whom she left unwell, her Child also.

9. Cloudy, and Sunshine Alternately, raw, wind WSW. Charles West call'd—HD. gone to Ministers Meeting 'tho far from well—Betsy Emlen, the two

19. James Lackington, *Memoirs of the First Forty-five Years of His Life* (London: 1791 [Watt, *Bibliotheca Britannica*]).

Saltars, call'd, Molly went out with them,—Nancy Morgan here after dinner, with her little fatt daughter Becky—MS. went this evening to Sallys, clear and cold, wind N.W.—about noon to day it snow'd fast, the sun shone at the same time.—Saml. Preston and Benny Wilson sup'd with us.

10. Clear cold morning wind S.W.—John Drinker call'd, HD. MS. MD. gone to meeting,—William, Sally and her daughter Elizah. sett off after 11 for Clearfield. S. Preston call'd, he show'd us a poetical letter from Saml. Stanton a Yankee who is settled in the woods near him—I have seen peices of his compossing, which were by no means the most contemptible—Considering—Molly Smith, Neighr. Waln, Nancy Skyrin, H. Mott, Peggy and Hannah Saltar, Docr. Redman, James Logan and James Harris call'd before dinner.—the air to day is sharp and penetrating, very unfitt for Billy to encounter, 'tho the Carriage is nearly close. I hope he will escape taking cold—I mist him at dinner, as it is a rare thing for him to be absent at that time. Some would think that Sally run a risk by spending a day so far from home at this time, but she seems free from fear or apprhension—Sister took tea at Robt. Stevensons this Afternoon. Molly gone to S. Emlens—Neighr. Waln, and her grand Son R Wells spent an hour with me,—William heard the cry of fier a little before day this morning we have not yet heard where it was.—WD. and SD. did not come home 'till near sun sett.—Several Men in the back parlor this evening with HD. on business. John Cannon, S. Preston &c.—Enoch Evans and his Neighbour William Rodgers and Saml. Emlen were here this evening.

11. Saml. Emlen breakfasted here. Henry and Hannah came to town forenoon. Henry din'd here—Sally Smith and Sally Large here before dinner, Molly walk'd out with them—Sally Downing here also, E. Downg. in the Afternoon—HD. James Pemberton, David Bacon, Jonathan Evans &c. had a conference this Afternoon in our back parlor, with Hannah Burrows a Mulatto Woman who has, for some time past, made her appearance frequently in our meetings as a preacher or teacher—Henry and Hannah went home towards evening—Nancy Skyrin and Daughter took tea with us—Molly went home with Nancy, intending to spend the evening at Ebenr. Larges.—Peggy and Han. Saltar left Philada. this Afternoon.

12. Clear morning cloudy after—wind N.E. Henry and Hannah came to town after breakfast, they went home after dinner—HD. drank tea at Saml. Pleasants, S. Preston took tea, with William and me, Sally Large, Sally Smith and Betsy Emlen, Richd. Smith, Saml. Rhoads and Walter Franklin took tea with Molly in back parlor.—Saml. Emlen call'd twice or thrice—rain this evening.

March 13. Clear temperate, wind S.W.—I thought it rain'd hard this morning but observing the sun shone bright, concluded it was a thaw, but knew not of what, 'till looking out at the window saw the surface had been cover'd with snow, which had fallen in the night.—Anniversary of the decease of my dear Father.—Docr. Kuhn, Saml. Emlen here forenoon—rain about noon, snow afternoon. Saml. Preston din'd with us—Elizabeth Skyrin spent the day—it has been an unsettled Stormey day, since 10 in the morning.

14. clear and very cold. wind Westerly, I have not this Year heard the wind blow with so much violence as about midnight.—MDs birthday.—Saml. Emlen here this morning—George Fry came to town this Morning he is putting up our grape-vine in this Garden, it having been for some time past uncover'd, by his order, it seems a cold time, but he says it will not suffer by it—MS. out this Afternoon—Nathan Fields Wife call'd, on account of Huson Langstrths Widdow,—Honor Fry call'd after dinner.—little William Fisher call'd—John Cannon here this evening Saml. Emlen also—Sister went to see Sally, found her Maid Nancy Reed, sick in bed. clear cold evening.

15. First day: clear and cold, wind westerly, J Cannon breakfasted with us, he and HD. went after 9 o'clock in the Waggon to Clearfield, intending for Germantown meeting, after to dine with Henry—MS. gone to meeting—Molly not very well, she went in the Afternoon, R. Jones din'd with us.—J.C. and HD return'd about 5. P.M. Henry came with them, they, Nancy Skyrin and Daughter took tea here, John Skyrin call'd—Betsy Emlen and her brother Saml., Sally Smith and her brother John Sally Large and brother John, My daughter and her two Brothers, here this evening—What a favour it is, to a young woman to have a good Brother, or brothers—S. Preston call'd—H.S.D. lodges here to night, cold this evening—It has been remarked that a greater number have died and been ill of the pleurisy this winter than, some say, any other since thier rememberance—I ask'd Docr. K—the other day, if it was not the Yallow fever that Nancy had last fall, he answer'd in the negative. Notwithstanding all my conjectures.

16. Sun shine this morning wind N.E. snow'd fast before noon, Sammy Smith &c call'd—Billy Saltar, Saml. Smith of B. County and HSD. din'd with us—Henry went homeward after dinner in the rain, MS. spent the Afternoon with Sally.—John and Honor Fry took tea with us, Sammy Rhoads spent the evening—Jacob Downing call'd.—John Cannon and Saml. Preston &c in the front room this evening with HD. on business—cloudy evening.

17. clear, more moderate, wind S.W.—HD. MS. and MD. at meeting. Saml. Emlen junr. call'd, he is going to Burlington, expected HSD. here, to go as far as Bristol with him—Our old Neighbor Johanna Hazelhurst paid us a morning visit, they expect to return to their former dwelling in second street, in three or four weeks.—Sally Hopkins gone out with Molly after meeting. James Logan, S. Preston call'd—Abraham Gibbons and Jos. Trimble din'd

with us—Widdow Durden call'd.—about noon, William concluded to loose blood, as he feels an uneasiness at his breast, and continues to bring up bloody phegm, Dr. Kuhn desir'd him, if those indications took place, not to omitt it, 'tis now near six months since he had a vain open'd. About one o'clock Frederick took 7 ounces, he feels weak since, yet I trust it was right.—Hannah Thornton call'd before dinner—it is meeting for Sufferings &c—I sent for Docr. Kuhn to look at Williams blood, he came, approv'd his having lost it, 'tho it is very little inflamed.—Sally Downing and her Children took tea with us. Jacob here also, R. Jones call'd, Henry came to town after dinner, he left us before tea, he intends to morrow for N. Bank. A Committee of Friends in our front room this evening I spent an hour this evening at Neighr. Walns, she having a bad cold.—A Stable in Brewers Alley was burnt down this Afternoon, we heard nothing of it at the time—S. Emlen here this evening—Molly spent this Afternoon with her Sister Nancy, the evening at S. Emlens.

18. clear and mild—William Blakey and Samuel Smith of Bucks county breakfasted with us—S. Preston call'd—WD. more unwell than usual after bleeding. he took a short walk this forenoon, spit a little blood. David Cumming din'd here—I intended going this Afternoon to visit Sarah Fisher, but was prevented by rain—Molly expected Company, who were detain'd by the same cause—it held up after, when Molly went to Nancys, Sister to Sallys, who was very bad last night with sick head ach, she is something better this evening—Ben Wilson took tea with us, he, WD. and self, amused ourselves most of this evening reading Hogarths cuts, they are very descriptive, comic and moral,—Stormy this evening with much rain—Molly sent Sam. Sprigs for her night cloaths, proposing to stay all night with her Sister—we have had much wett weather lately—the roads are very bad.

March 19. Sunshine cold, wind westerly. John Musser, Saml. Emlen, Billy Saltar &c call'd, Peggy and Hannah Saltar came to bid us farewell, they are going home to day. Sally Downing had a good night, and is better, which is matter of consolation to me.—Huldah Mott, and Betsy Emlen call'd on Molly about noon to ride with them, she return'd to dinner—sent home Hogarths prints which Molly borrow'd of John Fry, he asks fifteen Guineas for them, as they are said to be from the original paintings, engrav'd,—I went, cold as it is, to see Sally, she is in her Chamber 'tho much better, expects to come down tomorrow, Nancy Morgan and Nancy Skyrin there,—Jacob came home with me—James Logan and Saml. Smith of B Cy. here while I was out.

20. unsettled, very cold.—wind S.W—Molly Evans, Henry and Hannahs Maid came to town Yesterday with George Fry, she wishes to return to day, as her mistress is alone, James took her in our Chaise, found the road excessively bad, as he says—Dr. Redman here before dinner; Jacob Tomkins call'd for an order to bury a young man of the name of Clements.—Joseph Drinker, and

Saml. Smith BCy—here after dinner. William Blakey and Wm. Richardson also—Joseph Reed from the Jersy's here Afternoon, he took my acknowledgment of a deed. William and Sarah Bleaky, John and Rachel Watson, Nancy Skyrin and Child took tea here, W. and S.B. went towards evening to S. Pleasants, John and Rachel lodges here—John Skyrin, John Webb, call'd—HD. out this evening during his absence, Thos. Fisher, John Drinker, Thos. Stewardson and Joseph Sansom were here, expecting to meet HD. who did not return 'till after their departure. very cold this evening read a pamphlet, intitled a Kick for a Bite, by Peter Porcupine,[20] rather Scurrilous.

21st. more moderate wind S.W.—it snow'd yesterday—John and Rachel Watson breakfasted, John Hoskins, Saml. Smith BC—— &c call'd—Saml. Trimble came, he lodges here. Sister out this forenoon—Billy Beakey junr. call'd—Joseph and Hannah Trimble, Sammy Trimble John Shoemaker, and Joseph Brinton din'd here.—Widdow Delaplane call'd to pay Sister a ground-rent. I went to see how Sally fair'd this Afternoon, found her at work and Chearful, S Swett, S Perot, John and Nancy there.—When I came home found Joseph Brinton and his Sister Mary Moore at our house, they lodge here. MM. brought a letter from her Husband Robert Moore to WD.—none here this evening but our 5 lodgers.

22. First day: Our Spring meeting. Moderate wind S. West. heavy rain about 10 o'clock—Jacob Lindley, Eli Yarnel and our lodgers breakfasted here—Abraham Gibbons, Daniel Smith, William Savery here after breakfast—Amos Harvey, Ruth Walmsley, lately married to Thos. Walmsley of Bybery, Joseph Brinton, and Mary Moore din'd with us—John Drinker here in afternoon meeting time wrighting with HD.—they, R. Waln and Molly Drinker went to the funeral of Hannah Mitchel, youngest daughter of Abraham Mitchel deceased. her Sister Nancy, was one of my early friends and school mate.—John and Rachel Watson, Deborah Guest and Jane Cope took tea with us—George Churchman &c &c call'd—read an Essay concerning the restoration of Primitive Christianity by Thomas Beaven.[21]

March 23. A warm Morning wind S.E. John Watson on a Committee to meet at 7 o'clock, they were all gone out, when I came down, Oliver Paxon and G. Churchman, breakfasted here—Patrick Casody call'd—Sally Downing and her Children here in meeting time, Jacob call'd for her.—I read this forenoon, A Tender Salutation in gospel love, written principally for the use of his Rela-

20. Peter Porcupine [William Cobbett], *Kick for a Bite; or, Review upon Review; with a Critical Essay, on the Works of Mrs. S. Rowson; in a Letter to the Editor, or Editors, of the American Monthly Review* (Philadelphia: T. Bradford, 1795 [*NUC*]).

21. Thomas Beaven, *An Essay Concerning the Restoration of Primitive Christianity, in a Conduct Truly Pious and Religious* (London: J. Sowle, 1723 [*Brit. Mus. Cat.*]).

tions, by Thomas Colly.[22] an excellent little piece it is.—I pluck'd several Crocus's from our Garden, they are the first flowers I have seen this Spring. HSD. came to town this morning he return'd home from N. Bank on seventh day last, he din'd here—Jos. Brinton din'd here and bid us farewel, he sets of this Afternoon—Sister out, and Molly gone to Nancys—Henry left us about 5 o'clock, he intends tomorrow for North Bank—Hannah Trimble Sister to Richd Thomas call'd.—William Richardson call'd to pay the quoto for Bucks quarter.—Molly Moore has left us, and gone homeward—J. and R Watson & S Trimble sup'd.

24. Warm, tryingly so to some, wind S.W.—Willm. and Sarah Blakey and Son Billy came here this Morning to sett off with John and Rachel as their waggon and horses are kept in our Stable,—Saml. Smith and Saml. Trimble went also homeward, Peter Yarnel, George Churchman and others here—E Emlen call'd on Molly to go to meeting.—'tis said by some of the physicians, that this is rather a sickly time, pleurisieys, inflamatory rheumatisms, a rash among the Children, resembling the Measles, &c are now prevalent.—Owen Biddle and Benn. Swett came for Horse and Chaise to go into Chester County to James Gibbon's—J Logan call'd—William, Nancy and little Elizath. went out in the Carriage after 11 o'clock—Josiah Bunting John Stabler and Susannah Swett din'd with us—Sally Smith call'd, Molly and Nancy went out with her—SS. and Nancy Skyrin took tea here—Jacob and Sally, John and Nancy, and Molly Lippencott spent this evening here—unwell to day.

25. Warm. wind Southerly.—Joseph Wharton call'd this morning I have not seen him, to speak to him, since his return from England, which is many years, he was going next door to visit his brother Isaac, who is ill in the Gout.—William went out in the Carriage to call on his Sister SD. to ride with him. Nancy, Betts and the Child, came this forenoon for Molly to walk with them.—William return'd to dinner, Sally Large and Sally Smith call'd on Molly to go with them to Clearfield to visit lonely Hannah, Mary, who had not din'd, put a bit of Gingerbread in her pocket, and went off with them. Tristum Needles din'd with us.—Sally Downing spent the evening here and Afternoon, Jacob and little Mary came for her.—Molly came home after night.—they went out without any Beaus to wait on them, but unexpectedly to Molly, George Benson, Richd. Smith, Sammy Rhoads, and Walter Franklin came after—the roads very bad, Horses rather naught.—J Drinker call'd this evening Benjn. Wilson sup'd with us. We have been favour'd with pleasent showers of rain—fine growing weather.

March 26. a fine warm Morning wind S.W.—William gone out to call on

22. Thomas Colley, *A Tender Salutation in Gospel Love, Written Principally for the Use of His Relations*, 2d ed. (London: James Phillips, 1794 [*Brit. Mus. Cat.*]).

Sally to ride—Benjn. Catheral call'd. WD. return'd before dinner, Sally Downing spent the Afternoon. B. Swett return'd from Chester County brought home the horse and Chaise—HD. engag'd with several in the back parlor this Afternoon—I spent the afternoon and evening with our Neighbor Sally Rhoads, WD. came there to tea, HD. in the evening—the wind came round to N.E. with rain. William came home in the rain, I hope he has not suffred by it as 'twas so short a distance—Saml. Emlen call'd.—a very great change in the weather from morning to evening.

27. The rain last night turn'd to a heavy sleet, which continu'd all night, and is deep this morning wind high at Northeast and Stormy—If Sally should call her friends out to day, it would be attended with difficulty. S. Preston din'd with us. William, Mary and Samuel held a discourse after dinner on the subjects of Love, Courtship and Marriage, but could not jump in judgement.—M. Carcado a french Gentleman took tea with us—Sammy Rhoads spent the evening—The northeast storm which commenc'd last night, has continu'd all this day—and now, near 11 o'clock does not appear to be the least abated. HD. spent this day at home, which he rarely does when in health. The Equinoctial storm sometimes comes on before the Sun crosses the Line, and sometimes after.—After the House was look'd over, and all our family retired but little Sall Dawson and self, who have constantly this winter, the last up, I set by the fier, she sleeping in a chair by me, the wind very high with rain, did not know what hour our dear Sally would want our assistance, and Jacob knock at the door. I wish'd I had been there, before the Storm began, and continu'd with her,—sat up 'till near midnight reading, and when 'tired, scribbled the following anti-sublime, Namby, pamby Iricisms.—

Late, sitting by myself alone,
Unto my Lonely self I said—
To be alone, and by myself,
I am not in the least afraid—

For when I'm by myself alone,
I'm happier far than in a croud,
And speaking softly to myself—
More pleasing is, than speaking loud—

But yet the converse of a friend—
A friend with whom I can converse,
In conversation, sans restraint,
Nor obligation to rehearse—

The joy and pleasures past discript'
Description can't describe the Joy
Felt, and enjoy'd by mutial friends
Whose conversations never cloy.—

Sounds without sense, but no matter, 'tis not to be review'd.

28th. The Northeast storm continus with a degree of violence, snow in the night and this morning The snows this winter have been very frequent, 'tho not very deep or lasting, S Preston call'd, HSD. came to town forenoon, yesterday he left N. Bank and came to Clearfield,—Henry is not one of the invulnerables, nor is he, in a general way, rash or imprudent, yet he is venturous and resolute—I am often concerned on his account least while looking after his buildings and Farm, going backward and forwards in all weathers, he may take cold &c &c.—Our Coachman James Duning, some days past was let blood, 'tho not much amiss—his Arm was bound up very tight, his coat sleve small, which I believe is the occasion of his arm swelling, it appears inflam'd, I was going to give him a dose salts, but Fredrick Halier to whom he went on the occasion said 'twas better left for a day or two longer—he put a plaster to it.—S Preston din'd with us, Saml. Emlen took tea, several call'd—Our Son Henry left us between 4 and 5 in the storm, and before he could possibly reach home it rain'd so fast that I expect he will be thoroughly wett—HD. and several others in front room this evening—read an Epic Poem intitled Aristocracy,[23] which was lost upon me, as my dull brain could not comprehend it, perhaps the peice itself is not very comprehensible.

29. First day: storm ceas'd last night, Sun shone out this morning wind westerly, not yet clear'd up. HD. and MD. at meeting—T. Stewardson din'd with us—Molly went this Afternoon to visit her Sisters—James Consulted docr. Physick on account of his Arm, the Doctor treated it as something serious, order'd him to loose 10 oz. blood from the other arm, and sent him a purge—his arm has been frequently poulticed.—HD. at meeting this evening as usual, clear.

30. Clear, wind northerly. Henry and Hannah came to town forenoon in Chaise, through extream bad roads. Hannah tells me, that the hurt she received about two months ago, by lifting a table, is quite well, which is a very pleasing curcumstance—S. Emlen here. Docr. Philip Physick call'd to visit James, pronounc'd his Arm much better.—Henry din'd with us—John Saltar here after dinner, I acknowledg'd a Deed before him, for the place at Frankford, sold to Docr. Edwards. Ray and Anne King, James Logan, Anna Skyrin and Child, Betsy Emlen and HSD. took tea with us.—Sister spent this afternoon with Sally, who still keeps up—and appears chearful—A Concourse of comers and goers, in and out the front room this day—read a romance or novel, which I have not done for a long time before—it was a business I followd in my younger days, not so much as many others, 'tho more than some

23. [David Humphries?], *Aristocracy, an Epic Poem* (Philadelphia: [Richard Alsop], 1795 [*Brit. Mus. Cat.*]).

others, it was intitled Interisting Memoirs, said to be writen by a Lady[24]—it is no very great affair, 'tho there are some good sentiments, and many moral reflections, some of them very good. not quite clear this evening.

31. rain again this morning—William Robinson judge of Court of common pleas—Billy Waln and Tommy Gillpin here forenoon, Sammy and Molly Smith, my husband and self acknowledg'd a Deed before them, for Langhorn Park, sold to Andrew Kennady.—Henry din'd here—H. Catheral came from Neighr. Waln's before dinner, in some agitation, for Sister or self to go there, as little H. Hartshorn was ill, in a fainting fitt as they thought, Sister went with her, Dr. Kuhn pronounc'd it an hysteric or nerveous affection, she is much better this evening—Saml. Emlen here HD. went with him to Saml. Hopkinss—After they were gone, T[ ]y. Pickering, Saml. Hodgdon, Saml. Fox and Samuel Preston came by appointment, sent Sally for HD. who presently came—they retired to the Coumpting Room.—Sammy Rhoads here this evening to bid Adieu, as he sits off tomorrow morning for New York, intending for New England.—Sister went to Sallys this evening. moonlight 'tho it does not appear to be quite clear.

April 1. Clear, wind S.W.—Enoch Evans, Sally Smith, Sally Large, little William Fisher &c call'd—Henry and Hannah din'd with us—Molly went out after dinner with Hannah—Sally Downing spent this Afternoon once more with us, unexpecedly by me. I left her reluctantly, having engag'd to visit my old friend Sarah Fisher and Daughters before Sarah came. Billy Drinker took tea there with us,—we came home by moon light—found Joseph Saltar at our house, he lodges here—Henry went after dinner to Clearfield, left Hannah in town, intends sitting off tomorrow for his farm.—Amsterdam at last actuly taken by the french, it is said to be great news.

2. Clear, wind S.W. chang'd to S.E.—Jh. Saltar breakfasted with HD. before I came down stairs—he went homeward before dinner,—Neighr. Waln and Saml. Preston call'd—William and self, took a walk this forenoon, being pleasant weather, to Jacob Downings, Sally troubled with a bad cough,—Nancy and Child there, Hannah Drinker and Molly also, expected there to dinner.—We went to Charles Jervis's, his daughter Betsy ill, appears to be far advanc'd in a decay, call'd at [S.] Fishers, stay'd but a short time, came home to dinner,—I went over after dinner to see Hanh. Hartshorn, who appears to be much in the way of B. Jervis but not so far gone—Betsy Devenshire call'd. Docr. Kuhn paid us an unexpected visit this Afternoon—John Musser call'd in the evening. Sally Rhoads spent the evening with us—Ben Wilson, Sam

24. A Lady [Susanna Harvey Keir], *Interesting Memoirs*, 2 vols. (London: A. Strahan and T. Cadell, 1785 [*NUC*]).

Preston call'd—Nancy, Hannah, and Molly, spent the Afternoon at S. Emlens.

April 3. rain'd last evening and most of the night. Sun shone this morning cloudy after, wind due west, good friday. Elnathan Davis din'd with us—Hannah Drinker, Sally Large and George Benson call'd after dinner, Hannah tells us that Olley Gamble who was to have Nursed Sally Downing, is ill in the pleurisy.—Sister gone to see Sally, she being in her Chamber, much oppressed by a cold and hard cough—not a day to count on, by my reckoning for her.—Jacob here Afternoon—Sister came home to tea informs of the death of Betsy Jervis junr. who departed about 3 o'clock P.M.—in the sixteenth year of her Age. I had no thought when I saw her yesterday that she was near her end. I spent this evening with Sally, she seems in pretty good spirits 'tho her cough is very bad, M. Wheeling Nancy Morgan and Polly Drinker there—HSD. return'd to Philada. this afternoon—S. Preston here this evening,—clear.

4. Clear fine day: wind westerly. Jams. Wilson Esqr. call'd—Sister looking for a Nurse for Sally. Patty Mullan willing to serve, but we think her too indispos'd having a blister on for a sore throat &c—William and Molly out in Carriage, Nancy Skyrin and daughter here fore-noon—Widdow Durdan paid a morning visit—S. Preston, and Nancy Rice call'd. Robt. Fletcher of Abinton, George Tappin, and a young man of the name of Tremper, both of New York state, Sam Preston and HSD. din'd with us. J Logan took tea—Molly and self went out after dinner, to Charles Jervis's, the Corps of his Daughter was laid out in the middle room, perhaps the very room, if not, the same house in which my Mother, Sister and self were born—she appear'd much taller then I expected, having lost part of her hight, by stooping dureing her indispossion, she was a pritty innocent girl, and is, I doubt not, taken in mercy; from a world of trouble—I came back to Jacob Downings, where we had call'd before,—Molly went to Nancys—Hannah Yerkes took tea with Sally and self in the Chamber, Sallys cough rather better 'tho still hard and frequent—Sister has been this evening looking for a Nurse, but has not yet succeeded—I came home in the evening Sister went to Sally—I read this evening in the Philadelphia Minerva, a new paper, of the Death of Dr. Charles Bensel, of Germantown, he died the 17. ultimo—little Oliver Wadsworth who lives at J Skyrins, was innoculated a week or 10 days past, he is likely to have the small pox very favourably.

5. First day: clear. wind S.W.—Willm. Savery and Stephen Maxfield call'd on HD this morning he went with them to visit the prisoners in our jail with whom, they and several other friends, held a meeting.—MS. HSD. and MD. at our Meeting This day is very warm, more so than any other this Spring, and coming so suddenly, it is the more felt by invalids; William is very sensible of its effects, feels very languid and has flushes come over him—S Swett din'd

with us. Sister gone after dinner to visit Sally who continues in her Chamber, she intends going also to C. Jervis's to stay with them 'till the burial goes—Augustine Jones call'd after dinner, he arrived here a day or two ago, from Portugal, Mate of the Vessel—Our little Peter is very unwell and feverish, complains of disorder'd bowels—B. Catheral call'd afternoon to inform us, that little Robt. Potts, had taken the measles, ask'd if he should call on Docr. Rush, I told him by all means, HD. was out.—'tis likely our little Petter is breeding 'em.—My husband and Sister, John Skyrin and Wife, Jacob Downing and Molly Drinker, were at the interment of Betsy Jervis after the Afternoon meeting—William Savery spoke at the grave.—I came to Jacob Downings after tea, found Sally complaining, she has pains, which probably, will not go of 'till worse comes on, we have sent Dr. S. word that she is unwell, Sister has been out again this evening looking for a Nurse, but has not yet found one to our mind. poor Sally is gone to bed, but I fear not to sleep, I am going to do the same in back room with Eliza:—rain this evening with thunder & lightening.

6. There was a time, that if either of my beloved Children were in the Situation that my dear Sally is at present, I could not have found in my heart to have made a memorandum; is it that as we grow in years our feelings become blunted & Callous? or does pain and experience cause resignation? 'tis now past 11 at night my dear afflicted child has just taken anodoyne from Dr. Shippen, she has been all this evening in afflictive pain 'tho unprofitable, I came here yesterday afternoon, went to bed at 11 o'clock Jacob call'd me up after two this morning when I had just fallen asleep, Sally being rather worse, before four o'clock Jacob went for Hannah Yerkes, After breakfast we sent for Dr. Shippen, he felt her pulse, said he hoped she was in a good way—he din'd with us, and as Sally did not wish his stay, he left us, saying he would return in the evening she continu'd in pain at times, all day, was worse towards evening, Neighr. Waln, H. Yerkes and Sister with us—sent for the Doctor who soon came, towards night we precieved that all things were not right, I did not venture to question the Doctor, but poor Sally was not sparing in that perticular.—she suffer'd much to little purpose,—when the Anodoyne was given, two Opium pills, the Doctor went to lay down, when all was quiet for a short time, but poor Sally who instead of being compos'd grew worse, the Doctor was call'd, when he came I quited the room, knowing that matters must 'eer long come to a crisis. I was down stairs in back parlor by myself an hour and half as near as I can judge, when observing that my dear Child ceas'd her lementation and a bustle ensu'd—with a fluttering heart I went up stairs, in a state of suspence, not knowing if the child was born, or Sally in a fitt, as I heard no crying of a Child.—It was mercy fully born, the Doctor blowing in its mouth and slapping it, it came too and cry'd—The Doctor then told us, that a wrong presentation had taken place; which with poor Sallys usual difficulties call'd for his skill more perticularly; by good management he

brought on a footling labour, which 'tho severe, has terminated by divine favour, I trust, safely,—HSD. went this morning to Clearfield, left Hannah in town.

7. heavy rain in the night with some thunder and lightning—wind N.E—Henry Downing, the second of the Name, was born the seventh of the fourth month, between one and two in the morning, on the third day of the week—Sally is this morning as well as can be, all things consider'd—the effects of the anodoyne not gone off. Neighr. Waln, Hannah Yerkes and Dr. Shippen left us after breakfast—no Nurse as yet obtain'd to our mind. The little one seems hart whole, 'tho the blood is much settled in his legs feet &c. his feet almost as blue as indigo—Sally sleeps sweetly this Afternoon, her cough very hard when she awoke, the child put to the breast this evening he is, as the Nurses say, very handy at the buseness—Patty Mullen came this evening very oppertunly, she nurs'd Sally with her two first Children—I left Jacobs this evening about nine o'clock came home in a mist, I have been absent 50 hours, and sleep'd but two in that time, I feel at this present time much fatigued, bones ach, flesh sore, Head giddy &c. but have at same time much to be thankfull for—Jacob came home with me left sister there expecting to spend the night but she came after me—found Hannah S. Drinr. at our house she lodges here to night with Molly. little Peter very poorly, he was let blood by order of Dr. Rush, it is very buffy.

8. Cloudy, wind westerly—It was late last night when Sister and self retir'd, having had a conversation with S Dawson, relating to S.B. who has form'd an acquaintance with one of Gardners workmen, I fear we shall have more trouble with the bold Hussey. I arose early this morning caught cold coming home last night—Hannah stay'd with us 'till after dinner, then She and Molly went to see Sally and her Baby; they spent the Afternoon and evening with Nancy. J Logan &c. call'd. I went this Afternoon to Jacobs, found Sally amazingly well to appearence, I wish it may continue, as she is not ap't to be too carefull. The dear little babe is brused in many places, in its lower parts—it eats and sucks well, but is hurt when the legs and feet are handled.—Dr. Rush call'd to see little Peter, says he is better, talk'd of innoculating them tomorrow, which I cannot say I approve of, as the child is very poorly this evening & feverish, it is the pleurisy he has had—and the measels are in our Neighbourhood, which we suppose neither of our Negro boys have had—Sally Dawson has cut across her wrist a large gash, [diverting] herself with a dull knife and a stick.—I generally have some such cookery in hand.—S.B.—begins I fear to shew herself in her true colours, there is such ogleing between her and a fellow opposite our kitchen, and we have been inform'd that he has been talking with, and kissing her in our Yard—She has given me much uneasiness.—Jemmy Smith here forenoon, we have been expecting HSD. to day, but he is not arrived.

9. cold. wind N.W. Dr. Rush here forenoon, order'd little Peter's loosing 6 ounces more, blood, and sent him fever powders.—Hannah S Drinker din'd here,—Augustine Jones call'd.—Becky Thompson here after dinner, Saml. Emlen here also—Sally Zane drank tea with us—Sister gone this evening to see Sally, A Skyrin and Daughter were here in forenoon—Molly went out with Hannah, We have not seen Henry since second day last, when he went to Clearfield, we expected him back the next day—have since conjectur'd that he may be gone to North Bank, but as he did not mention, any such intention, and the roads being so very bad, we know not what to think—intend sending James tomorrow to Clearfield to enquire.—I read this evening a little Book intitled A Word of remembrance and caution to the Rich.—by John Woolman.[25]—I believe there are few, if any, who live up to JWs plan or rule, yet I think there are some who go a great way towards it.

10. cold sour weather, hard frost last night, wind N. West—Our apricott tree in bloom, the others not so forward, they are in danger of being hurt.—a little snow fell this morning Saml. Emlen Senr. here, brought Molly a card of invitation to his sons marriage on fifth day next, at Oxmead near Burlington—Sally Smith call'd.—James gone to Clearfield to enquire after Henry—little Peter very poorly—Dr. Rush has order'd a purge to be given him this Afternoon, it was dinner time when he call'd, and a blister to be laid on his side at bed time. I have sent for Ailce wright, to set up with him to night.—James return'd before dinner, found Henry well at Clearfield.—Hannah S. Drinker here after dinner—Sally Rhoads here this Afternoon, Molly gone this evening to see Sally—I have been for two days past oppress'd by a cold on my breast and a Cough.—put the blister on Peters right side about 10 o'clock. HD. and MS. gone this evening to see Sally.

11. Cold and very clear, wind N.W. frost last night. very unsettled weather have we had this Spring, frequent sudden transitions from cold to heat, and vice versa. As our little Peter had taken physick and had a blister apply'd, I could not be easy to leave him to the care of Ailce, his situation appeard to me critical, he was a little flighty in the night.—about two o'clock he complain'd of the blister making his side sore.—before 4, he seem'd better, I then went to Bed, and Ailce I believe did the same as soon as my back was turn'd—this morning I cut the blister, which did not rise as well as could have been wish'd, yet sufficient to be of some service to him, the Doctor says he is better this morning 'tho the disorder is not broke. Raynold Keen Senr. judge of court common pleas here this Morning I acknowledg'd a Deed before him.—Elizh. Downing came to spend the day with us.—Neighr. Waln spent an hour after dinner—Saml. Emlen call'd, he inform'd us of the death of Peter Yarnels

25. John Woolman, *A Word of Remembrance and Caution to the Rich* (Dublin: R. M. Jackson, 1793 [*Brit. Mus. Cat.*]).

wife—Caty Decon and little Mary came for Elizabeth—John Courtney and family mov'd from Clearfield to Philadelphia. Mary left Sall's Child, with Geo[ ] Frys wife.—The weather rather more moderate this evening Jams Logan and Ben Wilson spent part of this evening John and Nancy Skyrin, and Hannah S Drinker also. they have past great part of this day with Sally—Hannah in the dumps, not having seen Henry lately. Our little black boy sleeps finely, I hope 'tis restorative. How many vicissitudes do I pass through, in the small sphere in which I daily move,—declineing health and strength has been my lott for a long time past, I yet have abundant cause of thankfullness—If life is a blessing, and it is generally thought so to be,—I have been much favour'd, as I am now near four years older than my dear father was when remov'd hence, and near 14 more than my beloved Mother.—May I be thankfull for the time past, and endeavour to be resigned to what may occur in the little, that in all probability, remains, To leave those I love happy, seems the wish next my heart, but what do I say! true happiness or unmixt filicity is inconsistant with humanity—and not to be mett with in this state of probation—to leave them resigned to the will of providence should be the wish.

April 12. First day: Clear. wind NE. chang'd to S.W—HD. MS. MD at meeting—Dr. Rush call'd—Peter rather better, S Swett and Elijah Waring din'd with us—SS. Nancy Skyrin and Child, Hanh. Drinker, S. Preston and E. Downing took tea with us.—William Crage Merchant dead of a mortification in his Leg and foot, said to have been occasion'd by a small cut by a penknife scraping his foot after washing them—Jacob Downing sup'd here. Peter not so well as in the morning a dose of phisick sent, and given at one o'clock has not yet work'd—'tis past 10, his blister has not run well, and Ailce has neglected coming. Poor Olivia has finish'd her course this Afternoon, she will be much miss'd having been one of the first and best Nurses in the City. Sall Brant stays with little Peter to night.

13. rain most of the night, and this morning a Southeast storm—Dr. Rush call'd—he sent Peter two small opening pills, S Preston &c call'd—Henry Kendle from New York took tea with us—Thomas Stewardson, Hannah S Drinker and Sally Large came in the evening, they spent an hour. HK. went with them—Hannah talks of going tomorrow home to look for her husband—Sister gone to pay Sally Downing an evening visit. The Sun sett beautifully clear—Jacob came home with MS. all seems in a good way at their house—'tis about a week since we mov'd into back parlor—we avoid the morning Sun, and have the pleasure of seeing the trees put fourth, and the Garden in bloom—the south west wind also.

April 14. Clear fine day, wind westerly. Dr. Rush call'd, Peter bravely—Saml. Emlen and Saml. Rodman call'd—William, Nancy and little Elizabeth went out rideing this morning. Sally Rhoads, Sally Smith and Sally Large call'd—Richd. Smith and Hannah Drinker went to Clearfield in our Chaise this morning Richd. return'd before dinner, left Hannah there—Henry gone to his farm, he brought a letter from HSD. to me informing that it had not been in his power to come to town for Hannah, but wish'd she might have our Carriage if wanted—I suspect he has been indispos'd, which has prevented his coming, and being under the necessity of going to North Bank took the first oppertunity—Docr. Redman call'd at dinner time—Hannah Yerkes spent an hour after dinner, Saml. Emlen call'd. Huldah Mott and little Harriot also—Sally Rhoads, Betsy Fisher, Caroline Shoemaker Betsy Giles, Sally Smith and Richard Smith and self, took tea with Molly in front parlor Sammy Fisher there in the evening John Parish with HD. and Sister in the back parlor—Will[,] Ellis &c call'd—after they were gone, Molly went with me to see Sally, found her bravely, mett HD. there, came home in a few minutes, dress'd Peters Blister—Sally Dawson complains of a pain in her side, made a plaster of molasses and flour of sulpher and apply'd to it—did not go to bed 'till near midnight—John Parish came to inform HD. that he had received a letter from Richd. N——s wife giving him an account of her husbands indispossion and derangement, his family in great distress &c.

April 15. Clear, wind N.E. Dr. Rush call'd—Our old friend Charles West departed this life early this morning he has been for many years a steady Elder of our up town meeting. Aged 70 years.—James and Hetty Smith call'd between 10 and 11. in their Carriage, for Molly Drinker, who went with them towards Burlington, expecting to be, tomorrow, present at the Nuptils of Saml. Emlen junr. and Susanna Dillwyn—Ostin Jones call'd—HSD. came to town from North Bank just before dinner, he left us Afternoon and intends going with Hannah, early tomorrow morning from Clearfield towards Burlington.—Nancy Skyrin, her Child and John Saltar took tea with us. Eliza Downing spent the day here, I went home with her in the evening stay'd there 'till near 10 o'clock.—R. Jones call'd this Afternoon.—Molly Morris was buried yesterday, she nurs'd me, with my last Child, near fourteen years ago—she was exellent in her way—little Peters blister looks very sore, he is otherwise bravely.

16. pleasant morning wind Southerly, looks likely to change, Betsy Fordham call'd—Anna Hopkins call'd, an errand from her Grandmother to Sister—rain about noon—J. and Hetty Smith stop'd at our door this Afternoon at 6 o'clock, returning from Wedding, expeditious doings—they say, that Molly Drinker &c intend homeward tomorrow—Henry and Hannah came into meeting between 10 and 11, they must have left Clearfield by times this morning—No one, either Breakfasted, din'd or tea'd with us this day: R. Waln here this evening—Sammy Preston call'd, said that R. James, who is ill, wish'd to see me. Sister gone to Jacobs'—John and Nancy call'd this evening she had spent the Afternoon at [T.] Copes.

April 17. rain in the night, clear Morning wind. S.E—Jacob Lindley breakfasted here, Nurse Patty call'd away from Sally early this morning by [ ] Travis, to whose wife she was engag'd—Sister out, looking for another Nurse for SD—William gone out on the old Mare, 'tis many months since he has been on horse back, and 'twas this week the Mare was brought from her Colt, has not been used since she cut her leg. I received a Note this Afternoon from Nancy Skyrin intimating R. Thompsons desire that I would visit her Mother. After 10. I went there, found RJ. in bed rather better then she had been, 'tho low and oppress'd by the Asthma, a disorder she has been many years afflicted with—we were pleas'd to see each other, our meetings laterly have not been so frequent as formerly, oweing to indispossion &c. I went from JTs down to Nancys, found her busy seeing her House clean'd—then went to Sallys, mett Sister there—she has engag'd a Nurse Perkins who they expect there before dinner, E. Downing came home with me; Dr. Rush here before I went out, we had some discourse relating to a particular religious tennet, deem'd by many erroneous. he promised to lend me a volume on the subject. Great feasting to day, and fireing of Guns &c. on account of the successes of the french.[26]—Willm. Bleakey call'd—James Moon of Middletown call'd, he is in his 82 year, and rides to town with ease.—HD. gone to C. Wests funeral—Jos Sansom call'd—Molly England and Leonard Snowdens wife waited here to join the procession as it past our door,—I counted upwards of 300 persons, his wife was not there—How solemn and affecting must be the parting of Man and wife, after living 40 years together, was an observation of WDs and a very just one, To be seperated from a near friend and companion and father of her Children must be one of the greatest tryals in this life, to an affectionate wife.—John and Nancy, and two Men, who came to sell land, took tea here.—John Thompson's Henry came for our Bed Chair, said R. James was worse, S Preston here this evening said JT. told him he did not expect she would live 'till morning—I went out this evening with John and Nancy, intending to go to J Smiths, but found the weather so chang'd, so cold, I turn'd back.—Molly Drinker and others of the company, not return'd as was expected.

18. Morning cool, and clear, wind N.W—William gone out on mare, rather too early, S. Preston call'd, says R. James appears to be better, but J Thompson thinks she cannot continue 'till another day, being much oppress'd, and unable to discharge the phlegm.—Eliza Downing come to spend this day with us, Neighr. Waln and little Susan Hartshorn call'd, Nancy Skyrin and Daughter also—James Logan, he return'd last evening from Burlington, says, Molly

26. French, Dutch, and American citizens celebrated the French "capture" of Amsterdam with an artillery salute and a procession to the home of the French minister at Twelfth and Market streets, where the minister delivered an address and the flags of the three countries were ceremoniously joined under a civic crown. At night there was a festive dinner at Oeller's Hotel (Scharf and Westcott, *Philadelphia,* 1:482; see above, Jan. 6).

Drinker and others, intend homeward to day—she accordingly came, between 5 and 6. afternoon, with Sally Smith, Betsy Emlen, and Richd. Morris in Emlen's Carriage, Richd. Smith and Jonan. [Harvey] in Chaise with them. Henry and Hannah set off from Burlington this morning for North-Bank—Molly says she has had a very pleasent time while abroad—Sister has been visiting the sick and others to day, Sally Penington, B. Burge, Thos. Say, Ruth Woodcock, Rebecca James, a long walk put all togeather. Eliza, went home unwell, we think she may have taken the measles.—Hannah and Henry came here after candle light, we had a dish tea made for them—they went to J Smiths to lodge as usual, Saml. Preston bid farewell to day.—Sister gone to set up this night with Neighr. James, believing it may be her last.

19. First Day. a fine cool morning wind N.W.—a young man call'd this morning by desire of Betsy Foulke, to inform us of the departure of Reba. James about 9m. past 5 this morning 'tis now near 8. and sister not return'd from J Thompsons; she came soon after, confirm'd the account—HD. and HSD. went to morning meeting. S Swett din'd.—Nancy Skyrin and Child and SS. took Coffee with us, My husband, who generaly takes a very light dinner on this day of the week, thought a dish of Coffee might settle his head, as he had been troubled with the head-ach most of the day, was taken with a sick stomach suddenly while eating, a very unusual affection with him, he brought up what little he had taken, and seems much better this evening Hannah S Drinker, Sally Smith and Sally Large here this evening they went away with Nancy Skyrin, Molly also, to lodge with Nancy as John Skyrin is gone to Chester.—Capt. Whetheral is there, lately return'd from Sea—I went this evening Henry with me, to visit Sally, found her and babe midling—Jacob came home with me, Henry sup'd with us—S. Emlen &c. call'd.—Sally Johnson here this Afternoon, ask'd if SB could spend a day with her this week, to which I consented, told her of her daughters late conduct wish'd she would take her and Child of our hands, that she had a year to serve from this month, which would have been of more worth to us, had she been a virtuous girl, than any other two years of her time, a girl in her place would cost us 8 or 9/P week, that she is as capable, or perhaps more so, then any one we could hire; I was afraid of her bad example to our other little girl &c—she appeard more angry than griv'd, said she should not care if the childs brains were beat out &c—she would never have anything to do with it—I told her we would make no account of the expences we had already been at of Sallys laying in and board, the childs nursing since &c. she said she would take her daughter provided they, nither of 'em, should ever have any thing to do with the Child—she went away rather out of humor—when HD. come home we related the above to him, concluded were we to turn her off, upon her mothers terms, she would be in the high road to further ruin—he call'd her into the parlor this evening and talk'd closely to her, told her he had a right to send her to the work house and sell her for a servent, that it was in pity to her, and in hopes of her reformation

that he did not send Joe to prision, she had always had a good example in our house, if she did not mend her conduct she should not stay much longer in it &c. she cry'd but said nothing—How it will end, or what we shall do with her, I know not,—set aside this vile propensity, she is one of the most handy and best servants we have ever had—and a girl of very pritty manners.

20. pleasent cool morning wind N.W.—William rode out on Horseback.—Neighr. Waln came over to know if I would go with her to John Thompsons, agree'd, Nancy Skyrin, who was here went with us—it was paying the last visit, to the remains of an Old friend and Neighbour, in whose company I have spent many agreeable hours—Patty Smith there, Chalkleys wife and Children also—John Thomsons Children in the Measles.—mett Becky and Betsy Shoemaker and others there—went down a few minuets to Nancys, stop'd a little time at Jacob Downings—came home before dinner—HD. Billy Savery and Jos. Sansom gone this Afternoon to Clearfield, to Germantown &c. in our Carrige—Richd. Morris, Jonan. Hearvey, and Richd. Smith call'd this forenoon—E Skyrin spends the day with us—Sally Zane call'd, says H Pemberton is better—Nancy Skyrin took tea, John Skyrin and John Cannon here this evening E. Downing is very poorly—HD. went to John Thompsons this evening—Henry & Hannah went home this forenoon.

21 st. HD. MS. MD. gone to meeting, James gone to Clearfield with grass seed &c. Saml. Emlen, Sally Large call'd—Sally Johnson call'd, HD. desir'd her to come again on fifth day next, being himself at that time engaged H Mott, B. Emlen call'd—the little Downings better.—Ellis Cleaver call'd about black Horse,—S. Swett din'd and tea'd here.—HD. MS. Nancy and Molly, went this Afternoon to the funeral of Reba. James—our James attended at grave yard with the Carriage. Walter Franklin call'd this evening to see Molly, who was out.—John Cannon sup'd with us—Sister tea'd with Bulah Burge.

22. Clear cool morning Wind N.E. E. Downing very poorly. Dr. Rush here about noon, he innoculated the two Peters, Woodard and Savage—Hannah Catheral din'd here, Saml. Emlen took tea—two bearded men call'd—I spent most of this day, making peach blossom Syrup—John Cannon here this evening John Willcox ill, he borrow'd our bed-Chair.

April 23. Clear and cool, wind N.E—Author Donaldson and others call'd—S Johnson here, on account of her troublesome Daughter—After discorseing with HD. she had a conference with Sally, whom she says has promis'd amendment &c—William, Nancy and Molly gone to Clearfield to dine with Hannah, Henry in town—S. Swett spent the day with us—she, John Saltar, and HSD. din'd here—William and Molly returnd to tea. John and Nancy came in the evening I went with 'em to see Sally who is bravely—Eliza red with the Measles: I hope in a good way—John Cannon here this evening John Drinker also.

24th. Cool and clear—wind N.E—Saml. Emlen call'd he set longer than usual—Nancy Skyrin and Child here forenoon. HD. din'd at J Skyrins, I examin'd our black boys Arms, think they have not taken the infection—Sister out this Afternoon, Betsy Emlen call'd in their Carriage for Molly to ride with her, she gone to Nancys, where she went for her—Sammy Fisher came home with Sister, he spent an hour—E Downings throat sore—Tommy Stewardson call'd, rain this evening.

25. rain in the night, cloudy morning wind N.E—Jacob Downing call'd—HSD. came to town after dinner, he went home before tea—Saml. Emlen and Ben Wilson took tea with us.—rain this evening—I think I can observe to day, something where the puncture was made in the boys Arms—some signs that they have taken the infection, 'tho small signs.

April 26. First day. cloudy, rain in the night—wind still at N.E—where it has been for 5 days past—Saml. Emlen call'd before meeting—Sally Rhoads took tea, Nancy Skyrin and Child here, John came in the evening John Drinker call'd—A Saml. Heart, lately from Great Britain, was yesterday at work a short time in our Garden, HD. has recommended him to several as a Gardiner—he has a Wife and six Children, the eldest a daughter of 14 years, who has, as she says, never spoke a word in her life, a true object of Charity, those are the people, that, in my oppinion, ought to be perticularly attended to,—Molly spent this evening at J Smiths, the evening at S. Emlens.

27. rain forenoon, wind N.E—John Cannon breakfastd with me, Richd. Morris call'd—rain most of the Afternoon and evening Dr. Rush call'd before dinner, says the boys have taken the small pox, he expects they will sicken on fourth day next.

28th. rain in the night, heavy rain this morning. wind at last changed to west and N.W. variable—Nancy Skyrin call'd before meeting—boys took their last powder—James Logan and A Skyrin call'd after meeting—Caleb Crissons Son John, and Jeremiah Warders Daughter Mary, were merried, at meeting to day.—John Cannon, Elijah Waring and Hannah Catheral din'd here—A black woman, named Reba. Gibbs, and her daughter Patience, a girl of 12 years old. came from the lower Counties, from Warner Mifflin, the girl sent up for John Skyrin, we gave them their dinner, then sent them there.—Sally Smith and Sally Large call'd—Molly gone to Nancys, I went this Afternoon into [Jsh.] Whartons to see his little Son Francis, who is recovering of the Measles—mett Becky Shoemaker there.—Saml. Smith and Billy Savery call'd here this evening—I spent an hour at Neighr. Walns, then went to Jacob Downings, he came home with me.

April 29. rain in the night, and this Morning clear before noon. wind N.W.—Dr. Rush here, says the boys are a little feverish—Walter Franklin and Jonathan Hearvey call'd on Molly to go this Afternoon to Clearfield. Betsy Emlen, Sally Smith, and Sally Large and WF were to go in Emlens Carriage, MD. agree'd to go with JH. in a Chaise—I should have been better pleas'd that the Girls had gone alltogeather in the four wheel'd Carriage, as the roads are bad &c—S. Brant gone this Afternoon with her mother, to spend it at her step-fathers' near the Canall, he is a manager there, she brought a Chaise for her, promisd to return with her by dusk—which she did—Molly &c did not return 'till near 10 o'clock, moon light—I went after dinner to see Sally, she has been troubled with pain in her face and toothach, found her better, and Elizah, I hope recovering of the Measles,—E. Jervis there, she came home with me, I then went over to visit little H. Hartshorn, who has also had the measles, came home to tea—Peter Yarnel, Saml. Emlen, Betsy Jervis, Nancy Skyrin and Child took tea here.—Nichs. Waln came to see us this Afternoon—Dr. Jardine came from North Bank to Clearfield this Afternoon with Henry, left HSD. at home, and came to town in his Chair, he is to have the Horse to return to North Bank when he calls for him—John Skyrin here for Nancy this evening—William, Nancy, & little Elizabeth rode out this Afternoon—John Buncle,[27] has been, more in my mind this evening than any thing better, or worse.

April 30. Sunshine, 'tho hazey, not yet settled weather. wind N.E—Betsy Watson call'd—G. Fry came to town for Horse &c—Dr. Jardine call'd for HSDs Horse—William went out twice, short walks—Nancy Skyrin and her daughter took tea, Ostin Jones call'd, to say farewell, the Vessel, of which he is mate sails in an hour or two.—Reynold Keen here this Afternoon, I acknowledg'd a Deed before him, he being Judge of Ct. Common Plees. Jacob Downing, John and Nancy Skyrin and Molly, went this evening from hence to Jacobs.

May 1st. Sunshine, weather not settled, wind N.E. Huldah Mott and Betsy Emlen, call'd on Molly to ride with them—Neighr. Waln here fore noon—Nancy Skyrin call'd after dinner, then went to pay S Downing a visit, it being visiting time, as 'tis calld. Dr. Rush call'd—Betsy Emlen, Sally Smith and Sally Large took tea with Molly, Walter Franklin with them in front parlor this evening—Sister out, she drank tea with H Pemberton—James took the Sorril Horse to Clearfield to day—I went between 8 and 9 o'clock, William

27. See below, May 22.

with me, to Jacob Downings, mett with 6 or 8 visittors in Sallys Chamber—Sally better, 'tho not well.

2. Sun shine, 'tho not clear, wind N.E—J Skyrin here this morning HSD. came to town before breakfast. William, Molly, Nancy and Child, went out in Carriage this morning T. Stewardson call'd—Dr. Rush call'd—I pick'd a Tulip from our Garden with eight leaves, which I look on as a Curiosity, never having seen one before with more than six leaves.—sent the Cart, loaded with rolling Stone &c to Clearfield, Henry set off Afternoon for home on foot.—Joshua and Caty Howel an their Son Neddy, Saml. Emlen, Saml. Smith, Reba. Jones and HD. had a conference this Afternoon in our front parlor, on a Business relative to Edwd.—Nancy Skyrin, Saml. Emlen and James Logan took tea with us.

3. First day: Overcast, wind N.E—HD. MS. and MD. gone to meeting—S Swett din'd here, she and Nancy took tea—we caught a fine red bird in our yard, forenoon, put him in a Cage, where he appear'd quite contented, some one has lost a pet, I should be best pleas'd, was he in the poss[ess]ion of his right owner—Sister went to see Sally,—I went to Neighr. Rhoads who is unwell, her Daughter E.F has been very ill, is now better. a few small pox have made their appearance on our black boys, that look as if they would come to nothing.—Molly spent the evening at Saml. Emlens—Nancy Skyrins black girl Patience, is thought by Dr. Kuhn to have the itch, which is matter of no small thought to Ann and myself also, she has it not in a great degree, Nancy is useing means to cure it—Poor Richd. N——s——t. and family came to the City Yesterday, his Wife and Children are, for the present, at John Parishs—he is taken to the Hospital.

4. clear and pleasent, wind N.W. HD. MS. MD. gone to quarterly meeting—William went out forenoon on old Mare, to his dissapointment found her lame—Dr. Rush, Jonan. Harvey &c call'd—Daniel Drinker din'd here, he, HD. and William set off after 3 o'clock for Clearfield, cloudy—S. Emlen call'd, he paid 50 Dollars which he had borrow'd some days ago, he desires it may be expunged from the book of memory—I assur'd him it should be as much as was necessary—HD. &c return'd to tea, S Swett call'd—went this evening William with me to see Sally, found things there in good plight—came home to supper, Benn. Wilson sup'd with us.

5. heavy rain in the Night, Clear pleasent morning wind S.E—John Drinker call'd—HD. and Son Willm. rode out after dinner—Henry and Hannah came to town, they din'd at J Skyrins—I spent this Afternoon at S. Emlen's, call'd at Jacob Downings.—Molly Drinker, Betsy Emlen, Sally Smith, Sally Large, George Benson, Richd. Smith, Richd. Morris and Jonan. Hervey, were all at Grays Ferry this Afternoon, as Molly this evening informs me—which I,

by no means approve,—Friends Children going in companyes to public houses, is quite out of Character. Our James Duning has been for some time past very strange in his behaviour, sometimes talks of leaving us, 'tho he says he has no cause for so doing, then changes his mind and appears easy—this evening Benn. Oliver ask'd to speak with HD. told him, James was at his house crying, that he could not find out what ail'd him, but said his conduct was very strange—James came in sometime after and ask'd my husband if he would forgive him, what hast thou done amiss? he said he had sometimes overfed the Horses, at another time suffer'd them to run away—poor fellow: I fear he has something at heart that we know not off—he never was faulted for the above matters, one we look'd on as an accident, the other, knew nothing of—if it was so.

6. Clear, rather warm, wind S.E—Dr. Rush call'd—Henry Breakfasted here, Hannah call'd—Sally Hopkins, Nancy Skyrin and a Peggy Smith, a mantua maker, at work for Molly, din'd here—Anna Wells, Joseph Bringhurst John Drinker &c call'd—little E. Skyrin spent the day—Nancy is in trouble, she is apprehensive that Betsy Dawson has caught the itch off the Negro girl—Jacob and Sally here this Afternoon, the first of Sallys being out, since the birth of her Son—Saml. Smith and wife from B. County call'd—We were, this Afternoon inform'd of the Death, of our worthy friend John Pemberton, who died the 31st. of the first month, this year, at Pyrmont in Germany, the particulars of his sickness &c. have not yet heard—poor Hannah, I feel for her, she has lost, it may be truly said, one of the best of Husbands.—his death is matter of concern to our Son William, who lov'd him well, as did all our family, my husband particularly—Our Coachman James, this morning settled with his Master, made up a little bundle, and brought in the keys of Coachhouse and Stables, came into the parlor to bid us farewell, with tears in his eyes, I ask'd him where he was going? Any where, he said where he was not known,—We were uneasy on his account as he had eat nothing, or next to nothing for two days past, I desired him to set down in the window, he did so, and weep't much, He told us he had acquainted his master with the crime that lay heavy at his heart,—We could not consent to his going away, we knew not where, I asked my husband who was in the coumpting house, what mighty fault James had been guilty of, he said he could not make out what he would be at, what he had said to him was unintellgible, I gave him a glass of wine and water, Billy added 13 drops Liquid ladunum, and a peice bread, which I insisted on his eating, and then to go to his Chamber and lay down for a short time, that I did believe he would be the better for it, he told us that he had been some days ago at the Sweeds-Church, where the minister said something that pierc'd his heart,—poor fellow! his nerves appear to be much affected, he is but 23 or 4. years of age, a stout young Man near 6 feet high.—He came down to dinner, said he was much better, then went to take care of his horses, and appear'd to be reinstated—he went to bed, appearently compossed after taking

3 or 4 assafatida pills: but when Billy went up, sometime after, to enquire how he was, he found him on his knees by the bedside—I feel much for the poor young man, in a strange land, his parents are, he expects, living in Ireland, he told my husband last night, he was afraid he should brake their hearts.—John and Nancy, has had a rumpus, this evening with Thos. Dawson, on account of Betts—There is great trouble with Servants sometimes, more especially with some, when we are thoughtful for their wellfare.

7. clear and warm, wind S.W. James at work in the Garden, a thing not usual with him, he appears bravely.—James Logan, Saml. Emlen junr. &c call'd—Jacob, Sally, and W Drinker went this Afternoon to Clearfield. Henry came to town, he mett them,—he and Hannah and Nancy Skyrin took tea with us, HSD went home towards evening—he intends tomorrow for North Bank, he left Hannah here, Ben. Wilson here this evening he carried E Skyrin home in his Arms—Thos. Morris, John Drinker, Joseph Bringhurst and HD. in front parlor this evening busy correcting the discipline—warmest day as yet, John Skyrin call'd—I finish'd reading the following peices bound in one 8.oo Volume Vizt.—lent me by Docr. Rush—The Everlasting Gospel &c. concerning Eternal Redemption &c by Paul Siegvolck a German.[28]—The three Woe Trumpets; of which the first and second are already past; and the third is now begun: &c. By Elhanan Winchester being the substance of two discourses &c.[29]—The present state of Europe compared with antient prophecies A Sermon preach'd by Joseph Priestley &c[30]—The Lord Jesus Christ worthy of the love of all Men, demonstrated in two discourses—by E. Winchester,[31] and A Sermon deliver'd by the same, in London.

8. clear, wind S.W. very warm day. Wm. Shannon lately from Ireland breakfasted with us—John Hillborn and Hannah Catheral din'd here—Sally Rhoads took tea, Neighr. Waln &c call'd—Joseph Bringhurst, John Drinker &c in front parlor with HD. this evening—Sister gone with S. Rhoads to visit our afflicted friend H. Pemberton, John Hillborn lodges here. About 5. Afternoon, William and Mary sett off from our door, with designs to take in Nancy and Child, It look'd very like a gust coming on—they had not been gone ten minuits, before it blew with violence, but as they were then at J

28. Paul Siegvolck [George Klein-Nicolai], *The Everlasting Gospel, Commanded to Be Preached by Jesus Christ, Judge of the Living and the Dead, unto All Creatures . . . Concerning the Eternal Redemption Found Out by Him, Whereby Devil, Sin, Hell and Death, Shall at Last Be Abolished . . .*, trans. John S[echla] (Germantown, Pa.: Christopher Sower, 1753 [*NUC*]).

29. Elhanan Winchester, *The Three Woe Trumpets, of Which the First and Second Are Already Past, and the Third Is Now Begun . . .* (London, [1793?]; Boston: Folsom, 1794 [*NUC*]).

30. Joseph Priestley, *The Present State of Europe Compared with Antient Prophesies: A Sermon, Preached at the Gravel Pit Meeting in Hackney, February 28, 1794 . . . With a Preface, Containing the Reasons for the Author's Leaving England* (London: J. Johnson, 1794 [*NUC*]).

31. Elhanan Winchester, *The Lord Jesus Christ Worthy of the Love of All Men, Demonstrated in Two Discourses . . .* (London: T. Gillet, 1791 [*Brit. Mus. Cat.*]).

Skyrins they turn'd back—and came in just before the heavy rain, thunder and lightening—one very hard clap.

May 9. Clear and cool. wind N.W. Hannah Drinker and Sally Large here forenoon—John Hillborn din'd, he went away after dinner—Hannah Drinker, Sally Large, Billy and Molly went after dinner to Clearfield—William return'd rather late, left the others there—he brought me a letter from HSD. wrote yesterday, before he set off for North-Bank, informing, that Geo. Fry and wife, were tired of their Nursery &c—where we shall put it, are yet undertermin'd—A Skyrin and Child took tea here. Joseph Bringhurst and John Drinker, busy with HD. in front parlor—Sally Downing and her two little girls were here forenoon, Sally, 'tho she looks well, is very weak, and has a bad cough.—Billy tells me that James went into the woods, while they were at Clearfield and stay'd so long as to occasion their returning home rather later than was proper, he is exceeding low this evening is desirous of going away, some where, he knows not where, he would set off this evening if we would consent—says his heart is very heavy, that he is a great sinner, and has been too well [treated] in this house, &c—he appears to wish to be alone, says he thinks if we would consent to his going away, he might return in a few days better—WD. gave him 15 drops Liquid Laudanum in a glass wine, with a small cake, he took the wine, but would not eat.—I proposed to HD. after he was gone to bed, to send tomorrow for a phisician.—John Skyrin here this evening Sister visited Richd. Nisbets wife and Children this Afternoon—Saml. Lheman call'd. he paid me ground-rent for MS.—during the thunder storm Yesterday Afternoon, a house in Southwark was struck, where the shingles were removed, the roof, with several parts of the house considerably damaged. There were several women setting in the door—who providentially sustain'd no injury.—Benn. Oliver came in after 10 o'clock to know how James was, he, is his Confidential friend, he hinted that James had told him of something, that if it was true, was very bad, but he could not belive it, he look'd on it, as the effect of his low state of mind, which made the worst of every thing—he further said, that he talk'd of hanging or shooting himself—what the crime was he did not say, supposing, as I thought we knew it, nor did I urge him, not knowing of what nature it might be—he said Mr. Drinker knew what it was,—if thats the case, I trust 'tis nothing very criminal, as HD. seems to pity him.—between ten and eleven o'clock we were Alarmed by the cry of fier, were inform'd it was near the Playhouse.—How many distressing occurances there are in this World, to a feeling mind—My dear, Billy seems very poorly this evening on account of James.

10. First day: the wind N.E. this morning with some rain—HD. MS. at meeting. James, when I was up stairs, about eleven o'clock, went out, with a little bundle in his hand, stop'd in the entry, and said to Billy, The Lord bless you all, Billy ask'd him where he was going, desired him to stay and endeavour

to compose himself—he said he would not, and went off.—he had told my Husband this morning that he was going to his brothers—how that may be, we know not, as he had said some time ago, that he would not go to his brothers on any account—he has left most of his linnen &c in his closet, and some of his upper Cloaths at Benjn. Olivers.—The fire last night is said to be a Stable burnt down near the New Prison.—Gave our black boys, each a dose of Rheubarb, sent by the Doctor—they have had the small pox favourably, the bigest has had it, as the Doctors would say, beautifully, HD. went after dinner to visit Hannah Pemberton—Sister to see Hannah Hartshorn, Saml. Emlen here before Afternoon or evening Meeting, it begins now, at four o'clock—our little ES. here, Nancy stop'd here in her way home from Clearfield, their Horse fell down in a muddy place, they were under the necessity of geting out, and ungearing him—HSD. arrived at Clearfield about 4 PM. Molly, Hannah &c. well—James Smith here afternoon, John and Nancy, Daniel Drinker and Peter Barker sup'd with us—B. Oliver came in late this evening said James call'd at his house after he left us, told him he knew not where he was going.—I spent the fore part of this Afternoon writing the latter, in meeting time, reading, some expressions of Elizabeth Rathbone at different periods during her last illness. And an account of the sickness and death, of our friend Job Scott, of Rhode-Island—who died of the small-pox, the 22 of the eleventh month 1793. at Ballitore in Ireland.

11. Thunder early this Morning a steady rain for some hours after. wind S.W. John Drinker call'd—Simon Shewbart to pay MS. a ground rent—Dr. Redman spent an hour,—I did wonders this Afternoon in the visiting way—my first inducement was to go see my friend H. Pemberton in her trouble, P.P. and H.Y. there &c—took tea there, went from thence to J Smiths a long walk, stay'd but a short time, then went, Jonney Smith with me, to J Skyrins, Nancy gone to our house, Johney came home with me, Nancy was gone to her Sister Sallys—Sally Rhoads came in this evening to take leave of us, as she is moveing out of our Neighbourhood to a house up Arch-street, where she expects to be fix't in a day or two—John Drinker, John Elliott, Thos. Morris and HD. busy in front parlor this Afternoon. William went this evening to Jacob Downings, came home after night. very warm, looks like a gust, thunder &c.

May 12. Cloudy, wind N.E. HD. MS. at meeting—Susanh Swett din'd here—Jos. Bringhurst, John Elliott and Bancroft Woodcock and SS. took tea with us—Molly Drinker not yet return'd from Clearfield—went after night, with William to Jacob Downings, found Sally and her babe by themselves, an uncommon curcumstance—William rode out yesterday afternoon, two miles on the old Mare, he has been more unwell this Spring, than the latter part of the winter.

13. Wind N.E. with some rain, chang'd by noon—HSD. came to town, he

din'd with us—Jacob Downing, John Skyrin and James Logan call'd—went over to see Hannah Hartshorn, who is in a very weak state. A thunder shower this Afternoon. John Elliott, J Drinker, Joseph Bringhurst and Thos. Morris with HD. in front parlor, busy'd as usual, J Drinker and HSD. took tea with us—Henry I expect will lodge here, he was just setting off for home, when the rain came on which stop'd him—Polly Betton was here the day before yesterday settled with, and paid her off.

14. Clear and cool, wind N.W. HSD. and Wm. Saltar breakfasted with us.—Tommy Fisher call'd—Sally, Nancy, and their Daughters here forenoon, Abey Marshall and her Sister call'd to see Molly, who is not yet return'd from Clearfield—Billy Saltar and HSD. din'd here—Henry went home after dinner—S. Hartshorn sent for me after dinner, she was alone with her Daughter Hannah who she thought, appear'd rather lower than usual, but recover'd soon after to her common state. Sally Downing here this Afternoon—I went after tea, to visit M. Foulk who has been lately ill, but is now better, Patty Smith &c there—HD. come there to me, we went to Jacobs, their little Boy much grip'd. Elliston and Sally Perot there—Sammy Rhoads here this evening, he's lately return'd from New England. this has been a very pleasent day. William rode out, on the mare, three or four miles—he walk'd out this evening.

15. very fine weather, the wind at S.W. William went two or 3 miles, on Horse back,—Sally Downing gone with Sally Perot in their Carriage to Clearfield. they return'd home to dinner—Jacob call'd, he told us, that Sally left her Sister Molly unwell with headack, a disorder she is but seldom troubled with—she came home this evening with Hetty Smith, Sally Smith and Sally Large also.—Molly is but poorly, 'tho no so bad as I expected—The comittee in front Parlor again to day. I thought they had finish'd Neighr. Waln and John Drinker here this evening Sally Downing and Nancy Skyrin were here this Afternoon, Sally is far from well, her young maid Nancy Reed gone away—Tommy Fisher and his Son William here this evening I wrote this Afternoon to M. Penry—George Fry's wife parted with the poor little yallow one, to a Negro woman in the Neighbourhood 'till we can otherwise dispose of it—Saml. Heart at work in our Garden—James Logan call'd—Edward Garriges put up a Venitian Door to the back of our entry.

16. heavey rain between 11. and 12 last night—a fine clear morning wind N.W. William rode on horseback 4 miles, HSD. came to town—Molly and self went out about 10 o'clock went to Saml. Shoemakers up market street, spent and hour or more with Becky—call'd at Hannah Pembertons, who is poorly, came home to dinner—Sally and Nancy here after dinner, Henry din'd here and went home after tea, Sammy Rhoads here this evening, Molly abroad—the weather cool.

May 17. First day: Clear, wind N.E—chang'd to S.W.—HD. MS. and MD. at meeting—S Swett din'd, she, Nancy Skyrin and [J] Logan took tea—Sally Smith here, she and Molly went to S. Emlens—Peggy Wharton, Owen Biddle here this evening—J Skyrin came for Nancy—smart Shower about 10 this evening.

18. cloudy, wind N.E—fort malade cet matin—dull weather most of this day, moon chang'd A.M. we have had a very unsettled Spring, Northeast winds chiefly prevailing.—Isaac Potts, Betsy Fordham, &c call'd—Benjn. Oliver with a John Bowding here this evening HD. hir'd the latter as Coachman &c. at 75/ – P month, washing and board—he is to come tomorrow—no intelligence yet, of poor James Dunning—William went this cool evening to his Sister Sallys, Molly to Nancys.

19. Cloudy day, several small rains, wind N.E. and S.E. Peter Yarnel, and Saml. Emlen here before meeting—Anna Wells and her two Sons here forenoon—Hannah Catheral din'd with us—A meeting to be held this Afternoon at the North meeting house, Appointed by Peter Yarnel, for the young people of our Society, to begin at the fourth hour, Nancy Skyrin, Anna Wells, and Molly Drinker went from hence to attend it.—It held 'till after 7 o'clock.—John and Nancy Skyrin and Betsy Foulk drank tea with us—John Drinker and Isaac Potts here this evening—Sally Dawson gone off this evening we suppose to her Fathers, by the advice of her naughty Sister Betts, sent Sam Sprigs to look for her there, he found the door shut, and they gone out—I am uneasy to [look] her out, as we are not sure where she is,—'tho not in much doubt about it.

20. cloudy, wind S.E. chang'd to S.W.—Peggy Smith here, at work for Molly.—S. Dawsons Step-Mother here this morning says Sall is at their house, they found her when they came home, in bed with her little Sister, it was near eleven when they came home, would have brought her, but thought it too late, she had complain'd that Billy struck her.—he told her it was very true, but it was a week ago, he gave her a blow, the only time he ever touch'd her,[32] that she deserv'd much more then he gave her—It was a new thing to Sall, for him to strike her, she has never been beat since she liv'd with us, more than a light slap on her cheek—'tho she has often deserv'd it, her mother says she beleives it is her Sister Betts doings, says she will send her home with a good scolding—I fear she will be a troublesom bargin to us.—Sally Hopkins and Sally Smith call'd before dinner.—Molly Drinker, [S] Smith, Sally Large and Walter Franklin, in Largess Carriage, Sammy Rhoads and Betsy Emlen in a chair—Richd. Morris on Horse-back went this Afternoon to Clearfield—Thos. Dawson's Wife brought Sall home this Afternoon, she does not advocate

32. The words "in his life" crossed out.

her conduct, but hopes she'l mend her manners—I went this Afternoon to Sallys, found her and Children bravely, call'd at Sarah Fishers, came home, and went out again, to visit my old friend Rebecca Say who' I found ill, in her bed, she was very glad to see me, appears resigned to the will of her Maker.—I came home to tea—This has been a trying day to William &c. several in front parlor this evening with HD.—John Drinker call'd—lightening to the Westward.

21st. a gust of thunder lightening, rain and hail a little before midnight, cloudy this morning wind S.W—heavy rain about one o'clock, Sally Downing, and Daughter Elizah., Nancy Skyrin and her Daughter were detain'd here by the rain, they, William Blakey, David Cumming and Pegg Smith din'd here—Saml. Smith of B. County here forenoon I went over before dinner to see Hannah Hartshorn whom I think, is now, going fast—she appears low, 'tho setting up in a Chair, her poor Mother in great trouble—Jacob Downing call'd. HD. went this Afternoon to Clearfield, John Drinker with him as far as Fair hill, which place he has taken on a long lease—It is now[33] meeting for Suffering, many friends in town—John Fry call'd—Saml. Smith lodges here—Billy better. read, The Robbers, a Tragedy, translated from the German[34]—'tis long since I read a play before.

22. rain in the night, cloudy morning wind S.W.—James Logan call'd—Benjn. Swett breakfasted, James Jackson and George Churchman din'd with us.—Enoch Evans and Willm. Blakey call'd—John Simpson, Saml. Smith and Nancy Skyrin drank tea. I went with Nancy this evening to Jacob Downings to see little Mary, who has taken the Measles—Nancy and Jacob came back with me, she sup'd here, Sl. Smith went homewards after tea—finish'd reading some days ago, the life of John Buncle Esqr. in two Octo. Volls.[35] which I think may be call'd a Medley, many good remarks, and sensible observations—with, as I think, some absurdities, in the second volume especialy, the first I prefer.—James Lackington in his Memoirs says that it was written by a Thomas Amory, Esqr. who was living in the year 1788. at the great age of 97.—It looks as if I spent most of my time reading, which is by no means the case, a book is soon run over, and 'tho I seldom make mention of any other employment, yet I believe I may say, without vanity, that I was never an indolent person, or remarkably Bookish, tho more so for 5 or 6 years past, than at any other period since I was married,—haveing more leisure—when

33. The words "our quarter" crossed out.
34. Frederick Schiller, *The Robbers, a Tragedy in Five Acts*, trans. Lord Woodhouselee (London: G. G. J. and J. Robinson, 1792 [*NUC*]).
35. Thomas Amory, *The Life of John Buncle, Esq; Containing Various Observations and Reflections, Made in Several Parts of the World, and Many Extraordinary Relations* (London: J. Johnson and B. Davenport, 1746 [*NUC*]).

my Children were young I seldom read a volume; but was I at present favour'd with health, I should delight in it. As it is I often find it a consolation.

23. Cloudy with rain, wind Westerly. Jacob Downing call'd—Benjn. Swett din'd with us HD. &c. went this Afternoon to the President on Indian Affairs—Betsy Jervis took tea with us, she went with Sister to Jacob Downings—Dr. Rush here this evening. Samuel Moore came this Afternoon from Clearfield with Cart, he says, Henry return'd yesterday from North bank, where he has been since third day last. Polly Betton here this evening she took her Chest &c.

24. First Day: Whitsunday as 'tis call'd—cleard up last night, a fine cool pleasent morning wind N.W. I have heard that it is a remark of the Indians, that such weather as prevails on the second three days, that is, the 4th. 5. and 6th. of the Moons age, denotes the weather, fair or foul, that is to be expected during that month or moon—we have now an oppertunity of making the trial, this is the sixth day of the Moons age, and the first fair, since the change. My Husband, Jacob Downing and his daughter Eliza. went after breakfast to Clearfield, intending for Germantown meeting—John and Nancy Skyrin, Oliver, call'd before meeting, Molly Smith also, MS. and MD. gone, WD. and self at home, S. Swett and Ben Wilson din'd with us—Saml. Emlen and A Skyrin call'd after meeting—Betsy Emlen & N. Skyrin took tea here, Nancy's little one, and Betsy Emlens Harriott here also—Isaac Potts spent an hour—MD. EE. SS. SL.—SR. WF. GB. and [J]H. in front parlor this evening—HD. and Jacob return'd after tea.

May 25. Clear and cool, wind N.E—HSD. came to town this morning Sister gone to visit the Almshouse, Molly out, William gone on horseback—I went after dinner to see Reba. Say, thought her better then when I saw her last. call'd at Jacob Downings, Mary not ill, but an appearence on her Neck as tho the blood had settled in spots—the Measles are gone off, the Doctor said this morning she was bravely, this appearance has occur'd since he saw her.—Sister gone this Afternoon to Clearfield with Hetty Smith—and James Logan—Molly and self a few minutes at Neighr. Walns—Nicholas Waln here this Afternoon, Joseph Bringhurst call'd—Dr. Rush introduced a Scotch Gentleman of name Thomas Wilson, the latter took tea with us—WD. took a ride by himself to Middle Ferry, John had been out with Daniel Trotters Wife who is in poor health, when they return'd William went.—Molly spent the Afternoon at Phebe Morris's visiting Betsy Mifflin—very cool this evening.

26. Cloudy, wind Southerly.—Henry and Hannah came to town this morning HD. and Sister gone to meeting monthly, Roger Hunt, Nancy Skyrin &c call'd before meeting, S Swett and HSD. din'd here—HD. and William went from home at 4 o'clock for Clearfield, they return'd to tea—Nancy Morgan,

Anna Wells and Nancy Skyrin took tea here—HSD. and S Swett also—Nancy went yesterday in Chaise with her husband to Gloucester-point, Issey Pleasents &c with them—Walter Franklin and Sammy Rhoads here this evening William and self, paid Sally Downing an evening visit—Joshua Cliborn the larger, here this evening.

27. a fine clear pleasent morning wind S.W.—William went out by himself in the Chaise, with the old mare, 10 Miles, round Point and Frankford roads, came home to dinner—John Drinker call'd while we were at Dinner, was desireous of a passage to Fairhill for himself and Joshua Smith, it did not suit to wait 'till our Children were ready to go to Clearfield—William and Molly went, they did not overtake them, but brought 'em home when returning. I went to H Pembertons, spent an hour with her, Nancy Skyrin call'd there for me, we went to visit M. Pleasants, took tea with her—look'd over their New House, near ninth street in Market Street, nearly opposite the large building, now finishing for the President. SPs is a very neat and convenient house, the prospect from it beautiful—we went after tea to Jams Pembertons the next Door, Phebe unwell, in her Chamber.—came home by moon light John Skyrin with us, tired by so long a walk—Jacob Downing here this evening J Logan drank tea here—Sally Rhoads, and M Lippencott call'd.

28. Pleasent and clear, wind Southerly. HD. and Son Wm. went out in Chaise to the Cannal, WD. walk'd in R. Morriss Garden, they return'd before dinner—Jacob, Sally and their 3 Children, Nancy and her one, and John Thomas, were here this Afternoon, John Saltar and Nathan Shepard call'd, the former din'd with us—I step'd over after dinner to P. Hartshorn to see Hannah—William set off at half past three, in the Carriage, to call on Sally and the Children to go to Clearfield—Henry came to town this Afternoon, stay'd about an hour, then went homeward.—William Ashbridge took tea with us, he has lately return'd from Ireland—made his home while in Dublin, five or 6 Weeks, at Joseph Sandwiths—Saml. Emlen call'd this Afternoon, William &c return'd after 8 o'clock, a cloudy evening, and Easterly wind, how improper! WD. in his present weak state of health, Sally from her little babe, and the first time of little Marys going out, since the Measles. Molly spent the evening at Nancys.—I have been pleas'd by reading, the Morals of Confucius a Chinese philosopher who flourished about five hundred and fifty years before the coming of Christ[36]—said to be one of the choicest peices of Learning remaining of that Nation—a sweet little peice it is—If there were such men in that day, what ought to be expected in this more enlighten'd Age!—rain this evening.

36. *The Morals of Confucius, a Chinese Philosopher, . . . Being One of the Choicest Pieces of Learning Remaining of That Nation,* trans. and abridged from the Latin trans. by the Reverend Fathers Prospero Intorcetta, Philippe Couplet, and others (London: Randal Taylor, 1691 [*Brit. Mus. Cat., NUC*]).

29. It rain'd fast last night when we retired—very heavy at four this morning and continu'd raining after we arose. wind S.E—Henrys Scip came to town for Biscuit—says, his master left home this morning for North-bank. Jacob Downing here afternoon,—Molly went after dinner to set with her Sister Nancy—rain again this Afternoon and evening cloudy all day.—Joshua Clibborn [Maijor] here this evening John Skyrin came home with Molly.

30. Hazey. wind S.E—John Saltar and wife, here this forenoon, they acknowledg'd a Deed before Joseph Ellis Esqr. who was here also to Nathan Shepherd who was also present—HD. and self acknowledgd a Deed to John Saltar.—they went away before Dinner, Jacob Downing call'd, and Walter Franklin also. An account in this mornings paper of three Men who lost their lives fighting, yesterday in Southwark[37]—Had such an affair happen'd 30 or 40 years ago, the whole town would have been in an uproar, but we heard nothing of it 'till we saw the account in the News-paper. Jacob, Sally and their Daughters were here this afternoon, they wish'd me to go with them to the Statehouse Yard, and to Peels Museam[38] which is keep't in the State house,—I declin'd the motion, but Molly excepted it, and went with them—Nancy Skyrin, her Daughter and Oliver, spent this Afternoon with us, and evening also, detain'd by a heavy rain.—several friends in front Parlor this evening with HD—HD. WD. and MS. went out in Carriage this afternoon, MS. stop'd at Saml. Whartons, HD. and Son went to the house of Employment—they came home to tea—Sally Wharton agree'd to spend next third day with us, we are to send for her—Saml. Emlen call'd—John Skyrin came this evening, he, Nancy, the Child with Sam went home in the rain—Molly was much pleas'd this Afternoon, viewing the cureosities in the Museim.—My Husband and Son call'd when they were out this Afternoon, to see Hannah Pemberton, and went after to SWs for Sister.

31st. First day: much rain in the night, clear this morning wind N.W. tho it dont appear settled weather.—Oliver Wadsworth came to inform that Eliz[h]. Skyrin is very unwell, feverish and red in the face, her mother suspects she is breeding the Measles—John Collins call'd this morning Jacob and Sally with their Daughter Eliza[h]. call'd in their way to meeting. HD. MS. MD. gone to meeting. WD. and self at home. Jacob and Sally call'd after, they left Eliza to dine here went themselves to dine at John Skyrins—Benjn. Catheral and his

37. On May 29 a fight broke out between some French crewmen of the privateer brig *Brutus* and workers at a Southwark ropewalk. Two crewmen and one worker were killed. The fight and subsequent rioting necessitated calling out troops to patrol the area (*Gazette of the United States and Daily Evening Advertiser,* May 30, 1795; *The Philadelphia Gazette and Universal Daily Advertiser,* May 30, 1795).

38. Charles Willson Peale's museum, located in Philosophical Hall, housed both works of art and natural history. Portraits of Revolutionary War heroes were displayed along with exotic stuffed birds, animals, and artifacts from the world over. The museum also sponsored lectures, exhibitions, and concerts (Sellers, *Mr. Peale's Museum*).

puples the Potts's call'd—William poorly to day. HD. MD. and Eliza, at meeting this Afternoon.—HD. went before, to J Skyrins to see the little Girl, found her ailing, tho not ill.—I read this Afternoon, a phamplet intitled A few reasons for leaving The National Established Mode of Worship, addressed principally to those who attend the place call'd St. Giles's Church, Reading. by John Spalding.[39] he departed this life 29 of the 1st. month 1795, was intered in friends Burial ground at Reading the 6. of 2d. mo.—It is common in the Old Countries to keep the bodies of their dead, eight or ten days, Here we hurry them into the grave, in one, two, or three days, indeed in some seasons, it appears necessary, but the Season be it what it may, makes little odds in the Custom! mores the pity.—Saml. Emlen took tea with us—James Logan, John James and Neighr. Waln here this evening—Hetty Smith &c came this evening from Clearfield, brought us some peas, and sent word that Henry came home from N. Bank this Afternoon—HD. and self went this evening to Jacobs, Sally out,[40] but she came presently home as it was too cold for me, to go down to J Skyrins—Sally inform'd us, that Dr. Kuhn had been there, and said, that he could not tell, untill tomorrow, wether little Elizah. Skyrin had the measles or not, that if she had taken them the Symptoms were light.

June 1st. cool pleasent morning wind N.W.—HD. call'd at J Skyrins, found the Child much as last night,—A German Breakfasted with us—John Drinker and Josh. Bringhurst here forenoon—Sister gone to Alms-house &c. Huldah Mott and Betsy Emlen call'd in their Carriage for Molly, it did not suit her to go.—William walk'd out this cool morning Dr. Redman spent an hour before dinner. HD. MD. and Eliza Downing went this Afternoon to Clearfield.—John Drinker went with them as far as Fairhill—Sally Downing here this Afternoon—I went after tea to J Skyrins, call'd in the way at John Thompsons—he went with me to J Skyrin, the Child much better to night,—the Doctor apprehends that she has the intermitting fever, not the Measles.—John Skyrin came home with me. Owen Biddle here this evening—Sally Large and Jonathan Harvey here—cool evening—We have had a fier made in our parlor, every morning this Spring, two or three excepted. A fine clear cool moonlight night.

2. Clear, wind S.W. clouded over after, about 9 o'clock, sent for Sally Wharton, she came, but was hindred going to meeting, as she intended, by rain—HD. and MS. went. Henry and Hannah came to town, Sally Rhoads call'd after meeting—Hannah Catheral Sally Wharton and HSD. din'd with us—Sally Smith and Sally Large call'd William Brown and S.W. drank tea—

39. John Spalding, *A Few Reasons for Leaving the National Established Mode of Worship, Addressed Principally to Those Who Attend at the Place Called St. Giles's Church, Reading* (London: James Phillips, 1794 [*Brit. Mus. Cat.*]).

40. The word "we" crossed out.

Isaac Howel here Afternoon, I acknowledged a Deed before him—Rachel Drinker, Polly Cope, her Child and husbands Sister call'd—A very heavy rain with wind this Afternoon, prevented Henry and Hannah from going home—it clear'd up about Sunsett, when our friend S. Wharton went home—she is, to me, as one raised from the dead,—she looks, all things considered, extrodinary well, 'tho her present situation is very precarious.—James Logan and Hannah S Drinker came here towards evening—Walter Franklin and Jonan. Hearvy here.—Richd. Nisbet junr. came this evening to tell me, that his mother would open a school tomorrow in Arch Street,—fine clear full moon light night.

3. Clear and cool, wind W.S.W. William walk'd this morning to Robt. Stevensons, and to the State-House Yard. H Mott and E. Emlen call'd in their Carriage for Molly, she way busy'd, and did not go—Sally Smith and Sally Large, who were here went with them—Henry and Hannah left town early—A Wooden building which stands behind G. Frys house, in the Garden, is to be removed to day, to the side of GFs present Habatation—I was taken sick suddenly while eating my dinner, very sick, obliged to leave the table, and drink warm water as soon as I could get it. I soon became something better, 'tho far from being as well as before—William, his Sister Sally, and her Daughters and prehaps Jacob, are gone this Afternoon to Clearfield—Molly gone with T. and M. Cope, his Sister, Walter Franklin, and Joshua Clibborn the lesser, to walk to the House of Employment. they came here afterwards to tea—James Logan call'd—Sister went this evening to Sallys—HD. to Niegr. Walns. I took medicine, being more than usualy unwell.

4. Sunshine, wind N.E—Betsy Fordham came to work.—Betsy Emlen here this morning S. Swett spent the day—Elijah Waring call'd—he bid us farewell, is going to England in the William Penn—Nancy and her Daughter here forenoon, the Child far from well,—Molly Field and C. Harrison spent the Afternoon with Molly—A man call'd to visit little Peter, who lives near his parents—Joshua Clibborn minor, Walter Franklin and Richd. Smith here this evening—Danl. Drinker call'd—HD. out, he call'd at Sally Rhoadss her Son has been extreemly ill, he was let blood four times and blistered, in 24 hours, as I was inform'd, he is now better.—this has been a fine pleasent day, of the sort we have laterly had but few.

5. a fine day. wind N.W—William went in the Chaise to Clearfield, his Uncle John with him as far as Fair Hill, Isaac Howel, judge of Coart common pleas, here this morning I acknowledg'd two Deeds before him.—Molly gone this morning with Sally Smith, Sally Large and Tommy Tylee, in Smith's Carriage, to Clearfield—Neigr. Waln and little grand Son,—Danl. Drinker, Sally Downing were here fore noon—Nicholas Waln came this Afternoon to take leave, as he setts of tomorrow for Chester or New Castle to the Vessel, at one of which

places he expects to embark in Ship William Penn for London—John and Nancy Skyrin with their child, stop'd here, after having rode 10 miles round, Billy Saltar took tea with us—W.D. return'd sola in Chaise after sunset, there was 11 visitors at Clearfield beside himself.—I went after tea to Jacob Downings, Sally out, then went with Nancy Morgan to the french Clockmakers, next door but one to them, to see a very curious Clock and Organ, that did belong to the Queen of France, said to have cost origanly 1000 Gunies, plays twenty different tunes, stands on two large fluited mahogany pillars guilt—bought in france by Govr. Morris, for Robt. Morris of this City, for 500 pounds, as we were inform'd. I went this evening with my Husband to Isaac Howels, to acknowledge a deed, call'd in our way home at Joseph Yerkes's.

June 6. very fine Morning wind S.W.—Danl. Drinker Polly Henry Drinker here this morning they sett off with my husband, and were to call for Saml. Emlen, to go to Chester with Nichs. Waln,—HD. and some others intend for Willmington, on busyness with J[o]. Dickenson. I went this morning to see how Nancy and Child were, as she had sent me word last night, that she was indispos'd—mett Dr. Kuhn there—Nancy and child better—came home to dinner—William and Mary went this Afternoon in the Chaise to Clearfield. came home after sun set, they brought a smal quantity Strawberries &c.—Sally Downing, Nancy Skyrin and little Elizath. spent this Afternoon with us,—Polly Cope and hir Sister in law call'd—William went this evening to Sally's—Othneal Alsop lodges here to night, as HD. is absent, and robberies have been more frequent laterly than for a long time past—A Nest of thives have been, within these few days, detected, stolen goods discover'd, and great number of keys in their posesion,—'tis supposed that it was this gang, that, lately, broke open and rob'd the store of John and Elliston Perot.—Yesterday, the supreme court of the united States, which had been for some time past employ'd in trying those concerned in the late insurrection to the westward, adjourned. two were found guilty of treason, and condemned to be executed here on the 17th. instant[41] The trial of two others was postponed till the next court. The others were acquited. It is, I believe, 7 or 8 years since an unhappy youth, who lived in our Neighbourhood was executed, I have an idea that two Men were since, hang'd for murder.

June 7. First Day: fair, wind N.E—Nancy went her child and black girl to spend the day with us, JS. and herself intending for Clearfield—Sally Downing and Eliza call'd in their way to meeting, She and her two Daughters and S Swett din'd here. Jacob and B.W gone to Clearfield—Sister and Molly went

41. Twenty men involved in the Whiskey Rebellion came to trial before the United States Circuit Court in Philadelphia. Only two, John Mitchell and Philip Wiegel (also spelled Vigol), were found guilty of treason. President Washington later pardoned them (Baldwin, *Whiskey Rebels*, 257, 262–64; Wharton, *State Trials*, 164–84).

to morning meeting—Caty Deacon brought little Henry Downing after dinner, he is two months old this day, a fine Child. I have all my grand-Children with me this Afternoon, few as they are, 'tis but seldom that I see them all togeather—Sally Smith call'd—Saml. Emlen before Afternoon meeting—Sally Downing, S Swett, and the Children stay'd till after tea—John and Nancy stop'd at our door she stay'd with us, till he came back in the evening for her and Child—H.D. return'd from Willmington before tea—Saml. Pleasants came to town with him—Nichs. Waln, David Bacon, E. Waring; Nancy Penn, her Neice &c. went on board the Will Penn at Chester, yesterday Afternoon.

8. A pleasent cool day 'tho the wind is Easterly. Isaac Potts here fore noon—William took a very short ride on the Mare, as far as Callohill and fourth Streets, he went after dinner, Peter Woodard with him, in the Chaise to Clearfield, came home rather too late, is poorly this evening—Betsy Jervis and A Skyrin took tea here—I went home with Nancy, for sake of the walk, return'd about dusk sola—Sally Downing and Molly spent this Afternoon at Saml. Fishers, Sarah Fisher and her Son James here this evening—H.D. received a Letter from John W. DeBrahm, Georgia, with a phial of Elemental Condensation,[42] for Williams use, 20 drops to be taken at a time—early in the morning—when he has taken sufficient, we are to return what remains in the vial.

June 9. Clear, wind S.W—HD. and daughter Molly went to meeting—We are busy House cleaning, preparing for whitewashing. HSD. came to town this morning HD. was yesterday afternoon at H Pembertons, with several others, he is one of JPs Executors, the Will was open'd, a very long one, a great number of legacys left to indifferent persons,—I went over to see Hannah Hartshorn, who is I think going fast. Huldah Mott and Betsy Emlen call'd after meeting, Molly went out with them—Henry din'd with us, he went home in the Afternoon. Nancy took tea with us—I went home with her, Molly also, Dolly Large, and Walter Franklin there, Waltar came home with us. HD. son William and Daughter Molly took a ride the five miles round, came home to late tea.

10 Clear, wind S.W—Sally Downing here this morning HD. and Tommy Stewardson went to Frankford forenoon, return'd to dinner—T. Stewardson took tea here, Nancy, Molly, William and little Elizath. rode out this Afternoon, the old five miles round, they return'd to tea, James Logon here also—John Drinker, T. Stewardson, &c. busy with HD. in front parlor this After-

42. Most likely a vial of water from deep in Indian territory. DeBrahm, the Drinkers' friend and neighbor at Clearfield, was a mystic who considered water, particularly water from before the Biblical flood or water on the American continent that was unspoiled by Europeans, to be the "unblended element" (John Gerar William DeBrahm, *VII. Arm of the Tree of Knowledge* [Philadelphia: Zachariah Poulson, 1791], 55–57; see below, July 6).

noon—I went home with Nancy. J Logan with us—Capt. Wetheral came home with me. Warm.

11. rain most of last night. heavey rain this morning without thunder or Lightening—wind N.E—continued raining most of this day, No one here that I recolect but Betsy Fordham who is still at work for us. No one, I mean in the parlor, but Dr. Rush this evening many have been in the Coupting Room—A cold raw North east wind with rain this evening My Husband is setting by a comfortable fire smoking his Pipe—The Season has been remarkable for three months past—cool easterly winds.

June 12. rain'd most of the night, and this Morning—cloudy all day: wind N.E—a fier all day in back parlor—I arose between 3 and 4. this morning with a very sick stomach—call'd Sally up, drank near a pint of tipid water, it had not the desired effect or at least the effect I look'd for, but tended to settle my Stomac, I lay down again before 5. and dosed till the usual time of riseing, poorly all day,—Pearson Mitchle, Jacob Downing &c. call'd—HSD. came to town after dinner.—G. Fry here to day with Cart for Chairs, marketing &c. he brought us down, Peas and Strawberries—Dolly Large and Nancy Skyrin call'd in Larges Carriage for Molly to go with 'em to Giddion Wellss Sally Smith and Sally Large here, the latter went with them—J Downing call'd. HD. went to HPs this evening—Sammy Rhoads and Walter Franklin call'd this evening SR. appears to be recover'd, but does wrong to be out such inclement weather,—Ben Wilson and Thos. England, a young Man from Ireland here this evening Henry went home before tea in his Chair—Jacob Downing came home with Molly Sally D. and Nancy M was with them at GWs.

13. rain again in the night and this morning wind N.E. Thos. English breakfasted here,—a John Wall, a Lad from England went this forenoon with HD to Clearfield, has thoughts of serving our Son Henry on his farm, if it suits—Henry left Clearfield for North-bank this Morning before his father arrived there—my husband left the lad at Clearfield,—Hannah came to town with him before dinner Sister out this Morning—Sally Downing and her Daughters, Nancy Skyrin and her's, and Hannah S.D. here after dinner.—James Logan Sally Smith, Sally Large, Betsy Emlen took tea with Molly in the front parlor, Nancy Skyrin, B. Fordham with us in the back—Saml. Emlen, Richd. Nesbit, John Drinker, Daniel Drinker and Thos. Stewardson call'd—Saml. Rhoads and George Field with the Girls this evening.

14. First day: cloudy, wind N.E—HD. sent John Bowing, and Peter Woodward to Clearfield to Assist in getting in the hay—'tis a twelve month this day since I went there to reside for the Summer season—Joseph Smith from Burlington breakfasted with us.—HD. MS. MD. went to meeting—Sally

Downing and Daughter Eliza, call'd after meeting—S Swett din'd with us—sun shone afternoon—John Collins call'd—Neighr. Waln, Saml. Emlen before Afternoon meeting—Nancy and Child came in Afternoon—Josh. Bringhurst call'd—Jacob and Sally Downing sup'd here—clear evening—S.B.s Sister Letty came for her to go see her Sister Betsy whom she reported was dieing, Sally went, but on her return inform'd otherwise.

15. Clear and cool. wind N.W.—S.W. Afternoon—we have had a fire in parlor and day—and this evening I went to J Skyrins with a short cloath cloak on—Billy, Sally, and her two daughters rode to the middle ferry forenoon—our dear Son Billy very poorly and feverish this evening chilly in the Afternoon—he has, I expect, taken cold—James Dunning came to town from his Brothers, he appears better—We are pleas'd to see him in the land of the liveing—Nancy Skyrin was here forenoon—I mett Sally there this evening—Polly Foulk and Tabby Fisher had been there Sally, John and Molly, came home with me.

June 16. Clear, wind S.W—chang'd to N.E. with rain—Nancy call'd with her Child—left her with me, and went to meeting—Saml. Emlen and Betsy Foulke Huldah Mott and Betsy Emlen call'd after meeting. Nancy Skyrin stay'd dinner, detain'd by rain—Becky Jones and George Churchman call'd—Joseph Saltar from Atsion, drank tea, sup'd and lodg'd with us—Tabby Fisher call'd Afternoon—Johnny Smith came to know if any of our family were going to day to Clearfield, if so Hannah would go home with them, but as one of our Carriage Horses was lame, she went with J Logan in her fathers Carriage—Henry came from North bank to Clearfield yesterday—Richd. Nesbet, Peggy Wharton &c. here this evening Isaac Wharton afterwards—Molly went this evening to Js. Smiths, Hetty and her Daughter Sally are poorly—rain this evening—Sister and self were up last night with William, he was sick at Stomach, and puked—he was better in the morning.

17. Cloudy, wind N.E. James Logan call'd before dinner, Neighr. Waln after, The two insergents who were to have been executed this day, are respited.—Josh. Drinker here this evening John Drinker call'd—William took a short ride on Mare towards evening John Saltar here this evening his brother Joseph went homeward before dinner—Henry and Hannah came to town towards evening—Billy went out after night to Jacob Downings—Henry and Hannah came at 10 o'clock to lodge with us to night.—read a pamphlet intitled, Rewards and Punishments, or Satans Kingdom Aristocratical, rote by a John Cox, a Philadelphian[43]—in poetry—not much to the credit of JC. as a

43. John Cox, *Rewards and Punishments, or Satans Kingdom Aristocratical; To Which is Subjoined a Voyage to London, and an Acrostic* (Philadelphia: printed for the author, 1795 [*NUC*]).

poet or to Philadelphia, 'tho the young man may mean well, and might, have prehaps have done better in prose.

June 18. Clear. wind S.W—Henry and Hannah breakfasted with us—they are to be guest to day at the Marriage of Joseph Morris Son of Thos. Morris and Abigal Marshal daughter of Charles Marshal at the Market street meeting house—Saml. Smith of B. County came with his horse, it is meeting for Suffering—Nancy Skyrin and daughter call'd—she was ill last night with the Colick, 'tho she is out to day—Joshua Sharpless, Benjan. Ring, John Kinsey and John Collins din'd here—I spent a few minuits forenoon at Neighr. Walns—Molly at fifth day meeting this morning—William, Nancy, Molly and little ES—went this Afternoon to Clearfield, return'd to late tea. Thos. Stewardson and Sally Downing at tea also—I perused our friend JPs Will 22. pages—he has left a great part of his estate to Charitable uses &c. J Skyrin here this evening John Thomas also—Henry and Hannah came home about 10—a clear and warm evening.

19. Clear and warm, wind S.W—Henry and Hannah and Saml. Smith breakfasted with us—Saml. went home, H and H. din'd with us, they went home this Afternoon, Nancy Skyrin and John Kinsey took tea here—John has left the union farm and come again to reside in Bs. County. I am of the oppinion that if he lives seven years longer, he will be sorry that he has so done—Sarah Lewis, widdow of Jacob Lewis and Daughter of George Mifflin departed this life last night aged 77 years, she was an agreeable Chearful old friend, and only think! I knew her Grand-father, Hugh Cordary, a little old man, who I remember seeing, when I was a Child at our old meeting house at corner of market and second streets.—I went with Nancy this evening to Jacob Downings, they are getting ready to set off tomorrow morning for Downingstown with their family—Jacob and Sally came home with me, It has been a very warm day, We must think of going, also, in the country, on Williams account, or this separation of families is very disagreeable to me—Othenial Alsop has hurt his back, by a fall, not badly hurt, but so as to be absent from the Coumpting house—Harmon Husbands was bury'd this Afternoon, he was famous in the late inserrection and has been a prisoner here for some time past. I belive he did not die in prison.

20. Clear, wind S.E—Jacob Downing and family breakfasted with us—they sett off about 8 o'clock for the Valley—Sally, her 3 Children and Caty Deacon in the Carriage, Jacob goes in the Chaise with their little maid Anne, they expect to lodge to night at Richd. Thomas's, and go to their own House, which is 4 miles further, tomorrow morning cloudy with some rain before noon—My precarious state of health, makes me feel rather dull, parting with my Children,—John Kinsey din'd and took tea—he came this evening for his Horse, and went homeward—B. Wilson here this evening Betsy Fordham

sewing for us for the present—I have been busy with her for near three weeks, and am almost tir'd of confindment—not that I shall go, much, or any more, abroad—Molly has been for some days past, at times reading while we work'd, three romantic Volls. intitled The Mysteries of Udolphia[44]—A tremendious tale—but not quite like the old fashon Gothick stories that I was fond of when young, 'tis seldom I listen to a romance, nor would I encourage my Children doing much of that business—Jacob Downings black Man Ebenezar is to lodge here 'till his master returns which I expect will be on second day next.

21. First day: rain in the night, clear morning wind S.E—George Fry here, complaining to HD. I belive without much cause—there are two small families under one Roof, and 'tho room enough, they cant agree—Saml. Emlen call'd before meeting, Sammy Rhoads call'd, HD. MS. MD. went to meeting—S Swett and A Skyrin din'd with us, and spent the Afternoon, Nancy went to Afternoon meeting with Molly—J Skyrin call'd. Molly and self went towards evening to Hannah Pembertons, found her alone—HD. came to us—we came home by moon light—walk'd through the Market place, which has been for some years past, illuminated by Lamps,—I saw, for the first time, Cooks grand Edifice,[45] at corner of market and third streets, where Charles Jones's old house stood—it cuts a dash—indeed—and the New Presbyterian Meeting house, I belive they now call it Church—built within a year or two, the Appearance is something grand, tho the situation not so—the four pillers, the largest I have seen[46]—We call'd at J Skyrins, Nancy had been documenting her Daughter and was in trouble for[47] having done her Duty—The appearence of a gust hurried us home—it rain'd soon after, lightned but little thunder—understood by Sister, when we came home, that John Drinker was taken ill this afternoon of a vomitting &c, and cramp in his Stomac, had taken ladanum, and seem'd better—Our John return'd about 8 this evening from Downing town, they all got safe up, and he left them well.

22. Clear wind S.W—S. Swett din'd and tea'd, she try'd a Callico gown on me—Dr. Rush spent part of the Afternoon and took tea with us—Docr. Redman here before dinner—Sally Dawson unwell—Saml. Pleasants, Robt.

44. Ann [Ward] Radcliffe, *The Mysteries of Udolpho,* 3 vols. (Dublin: 1794 [Averley, *18th-Cen. Brit. Books,* 3:3303]).

45. Joseph Cooke, a jeweler, erected a four-story block of buildings on the southeast corner of Market and Third in 1794 in the hope that the "magnetism of its magnificance" would attract both commercial and residential customers (Joseph Jackson, *Market Street Philadelphia* [Philadelphia: Patterson & White Co., 1918], 36).

46. The new First Presbyterian Church, built in 1794 at the corner of Market and Bank streets, was one of the first churches in Philadelphia based on Greek motifs. Four pillars with Corinthian capitals supported a pediment, and eighty marble steps led up to the main floor. It replaced the former meetinghouse, known as Old Buttonwood (Scharf and Westcott, *Philadelphia,* 2:1270).

47. The word "doing" crossed out.

Stevenson call'd, Jacob Downing return'd this evening he makes his home with us, dureing the absence of his family—Molly spent this Afternoon at Saml. Emlens—HD. and self took a walk to J Skyrins, John Drinker abroad, and of course better—HSD. came to town before noon, he din'd with us—went out before evening—intends tomorrow for North bank—William went in Chaise John drove him, to Clearfield—return'd after sun set—Nancy went Afternoon with her Child and Maid Betts, to the State House Yard.

23. Clear morning wind S.W—HD. MS. MD. went to monthly meeting Saml. Emlen call'd—Saml. Moore came with Cart, sent two beds &c to Clearfield, preparatory to my, and Sons going there,—gave S. Dawson a dose of Castor Oyl, by direction Dr. Rush—black Cato came this Afternoon to white wash—Jacob Downing din'd with us, he is now one of our family—HD. Billy, Nancy, Molly and little Elizabeth rode out this Afternoon to the lower ferry &c.—Neighr Waln spent an hour—Nancy Skyrin and Daughter took tea with us—MS. out this Afternoon—MD. went home with Nancy—fine weather.

24. rain, wind N.E—rain again about noon—and very heavy rain Afternoon—the wall of one Chamber, which had just been whitewash'd, injured by the house leaking. Joshua Smith, who happen'd to be here, mending the kitchen hearth, examin'd the leak, found part wanted pointing, which he is soon to repare—a Carpenter is at work in back parlor, mending in some places—J Logan call'd forenoon—between 10 and 11 A.M—Neighr. Waln sent for me, Hannah Hartshorn having chang'd in the night—and they thought her near the cloase—I went in back Chamber to Sucky, who was in deep distress, she desired me after some time to go into front Chamber to enquire if she was gone—just as I came into the room she expired, between 11 and 12 o'clock—the conflict, I believe, was light—her Aunt Hannah Catheral, and Becky Jones were there, she has been near a twelve month, in a decline. Would have been 14 years of age, had she lived 'till 8th. month next—she was an innocent good little girl, the tryal is great to her poor mother, who has always been anxious for, and very fond of, her Children—I stayd till Molly Humphriss came to lay her out, a Solumn scene, which I did not stay to be a witness too, came home dinner time—It is still raining 10. at night.

25. rain'd most of the night, prehaps all, between one and two it rain'd exceedingly hard continu'd till near day brake, then slack'd a little—The heavy rain, and a feverish dispossition keep't me wakeing till long after day light—setting up in bed, takeing a pinch of snuff I observed the great obscureness of that time—thoughts crouded on my mind, for when I lay awake, 'tis not in a stupid or thoughtless state—I have been favour'd laterly to sleep better than some years past, which I look on a great blessing—I could not, I say, but observe that notwithstanding the obscureity of the night, the day dawn'd at its

usual time—beautifully dawn'd—No obstruction in the coarse of nature or providence—what humble, thankful creatures ought we to be, knowing and acknowledgeing our dependence on our Creator and Mercyful father,—arose near nine, still raining, wind N.W. went over after breakfast to Neighr. Hartshorns, several persons there—H. Catheral had something consolatory to offer to S.H—I offer'd the use of our front parlor for company at the funeral which is to be at 6 this evening—Neigr. Waln desir'd I would stay with her daughter during the absence of the family at the time of the interrement, as it was not thought proper for her to attend the last sceane, the weather being very damp and [cloudy] and she has been long confin'd—I came home to dinner—A Man call'd with two Books of paper hangings for us to chuse, they were all too gay, save one, which was not quite to our minds—Sister went after dinner over to P. Hartshorns—before 5. I went, and stay'd with Sucky, 'till they return'd—stay'd tea there—it raind most of the Afternoon, I came home towards evening Waltar Franklin, Richd. Smith, Sally Smith and Sally Large here this evening—Molly went out with them.

26. clear and cool, wind N.W—after so much rain and damp, thought it advisable to have a fier in the parlor, and tho past mid summer it is agreeable to William and self, and not disagreeable to others—John and Nancy Skyrin, their Child and Girl Betsy, sett off from hence about nine o'clock for Bristol, they have taken lodgings at Widdow Merriotts, where I lodg'd 24 years ago when in a low state of health—Nancy proposes staying some weeks there with her maid and Child—John return'd towards evening he left them bravely—John has Sam and Patience at home with him—S Merriott had been ill of Billious Colick,—her Sickness will make things less agreeable and Convenient to Nancy—James Logan, Jenny and Susan Stevenson, Saml. Emlen, Sally Rhoads, Betsy Emlen call'd before dinner—H. Catheral din'd with us, she seems lame, and otherwise poorly,—Richd. Nesbit, John Skyrin, Ben Wilson &c here this evening Jacob din'd out—Our old friend and Aquaintance Rebecca Say, departed this life about 10 this Morning aged 78 or 79—a well minded inofensive woman—From Dunlap and Claypooles Advertiser, A curious Fact.—Brown in his paper, calls it A Phenomenon in natural History—vizt. a few days ago some Hay Makers in a field near Germantown, took up a land Tortoise, which had every appearance of venerable age, on a closer inspection was read on its belly in fair characters George the 1st. 1717.—read two Volls. duodecimo. containing a great veriety of Anecdotes &c. good, bad and indifferent, borrow'd of JL.—fine clear night.

27. clear cool morning Jacob Downing left us after breakfast in Billys Sulkey, to visit his beloveds, he has a fine day for traveling. W. C.——n. rather abusive to HD. he has propogated an untruth, and instead of honestly owning it, flew into a passion of defience—I hope HD. will follow it up.—HD. and Son William went this afternoon to Clearfield, they came home to tea, brought

Rassberries and other vigatables with them, HSD. arrived at Clearfield, from Northbank, while his father &c were there—Hetty Smith and Hannah S Drinker were gone to Mayos Vendue at Germantown. Sammy Rhoads here this evening Molly went out with him I took tea with my Afflicted Neighr. Sucky Hartshorn, Richd. Nesbet here this evening—HD. went to visit H. Pemberton—Sally Hopkins here this Afternoon, as Henry rode through Bristol to day, Nancy saw, and call'd him—she is, she says well, but her little one poorly—S. Merriott I expect is better, as Henry says, he saw an ancient woman setting there with a Cloak on—John Skyrin here this evening he intends going tomorrow Bristol.

28. First day: clear cool and pleasent, wind NW. puss setting comfortably very near the fier—HD. MS. MD. at meeting. A note came desiring HD. to invite at meeting to the burial of R. Say. at two o'clock this Afternoon—This day is very like a fine day, in the month of March, only that the trees are full of leaves and some of them loaded with fruit. Our Yard and garden looks beautifully—S. Swett din'd, HD. MS. MD. went to the funeral of R. Say—William Shannon and Son, S.S. and E Emlen took tea with us—Sally Smith here, Molly went out this evening with her and Betsy Emlen,—S.B. visited her Sister Betsy—John Skyrin call'd this evening he came from Bristol, he left Nancy pretty well, the Child disordred in her bowels—this division of Families, occasions a great going too and fro—but they seem not to dislike it, and prehaps 'tis for the best.

June 29. Clear. wind S.W. warmer. HSD. came to town, he informs us, that little Caty Clearfield is very unwell, her bowels much disordred, I suppose she is teething—Saml. Smith of B. County brought his horse, Wm. Blackey came with Oats, J Logan spent an hour, Neighr. Waln also. Roger Dicks and John Pierce din'd with us—J Logan and Jacob Downing took tea with us—Jacob came to town this evening left Sally and the Children well.—Henry went home ward before tea, I sent by him Medicine &c. for the poor little Child—Molly went this Afternoon with Betsy Emlen, Sally Smith and Sl. Rhoads to visit Sally Large three miles off, on the Frankford road.—Wm. Bleakey and Saml. Smith went homeward this Afternoon, fine evening Cato and his wife at work Sister up stairs *all day*. I went to bed with my mind oppress'd.

30. Slep't none 'till after day, arose none the later, warm day, wind southerly, painters at work in front parlor, rain'd before noon—the painters quit their work—James Logan here.—Abraham Griffith aged 82. George Churchman, S Swett and Jacob Downing din'd here, John Drinker call'd—S.S. Jn. Skyrin, and Thos. Potts junr., from Bay of Hondorus, older brother to James and Robt. Potts, took tea here. I spent an hour with Neighr. Waln this evening moon light. On sixth day last, Saml. W. Stockden of Trenton lost his life, by the horse taken fright, as he was riding in a Chaise with his little boy, he

was thrown out, and it is suppos'd struck his head against some hard substance, and surviv'd the blow but about two hours, the Child was not hurt.

July 1. fourth day: Cloudy, wind S.E—the painters at work, and William *hear*, they left off before dinner, as it has turn'd out a rainey day—Saml. Moore from Clearfield brought a few lines from Hannah—informing, that Henry was taken this Morning with a Chill, and the fever was come on, I sent him what I thought proper, for the present, shall be thoughtfull 'till I hear again from him, The Stone cutter here this Afternoon measuring for a new Hearth in back parlor Chimney—Jacob and Molly sup'd togeather, William taking bran tea for a cold, which he has caught this damp weather.—HD. preparing to sett off very early tomorrow Morning for Chester County to the intended boarding-school—A steady rain most of this day, heavy shower 10. at night.

2. rain in the night, Cloudy morning wind, N.E—Sun shone out about 9 o'clock. We were invited to the burial of Molly Hudson this Afternoon—rain again afternoon—two Men papering front parlor, painters at work in the entry and stair case, giving the first Coat—received a note from Henry, telling us, that his fever went off with a copeous sweat, that poor little Caty was dead—Jacob Morris, a black boy, whose Mother had her to nurse brought the note, and came for a—Shroud to bury her in—After dinner, George Fry came to town with the Cart, to take a Table up for himself, he brought us vigatables, and a letter from Henry, telling us that he felt as well as usual, but very weak, desir'd I would send him an Emetic—which I did 'tho with reluctance, sent to Dr. Kuhn for it—It was an ounce of Antimonial Wine.—I shall feel anxious 'till I know its effect—John Drinker, Isaac Potts call'd—Neighr. Waln came this evening for Sister to go with her to visit Hannah Catheral who is indisposed. HD. having all things ready to go into Chester County, arose at 4 this morning—found Thos. Stewardson and Jona. Evans at our front door ready to go with him, they concluded the day was rather unpromissing and drop'd the journey for the present so much rain had made the roads bad. and more rain threatening. When HD. was retireing, he made a discovery, of an accident which had happen'd on our Bed—and 'tho I liked it not, yet I did not feel all that disgust &c. that some others did, but help'd S. Brant to reinstate matters, and prepare a more sutable situation for the distress'd party and those that were near her.

3. Cloudy, cool, wind N.E—Saml. Moore here, early this morning he brought plants for Jacob Downing, and Curr[ ]ts for us—heard nothing from Henry, by him—much rain, and Easterly winds have prevail'd in an uncommon manner, I think, for four months past—HD. and Daughter Mary sett off between nine and ten this morning for Clearfield—We were invited to the funeral of Docr. Rush's Mother, an antient woman, it was I belive his wifes

brother that lost his life lately near Bristol—We have a fire in parlor, and find it no ways incomodious, but rather necessary, as it takes off the damp, and smell of the paint—our dear William being here, in the scent of the paint, is not the thing.—We sent beds up to the place some time ago, and should, in all probability have been there ourselves, that is, WD. and self, but the wet weather and bad roads &c. have prevented.—Many in the Country have the chills and fever. H. Mott and B. Emlen call'd in their Carriage for Molly to ride with them, she was gone—James Logan, James Smith call'd this Afternoon, Jacob Downing sett off about one o'clock in Sulkey to visit his family—HD. and Molly did not return to dinner—Johnny Smith call'd to know if they were return'd, his father intending to go up there this Afternoon—MS. gone to meet the comittee of twelve—The paper hangers came after dinner, they are still at work in the entry—HD. and MD. came home after dinner, left Henry with fever coming on, a chill had preceeded it—he took the vomitt last night and bark &c since—John Skyrin and Sammy Rhoads here this evening—I step'd over to Neighr. Walns. clear night.

July 4. Clear. 'tho the wind continues at N.E—Anniversary of Independence, 19 Years.—General Orders in News-paper this forenoon, for a fuss and to do,—I think, orders for peace and quietness, would be more commendable and consistant, in a well regulated Government or State,—those days seldom pass over without some melancholy accident occuring from riotous doings—Henrys maid Molly, came to town early this morning she could not exactly tell how he was—his indispossition calls me there, 'tho there are many things on the other hand would detain me here, but think I must prepare to go.—We were invited to the burial of Benjn Hornor's wife, Sally Potts that was,—this is a call that we frequently hear,—more deaths, I think, than are common to this Month. I did use'd to think June, one of the healthyest months in the year, especially to Adults.—It was suspected, that a designe, to burn John Jay, in Effigee, was in agatation, but, Benjn. Chew, who was here forenoon, says, he believes that intention is suppress'd.[48]—Billy set off after dinner in Chaise,

48. Benjamin Chew was mistaken (see below, July 6). Democratic-Republican party leaders in Philadelphia organized a demonstration, parading a transparency of John Jay through the streets to the Kensington section of Philadelphia County, where they burned it. Jay had negotiated a controversial treaty with Great Britain in May. Though President Washington had attempted to keep the treaty's provisions private until the Senate had finished considering it, a copy of the treaty was leaked to Philadelphia's Democratic-Republican newspaper *The Aurora,* which published it on July 1. The treaty severely limited American trade with countries at war with Great Britain, and required the U.S. to give assurances that its ports would not be used as a base of operations by enemy privateers against the British. In return, Great Britain, which should have surrendered its posts in the Northwest following the 1783 treaty, agreed to do so by June 1796. The treaty left additional issues to arbitration and failed to address still others, such as the impressment of American sailors and compensation for slaves freed by the British. The publication of the treaty led to organized protests across the country. As Jay himself wryly noted, he could have found his way across the country by the light of his burning effigies, in which he was represented selling his country for British gold

HD. and self in the Carriage, we arrived at Clearfield between three and four, I was taken very sick, soon after I came, drank near a pint of warm water—was too unwell to take any thing else this evening Ben. Wilson here at tea,—My husband left us after tea, Ben stay'd till dusk—Hannah's maid Mary came up from town, she says there is an appearence of a riot, or mob, not very intilligent—I wish there may not be sad doings—Henry looks pale and sickly, 'tho in good Spirits.

5. First Day: Cloudy. wind I believe N.E—no vain here, I am at a loss to arsertain the point—Arose unwell, between 7 and 8. none up, but Mary and Sip, I expect my husband &c. are now on their way to Middletown meeting Chester County, Johnny Smith paid us a morning visit, he went home to dinner, as his father would otherwise be alone—Hetty Smith and her Daughter Sally and Ricd. Smith &c. are gone to Shrewsberry, to the Sea side, to stay two or three weeks.—I went to see little Catys grave, it appears to be decently done up—I told SB. yesterday, a little while before I left home, of the death of her Child, and took that oppertunity to talk to her on that and some other Subjects, she shed a few tears, but all, appeard to be got over in a little time after. HSD. has mist the Chill and fever to day, and by proper care, I trust, it will not return. I walk'd in the Garden this evening to look at the Alterations George has been making Jonathan Roberts spent part of this Afternoon with us—an appearence of rain took him home sooner then he intended—A pleasent shower this evening with some thunder. A fine Rainbow after.

July 6. Clear and plesant, wind Southerly—Hannah and William went to town after breakfast—Henry and self constitute the family at present, he takes the bark to day, I feel better than since I left home, comfortable, and I hope I may say thankful—Ray[nar]d Tyson call'd about lime—Henry and self din'd ensamble. he spent the forenoon reading, myself writing. Ben Wilson came up late in the Afternoon, he gave me the pleasing information, that he had seen John Skyrin, and that Nancy and the Child were bravely, he said there had like to have been a riot in the city on on seventh day night, threats had been thrown out of burning John Jays Effigy before the Presidents Door, that the light horse were parading all day, at 10. at night, when they had all, but 4 or 5 retired, they were told that a mob with the Effigy were coming from Kingsington, they then about calling the other light horse to come out, and when a few more of them had got togeather they went towards Kingsington and mett them coming with the figure, headed by one Coats,—Morrell, one of the light

---

(Marcus and Perry, *Supreme Court,* 7; DeConde, *Entangling Alliances,* 101–27; J. C. Miller, *Federalist Era,* 164–67; accounts of the July 4 parade are in R. G. Miller, *Federalist City,* 71–72, and Scharf and Westcott, *Philadelphia,* 1:480–81; on the use of effigies in Philadelphia parades see S. G. Davis, *Parades and Power,* 74–76).

Horse, spake civilly to him—but they soon had stones & brick-bats sent at them, and were beat off, Morrell 'tis said, is much hurt—The Mob came into the City, went quietly up one street and down another, without making any noise, with the Cart weels muffled, then went back to Kingsington where they burnt the Effigy after midnight.—tis well 'twas no worse. William and Hannah came home to tea. B.W. went away about dusk—Jacob Downing is return'd to town, he left Sally and the Children well, which is satisfactory—Molly was rideing out with Betsy Emlen,—William brought up several book, among the rest one, which I read, this evening a pamphlet, wrote by our old friend. John Gerar William de Brahm. he calls it, Sum of Testimonies of Truth—God in his extension &c. God in his concentration &c.[49]—An honest minded man, and of coarse a good hearted Man, I believe him to be, and a sensible Man. Yet there are few, in my oppinion beside himself, who can make out, or Comprehend these testimonies—some would say, that they believ'd he did not understand them himself.—I should like to see the oppinion of the reviewers on this book.—The printer has sent, by John's orders, several Dozen of those pamphlets to my husband, and to others. It thunders, and seems as tho a gust is coming on, 'tis about 11 o'clock—I expect HD. will be in town tomorrow. received a letter this day from M. Penry.

7. Clear and cool. wind N.W—a thunder gust about midnight—I arose and went in to Williams Chamber, took the lamp in my hand, spilt the Oyl, which I had not observ'd in the lamp plate,—made bad work on both the flours, and my cloaths, waked William, upon the whole did much more, apperent, harm then good, the windows, of the room, where I lodge, shook with the thunder, and as we were, each of us alone, I felt easyest to go to him, William and Henry went to town after breakfast, the wind very high, tho, not cold, spent this Afternoon up stairs writing, as I have but little work here as yet—Hannah making Current Jelly—William and Henry return'd to tea. they tell me, my husband return'd home in good health, before dinner, that he expects to be here tomorrow.

8. Clear, wind—I cannot tell how, but believe 'tis Easterly. William and Henry rode out forenoon, Henry continues to take the bark, the fever has favourably keep't off—*rather disagreeable sensations this Afternoon*—William not so well as at some other times, Hannah gone this Afternoon to Dr. Logans William & self took a walk up the road to the extent of our land, last summer I call'd it, to the end of the corn field, 'tis now wheat—we came home just about sunset—Dr. Logan came home with Hannah after tea. I was taken very sick suddenly while he was here, went up to my Chamber without saying any thing. came down, after a short time something better, tho not relieved—No

49. John Gerar William deBrahm, *Sum of Testimonies of Truth* ([Philadelphia?], 1795 [*NUC*]).

body from home to day, as was expected—Henry preparing for North bank tomorrow.

9. Clear and pleasent, HSD. left home early this morning before I came down stairs, for North bank and Atsion—he took a quantity of bark with him, William and Hannah went to town after breakfast in Chaise, she intends to stay a few days with her father and the Children, as her Mother and Sister is absent. It is a very fine day. I am here by myself—Mary and Sip in the Kitchen, am rather better than yesterday, 'tho far from well, Billy poorly, I din'd by myself, on cold leg lamb, bacon, eggs and beans, 'tis not the first time that I have din'd Sola.—to me 'tis not, at times disagreeable, there are some things that we may easily reconcile, and by so doing they become pleasent—I have been very busy all this day, reading, mending Stockings & taking extracts—Caroline and Anna Shoemaker here this Afternoon on a visit to Hannah, they stay'd sometime with me, and went visiting elsewhere—HD. WD. Jacob Downing and John Skyrin drank tea here, my husband came up with William in the Chaise—Jacob and John went away after Sunset—HSD. left Philadelphia about 8 o'clock AM. for Atsion—he cross'd the river.[50]—It was walking in the Sun in the City, the beginning of last week that, he thinks, gave him the Chills & fever.

10. Clear and warm—Betsy Jervis and M. Drinker, came up in the Carriage for my Husband, they arrived here before I was downstairs about 7 o'clock, they breakfasted with us, then went to town, William and self here—I spent part of the morning reading. William and self had an Affecting conversation, touchant mon fils et son frere—a worthy fellow. My heart was much softened and melted:—Afterward, reading in the pleasures of memory, I shed more tears, than I have done for Years, at one time, 'tho I have often been sufficiently distress'd, had they been ready—a very still warm evening William and self walk'd to Catys Grave, then took the walk of yesterday, came home to tea after sun set—not a leaf could we see stiring,—I read to day the Pleasures of Memory with some other Poems, I wish I knew the author[51]—'tis an exceeding beautiful little peice, the author a person of great Sensibility I venture to say—Our little family, which consists of 8 persons, besides 4 grand Children, are divided at present, in five different parts of the State, HD. MS. and MD. at home in the City, S.D. in the Vally. A.S. at Bristol, H.S.D. I expect is at North bank, WD. and ED. here at Clearfield. grand Children with their mothers.

July. 11. Sun Shine, heavy air, warm—wind NE—William left me about 9

50. The line "in the heat of the Day, which was not quite right" crossed out.

51. [Samuel Rogers], *The Pleasures of Memory, in Two Parts, with Some Other Poems* (London: J. Davis, 1792; Boston: Manning and Loring, 1795 [*Brit. Mus. Cat.*; Evans, *Am. Bibliography*]).

o'clock, went by himself in Chaise to town—I have work, and a book, to amuse me—dined Sola, employ'd myself, being alone, after dinner making extracts from Winchesters Lectures.[52] After sunset, my husband and William came up—we walk'd in the Garden, and took tea late. They had been to Germantown, and engaged Jestes Fox to be here tomorrow to bleed William by Dr. Kuhns direction whom he consulted to day, while in town—Jacob Downing left the City about noon for his family Seat—John Skyrin took Molly in a Chaise with him for Bristol, where she proposes spending a week with her Sister Nancy, it was about 5 o'clock when they left town, to go twenty miles, imprudent doings; Sister is the only person, in our big house, Servants excepted, and a Capital coward is she,—Othenial Alsop is to lodge there—Betsy Greeves, formerly Paschall, was this morning buried, she died yesterday, a few days after a premature delivery, 'tis said, she had hurt herself by a fall lately.—James Morris, Son of Joseph Morris deceased was buried to day at White Marsh. How frequent are those Summonses—I understand that our Neighr. Suky Hartshorn with her Children are gone to day to S. Merriots Bristol, my two Daughters the Child and her maid are also there, I wish there may be convenient room for them all, room I know there is, but such as may be agreeable to all parties, is the thing to be wished—My dear W.D. seems rather low spirited this evening, he has been for a considerable time past stationary, could I see him gaining strength, it would be cause of thankfull-ness.

July 12. First day. clear, not quite so hot as yesterday, wind S.W—John came up with Carriage for his master, left us after breakfast as HD. did not chuse to be absent from our meeting, two first days running—sent Samuel Moore with the Chaise for J Fox, he came about one o'clock—bleed William, in an expert and easy manner, but did not take, as I think, the quantity order'd—he stay'd dinner with us, Saml. took him home about 3 o'clock—Benjn. Buck spent part of this Afternoon with us—I am disapointed this evening in not seeing my Son Henry, fearing he may have a return of the Chills and fever while abroad. warm evening teas'd by the flies and Bugs, that are allured by the light of the Candle, some say, that when they come into the house in such numbers, 'tis a sign of rain, but I believe tis not always the case—William appears none the worse for bleeding.

13. Sun Shine, air not clear, very warm—William had a good night Henry not yet return'd, Saml. Moore went to town between 9 and 10. o'clock with vigatables &c. came back to dinner, says my husband and Sister are well, that

52. Elhanan Winchester, *A Course of Lectures, on the Prophecies That Remain to Be Fulfilled, Delivered in the Borough of Southwark, as Also, at the Chapel in Glasshouse-Yard, in the Year 1789* ([London]: Printed for the Philadelphian Society; and included in a periodical work . . . called the Philadelphian Magazine, [1789] [*Brit. Mus. Cat.*]).

the Painters are at work in the little back room—The black woman who nurs'd little Caty was here after dinner, to be paid for her trouble—she brought her cloaths home, which I gave her—she is to call to morrow, when we hope HSD. will be at home, he knows when she went to them.—William with Samuel to drive,[53] went about 6 this evening to take an airing, after a very warm day, he is rather disordred in his bowels, while he is absent, I read the Minerva[54]—have given over looking for HSD. to night—The fire flies are very numerous and very pritty—in the lawn before our door, they are latter in the season than usual, I think, the end of May or beginning of June, was the time, most common, for them to shew themselves.

14. clear. wind N.W—tho tis not cool—I was taken this morning with something of the Cholera Morbus, was ill for an hour or two, have fasted all day, and am something better—I believe it was occasion'd by my taking a tumbler of new milk last night after eating some Rassberries, the hot weather might have contributed thereto. HSD. came home after breakfast—he has been favour'd with health during his Absence, which to me, is an agreeable disopointment, as I thought he[55] went away in rather a critical situation—he saw Nancy and her Daughter and Molly at Bristol, who were bravely. They had been the day before, I think it was, to his farm at North bank, HSD. was not there, but had gone some little distance from thence before they arrived: John Skyrin, Israel Pleasants, and Walter Franklin were with them.—Henry went to town after dinner, talks of staying all night—William took a ride this evening Samuel with him—I feel very la, la, Billy but poorly—Henry return'd to us this evening I was pleas'd to see him he brought me several necessarires, that I stood in need of, such as Oat-meal &c—he left his Father & Aunt well,—J Downing is return'd, Henry forgot to enquire after his family, but we may conclude, that they are well, or he would have heard,—Sally Fisher her Daughters Hannah and Hetty, and son William, came over about Dusk, they stay'd but a short time, as it was late, she was so kind as to send me, a dose of Cholic Ellixer, which came very oppertunely—as I stand in need of something to take of my present sensations—I feel more happy this evening than for some days past, having heard of the well fair of our family, and having both my Sons with me. I paid the black woman, Sally Morris 2″1″3″ for nursing little Caty near 7 weeks at 6/– p week—Henry paid Betsy Fry, some time ago, the same sum, for the same service, for between 5 and 6. weeks at 7/6 p.—many are, the number of poor little Infants that go out of the world, for want of perticular care, 'tho I have no reason to suppose this child was neglected, I paid Mary Courtney, between 8 and 9 pounds for nursing it &c, she did her

53. The word "him" crossed out.

54. Archibald Woodruff and William Peckin had established the *Philadelphia Minerva*, a weekly literary newspaper, on Feb. 7. The newspaper, which also carried items of local news, would cease publication in July 1798 (Brigham, *Newspapers*, 2:924).

55. The word "left" crossed out.

duty by it, I doubt not, and Betsy Fry appear'd to take good care of it—And Sally Morris, I do believe did her best, she has had several Children of her own, her family were very fond of it and I was told they weep'd much when it died—I should have taken it home,[56] it suited, and brought it up, or had it brought up in our family, but a fear of bringing the parrents togeather, or reviveing the former likeing to the sire, as the mother is still in our house, but tis gone, and no doubt but all's for the best.

July 15. Clear, cooler, wind:—rather better to day tho not as I could wish—I came up here without work, intending to assist HD. to make her petites choses, but they were not here, so I am left at leisure to read, or do any thing I please, pick't up in front parlour, a Novel, intitled, the Casket, or double discovery,[57] which I read, and discover'd while reading that I had perused it formerly, so it turn'd out, a trible discovery, no great things, much like the generality of them—Henry has brought me a book from town, which I expect will please, and suit me, much better—and when Molly returns home, I shall have work sent me.—My husband came up to tea with us, sent John back empty—William and Henry took a ride in chaise this evening.

16. A Joseph Clark, to whome Jacob Downing had sold his Coachee, came for it this morning he was here, on first day last, to look at it,—My husband and Son Henry went to town after breakfast—tis a fine cool day, 'tho I believe the wind is N.E—I find myself but poorly this morning—two Masons are at work here to day, under pining, I think they call it, the wooden house that was lately moved, and pointing some part of the roof of this house—they eat here—William is out with them—HD. says that I must go home to morrow to acknowledge a deed &c. If I can make up my mind to go to Downingstown, I think I shall not return here beforehand—My Son Henry, this evening cracking the stone of an apricott, jamm'd a bit of the shell between two of his teeth, he was a long time endeavouring to get in out without effect, went to bed with it, but got rid of it before he slep't—the flies are so numerous here, that if I set still reading, or writing for an hour, I find it necessary to wash my face and hands, the reason is obvious, it might be, also, proper to change my Cap and Neckerchief, but that is not so soon done—William and self took a walk this fine evening, left the masons at supper, to Thos. Fishers, the Sun was set when we got there, so that our stay was short, we were at home about dusk—No body from town to night, spent most of this evening reading to my Son, it is a beautiful serene night,—My mind is thro' mercy, in better state than my body, it feels light and free just now, 'tho I am very far from being well.—not light minded I trust, neither.

56. Words crossed out.
57. *The Casket; or, Double Discovery; a Novel,* 2 vols. (London: Lowndes, 1785 [Watt, *Bibliotheca Britannica*]).

17. Cool morning hazey—wind S.W—Isaac Child finish'd pointing the roof of the old house &c. Billy paid him—Henry and Hannah came up about 10 o'clock forenoon, they din'd and spent the day here, but went to town again in the evening she is to loose blood tomorrow, by Dr. Kuhn's direction. My Husband and Reynold Keen came up to tea with us, HD. and self acknowledg'd a Deed before him—they also went away after tea. W.D. was taken sick while at dinner, went out and was releived by losing his dinner, he seems as well this evening as usual—he and I took a short walk, after we return'd, I read to him, a Pamphlet, wrote by one Richard Brothers, (who is, now, famous in London) intitled A Revealed Knowledge of the Prophecies & times[58]—wrote, as he says, under the direction of the Lord God. &c &c.

18. warm, flying cloudy—a little sprinkling of rain forenoon—wind Southerly—H.S.D. came home about 10. A.M. they are cradling Barley here to day—HD. and MS—concluded that it was not proper for WD. and self to come home yet, to prepare for our jaunt to Downingstown, as they were still painting at our house, and like to be so doing, for some time longer, the smell of the second coat of paint is much more heavy than the first.—I have been reading this morning a Testimony of the Authenticity of the Prophecies of Richard Brothers, and of his Mission to recall the Jews. By Nathaniel Brassey Halhed, M.P.[59]—Halhed, who is a member of Parliament, and a man of very good understanding, if we may judge by his writing, I mean his language,—insists that Brothers is a true Prophet, and sent of the Lord—Brothers says of himself, that he is, The Man (God Almighty's Nephew) that will be revealed to the Hebrews as their Prince, to all Nations as their Governour, according to the covenant to king David, immediately under God. &c. &c.—We had a very pleasing Shower of rain after dinner, not quite sufficient to lay the dust—William and self were walking in the Garden when the rain came on—he and Henry went out in the Chaise about 5 o'clock—while they were gone, being alone, I finish'd reading another pamphlet intitled, Sound Argument dictated by Common sense, in answer to N.B. Halhads testimony &c. relative to Brothers and his pretended Mission to recall the Jews. By George Horne

58. Richard Brothers, *A Revealed Knowledge of the Prophesies and Times, Particularly of the Present Time, the Present War, and the Prophesy Now Fulfilling . . . Book the First, Containing, with Other Great and Remarkable Things, the Restoration of the Hebrews to Jerusalem by the Year 1788, under Their Revealed Prince and Prophet Wrote by Himself* (London, 1794 [*Brit. Mus. Cat.*]). Brothers (1757–1824), a former British naval officer, announced himself to be a descendant of David with a claim to the crown of England, which he considered a new Israel. In 1795 he entered first Newgate prison, then an insane asylum, where he remained until 1806 (E. P. Thompson, *The Making of the English Working Class* [New York: Vintage, 1966], 117–19; *DNB*).

59. Nathaniel Brassey Halhed, *Testimony of the Authenticity of the Prophecies of Richard Brothers, and of His Mission to Recall the Jews* (London: H. D. Symonds, 1795 [*Brit. Mus. Cat.*]).

D.D.[60]—this peice, prehaps, not much inferior to the other, but in my Opinnion much more to the purpose.—I also read a fourth pamphlet.—A Calculation on the commencement of The Mellenium (which Richd. Brothers says will take place on the 19th. of November next at or about sunrise in the latitude of Jerusalem) with Observations on Dr. Horn's pamphlet &c. togeather with a speach deliver'd in the House of Commons respecting the confinement of Brothers the Prophet. By Natl. B. Halhed M.P.[61]—This same Brothers, undertakes to foretell many very extrodinary things, such as, A fatal catastrophe to the Emperor of Germany, and the Princes of the Empire. The Empress of Russia, The Pope, The Kings of England, France, Spain Prussia, and Serdinia.—'tis wrote that on the 20th. of Feby. he addres'd the King in the following words vizt. The Lord God commands me to say to you, George the third, King of England, that immediately on my being revealed in London to the Hebrews, as their Prince, and to all nations as their governor, your Crown must be deliver'd up to me, that all your power and authority may cease."—My Sons return'd to late tea,—We saw several Sky Rockets thrown from the City this evening.

19. First day: very warm[62]—HSD went to meeting, William and self as usual at home, no one here to day, either from Town or Country—William and Henry rode out towards evening it has been a plesant day,—I mett with and perused, a pamphlet of Letters to a Philosophical Unbeliever part the III. containing An Answer to Paines Age of Reason, By Joseph Priestly L.L.D. F.R.S. &c.[63]

20. Warm. William was unwell in the night—better this morning he is gone to town after breakfast, I fear he will be try'd by the heat—After he was gone, and Henry to the wheat field, I amus'd myself, having little to do, by reading Inkle and Yarico,[64] a Dramatic peice, but little worth—Henry and self, dinn'd by ourselves,—My husband and William came up to late tea, Henry went to town soon after they came; he intends returning tomorrow—we walk'd in garden this evening I have not been further for several days.

60. George Horne, D.D. [Walley Chamberlain Oulton], *Sound Argument Dictated by Common Sense, in Answer to Nathaniel Brassey Halhed's Testimony of the Authenticity of the Prophecies of Richard Brothers, and His Pretended Mission to Recal the Jews* (Oxford: T. Boosey et al., [1795] [*Brit. Mus. Cat.*]).

61. Nathaniel Brassey Halhed, *A Calculation on the Commencement of the Millennium, and a Short Reply to Dr. Horne's Pamphlet, Entituled, "Sound Argument Dictated by Common Sense"* . . . (Philadelphia: Robert Campbell, 1795 [*NUC*]).

62. The sentence "William was unwell in the night, better this morning he is gone to town for breakfast" crossed out.

63. Joseph Priestley, *Letters to a Philosophical Unbeliever, Part III, Containing an Answer to Mr. Paine's Age of Reason*, 2d ed. (Philadelphia: Thomas Dobson, 1795 [Evans, *Am. Bibliography*]).

64. George Colman the Younger, *Inkle and Yarico: An Opera, in Three Acts. As Performed at the Theatre-Royal in the Hay-Market, on Saturday, Aug. 11, 1787* (London: G. G. J. and J. Robinson, [1787] [*Brit. Mus. Cat.*]).

21st. warm morning My husband left us after breakfast, WD and self here—he brought up with him last evening A Second part of Richd. Brotherss Prophecies,[65] upwards of 100 pages, quotations from Scripture &c. I read it this forenoon, many are the denunciations of woe and Distruction to all Europe, that it contains, judgments that shall shortly come to pass—himself, he highly extols, says that nothing human can hurt or have any power over him &c.—I think him a very mistakeing Man to say no worse—but cannot account for Halhed's approbating and supporting him—No Henry to night, William and self took a plesant walk, as far as Millers, come home before dusk, but did not take tea 'till Candle light—I have been taking extracts this evening from Brotherss book, being much, since I came up here, in the reading and writing humour, and having little or no work with me, The Servant girl here, is a kind of house-keeper, that I have a time of great leisure.

22. Very warm. My Husband came up this morning with the Carriage to take us home, I found him here when I came down stairs at 7 o'clock. Nancy Skyrin he informs me is but poorly, she talks of returning to the City this week,—We left Clearfield about 10. were at home long before dinner time. papering and painting not yet finish'd—HSD. went home this evening by himself, Hannah still in town—Several here this Afternoon, John Kinsey, John Skyrin, John Musser and Joseph Swift &c—this is a very warm evening either in town or country. We were eighteen days at Clearfield, have come home in the hotest of the weather, 'tho it dont make much odds to me—Tabby and Becky Fisher and Neighr. Waln here this evening—great complaints of the heat—Hetty Smith &c not yet return'd from the Shore. They have been oversett and their Carriage much shatter'd—but how much hurt, we have not yet heard, I hope not materialy—those excurtions are often attended with more perplexity than pleasure, I have frequently found that to be the case—yet it is not so to many others, they are of a different opinion.

July 23. Excessively warm. wind S.W.—John Skyrin Jacob Downing as usual, warmer than any day yet this Summer—R Waln here fore noon—About 7 this evening a gust came from the South east with sharp lightning & loud thunder, it rain'd about an hour—it has been much wanted, we may prehaps be favour'd with more to night as it is still cloudy—Neighr. Waln here during the gust—A town meeting this evening held at State house Yard,[66] about the time of the thunder Storm.

65. Richard Brothers, *A Revealed Knowledge of the Prophecies and Times, Particularly of the Present Time, the Present War, and the Prophecy Now Fulfilling . . . Book the Second, Containing, with Other Great and Remarkable Things, Not Revealed to Any Other Person on Earth, the Sudden and Perpetual Fall of the Turkish, German, and Russian Empires . . .* (London, 1794 [*Brit. Mus. Cat.*]).

66. According to various reports, anywhere from five hundred to six thousand people attended the meeting, at which the city's Democratic-Republican leaders prepared an address urging President Washington not to sign the Jay treaty (Miller, *Federalist City*, 72; Scharf and Westcott, *Philadelphia*, 1:481).

24. It rain'd last night from 11 o'clock till one this Morning a fine steady soaking rain without thunder—I was up two or three times in the night it was so very warm—HD. also up in the night. Cloudy this morning wind N.E—unsettled—HD. took a dose Phisick—this morning having been disorder'd in his bowels by the heat as I think.—Ostin Jones here at 9 o'clock just came on shore from St. Bartholemews, mate of the vessel, all well, he says, on board, he gave me ½ Doz. Oranges—HSD. came to town, he lodges at J Smiths, as Hannah continues in town, her Father gone to meet his wife &c—Neighr. Waln here twice to day, she spent the evening and sup'd here—A thunder Gust again this evening RW. frequently comes over to us at the time of a gust—HSD. here this evening—I have felt very [ ] and poorly today. HD. also unwell. The farmers have great reason to rejoice at those seasonal and plentiful rains, unless 'tis those who have their Grass down, which is at present our case at Clearfield.—During the thunder storm of last evening the lightning struck two or the Houses of this City, without doing much damage—The Corporation of the City have lately provided watering carts for the watering and cleaning of the Streets, but the number is not yet sufficient.

July 25. rain again in the night, clear this morning wind N.W—Nancy, Molly, the Child and Betsy came here about 11 o'clock, J. Skyrin is coming in the Stage, he was overtaking in the rain last evening—in his way to Bristol, the Carriage very wett, they put boards in the bottom to day—Nancy &c and HSD. din'd with us—Nancy and her Child &c. have been 4 weeks at Bristol, she thought that the loss of a few ounces of blood might be of service to her, as she is unwell and feels heavy, as she spends this day with us, I have sent for Docr. Kuhn to ask his opinion—Jacob Downing left us after dinner for Downingstown. Joseph Read from New Jersey here fore noon acknowledg'd a deed before him—Saml. Emlen, a Son of Isaac Jackson &c call'd—William and Henry left home about 6 o'clock in the Chaise, they did not return 'till after night, they had been to Clearfield, did not tell us of their intention, or we should have opposed it, as 'tis very wrong for WD to be out, in the night air. Dr. Kuhn told him this day, that he had not felt his pulses, better since his indispossion—John, Nancy &c went home after tea, Nancy Murry, Hannah S Drinker and Sammy Rhoads here this evening—John Skyrin came this Afternoon from Bristol with Saml. Rhoads. HD. went this evening to visit Dickey Collins, who is ill at Boyer Brooks, of an inflamitory fever—the air is chang'd 'tis much cooler then for several days past, which is a very favourable circumstance—In a Moral and Physical peice, inserted in this days paper, relative to the late hot weather 'tis said, that twenty persons have probably died in a weeks time by drinking cold water, and some necissary cautions given.

26. First day: Cloudy, wind N.E—about 9 o'clock I went down to J Skyrins, mett Fredrick Hailer there, he bleed Nancy, after a short conflict with her, her Arm was twice tied up, before she could comply—I spent the day with her,

she finds herself much better for the opperation, John came home with me after night, Danl. Drinker here. HD. MS. MD. were at meeting this morning HD. MD. in the Afternoon—Ben Wilson and one Stevens, a Bookseller, dined here—Saml. Pleasents took tea, John Drinker and Joseph Bringhurst here towards evening cool and pleasent.

27. Cloudy, wind N.E—before we had been an hour down stairs, My husband sign'd two orders for burials, one a child of 2 years old and a young woman of nineteen, heard also this morning of one being ill, of a stroke from the Sun, several this summer have been taken in that way, HSD. went home to Clearfield at four this morning—Hannah still in town, rain most of this day, very heavy and steady in the Afternoon, it may allay the heat, and cool the air, and prove a great favour to this City, as many have been, and are, ill of fevers.

28. pleasent morning wind N.W.—MS. HD. went to monthly meeting, Nancy Skyrin and Daughter came here in meeting time, they din'd with us.—John Skyrin and Thos. Potts call'd, Billy took a ride of one or two miles, an old mare towards evening J Logan, John Broadhead, John Drinker call'd—William and self took a walk, as it is a fine moonlight night, to see Hannah Pemberton; came home between 9 and ten—Jacob Downing not yet returnd, 'tis out of the usual time—had he come to night—Nancy &c intended to have set off tomorrow to visit Sally at Downing's—one William Thompson, a young man, at Hezekiah Williams's is said to be very ill of the Yallow fever—the late favourable rains may prevent it from spreading—tis an aweful visitant.

29. very pleasent we were invited to day to the funeral of William Thompson—Jacob Downing came after dinner left his family well, but dear little Eliza something disordred in her bowels—Nancy, Billy, Molly and little ES—went this afternoon to Clearfield, their father set off with them, to go as far as eighth street, where he has business, they came here to tea, Margt. Elliott John Skyrin and Jacob Downing tea'd also—HSD. went from Clearfield, after breakfasting there, to North Bank, on second morning last, when he left us so early—and prehap was in the heavy rain. I did not hear 'till this evening that he was gone—Hannah S. Drinker and Sally Smith here afternoon. Sally has return'd before her mother—we are thinking of setting off tomorrow for the Vally, to visit Sally, so triffling a journey, as it would appear to some, to me is a mountain, such a consumate coward am I—and indeed the leaving home has some weight in the scale, and not a little, at this sickly season—the wind is easterly this evening and prehaps we may be stop'd tomorrow, by rain.

30. It began to rain this morning about 4 o'clock, continued all day, with short intermissions, several very smart showers, 'tis raining and blowing at present near 11 at night—Sammy Rhoads and Walter Franklin took tea here—

Nancy is disapointed, not going to visit her sister, but 'tis likely all is for the best.

July 31 cloudy, and very damp, wind W.N.W.—where is my Son Henry? I was thoughtful of him last Stormy night, he is I expect either at North bank, or alone at Clearfield—Dr. Redman, Saml. Emlen, Jon. Skyrin call'd—Nancy and her Daughter spent the day here. Sally Smith and Sally Large, Walter Franklin and Jonan. Hervey here this evening it continues cloudy.

Augt. 1. rainey morning wind N.E—last night, or rather one this morning I was awakened by a great noise, and a hard blow on my head, when lo! the cord that held up the cornice, had given way, and down it came upon us. The hurt I received is triffling, my husband none, this shall never be put up again says he;—so farewell to raised Teasters.—I believe there are very few of them now in use, this is near 49 years old, made for my dear mother before the birth of her last Child. Post bedsteads, which are a very old fashon, are now in general use.—Isaac Howel here forenoon, HD. and self acknowledg'd a deed before him. this is our quarterly meeting, HD. gone there—about one P.M. a gust of thunder &c. came from the eastward, not very sharp, Neighr. Waln here—clear'd away after dinner, but is rather warm. abundance of water has fallen within two days—A caution to snuff-takers[67]—this forenoon when filling my snuff-box from the bottle, I observed several shineing particles—upon examineing found, that I had broke a blister of glass within the bottle,—I loosen'd all the Snuff below the blister, and threw it away.—When buying a bottle of snuff, it would be well to examine it; The blisters within, are easily seen on the outside—Those who buy it by the Ounce or penny worth, run a risk.—I remember to have heard some one say, that the snuff-makers did put a quantity of pulverized glass in their snuff, to render it the more pungent—I doubt not, but this absurd idea arose from finding those small particles of glass, occasion'd by breaking the blisters within.—rain again this Afternoon, clearer this evening Nancy Skyrin and Child, Neigr. Waln &c. took tea with us—John Skyrin and J Downing here—our Son Henry came to town this Afternoon, glad was I to see him, he left North-bank yesterday, and with some difficulty arrive'd at Clearfield to day, was under the necessity of lodging by the way, the waters are so high and Bridges carried away, &c. that it is difficult traveling—he has had no return of the Ague, but appears in good health; Nancy better—Billy took it into his head this cloudy and damp Afternoon, to go out on the Mare, he rode a mile or two—it rain'd hard soon after his return.—"The late plentiful and continu'd rains have swelled the river Schuylkill to a very unusual hight,—the voilence of the fresh has entirely destroy'd the Bridge of the middle Ferry, and the water increased so rapidly as to overflow the first floor of the Ferry House to the depth of three feet, besides

67. ED was a longtime snuff user. See below, Dec. 2, 1803, and Apr. 15, 1806.

doing considerable damage." The full moon is shineing clear, yet it does not appear to be settled weather yet.

Augt. 2. First day: sun shines hot—wind N.E—Saml. Emlen inform'd my husband yesterday, of the death of Nelly Haydock, who departed this life on fifth day last, she was the youngest but one, of our friend Henry Haydocks six daughters, New York. HD. MD. went to meeting, MS. WD. ED. at home, Ruth Walmsley and Hannah Thornton din'd here—Henry and Hannah, Sally Smith and Sally Large and James Logan took tea with us. Ja Downing set off early this morning for the Vally—Jams. Fisher here this evening—A lad from J Smiths to inform Hannah that her Father and Mother were come home, she was gone with Molly &c. to S. Emlens.

3d. rain, rain, rain, we are never satisfied, some of us, full or fasting—'tis well we have not power over the elements &c.—It has rain'd, I believe, most of the night, very hard towards morning wind N.E—HD. gone to quarterly meeting—MS. & MD. were prevented going, by heavy rain—none, but our own family, din'd here—R. G——s——b was taken forceably out of meeting this morning—HSD. here after dinner—Molly gone to spend the Afternoon with Anne Wells, at Neighr. Walns.—S Emlen here this evening rain all day with very little cessation, I spent great part of this day up stairs, sewing and reading.

4. Cooler. wind S.W—unsettled—Molly and Sally Dawson gone to youths meeting—HSD. call'd—I have this morning finish'd reading four Octavo Volls. containing 42 lectures, on the Prophecies That remain to be fulfilled. deliver'd at the Chapel in Glass-House Yard London—in the year 1790 By Elhanan Winchester.[68]—I have been pleased with, and much interested in those lectures while reading them, but forbear making any conclusions; knowing that good Men of differant denomanations have different ideas of those things that are (in my opinion,) incomprehensible, and in the opinion of most, not easily understood.—I have taken several extracts from them.—The paper of this morning informs us, that the communication in the usual mode between the city and country west of Schuylkill, is entirely cut off, owing to the late rains, That the Bridges and Boats are all carried away, and most of them either lost or destroy'd.—So that we need not look for Jacob Downing as yet, or expect to hear from his family,—many will undoubtedly, be, as much or more, disappointed;—we are selfish creatures, and in many respects 'tis right, I think, that it should be so, if we do not carry it too farr, Those whom the God of Nature, has put immediately under our care, ought to be more perticularly cared for, by us; this, I think, cannot be call'd blamable selfishness. Our two Peters went, this Afternoon, to Negros meeting, with their master—Betsy Jervis,

68. See above, July 11.

John and Nancy Skyrin and Child drank tea with us. HD. and self went this evening to Jams. Smiths. Hetty thinks herself better for the jaunt.—Henry and Hannah left town before tea,—We call'd at J Skyrins in our way home, found Betsy Dawson ill of vomitting &c.—she was unwell this Afternoon while here—J Smiths New building at Summer Ville, lately raised, was by the late rain &c. beat down, the raising and great part of the new Wall.—When we came home, we very unexpectedly found Jacob Downing here, he don't own, or say, that the roads are so bad as reported—The turn-pike road is considerably damaged, and much destruction in many places, one or two new Houses in this City, either by the wind or rain have in part fallen down—Molly spent the Afternoon with Anna Wells, at S. Emlens, Saml. Rhoads came home with her. Neigr. Waln here this evening—This Evenings paper,[69] says, that The rains for a few days past have been greater and the floods higher than were before know in Pennsylvania. The Mails and the public stages which set out yesterday for different parts of the United States were all obliged to return to the City, finding the roads impassable. The Mails due this morning had not arrived when this Gazett was put to press.

5. Cloudy morning wind S.E—The painters here, they painted part of the front of the House, but gave over, as rain came on, heavy rain after dinner, Neighr. Waln here—HD. went this Afternoon to the funeral of Leonard Dorsey—John Ferree and Daughter Lidia Brinton and James Logan drank tea with us—John and his daughter are on their way to Shrewsbury, to the Sea shore, for her health, as she is far from well. John and Nancy Skyrin, Jona. Harvey and Thomas Stewardson were here this evening. An account in this days paper of the Death of the Dauphin of France, who died the 8th. June last.[70] William, Molly and self went on the top of our House this Afternoon to see a french Vessel fireing her Guns, which were return'd by a Salute from one of the Wharves. The plasterer was pointing our chimneys when we went up.

Augt. 6: clear. wind S.W—Richd. Collens was here a day or two ago, he appears to be recovering, 'tho very much reduced—after seven bleeding, blistering &c. HD. received a letter this morning from Joseph Trimble, Chester county, inviting him and others to the funeral of his Father, William Trimble tomorrow, he was in his 90th. year.—little E. Skyrin unwell with disordred bowels, B. Dawson still poorly—Saml. Emlen junr. Polly Noble, Sammy Fisher, John Skyrin &c called—H.S.D. who came to town forenoon din'd with us—he left town towards evening Sister gone this evening to visit Molly Smith, who is lame of a strain'd Ancle. Tis a very warm evening Sammy

69. The *Philadelphia Gazette and Universal Daily Advertiser*.

70. A dispatch from France dated June 15 reported the death of the imprisoned Louis-Charles, the ten-year-old son of Louis XVI and Marie Antoinette (Scott and Rothaus, *French Revolution*, s.v. "Louis XVII"; *Philadelphia Gazette and Universal Daily Advertiser*, Aug. 5, 1795).

Rhoads here.—Sally Smith and Tommy Tylee call'd, Molly &c went out with them.—for a few days past, it has been talk'd here that Malignant fever prevails in New York. I hope it is without much foundation.

7. Clear. not unpleasant tho warm, wind S.W.—John Nancy and Child came forenoon—Hannah Sansom, whom I have not seen for a long time, call'd this morning She mention'd a french Man and his Sister who lives near us, as being in need of help—Jos. Bringhurst call'd. James and Saml. Fisher and several others in front room with HD. on landed business—John, Nancy and Child din'd with us.—Nancy, Molly and Sally Smith went in our Waggon to E. Larges, about 3 miles on the Frankford road. J Skyrin was to have gone with them, but came here after they were set[71] off, little Elizath. stays with us, she is in good Spirits tho unwell,—Nancy &c. came home after night—Hetty Smith went with them,—My husband has not been out of the House this day, 'tho not unwell, which is rather extrodinary, it has been a very warm day, for one reason;—I have been reading a small volume wrote by Mrs. Barbauld and Dr. Aiken—intitled Evenings at Home; or the Juvenile Budget opened, consisting of a veriety of miscellaneous pieces for the instruction and amusement of young persons.[72]—I think it is well calculated for that purpose.

8. hazey morning forebodes great heat—wind S.W—Raynold Keen junr. breakfasted with us.—One Peter Notley a servant of Saml. Walace, who has been in the woods with his master, my husband and Henry, more than once, a very handy cleaver fellow, he died yesterday suddenly by drinking cold water.—It has been the fate to day and yesterday, as we have heard, of many others.—HSD. came to town after dinner, went back before tea. HD. Nancy, William, Molly and the Child took a ride towards evening they came back to tea here, Neighr. Waln also,—Elizath. Skyrin delighted with riding up and down our Yard in Charles's Coach—My husband and self took a walk this warm evening to Hanh. Pembertons, she declines going to Downingstown with me, as was talk'd off, thinks the weather too hot, and the journey too long.—We stop'd, for a minute, on our way home, at a book auction.—William and Mary walked thirteen squar's after night this very hot evening, he is too apt to overdo matters of this sort.—From the Gazette of this evening—We are sorry to learn by letters from New York, that a Malignant fever has made its appearance in that City.—The Mercury in the thirmometer, in the shade, this day at 2 o'clock stood at 87 degrees.

Augt. 9. First day: very warm, wind S.W.—rain in the night, Jacob Downing

71. The word "out" crossed out.

72. John Aitkin and Anna Laetitia Barbauld, *Evenings at Home; or, The Juvenile Budget Opened, Consisting of a Variety of Miscellaneous Pieces, for the Instruction and Amusement of Young Persons* . . . 2d ed. (London: J. Johnson, 1794–98 [*Brit. Mus. Cat.*]).

sett off to visit his family, which he does, regularly once a week, very early this morning—HD. MS. MD. went to meeting—Sally Rhoads, John Skyrin and B. Wilson call'd before meeting.—S Swett and B Wilson din'd here, George Fry also—not quite so warm to day as yesterday—HD. MD. gone to Afternoon meeting—S. Brants mother stop'd in Chaise to see her.—John and Nancy Skyrin, the Child and Betsy Dawson went this Afternoon to Clearfield, intending to stay there for a week or ten days, if Nancy continues well enough—JS. comes back—I spent an hour this evening with Neigh. Waln at her door, a fine Shower fell, which has cool'd the air,—a Clear evening the Stars remarkably bright—J Skyrin came home after night, he brings a good report of Nancy and the Child. I read this evening A Salutation (8 pages) of Brotherly love, from the monthly-meeting of Friends in this City, To the members of our Society,[73]—which my Husband read this morning in our meeting—'tis a peice, that I think, will be generaly approved among us and no doubt, by many others—I have, I believe, given over the thoughts of going to Downingstown to see my dear Sally, and her three precious children, bad roads, Nancys situation; and add to those two good reasons,—my fears of traviling &c.

Augt. 10. Clear and warm, wind S.W.—William rode out this morning in Chaise, Peter with him, Zebulon Heston call'd,—Hannah Sansom and French Man, who lives in our Alley, here forenoon—HSD. came to town, he din'd here—rain with some thunder Afternoon, R. Waln here. Henry stays with us to night, he came on Horse back, and as it continues to rain, I prevail'd on him to stay. What sort of an Autumn, does a rainy spring and Summer, bring?

11. Clouly, wind S.E—S. Emlen eat a late breakfast here, HD. MS. MD. and HSD. went to meeting—rain about one o'clock, Henry went homeward between 5 and six, it rain'd at the time—poor R—— N—— was taken this morning again, to the Hospital.—Betsy Emlen took tea, she, Waltar Franklin, and Richd. Smith in front parlor this evening.

12. rain in the night, Cloudy most of this day with frequent small rains, wind S.E—J Logan call'd—The Indian rule relative to the moon, and weather has not held good this moon.—Sister waited on M. Aimes, on Nancys account.—From the Gazette. Various concuring accounts confirm the report some days since circulated, that a Malignant fever prevails in New York. The general opinion is that it was brought there by a Spanish Vessel—The committee of health say that no more than eight persons have died of it there, Sailors excepted.—tis also said, that it is very sickly at Boston.—John Skyrin here this

73. *A Further Salutation of Brotherly Love, from the Monthly-Meeting of the Friends of Philadelphia to the Members of our Religious Society, in and near the Said City* (Philadelphia: Jacob Johnson, 1795 [*NUC*]).

evening he says, they are well at Clearfield—he has been there this Afternoon. It is raining now, near 11 o'clock at night.

13. rain most of the night and this morning, wind N.E—Nurse Patty Jones called forenoon she says Nancy has made a little mistake in her account of time, I would not give into it, and told her, that I should say nothing to Nancy about the matter, at least at present, but depend on her the month through,—Thos. Stewardson dined with us, Robt. Stevenson and Sally Zane took tea—Neighr. Waln and grandson Richd. called—Sammy Rhoads here towards evening Molly went out with him and S.Z—A Billy Parker call'd with copys of survays—The damage done by the late freshes at, and near, Newark, are great indeed: what with the loss of the Farmers and the injury done to Mill-[seats], forges &c. the total damage in those parts may not be computed at less than one hundred thousand pounds.—J Downing left us on first day last, he is not yet return'd, his dear little boy was poorly when he left them last week—Betsy Fordham call'd this evening with Shirts she has made for HD.—MD. received a broad hint this evening from her Father.

14. Cloudy. wind S.E—the moon chang'd about noon—at one o'clock it blew up strongly from N E. with rain—Sally Smith here forenoon, she and her Mammy were yesterday at Clearfield, informs, they were pretty well there, Henry not yet gone to N. Bank. Saml. Moore came with the Cart—I have not yet seen him, Jacob Tomkins call'd—We dispatch'd S. Moore after Dinner with nesessaries—Sally Smith here Afternoon, Molly went out with her to S Emlens &c—A clear night, unexpectedly so to me as I thought I foresaw a more lengthey storm from the Eastward—it is much cooler, many, without care, may feel the effect of this change in the weather.—I have read two Vols. intitled Variety, A Collection of Miscellanies, in verse and prose. printed in Dublin[74]—several good peices, none the reverse—religious and moral—William more poorly, occasion'd by the damp, and present change in the weather.

15. Clear and cool. wind N.W—John C. Miller from Scotland, breakfasted with us—Several with HD. in front parlor this morning on business—My Husband and William set off about 10 o'clock for Clearfield, with Sundries for our Children—the wind chang'd before noon to N.E—it is warmer and still unsettled—HD. returned to dinner, he came with Thos. Fisher in his Carriage, left ours to bring Wm., Nancy, her child and maid home this afternoon—John Skyrin call'd—After a busy afternoon with my Needle, I read An Appeal To the serious and candid Professors of Christianity &c. By Joseph Priestly. and an account of the Tryal of Mr. Elwall. &c.[75]—William Nancy &c.

74. *Variety: A Collection of Miscellanies, in Verse and Prose, with Original Poetry and Fugitive Pieces*, 2 vols. (Dublin: R. N. Butler, 1795 [*Brit. Mus. Cat.*]).

75. Joseph Priestley, LL.D., *An Appeal to the Serious and Candid Professors of Christianity . . . and an Account of the Trial of Mr. Eliwall, for the Heresy and Blasphemy, at Stafford Assizes* (Philadelphia: Thomas Dobson, 1794 [*Brit. Mus. Cat.*]).

arrived safe here to tea. Nancy and Child are better than when they left us—Thos. Stewardson and J Skyrin took tea here also—John Ryerson here this evening Molly Lippencot and Hannah Cope paid Molly an evening visit: A cool pleasent clear night.—The President of the United States has ratified the Treaty of Amity, Commerce and Navigation, between his Britanic Majesty and the United States of America.

16. First Day: clear and cool, wind S.W.—my husband, John Drinker, Thos. Stewardson and Owen Biddle, set off about 9 o'clock for Darby meeting, to proceed after to the intended boarding School &c.—HD. is not quite well, he took Rheubarb with him—MS. MD. went to meeting—S. Swett din'd with us—Molly went to Afternoon meeting, Betsy Emlen came home with her—Nancy Skyrin and SS—took tea with us. J Skyrin here this evening—Sammy Rhoads' here, he went with Molly to Saml. Emlens—I have been rather more unwell to day than usual—Israel Whelins Man, brought Jacob Downings smal trunk here this Afternoon, he says, he left them all well, and that Jacob intends coming to town tomorrow I suppose his horse is lame, as we heard he had run a nail in his foot, near the ferry, the day he left us, the rain and bad roads also have detain'd him. Othniel Alsop lodges here to night—HD. and our Man John being absent.

17. cool clear morning wind S.W—Jacob Downing came home before breakfast from the Buck—he left his family yesterday—Thos. Dawson called—Molly went with Molly Lippencot and Sally Smith to visit Abby Marshal now Morris.—A light gust of rain and thunder this afternoon—Jacob, John, Nancy, and Benn. Wilson here this evening—The French Embassador, unloaded two pistoles in and about his Head, but was not dead this afternoon.

18. Clear and warm. wind N.W—S. Emlen and Peter Yarnel call'd. before meeting. S. Swett and Jacob din'd with us,—Molly went rideing with Sally Emlen, H. Mott &c. Betsy Emlen—B. Emlen, S. Swett, John and Nancy took tea here, Dr. Redman called—William went out two miles on mare—several young foulks here this evening—I went over forenoon to P. Hartshorns, they return'd yesterday from Bristol, Suckey not well.

19. Clear and warm, wind S.W—Josh. Ball called with a paper relative to the president and the treaty[76]—WD. put his hand to it—HD. return'd home just before dinner.—William and Mary, took a ride the five miles round this Afternoon in the Chaise—Docr. Kuhn call'd, advised William to take a dose

76. Probably the address presented to President Washington on Aug. 20 by merchants and traders who favored ratification of the Jay treaty. This address carried 412 signatures; the address drawn up on July 22 by opponents of the treaty had 413 (*Gazette of the United States and Daily Evening Advertiser*, Aug. 19, 1795; Miller, *Federalist City*, 73).

Castor Oyl tomorrow, as he has been, a day or two, disorder'd in his bowels.— Henry's Neighbour Porter from Richland, call'd this evening he says that Docr. Jardine and Wife are both ill of a belious fever, he was to call on Docr. Rush to visit them, that our Son came from thence this morning—He is, I trust, at present, at home Clearfield—HD. Molly and self, went after night, to visit Nancy—she is poorly, sleeps very little and feels very uneasy—Benn. Wilson came home with us. The french Consel who shot himself, a day or two ago, is, tis said still alive, but badly mangled.

20. Clear and warm, wind S.W—the Painters again at work in back parlor, tis a tedious Job—by some mismanagement the paint would not dry, he was obliged to take it off, and after some time to give it another coat.—Saml. Smith from B. County, here, it is our meeting for Sufferings,—I have been pleas'd, by reading Cato Major; or a Treatise on Old Age, by M. Tullius Cicero. with Explanatory Notes from the Roman History, by the Honourable James Logan Esqr. &c.[77] father to our James Logan—those Notes are very entertaining as they are a kind of Roman History in miniature—Saml. Smith and Jacob Downing dined here.—WD. has taken a dose of Castor Oyl, he eat no dinner,—Molly went in the Carriage to call on Nancy to go to Clearfield— signs of a gust prevented them from proceeding—and John came back empty, left Molly at John Skyrins.—I went over to Neighr. Walns towards evening— two of our Neighr. Gardener's Daughters were married this evening Nelly and Nancy.—Walter Franklin and Sammy Rhoads here this evening Molly out. rain this Afternoon and evening—HD. most of this day at meeting—Molly came home near 10 o'clock, J Skyrin with her.—in a heavy shower and very dark; she should have stay'd where she was.

21. rain in the night and this morning wind N.E—George Churchman breakfasted with HD. before I came down stairs—HD. gone to meeting—Dr. Kuhn here forenoon, order'd William a dose Salts, as the disorder in his bowels still continues—cloudy all day with frequent rains—Williams bowels much disorder'd, fluxey—Saml. Smith came for his Horse, and is gone homewards.—I have spent most of this day up stairs with my Son—Thos. Stewardson took tea with us.

22. cloudy all day. wind N.E—rain towards evening. Docr. Kuhn here Morning and evening William took another dose salts, an ounce yesterday, ½ ounce to day neutral salts—he is feverish, the disorder not so much check'd as I expected it would have been—'tho it does not, yet amount to an inveterate decentry, it is much of that nature—HSD. came to town forenoon, he din'd with us—went home after dinner—Jacob Downg., Sally Smith took tea—

77. Marcus Tullius Cicero, *M. T. Cicero's Cato Major, or His Discourse of Old-Age*, trans. James Logan (Philadelphia: B. Franklin, 1744 [Evans, *Am. Bibliography*]).

Neighr. Waln, Walter Franklin, James Logan and Richd. Smith, here this evening William took 17 drops of liquid Laudunum.

Aug't. 23. first day Cloudy: wind N.E—William was in considerable pain in the night, Sister and self were up with him—at four in the morning gave him 10 drops more Laudunum—he sleep'd a little in the morning Doctor here after breakfast, order'd a decoction of bark to be given every hour, and an injection to be administred—he threw up the bark, the other produced nothing with it—HD. and MD. gone to meeting—no one din'd with us but JD—S. Emlen here after dinner—Jacob and John Skyrin took tea here—William took 9 doses of the bark, he has been very sick at Stomac, and has spent a trying day, but we hope he is rather better this evening Molly gone to Nancys, Sammy Rhoads called—I gave my William another levement this evening he is very weak and low, more so than he has yet been in this sickness, and I feel very poorly myself—My husband took a dose Rhubarb this evening being unwell in his bowels, tho not so as to be confined—He has been this evening to Hannah Pembertons.—she sent for him, has heard of the death of her Brother Isaac Zane, who departed lately, at Marlbro Iron Works in Virginia—which works he formerly own'd.

24. wind S.E—rain about 9 o'clock, Doctor here, says Willm. has little or no fever, he ordred another injection and a dose Castor Oyl, also the decoction of bark to be given regularly every two, yesterday he took it every hour, We were up with him in the night, and as his bowels were much pain'd, gave him 24 drops Laudanum.—Sent John with Carriage for Nancy and Child, they spent the day with us—Docr. Redman and James Logan called—The bells muffled this morning for William Bradford Atturney General.—James Mifflin called to look at the fruit Trees in our Yard—Docr. Kuhn here this evening he seems thoughtfull on WD.s account, or at least I think so, rain again this evening—Joseph Bringhurst and Saml. Emlen here this Afternoon—James Logan here in the evening with a receipt for Williams disorder—John Skyrin came after tea for his wife and Child—James Smith call'd in the evening, gave WD. another Levement, bath'd his bowels with Stees's Opodeldoc[78] and gave 25 drops liquid Laudanum—I think he has no small degree of fever to night—William Bradford died near Frankford, the funeral past our door this evening—prehaps twenty Carriages attended.

25. warm. wind variable, inclining to westward—John Parish call'd—HD. M D. went to meeting—Ml. Callanan call'd, he arrived yesterday from London—

78. Paracelsus, the famous sixteenth-century chemist and physician, coined the word *opodeldoc* to describe various medical plasters. By the 1720s the term had come to mean soap liniment. Dr. Steers, a British physician, marketed Steers' Opodeldoc, a patent medicine containing ammonia, as a remedy for bruises, sprains, cuts, burns, etc. (Griffenhagen and Young, "Patent Medicines," 161).

Dr. Kuhn ordred several opperations to be perform'd on our dear patient to day—Fredrick, bleed him after nine, an injection administred before ten, gave him a dose Castor Oyl before eleven.—his blood is very much inflamed, I fear the Doctor apprehends an obstruction in his bowels, he is calm and in good spirits.—the Oyl work'd—he discharged a quantity of green bile—Nurse Waters din'd here—My beloved Son has undergone much this day—HD. James Logan, A Skyrin and her Child and Molly, went this Afternoon to Clearfield—Michel Callanan called after dinner.—Dr. Kuhn came in the Afternoon, William as well as he could expect,—and that is far from well.—HSD. came to town after dinner he expects Hannah this evening—Eliston Periot call'd. Peggy Elliot also—Henry went home by Moon light as Hannah did not come—J Logan, S. Emlen, the two Saltars, and Sally Smith here this evening a fine pleasent evening rather warm, HD. gone to H. Pembertons—gave WD. un Levement—the disorder returns, tho the fever is not high.

26th. Clear and warm, wind NNE—Sister and self up in the night with our dear distress'd—he was in pain and constant urging—I repeated what had been done in the evening—and used the Opodeldoc—by his desere, I lay down in the next room, but at four o'clock Sister, who lays in the room with him, called me again, as he had been in constant pain all night, we gave 25 drops Laudanum with 20 [ditto] of antimonial wine,[79] we wish'd to omitt it if possiable or should have given it earlyer—Doctor called as usual this morning—said he did not expect to find him so unwell, but rather thought by his feeling last night, that he would have been better this morning—he ordred the bark in decoction to be given, again, every hour, and nothing else at present; he seems easier this morning as he generaly does when under the Effects of an anodoyne—James Saltar here this Morning—John Skyrin called, he says Nancy is unwell from a sleepless night and uneasy sensations.—William has taken a few spoonsfull of boiled bread and milk which appears, as yet, to set easy on his stomac—No body din'd here,—We have gone on very regularly to day, and William seems better, pepper mint water, peaches, and a little bread and milk, and bathing with opodoldoc &c. what a favour he is better, last night he was ill indeed.—Hannah and Peggy Saltar and their brother James call'd, they went home to day.—Henry and Hannah took tea with us—John and Nancy and Sammy Rhoads here this evening—Doctor called Afternoon,[80] he hopes the disorder is overcome,—William has been, mercyfully, easier most of this day—last night 'twas not easy to say, which way the Scale would turn,

79. Antimony is a native metal widely used in the eighteenth century, primarily as an emetic. Tasteless when combined with other ingredients, it was commonly given to children instead of preparations calling for quinine or bark, which were difficult to administer. Antimonial wine (tartrate of antimony dissolved in distilled water and combined with sherry) was often given in doses of one or two ounces (Estes, "Therapeutic Practice," 368, 381; Haller, "Tartar Emetic," 236, 238, n.5; see above, July 2).

80. The word "says" crossed out.

had it been the other way, what a different situation should we have been in this night—Having been laterly up in the night for hours together, I have observed a Solatery tree-frog, who has taken up his aboad in one of the trees in our yard, who begins to croke or chip, (his noise being more like an inseect than a common frog) at the close of day, and leaves off, a little after the dawn, his noat becomes weaker and weaker as the day advances, as tho he was singing himself to sleep—It seems to me that he continues his noise all night without intermission, but of this I am not certain.—I am ordered by the Doctor to give my dear William a dose of the decoction of bark every hour, 'tis surprising how fast the hours pass when each hour is to be attened too—some would say other wise, but to me, twelve or 24 hours appear to have a degree of length, but when something is to be done at the end of each hour, they seem to fly astonishingly fast.

27. A little over cast, wind S.E—we were up again in the night with William, he went to bed clear of pain, and we omited the Anodyne &c. about one o'clock Sister call'd me up, the pain &c had return'd.—We then gave him laudanum and Antimonial wine and &c.—Doctor called this morning order'd another injection with Castor Oyl in lieu of sweet Oyl, and to give the bark steadily, rub his bowels with Opodeldoc and let him eat good peaches.—Saml. Emlen with an Hibernian, and HSD. called—none din'd but Jacob Downing.—the Doctor, this afternoon, pronounces Williams pulses very good, and he much better, notwithstanding bad appearances—H Mott took tea with us.—Henry went home after night on horse back, Hannah in town.—Ben Wilson &c here this evening Molly spent the evening at J Skyrins, Hannah Drir. there—William not so well to night as during the day—he took an injection and Anodine as order'd, his bowels still very much disorder'd—bloody mucus.

28. Over cast. wind Southerly, when the sun braks out 'twill undoubtedly be very warm—S. Emlen breakfasted here, he is going by water to Burlington—Dr. Kuhn here as usual this Morning he ordred another dose Castor Oyl, larger than formerly, as Williams disorder continues, his evacuations have as bad an appearance as ever, 'tho not so frequent. The Oyl produc'd a large quantity of figured feces, a very favourable circumstance 'tho accompayn'd with mucus—Hannah Drinker spent the morning and din'd here, Danl. King James Logan &c. called.—Extract from Browns evening paper under the London head—"Many hundred of the desciples of Mr. Brothers in this City, express not only their suprize, but concern, that their masters prophecies have failed, not considering that in their being fulfilled their own destruction was certain!"[81] Our John took Hannah &c. home this Afternoon, Molly gone to J Smiths, J Logan, Sarah Fisher, Ben Wilson here this evening.

81. *Philadelphia Gazette and Universal Daily Advertiser,* Aug. 27, 1795; see above, July 17.

Augt. 29. warm, wind S.W—The Doctor ordered the decoction of bark to be given steadily to day—Eli Elmer breakfasted with us—Saml. Moore from Clearfield here fore noon, says his wife Jemima who has been ill, is better.—William has spent this day with very little pain, tho we have proof this evening that the disorder is not quite removed, or it has left his bowels in a very weak state, he has taken 13 doses of the decoction of bark. Doctor here this evening—Jb. Downing set off this Afternoon to visit his family—little E. Skyrin was sent to see us—Betsy Emlen, Sally Smith and Sally Large here this evening Neighr. Waln here also.

30. First day: very warm, wind southerly—John Drinker, Saml. Emlen junr. and Docr. Kuhn called, desired us to continue the bark—William takes the essence of one and a third ounce p day—his evacuations are at times as bad as ever, but not with pain, nor near so frequent—our dear Nancy far from well, and within 10 or 12 days of her trouble—I have not seen her here for several days past. Susana. Swett din'd with us—William better this Afternoon, more favourable appearences.—Docr. Kuhn with several other physicians were call'd togeather to take into consideration the expediency of stoping the Stages between us and New-York, on account of the fever that prevails there; it was concluded unnecessary at present. Dl. Trotter took tea here—Doctor call'd this evening says William has no fever, that his pulse is good—This fluxey disorder is prevalent in many parts of our City.—H.D. Molly and self took a walk this evening very fine full moon light. William, I hope, so much on the mending way as to admitt my leaving him with his Aunt, who will take equal care. We went to H. Pembertons, Sally Zane sets off on third day next for Marlbro in Virginia, upwards of 200 miles; she intends lodging in her way with Sally Downing. We went after to see our poor Nancy, who is in a [grunting] way, tho as chearful as she can, came home after 9 o'clock—Sally Rhoads, Tabby and Becky Fisher, were here while we were out—found Betsy Jervis here, she is in trouble, they have sold their House for a good price, but Charles talks of going into the Country in a few days, which is matter of grief to his Sister.—John Nixons wife buried this afternoon, she was formerly Betsy Davis, I went with her to school—My dear William is, I trust on the recovery—two or three days in last week I was in much distress, on his Account more than I own'd at the time, may I be sufficiently thankful if he is spared us.

31. very warm, wind S.E—Sister called me up in the night to William, who was very low and weak, scarcely any pulse, we rub'd his feet with brandy his temples with Lavender water, gave him pepper mint water to take, after a little time he was better, but had a discharge of mucus, which shews how weak his bowels still continue. The Doctor called this morning ordred a continuation of the bark with 10 drops Elixer Vitriol in each other dose; sent John for Nancy and the Child—they took a short ride, and came here just before a little storm

of wind and smart shower of rain, about 11 o'clock, HD. gone to ministers meeting, HSD. came to town little before noon, wet to the skin, as is common to him, had to change all his cloaths.—he does not appear to have taken cold—John Saltar here fournoon, very heavy rain between 12 and one, James Logan here—John and Nancy Skyrin and HSD—dined with us—Henry went home after dinner in his chaise in the rain, we sent Nancy home before dusk—Doctor Call'd this evening William is without fever, 'tis no wonder he is weak, the state he was in before he was taken with this disorder, the physick he has taken since, and lack of food for near two weeks, bleeding &c. Sammy Rhoads and Ben Wilson here this evening William took 15 drops Laudanum.

Sept. 1. Cloudy, wind variable inclining to the north. very heavy rain in the night, rain this morning—HD. MS. and MD. gone to meeting—Williams bowels much disorderd this morning tho without pain—Neighr. Waln here—Doctor Redman call'd to see William—Hannah Catheral dined here—WD. eat an hearty dinner all things considerd of roast veal and beats, an improper dinner in my opinion, he has not had an appetite before for two weeks & upwards. H.S.D. came to town this Afternoon, Micl. Callanan called. A proclamation published in this days paper by the Governour, prohibeting all intercorse, for a month to come, between us and New York, and the same with respect to Norfolk in Virginia, where, 'tis said an infectious fever, also, rages at present.—The Doctor call'd this evening he looks on William as recovering—'tho his bowels still continue very weak—The report of the Committee of health in New-York is much more favourable that common report, and I am much more inclined to believe it.—That since their report of the 28 instant 6 persons have died, dated Augt. 31.—Henry lodges here to night, he intends setting off very early tomorrow morning with Edward Garragus to North Bank.

2. heavy rain early this morning wind N.E—Doctor call'd order'd the bark and Elixer [vitriol]—the rain hindred Henry going as intended this morning he went home to Clearfield—We sent for Nancy and Child, they spent the day with us.—left us before tea to take a ride, J Skyrin with them—Danl. King and wife here on business—Molly went after dinner with H Mott and Betsy Emlen to take a ride—Sister out this afternoon—Our old Neighbour Edwd. Stiless Son, who came lately, to reside in his fathers house in this Neighbourhood, from Bermuda for his health, was buried this Afternoon.—Molly gone this evening to J Smiths, Jn. Drinker took tea here—Sister went this evening to visit our poor french Neighbours in the Alley—John and Nancy went to E Larges, they stop'd here, and walk'd home—the Doctor has forsaken us this evening which is no bad sign—William is we trust recovering 'tho in a weak state, without much pain.

Sepr. 3. very cool this morning wind N.W—the Doctor has advised William to take a ride—he was up in the night, The disorder, or the relic's of it yet continues—HSD—came to town forenoon, he took an early dinner, then went with Edd. Garragus towards North Bank—We sent for Nancy and Child, they stop'd for William who went with them the 10 miles round, Frankford and point—he seems better for the ride.—Molly Drinker went after dinner with Sally Smith to Clearfield, to stay with Hannah during Henrys absence,—I sent a note to B. Burge and S. Rawle forenoon, with a medicine, by the Doctors desire, S. Rawle's Son ill in the Flux—My husband received a letter yesterday, or the day before from Robt. Bowne merchant New-York of 26th. Ultimo wherein he says, that old Docr. Bard's sentiments were, that the number of sick, and deaths in that city, were no more than has been common in this season—John Kinsey din'd and took tea with us. Pelatiah Webster was bury'd this evening Aged 70 years. John and Nancy Skyrin sup'd here, the walk here and back again in so short a time, was rather too much for Nancy—Neighr. Waln here this evening.

4. Cool, wind N.W—Doctor call'd after 9 o'clock, William was sleeping, he did not see him, desir'd the bark continu'd. we sent near noon for Nancy and Child they stop'd and took in William—Sally Rhoads here forenoon,—Saml. Moore was here this morning as he has been for several days past with the Cart, to take Dung from our Stable yard to Clearfield—sent provisions by him, for our Children.—William, Nancy &c. return'd before dinner, they had rode 10 miles down in the Neck &c. Nancy and H.S.D. din'd here, Hannah Yerkes call'd after dinner: Sistor gone to meet the committee of twelve—William was setting at the door to day—Henry went home after dinner. Our french Neighbors Malerive and his sick Sister, came in this Afternoon full of thanks—she appears to be very weak and low, looks consumptive, ask'd if she might walk now and then in our Garden, as she was unable to go much further—to which we readily consented.—Sister went over this evening to see the widdow of James Stiles and her mother, they took the visit very kind, as they are Strangers and in trouble—John and Nancy Skyrin Patience and the Child went home after night, Nancy complaining—Saml. Emlen here—John Kinsey took tea.

5. Cool, wind N.N.E—Doctor calle'd, advis'd a continuation of the bark—tho not so frequently—William took a little cold while out yesterday, which makes against him—Debby Field here forenoon, Sister out—Our french Neighbors here, she insisted on my excepting of her staff,—which as it was not of much value, I could not refuse, for a keep-sake I suppose—sent for Nancy and Child after dinner, they arrived when HD. and his Son William set off for Clearfield after 3 o'clock. I had rather he had stay'd at home, as the wind is easterly.—Peter Savage, little Peters father was here fore noon from Virginia—Joshua Smith here, I have amused myself, by fitts and spurts, while in the Chamber with Billy, by reading A little plain English, a book so

intitled, by Peter Porcupine,[82] A very nerveous and sarcastic peice. The whole Duty of Woman, by a Lady[83]—a little peice which I have read more than once before, and always with pleasure and satisfaction.—Also an Arabian Tale, as at some times I can read anything.—and a peice printed in London in 1734. in verse, intitled, Discontent. the Universal Misery. in an epistle to a Friend—It put me in mind of Mat. Priors Ladle, "That cruel something unpossessed" &c.[84]—My husband and Son return'd to tea, brought our daughter Mary home. and Sally Smith—Henry went home after tea rode in the night, unwisely.—Polly Pleasants spent the Afternoon with us—her husband came in the evening John and Nancy Skyrin also here—they went home long after night with the Child—Saml. Emlen here Afternoon—Nancy Skyrin has been frequently here laterly she rides here and walks home after night, poor Child, when I follow her to the door, I think each, will be the last time we shall see her here; for many weeks at least.

Sepr 6. First day—cloudy, wind N.E—began to rain before ten, heavy rain before noon—Doctor here, this Morning Williams pulse rather quicker from the cold he has taken—his bowels much better. Saml. Emlen here before meeting HD. MS. MD. went to meeting—Our family din'd by themselves—I read this forenoon, a little old book that belonged to my Grandfather, intitled The Life and Death of Riches and Poverty, or the ready way to true Content &c. printed in Dublin in 1710.[85]—'tis a week to day, or yesterday, since Jacob Downing left us—I wish much to hear from Sally and her little ones.—My husband and Molly at Afternoon meeting. It has been cloudy all day, with several rains—William unwell and feverish—I went into Isaac Whartons this evening Peggy lays in, her Daughter Rebecca, near a week old.—Jacob Downing return'd this evening after 9 o'clock, he left Sally and the Children well, Sally Zane lodged there last 3d. day night.

82. Peter Porcupine [William Cobbett], *A Little Plain English, Addressed to the People of the United States, on the Treaty, Negociated with His Britannic Majesty, and on the Conduct of the President Relative Thereto; In Answer to "The Letters of Franklin"; With a Supplement* . . . (Philadelphia: Thomas Bradford, 1795 [*Brit. Mus. Cat.*]).

83. A Lady [William Kenrick], *The Whole Duty of Woman* . . . (London: R. Baldwin, 1753 [*NUC*]).

84. *Discontent, the Universal Misery, in an Epistle to a Friend* (London, 1734). Matthew Prior's poem "The Ladle," written in 1703 and first published in 1704, tells of a farm woman's desire for a ladle for her silver dish, and the disastrous form in which her wish is fulfilled. The moral of the poem, based on Ovid and on a seventeenth-century English story by Edmund Gayton, is that no matter how much peace and plenty a person has, he or she still wishes for "That cruel *Something* unpossess'd" (line 165; Averley, *18th-Cen. Brit. Books; The Literary Works of Matthew Prior*, ed. H. Bunker Wright and Monroe K. Spears, 2d ed. [Oxford: Clarendon Press, 1971], 1:202–7, 2:889).

85. *Life and Death of Riches and Poverty; or, The Ready Way to True Contentment* (Philadelphia: W. Bradford, 1754). ED's edition cannot be located (Roger P. Bristol, *Supplement to Charles Evans' Bibliography* [Charlottesville: University Press of Virginia, for the Bibliographical Society of America and the Bibliographical Society of the University of Virginia, 1970], 96).

7. rain in the night and this morning wind N.E—William had a good night. Richd. Downing and his Son Thomas here forenoon, they din'd with us—Saml. Emlen called—the Doctor did not call to day—William a little fiverish to night—Sammy Rhoads here in evening HD. and self went to see Nancy, she appears more unwell than usual, I do not feel easy to leave her, but must trust this one night—rain again this evening.

8. very heavy rain towards day, continues cloudy and raining this morning wind S.W—HD. MS. MD. at meeting this morning Docr. Kuhn called, says WDs pulse are rather quick, ordered a continuation of the decoction of bark—Nancy better this morning—George Fry came with vigatables, and for necessaries for HSD—informs they are all well.—Saml. Pleasants called—Molly dined at John Skyrins—read a peice intitled, the Philadelphia Jockey Club, or Mercantile Influence Weighed, consisting of Select characters taken from the Club of Addressers. By Timothy Tickler.[86]—23 low scurolous pages.—HSD. came to town after dinner, went away before tea—Betsy Emlen and Sally Smith spent the Afternoon and evening with Molly—I went over to see Sucky Hartshorn, whom I have not seen before, since her return from Bristol, she appears still to be in great trouble for the loss of her little girl.—A Committee in our front parlor this evening with Becky Griscomb, John Webb, Joseph Drinker and Wife, Sarah Bacon, Thos. Morris, HD. &c.—Samuel Emlen and John DeMarsillac here this evening—John and Nancy Skyrin, and Jacob Downing sup'd here. I did not expect to see Nancy this evening Walter Franklin came in the evening to the girles—very warm.

9. Clear, wind due East—William took laudanum, 15 drops last night, he is better this morning—Garret breakfasted here,—Jenny Roberts Tayloress came to work this morning for our black boys.—sent John with the Carriage for Nancy by her own desire, she, her husband, and Child dined here—William, Nancy and Molly went out four miles afternoon—Molly Penry from Lititz came here this Afternoon in the Lancaster Stage, she proposes staying some time with us, till her Cosen Peggy Stocker sends for her.—Dr. Rush, Joshua Edwards, Thos. Stewardson, Neighr. Waln. Sally Smith, Nancy Thatcher, &c call'd—our french Neighbours also, to inform us they are going to move from the Alley—M Penry stop'd last evening as they past by Sallys door, saw her and her little Son, well. HSD. came to town Afternoon, went home in an hour or two after. I feel myself very unwel this evening—William poorly—a fine clear night.

10. Clear and warm, wind S.W—M Penry spent the day with us at home—

86. Timothy Tickler [pseudonym], *The Philadelphia Jockey Club; or, Mercantile Influence Weighed, Consisting of Select Characters Taken from the Club of Addresses* (Philadelphia: printed for the purchasers, 1795 [*NUC*]).

WD lowish, Doctor call'd, says he is feverish desires him to quit the bark for two or 3 days—MP. and JD. at dinner—we sent again for Nancy, she came, and is chearful—walk'd home in the evening she did not desire me to go home with her, tho I was desireous of so doing—but as M. Penry is here, and Nancy seem'd to appear easy, I stay'd at home—John went for Henry and Hannah, they came in the evening—Thos. Fisher, Thos. Stewardson called—James Logan and MP. took tea—Molly this evening at Saml. Emlens.

11. Clear and warm, wind westerly—I have a distressing pain in my Ear this morning a pain I sildom have been troubled with. HD. went down to see Nancy, found her complaining—Peggy Stocker called this forenoon in her Phaeton for Molly Penry, took her home with her, and came to town with intent of lodging there.—HSD. here this forenoon—Billy seems better after a good nights rest—I have had discourse with my old acquaintance MP. on various subjects. sent Molly to dine with Nancy, and to stay there. Billy sent for Dr. Kuhn for me, he came after dinner, said I had a fever and advis'd me to loose 10 oz blood, and apply liquid laudanum to my ear. Nancy had sent me word that she was worse, I could not think of following the Doctors advise, however necessary, but went down to J Skyrins, Nancy was very unwell all the afternoon and evening we sent for Hannah Yerkes, her pains were frequent, but not of the right kind, at about 11 o'clock they prevailed on me to go to bed in the front room. Nancy undressed and went also to her bed—I lay all night in a degree of pain my ear throbbed much and I felt weak 'tho feverish. sleep'd very little during the night, a little after day I arose, and dressed myself, but finding all quiet lay down in my cloaths, waiting to hear some stiring in next Room, but being very much tired I fell asleep, a little after seven, Molly came into my room, and inform'd me, that Nancy was delivered just before, that they had sent out in the night, as quietly as possibly, for M. Aimes, and Hetty Smith, Nancy was very ill, a hard tedious time is agreed on all hands—I look on it now, when all is over, a favour to me that I did not know of her great distress at the time,—I had not an idea that she would be so soon deliver'd, tho she had been so long very unwell, being used to lingering tedious times—I was so weak and poorly when I came into Nancys room, I could hardly stand, and quite deaf of my right ear, but truly rejoiced and I trust thankful, that all was well over.

12. Eleanor Skyrin, was born September the 12, 1795. a little before 7 o'clock in the morning, on the seventh day of the week. An old saying of the Nurses, "No Moon, No Man."[87] our dear little one was born 18 hours before

87. "No moon no man" was a popular maxim of English folklore referring to the sex of the child. It was even believed in certain parts of England that a child born between the interval of the old moon and the appearance of the new moon would not reach puberty (G. L. Apperson, *English Proverbs and Proverbial Phrases: A Historical Dictionary* [London, 1929; reprint, Detroit: Gale Research Co., 1967]).

the moon changed—there is, I believe, but little in the saying—HSD. called this morning Hy. Smith went away with him, Hannah Yerkes stay'd dinner, then went home—Patty Jones, who was to have nursed Nancy, when we sent for her let us know that her Eyes were so sore that she could not attend—We have been all day at times, looking out for a Nurse but have not yet succeeded. Molly Drinker was up all night, and is tired and poorly this morning A new scene to Molly, she is gone home, Sister is out looking for a Nurse. HD. has been twice here this forenoon, he and Jacob Downing sett off after an early dinner for Downingstown. Nancy has spent this day better than could have been expected—Hannah S. Drinker took tea with us there. Sister came in the afternoon with Nurse Howel, who appears to be agreeable—I left Nancy about nine o'clock to the care of her Nurse—and came home Sam Sprigs with me, William has been very unwell for two or three days past. John R. Alsop lodges here to night, as HD. JD. and our man John are absent.

13. First day: rain in the night and this morning wind S.E—sent to know how Nancy fared, she had a good night, but the babe is unwell, its Stomac sick, Dr. Kuhn was here when Peter came with the message, he advised to guard against overloading its stomach with any kind of food, but the breast.—My Son William poorly, he has not recover'd the cold taken after the flux, myself very unwell—MS. went to meeting, Molly has not sufficiently recovered the fatigue of Yesterday and night before, to go out in the rain this morning Saml. Emlen called after meeting—R.G. very troublesom and talkative this forenoon in meeting—Sister, William, Molly and self dined togeather.—Molly went to afternoon meeting, and afterward down to J. Skyrins. Neighr. Waln took tea with us—Saml. Smith called, cloudy all day—Thos. Dawson and wife here this evening.

14. Cloudy, wind S.W. very unfavourable weather for invalides Jenny Roberson here at work—H. Yerkes, and Hannah S Drinker dined with us, they both had been to visit Nancy, by their accounts and the messenger I sent she is bravely, which I look on as a great favour. I have been unwell this morning William also,—Owen Biddle and Benn. Wilson here fore noon, Ben has been for some days past unwell, which is uncommon.—Hetty Smith and William Lippincotts Wife, called in the Carriage for Hannah—Saml. Fisher called to pay a sum money to O.A. My husband and Jacob Downing returned from the Valley after dinner, they left Sally and the Children well. The prevailing fever in New-York, which some time ago was thought much abated, is now said rather to increase than otherwise—HSD. intended for North Bank this morning. Molly Penry and B. Wilson here this evening HD. and self went to see Nancy, I found it difficult to get there, I am so weak and giddy headed.—Nancy bravely in some respects, not so well in others. a very warm evening.

15. Misty morning wind S.W—expect a warm day. HD. MS. MD. gone to

meeting—Nancy had a good night. We were invited to the burial of Francis Rawle, eldest son of Wm. Rawle, he was ill of the flux at same time that my dear William was suffering under the same painful disorder, how many things occur to bring us to our feelings. S. Swett and Jacob Downing dined—S. Swett, William Drinker, Molly Drinker and Eliza Skyrin went out in Coachee after 4 o'clock round Frankford and Point. Docr. Redman called at dinner time—Molly spent this Afternoon at S. Emlens—I went, Jacob with me to see Nancy, whom we found in a favourable way, Hannah S Drinker there.—John Drinker &c called here a very warm day, Jenny Roberson left us this evening after working for our black boys five days.

16. Clear and warm, wind S.W—Extract from last evenings paper vizt. "Sundries letters by the mail to day, mention the encrease of the malignant fever in New-York, and of its appearing in several parts of the City.[88]—Anna Wells and her son Robert here forenoon, Sister out this morning—Billy Saltar and JD. dined here. Saml. Smith here after dinner—good accounts from Nancy—Docr. Kuhn called repeated his advice to me to lose eight ounces blood, but the hot weather &c. serve as an excuse to put it off for the present. James Logan called. I read three pamphlets left with me by M. Penry. Periodical Accounts relating to the Missions of the Church of the United Brethren established among the Heathen, the Negroes in south America, Greenland, Hottentots at the Cape of good Hope. &c.[89] their task is arduous, they are, I doubt not, of service to many of those barbarous People—Sammy Rhoads called after dinner to ask Molly to go with him to visit Sally Large at their place near Frankford, Molly was engaged to go with her Brother William to take Hannah home to Clearfield.—they sett off about 4 o'clock, came back after sun set—John De Marsillac here at tea. HD. and self went this evening as usual, to visit our Daughter Ann, she and children are tolerabley well, Saml. Rhoads and Betsy Emlen here this evening this has been very warm day.

17. Clear, very warm, wind S.W—My right ear much disordered, and I am otherwise unwell; was I sure my ear would come too, I should be rather amused then otherwise by the disorder. The drum of the ear is rightly so called, as I am assured it is a musical machene.—if any one speaks aloud, or any sudden noise occurs, it vibrates on my ear, as on the string of a musicial instrument; but, unless at perticular times, or accidentual noises I am deaf with that ear, and when any one at my right side speaks to me, in a low voice, it appears to be on my left, as the sound enters that ear.—Nancy sent her

88. Approximately 750 persons in New York died of yellow fever in the summer and autumn of 1795 (Duffy, *Public Health*, 101–4).

89. *Periodical Accounts Relating to the Missions of the Church of the United Brethren, Established among the Heathen* (London: Brethren's Society for the Furtherance of the Gospel, [c. 1790] [*Brit. Mus. Cat.*]).

daughter Elizath. to spend this day with us—John DeMarsillac, Saml. Emlen and Thos. Stewardson dined with us.—William and Molly, went after dinner to take a ride, little E. Skyrin with them. Molly has a cold, and is hoarse.—I have read since dinner a peice called The Democratiad a Poem, in retaliation for the Philadelphia Jocky Club,[90] in verse.—prose in plain terms is better than ambiguous verse.—I went to Isaac Whartons this evening Peggy &c. well, I waited on E Skyrin home this evening Peter Woodard carried her—and Sally Dawson went also with me, as a kind of support, Nancy not so well to night, as hitherto, disordered in her bowels—John Skyrin came home with me—Billy walk'd out after night, two or 3 squars, came home in a heat;—wrong to go in the night air.

Sepr. 18. still very warm, wind S.W—Saml. Smith of B Cy. and Jacob D. at breakfast. Saml. Smith of Philada. called—Sally Smith called this morning those three Smiths are no ways related—it is, I believe, the most common name in Europe and North America—Molly went to Nancys fore noon found her better than last night.—Report of the New-York committee of health, That since their report of the 13th. instant Forty three persons have died of the present Epidemic. dated sepr. 16. forty three in three days, 14 or 15 p day—Jacob Downing left us, just before dusk, for the Valley—intending to lodge at the widdow Millers at the Buck, 11 miles. Sally Rhoads took tea with us—Saml. Moore from Clearfield came this forenoon with the Cart with some things for us, he took back several necessaries for Henry, he is not yet returned from N. Bank—I came this evening just after night to John Skyrins, it began to rain very fast about 8 o'clock, continued; 'till bed time, my night cloaths were sent me, and here I have concluded to stay this night, as it would be unsafe for me, in my present state of health, to venture out in the wind and rain after such hot weather. I sleep't with Nancy.

19. Clear'd up cool. wind N.W—I came home after breakfast, found all as usual—Sally Hopkins and Sally Smith here this morning—Hetty Smith and J Logan were at Clearfield yesterday, they came away rather lateish, Henry was not returned from N. Bank, He is generaly punctual to the time of returning. I cannot think what detains him—J Logan caught cold, has been since ill, is now better,—Molly Kelly called this morning says she will be ready on second day next to go to Clearfield to put up Hannahs bed—Sally Hopkins dined here,—Henry's Neighbour Porter called, he informs us that Henry is well, and intends homeward to day—[T.] Morris &c called—Sammy Rhoads here this evening he went with me to J Skyrins, left me there and return'd again to our house—Nancy and Child not quite well, Nurse apprehends it is breeding a sore mouth—We have had a little fire all day in back room—it is could enough

90. A Gentleman of Connecticut [Lemuel Hopkins], *The Democratiad, a Poem, in Retaliation for "The Philadelphia Jockey Club"* (Philadelphia: T. Bradford, 1795 [*NUC*]).

I think for frost, such sudden transitions from heat to cold may occasion, without care many disorders—I hope the change may be salutary to the inhabitants of New-York.

Sepr. 20. First day: a fine clear cool morning wind Southerly.—HD. MS. MD. at meeting.—A Man called this forenoon to enquire for Jacob Downing, said the Committee of health, of which he is a member, were to meet this Afternoon, that several New Yorkers had come into this City, that the Committee were to meet on that account to conclude how they should be disposed off—John Drinker call'd—rain after morning meeting for a short time—Molly went to afternoon meeting, she spent the evening at J Skyrins—John came home with her.

21. Clear and cool. wind N.W—we moved from back room to back parlor, find a fire comfortable, and most who came in acknowledge it, 'tho few have yet indulged in it.—Molly went after breakfast, with Sally Smith and Molly Kelly to Clearfield—HSD. came to town forenoon, he says, in his last stay at North-bank, he enjoyed his health, and spent the time he was there much to his satisfaction, he dined with us, went home after tea—Samuel Emlen &c. called—the Committee of health, sent twice here to day for Jacob Downing who is not yet returned—Sally Brants mother called in Chaise for Sally to go visit her sister Nancy Birtch, who she says is likely to die. 'Tis reported that 30 or 40 persons die daily at New-York, and that great numbers of the inhabitants have removed from thence. Their Committee of health say, 14 or 15 in 24 hours.—those among us, who do not sympathize with them, must be unfeeling indeed—HD. and self went this evening to see Nancy, she has had the head-ach to day, but is better this evening HD. went from JSs to visit James Logan, who is better, he came back for me—Molly came home coughing, she took cold some days since, and is continualy renewing it by carelesssness and dressing too lightly.—very cool this evening—a little rain fell after dinner.

Sepr. 22. Clear and cool, wind N.W—Mark Willcox breakfasted here, HD. MS. and MD. gone to monthly meeting. Molly Penry spent an hour with me this forenoon—Honor Fry and a Daughter of Willm. Crages called—William went out on the Mare this morning rode a mile or two, came home in good spirits—Jacob Downing return'd while we were at dinner—S Swett dined here, she and John James took tea with us—HSD. in town Afternoon, he left all well, soon went back again—Samuel here with the Cart preparing for Hannahs *Accouchement*. Betsy Emlen, Sally Smith here after meeting, Molly went out with them.—R.G. carried out of meeting again this forenoon, but not yet excummunicated—HCs Clerkship renounced, or given up in writing,!!![91]—Sister out this Afternoon, she called at Nancys, found them favoured with health—We do not learn from the accounts from New York that the raging fever there, is any ways abated, 'tho there has been a spell of cool weather for several days past.

23. Clear, cool and pleasant, wind N.W.—William rode out twice to day, Morning and afternoon, 2 or 3 miles each time, Sally Smith called—HSD. came to town forenoon, he and Hannah Catheral dined here, he went home Afternoon. Elizath. Skyrin spent the day with us—Benn. Wilson, Michel Callanan, Hannah Catheral and Thos. Stewardson took tea here—Saml. Emlen took a pipe,—Saml. Rhoads spent the evening Neighr. Waln called—M. Malerive and his Sister paid us a visit, they have revoved from our Alley, gave me a card of direction to their present aboad, at a Grocers in second street No. 170.—This morning about 3 o'clock, Sister, who lodges front, came into our Chamber, she had been akawned by the cry of fier,—we did not arise, It was a Hatters shop or shed on Vine street warfe, which was consumed, and little other damage done.—Jacob Downing walked eighteen or 20 miles to day, with one other of the Committee of health, to different posts—his feet were blistered, and no wonder.

Sepr. 24. fine morning wind S.W—Benn. Wilson Michel Callanan and William Drinker, sett off before 11 o'clock for Clearfield, intending to dine with Henry, M Penry spent part of the forenoon and dined here, she went with me after dinner to see Nancy, who was lay'd down. MP. went away, I spent the Afternoon and evening there, HD. Dolly Large and her daughter there—Nancy and Child bravely, came home after 8 o'clock Sam. with me, found my Son at home and bravely, finished reading a Romance or Novel, entitled, The Banished Man, in two Volums, By Charlotte Smith;[92] A string of probibilities, part truth, part fiction, wherein some scetches of the authors life is set fourth.—'tis said that she suported herself and three of four Children by this sort of writeing.—Sam Sprig came between 9 and 10. to inform us that Nancys Nurse was sent for to Capt. Strongs Daughter to whom she is engaged, Sister went late as it is, to Nurse Fisher up Chesnut street, who had promised to come to Nancy when her Nurse was called, but found her ill of a fever; so that I was under the Necessity of going to spend the night with my daughter, who has lain in 12 days, she and her babe are, through mercy, as well as can be expected, the baby lay with its Mother for the first time, Myself on the trundle

91. Hannah Catherall had been the clerk of the Philadelphia Northern District Women's Monthly Meeting since 1778 (J. M. Moore, *Friends in the Delaware Valley*, 258; Philadelphia Northern District Women's Monthly Meeting Minutes, 1791–96, microfilm, Friends Historical Library, Swarthmore College, 244, 264; see below, Jan. 24, 1797).

92. Charlotte [Turner] Smith, *The Banished Man: A Novel*, 2 vols. (London: T. Caddel, Jun., and W. Davies, 1791 [*NUC*]).

Bed with Hope Sharp, we past the night quite as well as we expected: the Child is a quiet one, but Nancy has caught cold, has the head-ach and Coughs.

25. hazey. wind S.W—Nancy rather better to day, John Skyrin gone to Almond Street to look for a Nurse Owen there, he returned without seeing her—HD. called—Molly Drinker came after dinner, tells me that Docr. Kuhn was at our house this forenoon, he advised William to lose 7 or 8 ounces blood, which was complyed with after dinner; I prefere bleeding in a morning, when it is convenient,—Billy rode out in the forenoon—[T]. Morris, S.Emlen, J Logan at our house—Sister was out looking for a Nurse; she has some expectation of a Nurse Easely calling on her this evening—I have spent this day in attendence on the little one, sewing over a new pair mittens, and reading An Address To the Youth of Norwich. by Joseph Phipps.[93] And 'tho I have not been idle, our foulk at home are more busy preparing for our yearly meeting. Molly came to J Skyrins this evening to stay all night with Nancy, as Nurse Easely cannot yet attend—it was with reluctance I left my daughter, as she is but poorly, with so young and inexperienced an attendant. HD. desired I would come home, J Skyrin came with me at 10 o'clock. I expected to have found friends from the Country, but none are yet come, William as well as I expected to find him, and indeed better, a fine clear moon light night. HSD. was in town to day, he dined here, went home in the Afternoon.

26. rather raw, wind N.E—Nurse Easely called this morning to tell us, she could attend Nancy, but as Sister had engaged a Nurse Davis who we expect every hour, she breakfasted with us and went[94] away, the other is not yet come, we know not which is the best, both being strangers to us.—Saml. Trimble his Wife and Son in Law Pierce, breakfasted here—I went after breakfast to Nancy, Nurse Davis came soon after—I had dressed the Child, the youngest I ever p[re]mormed that office for before—Nancys cold oppressive, I came home to dinner, John Cornell from New-York county, Samuel Trimble and Wife, and J Downing dined here, a young woman who left her horse here and Saml. Smith called—Saml. took tea with us—J. Drinker and Jos. Bringhurst spent this Afternoon and part of the evening in our front room writing—I went this evening to see how Nancy and her new nurse Ge[e]'d togeather, as she does not appear to be entirely, the thing, HD. went with me, he left me there, and went to an adjournment of a Committee, Hope Sharp in bed with pain in her bones and head, but no fever, I advised Cammomile tea,[95] to night, and a dose Castor Oyl tomorrow, our Othniel Alsop unwell, he is absent from Coumpting house.—A Young Man named Gilbart Watson died this morning at Abraham

93. Joseph Phipps, *An Address to the Youth of Norwich* (London: James Phillips, 1776 [*Brit. Mus. Cat.*]).

94. The word "home" crossed out.

95. Chamomile was recommended for various stomach and intestinal disorders, jaundice, and quartan ague (Blackwell, *Curious Herbal*, vol. 2, pl. 298).

Carliles, in our neighbourhood, a relation of his wife, of a billious fever—The Man that bleed our Son yesterday, told him that he had bleed this young man 23 times in a week, and we understand that the operation has been preformed 2 or 3 times since.—I must own that I have been thoughtful of the lancet used the same day for him and my Son. Sammy Downing here to night, he says Sally and Children are well,—Saml. Trimble and Wife and John Watson sup'd and lodged here, Robt. Moore and wife also—Rachel Watson is with her daughter who is ill of a Quinsey at Springfield.—The late advices from New York State, that Notwithstanding the numbers that have fled from thence, the disorder continues to gain ground and deaths to increase, twenty 'tis said die in a day; some say, many more.

Sepr. 27. First day: rain this morning wind variable, inclining to the East—some others besides our lodgers breakfasted with us.—William Blakey, Henry Artherton, Capt. Folkner &c. here going to the funeral of Gilbert Watson before morning meeting—HD. MS. gone to meeting—Thos. Lightfoot and some of our lodgers dined here—Joseph Bringhurst &c called—HD at home this Afternoon writeing—HD. and MS. went to evening meeting—Our Afternoon meeting begin from this time at ½ past two for the winter season, and evening meetings are held—I read, in meeting time, another of M. Penrys Moravian Pamphlets or Periodical Accounts from their Missioneries, among the Hottentots at the Cape of good hope.—A Young Man, a Jew was buryed this Afternoon from the third house from us, toward race street, who came within these two last weeks from New York, some say he died of a Consumption, others say otherwise. Cloudy all day, heavy rain before evening meeting broke up—Saml. Smith of B County called—I sent this evening to enquire after Nancy—she sent word that her head ached badly and Elizabeth was poorly.

28th. Clear and warm, wind S.W—S. Brant sent for, her Sister said to be dieing—Joshua Way and A Hervey called—Sammy Downing gone homewards—William rode out on the mare a mile or two, better accounts from Nancy this morning myself unwell,—HSD. came to town forenoon he left Hannah well—John Balderstone and Horse came to dine and lodge with us.—5 or 6 dined here—John Courtney called to borrow 20 pounds HD. gone to meeting—Enoch Evans, Jos Pusey, and several others called after dinner—a Number of Strangers at tea.—David Watson came with John Balderston, he lodges here—Betsy Foulke called—Jacob Downing went with me to J. Skyrins, Nancy and her Children bravely, a very fine evening On sixth day last. 31. persons died of the Epidemic fever in N. York, no accounts from the Committee of health—SBs Sister dead, she went there after dinner, her mother brought her home in the Chaise, she asked my husband for an order to bury her in friends burying ground, it was granted, tho they have no claim to such indulgence, M. Malerive and his Sister were here this Afternoon; poor folk, I pity them; Strangers in a strange land, without money, and unaquainted with our language.

29. Cloudy. wind N.W—Pearson Mitchel &c. besides our lodgers breakfasted here, Jacob and Sarah Lunday call'd. HD. and Sister gone to meeting, J Logan called, ten dined here, several whose names I do not know—RG. has been troublesom at meeting, as usual, to day, was therefore took to Jail—a guard of 2 or 3 friends were set at the meeting house gate to prevent her enterance, which they found a difficult business, and therefore thought fitt to confine her.—Our Sall Brant went this Afternoon to the funeral of her Sister.—Danl. and Richd. Trimble and four others took tea here. Phebe Smith and another with her called—Jona. Evans &c &c called—Rachel Watson and William Newbold came this Afternoon, Rachel lodges here—O. Biddle's Daughter Sally was buryed this afternoon Jany. Downing and Molly Thomas who dined here went with Molly after meeting to visit Nancy. Hope Sharp was ill last night of nettle-rash, Nancy was frightned in the night, by Betts coming suddenly and violently into the room to inform her of Hopes indispossion, she is bravely this morning H.S.D. dined with us, he went home after meeting—My husband is gone to bed poorly, over done, too much setting and attention—This morning between 7 and 8 o'clock a fier broke out in a wooden house at the corner of Arch and eighth streets which was not extinguished till the building was nearly destroyed and the adjoining buildings which were also wood, were greatly injured—Jenny Downing inform's us, that Henry Downing cut his first tooth fifth day last.

30. cool. wind N.E—I was unwell most of the night and frequently up—did not come down stairs till after HD. and some of our friends were gone to select meeting, which begins at 8 o'clock—Danl. and Richd. Trimble here—HSD. came to town—Nancy sent Oliver to request the Carriage to take her out—she has lain in but 18 days, has had a cold, and this day, in my oppinion, unfitt to go out for the first time, I therefore refused—William walked out—Betsy Emlen here, Molly went out with her. No body dined with us this day but Robt. Moore and Jacob Downing—Molly gone to afternoon Meeting. HD. and Son William went about 3 o'clock to take a ride in waggon—HD. poorly—William more that usualy weak, the Mens meeting begins at 4 o'clock, after riding to the middle ferry, William left his father at fourth street meeting house, then took a short ride by himself, called to look at the Panorama, at the upper end of Market street. It is a view of the Cities of London and Westminster, with the three bridges &c. The painting, they say, contains nearly 3,000 square feet of canvas. Being in a circle gives every object its proper bearing, and exhibits it in its true point of compass, appearing as learge and in every respect the same as the reallity. so says the advertisement or nearly so; William

reports it very beautifull, and well worth going to view[96]—Hannah S Drinker in town to day, she was at Nancys, but we did not see her—Mary Moore, Susannah Brinton, wife to Joseph, William Scarlet, Soloman Merideth and two or three others took tea here, John Needles and several others called—A Committee of 17 men, mett in our front parlor this evening to settle the Yearly meeting Accounts.—Molly spent this evening at S. Emlens.

Octor. 1st. Clear and pleasant, 'tho the winds at N.E—none but our own lodgers at breakfast—The Pine and third streets meetings where the business is transacted are so far from us that we have fewer call on us at this time, than otherwise would, HSD. came to town to get his Chaise mended, he is in a hurry to return, as Hannah is nearly Solas, and at this time, perticularly, he does not choose to leave her alone for any length of time—HD. MS. MD. at meeting—William gone out in Chaise, Peter with him, they went the 10 miles round Frankford and Point—Thos. Morris called.—Robt. Moore, only, at Dinner, John Ryreson &c called—John Kinsey and John Pickering, my husband, Sister and William, went out in the Carriage to take an airing before meeting, HD. stopped at Pine street meeting house, M.S. and WD extended their ride five miles afterward—The accounts from New-York are, that the fever is considerably abated. Abia Park, David Watson and two others took tea—Esther Trimble, my husband and self went this evening to see Nancy, HD. left us and went to meeting. Nancy is bravely, J Skyrin came home with us—Billy better, myself poorly.

2. clear and cool, wind N.E—family at meeting William set off with Peter in the Chaise about 11 o'clock inclining for Clearfield, I advised against it as the weather is rather unpromising, he went notwithstanding, and returned before dinner—Rachel Richards and Jane Temple called—Eliza Skyrin came to spend the day with us—she is not well—Joshua Sharpless and Jonathan Pettit, M. Moore and others dined with us—Sally Smith here. she went to meeting with Molly—William Saltar and Esther Trimble took tea—Sam came for the Child after night, she is more unwell than her mother is sensiable of—she has had several bad evacuations to day, some of a sanguinary appearence—I sent a note to Nancy—Martha Livezey and Neighr. Waln were here before meeting time after dinner. Josiah Reeve, Richd. Hartshorn here in the evening William Newbold suped with others here—Willm. Saltar in town on business, came here to lodge as usual.

3. Clear, wind S.E—Abraham Gibbons, Jacob Ritter, Billy Saltar and one more, beside our other lodgers breakfasted here—John Rireson called—Jacob

96. Edward Savage, an American painter who had studied in London between 1791 and 1794, had brought his panorama to Philadelphia from New York in July (Peale, *Selected Papers*, 2:114, 117, n.6).

Downing left us this morning after breakfast for Downingstown—Molly Thomas with him—Nancy Skyrin who has lain in three weeks to day—went out in the Carriage with William and little Elizath. who is better—they were stoped at Arch street corner by a cart and horse that were fallen down, the Cart partly on the horse, John back'd—and came round Arch and second street—William Blakey with some of our lodgers dined here. Billy walked out this afternoon—Sister and Molly at meeting—Myself at home sola which is frequently the case mending Stockings and reading each by turn, as it suits my humour—John Watson, Saml. Trimble, Robt. Moore came from Pine street after 6, to tea, went back at 7. HD. did not come home till ten, when the rest returned also—the Yearly meeting concluded.

4. First Day: rain this morning cleard measurably away before 8 o'clock wind S.E—William Blakey and wife, Susannah Brinton, Phebe Smith, Joice Buckman and our lodgers breakfasted with us.—They all left us before 9 o'clock—We have had first and last ten lodgers this week Jacob Downing included.—William poorly disorderd in his bowels and feverish—he took too long a walk last night.—Peter Yarnel, S. Swett, Ruth Walmsley, Hannah Thornton dined here—Thos. Walmsley came after dinner, HD. M.D. went to Afternoon meeting—Edwd. Hallock, John Cornell, and SS. took tea with us. Warner Mifflin and Wife, and John Parish came after tea—A Meeting appointed by Deborah Darby for the black people, was held this evening at the North House—our two black boys there—After meeting came here, Warner and Nancy Mifflin, Peggy Elliot, Philenia Lay, Joseph Cloud and Mark Miller, they all suped here—William very unwell this evening Sick at stomach, he took warm water which puk'd him—he went to bed rather better.

5. Clear, wind Southerly. Christopher Smith breakfasted. George Churchman called—One Huggens called for 170 dollars for five Oxen, HD. out—HSD. came to town with his Mother Smith—they went out again soon after dinner—Docr. Shippen has been to Clearfield a day or two ago, he ordered Hannah to lose blood, which Jestes Fox performed—James Logan went forenoon with William in Chaise to Clearfield, they returned before dinner—Nurse Waters called—HD. and Billy went again after dinner to Clearfield in waggon, M Penry spent an hour—Molly gone Afternoon to assist in waiting on Nancys visitors. A man was buried this morning from the same house, 3 or 4 doors from us, where a Jew was taken from yesterday week—Jacob Rutter told my Son Henry and M Penry, that he was assured it was the Yallow fever he died off but I hope otherwise—We sent our little Sally last night with something for Betty Newton who lives there, she saw the Corps laid out, we had heard nothing of the death before—HD. and WD. returned to tea, Saml. Emlen called this evening cloudy—HSD paid some time ago 11/3 to black Jacob Morris for his Attendence on Caty Clearfields funeral—J Skyrin came

home with Molly Jacob Downing return'd to town late this evening he left all his family well. rain about 9 at night.

6. rain most of the night, clear'd up with a Northwester. HD. MS. MD. at the adjournment of monthly meeting One Townsend from Redstone, and S Swett dined with us—Saml. Smith and R. Jones called—Molly gone to Nancys this Afternoon. SS. stay'd tea—she went home in the evening MS. went over to Neighr. Waln's—I have read some account of the Life of Thomas Newton DD. Lord Bishop of Bristol and Dean of St. Pauls, with Anecdotes of several of his Friends.[97]—very entertaining.

7. Clear, wind westerly—Saml. Moore here forenoon, for Chickens and Candles &c—says they are all well at Clearfield. Hetty Smith has been for some days past waiting on Hannah. Henry went yesterday to Dunkss ferry for the Nurse, whom he brought home with him, to be in readiness for the important time, which is every day expected—Molly again at Nancys this Afternoon—Saml. Emlen here after dinner he took a short nap in his chair while William slept on the Sopha—Betsy Emlen and Billy Mott came this evening to see Molly, they went down to J Skyrins to her—several called—I spent an hour or two looking over, what Bishop Newtown has wrote on the Prophecies, I believe I shall not peruse them 'tho I doubt not but it is well worth reading, but as it is a lengthy work, and I have much lately on that subject, I shall at present omitt it—Jacob, came home with Molly at 10 o'clock, Elizath. Skyrin is unwell, sick stomac, has been vomitting.—The fever in New-York which had abaited considerably sometime past, has again increased, 27 deaths are reported the 5th instant since the day before.

8. A steady rain this morning tho the wind is N.W—Saml. Emlen breakfasted with us, Othniel Alsop dined. Neighr. Waln took tea, William Savery called—cloudy all day, clear this evening little E. Skyrin feverish all night, and poorly today when J Downing dined there, but this evening her Grandfather visited her and found her better and chearful—Sammy Rhoads and Walr. Franklin spent the evening—There are numbers now sick in different parts of this City, and in many parts of the country very much so, less so in the City, than the country.

Octor. 9. Clear wind N.W—John Brittons wife up town was buried this forenoon, she died, 'tis said of a billious fever, many have billious fevers at present, but whether they are of the Malignant or infectious kind, I know not, the fears of some are raised—but the Physiciand say there is no contagious

97. *The Works of the Right Reverend Thomas Newton, with Some Account of His Life, and Anecdotes of Several of His Friends, Written by Himself,* 6 vols. (London: John, Francis, and Charles Rivington, 1782 [*NUC*]).

fever now in our City.—M. Malerive and Sister called to see us,—Bety. Emlen came to tell Molly she would go with her to Atsion &c.—Molly Penry and HSD. dined with us—Hannah Yerkes here this Afternoon, Saml. Emlen also—Henry went home towards evening M Penry and J Logan took tea here. My husband, Daughter Molly and Betsy Emlen set off about 4 o'clock Afternoon to cross the river, and John with the Carriage: they intend for Haddonfield this evening Evesham tomorrow, Atsion on first day, where Peter Yarnal has appointed a meeting—I do not expect them home till second or third day next—Eliz Skyrin spent this day with us—she is pale and unwell, I judge she has worms—Hannah S Drinker keeps up longer than I expected—Je donnez a [J]L quelque chose pour un pover francioes—we have understood that it is very sickly at Haddonfield and Evesham, which makes me thoughtful on account my husband, Molly &c.

10. Hazey. wind NE—Jacob Downing marketed for us—received a note from Nancy informing that Elizath. is unwell with lax and vomitting. HSD. came to town forenoon with Esther Smith—he went with me to see Nancy—gave Elizath. spiced Rhubarb, I stayed dinner there—came home about three o'clock. Henry and E Smith went back to Clearfield toward evening rain after night—my thoughts are much on Hannah.

11. First day: Much rain in the night, cloudy this morning wind Southerly—Ben Wilson here before Morning meeting—Neighr. Waln came over, she went with Sister to meeting—no other of our family there—HD. and Molly in Jersey—Ben Wilson dined with us, J.D. out at dinner—Nancy sent word that Elizah. was ill in the night, better this morning—we have had rain and Sun shine alternately several times to day—read this forenoon a Short Historical Account of the Life of the Archbishop of Cambray[98]—A truely good man I believe—Noke brought a letter from Sally Zane, Virginia, to HD—Jacob came home to supper, he thought he saw Henrys Chaise with two men in it a little before dusk driving down second street, 'tis not unlikely that he is come for Doctor &c as the moon changes tomorrow and Hannah at her full time—I told him if the weather was unfair, or if they sent towards, or in the night, not to come for me, as it would be very improper for me to go in such case. I shall think of them 'till I hear how they fare.

98. Probably "The Life of Salignac De la Mothe Fenelon, Archbishop of Cambray," in *The Adventures of Telemachus, the Son of Ulysses, from the French of Salignac de la Mothe-Fenelon, by the Celebrated Jn. Hawkesworth LL.D., Corrected & Revised by E. Gregory, With a Life of the Author,* 2 vols. (London: C. and G. Kearsley, 1795). *Telemachus* was one of the most popular French works read in Philadelphia during the eighteenth century (Watt, *Bibliotheca Britannica;* Howard Mumford Jones, "The Importation of French Books in Philadelphia, 1750–1800," *Modern Philology* 32 (1934–35): 160; Edwin Wolff II, *The Book Culture of a Colonial American City: Philadelphia Books, Bookmen, and Booksellers* [Oxford: Clarendon Press, 1988], 53–54, 164, 165).

12. Clear, wind S.W—Jacob Downings old boy Dan Stonemitts, came here early this morning by water, from Daniel Trimbles, he is now 16 years old and free, he is on his way to Richmond in Virginia to visit his mother.—one Benjn. Elliott called with a letter from John Cannon.—Saml. Emlen called—HSD. came to town forenoon, it was not his Chaise that Jacob saw last evening Hannah is still about house—George Frys wife was brought to bed of a daughter last seventh night at Clearfield.—Benn. Wilson called—James Logan and Sarah Fisher here this forenoon—Henry and Jacob dined, Henry went home after dinner—Nancy sent me word that Eliz[h]. was so poorly that if I would come down, she would send for the Doctor tho she was no worse than when I last saw her, I believe I must leave it 'till evening as Molly is from home, and company expected here.—Sarah Fisher, Betsy Fisher and Becky spent the Afternoon and part evening My husband and daughter returned from Jersey this Afternoon, Betsy Emlen with them—Mollys throat very sore and inflamed, she took cold the day she left home, they lodged at John Hopkins Haddonfield, the first night, Billy Hopkins was just recovering of a billious fever, their Doctor called it the bilious remitting fever—he was to have past the second meeting to day with a Nancy Morgan, if his sickness did not prevent;—they had a meeting at Evesham, and dined at Rehoboam Braddocks, lodged the second night at Atsion, where Molly was very poorly, on first day held two meetings at Joseph Saltars, Molly did not attend the second, but went to bed in the Afternoon, had a high fever in the night, could scarcely swallow.[99] she took, by P. Yarnels advice, a dose Castor-Oyl, had a poor night, On Second day her father thought her too unwell to come home, he had thoughts of leaving her there or at B. Swetts, but she was not free to stay behind, and glad am I she did not—the loss of 7 or 8 ounces blood this morning might have been of service—since she returned this evening her throat has been bathed, and gargeled several time, her feet bathed in warm water, and she seems much better tho feverish.—I did not approve her going this little journey, not being quite well when she left me, and the people round the Country are very sickly—they say that scarcely one family in Haddonfield, but some are sick in it,—It looks like to be a warm Ellection tomorrow, a great stir among the Democrates.[100]—Sammy Fisher was here this evening.

13. Clear and pleasant, wind S.W—Molly had a good night considering—her throat swelled and inflamed this morning tho less fever. HD. MS. gone to meeting—Sally Parish called after meeting, her brother George had been troublesome, HD. took him to task, which set R. Griscomb a going in the old way, in meeting—Saml. Emlen and Betsy Emlen called—Dr. Kuhn, whom I

99. The words "on Second day" crossed out.

100. Elections were slated for Oct. 13 for Philadelphia's six state assembly seats and one state senate seat. Though the Democratic-Republican challengers appealed to popular opposition to the Jay treaty, the Federalist incumbents would carry the day (Miller, *Federalist City*, 74–77).

sent for, came before dinner, he ordered a dose Castor Oyl for Molly, and 10 ounces blood to be taken. William, Nancy and little Elizath. took a ride this Morning—Betsy Fishers Nurse and child here to enquire how was Molly—Fredrick bleed her about one o'clock, he made a very small orifice which occasioned the blood to flow so slowly, and drible for so long time, that she became sick and fainty, but by taking lavender compound[101] &c. she recovered—S. Swett dined here—William went out in Chaise after dinner, Peter with him, he gave in his Vote for that part he thought the best of the two. Sister gone this afternoon to Robt. Stevensons, his daughter Hannah Smith was delivered last week of her first Son. Neighr. Waln here this evening—Molly has spent this day in her Chamber, she has a fever to night, tho I hope she is some thing better—Doctor calls it an inflamatory sore throat, he hopes it will not gather—Sammy Rhoads here this evening—William, indiscreetly, out after night.—Saml. Moore from Clearfield here this afternoon for beer &c. says Hannah is not quite well—I am surprized at her keeping up so long.—There is a great noise in the street to night, druming and huzzaing, I wish it may not be a riotous Ellection.

14. a little foggy—wind S.W—The Ellection for the City—the federal ticket got the day by 600 votes odds—county lost it—About 5 o'clock this morning our Son Henry knocked at out door Sister heard and answer'd him, he then went to look for Dr. Shippen, who was engaged at another place, he then went in quest of Dr. Way, who was gone to Chester—he called on Dr. Wister who recommended him to a Docr. Dunlap, whom I have heard since, and before is well thought of in[102] that line of business, he soon mett with him, and they came here in the Carriage, Sally Lippencott came also,—The Doctor, SL, HSD, and myself left our door at eight o'clock, arrived at Clearfield before 9—found poor Hannah complaining in the Easy-Chair[103]—The Germantown Midwife, Englee there—Hannah was delivered about one o'clock, after being

101. Mild cordials of lavender flowers, water, alcohol, and other flowers and spices were drunk or rubbed on the temples and forehead to soothe the nerves (W. Lewis, *New Dispensatory*, 385–87).

102. The word "his" crossed out.

103. Easy chairs were originally designed to be used by sick or aged persons. By the late eighteenth century the term was used to denote both the ornate lounge chairs found in affluent homes and the more specialized chairs used for lying-in women, the sick, and the aged. The chair noted by ED may have been similar to one illustrated in Charles White's *Treatise on the Management of Pregnant and Lying-in Women* (1773; first American edition, 1793). It shows a wheeled chair similar to a present-day recliner, with a frame on the back, possibly to support a chamber pot. White recommended it for fatigued women so they could rest during labor without having to be put to bed. Some Anglo-American women of this period did give birth in special chairs, but the more common position was reclining in bed (Patricia F. Kane, *300 Years of American Seating Furniture: Chairs and Beds from the Mabel Brady Garvan and Other Collections at Yale University* [Boston: New York Graphic Society, 1976], 227; White, *Management of Pregnant and Lying-in Women,* 108–10 and plate 1; Claire Elizabeth Fox, "Pregnancy, Childbirth, and Early Infancy in Anglo-American Culture, 1675–1830" [Ph.D. diss., University of Pennsylvania, 1966], 137–44).

between two and three hours ill, the Doctor said it was a severe labour, but not more so than was common with a first child, dear girl, I felt much for her, but I have been accostomed to severer labours.—William Drinker, Son of Henry and Hannah Drinker was born the 14 day October at about one o'clock P.M. on the fourth day of the week 1795. at Clearfield—a fine strong boy, as far as one can judge. My husband and Son William came up about and hour before the child was born, they stayed dinner. After dinner HD. drove Dr. Dunlap to town in the Chaise. Sally Lippencott, William Drinker and self returned in our Carriage, left Hetty Smith with her daughter—got home about 5 o'clock,—left Hannah as well as could be expected, she has a very good Nurse, Elizabeth Kemble, from Dunks's ferry, who Nursed Hetty Smith with Hannah, and several other of her Children—J Logan was at our house when we came home, Jacob Downing and Sister dined togeather. Sally Hopkins from Haddonfield here to day—Samy. Rhoads called. One Jonathan Gibbs died this Afternoon in Race street, 'tis said, of the Yallow fever.—'Tis a warm night Mollys throat better, 'tho she is not clear of fever. Dr. Kuhn was here while I was abroad.

15. Steady rain with wind this morning wind S.E—Dr. Kuhn called, ordered boiling water poured on Cream of tarter for Mollys drink—her throat is not yet well—Our old Neighbour Stiles is to be buried this afternoon, she died yesterday, cloudy most of this day, with frequent rains, clear'd up after night Neighr. Waln here—Molly Lippencott spent the evening with Molly up stairs—her brother came for her.—I have spent great part of this day above with Molly.

16. Clear and cool, wind westerly—Je suis Malade. sent John for Nancy and Children, they came about 11 o'clock. the first visit from the little Stranger Elleanor. William Nancy and Elizath. took a ride—Saml. Emlen, Sally Smith and Sally Large called—Dr. Dunlap called forenoon to enquire after Hannah—Molly Drinker came down stairs this morning, she has been confined three days, Dr. K. called, Betsy Emlen called—M. Penry, Nancy Skyrin and Jacob Downing dined here—My husband and William went after dinner to Clearfield, they took a Sweep up with them, who swep't three chimneys, they return'd to tea—J Skyrin at tea—Saml. Moore in town with Cart for chickens &c. Hannah and Child well—Robt. Stevenson called—Isaac Potts here Afternoon, he says his Niece Duffield is ill of a billious fever, somewhat putrid.—by the last accounts from New York 9 died in a day. it is to be hoped, that it abates—Jacob Downing set off to visit his family this Afternoon—Elijah Waring, who went to Great Britain in the William Penn about four months ago, and lately return'd in the same Vessel, spent part of the evening here, as did Sammy Rhoads also.

17. Appearences of a rosey morning which soon vanished, and rain followed

most of the forenoon, wind westerly—became very cold afternoon, Joseph Bringhurst here forenoon, WD. took a little cold, Henry came to town after dinner, left Hannah and Child well—the accounts from Nancy to day is that her little Elleanor has a very sore mouth. Henry made but an hours stay—J Logan took tea here. HD. went to see Hannah Pemberton.

18. First Day: Clear morning wind S.W—became cloudy and raw afterwards. HD. MS. MD. went to meeting. S. Swett and Thos. Stewardson dined with us Benn. Catheral called—Elijah Waring called after dinner, Peggy Wharton spent an hour in afternoon meeting time.—Saml. Emlen called—Huldah Mott and Betsy Emlen came after meeting. Betsy spent the Afternoon, I went to J Skyrins, Nancy had desired to see me, as her little one was unwell—I took tea there, and stay'd till 9 at night, Sam came home with me.—Cry of fire, bells rang, near 10 o'clock, have not heard where it was.

19. Cold and raw, wind variable inclining to East—John and Nancy Skyrin and little Elizath. set off from hence for Clearfield, to visit Hannah and the young Stranger, Jenny Stevenson and a female Cousin of hers from New York, called forenoon—John and Nancy returned before dinner, Nancy left her daughter here, and came herself again after dinner, she and self went to Shops, a business that I have not been in for several years before—I purchased three painted glass muggs, one for each of my daughters,—went home with Nancy, then about dusk came home to tea—Neighr. Waln here this evening Jacob Downing returned Afternoon, left Sally and the Children well, his mother very poorly. Molly out this evening—Walter Franklin called.

20. A fine pleasant clear morning wind S.W—changed before noon cloudy. wind N.W—HD. MS. MD. at meeting William and Peter out in Chaise,[104] W.D. mett Henry on foot 2½ miles from town took him in, and sent Peter home from the towns end, then rode together about the City, came here before meeting was done—Nancy and her daughter Elizath. came this morning she wished me to come to their house after dinner, as she intends to send for Dr. Kuhn to look at Elleanors mouth, as it continues sore—HSD. dined here, he went home after dinner—I spent the Afternoon with Nancy, the Doctor came, he recommended a little cool water two or three times a day, and bolemonac[105] and Molasses mix't in an electuary to rub gently in her mouth. I came home after tea, by moon light, Sam with me—A very great rumpus this afternoon in meeting with R.G.—she was twice carried out forcibly. A Letter in this days paper from Dr. W P. Smith of New-York, informing, That he considers the Yallow-fever now absolutely extinguished and departed from

104. The word "they" crossed out.
105. Probably bole armeniac, earth imported from Armenia and used as an astringent (Estes, "Therapeutic Practice," 369).

that City &c.—Josh. Bringhurst called—B. Wilson spent the evening and suped with us.

21. Clear, wind N.W—changed to N.E—HD. left us about noon, in the Chaise, for John Watsons Middle-town, intending tomorrow to Henrys place North-Bank, where he expects to meet his Son, who left Clearfield, as Sam Moore informes us this morning:—William was to have gone with his Father, but having a Cough, and the weather being too cold, he declined it—Nancy and her Daughter Elizath. dined with us. M. Penry spent the forenoon with me, she dined with Hannah Sansom—Sister paid a visit to M. Malerive and his Sister.—Jams. Logan took tea here. Sammy Rhoads here twice—Molly gone out with him &c. this evening—Jacob Downing and Molly came home after 10. I should have been better pleased had they spent the evening at home. Jacob lodges in Mollys chamber to night: Molly with me, as her father is absent.

22. cloudy, wind inclining to N.E—Sister out this fore noon, Molly ironing, black Rachel scrubing stairs &c. Saml. Emlen called—No body dined or teaed—Neighr. Waln and Sammy Rhoads spent part of the evening John Wilson called, cloudy all day.

23. rain in the night, and again this morning wind N.E—my husband and Son Henry, measurebly exposed to the weather, 'tis well William went not with his father—HD. breakfasted at North bank, left Henry there and came home to a late dinner about 3 o'clock, he lodg'd last night at North bank—Molly spent the Afternoon and evening with Nancy—James and Hetty Smith here this evening Jacob Downing took the bed Chair down to his store in order to send to Downingstown for the use of his Mother, who is much oppressed by an Asthma;—I have read a romance, three Vollums intitled the Minstrel or Anecdotes of distinguished personages in the fifteenth Century.[106]

24. Clear, wind N.W—Jacob Downing and Molly Drinker sett off, a little before 11 o'clock in the Chaise, to visit Sally &c. they should have moved two hours sooner, as it is 33 miles. William and Ann, gone in Carriage to Clearfield. little ES. stays with us—MD. gone to visit Jams. Pemberton, who has been for several days past considered dangerously ill—Saml. Emlen and Betsy Foulk called—Jon. Shoemaker dined here, Nancy Skyrin also, William and she returned while we were at dinner—James Logan and Dr. Redman here before dinner—Ben Wilson took tea with Sister, William and self went this Afternoon to H. Pembertons HD. came there to tea with us—James Pemberton, said to be worse—WD. and self, came home after 7 o'clock HD—

106. *The Minstrel; or, Anecdotes of Distinguished Personages in the Fifteenth Century* . . . (London: Hookham and Carpenter, 1793 [*NUC*]).

before—found Josh. Norris here on business with HD—a little rain this evening which is very pleasent.

October 25. First day: a fine morning clear and mild, wind westerly, inclining to the south, or W.S.W—I have suffered this morning from a weakness under which I daily labour more or less—John Drinker called, Sush. Swett dined here—Nancy and her Children came after dinner—she left them with me, while she went to Afternoon Meeting, Suckey Sanson and daughter, John and Nancy Skyrin came after meeting, stay'd but a short time, Nancy did not like to keep her young child out towards evening—SS. only took tea here—HD. at Saml. Emlens junr. who has, last week settled in his fathers house at the corner of Keys Alley second street—I have read this day a volume, consisting of 14 long letters from Baron Haller to his Daughter, on the Truths of the Christian Religion &c. translated from the German.[107] disagreeable intilligence from Peter Woodard this evening relating to SB. her conduct &c.

26. very fine clear morning wind N.W. Js. Logan called—Nancy Skyrin and Elizath. here forenoon—she left the Child, and went home, returned after dinner, went with her Father and brother William to Clearfield—HSD. dined here—Saml. Emlen called said Js. Pemberton was better—Henry went home Afternoon—Sister has an oppressive cold—Betsy Jervis and Benjn. Chew took tea with us—Joseph Sanson here this evening with a plan for the intended boarding School—O. Alsop spent part of the evening in back parlor with us.—The Committee of health appointed here to prevent any from New-York entering our City, &c. have dissolved themselves,—perhaps prematurely, as in the report of yesterday there was but 4 died, but the accounts of this day are, that 10. died, by last report, of the Epidemic;—A few days ago they prounonced the fever extinguished.—No J Downing or M Drinker to night.

Octor. 27. clear, wind N.E—changed afternoon to S.W—HD. gone to monthly meeting—Sisters cough to bad to go out, tho better than yesterday—Saml. Smith, Isaac Potts, Neighr. Waln and A Skyrin called before meeting—Nancy and S. Swett, who went home with her to dine, called after—R. Griscomb taken out of meeting—M. Penry dined here—William rode out on the Mare, forenoon and Afternoon—he called at Saml. Pleasents; J Pemberton continues in a doubtful way—HSD. came to town forenoon, he dined at J Skyrins, went home Afternoon, Jacob Downing and M. Drinker returned after candle light about 6 o'clock, they left all well, M Downing Senr. excepted, who continues very poorly—John Elliot called, HD. at the adjournment of the monthly meeting—Danl. Trimble suped here, moon light.

107. [Baron Albrecht von Haller], *Letters from Baron Haller to His Daughter, on the Truths of the Christian Religion; Translated from the German* (London: J. Murray, 1780 [*Brit. Mus. Cat.*]).

28. Foggy morning wind S.W—Molly Kelly at work here, making white Curtains for Green Chamber—she informed us of the death of Hannah Norton widdow Daughter of Lydia Noble, she has been ill but 3 or 4 days something of a paralytic stroke, was let blood upwards of 20 times—by direction of Dr. Physick—Marmaduke Cooper, her mothers brother lays dead in Jersey[108] by a bilious disorder which has prevailed much this fall, in and about Haddonfield and other parts of Jersey—William, Mary, Ann Skyrin and her Daughter Elleanor set off for Clearfield about 11 o'clock. I spent a few minuits at Neighr. Walns,—William &c. came home to dinner, Nancy and children stayed dinner—Sammy Rhoads spent the evening.

29. a little hazey this morning turn'd out a beautiful day, wind S.W—the last four days have been delightfull, temperate with a cloudless sky, for those in health, how pleasing! but perhaps they are, some of them, the last to discern it:—HD. went, this morning to the funeral of the widdow Norton. Molly out forenoon, William out in Chaise with Peter. I went about noon to J Skyrins, dined there, and spent the Afternoon and evening John came home with me—A Committee of friends here this evening in back parlor, 8 or 10. on business concerning the Indians &c.—Neighr. Waln with Sister in front Room—Jacob went with Molly to S. Emlens this evening—A large Company at Clearfield this forenoon, female Visitants—HD. was informed yesterday, of the Marriage of Samuel Preston to a Mercia Jinkins, before witnesses at Stockport.—No death reported in New York for twenty four hours, nor none taken down by the disorder—the Committee there are disolved. A merciful alteration, how thankful should we be, that have escaped the infection in our City.

30. fine day, tho a little hazey, wind S.W—William went in the Chaise, Peter with him, to Clearfield—came home to dinner, his brother set off yesterday for Northbank, many are the journeys he necessarly takes to his Farm, and must continue 'till they are setteled there.—this is his birthday 25 years.—little E. Skyrin spent the day, John, Nancy and Jacob took tea. James Logan called—George Harris's daughter from Maurices river a young man with her brought a letter for HD—Molly Penry and Benjn. Henry here this evening I am oppressed by a cold &c.—Molly Drinker gone this evening to visit Betsy Giles, HD. spent this Afternoon at Benjn. Chews on an arbitration—William, walked out this evening—Jacob Downing was invited to day to the funeral of his Aunt Jane Roberts, his fathers Sister, and widdow of John Roberts who was executed with Abraham Carlile about 17. years ago. she died at her dwelling within 2 or 3. miles of Downingstown.

31. Cloudy, wind westerly, more than usualy unwell to day: George and

108. The word "of" crossed out.

Saml. in town with the Cart, with and for necessaries, M. Penry dined and spent the day—she lodges here to night—A Committee mett in back parlor this evening John Parish, Warner Miffin, Thos. Harrison, Jos. Samson, John Biddle, William Savery, Saml. Howel, Thos. Wister, John Elliot and HD.—rain most of the Afternoon, clear this evening wind high—Jacob set off late in the forenoon for Downingstown, intending tomorrow to attend the funeral of his Aunt Roberts—M. Malerive called—I expect my Son Henry will travel this rainy Afternoon homewards—Sister spent this day up stairs, her cough not left her, nor is it likely it will sudenly, the way she manages herself.

Novr. 1st. First Day: Cloudy and rather cold, wind Westerly unsettled—between 12 and one this morning I had not sleep't, the wind was high, when I heard a door slam with force, twice, I was sure it was some door in the back part of our house, I arose and dressed myself, having a candle burning in our chimney—went through Mollys room, and in the Nursery where Sister lodged last night, called little Salley up, took her with me, a fine safeguard,—examined all below, found every thing in Statu-quo, as I had left it, went to bed again, soon after heard the slaming frequently repeated, lay considering what it could be, when it occur'd, that it was the New Venetian door on the outside of the back entry door, that had been left unfastned—My husband this morning took it off the hinges, as 'tis not necssary in the winter, M. Penry went out after breakfast, HD. and MD. gone to morning meeting, Sister not well enough to go abroad. Sally Smith and Sally Large called in Carriage for Molly to go with them to Clearfield, but I was pleased that she was gone to meeting—Joshua Clibborn the larger, dined with us. Sister most of the day up stairs, Nancy and her Children came after dinner, she left them and B Dawson with me, and went with Molly to afternoon meeting. came after and took them home before tea. The same Committee that mett here last night, were here again this evening Sammy Rhoads and Neighr. Waln spent part of the evening in front parlor, with Molly, Billy and self.

Novemr. 2. unsettled, wind N.E—HD. and MS. gone to quarterly meeting—Nancy Skyrin called in her way thither, she returned after the first meeting broke up, Molly went out with her—R.G—carried out of meeting as usual—Augustine Jones called—he arrived a day or two past from St. Eustatia by way of Boston—William gone out forenoon on the Mare, the weather not suitable—Saml. Moore here from Clearfield, he dined here, as he generally does—he says Henry returned home last evening all well—Jonathan Evans dined with us—rain after dinner—Read a Duoducimo Vollume intitled Slavery, or the Times. By the author of Monmouth The danish Massacre.[109] sister

109. [Anna Maria Mackenzie], *Slavery; or, The Times, in Two Volumes, by the Author of Monmouth, the Danish Massacre, &c.* (London: G. G. J. and J. Robinson and J. Dennis, 1792 [*Brit. Mus. Cat.*]).

out Afternoon—Jacob Downing returned long after night. Sally and Children well, but his Mother very much otherwise, Richd. Trimble spent the evening.

3. rather unsettled, wind variable inclining to East. HD. went early to meeting, MD. and Nancy, who called here, went to Youths meeting, William was preparing to go to Clearfield, when his brother came in, he then changed his mind, and Henry went with him to take a shorter ride. Saml. Moore here again to day, he brings Hay, and takes back Dung—Read a Pamphlet of 100 pages, containing ten Letters, addressed to Mr. Paine, In Answer to his Pamphlet entitled The Age of Reason: containing some clear and satisfying evidences of the truth of Divine Revelation; and especially of the Resurrection and Asscension of Jesus. By E. Winchester.[110] HSD. dined here, he went home before tea, Sister out Afternoon Nancy and Daughters here after dinner, stay'd but an hour. Betsy Emlen, Sally Smith, Sally Large, Sally Waln and Nancy Howel took tea with Molly—Ricd. Smith called in the evening—Sally Johnson in her Chaise with her son John called after dinner for SB to visit her Sister Betsys Husband, Adam Franks, who she said was near his end. I saw no good purpose her going could answer, as by her account his fever is belious.

Novr. 4. Moderate morning wind variable, John Kinsey breakfasted, Gervis Johnson a young Man from Ireland here, Isaac Potts &c called—HSD. came to town after breakfast. William, Molly, Nancy Skyrin and her daughter Elizath. set off about 11 o'clock for Clearfield. they returned to dinner, Nancy went home, HSD. and Jacob Dined—Henry went home towards evening—Nancy called on Molly, they went to visit Honor Fry.—SR. knock'd at the door this evening HD. went to the door!—John Kinsey and a Committee of the Union Farm mett this evening in the compting house—Sister has been out three Afternoons successively which is rather uncommon—William went out this Afternoon, he took tea at Hannah Pembertons, did not come home 'till after 8 at night—John and Nancy came home with Molly. Stay'd but a short time—Our old Coach-man James Dinning, was here this morning he appears to be quite recovered, talks of going home to Ireland this fall—or we should have been pleased to have employed him again—Sally Wharton sent a note to HD. requesting the loan of our Carriage tomorrow to go to Frankford, HD. was sorry it so happened, but intends going himself to Abington quarterly meeting, has engaged to take several friends with him.

5. clear and temperate, wind S.W—We were awaken'd this morning between one and two o'clock by the cry of fire, the light shining strongly into our

110. Elhanan Winchester, *Ten Letters Addressed to Mr. Paine in Answer to His Pamphlet, Entitled "The Age of Reason," Containing Some Clear and Satisfying Evidences of the Truth of Divine Revelation, and Especially of the Resurrection and Ascension of Jesus* (Boston: John W. Folsom, 1794 [Evans, *Am. Bibliography*]).

Chamber; it proved to be the shop of one Cox a chair maker, on the north side of Coombs Alley, it was not got under till several wooden buildings and other property were destroyed, Wm. Lippencotts back buildings, a tenenment on Thommy Morgans lot &c. Nancy Morgan and her Children came before 4 o'clock to Neighr. Hartshorns, their furniture was moved out of their dweling house, as was some other families—We were up two or three hours—Jacob Downing very busy there—Isaac Pots, very kindly, came here while the fire was rageing to enquire for Jacob, said he did not know but his House was in danger, but it proved otherwise—we retired after it was out for a few hours.—As I stood at our door about two in the morning I had the pleasure, if at such a time any thing could be pleasent, of seeing the moon rising in its last quarter, a sight I seldom enjoy—HD. did not go as he intended to Abinton. as one or more of those that ware going with him were unwell &c—S. Emlen called this morning—A Doctor who lives near Quibbletown dined with us—Nancy and her Children here this Afternoon, she and I went over to Neigr. Walns, for a short time to enquire how A Morgan was after her fright—she was sleeping—Nancy went home early—Richd. Thomas and Saml. Downing took tea with us—Sister out again this Afternoon. Saml. Moore here Afternoon from Clearfield, I sent a note by him to Henry, he expected his Father and others on their return from Abington to have dined with him to day—Sammy Rhoads here this evening Molly just going out, he went with her.

6. Clear and moderate wind N.E—Sammy Downing breakfasted with us—Gervis Johnson employed in our Compting house, Othniel going to leave us—John Marshal called, Jos. Bringhurst and John Parish called—Jacob Downing set off after 12 in Sulkey for the Valley, R. Thomas and Saml. Downing gone also. HD. was let blood this forenoon feeling himself not quite well, and being used to it fall and Spring—John Skyrin left Philadelphia for New-York &c this morning Molly Drinker very poorly to day—Sam Moore in town he says, HSD. left Clearfield for North Bank this morning—Nancy here after dinner, she came again to tea with us—Sister out again this Afternoon—The Committee on Indian affairs mett here again this evening back parlor, Walter Franklin spent part of this evening with William Mary and self, in Compting Room.

7. Hazey, wind S.W—Jos. Sanson called—William rode out forenoon on Mare 3 or 4 miles, we have been much alone to day, I mean without company, Nancy took tea with us—Tommy Wister called this evening—Molly read to William and self, this Afternoon, a letter from T. Eddey of New York, giving an account of a Satisfactory visit which he and some others have lately made to the Indians at a Treaty with them.[111]

111. Thomas Eddy was one of three New York Quakers who had traveled to Indian communities on the frontiers of New York that summer to witness treaty negotiations between U.S. commissioners and the Cayuga and Onondaga Indians over disputed land (*Friends' Review* 5 (1852): 778–80, 788–90, 803–5, 820–22; 6 (1853): 3–5, 20–22, 34–35, 53–54; Kelsey, *Friends and the Indians*, 114–15).

8. First day: A Charming morning wind S.W—'tis what some call an Indian Summer or weather breeder—Thos. Wister and M Penry called before meeting—William and Peter sett off for Clearfield about 11 o'clock, 'tho he does not approve riding on first days, yet as it is probable we shall not have many such days this fall, he concluded to embrace it, the roads are remarkably good—he returned to dinner. Hannah S Drinker came down to dinner today, the first of her leaving her Chamber—S Swett and M. Penry dined with us—Nancy and Children came after dinner, she went to Afternoon meeting with Molly—Eliza and Susan Smith, and Becky Hartshorn three little Girls called to see us.—I have read to day a small volume, of some account of the Life and religious Exercises of Mary Neale, formerly Mary Peisley. principally compiled from her own writings[112]—S Swett and A Skyrin &c. took tea with us—Neighr. Waln here this Evening Sister out. Sammy Rhoads here Molly out with him this evening T. Harrison called.

9. rain most of the night, and this morning wind S.W—changed Afternoon to NW. but still continues raining. I have had an uneasy day so far, on account of my dear MD. &c John C. Miller, scotch Gentleman, lately returned from woods was here, Peggy Smith at work here for Molly &c. cloudy wind high, Sammy Rhoads here this evening Molly up stairs with Peggy Smith.

10. fine Morning wind N.W—HD. MS. MD. gone to meeting, William rode a mile, found the Air too cold, and soon returned—A French Man of the Name of Caraceaux or something very like it, called this forenoon with a petition setting fourth, that his House had been burnt, his property taken from him, and himself made prisoner in St. Domingo—on his being lately set at liberty, he came here in distress &c. Sammy Rhoads called in meeting time to enquire how Molly was,—she was at meeting, if it should be an adieu I should not wonder at it.—Nancy Skyrin called after meeting, and Sally Rhoads also.—John Hallowell and Becky Parker were married this morning at the North meeting House—Sister out this Afternoon Sall Dawsons step mother called—John C. Miller, George Roberts, Joseph Swift, Jams. and Saml. Fisher, in back parlor, on business with HD—T. Stewardson, William Savery and Saml. Emlen called—J. Miller, J Swift, G. Roberts, J Fisher and Jams. Logan took tea here—Jacob Downing returned this Afternoon, he left his mother better, Sally and Children midling, little Mary and Henry have had bad colds, the latter very bad, so that they were awake with him one whole night he was so much oppressed; they gave him Caster Oyl &c. he was better when his father left him. Molly has orders to dismiss!

11. Clear, wind Southerly; George Fry at work in our town Garden, triming

112. *Some Account of the Life and Religious Exercises of Mary Neale, Formerly Mary Peisley, Principally Compiled from Her Own Writings* (Dublin: J. Gough, 1795 [*NUC*]).

the trees &c. Robt. Stevenson A Skyrin and her daughter Elizath. here forenoon; Benjn. Wellby or some such name, from the back woods, HSD. dined with us—Henry went home Afternoon, Nancy Skyrin took tea here—Molly out this evening William also out taking a night walk, of which do not approve, My husband abroad on an appointment. William took two rides to day,—settled with Peggy Smith this evening she has been three days.—Ben Wilson spent evening.

12. raw and Cloudy, wind N.E—Saml. Emlen here early this morning Nancy Skyrin and Children and Maid Betsy spent this day, she, Jacob and HSD. dined here. Henry went home towards evening Saml. Rhoads spent the evening rain this evening MS. went to see S Swett who is unwell.

13. Hazey, wind N.E—James Logan here forenoon HSD. came to dinner, he went home after, I walk'd out this forenoon to visit Sally Emlen, whom I had not seen for a long time, her Daughter very unwell in her Chamber a blister on her side and otherwise unwell—from thence I went down to John Skyrins, dined and spent the day with Nancy, Becky Thompson and Anna Wells there this Afternoon—HD. came for me in the evening he had been to visit J.W DeBrahm at John Elliots, he has lately arrived from South Carolinia. Wm. Savery called this evening Betsy Howel and Hannah Hopkins called on Sister and self while I was out, for a subscription for the relief of the poor this winter, 18 young women have embarked in this business,[113] HD. ordred Molly to put down 20 dollars in her own name, which she had rather been excuse'd from.

14. Clear, wind N.E—Jacob Downing did not intend to have gone to the Valley this week, but as he had left his mother and two Children unwell he concluded to go, he set off about 11 o'clock A.M.—this has been but a sad day to me. weather temperate, Benjn. Chew took tea and spent part of the evening—Ben Oliver here this evening he agree'd to go in a week or 10 days to Virginia for Sally Zane, from whom HD. received a letter this day, I have been reading the minuts of the last yearly meeting, when a large Committee was nominated; to raise a Subscription &c. to be laid out for the benifit and civilization of the Indians, to build saw mills &c. to teach them handy crafts, reading, writing &c &c. A considerable sum will undoubtedly to raised, for their help in many ways, MS. went to see S Swett, who continues poorly.

15. First Day: rather raw, wind N.E—HD. John Drinker and his Son

113. This was probably the Female Society for the Relief and Employment of the Poor, founded in 1795 by Anne Parish. Margaret Haviland, " 'Inasmuch as ye have done it unto me': Quaker Women and Benevolence in Philadelphia, 1790–1820," paper presented at the College of Physicians, Philadelphia, Mar. 30, 1990.

Henry, went in our Carriage to Clearfield and to Germantown meeting, they dined at HSDs—Hannahs Nurse left her to day, she was sent for. they returned before dark. S.R. called this forenoon in meeting time, parler avac moy, he had done the same with HD. on sixth day last, of which I was entirely ignorent. matters are, I expect, concluded—I sincearly wish we may do better—Molly Penry dined here. Nancy Skyrin took tea, she had been to Afternoon meeting. Joseph Bringhurst here towards evening Neighr. Waln spent part of the evening.

16. N.E—storm to day, with steady rain, of which our Puss gave notice, or foretold last night,—*A dull day*, tout a fait—I spent it cutting out underments for our blacks and whites, in the kitchen—No one called on us to day, save those that came to the Compting house—Saml. Fisher spent most of the evening there with HD—rain all day and this evening very heavy at near 11 o'clock 'tis likely 'twill clear up about midnight, cold high wind—S Swett rather better.

17. Stormy with rain most of the night, cloudy morning wind N.W—HD. and Sister at preparative meeting, James Logan here this forenoon—Jacob Downing returned before dinner, he left his family bravely—Nancy Skyrin took tea here—Sammy Downing suped and lodged here—he came to town with JD—cleared up about noon, moderate.

18. Clear a bluster wind NW—Richd. and Saml. Downing breakfasted with us—Saml. Canby, and another called—HSD. in town, WD. Nancy, and her little Eleanor and Betts Dawson went to Clearfield, intending to take Hannah and her little William out airing, and to dine there—Sammy Downing, Henry, and Jacob dined here—Richd. and Saml. Downing gone homeward—Henry also after dinner—M Penry called to bid farewell, as she intends leaving the City on sixth day next. little E Skyrin spent this day here—Our Children returned from Clearfield about sunset—Anna Wells and Nancy Skyrin took tea here. Gideon Wells came in the evening Ben Wilson also. Henry intends going tomorrow to North-bank—clear.

19. Not quite clear, wind NE. changed to S.W—John C. Miller breakfasted with us—Molly Penry called again this Morning she goes tomorrow in the Stage, propposses lodging with Sally Downing in her way through Downgs. town. Sally Johnson called to entread for an order to bury her grandchild in friends burying ground, which was granted—Saml. Emlen called—William rode out on Mare. MS. visited S Swett forenoon, William came home to dinner. William Blakey and Saml. Smith of B County dined here. Docr. Redman and James Logan called—N. Skyrin here after dinner—S.Brant went to the funeral of her Nephew or Neice—Sally Smith came this evening to know if Molly would go with her tomorrow to Clearfield. Saml. Smith sup'd and

lodged here—I have read this evening A Poem intitled The Fair Circassian,[114] imitated from the Songs of Solomon, a piece I disapprove. I saw this poem when I was a young woman and would not then read it,—Am sorry it is republished in 95.

Novr. 20. Clear and cold wind N.W—Saml. Smith left us this morning—Peggy Smith at work here to day—Molly Drinker went in the Carriage between 10 and 11. to call on Sally Smith, intending to spend the day at Clearfield—Docr. Redman and Thos. Morris called at dinner time. John C. Miller and John Skyrin took tea here—JS. returned this Morning from New York &c.—Nancy and her two Daughters were here this Afternoon—Molly returned home after Candle light. *Thos. Fisher* was at Clearfield this Afternoon, he left it a considerable time before the Girls set off. When they were returning home, they observed at the upper end of fourth street a number of people assembled, and T. Fishers Carriage standing without the Horses and the Standards broken, on enquiry, they were informed that the Gentleman was much hurt, and taken into a House hard by, that the Horses had run off, and the Coachman was gone after them. I sent this evening to J Smiths to enquire, word was brought, that T. Fisher was much hurt, 'tho not dangerously, his two youngest Sons who were with him not much hurt.—Our dear William is this evening drinking bran tea, sweet'ned with Honey, for a cold he has taken. cold weather, sildom fails to affect his weak breast.

21st. Steady rain this morning wind Southerly, held up a little about nine o'clock, Jacob Downing set off in the Chaise for the Valley, wind changed to N.E—cloudy with rain at times all day—We are to send John to Downingstown tomorrow or next day, with the Carriage if it clears up, to assist in bringing the family home—HD. went to day to T. Fishers, to know how he is after the fright &c. received yesterday—He is as well as could be expected, has been twice bleed. one of the bones in his fore arm broke, and his side much brused—The accidint happen'd by a Naughty boy beating a hoop against the Horses legs, frighted one of them so that they run the Carriage up the side of a bank and overset it, then both broke loose from it and run away.—The last time that Jacob Downing went to visit his family, he went in the Sulkey, Richd. Thomas and Saml. Downing in a Chair, when they were within 12 miles of home, the Swingeltree of the Chair gave way and fell against the Horses legs, set him runing with violence, Jacob was before, with a top to the Sulkey and was not aware of their coming behind him, which they could not avoid, the Sulkey was turned upside down with Jacob under it, he was a little brused, and the Sulkey broke almost in peices—Richd Thomas had his leg

114. Samuel Croxall, *The Fair Circassian: A Dramatic Performance Done from the Original, by a Gentleman-Commoner of Oxford,* 6th ed. (New York: Hugh Gaine, 1754); a verse adaptation of the Song of Solomon (Evans, *Am. Bibliography*).

badly hurt and has been lame ever since.—George Roberts, Joseph Swift, James and Saml. Fisher and John C. Miller mett HD. this Afternoon in back parlor.—WD. and self in the Compting Room with Gervis and Othniel—they went away before five; G. Churchman took tea with us. HD. gone this evening to H. Pembertons.

22. First day: Cold and raw—wind Northerly—the Sun peep'd out about 11 o'clock, sent John off with the Carriage towards Downingstown. cloudy again and cold—none went to meeting this morning but HD. who never misses when he can possiably help it.—Molly went Afternoon, Nancy came with her maid and Children after dinner intending for meeting but little Eleanor was taken with a twitching or kind of spasm which detained her mother here; she became better after a time and went to sleep. John and Nancy Skyrin took tea with us. they went home pack and package, after candle light—I have been in pain all this day.

23. Cold, sunshine, then cloudy, raw, wind N.W—Saml. Emlen, Neighr. Waln and Docr. Redman called—Molly Drinker spent the day out, she dined with Nancy. Henry came to town forenoon, dined here, went home after noon—John Skyrin came forenoon, he says, Eleanor is as yesterday, when they attempt to dance or raise her quickly up she struggles and the blood flies in her face in an unusal manner, I am fearful the little lamb, has mett with a hurt, that her mother knows not of, and advised her to send for the Physician. David Cumming spent the evening and suped—James Logan called—the weather is moderated, so much the better for our Childrens return.

24. Clear and cool wind N.W—HD. MS. went to monthly meeting, Nancy Skyrin called in her way to meeting—Henry came to town, he intends to apply for a Certificate for his removeal to Bucks County.[115]—Sam Moore brought a load of Henrys goods from Clearfield yesterday, and another this forenoon, which he put in our front parlor, ready packed up in Matts to go from hence to North-bank by water. After the first meeting broke up Nancy Skyrin called. R.G. had been exclaiming, in a friendly stile, against several, then, in meeting, HD. and Isaac Potts among the rest, whom she called instigators—and threatened them with having their names soon in print &c.—S. Emlen called for a short time, he returned to meeting. We expected company to dinner who did

115. Henry S. Drinker wished to change his family's memberships from his parents' monthly meeting in Philadelphia's Northern District to the Falls Monthly Meeting in Bucks County, Pa., where he and his family lived at North Bank, their farm. In such circumstances, Quaker discipline required a certificate of removal, which served as both a credential and a recommendation. Monthly meetings frequently investigated the behavior of the applicant before granting the certificate. The Falls meeting received the certificates of both HSD and his son, William, in March 1796 and that of HSD's wife, Hannah, in January 1797 (Brinton, *Quaker Practice*, 69; Soderlund, *Quakers & Slavery*, 190; Hinshaw, *American Quaker Genealogy*, 2:993).

not come—HSD dined here—Samuel brought another load of furniture this Afternoon. Henry went home before tea. M. Malerive paid us a visit this Afternoon—Nancy and her Daughters came to meet Sally and hers, on their return, it was an hour after candle light when they arrived all in good health but dear little Henry who has a cough—Jacob, Sally, their three Children, and two maids are to stay here 'till their own House is put in order for their reception, their Negro boy Dan, who Jacob has lately purchased, is on his way in R Downings Waggon, Molly spent the Afternoon and evening at Geddion Wellss—Ben Wilson spent the evening here—We have a large family, at present.—Casper Morris and Betsy Giles married this evening.

25. Clear and cool. wind N.W—Catty Deacon and Anna went this morning to clean and make fires in Jacobs House, Sally and the Children went home this evening—Molly Kelly put up three suits Curtains for us, one of them a new white suit in our Chamber, she dined here; We sent S Swett her dinner as usual, she says she is better, but Sister thinks her very poorly. Neighr. Waln, Nancy Morgan and Anna Wells called—John Warders wife called to speak with Sally Downing concerning a Nurse, Sally Smith, T. Stewardson called. James Logan took tea or water with us—Nancy Skyrin spent this morning here.

26. Cool, hazey, wind N.W—H.SD. came to town this Morning went back before dinner. John went up with the Carriage, Henry and all his family came to town to J Smiths, only Scipio, who is here with us—Hannah expects to stay some days at her fathers before they go home to North-bank.—Peter Woodard fell down the hold of the Vessel in which Henry is sending his goods &c. he hurt his side a little, I bathed it with Steers Opodeldoc, and hope the hurt is of little consequence. Benjn. Chew took tea here, Sally Smith came for Molly to go with her to Betsy Emlens—HSD. spent the evening here. I spent an hour or two at Sammy Fishers, his wife in her Chamber, very poorly, Sally Rhoads there—Saml. Fisher came home with me—An account in this days paper of the Death of Lawrence Embree of N. York.

27. Cloudy, wind NE—rain afternoon, George and Samuel here to day helping to put HSDs Goods on board. Henry in and out many times very busy. As Peter complained this morning of the pain in his side, 'tho he eat an hearty breakfast, we sent for Lewis Guilliams, Fredrick out of town, to bleed him, he took 8 or 10 ounces—said Fredrick was married last night to a widdow in the Country, aged fifty years, with seven Children, he has Courage. gave Peter a dose of Castor Oyl, he appears near well this Afternoon. John Skyrin and HSD. took tea here, Walter Franklin spent the evening.

28. Clear, wind N.W—Saml. Emlen breakfasted here before I came down stairs. HSD. here this Morning Molly out after breakfast. Saml. Andrew Law

from Connecticut, Henry and Hannah Drinker with their little Son and Maid Mary, Saml. Moore, Sipio &c. dined here,—the first visit paid us by the dear little boy—Nancy with her two Daughters and Betts came after dinner—they went all together to visit Sally, as she has never, yet, seen Nancys or Hannahs little ones—Sally Hopkins and James Hopkinss daughter Betsy [were] here this Afternoon—Sister at Neighr. Walns this evening James Logon came home with Molly from Saml. Emlens junr.—cloudy.—pouver Mairia.

Novr. 29. First day: cloudy. wind N.E—HD. MS and MD. went to meeting, rained when it broke up—No one dined here, this has been a quiet Solumn day so far—rain the evening HD. gone to meeting.—last night was married, Jenny Stevenson Eldest daughter of our friend Robt. Stevenson, to Jacob Clarkson son of Dr. Gladious Clarkson deceased—Henry Sibble a Lad from East-town called to see us, he is Son to Jane Sibble formerly Boon, she lived with us near four years, tended Molly when an Infant, she married one of Major Crammonds Orderly Men Philip George Sibble an Anspach, he deserted from the troop when they left this City, as did many more of his Countrymen, he is now in business at Easttown as a Physician, sells medicine, and makes mony fast, German like.

30. Clear, wind high at N.W—Our Son Henry went after breakfast towards his Farm, expecting to find his goods and Furniture there on his arrival. Hannah and Child stays at her Fathers during his absence—Our old Friend John De Brahm, dined with us, the first visit he has paid us since his arrival from Georgia, having been indisposed—Sally Smith called for Molly to go with her to visit Suckey Emlen—John Drinker here this evening he has been busy to day at H. Pembertons, where my husband found him, they took tea there, William took a walk there also—Sally Brant began a quarters Schooling this Afternoon at her old Mistress Prices—John Watson junr. and his Cousin Rachel Paxon were here this Afternoon, he brought two rocking Arm Chairs to town, which had been bespoak in their neighbourhood, he put up his waggon and Horses in our Stable, then went away, he sent the chairs to the owners—John called again this evening.

Decemr. 1st. fine morning wind Southerly inclining to East. John Watson and Rachel Paxon set off from hence this morning ten o'clock, HD. MS. gone to meeting, Nancy called in her way thither. William rode out forenoon on the mare—Sally Downing with her two Daughters came, she left the Children with me, and went out with Molly. Saml. Emlen and Nancy Skyrin called after meeting. Dr. Redman called; Our two little Downings dined with us—Daniel Drinker and Saml. Pleasants took tea here, John Parish here also. Neighr. Waln and Othniel Alsop spent the evening. Clement Remington and Saml. A Law were here this evening Sister at Jacobs, Molly at J Skyrins. HSD. returned from North bank this Afternoon. I have read two pamphlets, one of them transacted and printed upwards of 160 years ago. Facts—*Abominable.* the other bound up with the first not so bad, but of the same nature.

2. clear morning wind S.W—varied afterwards very high and blustering—HSD. here this forenoon, Sister out, she brought Mary Downing home, who spent the day with us—James Logan here this forenoon, HSD. took tea with us—Elijah Waring and Saml. A Law spent the evening—Were I to make a memorandum when ever I felt my self indisposed, I should daily say I was unwell, but when more than commonly so, I may of a truth say, very poorly, which is the case at present,—'tho at same time I might be much worse, therefore ought to be thankfull—Our dear William I think is better than he has been for a long time past, his breast rather stronger.

3. temperate wind S.W—Our Son Henry breakfasted here, he went this forenoon to Clearfield—Huldah Mott and Betsy Emlen were here this forenoon. EE. and MD. had high words together, which ended in a farewell parting, or at least it appear'd so, I have no wish it should be otherwise—"Let envy alone, and it will punish itself."—We had the satisfaction to day of the company of all our Children to dine with us, which in the whole amounted to no more than 14 Grand children included. Henry returned before dinner—John, Nancy, and their Elizath. spent the Afternoon and evening the others were engaged and left us sooner—Saml. A Law sup'd here. Nathen Shepherd, Saml. Emlen and others called. Molly wrote this evening to Sally Saltar Atsion.

4. clear temperate morning John DeBrahm here after breakfast. HSD. called—Hannah Catheral here forenoon. Sister with the Committee of twelve this Afternoon. Micl. Callanan here—John Collins for an order to bury an apprentice of William Garrigus—Jacob Downing here this evening to invite us to dine with him and others at his house tomorrow. Sister at Neighr. Walns this evening HD. as usual on an appointment. Richd. Smith and Sally Smith came here late this evening the latter to inform Molly that she expected EE. at their house tomorrow to make enquries and accusations.

5. Clear, wind westerly: HSD. called, A Skyrin and her daughter Elizath. also,—Sally Smith and Sally Large, George Field with them, were here this forenoon, giving an account of their Rumpus with EE. at J Smiths, they have shaken hands with her, as the saying is. Malerive and his Sister here before dinner. My husband, John and Nancy Skyrin, WD. and H.S.D. dined at Jacob Downings, Hannah could not go, as her Child is unwell.—John Drinker called here,—Molly spent this Afternoon at John Fields. George Roberts here, he and others mett in compting house on business with HD. David Cumming here this evening Our dear little Henry Downing was innoculated for the small pox this forenoon by Docr. Kuhn.—I have read a volume,

medical, entitled Natures Assistant to the Restoration of health in a variety of complaints &c. By J Hodson MD.[116] wherein he ascribes great success to his many Nostrums, for a variety of disorders.

Decemr. 6. First day: Clear, wind N.W—HD. stay'd all day at home, he took medicine, haveing been for some days past somewhat indisposed. MS. MD. went to meeting, Jacob Downing called he left his daughter Eliza here, as Molly was gone, and she could not go by herself—William Cooper and E. Downing dined with us—Sally Downing called after dinner, Nancy Skyrin also, she left her daughter ES. with me, Sally took both hirs to meeting with her.—they all called after meeting, Hannah S. Drinker her maid and Son came,—John Drinker, William Lippencott, Hannah S Drinker and Sally Smith took tea here—Saml. Emlen and William Savery called—one Viceree called.—Saml. A Law here this evening he goes away tomorrow. Molly spent the evening at Nancys, Walter Franklin came home with her. [S]L. and SS. were there also.

7. Cloudy, wind NE—HSD. here this morning very busy preparing for their departure tomorrow if the weather premitts. Hannah was here after dinner, she bid fare well—Henry, has sold Scipio to George Emlen, and we have given him our little Peter Savage, I hope he will be a good boy, 'tho he is but little worth at present—M. Pleasants and her Daughter Molly spent the Afternoon with us. rain most of the Afternoon and evening HSD. here.

8. Rain this morning wind N.E—cloudy most all day. H.S.D. here this morning No going home to North bank this day,—The Committee on Indian Affairs mett at nine o'clock in front parlor, they continued 'till dinner time—Saml. Emlen called—Benjn. Swett, John Pearce, Joseph Slone, and James Cooper, dined here. No one went to meeting from our house to day—Sister a little rheumatic. Molly out this Afternoon. H.S.D. William Cooper and Thos. Stewardson took tea with us. J Logan, C. Remington, Jacob and Thos. Downing here this evening—MS. went to James Smiths.

Decr. 9. wind very high in the night. Calmer this morning, wind S.W—a fine cool day, agreeable for our Son and his little family to go home—they left J Smiths about 10 o'clock, Hetty Smith, Hannah and her lettle Son, and their Maid Mary Evens, in our Carriage drove by John, little Peter Savage went in the Chair with his Master, they expect to get home to a dish of Coffee in the Afternoon—If it is hard to part with a beloved Son, it must be more so to part with a Child-bareing Daughter, prehaps equaly beloved. William went

116. James Hodson, M.D., Swedenborg Minister, *Nature's Assistant to the Restoration of Health; To Which Is Added a Short Treatise on the Venereal Disease,* 7th ed. (London: J. Matthews, [1790] [*Brit. Mus. Cat.*]).

out on old mare, found it too cold, and soon returned—My Husband dined to day at Hanh Pemberton Alexander White &c—there—Sally Zane returned last evening from Virginia—Sally Downing and Nancy Skyrin were here twice to day, the latter and her husband and daughter Elizath. took tea here and spent the evening—they had a religious visit paid them this forenoon by Deborah Derby, Rebecca Young, Ruth Ann Rutter and Samuel C Clark. R. Griscomb paid HD. a visit of accusation this forenoon in the Compting house. Gervis Johnson gently moved her out.—Molly received a card of invitation from G. and A. Wells, to supper with them this day week.

10. Hazey, temperate morning wind westerly. Nancy Skyrin and her Children spent most of the day dined with us—William rode out this morning found it agreeable—read this forenoon a small pamphlet—called The Court Secret: A Melancholy Truth, now first translated From the Original Arabic, the date omitted.[117] I believe it to be old.—Saml. Emlen and Sally Downing called—Nancy stay'd tea and spent most of the evening Neighr. Waln, James Smith, James Logan and Walter Franklin here this evening.

11. Clear and temperate, wind N.W—Saml. Emlen called, Sally Downing, Nancy Skyrin, Sally Smith and Sally Large called. Jacob Ritter brought me a letter from my friend M Penry, with some medical directions. Sister out this Afternoon, The Indian Committee mett in back parlor. William, Mary, and self, spent the evening reading and at work in the Compting house, Sister went over to set with Neighr. Waln—David Evans came for an order to bury a Child of Isaac Peningtons—Jemmy Smith came to settle the time of his and my husbands going tomorrow to North bank. It is 12 months this day since Henry was married, he is now on his farm with a fine Son near two months old. John returned last night with the Carriage he brought a letter from our Son informing us of their safe arrival just before sunset, all in good health.—Molly Jervis daughter of our Cousine Charles Jervis was married last night to John Gardener, I dont know the young man but have heard him well spoken of—Marriages have been, laterly, very frequent and numerous in, and out, of our society. uncommonly so.

12. rather overcast, wind Easterly. HD. and James Smith left our door in JSs carriage about 11 o'clock. A.M. for North-bank. I am apprehensive they will have dull weather, should it turn out otherwise, a little relaxation from business may be useful to HD—I am not acquainted with the extent of my husbands great variety of engagements, but this I know, that he is perpetualy and almost ever employed; the Affairs of Society and the public, and private, out of his own family, or his own concerns, I believe takes up ten twelfths of

117. [George, Lord Lyttelton?], *The Court-Secret: A Melancholy Truth, Now First Translated from the Original Arabic* (London: T. Cooper, 1741 [*NUC*]).

his time, if benevolence and beneficence will take a man to Heaven, and no doubt it goes a great way towards it, HD. stands as good, indeed a better, chance than any I know off.—Molly gone out this forenoon, W.D. gone to visit friend Swett, MS. WD. and self dined together. Molly dined at Jacob Downings, she came home after dinner. It began to rain this Afternoon sooner than it was probable, that HD. and JS. were at their journeys end.—Emlens little Harriot, brought a letter this Afternoon from EE. to MD. scurrilous and abusive, demanding all the notes and letters that she had wrote her—Molly after, calmly, reading the letter, told Hariott, she had no answer to send.—Molly went down to see her Sister Nancy, who she found in bed ill with the sick head ach. she called towards evening at Er. Larges, John Large came home with her. I sent Peter this evening to enquire how Nancy was, he brought me the pleasing account that she was setting up, much better, and expected to eat a little supper.—Gervis Johnson lodges here to night.—Molly with me during my husbands absence.

13. First Day. rain in the night. cloudy morning wind S.W—MS. went to meeting, Saml. Emlen called after. and Saml. Emlen junr. before dinner—MD. went to Afternoon meeting. MS. to Jacob Downings, to know if their little boy had yet sicken'd for the small pox. I have been reading a small peice on Natural Philosophy; few subjects more amusing.—last spring I read three Octavo Volumes of Goldsmiths Natural History,[118] the fourth was misslaid, so that a stop was put at that time to my amusement, there are five more 8 in all,—The first volume on the Earth &c., I like the best, it is both entertaining and instructive, the second on Man, is very interesting, the 3d. on Beast, and all the others on animated Nature are, I doubt not, very pleasing and amusing—.

I stay much at home, and my business I mind,
Take note of the weather, and how blows the wind,
The changes of Seasons, The Sun, Moon and Stars,
The Setting of Venus, and riseing of Mars.
Birds, Beasts and Insects, and more I cold mention,
That pleases my leisure, and draws my attention.
But respecting my Neighbours, their egress, and Regress,
Their Coaches and Horses, their dress and their Address,
What matches are making, whos plain, or Whos gay,
I leave to their parents, or Guardians to Say:
For most of those things, are out of my *Way*.
But to those, where my love and my duty doth bind
More than most other Subjects, engages my Mind.

—and I am not ashamed to own it.—Sister came home to tea, little Henry

118. See above, Feb. 25.

continues well yet, John Skyrin called after meeting, Molly went home with him—Neighr. Waln and Susan Hartshorn junr. spent the evening, Pattison Hartshorn came over to them—Edwd. Bonsel brought a letter here this evening for Jacob Downing from his brother Richd. giving an account of the decease of their mother Mary Downing, she died sometime in last night, we know not yet the perticulars.—John Smith came home with Molly.

14. I past, almost, a sleepless night, rain most of the night and this morning wind N.W—received a letter from HSD. this morning requisting his Burow-table might be sent—Jacob Downing, by our Johns missconduct, and other neglect, did not get away 'till near five this Afternoon, he then sett off in our Carriage by himself, intending to lodge at the buck, and proceed very early tomorrow morning towards his fathers—cloudy most of the day—A Letter brought from Reb[a]. Griscomb to HD—Gervis Johnson called this evening HD. and James Smith his wife with them came home after night, they left Henry and family well, Hannah, no doubt, in trouble parting with her Mammy. My husband, last night run a nail in the forefinger of his left hand near the middle joint, opening a case that held a looking-glass, it was swell'd, and had a poltice on when he came home, we renewed the poltice this evening—he says it feels easy 'tho—stiff—We all wished him to take advice, 'tho there is no apparent danger, yet as we have frequently heard of very serious consequences, occuring from slight appearences, could not, but be uneasy—James Logan took tea here, Molly read EEs letter to him. I have been surprised at the Calmness, patience and evenness of temper, with which Molly has born, the envy, malice and abuse of that little v-x-n—clear and cold this evening How carefull Young Girls should be, how, and with whom they form an intimate acquaintance.

Decemr. 15. wind high in the night, variable this morning cloudy. David —— here this morning talking about Quibbletown Mill—Nancy Skyrin called in her way to meeting. HD. MS. MD. gone to meeting—William wrote to Henry.—William Cooper dined here, James Logan called—John and Nancy Skyrin and John Jones of Peach-[b]ottom took tea here—Ben Wilson suped—I spent this evening with Sally Downing, Nancy Morgan there—there are but three eruptions come out as yet on the Child, they are very like the small pox, he is chearful and appears to ail little. Molly went with Peggy Wharton, Sally Rawle and Sally Perot, to visit Caroline Shoemaker, who lays in with her second Child a daughter.

16. Clear, wind westerly—George Fry from Clearfield, brought vigatables—Nancy Skyrin and Daughter Eliza[h]. here forenoon, she left the Child to spend the day with us. Hope Sharp came for her in the evening Peter went with them, he brought word back that little Eleanor was ill in a fitt of the Colic—I sent him an hour or two afterwards to enquire how she was, as I could

not with propriety go out this cold evening having a sore-eye &c. he brought word back that she was rather better—Sister was out this Afternoon—John Muscer here this evening—Molly gone with Sally Smith and Sally Large to sup at Gedian Wellss with a large Company.—HD. gone this evening to Hannah Pembertons—William walked out twice, a coldish day this has been. Cry of fire this evening a Chimney in Arch-Street. Jacob Downing returned after dusk from the funeral of his Mother, we have not yet seen him, Rd. Thomas came with him—William wrote to Henry to night. Molly came home about mid-night, never so late out before, they walk'd home, as did many others, Richd. Morris waited on Molly home—there was upwards of thirty in company—she is not displeased that she went, but wishes not to go again to such late entertainment knowing it is disagreeable to her parents.

Decr. 17. a pleasant temperate winter morning wind S.W—Setting up late last night for my Daughter, I finish'd knitting a third pair of coarse large cotton Stockings for self—it is an employment I once was very fond of, when my boys were little, but having a pain in my breast the Doctor advised against it, as affecting the Nerves, 'tis many years since I have done much in that way till lately, the relish returnd. William out this morning, I am much delighted, and I trust thankful, to see him so much on the recovery as he appears to be at present—I went after dinner to visit our grand Son, he is more feverish, and a few more small pox coming out, this is the 13th. day,—Sally informed me that Rachel James was coming to our house—I therefore came home sooner than I intended, found her here. John James came after, they took tea, and spent part the evening Sister went after they were gone to Sallys—Sally Smith called here this Afternoon—Nancy Skyrin and Sally Large sent Oliver Wadsworth for Molly this evening Peter and Oliver went with her to JSs—James Fisher called this evening Jacob came home with Sister, JS. with Molly.

18. 'tis said that it snow'd in the night, there is not the least vestage or appearence of it this morning clear wind high at N.W—'tho not very cold—William walked out forenoon, to purchase a Cane, and call on SR.—Betsy Jervis and Nancy Skyrin and child took tea here, Saml. Emlen called WD. and MD. had a conference with him in the Compting room, shewed him his Daughters letter.—Our dear little Henry Downing was so unwell to day as to refuse the breast, he is feverish and has but 4 or 5. small pox come out, the Doctor thinks that his teeth cutting is part of the cause of the fever—he ordered them to get his Gums lanced.—He is a very fine Child remarkabley good tempered, and forward of his Age he is now turned of 8 months, and tis several weeks that he has spoken many words very plainly, such as Aunty, Cattey and Eisey for Eliza, &c William went this cool evening to J Downings, John Skyrin came for Nancy. Docr. John Watson from bucks county suped and lodges here to night—Jacob came after ten for Sister, who intends to

spend the night with Sally and her Son, Molly spent the Afternoon at E. Larges.

Decr. 19. Clear and cool, wind N.W—I went to see our little Henry. Dr. Kuhn there—the child appears very poorly a rash came out on him last night, it seems to me to be out of season, and he has still a fever, a great flush in his cheeks, very cold hands and feet, sick stomach, frequently puking—this evening Sister was there, he has been since evening and taking a nap, chearful and rather better—Molly went this forenoon to Anna Wellss—James Logan here—Nancy Ward formerly Quick, and a young woman with her, John Musser, Danl. Drinker, Neighr. Waln, here this evening Sally Smith and Sally Large also—they report, that the difference they and MD. has had with EE—is much talked of—poor Elizabeth! she has exposed herself very much by her malice and violence—Molly received a letter from Sally Salter, Peter took S. Swett her dinner, she told him she was now bravely, that there was no longer occasion of bringing it, as her Neice, and Neices daughter were come to live with her—I was pleased when I first heard of her intention to have company, it is several years she has lived quite alone day and night, we have long thought, that for a person of her age it was very improper, and have more than once mentioned it to her, which always seemed to displease her—I have often observed that old Women who have been accustomed to live alone, very much dislike the thoughts of a companion in the house with them, 'tis strange it should be so, but they do not like to be, in the least, put out of their usual way.—Peter informed Sister this evening of fresh appearences of Mal conduct in S.B—if tis true, we must bid her adieu.—Our old friend and acquaintance Joshua Howel was taken ill today, or last evening with a Spitting up of blood, Samuel Smith called to inform us of it,—We sent this evening to enquire how he was, was told that he had brought up above a pint, in the corse of the day—but they hoped he was a little better this evening he has been twice bleed.

Decr. 20. First day. a steady Snow this morning wind N.E—Our little Henry had a good night and is better this morning HD. and MS. went to meeting—No one dined here—it left of Snowing after dinner—continues cloudy—HD. MD. went to Afternoon meeting—HD. took tea at Jacob Downings, then went to evening meeting, he called at Joshua Howels, who has had 40 ounces of blood taken from him, they hope he is better—I have generaly made it a practice to read at the end of the year,[119] the Almanac for the succeeding year, Poulsons for 96. has several good things in it.—William Cooper called this evening stay'd a short time and took a french leave.

21. overcast, wind N.W—Saml. Emlen called—received a letter this morning from our Son Henry—they are all favour'd with health, Willm. Parsons who

119. The words "to read" crossed out.

brought it, dined here, Docr. Redman called before dinner, Billy Saltar took tea here, his Sisters, Sally and Betsy are come to town with him, HD. at H Pembertons this Afternoon, Molly gone to her Sister Nancys—cold and raw. Cadr. Evans and Nicholas—here this evening John Drinker called—John Skyrin came home with Molly—Billy Saltar sup'd and lodges here.

22. Clear, wind N.E—Wm. Parsons went off after breakfast with letters and several other Articles for HSD—Wm. Saltar breakfasted here. HD. MS. went to monthly meeting—R.G. vociferated there—Betsy Saltar called this forenoon; she cleared up to our satisfaction, EE tale—her Sisters Sally is poorly at S. Emlens—Betsy Robinson came here to her, they intend sitting of tomorrow or next day, in the Stage for New-York, EE. goes with them—Cadr. Evans here fore noon, *Sally Downing* also,—Daniel Drinker dined here—Saml. Emlen called—A Skyrin came after dinner with her eldest daughter, and a curious new-made grand-daughter, she left them here, and went with A Morgan to spend the Afternoon at Gedion Wellss—Sister went this evening to visit Mercy Carlile—Sam came for the Child after night. Billy Saltar suped and lodg'd here.

23. Cloudy most of the day, wind S.E—Wm. Saltar breakfasted—John and Elizath. Saltar, HD. and self acknowledged a Deed this Afternoon in our Compting house before Judge Smith of New Jersey, we had acknowledged one before for the same uses and purposses, but as it was supposed there was some mistake or omission in it, it was thought proper to draw and execute another—Docr. Vermeule of New-Jersey took tea here,—Molly Taylor called after dinner for MS. to go with her to visit and hand out something to several poor widdows, by order of the monthly meeting—Walter Franklin and Richd. Morris, spent the Evening here.

24. rain most of the night, and this morning wind S.W—clear'd away about noon, very damp. Saml. Emlen called this fore noon, says his Daughter and the Salters &c. set off in the Stage this morning in the rain, roads very bad—Leonard Snowden called, Neighr. Waln spent part of the evening—Docr. Vermule also.—Nancy Skyrin went this Afternoon with Nancy Morgan &c. to visit Hetty Eddy. cloudy this evening.

25. Called Christmass day: many attend religeously to this day, others spend it in riot and dissipation, We, as a people, make no more account of it than another day. rain in the night, cloudy all day, wind N.W—changed after night to N.E—Saml. Emlen and James Logan called this morning—Nancy Skyrin and her Children spent the Afternoon—John and Nancy sup'd.

26. rain in the night, cloudy all day: wind Easterly in the morning Southerly at night—Willm. Cooper dined here—I was taken very unwell after dinner

with griping vomitting &c. suffered much in the course of an hour by the obstruction in my bowels, sent for Docr. Kuhn, he read a piece I received from MP., and advised the use of it, and recommended to William and self, to loose 8 or 10 ounces blood, each, tomorrow morning—I lay on the bed upwards of an hour, felt better, and came down to my work as usual: little did I think, a few hours ago, that I should be able to do so.—Isaac Potts and Sammy Fisher spent part of the evening—We have not heard from our Children this day.

27: First day: A fine clear temperate day—wind N.W—HD. and Daughter Mary went to meeting, MS. tarried at home, to attend to William and his Mother. We each had a vein open'd by Fredrick Hailer—Williams blood better than common, mine inflamed, black and buffey—Othniel Alsop and Isaac Grifith called after meeting—Docr. Kuhn also called, Williams pulse better since bleeding, little or none alteration in mine. O. Alsop dined here. HD. went to the funeral of John Elliots Son, who was carried to the market Street meeting house—A Skyrin with her maids and Children came after dinner, she and Molly went to afternoon meeting, left the Children with us, they came back to tea, they went in the evening to visit Betsy Fisher, who has been long unwell in her Chamber.—I read to day, a large Pamphlet, entitled A Vindication of Mr. Randolphs Resignation.[120] some say it does not make good the Title. for my part I look not on myself as a competent Judge. HD. gone this evening to Molly Foulks—Saml. Fisher came home with my Daughters, he waited on Nancy and her Children home, Molly went with them, John Skyrin came after they were gone, he came again home with Molly.

28. a fine clear day, wind S.E—J Logan called. Benjn. Tucker called—Nancy and Molly went this Afternoon to visit at Charles Jerviss a bride visit to Molly Gardiner—Sister on a Committee—Isaac Potts called—Neighr. Waln and grand-daughter Becky Hartshorn here this evening Elliston Perot also, they were amused looking at J Skyrins perspective views which he has lately received from England—Molly heard while abroad, not at CJs, of verses made on her, by EE—not much to the authors credit.

29. Clear fine morning wind S.W—chang'd afternoon cold and raw wind N.E—HD. MS. went to meeting, our Neighbour Johanna Hazelhurst spent an hour this morning, she enquired the charectar of our driver John Bowing, we could not say much in his favour, nor did we say more against him then was proper—If every one, would give the true state of those matters as near as they could with propriety, neither worse or better than they deserve, I belive they would be better served in that necessary branch of House-keeping. William

120. Edmund Randolph, *A Vindication of Mr. Randolph's Resignation* (Philadelphia: Samuel H. Smith, 1795 [Evans, *Am. Bibliography*]).

walked out this forenoon, he paid several visits, and too long a walk again this Afternoon, he is pleased that he is able so to do, but I fear he will some time over do it.—Gervis Johnson returned to day from Brumswick &c. he and Thos. Potts are both at present employed in our Compting house.—Sally Smith and Sally Large were here Yesterday Afternoon the former informed us that she was to set off this morning with her cousin Richd. Smith for North-bank. William sent a book and some papers to his Brother.—Isaac Potts and Saml. Hopkins were here this evening Molly spent the Afternoon at Robt. Stevensons on a visit to his daughter Jane, a brides visit 'tho rather out of Season, Nancy Skyrin was to have gone with her, but has the Head-ach, she was here forenoon, before and after meeting. Sister out this Afternoon visiting the poor. I have this day began to make use of a active medicine, should it prove salutary, I shall have great cause of thankfulness.

30. rain in the night, cloudy morning wind N.E—about 3 o'clock this morning a fire broke out in the House occupied by the Widdow Sewel, at the corner of Elm and thirds streets, the roof was consumed—My husband and self heard nothing of it, Sister and Molly heard the cry of fire for a short time but did not rise—HD. has had an appearance of blood in his spittle, which is not a new thing with him, but nevertheless alarming. I have heard within a week past of 5 or 6. persons that have spit blood. G. Johnson was one of them. he is now bravely. J Logan called forenoon. Nancy Skyrin and her Daughter Elizabeth spent the Afternoon and evening with us—John Skyrin came in evening—heavey air.

Decemr. 31. Cloudy, wind S.E—heavy air and damp—sent for Dr. Kuhn, being very unwell, he came, said my pulse were better than when he last saw me, ordred me to take tomorrow, a table spoonful Castor Oyl, every three hours 'till I have taken 5 or 6 doses, if my stomach will bare it, in order to remove the obstruction in my bowels. I feel some dread on the occasion—HD. took 3 opening pills last night, he is bravely, I hope, today, no more of the sanguinary appearence since in his spittle rain Afternoon Molly poorly, she lay down, arose again towards evening better—John Cannon and John Drinker took tea with us—J. Cannon came from Hartslog Huntington County. A Senator—Richd. and Sally Smith returned this evening from North-bank, they left Henry and family well,—brought a letter for William.—But 4 hours of the year 95, to come, Bells ringing out the old year as they say—to a thoughtful mind it is a serious consideration.[121]

121. On the outside back cover of the manuscript volume for 1795 are the following numbers:

4007
1795
5802   5812